Brill's New Pauly

ANTIQUITY
VOLUME 8

LYD-MINE

Brill's New Pauly

Brill's

Encyclopaedia of the Ancient World

New Pauly

Edited by
Hubert Cancik and
Helmuth Schneider

English Edition
Managing Editor *Christine F. Salazar*

Assistant Editors *Simon Buck, Michael Chase,*
Tina Chronopoulos, Fem Eggers, Susanne E. Hakenbeck,
Tina Jerke, Ingrid Rosa Kitzberger, Sebastiaan R. van der
Mije, Antonia Ruppel, Reinhard Selinger and *Ernest Suyver*

ANTIQUITY
VOLUME 8

LYD-MINE

BRILL
LEIDEN - BOSTON
2006

© Copyright 2006 by Koninklijke Brill NV, Leiden, The Netherlands

Koninklijke Brill NV incorporates the imprints Brill Academic Publishers, Martinus Nijhoff Publishers and VSP.

Originally published in German as DER NEUE PAULY. Enzyklopädie der Antike. Herausgegeben von Hubert Cancik und Helmuth Schneider. Copyright © J.B. Metzlersche Verlagsbuch-handlung und Carl Ernst Poeschel Verlag GmbH 1996ff./1999ff. Stuttgart/Weimar

Cover design: TopicA (Antoinette Hanekuyk)
Front: Delphi, temple area
Spine: Tabula Peutingeriana

Translation by protext TRANSLATIONS B.V.

Data structuring and typesetting:
pagina GmbH, Tübingen, Germany

The publication of this work was supported by a grant from the GOETHE-INSTITUT INTER NATIONES.

ISBN (volume) 90 04 12271 0
ISBN (set) 90 04 12259 1

This book is printed on acid-free paper.

PRINTED IN THE NETHERLANDS

Table of Contents

Notes to the User

Arrangement of Entries

The entries are arranged alphabetically and, if applicable, placed in chronological order. In the case of alternative forms or sub-entries, cross-references will lead to the respective main entry. Composite entries can be found in more than one place (e.g. *a commentariis* refers to *commentariis, a*).

Identical entries are differentiated by numbering. Identical Greek and Oriental names are arranged chronologically without consideration of people's nicknames. Roman names are ordered alphabetically, first according to the *gentilicium* or *nomen* (family name), then the *cognomen* (literally 'additional name' or nickname) and finally the *praenomen* or 'fore-name' (e.g. *M. Aemilius Scaurus* is found under *Aemilius*, not *Scaurus*).

However, well-known classical authors are lemmatized according to their conventional names in English; this group of persons is not found under the family name, but under their *cognomen* (e.g. Cicero, not Tullius). In large entries the Republic and the Imperial period are treated separately.

Spelling of Entries

Greek words and names are as a rule latinized, following the predominant practice of reference works in the English language, with the notable exception of technical terms. Institutions and places (cities, rivers, islands, countries etc.) often have their conventional English names (e.g. *Rome* not *Roma*). The latinized versions of Greek names and words are generally followed by the Greek and the literal transliteration in brackets, e.g. *Aeschylus* (Αἰσχύλος; *Aischýlos*).

Oriental proper names are usually spelled according to the 'Tübinger Atlas des Vorderen Orients' (TAVO), but again conventional names in English are also used. In the maps, the names of cities, rivers, islands, countries etc. follow ancient spelling and are transliterated fully to allow for differences in time, e.g. both Καππαδόκια and *Cappadocia* can be found. The transliteration of non-Latin scripts can be found in the 'List of Transliterations'.

Latin and transliterated Greek words are italicized in the article text. However, where Greek transliterations do not follow immediately upon a word written in Greek, they will generally appear in italics, but without accents or makra.

Abbreviations

All abbreviations can be found in the 'List of Abbreviations' in the first volume. Collections of inscriptions, coins and papyri are listed under their *sigla*.

Bibliographies

Most entries have bibliographies, consisting of numbered and/or alphabetically organized references. References within the text to the numbered bibliographic items are in square brackets (e.g. [1.5 n.23] refers to the first title of the bibliography, page 5, note 23). The abbreviations within the bibliographies follow the rules of the 'List of Abbreviations'.

Maps

Texts and maps are closely linked and complementary, but some maps also treat problems outside the text. The authors of the maps are listed in the 'List of Maps'.

Cross-references

Articles are linked through a system of cross-references with an arrow → before the entry that is being referred to.

Cross-references to related entries are given at the end of an article, generally before the bibliographic notes. If reference is made to a homonymous entry, the respective number is also added.

Cross-references to entries in the *Classical Tradition* volumes are added in small capitals.

It can occur that in a cross-reference a name is spelled differently from the surrounding text: e.g., a cross-reference to Mark Antony has to be to Marcus → Antonius, as his name will be found in a list of other names containing the component 'Antonius'.

List of Transliterations

Transliteration of ancient Greek

α	a	alpha
αι	ai	
αυ	au	
β	b	beta
γ	g	gamma; γ before γ, κ, ξ, χ: n
δ	d	delta
ε	e	epsilon
ει	ei	
ευ	eu	
ζ	z	z(d)eta
η	ē	eta
ηυ	ēu	
θ	th	theta
ι	i	iota
κ	k	kappa
λ	l	la(m)bda
μ	m	mu
ν	n	nu
ξ	x	xi
ο	o	omicron
οι	oi	
ου	ou	
π	p	pi
ϱ	r	rho
σ, ς	s	sigma
τ	t	tau
υ	y	upsilon
φ	ph	phi
χ	ch	chi
ψ	ps	psi
ω	ō	omega
ʽ	h	spiritus asper
ᾳ	ai	iota subscriptum (similarly ῃ, ῳ)

In transliterated Greek the accents are retained (acute ´, grave `, and circumflex ˆ). Long vowels with the circumflex accent have no separate indication of vowel length (makron).

Transliteration of Hebrew

א	a	alef
ב	b	bet
ג	g	gimel
ד	d	dalet
ה	h	he
ו	w	vav
ז	z	zayin
ח	ḥ	khet
ט	ṭ	tet
י	y	yod
כ	k	kaf
ל	l	lamed
מ	m	mem
נ	n	nun
ס	s	samek
ע	ʿ	ayin
פ	p/f	pe
צ	ṣ	tsade
ק	q	qof
ר	r	resh
שׂ	ś	sin
שׁ	š	shin
ת	t	tav

Pronunciation of Turkish

Turkish uses Latin script since 1928. Pronunciation and spelling generally follow the same rules as European languages. Phonology according to G. Lewis, Turkish Grammar, 2000.

A	a	French a in *avoir*
B	b	b
C	c	j in *jam*
Ç	ç	ch in *church*
D	d	d
E	e	French ê in *être*
F	f	f
G	g	g in *gate* or in *angular*
Ğ	ğ	lengthens preceding vowel
H	h	h in *have*
I	ı	i in *cousin*
İ	i	French i in *si*
J	j	French j
K	k	c in *cat* or in *cure*
L	l	l in *list* or in *wool*
M	m	m

Geneva, MAH	Geneva, Musée d'Art et d'Histoire	Palermo, MAN	Palermo, Museo Archeologico Nazionale
Ger.	German	Paris, BN	Paris, Bibliothèque Nationale
Gk.	Greek	Paris, CM	Paris, Cabinet des Médailles
Hamburg, MKG	Hamburg, Museum für Kunst und Gewerbe	Paris, LV	Paris, Louvre
		pl.	plate
Hanover, KM	Hanover, Kestner-Museum	plur.	plural
HS	sesterces	pon. max.	pontifex maximus
Imp.	Imperator	pr(aef).	praefatio
inventory no.	inventory number	praef.	praefectus
		procos.	proconsul
Istanbul, AM	Istanbul, Archaeological Museum	procur.	procurator
		propr.	propraetor
itin.	itineraria	Ps.-	Pseudo
Kassel, SK	Kassel, Staatliche Kunstsammlungen	Q.	Quintus
l.	lex	qu.	quaestor
l.	line	r	recto
L.	Lucius	rev.	revised
l.c.	loco citato	Rome, MC	Rome, Museo Capitolino
Lat.	Latin	Rome, MN	Rome, Museo Nazionale
leg.	leges	Rome, VA	Rome, Villa Albani
lib.	liber, libri	Rome, VG	Rome, Villa Giulia
ling.	linguistic(ally)	Rome, MV	Rome, Museo Vaticano
loc.	locative	S.	Sextus
London, BM	London, British Museum	s.v.	sub voce
		SC	senatus consultum
M'.	Manius	sc.	scilicet
M.	Marcus	schol.	scholion, scholia
Madrid, PR	Madrid, Prado	Ser.	Servius
Malibu, GM	Malibu, Getty Museum	serm.	sermo
		s(in)g.	singular
masc.	masculinum, masculine	Sp.	Spurius
Moscow, PM	Moscow, Pushkin Museum	St.	Saint
		St. Petersburg, HR	St. Petersburg, Hermitage
MS(S)	manuscript(s)	T.	Titus
Munich, GL	Munich, Glyptothek	t.t.	terminus technicus
Munich, SA	Munich, Staatliche Antikensammlung	The Hague, MK	The Hague, Muntenkabinet
Munich, SM	Munich, Staatliche Münzsammlung	Thessaloniki, NM	Thessaloniki, National Museum
Mus.	Museum, Musée, Museo		
N.	Numerius	Ti., Tib.	Tiberius
n.d.	no date	tit.	titulus
Naples, MN	Naples, Museo Nazionale	tr. mil.	tribunus militum
neutr.	neutrum, neuter, neutral	tr. pl.	tribunus plebis
New York, MMA	New York, Metropolitan Museum of Arts	Univ.	Universität, University, Université, Università
no.	number	v.	verse
nom.	nominative	v	verso
NT	New Testament	Vienna, KM	Vienna, Kunsthistorisches Museum
Op., Opp.	Opus, Opera	vir clar.	vir clarissimus
opt.	optative	vir ill.	vir illustris
OT	Old Testament	vir spect.	vir spectabilis
Oxford, AM	Oxford, Ashmolean Museum	vol.	volume
p.	page		
P	Papyrus		
P.	Publius		

3. Abbreviations used in the Bibliographies

This list contains abbreviations of English, German, French, Italian and Latin words used in the bibliographies.

Abh.	Abhandlung
Acad.	Academia, Académie, Academy
Act.	acta, acts, actes
Akad.	Akademie
Akt.	Akten
Alt.	Altertum
ant.	antike
Anz.	Anzeiger
app./App.	appendix, appendices/Appendizes
Arch./arch.	Archäologie/archäologisch
archa.	archaisch
AT	altes Testament
att.	attisch
Bed.	Bedeutung
Beih.	Beiheft
Beil.	Beilage
Beitr.	Beitrag
Ber.	Bericht
Bull.	Bulletin, Bullettino
byz.	byzantin(ist)isch
Cat.	Catalogue, Catalogo
Cod.	Codex, Codices, Codizes
Coll.	Collectio
Congr.	Congress, Congrès, Congresso
Const.	Constitutio
Corp.	Corporation
Diss.	Dissertation
dor.	dorisch
ed.	edidit, editio, editor, edited (by)
edd.	ediderunt
edn.	edition
Einf.	Einführung
Ergbd.	Ergänzungsband
Ergh.	Ergänzungsheft
ES	Einzelschrift
Ét.	Études
Etym.	Etymologie
exc.	excerpta
Festg.	Festgabe
Forsch.	Forschung(en)
FS	Festschrift
Geogr.	Geographie
Ges.	Gesellschaft
Gesch.	Geschichte
Gramm.	Grammatik
gloss.	glossaria
gr(iech).	griechisch
GS	Gedenkschrift
H.	Heft
Hab.	Habilitation
Hdb.	Handbuch
hell.	hellenistisch
Hs.	Handschrift
HWB	Handwörterbuch
Inschr.	Inschrift
Inscr.	Inscriptiones
I(n)st(it).	Institut, Institute, Istituto
Jb.	Jahrbuch
Jbb.	Jahrbücher
Jh.	Jahrhundert
Journ.	Journal
Jt.	Jahrtausend
Kat.	Katalog
klass.	klassisch
Komm.	Kommentar
Kongr.	Kongreß
KS	Kleine Schriften
Lex.	Lexicon, Lexikon
MA	Mittelalter
Mél.	Mélanges
Mitt.	Mitteilungen
Nachr.	Nachrichten
N.S.	Neue Serie, New Series, Nouvelle Série, Nuova Seria
öst.	österreichisch
Proc.	Proceedings
Prov.	Provinz
Rel.	Religion
Rev.	Review, Revue
Rhet.	Rhetorik
Riv.	Rivista
repr.	reprint
röm.	römisch
SB	Sitzungsbericht
Ser.	Serie, Series, Série, Seria
Soc.	Society, Societé, Società
Stud.	Studia, Studien, Studies, Studi
suppl./Suppl.	supplement/Supplement
suppl. vol(s)	supplementary volume(s)
Top.	Topographie
tract.	tractatus
Trag.	Tragödie, Tragiker
trans.	translation, translated (by)
Übers.	Übersetzung, übersetzt
Unt.	Untersuchung
Verh.	Verhandlung
WB	Wörterbuch
wiss.	wissenschaftlich
Zschr.	Zeitschrift

4. Bibliographic Abbreviations

A&A
  Antike und Abendland
A&R
  Atene e Roma
AA
  Archäologischer Anzeiger
AAA
  Annals of Archaeology and Anthropology
AAAlg
  S. GSELL, Atlas archéologique de l'Algérie. Édition spéciale des cartes au 200.000 du Service Géographique de l' Armée, 1911, repr. 1973
AAHG
  Anzeiger für die Altertumswissenschaften, publication of the Österreichische Humanistische Gesellschaft
AArch
  Acta archeologica
AASO
  The Annual of the American Schools of Oriental Research
AATun 050
  E. BABELON, R. CAGNAT, S. REINACH (ed.), Atlas archéologique de la Tunisie (1 : 50.000), 1893
AATun 100
  R. CAGNAT, A. MERLIN (ed.), Atlas archéologique de la Tunisie (1: 100.000), 1914
AAWG
  Abhandlungen der Akademie der Wissenschaften in Göttingen. Philologisch-historische Klasse
AAWM
  Abhandlungen der Akademie der Wissenschaften und Literatur in Mainz. Geistes- und sozialwissenschaftliche Klasse
AAWW
  Anzeiger der Österreichischen Akademie der Wissenschaften in Wien. Philosophisch-historische Klasse
ABAW
  Abhandlungen der Bayerischen Akademie der Wissenschaften. Philosophisch-historische Klasse
Abel
  F.-M. ABEL, Géographie de la Palestine 2 vols., 1933 – 38
ABG,
  Archiv für Begriffsgeschichte: Bausteine zu einem historischen Wörterbuch der Philosophie
ABr
  P. ARNDT, F. BRUCKMANN (ed.), Griechische und römische Porträts, 1891 – 1912; E. LIPPOLD (ed.), Text vol., 1958
ABSA
  Annual of the British School at Athens
AC
  L'Antiquité Classique
Acta
  Acta conventus neo-latini Lovaniensis, 1973

AD
  Archaiologikon Deltion
ADAIK
  Abhandlungen des Deutschen Archäologischen Instituts Kairo
Adam
  J.P. ADAM, La construction romaine. Matériaux et techniques, 1984
ADAW
  Abhandlungen der Deutschen Akademie der Wissenschaften zu Berlin. Klasse für Sprachen, Literatur und Kunst
ADB
  Allgemeine Deutsche Biographie
AdI
  Annali dell'Istituto di Corrispondenza Archeologica
AE
  L'Année épigraphique
AEA
  Archivo Espanol de Arqueología
AEM
  Archäologisch-epigraphische Mitteilungen aus Österreich
AfO
  Archiv für Orientforschung
AGD
  Antike Gemmen in deutschen Sammlungen 4 vols., 1968–75
AGM
  Archiv für Geschichte der Medizin
Agora
  The Athenian Agora. Results of the Excavations by the American School of Classical Studies of Athens, 1953 ff.
AGPh
  Archiv für Geschichte der Philosophie
AGR
  Akten der Gesellschaft für griechische und hellenistische Rechtsgeschichte
AHAW
  Abhandlungen der Heidelberger Akademie der Wissenschaften. Philosophisch-historische Klasse
AHES
  Archive for History of Exact Sciences
AIHS
  Archives internationales d'histoire des sciences
AION
  Annali del Seminario di Studi del Mondo Classico, Sezione di Archeologia e Storia antica
AJ
  The Archaeological Journal of the Royal Archaeological Institute of Great Britain and Ireland
AJA
  American Journal of Archaeology
AJAH
  American Journal of Ancient History

AJBA
  Australian Journal of Biblical Archaeology
AJN
  American Journal of Numismatics
AJPh
  American Journal of Philology
AK
  Antike Kunst
AKG
  Archiv für Kulturgeschichte
AKL
  G. MEISSNER (ed.), Allgemeines Künsterlexikon: Die
  bildenden Künstler aller Zeiten und Völker, ²1991
  ff.
AKM
  Abhandlungen für die Kunde des Morgenlandes
Albrecht
  M. v. ALBRECHT, Geschichte der römischen Litera-
  tur, ²1994
Alessio
  G. ALESSIO, Lexicon etymologicum. Supplemento ai
  Dizionari etimologici latini e romanzi, 1976
Alexander
  M.C. ALEXANDER, Trials in the Late Roman Repub-
  lic: 149 BC to 50 BC (Phoenix Suppl. Vol. 26), 1990
Alföldi
  A. ALFÖLDI, Die monarchische Repräsentation im
  römischen Kaiserreiche, 1970, repr. ³1980
Alföldy, FH
  G. ALFÖLDY, Fasti Hispanienses. Senatorische
  Reichsbeamte und Offiziere in den spanischen Pro-
  vinzen des römischen Reiches von Augustus bis Dio-
  kletian, 1969
Alföldy, Konsulat
  G. ALFÖLDY, Konsulat und Senatorenstand unter
  den Antoninen. Prosopographische Untersuchungen
  zur senatorischen Führungsschicht (Antiquitas 1,
  27), 1977
Alföldy, RG
  G. ALFÖLDY, Die römische Gesellschaft. Ausge-
  wählte Beiträge, 1986
Alföldy, RH
  G. ALFÖLDY, Römische Heeresgeschichte, 1987
Alföldy, RS
  G. ALFÖLDY, Römische Sozialgeschichte, ³1984
ALLG
  Archiv für lateinische Lexikographie und Gramma-
  tik
Altaner
  B. ALTANER, Patrologie. Leben, Schriften und Lehre
  der Kirchenväter, ⁹1980
AMI
  Archäologische Mitteilungen aus Iran
Amyx, Addenda
  C.W. NEEFT, Addenda et Corrigenda to D.A. Amyx,
  Corinthian Vase-Painting, 1991
Amyx, CVP
  D.A. AMYX, Corinthian Vase-Painting of the Ar-
  chaic Period 3 vols., 1988

Anadolu
  Anadolu (Anatolia)
Anatolica
  Anatolica
AncSoc
  Ancient Society
Anderson
  J.G. ANDERSON, A Journey of Exploration in Pontus
  (Studia pontica 1), 1903
Anderson Cumont/Grégoire
  J.G. ANDERSON, F. CUMONT, H. GRÉGOIRE, Recueil
  des inscriptions grecques et latines du Pont et de l'Ar-
  ménie (Studia pontica 3), 1910
André, botan.
  J. ANDRÉ, Lexique des termes de botanique en latin,
  1956
André, oiseaux
  J. ANDRÉ, Les noms d'oiseaux en latin, 1967
André, plantes
  J. ANDRÉ, Les noms de plantes dans la Rome an-
  tique, 1985
Andrews
  K. ANDREWS, The Castles of Morea, 1953
ANET
  J.B. PRITCHARD, Ancient Near Eastern Texts Relat-
  ing to the Old Testament, ³1969, repr. 1992
AnnSAAt
  Annuario della Scuola Archeologica di Atene
ANRW
  H. TEMPORINI, W. HAASE (ed.), Aufstieg und Nie-
  dergang der römischen Welt, 1972 ff.
ANSMusN
  Museum Notes. American Numismatic Society
AntAfr
  Antiquités africaines
AntChr
  Antike und Christentum
AntPl
  Antike Plastik
AO
  Der Alte Orient
AOAT
  Alter Orient und Altes Testament
APF
  Archiv für Papyrusforschung und verwandte Gebie-
  te
APh
  L'Année philologique
Arangio-Ruiz
  V. ARANGIO-RUIZ, Storia del diritto romano, ⁶1953
Arcadia
  Arcadia. Zeitschrift für vergleichende Literaturwis-
  senschaft
ArchCl
  Archeologia Classica
ArchE
  Archaiologike ephemeris
ArcheologijaSof
  Archeologija. Organ na Archeologiceskija institut i
  muzej pri B'lgarskata akademija na naukite

ArchHom
    Archaeologia Homerica, 1967ff.
ArtAntMod
    Arte antica e moderna
ARW
    Archiv für Religionswissenschaft
AS
    Anatolian Studies
ASAA
    Annuario della Scuola Archeologica di Atene e delle
    Missioni italiane in Oriente
ASL
    Archiv für das Studium der neueren Sprachen und
    Literaturen
ASNP
    Annali della Scuola Normale Superiore di Pisa, Clas-
    se di Lettere e Filosofia
ASpr
    Die Alten Sprachen
ASR
    B. ANDREAE (ed.), Die antiken Sarkophagreliefs,
    1952 ff.
Athenaeum
    Athenaeum
ATL
    B.D. MERITT, H.T. WADE-GERY, M.F. McGRECOR,
    Athenian Tribute Lists 4 vols., 1939–53
AU
    Der altsprachliche Unterricht
Aulock
    H. v. AULOCK, Münzen und Städte Pisidiens
    (MDAI(Ist) Suppl. 8) 2 vols., 1977–79
Austin
    C. AUSTIN (ed.), Comicorum graecorum fragmenta
    in papyris reperta, 1973
BA
    Bolletino d'Arte del Ministero della Publica Istruzi-
    one
BAB
    Bulletin de l'Académie Royale de Belgique. Classe
    des Lettres
BABesch
    Bulletin antieke beschaving. Annual Papers on Clas-
    sical Archaeology
Badian, Clientelae
    E. BADIAN, Foreign Clientelae, 1958
Badian, Imperialism
    E. BADIAN, Roman Imperialism in the Late Repub-
    lic, 1967
BaF
    Baghdader Forschungen
Bagnall
    R.S. BAGNALL ET AL., Consuls of the Later Roman
    Empire (Philological Monographs of the American
    Philological Association 36), 1987
BalkE
    Balkansko ezikoznanie
BalkSt
    Balkan Studies

BaM
    Baghdader Mitteilungen
Bardenhewer, GAL
    O. BARDENHEWER, Geschichte der altkirchlichen Li-
    teratur, Vols. 1–2, ²1913 f.; Vols. 3–5, 1912–32;
    repr. Vols. 1–5, 1962
Bardenhewer, Patr.
    O. BARDENHEWER, Patrologie, ³1910
Bardon
    H. BARDON, La littérature latine inconnue 2 vols.,
    1952 – 56
Baron
    W. BARON (ed.), Beiträge zur Methode der Wissen-
    schaftsgeschichte, 1967
BASO
    Bulletin of the American Schools of Oriental Rese-
    arch
Bauer/Aland
    W. BAUER, K. ALAND (ed.), Griechisch-deutsches
    Wörterbuch zu den Schriften des Neuen Testamen-
    tes und der frühchristlichen Literatur, ⁶1988
Baumann, LRRP
    R.A. BAUMAN, Lawyers in Roman Republican Poli-
    tics. A study of the Roman Jurists in their Political
    Setting, 316–82 BC (Münchener Beiträge zur Papy-
    rusforschung und antiken Rechtsgeschichte), 1983
Baumann, LRTP
    R.A. BAUMAN, Lawyers in Roman Transitional Poli-
    tics. A Study of the Roman Jurists in their Political
    Setting in the Late Republic and Triumvirate (Mün-
    chener Beiträge zur Papyrusforschung und antiken
    Rechtsgeschichte), 1985
BB
    Bezzenbergers Beiträge zur Kunde der indogerma-
    nischen Sprachen
BCAR
    Bollettino della Commissione Archeologica Comu-
    nale di Roma
BCH
    Bulletin de Correspondance Hellénique
BE
    Bulletin épigraphique
Beazley, ABV
    J.D. BEAZLEY, Attic Black-figure Vase-Painters,
    1956
Beazley, Addenda²
    TH.H. CARPENTER (ed.), Beazley Addenda, ²1989
Beazley, ARV²
    J.D. BEAZLEY, Attic Red-figure Vase-Painters,
    ²1963
Beazley, EVP
    J.D. BEAZLEY, Etruscan Vase Painting, 1947
Beazley, Paralipomena
    J.D. BEAZLEY, Paralipomena. Additions to Attic
    Black-figure Vase-Painters and to Attic Red-figure
    Vase-Painters, ²1971
Bechtel, Dial.¹
    F. BECHTEL, Die griechischen Dialekte 3 vols.,
    1921–24

Bechtel, Dial.²
F. BECHTEL, Die griechischen Dialekte 3 vols.,
⁴1963
Bechtel, HPN
F. BECHTEL, Die historischen Personennamen des
Griechischen bis zur Kaiserzeit, 1917
Belke
K. BELKE, Galatien und Lykaonien (Denkschriften
der Österreichischen Akademie der Wissenschaften,
Philosophisch-Historische Klasse 172; TIB 4), 1984
Belke/Mersich
K. BELKE, N. MERSICH, Phrygien und Pisidien
(Denkschriften der Österreichischen Akademie der
Wissenschaften, Philosophisch-Historische Klasse
211; TIB 7), 1990
Bell
K.E. BELL, Place-Names in Classical Mythology,
Greece, 1989
Beloch, Bevölkerung
K.J. BELOCH, Die Bevölkerung der griechisch-römi-
schen Welt, 1886
Beloch, GG
K.J. BELOCH, Griechische Geschichte 4 vols.,
²1912–27, repr. 1967
Beloch, RG
K.J. BELOCH, Römische Geschichte bis zum Beginn
der Punischen Kriege, 1926
Bengtson
H. BENGTSON, Die Strategie in der hellenistischen
Zeit. Ein Beitrag zum antiken Staatsrecht (Münche-
ner Beiträge zur Papyrusforschung und antiken
Rechtsgeschichte 26, 32, 36) 3 vols., 1937–52, ed.
repr. 1964–67
Berger
E.H. BERGER, Geschichte der wissenschaftlichen
Erdkunde der Griechen, ²1903
Berve
H. BERVE, Das Alexanderreich auf prosopographi-
scher Grundlage, 1926
Beyen
H. G. BEYEN, Die pompejanische Wanddekoration
vom zweiten bis zum vierten Stil 2 vols., 1938–60
BFC
Bolletino di filologia classica
BGU
Ägyptische (Griechische) Urkunden aus den Kaiser-
lichen (from Vol. 6 on Staatlichen) Museen zu Berlin
13 vols., 1895–1976
BHM
Bulletin of the History of Medicine
BIAO
Bulletin de l'Institut français d'Archéologie Orien-
tale
BiblH&R
Bibliothèque d'Humanisme et Renaissance
BiblLing
Bibliographie linguistique / Linguistic Bibliography
BIBR
Bulletin de l'Institut Belge de Rome

Bickerman
E. BICKERMANN, Chronologie (Einleitung in die Al-
tertumswissenschaft III 5), 1933
BICS
Bulletin of the Institute of Classical Studies of the
University of London
BIES
The Bulletin of the Israel Exploration Society
BiogJahr
Biographisches Jahrbuch für Altertumskunde
Birley
A.R. BIRLEY, The Fasti of Roman Britain, 1981
BJ
Bonner Jahrbücher des Rheinischen Landesmuse-
ums in Bonn und des Vereins von Altertumsfreunden
im Rheinlande
BKT
Berliner Klassikertexte 8 vols., 1904–39
BKV
Bibliothek der Kirchenväter (Kempten ed.) 63 vols.,
²1911–31
Blänsdorf
J. BLÄNSDORF (ed.), Theater und Gesellschaft im Im-
perium Romanum, 1990
Blass
F. BLASS, Die attische Beredsamkeit, 3 vols.,
³1887–98, repr. 1979
Blass/Debrunner/Rehkopf
F. BLASS, A. DEBRUNNER, F. REHKOPF, Grammatik
des neutestamentlichen Griechisch, ¹⁵1979
Blümner, PrAlt.
H. BLÜMNER, Die römischen Privataltertümer
(HdbA IV 2, 2), ³1911
Blümner, Techn.
H. BLÜMNER, Technologie und Terminologie der
Gewerbe und Künste bei Griechen und Römern,
Vol. 1, ²1912; Vols. 2–4, 1875–87, repr. 1969
BMC, Gr
A Catalogue of the Greek Coins in the British Mu-
seum 29 vols., 1873–1965
BMCByz
W. WROTH (ed.), Catalogue of the Imperial Byzan-
tine Coins in the British Museum 2 vols., 1908, repr.
1966
BMCIR
Bryn Mawr Classical Review
BMCRE
H. MATTINGLY (ed.), Coins of the Roman Empire in
the British Museum 6 vols., 1962–76
BMCRR
H.A. GRUEBER (ed.), Coins of the Roman Republic
in the British Museum 3 vols., 1970
BN
Beiträge zur Namensforschung
Bolgar, Culture 1
R. BOLGAR, Classical Influences on European Cul-
ture A.D. 500 – 1500, 1971
Bolgar, Culture 2
R. BOLGAR, Classical Influences on European Cul-
ture A.D. 1500–1700, 1974

Bolgar, Thought
R. BOLGAR, Classical Influences on Western Thought A.D. 1650–1870, 1977

Bon
A. BON, La Morée franque 2 vols., 1969

Bonner
S.F. BONNER, Education in Ancient Rome, 1977

Bopearachchi
O. BOPEARACHCHI, Monnaies gréco-bactriennes et indo-grecques. Catalogue raisonné, 1991

Borinski
K. BORINSKI, Die Antike in Poetik und Kunsttheorie vom Ausgang des klassischen Altertums bis auf Goethe und Wilhelm von Humboldt 2 vols., 1914–24, repr. 1965

Borza
E.N. BORZA, In the shadow of Olympus. The emergence of Macedon, 1990

Bouché-Leclerq
A. BOUCHÉ-LECLERQ, Histoire de la divination dans l'antiquité 3 vols., 1879–82, repr. 1978 in 4 vols.

BPhC
Bibliotheca Philologica Classica

BrBr
H. BRUNN, F. BRUCKMANN, Denkmäler griechischer und römischer Skulpturen, 1888–1947

BRGK
Bericht der Römisch-Germanischen Kommission des Deutschen Archäologischen Instituts

Briggs/Calder
W.W. BRIGGS, W.M. CALDER III, Classical Scholarship. A Biographical Encyclopedia, 1990

Bruchmann
C.F.H. BRUCHMANN, Epitheta deorum quae apud poetas graecos leguntur, 1893

Brugmann/Delbrück
K. BRUGMANN, B. DELBRÜCK, Grundriß der vergleichenden Grammatik der indogermanischen Sprachen, Vols. 1–2, 1897–1916; Vols. 3–5, 1893–1900

Brugmann /Thumb
K. BRUGMANN, A. THUMB (ed.), Griechische Grammatik, ⁴1913

Brunhölzl
F. BRUNHÖLZL, Geschichte der lateinischen Literatur des Mittelalters 2 vols., 1975–92

Brunt
P.A. BRUNT, Italian Manpower 222 B. C. – A. D. 14, 1971

Bruun
C. BRUUN, The Water Supply of Ancient Rome. A Study of Imperial Administration (Commentationes Humanarum Litterarum 93), 1991

Bryer/Winfield
A. BRYER, D. WINFIELD, The Byzantine Monuments and Topography of Pontus (Dumbarton Oaks Studies 20) 2 vols., 1985

BSABR
Bulletin de Liaison de la Société des Amis de la Bibliothèque Salomon Reinach

BSL
Bulletin de la Société de Linguistique de Paris

BSO(A)S
Bulletin of the School of Oriental (from Vol. 10 ff. and African) Studies

BTCGI
G. NENCI (ed.), Bibliografia topografica della colonizzazione greca in Italia e nelle isole tirreniche, 1980 ff.

Buck
A. BUCK (ed.), Die Rezeption der Antike, 1981

Burkert
W. BURKERT, Griechische Religion der archaischen und klassischen Epoche, 1977

Busolt/Swoboda
G. BUSOLT, H. SWOBODA, Griechische Staatskunde (HdbA IV 1, 1) 2 vols., ³1920–26, repr. 1972–79

BWG
Berichte zur Wissenschaftsgeschichte

BWPr
Winckelmanns-Programm der Archäologischen Gesellschaft zu Berlin

Byzantion
Byzantion. Revue internationale des études byzantines

ByzF
Byzantinische Forschungen. Internationale Zeitschrift für Byzantinistik

ByzZ
Byzantinische Zeitschrift

Caballos
A. CABALLOS, Los senadores hispanoromanos y la romanización de Hispania (Siglos I al III p.C.), Vol. 1: Prosopografia (Monografias del Departamento de Historia Antigua de la Universidad de Sevilla 5), 1990

CAF
T. KOCK (ed.), Comicorum Atticorum Fragmenta, 3 vols., 1880–88

CAG
Commentaria in Aristotelem Graeca 18 vols., 1885–1909

CAH
The Cambridge Ancient History 12 text- and 5 ill. vols., 1924–39 (Vol. 1 as 2nd ed.), vols. 1–2, ³1970–75; vols. 3,1 and 3,3 ff., ²1982 ff.; vol. 3,2, ¹1991

Carney
T.F. CARNEY, Bureaucracy in Traditional Society. Romano-Byzantine Bureaucracies Viewed from Within, 1971

Cartledge/Millett/Todd
P. CARTLEDGE, P. MILLETT, S. TODD (ed.), Nomos, Essays in Athenian Law, Politics and Society, 1990

Cary
M. CARY, The Geographical Background of Greek and Roman History, 1949

Casson, Ships
L. CASSON, Ships and Seamanship in the Ancient World, 1971

Casson, Trade
  L. CASSON, Ancient Trade and Society, 1984
CAT
  Catalogus Tragicorum et Tragoediarum (in TrGF
  Vol. 1)
CatLitPap
  H.J.M. MILNE (ed.), Catalogue of the Literary Pa-
  pyri in the British Museum, 1927
CCAG
  F. CUMONT ET AL. (ed.), Catalogus Codicum As-
  trologorum Graecorum 12 vols. in 20 parts, 1898–
  1940
CCL
  Corpus Christianorum. Series Latina, 1954 ff.
CE
  Cronache Ercolanesi
CEG
  P.A. HANSEN (ed.), Carmina epigraphica Graeca
  (Texts and Commentary 12; 15), 1983 ff.
CeM
  Classica et Mediaevalia
CGF
  G. KAIBEL (ed.), Comicorum Graecorum Fragmen-
  ta, ²1958
CGL
  G. GÖTZ (ed.), Corpus glossariorum Latinorum, 7
  vols., 1888–1923, repr. 1965
Chantraine
  P. CHANTRAINE, Dictionnaire étymologique de la
  langue grecque 4 vols., 1968–80
CHCL-G
  E.J. KENNEY (ed.), The Cambridge History of Clas-
  sical Literature. Greek Literature, 1985 ff.
CHCL-L
  E.J. KENNEY (ed.), The Cambridge History of Clas-
  sical Literature. Latin Literature, 1982 ff.
Chiron
  Chiron. Mitteilungen der Kommission für alte Ge-
  schichte und Epigraphik des Deutschen Archäolo-
  gischen Instituts
Christ
  K. CHRIST, Geschichte der römischen Kaiserzeit von
  Augustus bis zu Konstantin, 1988
Christ, RGG
  K. CHRIST, Römische Geschichte und deutsche Ge-
  schichtswissenschaft, 1982
Christ, RGW
  K. CHRIST, Römische Geschichte und Wissen-
  schaftsgeschichte 3 vols., 1982–83
Christ/Momigliano
  K. CHRIST, A. MOMIGLIANO, Die Antike im 19.
  Jahrhundert in Italien und Deutschland, 1988
CIA
  A. KIRCHHOFF ET AL. (ed.), Corpus Inscriptionum
  Atticarum, 1873; Suppl.: 1877–91
CIC
  Corpus Iuris Canonici 2 vols., 1879–81, repr. 1959
CID
  Corpus des inscriptions de Delphes 3 vols., 1977–92

CIE
  C. PAULI (ed.), Corpus Inscriptionum Etruscarum,
  Vol. 1–2, 1893–1921; Vol. 3,1 ff., 1982 ff.
CIG
  Corpus Inscriptionum Graecarum 4 vols., 1828–77
CIL
  Corpus Inscriptionum Latinarum, 1863 ff.
CIL III Add.
  M. SASEL-KOS, Inscriptiones latinae in Graecia re-
  pertae. Additamenta ad CIL III (Epigrafia e antichità
  5), 1979
CIRB
  Corpus Inscriptionum regni Bosporani, 1965
CIS
  Corpus Inscriptionum Semiticarum 5 parts, 1881–
  1951
CJ
  Classical Journal
CL
  Cultura Neolatina
Clairmont
  C.W. CLAIRMONT, Attic Classical Tombstones 7
  vols., 1993
Clauss
  M. CLAUSS, Der magister officiorum in der Spätan-
  tike (4.–6. Jahrhundert). Das Amt und sein Einfluß
  auf die kaiserliche Politik (Vestigia 32), 1981
CLE
  F. BÜCHELER, E. LOMMATZSCH (ed.), Carmina La-
  tina Epigraphica (Anthologia latina 2) 3 vols.,
  1895–1926
CM
  Clio Medica. Acta Academiae historiae medicinae
CMA
  Cahiers de l'Institut du Moyen Age grec et latin
CMB
  W.M. CALDER III, D.J. KRAMER, An Introductory
  Bibliography to the History of Classical Scholarship,
  Chiefly in the XIXth and XXth Centuries, 1992
CMG
  Corpus Medicorum Graecorum, 1908 ff.
CMIK
  J. CHADWICK, Corpus of Mycenaean Inscriptions
  from Knossos (Incunabula Graeca 88), 1986 ff.
CML
  Corpus Medicorum Latinorum, 1915 ff.
CMS
  F. MATZ ET AL. (ed.), Corpus der minoischen und
  mykenischen Siegel, 1964 ff.
CodMan
  Codices manuscripti. Zeitschrift für Handschriften-
  kunde
Coing
  H. COING, Europäisches Privatrecht 2 vols., 1985–
  89
CollAlex
  I.U. POWELL (ed.), Collectanea Alexandrina, 1925
CollRau
  J. v. UNGERN-STERNBERG (ed.), Colloquia Raurica,
  1988 ff.

Conway/Johnson /Whatmough
  R.S. CONWAY, S.E. JOHNSON, J. WHATMOUGH, The Prae-Italic dialects of Italy 3 vols., 1933, repr. 1968
Conze
  A. CONZE, Die attischen Grabreliefs 4 vols., 1893–1922
Courtney
  E. COURTNEY, The Fragmentary Latin Poets, 1993
CPF
  F. ADORNO (ed.), Corpus dei Papiri Filosofici greci e latini, 1989 ff.
CPG
  M. GEERARD (Vols. 1–5), F. GLORIE, (Vol. 5), Clavis patrum graecorum 5 vols., 1974–87
CPh
  Classical Philology
CPL
  E. DEKKERS, A. GAAR, Clavis patrum latinorum (CCL), ³1995
CQ
  Classical Quarterly
CR
  Classical Review
CRAI
  Comptes rendus des séances de l'Académie des inscriptions et belles-lettres
CRF
  O. RIBBECK (ed.), Comicorum Romanorum Fragmenta, 1871, repr. 1962
CSCT
  Columbia Studies in the Classical Tradition
CSE
  Corpus Speculorum Etruscorum, 1990 ff.
CSEL
  Corpus Scriptorum ecclesiasticorum Latinorum, 1866 ff.
SCIR
  Corpus Signorum Imperii Romani, 1963 ff.
Cumont, Pont
  F. CUMONT, E. CUMONT, Voyage d'exploration archéologique dans le Pont et la Petite Arménie (Studia pontica 2), 1906
Cumont, Religions
  F. CUMONT, Les Religions orientales dans le paganisme romain, ³1929, repr. 1981
Curtius
  E.R. CURTIUS, Europäische Literatur und lateinisches Mittelalter, ¹¹1993
CVA
  Corpus Vasorum Antiquorum, 1923 ff.
CW
  The Classical World
D'Arms
  J.H. D'ARMS, Commerce and Social Standing in Ancient Rome, 1981
D'Arms/Kopff
  J.H. D'ARMS, E.C. KOPFF (ed.), The Seaborne Commerce of Ancient Rome: Studies in Archaeology and History (Memoirs of the American Academy in Rome 36), 1980

Dacia
  Dacia. Revue d'archéologie et d'histoire ancienne
Davies
  J.K. DAVIES, Athenian Propertied Families 600–300 BC, 1971
DB
  F. VIGOUROUX (ed.), Dictionnaire de la Bible, 1881 ff.
DCPP
  E. LIPIŃSKI ET AL. (ed.), Dictionnaire de la Civilisation Phénicienne et Punique, 1992
Degrassi, FCap.
  A. DEGRASSI, Fasti Capitolini (Corpus scriptorum Latinorum Paravianum), 1954
Degrassi, FCIR
  A. DEGRASSI, I Fasti consolari dell'Impero Romano, 1952
Deichgräber
  K. DEICHGRÄBER, Die griechische Empirikerschule, 1930
Delmaire
  R. DELMAIRE, Les responsables des finances impériales au Bas-Empire romain (IVᵉ-VIᵉ s). Études prosopographiques (Collection Latomus 203), 1989
Demandt
  A. DEMANDT, Der Fall Roms: die Auflösung des römischen Reiches im Urteil der Nachwelt, 1984
Demougin
  S. DEMOUGIN, Prosopographie des Chevaliers romains Julio-Claudiens (43 av.J -C.–70 ap.J.-C.) (Collection de l'École Française de Rome 153), 1992
Deubner
  L. DEUBNER, Attische Feste, 1932
Develin
  R. DEVELIN, Athenian Officials 684–321 B.C. 1949
Devijver
  H. DEVIJVER, Prosopographia militiarum equestrium quae fuerunt ab Augusto ad Gallienum (Symbolae Facultatis Litterarum et Philosophiae Lovaniensis Ser. A 3) 3 vols., 1976–80; 2 Suppl. Vols.: 1987–93
DHA
  Dialogues d'histoire ancienne
DHGE
  A. BAUDRILLART, R. AUBERT (ed.), Dictionnaire d'Histoire et de Géographie Ecclésiastiques 1912 ff.
DID
  Didascaliae Tragicae/Ludorum Tragicorum (in TrGF Vol. 1)
Diels, DG
  H. DIELS, Doxographi Graeci, 1879
Diels/Kranz
  H. DIELS, W. KRANZ (ed.), Fragmente der Vorsokratiker 3 vols., ⁹1951 f., repr. Vol.1, 1992; Vol. 2, 1985; Vol. 3, 1993
Dierauer
  U. DIERAUER, Tier und Mensch im Denken der Antike, 1977

Dietz
K. DIETZ, Senatus contra principem. Untersuchungen zur senatorischen Opposition gegen Kaiser Maximinus Thrax (Vestigia 29), 1980

Dihle
A. DIHLE, Die griechische und lateinische Literatur der Kaiserzeit: von Augustus bis Justinian, 1989

DiskAB
Diskussionen zur archäologischen Bauforschung, 1974 ff.

Dixon
S. DIXON, The Roman Family, 1992

DJD
Discoveries in the Judaean Desert, 1955 ff.

DLZ
Deutsche Literaturzeitung für Kritik der internationalen Wissenschaft

DMA
J.R. STRAYER ET AL. (ed.), Dictionary of the Middle Ages 13 vols., 1982–89

Dmic
F. AURA JORRO, Diccionario Micénico, 1985

Dörrie/Baltes
H. DÖRRIE, M. BALTES (ed.), Der Platonismus in der Antike, 1987 ff.

Domaszewski
A.V. DOMASZEWSKI, Aufsätze zur römischen Heeresgeschichte, 1972

Domaszewski /Dobson
A.V. DOMASZEWSKI, B. DOBSON, Die Rangordnung des römischen Heeres, ²1967

Domergue
C. DOMERGUE, Les mines de la péninsule Iberique dans l'Antiquité Romaine, 1990

Drumann /Groebe
W. DRUMANN, P. GROEBE (ed.), Geschichte Roms in seinem Übergange von der republikanischen zur monarchischen Verfassung 6 vols., 1899–1929, repr. 1964

DS
C. DAREMBERG, E. SAGLIO (ed.), Dictionnaire des antiquités grecques et romaines d'après les textes et les monuments 6 vols., 1877–1919, repr. 1969

Dulckeit /Schwarz /Waldstein
G. DULCKEIT, F. SCHWARZ, W. WALDSTEIN, Römische Rechtsgeschichte. Ein Studienbuch (Juristische Kurz Lehrbücher), 1995

Dumézil
G. DUMÉZIL, La religion romaine archaïque, suivi d'un appendice sur la religion des Etrusques, 1974

Duncan-Jones, Economy
R. DUNCAN-JONES, The Economy of the Roman Empire. Quantitative Studies, 1974

Duncan-Jones, Structure
R. DUNCAN-JONES, Structure and Scale in the Roman Economy, 1990

DVjS
Deutsche Vierteljahrsschrift für Literaturwissenschaft und Geistesgeschichte

EA
Epigraphica Anatolica. Zeitschrift für Epigraphik und historische Geographie Anatoliens

EAA
R. BIANCHI BANDINELLI (ed.), Enciclopedia dell'arte antica classica e orientale, 1958 ff.

EB
G. CAMPS, Encyclopédie Berbère 1984 ff.

Ebert
F. EBERT, Fachausdrücke des griechischen Bauhandwerks, Vol. 1: Der Tempel, 1910

EC
Essays in Criticism

Eck
W. ECK, Die Statthalter der germanischen Provinzen vom 1.–3. Jahrhundert (Epigraphische Studien 14), 1985

Eckstein
F.A. ECKSTEIN, Nomenclator philologorum, 1871

Edelstein, AM
L. EDELSTEIN, Ancient medicine, 1967

Edelstein, Asclepius
E.J. and L. EDELSTEIN, Asclepius. A Collection and Interpretation of the Testimonies, 1945

Eder, Demokratie
W. EDER (ed.), Die athenische Demokratie im 4. Jahrhundert v. Chr. Vollendung oder Verfall einer Verfassungsform? Akten eines Symposiums, 3. – 7. August 1992, 1995

Eder, Staat
W. EDER (ed.), Staat und Staatlichkeit in der frühen römischen Republik: Akten eines Symposiums, 12. – 15. Juli 1988, 1990

EDM
K. RANKE, W. BREDNICH (ed.), Enzyklopädie des Märchens. Handwörterbuch zur historischen und vergleichenden Erzählforschung, 1977 ff.

EDRL
A. BERGER, Encyclopedic Dictionary of Roman Law (TAPhA N.S. 43,2), 1953, repr. 1968

EEpigr
Ephemeris Epigraphica

EI
Encyclopaedia of Islam, 1960 ff.

Eissfeldt
O. EISSFELDT (ed.), Handbuch zum Alten Testament, ³1964 ff.

Emerita
Emerita. Revista de linguistica y filologia clasica

EncIr
E. YARSHATER (ed.), Encyclopaedia Iranica, 1985

Entretiens
Entretiens sur l'antiquité classique (Fondation Hardt)

EOS
Atti del Colloquio Internazionale AIEGL su Epigrafia e Ordine Senatorio: Roma, 14–20 maggio 1981, 2 vols., 1982

EpGF

M. DAVIES, Epicorum graecorum fragmenta, 1988

EpGr

G. KAIBEL (ed.), Epigrammata Graeca ex lapidibus conlecta, 1878

Epicurea

H. USENER (ed.), Epicurea, 1887, repr. 1963

EPRO

Études préliminaires aux religions orientales dans l'Empire Romain, 1961 ff.

Eranos

Eranos. Acta Philologica Suecana

Er-Jb

Eranos-Jahrbuch

Erasmus

Erasmus. Speculum Scientiarum. Internationales Literaturblatt der Geisteswissenschaften

Eretz Israel

Eretz-Israel, Archaeological, Historical and Geographical Studies

Ernout/Meillet

A. ERNOUT, A. MEILLET, Dictionnaire étymologique de la langue latine, ⁴1959

Errington

R.M. ERRINGTON, Geschichte Makedoniens. Von den Anfängen bis zum Untergang des Königreiches, 1986

ESAR

T. FRANK (ed.), An Economic Survey of Ancient Rome 6 vols., 1933–40

Espérandieu, Inscr.

E. ESPÉRANDIEU, Inscriptions latines de Gaule 2 vols., 1929–36

Espérandieu, Rec.

E. ESPÉRANDIEU, Recueil généneral des bas-reliefs, statues et bustes de la Gaule Romaine 16 vols., 1907–81

ET

H. RIX (ed.), Etruskische Texte (ScriptOralia 23, 24, Reihe A 6,7) 2 vols., 1991

ETAM

Ergänzungsbände zu den Tituli Asiae minoris, 1966 ff.

Euph.

Euphorion

EV

F. DELLA CORTE ET AL. (ed.), Enciclopedia Virgiliana 5 vols. in 6 parts, 1984–91

Evans

D.E. EVANS, Gaulish Personal names. A study of some continental Celtic formations, 1967

F&F

Forschungen und Fortschritte

Farnell, Cults

L.R. FARNELL, The Cults of the Greek States 5 vols., 1896–1909

Farnell, GHC

L.R. FARNELL, Greek Hero Cults and Ideas of Immortality, 1921

FCG

A. MEINEKE (ed.), Fragmenta Comicorum Graecorum 5 vols., 1839–57, repr. 1970

FCS

Fifteenth-Century Studies

FdD

Fouilles de Delphes, 1902 ff.

FGE

D.L. PAGE, Further Greek Epigrams, 1981

FGrH

F. JACOBY, Die Fragmente der griechischen Historiker, 3 parts in 14 vols., 1923–58, Part 1: ²1957

FHG

C. MÜLLER (ed.), Fragmenta Historicorum Graecorum 5 vols., 1841–1970

Fick/Bechtel

A. FICK, F. BECHTEL, Die griechischen Personennamen, ²1894

FiE

Forschungen in Ephesos, 1906 ff.

Filologia

La Filologia Greca e Latina nel secolo XX, 1989

Finley, Ancient Economy

M.I. FINLEY, The Ancient Economy, ²1984

Finley, Ancient Slavery

M.I. FINLEY, Ancient Slavery and Modern Ideology, 1980

Finley, Economy

M.I. FINLEY, B.D. SHAW, R.P. SALLER (ed.), Economy and Society in Ancient Greece, 1981

Finley, Property

M.I. FINLEY (ed.), Studies in Roman Property, 1976

FIRA

S. RICCOBONO, J. BAVIERA (ed.), Fontes iuris Romani anteiustiniani 3 vols., ²1968

FIRBruns

K.G. BRUNS, TH. MOMMSEN, O. GRADENWITZ (ed.), Fontes iuris Romani antiqui, 1909, repr. 1969

Fittschen/Zanker

K. FITTSCHEN, P. ZANKER, Katalog der römischen Porträts in den capitolinischen Museen und den anderen kommunalen Museen der Stadt Rom, 1983 ff.

Flach

D. FLACH, Römische Agrargeschichte (HdbA III 9), 1990

Flashar

H. FLASHAR, Inszenierung der Antike. Das griechische Drama auf der Bühne der Neuzeit, 1991

Flashar, Medizin

H. FLASHAR (ed.), Antike Medizin, 1971

FMS

Frühmittelalterliche Studien, Jahrbuch des Instituts für Frühmittelalter-Forschung der Universität Münster

Fossey

J.M. FOSSEY, Topography and Population of Ancient Boiotia, Vol. 1, 1988

FOst

L. VIDMANN, Fasti Ostienses, 1982

Fowler
  W.W. FOWLER, The Roman Festivals of the Period
  of the Republic. An Introduction to the Study of the
  Religion of the Romans, 1899
FPD
  I. PISO, Fasti Provinciae Daciae, Vol. 1: Die senato-
  rischen Amtsträger (Antiquitas 1,43), 1993
FPL
  W. MOREL, C. BÜCHNER (ed.), Fragmenta Poetarum
  Latinorum epicorum et lyricorum, ²1982
FPR
  A. BÄHRENS (ed.), Fragmenta Poetarum Romano-
  rum, 1886
Frazer
  J.G. FRAZER, The Golden Bough. A Study in Magic
  and Religion, 8 parts in 12 vols., Vols. 1–3, 5–9,
  ³1911–14; Vols. 4, 10–12, 1911–15
Frenzel
  E. FRENZEL, Stoffe der Weltliteratur, ⁸1992
Friedländer
  L. FRIEDLÄNDER, G. WISSOWA (ed.), Darstellungen
  aus der Sittengeschichte Roms 4 vols., ¹⁰1921–23
Frier, Landlords
  B.W. FRIER, Landlords and Tenants in Imperial Ro-
  me, 1980
Frier, PontMax
  B.W. FRIER, Libri annales pontificum maximorum.
  The origins of the Annalistic Tradition (Papers and
  Monographs of the American Academy in Rome
  27), 1979
Frisk
  H. FRISK, Griechisches etymologisches Wörterbuch
  (Indogermanische Bibliothek: Reihe 2) 3 vols.,
  1960–72
FRLANT
  Forschungen zur Religion und Literatur des Alten
  und Neuen Testaments
Fuchs/Floren
  W. FUCHS, J. FLOREN, Die Griechische Plastik, Vol.
  1: Die geometrische und archaische Plastik, 1987
Furtwängler
  A. FURTWÄNGLER, Die antiken Gemmen. Geschichte
  der Steinschneidekunst im klassischen Altertum 3
  vols., 1900
Furtwängler/Reichhold
  A. FURTWÄNGLER, K. REICHHOLD, Griechische Va-
  senmalerie 3 vols., 1904–32
Fushöller
  D. FUSHÖLLER, Tunesien und Ostalgerien in der Rö-
  merzeit, 1979
G&R
  Greece and Rome
GA
  A.S.F. GOW, D.L. PAGE, The Greek Anthology, Vol.
  1: Hellenistic Epigrams, 1965; Vol. 2: The Garland
  of Philip, 1968
Gardner
  P. GARDNER, A History of Ancient Coinage, 700–
  300 B.C., 1918

Gardthausen
  V. GARDTHAUSEN, Augustus und Seine Zeit, 2 parts
  in 6 vols., 1891–1904
Garnsey
  P. GARNSEY, Famine and Food Supply in the Graeco-
  Roman World. Responses to Risk and Crisis, 1988
Garnsey/Hopkins/Whittaker
  P. GARNSEY, K. HOPKINS, C.R. WHITTAKER (ed.),
  Trade in the Ancient Economy, 1983
Garnsey/Saller
  P. GARNSEY, R. SALLER, The Roman Empire, Econo-
  my, Society and Culture, 1987
GCS
  Die griechischen christlichen Schriftsteller der ersten
  Jahrhunderte, 1897 ff.
Gehrke
  H.-J. GEHRKE, Jenseits von Athen und Sparta. Das
  Dritte Griechenland und seine Staatenwelt, 1986
Gentili/Prato
  B. GENTILI, C. PRATO (ed.), Poetarum elegiacorum
  testimonia et fragmenta, Vol. 1, ²1988; Vol. 2, 1985
Georges
  K.E. GEORGES, Ausführliches lateinisch-deutsches
  Handwörterbuch 2 vols., ⁸1912–18, repr. 1992
Gérard-Rousseau
  M. GÉRARD-ROUSSEAU, Les mentions religieuses
  dans les tablettes mycéniennes, 1968
Germania
  Germania. Anzeiger der Römisch-Germanischen
  Kommission des Deutschen Archäologischen Insti-
  tuts
Gernet
  L. GERNET, Droit et société dans la Grèce ancienne
  (Institut de droit romain, Publication 13), 1955,
  repr. 1964
Geus
  K. GEUS, Prosopographie der literarisch bezeugten
  Karthager (Studia Phoenicia 13 Orientalia Lovani-
  ensia analecta 59), 1994
GGA
  Göttingische Gelehrte Anzeigen
GGM
  C. MÜLLER (ed.), Geographi Graeci Minores 2 vols.,
  Tabulae, 1855–61
GGPh¹
  F. ÜBERWEG (ed.), Grundriß der Geschichte der Phi-
  losophie; K, PRÄCHTER, Teil 1: Die Philosophie des
  Altertums, ¹²1926, repr. 1953
GGPh²
  W. OTTO, U. HAUSMANN (ed.), Grundriß der Ge-
  schichte der Philosophie; H. FLASHAR (ed.), vol. 3:
  Die Philosophie der Antike, 1983, vol. 4: Die helle-
  nistische Philosophie, 1994
GHW 1
  H. BENGTSON, V. MILOJCIC ET AL., Großer Histo-
  rischer Weltatlas des Bayrischen Schulbuchverlages
  1. Vorgeschichte und Altertum, ⁶1978
GHW 2
  J. ENGEL, W. MACER, A. BIRKEN ET AL., Großer His-

torischer Weltatlas des Bayrischen Schulbuchverlages 2. Mittelalter, ²1979

GIBM
C.T. NEWTON ET AL. (ed.), The Collection of Ancient Greek Inscriptions in the British Museum 4 vols., 1874–1916

Gillispie
C.C. GILLISPIE (ed.), Dictionary of scientific biography 14 vols. and index, 1970–80, repr. 1981; 2 Suppl. Vols., 1978–90

GL
H. KEIL (ed.), Grammatici Latini 7 vols., 1855–80

GLM
A. RIESE (ed.), Geographi Latini Minores, 1878

Glotta
Glotta. Zeitschrift für griechische und lateinische Sprache

GMth
F. ZAMINER (ed.), Geschichte der Musiktheorie, 1984 ff.

Gnomon
Gnomon. Kritische Zeitschrift für die gesamte klassische Altertumswissenschaft

Göbl
R. GÖBL, Antike Numismatik 2 vols., 1978

Goleniščev
I.N. GOLENIŠČEV-KUTUZOV, Il Rinascimento italiano e le letterature slave dei secoli XV e XVI, 1973

Gordon
A.E. GORDON, Album of Dated Latin Inscriptions 4 vols., 1958–65

Goulet
R. GOULET (ed.), Dictionnaire des philosophes antiques, 1989 ff.

Graf
F. GRAF, Nordionische Kulte. Religionsgeschichtliche und epigraphische Untersuchungen zu den Kulten von Chios, Erythrai, Klazomenai und Phokaia, 1985

GRBS
Greek, Roman and Byzantine Studies

Grenier
A. GRENIER, Manuel d'archéologie gallo-romaine 4 vols., 1931–60; vols. 1 and 2, repr. 1985

GRF
H. FUNAIOLI (ed.), Grammaticae Romanae Fragmenta, 1907

GRF(add)
A. MAZZARINO, Grammaticae Romanae Fragmenta aetatis Caesareae (accedunt volumini Funaioliano addenda), 1955

GRLMA
Grundriß der romanischen Literaturen des Mittelalters

Gruen, Last Gen.
E.S. GRUEN, The Last Generation of the Roman Republic, 1974

Gruen, Rome
E.S. GRUEN, The Hellenistic World and the Coming of Rome, 1984, repr. 1986

Gruppe
O. GRUPPE, Geschichte der klassischen Mythologie und Religionsgeschichte während des Mittelalters im Abendland und während der Neuzeit, 1921

Gundel
W. and H-G. GUNDEL, Astrologumena. Die astrologische Literatur in der Antike und ihre Geschichte, 1966

Guthrie
W.K.C. GUTHRIE, A History of Greek Philosophy 6 vols., 1962–81

GVI
W. PEEK (ed.), Griechische Vers-Inschriften, Vol. I, 1955

Gymnasium
Gymnasium. Zeitschrift für Kultur der Antike und humanistische Bildung

HABES
Heidelberger althistorische Beiträge und epigraphische Studien, 1986 ff.

Habicht
C. HABICHT, Athen. Die Geschichte der Stadt in hellenistischer Zeit, 1995

Hakkert
A.M. HAKKERT (ed.), Lexicon of Greek and Roman Cities and Place-Names in Antiquity c. 1500 B.C. – c. A.D. 500, 1990 ff.

Halfmann
H. HALFMANN, Die Senatoren aus dem östlichen Teil des Imperium Romanum bis zum Ende des 2. Jahrhunderts n. Chr. (Hypomnemata 58), 1979

Hamburger
K. HAMBURGER, Von Sophokles zu Sartre. Griechische Dramenfiguren antik und modern, 1962

Hannestad
N. HANNESTAD, Roman Art and Imperial Policy, 1986

Hansen, Democracy
M.H. HANSEN, The Athenian Democracy in the Age of Demosthenes. Structure, Principles and Ideology, 1991, repr. 1993

Harris
W.V. HARRIS, War and Imperialism in Republican Rome 327–70 B.C., 1979

Hasebroek
J. HASEBROEK, Griechische Wirtschafts- und Gesellschaftsgeschichte bis zur Perserzeit, 1931

HbdOr
B. SPULER (ed.), Handbuch der Orientalistik, 1952 ff.

HbdrA
J. MARQUARDT, TH. MOMMSEN, Handbuch der römischen Alterthümer, vols. 1–3, ³1887 f.; vols. 4–7, ²1881–86

HBr
P. HERRMANN, R. HERBIG, (ed.), Denkmäler der Malerei des Altertums 2 vols., 1904–50

HDA
H. BÄCHTOLD-STÄUBLI ET AL. (ed.), Handwörter-

buch des deutschen Aberglaubens 10 vols., 1927–42, repr. 1987

HdArch

W. Otto, U. Hausmann (ed.), Handbuch der Archäologie. Im Rahmen des HdbA 7 vols., 1969–90

HdbA

I. v. Müller, H. Bengtson (ed.), Handbuch der Altertumswissenschaft, 1977 ff.

Heckel

W. Heckel, Marshals of Alexander's Empire, 1978

Heinemann

K. Heinemann, Die tragischen Gestalten der Griechen in der Weltliteratur, 1920

Helbig

W. Helbig, Führer durch die öffentlichen Sammlungen klassischer Altertümer in Rom 4 vols., ⁴1963–72

Hephaistos

Hephaistos. Kritische Zeitschrift zu Theorie und Praxis der Archäologie, Kunstwissenschaft und angrenzender Gebiete

Hermes

Hermes. Zeitschrift für klassische Philologie

Herrscherbild

Das römische Herrscherbild, 1939 ff.

Herzog, Staatsverfassung

E. v. Herzog, Geschichte und System der römischen Staatsverfassung 2 vols., 1884–91, repr. 1965

Hesperia

Hesperia. Journal of the American School of Classical Studies at Athens

Heubeck

A. Heubeck, Schrift (Archaeologia Homerica Chapter X Vol. 3), 1979

Heumann/Seckel

H.G. Heumann, E. Seckel (ed.), Handlexikon zu den Quellen des römischen Rechts, ¹¹1971

Highet

G. Highet, The Classical Tradition: Greek and Roman Influences on Western literature, ⁴1968, repr. 1985

Hild

F. Hild, Kilikien und Isaurien (Denkschriften der Österreichischen Akademie der Wissenschaften, Philosophisch-Historische Klasse 215; TIB 5) 2 vols., 1990

Hild/Restle

F. Hild, M. Restle, Kappadokien (Kappadokia, Charsianon, Sebasteia und Lykandos) (Denkschriften der Österreichischen Akademie der Wissenschaften: Philosophisch-Historische Klasse 149; TIB 2), 1981

Hirschfeld

O. Hirschfeld, Die kaiserlichen Verwaltungsbeamten bis auf Diocletian, ²1905

Historia

Historia. Zeitschrift für Alte Geschichte

HJb

Historisches Jahrbuch

HLav

Humanistica Lavanensia

HLL

R. Herzog, P.L. Schmidt (ed.), Handbuch der lateinischen Literatur der Antike, 1989 ff.

HM

A History of Macedonia, Vol. 1: N.G.L. Hammond, Historical geography and prehistory, 1972; Vol. 2: N.G.L. Hammond, G.T. Griffith, 550–336 BC, 1979; Vol. 3: N.G.L. Hammond, F.W. Walbank, 336–167 BC, 1988

HmT

H.H. Eggebrecht, Handwörterbuch der musikalischen Terminologie, 1972 ff.

HN

B.V. Head, Historia numorum. A manual of Greek numismatics, ²1911

Hodge

T.A. Hodge, Roman Aqueducts and Water Supply, 1992

Hölbl

G. Hölbl, Geschichte des Ptolemäerreiches. Politik, Ideologie und religiöse Kultur von Alexander den Großen bis zur römischen Eroberung, 1994

Hölkeskamp

K.-J. Hölkeskamp, Die Entstehung der Nobilität. Studien zur sozialen und politischen Geschichte der Römischen Republik im 4.Jh. v. Chr., 1987

Hoffmann

D. Hofmann, Das spätrömische Bewegungsheer und die Notitia dignitatum (Epigraphische Studien 7) 2 vols., 1969 f. = (Diss.), 1958

Holder

A. Holder, Alt-celtischer Sprachschatz 3 vols., 1896-1913, repr. 1961 f.

Honsell

H. Honsell, Römisches Recht (Springer-Lehrbuch), ³1994

Hopfner

T. Hopfner, Griechisch-ägyptischer Offenbarungszauber 2 vols. in 3 parts, 1921–24, repr. 1974–90

Hopkins, Conquerors

K. Hopkins, Conquerors and Slaves. Sociological Studies in Roman History, Vol. 1, 1978

Hopkins, Death

K. Hopkins, Death and Renewal. Sociological Studies in Roman History, Vol. 2, 1983

HR

History of Religions

HRR

H. Peter (ed.), Historicorum Romanorum Reliquiae, Vol. 1, 1914; Vol. 2, 1906, repr. 1967

HrwG

H. Cancik, B. Gladigow, M. Laubscher (from Vol. 2: K.-H. Kohl) (ed.), Handbuch religionswissenschaftlicher Grundbegriffe, 1988 ff.

HS

Historische Sprachforschung

HSM
Histoire des sciences médicales
HSPh
Harvard Studies in Classical Philology
Hülser
K. HÜLSER, Die Fragmente zur Dialektik der Stoiker. Neue Sammlung der Texte mit deutscher Übersetzung und Kommentaren 4 vols., 1987 f.
Humphrey
J.H. HUMPHREY, Roman Circuses. Arenas for Chariot Racing, 1986
Hunger, Literatur
H. HUNGER, Die hochsprachlich profane Literatur der Byzantiner (HdbA 12, 5) 2 vols., 1978
Hunger, Mythologie
H. HUNGER (ed.), Lexikon der griechischen und römischen Mythologie, ⁶1969
Huss
W. HUSS, Geschichte der Karthager (HdbA III 8), 1985
HWdPh
J. RITTER, K. GRÜNDER (ed.), Historisches Wörterbuch der Philosophie, 1971 ff.
HWdR
G. UEDING (ed.), Historisches Wörterbuch der Rhetorik, 1992 ff.
HZ
Historische Zeitschrift
IA
Iranica Antiqua
IconRel
T.P. V. BAAREN (ed.), Iconography of Religions, 1970 ff.
ICUR
A. FERRUA, G.B. DE ROSSI, Inscriptiones christianae urbis Romae, 1922ff.
IDélos
Inscriptions de Délos, 1926 ff.
IDidyma
A. REHM (ed.), Didyma, Vol. 2: Die Inschriften, 1958
IEG
M. L. WEST (ed.), Iambi et elegi Graeci ante Alexandrum cantati 2 vols., 1989–92
IEJ
Israel Exploration Journal
IER
Illustrierte Enzyklopädie der Renaissance
IEry
H. ENGELMANN (ed.), Die Inschriften von Erythrai und Klazomenai 2 vols., 1972 f.
IF
Indogermanische Forschungen
IG
Inscriptiones Graecae, 1873 ff.
IGA
H. ROEHL (ed.), Inscriptiones Graecae antiquissimae praeter Atticas in Attica repertas, 1882, repr. 1977

IGBulg
G. MIHAILOV (ed.), Inscriptiones Graecae in Bulgaria repertae 5 vols., 1956–1996
IGLS
Inscriptions grecques et latines de la Syrie, 1929 ff.
IGR
R. CAGNAT ET AL. (ed.), Inscriptiones Graecae ad res Romanas pertinentes 4 vols., 1906–27
IGUR
L. MORETTI, Inscriptiones Graecae urbis Romae 4 vols., 1968–90
IJCT
International Journal of the Classical Tradition
IJsewijn
J. IJSEWIJN, Companion to Neo Latin Studies, ²1990 ff.
IK
Die Inschriften griechischer Städte aus Kleinasien, 1972 ff.
ILCV
E. DIEHL (ed.), Inscriptiones Latinae Christianae Veteres orientis 3 vols., 1925–31, repr. 1961; J. MOREAU, H.I. MARROU (ed.), Suppl., 1967
ILLRP
A. DEGRASSI (ed.), Inscriptiones Latinae liberae rei publicae 2 vols., 1957–63, repr. 1972
ILS
H. DESSAU (ed.), Inscriptiones Latinae Selectae 3 vols. in 5 parts, 1892–1916, repr. ⁴1974
IMagn.
O. KERN (ed.), Die Inschriften von Magnesia am Mäander, 1900, repr. 1967
IMU
Italia medioevale e umanistica
Index
Index. Quaderni camerti di studi romanistici
InscrIt
A. DEGRASSI (ed.), Inscriptiones Italiae, 1931 ff.
IOSPE
V. LATYSCHEW (ed.), Inscriptiones antiquae orae septentrionalis ponti Euxini Graecae et Latinae 3 vols., 1885–1901, repr. 1965
IPNB
M. MAYRHOFER, R. SCHMITT (ed.), Iranisches Personennamenbuch, 1979 ff.
IPQ
International Philosophical Quaterly
IPriene
F. HILLER VON GÄRTRINGEN, Inschriften von Priene, 1906
Irmscher
J. IRMSCHER (ed.), Renaissance und Humanismus in Mittel- und Osteuropa, 1962
Isager/Skydsgaard
S. ISAGER, J.E. SKYDSGAARD, Ancient Greek Agriculture, An Introduction, 1992
Isis
Isis

IstForsch
  Istanbuler Forschungen des Deutschen Archäologischen Instituts
Iura
  IURA, Rivista internazionale di diritto romano e antico
IvOl
  W. DITTENBERGER, K. PURGOLD, Inschriften von Olympia, 1896, repr. 1966
Jaffé
  P. JAFFÉ, Regesta pontificum Romanorum ab condita ecclesia ad annum 1198 2 vols., ²1985–88
JBAA
  The Journal of the British Archaeological Association
JbAC
  Jahrbuch für Antike und Christentum
JCS
  Journal of Cuneiform Studies
JDAI
  Jahrbuch des Deutschen Archäologischen Instituts
JEA
  The Journal of Egyptian Archaeology
Jenkyns, DaD
  R. JENKYNS, Dignity and Decadence: Classicism and the Victorians, 1992
Jenkyns, Legacy
  R. JENKYNS, The Legacy of Rome: A New Appraisal, 1992
JHAS
  Journal for the History of Arabic Science
JHB
  Journal of the History of Biology
JHM
  Journal of the History of Medicine and Allied Sciences
JHPh
  Journal of the History of Philosophy
JHS
  Journal of Hellenic Studies
JLW
  Jahrbuch für Liturgiewissenschaft
JMRS
  Journal of Medieval and Renaissance Studies
JNES
  Journal of Near Eastern Studies
JNG
  Jahrbuch für Numismatik und Geldgeschichte
JÖAI
  Jahreshefte des Österreichischen Archäologischen Instituts
Jones, Cities
  A.H.M. JONES, The Cities of the Eastern Roman Provinces, ²1971
Jones, Economy
  A.H.M. JONES, The Roman Economy. Studies in Ancient Economic and Administrative History, 1974

Jones, LRE
  A.H.M. JONES, The Later Roman Empire 284–602. A Social, Economic and Administrative Survey, 1964
Jones, RGL
  A.H.M. JONES, Studies in Roman Government and Law, 1968
Jost
  M. JOST, Sanctuaires et cultes d'Arcadie, 1985
JPh
  Journal of Philosophy
JRGZ
  Jahrbuch des Römisch-Germanischen Zentralmuseums
JRS
  Journal of Roman Studies
Justi
  F. JUSTI, Iranisches Namenbuch, 1895
JWG
  Jahrbuch für Wirtschaftsgeschichte
JWI
  Journal of the Warburg and Courtauld Institutes
Kadmos
  Kadmos. Zeitschrift für vor- und frühgriechische Epigraphik
KAI
  H. DONNER, W. RÖLLIG, Kanaanaeische und aramaeische Inschriften 3 vols., ³1971–1976
Kajanto, Cognomina
  I. KAJANTO, The Latin Cognomina, 1965
Kajanto, Supernomina
  I. KAJANTO, Supernomina. A study in Latin epigraphy (Commentationes humanarum litterarum 40, 1), 1966
Kamptz
  H. V. KAMPTZ, Homerische Personennamen. Sprachwissenschaftliche und historische Klassifikation, 1982 = H. V. KAMPTZ, Sprachwissenschaftliche und historische Klassifikation der homerischen Personennamen (Diss.), 1958
Karlowa
  O. KARLOWA, Römische Rechtsgeschichte 2 vols., 1885–1901
Kaser, AJ
  M. KASER, Das altrömische Jus. Studien zur Rechtsvorstellung und Rechtsgeschichte der Römer, 1949
Kaser, RPR
  M. KASER, Das römische Privatrecht (Rechtsgeschichte des Altertums Part 3, Vol. 3; HbdA 10, 3, 3) 2 vols., ³1971–75
Kaser, RZ
  M. KASER, Das römische Zivilprozessrecht (Rechtsgeschichte des Altertums Part 3, Vol. 4; HbdA 10, 3, 4), 1966
Kearns
  E. KEARNS, The Heroes of Attica, 1989 (BICS Suppl. 57)
Keller
  O. KELLER, Die antike Tierwelt 2 vols., 1909–20, repr. 1963

Kelnhofer
F. KELNHOFER, Die topographische Bezugsgrundlage der Tabula Imperii Byzantini (Denkschriften der Österreichischen Akademie der Wissenschaften: Philosophisch-Historische Klasse 125 Beih.; TIB 1, Beih.), 1976

Kienast
D. KIENAST, Römische Kaisertabelle. Grundzüge einer römischen Kaiserchronologie, 1990

Kindler
W. JENS (ed.), Kindlers Neues Literatur Lexikon 20 vols., 1988–92

Kinkel
G. KINKEL, (ed.), Epicorum Graecorum Fragmenta, 1877

Kirsten /Kraiker
E. KIRSTEN, W. KRAIKER, Griechenlandkunde. Ein Führer zu klassischen Stätten, ⁵1967

Kleberg
T. KLEBERG, Hôtels, restaurants et cabarets dans l'antiquité Romaine. Études historiques et philologiques, 1957

Klio
Klio. Beiträge zur Alten Geschichte

KlP
K. ZIEGLER (ed.), Der Kleine Pauly. Lexikon der Antike 5 vols., 1964–75, repr. 1979

Knobloch
J. KNOBLOCH ET AL. (ed.), Sprachwissenschaftliches Wörterbuch (Indogermanische Bibliothek 2), 1986 ff (1st installment 1961)

Koch/Sichtermann
G. KOCH, H. SICHTERMANN, Römische Sarkophage, 1982

Koder
J. KODER, Der Lebensraum der Byzantiner. Historisch-geographischer Abriß ihres mittelalterlichen Staates im östlichen Mittelmeerraum, 1984

Koder/Hild
J. KODER, F. HILD, Hellas und Thessalia (Denkschriften der Österreichischen Akademie der Wissenschaften, Philosophisch-Historische Klasse 125; TIB 1), 1976

Kraft
K. KRAFT, Gesammelte Aufsätze zur antiken Geschichte und Militärgeschichte, 1973

Kromayer/Veith
J. KROMAYER, G. VEITH, Heerwesen und Kriegführung der Griechen und Römer, 1928, repr. 1963

Krumbacher
K. KRUMBACHER, Geschichte der byzantinischen Litteratur von Justinian bis zum Ende des oströmischen Reiches (527–1453) (HdbA 9, 1), ²1897, repr. 1970

KSd
J. FRIEDRICH (ed.), Kleinasiatische Sprachdenkmäler (Kleine Texte für Vorlesungen und Übungen 163), 1932

KUB
Keilschrifturkunden von Boghazköi

Kühner/Blass
R. KÜHNER, F. BLASS, Ausführliche Grammatik der griechischen Sprache. Teil 1: Elementar- und Formenlehre 2 vols., ³1890–92

Kühner/Gerth
R. KÜHNER, B. GERTH, Ausführliche Grammatik der griechischen Sprache. Teil 2: Satzlehre 2 vols., ³1898–1904; W. M. CALDER III, Index locorum, 1965

Kühner/Holzweißig
R. KÜHNER, F. HOLZWEISSIG, Ausführliche Grammatik der lateinischen Sprache. Teil I: Elementar-, Formen- und Wortlehre, ²1912

Kühner/Stegmann
R. KÜHNER, C. STEGMANN, Ausführliche Grammatik der lateinischen Sprache. Teil 2: Satzlehre, 2 vols., ⁴1962 (revised by A. THIERFELDER); G.S. SCHWARZ, R. L. WERTIS, Index locorum, 1980

Kullmann/Atlhoff
W. KULLMANN, J. ALTHOFF (ed.), Vermittlung und Tradierung von Wissen in der griechischen Kultur, 1993

Kunkel
W. KUNKEL, Herkunft und soziale Stellung der römischen Juristen, ²1967

KWdH
H.H. SCHMITT (ed.), Kleines Wörterbuch des Hellenismus, ²1993

Lacey
W.K. LACEY, The Family in Classical Greece, 1968

LÄ
W. HELCK ET AL. (ed.), Lexikon der Ägyptologie 7 vols., 1975–92 (1st installment 1972)

LAK
H. BRUNNER, K. FLESSEL, F. HILLER ET AL. (ed.), Lexikon Alte Kulturen 3 vols., 1990–93

Lanciani
R. LANCIANI, Forma urbis Romae, 1893–1901

Lange
C.C.L. LANGE, Römische Altertümer, Vols. 1–2, ²1876–79; Vol. 3, 1876

Langosch
K. LANGOSCH, Mittellatein und Europa, 1990

Latomus
Latomus. Revue d'études latines

Latte
K. LATTE, Römische Religionsgeschichte (HdbA 5, 4), 1960, repr. 1992

Lauffer, BL
S. LAUFFER, Die Bergwerkssklaven von Laureion, ²1979

Lauffer, Griechenland
S. LAUFFER (ed.), Griechenland. Lexikon der historischen Stätten von den Anfängen bis zur Gegenwart, 1989

Lausberg
H. LAUSBERG, Handbuch der literarischen Rhetorik. Eine Grundlegung der Literaturwissenschaft, ³1990

LAW
  C. ANDRESEN ET AL.(ed.), Lexikon der Alten Welt, 1965, repr. 1990
LCI
  Lexikon der christlichen lkonographie
LdA
  J. IRMSCHER (ed.), Lexikon der Antike, ¹⁰1990
Le Bohec
  Y. LE BOHEC, L'armée romaine. Sous le Haut-Empire, 1989
Leitner
  H. LEITNER, Zoologische Terminologie beim Älteren Plinius (Diss.), 1972
Leo
  F. LEO, Geschichte der römischen Literatur. I. Die archaische Literatur, 1913, repr. 1958
Lesky
  A. LESKY, Geschichte der griechischen Literatur, ³1971, repr. 1993
Leumann
  M. LEUMANN, Lateinische Laut- und Formenlehre (HdbA II 2, 1), 1977
Leunissen
  P.M.M. LEUNISSEN, Konsuln und Konsulare in der Zeit von Commodus bis zu Alexander Severus (180–235 n. Chr.) (Dutch Monographs in Ancient History and Archaeology 6), 1989
Lewis/Short
  C.T. LEWIS, C. SHORT, A Latin Dictionary, ²1980
LFE
  B. SNELL (ed.), Lexikon des frühgriechischen Epos, 1979 ff. (1st installment 1955)
LGPN
  P.M. FRASER ET AL. (ed.), A Lexicon of Greek Personal Names, 1987 ff.
Liebenam
  W. LIEBENAM, Städteverwaltung im römischen Kaiserreich, 1900
Lietzmann
  H. LIETZMANN, Geschichte der Alten Kirche, ⁴/⁵1975
LIMC
  J. BOARDMAN ET AL. (ed.), Lexicon Iconographicum Mythologiae Classicae, 1981 ff.
Lippold
  G. LIPPOLD, Die griechische Plastik (HdArch III), 1950
Lipsius
  J.H. LIPSIUS, Das attische Recht und Rechtsverfahren. Mit Benutzung des Attischen Processes 3 vols., 1905–15, repr. 1984
Lloyd-Jones
  H. LLOYD-JONES, Blood for the Ghosts – Classical Influences in the Nineteenth and Twentieth Centuries, 1982
LMA
  R.-H. BAUTIER, R. AUTY (ed.), Lexikon des Mittelalters 7 vols., 1980–93 (1st installment 1977), 3rd vol. repr. 1995

Lobel/Page
  E. LOBEL, D. PAGE (ed.), Poetarum lesbiorum fragmenta, 1955, repr. 1968
Loewy
  E. LOEWY (ed.), Inschriften griechischer Bildhauer, 1885, repr. 1965
LPh
  T. SCHNEIDER, Lexikon der Pharaonen. Die altägyptischen Könige von der Frühzeit bis zur Römerherrschaft, 1994
LRKA
  Friedrich Lübkers Reallexikon des Klassischen Altertums, ⁸1914
LSAG
  L.H. JEFFERY, The Local Scripts of Archaic Greece. A Study of the Origin of the Greek Alphabet and its Development from the Eighth to the Fifth Centuries B.C., ²1990
LSAM
  F. SOKOLOWSKI, Lois sacrées de l'Asie mineure, 1955
LSCG
  F. SOKOLOWSKI, Lois sacrées des cités grecques, 1969
LSCG, Suppl
  F. SOKOLOWSKI, Lois sacrées des cités grecques, Supplément, 1962
LSJ
  H.G. LIDDELL, R. SCOTT, H.S. JONES ET AL. (ed.), A Greek-English Lexicon, ⁹1940; Suppl.: 1968, repr. 1992
LThK²
  J. HÖFER, K. RAHNER (ed.), Lexikon für Theologie und Kirche 14 vols., ²1957–86
LThK¹
  W. KASPER ET AL. (ed.), Lexikon für Theologie und Kirche, ¹1993 ff.
LTUR
  E.M. STEINBY (ed.), Lexicon Topographicum Urbis Romae, 1993 ff.
LUA
  Lunds Universitets Arsskrift / Acta Universitatis Lundensis
Lugli, Fontes
  G. LUGLI (ed.), Fontes ad topographiam veteris urbis Romae pertinentes, 6 of 8 vols. partially appeared, 1952–62
Lugli, Monumenti
  G. LUGLI, I Monumenti antichi di Roma e suburbio, 3 vols., 1930–38; Suppl.: 1940
Lustrum
  Lustrum. Internationale Forschungsberichte aus dem Bereich des klassischen Altertums
M&H
  Mediaevalia et Humanistica. Studies in Medieval and Renaissance Society
MacDonald
  G. MACDONALD, Catalogue of Greek Coins in the Hunterian Collection, University of Glasgow 3 vols., 1899–1905

MacDowell
  D. M. MACDOWELL, The law in Classical Athens (Aspects of Greek and Roman life), 1978
MAev.
  Medium Aevum
Magie
  D. MAGIE, Roman Rule in Asia Minor to the End of the Third Century after Christ, 1950, repr. 1975
MAII
  Mosaici Antichi in Italia, 1967 ff
MAMA
  Monumenta Asiae minoris Antiqua, 1927ff.
Manitius
  M. MANITIUS, Geschichte der lateinischen Literatur des Mittelalters (HdbA 9, 2) 3 vols., 1911–31, repr. 1973–76
MarbWPr
  Marburger-Winckelmann-Programm
Marganne
  M.H. MARGANNE, Inventaire analytique des papyrus grecs de médecine, 1981
Marrou
  H.-I. MARROU, Geschichte der Erziehung im klassischen Altertum (translation of Histoire de l'éducation dans l'antiquité), ²1977
Martinelli
  M. MARTINELLI (ed.), La ceramica degli Etruschi, 1987
Martino, SCR
  F. DE MARTINO, Storia della costituzione romana 5 vols., ²1972–75; Indici 1990
Martino, WG
  F. DE MARTINO, Wirtschaftsgeschichte des alten Rom, ²1991
Masson
  O. MASSON, Les inscriptions chypriotes syllabiques. Recueil critique et commenté (Études chypriotes 1), ²1983
Matz/Duhn
  F. MATZ, F. v. DUHN (ed.), Antike Bildwerke in Rom mit Ausschluß der größeren Sammlungen 3 vols., 1881 f.
MAVORS
  M.P. SPEIDEL (ed.), Roman Army Researches 1984 ff.
MDAI(A)
  Mitteilungen des Deutschen Archäologischen Instituts, Athenische Abteilung
MDAI(Dam)
  Damaszener Mitteilungen des Deutschen Archäologischen Instituts
MDAI(Ist)
  Istanbuler Mitteilungen des Deutschen Archäologischen Instituts
MDAI(K)
  Mitteilungen des Deutschen Archäologischen Instituts (Abteilung Kairo)
MDAI(R)
  Mitteilungen des Deutschen Archäologischen Instituts, Römische Abteilung

MDOG
  Mitteilungen der Deutschen Orient-Gesellschaft zu Berlin
MededRom
  Mededelingen van het Nederlands Historisch Instituut te Rome
Mediaevalia
  Mediaevalia
Mediaevistik
  Mediaevistik. Internationale Zeitschrift für interdisziplinäre Mittelalterforschung
MEFRA
  Mélanges d'Archéologie et d'Histoire de l'École Française de Rome. Antiquité
Meiggs
  R. MEIGGS, Trees and Timber in the Ancient Mediterranean World, 1982
Merkelbach/West
  R. MERKELBACH, M.L. WEST (ed.), Fragmenta Hesiodea, 1967
Mette
  H.J. METTE, Urkunden dramatischer Aufführungen in Griechenland, 1977
MG
  Monuments Grecs
MGG¹
  F. BLUME (ed.), Die Musik in Geschichte und Gegenwart. Allgemeine Enzyklopädie der Musik 17 vols., 1949–86, repr. 1989
MGG²
  L. FINSCHER (ed.), Die Musik in Geschichte und Gegenwart 20 vols., ²1994 ff.
MGH
  Monumenta Germaniae Historica inde ab anno Christi quingentesimo usque ad annum millesimum et quingentesimum, 1826 ff.
MGH AA
  Monumenta Germaniae Historica: Auctores Antiquissimi
MGH DD
  Monumenta Germaniae Historica: Diplomata
MGH Epp
  Monumenta Germaniae Historica: Epistulae
MGH PL
  Monumenta Germaniae Historica: Poetae Latini medii aevi
MGH SS
  Monumenta Germaniae Historica: Scriptores
MGrecs
  Monuments Grecs publiés par l'Association pour l'Encouragement des Etudes grecques en France 2 vols., 1872–97
MH
  Museum Helveticum
MiB
  Musikgeschichte in Bildern
Millar, Emperor
  F.G.B. MILLAR, The Emperor in the Roman World, 1977

Millar, Near East
  F.G.B. MILLAR, The Roman Near East, 1993
Miller
  K. MILLER, Itineraria Romana. Römische Reisewe-
  ge an der Hand der Tabula Peutingeriana, 1916,
  repr. 1988
Millett
  P. MILLETT, Lending and Borrowing in Ancient
  Athens, 1991
Minos
  Minos
MIO
  Mitteilungen des Instituts für Orientforschung
MIR
  Moneta Imperii Romani. Österreichische Akademie
  der Wissenschaften. Veröffentlichungen der Numis-
  matischen Kommission
Mitchell
  S. MITCHELL, Anatolia. Land, Men and Gods in Asia
  Minor 2 vols., 1993
Mitteis
  L. MITTEIS, Reichsrecht und Volksrecht in den öst-
  lichen Provinzen des römischen Kaiserreichs. Mit
  Beiträgen zur Kenntnis des griechischen Rechts und
  der spätrömischen Rechtsentwicklung, 1891, repr.
  1984
Mitteis/Wilcken
  L. MITTEIS, U. WILCKEN, Grundzüge und Chresto-
  mathie der Papyruskunde, 1912, repr. 1978
ML
  R. MEIGGS, D. LEWIS (ed.), A Selection of Greek
  Historical Inscriptions to the End of the Fifth Cen-
  tury B.C., ²1988
MLatJb
  Mittellateinisches Jahrbuch. Internationale Zeit-
  schrift für Mediävistik
Mnemosyne
  Mnemosyne. Bibliotheca Classica Batava
MNVP
  Mitteilungen und Nachrichten des Deutschen Paläs-
  tinavereins
MNW
  H. MEIER ET AL. (ed.), Kulturwissenschaftliche Bi-
  bliographie zum Nachleben der Antike 2 vols.,
  1931–38
Mollard-Besques
  S. MOLLARD-BESQUES, Musée National du Louvre.
  Catalogue raisonné des figurines et reliefs en terre-
  cuite grecs, étrusques et romains 4 vols., 1954–86
Momigliano
  A. MOMIGLIANO, Contributi alla storia degli studi
  classici, 1955 ff.
Mommsen, Schriften
  TH. MOMMSEN, Gesammelte Schriften 8 vols.,
  1904–13, repr. 1965
Mommsen, Staatsrecht
  TH. MOMMSEN, Römisches Staatsrecht 3 vols., Vol.
  1, ³1887; Vol. 2 f., 1887 f.

Mommsen Strafrecht
  TH. MOMMSEN, Römisches Strafrecht, 1899, repr.
  1955
Mon.Ant.ined.
  Monumenti Antichi inediti
Moos
  P. V. MOOS, Geschichte als Topik, 1988
Moraux
  P. MORAUX, Der Aristotelismus bei den Griechen
  von Andronikos bis Alexander von Aphrodisias (Pe-
  ripatoi 5 und 6) 2 vols., 1973–84
Moreau
  J. MOREAU, Dictionnaire de géographie historique
  de la Gaule et de la France, 1972; Suppl.: 1983
Moretti
  L. MORETTI (ed.), Iscrizioni storiche ellenistiche 2
  vols., 1967–76
MP
  Modern Philology
MPalerne
  Mémoires du Centre Jean Palerne
MRR
  T.R.S. BROUGHTON, The Magistrates of the Roman
  Republic 2 vols., 1951–52; Suppl.: 1986
MSG
  C. JAN (ed.), Musici scriptores Graeci, 1895; Suppl.:
  1899, repr. 1962
Müller
  D. MÜLLER, Topographischer Bildkommentar zu
  den Historien Herodots: Griechenland im Umfang
  des heutigen griechischen Staatsgebiets, 1987
Müller-Wiener
  W. MÜLLER-WIENER, Bildlexikon zur Topographie
  Istanbuls, 1977
Münzer¹
  F. MÜNZER, Römische Adelsparteien und Adelsfa-
  milien, 1920
Münzer²
  F. MÜNZER, Römische Adelsparteien und Adelsfa-
  milien, ²1963
Murray/Price
  O. MURRAY, S. PRICE (ed.), The Greek City: From
  Homer to Alexander, 1990
Muséon
  Muséon Revue d'Études Orientales
MVAG
  Mitteilungen der Vorderasiatischen (Ägyptischen)
  Gesellschaft
MVPhW
  Mitteilungen des Vereins klassischer Philologen in
  Wien
MythGr
  Mythographi Graeci 3 vols., 1894–1902; Vol. 1,
  ²1926
Nash
  E. NASH, Bildlexikon zur Topographie des antiken
  Rom, 1961 f.
NC
  Numismatic Chronicle

NClio
  La Nouvelle Clio
NDB
  Neue Deutsche Biographie, 1953 ff.; Vols. 1–6, repr. 1971
NEAEHL
  E. STERN (ed.), The New Encyclopedia of Archaeological Excavations in the Holy Land 4 vols., 1993
Neoph.
  Neophilologus
Newald
  R. NEWALD, Nachleben des antiken Geistes im Abendland bis zum Beginn des Humanismus, 1960
NGrove
  The New Grove Dictionary of Music and Musicians, ^{6}1980
NGroveInst
  The New Grove Dictionary of Musical Instruments, 1994
NHCod
  Nag Hammadi Codex
NHS
  Nag Hammadi Studies
Nicolet
  C. NICOLET, L' Ordre équestre à l'époque républicaine 312–43 av. J.-C. 2 vols., 1966–74
Nilsson, Feste
  M.P. NILSSON, Griechische Feste von religiöser Bedeutung mit Ausschluss der attischen, 1906
Nilsson, GGR,
  M.P. NILSSON, Geschichte der griechischen Religion (HdbA 5, 2), Vol. 1, ^{3}1967, repr. 1992; Vol. 2, ^{4}1988
Nilsson, MMR
  M.P. NILSSON, The Minoan-Mycenaean Religion and its Survival in Greek Religion, ^{2}1950
Nissen
  H. NISSEN, Italische Landeskunde 2 vols., 1883–1902
Nock
  A.D. NOCK, Essays on Religion and the Ancient World, 1972
Noethlichs
  K.L. NOETHLICHS, Beamtentum und Dienstvergehen. Zur Staatsverwaltung in der Spätantike, 1981
Norden, Kunstprosa
  E. NORDEN, Die antike Kunstprosa vom 6. Jh. v. Chr. bis in die Zeit der Renaissance, ^{6}1961
Norden, Literatur
  E. NORDEN, Die römische Literatur, ^{6}1961
NSA
  Notizie degli scavi di antichità
NTM
  Schriftenreihe für Geschichte der Naturwissenschaften, Technik und Medizin
Nutton
  V. NUTTON, From Democedes to Harvey. Studies in the History of Medicine (Collected Studies Series 277), 1988

NZ
  Numismatische Zeitschrift
OA
  J.G. BAITER, H. SAUPPE (ed.), Oratores Attici 3 vols., 1839–43
OBO
  Orbis Biblicus et Orientalis
OCD
  N.G. HAMMOND, H.H. SCULLARD (ed.), The Oxford Classical Dictionary, ^{2}1970, ^{3}1996
ODB
  A.P. KAZHDAN ET AL. (ed.), The Oxford Dictionary of Byzantium, 1991 ff.
OF
  O. KERN (ed.), Orphicorum Fragmenta, ^{3}1972
OGIS
  W. DITTENBERGER (ed.), Orientis Graeci Inscriptiones Selectae 2 vols., 1903–05, repr. 1960
OLD
  P.G.W. GLARE (ed.), Oxford Latin Dictionary, 1982 (1st installment 1968)
OIF
  Olympische Forschungen, 1941 ff.
Oliver
  J.H. OLIVER, Greek Constitutions of Early Roman Emperors from Inscriptions and Papyri, 1989
Olivieri
  D. OLIVIERI, Dizionario di toponomastica lombarda. Nomi di comuni, frazioni, casali, monti, corsi d'acqua, ecc. della regione lombarda, studiati in rapporto alle loro origine, ^{2}1961
Olshausen/Biller/Wagner
  E. OLSHAUSEN, J. BILLER, J. WAGNER, Historisch-geographische Aspekte der Geschichte des Pontischen und Armenischen Reiches. Untersuchungen Zur historischen Geographie von Pontos unter den Mithradatiden (TAVO 29), Vol. 1, 1984
OLZ
  Orientalistische Literaturzeitung
OpAth
  Opuscula Atheniensia, 1953 ff.
OpRom
  Opuscula Romana
ORF
  E. MALCOVATI, Oratorum Romanorum Fragmenta (Corpus scriptorum Latinorum Paravianum 56–58); vols., 1930
Orientalia
  Orientalia, Neue Folge
Osborne
  R. OSBORNE, Classical Landscape with Figures: The Ancient Greek City and its Countryside, 1987
Overbeck
  J. OVERBECK, Die antiken Schriftquellen zur Geschichte der bildenden Künste bei den Griechen, 1868, repr. 1959
PA
  J. KIRCHNER, Prosopographia Attica 2 vols., 1901–03, repr. 1966

Pack
R.A. PACK (ed.), The Greek and Latin Literary Texts from Greco-Roman Egypt, ²1965
Panofsky
E. PANOFSKY, Renaissance und Renaissancen in Western Art, 1960
Pape/Benseler
W. PAPE, G.E. BENSELER, Wörterbuch der griechischen Eigennamen 2 vols., 1863–1870
PAPhS
Proceedings of the American Philosophical Society
Parke
H.W. PARKE, Festivals of the Athenians, 1977
Parke/Wormell
H.W. PARKE, D.E.W. WORMELL, The Delphic Oracle, 1956
PBSR
Papers of the British School at Rome
PCA
Proceedings of die Classical Association. London
PCG
R. KASSEL, C. AUSTIN (ed.), Poetae comici graeci, 1983 ff.
PCPhS
Proceedings of the Cambridge Philological Society
PdP
La Parola del Passato
PE
R. STILLWELL ET AL. (ed.), The Princeton Encyclopedia of Classical Sites, 1976
Peacock
D.P.S. PEACOCK, Pottery in the Roman World: An Ethnoarchaeological Approach, 1982
PEG I
A. BERNABÉ (ed.), Poetae epici graeci. Testimonia et fragmenta. Pars I, 1987
Pfeiffer, KPI
R. PFEIFFER, Geschichte der Klassischen Philologie. Von den Anfängen bis zum Ende des Hellenismus, 1978
Pfeiffer KPII
R. PFEIFFER, Die Klassische Philologie von Petrarca bis Mommsen, 1982
Pfiffig
A.J. PFIFFIG, Religio Etrusca, 1975
Pflaum
H.G.PFLAUM, Les carrières procuratoriennes équestres sous le Haut-Empire Romain 3 vols. and figs., 1960 f.; Suppl.: 1982
Pfuhl
E. PFUHL, Malerei und Zeichnung der Griechen, 1923
Pfuhl/Möbius
E. PFUHL, H. MÖBIUS, Die ostgriechischen Grabreliefs 2 vols., 1977–79
PG
J.P. MIGNE (ed.), Patrologiae cursus completus, series Graeca 161 vols., 1857–1866; Conspectus auctorum: 1882; Indices 2 vols.: 1912–32

PGM
K. PREISENDANZ, A. HENRICHS (ed.), Papyri Graecae Magicae. Die griechischen Zauberpapyri 2 vols., ²1973 f. (1928–31)
Philippson /Kirsten
A. PHILIPPSON, A. LEHMANN, E. KIRSTEN (ed.), Die griechischen Landschaften. Eine Landeskunde 4 vols., 1950–59
Philologus
Philologus. Zeitschrift für klassische Philologie
PhQ
Philological Quarterly
Phronesis
Phronesis
PhU
Philologische Untersuchungen
PhW
Berliner Philologische Wochenschrift
Picard
CH. PICARD, Manuel d'archéologie grecque. La sculpture, 1935 ff.
Pickard-Cambridge/Gould/Lewis
A.W. PICKARD-CAMBRIDGE, J. GOULD, D.M. LEWIS, The Dramatic Festivals of Athens, ²1988
Pickard-Cambridge/Webster
A.W. PICKARD-CAMBRIDGE, T.B.L. WEBSTER, Dithyramb, Tragedy and Comedy, ²1962
Pigler, I
A. PIGLER, Barockthermen. Eine Auswahl von Verzeichnissen zur lkonographie des 17. Und 1 8. Jahrhunderts. 2 vols., ²1974; Ill. Vol.: 1974
PIR
Prosopographia imperii Romani saeculi, Vol. I-III, ²1933 ff.
PL
J.P. MIGNI (ed.), Patrologiae cursus completus, series Latina 221 vols., 1844–65 partly repr. 5 Suppl. Vols., 1958–74; Index: 1965
PLM
AE. BAEHRENS (ed.), Poetae Latini Minores 5 vols., 1879–83
PLRE
A.H.M. JONES, J.R. MARTINDALE, J. MORRIS (ed.), The Prosopography of the Later Roman Empire 3 vols. in 4 parts, 1971–1992
PMG
D.L. PAGE, Poetae melici graeci, 1962
PMGF
M. DAVIES (ed.), Poetarum melicorum Graecorum fragmenta, 1991
PMGTr
H.D. BETZ (ed.), The Greek Magical Papyri in Translation, Including the Demotic Spells, ²1992
Poccetti
D. POCCETTI, Nuovi documenti italici a complemento del manuale di E. Vetter (Orientamenti linguistici 8), 1979
Pökel
W. PÖKEL, Philologisches Schriftstellerlexikon, 1882, repr. ²1974

Poetica
  Poetica. Zeitschrift für Sprach- und Literaturwissen-
  schaft
Pokorny
  J. POKORNY, Indogermanisches etymologisches
  Wörterbuch 2 vols., ²1989
Poulsen
  F. POULSEN, Catalogue of Ancient Sculpture in the
  Ny Carlsberg Glyptotek, 1951
PP
  W. PEREMANS (ed.), Prosopographia Ptolemaica
  (Studia hellenistica) 9 vols., 1950–81, repr. Vol. 1–3,
  1977
PPM
  Pompei, Pitture e Mosaici, 1990 ff.
Praktika
  Πρακτικά της εν Αθήναις αρχαιολογικάς εταιρείας
Préaux
  C. PRÉAUX, L'économie royale des Lagides, 1939,
  repr. 1980
Preller/Robert
  L. PRELLER, C. ROBERT, Griechische Mythologie,
  ⁵1964 ff.
Pritchett
  K. PRITCHETT, Studies in Ancient Greek Topogra-
  phy (University of California Publications, Classical
  Studies) 8 vols., 1969–92
PropKg
  K. BITTEL ET AL. (ed.), Propyläen Kunstgeschichte 22
  vols., 1966–80, repr. 1985
Prosdocimi
  A.L. PROSDOCIMI, M. CRISTOFANI, Lingue dialetti
  dell'Italia antica, 1978; A. MARINETTI, Aggiorna-
  menti ed Indici, 1984
PrZ
  Prähistorische Zeitschrift
PSI
  G. VITELLI, M. NORSA, V. BARTOLETTI ET AL. (ed.),
  Papiri greci e latini (Pubblicazione della Soc. Italiana
  per la ricerca dei pap. greci e latini in Egitto), 1912 ff.
QSt
  Quellen und Studien zur Geschichte und Kultur des
  Altertums und des Mittelalters
Quasten
  J. QUASTEN, Patrology 2 vols., 1950–53
RA
  Revue Archéologique
RAC
  T. KLAUSER, E. DASSMANN (ed.), Reallexikon für
  Antike und Christentum. Sachwörterbuch zur Aus-
  einandersetzung des Christentums mit der antiken
  Welt, 1950 ff. (1st installment 1941)
RACr
  Rivista di Archeologia Cristiana
Radermacher
  L. RADERMACHER, Artium Scriptores. Reste der vor-
  aristotelischen Rhetorik, 1951
Radke
  G. RADKE, Die Götter Altitaliens, ²1979

Raepsaet-Charlier
  M-T. RAEPSAET-CHARLIER, Prosopographie des
  femmes de l'ordre sénatorial (l. – II. siècles) (Fonds
  René Draguet 4) 2 vols., 1987
RÄRG
  H. BONNET, Reallexikon der ägyptischen Religions-
  geschichte, ²1971
RAL
  Rendiconti della Classe di Scienze morali, storiche e
  filologiche dell'Academia dei Lincei
Ramsay
  W.M. RAMSAY, The Cities and Bishoprics of Phrygia
  2 vols., 1895–97
RAssyr
  Revue d'assyriologie et d'archéologie orientale
Rawson, Culture
  E. RAWSON, Roman Culture and Society. Collected
  Papers, 1991
Rawson, Family
  B. RAWSON (ed.), The Family in Ancient Rome. New
  Perspectives, 1986
RB
  P. WIRTH (ed.), Reallexikon der Byzantinistik, 1968
  ff.
RBA
  Revue Belge d'archéologie et d'histoire de l'art
RBi
  Revue biblique
RBK
  K. WESSEL, M. RESTLE (ed.), Reallexikon zur byzan-
  tinischen Kunst, 1966 ff. (1st installment 1963)
RBN
  Revue Belge de numismatique
RBPh
  Revue Belge de philologie et d'histoire
RDAC
  Report of the Department of Antiquities, Cyprus
RDK
  O. SCHMITT (ed.), Reallexikon zur deutschen Kunst-
  geschichte, 1937ff.
RE
  G. WISSOWA ET AL., (ed.), Paulys Real-Encyclopädie
  der classischen Altertumswissenschaft, Neue Be-
  arbeitung, 1893–1980
REA
  Revue des études anciennes
REByz
  Revue des études byzantines
REG
  Revue des études grecques
Rehm
  W. REHM, Griechentum und Goethezeit, ³1952,
  ⁴1968
Reinach, RP
  S. REINACH, Répertoire de peintures greques er ro-
  maines, 1922
Reinach, RR
  S. REINACH, Répertoire de reliefs grecs et romains 3
  vols., 1909–12

Reinach RSt
  S. REINACH, Répertoire de la statuaire greque et ro-
  maine 6 vols., 1897–1930, repr. 1965–69
REL
  Revue des études latines
Rer.nat.scr.Gr.min
  O. KELLER (ed.), Rerum naturalium scriptores Gra-
  eci minores, 1877
Reynolds
  L.D. REYNOLDS (ed.), Texts and Transmission: A
  Survey of the Latin Classics, 1983
Reynolds/Wilson
  L.D. REYNOLDS, N.G. WILSON, Scribes and Schol-
  ars. A Guide to the Transmission of Greek and Latin
  Literature, ³1991
RFIC
  Rivista di filologia e di istruzione classica
RG
  W.H. WADDINGTON, E. BABELON, Recueil général
  des monnaies grecques d'Asie mineure (Subsidia epi-
  graphica 5) 2 vols., 1908–1925, repr. 1976
RGA
  H. BECK ET AL. (ed.), Reallexikon der germanischen
  Altertumskunde, ²1973 ff. (1st installment 1968);
  Suppl.: 1986 ff.
RGG
  K. GALLING (ed.), Die Religion in Geschichte und
  Gegenwart. Handwörterbuch für Theologie und Re-
  ligionswissenschaft 7 vols., ³1957–65, repr. 1980
RGRW
  Religion in the Graeco-Roman World
RGVV
  Religionsgeschichtliche Versuche und Vorarbeiten
RH
  Revue historique
RHA
  Revue hittite et asianique
RhM
  Rheinisches Museum für Philologie
Rhodes
  P.J. RHODES, A commentary on the Aristotelian
  Athenaion Politeia, ²1993
RHPhR
  Revue d'histoire et de philosophie religieuses
RHR
  Revue de l'histoire des religions
RHS
  Revue historique des Sciences et leurs applications
RIA
  Rivista dell'Istituto nazionale d'archeologia e storia
  dell'arte
RIC
  H. MATTINGLY, E.A. SYDENHAM, The Roman Im-
  perial Coinage 10 vols., 1923–94
Richardson
  L. RICHARDSON (Jr.),   A New Topographical Dic-
  tionary of Ancient Rome, 1992
Richter, Furniture
  G.M.A. RICHTER, The Furniture of the Greeks,
  Etruscans and Romans, 1969

Richter, Korai
  G.M.A. RICHTER, Korai, Archaic Greek Maidens,
  1968
Richter, Kouroi
  G.M.A. RICHTER, Kouroi, Archaic Greek Youths,
  ³1970
Richter, Portraits
  G.M.A. RICHTER, The Portraits of the Greeks 3 vols.
  and suppl., 1965–72
RIDA
  Revue internationale des droits de l'antiquité
RIG
  P-M. DUVAL (ed.), Recueil des inscriptions gauloi-
  ses, 1985 ff.
RIL
  Rendiconti dell'Istituto Lombardo, classe di lettere,
  scienze morali e storiche
Rivet
  A.L.F. RIVET, Gallia Narbonensis with a Chapter on
  Alpes Maritimae. Southern France in Roman Times,
  1988
Rivet/Smith
  A.L.F. RIVET, C. SMITH, The Place-Names of Ro-
  man Britain, 1979
RLA
  E. EBELING ET AL. (ed.), Reallexikon der Assyriolo-
  gie und vorderasiatischen Archäologie, 1928 ff.
RLV
  M. EBERT (ed.), Reallexikon der Vorgeschichte 15
  vols., 1924–32
RMD
  M.M. ROXAN, Roman military diplomas (Occasion-
  al Publications of the Institute of Archaeology of the
  University of London 2 and 9), Vol. 1, (1954–77),
  1978; Vol. 2, (1978–84), 1985; Vol. 3, (1985–94),
  1994
RN
  Revue numismatique
Robert, OMS
  L. ROBERT, Opera minora selecta 7 vols., 1969–90
Robert, Villes
  L. ROBERT, Villes d'Asie Mineure. Etudes de géo-
  graphie ancienne, ²1902
Robertson
  A.S. ROBERTSON, Roman Imperial Coins in the
  Hunter Coin Cabinet, University of Glasgow 5 vols.,
  1962–82
Rohde
  E. ROHDE, Psyche. Seelenkult und Unsterblichkeits-
  glaube der Griechen, ²1898, repr. 1991
Roscher
  W.H. ROSCHER, Ausführliches Lexikon der grie-
  chischen und römischen Mythologie 6 vols.,
  ³1884–1937, repr. 1992 f.; 4 Suppl. Vols.: 1893–
  1921
Rostovtzeff, Hellenistic World
  M.I. ROSTOVTZEFF, The Social and Economic His-
  tory of the Hellenistic World, ²1953

Rostovtzeff, Roman Empire
  M.I. ROSTOVTZEFF, The Social and Economic History of the Roman Empire, ²1957
Rotondi
  G. ROTONDI, Leges publicae populi Romani. Elenco cronologico con una introduzione sull' attività legislativa dei comizi romani, 1912, repr. 1990
RPAA
  Rendiconti della Pontificia Accademia di Archeologia
RPC
  A. BURNETT, M. AMANDRY, P.P. RIPOLLÈS (ed.), Roman Provincial Coinage, 1992 ff.
RPh
  Revue de philologie
RQ
  Renaissance Quarterly
RQA
  Römische Quartalsschrift für christliche Altertumskunde und für Kirchengeschichte
RRC
  M. CRAWFORD, Roman Republican Coinage, 1974, repr. 1991
RSC
  Rivista di Studi Classici
Rubin
  B. RUBIN, Das Zeitalter Iustinians, 1960
Ruggiero
  E. DE RUGGIERO, Dizionarío epigrafico di antichità romana, 1895 ff., Vols. 1–3: repr. 1961 f.
Saeculum
  Saeculum. Jahrbuch für Universalgeschichte
Saller
  R. SALLER, Personal Patronage Under the Early Empire, 1982
Salomies
  O. SALOMIES, Die römischen Vornamen. Studien zur römischen Namengebung (Commentationes humanarum litterarum 82), 1987
Samuel
  A.E. SAMUEL, Greek and Roman Chronology. Calendars and Years in Classical Antiquity (HdbA I 7), 1972
Sandys
  J.E. SANDYS, A History of Classical Scholarship 3 vols., ²1906–21, repr. 1964
SAWW
  Sitzungsberichte der Österreichischen Akademie der Wissenschaften in Wien
SB
  Sammelbuch griechischer Urkunden aus Ägypten (Inschriften und Papyri), Vols. 1–2: F. PREISIGKE (ed.), 1913–22; Vols. 3–5: F. BILABEL (ed.), 1926–34
SBAW
  Sitzungsberichte der Bayerischen Akademie der Wissenschaften
SCCGF
  J. DEMIAŃCZUK (ed.), Supplementum comicum comoediae Graecae fragmenta, 1912

Schachter
  A. SCHACHTER, The Cults of Boiotia 4 vols., 1981–94
Schäfer
  A. SCHÄFER, Demosthenes und seine Zeit 3 vols., ²1885–87, repr. 1967
Schanz/Hosius
  M. SCHANZ, C. HOSIUS, G. KRÜGER, Geschichte der römischen Literatur bis zum Gesetzgebungswerk des Kaisers Justinian (HdbA 8), Vol. 1, ⁴1927, repr. 1979; Vol. 2, ⁴1935, repr. 1980; Vol. 3, ³1922, repr. 1969; Vol. 4,1, ²1914, repr. 1970; Vol. 4,2, 1920, repr. 1971
Scheid, Collège
  J. SCHEID, Le collège des frères arvales. Étude prosopographique du recrutement (69 –304) (Saggi di storia antica 1), 1990
Scheid, Recrutement
  J. SCHEID, Les frères arvales. Recrutement et origine sociale sous les empereurs julio-claudiens (Bibliothèque de l'École des Hautes Études, Section des Sciences Religieuses 77), 1975
Schlesier
  R. SCHLESIER, Kulte, Mythen und Gelehrte – Anthropologie der Antike seit 1800, 1994
Schmid/Stählin I
  W. SCHMID, O. STÄHLIN, Geschichte der griechischen Literatur. Erster Theil: Die klassische Periode der griechische Literatur VII 1) 5 vols., 1929–48, repr. 1961–80
Schmid/Stählin II
  W. CHRIST, W. SCHMID, O. STÄHLIN, Geschichte der griechischen Litteratur bis auf die Zeit Justinians. Zweiter Theil: Die nachklassische Periode der griechischen Litteratur (HdbA VII 2) 2 vols., ⁶1920–24, repr. 1961–81
Schmidt
  K.H. SCHMIDT, Die Komposition in gallischen Personennamen in: Zeitschrift für celtische Philologie 26, 1957, 33–301 = (Diss.), 1954
Schönfeld
  M. SCHÖNFELD, Wörterbuch der altgermanischen Personen- und Völkernamen (Germanische Bibliothek Abt. 1, Reihe 4, 2), 1911, repr. ²1965)
Scholiall
  H. ERBSE (ed.), Scholia Graeca in Homeri Iliadem (Scholia vetera) 7 vols., 1969–88
SChr
  Sources Chrétiennes 300 vols., 1942 ff.
Schrötter
  F. v. SCHRÖTTER (ed.), Wörterbuch der Münzkunde, ²1970
Schürer
  E. SCHÜRER, G. VERMÈS, The history of the Jewish people in the age of Jesus Christ (175 B.C. – A.D. 135) 3 vols., 1973–87
Schulten, Landeskunde
  A. SCHULTEN, Iberische Landeskunde. Geographie des antiken Spanien 2 vols., 1955–57 (translation of the Spanish edition of 1952)

Schulz
F. Schulz, Geschichte der römischen Rechtswissenschaft, 1961, repr. 1975
Schulze
W. Schulze, Zur Geschichte lateinischer Eigennamen, 1904
Schwyzer, Dial.
E. Schwyzer (ed.), Dialectorum Graecarum exempla epigraphica potiora, ³1923
Schwyzer, Gramm.
E. Schwyzer, Griechische Grammatik, Vol. 1: Allgemeiner Teil. Lautlehre Wortbildung, Flexion (HdbA II 1, 1), 1939
Schwyzer/Debrunner
E. Schwyzer, A. Debrunner, Griechische Grammatik, Vol. 2: Syntax und syntaktische Stilistik (HdbA II 1,2), 1950; D. J. Georgacas, Register zu beiden Bänden, 1953; F. Radt, S. Radt, Stellenregister, 1971
Scullard
H. H. Scullard, Festivals and Ceremonies of the Roman Republic, 1981
SDAW
Sitzungsberichte der Deutschen Akademie der Wissenschaften zu Berlin
SDHI
Studia et documenta historiae et iuris
SE
Studi Etruschi
Seeck
O. Seeck, Regesten der Kaiser und Päpste für die Jahre 311 bis 470 n. Chr. Vorarbeiten zu einer Prosopographie der christlichen Kaiserzeit, 1919, repr. 1964
SEG
Supplementum epigraphicum Graecum, 1923 ff.
Seltman
C. Seltman, Greek Coins. A History of Metallic Currency and Coinage down to the Fall of the Hellenistic Kingdoms, ²1905
Sezgin
F. Sezgin, Geschichte des arabischen Schrifttums, Vol.3: Medizin, Pharmazie, Zoologie, Tierheilkunde bis ca. 430 H., 1970
SGAW
Sitzungsberichte der Göttinger Akademie der Wissenschaften
SGDI
H. Collitz et al. (ed.), Sammlung der griechischen Dialekt-Inschriften 4 vols., 1884–1915
SGLG
K. Alpers, H. Erbse, A. Kleinlogel (ed.), Sammlung griechischer und lateinischer Grammatiker 7 vols., 1974–88
SH
H. Lloyd-Jones, P. Parsons (ed.), Supplementum Hellenisticum, 1983
SHAW
Sitzungsberichte der Heidelberger Akademie der Wissenschaften

Sherk
R.K. Sherk, Roman Documents from the Greek East: Senatus Consulta and Epistulae to the Age of Augustus, 1969
SicA
Sicilia archeologica
SIFC
Studi italiani di filologia classica
SiH
Studies in the Humanities
Simon, GG
E. Simon, Die Götter der Griechen, ⁴1992
Simon, GR
E. Simon, 1 Die Götter der Römer, 1990
SLG
D. Page (ed.), Supplementum lyricis graecis, 1974
SM
Schweizer Münzblätter
SMEA
Studi Micenei ed Egeo-Anatolici
Smith
W.D. Smith, The Hippocratic tradition (Cornell publications in the history of science), 1979
SMSR
Studi e materiali di storia delle religioni
SMV
Studi mediolatini e volgari
SNG
Sylloge Nummorum Graecorum
SNR
Schweizerische Numismatische Rundschau
Solin/Salomies
H. Solin, O. Salomies, Repertorium nominum gentilium et cognominum Latinorum (Alpha – Omega: Reihe A 80), ²1994
Sommer
F. Sommer, Handbuch der lateinischen Laut- und Formenlehre. Eine Einführung in das sprachwissenschaftliche Studium des Latein (Indogermanische Bibliothek 1, 1, 3, 1), ³1914
Soustal, Nikopolis
P. Soustal, Nikopolis und Kephallenia (Denkschriften der Akademie der Wissenschaften, Philosophisch-Historische Klasse I 50; TIB 3), 1981
Soustal, Thrakien
P. Soustal, Thrakien. Thrake, Rodope und Haimimontos (Denkschriften der Österreichischen Akademie der Wissenschaften, Philosophisch-Historische Klasse 221; TIB 6), 1991
Sovoronos
J.N. Sovoronos, Das Athener Nationalmuseum 3 vols., 1908–37
Spec.
Speculum
Spengel
L. Spengel, (ed.), Rhetores Graeci 3 vols., 1853–56, repr. 1966
SPrAW
Sitzungsberichte der Preußischen Akademie der Wissenschaften

SSAC
Studi storici per l'antichità classica
SSR
G. GIANNANTONI (ed.), Socratis et Socraticorum Reliquiae 4 vols., 1990
Staden
H. v. STADEN, Herophilus, The Art of Medicine in Early Alexandria, 1989
Stein, Präfekten
A. STEIN, Die Präfekten von Ägypten in der römischen Kaiserzeit (Dissertationes Bernenses Series 1, 1), 1950
Stein, Spätröm.R.
E. STEIN, Geschichte des spätrömischen Reiches, Vol. 1, 1928; French version, 1959; Vol. 2, French only, 1949
Stewart
A. STEWART, Greek sculpture. An exploration 2 vols., 1990
StM
Studi Medievali
Strong/Brown
D. STRONG, D. BROWN (ed.), Roman Crafts, 1976
Stv
Die Staatsverträge des Altertums, Vol. 2: H. BENGTSON, R. WERNER (ed.), Die Verträge der griechisch-römischen Welt von 700 bis 338, ²1975; Vol. 3: H.H. SCHMITT (ed.), Die Verträge der griechisch-römischen Welt 338 bis 200 v. Chr., 1969
SVF
J. v. ARNIM (ed.), Stoicorum veterum fragmenta 3 vols., 1903–05; Index: 1924, repr. 1964
Syll.²
W. DITTENBERGER, Sylloge inscriptionum Graecarum 3 vols., ²1898–1909
Syll.³
F. HILLER VON GAERTRINGEN ET AL. (ed.), Sylloge inscriptionum Graecarum 4 vols., ³1915–24, repr. 1960
Syme, AA
R. SYME, The Augustan Aristocracy, 1986
Syme, RP
E. BADIAN (Vols. 1,2), A.R. BIRLEY (Vols. 3–7) (ed.) R. SYME, Roman Papers 7 vols., 1979–91
Syme, RR
K. SYME, The Roman Revolution, 1939
Syme, Tacitus
R. SYME, Tacitus 2 vols., 1958
Symposion
Symposion, Akten der Gesellschaft für Griechische und Hellenistische Rechtsgeschichte
Syria
Syria. Revue d'art oriental et d'archéologie
TAM
Tituli Asiae minoris, 1901 ff.
TAPhA
Transactions and Proceedings of the American Philological Association

Taubenschlag
R. TAUBENSCHLAG, The law of Greco-Roman Egypt in the light of the Papyri: 332 B. C. – 640 A. D., ²1955
TAVO
H. BRUNNER, W. RÖLLIG (ed.), Tübinger Atlas des Vorderen Orients, Beihefte, Teil B: Geschichte, 1969 ff.
TeherF
Teheraner Forschungen
TGF
A. NAUCK (ed.), Tragicorum Graecorum Fragmenta, ²1889, 2nd repr. 1983
ThGL
H. STEPHANUS, C. B. HASE, W. UND L. DINDORF ET AL. (ed.), Thesaurus graecae linguae, 1831 ff., repr. 1954
ThlL
Thesaurus linguae Latinae, 1900 ff.
ThlL, Onom.
Thesaurus linguae Latinae, Supplementum onomasticon. Nomina propria Latina, Vol. 2 (C – Cyzistra), 1907–1913; Vol. 3 (D – Donusa), 1918–1923
ThLZ
Theologische Literaturzeitung Monatsschrift für das gesamte Gebiet der Theologie und Religionswissenschaft
Thomasson
B.E. THOMASSON, Laterculi Praesidum 3 vols. in 5 parts, 1972–1990
Thumb/Kieckers
A. THUMB, E. KIECKERS, Handbuch der griechischen Dialekte (Indogermanische Bibliothek 1, 1, 1), ²1932
Thumb/Scherer
A. THUMB, A. SCHERER, Handbuch der griechischen Dialekte (Indogermanische Bibliothek, 1, 1, 2), ²1959
ThWAT
G.J. BOTTERWECK, H.-J. FABRY (ed.), Theologisches Wörterbuch zum Alten Testament, 1973 ff.
ThWB
G. KITTEL, G. FRIEDRICH (ed.), Theologisches Wörterbuch zum Neuen Testament 11 vols., 1933–79, repr. 1990
TIB
H. HUNGER (ed.). Tabula Imperii Byzantini 7 vols., 1976–1990
Timm
S. TIMM, Das christlich-koptische Ägypten in arabischer Zeit. Eine Sammlung christlicher Stätten in Ägypten in arabischer Zeit, unter Ausschluß von Alexandria, Kairo, des Apa-Mena-Klosters (Der Abu Mina), des Sketis (Wadi n-Natrun) und der Sinai-Region (TAVO 41) 6 parts, 1984–92
TIR
Tabula Imperii Romani, 1934 ff.
TIR/IP
Y. TSAFRIR, L. DI SEGNI, J. GREEN, Tabula Imperii

Romani. Iudaea – Palaestina. Eretz Israel in the Hellenistic, Roman and Byzantine Periods, 1994

Tod
M.N. Tod (ed.), A Selection of Greek Historical Inscriptions to the End of the Fifth Century BC, Vol. 1: ²1951, repr. 1985; Vol. 2: ²1950

Tovar
A. Tovar, Iberische Landeskunde 2: Die Völker und Städte des antiken Hispanien, Vol. 1 Baetica, 1974; Vol. 2: Lusitanien, 1976; Vol. 3: Tarraconensis, 1989

Toynbee, Hannibal
A.J. Toynbee, Hannibal's legacy. The Hannibalic war's effects on Roman life 2 vols., 1965

Toynbee, Tierwelt
J.M.C. Toynbee, Tierwelt der Antike, 1983

TPhS
Transactions of the Philological Society Oxford

Traill, Attica
J. S. Traill, The Political Organization of Attica, 1975

Traill, PAA
J. S. Traill, Persons of Ancient Athens, 1994 ff.

Travlos, Athen
J. Travlos, Bildlexikon zur Topographie des antiken Athen, 1971

Travlos, Attika
J. Travlos, Bildlexikon zur Topographie des antiken Attika, 1988

TRE
G. Krause, G. Müller (ed.), Theologische Realenzyklopädie, 1977 ff. (1st installment 1976)

Treggiari
S. Treggiari, Roman Marriage. Iusti Coniuges from the Time of Cicero to the Time of Ulpian, 1991

Treitinger
O. Treitinger, Die Oströmische Kaiser- und Reichsidee nach ihrer Gestaltung im höfischen Zeremoniell, 1938, repr. 1969

Trendall, Lucania
A.D. Trendall, The Red-figured Vases of Lucania, Campania and Sicily, 1967

Trendall, Paestum
A.D. Trendall, The Red-figured Vases of Paestum, 1987

Trendall/Cambitoglou
A.D. Trendall, The Red-figured Vases of Apulia 2 vols., 1978–82

TRF
O. Ribbeck (ed.), Tragicorum Romanorum Fragmenta, ²1871, repr. 1962

TRG
Tijdschrift voor rechtsgeschiedenis

TrGF
B. Snell, R. Kannicht, S. Radt (ed.), Tragicorum graecorum fragmenta, Vol. 1, ²1986; Vols. 2–4, 1977–85

Trombley
F.R. Trombley, Hellenic Religion and Christianization c. 370–529 (Religions in the Graeco-Roman World 115) 2 vols., 1993 f.

TU
Texte und Untersuchungen zur Geschichte der altchristlichen Literatur

TUAT
O. Kaiser (ed.), Texte aus der Umwelt des Alten Testaments, 1985 ff. (1st installment 1982)

TürkAD
Türk arkeoloji dergisi

Ullmann
M. Ullmann, Die Medizin im Islam, 1970

UPZ
U. Wilcken (ed.), Urkunden der Ptolemäerzeit (Ältere Funde) 2 vols., 1927–57

v. Haehling
R. v. Haehling, Die Religionszugehörigkeit der hohen Amtsträger des Römischen Reiches seit Constantins I. Alleinherrschaft bis zum Ende der Theodosianischen Dynastie (324–450 bzw. 455 n. Chr.) (Antiquitas 3, 23), 1978

VDI
Vestnik Drevnej Istorii

Ventris/Chadwick
M. Ventris, J. Chadwick, Documents in Mycenean Greek, ²1973

Vetter
E. Vetter, Handbuch der italischen Dialekte, 1953

VIR
Vocabularium iurisprudentiae Romanae 5 vols., 1903–39

VisRel
Visible Religion

Vittinghoff
F. Vittinghoff (ed.), Europäische Wirtschafts- und Sozialgeschichte in der römischen Kaiserzeit, 1990

VL
W. Stammler, K. Langosch, K. Ruh et al. (ed.), Die deutsche Literatur des Mittelalters. Verfasserslexikon, ²1978 ff.

Vogel-Weidemann
U. Vogel-Weidemann, Die Statthalter von Africa und Asia in den Jahren 14–68 n.Chr. Eine Untersuchung zum Verhältnis von Princeps und Senat (Antiquitas 1, 31), 1982

VT
Vetus Testamentum. Quarterly Published by the International Organization of Old Testament Scholars

Wacher
R. Wacher (ed.), The Roman World 2 vols., 1987

Walde/Hofmann
A. Walde, J.B. Hofmann, Lateinisches etymologisches Wörterbuch 3 vols., ³1938–56

Walde/Pokorny
A. Walde, J. Pokorny (ed.), Vergleichendes Wörterbuch der indogermanischen Sprachen 3 vols., 1927–32, repr. 1973

Walz
C. Walz (ed.), Rhetores Graeci 9 vols., 1832–36, repr. 1968

WbMyth
H.W. HAUSSIG (ed.), Wörterbuch der Mythologie, Teil 1: Die alten Kulturvölker, 1965 ff.

Weber
W. WEBER, Biographisches Lexikon zur Geschichtswissenschaft in Deutschland, Österreich und der Schweiz, ²1987

Wehrli, Erbe
F. WEHRLI (ed.), Das Erbe der Antike, 1963

Wehrli, Schule
F. WEHRLI (ed.), Die Schule des Aristoteles 10 vols., 1967–69; 2 Suppl. Vols.: 1974–78

Welles
C.B. WELLES, Royal Correspondence in the Hellenistic Period: A Study in Greek Epigraphy, 1934

Wenger
L. WENGER, Die Quellen des römischen Rechts (Denkschriften der Österreichischen Akademie der Wissenschaften. Philosophisch-Historische Klasse 2), 1953

Wernicke
I. WERNICKE, Die Kelten in Italien. Die Einwanderung und die frühen Handelsbeziehungen zu den Etruskern (Diss.), 1989 = (Palingenesia), 1991

Whatmough
J. WHATMOUGH, The dialects of Ancient Gaul. Prolegomena and records of the dialects 5 vols., 1949–51, repr. in 1 vol., 1970

White, Farming
K.D. WHITE, Roman Farming, 1970

White, Technology
K.D. WHITE, Greek and Roman Technology, 1983, repr. 1986

Whitehead
D. WHITEHEAD, The demes of Attica, 1986

Whittaker
C.R. WHITTAKER (ed.), Pastoral Economies in Classical Antiquity, 1988

Wide
S. WIDE, Lakonische Kulte, 1893

Wieacker, PGN
F. WIEACKER, Privatrechtsgeschichte der Neuzeit, ²1967

Wieacker, RRG
F. WIEACKER, Römische Rechtsgeschichte, Vol. 1, 1988

Wilamowitz
U. v. WILAMOWITZ-MOELLENDORFF, Der Glaube der Hellenen 2 vols., ²1955, repr. 1994

Will
E. WILL, Histoire politique du monde hellénistique (323–30 av. J. C.) 2 vols., ²1979–82

Winter
R. KEKULÉ (ed.), Die antiken Terrakotten, III 1, 2: F. WINTER, Die Typen der figürlichen Terrakotten, 1903

WJA
Würzburger Jahrbücher für die Altertumswissenschaft

WMT
L.I. CONRAD ET AL., The Western medical tradition. 800 BC to A.D. 1800, 1995

WO
Die Welt des Orients. Wissenschaftliche Beiträge zur Kunde des Morgenlandes

Wolff
H.J. WOLFF, Das Recht der griechischen Papyri Ägyptens in der Zeit der Ptolemaeer und des Prinzipats (Rechtsgeschichte des Altertums Part 5; HbdA 10, 5), 1978

WS
Wiener Studien, Zeitschrift für klassische Philologie und Patristik

WUNT
Wissenschaftliche Untersuchungen zum Neuen Testament

WVDOG
Wissenschaftliche Veröffentlichungen der Deutschen Orient-Gesellschaft

WZKM
Wiener Zeitschrift für die Kunde des Morgenlandes

YCIS
Yale Classical Studies

ZA
Zeitschrift für Assyriologie und Vorderasiatische Archäologie

ZÄS
Zeitschrift für ägyptische Sprache und Altertumskunde

ZATW
Zeitschrift für die Alttestamentliche Wissenschaft

Zazoff, AG
P. ZAZOFF, Die antiken Gemmen, 1983

Zazoff, GuG
P. ZAZOFF, H. ZAZOFF, Gemmensammler und Gemmenforscher. Von einer noblen Passion zur Wissenschaft, 1983

ZDMG
Zeitschrift der Deutschen Morgenländischen Gesellschaft

ZDP
Zeitschrift für deutsche Philologie

Zeller
E. ZELLER, Die Philosophie der Griechen in ihrer geschichtlichen Entwicklung 4 vols., 1844–52, repr. 1963

Zeller/Mondolfo
E. ZELLER, R. MONDOLFO, La filosofia dei Greci nel suo sviluppo storico, Vol. 3, 1961

ZfN
Zeitschrift für Numismatik

Zgusta
L. ZGUSTA, Kleinasiatische Ortsnamen, 1984

Zimmer
G. ZIMMER, Römische Berufsdarstellungen, 1982

ZKG,
Zeitschrift für Kirchengeschichte

ZNTW
Zeitschrift für die Neutestamentfiche Wissenschaft und die Kunde der älteren Kirche

ZpalV
  Zeitschrift des Deutschen Palästina-Vereins
ZPE
  Zeitschrift für Papyrologie und Epigraphik
ZKG
  Zeitschrift der Savigny-Stiftung für Rechtsgeschich-
  te. Romanistische Abteilung

ZRGG
  Zeitschrift für Religions- und Geistesgeschichte
ZVRW
  Zeitschrift für vergleichende Rechtswissenschaft
ZVS
  Zeitschrift für Vergleichende Sprachforschung

5. Ancient Authors and Titles of Works

Abd	Abdias	Anth. Gr.	Anthologia Graeca
Acc.	Accius	Anth. Lat.	Anthologia Latina (Riese
Ach.Tat.	Achilles Tatius		²1894/1906)
Act. Arv.	Acta fratrum Arvalium	Anth. Pal.	Anthologia Palatina
Act. lud. saec.	Acta ludorum saecularium	Anth. Plan.	Anthologia Planudea
Acts	Acts of the Apostles	Antiph.	Antiphon
Aet.	Aetius	Antisth.	Antisthenes
Aeth.	Aetheriae peregrinatio	Apc.	Apocalypse
Ael. Ep.	Aelianus, Epistulae	Apoll. Rhod.	Apollonius Rhodius
NA	De natura animalium	Apollod.	Apollodorus, Library
VH	Varia historia	App. B Civ.	Appianus, Bella civilia
Aen. Tact.	Aeneas Tacticus	Celt.	Celtica
Aesch. Ag.	Aeschylus, Agamemnon	Hann.	Hannibalica
Cho.	Choephori	Hisp.	Iberica
Eum.	Eumenides	Ill.	Illyrica
Pers.	Persae	It.	Italica
PV	Prometheus	Lib.	Libyca
Sept.	Septem adversus Thebas	Mac.	Macedonica
Supp.	Supplices	Mith.	Mithridatius
Aeschin. In Ctes.	Aeschines, In Ctesiphontem	Num.	Numidica
Leg.	De falsa legatione	Reg.	Regia
In Tim.	In Timarchum	Sam.	Samnitica
Aesop.	Aesopus	Sic.	Sicula
Alc.	Alcaeus	Syr.	Syriaca
Alc. Avit.	Alcimus Ecdicius Avitus	App. Verg.	Appendix Vergiliana
Alex. Aphr.	Alexander of Aphrodisias	Apul. Apol.	Apuleius, Apologia
Alci.	Alciphron	Flor.	Florida
Alcm.	Alcman	Met.	Metamorphoses
Alex. Polyh.	Alexander Polyhistor	Arat.	Aratus
Am	Amos	Archil.	Archilochus
Ambr. Epist.	Ambrosius, Epistulae	Archim.	Archimedes
Exc. Sat.	De excessu Fratris (Satyri)	Archyt.	Archytas
Obit. Theod.	De obitu Theodosii	Arist. Quint.	Aristides Quintilianus
Obit. Valent.	De obitu Valentiniani (iunioris)	Aristaen.	Aristaenetus
Off.	De officiis ministrorum	Aristid.	Aelius Aristides
Paenit.	De paenitentia	Aristob.	Aristoboulus
Amm. Marc.	Ammianus Marcellinus	Aristoph. Ach.	Aristophanes, Acharnenses
Anac.	Anacreon	Av.	Aves
Anaxag.	Anaxagoras	Eccl.	Ecclesiazusae
Anaximand.	Anaximander	Equ.	Equites
Anaximen.	Anaximenes	Lys.	Lysistrata
And.	Andocides	Nub.	Nubes
Anecd. Bekk.	Anecdota Graeca ed. I. Bekker	Pax	Pax
Anecd. Par.	Anecdota Graeca ed. J.A. Kramer	Plut.	Plutus
Anon. De rebus bell.	Anonymus de rebus bellicis (Ireland 1984)	Ran.	Ranae

Thesm.	Thesmophoriazusae
Vesp.	Vespae
Aristot. An.	Aristotle, De anima (Becker 1831–70)
An. post.	Analytica posteriora
An. pr.	Analytica priora
Ath. Pol.	Athenaion Politeia
Aud.	De audibilibus
Cael.	De caelo
Cat.	Categoriae
Col.	De coloribus
Div.	De divinatione
Eth. Eud.	Ethica Eudemia
Eth. Nic.	Ethica Nicomachea
Gen. an.	De generatione animalium
Gen. corr.	De generatione et corruptione
Hist. an.	Historia animalium
Mag. mor.	Magna moralia
Metaph.	Metaphysica
Mete.	Meteorologica
Mir.	Mirabilia
Mot. an.	De motu animalium
Mund.	De mundo
Oec.	Oeconomica
Part. an.	De partibus animalium
Phgn.	Physiognomica
Ph.	Physica
Poet.	Poetica
Pol.	Politica
Pr.	Problemata
Rh.	Rhetorica
Rh. Al.	Rhetorica ad Alexandrum
Sens.	De sensu
Somn.	De somno et vigilia
Soph. el.	Sophistici elenchi
Spir.	De spiritu
Top.	Topica
Aristox. Harm.	Aristoxenus, Harmonica
Arnob.	Arnobius, Adversus nationes
Arr. Anab.	Arrianus, Anabasis
Cyn.	Cynegeticus
Ind.	Indica
Peripl. p. eux.	Periplus ponti Euxini
Succ.	Historia successorum Alexandri
Tact.	Tactica
Artem.	Artemidorus
Ascon.	Asconius (Stangl Vol. 2, 1912)
Athan. ad Const.	Athanasius, Apologia ad Constantium
c. Ar.	Apologia contra Arianos
Fuga	Apologia de fuga sua
Hist. Ar.	Historia Arianorum ad monachos
Ath.	Athenaeus (Casaubon 1597) (List of books, pages, letters)
Aug. Civ.	Augustinus, De civitate dei
Conf.	Confessiones
Doctr. christ.	De doctrina christiana

Epist.	Epistulae
Retract.	Retractationes
Serm.	Sermones
Soliloq.	Soliloquia
Trin.	De trinitate
Aur. Vict.	Aurelius Victor
Auson. Mos.	Ausonius, Mosella (Peiper 1976)
Urb.	Ordo nobilium urbium
Avell.	Collectio Avellana
Avien.	Avienus
Babr.	Babrius
Bacchyl.	Bacchylides
Bar	Baruch
Bas.	Basilicorum libri LX (Heimbach)
Basil.	Basilius
Batr.	Batrachomyomachia
Bell. Afr.	Bellum Africum
Bell. Alex.	Bellum Alexandrinum
Bell. Hisp.	Bellum Hispaniense
Boeth.	Boethius
Caes. B Civ.	Caesar, De bello civili
B Gall.	De bello Gallico
Callim. Epigr.	Callimachus, Epigrammata
Fr.	Fragmentum (Pfeiffer)
H.	Hymni
Calp. Ecl.	Calpurnius Siculus, Eclogae
Cass. Dio	Cassius Dio
Cassian.	Iohannes Cassianus
Cassiod. Inst.	Cassiodorus, Institutiones
Var.	Variae
Cato Agr.	Cato, De agri cultura
Orig.	Origines (HRR)
Catull.	Catullus, Carmina
Celsus, Med.	Cornelius Celsus, De medicina
Celsus, Dig.	Iuventius Celsus, Digesta
Censorinus, DN	Censorinus, De die natali
Chalcid.	Chalcidius
Charisius, Gramm.	Charisius, Ars grammatica (Barwick 1964)
1 Chr, 2 Chr	Chronicle
Chron. pasch.	Chronicon paschale
Chron. min.	Chronica minora
Cic. Acad. 1	Cicero, Academicorum posteriorum liber 1
Acad. 2	Lucullus sive Academicorum priorum liber 2
Ad Q. Fr.	Epistulae ad Quintum fratrem
Arat.	Aratea (Soubiran 1972)
Arch.	Pro Archia poeta
Att.	Epistulae ad Atticum
Balb.	Pro L. Balbo
Brut.	Brutus
Caecin.	Pro A. Caecina
Cael.	Pro M. Caelio
Cat.	In Catilinam
Cato	Cato maior de senectute
Clu.	Pro A. Cluentio
De or.	De oratore

Deiot.	Pro rege Deiotaro
Div.	De divinatione
Div. Caec.	Divinatio in Q. Caecilium
Dom.	De domo sua
Fam.	Epistulae ad familiares
Fat.	De fato
Fin.	De finibus bonorum et malorum
Flac.	Pro L. Valerio Flacco
Font.	Pro M. Fonteio
Har. resp.	De haruspicum responso
Inv.	De inventione
Lael.	Laelius de amicitia
Leg.	De legibus
Leg. agr.	De lege agraria
Lig.	Pro Q. Ligario
Leg. Man.	Pro lege Manilia (de imperio Cn. Pompei)
Marcell.	Pro M. Marcello
Mil.	Pro T. Annio Milone
Mur.	Pro L. Murena
Nat. D.	De natura deorum
Off.	De officiis
Opt. Gen.	De optimo genere oratorum
Orat.	Orator
P. Red. Quir.	Oratio post reditum ad Quirites
P. Red. Sen.	Oratio post reditum in senatu
Parad.	Paradoxa
Part. or.	Partitiones oratoriae
Phil.	In M. Antonium orationes Philippicae
Philo.	Libri philosophici
Pis.	In L. Pisonem
Planc.	Pro Cn. Plancio
Prov. cons.	De provinciis consularibus
Q. Rosc.	Pro Q. Roscio comoedo
Quinct.	Pro P. Quinctio
Rab. perd.	Pro C. Rabirio perduellionis reo
Rab. Post.	Pro C. Rabirio Postumo
Rep.	De re publica
Rosc. Am.	Pro Sex. Roscio Amerino
Scaur.	Pro M. Aemilio Scauro
Sest.	Pro P. Sestio
Sull.	Pro P. Sulla
Tim.	Timaeus
Top.	Topica
Tull.	Pro M. Tullio
Tusc.	Tusculanae disputationes
Vatin.	In P. Vatinium testem interrogatio
Verr. 1, 2	In Verrem actio prima, secunda
Claud. Carm.	Claudius Claudianus, Carmina (Hall 1985)
Rapt. Pros.	De raptu Proserpinae
Clem. Al.	Clemens Alexandrinus
Cod. Greg.	Codex Gregorianus
Cod. Herm.	Codex Hermogenianus
Cod. Iust.	Corpus Iuris Civilis, Codex Iustinianus (Krueger 1900)
Cod. Theod.	Codex Theodosianus
Col	Letter to the Colossians
Coll.	Mosaicarum et Romanarum legum collatio
Columella	Columella
Comm.	Commodianus
Cons.	Consultatio veteris cuiusdam iurisconsulti
Const.	Constitutio Sirmondiana
1 Cor, 2 Cor	Letters to the Corinthians
Coripp.	Corippus
Curt.	Curtius Rufus, Historiae Alexandri Magni
Cypr.	Cyprianus
Dan	Daniel
Din.	Dinarchus
Demad.	Demades
Democr.	Democritus
Dem. Or.	Demosthenes, Orationes
Dig.	Corpus Iuris Civilis, Digesta (Mommsen 1905, author presented where applicable)
Diod. Sic.	Diodorus Siculus
Diog. Laert.	Diogenes Laertius
Diom.	Diomedes, Ars grammatica
Dion. Chrys.	Dion Chrysostomus
Dion. Hal. Ant. Rom.	Dionysius Halicarnasseus, Antiquitates Romanae
Comp.	De compositione verborum
Rhet.	Ars rhetorica
Dionys. Per.	Dionysius Periegeta
Dion. Thrax	Dionysius Thrax
DK	Diels /Kranz (preceded by fragment number)
Donat.	Donatus grammaticus
Drac.	Dracontius
Dt	Deuteronomy = 5. Moses
Edict. praet. dig.	Edictum perpetuum in Dig.
Emp.	Empedocles
Enn. Ann.	Ennius, Annales (Skutsch 1985)
Sat.	Saturae (Vahlen ²1928)
Scaen.	Fragmenta scaenica (Vahlen ²1928)
Ennod.	Ennodius
Eph	Letter to the Ephesians
Ephor.	Ephorus of Cyme (FGrH 70)
Epicurus	Epicurus
Epict.	Epictetus
Eratosth.	Eratosthenes
Esr	Esra
Est	Esther
Et. Gen.	Etymologicum genuinum
Et. Gud.	Etymologicum Gudianum
EM	Etymologicum magnum
Euc.	Euclides, Elementa
Eunap. VS	Eunapius, Vitae sophistarum
Eur. Alc.	Euripides, Alcestis
Andr.	Andromache

Bacch.	Bacchae	Mart.	De virtutibus Martini
Beller.	Bellerophon	Vit. patr.	De vita patrum
Cyc.	Cyclops	Hab	Habakkuk
El.	Electra	Hagg	Haggai
Hec.	Hecuba	Harpocr.	Harpocrates
Hel.	Helena	Hdt.	Herodotus
Heracl.	Heraclidae	Hebr	Letter to the Hebrews
HF	Hercules Furens	Hegesipp.	Hegesippus (= Flavius Josephus)
Hipp.	Hippolytus	Hecat.	Hecataeus
Hyps.	Hypsipyle	Hell. Oxy.	Hellennica Oxyrhynchia
Ion	Ion	Hen	Henoch
IA	Iphigenia Aulidensis	Heph.	Hephaestio grammaticus (Alexandrinus)
IT	Iphigenia Taurica		
Med.	Medea	Heracl.	Heraclitus
Or.	Orestes	Heraclid. Pont.	Heraclides Ponticus
Phoen.	Phoenissae	Herc. O.	Hercules Oetaeus
Rhes.	Rhesus	Herm.	Hermes Trismegistus
Supp.	Supplices	Herm. Mand.	Hermas, Mandata
Tro.	Troades	Sim.	Similitudines
Euseb. Dem. evang.	Eusebios, Demonstratio Evangelica	Vis.	Visiones
		Hermog.	Hermogenes
Hist. eccl.	Historia Ecclesiastica	Hdn.	Herodianus
On.	Onomasticon (Klostermann 1904)	Heron	Hero
		Hes. Cat.	Hesiodus, Catalogus feminarum (Merkelbach /West 1967)
Praep. evang.	Praeparatio Evangelica		
Eust.	Eustathius	Op.	Opera et dies
Eutr.	Eutropius	Sc.	Scutum (Merkelbach /West1967)
Ev. Ver.	Evangelium Veritatis		
Ex	Exodus = 2. Moses	Theog.	Theogonia
Ez	Ezechiel	Hsch.	Hesychius
Fast.	Fasti	Hil.	Hilarius
Fest.	Festus (Lindsay 1913)	Hippoc.	Hippocrates
Firm. Mat.	Firmicus Maternus	H. Hom.	Hymni Homerici
Flor. Epit.	Florus, Epitoma de Tito Livio	Hom. Il.	Homerus, Ilias
Florent.	Florentinus	Od.	Odyssea
Frontin. Aq.	Frontinus, De aquae ductu urbis Romae	Hor. Ars P.	Horatius, Ars poetica
		Carm.	Carmina
Str.	Strategemata	Carm. saec.	Carmen saeculare
Fulg.	Fulgentius Afer	Epist.	Epistulae
Fulg. Rusp.	Fulgentius Ruspensis	Epod.	Epodi
Gai. Inst.	Gaius, Institutiones	Sat.	Satirae (sermones)
Gal	Letter to the Galatians	Hos	Hosea
Gal.	Galenus	Hyg. Poet. Astr.	Hyginus, Astronomica (Le Bœuffle 1983)
Gell. NA	Gellius, Noctes Atticae		
Geogr. Rav	Geographus Ravennas (Schnetz 1940)	Fab.	Fabulae
		Hyp.	Hypereides
Gp.	Geoponica	Iambl. Myst.	Iamblichus, De mysteriis
Gn	Genesis = 1. Moses	Protr.	Protrepticus in philosophiam
Gorg.	Gorgias	VP	De vita Pythagorica
Greg. M. Dial.	Gregorius Magnus, Dialogi (de miraculis patrum Italicorum)	Iav.	Iavolenus Priscus
		Inst. Iust.	Corpus Juris Civilis, Institutiones (Krueger 1905)
Epist.	Epistulae		
Past.	Regula pastoralis	Ioh. Chrys. Epist.	Iohannes Chrysostomus, Epistulae
Greg. Naz. Epist.	Gregorius Nazianzenus, Epistulae	Hom. ...	Homiliae in ...
Or.	Orationes	Ioh. Mal.	Iohannes Malalas, Chronographia
Greg. Nyss.	Gregorius Nyssenus	Iord. Get.	Iordanes, De origine actibusque Getarum
Greg. Tur. Franc.	Gregorius of Tours, Historia Francorum		
		Iren.	Irenaeus (Rousseau/Doutreleau 1965–82)

Is	Isaiah
Isid. Nat.	Isidorus, De natura rerum
Orig.	Origines
Isoc. Or.	Isocrates, Orationes
It. Ant.	Itinerarium, Antonini
Aug.	Augusti
Burd.	Burdigalense vel Hierosolymita-num
Plac.	Placentini
Iul. Vict. Rhet.	C. Iulius Victor, Ars rhetorica
Iuvenc.	Iuvencus, Evangelia (Huemer 1891)
Jac	Letter of James
Jdt	Judith
Jer	Jeremiah
Jer. Chron.	Jerome, Chronicon
Comm. in Ez.	Commentaria in Ezechielem (PL 25)
Ep.	Epistulae
On.	Onomasticon (Klostermann 1904)
Vir. ill.	De viris illustribus
1 – 3 Jo	1st – 3rd letters of John
Jo	John
Jon	Jona
Jos. Ant. Iud.	Josephus, Antiquitates Iudaicae
BI	Bellum Iudaicum
Ap.	Contra Apionem
Vit.	De sua vita
Jos	Joshua
Jud	Letter of Judas
Julian. Ep.	Julianus, Epistulae
In Gal.	In Galilaeos
Mis.	Misopogon
Or.	Orationes
Symp.	Symposium
Just. Epit.	Justinus, Epitoma historiarum Phi-lippicarum
Justin. Apol.	Justinus Martyr, Apologia
Dial.	Dialogus cum Tryphone
Juv.	Juvenalis, Saturae
1 Kg, 2 Kg	1, 2 Kings
KH	Khania (place where Linear B tables were discovered)
KN	Knossos (place where Linear B ta-bles were discovered)
Lactant. Div. inst.	Lactantius, Divinae institutiones
Ira	De ira dei
De mort. pers.	De mortibus persecutorum
Opif.	De opificio dei
Lam	Lamentations
Lex Irnit.	Lex Irnitana
Lex Malac.	Lex municipii Malacitani
Lex Rubr.	Lex Rubria de Gallia cisalpina
Lex Salpens.	Lex municipii Salpensani
Lex Urson.	Lex coloniae Iuliae Genetivae Ur-sonensis

Lex Visig.	Leges Visigothorum
Lex XII tab.	Lex duodecim tabularum
Lib. Ep.	Libanius, Epistulae
Or.	Orationes
Liv.	Livius, Ab urbe condita
Lc	Luke
Luc.	Lucanus, Bellum civile
Lucil.	Lucilius, Saturae (Marx 1904)
Lucr.	Lucretius, De rerum natura
Lucian. Alex.	Lucianus, Alexander
Anach.	Anacharsis
Cal.	Calumniae non temere creden-dum
Catapl.	Cataplus
Demon.	Demonax
Dial. D.	Dialogi deorum
Dial. meret.	Dialogi meretricium
Dial. mort.	Dialogi mortuorum
Her.	Herodotus
Hermot.	Hermotimus
Hist. conscr.	Quomodo historia conscribenda sit
Ind.	Adversus indoctum
Iupp. trag.	Iuppiter tragoedus
Luct.	De luctu
Macr.	Macrobii
Nigr.	Nigrinus
Philops.	Philopseudes
Pseudol.	Pseudologista
Salt.	De saltatione
Somn.	Somnium
Symp.	Symposium
Syr. D.	De Syria dea
Trag.	Tragodopodagra
Ver. hist.	Verae historiae, 1, 2
Vit. auct.	Vitarum auctio
Lv	Leviticus = 3. Moses
LXX	Septuaginta
Lydus, Mag.	Lydus, De magistratibus
Mens.	De mensibus
Lycoph.	Lycophron
Lycurg.	Lycurgus
Lys.	Lysias
M. Aur.	Marcus Aurelius Antoninus Augus-tus
Macrob. Sat.	Macrobius, Saturnalia
In Somn.	Commentarii in Ciceronis som-nium Scipionis
1 Macc, 2 Macc	Maccabees
Mal	Malachi
Manil.	Manilius, Astronomica (Goold 1985)
Mar. Vict.	Marius Victorinus
Mart.	Martialis
Mart. Cap.	Martianus Capella
Max. Tyr.	Maximus Tyrius (Trapp 1994)
Mela	Pomponius Mela
Melanipp.	Melanippides

Men. Dys.	Menander, Dyskolos
Epit.	Epitrepontes
Fr.	Fragmentum (Körte)
Pk.	Perikeiromene
Sam.	Samia
Mi	Micha
Mimn.	Mimnermus
Min. Fel.	Minucius Felix, Octavius (Kytzler 1982,²1992)
Mk	Mark
Mod.	Herennius Modestinus
Mosch.	Moschus
Mt	Matthew
MY	Mycenae (place where Linear B tables were discovered)
Naev.	Naevius (carmina according to FPL)
Nah	Nahum
Neh	Nehemia
Nemes.	Nemesianus
Nep. Att.	Cornelius Nepos, Atticus
Hann.	Hannibal
Nic. Alex.	Nicander, Alexipharmaca
Ther.	Theriaca
Nicom.	Nicomachus
Nm	Numbers = 4. Moses
Non.	Nonius Marcellus (L. Mueller 1888)
Nonnus, Dion.	Nonnus, Dionysiaca
Not. Dign. Occ.	Notitia dignitatum occidentis
Not. Dign. Or.	Notitia dignitatum orientis
Not. Episc.	Notitia dignitatum et episcoporum
Nov.	Corpus Iuris Civilis, Leges Novellae (Schoell/Kroll 1904)
Obseq.	Julius Obsequens, Prodigia (Rossbach 1910)
Opp. Hal.	Oppianus, Halieutica
Kyn.	Cynegetica
Or. Sib.	Oracula Sibyllina
Orib.	Oribasius
Orig.	Origenes
OrMan	Prayer to Manasseh
Oros.	Orosius
Orph. A.	Orpheus, Argonautica
Fr.	Fragmentum (Kern)
H.	Hymni
Ov. Am.	Ovidius, Amores
Ars am.	Ars amatoria
Epist.	Epistulae (Heroides)
Fast.	Fasti
Ib.	Ibis
Medic.	Medicamina faciei femineae
Met.	Metamorphoses
Pont.	Epistulae ex Ponto
Rem. am.	Remedia amoris
Tr.	Tristia
P	Papyrus editions according to E.G. TURNER, Greek Papyri. An Introduction, 159–178

P Abinn.	Papyrus editions according to H.I. BELL ET AL. (ED.), The Abinnaeus Archive papers of a Roman officer in the reign of Constantius II, 1962
P Bodmer	Papyrus editions according to V. MARTIN, R. KASSER ET AL. (ED.), Papyrus Bodmer 1954ff.
P CZ	Papyrus editions according to C.C. EDGAR (ED.), Zenon Papyri (Catalogue général des Antiquités égyptiennes du Musée du Caire) 4 vols., 1925ff.
P Hercul.	Papyrus editions according to Papyri aus Herculaneum
P Lond.	Papyrus editions according to F.G. KENYON ET AL. (ED.), Greek Papyri in the British Museum 7 vols., 1893–1974
P Mich	Papyrus editions according to C.C. EDGAR, A.E.R. BOAK, J.G. WINTER ET AL. (ED.), Papyri in the University of Michigan Collection 13 vols., 1931–1977
P Oxy.	Papyrus editions according to B.P. GRENFELL, A.S. HUNT ET AL. (ED.), The Oxyrhynchus Papyri, 1898 ff.
Pall. Agric.	Palladius, Opus agriculturae
Laus.	Historia Lausiaca
Pan. Lat.	Panegyrici Latini
Papin.	Aemilius Papinianus
Paroemiogr.	Paroemiographi Graeci
Pass. mart.	Passiones martyrum
Paul Fest.	Paulus Diaconus, Epitoma Festi
Paul Nol.	Paulinus Nolanus
Paulus, Sent.	Julius Paulus, Sententiae
Paus.	Pausanias
Pelag.	Pelagius
Peripl. m. eux.	Periplus maris Euxini
Peripl. m.m.	Periplus maris magni
Peripl. m.r.	Periplus maris rubri
Pers.	Persius, Saturae
1 Petr, 2 Petr	Letters of Peter
Petron. Sat.	Petronius, Satyrica (Müller 1961)
Phaedr.	Phaedrus, Fabulae (Guaglianone 1969)
Phil	Letter to the Philippians
Phil.	Philo
Philarg. Verg. ecl.	Philargyrius grammaticus, Explanatio in eclogas Vergilii
Philod.	Philodemus
Phlp.	Philoponus
Philostr. VA	Philostratus, Vita Apollonii
Imag.	Imagines
VS	Vitae sophistarum
Phm	Letter to Philemon
Phot.	Photius (Bekker 1824)

Phryn.	Phrynichus	Men.	Menaechmi
Pind. Fr.	Pindar, Fragments (Snell/Maehler)	Merc.	Mercator
Isthm.	Isthmian Odes	Mil.	Miles gloriosus
Nem.	Nemean Odes	Mostell.	Mostellaria
Ol.	Olympian Odes	Poen.	Poenulus
Pae.	Paeanes	Pseud.	Pseudolus
Pyth.	Pythian Odes	Rud.	Rudens
Pl. Alc. 1	Plato, Alcibiades 1 (Stephanus)	Stich.	Stichus
Alc. 2	Alcibiades 2	Trin.	Trinummus
Ap.	Apologia	Truc.	Truculentus
Ax.	Axiochus	Vid.	Vidularia
Chrm.	Charmides	Plin. HN	Plinius maior, Naturalis historia
Cleit.	Clitopho	Plin. Ep.	Plinius minor, Epistulae
Crat.	Cratylus	Pan.	Panegyricus
Crit.	Crito	Plot.	Plotinus
Criti.	Critias	Plut.	Plutarchus, Vitae parallelae (with
Def.	Definitiones		the respective name)
Demod.	Demodocus	Amat.	Amatorius (chapter and page
Epin.	Epinomis		numbers)
Ep.	Epistulae	De def. or.	De defectu oraculorum
Erast.	Erastae	De E	De E apud Delphos
Eryx.	Eryxias	De Pyth. or.	De Pythiae oraculis
Euthd.	Euthydemus	De sera	De sera numinis vindicta
Euthphr.	Euthyphro	De Is. et Os.	De Iside et Osiride (with chapter
Grg.	Gorgias		and page numbers)
Hp. mai.	Hippias maior	Mor.	Moralia (apart from the sepa-
Hp. mi.	Hippias minor		rately mentioned works; with p.
Hipparch.	Hipparchus		numbers)
Ion	Ion	Quaest.	Quaestiones Graecae (with
La.	Laches	Graec.	chapter numbers)
Leg.	Leges	Quaest. Rom.	Quaestiones Romanae (with ch.
Ly.	Lysis		numbers)
Men.	Menon	Symp.	Quaestiones convivales (book,
Min.	Minos		chapter, page number)
Menex.	Menexenus	Pol.	Polybius
Prm.	Parmenides	Pol. Silv.	Polemius Silvius
Phd.	Phaedo	Poll.	Pollux
Phdr.	Phaedrus	Polyaenus, Strat.	Polyaenus, Strategemata
Phlb.	Philebus	Polyc.	Polycarpus, Letter
Plt.	Politicus	Pompon.	Sextus Pomponius
Prt.	Protagoras	Pomp. Trog.	Pompeius Trogus
Resp.	Res publica	Porph.	Porphyrius
Sis.	Sisyphus	Porph. Hor.	Porphyrio, Commentum in Horatii
Soph.	Sophista	comm.	carmina
Symp.	Symposium	Posidon.	Posidonius
Thg.	Theages	Priap.	Priapea
Tht.	Theaetetus	Prisc.	Priscianus
Ti.	Timaeus	Prob.	Pseudo-Probian writings
Plaut. Amph.	Plautus, Amphitruo (fr.according	Procop. Aed.	Procopius, De aedificiis
	to Leo 1895 f.)	Goth.	Bellum Gothicum
Asin.	Asinaria	Pers.	Bellum Persicum
Aul.	Aulularia	Vand.	Bellum Vandalicum
Bacch.	Bacchides	Arc.	Historia arcana
Capt.	Captivi	Procl.	Proclus
Cas.	Casina	Prop.	Propertius, Elegiae
Cist.	Cistellaria	Prosp.	Prosper Tiro
Curc.	Curculio	Prov.	Proverbs
Epid.	Epidicus	Prudent.	Prudentius

Ps (Pss)	Psalm(s)
Ps.-Acro	Ps.-Acro in Horatium
Ps.-Aristot. Lin. insec.	Pseudo-Aristotle, De lineis insecabilibus
Mech.	Mechanica
Ps.-Sall. In Tull.	Pseudo-Sallustius, In M.Tullium Ciceronem invectiva
Rep.	Epistulae ad Caesarem senem de re publica
Ptol. Alm.	Ptolemy, Almagest
Geog.	Geographia
Harm.	Harmonica
Tetr.	Tetrabiblos
PY	Pylos (place where Linear B tablets were discovered)
4 Q Flor	Florilegium, Cave 4
4 Q Patr	Patriarch's blessing, Cave 4
1 Q pHab	Habakuk-Midrash, Cave 1
4 Q pNah	Nahum-Midrash, Cave 4
4 Q test	Testimonia, Cave 4
1 QH	Songs of Praise, Cave 1
1 QM	War list, Cave 1
1 QS	Comunal rule, Cave 1
1 QSa	Community rule, Cave 1
1 QSb	Blessings, Cave 1
Quint. Smyrn.	Quintus Smyrnaeus
Quint. Decl.	Quintilianus, Declamationes minores (Shackleton Bailey 1989)
Inst.	Institutio oratoria
R. Gest. div. Aug.	Res gestae divi Augusti
Rhet. Her.	Rhetorica ad C. Herennium
Rom	Letter to the Romans
Rt	Ruth
Rufin.	Tyrannius Rufinus
Rut. Namat.	Rutilius Claudius Namatianus, De reditu suo
S. Sol.	Song of Solomon
Sext. Emp.	Sextus Empiricus
Sach	Sacharia
Sall. Catil.	Sallustius, De coniuratione Catilinae
Hist.	Historiae
Iug.	De bello Iugurthino
Salv. Gub.	Salvianus, De gubernatione dei
1 Sam 2 Sam	Samuel
Schol. (before an author's name)	Scholia to the author in question
Sedul.	Sedulius
Sen. Controv.	Seneca maior, Controversiae
Suas.	Suasoriae
Sen. Ag.	Seneca minor, Agamemno
Apocol.	Divi Claudii apocolocyntosis
Ben.	De beneficiis
Clem.	De clementia (Hosius ²1914)
Dial.	Dialogi
Ep.	Epistulae morales ad Lucilium
Herc. f.	Hercules furens

Med.	Medea
Q Nat.	Naturales quaestiones
Oed.	Oedipus
Phaedr.	Phaedra
Phoen.	Phoenissae
Thy.	Thyestes
Tranq.	De tranquillitate animi
Tro.	Troades
Serv. auct.	Servius auctus Danielis
Serv. Aen.	Servius, Commentarius in Vergilii Aeneida
Ecl.	Commentarius in Vergilii eclogas
Georg.	Commentarius in Vergilii georgica
Sext. Emp.	Sextus Empiricus
SHA Ael.	Scriptores Historiae Augustae, Aelius
Alb.	Clodius Albinus
Alex. Sev.	Alexander Severus
Aur.	M. Aurelius
Aurel.	Aurelianus
Avid. Cass.	Avidius Cassius
Car.	Carus et Carinus et Numerianus
Carac.	Antoninus Caracalla
Clod.	Claudius
Comm.	Commodus
Diad.	Diadumenus Antoninus
Did. Iul.	Didius Iulianus
Gall.	Gallieni duo
Gord.	Gordiani tres
Hadr.	Hadrianus
Heliogab.	Heliogabalus
Max. Balb.	Maximus et Balbus
Opil.	Opilius Macrinus
Pert.	Helvius Pertinax
Pesc. Nig.	Pescennius Niger
Pius	Antoninus Pius
Quadr. tyr.	Quadraginta tyranni
Sev.	Severus
Tac.	Tacitus
Tyr. Trig.	Triginta Tyranni
Valer.	Valeriani duo
Sid. Apoll. Carm.	Apollinaris Sidonius, Carmina
Epist.	Epistulae
Sil. Pun.	Silius Italicus, Punica
Simon.	Simonides
Simpl.	Simplicius
Sir	Jesus Sirach
Scyl.	Scylax, Periplus
Scymn.	Scymnus, Periegesis
Socr.	Socrates, Historia ecclesiastica
Sol.	Solon
Solin.	Solinus
Soph. Aj.	Sophocles, Ajax
Ant.	Antigone
El.	Electra
Ichn.	Ichneutae
OC	Oedipus Coloneus

OT	Oedipus Tyrannus	1 Thess, 2 Thess	Letters to the Thessalonians
Phil.	Philoctetes	Thgn.	Theognis
Trach.	Trachiniae	Thuc.	Thucydides
Sor. Gyn.	Soranus, Gynaecia	TI	Tiryns (place where Linear B tablets
Sozom. Hist.	Sozomenus, Historia ecclesiastica		were discovered)
eccl.		Tib.	Tibullus, Elegiae
Stat. Achil.	Statius, Achilleis	1 Tim, 2 Tim	Letters to Timothy
Silv.	Silvae	Tit	Letter to Titus
Theb.	Thebais	Tob	Tobit
Steph. Byz.	Stephanus Byzantius	Tzetz. Anteh.	Tzetzes, Antehomerica
Stesich.	Stesichorus	Chil.	Chiliades
Stob.	Stobaeus	Posth.	Posthomerica
Str.	Strabo (books, chapters)	Ulp.	Ulpianus (Ulpiani regulae)
Suda	Suda = Suidas	Val. Fl.	Valerius Flaccus, Argonautica
Suet. Aug.	Suetonius, Divus Augustus (Ihm	Val. Max.	Valerius Maximus, Facta et dicta
	1907)		memorabilia
Calig.	Caligula	Varro, Ling.	Varro, De lingua Latina
Claud.	Divus Claudius	Rust.	Res rusticae
Dom.	Domitianus	Sat. Men.	Saturae Menippeae (Astbury
Gram.	De grammaticis (Kaster 1995)		1985)
Iul.	Divus Iulius	Vat.	Fragmenta Vaticana
Tib.	Divus Tiberius	Veg. Mil.	Vegetius, Epitoma rei militaris
Tit.	Divus Titus	Vell. Pat.	Velleius Paterculus, Historiae
Vesp.	Divus Vespasianus		Romanae
Vit.	Vitellius	Ven. Fort.	Venantius Fortunatus
Sulp. Sev.	Sulpicius Severus	Verg. Aen.	Vergilius, Aeneis
Symmachus, Ep.	Symmachus, Epistulae	Catal.	Catalepton
Or.	Orationes	Ecl.	Eclogae
Relat.	Relationes	G.	Georgica
Synes. epist.	Synesius, Epistulae	Vir. ill.	De viris illustribus
Sync.	Syncellus	Vitr. De arch.	Vitruvius, De architectura
Tab. Peut.	Tabula Peutingeriana	Vulg.	Vulgate
Tac. Agr.	Tacitus, Agricola	Wisd	Wisdom
Ann.	Annales	Xen. Ages.	Xenophon, Agesilaus
Dial.	Dialogus de oratoribus	An.	Anabasis
Germ.	Germania	Ap.	Apologia
Hist.	Historiae	Ath. pol.	Athenaion politeia
Ter. Maur.	Terentianus Maurus	Cyn.	Cynegeticus
Ter. Ad.	Terentius, Adelphoe	Cyr.	Cyropaedia
An.	Andria	Eq.	De equitandi ratione
Eun.	Eunuchus	Eq. mag.	De equitum magistro
Haut.	H(e)autontimorumenos	Hell.	Hellenica
Hec.	Hecyra	Hier.	Hiero
Phorm.	Phormio	Lac.	Respublica Lacedaemoniorum
Tert. Apol.	Tertullianus, Apologeticum	Mem.	Memorabilia
Ad nat.	Ad nationes (Borleffs 1954)	Oec.	Oeconomicus
TH	Thebes (place where Linear B tables	Symp.	Symposium
	were discovered)	Vect.	De vectigalibus
Them. Or.	Themistius, Orationes	Xenoph.	Xenophanes
Theoc.	Theocritus	Zen.	Zeno
Theod. Epist.	Theodoretus, Epistulae	Zenob.	Zenobius
Gr. aff. Cur.	Graecarum affectionum curatio	Zenod.	Zenodotus
Hist. eccl.	Historia ecclesiastica	Zeph	Zephania
Theopomp.	Theopompus	Zon.	Zonaras
Theophr. Caus.	Theophrastus, De causis plantarum	Zos.	Zosimus
pl.			
Char.	Characteres		
Hist. pl.	Historia plantarum		

List of Illustrations and Maps

Illustrations are found in the corresponding entries.
ND means redrawing following the instructions of the
author or after the listed materials.
RP means reproduction with minor changes.

Some of the maps serve to visualize the subject matter
and to complement the articles. In such cases, there will
be a reference to the corresponding entry. Only literature that was used exclusively for the maps is listed.

Macedonia

Macellum

Magic

Mago

Manching

Marble

Marzabotto

Masks

Masonry

Massalia

Mastaba

Mathematics

Mauryas
The development of the Mauryan empire in the 4th–3rd cents. BC
ND: K. KARTTUNEN/EDITORIAL TEAM

Mausoleum
Mausoleum; hypothetical reconstruction of east side
ND after: W. HOEPFNER, Zum Maussolleion von Halikarnassos, in: AA 1996, fig. 7.

Mausoleum Augusti
Rome, Mausoleum Augusti (schematic front elevation)
ND after: J. GANZERT, Das Kenotaph für Gaius Caesar in Limyra, 1984, Beilage 22.

Mausoleum Hadriani
Mausoleum Hadriani (Castel Sant'Angelo): ground-plan of the southern half
ND after: F. COARELLI, Rom. Ein archäologischer Führer, 1975, 322.

Menelaus [6] of Alexandria
ND after: J. MAU, s. v. Menelaos [6], KlP 3, 1211.

Mesopotamia
Mesopotamia and the adjacent regions (3rd millennium – 6th cent. BC)
ND: J. OELSNER

Messapian pottery
Vessel shapes in Messapian pottery
ND after: D. YNTEMA, Messapian Pottery. Analyses and Provisory Classification, in: BABesch 49, 1974, 8.

Messene
Messene, Asklepieion (ground-plan)
ND after: P. THEMELIS, Damophon von Messene – Sein Werk im Lichte der neuen Ausgrabungen, in: AK 36–37, 1993–94, 29, Abb. 2.

Metallurgy
Ore-washing plant at Laurium (ground-plan)
ND after: J. F. HEALY, Mining and Metallurgy in the Greek and Roman World, 1978, 146.

Migration of the peoples
Migrations of Germanic tribes and their incursions into the Roman Empire during the 3rd cent. AD
ND: K. TAUSEND
Migrations of Germanic tribes between the 2nd and the 6th cents. AD
ND: K. TAUSEND
Germanic kingdoms and settlement areas c. AD 476
ND: K. TAUSEND

Miletus
Millawa(n)da (?) / Miletus: settlement areas (c. 19th–6th cents. BC)
ND: R. SENFF/EDITORIAL TEAM TÜBINGEN
Miletus (7th cent. BC – 6th cent. AD)
ND: B. F. WEBER

Mills
Prehistoric saddlestone mill
ND after a design of D. BAATZ
Late Hellenistic hand-mill
ND after a design of D. BAATZ
Lever mill (reconstruction)
ND after: D. M. ROBINSON, J. W. GRAHAM, Excavations at Olynthos. The Hellenic House, 8, 1938, 328, Abb. 34.
Donkey mill, 1st cent. AD (reconstruction)
ND after a design of D. BAATZ
Fast-turning grinding mechanism, its components based on the find at Zugmantel, Taunus (2nd half 2nd cent. AD).
ND after a model of D. BAATZ
Water-mill with fast-turning grinding mechanism (from 2nd cent. AD onwards); reconstruction.
ND after a model of D. BAATZ

Mineral resources
Mineral resources in the Aegaean area (c. 4000 – after 1100 BC)
EDITORIAL TEAM TÜBINGEN/ND after TAVO (Autor: S. Schöler, © Dr. Ludwig Reichert Verlag, Wiesbaden)
Lit.: S. SCHÖLER, Mineralische Rohstoffe in vorgeschichtlicher und geschichtlicher Zeit, TAVO A II 2, 1990.
F. TICHY, DNP 2, 1997, s. v. Bodenschätze.

List of Authors

Aigner-Foresti, Luciana, Vienna	L.A.-F.	Dorandi, Tiziano, Paris	T.D.
Albiani, Maria Grazia, Bologna	M.G.A.	Döring, Klaus, Bamberg	K.D.
Albrecht, Ruth, Hamburg	R.A.	Dräger, Paul, Trier	P.D.
Alonso-Núñez, José Miguel, Madrid	J.M.A.-N.	Drew-Bear, Thomas, Lyon	T.D.-B.
Ameling, Walter, Jena	W.A.	Dreyer, Boris, Göttingen	BO.D.
Andreau, Jean, Paris	J.A.	Drögemüller, Hans-Peter, Hamburg	H.-P.DRÖ.
Auffarth, Christoph, Tübingen	C.A.	Drougou, Stella, Thessaloniki	S.DR.
Baatz, Dietwulf, Bad Homburg	D.BA.	Duridanov, Ludmil, Freiburg	L.D.
Badian, Ernst, Cambridge, MA	E.B.	Dürkop, Martina, Potsdam	MA.D.
Baltes, Matthias, Münster	M.BA.	Eck, Werner, Cologne	W.E.
Banholzer, Iris, Tübingen	I.BAN.	Eder, Walter, Bochum	W.ED.
Barceló, Pedro, Potsdam	P.B.	Ego, Beate, Osnabrück	B.E.
Baroin, Catherine, Paris	CA.BA.	Eigler, Ulrich, Trier	U.E.
Baudy, Gerhard, Konstanz	G.B.	Eleuteri, Paolo, Venice	P.E.
Baumbach, Manuel, Heidelberg	M.B.	Elvers, Karl-Ludwig, Bochum	K.-L.E.
Baumeister, Theofried, Mainz	TH.BA.	Engels, Johannes, Cologne	J.E.
Beck, Hans, Cologne	HA.BE.	Errington, Robert Malcolm, Marburg/Lahn	MA.ER.
Becker, Andrea, Berlin	AN.BE.	Esders, Stefan, Bochum	S.E.
Belke, Klaus, Vienna	K.BE.	Euskirchen, Marion, Bonn	M.E.
Benedetti Conti, Marina, Pisa	M.B.C.	Falco, Giulia, Athens	GI.F.
Berger, Albrecht, Berlin	AL.B.	Felber, Heinz, Leipzig	HE.FE.
Birley, A.R., Düsseldorf	A.B.	Fischer Saglia, Gudrun, Munich	G.F.S.
Bleckmann, Bruno, Bern	B.BL.	Fitschen, Klaus, Kiel	K.FI.
Bloedhorn, Hanswulf, Jerusalem	H.BL.	Flamant, Jaques, Venelles	J.F.
Blümel, Wolfgang, Cologne	W.BL.	Folkerts, Menso, Munich	M.F.
Böck, Barbara, Berlin	BA.BÖ.	Fornaro, Sotera, Sassari	S.FO.
Bodnár, István, Budapest	I.B.	Frank, Karl Suso, Freiburg	K.-S.F.
Bonfante, Larissa, New York	L.B.	Franke, Thomas, Bochum	T.F.
Bove, Annalisa, Pisa	A.BO.	Frateantonio, Christa, Gießen-Erfurt	C.F.
Bowie, Ewen, Oxford	E.BO.	Frede, Michael, Oxford	M.FR.
von Bredow, Iris, Stuttgart	I.v.B.	Freitag, Klaus, Münster	K.F.
Brentjes, Burchard, Berlin	B.B.	Frey, Alexandra, Basle	AL.FR.
Bringmann, Klaus, Frankfurt/Main	K.BR.	Freyburger, Gérard, Mulhouse	G.F.
Brisson, Luc, Paris	L.BR.	Frigo, Thomas, Bonn	T.FR.
Brock, Sebastian P., Oxford	S.BR.	Fritscher, Bernhard, Munich	B.FR.
Brodersen, Kai, Newcastle and Mannheim	K.BRO.	Fündling, Jörg, Bonn	JÖ.F.
Burckhardt, Leonhard, Basle	LE.BU.	Funke, Peter, Münster	P.F.
Burian, Jan, Prague	J.BU.	Furley, William D., Heidelberg	W.D.F.
Cabanes, Pierre, Clermont-Ferrand	PI.CA.	Gaggero, Gianfranco, Genova	G.GA.
Campbell, J.Brian, Belfast	J.CA.	Galsterer, Hartmut, Bonn	H.GA.
Camporeale, Giovannangelo, Florence	GI.C.	Garnsey, Peter, Cambridge	P.GA.
Cartledge, Paul A., Cambridge	P.C.	Gärtner, Hans Armin, Heidelberg	H.A.G.
Charpin, Dominique, Paris	D.CH.	Gatti, Paolo, Triento	P.G.
Cobet, Justus, Essen	J.CO.	Gauly, Bardo Maria, Kiel	B.GY.
Courtney, Edward, Charlottesville, VA	ED.C.	Giaro, Tomasz, Frankfurt/Main	T.G.
Damschen, Gregor, Halle/Saale	GR.DA.	Giesen, Katharina, Tübingen	K.GIE.
Daverio Rocchi, Giovanna, Milan G.D.R.	L.d.L.	Gippert, Jost, Frankfurt/Main	J.G.
	S.d.V.	Gizewski, Christian, Berlin	C.G.
Decker, Wolfgang, Cologne	W.D.	Glei, Reinhold F., Bochum	R.GL.
Dietrich, Albert, Göttingen	A.D.	Gniers, Andrea Maria, Basle	A.M.G.
Dietz, Karlheinz, Würzburg	K.DI.	Gordon, Richard L., Ilmmünster	R.GOR.

Goulet-Cazé, Marie-Odile, Antony	M.G.-C.
Graßl, Herbert, Salzburg	H.GR.
Greschat, Katharina, Mainz	K.GRE.
Groß-Albenhausen, Kirsten, Frankfurt/Main	K.G.-A.
Grünewald, Thomas, Duisburg	TH.GR.
Gulletta, Maria Ida, Pisa	M.I.G.
Günther, Linda-Marie, Bochum	L.-M.G.
Gutsfeld, Andreas, Münster	A.G.
Habermehl, Peter, Berlin	PE.HA.
Haebler, Claus, Münster	C.H.
Hahn, Johannes, Münster	J.H.
Halbwachs, Verena Tiziana, Vienna	V.T.H.
Halfwassen, Jens, Cologne	JE.HA.
Harder, Ruth Elisabeth, Zürich	R.HA.
Hecker, Karl, Münster	K.HE.
Heimgartner, Martin, Basle	M.HE.
Heinze, Theodor, Geneva	T.H.
Herz, Peter, Regensburg	P.H.
Heucke, Clemens, Munich	C.HEU.
Hidber, Thomas, Göttingen	T.HI.
Hild, Friedrich, Vienna	F.H.
Hitzl, Konrad, Tübingen	K.H.
Höcker, Christoph, Zürich	C.HÖ.
Hoesch, Nicola, Munich	N.H.
Holzhausen, Jens, Berlin	J.HO.
Hübner, Wolfgang, Münster	W.H.
Hünemörder, Christian, Hamburg	C.HÜ.
Hunger, Hermann, Vienna	H.HU.
Hurschmann, Rolf, Hamburg	R.H.
Huß, Werner, Munich	W.HU.
Inwood, Brad, Toronto, ON	B.I.
Jacobs, Bruno, Vienna	BR.JA.
Jameson, Michael, Stanford	MI.JA.
Jansen-Winkeln, Karl, Berlin	K.J.-W.
John, James J., Ithaca, NY	J.J.J.
Johne, Klaus-Peter, Berlin	K.P.J.
Johnston, Sarah Iles, Columbus, OH	S.I.J.
Jung, Reinhard, Vienna	R.J.
Kahl, Jochem, Münster	J.KA.
Kaizer, Ted, Oxford	T.KAI.
Kalcyk, Hansjörg, Petershausen	H.KAL.
Kaletsch, Hans, Regensburg	H.KA.
Käppel, Lutz, Kiel	L.K.
Karttunen, Klaus, Helsinki	K.K.
Kehne, Peter, Hannover	P.KE.
Kessler, Karlheinz, Emskirchen	K.KE.
Kierdorf, Wilhelm, Cologne	W.K.
King, Helen, Reading	H.K.
Kinzl, Konrad, Peterborough	K.KI.
Klodt, Claudia, Hamburg	CL.K.
Klose, Dietrich, Munich	DI.K.
Kohler, Christoph, Bad Krozingen	C.KO.
Kolb, Anne, Zürich	A.K.
Kowalzig, Barbara, Oxford	B.K.
Krafft, Fritz, Marburg/Lahn	F.KR.
Kramolisch, Herwig, Eppelheim	HE.KR.
Krapinger, Gernot, Graz	G.K.
Krauss, Rolf, Berlin	R.K.

Kuchenbuch, Ludolf, Hagen	LU.KU.
Kühne, Hartmut, Berlin	H.KÜ.
Kundert, Lukas, Basle	LUK.KU.
Kunz, Heike, Tübingen	HE.K.
Kutsch, Ernst, Vienna	ER.K.
Lafond, Yves, Bochum	Y.L.
Lamboley, Jean-Luc, Grenoble	J.-L.L.
Latacz, Joachim, Basle	J.L.
Lausberg, Marion, Augsburg	MA.L.
Le Bohec, Yann, Lyon	Y.L.B.
Leisten, Thomas, Princeton, NJ	T.L.
Leonhardt, Jürgen, Marburg/Lahn	J.LE.
Leppin, Hartmut, Frankfurt/Main	H.L.
Letsch-Brunner, Silvia, Zürich	S.L.-B.
Ley, Anne, Xanten	A.L.
Lezzi-Hafter, Adrienne, Kilchberg	A.L.-H.
de Libero, Loretana, Hamburg	
Lienau, Cay, Münster	C.L.
Liwak, Rüdiger, Berlin	R.L.
Lohmann, Hans, Bochum	H.LO.
Lohwasser, Angelika, Berlin	A.LO.
Lombardo, Mario, Lecce	M.L.
Losemann, Volker, Marburg/Lahn	V.L.
Lütkenhaus, Werner, Marl	WE.LÜ.
Luz, Ulrich, Göttingen	U.L.
Maharam, Wolfram-Aslan, Munich	W.-A.M.
von Mangoldt, Hans, Tübingen	H.v.M.
Markschies, Christoph, Berlin	C.M.
Martini, Wolfram, Gießen	W.MA.
Mastrocinque, Attilio, Verona	A.MAS.
Maul, Stefan, Heidelberg	S.M.
Mehl, Andreas, Halle/Saale	A.ME.
Meier, Mischa, Tübingen	M.MEI.
Meiser, Gerhard, Halle/Saale	GE.ME.
Meißner, Burkhard, Halle/Saale	B.M.
Meister, Klaus, Berlin	K.MEI.
Meriç, Recep, Izmir	R.M.
Messina, Aldo, Triest	AL.MES.
Meyer †, Ernst, Zürich	E.MEY.
Michel, Raphael, Basle	RA.MI.
Miller, Martin, Berlin	M.M.
Mommsen, Heide, Stuttgart	H.M.
Montanari, Ornella, Bologna	O.M.
Muggia, Anna, Pavia	A.MU.
Müller, Christian, Bochum	C.MÜ.
Müller, Walter W., Marburg/Lahn	W.W.M.
Nadig, Peter C., Duisburg	P.N.
Nauerth, Claudia, Heidelberg	CL.NA.
Nesselrath, Heinz-Günther, Göttingen	H.-G.NE.
Neudecker, Richard, Rome	R.N.
Neumeister, Christoff, Frankfurt/Main	CH.N.
Niehoff, Johannes, Budapest	J.N.
Nielsen, Inge, Hamburg	I.N.
Niemeyer, Hans Georg, Hamburg	H.G.N.
Nissen, Hans Jörg, Berlin	H.J.N.
Nünlist, René, Providence, RI	RE.N.
Nutton, Vivian, London	V.N.
Oakley, John H., Williamsburg, VA	J.O.

Oelsner, Joachim, Leipzig	J. OE.	Seidlmayer, Stephan Johannes, Berlin	S. S.
Olshausen, Eckart, Stuttgart	E. O.	Senff, Reinhard, Bochum	R. SE.
Pahlitzsch, Johannes, Berlin	J. P.	Smolak, Kurt, Vienna	K. SM.
Parker, Robert, Oxford	R. PA.	Sonnabend, Holger, Stuttgart	H. SO.
Patzek, Barbara, Essen	B. P.	Spickermann, Wolfgang, Bochum	W. SP.
Paulus, Christoph Georg, Berlin	C. PA.	Stanzel, Karl-Heinz, Tübingen	K.-H. S.
Peter, Ulrike, Berlin	U. P.	Starke, Frank, Tübingen	F. S.
Petersen, Silke, Hamburg	S. P.	Stegmann, Helena, Bonn	H. S.
Petzl, Georg, Cologne	G. PE.	Stein-Hölkeskamp, Elke, Cologne	E. S.-H.
Phillips, C. Robert III., Bethlehem, PA	C. R. P.	Stenger, Jan, Kiel	J. STE.
Pingel, Volker, Bochum	V. P.	Stol, Marten, Leiden	MA. S.
Plontke-Lüning, Annegret, Jena	A. P.-L.	Strauch, Daniel, Berlin	D. S.
Podella, Thomas, Lübeck	TH. PO.	Strobel, Karl, Klagenfurt	K. ST.
Polfer, Michel, Luxemburg	MI. PO.	Stroh, Wilfried, Munich	W. STR.
Pollmann, Karla, St. Andrews	K. P.	von Stuckrad, Kocku, Erfurt	K. v. S.
Portmann, Werner, Berlin	W. P.	Stumpf, Gerd, Munich	GE. S.
Prato, Giancarlo, Cremona	G. P.	Takacs, Sarolta A., Cambridge, MA	S. TA.
Prayon, Friedhelm, Tübingen	F. PR.	Temporini – Gräfin Vitzthum, Hildegard, Tübingen	
Prescendi, Francesca, Geneva	FR. P.		H. T.-V.
Quack, Joachim, Berlin	JO. QU.	Thür, Gerhard, Graz	G. T.
Rathmann, Michael, Bonn	M. RA.	Tichy, Franz, Erlangen	F. TI.
von Reden, Sitta, Bristol	S. v. R.	Tinnefeld, Franz, Munich	F. T.
Renger, Johannes, Berlin	J. RE.	Todd, Malcolm, Exeter	M. TO.
Rhodes, Peter J., Durham	P. J. R.	Toral-Niehoff, Isabel, Freiburg	I. T.-N.
Riedweg, Christoph, Zürich	C. RI.	Touwaide, Alain, Madrid	A. TO.
Rist, Josef, Würzburg	J. RI.	Trapp, Michael, London	M. T.
Rix †, Helmut, Freiburg	H. R.	Treggiari, Susan, Stanford	SU. T.
Robbins, Emmet, Toronto, ON	E. R.	Uggeri, Giovanni, Florence	G. U.
Roberts, Michael, Middletown	M. RO.	Untermann, Jürgen, Pulheim	J. U.
Rosen, Klaus, Bonn	K. R.	Uthemann, Karl-Heinz, Amsterdam	K. U.
Rudolph, Kurt, Marburg/Lahn	KU. R.	Vassis, Ioannis, Athens	I. V.
Ruffing, Kai, Marburg/Lahn	K. RU.	de Vido, Stefania, Venice	
Rüpke, Jörg, Erfurt	J. R.	Visser, Edzard, Basle	E. V.
Saffrey, Henri D., Paris	H. SA.	Wagner-Hasel, Beate, Darmstadt	B. W.-H.
Sallaberger, Walther, Leipzig	WA. SA.	Walde, Christine, Mainz	C. W.
Salsano, Deborah, Catania	D. SA.	Waldner, Katharina, Erfurt	K. WA.
Sartori, Antonio, Milan	A. SA.	Wandrey, Irina, Berlin	I. WA.
Šašel Kos, Marjeta, Ljubljana	M. Š. K.	Wartke, Ralf-B., Berlin	R. W.
Savvidis, Kyriakos, Bochum	K. SA.	Weiß, Peter, Kiel	P. W.
Sayar, Mustafa H., Cologne	M. H. S.	Weißenberger, Michael, Greifswald	M. W.
Schanbacher, Dietmar, Dresden	D. SCH.	Welwei, Karl-Wilhelm, Bochum	K.-W. WEL.
Scherf, Johannes, Tübingen	JO. S.	Wermelinger, Otto, Fribourg	O. WER.
Schiemann, Gottfried, Tübingen	G. S.	West, Martin L., Oxford	M. L. W.
Schindler, Alfred, Heidelberg	AL. SCHI.	Westbrook, Raymond, Baltimore	RA. WE.
Schlapbach, Karin, Zürich	K. SCHL.	Wick, Peter, Basle	P. WI.
Schmidt, Peter Lebrecht, Konstanz	P. L. S.	Wiegels, Rainer, Osnabrück	RA. WI.
Schmitt, Tassilo, Bielefeld	TA. S.	Wiesehöfer, Josef, Kiel	J. W.
Schmitz, Winfried, Bielefeld	W. S.	Wiggermann, Frans, Amsterdam	F. W.
Schneider, Helmuth, Kassel	H. SCHN.	Will, Wolfgang, Bonn	W. W.
Schneider, Notker, Cologne	NO. SCH.	Willers, Dietrich, Bern	DI. WI.
Schneider, Rolf Michael, Cambridge	R. M. S.	Wirbelauer, Eckhard, Freiburg	E. W.
Schön, Franz, Regensburg	F. SCH.	Zahrnt, Michael, Kiel	M. Z.
Schönig, Hanne, Halle/Saale	H. SCHÖ.	Zimbrich, Ulrike, Frankfurt/Main	U. ZI.
Schottky, Martin, Pretzfeld	M. SCH.	Zimmermann, Bernhard, Freiburg	B. Z.
Schulzki, Heinz-Joachim, Freudenstadt	H.-J. S.	Zimmermann, Martin, Munich	MA. ZI.
Schwertheim, Elmar, Münster	E. SCH.	Zucca, Raimondo, Rome	R. Z.

L

Lydae (Λύδαι; *Lýdai*). Place in → Lycia (see map) on the south-west coast of Asia Minor on the Gulf of Telmessus, 2,4 km west of Fethiye (Ptol. 5,3,2; GGM 1, 494f. no. 259f., Κλύδαι; *Klýdai*). The identification has been secured by inscriptions (TAM 2,1 no. 41, 49). Extended Imperial and early Byzantine ruins on the cape Kapı Dağ (possibly the ancient Cape Artemisium: Str. 14,2,2) as well as the nearby Tersane Adası.

G.E. BEAN, s.v. L., PE, 536; Id., Kleinasien 4, 1980, 43–45; P.ROOS, Topographical and Other Notes on South-Eastern Caria, in: OpAth 9, 1969, 59–93; V.RUGGIERI, Due complessi termali nel golfo di Macris (Fethiye), in: Orientalia christiana periodica 57, 1991, 179–198.   H.LO.

Lydda (Λύδδα/*Lýdda*, Hellenized form of Hebrew *Lod*, derived from it Arab. *Ludd*). City in Palestine, south-east of Jaffa (→ Ioppe) on the edge of the coastal plain on the road to Jerusalem. L. is first mentioned in the list of Palestinian cities conquered by Thutmosis III in the 15th cent. BC. The founding of L., which is ascribed to the tribe of Benjamin in 1 Chr 8:12, possibly goes back to the resettlement of the city in post-exilic times by the tribe of Benjamin (Esr 2:33, Neh 7:37 and 11:35). In the Hellenistic period it was still outside of the borders of Juda; in 145 BC, L. was added to the territory of the → Hasmonaeans by the Seleucid → Demetrius [8] II. L.'s significance was based on its position at the crossroads of the road which led from Egypt to → Damascus, the *via Maris*, and the road from Jaffa to Jerusalem, as well as on the fertility of the surrounding land. After it was raised to the chief city of one of the Judaean toparchies, → Cassius [I 10] sold the residents of L. into slavery because they could not raise the tribute he demanded. → Antonius [I 9] revoked the measure shortly afterwards. In the course of the First Jewish War, Vespasian captured the city in AD 68 and settled Jews there who were loyal to Rome. The Apostle Peter healed Aeneas in L., whereupon the population of the city converted to Christianity (Acts 9:32–35). Probably under → Septimius Severus, L. became a Roman colony with the name Diospolis. Aetius is the first historically documented bishop of L. as participant at the Council of Nicaea (AD 325). The city attained special significance from the 6th cent. at the latest as the birth place and burial place of St. George. After the Arab conquest in 636, L. lost significance considerably because of the founding of the nearby Ramla.

M.GÖRG, s.v. Lydda, Neues Bibel-Lex. 2, 676f.; D.PRINGLE, The Churches of the Crusader Kingdom of Jerusalem 2, 1998, 9–27; M.SHARON, s.v. Ludd, EI 5, 798–803.   J.P.

Lydia (Λυδία; *Lydía*).
I. GEOGRAPHY II. HISTORY III. CULTURE

I. GEOGRAPHY
Region in western Asia Minor; its southern border with Caria is formed by the → Mes(s)ogis and the → Maeander, its eastern border with Phrygia by the confluence of the → Lycus [18] and the Maeander, the upper course of the → Hermus [2] and the Dindymus mountains (modern Murat Dağı) and its northern border with Mysia by the → Caicus [1]) and the Temnus (Demirci Dağı) and mountain ranges further west. Aeolis and Ionia are offshore in the west, sharing with L. the climate, soil conditions and vegetation. L. is structured by three rivers which flow into the Aegean: the Hermus, the → Caystrus [1] and the Maeander. Between the mountain ranges of Tmolus, rising to more than 2,000 m, and Mesogis mountains rising to more than 1,600 m, the river valleys form fertile plains, where the most important cities are located.

II. HISTORY
A. END OF THE 2ND MILLENNIUM AND DARK AGES
B. ARCHAIC PERIOD: MERMNADAE C. PERSIAN
RULE (546–334 BC) D. ALEXANDER AND HELLENISM E. LYDIA AS PART OF THE PROVINCE OF ASIA
F. LATE ANTIQUITY AND CHRISTIANITY

A. END OF THE 2ND MILLENNIUM AND DARK AGES
In the 13th cent. BC, one of the Arzawa countries (→ Arzawa) in western Asia Minor (→ Asia Minor III. C.) was the Hittite vassal kingdom of → Mira, which, together with the 'Land of the River Šēḫa' adjacent to the north, covered a large part of L. It is likely that one of the princes of this country is depicted on the rock relief at Karabel [1]. Whereas written documents allow the tracing of the late Hittite principalities in south-east Asia Minor and northern Syria into the 8th/7th cents., there are no equivalent sources for western Asia Minor. Consequently, L.'s history in the 'Dark Ages' remains dark for the time being [2].

Assuming a period of rule of 505 years prior to the presumed date of their deposal by → Gyges, the Lydian dynasty of the → Heraclidae (Hdt. 1,7), who have been identified for this period, probably dates back to the early 12th cent. BC, i.e. the period of the Aegean migration (→ Dark Ages [1]). This seems to fit in with certain findings from → Sardeis. From the Submycenaean/Protogeometric period onwards, the ancestors of the Maeonians/Lydians were most likely gradually pushed further into central L. by native Greeks (→ Colonization II.). Connected to the Heraclids, who were only named thus by the Greek, seems to be the legend of Hercules and → Omphale (Greek interpretation of the couple → Cybele and her paredros Attis or Masnes [3] or

Sandon?); the last king of the Heraclids was called → Candaules, a reference to Hermes or Hercules (Hipponax fr. 4 D.), possibly a religious epithet of the king otherwise named → Myrsilus by the Greeks, after his father Myrsus (Hdt. 1,7). Furthermore, → Atys [1] is cited as the Lydian ancestral king, together with his (eponymous) sons Lydus and Tyrsenus (Hdt. 1,94; Dion. Hal. Ant. Rom. 1,27), thus providing a genealogical anchor in L. for the problematic tradition of the emigration of the Tyrseni from L. (not historical: [4]), caused by a great famine. The epichoric Lydian tradition (Xanthus, *Lydiaka*, FGrH 765; Nicolaus of Damascus FGrH 90 F 44ff.) knows of two other dynasties apart from the royal house: the Tylonids, descendants of the legendary Tylon [5], sometimes equated with the Heraclids, and the historical → Mermnadae [6]. The last king of the earlier dynasty was called Sadyattes (Candaules in Hdt. 1,7ff.), the unconnected stories attributed to some of these kings are mainly of mythological, particularly (cultic-) aetiological content; only the later kings just prior to Gyges gain historical profile. This entire complex of traditions has as yet largely eluded historical clarification [7; 8].

B. Archaic period: Mermnadae

For the history of L. at the time of the Mermnad kings, cf. → Gyges, → Ardys [1], → Sadyattes II, → Alyattes, → Croesus, and → Atys [2].

C. Persian rule (546–334 BC)

The uprising against the Persian governor Tabalus (546/5), instigated by the Lydian Pactyer after → Cyrus' [2] withdrawal and supported by the Aeoles and Iones, was brutally suppressed by Mazares and Harpagus (Hdt. 1,154ff.; [9]).

L. became the core territory of Satrapy II *Sparda* (= Sardis), also largely responsible for the administration of the coastal regions of Satrapy I *Yauna* (Aeolis, Ionia and Caria). 499 BC saw the outbreak of the → Ionian Revolt with the burning of Sardis including the temple of Cybebe (Cybele)this was later used as an argument by the Persians for their destruction of Greek temples (Hdt. 5,102,1). The Persian → Royal Road, replacing the ancient roads, ran for 525 km, a fifth of its entire length, through Lydian and Phrygian territory (Hdt. 5,52f.).

L. remained largely untouched by the → Persian Wars, the → Delian League and the → Peloponnesian War; only the coastal regions of the satrapy were lost to Athens from 479, then to Sparta from 412 to 404 and once again from 400 to 394. For L.'s history under the rule of Persian satraps in the 5th and 4th cents. BC, cf. → Pissuthnes, → Tissaphernes, → Cyrus [3], → Struthas, → Hecatomnus, → Tiribazus, → Autophradates [1] and → Orontes. The Lydian feudal lords with their latifundia (Hdt. 7,27ff.) were replaced by the satraps and other high-ranking Persians, who managed the domains of the great king as well as their own estates, and also by exiled Persophiles from Greece (Thuc.

1,138,5; Xen. An. 2,1,3; 7,8,8; 8,17). The estates were fortified with towers and protected by military garrisons (Xen. An. 7,8,7–24; [10]); alongside agricultural production, they played a vital role in ensuring the country's civil control and military security. The creation of plantations, botanical gardens and zoos (*parádeisoi* [11]), an ancient Lydian tradition (Ath. 12,515e), was intensified under Persian rule on behalf of the great king (ML 12; Xen. An. 1,2,7; Xen. Oec. 4,20ff.; Diod. Sic. 14,80,2). An 'Achaemenid colonization' in the 5th/4th cents. is to some extent only manifest for the Hellenistic-Roman period [12]. Around 400 BC, Assyrian hoplites and Hyrcanian cavalry served as protecting forces in the Caicus valley (Xen. An. 7,8,15); the settlers from Hyrcania were given their land tenures in the 'Hyrcanian plain' (the central Hermus plain), but maybe only under the → Seleucids (Str. 13,4,13). It is possible that a small congregation of exiled Jews (Abd 20) came to *Sefarad* (= Sparda = L.) as early as the 5th cent. BC.

D. Alexander and Hellenism

In 334 BC, more than 200 years of Achaemenid rule in L. came to an end. → Alexander [4] the Great permitted the Lydians to live by their traditional laws (Arr. Anab. 1,17,4), and granted them (local) self-government. Alexander's edict was in line with his policy of winning the support of non-Greek groups within his empire. On the other hand, in Lydia too the former Persian estates were confiscated for Alexander and the Macedonians, and the Lydian population continued to be liable for taxes (Arr. Anab. 1,17,4; [13]).

During the Wars of the → Diadochi, → Antigonus [1] Monophtalmos took possession of L. in 319 (Diod. Sic. 18,52,5f.), after it had been briefly under the control of → Eumenes [1] in 320 [14]. In 301, L., together with the rest of western Asia Minor, fell to → Lysimachus [2] and after the latter's death in 281 to → Seleucus I. After that, it remained part of the Seleucid kingdom until 190/189. The Seleucid part of Asia Minor, including Ionia, was administered by the governor general in Sardis [15]. During the 3rd cent. BC, L. was often a theatre of war: cf. → Eumenes [2], → Antiochus [2], → Seleucus II, → Achaeus [5] and → Antiochus [5].

In its settlement geography, L. was from the Hellenistic period onwards characterized by a great number of *katoikiai* (military colonies; → *katoikos*) to secure the much fought-for region: Seleucus I made the start in 281 with Thyatera, Antiochus I founded Stratoniceia on the Caicus, followed by further *katoikiai* set up by the Seleucids in the 3rd cent. and the Attalids in the 2nd cent. (→ Attalus, with stemma): in the 'Hyrcanian plain' (Tac. Ann. 2,47), in Magnesia [3] (OGIS 229; StV 492; [16]), Mostene, Nacrasa and elsewhere. The *katoikiai* of the 'Macedonians' (their dedication [17]; see also [18]) either formed a *koinón* with the citizenry of the community on whose territory they settled, or remained for an extended period as separate entities alongside these communities ('the Macedonians in ...');

in remote eastern L., they retained their own tribal constitution, as e.g. even in Roman times the Mysomacedonians and Mysotimolitae, former Seleucid or Attalid mercenaries (Plin. HN 5,111; [19; 20; 21; 22]).

At the end of the 3rd cent., viceroy → Zeuxis was allegedly ordered by → Antiochus [5] Megas to admit 2,000 Jewish families from Babylonia to L. and Phrygia (Jos. Ant. Iud. 12,148–153, regarding the historicity [23; 24; 25]). In 202/1, Zeuxis showed considerable reluctance in providing Philip V with the support for his operations in Asia Minor, which the latter expected by virtue of his alliance with Antiochus [5] (StV 547) [26]. As part of the Seleucid territories in Asia Minor ceded by Antiochus [5] in 188 (Pol. 21,42f.; Liv. 37,45; 38,38f.), L. fell to → Eumenes [3].

For L., the renewal of Attalid rule (188–133; → Attalus, with stemma) brought the foundation of new towns such as Philadelphia (Str. 12,8,18; 13,4,10) and Apollonis [27], and in 168 the endowment of the 'Eumeneia' festival in gratitude for the salvation from a Galatian uprising (OGIS 305; [28]). Cf. → Attalus [5], → Prusias II.

E. Lydia as part of the province of Asia
1. Roman Republic 2. Roman Imperial period

1. Roman Republic
With → Attalus' [6] III testament, the kingdom of Pergamum fell to Rome in 133 BC; in 129 Rome turned the western core territory with L. into the province of → Asia [2], after having overpowered → Aristonicus [4], the pretender to the throne. From 123 onwards, this fertile region, devoid of tax-exempt cities, was plundered. However, the massacre of Italians in Asia in 88 ('Ephesian Vespers') and the First → Mithridatic War concerned L. only rather peripherally: Magnesia on the Sipylum, Thyatera, Hypaipa in the Caystrus valley, Tralleis. During the Roman Civil Wars, the cities were once again forced to pay contributions.

2. Roman Imperial period
In the first two centuries of the Imperial period, L. experienced economic and cultural bloom as a result of increased urbanization and improved urban infrastructures. Imperial munificence alleviated the large-scale damages caused by earthquakes – 24 BC in Thyatera (Suet. Tib. 8), AD 17 in 12 cities in Asia, 7 of them in L. (Tac. Ann. 2,47). The building activity by the local elites resulted in large buildings for the common welfare [29]. The devastating epidemics of the 2nd cent. AD did not spare L. Imperial visits brought with them privileges [30]: Hadrian visited Thyatera and Sardis in 123/4 [31], Caracalla in Thyatera and Philadelphia in 215.

The → ruler cult (Roma and Augustus) [32], organized on the basis of the provincial assembly of Asia, was in L. the responsibility of the elected high priest (archiereús Asías of the Sardis temples) [33]. L. was divided between four conventus iuridici in Asia: Sardis, Smyrna, Ephesus, Pergamum (Plin. HN 5,111; 120; 126; Str. 13,4,12).

Outside of the cities and their territories, the former royal land of Persian and Hellenistic times continued to exist in form of imperial domains and private estates; large tracts of land, though, were in the hands of indigenous free small farmers. The fact that L. had for long been a part of large multinational states, is reflected in its population: various katoikiai of different origins, instituted by Achaemenids, Seleucids and Attalids, Jewish congregations in Sardis, Thyatera and other Lydian cities, Greek immigrants and also, even if smaller in number, Italians; the indigenous Lydian population, who mainly inhabited the many small towns, katoikiai and kōmai which had partly developed around sanctuaries or local manors, and which mostly only acquired urban character and began to issue coins in the Imperial period [34; 35].

F. Late antiquity and Christianity
With the provincial reforms under → Diocletianus (see map there) in 297, the old geographical name was revived as the name of the new province of L. (as one of seven within the dioecesis IV Asiana); however, with the judicial districts of Thyatera and Sardis, it only covered a part of the original L. Its metropolis ('capital') was Sardis. In 399, L. was laid waste by hordes of Ostrogoths from Phrygia (Greuthungi), led by Tribigild and the magister militum Gainas (Zos. 5,18; [36]). L.'s economic decline in the early 6th cent. is illuminated by a ruling of Demosthenes, the praefectus praetorio per orientem, in favour of the governor of L. regarding the tax liability after the flight of joint owners of an estate; the appointment of a special agent tasked with suppressing the scourge of banditism (biokōlýtēs, 'preventer of violence') around 548 did not improve the situation [37].

The basis for Christianity in L. [38] was laid by the missionary journeys of the Apostle → Paulus. Three of the seven churches in the province of Asia mentioned in Apc. are located in L.: Sardis, Thyatera, Philadelphia (Apc. 2:18; 3:1; 3:7); Christian inscriptions dating from earlier than the 4th cent. are rare. During the reigns of the emperors Antoninus Pius and M. Aurelius, the apologete → Meliton [3] was bishop of Sardis (d. 190). The indigenous non-Greek population in the eastern part of L., bordering on Phrygia, proved particularly open to Christian heresies (→ Montanism, → Novatianus). The Quartadecimans, to whom Meliton had belonged, and who were declared heretics from 325, were prosecuted in L. especially in the 5th cent. A revival of pagan cult in L. (Sardis) under emperor Iulianus [11] in 362 was doomed to failure (Eunap. VS 501; 503); in Justinian's time, followers of pagan cults were only found in the mountainous region of Mes(s)ogis [41] which was far away from the cities; this was due to the zealous Christian proselytism of the (Monophysite) bishop → Iohannes [26] ([39; 40]). Until 1389, the Metropolite of Sardis was ranked sixth after the patriarch of Constantinople.

III. Culture
A. Society, economy, military organization
B. Material culture, everyday life
C. Religion D. Art and craft

A. Society, economy, military organization

Several large families determined the feudal character of Lydian society, an aristocracy involved in horse breeding on estates that were partly run by serfs of the rural population. The Mermnadae were related by marriage to the Median royal house (Hdt. 1,73,4) and also to the Basilids in Ephesus (Melas, Pindarus, Ael. VH 3,26) and maintained political and social relations with aristocrats in Lesbos (Alcaeus fr. 42 D.), including Sappho's circle (fr. 98 D.). Alcman spoke with pride of his hailing from Sardis (fr. 13 D.), and the vernacular in Ephesus contained Lydian words (used as a stylistic device by Hipponax, e.g. fr. 42 MASSON; [42]).

→ Gyges (Archilochus fr. 22 D.) and also → Croesus owed their proverbial wealth to the river → Pactolus, carrying gold down from Mt. Tmolus (Hdt. 1,93,1; archaeological evidence of gold washeries), and even more so to the mines in Mysia (near Pergamum, Aristot. Mir. 834a), furthermore to the gold imported from the Black Sea region, probably by Milesians, for the minting of coins (Aristeas FGrH 35 F 4), as well as generally to the tributes paid by their subsidiary territories, in particular the Greek coastal towns (Hdt. 1,6). Special taxes were levied on certain trade groups to finance large building projects (tomb of Alyattes, Hdt. 1,93,2f.). The ancient Lydian feudal economic and social structure persisted throughout the Persian and the Hellenistic periods, and, under different circumstances, even in Roman times.

The Lydian aristocracy provided the war-charioteers (who became obsolete in the 6th cent. BC; Sappho fr. 27a,19f. D.) and the cavalry (Hdt. 1,27; 80); Greeks obliged to perform military service also fought as hoplites. Carian and Ionian mercenaries were also recruited (Hdt. 2,152; Diod. Sic. 1,66,2). The Lydian army also included a unit of 'Egyptian' auxiliaries (Xen. Hell. 3,1,7; Xen. Cyr. 31,45). Lydian weapons were similar to those of the Greeks (Hdt. 7,74); Assyrian siege technology with earth ramps was used in the siege of Smyrna (c. 600 BC) [43; 44].

Apart from the aristocracy, there are references to a class of traders and artisans: to the Ionians, the Lydians appeared as the first retailers (Hdt. 1,94,1) and innkeepers (operators of caravanserais? cf. Nicolaus Dam. FGrH 90 F 44 on → Ardys [1]). Archaeological evidence of workshops for processing gold, ivory, leather and wool has been found in Sardis. In Asia Minor, the Lydians were seen as the inventors of coin minting (→ Coinage, Coins).

B. Material culture, everyday life

The Lydians had a reputation for a hedonistic way of life (tryphḗ); Ionians and Athenians, who imitated them, were accused of being soft (habrosýnē) or mocked for suffering from the 'Lydian disease' (lydopatheís, Anac. 481 PMG) [45]. Luxury articles from Lydia included jewellery, colourful Sardian mitras (Sappho fr. 98a, 10ff. D.), generously cut chitons, soft boots (Hdt. 1,155,5; Hom. h. 3,147) and also the famous perfumed ointment bákkaris (Ath. 15,690 a-d). Dice games were seen as a Lydian invention (Hdt. 1,94,2). With regard to sexuality, there were several customs, condemned by the Greeks as signs of Oriental luxuriance, that were attributed to the Lydians; these included the service of eunuchs at the Lydian royal court (Hdt. 3,48), the alleged invention of female sterilization (Ath. 12,515d: from Xanthus); the premarital prostitution of girls (Hdt. 1,93,4; 94,1) is probably a Greek misunderstanding of certain forms of Oriental temple prostitution (Str. 11,14,16; 12,3,36; 8,6,20).

C. Religion

The Hittite-Hurrite goddess Kubaba, received in Phrygia as matar kubeleja ('mountain mother'), in L. as Kuvav, appears in Greek as → Cybele or Cybebe; the Mḗtēr Oreía ('mountain mother') is also fixed geographically: e.g. amongst others as Mḗtēr Sipylḗnē or Dindymḗnē (→ Asia Minor IV. E.) [46]. Also adopted from Phrygia were the cults of Argistis as part of the myth of Attis and Cybele (→ Attis), of the vegetation god → Sabazius and of → Ma (for the regulations of her mysteries, see inscription of 366 BC [47]). In L., Sandon is seen as Cybele's companion (Luwian-Cilician: Santaš), equated with Hercules by the Greeks (Nonn. 34,192). Also in epichoric inscriptions, the wine god Baki (Dionysus, → Bacchus), as well as Pldans (Apollo) and Artimus (Artemis) are only known by their Greek names – it is contentious whether these had been transferred to indigenous deities or whether the deities themselves had been adopted from the Greek pantheon. Without a Greek equivalent is the Anatolian (Phrygian-Lydian) moon god → Men, whose cult spread across all of Asia Minor as far as Greece in the Hellenistic period. In addition, there was a Lydian horse goddess called Pirva [3. 79]. The Lydian kings held the Greek sanctuaries in high regard: this is shown by precious votive offerings by Gyges, Alyattes and Croesus, particularly in Delphi (Hdt. 1,25; 50ff.; 92), by the deposit of large sums of money in the temple of Apollo in Didyma (Hdt. 5,36) or by the assignment of confiscated property of enemies (Hdt. 1,92,2ff.; Nicolaus Dam. FGrH 90 F 65) to the temple of Artemis in Ephesus, which had an affiliated cult in Sardis. The spread of Iranian cults in L., e.g. that of → Anaetis in the valleys of the Hermus and Caystrus (→ Hiera Kome, Hypaipa, Paus. 5,27,5f.), dates back to Persian military settlers. Alongside Persian and Greek cults, the ancient Anatolian and rural cults [48] had followers in L. until the end of antiquity; in inscriptions, the deities appear as 'lords' of their temple territories; strange phenomena (an Anatolian substrate?) are the eastern Lydian so-called confession or atonement inscriptions (mid–1st to 3rd cent. AD) [49; 50; 51].

D. ART AND CRAFT

The influence of eastern Greek culture was very strong in the 7th and 6th cents. BC. Oriental motives were adopted from this, and not directly from the Late Hittite or Assyrian spheres. Typical features of this art are: Lydian ceramics with light-coloured glaze and colourful stripes, and 'marbled ware'; a special form is the *lydion*, a small vessel for the *bákkaris* ointment [52; 45. 114ff.]. Lydian ivory carvings on horse harnesses (Hom. Il. 4,141ff.), statuettes (6th cent.); Lydian ivory carvers were employed at the palace of Darius in Susa. Lydian architectural terracottas (relief friezes) also show Greek influence [53]. Typical for the textile production were purple chitons (Hdt. 1,50,1), purple and 'Sardian'-red blankets and carpets (Ath. 2,48b; 12,514c), appreciated by the Greeks as well as by the Great King; garments embroidered with gold platelets in the Oriental fashion, material interwoven with gold threads (in the Hellenistic period). So far, products of Lydian goldsmiths – with the exception of small finds, some of Greek provenance [54] – are predominantly attested by literary evidence (Hdt. 1,50f.). The precious votive offerings of the Lydian kings were mainly commissioned works by Ionian artists: gold and silver kraters by Glaucus of Chios (Hdt. 1,25) and Theodorus of Samos (Hdt. 1,51). Ionian artists also created the column drums with figurative reliefs at the archaic temple of Artemis in Ephesus, a donation by Croesus (Hdt. 1,92, votive inscription) and also a Cybele naiskos in Sardis (mid–6th cent.) [45. 110f.]. After the Persian conquest, Greek and Lydian workshops continued to work on Persian orders: craftsmen from 'Sparda' and 'Yauna' (L. and Ionia) worked at Persian palaces in Pasargadae, Susa and Persepolis. The so-called 'pyramid tomb' (fragment) in Sardis displays an Achaemenid-Greek style mixture like the tomb of Cyrus in Pasargadae; it was possibly the burial place of a Lydian satrap (4th cent. BC?) [55].

Architecture typical of Asia Minor is represented by the monumental tumuli of the Lydian royal necropolis of Bintepe near → Gygaia limne: brick-built krepis, tomb chamber with anteroom in skilful square stone masonry, some with dromos; the largest tumulus is that of Alyattes (355 m in diameter, 59 m in height, 1,115 m in circumference), crowned originally by five stone pillars bearing inscriptions (Hdt. 1,93); Gyges' tumulus (Karnıyarıktepe) (Hipponax fr. 42 MASSON), with wall graffiti *Gu-gu* [56].

For the Lydian language and script, see → Lydian, for the development and the characteristics of Lydian music, see → Music.

→ Asia Minor (with maps)

1 J.D. HAWKINS, Takasnawa, King of Mira, 'Tarkondemos', Karabel, and Boğazköy Sealings, in: AS 48, 1998

2 E. AKURGAL, Das dunkle Zeitalter Kleinasiens, in: S. DEGER-JALKOTZY (ed.), Griechenland, die Ägäis und die Levante während der 'Dark Ages', 1983, 67–78   3 G.M. A. HANFMANN, Lydiaka II: Tylos and Masnes, in: HSPh 63, 1958, 65–88   4 R. DREWS, Herodotus 1.94, in: Historia 41, 1992, 14–39   5 H. HERTER, Von Xanthos dem Lyder zu Aineias aus Gaza, in: RhM 108, 1965, 189–212   6 O. SEEL, Herakliden und Mermnaden, in: Navicula Chiloniensis. FS F. Jacoby, 1956, 37–65   7 Id., Lydiaka, in: K. MRAS (ed.), FS A. Lesky (WS 69), 1956, 212–236   8 H. HERTER, Lyd. Adelskämpfe (1966), in: Id., KS, 1975, 536ff.   9 V. LA BUA, Gli Ioni e il conflitto lidio-persiano, in: Miscellanea Greca e romana 5, 1977, 1–64   10 O. LENDLE, Kommentar zu Xenophons Anabasis, 1995, 482f.   11 CH. TUPLIN, The Parks and Gardens of the Achaemenid Empire, in: Id. (ed.)., Achaemenid Studies, 1996, 80–131   12 M.V. SEKUNDA, Achaemenid Colonization in L., in: REA 87, 1985, 7–30   13 A.B. BOSWORTH, A Historical Commentary on Arrian's History of Alexander, vol. 1, 1980, 130   14 BENGTSON 1, 171f.   15 BENGTSON 2, 12ff.   16 IK 8, 1978, 23–130   17 L. ROBERT, Hellenika 6, 1948, 22ff.   18 G.M. COHEN, Katoikiai, Katoikoi, and Macedonians in Asia Minor, in: AncSoc 22, 1991, 41–50   19 JONES, Cities, 44f.   20 MAGIE, 972ff.   21 E. BIKERMAN, Institutions des Séleucides, 1938, 80ff.   22 G.M. COHEN, Seleucid Colonies, 1978   23 BENGTSON 2, 110ff.   24 L. ROBERT, Nouvelles inscriptions de Sardes, 1963, 27ff.   25 A. KRAABEL, Judaism in Western Asia under the Roman Empire, 1968, 198–203   26 E. OLSHAUSEN, s.v. Zeuxis, RE 10 A, 382f.   27 ROBERT, Villes, 31–40   28 NILSSON, GGR 2, 173   29 E. WINTER, Staatliche Baupolitik und Baufürsorge in den röm. Prov. des kaiserzeitlichen Kleinasien, 1996   30 H. HALFMANN, Itinera Principum, 1986   31 P. WEISS, Hadrian in L., in: Chiron 25, 1995, 213–224   32 S.R. F. PRICE, Rituals and Power, 1984, 259ff.   33 J. DEININGER, Die Provinziallandtage der röm. Kaiserzeit, 1965, 38ff.   34 MITCHELL 1, 180ff.   35 CH. SCHULER, Ländl. Siedlungen und Gemeinden im hell. und röm. Kleinasien, 1998   36 A. DEMANDT, Die Spätant. (HdbA 3,6), 1989, 158f.   37 JONES, LRE 1, 294; 2, 814   38 A. VON HARNACK, Die Mission und Ausbreitung des Christentums in den ersten drei Jh., 1924, 732ff., 780ff.   39 JONES, LRE 2, 939   40 MITCHELL 2, 88–95, 118f.   41 C. FOSS, Byzantine and Turkish Sardis, 1976, 28ff.   42 G.L. HUXLEY, The Early Ionians, 1966, 111f.   43 J.M. COOK, Old Smyrna, 1948–1951, in: ABSA 53/54, 1958/9, 24f.   44 E. AKURGAL, Alt-Smyrna, 1983, 74f.   45 J. BOARDMAN, Kolonien und Handel der Griechen, 1981, 114   46 MITCHELL 2, 19ff.   47 L. ROBERT, Une nouvelle inscription de Sardes, in: CRAI 1975, 307–330   48 G. PETZL, Ländliche Religiosität in L., in: E. SCHWERTHEIM (ed.), Forsch. in Lydien, 1995, 37–48   49 P. HERRMANN, E. VARINLIOĞLU, Theoi Pereudenoi, in: EA 3, 1984, 1–17   50 M. RICL, The Appeal to Divine Justice in the Lydian Confession Inscriptions, in: E. SCHWERTHEIM (ed.), Forsch. in Lydien, 1995, 67–76   51 MITCHELL 1, 191ff.   52 E. AKURGAL, Die Kunst Anatoliens von Homer bis Alexander, 1961, 150ff.   53 E. HOSTETTER, Lydian Architectural Terracottas, 1994   54 J.C. WALDBAUM, Metalwork from Sardis, 1983   55 S. HORNBLOWER, Asia Minor, in: CAH² 6, 217f.   56 G.M. A. HANFMANN, Letters from Sardis, 1972, 154 with fig. 107.

GEOGRAPHY: J. KEIL, A.v. PREMERSTEIN, Ber. über eine Reise in L. und den angrenzenden Gebieten Ioniens, Denk-

schriften der Akad. der Wiss. in Wien 53/2, 1908; 54/2, 1911; 57/1, 1914; W. M. RAMSAY, The Historical Geography of Asia Minor, 1890; A. PHILIPPSON, Top. Karte des westl. Kleinasien, 1910; W. WARFIELD, in: Sardis 1, 1922, 175–180.
INSCRIPTIONS: P. HERRMANN, Neue Inschr. zur histor. Landeskunde von L. ... , Denkschriften der Akad. der Wiss. in Wien 77, 1959; 80, 1962; P. HERRMANN, J. KEIL, in: TAM 5,1–2, 1981–1989.
HISTORY, CULTURE: L. ALEXANDER, The Kings of L., 1913; L. A. BORSAY, L., thesis Pittsburgh 1965 (1979); L. BÜRCHNER, J. KEIL, s.v. L., RE 13, 2122ff., 2161ff.; R. DUSSAUD, La Lydie et ses voisins, 1930; Id., Prelydiens, Hittites et Achéens, 1953; C. FOSS, Sites and Strongholds of Northern L., in: AS 37, 1987, 81–101; J.-D. GAUGER, s.v. L., KWdH, 418f.; A. GOETZE, Kleinasien (HdbA 3,1,3,3,1), 1957, 206ff.; G. M. A. HANFMANN, Sardis und Lydien, AAWM 1960, 6; S. HORNBLOWER, Asia Minor, in: CAH² 6, 1994, 209–233; J. KEIL, Die Kulte L.s, in: W. H. BUCKLER et al. (ed.), Anatolian Studies. FS W.H. Ramsay, 1923, 239–266; MAGIC; S. MAZZARINO, Fra oriente e occidente, 1947; M. J. MELLINK, The Lydian Kingdom, in: CAH² 3/2, 1991, 643–655; MITCHELL; J. G. PEDLEY, Ancient Literary Sources on Sardis, 1972; G. RADET, La Lydie au temps des Mermnades, 1892; C. ROEBUCK, Ionian Trade and Colonization, 1959, 50ff.; R. SCHUBERT, Geschichte der Könige von L., 1884; C. TALAMO, La Lidia arcaica, 1979.   H.KA.

Lydiadas (Λυδιάδας; *Lydiádas*).
[1] Son of Eudamus from Caphyae (?, cf. Syll.³ 504) [1. 401] or from Megalopolis; as tyrant of the latter, L. joined the city in 235 BC to the Achaean League (→ Achaeans with map) (Pol. 2,44,5; Plut. Aratus 30; [1. 158; 3. 71f.; 87]), he served as its *stratēgós* in 234/3, 232/1 and again in 230/229. L.'s rivalry with → Aratus [2] escalated when Argus joined the League under → Aristomachus [4]; in the war against → Cleomenes [6] III of Sparta, which L. pursued vigourously, he died in the summer of 277 BC in the area of Megalopolis (Pol. 2,51,3; Plut. Aratus 36f.; Plut. Cleomenes 6,4–7) [3. 137f.; 193].
[2] L. from Megalopolis, probably grandson of L. [1], sent by the Achaean League to Rome in 180 BC, together with → Callicrates, as representatives of → Lycortas' moderate pro-Roman faction [11] (Pol. 24,10) [4. 137f.].

1 H. BERVE, Die Tyrannis bei den Griechen, 1967
2 ERRINGTON   3 R. URBAN, Wachstum und Krise des Achäischen Bundes, 1979   4 J. DEININGER, Der polit. Widerstand gegen Rom in Griechenland, 1971.   L.-M.G.

Lydian Lydian, belonging to the → Anatolian languages, is the language of the Lydians and is transmitted in its own alphabetical script, which is written either left-to-right or right-to-left (→ Asia Minor V., with map). Around 100 inscriptions are known today (including several graffiti and inscriptions on seals and coins), the majority of them, including two Lydian-Greek and two Lydian-Aramaic bilingual inscriptions, stemming from the 5th–4th/3rd cent. BC, while some of the graffiti and coins are older (no earlier than the late 8th/early 7th cent.). The main finding place is → Sardes. Additional finds are from the Caystrus and the Hermus valleys, from Smyrna/Bayraklı, Ephesus, and Carian Aphrodisias. The most important group of texts, both in number and size, consists of tomb inscriptions and dedications on steles, among them six in verse (see [1]). Two inscriptions are declarations of ownership, one inscription contains orders of a priest by the name of Mitradaśta. The entire material, supplemented by around 50 glosses from Greek authors (among them Lydian words from the common vernacular by → Hipponax) is summarized in [2; 3] complete with an outline of Lydian grammar. On Lydian personal names in secondary Greek transmission, see [4].

Lydian is not closely related to → Hittite, but rather to → Carian, → Luwian, → Palaic, and → Sidetan as is indicated by common innovations (e.g. the expansion of the suffix -*i*- to consonant-stem adjectives, the unique continuation of proto-Anatolian pl. acc. *commune* *-*nz* [in stems end- ing in vowels] > Lydian -*s*). However, it probably separated from this shared proto-West-Anatolian language phase earlier than the others since it shows a number of peculiar innovations. Among them are the disappearance of the Proto-Indo-European/proto-Anatolian laryngeal *h₂ (*eśa*- : Cuneiform Luwian *ḫamsa*(/*i*)-, Hittite *ḫassa*- 'grandchild') and of the vowel in the absolute final position (e.g. present tense third singular -*t*/-*d* < *-*ti*/*-*di*), the phonetic shift *uṷa > *o* (as in *kod* 'how' < *kuṷad alongside *qed* [*kṷed*] 'what' < **ku̯ad*, both < Proto-Indo-European *kʷod), and the (conditioned) emergence of *l*/*λ* < cerebralized *d (generalized in the past third singular -*l* for *-*da* and *-*ta*), which must be distinguished from the common Anatolian *d*/*l* change due to assimilation / dissimilation (as in the Lydian personal name Ἀδυάττης/Ἀλυάττης, Greek secondary transmission). Specifically Lydian innovations in the morphological realm include the nominal endings singular nom./acc. neut. -*d* (after pronouns) and dat. -*λ* (actually an enclitic pronoun = *λ* 'to him/her' = Palaic, Cuneiform Luwian, Hieroglyphic Luwian =*du*). cf. [5]; methodologically not convincing [6].

Lydian language material cannot be identified in the Hittite transmission. Another problem lies in the location and extent of the Lydian language area in the 2nd millennium BC, since the future → Lydia has been shown to be Luwian-speaking at that time (see → Mirā; → Sēḫa); cf. [7. 384¹⁰].

1 H. EICHNER, Die Akzentuation des Lydischen, in: Sprache 32, 1986, 7–21   2 R. GUSMANI, Lyd. WB, 1964
3 Id., Lyd. WB, Supplement, 1980–1986   4 L. ZGUSTA, Kleinasiat. PN, 1964.   5 N. OETTINGER, Die Gliederung des anatol. Sprachgebietes, in: ZVS 92, 1978, 74–92   6 R. GUSMANI, Zur Komparation des Lydischen, in: ZVS 95, 1981, 279–285   7 F. STARKE, Schriften und Sprachen in Karkamis, in: FS W. Röllig, 1997, 381–395.   F.S.

Lydias (Λυδίας; *Lydías*). Navigable river in → Macedon (supplied by the nowadays dried Lake Loudias), which connected → Pella with the sea (Str. 7, fr. 20; 22). Mentioned already by Hecat. FGrH 1 F 147 and Scyl. 66. The mouth appears to have shifted to the north in antiquity, since Hdt. 7,127 reports a common mouth of the L. and the → Haliacmon.

F. PAPAZOGLOU, Les villes de Macédoine, 1988, 101f., 125 map 2.   MA.ER.

Lydios see → Brigandry

Lydus (Λυδός; *Lydós*).
[1] Mythological king of Lydia, son of → Atys [1], brother of Tyrsenus (→ Tyrrhenus). Eponym of the Lydian people (→ Lydia) (formerly Maeon: Hom. Il. 2,864): Hdt. 1,94; Str. 5,219; Tac. Ann. 4,55. According to Hdt. 1,171 L., Mysus and → Car were brothers, which expresses the tribal kinship of the Lydians, Carians and Mysians (→ Carian, → Mysia).   L.K.
[2] (ὁ Λυδός/*ho Lydós*, 'the Lydian'). Attic black-figured vase painter, before 560–540/530 BC; a bit older than → Amasis and → Execias, he, together with them, belongs among the leading masters of black-figured vase painting during its height. In his two artist's signatures he calls himself 'the Lydian', but his drawing style is deeply rooted in the Attic tradition. While originally still indebted to the animal frieze style, he soon developed a powerful style of figure painting, in which he masterfully depicted compositions in motion: e.g. → Hercules' battle against Geryoneus on a hydria in Rome (VG, M. 430), the → Gigantomachy on the signed dinos of the Acropolis (Athens, NM, Akr. 607) or the return of → Hephaestus to the Olympus on a monumental colonette crater in New York (MMA, 31.11.11). L. preferred scenes from mythology, but also portrayed the lament for the dead with impressive passion; everyday life (e.g. images of athletes) can mainly be found in side friezes. About 130 vessels of all current forms have been assigned to him, which, however, come from different potters, among them → Nicosthenes and maybe Colchos; they were found mainly in Athens but also bear witness to extended trade. Numerous subordinate painters share above all the style of animal friezes with L., so that his own personal work cannot always be clearly differentiated from workshop pieces.
→ Black-figured vases

BEAZLEY, Addenda², 29–32; A. KOSSATZ-DEISSMANN, Satyr- und Mänadennamen auf Vasen, in: J. FREL (ed.), Greek Vases in the J. Paul Getty Museum 5, 1991, 131–137, fig. 2 a-d; M.B. MOORE, L. and the Gigantomachy, in: AJA 83, 1979, 79–99; M. A. TIVERIOS, Ho Lydos kai to ergo tou, 1976.   H.M.

[3] Iohannes L.
A. LIFE B. WORK

A. LIFE
Born in Philadelphia in Lydia in AD 490, died in Constantinople around AD 560, East Roman official and man of letters. After receiving the foundations of a solid Greek classical education in his hometown, he studied philosophy in Constantinople from 511 with the Neoplatonist → Agapius and soon received an office in the praetorian prefecture (see → Praefectus praetorio), in whose service he remained for 40 years. Since he knew Latin, he was responsible for composing documents in this language, among other things. In *c.* 543 he was also given a teaching position at the imperial school on the Capitol of Constantinople.

B. WORK
Of L.'s literary work, three treatises of antiquarian character are extant (on the chronological order: [3. 10]). His excellent knowledge of the ancient sources in the Greek and Latin languages made him especially capable of this. In the probably earliest work 'On the Months' (Περὶ μηνῶν/*Perì mēnôn*, Latin *De mensibus*) he compiled material on the Roman calendar and its holidays from the time of the monarchy onwards. He also mentions some pagan festivals which were still celebrated in his time with the approval of emperor → Iustinianus [1] I. But in the case of the Brumalia (festival in honour of Dionysus from 24 November until the winter solstice) he points out that they were not approved of by the Church. Probably also while he was still in office he composed a work 'On the Omens' (Περὶ διοσημειῶν; *Perì diosēmeiôn*, Latin *De ostentis*), a treatise on omens of all kinds compiled from ancient astrological works, but also containing information on interpreting weather signs (thunder and lightning) as well as earthquakes.
Only after he had left public service (551) L. began, in 554, to write his most important work, 'On the Offices of the Roman State' (Περὶ ἀρχῶν τῆς Ῥωμαίων πολιτείας/*Perì archôn tês Rhōmaíōn politeías*, Latin *De magistratibus*), a historical representation of Roman bureaucracy. In the 1st book he describes its development according to the requirements of each epoch from Rome's beginnings until L.'s time. Bk. 2 and especially bk. 3 deal with the development of the administrative body to which L. himself belonged, the praetorian prefecture, from its inception under Augustus until his own time. L. praises its excellent organization and its formation by an educational elite in former times and regrets its gradual decline from the 4th cent., which is supposed to have reached a low under his former superior Flavius → Iohannes [16], 'the Cappadocian'. Even though L. praises emperor Justinian I expressly because of his restorative governmental programme, he still expects him to act more decisively against the decline of the administrative body.

Although L.'s literary work fits into the tradition-friendly tendencies which marked Justinian I's rule, it does not show any inclination of the author to adopt the emperor's programme of Christian renewal. L. is almost completely silent about anything Christian and suggests only through the abstention from open propagan propaganda that he was at least officially not a 'pagan'. But he regrets only too clearly, in looking back on pagan traditions, present negative developments.

1 ODB 2, 1061f.   2 PLRE 2,612–615 (Lydus 75)
3 M. MAAS, John Lydus and the Roman Past, 1992.   F.T.

Lygdamis (Λύγδαμις; *Lýgdamis*).
[1] Aristocrat from → Naxos, assisted → Peisistratus after the second exile (*c.* 546 BC) in regaining rule in Athens from Eretria (Hdt.1,61,4; [Aristot.] Ath. Pol. 15,2). In appreciation, the latter subjected Naxos and installed L. as tyrant there (cf. Hdt. 1,64,1f.; [Aristot.] Ath. Pol. 15,3), who in turn supported → Polycrates in seizing power in Samos in the 530s (Polyaenus, Strat. 1,23,2). L. was overthrown by the Spartans (Plut. Mor. 859d), probably *c.* 524 in the expedition against Samos.

H. BERVE, Die Tyrannis bei den Griechen, 1967, 78f.;
L. DE LIBERO, Die archa. Tyrannis, 1996, 236–243.

[2] Father of → Artemisia [1] (Hdt. 7,99,2; Paus. 3,11,3 *et al.*), probably like her dynast of → Halicarnassus under Persian sovereignty.

H. BERVE, Die Tyrannis bei den Griechen, 1967, 120.

[3] Son of Pisindelis, grandson of Artemisia [1] (Suda, s.v. Ἡρόδοτος; differently [1]), also attested by inscriptions as dynast of → Halicarnassus (Syll.³ 45). His rule ended after fierce conflicts (Suda s.v. Ἡρόδοτος; s.v. Πανύασις *c.* 450 BC (IG I³ 259 is no certain *terminus ante quem*: [3. 96–99]).

1 BELOCH, GG, vol. II,2, 1–2   2 H. BERVE, Die Tyrannis bei den Griechen, 1967, 121   3 W. MCLEOD, Studies on Panyassis, in: Phoenix 20, 1966, 95–110.

[4] L. from → Syracusae, in 648 BC victor in the first → pankration competition in → Olympia (Paus. 5,8,8; Philostr. Gymnastikos p. 268 K..; Eus. Chronicorum liber I, Olympiades Ionum 33); Pausanias knew of L.'s tomb in Syracusae.

L. MORETTI, Olympionikai, 1957, 65.   W.K.

Lygdamus Name given by the anonymous author to the narrator of six love elegies transmitted in the *Corpus Tibullianum* (3,1–6; → Tibullus), which seem rather amateurish in style as well as in their train of thought. The small cycle suggests a situation uncommon for Roman love elegy, that the wife of L., Neaera, turned to another man, whereupon L. reacts by wooing, hoping, lamenting, and finally resigning. It must remain open whether this story may be interpreted autobiographically (thus [4. 84]). In any case, the anonymous author uses themes and formulations throughout that can be found in Catullus (named explicitly in 3,6,41) and in Roman love elegies. It is generally accepted that L. is the one on the receiving end in regard to → Catullus, → Propertius and → Tibullus. Contested is his relationship to → Ovidius: one side [4] assumes that Ovid is the recipient, but must then try to explain why a poet of Ovid's rank would keep referring throughout his entire oeuvre (from the *Amores* to the *Tristia*) to the small and poetically inferior work of the anonymous author. The other side (e.g. [1; 2]) represents the opposite view which seems altogether more plausible right from the beginning.

This controversy is closely linked to the much discussed problem of the anonymous' dating. Tib. 3,5,18 describes L.'s year of birth with the phrase known from Ov. Tr. 4,10,65 *cum cecidit fato consul uterque pari* ('when both consuls fell, struck by the same fate'). If one takes this as an autobiographical information also of the author, he would have been of the same age as Ovid, who was born in 43 BC [4]. [5], on the other hand, proposed in 1954 to refer the phrase to the death of Galba and Titus Vinius in January of the Year of Three Emperors (AD 69) and to date the work into the Flavian period. Against arguments based on verse technique [4] a more probable view is presented by [1] and [2] who identified analogies in lexical use and in the use of motifs with authors of the Flavian period (Martial and Statius), thus confirming the latter temporal classification.

A late dating of L.'s poems implies that the creation of the *Corpus Tibullianum* must be regarded as a 'multistage process' [1. 1ff.]: to bks. 1 and 2, by Tibullus himself, the only partially Tibullian poems of the → Sulpicia cycle would have been added still in the Augustan period, then, towards the end of the 1st cent. AD, L. and the → Panegyricus Messallae. Due to the inclusion into a corpus attributed to Tibullus the poems of the 3rd bk. outlasted late antiquity and the Middle Ages. Doubts about their authenticity which have surfaced in the early modern age (regarding L. first in 1786 by VOSS) have resulted in a decreased educated and scientific interest in them.

1 H. TRÄNKLE, Appendix Tibulliana, 1990 (with commentary).   2 B. AXELSON, L. und Ovid, in: Eranos 58, 1960, 93–111 (= Id., KS zur Lat. Philol., 1987, 283–297)
3 Id., Das Geburtsjahr des L., in: Eranos 58, 1960, 281–297 (= Id., KS, 298–309)   4 K. BÜCHNER, Die Elegien des L., in: Hermes 93, 1965, 65–112   5 B. HAGEN, Stil und Abfassungszeit der L.-Gedichte, thesis Hamburg (unpublished), 1954.   CH.N.

Lydus Slave and eunuch of → Drusus [II 1], the son of Tiberius. Aelius [II 19] Seianus instigated L.'s poisoning of Drusus in AD 23. When Apicata, the wife of Seianus, testified about her husband in 30, L. was also convicted and executed. PIR² L 465.   W.E.

Lykaios (Λύκαιος). Epiclesis of → Zeus.

Lykeios (Λύκειος; *Lýkeios*). The epiclesis L. (*Lýkios* for the first time in the Imperial period) characterizes a local and functional peculiarity of → Apollo. The etymological explanations mirror the religious philological hypotheses: the derivation from 'wolf' (λύκος/ *lýkos*) resulted in L. becoming a totem animal [3. 221] or allowed people to assume, according to the pattern of natural magic, that it could magically fend off the enemy of the herds. Importation of gods is behind the interpretation that Apollo was the *Lycian* god (Hom. Il. 4,101; [2. 445–448]). Even less valid is the derivation from Greek √λυκ, 'to shine', that was put forward at the end of the 19th cent. as a model example of natural mythology, although the link between Apollo and the sun god is already attested from the 5th cent. BC (Aesch. TrGF III fr. 23; Hdt. 9,92–96 ([1. 75f.]); Eur. Phaeton fr. 781). All these interpretations can already refer to ancient derivations; cf. the interpretation catalogues of the ancient commentators Serv. Aen. 4,377; Macrob. Sat. 1,17,36–38; Eust. Hom. Il. 4,101. The epiclesis L. is therefore already ambiguous for the Greeks.

Central to religious history, however, appears to be the early local foundation myth of the political sphere, especially in Argus, as a league of young men who represent themselves in the wolf. Apollo L. is the god of the ephebes (→ Ephebeia). The cult in the main temple of the city on the agora of Argus was dedicated to him (Soph. El. 6f.; Paus. 2,19,3–8); there he was the reason for, and refuge of, civilization (fire of the cultural hero → Phoroneus) as well as of the political culture, for he also protected the public treaties of the city.

→ Apollo (with map); → Argus [II 1]; → Ephebeia

1 W. BURKERT, Euenios der Seher von Apollonia und Apollon L., in: Kernos 10, 1997, 73–81   2 W. FAUTH, s.v. Apollon, in: KlP 1, 1964, 441–448   3 GRAF, 220–227   4 M. JAMESON, Apollon L. in Athens, in: Archaiognosia 1, 1980, 213–235.   C.A.

Lymax (Λύμαξ; *Lýmax*). Northern tributary of the Neda, about 2 km east of Phigaleia in Arcadia (Paus. 8,41,2; 4; 10), modern stream of Dragogi.

E. MEYER, s.v. L., RE 13, 2468; Id., s.v. L., RE Suppl. 9, 396.   E.MEY.

Lymphae (also *Lumphae*: Prisc. Institutio de arte grammatica 2,36,22). Italian name for water goddesses. The name should be regarded as close, from the point of view of content and language, like Oscan *diumpaís*, to Greek *nýmphai* (→ Nymphs) [1] to which it is partly used as a parallel: CIL V 3106 (Vicetia), Aug. Civ. 4,34; Paul. Fest. 107,17 L. As an equivalent of Greek *nymphóleptos*, 'raging', Latin *lymphatus* is created (Varro, Ling. 7,87; Paul. Fest. 107,17–20 L.). The cult worship of the *lymphae* attested by inscriptions – e.g. CIL III 6373 (Salonae), XI 1918 (Perusia) and pri-

marily X 6791, 6796, 6797 (= I² 1624) from the sanctuary of the Nymphae Nitrodes on Ischia – is based on their relationship with agriculture as donors of water (Varro, Rust. 1,1,6; Aug. Civ. 4,22). As individual *lymphae* a *lympha* → Iuturna and the *lymphae* Commotitiae in the lake of → Cutilia are mentioned (Varro, Ling. 5,71).

→ Sea gods; → Personification

1 WALDE/HOFMANN, s.v. lumpa   2 G. WISSOWA, Rel. und Kultus der Römer, ²1912, 223f.   JO.S.

Lynceus (Λυγκεύς/*Lynkeús*, related to λύγξ, 'lynx').
[1] Son of → Aphareus [1], king of Messene, and of Arene; brother of → Idas (L. is always mentioned together with him; the pair of brothers is called Apharetidae). The brothers take part in the journey of the → Argonauts (Apoll. Rhod. 1,151) and in the Calydonian hunt (Apollod. 1,67; Ov. Met. 8,304). They are said to have abducted Helene and delivered her to Theseus (Plut. Theseus 31,1). In the battle with the Dioscuri, L. dies at the hands of Polydeuces (various versions of the battle: → Dioscuri; → Idas). His tomb was displayed in Sparta (Paus. 3,13,1). L. has superhuman vision that penetrates all solid objects and reaches deep into the earth and far into the distance. In the euhemeristic explanation of this vision in Palaephatus 9, L. is the archegete of mining. His vision is proverbial (e.g. Aristoph. Plut. 210; Pl. Ep. 7,344a; Aristot. Protrepticus B 105 DÜRING; Orph. A. 1193; Hor. Epist. 1,1,28; Plot. 5,8,4,25).

L. JONES ROCCOS, s.v. Lynkeus (1) et Idas, LIMC 6.1, 319f.

[2] Son of Aegyptus and Argyphie (Apollod. 2,21), husband of the Danaid → Hypermestra [1]. L. is the only one of the 50 brothers on the wedding night to the 50 daughters of → Danaus in Argus who is not killed by his wife (according to the version in Apollod. 2,21 because he did not touch her – possibly a connection between L.'s name and the idea in Plin. HN 28,122: the medical use of the nails and skin of the lynx inhibits libido?). According to Paus. 2,25,4f., L. saves himself on the wedding night by going to Lyrceia from where he sends his wife torchlight signs (aition of a torch festival of the Argives). Lyrceia is said to have originally been called Lynceia; the change was explained by L.'s son or grandson Lyrcus (ibid.; others [1. 24; 2. 272] assume, however, that L. was originally called Lyrceus or Lyrcus). L. has a son → Abas [1] by Hypermestra and becomes the successor of Danaus (Paus. 2,16,1f.); according to another version he kills Danaus and the other Danaids (schol. Eur. Hec. 886; Archil. IEG fr. 305). L. was buried together with Hypermestra in Argus (Paus. 2,21,2). His statue stood in Delphi (ibid. 10,10,5).

1 U. v. WILAMOWITZ-MOELLENDORFF, Aischylos. Interpretationen, 1914   2 PRELLER/ROBERT II⁴.

[3] Companion of Aeneas in Italy, killed by Turnus (Verg. Aen. 9,768).   K.SCHL.

[4] Samian, brother of the historiographer → Duris [1], student of the Peripatetic → Theophrastus. L. wrote a series of (probably more anecdotally oriented) works (Τέχνη ὀψωνητική/'The Art of Buying Fish', Ἐπιστολαὶ δειπνητιχαί/'Meal Letters', Ἀπομνημονεύματα/'Memories' or Ἀποφθέγματα/'Sayings'), one of which was in any case a work 'On Menander' (Περὶ Μενάνδρου). As a comedian he is said to have even defeated Menander [1. test.]; of these plays, only a fragment from the 'Centaurs' (Κένταυρος) encompassing 22 trimeters is still extant, in which a man from Perinthus in a conversation with a cook criticizes the Attic 'nouvelle cuisine' and demands more nutritious meals.

1 PCG V, 1986, 616f.   H.-G.NE.

Lyncon montes Mountain massif in the Epirote part of the → Pindus, up to 2,249 m high, whose northern foothills are directed towards Macedonia and whose southern ones towards Thessaly source area of the Aous (modern Viotsa). According to Liv. 32,13,2f., thickly wooded with wide tablelands and perennial springs.

N. G. L. HAMMOND, Epirus, 1967, 280f.; PHILIPPSON/ KIRSTEN 2, 69–76.   D.S.

Lyncus (Λύγκος; *Lýnkos*). Upper Macedonian region north of → Eordaea and Orestis whose inhabitants were called *Lynkēstaí*. In the 5th cent. BC, L. was not yet integrated by the Macedonian Argead kings into their region of power (Thuc. 2,99,2; 4,83,1), which probably did not occur until under Philip II, who possibly founded the important city of → Heraclea [2]. The *via Egnatia* passed through L. [1. 14–22].

1 L. GOUNAROPOULOU, M. B. HATZOPOULOS, Les milliaires de la voie egnatienne... , 1985.

F. PAPAZOGLOU, Les villes de Macédoine, 1988, 256–258 (with map).   MA.ER.

Lynx (λύγξ/*lýnx*, λυγχίον/*lynkíon*, according to Ael. NA 7,47, the young was called σκύμνιος/*skýmnios*; Latin *lynx* or *chama*). The swamp lynx, a small species of cat [1. 1,81f.], and the desert lynx or caracal (*Lynx caracal*; probably meant in Plin. HN 8,72) are attested on Egyptian representations (e.g. a swamp lynx? on a middle Minoan fresco from Hagia Triada on Crete together with a → cormorant [1. 1,66, Fig. 17]). The northern lynx (*Lynx lynx*) from the predatory family of the cats is mentioned by Aristotle (Hist. an. 2,1,499b 24f.: has only half of the cuboid bone; 500b 15: urinates backwards; 5,2,539b 22f.: mates πυγηδόν, backside against backside) without precise description. Plin. HN 8,70 knows the northern lynx as *chama*, 'which the Gauls called Rufius' [1. 1,83] or 11,202 as *lupus cervarius*. Not the characteristic tufts of hair on the ears but the spotted fur (Verg. G. 3,264; Verg. Aen. 1,323) are emphasized, as well as its alleged cowardice that was based on timidity with regard to humans (Hor.

Carm. 2,13,40: *timidos lyncas* and 4,6,33f.: *fugaces lyncas*) and its outstanding vision (Plin. HN 28,122; cf. → Lynceus [1]). With regard to folk medicine, Pliny (HN 28,122) knows from the Aegean island of Carpathus of the ash from the burnt claws and the skin used in drinks as an agent against lecherousness in men and (sprinkled on the skin) against the lasciviousness of women. The urine that the lynx immediately covered over with soil is said to assist against urgency of urination and against pain in the collar bones. This burying was interpreted as resentful hiding of the lynx stone λυγγούριον/*lyngoúrion* that supposedly originated from urine, a type of → amber (Plin. HN 37,34 and 52f.: against Theophr. De lapidibus 28 and the medical indication e.g. in Dioscorides 2,81,3 WELLMANN = 2,100 BERENDES).

1 KELLER

A. STEIER, s.v. Luchs, RE 13,2476.   C.HÜ.

Lyons tablet see → Tabula Lugdunensis

Lyppeus (spelled as in Stv II 309; on coins Λυκκείου/ *Lykkeíou* or Λυκπείου/*Lykpeíou*, HN 236; [1. 199–201, pl. XXXVII; 2. 71]). L., king of → Paeonia (359–335 BC), fought alongside Cetriporis of Thrace and Grabus of Illyria (356) against → Philippus II of Macedonia, but joined the latter as an ally after the defeat (Isoc. Or. 5,21; Diod. Sic. 16,22,3: not mentioned by name); Stv II 309 (alliance with Athens of July 356).

1 H. GAEBLER, Mz. Nordgriechenlands, vol. 3.2, 1935
2 H. KRAHE, Die Sprache der Illyrier, 1955.   BO.D.

Lyra see → Musical instruments

Lyrbe see → Seleucia

Lyrceia, Lyrceum (Λυρχεία, Λύρχειον; *Lyrkeía, Lýrkeion*). Settlement *c.* 12 km north-west of Argos in the Inachus valley (Paus. 2,25,4f.; Str. 6,2,4), located either on the site of the ruins of Skala, or on the site of the modern Lyrkeia (formerly Kato Belesi), or east of the modern Sterna on the left bank of the Inachus. The pre-Homeric city was probably sited near Melissi (Mycenaean necropolis). Following Argos' rise, L. remained a politically dependent → *kṓmē*. According to Str. 8,6,7 [1. 70], the river → Inachus [2] rose from the mountain range also named L., which formed the border with Arcadia. Therefore, Argos is poetically referred to as Lyrcean. An important pass crossed those mountains to Arcadia in 294 BC, the location of a battle between → Demetrius [2] Poliorcetes and the Spartans (Plut. Demetrius 35,1; Polyaenus, Strat. 4,7,9).

1 R. BALADIÉ, Le Péloponnèse de Strabon, 1980, 69f.

I. PAPACHRISTODOULOU, Lyrkeia-Lyrkeion, in: AAA 3, 1970, 117–120; PRITCHETT 3, 1980, 12–17; R. A. TOMLINSON, Argos and the Argolid, 1972, 38–40.   Y.L.

Lyric poetry
I. GREEK   II. LATIN

I. GREEK
A. DEFINITION, CHARACTERISTICS
B. TRANSMISSION   C. GENRES   D. POET AND RECITATION   E. OTHER

A. DEFINITION, CHARACTERISTICS

The term lyric poetry (LP) encompasses the entirety of Greek poetry from the 7th to the mid–5th cent. BC with the exception of stichic hexameter poetry and drama. The word *lyrikós* (λυρικός) is related to *lýra* (λύρα), lyre, and initially refers to poetry that is sung to the accompaniment of a string instrument or, in a broader sense, to all poetry sung to musical accompaniment. This also includes elegiac distichs, which were usually or even without exception accompanied by an *aulós* (→ Elegy, → Music), epinician poetry, accompanied by a *lýra* or an *aulós* (e.g. Pind. Ol. 3,8; Ol. 7,12) and the → iambe (which may or may not have been accompanied by music). The term *lyrikós* originated, comparatively late, in Hellenistic times: Philod. De Poematis 2,35 divides poetry into 'comic, tragic and lyric' (τὰ κωμικὰ καὶ τραγικὰ καὶ λυρικά).

As the term → *mélos* ('song') already occurs in → Archilochus, the term 'melic' is sometimes used today to distinguish LP from iambic or elegiac poetry. This, however, does not take into account that elegies were sung also. Hereafter, the term LP is used mainly in the more narrow sense of the word (as Greek poetry sung to a lyre). While the distinction between choral and monodic poets can sometimes be helpful, it can also be misleading: Greek poets cannot exclusively be assigned to one or the other of the two groups. Today, a number of works that had hitherto been interpreted as choral pieces are also increasingly thought to have been performed by soloists [1]. Furthermore, it is difficult to distinguish between the first-person narrator typical for this type of poetry, and the poet himself: up until recently comments made in the first person have been interpreted as the poet's personal point of view [2], an interpretation that was reinforced by the tradition (prevalent from the antiquity to the 19th cent.) of drawing conclusions about a poet's biography from his work [3; 4]. But it is just as probable that the 'I' of early LP was a convention and expressed the attitudes of the audience. In the case of publicly performed poetry, some scholars even went as far as trying to exclude the poet as an individual almost altogether [5]. The fact that most of the historical evidence consists of fragments makes it even harder to resolve this issue.

What all lyric forms have in common are artful metrical patterns, sometimes strophic ones – often in three stanzas, the third stanza being a variation on the first two identical ones (e.g. Sapphic and Alcaic strophes). Sometimes the structure is triadic (a musical rather than choreographic structural principle) with identical strophe and antistrophe, followed by a varying epode [6; 7]

(→ Metre). All poets from the 7th to the 5th cent. BC (with the exception of Solon) used non-Attic dialects: → Sappho and → Alcaeus [4] used local → Aeolic, → Anacreon [4] used → Ionic. Similar to the way in which elegies, which can be found on the mainland (Tyrtaeus) and in Asia Minor, used the 'international' language of the hexameter, choral LP uses a literary *koiné*, which, depending on the poet's geographical origin, is more or less influenced by Doric tradition.

B. TRANSMISSION

→ Writing had been introduced in Greece in the 8th cent. BC and played an equally important role in the preservation of lyric and epic poetry. The book trade, which was most likely instituted in the 5th cent. BC, made the collection of texts easier. The Peripatetics (→ Peripatos) started the scholarly research on the lyric poets: → Dicaearchus wrote about → Alcaeus [4]; → Chamaeleon [1] and others about → Alcman, → Stesichorus, → Anacreon [4], → Simonides, → Ibycus and → Lasus [1]. The Alexandrians established a → canon [1 III] of nine lyric poets of archaic and classical times and subdivided the work of each poet according to genres into books. In chronological order these nine poets were: Alcman, Alcaeus, Sappho, Stesichorus, Ibycus, Anacreon, Simonides, Bacchylides and Pindar. The canon was compliant with availability in the library of → Alexandria [1] and seems to be based on works with which the Peripatetics were occupied, but additions (Bacchylides) and exclusions (Lasus) occurred. Two anonymous epigrams, Anth. Pal. 9,184 and 571, from the 1st cent. BC or AD (FGE 341), first mention this canon. According to Quint. Inst. 10,1,61 'Pindar was by far the leading one of the nine lyric poets' (*novem lyricorum longe Pindarus princeps*); Petron. 2 mentions 'Pindar and the nine lyric poets' (*Pindarus novemque lyrici*), which leads to the assumption that → Corinna was sometimes also counted as one of them. Apart from Pindar's *epinicia* and the Theognidea (→ Theognis) no complete books of poetry are in existence; on the other hand, non-authentic material was collected and accredited to famous names such as Anacreon and Simonides. The Alexandrians seem to have been in the possession of at least 100 scrolls of papyrus containing LP with an average of more than 1,000 verses each. Of this mass of text only a single assuredly complete poem by Sappho, for example, as well as relatively small amounts of text by other poets are extant, none of which have a manuscript tradition. The bulk of our knowledge about this flourishing kind of poetry arises only from short quotations by ancient authors, who render brief passages for the most diverse reasons. The discovery of papyri in the 20th cent. however has contributed considerably, if fragmentarily, to our knowledge about the majority of the poets.

C. GENRES

In Homer, various types of LP are mentioned: the sung → paean (Hom. Il. 1,472–73; 22,391), the → threnos (ibid. 24,720ff.), the → Linus song (ibid. 18,570, see also → Ailinos) and the → hymenaeus (ibid. 18,493). Much as in the case of epic poetry, there was without doubt a case history of individually as well as jointly sung folk songs. But for us the development of the individual metric types only starts with the first poets who emerged from the anonymity of the time preceding the 7th cent. BC. The classification of types reflects Alexandrian terminology, not however the rules of composition that the poets themselves consciously applied [8; 9]. The fundamental principle of distinction in that case is the differentiation between songs honouring gods and songs honouring people. The historical perspective however is not considered here: the → epinikion for example is supposed to honour mortals, but poets commonly refer to it as *hýmnos*, which reminds us of the fact that it is a secularized form with religious undertones whose ethos is strongly influenced by its development.

D. POET AND RECITATION

The differentiation between personal and public poetry, which focuses on the difference between target audiences, turns out to be more helpful than the traditional distinction between monody and choral LP. Some poets wrote for a general audience, other more for a selected group, yet others for both. Alcman's *partheneia* were doubtlessly performed by a chorus during religious festivals and publicly recited in Sparta, where marriageable girls were introduced to the community with jests and banter in a rite of passage. The group speaks, the personal element is rather restricted; this however should not lead to the assumption that therefore all of Alcman's extant verse was choral LP. The only longer fragment of a *partheneion* (1 PMGF) gives a foretaste of the elaborate *epinicia* of Pindar. In addition to that there is a myth, gnomic ethical deliberations, theological reflections and more detailed information about the occasion and the performance, although it remains a mystery which local celebration in Sparta itself is referred to. For the most part, non-epicinian poetry was relevant only on a local level and therefore less likely to be preserved, while Pindar's *epinicia* are extant because the celebrations in question, the athletic festivals, were panhellenic.

Public celebrations also seem to have been the stage for Stesichorus' poetry on epic themes. His name in itself gives an indication that he probably deployed a chorus for his performances; but the more we learn about the likely length of his poems and the nature of the recently discovered papyrus fragments (57–587 PMGF), the more likely it seems that their author is a cithara player in the tradition of → Terpander, for example an *aoidós* (ἀοιδός) (→ Aoidoi) as in Homer. Considering the remarkable number of speeches in the poems, it may be assumed that members of the chorus played individual parts. In that case, Stesichorus would be an important forerunner of tragedy. He is credited with the invention of the triadic form, which in itself

does not necessarily imply (see above) a choral performance. Stesichorus apparently was the first to use the dactylic epitritos [10]; this fusion of cola with two short syllables and one short syllable is also found in the *asynarteta* of Archilochus, which might also have been sung.

Ibycus has so far normally been grouped with the poets of choral LP. It is hard to imagine, however, that the hymn to Polycrates in fr. 5151 PMGF was sung by a chorus; nor can we just conclude that a triadic structure necessarily implies that a chorus was performing (cf. Pind. fr. 123 MAEHLER). The other relevant fragments of Ibycus (fr. 286–288 PMGF) were deeply erotic and probably intended for the court in Samos (as were the songs of the younger Anacreon, whose preference for three-part compositions is shared by Ibycus [11. 325, 334]).

Greek choral LP reaches its peak in the late 6th and the 1st half of the 5th cent. BC in the works of Simonides, Pindar and Bacchylides. These poets were paid by patrons, mostly affluent aristocrats of the entire Greek world: they commissioned poets to celebrate their victories in the more important games (→ Sports festivals) in order to show their wealth and to gain fame. In many cases this type of choral LP (→ dithyramb in honour of Dionysus, → paean, → hyporchema, → prosodion/procession songs, → partheneion) is intended for city festivals, while *epinikia* mainly serve the purpose of praising individual people and are not intended as accompaniment for rituals performed in honour of gods. Compared to Pindar, Bacchylides' narrative style (as well as his disposition for extensive speeches) is detached, and reminiscent of Stesichorus. It is unclear whether the victory songs were choral or monodic; the occasion was doubtlessly public [1; 3; 4]. These songs are a continuation of the old and important tradition of public praise and admonition (→ Encomium), which first appears in the invectives of Archilochus.

Public celebrations were probably the stage for longer Greek → elegies [12], and some of them (e.g. Simonides 10–14 IEG II) may have been performed during tournaments. Shorter elegies on the other hand were sung at symposia (→ Banquet), which are also the most likely place for the performance of the majority of early monodic or personal LP – this applies to Archilochus, Alcaeus or Anacreon. The metric structure of personal LP for this kind of occasion, in front of a small audience, is for the most part simpler than that of elaborate sung performances in public. The music (such as elegiac distichs or Aeolian strophe) could be repeated from one song to the next. Eating and drinking revelries are frequently chosen as subjects by these poets whose works were performed by companions of kindred spirit (*hetaîroi*) [13]. Irrespective of whether the subject is love, war, politics or communal revelries, the poems, like all Greek literature, have a tendency to generalize. Gnomic elements (→ Gnome) were customarily included. Although every poet makes personal references to contemporaries, the songs have a tendency to identify the singer with the group, and thus can be performed by others at different occasions. Among the extant fragments of Greek LP is a collection of anonymous drinking songs (→ Skolion; fr. 884–917 PMG), which were sung at gatherings.

The poetry of Sappho is very likely to have been sung among women in Mytilene; it gives us a little insight into the world of women in addition to the world of male warriors. Aphrodite rather than Dionysus holds the place of honour here. The exact nature of Sappho's circle is still fiercely discussed: some see her as an educator, others as a priestess, yet others simply as a singer of homoerotic passion (→ Women authors). Nowhere else was the tendency to interpret poetry from a biographical point of view stronger than with Sappho. According to the classification of the Alexandrian philologists, one of her books of poems contained *epithalamia* [14], at least some of which must have been choral.

E. Other

Countless names of poets have been passed down, sometimes without clearly attributable fragments (Poetae Melici Minores 696–846 PMG). It is remarkable that dithyramb poets (→ Cinesias, → Melanippides, → Philoxenus, → Timotheus) clearly dominated in the late 5th cent. BC, when the total number of choral genres decreased and the choral element in tragedies declined as well. These dithyramb poets were an avantgarde and a challenge for traditional Athenian dramatists: their compositions served as an experimental playground for a new kind of music, in which the absence of strophic responses, elaborate musical solos and dance movements and the mixing of keys became more important than the words to which all other elements of song had hitherto been subordinate. LP performed by individuals, the traditional custom of singing after meals went out of use in Athens, as we know from Aristoph. Nub. 1353ff. Metric complexity tapered off towards the late-classical period.

While songs as well as written poetry in the simple metres of the archaic epoch exist in Hellenistic times [6. 138–152], it was the epigram that became the most important poetic medium of personal expression and was still recited in Ptolemaic times during symposia; as such it is the only poetic form of the *Anthologia Graeca* [15; 16]. Also extant are numerous → folk songs from various periods (Carmina Popularia 847–883 PMG). There is a close connection between these and various → work songs.

→ Lyric poetry; → Metre; → Music; → Songs

1 M. DAVIES, Monody, Choral Lyric, and the Tyranny of the Handbook, in: CQ n.s. 38, 1988, 52–64   2 B. SNELL, Die Entdeckung des Geistes, ³1955, 83–117   3 M. LEFKOWITZ, The Lives of the Greek Poets, 1981   4 Id., First-Person Fictions: Pindar's Poetic 'I', 1991   5 E. BUNDY, Studia Pindarica (Univ. of California Publications in Classical Philology 18, 1962 (repr. 1986), 1–92   6 M. L. WEST, Greek Metre, 1982, 32–33   7 Id., Stesichorus, in: CQ n.s. 21, 1971, 302–314   8 H. W. SMYTH, Greek Melic Poets, 1900 (repr. 1963), XXIII–CXXXIV   9 A. E.

HARVEY, The Classification of Greek Lyric Poetry, in: CQ n.s. 5, 1955, 157–175   10 M. HASLAM, Stesichorean Metre, in: Quaderni Urbinati 17, 1974, 7–57   11 H. FRÄNKEL, Dichtung und Philos. des frühen Griechentums, ²1962   12 E. BOWIE, Early Greek Elegy, Symposium and Public Festival, in: JHS 106, 1986, 13–35   13 W. RÖSLER, Dichter und Gruppe, 1980   14 D. L. PAGE, Sappho and Alcaeus, 1955 (repr. 1987), 119–126   15 A. CAMERON, Callimachus and his Critics, 1995, 24–103   16 R. HUNTER, Theocritus and the Archaeology of Greek Poetry, 1996, 1–13.

EDITIONS: E.-M. VOIGT, Sappho et Alcaeus, 1971; IEG; PMG; PMGF; D. A. CAMPBELL, Greek Lyric 1–5, 1983–93.

BIBLIOGRAPHY: D. A. CAMPBELL, The Golden Lyre: The Themes of the Greek Lyric Poets, 1983; R. L. FOWLER, The Nature of Early Greek Lyric, 1987; H. FRÄNKEL, ²1962 (s. [11]); B. GENTILI, Poesia e pubblico nella Grecia antica, ³1995; D. E. GERBER, Greek Lyric Poetry Since 1920, Part I, in: Lustrum 35, 1993, 7–179; Part II, in: Lustrum 36, 1994 7–188, 285–297; D. E. GERBER (ed.), A Companion to the Greek Lyric Poets, 1997; J. HERINGTON, Poetry into Drama: Greek Tragedy and the Greek Poetic Trad., 1985; G. M. KIRKWOOD, Early Greek Monody, 1974; W. RÖSLER, 1980 (s. [13]).   E. R.

II. LATIN
A. THE ROMAN CONCEPT OF LP   B. THE LATIN LYRIC POETS   C. LATIN LP IN THE MIDDLE AGES AND IN MODERN TIMES

A. THE ROMAN CONCEPT OF LP

Following Greek theory, Cicero distinguished melic poetry from drama, epic poetry and dithyramb among the various genres of poetry; he used the term *melicum poema* ('melic poem', Cic. Opt. Gen. 1) or talks about the *poetae λυρικοί* (*lyrikoí*, 'lyric poets', Orat. 183). While the term *mélos* (for *carmen*) remained a foreign word in Latin, the term *lyricus* (like the loan-word *lyra*) became part of the Latin vocabulary after Cicero [3. 11–13]. Under the influence of the Alexandrians, who paid little heed to the performance practices of older LP, Latin LP, from Augustan times at the latest, refers almost exclusively to written poetry (against [8]). The distinction between monodic and choral LP is no longer made.

According to ancient theories, form is the primary defining characteristic of LP, i.e. Latin LP initially encompasses poems in Aeolic poetic metres as well as those in lyric iambs, trochees, anapaests, iambs (excluding the → canticum in dramas); → Horatius [7] also uses forms of iambographic epodes for his *Carmina*. The borders between form and genre in poetry had become obscured since Hellenistic times anyway. → Catullus for example used Sapphic verse for invectives, *choliambi* for love poems and hexameters for an epithalamion [4], and later on → Martialis interprets Catullus' short polymetric poems as → epigrams [7. 77]. Thus the criterion of theme is added to that of form: erotic, sympotic, poetologic and (to a limited extent) political themes take centre stage. But satires and invectives – when composed in lyric metres – can also be considered part of Latin LP.

The complicated Greek metric systems were simplified in Latin LP: Aeolic verse becomes monostichic (e.g. glyconics, pherecratics; thus Catullus, Horace, later also → Prudentius, → Boethius); the strophes are only bior quadri-nominal; the triadic structure is dropped.

Horace adopts the Alexandrian selection of the nine lyric poets (*lyrikoì poiētaí*), whom he explicitly considers as models, and puts → Pindarus at the top of his 'catalogue of lyric poets' (Carm. 4,9,6–12); that is exactly where Pindar can be found in Quintilian's canon of exemplary lyric poets (Inst. 10,1,61; 8,6,71). Alexandrian theory and editorial practices are probably also behind Horace's classification of lyric genres in Carm. 4,2,10–24 (dithyramb, hymn, epinikion, threnos) and in Ars 83–85 (hymnus, encomium, scolion [5. 142]), which do not consistently correspond to the genres of Latin LP; but the scope of genres used continues to be essentially determined by pre-Hellenistic Greek tradition (→ Symposium literature, erotic poems, → Hymn, → Epithalamion, paraklausithyron, propemptikon, epicedium, etc.). Apart from these artistic forms of written poetry, Latin LP also encompasses different forms of the art and folk song (→ Songs).

B. THE LATIN LYRIC POETS

Apart from relics of other neoteric poetry, the reception of older Greek melic poetry (with Alexandrian vowel shift) in Latin LP only becomes discernible in Catullus' short *polymetra* as well as in the *epithalamia*. But it is → Horatius who claims to be the 'player of the Roman lyre' (*Romanae fidicen lyrae*) and to have introduced older Greek LP in Rome under the name of *Alcaeus Latinus*; through his classicizing imitation of, and excellence in, occidental LP he indeed opens up a new field (see below). Quintilian ranks Horace first among the *lyrici*, and → Caesius [II 8] Bassus is the only other one he names in this category of poets (inst. 10,1,96). As Horace adopts the old kind of poetry as written 'literature' and (with the exception of the *Carm. saec.*) writes poetry purely for reading, he can freely combine various forms as well as individual motives and formulations of Greek LP, and for example imitate Pindar using Sapphic verse [5. 142f.].

After Horace, LP is found only sporadically and in most cases as part of poetry books (→ Poetry book, often in the form of Horace-→ *imitatio* (Statius, *Silvae*; Prudentius; Martianus Capella; Ennodius Carm. 1,4,7 and 17; Ausonius; Claudianus, *Carmina minora*; Paulinus of Nola; Sidonius Apollinaris; Venantius Fortunatus), partly using new forms (stichic use of verse, which is only used in strophes in Catullus and Horace). At the same time, Latin LP experiences a diversification of themes: apart from poetry written to celebrate friendship and casual occasions, it encompasses religious and philosophical themes (Boethius); thus Hilarius of Poitiers is able to apply Horace's' lyric measures to Christian strophic songs and introduces them into Christian hymnic poetry (like Ambrose, Prudentius, Sedulius *et al.*). These lyric forms are now put into rhythm and sung (→ Songs).

C. LATIN LP IN THE MIDDLE AGES AND IN MODERN TIMES

In the clerical poetry of the Middle Ages, Latin Christian LP as well as archaic art forms continue to be in use (Maroboduus, Hildebert of Lavardin, Abelard, Adam of St. Victor [6]). In the secular world, it is mainly the Carolingian poet laureates (Paulus Diaconus, Alcuin, Theodulf of Orléans, Modoin, Walafrid Strabo, Gottschalk, *et al.*) and the Goliard poets (Hugo Primas, the Archipoeta, Walter of Châtillon; *Carmina Burana*) who pick up on archaic forms and motives. Classical Latin LP is set to music [6]. The Middle Ages introduce rhyme (which was alien to the Romans) into poetry, which, compared to archaic LP, expands the variety of forms considerably.

By way of the Latin grammar schools, the term *lyricus* (in addition to *melicus*) enters the poetic theory of the Renaissance. Following the judgement of Horace and Quintilian, Pindar is celebrated as a lyric poet. It is, however, Latin LP, and above all that of Catullus and Horace, that forms the basis for the appreciation of LP and for the Latin LP of the humanists, who subsequently tend to project Horace's ideas about LP back onto the old Greek lyric poets [5. 145]. From the 17th to the 20th cent., the poetry of European classicism adopts the Latin lyric poets (French *pléiade*, German *Ode*, etc.). Rather than hark back directly to Greek forms, even the *imitatio* of Greek LP more frequently picks up the formal elements that Catullus and Horace developed. Apart from form (strophic structure, Alcaic, Archilocian, Asclepiadian, Sapphic strophe; Pindaric ode; rhymelessness), subject matter is increasingly perceived as a criterion of LP (turn of thought, emotional depth). Due to this development and to the fact that from the 16th cent. European literary theory (with the exception of France) championed the doctrine of a triad of genres, Roman elegiac love poetry (→ Elegy) and iambic poetry are also subsumed under the term LP. Thus even Catullus, who was perceived as an epigrammatic poet since the Renaissance (according to the judgement of Martial), can again be considered a lyric poet in the 19th cent. The common 20th-cent. extension of the term to include Virgil's *Eclogues* and elegiac love poetry (cf. e.g. [1]) is not archaic. LP in the Latin language (in various archaic metres) is still cultivated in the 20th cent. [2].

→ Lyric poetry; → Metre; → Music; → Middle Latin II; → Songs

1 K. BÜCHNER, Die röm. L., ²1983   2 J. EBERLE (ed.), Viva Camena, Latina huius aetatis carmina, 1961   3 H. FÄRBER, Die L. in der Kunsttheorie der Ant., 1936   4 T. FUHRER, The Question of Genre and Metre in Catullus' Polymetrics, in: Quaderni urbinati N.S. 46, 1994, 95–108   5 T. GELZER, Die Alexandriner und die griech. Lyriker, in: Acta antiqua Academiae Scientiarum Hungaricae 30, 1988, 129–147   6 F. MUNARI, Trad. und Originalität in der lat. Dichtung des XII. Jh., in: Romanistische Forsch. 69, 19, 305–331 (= Id., KS, 1980, 131–157)   7 B. W. SWANN, Martial's Catullus, 1994   8 G. WILLE, Musica Romana, 1967.   T.FU.

Lyrnessus (Λυρνεσσός; *Lyrnessós*). Settlement in the Mysian-Trojan border region not localized exactly. Attempts to locate it are based especially on Homer (Il. 2,690f.; 19,60; 20,92; 20,191; Str. 13,1,7; 61) and Pliny (HN 5,122), in whose time L. was destroyed. Older localizations: near Antandrus [1. 217–221], near Havran [2. 301], recently on the Ala Dağ [3. 70f.]. According to Hom. Il. 2,689ff. and 19,60, L. was destroyed by Achilles, who also killed king Mynes and abducted → Briseis. Now in detail [3. 66–71].

1 W. LEAF, Troy, 1912 2 H. KIEPERT, in: Zschr. der Ges. für Erdkunde zu Berlin 24, 1889 3 J. STAUBER, Die Bucht von Adramytteion 1 (IK 50), 1996.   E.SCH.

Lysagoras (Λυσαγόρας; *Lysagóras*) from Paros, son of Teisias. According to Herodotus (6,133,1), the original motive for the Paros expedition by → Militiades in 489 BC was personal grudge against L., who supposedly had previously slandered Militiades to the Persian commander → Hydarnes [2]. A source hostile to Militiades is presumably the basis for the report [1].

1 K. H. KINZL, Miltiades' Parosexpedition in der Geschichtsschreibung, in: Hermes 104, 1976, 280–307.   HA.BE.

Lysander (Λύσανδρος; *Lýsandros*).
[1] Spartiate, son of Aristocritus. Reports that the family, which traces its family tree back to Hercules and was connected to king Libys of Cyrene through hospitality (Diod. Sic. 14,13,5–6; Paus. 6,3,14), was impoverished (Plut. Lysander = Lys. 2,1) and that L. was considered a *móthax* (foster-brother of a citizen's boy, → *móthakes*) (Phylarchos FGrH 81 F 43; Ael. VH 12,43), appear to be based on deliberate defamation. L. became fleet commander (*naúarchos*) of the Spartan fleet in Rhodes (→ Peloponnesian War) in spring 407 BC, sailed with 70 triremes to Ephesus and, after clever negotiations with Cyrus [3] the Younger, received large Persian subsidies (Xen. Hell. 1,5,1–8; Diod. Sic. 13,70; Plut. Lys. 3–4). He won numerous Spartan partisans as personal followers and in the spring of 406 inflicted losses on the Athenian fleet at Notion in the absence of → Alcibiades [3], who was deprived of his command thereupon (Xen. Hell. 1,5,11–15; Hell. Oxy. 4,1–4 BARTOLETTI; Diod. Sic. 13,71; Plut. Lys. 5). After the severe defeat of the Spartan fleet under the command of L.'s successor Callicratidas [1] at the Arginusae islands (in the middle of the summer of 406) L. became *epistoleús* ('vice commander') of the new nauarch Aracus and actually took over the fleet command again. He destroyed the Athenian sea power in September 405 through a surprise attack at → Aegospotami (Xen. Hell. 2,1,7–32; Diod. Sic. 13,105–106; Plut. Lys. 9,6–13,2 [1. 594ff.]). L.'s special position after this victory and the power of Sparta at that time are symbolized by the victory monument in Delphi (Paus. 10,9,7).

In the autumn of 405, L. put an end to the remaining Athenian rulership in the Aegean (except for Samos) and blockaded Athens from the sea until it surrendered in the spring of 404 (Xen. Hell. 2,2,1–23; Diod. Sic. 13,107; Plut. Lys. 13–14). Then he subjugated Samos, where he (probably after another stay in the summer of 404) was the first Hellene to receive 'god-like honours' from Samian oligarchs whom he had returned to Samos (Duris, FGrH 76 F 26 and 71; Paus. 6,3,14–15; [2. 3ff.; 3. 871]). His operations in Thrace to consolidate the Spartan sphere of control are difficult to date (probably in the summer of 404) (Plut. Lys. 16,1).

In *c.* June/July 404 or a bit later L. supported the seizure of power by the Thirty in Athens (→ Triakonta; Xen. Hell. 2,3,2–3; 2,3,11–14; Diod. Sic. 14,3,4–7; Plut. Lys. 15,1–2), whom he, from the beginning, gave a free hand to pursue their opponents [4. 27f.]. In a series of poleis he constituted, according to Diod. Sic. 14,13,1, → dekadarchia [1] in agreement with the ephors, who for the time being (until oligarchies would be established?) should guarantee the loyalty of the new league comrades but also strengthen his own position in Sparta. After the overthrow of the Thirty, L. was able to have the new Athenian administrative body of the so-called Ten be recognized in Sparta and himself as *harmostés* with his brother → Libys, who was appointed *naúarchos*, be sent to Athens. King → Pausanias, however, was not ready to accept L.'s dominating role and supported, together with → Agis [2] II. (Plut. Lys. 21), that the factions of the Athenian Civil War reconcile in order to consolidate Sparta's hegemony, while L. wanted to fight the Athenian 'democrats' without compromises [5. 80ff.].

Even though L. was defeated in this conflict and the *dekadarchiai* were dissolved (Xen. Hell. 3,4,2), he remained influential at first. In the year 400 he successfully supported → Agesilaus' [2] II. claim to the Spartan royal crown (Xen. Hell. 3,3,1–4; Plut. Lys. 22; Plut. Agesilaus 3). He achieved that Agesilaus got the command in the Persian War in Asia Minor in 396 (Xen. Hell. 3,4,2–4), but Agesilaus soon relegated him to the background [6. 180ff.; 7. 87ff.]. It is not possible to verify that L., after his return, planned to constitute an elected monarchy in Sparta in order to gain power himself (Diod. Sic. 14,13,2–8; Plut. Lys. 24–26; Plut. Agesilaus 20). Allegedly incriminating evidence was not published. L. fell in the autumn of 395 before Haliartus in the battle against Thebes (Xen. Hell. 3,5,6; 3,5,17–25; Diod. Sic. 14, 81, 1–2; Plut. Lys. 27–28).

Just as other Spartan leaders, L. was not able to develop a promising concept to stabilize the Greek world after 404 and in the end remained bound to the mechanisms of political events in Sparta. High-flying imperial plans can hardly be derived from Xenophon (Hell. 3,4,2).

1 B. BLECKMANN, Athens Weg in die Niederlage, 1998 2 CHR. HABICHT, Gottmenschentum und griech. Städte, ²1970 3 A. B. BOSWORTH, in: CAH 6, ²1994 4 G. A. LEHMANN, Oligarchische Herrschaft im klass. Athen,

1997 5 R. J. BUCK, Thrasybulus and the Athenian Democracy, 1998 6 P. CARTLEDGE, Agesilaos, 1987 7 CH. D. HAMILTON, Agesilaus and the Failure of Spartan Hegemony, 1991.

J.-F. BOMMELAER, Lysandre de Sparte, 1981; D. LOTZE, Lysander und der Peloponnesische Krieg, 1964.
K.-W.WEL.

[2] Athenian who was installed as governor in → Leucas in 314 BC in the course of → Cassander's expansion towards Epirus (cf. Diod. Sic. 19,67,5). In 312 L. fell in an attack with Cassander's *stratēgós* from Acarnania, Lyciscus [4], against Alcetas [3] near Eurymenae (Diod. Sic. 19,88,5).

PA 9281; TRAILL, PAA 612365.
BO.D.

[3] Spartan, descendant of L. [1] (Paus. 3,6,7), influential follower of → Agis [4] IV; as one of the → *éphoroi* 243/2 BC he proposed the latter's reform programme in the → *gerousía* and in the public assembly, drove → Leonidas II out and installed Cleombrotus [3] II as king (Plut. Agesilaus 6; 8–9; 11). After his year in office he had the kings dismiss the new ephors, but was deceived by Agesilaus, the uncle of Agis [4] IV., and went into exile (Plut. l.c. 12–13; 19).
K.-W.WEL.

Lysandra (Λυσάνδρα; *Lysándra*). Daughter of → Ptolemaeus I and → Eurydice [4], sister of Ptolemy Keraunos. She probably only married Alexander, the son of → Cassander, after 297/6 BC (FGrH 260 F 3,5). After his death in 294/3 she married → Agathocles [5], the son of Lysimachus [2] (Plut. Demetrius 31,5; Paus. 1,9,6 probably erroneously assume the date 299, which made a split into two persons necessary, PP VI 14529 and 14530; the formulation by Plutarch, however, speaks against this possibility). Thus Agathocles secured for himself a claim to Macedonia and the connection with Egypt. After the murder of Agathocles, L. fled with her children and brothers to Seleucus I, which should not, however, be seen as the decisive reason for the war against Lysimachus.
→ Diadochi

J. SEIBERT, Historische Beiträge zu den dyn. Verbindungen in hell. Zeit, 1967, 75f.; H. HEINEN, Unt. zur hell. Geschichte, 1972, 6; 13; 51f.
W.A.

Lysandridas (Λυσανδρίδας; *Lysandrídas*).
[1] (Plut.: Λυσανορίδας; *Lysanorídas*). Spartan, one of the three → *harmostai* of the Spartan occupation in Thebes, who could not prevent this polis from being liberated by → Pelopidas in 379 BC. L. was condemned to a big fine in Sparta and left the Peloponnese (Plut. Pel. 13; Theopomp. FGrH 115 F 240; cf. Xen. Hell. 5,4,13; Diod. Sic. 15,27).
K.-W.WEL.
[2] L. from Megalopolis (→ Megale Polis); in 223/2 BC L. wanted to lead his fellow citizens, who had fled, back into the city that had been conquered by → Cleomenes [6] III. The price for the return would have been leaving the Achaean League. However, → Philopoemen prevented this (Plut. Cleomenes 24,2–9).

R. URBAN, Wachstum und Krise des Achäischen Bundes, 1979, 199f.
L.-M.G.

Lysanias (Λυσανίας; *Lysanías*).
[1] Tetrarch of Abilene who was introduced by the evangelist Luke (Lc 3:1) for the purpose of synchronization, in the 15th year of the emperor Tiberius = October 27 – September AD 28. He must have died before 37, since Caligula gave his territory to → Herodes [8] Agrippa I at that time.

L. BOFFO, Iscrizioni Greche e Latine per lo studio della Bibbia, 1994, 171ff.; PIR² L 467.
W.E.

[2] Greek grammarian from Cyrene who lived in the 3rd cent. BC. Known as the teacher of → Eratosthenes [2] (Suda s.v. Ἐρατοσθένης). His work Περὶ ἰαμβοποιῶν ('On Iambic Poets') has been attested for certain; numerous fragments are extant in Ath. 7,304b and 14,620c. Besides he is mentioned in several scholia on Homer (schol. Hom. Il. 9,378; 16,558; 21,262) and Euripides (schol. Eur. Andr. 10) [1] [2]. L.'s lexicographical activity is attested by Ath. 11,504b and EM s.v. ὑπερικταίνοντο.

1 A. BAUMSTARK, Beitr. zur griech. Litt.-Gesch., in: Philologus 53, 1894, 687–716, esp. 708–716 2 A. GUDEMAN, s.v. L., RE 13, 2508–2511.
M.B.

Lyseis see → Zetemata

Lysias (Λυσίας; *Lysías*).
[1] Attic → *logographos*, 459/8 or *c.* 445 to *c.* 380 BC
A. LIFE B. WORK C. CHARACTERISTICS AND RECEPTION

A. LIFE
The main biographical facts can be gathered from L.'s speeches (esp. or. 12), from which the later *vitae* (Dion. Hal. de Lysia; Ps.-Plut. Mor. 835c ff.) and Byzantine learning (Phot. Bibl. 262; Suda s.v. L.) drew partly. Born probably around 445, L. left Athens at the age of 15 and together with his older brother Polemarchus settled in the Panhellenic colony of → Thurii, which had been founded in 444 (the archaic assessment of his year of birth as 459/8 was most likely a combination of references to his age and the foundation year of Thurii). After returning from Thurii, where he is said to have studied rhetoric with → Teisias (412: anti-Athenian sentiment in Lower Italy after the defeat at Syracusae), L. was possibly active as a teacher of rhetoric (Cic. Brut. 48 referring to Aristotle) and maybe already as a *logographos*, although his economic situation (joint inheritance of the weapon manufacturing business of his father, the wealthy → *métoikos* Cephalus, cf. Plato's 'Republic') certainly did not necessitate this; he is also said to have composed specialized rhetorical works (Plut. Mor. 836b; Marcellinus ad Hermog. WALZ 4,352). As democratic-minded and moreover very affluent metics, L. and his brother became

victims of the Thirty (→ Triakonta, 404/3): Polemarchos was murdered, L. managed to escape to Megara, but the fortune was lost for the most part. With the little that had been saved, L. generously supported the democratic opposition that was forming in Boeotian exile; because of this they wanted to honour him with the citizenship after the restoration of democracy in Athens; an injunction (→ Paranomon graphe) by → Archinus defeated that plan, and L. remained a *métoikos* with → *isotéleia*. From that time on, he was active as a speechwriter and also appeared as an orator himself (e.g. 388: *Olympiakós lógos* = or. 33). The last of his speeches that can be dated approximately (fr. 78 THALHEIM) takes us to the end of the 80s; his year of death is unknown.

B. WORK

Of the 425 speeches that were attributed to L. in antiquity (Dion. Hal. and Caecilius [III 5] of Cale Acte believed 233 to be genuine) 172 titles and numerous fragments are extant. Almost completely preserved are 31 speeches as well as the introductory parts of a further three which are quoted by Dion. Hal. (Lys. or. 32–34) and the so-called *Erōtikós* (or. 35), a speech of the sophistic school, which is quoted and criticized in Pl. Phdr. 231a ff. but could of course also be attributed to Plato himself. Apart from two speeches that are categorized as *génos epideiktikón* ('festive' or 'ceremonial speech': or. 2; 33) and one categorized as *génos symbouleutikón* ('advisory' or 'political speech': or. 34), they are court speeches, which L. wrote for the prosecution or the defence in state or private lawsuits. Apart from purely private matters (e.g. or. 1, 3, 4, 7, 24), there are cases in which politics plays a pivotal role. They include the oligarchic intermezzo of 404/3 (or. 12 'Against Eratosthenes', delivered by L. himself; or. 13 'Against Agoratus'; cf. also the *dokimasia* speeches 16, 25, 26, 31; → *dokimasia*) as well as events in everyday political life in the 90s and 80s of the 4th cent. BC., e.g. desertion (or. 14 and 15), malpractice (or. 30), unlawful gain (or. 19, 28, 29), bribery in office (or. 21), profiteering (or. 22) and others. Part of the corpus are two speeches which are doubtlessly not authentic (or. 6 and 20) as well as some others whose authenticity has been called into question (or. 2, 8, 9, 14, 15). A more recent theory (DOVER), according to which almost all speeches are interpreted as joint products of composite authorship (logographers, client, subsequent reviser), has been refuted (USHER, WINTER).

C. CHARACTERISTICS AND RECEPTION

While L.'s speeches are valuable sources of the history and politics as well as of private and business life in the Attic state between 404 and 380, their evaluation demands a careful analysis of the purpose of the particular argument and of the chosen strategy of persuasion. Only in the 20th cent. closer attention was paid to this, although the ingenious finesse behind the apparent naturalness and unpretentiousness of L.'s style had al-ready been felt in antiquity. His technique of persuasion is based firstly on the subtle construction of what seems at first sight an irrefutable (pseudo-) argument; secondly, on the almost perfectly hidden suggestivity of his seemingly honestly-artless *narrationes;* thirdly, on ethopoiia, which does not refer to the adaptation of diction to the real character of a particular orator, but to the orator's plausible presentation as – depending on the requirements – a shrewd or naive, dauntless or anxious, but in any case likeable person. The language and style of L. have been praised from antiquity (Dion. Hal. in particular) because of the purity of their → Attic character, the simplicity of expression, the economic use of rhetorical ornaments, their brevity, clarity and ostensiveness, and the resulting grace (*cháris*), which Dion. Hal. calls the ultimate criterion for the authenticity of a speech (Dion. Hal. de Lysia 11). What is missing, however, is the stirring passion and fulminating power, which can be felt with Demosthenes [2] for example. While L. was the chosen paragon of some orators (Charisius, Hegesias, cf. Cic. Brut. 286; or. 226) even in Hellenistic times, the pinnacle of his appreciation as a canonical model of style (→ Canon III.) only started with the → Atticism of the 1st cent. BC, when esp. Roman followers of this school of style ranked L. even above Demosthenes; Caecilius preferred him to Plato, a verdict that Auctor *De sublimitate* (32,8; → Ps.-Longinus) refuted in the early days of the Imperial period. Hermogenes (De ideis 2,9 = p. 376f. RABE and 2,11 = p. 395f. R.) still rates L. very favourably; according to the Suda he was commented on repeatedly during the Imperial period.

→ Rhetoric

COMPLETE EDITIONS: TH. THALHEIM, ²1913; K. HUDE, 1912; L. GERNET, M. BIZOS, 1924–1926 (²1955; with French transl.); W. R. M. LAMB, 1930 (²1967; with Engl. transl.); U. ALBINI, 1955 (with Italian transl.); E. MEDDA, 1991–1995 (with Italian transl.); German transl.: U. TREU, 1983.
EDITIONS, COMMENTARIES AND TRANSLATIONS OF SELECTED SPEECHES: M. H. HANSEN, 1982 (or. 1, 3, 10, 13, 24, 30); M. J. EDWARDS, S. USHER, 1985 (or. 1, 10, 12, 16, 22, 24, 25); G. AVEZZÙ, 1985 (or. 1, 2); J. L. CALVO MARTÍNEZ, 1988 (or. 1–15); C. CAREY, 1989 (or. 1, 3, 7, 14, 31, 32); M. WEISSENBERGER, 1987 (or. 16, 25, 26, 31).
INDIVIDUAL SPEECHES (MORE RECENT EDITIONS): or. 1: P. VIANELLO DE CORDOVA, 1980; or. 10: M. HILLGRUBER, 1988; or. 12: G. AVEZZÙ, 1991; Id., 1992; or. 16: V. UGENTI, 1991.
BIBLIOGRAPHY: BLASS, 1, 339–644; K. J. DOVER, L. and the Corpus Lysiacum, 1968; P. GRAU, Prooemiengestaltung bei L., 1971; H. M. HAGEN, Ethopoiia, 1966; K. SCHÖN, Die Scheinargumente bei L., 1918; M. L. SOSOWER, Pal. Gr. 88 and the Manuscript Tradition of L., 1987; S. USHER, L. and his Clients, in: GRBS 17, 1976, 31–40; TH. N. WINTER, On the Corpus of L., in: CJ 69, 1973, 34–40.
ON SEPARATE SPEECHES: or. 1: G. HERMAN, Tribal and Civic Codes of Behaviour in L., in: CQ 43, 1993, 406–419; M. WEISSENBERGER, Die erste Rede des L., in: AU 36(3), 1993, 55–71; or. 6: M. CATAUDELLA, Su Ps.-L. 6 (Contra Andocidem), cronologia e interpretazione, in: Anales de

Historia Antigua y Medieval 20, 1977–1979, 44–56; or. 7: E. HEITSCH, Recht und Taktik in der siebten Rede des L., in: MH 18, 1961, 204–219; or. 9: D. M. MacDOWELL, The Case of the Rude Soldier (L. 9), in: G. THÜR (ed.), Symposion 1993, 1994, 153–164; or. 12: P. KRENTZ, Was Eratosthenes Responsible for the Death of Polemarchos?, in: PdP 39, 1984, 23–32; TH. C. LOENING, The Autobiographical Speeches of L. and the Biographical Trad., in: Hermes 109, 1981, 280–294; or. 21: TH. SCHMITZ, Die 21. Rede des L. und ihre Aktualität, in: AU 38(3), 1995, 72–96; or. 22: TH. J. FIGUEIRA, Sitopolai and Sitophylakes in L.'s 'Against the Graindealers', in: Phoenix 40, 1986, 149–171; or. 24: C. CAREY, Structure and Strategy in L. XXIV, in: G&R 37, 1990, 44–51; or. 25: T. M. MURPHY, L. 25 and the Intractable Democratic Abuses, in: AJPh 113, 1992, 543–558; or. 30: ST. TODD, L. against Nikomachos, in: L. FOXHALL, A. D. E. LEWIS (ed.), Greek Law in Its Political Setting, 1996, 101–131; or. 33: H.-G. KLEINOW, Die Überwindung der Polis im frühen 4. Jh. v.Chr. Zu den panhellenischen Reden bei L., 1981; or. 35: A. W. H. ADKINS, The 'Speech of L.' in Plato's Phaedrus, in: R. B. LOUDEN, P. SCHOLLMEIER, (ed.), The Greeks and Us. Essays in Honor of A.W.H. Adkins, 1996, 224–240; H. GÖRGEMANNS, Ein neues Argument für die Echtheit des lysianischen Erotikos, in: RhM 131, 1988, 108–113.

                                                                    M.W.

[2] Athenian, voted *stratēgós* in a by-election in 406/5 BC, in command of the 15 triremes of the right wing in the battle of → Arginusae. His ship was sunk by the Spartan nauarch → Callicratidas [1]. Like his colleagues, L. was afterwards removed from office, tried and executed (Xen. Hell. 1,6,30; 7,1–35; Diod. Sic. 13,74,1; 99,3; 101–2; Philochorus FGrH 328 F 142).

DEVELIN, 1849.   HA.BE.

[3] In 286 BC, as an officer of Seleucus I, he prevented Demetrius [2] Poliorcetes, who had been expelled from Asia Minor, from crossing the Taurus mountains into Syria(Polyaenus, Strat. 4,9,5).

[4] The Macedonian L., whose identity as *próxenos* (→ Proxenia, proxenos) was attested in Delphi in 248/7 BC, was the son of Philomelus and a dynast in southeast Phrygia; probably founded some cities there (Lysias, Philomelium) and in 225 fought against Attalus I of Pergamum (SGDI 2736; OGIS 272; 277). If L. is identical with Lysanias, he helped Rhodes in 226 after it had been damaged by an earthquake (Pol. 5,90,1). L.'s son Philomelus made an endowment to the Apollo sanctuary in Didyma and together with Termessus pillaged the urban area of Isinda in 189 ([1. 277]; Pol. 21,35,2) [2. 156].

    1 A. REHM, Inschr. von Didyma, 1958   2 ROBERT, Villes.

[5] As a member of a delegation of Antiochus [5] III in Rome, he tried to elicit the Senate's opinion on the pursuits of his master in Asia Minor and in Thrace and in 196 BC negotiated with T. → Quinctius Flamininus in Corinth and in Lysimacheia (Pol. 18,47,1–4; 50,1–3; App. Syr. 6,21–23).

[6] Became administrator of the western half of the empire under Antiochus [6] IV in 165 BC and was defeated

by → Judas [1] Maccabaeus (1 Macc 3:32f.; 4:26–35; Jos. Ant. Iud. 12,313–315). After Antiochus' death he became chancellor and guardian of Antiochus [7] V and took Bethsura and in 163/2 → Jerusalem, whose fortification he destroyed. He killed the high priest Menelaus, but endorsed the Jewish cult because Philippus, whom Antiochus IV had probably made chancellor, had risen against him. L. was victorious over Philippus (1 Macc 6:28ff.; 2 Macc 11:22–33; 13,14; Jos. Ant Iud. 12,360–386; 20,235). In Rome L. tried to excuse the murder of Cn. Octavius by → Leptines [6] (Pol. 31,11(19),1–2; Zon. 9,25). L. and Antiochius V were killed by Demetrius [7] I. in 162 (1 Macc 7:1–4; Jos. Ant. Iud. 12,389f.; App. Syr. 47,242).

E. BEVAN, The House of Seleucus, 1902; WILL.   A.ME.

[7] **L. Aniketos** (Middle Indian *Lisi(k)a*). One of the late Indo-Greek kings, probably in the Paropamisadae (modern eastern Afghanistan) at the end of the 2nd or in the 1st cent. BC; historical evidence only in the form of his coins.

BOPEARACHCHI, 93–95, 266–270.   K.K.

[8] Son of Pyrrhandrus, sculptor from Chios. The fact that his quadriga with Apollo and Artemis was re-erected at the Palatine by Augustus was seen as proof of his fame in antiquity. In Lindus, his inscription can be read on two bases from the 2nd cent. BC, one bearing the rudiments of a statue of Hercules.

OVERBECK, no. 2100; LIPPOLD, 352; G. A. MANSUELLI, s.v. L. (2), EAA 4, 1961, 754.   R.N.

[9] Greek physician of the 1st cent. BC or AD, inventor of a remedy for an ulcerated artery (Gal. De compositione medicamentorum secundum locos 7,2 = 13,49 K.). A MS of → Caelius [II 11] Aurelianus (De morbis chronicis 2,59; 2,111, 4,79: CML 6,1,578 611, 819) attributes similar remedies against bleeding, colds, and stomach problems to the four-book work 'On Chronic Diseases' by a certain *Lucius*, whose name some editors emend to *Lysias*. Since Soranus Gynaecia 3,2, however, refers to a Lucius, follower of Asclepiades, as the author of a homonymous work in 3 bks., the argument for this emendation is not cogent.   V.N.

Lysicles (Λυσικλῆς; *Lysiklês*). L. was a friend of → Pericles and like the latter supported aggressive Athenian policy in relation to Sparta (Aristoph. Equ. 765: predecessor of Cleon). A L. was (in 432 BC?) the petitioner for a decree regarding naval weapons and regarding Apollo of Delos (IG I² 128 l. 3; supplements in SEG 21, 37, IG I³ 130a). After 429 BC, L. married Pericles' widow → Aspasia (Plut. Pericles 24), in 428/7 as a *strategos* he fell in battle in Caria (Thuc. 3,19,1f.). Aristophanes has him appear in the 'Equites' as a small cattle wholesaler (Aristoph. Equ. 132 with schol.).

PA 9417; TRAILL, PAA 614815.   W.W.

Lysicrates monument see → Athens

Lysidice (Λυσιδίκη; *Lysidíkē*).
[1] Daughter of → Pelops and → Hippodamia [1], wife of Mestor, mother of Hippothoe (Apollod. 2,50). According to a tradition dismissed by Paus. 8,14,2, the mother of → Amphitryon and hence the wife of Alcaeus. According to schol. Pind. Ol. 7,49, the wife of Electryon, mother of → Alcmene (cf. also Plut. Thes 7,1 and schol. Pind. Ol. 7,50). All the husbands of L. who appear in the tradition are sons of → Perseus.
[2] On the François Vase (570–565 BC), the epigraphical name of one of the female companions of → Theseus and → Ariadne on the return journey form Crete [3].
[3] Daughter of the Lapith → Coronus, wife of the Telamonian → Ajax [1], mother of Philius (Tzetz. schol. Lycoph. 53).

1 H. LAMER, s.v. L., RE 13, 2544–2550   2 SCHIRMER, s.v. L., ROSCHER 2, 2211   3 R. WACHTER, The Inscriptions on the François Vase, in: MH 48, 1991, 88–113.   K.WA.

Lysimache (Λυσιμάχη; *Lysimáchē*). Daughter of → Abas [1], granddaughter of → Melampus (according to Antimachus in schol. Eur. Phoen. 150, daughter of Cercyon, granddaughter of Poseidon), wife of the Argive king Talaus, mother of → Adrastus [1], Parthenopaeus, Pronax, Mecisteus, Aristomachus and Eriphyle (Apollod. 1,103).   K.WA.

Lysimachia (Λυσιμάχεια; *Lysimácheia*).
[1] City founded by one of the Diadochi Lysimachus, in 309 BC – in place of the city of Cardia destroyed by him – as the capital city of Thracian Chersonesus and the seat of government (Str. 7, fr. 51; Liv. 23,38,11; Ptol. 3,11) there on the southern coast of → Melas Kolpos near modern Bakla Burnu. In the Hellenistic period L. was the most important trans-shipment harbour for the Thracian hinterland. Important coin minting centre: the gold and silver coins issued by L. were for a long time the leading currency in the Balkans and in the northern Pontic regions. After the defeat of Lysimachus [2], Seleucus I attempted to extend his rule to Europe in 280 BC but was murdered by Ptolemy Ceraunus in L. (Iust. 17,1; App. B Civ. 4,88). In 278 BC, Galatae threatened L. but were driven out (Liv. 38,16; Iust. 25,1; Diog. Laert. 2,141). After a short interlude of Egyptian influence around the middle of the 3rd cent. BC, L. became a member of the Aetolian League (Pol. 18,3,11; 15,23,8). In 200 BC, Philip V captured L. and additional cities of the Chersonesus which led to fruitless protests in Rome on the part of the Aetolians. Shortly afterwards, L. was attacked by Thrace and destroyed (Liv. 38,8; Pol. 18,4,5; 51,7). In 196 BC, Antiochus [5] III captured L. (Pol. 18,48,3f.; Liv. 36,71,5) and rebuilt it completely; apart from the former inhabitants he also brought in numerous new settlers and financed an economic and military beginning. Shortly afterwards, conquered by Cornelius [I 72] Scipio, L.

was ceded to Pergamum in 188 BC (Pol. 21,46,9). About 144 BC, the Thracian Caeni under their king → Diegylis captured L. and ultimately destroyed it (Diod. Sic. 33,14).   I.v.B.
[2] City in Aetolia 3 km south of the modern town of Lysimachea and south-west of the homonymous lake. East of L. the Klisura Gorge is located, the narrow section on the route from the Gulf of Patrae to the inland plain. The foundation of or rather the renaming of an existing city (name unknown) as L. occurred between 284 and 281 BC in honour of king → Lysimachus [2]. L., a member of the Aetolian League (→ Aetolians, with map), is mentioned in connection with the military campaigns of Philip V (Pol. 5,7,7) and Antiochus III (Liv. 36,11,7). Str. 10,2,22 refers to L., following Apollodorus, as no longer in existence. The well-preserved wall-ring and the city have hardly been investigated [3]. Inscriptions: [1] IG IX 1²,1, 130, p. 83; [2].

1 BCH 45, 1921, 24 IV 74   2 G. KLAFFENBACH, Neue Inschriften aus Aitolien, in: SPrAW 1936, 364
3 PRITCHETT 6, 136.

H.G. LOLLING, Reisenotizen aus Griechenland, ed. by B. HEINRICH, 1989, 223–225; D. STRAUCH, Römische Politik und griechische Tradition, 1996, 318f.   D.S.

Lysimachides (Λυσιμαχίδης; *Lysimachídēs*). Greek grammarian of the Augustan period (born in *c.* 50 BC). L. is considered to be the critic of his contemporary → Caecilius [III 5] of Cale Acte [1. 168]. Of his work 'On the Athenian Months' (Περὶ τῶν Ἀθήνησι μηνῶν), three records are extant in → Harpocration's [2] 'Lexicon on the Ten Orators' (FGrH 366).

1 E. OFENLOCH, Caecilii Calactini fragmenta, 1907.   M.B.

Lysimachus (Λυσίμαχος; *Lysímachos*).
[1] Athenian, son of Aristides [1], born around 480 BC, is a dialogue partner in → Plato's *Láchēs* (178ff.), where he is represented as the prototype of the unsuccessful son of a celebrated father. A decree mentioned by Demosthenes (20,115; cf. Plut. Aristides 27), according to which L. is said to have been granted support from the state because he was penniless after the death of his father, is probably a construction from the 4th cent.

DAVIES 1695 III–IV.   E.S.-H.

[2] General of Alexander, one of the Diadochi.
A. DESCENT   B. SERVICE UNDER ALEXANDER THE GREAT   C. FROM THE DEATH OF ALEXANDER THE GREAT (IN 323) TO IPSUS (IN 301)   D. FROM IPSUS TO CURUPEDION (281)

A. DESCENT
L., son of Agathocles from Pella, from the Macedonian higher nobility, born in 361 BC (Hieronymus [6] of Cardia near [Lucianus], Macrobii 11). The later accusation against his father, that he came from the

slave class of the → *penéstai*, is based on slander on the part of the historian Theopompus.

B. Service under Alexander the Great

L. was a *sōmatophýlax* (→ Somatophylakes) of Alexander [4], perhaps already of → Philippus II, but is never attested as holding positions of command. He took part in two lion hunts and this was later spun out as material for a novella (especially Iust. 15,3; correct Curt. 8,1,17). Inferring from Arrian (Anab. 5,13,1), he fought against the Indian king → Porus on Alexander's side. He was wounded in India in 326, but in the autumn of that year he became one of the *triḗrarchoi* (→ Trierarchia) of the → Hydaspes fleet (Arr. Ind. 18,3). With other *sōmatophýlakes* he attempted to prevent the killing of → Cleitus [6] (Curt. 8,1,46). In Susa he was certainly one of those who were honoured with a golden wreath and married to the daughters of Iranian princes (Arr. Anab. 7, 4–5). We cannot determine whether he was the L. who campaigned against → Callisthenes [1] (Plut. Alexander 55,1–2). He was neither a student of Callisthenes nor interested in philosophy (thus in Iust. 15,3,6, from a eulogy). Arrianus (7,3,4) distinguishes the L. to whom → Calanus [1] gave his horse from this officer. L. is mentioned at the banquet of → Medius [2] – and quite often in the fictitious tradition of the last days of the king – as being on his side.

C. From the death of Alexander the Great (in 323) to Ipsus (in 301)

After Alexander's death, L. was allocated Thrace as a satrapy and perhaps the west coast of the Black Sea (Arr. FGrH 156 F 1,7; Diod. Sic. 18,3,2) and this was confirmed by → Antipater [1] in the agreement of → Triparadeisos in 320 (→ Diadochi). He married Antipater's daughter → Nicaea, who bore him Agathocles [5] and Eurydice [5]. The marriage still existed (not as though the only one) after 301 (Str. 12,4,7). In Thrace the Macedonian sovereignty that had been achieved by Philip II collapsed under Alexander (Curt. 10,1, 44ff.). The task of restoring it appears to have occupied L. unsuccessfully for the next twenty years. In 323 he fought against the Odrysian prince → Seuthes but the battle was undecided and it left Seuthes independent. Perhaps an alliance was achieved temporarily: according to Pausanias (1,10,5), L. had an Odrysian concubine (cf. however Polyaenus, Strat. 6,12).

During the next few years L. managed to occupy several Greek cities. In 315 he took part in the coalition that made demands in the form of an ultimatum to → Antigonus [1] but not in the ensuing war against him. When the Greek cities broke away from L. in 313, they were supported by Antigonus and Seuthes. L. recaptured all of them apart from → Callatis, defeated Seuthes (who, however, remained independent) and an officer of Antigonus but nevertheless kept away from war against Antigonus. He was involved in the truce of 311 but did not take part in the subsequent wars between the → Diadochi. In 305 he, together with → Cassander [2], → Ptolemaeus [1] and → Seleucus [1] assumed the title of king in the retinue of Antigonus and in 304 together they supported Rhodes – which was besieged by Antigonus' son → Demetrius [2] (Diod. Sic. 20,53,4) – with grain.

Demetrius' successes in Greece (303–302) were the turning-point for L. If in his prime he had barely shown any political ambitions, he now, at the age of almost 60, stepped onto the world stage in a leading role. With the help of → Prepelaus, who had been placed at his disposal by Cassander, he invaded Asia. Their successes forced Antigonus to recall Demetrius from Greece and gave Seleucus time to lead an army from the Indian border to Phrygia and to ally with L. In the battle of → Ipsus in 301 BC, Demetrius allowed himself to be enticed away from the field, and Antigonus lost the battle and his life. His kingdom was divided up among the victors but Demetrius remained the lord of the sea and the coastal towns.

D. From Ipsus to Curupedion (281)

L. now sent → Amastris [3] – whom he had married before Ipsus – back to Heraclea [7] and married Ptolemy's daughter → Arsinoe [II 3], who bore him a Ptolemy and two additional sons (Iust. 24,3).

In Thrace there continued to be nothing but setbacks. First L.'s son → Agathocles [5] and then he himself were taken prisoner (in 292, by → Dromichaites). On both occasions ransom had to be won by ceding the entire newly acquired area. Seuthes remained independent, and in → Cabyle a small dynast became independent as king (IGBulg 3,1731). In Asia L. had more success. His share of the former kingdom of Antigonus comprised almost the whole of Asia Minor, with previously undreamt-of wealth. → Lysimacheia [1] which he had already founded in 309 for protection against Antigonus, became the junction of L.'s kingdom. There he began in great style to mint gold and silver coins, without exception with Alexander's head on the averse, in order to emphasize his own legitimacy as successor. The treasures of Asia made it possible for him to recruit a large army with which he decisively and unscrupulously intervened in politics. He was gradually able to occupy the coastal towns of Asia Minor, especially after Demetrius had left Asia after Cassander's death (in 297). He put the Ionian League under the control of Milesian 'friends' (*phíloi*, see → Court titles) as *stratēgoí* (Syll.[3] 368; SEG 35,926). The towns were ruled justly but high-handedly and had to pay high taxes. In most of them he had himself deified.

In 294/3, L. had to acknowledge Demetrius as king in Macedonia because he was caught up in Thracian wars (Iust. 16,1,19). His son-in-law → Antipater [2], who had been expelled by Demetrius, fled to him. L. did not see his chance come until 288: he murdered Antipater so that he could claim the succession for himself, and in an alliance with the king of Epirus, → Pyrrhus, he invaded Macedonia and drove out Demetrius who, deserted by his army, tried his luck with a mercenary army in Asia. There he found much favour among the towns but was overpowered by Agathocles in a positional warfare. In 286 he surrendered to Seleucus who imprisoned him. L. offered Seleucus a large sum of money for the killing of Demetrius, but Seleucus refused to give up a useful pawn (Diod. Sic. 21,20; Plut. Demetrius 51,3). The towns were occupied again and subjected to an even harsher exploitation.

Now L. had his hands free to attack Pyrrhus: he was able to extend his rule over the whole of Macedonia and almost the whole of Thessaly and then devote himself to Asia again. Attacks on → Zipoetes of Bithynia failed but he was able to acquire Heraclea [7]: when the two sons of Amastris called for his help after her death, he appeared as a friend in the city in 284, but then he had them arrested and executed as the murderers of their mother.

At the height of his power, he was struck by catastrophe. Agathocles, for a long time chosen to be the heir to the throne, was accused by Arsinoe – who wanted to secure the succession for her eldest son – of conspiracy. We do not know whether he was innocent or was planning a *coup d'état* to forestall Arsinoe's plan. As it was politically out of the question to bring him before a court, L. had him murdered in 282. His wife → Lysandra and his friends fled to Seleucus, several of the officers appointed by Agathocles offered to defect to Seleucus, and the towns hoped to be liberated from the oppression of L. In this way Seleucus was able to occupy Asia Minor almost without resistance. In 281, a battle occurred at → Curupedion in which L. lost his kingdom and his life and Seleucus became the lord of almost the entire empire of Alexander.
→ Diadochi and Epigoni; → Diadochi, wars of the; → Hellenistic states

HECKEL, 267–75 (until Alexander's death); F. LANDUCCI GATTINONI, Lisimaco di Tracia, 1992; H. S. LUND, Lysimachus, 1992.

[3] An Acarnanian who was involved in the education of → Alexander [4] the Great, he followed him to Asia and according to → Chares [2] is said to have exposed him to risk in the Antilebanon because of his own debility. (Plut. Alexander 5,8; 24,10–12). We cannot determine whether he or L. [2] campaigned against → Callisthenes [1] (Plut. Alexander 55, 1–2). Nor can L. be the L. who according to Arrian (Anab. 7,3,4) is not identical to L. [2], to whom → Calanus gave his horse before his death.

BERVE 2, no. 481.   E.B.

[4] Son of Ptolemy II and Arsinoe [II 2], probably murdered shortly before → Magas [3] after Ptolemy IV had come to power; nothing definite is known about his further activities and status (strategy of Cyprus? *strategos* in Egypt?).

R. BAGNALL, The Administration of the Ptolemaic Possessions outside Egypt, 1976, 42ff.; F. W. WALBANK, A Historical Commentary on Polybius 2, 1967, 481.

[5] Grandson of Lysimachus [2], son of Ptolemy (PP VI 14541), around 220 BC dynast in Lycian → Telmissus and probably as such the successor of his father as the owner of the Ptolemaic *dōreá* ('gift') Telmissus. His son Ptolemy was on the side of → Antiochus [5] III by 193.

M. WÖRRLE, Epigraph. Forsch. zur Geschichte Lykiens II, in: Chiron 8, 1978, 222f.; Id., Epigraph. Forsch. zur Geschichte Lykiens III, in: Chiron 9, 1979, 84ff.; J. KOBES, Kleine Könige, 1996, 79; 149.   W.A.

[6] Greek mythographer and grammarian; we can estimate that he lived around 200 BC on the basis of his knowledge of the periegete → Mnaseas of Patara [3. 33]; in schol. Apoll. Rhod. 1,558 and schol. Soph. OC 91 he is probably mentioned because of his work as an (Alexandrian) scholar 'of the Alexandrians' (ὁ Ἀλεξανδρεύς); however, as L. could also be the author of the work *Aigyptiaká* [3. 35] (which according to Jos. Ap. 2,14 has anti-Semitic tendencies), we cannot exclude the possibility that the name also refers to L.'s origin. In at least three bks. of travel legends (Νόστοι) and in a 'Collection of Theban Marvellous Stories' (συναγωγὴ τῶν Θηβαϊκῶν παραδόξων or Θηβαϊκὰ παράδοξα) consisting of at least 13 bks., L. presents in an exhaustive depiction (in the travel legends we encounter, apart from the actual wanderings of the heroes of Troy, for example, also Laocoon and the story of Aeneas and Antenor), with precise indication of his sources and without his own additions, the oldest and most reliable Greek legendary stories, placing them alongside each other in a concordance-like manner [1; 2]. The scholia regarding Euripides, Apollonius Rhodius, Lycophron, Sophocles and Pindar, just like → Eustathius, → Servius (Serv. Aen. 2,211) and the commentary of → Didymus [1] Chalcenterus and → Theon, prove L.'s achievement. The two books 'On the Plagiarism of Ephorus' (Περὶ τῆς Ἐφόρου κλοπῆς) are probably a by-product of his work on the mythographies.

1 FHG 3, 334–342   2 FGrH 3 B 382   3 A. GUDEMAN, s.v. L., RE 14, 32–39.   GR.DA.

[7] L. of Cos Greek physician, active at the end of the 2nd or the beginning of the 1st cent. BC. A Hippocratic, he wrote a work in 20 bks. in which he explained difficult concepts from the Hippocratic writings (→ Hippocrates [7]). In three additional works he opposed the explanations offered by the Herophilean → Cydias [4] and the Epicurean → Demetrius [21]. L. is probably to be identified with the Hippocratic Silimachus (Caelius Aurelianus, De morbis chronicis 1,57) who described an epidemic of *incubus* in Rome, and with Salimachus (ibid. 3,138). Among the sources for animal remedies in bk. 28 of his natural history, Pliny the Elder mentions a certain L. He reports in HN 25,72 that the plant *lysimachea* owes its name to L., but as it was already known to → Erasistratus, this is either an error or Pliny is referring to a much older homonymous physician.
                                                    V.N.

[8] Tragedian of the 2nd cent. BC (TrGF I 132). B.Z.

Lysimeleia (Λυσιμέλεια λίμνη; *Lysiméleia límē*). According to Thucydides (6,101,1ff.; 7,53,2), L. refers to the southern part of the swamp area in the alluvial plain of → Syracusae between the necropolis of Fusco, the Anapus and the north-western edge of the Great Harbour in the confluence region of minor watercourses (modern Canale Regina and Canale Pisimotta); cf. Theoc. 16,84, (Syracusae as 'great city on the waters of the L.'). Identification of the L. with the swamp of Syrako is nevertheless contentious [1. 1f. and n. 10f.].

1 H.-P. DRÖGEMÜLLER, Syrakus, 1968. H.-P.DRÖ. and E.O.

Lysinia Pisidian town on the north-western bank of the Lake of Burdur/Turkey, remains on the hill of Üveyik Burnu near Karakent [2]. Its (probably Greek) name has been deduced from the ethnicon ΛΥΣΙΝΙΕΩΝ of the coins; the few literary records provide distorted forms. Attested for the first time on the occasion of the campaign of → Manlius Vulso (in 189 BC) to whom L. surrendered (Pol. 21,36; Liv. 38,15,8); L. is missing from the Byzantine diocese lists. Meagre coin minting under Septimius Severus [1].

1 AULOCK 1, 35f., 109f. 2 G. E. BEAN, Notes and Inscriptions from Pisidia 1, in: AS 9, 1959, 78–81.

W. RUGE, s.v. L., RE 14, 40f. P.W.

Lysiodia see → Simodia

Lysippe (Λυσίππη; *Lysíppē*). Daughter of → Proetus and Stheneboea (Apollod. 2,25–26). Because she sinned against the gods, L. goes mad together with her sisters → Iphianassa [1] and → Iphinoe, but is then cured by → Melampus (Apollod. 2,26–29; cf. Hes. Cat. fr. 37,10–15; 131; 133). K.WA.

Lysippides Painter Attic black-figure vase painter from the late archaic period, *c.* 530–510 BC; named after a → kalos inscription (*Lysippídēs*) on one of his amphorae. The LP is the most important student of → Execias, from whom he adopted not only his drawing technique but also some subjects (e.g. Ajax and Achilles playing board games); otherwise he favours the feats of → Heracles. About 30 vases have been ascribed to the LP, mostly amphorae and eye-bowls. His neck and belly amphorae (see → Pottery with fig.), the shapes, manner of decoration and ornaments of which also go back on Execias, initiated the great series of late black-figure standard amphorae. Remarkable is his collaboration with the → Andocides Painter, who is considered the inventor of red-figure painting. On six 'bilingual' amphorae and one bowl, the various techniques are contrasted on the front and back respectively. Comparison is sometimes all the more invited because of concurrent subjects. It was long strongly disputed whether the same painter, here and in the case of

other → bilingual vases used two different techniques. COHEN [4. 1–193] however was able to show that the discrepancy between the LP's tradition-bound painting technique and the uninhibited and sensitive red-figure images, despite mutual adaptations, can be explained only by the different characters of two masters. Both worked with the potter Andocides.

1 BEAZLEY, ABV, 254–257 2 BEAZLEY, Paralipomena, 113f. 3 BEAZLEY, Addenda², 65–67 4 B. COHEN, Attic Bilingual Vases and their Painters, 1978, 1–104 5 M. ROBERTSON, The Art of Vase-Painting in Classical Athens, 1992, 10–15. H.M.

Lysippus (Λύσιππος; *Lýsippos*).
[1] Poet of the Old Comedy who perhaps as early as the 430s BC won at the → Dionysia [1. test. *2] and about whom further victories are attested in 409 and later [1. test. 3]. Only three titles of plays are extant; fragments (apart from three without a title) are only attributed to the 'Bacchae' (Βάκχαι): In fragment 1 a man by the name of Hermon (who had been thrown into a well by his father) talks to his brother.

1 PCG V, 1986, 618–622. H.-G.NE.

[2] Bronze sculptor from Sicyon. With his enormous productivity (1,500 statues) and long period of creativity (*c.* 372 to 306 BC), L. is characterized in the ancient tradition as an innovator who by proportioning and attention to detail succeeded in creating → sculpture that was true to life in a manner not previously achieved. The tradition regarding his *c.* 50 works is rich but unreliable; among the diverse subjects male statues are favoured. Their body canon with a smaller head and slimmer body compared to the canon of → Polyclitus was represented by the lost statue of → Kairos and can be seen in the statue of the *Apoxyómenos* ('scraper', an athlete who scrapes sand and oil off himself). It was attributed to L. with the aid of the inscription on a copy (Rome, MV). Further statues of athletes and statues of honour are only attested by Pausanius or through inscriptions on bases. A statue of Troilus (winner in the chariot race of 372 BC) marks the beginning of his creative period. We can gain an idea of the statue of Agias, which is also merely attested in inscriptions in Pharsalus, with the help of a repetition in the family group of Daochus in Delphi (after 338 BC) (differently: [1]).

Many portraits of L. remain unknown, for instance that of the musician → Praxilla, which is probably identical with a *temulenta tibicina* (Plin. HN 34,63). His seated bronze statue of Socrates in the → Kerameikos is associated with portrait type B. The portrait of Seleucus Nicator has been attested and identified by an inscription. L. was soon considered the only authorized portraitist for Alexander [4] the Great, capturing his personality through the position of the head, the gaze and the movement of the hair. The portrait type of Alexander named after a Herm copy in the Azarra collection (Madrid PR) and a type of statue with a lance passed down in small bronzes, have generally been attributed to him. The group compositions of L. were famous, ranging from quadrigas via the *Turma Alexandri* to the lion hunt. The *Turma Alexandri* portrayed 25 Macedonians who had died in the battle at the Granicus. The depiction of the lion hunt in which → Craterus [1] (who commissioned the work) had saved the life of Alexander, was completed in 318 BC by L. and → Leochares, and erected in Delphi; a relief base in Messene gives us an idea of the composition.

Of the numerous depictions of gods by L., some were of colossal size, as in Tarentum a Zeus and a seated → Heracles statue, both in bronze. Epigraphically, the type of Hercules Farnese is attributed to L. Further statues of Heracles and Zeus, also in groups, and of other gods, are mentioned in the literature, but cannot be reliably identified in copies. An Eros with bow that L. sculpted in Thespiae is preserved in copies. Besides authentic works, imitations were already traded in antiquity, one of which is a small-scale Heracles Epitrapezios, which in the Imperial period is cited as a famous collector's item. Because of the innovative power of his work, L. had several students, among them also his sons. In the history of art, L. is regarded as the sculptor who overcame Greek Classicism and was a precursor of Hellenism.

1 W. GEOMINY, Zum Daochos-Weihgeschenk, in: Klio 80, 1998, 369–402.

J. CHAMAY (ed.), Lysippe et son influence. Études de divers savants, 1987; R. CITTADINI, La Prassilla di Lisippo, in: MEFRA 107, 1995, 1165–1180; J. DÖRIG, Lysippe et Alexandrie, in: Alessandria e il mondo ellenistico-romano, 1995, 299–307; C.M. EDWARDS, Lysippos, in: YClS 30, 1996, 130–153; A. GIULIANO, EAA 4, 1961, 654–660; LIPPOLD, 276–286; LOEWY, Index; J. MARCADÉ, Recueil des signatures de sculpteurs grecs, 1, 1953, 66–75; P. MORENO, Testimonianze per la teoria artistica di Lisippo, 1973; Id., Lisippo, 1, 1974; Id., Vita e arte di Lisippo, 1987; Id., Scultura ellenistica, 1994, 23–123; Id. (ed.), Lisippo. L'arte e la fortuna (Catalogo della mostra Roma 1995), 1995; A.M. NIELSEN, »Fecit et Alexandrum multis operibus«. Alexander the Great and L., in: Acta archaeologica 58, 1987, 151–170; OVERBECK, Index; B.S. RIDGWAY, Fourth-Century Styles in Greek Sculpture, 1997, 286–320; L. TODISCO, Scultura greca del IV secolo, 1993, 112–131.   R.N.

Lysis (Λύσις; *Lýsis*). Pythagorean of Tarentum, who according to Aristoxenus fr. 18 WEHRLI, at a young age escaped together with → Archippus [2] the arson attack on the Pythagoreans in Croton dated at around 450 and 440 or 415; he is said to have then migrated to Greece and to have become the teacher of → Epaminondas in Thebes (cf. Aristox. ibid.; Dion Chrys. or. 49,5 etc.; [1]). L.'s pseudepigraphic letter to → Hipparchus [3], in which the latter is urged to adhere to Pythagoras' instructions and not to make the 'treasures' of his philosophy accessible to the public, enjoyed great popularity in antiquity. The letter was probably written to authenticate the falsified 'Memories' (ὑπομνήματα) of Pythagoras whose alleged origin is outlined in the final

part, and was probably originally published together with these (see [2; 3]).
→ Pythagorean School; → Pseudepigraphic literature

1 P. LÉVÊQUE, P. VIDAL-NACQUET, Épaminondas pythagoricien, in: Historia 9, 1960, 307f.   2 W. BURKERT, Hell. Pseudopythagorica, in: Philologus 105, 1961, 17–28   3 A. STÄDELE, Die Briefe des Pythagoras und der Pythagoreer, 1980, 203–251.

H.A. BROWN, Philosophorum pythagoreorum collectionis specimen, 1941, 76–87; H. THESLEFF, The Pythagorean Texts of the Hellenistic Period, 1965, 110–115.
                                                                            C.RI.

Lysistratus (Λυσίστρατος; *Lysístratos*).
[1] from Chalcis. Tragedian, after 85 BC he was victorious at the Amphiaraia (→ Amphiaraus) and → Romaia in Oropus. His works are not extant.   B.Z.
[2] Bronze sculptor from Sicyon, brother and collaborator of → Lysippus [2]. By making plaster casts of living people, L. is said to have improved the similarity of portraits to their subjects, to have based his work on clay models and to have made plaster casts of statues. Of his works, tradition only mentions a statue of Melanippe. Two pedestals in Thebes and Tanagra with an extant signature cannot be associated with L. with certainty because of the differing ethnicon.

LIPPOLD, 286; OVERBECK, no.1513–1515; EAA 4, s.v. L., 1961, 753; L. TODISCO, Scultura greca del IV secolo, 1993, 131.   R.N.

Lysitheides (Λυσιθείδης; *Lysitheídēs*).
[1] A pro-Persian Greek of the 5th cent. BC, rendered great services to the army of Xerxes and is said to have introduced to it → Themistocles who had fled from Greece (Diod. Sic. 11,56,4–8; however in Plut. Themistocles 26,4 Nicogenes is mentioned instead of L.).
[2] Rich Athenian (Dem. Or. 21,157) from the deme of Cicynna who owned land in the mining area of Attica; student of → Isocrates and honoured with a golden wreath for political achievements and donations to Athens (Isocr. Or. 15,93); in *c.* 372 and 369/8 BC a private arbitrator on two occasions (Dem. Or. 52,14f. and 52,30); in 355 trierarch of the ship on which an Athenian delegation travelled to → Maussolus from Halicarnassus (Dem. Or. 24 hypoth. I 3; Dem. Or. 24,11–14; IG II² 150,4).

PA 9395; DAVIES 9461, p. 356f.   J.E.

Lyson Greek family name.
[1] L. of Lilybaeum. In 72 BC friend of Cicero, host of → Verres who created a statue for him (Cic. Verr. 2,4,37). Cic. Fam. 13,34 is a letter of recommendation for L.'s son.
[2] L. of Patrae. Host of Cicero, in 50 BC looked after his sick secretary Tiro (Cic. Fam. 16,4,1f.). L. was a Pompeian in the Civil War and in 46 or 45, after Caesar's victory, he asked for his pardon (13,19; 24).   JÖ.F.

[3] Greek bronze sculptor. Pliny lists L. in a general list of sculptors. L. created a statue of Demos on the Athenian Agora that is not extant.

G. A. MANSUELLI, s.v. L. (2), EAA 4, 1961, 753; OVERBECK, no. 1932,4; 2068. R.N.

Lyssa (Λύσσα, Λύττα; *Lýssa, Lýtta*). Personification of (battle) rage and madness. She appears as an independent person for the first time in 5th-cent. tragedy; according to Eur. HF 822–899 she is descended from → Nyx and the blood of → Uranus that the latter sheds when he is castrated by Kronos. Homer mentions the state of *lyssa*, but she is not a person (Hom. Il. 8,299; cf. also 9,239; 304f.). As such she appears for the first time in Aeschylus in the *Xántriai* (TrGF III fr. 169) where she spurs on the → Minyades – struck with madness by → Dionysus – to kill a human being whom they consider to be a sacrificial animal. In Aesch. PV 883 → Io considers her madness to be due to the influence of L. → Orestes is not only pursued by the Erinyes (→ Erinys) but also by L. (Aesch. Cho. 288); in Eur. Or. 254, 326, 400f. *et passim*, the fury of Orestes is described as the effect of L. In Euripides' 'Heracles', L. appears in the form of a huntress riding on a chariot. Her eyes sparkle and her face is framed by snakes (Eur. HF 880–885). This depiction is reminiscent of → Gorgo [1]. In Euripides' 'Bacchae', L. acts on behalf of → Dionysus: she confuses the powers of → Pentheus' reason (Eur. Bacch. 851) and she sets her dogs on the daughters of Cadmus to spur on them to kill Pentheus (ibid. 977). Poll. 4,142 mentions the mask of L., which suggests that she was a common stage character. Sophocles (TrGF IV fr. 941,4) mentions L. as a name of Cypris (→ Aphrodite) L. (cf. also Pl. Leg. 839a; Thec. 3,47). The term *lyssa* was also used as a description for rabies in dogs (Xen. An. 5,7,26; Plin. HN 29,100). L. herself could be represented as a dog.

A. KOSSATZ-DEISSMANN, s.v. L., LIMC 6, 322f. (with bibliography); K. H. LEE, The Iris-L. Scene in Euripides' Heracles, in: Antichthon 16, 1982, 44–52; SCHIRMER, s.v. L., ROSCHER 2, 2213f.; J. SCHMIDT, s.v. L., RE 14, 69–71. K.WA.

Lystra (Λύστρα; *Lýstra*), modern Hatunsaray; southwest of Iconium (Turkey). Founded by Augustus as a Roman colony in the province of → Galatia [1. 51–53, 153–156, 195–197]. Christianized by the Apostle Paul during his 1st and 2nd missionary journey (Acts 14:6–20; 16:1–3; 2 Tim 3:11). Around 370 annexed to the new province of Lycaonia. Attested as a diocese (suffragan of → Iconium) from 380 [2. 200].

1 B. LEVICK, Roman Colonies in Southern Asia Minor, 1967 2 BELKE. K.BE.

Lytaea (Λυταία; *Lytaía*). One of the → Hyacinthides. L., together with her sisters Antheis, Aigleis and Orthaea, is sacrificed in Athens on the grave of Geraestus, the Cyclops, when the city is under siege by Minos and suffering from hunger and plague (Apollod. 3,212; cf. Diod. Sic. 17,15,2). J.STE.

Lytron (λύτρον/*lýtron*, mostly used in the plural λύτρα/*lýtra*). The ransom for → prisoners of war was called *lytron* in Greek (similarly: ἄποινα/*ápoina*). The expression was also used for buying the freedom of victims of → piracy. Buying the freedom of prisoners was, alongside exchanging prisoners, enslaving or killing, a common practice in Greek warfare from Homeric (Hom. Il. 6,425ff.; 11,106) to Hellenistic times. According to DUCREY [1], selling into slavery was, of course, more common than buying a person's freedom, the terms and prices of which varied according to the circumstances. The release of prisoners could be bought on the basis of a special agreement between the poleis involved, within the framework of a peace treaty (Thuc. 5,18,7; in 421 BC), or on the basis of an individual initiative (cf. e.g. Dem. Or. 53,6–10); the money mostly had to be provided by the affected person himself. Sums of a *mina* (Androtion, FGrH 324, fr. 44; 408/7 BC), two *minai* (Hdt. 5,77,3; 505 BC) or a talent (Aeschin. Leg. 100; in 346 BC) per person are mentioned. But higher sums also occurred; they could be graded according to military rank, economic performance or status (Xen. Hell. 4,8,21). If prisoners were released without a ransom – frequently as a means of diplomacy to draw those affected over to their own side – this was especially emphasized, since it obviously rarely happened (Xen. Hell. 7,2,16; Pol. 5,10,4: in 338 BC).

1 P. DUCREY, Le traitement des prisonniers de guerre dans la Grèce antique, des origines à la conquête romaine 1968, 238–246 2 W. K. PRITCHETT, The Greek State at War 5, 1991, 245–312. LE.BU.

M

M (linguistics) The letter M in Greek and Latin designates a voiced labial nasal. In Latin words final -*m* was probably almost silent after the nasalization of the preceding vowel, which can be seen on the one hand in the regular slurring of word final 'vowel + -*m*' with the following word's initial vowel in the → metre, on the other hand in its orthographic neglect in the inscriptions of the 3rd and early 2nd cents. BC. Even though -*m* was written consistently again since the middle of the 2nd cent. BC, Priscian and Quintilian attest to continued validity of the special pronunciation of final -*m* [1].

In inherited Greek and Latin words, *m* continues Proto-Indo-European *m*, cf. Greek Doric μᾱ́τηρ/*mā́tēr*, Lat. *māter* < **mátēr*, Greek θυμός/*thymós*, Lat. *fūmus* < **dhu₂₂mó-*. The phonological developments of *m* in both languages are parallel for the most part: word-initially Greek μ-, Latin *m*- also represent *sm*- (Greek μιχρός/*mikrós*, compare σμιχρός/*smikrós*, Lat. *mīrus* < **smei-ro-* to the root **smei-*) [2. 309f.; 3. 144, 190]. Geminates arise from 'labial + *m*' (Greek ὄμμα/*ómma*, γέγραμμαι/*gégrammai*, κέκομμαι/*kékommai* to **op-* (< **okᵘ-*), γράφω/*gráphō*, κόπτω/*kóptō*, Lat. *summus* < **supmo-*, in Aeolian Greek furthermore from *sm* (ἔμμι/ *émmi* versus Attic [ēmi] εἰμί/*eimí* from **esmi*) [2. 322f.; 3. 201], *m* in Latin also by assimilation from labial before *n* (*somnus* < **suepno-*). In both languages inherited *m* becomes *n* before *i̯* (Greek βαίνω/*baínō*, Lat. *venio* < **gʷṃ-i̯e/o-*) [2. 309; 3. 214], initially before *r* and *l* it becomes *b* (Greek βροτός/*brotós* < **mrotó-* < **mṛtó-*, Lat. *brevis* < **mreǵʰu̯i-*, Greek βλάξ/*bláx*, Lat. *blandus* < **mlāndo-* to root **mla₂₂* [2. 323f.; 3. 190; 4. 112] and Latin *m...m* becomes *f...m* by means of distant dissimilation (*formīca* versus Greek μύρμηξ/*mýrmēx*) [3. 191]. Proto-Indo-European *ṃ*, the syllabic variant of the *m* phoneme, appears in Greek as α before consonants or αμ before vowels, in Lat. as *em* (Greek πόδα/*póda*, Lat. *pedem* < **pod-/ped-ṃ*) [2. 342f.; 3. 58].

1 ThlL VIII 1, 18.47–50   2 SCHWYZER, Gramm.
3 LEUMANN 4 G. MEISER, Histor. Laut- und Formenlehre der lat. Sprache, 1998.   GE.ME.

M. Abbreviation of the Latin personal name → Marcus and (already in antiquity with an apostrophe: M') → Manius. As a numerical sign, M stands for the number 1,000, but it was not derived from *mille* (Latin word for thousand), rather it came about by reforming the Greek letter Φ (*phi*), which was not adopted into the Latin → alphabet (see → D as a numerical sign).   W.ED.

Ma (Greek Μᾶ/*Mâ*, Lat. Ma-Bellona).
One of a number of powerful Anatolian deities, whose cult was concentrated on the great temples (cf. → Anaitis in Zela, → Cybele/*Mếtēr* in Pessinus, → Men Pharnaku in Cabira). The basic meaning of the word

[1], widespread as a feminine proper name, is 'mother'.
A. TEMPLE AND CULT IN ANATOLIA B. ROME

A. TEMPLE AND CULT IN ANATOLIA

The original centre of the cult was → Comana [1]/Hierapolis in Cappadocian → Cataonia. The local temple was already significant at the time of Suppiluliuma I (*c.* 1355–1320 BC) (→ Hattusa B. 3). A second 'temple state' arose in → Comana [2]/Hierocaesarea Pontica. Both were situated on the Persian Royal Road, but off the important Roman roads.

M. was associated with war and victory: its other epithet is ἀνίκητος/*aníkētos*, 'invincible'; it is also described as ἡ νικηφόρος/*hē nikēphóros*, 'the bringer of victory'. After the conquest of the region by Alexander [4] the Great, the distinctive features of the cult were defined according to the Greek model: → Orestes and → Iphigenia are supposed to have brought the rites and the statue of → Artemis Tauropolos from Scythia to Comana [1] and to have dedicated their hair there (Greek κομά-ειν/*komá-ein*, 'let the hair grow as a vow') (Str. 12,2,3; Cass. Dio 36,11). Strabo identifies M. with → Enyo, Plutarch also with → Semele and → Athena (Plut. Sulla 9,7,457c). All this, together with the 'sacred → prostitution' institutionalized in the temples during feast days (Str. 12,3,36), indicates a deity that is associated with the transition to normative adulthood for both genders: what war is for the young men, defloration is for the girls.

Strabo paints a static picture of the cult in the late first cent. BC, although the Romans had already intervened repeatedly in the Pontian Comana [2] (App. Mith. 9,64; 17,114; Str. 12,3,34; 12,8,9; Cic. Fam. 15,4,6). The high priests of both temple complexes ranked second only after the kings; at the *éxodos*, the festive 'going out' of the deity from her temple in → Hierapolis [1] – magnificent festivities, which took place twice a year and even attracted pilgrims from far and wide (Str. 12,3,36) –, they wore the royal tiara (Str. 12,3,32). In both temples there were at the time at least 6,000 → *hierodouloi* of both sexes (Str. 12,2,3; 12,3,34); the θεοφόρητοι/*theophórētoi*, those 'possessed by the god' are to be differentiated from them. The special status of the Pontian Comana was marked by the prohibition pertaining to the consumption of pork (Str. 12,8,9). After Cappadocia had become a Roman province (AD 34/5), the position of power of the office of the high priesthood seems to have decreased as a result of its distribution amongst leading local families [2].

Outside the two Comanas there is only scant evidence of the cult in Anatolia, yet it had already gained a wide circulation under the → Achaemenids [2]: in an inscription from Sardes, → Artaxerxes [2] II. forbids the → *neōkóroi* of 'Zeus' (→ Ahura Mazdā) to take part in the rituals of → Sabatius, of → Agdistis and of M. in the 4th cent. BC [3].

B. ROME

When the Romans encountered M. during the → Mithridatic Wars, they identified the goddess with → Bellona, later with → Virtus (CIL XIII 7281). The violence of the deity made a strong impression on Sulla (Plut. Sulla 9,7,457c). The peculiarities of the cult that shocked the Romans the most are not mentioned by Strabo: being possessed in a state of trance, foretelling of the future and self-injury (Juv. 4,123–125; Lactant. Div. inst. 1,21,16). The fact that Artaxerxes [2] II. (see above) associated M. with Sabazius and Agdistis, suggests that these elements were already part of the original cult, even if they also possibly remained restricted to the *theophórētoi* (= *fanatici*) and special occasions. The body becomes the location, where the boundary between gods and humans can temporarily be transcended: The Roman concentration on the exotic nature of the cult and the widespread confusion of *gálloi*, *fanatici* and other non-Roman priests (Apul. Met. 8,25,3; 8,27–29; → Metragyrtae) represent strategies of marginalizing religious concepts, which were regarded as un-Roman by the Roman elite.

1 ZGUSTA, s.v. M.   2 R. P. HARPER, Tituli Commanorum Cappadociae, in: AS 18, 1968, 104, no. 206
3 L. ROBERT, Une nouvelle inscription grecque de Sardes, in: CRAI 1975, 306–331.

A. HARTMANN, s.v. M., RE 14, 77–91; P. DEBORD, Aspects sociaux et économiques de la vie religieuse dans l'Anatolie gréco-romaine (EPRO 88), 1982.   R.GOR.

Maʿīn see → Minaei

Maat

Maat (mȝ͑.t) is an intellectual concept that was a central component of religion and society in ancient Egypt. The basic principles of *maat* are order, justice, truth and communal action. *Maat* is given by the creator god to the king who makes *maat* rule on earth but also gives it back to the creator god. As a principle that creates order, *maat* contributes to the course of the world. Presented as a deity, *Maat* as the daughter of the → sun god keeps the course of the sun in motion and thus also guarantees the order of the cosmos. In addition *maat* has a significant role in the judgement of the dead.
→ Egyptian law; → Ruler

1 J. ASSMANN, Maʾat. Gerechtigkeit und Unsterblichkeit im Alten Ägypten, 1990   2 M. LICHTHEIM, Maat in Egyptian Autobiographies and Related Studies, 1992.   J.KA.

Mabartha

Mabartha (Aramaic *maʿbartā*, 'ford, passage'; Greek Μαβάρθα/*Mabártha*; Latin Mamortha). Name of a place or landscape in Palestine between Ebal and Garizim, near → Neapolis (Talmud: jTaan 4,68c,74–d,1; Jos. BI 4,449; Plin. HN 5,69).   TH.PO.

Macae

Macae (Μάκαι; *Mákai*).
[1] According to Ptol. 6,7,14, a people in eastern Arabia in the hinterland of the bays around modern Rāʾs

Musandam on the road from Hormuz. Also mentioned in Str. 13,765f., Plin. HN 6,98.152 and Mela 3,79; according to them, the M. settled opposite the Carmanian foothills. According to Arr. Ind., Μαχέτα/*Makéta* (Rāʾs Musandam) was an important trading centre for the spice trade (→ Spices) on the Persian Gulf.   I.T.-N.
[2] (*Macae*). A large nomadic tribe or tribal league that had its central grazing areas west of the region of the → Nasamones (on both sides of the river → Cinyps) (Hdt. 4,175; Ps.-Scyl. 109 [GGM 1,84f.]; Diod. Sic. 3,49,1; Plin. HN 5,34; Sil. Pun. 2,60; 3,275). Ptolemy calls the M. *Makaîoi Syrtîtai* (Μακαῖοι Συρτῖται, 4,3,27) but nevertheless localizes them (under the name Μαχχόοι/*Makkóoi* or Μαχόαι/*Makóai*) in the interior of Libya (4,6,18) – perhaps because in summer they moved with their herds to the mountains south-west of the Great Syrte. During the period of the attempt by → Dorieus [1] to establish himself at the Cinyps, they called upon the Carthaginians for aid. Together with them they prevented the Greeks from expanding further on African territory (Hdt. 5,42,3). If the M. are identifiable with the Μαχχοῖοι/*Makkoîoi* of Pol. 3,33,15, troops of the M. served in Hannibal's army. Silius calls the M. *Cinyphii Macae* (3,275; cf. 2,60) and has them being armed with boomerangs (*cateiae*) (3,277; cf. also Sil. 5,194; 9,11; 9,89; 9,222; 15,670; also Liber generationis 1, Chron. min. 1, 102,145; SEG IX 356, l. 50f.; 414, l. 1; Excerpta Barbari Scaligeri p. 202,16; Chronica Alexandrina, Chron. min. 1, 102,117).

J. DESANGES, Catalogue des tribus africaines..., 1962, 106f.   W.HU.

Macareae

Macareae (Μακαρέαι; *Makaréai*). Town west of → Megale Polis, belonging to its region, in the plain to the left of the Alpheius, in ruins at the time of Pausanias (8,3,3; 27,4; 36,9); remains not known.   Y.L.

Macar(eus)

Macar(eus) (Μάκαρ/*Mákar*, Μακαρεύς/*Makareús*; Latin Macareus). Mythical king of Lesbos who resettled this island after it was depopulated through the Deucalian flood (→ Deucalion) and thus gave it the name of Macaria; Lesbos is already called 'seat of Macar' by Homer (Hom. Il. 24,544; H. Hom. 1,37). In the last-mentioned reference, the information 'son of Aeolus' is added; this patronymicon was probably a reflection of the Aeolian settlement of Lesbos.

The most detailed depiction of M. is provided by Diod. Sic. 5,81f.: according to this, M. was a grandson of Zeus (already represented in this way in Hesiod) and originally lived in Achaean Olenus that was at that time still settled by Ionians; M.'s followers are therefore called Ionians. On Lesbos, M. enacts good laws and creates in the eastern Aegaean an island kingdom that he has his sons rule as governors; his daughters Mytilene and Methymna give their names to the two main cities of Lesbos. Aelianus knows of the story of a priest of Dionysus, M. of Mytilene, who had killed a stranger in his temple and was therefore executed together with his family (Ael. VH 13, 2).

Contrasting with these details regarding M. that tend to be influenced by historical facts is a legendary tradition, according to which M. is the son of the god of the wind → Aeolus [2]. Like the other sons of Aeolus, M. is also said to have been married to one of his sisters (Hom. Od. 10,1–7); for her the name → Canace is passed down to us in later texts. This relationship is the material for Euripides' tragedy 'Aeolus' (TGF fr. 14–41; additional extant literary expansion in Ov. Epist. 11); here, however, incest is no longer accepted but Aeolus forces his daughter to commit suicide because of her love for M., whereupon M. also kills himself (Hyg. Fab. 242).

M. van der Kolf, s.v. Makareus, RE 14, 617–622; M. Labate, La Canace ovidiana e l'Eolo di Euripide, in: ASNP 3, 7.2, 1977, 583–593; S. Jäkel, The Aiolos of Euripides, in: Grazer Beiträge 8, 1979, 101–118.   E.V.

Macaria (Μαχαρία; *Makaría*).

[1] Daughter of → Heracles and → Deianira; sacrifices herself voluntarily in the war of the Athenians and the → Heraclidae against → Eurystheus to secure victory (→ Human sacrifices): first referred to in this way in Eur. Heracl., but without mentioning her name; possibly already in Aeschylus or in Athenian local myth [1. XVI, XXXI–XXXIII, 111f.]

1 J. Wilkins (ed.), Euripides, Heraclidae, 1993 (introduction and commentary).   L.K.

[2] Spring in → Tricorythus in the north of the plain of Marathon, named after the daughter of Hercules, M. [1], who had sacrificed herself in the battle against Eurystheus, modern Megalomati near Kato Souli. Evidence: Paus. 1,32,6; Str. 8,6,19; schol. Aristoph. Equ. 1151; schol. Pl. Hp. mai. 1,293a; Zenob. 2,61.

W.M. Leake, Die Demen von Attika, 1840, 80; A. Milchhoefer, Karten von Attika. Erläuternder Text 3/6, 1889, 49; W. Wrede, s.v. M. (5), RE 14, 624.   E.MEY. and H.LO.

[3] The particularly fertile lower Messenian plain through which the Pamisus flows (Str. 8,4,6).

F. Bölte, s.v. M. (6), RE 14, 625f.   C.L. and E.MEY.

Macarius (Μαχάριος; *Makários*).
I. Greek   II. Roman

I. Greek
[1] Spartiate, in 426/5 BC he took part in the council of war of Eurylochus [2] in the campaign of the armed forces of Spartan allies against → Naupactus and the → Acarnanians and fell in battle at Olpae (Thuc. 3,100,2; 109,1).

J. Roisman, The General Demosthenes and his Use of Military Surprise, 1993, 27ff.   K.-W.WEL.

[2] **M. of Alexandria** According to the → *Historia monachorum in Aegypto* [1. § 23], a certain M. (4th cent. AD) was the first to build a hermitage in Sketis –

there he bears the epithet ὁ πολιτικός (*ho politikós=* *urbanus*, 'the town dweller') – according to Sozom. Hist. eccl. 3,14,1 because he came from Alexandria. Some hagiographic episodes from the life of M. are passed down to us in the *Historia Monachorum* (§ 23,2–4) and a whole additional number of these in the *Historia Lausiaca* by → Palladius (Pall. Laus. § 17 and above all § 18). Further information about his life comes from a Coptic [2] and a Latin *vita* [3] as well as diverse Greek traditions. [4].

The Latin texts passed down to us under his name (monastic rule, CPL 1842, and two letters, CPL 1843 and 1843a) probably come from the Gallic monasticism of the 5th to 8th cents; the Greek and Syrian texts attributed to him were also presumably not written by him (CPG 2, 2400–2402).

→ Monasticism

1 A.-J. Festugière (ed.), Historia monachorum in Aegypto (Subsidia Hagiographica 34), 1961, 123f. 2 E. Amélineau (ed.), Bibliotheca Hagiographica Orientalis 577, 1910, 235–261   3 Soc. des Bollandistes, Bibliotheca Hagiographica Latina, ²1992, 5099, 5099c 4 F. Halkin (ed.), Bibliotheca Hagiographica Graeca, ³1957, 999y, 999yb, 999z–999zc.

Sources: CPG 2, 2400–2403; CPL 1842–1843a.
Bibliography: E. Amélineau, Histoire des monastères de la Basse Égypte, in: Annales du Musée Guimet 25, 1894, 235–261; G. Bunge, Évagre le Pontique et les deux Macaire, in: Irénicon 56, 1983, 215–227; W. Strothmann, Die syrische Überlieferung der Schriften des M. (Göttinger Orientforsch. 21/1–2), 1981.

[3] **M. Magnes** Author of an *Apokritikòs è monogenés* (Ἀποκριτικὸς ἢ μονογενής), written in the 2nd half of the 4th cent., which was edited in 1876 by C. Blondel (and posthumously by P. Foucart) from an Athenian MSS that has since been lost [1]; in addition, fragments are extant (among others from a homily on genesis: CPG 3, 6116). The key word *Monogenés* from the title refers to the title of Christ (cf. 3,8; 3,9; 3,13f.; 3,23 and 3,27). The text purports to be a word-for-word record of a disputation between the author and a scholarly Greek critic of Christianity; in all probability, passages from an excerpt from the work *Katà Christianôn* (Κατὰ Χριστιανῶν) by → Porphyrius are used. The author is perhaps identical to a bishop of Magnesia (on the Maeander?) attested in → Photius (Bibl. cod. 59).

1 C. Blondel (ed.), Macarii Magnetis quae supersunt ex inedito codice, 1876   2 J.B. Pitra (ed.), Spicilegium Solesmense 1, 1852, 302–335.

Sources: CPG 3, 6115–6117.
Bibliography: T.D. Barnes, Porphyry Against the Christians: Date and the Attribution of Fragments, in: Journ. of Theological Studies 24, 1973, 424–442; A.v. Harnack, Kritik des Neuen Testaments von einem griechischen Philosophen des 3. Jh. (TU 37/4), 1911; J. Palm, Textkritisches zum 'Apokritikos' des M. Magnes, 1961; G. Schalkhausser, Zu den Schriften des M. von Magnesia (TU 31/4), 1907; R. Waelkens, L'économie, thème apologétique et principe herméneutique dans l'Apocriticos de Macarios Magnés (Recueil de travaux d'histoire et de philologie. 6ᵉ sér. Fasc. 4), 1974.   C.M.

[4] M. the Egyptian see → Symeon [1]

II. ROMAN

[5] One of the two special envoys of the emperor
→ Constans [1] who distributed donations in North
Africa after AD 343 and who was to end the division
between Donatists (→ Donatus [1]) and Catholics.
While he was taking the appropriate steps, violent riots
occurred in → Bagae and Vegesela (Numidia), in the
course of which → Marculus was executed. The Donatist side later referred to the campaign by the abusive
name *Macariana tempora* ('Macarian times') as the
epitome of the Catholic- Imperial persecution of the
Donatists. Most important source: Optatus of Mileve,
Contra Parmenianum 3,1–10.

> A. MANDOUZE, Prosopographie chrétienne du Bas-Em-
> pire, vol. 1: Afrique, 1982, 655–658; S. LANCEL, J.S. Alex-
> ander s.v. Donatistae, Augustinus-Lexikon, vol. 2, 606–
> 638   AL.SCHI.

Macartatus (Μακάρτατος; *Makártatos*).
[1] The Athenians M. and Melanopus fell in battle in
458/7 or *c.* 410 BC as cavalrymen in the battle against
the Lacedaemonians and Boeotians in the border territory between Tanagra and Eleon. Pausanias (1,29,6)
saw a stele dedicated to the two of them in the → Kerameikos. A remnant of the base of this stele appears to
have been found (IG I³ 1288).

> PA 9658; TRAILL, PAA 631475.

[2] Athenian, sold (probably before 378 BC) his estate
in Prospalta, bought a trireme and journeyed to Crete.
As a result, the Athenians feared for peace with Sparta.
During the journey, M. lost his ship and his life; legal
proceedings were conducted regarding his inheritance
(Isaeus 11,48f.; Lys. fr. 86 THALHEIM) [1; 2].

> 1 DAVIES, 85f.   2 L. CASSON, A Trireme for Hire (Is.
> 11.48), in: CQ 45, 1995, 241–245.
>
> PA 9660; TRAILL, PAA 631490.

[3] Son of → Theopompus of Oeon and of the sister of
M. [2] who was appointed as heir to M. who had died
childless (Isaeus 11,49). After the death of his father, he
inherited – as he had in the meantime returned to the
family of his natural father – the estate of Hagnias that
had been the subject of dispute in several legal proceedings and that was contested again around 340 BC in a
court case ([Dem.] Or. 43).

> 'PA 9659; TRAILL, PAA 631480.   W.S.

Maccabean Revolt see → Judas [1]; → Jewish Wars;
→ Maccabees

Maccabees (Μακκαβαῖοι; *Makkabaîoi*). Jewish priestly
family from Modeïn north-west of Jerusalem (named
after its historically most important representative
→ Judas [1] Maccabaeus); also called → Hasmonaeans.
From 167 BC onwards the M. led the Jewish uprising

against the religious persecution of → Antiochus [6] IV
and his Hellenizing Jewish party liners (so-called Maccabean Revolt). After the recapture of → Jerusalem and
the rededication of the → Temple (III.) for the traditional Jewish cult in 165 BC, this resulted, despite some
temporary setbacks, in the founding of an independent
Jewish state under the leadership of the M.-Hasmone-
ans as the ruling dynasty (from 141 BC hereditary high
priestly office, and at the latest from → Alexander [16]
Iannaeus, 103–76, also the kingship).

The increasing weakness and the confusion surrounding the throne of the → Seleucids facilitated the
extension of Hasmonean sovereignty over almost all
Palestine and several of the neighbouring regions. Thus,
the largest Jewish-Israelite state body since the monarchy of David and Solomon in the 10th cent. BC was
created. Partly rescinded by the new Roman sovereigns
after 63 BC, the Maccabean-Hasmonean expansion
into non-Jewish settlement areas did, however, form
the basis of ethnic-religious distribution of the population in the Roman province of Judaea in the 1st cent.
AD.

Seleucid religious persecution and the Maccabean
movement had far-reaching historical effects, particularly in the religious sphere. Significant impulses for the
development of → Judaism and → Christianity resulted
from this religious and political development in the 2nd
cent. BC (i.a. the ideal of martyrdom, the belief in the
resurrection, apocalyptic messianism, → Messiah) and
have left their traces in Jewish literature (book of
Daniel, Maccabees) and liturgy (feast of Chanukkah).
Accordingly, modern research has been primarily concerned with the history of thought of the political
events, especially after the internal Jewish component
of the religious conflict had been examined by [1].
→ Judaism (C.); → Jewish Wars

> 1 E. BICKERMANN, Der Gott der Makkabäer, 1937.
>
> B. BAR-KOCHVA, Judas Maccabaeus, 1989; K. BRING-
> MANN, Hell. Reform und Religionsverfolgung in Judäa,
> 1983; TH. FISCHER, Seleukiden und Makkabäer, 1980;
> M. HENGEL, Judentum und Hellenismus, ²1973; F. G. B.
> MILLAR, The Background of the Maccabean Revolution,
> in: Journal of Jewish Studies 29, 1978, 1–21; SCHÜRER,
> vol. 1; E. WILL, CL. ORRIEUX, Ioudaïsmos – Hellénismos,
> 1986.   JÖ. GE.

Maccala (Μάκκαλα; *Mákkala*). According to Ptol.
6,7,41, a city in → Arabia Felix. We should probably
reject the obvious identification with the modern harbour town of Mukallā/Yemen on the south coast, as it is
inconsistent with the sequence of place names in Ptolemy. It corresponds rather with Manqal in the hinterland of *Mélan óros* (Μέλαν ὄρος, Arabic *as-Saudā'*).

> H. v. WISSMANN, Zur Geschichte und Landeskunde von
> Altsüdarabien (SAWW, Phil.-histor. Klasse 246), 1964,
> 417 (map).   I.T.-N.

Maceda (Hebrew *Maqqēdā*; LXX, Euseb. On. 126,22
Μακηδά/*Makēdá*; Jos. Ant. Iud. 5,61 Μακχίδα/

Makchída; Egyptian *mkt*). Town in the southern part of the western Judaean hill country, known because of a cave (Jos. Ant. Iud. 10,10ff.) and under Josiah belonging to the district of Laḥiš (Jos. Ant. Iud. 15,41); according to Euseb. On., 8 *milia passuum* east of Eleutheropolis (= Bēt Ǧibrīn), therefore possibly to be identified with Bēt Maqdum 11 km south-east of Bēt Ǧibrīn.

> K. ELLIGER, Josua in Juda, in: Palästina Jahrbuch 30, 1934, 55–58.   ER.K.

Macedo

[1] According to the Digesta (14,6,1), under Vespasian a M. who was being pressured by his creditors is said to have killed his father so that he could settle his debts. A → *senatus consultum* was therefore enacted stating that there was no option – even after the death of the father – for a creditor to bring a suit against sons who are under the authority of their father and have taken up a loan [1.; 2. 443f.]. Naming a *senatus consultum* after a person affected instead of after the magistrate putting in an application nevertheless appears to be very remarkable.

> 1 PIR² M 9   2 R. TALBERT, The Senate of Imp. Rome, 1984.

[2] Leader of Osrhoenian archers who is said to have played a part at Mainz immediately after the murder of the emperor → Severus Alexander. PIR² M 10.   W.E.

Macedon (Μακεδών; *Makedṓn*).

Tribal hero and eponym of the Macedonians. There are several genealogies:

[1] Son of Zeus and Thyia (the daughter of → Deucalion), brother of → Magnes [1] (Hes. fr. 7). His wife is Oreithyia, his sons are, among others, Europus (Steph. Byz. s.v. Εὐρωπός), Pierus, Amathus: also eponyms for Macedonian cities (schol. Hom. Il. 14,226).

[2] Son of Aeolus, the son of → Hellen and brother of Dorus and Xuthus; thus M. links his people with the Hellenic genealogies (Steph. Byz. s.v. Μακεδονία).

[3] Son of → Lycaon; thus link with the Pelasgians (Ael. NA 10,48; Apollod. 3,97: Μάκεδνος).

[4] Son of → Osiris; M. accompanies his father with his brother Anubis on his campaign of conquest around the world and is left behind by him in Macedonia as its ruler.   AL.FR.

Macedonia, Macedones (Μακεδονία/*Makedonía*, Μακεδόνες/*Makedónes*, Lat. *Macedonia*, *Macedones*).

I. GEOGRAPHY, ECONOMY, ETHNOGENESIS II. POLITICAL HISTORY III. POLITICAL, SOCIAL AND MILITARY STRUCTURES IV. TOWNS V. PROVINCE, DIOCESE AND THEMA VI. ARCHAEOLOGY

I. GEOGRAPHY, ECONOMY, ETHNOGENESIS

The core territory of the ancient Macedonian state was in the plains immediately to the east and north of the Olympus mountain range. Beginning with the 7th cent. BC, the Macedones conquered from their capital → Aegae [1] step by step Pieria (south of the lower → Haliacmon), Bottiaea (between Haliacmon and → Axius), → Almopia, Mygdonia (located in lowlands of lake → Bolbe), Crestonia (to the north of Mygdonia), Anthemus (south of Mygdonia); later, the areas → Elimea, → Eordaea, → Lyncus, Orestis and → Pelagonia in upper M. were conquered, or added to the state by other means. The general area was united politically only in the 4th cent. BC under → Philippus II, it functioned as a bridge, or, depending on the viewpoint, as a buffer zone between the non-Greek tribes on the Adriatic coast to the west, in Thrace to the east as far as the lower Ister (Danube), and the multitude of the small Greek states (*póleis*) in the Aegaean. There were four important roadways crossing M.: from the → Ister [2] via the Morava valley and the Axius valley, from the Adriatic Sea via Lyncus, from Thrace via Mygdonia and from the south via → Tempe. High mountain ranges, especially to the west and south, separate M. from her neighbours.

Since M. is partially located in continental climate zones, as well as being influenced by the Mediterranean Sea in coastal areas, the area brought forth typical products of both zones: horses, cattle and sheep or goats as well as timber for ships, in addition to grain, fruit, olive oil and wine. There also was mining of iron, silver and gold in the mountains (→ Gold, with map, e.g. → Pangaeum).

At the time of the Macedonian conquests, the population was of different origins, but Hes. fr. 5 already considered them a Greek tribe of horse lovers, descendants of Zeus, residing in the areas around Pieria and Olympus. The first royal dynasty, the → Argeadae, claimed descent from the Temenidae of Argos [II 1] in the Peloponnese. Thus, Alexander [2] was able to convince the judges in Olympia of his Greek origin (Hdt. 5,22). If in later disputes, especially during the controversies with Athens in the 4th cent., some of the southern Greeks maintained the Macedonians – with the exception of the royal house – were not Greek at all (cf. Isocr. Or. 5,107), the argument was not only based on current political interest. Rather, it reflects the historically somewhat obscure genesis of the Macedonian state, as well as the different political and social structures when compared with the *póleis*. The latter mostly could point to a much longer political history, and the Athenians even claimed to be autochthonous, i.e. they had always been there. No Greek state of the period had an all-powerful royalty, and the Macedonian dialect (→ Macedonian), while probably being basically Greek, was intermingled with Illyrian and Thracian words and phrases and therefore was considered unintelligible, therefore non-Greek [1; 2]. The ethnogenesis of the Macedonians indeed was much younger and much more complex than that of the southern Greek states.

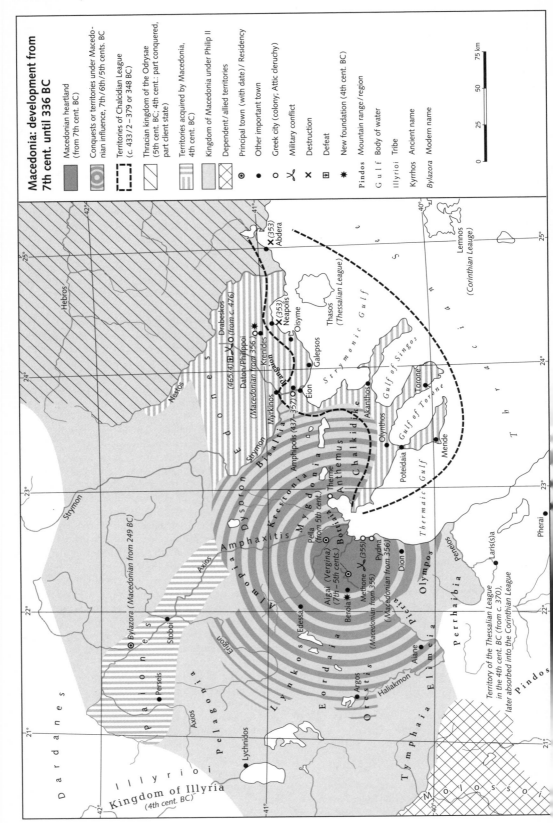

Macedonia: development from 7th cent. until 336 BC

Macedonian heartland (from 7th cent. BC)

Conquests or territories under Macedonian influence, 7th/6th/5th cents. BC

Territories of Chalcidian League (c. 433/2 – 379 or 348 BC)

Thracian kingdom of the Odrysae (5th cent. BC; 4th cent.: part conquered, part client state)

Territories acquired by Macedonia, 4th cent. BC)

Kingdom of Macedonia under Philip II

Dependent / allied territories

⊙ Principal town (with date) / Residency

● Other important town

○ Greek city (colony; Attic cleruchy)

✗ Military conflict

✗ Destruction

⊞ Defeat

✳ New foundation (4th cent. BC)

Pindos Mountain range / region

G u l f Body of water

Illyrioi Tribe

Kyrrhos Ancient name

Bylazora Modern name

0 25 50 75 km

Lemnos

Abdera ✗ (353)

Hebros

Drabeskos

Daton/Philippoi ✗○ (from c. 476)
(465/4) ⊞ ✳ Krenides
(Macedonian from 356)

Nestos

Neapolis ✗ (353)

Oisyme

Thasos (Thessalian League)

Galepsos

Strymonic Gulf

Gulf of Singos

Myrkinos
Eion
Amphipolis (437–357)
(Macedonian from 357)

Strymon

Bisaltia

Akanthos

Gulf of Torone

Torone

Strymon

Dysoron

Krestonia

Olynthos

Mende

Poteidaia

Amphaxitis

Axios

Mygdonia (from 5th cent.)

Therme

Anthemus

Chalkidike

Thermaic Gulf

T h r a c i a

25°

24°

23°

Pella (from 5th cent.)

Bottiaia

Almopia

Eordaia

Paiones

Bylazora (Macedonian from 249 BC)

Stoboi

Perseis

Axios

Pelagonia

Erigon

Lynkos

Orestis

Argos

Aiane

Halliakmon

Lychnidos

Aigai (Vergina) (7th–5th cents.)

Beroia ✳

Methone ✗ (355)
(Macedonian from 356)

Edessa

Pydna

Dion

Pieria

Elimeia

Olympos

Peneios

Laris(s)a

Pherai

Perrhaibia

Tymphaia

Pindos

Territory of the Thessalian League in the 4th cent. BC (from c. 370), later absorbed into the Corinthian League

(Corinthian League)

D a r d a n e s

I l l y r i o i

Kingdom of Illyria (4th cent. BC)

M o l o s s o i

42°

41°

40°

21°

22°

23°

24°

25°

II. Political History

A. Developments from the 7th cent. until 359 BC   B. Macedonia under Philip II and Alexander the Great   C. Hellenistic period D. Under Roman rule   E. Late antiquity and Byzantine Era

A. Developments from the 7th cent. until 359 BC

The historical development of M. can only be traced by kings and conquests. The list of kings in Hdt. 8,137 comprises but six names before Alexander [2] I, 'the Philhellene' (around 498–454 BC): Perdiccas, Argaeus, Philippus, Aeropus, Alcetas as well as Amyntas, the father of Alexander. The list barely goes back to before the middle of the 7th cent. BC. The Macedonians themselves had no information on the period before → Perdiccas; → Amyntas, or probably rather Alexander, concluded a treaty with the Persian empire under Darius and Xerxes when it expanded to Europe. It appears likely that Alexander expanded his reign beyond Mygdonia to the Strymon after the failure of Xerxes' campaign in 479, and began exercising a more pronounced influence in upper M. (Thuc. 2,99,2).

In the period between the death of Alexander I (about 454 BC) and the succession of Philipp II to the throne (359), M. suffered from her marginal situation. When Athens rose to be a naval power in the Aegaean in the 5th cent. BC, trade in Macedonian shipbuilding timber brought additional wealth, but M. also was drawn into the controversies between the southern Greeks, especially during the → Peloponnesian War (431–404). → Perdiccas II and → Archelaus [1] encountered serious difficulties, especially because of the way Athens was conducting war on Chalcidice, but also because of their own attempts to include the largely independent domains in upper M. in the state of the Argeads. Archelaus finally took a new political departure by implementing a state investment program, improving the infrastructure by which especially the army would benefit – there was more support than ever for road-building, arsenals, forts and military bases (Thuc. 2,100). He also instituted Macedonian festivals based on Greek models in → Dion [II 2]. The expansion of the centrally located town of → Pella to a royal residence is also due to him. After his murder (399 BC), the Illyrians threatened the existence of M. as did several Greek states – Athens, Sparta, Thebes and the Chalcidian League, too – until Philip II was able to defeat the Illyrians decisively, immediately after his accession to the throne (359) when he began to consolidate the Macedonian state systematically and to turn it into the most important power in the Balkan region.

B. Macedonia under Philip II and Alexander the Great

Up until the murder of Philip II in 336 BC, a power structure had emerged in M. which remained in place basically until 196 BC, when it began to be dismantled

under Roman hegemony. Central issues for Philip were secure borders, which he achieved by political and social consolidation in the interior, as well as by elimination of enemies lurking immediately beyond the borders. In the east, the lines were advanced to the Nestus, Chalcidice was integrated into M. after the destruction of → Olynthus; to the north, the → Paeones in the Axius valley were defeated and integrated, in the west the Illyrians were subdued; and by the marriage with → Olympias, a dynastic link with the Epirote Molossi (→ Epirus) was created. In the south, Thessalia was organized as a secure buffer zone towards Greece, in the pursuit of which Philip possibly became archon of the Thessalian League for a time. After the battle of → Chaeronaea (338) M. could also dictate to most Greek states, but Macedonian dominance was formally hidden by the establishment of a league headed by the king of M. (→ 'Corinthian League'). In the interior, an effective army was created, which offered possibilities for service and advancement to individual Macedonians, furthering the integration of the independence-minded princes of upper Macedonia. In the border areas of the west, as well as in the areas of 'New Macedonia' in the east (especially in Chalcidice and in Mygdonia, around Amphipolis and especially around Philip's new foundation Philippi), personal allegiances were created by royal land grants to Macedonians and others willing to settle there. These grants promoted the inner consolidation of the state and formed a basis of loyalty towards the royal house without which Alexander the Great's conquests (→ Alexander [4], with map) would hardly have been possible.

C. Hellenistic period

Alexander's sudden death in Babylon in 323, after he had subdued the Persian empire with his Macedonian army, advancing as far as India, was a disaster for M. Replacements for his fighting troops had time and again been sent from M. Alexander's death set in motion an extended period of competition for dominance amongst his former generals in the conquered territories and in M. (→ Diadochi, Wars of the). The last members of the Argead house were murdered in M. in 310 BC, and only after 30 years of civil war and political chaos did the grandson of Alexander's officer Antigonus [1] Monophthalmus, Antigonus [2] Gonatas, emerge victoriously in 276 as the founder of a new dynastic line (→ Antigonus, with stemma). The political history of the reign of the Antigonids, who ruled until 168 BC, was characterized by 1) the strife to re-establish and maintain the rule over the Greeks, who increasingly were disinclined to tolerate this dominance, and who time and again were aided by the other monarchs which had emerged from Alexander's empire: the Ptolemies in Egypt (→ Ptolemaeus) and the Seleucids in Syria and Asia Minor (→ Seleucus, see also → Hellenistic states with map); and, 2) the fight against Rome, which → Philippus V had carelessly provoked in 215 BC by entering a co-operative treaty with → Hannibal

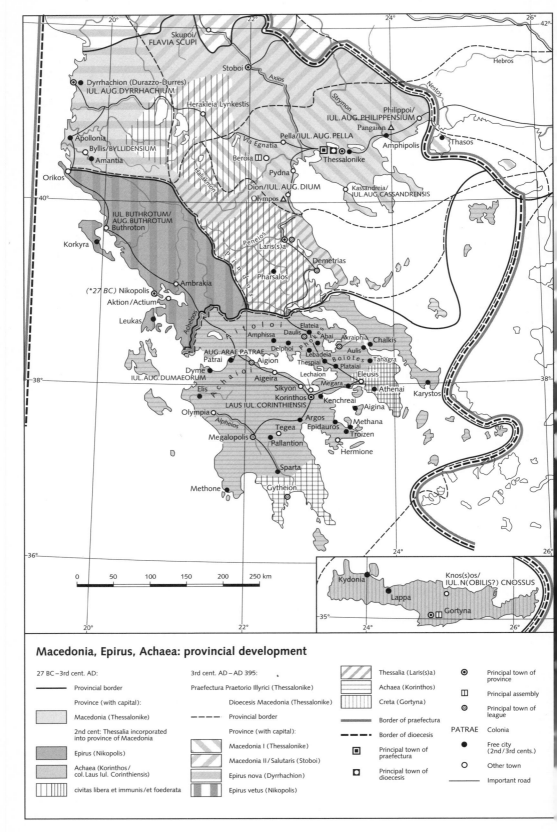

Macedonia, Epirus, Achaea: provincial development

27 BC–3rd cent. AD:

—— Provincial border

Province (with capital):

Macedonia (Thessalonike)

2nd cent: Thessalia incorporated into province of Macedonia

Epirus (Nikopolis)

Achaea (Korinthos/col. Laus Iul. Corinthiensis)

civitas libera et immunis/et foederata

3rd cent. AD – AD 395:

Praefectura Praetorio Illyrici (Thessalonike)

Dioecesis Macedonia (Thessalonike)

– – – Provincial border

Province (with capital):

Macedonia I (Thessalonike)

Macedonia II/Salutaris (Stoboi)

Epirus nova (Dyrrhachion)

Epirus vetus (Nikopolis)

Thessalia (Laris(s)a)

Achaea (Korinthos)

Creta (Gortyna)

——— Border of praefectura

– – – Border of dioecesis

Principal town of praefectura

Principal town of dioecesis

Principal town of province

Principal assembly

Principal town of league

PATRAE Colonia

● Free city (2nd/3rd cents.)

○ Other town

—— Important road

[4], causing three wars (→ 'Macedonian Wars'). In the course of the first war (214–205), which ended with the peace of compromise of Phoenice, the Roman intention had been to stop Phillips' aiding Hannibal. In the second war (200–196), which can be seen as a continuation of the war against Hannibal, Rome specifically aimed at dismantling Macedonian power outside of her traditional borders. After the battle of → Cynoscephalae in Thessalia (197), the Romans under T. → Quinctius Flamininus declared Thessalia and Orestis as independent, as well as all other outer Macedonian territories. Flamininus used this measure very effectively when he proclaimed 'freedom for the Greeks' at the Isthmian games of 196. After an interval of an increasingly tension-ridden alliance with Rome and her allies, the Macedonian monarchy came to an end with the third war (171–168), which ended with the defeat of → Perseus by Aemilius [I 32] near Pydna.

D. Under Roman rule

At first, Rome divided M. into four regions (*merídes*) which were supposed to administer themselves by assemblies in → Amphipolis, → Thessalonica, → Pella and → Heraclia [2], but they were prohibited from having contacts with each other. This rather unrealistic regulation caused notable unrest and finally provoked a rebellion (150–148 BC). After Q. Caecilius [I 27] Metellus (Macedonicus) had subdued the rebellion, M. was administered as a Roman province while the four *merídes* were retained only as judicial districts. When the province was organized, those parts of southern Illyria which had been annexed by Perseus' ally → Genthius in 187 were added to the new *provincia Macedonia*. The result was a very large province that stretched from the Adriatic Sea near Apollonia to the river Nestus. The → *via Egnatia*, constructed soon afterwards, connected the Adriatic ports of Apollonia and Epidamnus (Dyrrhachium) with the seat of the Roman governor in → Thessalonica; it was extended later to Byzantium [3].

Originally, M. was a border province and served as a protective area for Greece. The governor also had responsibilities involving public order in Greece. During the Roman Civil War, M. served as a deployment area of troops for Pompeius against Caesar (battle of → Pharsalus, 48 BC) as well as for Caesars' murderers against Mark Antony and the later Augustus (battle near → Philippi, 42 BC). However, as Roman military activities advanced to the Danube during the reign of Augustus, and because of the organization of the new border province of Moesia in AD 45/6, M. lost its central protective function on the Balkans, a function it had occupied for centuries, and was downgraded to a senatorial province (Cass. Dio, 60. 24; see also → Achaia, → Epirus, → Thessalia).

E. Late antiquity and Byzantine era

Under Roman dominance, M. could only be as secure as the empire itself. Already in 196 BC, T. Quinc-

tius Flamininus had advocated the necessity for a continuation of the Macedonian kingdom with the argument that Greece needed protection from the Balkan tribes (Pol. 18,37,8f.), a function which was maintained up to the creation of the province of Moesia (cf. Cic. Pis. 38). From the 3rd cent. AD onwards, M. suffered also, since the border on the Ister (Danube) was frequently penetrated by Sarmatian and Germanic tribes. Already under Gallienus or Claudius Gothicus (268 or 269), → Goti and other tribes invaded M., laid siege to Cassandria (→ Potidaea) and → Thessalonica and continued plundering along the *via Egnatia* towards the west (Zos. 1,43) M. was affected worst after the battle of Adrianople [3] (378), when the victorious Goti invaded the entire Balkan region plundering and devastating, even swarming as far as the area of Thessalonica (Zos. 4,24f.). Also, later, M. could not be protected from the Goti of Alaricus who in 397 were even permitted to settle on Macedonian soil for a few years (Claud. Bellum Geticum 497). Under the emperor Zeno, there were battles in M. with and between the two Gothic chieftains Theodoric (son of Triarius) and Theodoric ('the Great'; son of Theodemir), who had been named king of the Goths in AD 474 after the battle of → Cyrrhus [1] (Iord. Get. 287f.).

Justinian supposedly, as elsewhere, undertook a massive reconstruction of the military infrastructure (Procop. Aed. 4,4), yet these efforts, if they took place at all, could not prevent Slavs and Avars from appearing near Thessalonica already before the end of the 6th cent., threatening Macedonian cities in the following century and settling in the countryside (Miracula Sancti Demetrii [10]). Only in the 8th cent., a more effective Byzantine administration was re-established with the organization of the Macedonian → *thema* (Theophanes 475,22).

III. Political, social and military structures

Before 168 BC, the monarchs' administration controlled life in M., and royalty as an institution never seems to have been questioned at all. This is mainly due to the symbiotic relationship between king and nobility, but the popular appearance of the kings was a factor as well. They should be accessible to the common man, and normally were, since there was no popular representative body in regular sessions in M. The state was governed by the kings and influential noblemen; the latter also had their say in questions of succession, even if there was an adult son of the deceased ruler who could succeed him. The king's 'companions' (*hetaîroi*) or later simply 'friends' (*phíloi*), chosen by himself, were his advisors. The king also managed foreign policies since he concluded treaties in his own name, negotiating them himself, and also because he entered into political marriages (once, or several times, depending on inclinations). The permanent bond of the nobility to the court – during the early period there were local royal houses in upper M. (such as in Elimea, Orestis, Lyncus or Pelagonia) who only lost their importance under Philip II but not their influence – was effected especially by military service (increasingly successful beginning with the reign of Philip II, which heightened the reputation and the attractiveness of such service considerably), as well as by membership of the noble youth in the corps of pages founded by Philip II. Such bonds were strengthened further by generous land grants in the conquered areas of new M., which were at first treated as royal lands, to meritorious or influential personalities

Cavalry had already been of central importance in the Macedonian military as early as under Alexander I. It appears that before the reorganization of the infantry phalanx under Philip II, there was no systematic training of infantry. Philip introduced the Theban model, as well as uniform armament with the → sarissa, a lance of 5 m length, also with a helmet, shin guards, sword and shield. Normally, the army consisted of 20,000–30,000 men (more in emergencies) who at certain times, especially in the 4th and 3rd cents. BC, became professional fighters who nearly always would be able to carry the day against the soldiers of the smaller Greek states. During campaigns, the king himself led the army, his 'friends' acting as high-ranking officers. M. never had a considerable navy. In all other respects, the state was governed centrally by the king. Any administrative officials known to us seem to have been royal appointees. Taxes were mainly levied on harvests which yielded 200 talents annually under Perseus (Plut. Aemilius Paulus 28,3), they were centrally organized by the royal administration which disposed of the income. Mining and exports of wood were royal monopolies. Towns possibly had access to port- and market fees.

It appears that also cultural life was determined by the royal court where the kings liked to show themselves as patrons of artists and intellectuals. Euripides [1] wrote his 'Bacchae' during a sojourn in Pella; and Aristoteles [6] served as a tutor for the young Alexander [4] (the Great). This influence continued when the cities in M. began to bloom with increasing wealth in the 3rd and 2nd cents. BC, giving rise to a cultural infrastructure there as well (theatres, gymnasia, temples, all with corresponding local events) which should not be neglected. In the areas of architecture and painting, where excavations continue to make new discoveries, it can be shown that there was a sensibility for high artistic quality no later than the end of the 5th cent. BC. At that time, Archelaus hired the painter → Zeuxis to decorate his new palace in Pella. There are high-quality burial objects especially from Sindos and Derveni (in the museum of Thessalonica), as well as the peristyle houses with ornate mosaics in Pella and the painted burial structures, especially the 'royal tombs' in Vergina (→ Aegae [1]), which clearly document these achievements (see below VI. Archaeology).

IV. Towns
An important long-term development in M. was urbanization and the concurrent adaptation of life in the cities for many Macedonians. This development dominated most parts of the Greek world, and it is characteristic for Graeco-Roman culture. The list of theorodókoi from Epidaurus (about 360 BC) speaks of recognized municipalities in M. giving shelter to the sacred ambassadors (theōroí) of Asclepius (IG IV² 1, 94) only in addition to old Greek colonies and the king himself. Towards the end of the 3rd cent., a corresponding list of theōrodókoi from Delphi mentioned 31 communities in M., many of them inland [4]. The number of urban centres with a degree of autonomous administration grew substantially from about the time of Philip II. Apparently he tried to include the towns he conquered into the Macedonian state (e.g. → Amphipolis) as first ruler, in addition to founding settlements in the conquered territories either conceived as póleis (e.g. → Philippi, → Apollonia [3], → Heraclia [2]), or by creating the economic basis for a later formation of póleis by generous land grants to Macedonians (e.g. → Calindoea).

Urban centres required a local administration, which in most Greek póleis (not having to deal with a superior territorial power during their initial phase) was effected in the 4th cent. BC by a people's assembly (ekklēsía), headed by a smaller council (boulé) as well as by officials who were in office only for short periods (e.g. one year) and on an unsalaried basis. Such a 'democratic' system already existed in Amphipolis when Philip II conquered the town. He accepted the system as being suitable for local administration, however with a royal supervisor when needed (sometimes referred to as epistátēs), or a garrison commander to keep matters in check when the state as a whole was affected. The advantage was cost-efficiency and satisfaction on the part of the local residents not at being patronized in purely local matters by a central administration. Local administration was an area where local pride could develop, where local autonomy could be exercised, however, this system also provided the advantages of the monarchic territorial state in which the poorer classes could profitably serve in the military and where the upper classes were able to enjoy a wider arena for their political ambitions.

As Philip II had shown the way, his son Alexander followed him by making the foundation of Greek póleis and the settlement of Greek colonists an imperialist tool in Asia, as did all of the Diadochi (→ Diadochi, Wars of the). The urban system blossomed under Alexander's Macedonian successors as it had never before, even inside M. new cities emerged, either as new foundations (e.g. Cassandria, Thessalonica) or as groupings of rural settlements concentrated as a town (e.g. Calindoea) [5. 91–106]. It was a slow process, with regional variants, and in the mountainous regions of upper Macedonia village-type or tribal structures of settlements and organizations continued for quite a while, perhaps they never completely dissolved (cf.. SEG 30, 568). Yet, at the end of the monarchy the towns had become the most important sub-unit of administration so that after the battle of → Pydna in 168 BC the victorious L. Aemilius [I 32] Paullus started the Roman administration of M. by requesting that each town send him ten negotiators (Liv. 45,29,1). Urban administrations were so well established that they could be turned into the basis of Roman provincial administration. A new kind of administrative office, *politárchēs*, was installed in many Macedonian cities of the Roman period and even though it appears that the very first *politárchai* were said to have been royal officials, their spread indicates tendencies towards standardized Roman provincial administration [6. 99f.]. After the Roman Civil Wars, the ranks of towns were increased by the foundation of colonies of Roman veterans in Dion, Cassandria, Philippi and near Pella, with a corresponding influx of Latin-speaking settlers. There was a provincial assembly (*koinón*) in → Berea [1] during the Imperial period.

Also in M., towns were not merely administrative units, but living spaces and cultural centres. The most important institution of this kind was probably the → gymnasium as a common Greek cultural institution which instilled in participants a feeling of cultural unity beyond town borders. The gymnasium best know to us was in Berea where a unique law was passed, probably shortly after 168 BC, providing us with detailed information [7]. Apparently there were many gymnasia, and during the monarchic period they did not function without occasional royal interference [8. vol. 2, no. 16]. The running of an urban gymnasium which offered not only physical but also intellectual, especially philosophical, challenges could not be kept up without a certain degree of openness towards other towns from the same cultural area.

No later than with the foundation of Thessalonica (in 315 BC), M. acquired an outstanding seaport which rapidly turned the town into one of the most important trade centres of the Mediterranean, at the same time providing an opening for the intellectual and religious movements of Hellenistic and Roman times. Already in the 3rd cent. BC, there is evidence of the new Egyptian deity → Sarapis in M., up until 187 his temple in Thessalonica was so wealthy that the king himself felt he had to regulate access to the treasures of the temple [9. vol. 2 no. 110]. Construction of the *via Egnatia* also improved connections with Italy, so that e.g. Cicero selected Thessalonica as his place of exile because of the good systems of information to and from this city (Cic. Att. 3,10–22, esp. 14,2). But simpler people also came to M. in the 2nd and 1st cents. BC, notably the Jews, who within the framework of the diaspora movement (→ Diaspora) were to provide the intellectual ground for the activities of the Apostle → Paul in Philippi, Berea and Thessalonica, causing the first Christian communities in Europe to be established there. Christianization as well as the acceptance of Egyptian cults constitutes a hallmark of the slow integration of M. into the cultural continuum of the eastern Mediterranean, 'Graeco-Roman civilization'. As soon as Christianity was supported in the empire in the 4th cent. AD, Macedonian bishops began to play an important role. Thus,

in the imperial Synod of → Nicaea (325) Stobi and Thessalonica were represented, or in the person of Acholius of Thessalonica, who had baptized the emperor Theodosius in 379/380 during his sojourn in Thessalonica and who served as an advisor during the preparations for the → Synod of Constantinople in 381. No later than at this time, M. had become an important central area of the Roman empire and was no longer a mere border province.

→ Balkan peninsula, languages; → Macedonian; → Macedonia

1 J. N. KALLÉRIS, Les anciens Macédoniens 1, 1954; 2, 1976 2 O. MASSON, s.v. Macedonian Language, OCD³, 905f. 3 L. GOUNAROPOULOU, M. B. HATZOPOULOS, Les milliaires de la voie egnatienne ... , 1985 4 A. PLASSART, Inscriptions de Delphes. La liste des Théorodokes, in: BCH 45, 1921, 1–87 5 G. M. COHEN, The Hellenistic Settlements in Europe, the Islands and Asia Minor, 1995 6 G. H. R. HORSLEY, The Politarchs in M. and Beyond, in: Mediterranean Archaeology 7, 1994, 99–126 7 PH. GAUTHIER, M. B. HATZOPOULOS, La loi gymnasiarche de Béroia, 1993 8 M. B. HATZOPOULOS, Macedonian Institutions under the Kings, 2 vols., 1996 9 MORETTI 10 P. LEMERLE, Les plus anciens recueils de saint Démétrius, 2 vol., 1979–1981.

E. N. BORZA, In the Shadow of Olympus, 1990; ERRINGTON; HM; F. PAPAZOGLOU, Les villes de Macédoine, 1988.   MA.ER.

MAPS: S. E. ALCOCK, Graecia capta, the Landscapes of Roman Greece, 1993; T. BECHERT, Die Provinzen des Röm. Reiches, 1999; K. BUSCHMANN et al., Östlicher Mittelmeerraum und Mesopotamien. Von Antoninus Pius bis zum Ende des Parthischen Reiches (138–224 n.Chr.), TAVO B V 9, 1992; ERRINGTON; B. GEROV, Die Grenzen der römischen Provinz Thracia bis zur Gründung des Aurelianischen Dakien, in: ANRW II 7.1, 1979, 213–240; R. GINOUVÈS (ed.), Macedonia from Philip II to the Roman Conquest, 1994; M. B. HATZOPOULOS, L. D. LOUKOPOULOS (ed.), Philip of Macedon, 1980; E. KETTENHOFEN, Vorderer Orient. Römer und Sasaniden in der Zeit der Reichskrise (224–284 n.Chr.), TAVO B V 11, 1982; Id., Östlicher Mittelmeerraum und Mesopotamien. Die Neuordnung des Orients in diokletianisch-konstantinischer Zeit (284–337 n.Chr.), TAVO B VI 1, 1984; F. PAPAZOGLU, Quelques aspects de l'histoire de la province de Macédonie, in: ANRW II 7.1, 1979, 302–369; I. PILLRADEMACHER et al., Vorderer Orient. Römer und Parther (14 bis 138 n.Chr.), TAVO B V 8, 1988; J. WAGNER, Östlicher Mittelmeerraum und Mesopotamien. Die Neuordnung des Orients von Pompeius bis Augustus (67 v.Chr. bis 14 n.Chr.), TAVO B V 7, 1983.

V. PROVINCE, DIOCESE AND THEMA

The Roman province of M. survived the administrative reforms, as they were begun by Aurelianus and completed by → Diocletianus (with map) and Constantine I, as part of one of the twelve dioceses (namely of Moesiae), however reduced in territory (cf. *Laterculus Veronensis*, AD 292–297; regarding the possible division of the diocesis of Moesiae into the dioceses M. and Dacia cf. [3. 134; 6. 21]). → Festus [4] Rufius comments (Breviarium 8,3) that the diocese of M. was subdivided into the provinces M., Thessalia, Achaia, Epiri duae, Praevalis and Crete [1. 13].

In the → *Notitia dignitatum* (379–408), for the first time the province of *Macedonia salutaris* is mentioned, partially located in the diocese of M., partially in the diocese of Dacia. In contrast with the dioceses of Dacia and Pannonia, the diocese of M. was headed by a → *vicarius*. With the division of the diocesis of Moesiae into the dioceses of M. and Dacia, also the province of M. was split up into the larger M. *prima* (Θεσσαλονίκη, Thessalonike) and the M. *salutaris* (Στόβοι, Stobi) to the northwest of it. M. *salutaris* was established about 386 [4. 768] and existed only for a few decades [2. 135]. It then became M. *secunda* (Στόβοι, modern Pustogradsko; [11. 987]; cf. Hierocles, Synekdemos 641,1 [5. 15]; a different version [11. 987]). Hierocles' work, originated in the beginning of the reign of → Iustinianus [1] at the imperial Roman court, is the most recent official source containing information on the administrative situation of M. The *Descriptio orbis Romani* of Georgios of Kypros (early 7th cent.) no longer mentions M. [7. 81–82]. In contrast with M. *prima*, which was under a κονσουλάριος/*konsoulários* (*consularis*) [5. 14], M. *secunda* was administered by a ἡγεμών/*hēgemón* (*praeses*) [5. 15]. Provincial structure under Byzantine rule was basically changed in favour of the theme system (→ *théma*) facing the growing threat of Arab, Slavic and Avar attacks. Jurisdiction of M. *secunda* continued during the 7th cent. on the territory of the prefecture of Illyricum (PG 116,1276).

The subscription lists of the 6th Ecumenical → Synod of Constantinople (680–681) and of the Quinisextum (692) show two titular bishops of Stobi are entered, but like many others they obviously remained without dioceses [8. 227f.]. Archaeological excavations indicate that Stobi was abandoned by its inhabitants near the end of the 6th cent. because of Slavic incursion, an earthquake and the increasing drought [10. 308–310]. The modern name Pustogradsko means 'abandoned town'. The prefecture of Illyricum was reduced to → Thessalonica and environs, also to the areas on the coast because of Slav immigration to the Balkan peninsula, which probably was the basis for the later theme division [7. 123]. In the enumeration of the provinces taken over by the Slavs and Avars (PG 116,1361b), M. is not mentioned since it probably had not been occupied in its entirety. The organization into themes, which were both army districts and civilian provinces, was continued on the Balkan peninsula until the end of the 8th cent. within the framework of renewed Hellenization. [9. 132]. The new *théma Makedonía tês Thráikēs* was created in west Thracian areas and was separated from the *thema* of Thracia between 783 (Theophanes 456,27f.) and 802 (Theophanes 475,22f.), its capital was → Adrianople [3].

1 M.-P. ARNAUD-LINDET, Festus, Abrégé des hauts faits du peuple romain, 1994, XVI n. 47, 13   2 J. BURY, The Notitia Dignitatum, in: JRS 10, 1920, 131–154   3 Id.,

The Provincial List of Verona, in: JRS 13, 1923, 127–151, esp. 134   4 F. GEYER, s.v. M., RE 14, 638–771   5 E. HONIGMANN, Le synekdémos d'Hiéroclès et l'opuscule de Georges de Chypre, 1939   6 A. JONES, The Date and Value of the Verona List, in: JRS 44, 1954, 21–29   7 P. LEMERLE, Philippe et la Macédoine orientale à l'époque chrétienne et byzantine, 1945   8 H. OHME, Das Concilium Quinisextum und seine Bischofsliste, 1990   9 G. OSTROGORSKY, Geschichte des byz. Staates, 1963   10 J. WISEMAN, The City in Macedonia Secunda, in: Villes et peuplement dans l'Illyricum protobyzantin, 1984, 289–314   11 P. SOUSTAL, B. SCHELLEWALD, L. THEIS, s.v. Makedonien, RBK, 983–1220.

E. CHRISTOPHILOPOULOU, Byzantini Makedonia, in: Byzantina 12, 1983, 10–63; Διεθνές Συμπόσιο: Βυζαντινή Μακεδονία (324–1480 μ.Χ.), Θεσσαλονίκη 29–31. Okt. 1992, 1995; B. FILOW, Die Teilung des aurelianischen Dakiens, in: Klio 12, 1912, 234–239; TH. MOMMSEN, Verzeichnis der röm. Prov. angesetzt um 297, in: Id., Gesammelte Schriften 5, 1908, 561–588; P. SOUSTAL, s.v. M., LMA 6, 152–154 (with bibliography).   L.D.

VI. ARCHAEOLOGY
A. LATE BRONZE AGE TO GEOMETRIC PERIOD
B. ARCHAIC TO ROMAN PERIODS

A. LATE BRONZE AGE TO GEOMETRIC PERIOD
Culture of the inhabitants of M. from the late Bronze Age to the early Iron Age is characterized by a changing combination of Mycenaean elements (up to Geometric) of the south with Balkanic ones of the north.

M. as well as → Epirus was not in the zone of Mycenaean palace states during the 2nd half of the second millennium. Normally, the inhabitants lived on man-made settlement hills (toumbas) which resulted from continuous settlement in some places from the Neolithic Age. Among the largest of them is the toumba of → Thessalonica, with a basis area of 1.3 ha and Hagios Mamas with 1.5 ha. The areas settled in the late Bronze Age were notably smaller. They all were smaller settlements compared to the southern Greek fortresses of → Tiryns (2 ha) and → Mycenae (3 ha; cf. also the settlement areas around the castles/palaces: → Pylos 12,4 ha, Tiryns 25 ha). At some Macedonian toumbas (Thessalonica and Assirus) the existence of substantial terracing and sometimes fortification measures could be shown.

The economy of the late Bronze Age in M., in the 14th and 13th cents. BC, was very different from the redistribution-oriented economy of the palaces (→ Mycenaean culture and archaeology) of the Mycenaean south. In M., there is no evidence of palaces and a state bureaucracy involving written documentation. There were communal reserve systems on the toumbas of Assirus and Thessalonica, among others, but not for extensive areas. There was cultivation of barley, emmer and einkorn, millet, some legumes, as well as linseed and poppies. There was viticulture, but no olives. Animal-based foods were derived from beef, sheep and goats as well as pigs in about the same measure. During

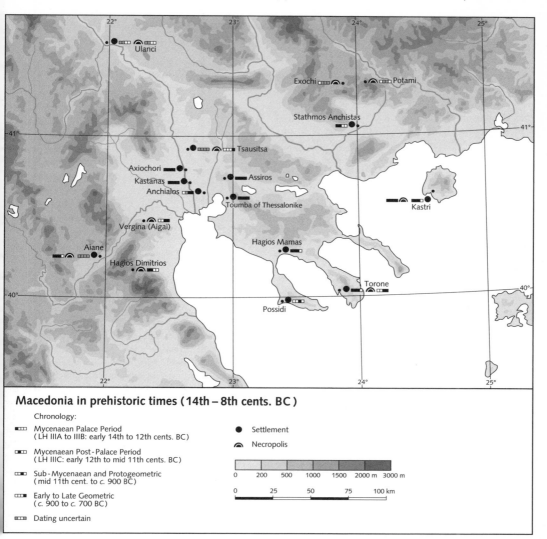

Macedonia in prehistoric times (14th – 8th cents. BC)

Chronology:

▪▫▫ Mycenaean Palace Period
      (LH IIIA to IIIB: early 14th to 12th cents. BC)

▪▫▫ Mycenaean Post-Palace Period
      (LH IIIC: early 12th to mid 11th cents. BC)

▫▫▫ Sub-Mycenaean and Protogeometric
      (mid 11th cent. to c. 900 BC)

▫▫▪ Early to Late Geometric
      (c. 900 to c. 700 BC)

▫▪▫ Dating uncertain

● Settlement

◠ Necropolis

0   200   500   1000   1500 2000 m 3000 m

0   25   50   75   100 km

the period of the Mycenaean palace states (→ Mycenaean culture and archaeology), an economic and eco-
logic crisis developed because of extensive monoculture
and overuse of animal resources which could only be
overcome very slowly (Kastanas).

Already before the middle of the 2nd millennium BC
there were contacts between the Peloponnese and M.:
Minyan ceramics in Hagios Mamas, a ring of gold wire
in Kastanas, early Mycenaean ceramics in → Torone on
the one hand, gifts in the pit graves of Mycenae of silver
from Chalcidice on the other hand. These contacts with
the south lead to an early acceptance of clay tile architecture in M., also, no later than the end of the 14th
cent., and to local productions of wheel-turned pottery
(in lesser numbers, when compared to the unpainted,
cut-decorated, incrusted or flat-painted handthrown
wares).

In the Bronze Age in western and northern M. the
dead were buried in box graves, in Castri on → Thasus

however there are low burial structures built for several
graves and in the north of eastern M. we find tumuli
(→ Tumulus). Traces of Mycenaean religious influences
are scant; we have but one anthropomorphous terracotta figurine from Ano Komi/Kosani and terracotta
animal figurines from Hagios Mamas.

The transition to the Iron Age at the end of the 2nd
millennium BC is characterized by strong regionaliza-
tion with varyingly intensive contacts to the Balkans
and to the southern Aegaean Sea. In Kastanas, e.g.
buildings change from southern clay brick to wooden
structures of Balcanic appearance. The extensive settlements in the flatlands at the foot of the Bronze Age
toumbas are characteristic for the Iron Age, e.g. Axiochori, Anchialos, Thessalonica.

Eating habits changed as the agrarian crises of the
late Bronze Age were overcome. Cattle became more
important than pigs, sheep and goats, gardens make
their appearance (Kastanas). Protogeometric ceramics

replaced the ceramics of Mycenaean style only slowly. An early Iron Age innovation is the so-called grey (wheel) ware.

Social inequality is seen in major differences in quality and quantity of bronze jewellery as well as iron weapons and implements of the graves in the tumuli of Vergina. While they are predominantly body burials, as well as those of Tsausitsa and also in the Iron Age burial structures of Kastri on Thasos, the necropolis of Torone is dominated by cremation burials. In the 'Iliad', the → Paeones, fighting under → Pyrichmes and → Asteropaeus on the side of the Trojans (Hom. Il. 2,848–850; 16,287–288; 21,140ff.), come from the wide-flowing Axius river, from Amydon (= Axiochori),.

ST. ANDREOU, M. FOTIADIS, K. KOTSAKIS, Review of Aegean Prehistory V: The Neolithic and Bronze Age of Northern Greece, in: AJA 100, 1996, 537–597; M. ANDRONIKOS, Βεργίνα. Tὸ νεκροταφεῖον τῶν τύμβων, 1969; W. A. HEURTLEY, Prehistoric Macedonia, 1939; B. HÄNSEL (ed.), Kastanas: Ausgrabungen in einem Siedlungshügel der Bronze- und Eisenzeit Makedoniens, 1975–1979, 6 vols. in the series: Prähistor. Arch. in Südosteuropa (PAS), 1983–1989; CH. KOUKOULI-CHRYSSANTHAKI, Προϊστορική Θάσος. Τα νεκροταφεία του οικισμού Καστρί. Δημοσιεύματα του αρχαιολογικού Δελτίου (supplement to AD) 45, 1992; D. MITREVSKI, Protoistoriskite zaednici vo Makedonija, 1997; J. K. PAPADOPOULOS, Euboians in Macedonia? A Closer Look, in: Oxford Journal of Archaeology 15, 1996, 151–181; K. RHOMIOPOULOU, I. KILIAN-DIRLMEIER, Neue Funde aus der eisenzeitlichen Hügelnekropole von Vergina, Griechisches Makedonien, in: PrZ 64, 1989, 86–151; Z. A. STOS-GALE, C. F. MACDONALD, Sources of Metals and Trade in the Bronze Age Aegean, in: N. H. GALE (ed.), Bronze Age Trade in the Mediterranean. Papers Presented at the Conference Held at Oxford in Dec. 1989 (Stud. in Mediterranean Archaeology 90), 1991, 249–288; K. A. WARDLE, Mycenaean Trade and Influence in Northern Greece, in: C. ZERNER et al. (ed.), Proc. of the International Conference Wace and Blegen. Pottery … 1939–1989, 1993, 117–141.   R.J.

B. ARCHAIC TO ROMAN PERIOD

The still sparse archaeological evidence comes primarily from central and eastern M. It includes dwellings with stone foundations and wooden walls, but also clay tile buildings (Axichori), later there are apsidal houses (Assirus). The most important information is presented by the necropoleis (e.g. Hagios Dimitrios, Sykia and Torone); they show tumuli (→ Tumulus) as their characteristic structure, body and cremation burials with numerous grave goods. Influences from the south of Greece as well as from central Europe and the Balkans can be noted. Ceramics show a continuation of the Bronze Age tradition. Parallel to the tradition, new kinds of ceramics are introduced: black ceramics with fluted decorations, grey wheelware with horizontal cannelures, matte ceramics mostly from western M. as well as protogeometric ceramics which extend to the 6th cent. BC. Weapons, mostly swords, are of iron, jewellery mostly of bronze: neck rings, violin-bow and spectacle fibulae, belt decorations, arm rings and pendants. Many patterns of jewellery remain in use into the 5th cent. BC. Settlements of the archaic and early classical periods usually are located on hills, as e.g. in → Aegae [1] (modern Vergina) and → Aeane. Later towns like → Pella prefer more level areas so that buildings, public places and sanctuaries can be on one level.

M. gained a growing degree of independence only in the classical period. In the 4th cent. BC in the field of metal work (→ Metallurgy) and production of → weapons, it became a leader, also in the field of → wall painting and → mosaic technology, – mostly by adaptation of primarily Attic art.

The most important form of burial was the chamber tomb [1]. Normally, it consists of an ante- and a main room; the ceiling is formed by a genuine → vault. The earliest examples date from the 2nd half of the 4th cent. BC and can be found in Vergina. → Grave painting, as developed in M., was unknown in southern Greece. The more elaborate chamber tombs have painted interiors as well as exteriors. Grave gifts consisted of vessels of precious and other metals, golden wreaths, carved ivory and → purple vestments.

Vergina, which now can be considered as clearly identified as the old Macedonian residence of → Aegae [1], was settled without interruption probably from about 1000 BC well into the Roman Imperial period. Remnants of the urban settlement explored thus far belong to the early 3rd cent. BC. To the southeast of the modern village the ruins of a two-storied palace were uncovered, probably from the 3rd cent. There are dining rooms and other representational rooms, whose mosaic floors partially still can be seen around a peristyle yard of 45m by 45m. Near the palace, remnants of a small sanctuary and of a rather small theatre were found. A field with more than 300 tumuli constitutes the necropolis of the period between 1000 and 700 BC. Many chamber tombs date from the 4th and 3rd cents., including the double-chambered so-called Tomb of Philip (fig. see → Funerary architecture) of 9,5 m by 4,5 m. Inside the grave, two golden larnakes (→ Sarcophagi; → Urn) were discovered. The larger one probably contained the skeletal remnants of Philip II of M. (see [2]). Next to the larnax was a large oak wreath of gold. The second, smaller larnax contained the cremated skeleton of a woman, wrapped in brocade material, as well as a fine golden diadem. Both rooms contained numerous burial gifts of gold, silver, iron and bronze, also splendid ivory objects: a magnificent shield, ornamented with glass and gold platelets, as well as ivory heads and reliefs which had decorated the wooden bases. The Tomb of Phillip is located near the Tomb of Persephone, which consists only of a very shallow covered chamber without a door, and the Princes' tomb, a double-chambered grave with a vaulted roof underneath a large tumulus of more than 110m diameter and 20m height.

→ Pella had been founded around 410 BC at the northern edge of the Macedonian plain and soon replaced Aegae as the capital of the Macedonian kingdom. A large agora of 250 m × 200 m was situated at the centre of a orthogonal pattern of streets with richly appointed residences, sanctuaries and fountains. Floor mosaics, executed in white, black and coloured natural pebbles, discovered in the houses show a wide variety of themes [3]. Some houses had painted walls. The oldest phase of an extensive palace complex in the north of town dates from the period of Philip II. Building continued in Pella up until the beginning of the 1st cent. BC. The town was abandoned in the 2nd cent. AD (→ Thessalonica).

→ Dion [II 2], located at the foot of Mount Olympus, was the southernmost town of the Macedonian kingdom and contained the most important sanctuary of M. Recent excavations exposed large portions of the well-preserved city wall, a Hellenistic and a Roman theatre, a stadium, several temples and remnants of the water supply. Outside of the town proper, several tombs of the Macedonian type were uncovered.

→ Aeane is located in Central M., southeast of Kozani on a hill. Several excavated large public buildings, an agora, a cistern and a large number of red-figured fragments suggest that Aeane was an important town even before the middle of the 5th cent. BC. Because of systematic destruction, i.e. the removal of stones after abandonment of the settlement in the 1st cent. BC, only few remnants of walls remain on the topmost level. The settlement hill is surrounded by extensive necropoleis and grouped burial sites. The burial sites are sometimes surrounded by walls. The three largest tombs show indications of a cult of the dead.

Lefkadia (ancient → Mieza) near → Beroea is one of the most important settlements at the western edge of the Macedonian plain; it possessed partial administrative autonomy even during Roman times. The existing ruins date from the Hellenistic period. The theatre from the 2nd cent. BC had about 1,500–2,000 seats. One building could be identified as the → Nymphaeum of the school of Aristotle. In the vicinity of Lefkadia six Macedonian chamber tombs from the Hellenistic period were discovered, with partially well-preserved paintings inside and out. The whole area indicates settlement was continuous from the late Bronze Age until the Roman period.

Near Derveni, to the northeast of Thessalonica, a Macedonian necropolis of the 4th and 3rd cents. BC is located. It appears that body and cremation burials were used simultaneously in chamber, box and pit tombs. The inside of the box and chamber tombs was stuccoed in the usual manner and painted with frescoes. Best known is the tumulus, established around 300 BC, which contained among the gifts a multipart silver table set, a bronze wine mixing vessel, richly decorated with plastic figures and reliefs (the so-called Derveni Crater), and the only papyrus of the classical period (4th cent. BC) found in Greece to-date (1964) with a commentary on Orphic teachings (→ Orphism) (the so-called Derveni papyrus).

Sindus to this date is only known by its necropolis. Most of the more than 100 graves can be dated from the archaic to the early classical period. Some burial sites, however, belong to the last quarter of the 5th cent. BC. Stone and wooden sarcophagi as well as boxes and simple earthen tombs were used without exception for individuals. Men were buried with the head towards the west, women with the head towards the east. Among the notable gifts there are golden masks and iron miniatures of furniture and carts. The area was not used as a necropolis in later times because pottery workshops with four kilns of the 4th cent. BC were discovered on the site.

With the building of the *via Egnatia* near the end of the 2nd cent. BC, the growing prosperity of Macedonian towns is shown in respect to population growth and economic progress. The capital of the Roman province of M., → Thessalonica, was subdivided into large *insulae*, a forum was built and the town was fortified with a wall. During the 2nd Tetrarchy (AD 305–306), there was a renewed period of prosperity: Thessalonica became the residence of the tetrarch Galerius [5] (palace, triumphal arch commemorating his victory over the Persians in AD 297, his mausoleum, expansion of the wall, hippodrome, splendid roads). Typical for the art of the period are portraits of dignitaries on funerary and honorary monuments. Similar aspects are also found in → Dion, → Beroea (funerary and honorary monuments, villas with floor mosaics as well as numerous inscriptions).

→ Philippi was elevated to colony status in 42 BC; Philippi was following Octavian's elevation to → Augustus; named Colonia Augusta Iulia Philippensium. Coinage is documented for this period, and there are splendid buildings: a forum and administrative buildings, thermal baths, gymnasium, theatre at the castle hill and villas. Sanctuaries and inscriptions near the end of the Roman period point to the existence of oriental and Egyptian cults of mysteries (e.g. Mithras). There is relatively early proof of Christianity. The Apostle → Paul visited the town in AD 49. The first Christian structure, dedicated to the Apostle Paul, was originally built at the hero's grave from Hellenistic time. The large basilica was constructed in the 6th cent. AD. The town lost much of its importance by earthquakes in the 6th and 7th cents., and by the incursions of barbarians in the 8th cent. AD.

→ Macedonia

1 B. GOSSEL, Maked. Kammergräber, thesis 1980 2 N. G. L. HAMMOND, The Royal Tombs at Vergina: Evolution and Identities, BSA 86, 1991, 69–82 3 D. SALZMANN, Unt. zu den antiken Kieselmosaiken, 1982; M. HATZOPOULOS, L. LOUKOPOULOS (ed.), Philipp von M., 1980; LAUFFER, Griechenland; I. VOKOTOPOULOU (ed.), Makedonen. Die Griechen des Nordens, 1994.; M. ANDRONICOS, Vergina. The Royal Tombs and the Ancient City, 1984; A. PEKRIDOU-GORECKI, Zum Fries des sogenannten Philippsgrab in Vergina, in: F. BLAKOLMER et al. (ed.), Fremde Zeiten. FS J. Borchhardt, vol. 2, 1996, 89–103.; PH. PETSAS, Pella. Alexander the Great's Capi-

tal, 1978.; D. PANDERMALIS, Ανασκαφή Δίου, in: To αρχαιο- λογικό έργο στη Μακεδονία και Θράκη 5, 1991, 137–144.; K. SIAMOPOULOS, Αιανή. Ιστορία – Τοπογραφία – Αρχαιολογία, 1974.; K. RHOMIOPOULOU, Lefkadia. Ancient Mieza, 1997.; P. THEMELIS, G. TOU-RATSOGLOU, Οι τάφοι τού Δερβενίου, 1997.; I. VOKOTO-POULOU et al., Σίνδος. Exhibiton catalogue, 1985.   H.v.M.

Macedonian A reliable verdict on the character and origins of Macedonian is hardly possible (μακεδονίζειν/ *makedonízein* 'to speak Macedonian', μακεδονιστί/ *makedonistí* 'in Macedonian') as it only survives in small fragments. In spite of a few recently found inscriptions possibly composed in Macedonian (among them a → *defixio* from Pella, 4th cent. BC), for now we depend entirely on the vocabulary left to us by Greek lexicographers and historians including around 140 glosses which were designated as Macedonian or used as such, which in part come from the collection of → Amerias, in addition to names of people of Macedonian origin as well as toponyms and hydronyms from ancient Macedon.

The Macedonian linguistic heritage can be divided *grosso modo* into two groups: the first includes words and names, which – even though they differ to varying degrees in phonology, word formation or meaning – have counterparts in Greek, e.g. Macedonian σαυτορία/ *sautoría* 'salvation', corresponding to Greek σωτηρία/ *sōtēría*; Macedonian ἰνδέα/*indéa* 'midday', cf. Greek ἔνδιος/*endios* 'at midday'; Macedonian ἀκρουνοί/ *akrounoí* 'boundary stones', cf. Greek ἄκρον/*ákron* 'point, end'; Macedonian ἀργίπους/*argípous* 'eagle', cf. Homeric Greek ἀργίπους/*argípous* 'fleet-footed'; Macedonian νικάτωρ/*nikátōr* 'victor' as a Hellenistic ruler title, in the plural as honorary designation of the royal Macedonian body guard (Akkadian *nicatoras*, Liv. 43,19,11), cf. Greek νικητήρ/*nikētḗr*; furthermore names that can be interpreted via the Greek, e.g. personal name Macedonian Ἀλέξανδρος/*Aléxandros* (already Mycenaean fem. *a-re-ka-sa-da-ra*), Macedonian Πτολεμαῖος/*Ptolemaîos* (already Homeric), place name Macedonian Εἰδομένη/*Eidoménē* and the river name Macedonian Ἁλιάκμων/*Haliákmōn*.

This group certainly contains loanwords from Greek, but only two layers of them are conceivable, one of them relatively young, which contains e.g. military technical terms such as ἑταῖροι/*hetaîroi* 'members of the royal cavalry troop', and another with only superficially Macedonized Greek names such as the personal name Macedonian Βίλιππος/*Bílippos* for Greek Φίλιππος/*Phílippos*, Macedonian Βερενίκα/*Bereníka* for Greek Φερενίκη/*Phereníkē*; place name Macedonian Βέροια/*Béroia* for Greek Φέροια/*Phéroia*. This points us to a phonetic characteristic of Macedonian which had already been noticed in antiquity: Macedonian β δ γ, probably [b d g], correspond to Greek φ θ χ [pʰ tʰ kʰ], thus they show voicing and the loss of aspiration of the Greek sound, e.g. Macedonian κεβαλά/ *kebalá*, κεβαλή/*kebalḗ* 'head', corresponding to Greek κεφαλή/*kephalḗ*; Macedonian ἀδῆ/*adê* 'heaven', corresponding to Greek αἰθήρ/*aithḗr*.

Words and names which do not look Greek belong to a second group, which might be connected to other Indo-European languages, thus possibly ἀβροῦτες/ *abroûtes* 'eyebrows', with -*t*-extension corresponding to early Avestan *bruuat̰.biiạm* (dat. dual) 'eyebrows' (unless corrupted from ἀβροῦϜες/*abroûFes* and then belonging to the first group), and in part appear non-Indo-European, e.g. ἄβαγνα/*ábagna* 'roses'; βαβρήν/ *babrḗn* 'olive oil sediment'.

Accordingly, the opinions on the genetic classification of Macedonian differ greatly; yet it is not disputed that it is a language of Indo-European origin. Unless it is seen as an independent Indo-European language, a connection to Macedonian's neighbouring languages, such as Illyrian or Thracian (which of course are just as inadequately known as Macedonian itself), is sought or – more often – to → Greek, in that it is either seen as being close to Greek or its sister language, or that a Greek dialect *sui generis* is seen in it whose relationships to other Greek dialects (including Thessalian or northwest Greek dialects) then are judged in various ways. The predominantly Greek character of Macedonian personal names and vocabulary could support the theory for an 'archaic dialect, close to that of the Greek »mountain tribes«', a dialect 'which, split off early, received foreign traits from the foreign surroundings and lower classes' [5. 70]. The non-Greek aspects of Macedonian vocabulary would then possibly be attributed to the adstrate or substrate languages (including Illyrian, Thracian), with whom Macedonian came into contact when penetrating new territory.

Undoubtedly Macedonian became more and more Hellenized in a long-lasting process, which first involved the upper classes, until it was completely replaced by Greek and died out. It is not possible to ascertain when this happened. Ancient Macedonian has no relationship with modern Macedonian, which along with Bulgarian belongs to the eastern group of the southern Slavonic languages.

→ Balkan peninsula, Languages (with map); → Greek (I. B.)

1 C. BRIXHE, A. PANAYOTOU, Le macédonien, in: F. BADER, Langues indo-européennes, 1994, 205–220 2 O. HOFFMANN, Die Makedonen, ihre Sprache und ihr Volkstum, 1906 3 J. N. KALLÉRIS, Les anciens Macédoniens. Ét. linguistique et historique, vol. 1, 1954; vol. 2,1, 1976 4 R. KATIČIĆ, Ancient Languages of the Balkans, vol. 1, 1976, 100–116 5 SCHWYZER, Gramm., 69–71.   C.H.

Macedonian dynasty Byzantine dynasty AD 867–1056, founded by → Basilius [5] I, who hailed from the province (*théma*) of Macedonia, after the murder of Michael III (→ Amorian dynasty). Basilius was succeeded in 886 by his second son Leo [9] VI (until 912), who was in turn first succeeded by his brother Alexander [20] (until 913), then his son Constantinus [9] VII (913–959; b. 905). Initially, various regents reigned in place of the young Constantine, then, from 920 onwards, his father-in-law Romanus I; only from January 945 did Constantine reign in his own right. His son Romanus II died early (in 963), leaving as his successor the underaged Basilius [6] II, for whom two emperors from other families – Nicephorus II and Iohannes [35] I – ruled until 976. When Basilius died childless in 1025, he was succeeded by his brother Constantine [10] VIII (until 1028). With the latter, the dynasty died out in the male line. Constantinus' daughter and heiress → Zoe, who died childless in 1050, passed the rule first to her first husband Romanus III, then to her second one Michael IV, then to her adopted son Michael V and finally to her third husband Constantinus [11] IX. (1042–1055). The latter was succeeded by → Theodora, Zoe's younger sister, whose death in 1056 marks the end of the dynasty.

The early Macedonian emperors made a considerable contribution to the reorganization of the Byzantine state by streamlining the administration, reforming the legislation and expanding the army, but also by promoting culture by going back to late-antique traditions. In visual arts, the controversial term → 'Macedonian Renaissance' has been coined, which can be transferred to the literary culture only with inclusion of important new impulses before and during the Amorian dynasty. In its foreign policy, the Macedonian dynasty (including the 'interim emperors') was very successful, especially in its wars against the → Arabs and the Bulgarians, who had been Christianized from 864 (→ Bulgari). Internally, the Macedonian emperors of the 10th cent. tried – ultimately unsuccessfully – to stem the growth of → large estates/ latifundia. This was one of the reasons why in the 11th cent. Constantinople's power as the centre of the empire waned; paradoxically, this boosted rather than hampered a renewed blossoming of culture, trade and commerce.

→ Constantinople; → Macedonian Renaissance

ODB 2, 1262f.; P. Schreiner, Byzanz, ¹1986, ²1994.
F.T.

Macedoniani Initially the term for the Arian factions (→ Arianism) gathered in the mid 4th cent. around bishop Macedonius of Constantinople († before AD 364). Later the name is applied to the → *pneumatomáchoi*, i.e. all those, also non-Arians, who deny the divinity of the Holy Spirit. The eponymous Macedonius – initially in constant competition with the Nicene bishop Paulus who had been exiled on several occasions – became bishop of Constantinople in 342. After Paulus' final expulsion (in 351), sole bishop; Macedonius supported the Arian church party of the Homoiousians (key statement: ὅμοιος κατ᾽ οὐσίαν/*hómoios kat'ousían*, 'the son is similar in nature to the father'), on whose side he took part in the Synod of Seleucea (in 359). Shortly afterwards a synod meeting in Constantinople deposed him in 360. The sources provide only vague information about the use of the term Macedoniani. It was probably

used at first for the party-liners of the Homoiousian type who stayed in Constantinople and the immediate vicinity after the dismissal of Macedonius. Noticeable for the first time in the West (*Tomus Damasi* [1]; cf. Jer. Chron. ad ann. 342), the Pneumatomachians are also called Macedoniani from 380 (thus [3. 41; 2. 237]; with Cod. Theod. 16,5,11 [4. 1073] insisted on 383), and the older name is visibly superseded. The Pneumatomachian ideas that were already on hand around 360 in the circle surrounding Macedonius probably form the background [2. 238].

1 EOMIA 1, 285 2 W.-D. Hauschild, Die Pneumatomachen, thesis Hamburg 1967, 236–239 3 F. Loofs, s.v. Macedonius und die Macedonianer, Realencyclopädie für protestantische Theologie und Kirche 12, ³1903 (repr. 1971), 41–48 4 P. Meinhold, s.v. Pneumatomachoi, RE 21, 1066–1101, esp. 1067–1078 5 W. Telfer, Paul of Constantinople, in: Harvard Theological Rev. 43, 1950, 31–92.
J.RI.

Macedonian Renaissance
A. Characteristics B. Literature C. Law

A. Characteristics
In Byzantine art history, Macedonian Renaissance (MR) usually refers to the classicist revival that took place mostly during the → Macedonian dynasty (867–1056). It takes its name from its founder emperor → Basilius [5] I (867–886), who was born in the *thema* of Macedonia. During that time Byzantium experienced its greatest expansion since Justinian. However, indications for a cultural Renaissance (including art) can be found as early as under Theophilus (829–842) (cf. the philosopher → Leon [10]) and especially under → Michael III (842–867; *Kaîsar* → Bardas 855/6 re-established the school in the Magnaura palace).

B. Literature
Three key figures dominate this period. With his so-called *Bibliothḗkē*, patriarch → Photius (c. 810–893) provided an extensive description of the books he had read (279 codices with information on 386 works) and thus created a mine of information pertaining to the literary history of many ancient works now lost. His gift for philological exegesis also comes through in his 329 *Amphilóchia*, where he discusses a wide range of biblical and theological issues. His 'Lexicon' was intended as a practical aid for writing and for reading ancient authors, esp. the Old Comedy, of which it had preserved many fragments.

→ Arethas, archbishop of Caesarea in Cappadocia (mid 9th cent. to 932/944), often had a significant role in the tradition of classical and Christian authors: he had MSS copied (and occasionally added scholia himself). At least eight of them have survived; they include Euclides [3], Plato (24 dialogues), Aristotle [6] ('Organon'), Lucian, Aelius Aristides [3], Christian apologetes (Clemens [3] of Alexandria, Justin, etc.), ecclesiastical law and theological treatises with Ps.-Aristotle.

Probably one of the most significant achievements of the emperor → Konstantinos [1] VII Porphyrogennetus (905–959) is the encyclopaedic compendium (53 entries, extant only in fragments) in which he systematically codified ancient and Byzantine knowledge on various subjects (history, reports of envoys, medicine, → Hippiatrica, agriculture, zoology, etc.).

The classicist tendencies of this period are reflected in poetry composed in the ancient style and in the arrangement of the *Anthologia Palatina* (→ Anthology [1]), a magnificent collection of ancient and early Byzantine → epigrams and poems, compiled by Konstantinos Kephalas around 900, expanded *c.* 50 years later and divided into 15 bks. Worth mentioning is further the → Suda, a gigantic 'encyclopaedia' of *c.* 30,000 lemmata, created at the end of the 10th cent.

In the first decades of the MR the *metacharaktērismós* was completed, i.e. the 'transliteration' of → majuscule MSS into → minuscule (first example 835). Noteworthy is the so-called philosophical collection (mid 9th cent.) comprising at least 12 codices mostly of philosophical content (Plato and Aristotle, including commentators, as well as one book with geographic, paradoxographic and epistolographic texts). Palaeographic and codicological considerations suggest they should be attributed to a single scriptorium, probably in Constantinople. Many important MSS (among them archetypes) of the tradition of classical authors date to the MR as well.

C. LAW

In this period the Justinianic Law was revived for political and administrative reasons and (supposedly) 'purged' of texts from the Isaurian period (→ Isaurian emperors): to the early Macedonian period belong i.a. the *Prócheiros Nómos* (between 870–879 or rather 907; private law including criminal law and distribution of war booty), the *Epanagogé*, (*Eisagōgḗ* not promulgated; including public law), which goes back to the patriarch Photius, the *Basiliká* (a systematization and collection of the Justinianic *Corpus Iuris* in Greek, completed and published by → Leo [9] VI in the first years of his government) and the collection of amendments (decrees) compiled under Leo VI. Afterwards, i.a. the *Epitome legum* (920; a compilation of legal literature from the 6th to the 9th cents.) and a series of compendia and commentaries, esp. on the *Basiliká*, were created. Relevant for ecclesiastical law is the compilation of the *Syntagma canonum* (882/3). Finally, historiography (→ Georgius [5] Monachos, → Symeon Logothetes, → Leon [11] Diakonos), hagiography (the → *Menologion* of Symeon Metaphrastes) and some evidence for popular literature should be mentioned as well.

→ Textual history

P. LEMERLE, Le premier humanisme byzantin, 1971; W. TREADGOLD, The Macedonian Renaissance, in: Id., (ed.), Renaissances before the Renaissance, 1984, 75–98; N. G. WILSON, Scholars of Byzantium, ²1996, 79–147.
P.E.

Macedonian Wars The name given to the three wars between Rome and the Macedonian kings → Philippus V (215–205 and 200–197 BC) and → Perseus (171–168).

A. THE FIRST MACEDONIAN WAR B. THE SECOND MACEDONIAN WAR C. THE THIRD MACEDONIAN WAR

A. THE FIRST MACEDONIAN WAR

The origin of the First Macedonian War lies in the competing interests of the two powers on the Adriatic-Illyrian coast. In 229/8, Rome conducted a successful war against the Illyrian kingdom of queen → Teuta in order to suppress → piracy, and established friendly relations with cities, tribes and dynasts in this region. In 219, a conflict developed between Rome and one of these dynasts, Demetrius of Pharus, resulting in the expulsion of the latter. In 217 → Philippus V tried to restore him to power as part of his politics to regain control of the Illyrian Adriatic coast, but in 216 he retreated when faced with the threat of a Roman naval intervention. The immediate cause of war was the co-operation agreement of 215 between → Hannibal [4] and Philip (Stv III 528). Rome tried to control the opposite Italian Adriatic coast by stationing a naval squadron in Oricus; furthermore, after Philip's capture of Lissus in 212 or 211, it entered into an alliance with the Aetolian League (Stv III 536; see → Aetolians, with map), which together with Sparta, Elis, and Messenia was already engaged in a war against Philip. After Aetolia's withdrawal from the war contrary to the contract in 206, Rome, too, broke off the war and concluded the peace treaty of Phoenice (Stv III 543: summer 205) on the basis of the status quo (thus, the territory of the Illyrian Atintanians remained in the Macedonian sphere of influence), in order to concentrate all forces on the final battle against Hannibal.

B. THE SECOND MACEDONIAN WAR

After the end of the Second Punic War (→ Punic Wars), Rome resumed the battle against Philip V despite the initial resistance of the people's assembly following some diplomatic preparations in Greece (autumn 200). Thus, it intervened in a conflict within the system of → Hellenistic states, which had been caused by the death of → Ptolemaeus IV (d. 204) and the resulting weakness of the Ptolemaic kingdom. Philip V and → Antiochus [5] III had begun to conquer the minor Ptolemaic territories, such as Koile Syria and scattered territories in Asia Minor and the Aegaean, and to this end had entered into a co-operation agreement (Stv III 547). Philip V took hold of the straits and western Asia Minor; he had come into conflict with a coalition under the leadership of → Attalus [4] I of Pergamum and Rhodes, in the spring of 200 joined by Athens, which was already at war with Philip for different reasons. Already at the end of 201, an Attalid-Rhodian legation had tried to get Rome involved in the war with reference to the

Macedonian-Seleucid treaty and was favourably received.

The Roman motives are controversial (a list of research opinions in [8. vol. 2, 382ff.]). M. HOLLEAUX' [11. 306ff.] hypothesis that the fear of a shift of power due to the impending division of the Ptolemaic kingdom had motivated Rome to enter the war is questionable. Aside from the fact that the existence [12] or the content [4; 5] of the Macedonian-Seleucid treaty is contentious: Rome was not interested in whether the balance of power in the eastern Mediterranean was upset, but solely in a reason to go to war against Philip, a reason which could not be deduced from the Phoenice peace treaty. It is clear that Rome did not take up arms in order to aid threatened allies, nor can the hypothesis [11] that Rome wanted to restore its reputation, damaged in the First Macedonian War in the eyes of the Greeks, be seen as sufficient motivation. Territorial demands and the gaining of fame and spoils of war were even less motivation (even though the latter may have favoured the disposition to decide for war [9]), and for sure Rome did not act for fear of the Macedonian power.

The main political motive was probably the intention to continue the war that had been interrupted by the peace of Phoenice with the aim to reduce Macedonia, like → Carthage, to the status of a medium-sized power no longer able to wage large-scale war. This could only be achieved by war, because it was obvious from the start that Philip would not be able to accept the ultimatum, which had first been passed to him indirectly, then directly in the summer of 200, demanding of him to cease all armed hostilities against Greeks and to submit to impartial arbitration in all matters of dispute with Attalus and Rhodes (Pol. 16,27–34). The military operations, started in the autumn of 200, brought no decision in the first two years of the war. Only in the summer of 198, T. → Quinctius Flamininus successfully forced Philip to abandon his blocking position at the river Aous near Antigonea and in October he achieved that the Achaean League switched allegiances (→ Achaeans, with map); the Aetolian League had already joined the anti-Macedon league in 199. The peace negotiations in the Locrian city of Nicaea in the winter of 198/7 remained without results because of the exaggerated demands by Rome's Greek allies. For that reason, the decision was reached in battle near Cynoscephalae in June 197 (cf. map in → Aetolians). Flamininus prevailed against Aetolian demands for the destruction of Macedonia in preserving the latter, but Philip was forced to give up all Greek possessions (Thessaly with Demetrias, Corinth and Chalcis), to surrender his fleet of six ships and to pay war reparations of 1,000 talents.

C. THE THIRD MACEDONIAN WAR

The 'freedom for all Greeks' proclaimed by Flamininus in the spring of 196 BC brought Roman eastern foreign politics into a field of tension between Philhellenism and (informal) hegemony (fundamental on this [6]; cf. [2]) got it involved in the complicated problems resulting from the realization of the principle of Greek freedom, i.a. in the war against Antiochus [5] III. (190–188). Rome was called upon to mediate in numerous internal and bilateral conflicts within the Greek world; it became unavoidable that discontentment grew, regardless of whether Rome declined the requested intervention or whether it decided upon a solution, which would disappoint at least one of the parties involved.

On the other hand, Macedonia recovered from its defeat and increased its status within Greece, especially after Perseus' accession to the throne in 179 BC. Many Greeks – e.g. in Thessaly, Boeotia and Aetolia set high hopes on the new king – and even the Achaean League considered an alliance with him. Perseus was careless enough to march an army – though in peaceful intent – to Delphi and to demonstrate his powers there (174). The virulent Roman mistrust was further stirred up in 172 by complaints and slander from → Eumenes [3] II of Pergamum. In any case, there had been an increasing inclination in Rome to evade the problems resulting from its hegemonic position by using its military power (brilliantly analyzed in [10]). Rome prepared the ground for war with diplomacy and propaganda (the proclamation of war, published in Delphi, is partially extant: Syll.³ 643). Without a valid legal reason, Rome went to war with the aim to destroy the potential rival, the presumed cause of the problems within the Greek sphere. Perseus was refused peace. After a lengthy successful defensive campaign, he was crushingly defeated by L. → Aemilius [I 32] Paullus in the battle of Pydna on 22 June 168. The Macedonian monarchy and the unity of the country were both abolished. Macedonia was split into four independent regions with the main settlements of Amphipolis, Thessalonica, Pella and Pelagonia. The four republics were forbidden to engage in → conubium and → commercium and to use their most important natural resources (mining for precious metals and wood for ship building) (Liv. 45,18), but still Rome refrained from annexations.

→ Macedonia, Macedones

1 E. BADIAN, Notes on Roman Policy in Illyria (230–201 B.C.), in: PBSR 20, 1952, 72–93   2 ID., Titus Quinctius Flamininus. Philhellenism and Realpolitik, 1970   3 CAH 8² (with sources)   4 R. M. ERRINGTON, The Alleged Syro-Macedonian Pact and the Origins of the Second Macedonian War, in: Athenaeum 49, 1971, 336–354   5 Id., Antiochos III., Zeuxis und Euromos, in: EA 8, 1986, 1–8   6 J.-L. FERRARY, Philhellénisme et impérialisme, 1988   7 H. G. GEHRKE, Geschichte des Hell., 1990, 110–112, 114ff., 206f., 208ff.   8 GRUEN, Rome   9 HARRIS 10 W. HOFFMANN, Die römische Politik des 2. Jh. und das Ende Karthagos, in: Historia 9, 1960, 309–344 11 M. HOLLEAUX, Rome, la Grèce et les monarchies hellénistiques au IIIᵉᵐᵉ siècle, 1921   12 D. MAGIE, The 'Agreement' between Philip V and Antiochos III for the Partition of the Egyptian Empire, in: JRS 29, 1939, 32–44 13 L. RADITSA, Bella Macedonica, in: ANRW I/1, 1972, 564–589   14 F. W. WALBANK, The Causes of the Third Macedonian War: Recent Views, in: Archaia Makedonia 2, 1977, 81–94.   K. BR.

Macedonicus Victor's epithet of Q. → Caecilius [I 27] Metellus M. (*cos.* 143 BC). K.-L.E.

Macedonius (Μακεδόνιος; *Makedónios*).
[1] Author of a → paean to Apollo and Asclepius passed down to us in inscriptions (1st cent. BC) in Delphi, created perhaps already around 300 BC [1; 2], in dactylic metre [3]. Probably not identical with M. [2] (thus still [4]). The content and structure of the paean closely follow the → Erythraean paean and → Isyllus; cf. → Ariphron.

> 1 W. PEEK, Att. Versinschr. (Abhandlungen der Sächsischen Akademie der Wiss. Leipzig, Philol.-histor. Klasse 69/2), 1980, 45f. (Text) 2 L. KÄPPEL, Paian, 1992, 200–206, 383f. (text, translation, interpretation, bibliography) 3 M. WEST, Greek Metre, 1982, 141 4 U. V. WILAMOWITZ-MOELLENDORFF, Griechische Verskunst, 1921, 133 n. 1. L.K.

[2] M. of Thessalonica. Epigrammatist of the 'Garland' of Philippus, of which three poems are extant: the ethnicon is only mentioned in the lemma of the sharp and vicious epigram Anth. Pal. 11,39; this could therefore suggest that another poet is the author of the colourless epigrams 9,275 and 11,27. Identification with the homonymous M. [1] (Coll. Alex. 138–140 = Paean 41 KÄPPEL), however, remains a hypothesis that is based on the rarity of the name M. in the period of → Philippus of Thessalonica (1st cent. AD).

> 1 L. KÄPPEL, Paian, 1992 2 GA II.1, 286f.; 2,317–319.

[3] High official at the imperial court, honorary consul (*cos. honorarius*), perhaps identifiable with a *curator dominicae domus* of AD 531. Elegant epigrammatist, probably communicated with → Paulus Silentiarios, who in Anth. Pal. 7,604 mentions a twelve-year-old girl (according to the lemma the daughter of Paulus) by the name of Macedonia. A total of 41 poems in the 'Cycle' of Agathias are extant: votive and love epigrams, as well as epideictic, protreptic, sympotic and satirical epigrams. M. does not know the funerary epigram: Anth. Pal. 7,566 is only a gloomy reflection on the *conditio humana*. The praises of love are sung with reference to traditional themes of the Hellenistic and particularly the Meleagrian epigram (apart from the one about pederasty): the inconstancy of woman (Anth. Pal. 5,247: the female protagonist of the poem bears the antiphrastic name *Parmenís*, 'Constancy'), arrows and wounds (5,224: a sober individual distichon, with which M., who normally writes six, eight or ten verses, beseeches Eros to stop shooting at him; 5,225, whose first verse became a proverb, cf. Apostolius, Coll. paroemiorum 7,3), the disfiguring effect of age (5,271, but in 5,227 he maintains emphatically that he as a lover will bear the 'tendril of wrinkles' of the beloved, cf. Paulus Silentiarios, Anth. Pal. 5,258).
The influence of Leonidas [3] of Tarentum is obvious in the votive epigrams, that of Palladas in the gnomic-satirical epigrams (cf. Anth. Pal. 10,71; 11,375), that of

Nonnus and above all of Homer (who is mentioned occasionally, cf. Anth. Pal. 9,625; 11,380) especially in the sympotic poems. M. handles the *imitatio* (together with the mythological cultural heritage a fundamental component of the epigram in the Justinianic period, cf. → Epigram I. G.) with sophisticated mastery, is not averse to neologisms and has real flashes of inspiration from time to time (cf. also Anth. Pal. 11,58; 11, 366).

> J. A. MADDEN, Macedonius Consul. The Epigrams, 1995 (ed., Engl. transl., comm.); Av. and A. CAMERON, The Cycle of Agathias, in: JHS 86, 1966, 17; B. BALDWIN, The Fate of Macedonius Consul, in: Eranos 79, 1981, 145–146; I. G. GALLI CALDERINI, Tradizione e struttura retorica negli epigrammi di Macedonio Console, in: Koinonia 9, 1985, 53–66. M.G.A.

[4] In AD 381 *comes sacrarum largitionum* (Cod. Theod. 11,30,39), by 382 → *magister officiorum*. He supported the Priscillianists (→ Priscillianus), which brought him into conflict with → Ambrosius. He protected fugitive members of the compulsory corporation of the *mancipes salinarum* ('salt leaseholders') from prosecution (Symmachus, Relat. 44). After the death of → Gratianus [2] he was accused and arrested (Symmachus, Relat. 36), although he attempted to take refuge in a church. Nothing is known about any sentence imposed on him.

> CLAUSS, 91, 167; PLRE 1, 526, 3. K.G.-A.

[5] *Vicarius Africae* in AD 413/14 (Possidius, Vita Augustini 20) and correspondence partner of → Augustinus (Aug. Epist. 152–155). M. issued an edict against the Donatists (ibid. 155,17; → Donatus [1]) and received from Augustine the first three books of the work *De civitate Dei* (ibid. 154, 2). PLRE 2, 697. K.P.J.

Macella (Μάκελλα/*Mákella*; Latin Macela, ILS 65, l. 4). Sicilian inland city, cannot be located. After the naval victory of Mylae in 260 BC, captured by C. → Duilius [1], in the Second → Punic War at times on the Punic side, in the Slave War in 102 BC a military base of Athenion [2]. Plin. HN 3,91 counts the *Magellini* among the *stipendiarii*. Evidence: Pol. 1,24,2; Liv. 26,21; Diod. Sic. 23,4,2; Cass. Dio fr. 93,4; Ptol. 3,4,14.

> BTCGI 9, 300–304. GI.F.

Macellum
A. TERMINOLOGY, DEFINITION AND TYPOLOGY
B. ORIGINS: ROME AND ITALY C. THE PROVINCES

A. TERMINOLOGY, DEFINITION AND TYPOLOGY
The term *macellum* is first attested in Plautus; we can assume that it is probably the Latinized version of the Greek word μάκελλος/*mákellos* ('market') which, however, was not used to refer to this institution before the Roman conquest of Greece and only rarely afterwards. A *macellum* was a public complex of buildings, which,

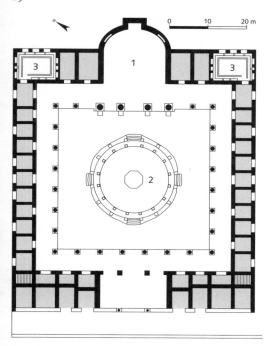

Puteoli (modern Pozzuoli): remains of macellum
(ground–plan).

1 Exedra
2 Tholos
3 Latrines

Multistorey porticoes
with shops (tabernae)

like a courtyard, was enclosed by walls. Along to the
walls, in most cases behind a portico, were little shops
or allotments for vendors. The courtyard was frequently quadratic, but could also be rectangular or
round. A central monument is often placed in the centre
of the courtyard, either a → tholos (see fig. no. 2) with
statues, a fountain or a water basin. DE RUYT distinguished two types of *macella*: 1. *macella* with a centre-
oriented ground plan in which the shops and porticoes
are evenly arranged around the courtyard (e.g. Corinth,
Cuicul), 2. axially oriented *macella*, in which the side
opposite the entrance is emphasized. This was often
achieved with a – sometimes apsidial – → exedra (see
fig. no. 1), flanked by large columns (e.g. Pompeii,
Puteoli, see fig., Thamugadi). Both types were already
known in Italy in Republican times. The *macellum* was
a grocery market, especially for meat, fish and specialty
foods, which were sold by individual merchants at
shops they rented. In that respect the *macellum* complemented the → forum. Although the model for the
macellum was probably the commercial, mercantile
→ agora of the Hellenistic cities, the size and function of
the *macellum* remained limited in comparison, because
the wholesale trade that was common at the *agoraí* was
not allowed here.

B. ORIGINS: ROME AND ITALY

It is probable that the *macellum* as a type was developed in Italy. The first *macellum* mentioned was erected
in Rome in the 2nd half of the 3rd cent. BC near the
Forum Romanum (Plaut. Aul. 264; 373; Pseud. 169;
Rud. 979; Amph. 1012; Liv. 27,11,16). Its purpose was
apparently to shift commerce away from the political
and religious centre. It remained the only *macellum* in
Rome until Augustus erected the *Macellum Liviae* and
Nero the *Macellum Magnum*; the old *macellum* was
subsequently overbuilt by Vespasian's *Forum Pacis*.
Italian *macella* were already erected in other cities in
Republican times; the earliest belong to the 2nd half of
the 2nd cent. BC (Pompeii, first phase, Morgantina,
Aletrium, Alba Fucens); more followed in the 1st cent.
BC (Brundisium, Firmum); the *macella* of Saepinum
and Puteoli date to the Imperial period.

C. THE PROVINCES

Most of the provincial *macella* were found in North
Africa, a fact that is explained by the large number of
relatively well preserved city facilities. The earliest
macellum here is found in → Leptis Magna (Augustan).
The majority was erected in the 2nd cent. AD and later
under the reign of Septimius Severus (e.g. Hippo
Regius, Thamugadi, Gightis). In the western and northern provinces, the existence of *macella* can in most cases
only be proven epigraphically; few facilities have been
archaeologically secured (e.g. Baelo, Viroconium and
Aquincum). In the east, *macella* have been preserved
mainly in Anatolia, dating from the 2nd cent. AD (e.g.
Aezani, Sagalassus, Perge). A total of about 80 *macella*
from all parts of the Roman Empire are known, attest-
ing the Romanization of the Mediterranean world. In
many places they were used into late antiquity. In Constantinople some *macella* were still in use as late as the
5th and 6th cents. AD.

A. BOËTHIUS, J. B. WARD-PERKINS, Etruscan and Roman
Architecture, 1970, *passim*; N. NABERS, Macella. A Study
in Roman Archaeology, thesis Princeton 1967; Id., The
Architectural Variations of the M., in: OpRom 9, 1973,
173–176; C. DE RUYT, M. Marché alimentaire des
Romains, 1983; J. B. WARD-PERKINS, From Republic to
Empire: Reflections on the Early Provincial Architecture
in the Roman West, in: JRS 55, 1970, 1–19.   I.N.

Macer

[1] **Licinius M., C.** see → Licinius [I 30]
[2] **Licinius M. Calvus, C.** see → Licinius [I 31]
[3] Correspondent of the younger → Plinius (Plin. Ep.
6,24). Probably identical to P. Calpurnius [II 11].
[4] [– – –]**cius Macer** *Cos. suff.* in AD 100 [1. 45, 94];
identification with other senators who bear the name
M. during this period is not possible: M., *curator viae
Appiae* in 95; M., Imperial legate in Dalmatia in 98; M.,
proconsul in Baetica. For the identification of this person, cf. also M. [3] and Q. Baebius [II 10] Macer, *cos.
suff.* in 103 and consular legate in the province of Dacia
in 113 (unpublished diploma).

1 FO² 2 W. Eck, s.v. Macer, RE Suppl. 14, 271f.
3 PIR² M 12–14.   W.E.

[5] Q. Baebius M. see → Baebius [II 10]

Maceria, Maceries see → Masonry

Macestus, Mecestus (Μέγιστος; *Mégistos*). Aside from the → Rhyndacus and the Tarsius, the largest river in northern Mysia (cf. Str. 12,8,11; Plin. HN 5,142; Pol. 5,77,8), modern Simav Çayı that like the Tarsius flows into the Rhyndacus north of → Miletupolis. → Attalus [4] I was encamped on the M., north of the Pelecas Mountains with the Galatian Aegosages on his campaign against Achaeus [5], when he experienced a lunar eclipse on 1 January 218 BC. A relief of Apollo Mekastenos is probably also reminiscent of this river [1].

1 F.W. Hasluck, Unpublished Inscriptions from the Cyzicus Neighbourhood, in: JHS 24, 1904, 20, no. 1.

A. Philippson, Reisen und Forschungen im westlichen Kleinasien 3 (Petermanns Geogr. Mitt. Ergh. 177), 1913, 3; L. Robert, Études Anatoliennes, 1937, 187 (repr. 1970); W. Ruge, s.v. M., RE 14, 773.   E.SCH.

Machaereus see→ Neoptolemus

Machaerion (Μαχαιρίων; *Machairíōn*). Name of the Spartan (or Mantinaean) who is said to have killed → Epaminondas in the battle of → Mantinaea (in 362 BC) (Paus. 8,11,5; the Athenian → Gryllus [2], who is also mentioned there, is ruled out as the perpetrator as he had, according to Ephorus, already fallen in battle: FGrH 70 F 85). According to Diodorus (15,86), Epaminondas was killed 'with a spear' (*dórati*) in the middle of the battle; Plutarch (Agesilaus 35), basing his views on the epigrammatist Dioscorides, however, mentions an Anticrates whose descendants call themselves *Machairíones* and who probably was given the honorary epithet M. because he had killed Epaminondas 'with a sword' (*machaírai*).   BO.D.

Machaerus (Μαχαιροῦς/*Machairoûs*, Hebrew M^ekawar, M^ekabar). Fortress situated east of the Dead Sea in southern Peraea, on the border with the Nabataean kingdom (→ Nabataei) which → Alexander [16] Iannaeus (103–76 BC) had built (modern Ruğm al-Mišnaqa). According to Plin. HN 5,16,72, M. was, apart from → Jerusalem, the strongest fortress in Judea. M. was completely destroyed during the Roman campaign in 63 BC by → Pompeius (Str. 16,763) and later by the proconsul of Syria → Gabinius [I 2] (57–55 BC) (Jos. Ant. Iud. 14,5,4; Jos. BI 1,8,5). Under → Herodes [1] the Great the fortress was renovated and additionally secured through the establishment of a town (modern Ḥirbat al-Mukāwir) (Jos. BI 7,6,2) [3]. In the Jewish War, M. was, aside from → Masada and Herodeion, a fortress held by the Zelots (→ Zelotus) even after the conquest of Jerusalem and did not surrender until AD

72 when it was given up to → Lucillius [II 2] Bassus, the governor of Judaea (Jos. BI 7,6,1). According to Jos. Ant. Iud. 17,5,2, John the Baptist was imprisoned and executed by → Herodes [4] Antipas in M. (cf. Mt 14:10; Mk 6:14ff.; M. is not mentioned there!). In the Byzantine period it was settled by Christians until the Arab conquest.

1 F.-M. Abel, Croisière autour de la Mer Morte, 1911, 31–37 2 C. Kopp, Die heiligen Stätten der Evangelien, ²1959, 175f. 3 Schürer 1, 511 4 A. Strobel, Machärus. Geschichte und Ende einer Festung im Lichte archäologisch-topographischer Betrachtungen, in: S. Wagner (ed.), Bibel und Qumran. FS für H. Bardtke, 1968, 198–225 5 Id., Das römische Belagerungswerk um Machärus: Topographische Untersuchungen, in: ZPalV, 90, 1974, 128–184.   I.WA.

Machairophoroi (μαχαιροφόροι; *machairophóroi*).
[1] In the Ptolemaic period, part of the royal guard and especially used for rural policing purposes and for the protection of high civil officials (later also for the → *kōmárchēs* or the *práktōr laographías*); the members of the guard did not necessarily have to be Egyptians (cf. e.g. OGIS 737). In the Imperial period the term is often simply used as a synonym for 'soldier(s)'; there were *machairophóroi* in the service of the imperial household and as bodyguards for officials who had to handle taxes and other monies. To provide for them, they had their own tax, the *opsṓnion toû machairophórou*.

J.J. Aubert, Transfer of Tax-Money, in: Bulletin of the American Society of Papyrologists 24, 1987, 127ff.   W.A.

[2] Attribute of the → Thraces, derived from their weapon, the *máchaira*, a single-edged sword with a curved blade, also called *skálmē*, erroneously considered to be an epithet for the tribe of the Dii (Diobessi) (Xen. Cyr. 6,2,10; Thuc. 2,96,1; 2,98,4; 7,27,1; Plin. HN 4,40).   I.v.B.

Machanidas (Μαχανίδας/*Machanídas*, cf. Syll.³ 551). As the guardian of → Pelops, dictator in Sparta from 211(?) to 207 BC (Liv. 27,29,9: *tyrannus Lacedaemoniorum*; [1. 408; 2. 65]); active opponent of the → Achaeans who were allied with → Philippus V in the First → Macedonian War; conquered Tegea in 209 and attacked Argus as well as Elis in 208 during the Olympic Peace, but was defeated in the battle of Mantinaea (late summer 207; Pol. 11,11–18; Plut. Philopoemen 10; [2. 66]). M. was killed on the edge of the battlefield by → Philopoemen himself (Pol. 11,17,4–18,4), who celebrated this act by dedicating a statue of the victor in Delphi (Syll.³ 625).

1 H. Berve, Die Tyrannis bei den Griechen, 1967 2 P. Cartledge, A. Spawforth, Hellenistic and Roman Sparta, 1989.   L.-M.G.

Machaon (Μαχάων; *Macháōn*). In Homer, M., like his brother → Podalirius, is the son of → Asclepius and like him is a 'good physician' and commander of 30 ships from Tricca, Ithome and Oechalia (Hom. Il. 2,729ff.) in Thessaly [1. 47ff.; 2. vol. 2, 17ff.; 3. vol. 1, 225ff.]; he cures Menelaus, who has been wounded by Pandarus, with herbs that Asclepius obtained from → Chiron (Hom. Il. 4,192ff.); M. himself is wounded by Paris with an arrow (ibid. 11,505ff.) and revived by Hecamede with a mixed drink and a bath in Nestor's tent (ibid. 11,613ff. 832ff.; 14,2ff.). According to Iliioupersis fr. 1 EpGF, M., like his brother, is the son of Poseidon, the first surgeon, and Podaleirius is the first representative of internal medicine and even of psychiatry or diagnostics [1. 47; 4. 32]. M. meets his death through → Penthesilea (Apollod. epit. 5,1) or through → Eurypylus [2] (Ilias parva fr. 7 EpGF).

M. and Podaleirius are professional army physicians who are elevated by the epic to the status of noble warriors (M. from Greek *máchesthai*, 'to fight' [3. vol. 2, 226 n. 1]) [2. vol. 2, 5ff.; 5. 97f.]; the original paternity (Asclepius or Poseidon) cannot be determined [2. vol. 2, 15ff.]. Achaeans displaced from Thessaly take M. with them to the Aeolis early on, and (through Nestor, who transports his bones, Paus. 3,26,9f.; 4,3,2) to the Peloponnese [1. 52ff.; 3. 226]. Here he receives Xanthe (otherwise Epione, Hes. Cat. 53) as his mother and Anticlea as his wife (Paus. 4,30,3). Through cult overlapping he becomes the father of the old healing gods → Gorgasus and Nicomachus, → Alexanor, → Sphyrus and Polemocrates (cf. Paus. 4,30,3; 2,11,5; 2,23,4; 2,38,6 [1. 54ff.; 2. vol. 2, 21; 7. 182ff.]). As M.'s sisters, the healing heroines → Aegle [5], → Aceso, → Hygiea, Iaso and Panacaea are mentioned [2. vol. 2, 87ff.]. On the other hand, the Asclepius cult on Cos (Aristid. 38,11ff. 19ff.) is young (4th cent. [2. vol. 2, 243; 3. vol. 2, 226]). M. in Greek and Roman art: [8. 150-152; 9].

1 U. v. WILAMOWITZ-MOELLENDORFF, Isyllos von Epidauros, 1886   2 EDELSTEIN, Asclepius   3 WILAMOWITZ 4 F. KUDLIEN, Der Beginn des medizinische Denkens bei den Griechen, 1967   5 S. LASER, Medizin und Körperpflege, 1983 (ArchHom S), 97ff.   6 W. KULLMANN, Die Quellen der Ilias, 1960   7 WIDE   8 M. VAN DER KOLF, s.v. M., RE 14, 144-152   9 D. PANDERMALIS, I. LEVENTI, s.v. M., LIMC 8.1, 777-780.   P.D.

Machares (Μαχάρης; *Macháres*). Son of Mithridates VI; M. went over to the Roman side as early as 70 BC as *amicus et socius* (Plut. Lucullus 24). He sent Lucullus (→ Licinius [I 26]) auxiliary troops and food at the siege of Sinope. In 65 he attempted to flee Mithridates from → Panticapaeum to the → Chersonesus [3], burnt the ships behind him in the harbour and committed suicide in view of the hopelessness of his situation (Memnon, FGrH 434 F 37f.; App. Mith. 102) or was murdered (Cass. Dio 36,50).

V. F. GAIDUKEVIČ, Das Bosporanische Reich, 1971, 318f.
     I.v.B.

Machatas (Μαχάτας; *Machátas*).
[1] Member of the Macedonian [1. 200] dynasty of → Elimea, brother of → Derdas [3], through his sister Phila brother-in-law of → Philippus II (Satyrus, FHG 3,161 fr. 5 in Ath. 557c). It is possibly this M. who is mentioned as the father of → Harpalus (Arr. Anab. 3,6,4; [2. 2,75-80 no. 143]), Philip (Arr. Anab. 5,8,3; [2. 2,384f. no. 780) and Tauron (IG XII 9, 197, 4; [2. 2,371f. no. 741]).
[2] Aetolian who was active on behalf of the Aetolian League in 220/219 BC on several occasions as an envoy in Sparta and then in Elis (Pol. 4,34-36).
[3] Epirote whose father Charops, in a plot against the Epirote League, which was allied with → Philippus V (→ Epirus), had effectively supported the Romans in the Second → Macedonian War in 198 BC in a militarily decisive situation (Liv. 32,6; 11; Diod. Sic. 30,5; Plut. Flamininus 4,5ff.). In 192, M. as envoy called on → Antiochus (Pol. 20,3). His son Charops made contact with senatorial circles as envoy in Rome, in 167 slandered pro-Macedonian confederate politicians in Rome (Pol. 27,15) before the outbreak of the Third Macedonian War (171-168), wanted the Senate to confirm his high-handed regulations in Epirus in Rome in 160 and died on the return journey in Brundisium (Pol. 32,5,4ff.) [3].

1 I. I. RUSSU, Macedonica, in: Ephemeris Dacoromana 8, 1938, 105-232   2 BERVE   3 TH. BÜTTNER-WOBST, s.v. Charops (11/12), RE Suppl. 1, 284f.   E.O.

Machimoi The term *máchimoi* (μάχιμοι, 'the pugnacious'; troops fit for action) was used by Greek authors primarily for non-Greek armies. Herodotus differentiates the *machimoi* from the retinue of the Persian army (Hdt. 7,186,1) and refers with this word to the class of professional warriors in ancient Egypt (2,164f.). In the Ptolemaic army, *machimoi* were the native soldiers who performed the duties of auxiliary, guard and police units until *c.* the end of the 3rd cent. BC, afterwards however, at the latest from the battle of Raphia in 217 BC, also constituted battle troops in their own units with Greek equipment (Pol. 5,65,9; 5,107,1).   LE.BU.

Machlyes Libyan nomads who according to Herodotus (4,178; 180) lived west of the Lotophagoi and east of the Ausees (on the Little Syrte?) and according to Pliny (HN 5,28; 7,15) in the neighbouring area of the → Nasamones on the Great Syrte. Pliny and his source Calliphanes – both incidentally see in the M. *androgynoi* (i.e. people of dual sexuality) – were probably wrong. Sources: Hdt. 4,178; 180 (Μάχλυες; *Máchlyes*); Nicolaus of Damascus FGrH 90 F 103q (Ἰαλχλευεῖς/ *Ialchleueîs* the MSS tradition SMA; Μαχλυεῖς/*Machlyeîs* corr. J. VOSSIUS); Plin. HN 5,28 (*Machroae*); 7,15 (*Machlyae*); Ptol. 4,3,26 (Μάχρυες; *Máchryes*); Coripp. Iohannis 3,410 (*Mecales*); Steph. Byz. s.v. Μάχρυες/ *Mákryes*.
→ Libyes, Libye

J. DESANGES, Catalogue des tribus africaines ... , 1962, 107; M. SCHWABE, s.v. Μάχλυες, RE 14, 157f.   W.HU.

Machon (Μάχων; *Máchōn*) from Sicyon or Corinth; lived at the time of → Apollodorus [5] of Carystus (3rd cent. BC) [1. test. 1] and was active as a writer in Alexandria, also the place of his death. M. wrote Χρεῖαι (*Chreîai*, 'Anecdotes') in iambic trimeter (of which a total of about 470 are extant in Ath. *Deipnosophistaí* XIII) about hetaerae, parasites and poets (Diphilus, Euripides, Philoxenus), as well as important political figures (Ptolemy, Demetrius Poliorcetes); the material, in which sex plays a certain role, comes from anecdotal prose works of the late 4th and 3rd cents. (e.g. → Lynceus of Samos). M.'s comedies were more highly regarded [1. test. 3]; because of them, he was considered almost an equal of the tragic → Pleias [1. test. 1], and they brought him the attention of → Aristophanes [4] of Byzantium [1. test. 1. 2]. The titles of two pieces (Ἄγνοια/'Ignorance'; Ἐπιστολή/'The Letter ') and two fragments are extant. In fr. 2, a cook speaks who describes gourmets as the essential basis of his art.

1 PCG V, 1986, 623f.   2 A.S. F. GOW, M., 1965.
H.-G.NE.

Macistum, -us (Μάκιστον, -ος; *Mákiston, –os*). Settlement in → Triphylia (western Peloponnese) on the southern foot of Mount Kaiapha, on whose territory was the sanctuary of 'Samian' Poseidon [1. 37–42] on the western tip of the mountain range as well as other sanctuaries along the Minthe range (modern Alvena) and in the coastal plain south of Mount Kaiapha. In around 400 BC, Xenophon still refers to M. as an existing city (Xen. An. 7,4,16; Xen. Hell. 3,2,25; 30); later, all knowledge of it is lost, and even the Hellenistic interpreters of Homer could no longer pinpoint its location. In the Hellenistic period, M. could possibly be identified with → Samicon [2]. Some interpreters of Homer equate M. with the equally unknown Πλατανιστοῦς/ *Platanistoûs* (Str. 8,3,16). Apollodorus (in Str. 8,3,13f.; 24f.) uses the regional name Μακιστία/*Makistía* to refer to Triphylia south of the river Alpheius, in contrast with Artemidorus (in Str. 8,3,15), who restricted it to the part south of Mount Kaiapha – both are artificial improvisations, of which at least the latter corresponds more closely to the known facts. According to schol. Eur. Or. 4 SCHWARTZ, Atreus and Thyestes lived in M. after their expulsion from Pisa. Hdt. 4,148 refers to M. as a Minyaean foundation (→ Minyae) after the expulsion of the Caucones (Str. 8,3,13f.; 16; 18; 21, a sanctuary of Hercules Μακιστιός; 6,1,6; 10,1,10; Aristot. fr. 611,55 R; Paus. 6,22,4; Plin. HN 4,20; Steph. Byz. s.v. Μάκιστος).

1 A.M. BIRASCHI, Strabone e Omero, in: Id. (ed.), Strabone e la Grecia, 1994, 25–57   2 F. CARINCI, s.v. Elide (1), EAA², 1994, 448f.   Y.L.

Mackerel (σκόμβρος/*skómbros*, σκομβρίς/*skombrís*, Latin scomber, κολίας/*kolías* with unexplained etymology according to [1], Latin *colias*), the predatory marine fish, *Scomber scombrus* L. of the sub-species of the *Scombroidea*, that is often confused with the → tuna because of its kinship with it. The mackerel, which according to Plin. HN 9,49 has a sulphury yellow colour in the water (*sulpureus color*), comes, according to Aristot. Hist. an. 7(8),13,599a 1–3, in large schools to spawn on the sea coasts. Its catch (details in Opp. Hal. 3,576–595) was profitable primarily in the Black Sea (Plin. HN 9,49), in the Sea of Marmara, in the Propontis (Aristot. ibid. 598a 24–26 and b 27f.), at Byzantium and Paros (Ath. 3,116b-c; Plin. HN 32,146), in the Straits of Gibraltar (Plin. HN 31,94) and at Carthage (Str. 3,4,6). Mackerel served mostly as a salted or pickled fish (Ath. 3,116a; 118d) or was used for the fish sauce *garum* (→ Fish dishes; → *Liquamen*) (Plin. HN 31,94; Martial. 13,102; Ath. 3,121a with a quotation from Str. 3,4,6) and was therefore very cheap in Athens (Aristoph. Equ. 1008) as well as in Rome (Plaut. Capt. 851). Catull. 95,8 and Mart. 3,50,9 and 4,86,8 are therefore able to describe poor literary works like the 'Annals' of Volusius as a loose wrapping (*laxae tunicae*) for mackerel. The nutritional value and taste were judged in various ways (schol. to Opp. Hal. 3,576; Ath. 3,121a and 7,321a). Columella 8,17,12 recommends, among other things, to use the entrails as fish feed in ponds for the breeding of marine fish.
→ Fishes

1 FRISK s.v. κολιάς, σκόμβρος   C.HÜ.

Macna (Μάκνα/*Mákna*, Ptol. 6,7,27) was situated at the site of the modern oasis of Maqnā on the Gulf of ʿAqaba.   A.D.

Macoraba (Μακοράβα; *Makorába*). According to Ptol. 6,7,32, city in north-western → Arabia Felix, already at an early time equated with → Mecca. Based on the southern Semitic root *mkrb* ('temple', 'sanctuary' but also 'altar'). In pre-Islamic Mecca there was a temple to the moon god Hubal, who was worshipped by the tribes in the neighbourhood.

H. V. WISSMANN, Zur Geschichte und Landeskunde von Altsüdarabien (SAWW, Phil.-histor. Klasse 246), 1964, 185, n. 380.   I.T.-N.

Macra River in the region of the Liguri Apuani near → Luna [3], border between the Augustan regions of Liguria and Etruria, modern Magra. Its upper reach was possibly called Audena. A river port lay towards the mouth (Ptol. 3,1,3; Liv. 39,32,2; 40,41,3; 41,19,1; Luc. 2,426f.; Plin. HN 3,48–50).

G. FORNI (ed.), Fontes Ligurum et Liguriae antiquae, 1976, s.v. M.; S. PESAVENTO MATTIOLI, Gli scali portuali di Luni nel contesto della rotta da Roma ad Arles, in: Centro Studi Lunensi, Quaderni 10–12, 1985–1987, 626–

628; R. RICCI, M.-Audena, in: Archivio storico per le province parmensi 43, 1991, 99–108; R. THOMSEN, The Italic Regions, 1947, 124f.   G.GA.

Macrianus

[1] *Rex* of the Alamanni in the Main-Neckar region, where he surrendered to → Iulianus [11] in AD 359 (Amm. Marc. 18,2,15–18). In 370, → Valentinianus [1] mobilized a Burgundian army (Amm. Marc. 28,5,8–13) against M., who had by then become more powerful. However, M. avoided capture in 372 by fleeing. *Rex* Fraomarius, appointed by the emperor to replace M., could not sustain his position for long (Amm. Marc. 29,4,2–7; 30,7,11). In 374, the emperor entered into a → *foedus* (Amm. Marc. 30,3,3–7) with M., who remained loyal from then on. In *c.* 380, M. died in the attack on the Franks under → Mallobaudes.

> B. GUTMANN, Studien zur röm. Außenpolitik in der Spätant., 1991, 9–41; PLRE 1, 527f. no. 1.   P.KE.

[2] Fulvius M. A member of the equestrian class, M. originally pursued a military career (SHA Tyr. Trig. 13,3); under → Valerianus he took on the office of *a* → *rationibus* in Egypt. According to Eusebius (Euseb. Hist. eccl. 7,10,4–7) he induced the emperor to persecute Christians. During the Persian campaign, and also wounded, M. was appointed by the emperor to oversee the military pay-office and grain supplies (Euseb. Hist. eccl. 7,10,8; Petrus Patricius, Excerpta de sententiis p. 264 N. 159 BOISSEVAIN; exaggerated SHA Tyr. Trig. 12,16). When Valerian came into Persian captivity in AD 260, M. gathered troops in Samosata and refused obedience (Petrus Patricius l.c.; Euseb. Hist. eccl. 7,23,1). On → Ballista's initiative, M. was offered the imperial purple, which he, however, declined, because of his age and infirmity, in favour of his sons Macrianus and Quietus (SHA Gall. 1,2,5; SHA Tyr. Trig. 12; 14,1; Euseb. Hist. eccl. 7,10,8; Zon. 12,24 D.). In 261, he died together with his elder son M. [3] in Illyricum in a battle against → Aureolus (SHA Gall. 2; 3,1; 3,6; SHA Tyr. Trig. 11,2; 12,13f.).

> KIENAST, 224f.; PFLAUM, vol. 2, 928ff. no. 350; PIR[2] F 549; PLRE 1, 528,2.   T.F.

[3] Iunior Imp. Caes. T. Fulvius Iunius Macrianus Augustus, elder son of Fulvius → Macrianus [2], served as military tribune under → Valerian's [2] (SHA Tyr. Trig. 12,10; Zon. 12,24 D.). After Valerianus' capture by the Persians, his father elevated him and his brother → Quietus to Augusti before 17 September 260; however, they were only recognized in the east (RIC 5,2, 589 f.; SHA Gall. 1,3–5; SHA Tyr. Trig. 12,10–12; POxy. 3476,12 f.; IGR III 27). On their march west, M. fell together with his father in Illyricum in the battle against → Gallienus' generals → Aureolus and Domitian in 261.

> KIENAST, 225; M. PEACHIN, Roman Imperial Titulature, 1990, 40f.; PIR[2] F 546; PLRE 528, no. 3.   T. F.

Macri campi Area in the Apennines 7 km west of Mutina in the Val di Montirone near modern Magreta (cf. the ancient place name!). A cattle market as early as pre-Roman times. The Roman garrison (from 176: Liv. 41,18,5ff.) developed into an important trading centre (Varro, Rust. 2, pr. 6; Columella 7,2,3; Str. 5,1,11: Μακροὶ Κάμποι/*Makroì Kámpoi*) that was abandoned in the mid 1st cent. AD [1].

> 1 E. GABBA, Mercati e fiere nell'Italia romana in: Studi Classici e Orientali 25, 1975, 141–163.
>
> NISSEN 2, 265; A. SABATINI, I Campi Macri, in: Rivista storica dell' Antichità 2, 1972, 257–260.   A.SA.

Macrina Born around AD 327, sister of → Basilius [1] the Great, Petrus of Sebaste and → Gregorius [2] of Nyssa. Daughter of the rhetor Basilius and Emmelia, granddaughter of M. the Elder (*c.* 270–*c.* 340). After the death of her bridegroom, M. lived an ascetic life on a family estate on the Iris in Pontus; died around 380. Her brother Gregorius wrote a biography of M. (*Vita M. iunioris*; Greg. Nyss. Opera ascetica 8,1, p. 370–414) and had her answer his theological questions as a teacher in his work *De anima et resurrectione* (PG 46, 12–160).   K.G.-A.

Macrinius

[1] M. M. Avitus Catonius Vindex Son of M. [4]. Began his career as an equestrian with the *quattuor militiae*, receiving the → *dona militaria* from Marcus [2] Aurelius in AD 169. Procurator of Dacia Malvensis. Entered the Senate, legate of Moesia superior, perhaps as praetorian; suffect consul probably in 175; consular governor of Moesia inferior before the year 177. Died at the age of 42, probably during his governorship of Moesia inferior (CIL VI 1449 = ILS 1107). PIR[2] M 22.   W.E.

[2] C. M. Decianus As governor of Numidia, this *vir clarissimus* defeated the → Bavares in AD 259/260 (CIL VIII 2615 = ILS 1194; cf. here CIL VIII 9047 = ILS 2767 and 20736). Afterwards he held the office of governor of the province of Noricum.

> PIR[2] M 23; B. E. THOMASSON, 189f. no. 69.

[2a] M. Regulus Equestrian *praefectus classis* in Pannonia AD 146; he came from Neviomagus, which probably refers to Ulpia Noviomagus in Germania inferior.

> W. ECK, P. WEISS, Die Sonderregelungen für Soldatenkinder, in: ZPE 135, 2001, 195–208; W. ECK, Ein Kölner in Rom? T. Flavius Constans als kaiserlicher Prätorianerpräfekt. FS Precht, Mainz 2002, 37–42.   W. E.

[3] C. M. Sossianus *Vir clarissimus, Curator rei publicae Kalamensium* in AD 283, thereafter *cos. suff.*; from 290–294 he served under the proconsul → Aurelius [II 3] Aristobulus as *legatus provinciae Africae* (CIL VIII 5332 = ILS 606; CIL VIII 608+11772 = ILS 637; CIL VIII 4645 = ILS 5714; CIL VIII 5290 = ILS 5477; ILAlg I 2048; AE 1933,60).

> PIR[2] M 24; PLRE 1, 849,1.   T.F.

[4] M. Vindex Equestrian, possibly from Germania inferior or Britain [1. 538; 2. 550]. Praesidial procurator of Dacia Porolissensis in AD 154; Praetorian prefect together with M. Bassaeus Rufus under Marcus Aurelius and Verus. He died in the war against the Marcomanni, and was honoured by Marcus [2] Aurelius with three statues at Rome. PIR² M 25.

1 A.R. BIRLEY, Senators from Britain?, in: EOS, vol. 2
2 W. ECK, Senatoren aus Germanien, Raetien, Noricum?, in: EOS, vol. 2.   W.E.

Macrinum Way station on the Adriatic coastal road in Picenum between Castrum Novum and Ostia Aterni (Tab. Peut. 6,1). The place name is probably corrupt, in connection with the mouth of the river called *Matrínos* by Str. 5,4,2 and Ptol. 3,1,17.

NISSEN 2, 431; N. ALFIERI, I fiumi adriatici, in: Athenaeum 37, 1949, 137f.   G.U.

Macrinus Imperator Caesar M. Opellius Severus M. Augustus. Roman Emperor AD 217–218. Born in 164 (Cass. Dio 78,40,3) or 166 (Chron. pasch. I p. 498 D.) in Caesarea Mauretania, of humble origins (Cass. Dio 78,11,1; SHA Opilius Macrinus (= Macr.) 2,1). M. initially worked as a lawyer, then as procurator of the *praef. praet.* → Fulvius [II 10] Plautianus, whose deposal he survived unharmed thanks to the intervention of L. → Fabius [II 6] Cilo (Cass. Dio 78,11,2). → Septimius Severus appointed him *praefectus vehiculorum per Flaminiam* (Cass. Dio 78,11,3), and in *c.* 208 keeper of the imperial wardrobe (SHA Diadumenianus Antoninus 4,1; Cass. Dio 78,34,2).

Under → Caracalla, M. served in several short-term procuratorial appointments, amongst them that of *res privata* (Cass. Dio 78,11,3; SHA Macr. 2,1; 7,2 regarding the priestly offices is probably fictitious); in 212, Caracalla made M. → *praefectus praetorio* (Aur. Vict. Caes. 22,1; Eutr. 8,21). From at the latest 216, M. fought alongside the emperor in the war against the Parthians (AE 1947,182; Cod. Iust. 9,51,1); in early 217, he received the *ornamenta consularia* and – together with his son – the title → *vir clarissimus* (Cass. Dio 78,13,1; CIL XV 7505).

As M. felt threatened by Caracalla, he took the initiative to depose the emperor (Cass. Dio 78,4,1–5; Hdn. 4,12,4–8), and had him assassinated by Iulius [II 92] Martialis on 8 April 217 (Cass. Dio 78,5,3–6,5; Hdn. 4,13,1–6). M. succeeded in keeping his own involvement secret; for that reason, three days after the assassination (11 April 217), the troops proclaimed him emperor, the first non-senator to be offered that title (Cass. Dio 78,11,6; Hdn. 4,13,7–8; 14,1–3). Without waiting for the Senate to confirm his acclamation, M. assumed the imperial title and gave the title of Caesar to his son Diadumenianus (Cass. Dio 78,16,2; 17,1; 19,1; Hdn. 5,2,1; SHA Macr. 7; Aur. Vict. Caes. 22,1; AE 1953, 54; 1954, 8; 1960, 36). In 218, M. was *cos. ord. II* (AE 1953, 11; 1964, 229). Out of necessity rather than desire, M. carried on with the war against the Parthians, but in the spring of 218 entered into an unfavourable peace with their king Artabanus [8] IV (Cass. Dio 78,26,2–27,3; Hdn. 4,15,1–9; SHA Macr. 8). M. refused the victorious epithet *Parthicus*, offered to him by the Senate. He succeeded in bringing Armenia back under Roman control (Cass. Dio 78,27,3–4). He attempted to rebalance the state budget (Cass. Dio 78,12,5–7) and to restore discipline within the army (Cass. Dio 78,12,1–9; 28,2; 31,1).

M.'s appointment of his son as Augustus and the payment of a donative to the mutinous troops (Cass. Dio 78,34,2) was too late a reaction to the general feeling of resentment; → Iulia [17] Maesa had already bribed the soldiers at Emesa to proclaim her grandson → Elagabalus emperor (Hdn. 5,4,1–4; Cass. Dio 78,30,2–36,5; SHA Macr. 9). On 8 June 218, M. was defeated in a battle at Antioch [1] by the insurgents; he escaped to Chalcedon and was murdered soon after. His name was subject to a *damnatio memoriae* (Hdn. 5,4,5–12; Cass. Dio 78,37,3–40,3; SHA Macr. 10).

KIENAST, 169f.; PFLAUM, 667–672 no. 248; PIR² O 108.   T.F.

Macris (Μάκρις; *Mákris*). Daughter of → Aristaeus [1], wet-nurse of → Dionysus on Euboea. After she was banished by Hera she lived on Corcyra, which was named M. after her, in a grotto which was later the place where → Iason and → Medea got married (Apoll. Rhod. 4,540; 990; 1130ff.).   L.K.

Macro see → Sutorius Macro

Macrobii (Μακρόβιοι; *Makróbioi*, Lat. *Macrobii*). [1] According to Herodotus, Cambyses had also the intention of campaigning against the 'long-living Ethiopians' (μακροβίους Αἰθίοπας, Hdt. 3,17,1), who lived on the 'southern sea' (νοτίη θαλάσση, Hdt. l.c.; cf. also Hdt. 3,21–23). Since this *notíēi thalássei* (νοτίη θαλάσση) of Herodotus' is lost in mythical darkness, it is useless to speculate on the locales of the 'long-living Ethiopians', who are occasionally incorrectly separated from the other Ethiopians. Some ancient authors have done so nevertheless, within the framework of their world view, e.g. Plin. HN 6,190: *ex adverso in Africae parte*; Anon. (Geographiae veteris scriptores Graeci minores 4, G. 38 HUDSON): Εἶτα ὁ... Ἀστάπους καὶ Ἀσταβόρας ... ἑνοῦνται ὡς εἰς τῷ Μεγάλῳ ποταμῷ κατὰ τοὺς Μακροβίους καλουμένους ('The Astapus and the Astaboras join as one river in the great river [Nile] by the so-called M.'). Mela 3,85 and Paus. 1,33,4 identify the M. by some right with the Meroitic Ethiopians.

D. HERMINGHAUSEN, Herodots Angaben über Äthiopien, 1964, 26–33; I. HOFMANN, A. VORBICHLER, Der Äthiopenlogos bei Herodot (Beitr. zur Afrikanistik 3), 1979, 45–50.   W.HU.

[2] Plin. HN 4,37 knows of an Apollonia on the Acte (→ Athos), whose inhabitants would be called *Macrobii*. In 7,27 he traces the longevity of the inhabitants of Mount Athos and their freedom from vermin back to the consumption of viper meat. Mela 2,32 (= Solin. 11,34) gives the name M. to the citizens of a city called Acrothoon on the peak of Mount Athos. Cf. Lucian Macrobii 5; Ael. VH 9,10.

B. LENK, s.v. M. (2), RE 14, 814.   M.Z.

Macrobius
[1] M., Theodosius
A. IDENTIFICATION B. WORKS C. INFLUENCE

A. IDENTIFICATION
There are three Latin works extant under the name Ambrosius Theodosius M., *vir clarissimus* and *illustris* (sometimes listed in reverse order): 7 bks. of *Saturnalia*(*Sat.*), 2 bks. of *Commentarii in Somnium Scipionis* (*Somn.*) and excerpts from *De differentiis et societatibus Graeci Latinique verbi*. Otherwise the author is unknown. However, the persons that appear in *Sat.* (Vettius Agorius → Praetextatus, Q. Aurelius → Symmachus and several Albini) are well-known Roman aristocrats from the late 4th cent. AD. On the basis of Praetextatus' date of death and of the anachronisms that M. himself acknowledges (Sat. 1,1,5), *Sat.* can be dated to the period of time immediately after 410 or later. If we look for the author among the three high-ranking officials that bear the name M. in the *Codex Theodosianus* (→ Codex II. C.), the only possibility is the *proconsul Africae* for the year 410 [11]. If, however, we adhere to the name Theodosius, only the *praef. praet.* for the year 430 permits acceptable identification [8]. Otherwise the son to whom the two primary works are dedicated must be identified with the *praef. urbi* for the year 463. Finally, the editor's note in the MS, which mentions a text revision by M.Plotinus Eustathius with the support of Memmius Symmachus (Boethius' father-in-law), leads to the conclusion that Eustathius is probably M.'s grandson.

B. WORKS
1. SATURNALIA 2. COMMENTARII IN SOMNIUM SCIPIONIS 3. DE DIFFERENTIIS ET SOCIETATIBUS GRAECI LATINIQUE VERBI

1. SATURNALIA
M. intends, as he says in his foreword, to provide his son with a collection of knowledge from various fields in order to save him from strenuous seeking. However, in order to design this 'repository' appropriately, he presents it in the form of a literary banquet under the auspices of Plato (→ Symposium literature). The *Saturnalia* faithfully apply the rules of the genre: a preface and a variety of subjects, a mixture of the serious and the entertaining; a range of topics that are brought freely into the conversation; character types: the drunk-

ard, the quarreller, the cynic; required motifs: the unexpected arrival of an uninvited guest, the argument, etc. Deviations from the usual topoi have a particular meaning: instead of a ridiculous guest, *three* admirable guests appear one after the other, which emphasizes the presence of *three* leaders of the pagan aristocracy in Rome as well as the good behaviour on the part of a gathering from which female dancers are excluded. Typical of the genre, on the other hand, are the famous *Quaestiones convivales*, which Apuleius (→ Ap(p)uleius [III]) and → Plutarchus collected (Does the chicken or the egg come first? Is there an even or an odd number of stars? ...), and the famous witticisms, cited in bk. 2. In addition, however, there is also a coherent treatise on the Roman → calendar up to its reform by Caesar.

Two topics take up an unusual amount of space: the religious-scientific treatise on the sun by Praetextatus at the end of bk. 1 and the representation of Virgil's universal superiority in bks. 3–6. Thus it gradually becomes clear what M. really cares about – *vetustas semper adoranda* ('old age, always worthy of admiration') and classical Roman religion, sublimated by Oriental sun theology. M. gravely insults Christianity, which was emerging as triumphant during his life-time, by ignoring it (BOISSIER). His work as a whole conveys the impression of an erudite yet polite and witty discussion among men of the world whose literary or (pagan) religious education is occasionally praised: M.'s education is impressive but second-hand.

2. COMMENTARII IN SOMNIUM SCIPIONIS
M. likewise dedicated the two books of the *Commentarii* on → Cicero's famous text to his son (already older, as the difficult topics show). In the revelations that Aemilius Scipio receives in his grandfather's and adoptive father's dream (Cic. Rep. 6,10ff.), M. recognised *universa philosophiae integritas*, philosophy in its entirety; he makes his commentary a veritable compendium of science and philosophy. After a short comparison between Scipio's dream and the vision of → Er in Plato's 'Republic', the text (albeit only half of it in all) is commented on sentence by sentence but much more freely than in other philosophical commentaries, and with extended digressions. For example, a short comment by Cicero on Aemilius' age at death (Macrob. In Somn. 1,5,2: 56 years = 7×8) is followed by a detailed mathematical discussion of the first ten numbers. Some chapters deal with the nature, origin and determination of the soul; two others address the Neoplatonic theory of the hierarchy of virtues and Plotinus' disapproval of suicide (ibid. 1,8). The description of the sky as it looks from the vantage point of the cosmos ('from above') is followed by a long discussion (ibid. 1,14–2,9) of astronomy, mathematical geography and the music of the spheres. Finally, an excerpt from Plato's 'Phaedo' that proves the soul's immortality using its ability to move itself leads to a discussion (already scholastic in nature) of Aristotle's objections and their refutation by the Platonists. Although he was a great admirer of Plato and Cicero (whose indubitable agreement with one another

he seeks to prove), M. refers above all to → Plotinus, whom he knows primarily through → Porphyrius. The fact that the 'investigation of sources' leads to a dead end shows the originality displayed by M., who formulates his thoughts in a comprehensible and even elegant manner in spite of his love of the mathematical and his limited formal philosophical learning.

3. DE DIFFERENTIIS ET SOCIETATIBUS GRAECI LATINIQUE VERBI

Some excerpts from this work on the differences and commonalities between the Greek and the Latin verb are preserved in various MSS (including the Cod. Parisinus Lat. 7186). M. retains the classical classification of the seven qualifications of the verb, but anticipates → Priscianus' work in the following century by means of an original method of systematic comparison of Latin and Greek verbs. At the same time, he introduces the category of *differentiae* ('differences'; → Differentiarum scriptores), of which → Isidorus [9] of Seville later made productive use.

C. INFLUENCE

The first citations from M.'s oeuvre can be found in → Boethius and → Cassiodorus. Most of our MSS go back to the Carolingian epoch. They became more numerous after that period. M. is discussed along with → Calcidius, one of the most widely-read authors of the Middle Ages, by Johannes SCOTUS ERIGENA, the Platonists from the School of Chartres, ABELARD, and THOMAS OF AQUINAS. Paradoxically, the work of this non-Christian who was focused on the past became a favourite book in the Christian Middle Ages. During the Renaissance 30 incunables by M. were published. Interest then trailed off and ceased completely during the Enlightenment era.

EDITIONS: 1 J. WILLIS, 2 vols., 1963. *Sat.:* 2 N. MARINONE, 1967 (with Italian transl.). *Commentarii:* 3 M. REGALI, 1983/1990 (with Italian transl.) 4 L. SCARPA, 1981 (with Italian transl.) 5 W. H. STAHL, 1952 (Engl. transl.). *De Differentiis:* GL 5,595–655 6 P. DE PAOLIS, 1990.
BIBLIOGRAPHY: 7 B. C. BARKER-BENFIELD, The Mss. of M.' Commentary on the Somnium Scipionis, thesis Oxford, 1975 8 A. CAMERON, The Date and Identity of M., in: JRS 56, 1966, 25–38 9 P. COURCELLE, Les lettres grecques en Occident de M. à Cassiodore, ²1946, 3–36 10 P. DE PAOLIS, Macrobio 1934-1984, in: Lustrum 28/29, 1986-87, 107–249 11 J. FLAMANT, M. et le néo-platonisme latin à la fin du IVème siècle, 1977 12 S. GERSH, Middle Platonism and Neoplatonism, 1986 13 K. MRAS, M.' Kommentar zu Ciceros Somnium, SB Preuß. Akad. Wiss. 1933, 232–286 14 M. SCHEDLER, Die Philosophie des M. und ihr Einfluß auf die Wissenschaft des Mittelalters, 1916 15 W. H. STAHL, Astronomy and Geography, in: TAPhA 73, 1942, 232–255 16 P. WESSNER, s.v. M., RE 14, 170–198.   J.F.

[2] East Roman official (→ *praepositus sacri cubiculi*, Chief of the Imperial Chamber), referred to in AD 422 in one of the laws of Theodosius II (Cod. Theod. 6,8,1), which elevates the rank of that office. PLRE 2, 698f.
F.T.

Macrocephali (Μακροκέφαλοι; *Makroképhaloi*, 'the large-headed'). Apparently a tribe west of → Colchis (Hes. fr. 153). But the name probably comes from the mythical or fictitious reports on the peoples on the → Pontos Euxeinos (cf. Str. 7,3,6 as an example of his mythical criticism), even though geographers continued to use it (Mela 1,19; Plin. HN 6,2). According to Scyl. 37 they are identical with the → Macrones.   I.v.B.

Macron (Μάκρων; *Mákrōn*). Attic red-figure vase painter, active around 490–470 BC. With the probably slightly older potter Hieron he founded one of the four great potteries of the 5th cent. (→ Codrus Painter). The overwhelming proportion of the at least 600 extant vases are kylikes (→ Vessels) and are often signed by the potter on the inside of the handle, an unusual place. Reliably M.'s signature is only known from the skyphos in Boston, MFA 13.186. Mostly only developed images bear captions; among them a few → kalos-inscriptions, for instance to Hippodamas. Besides the → Brygus Painter, M. is the only one who does not design entirely symmetrically the area below the handles of the vessel: a sleeping boy is opposed by a krater, a goat by a garland of palms, even Mount Nysa is used to fill the area under the handle. Later M. places outsized ivy leaves there, which form a striking Dionysiac interlude between the friezes. The typical themes, which accompanied him throughout his career, already become apparent in his early period: everyday scenes of symposium and → komos, of music school and → palaistra and of encounters between the sexes. His trade marks were figures of → Maenads: he gave their chitons such variable colouring and transparency, partly using relief, partly the paintbrush, that their moving limbs are lit up in endless variety. When they are not brandishing the great, leafy thyrsus, they are often holding their hands inside the sleeves of their chitons, far away from all contact with the outside world. The image of the Maenads dancing around Dionysus Dendrites on the vessel in Berlin, SM F 2290, belongs among the most impressive of those relating to the cult of the wine god left to us.

Among mythical images, M. favoured Trojan themes, as on a second vessel in Berlin, SM F 2291, on one side of which is depicted the abduction of → Helen by → Paris and on the other the events leading up to this. That the Trojan prince has awarded the prize to Aphrodite, surrounded by fluttering cupids, is clear from her expression. The most original representation by M., however, is found on a small bowl in Bochum, Univ.-collection S 1178: Heracles, unclothed, carries the vault of heaven in place of Atlas.

BEAZLEY, ARV², 458–482; BEAZLEY, Paralipomena, 377–379; BEAZLEY, Addenda², 243–247; N. KUNISCH, M., 1997.   A.L.-H.

Macrones (Μάκρωνες; *Mákrōnes*). Mountain people, already mentioned by Hecat. FGrH 1 F 206, who belonged to the 19th tax district under Darius [1] (Hdt. 3,94; 7,78; mentioned here between the Tibareni and the Mossynoeci). According to Xen. (An. 4,7,24; 8,1–22), their region lay south-west of → Trapezus. Modern Meryemana Deresi (righthand tributary of Maçka Dere) then formed the border river between M. and Scythae; the border fortress of the Colchi was located outside Cevrilik. Colchic influence can be deduced from the adoption of circumcision (Hdt. 2,104,3). According to Str. 12,3,18, the M. were later called → Sanni (*Machorones*, Plin. HN 6,11f.; he names both). Amm. Marc. 22,8,21 calls the M. 'a tribe, with which we have no dealings and that is therefore unknown to us'. Possibly identical with the → Macrocephali.

O. LENDLE, Kommentar zur Xenophons Anabasis, 1995, 273f.   I.v.B.

Mactaris (Neo-Punic *Mkt'rm*). City in the Roman province of Africa Byzacena (→ Africa [3]), about 150 km south-west of → Carthage, modern Maktar. M. was the centre of the Carthaginian district ('*rṣt Tšk't* ('territories of Tuschkat')) seized by → Massinissa at the end of the 50s of the 2nd cent. BC [1. 432]. Testimonials to Punic culture – for example over 200 neo-Punic inscriptions – are numerous [2. 273–292]. An important sanctuary of the city was dedicated to *Ḥtr-Mskr* (*Hoter Miskar*). The Roman names Saturnus, Apollo deus patrius and Liber Pater conceal the old Punic gods Baal Hammon, Reshep (?) and Shadrapa (→ Phoenician religion). The tophet stelae mention Baal Hammon but not Tinit. At the head of the public administration of the city were three → 'sufetes' (KAI 146) – a Numidian institution. Later these officials were called *III viri* (CIL VIII 1, 630 = Suppl. 1, 11827). Antoninus Pius or M. Aurelius gave the city the status of a *colonia* (CIL VIII Suppl. 1, 11801; 11804). Bishops are attested from AD 258 [3]. There is a large number of extant monuments. Inscriptions.: CIL VIII 1, 619–684; Suppl. 1, 11780–11909; Suppl. 4, 23398–23594; AE 1953, 48; 1993, 1727–1730; RIL 19–32.

1 HUSS   2 C. G. PICARD, Catalogue du Musée Alaoui. Nouvelle série 1,1, n.d. (= Cb 976–1052)   3 H. DESSAU, s.v. M., RE 14, 199.

A. BESCHAOUCH, M., civitas de droit latin sous Trajan, in: Bull. archéologique du Comité des travaux historiques, N.F. 23 (1990–1992), 1994, 203f.; J. GASCOU, La politique municipale de l'Empire romain en Afrique proconsulaire ... , 1972, esp. 147–151; S. LANCEL, G. CH. PICARD, s.v. Maktar, DCPP, 270f.; C. LEPELLEY, Les cités de l'Afrique romaine ... , vol. 2, 1981, 289–295; A. M'CHAREK, Aspects de l'évolution démographique et sociale à Mactaris aux IIᵉ et IIIᵉ siècles ap. J.C., 1982; G. CH. PICARD, Civitas Mactaritana (Karthago 8), 1957; K. VÖSSING, Untersuchungen zur römischen Schule – Bildung – Schulbildung ... , 1991, 102–115.   W.HU.

Mactorium (Μακτώριον; *Maktórion*). Sicilian city north of → Gela to which citizens of Gela fled when driven out at an uncertain time in a civil war against large estate owners. An ancestor of Gelon, Telines, succeeded in persuading them to return (Hdt. 7,153; cf. also Philistus, FGrH 556 F 3). According to Steph. Byz. s.v. Μακτώριον, M. is said to have been founded by an otherwise unknown Μόνων/*Mónōn* in the 7th/6th cents. BC. The name of a previous settlement survived in the Siculan proto-Latin root of the place name [1. 49¹⁵²]. M. should be pinpointed as lying near Butera (ADAMESTEANU) or rather near Monte Bubbonia (ORLANDINI) that is situated *c.* 20 km north of Gela.

1 G. ALESSI, Fortuna della Grecità linguistica in Sicilia, 1970.

BTCGI 9, 1991, 304–307.   D.SA.

Macynia (Μακυνία, Μακύνεια; *Makynía, Makýneia*, ethnicon Μακυνιεύς; *Makynieús*). Coastal town in west Locris north-west of Antirrhium in the region of Mamakou, possibly on the Paleokastro, at a short distance from Taphiassus (modern Klokova; Str. 10,2,4; 6; 21; Plin. HN 4,6; Steph. Byz. s.v. M.); remains of the city walls (from about the 4th/3rd cents. BC), probably built after the incorporation of M. into the Aetolian League (in 338 BC; → Aetolians). According to Plut. Quaest. Graec. 15, who cites Archytas [3], the epiclesis Ozolis for the West Locrians comes from the delicate fragrance of the flowers in M. (for different aetiologies → Locris). Inscriptions.: IG IX I² 13; 22.

W. A. OLDFATHER, s.v. M., RE 14, 816–818; L. LÉRAT, Les Locriens de l'ouest 1, 1952, 189–191; 2, 61; PHILIPPSON/KIRSTEN 2, 322; R. SCHEER, s.v. M., in: LAUFFER, Griechenland, 403.   G.D.R.

Madaba mosaic see → Medaba

Madates (Μαδάτης, Μαδέτης; *Madátēs, Madétēs*). Sheik of the Uxians (→ Uxii) who roamed the mountain range between Susiane and Persis and controlled the road to → Persepolis that leads over a pass. They were not subjects of the Persians, and supposedly even used to collect a road toll from them. Nevertheless, M. held a kind of office (in Curtius: *praefectus*) in the name of the Achaemenid imperial government. When M. refused in 330 BC to allow → Alexander [4] to march through, he was defeated by him but allowed to continue in his official post. M. had to pay an annual tribute of 100 horses, among other tributes (Arr. Anab. 3,17 and Curt. 5,3,4–13).

P. BRIANT, Rois, tributs et paysans, 1982.   P.HÖ.

Madaurus Numidian city of the later province of Africa proconsularis (→ Africa [3]), situated *c.* 25 km south of → Tagaste near modern Mdaourouch: Ptol. 4,3,30 (Μάδουρος; *Mádouros*); Iulius Honorius, Cosmographia B 44 (*Madauros*). According to Apul. Apol.

24, M. initially belonged to the kingdom of → Syphax, then to that of → Massinissa. In the Flavian period (AD 69–96), M. was the place of residence (*colonia*) of veterans [1. 2152]. The little town developed into a centre of Roman life. → Ap(p)uleius [III] was born there (Apul. Apol. 24; cf. also [1. 2115]), and → Augustinus studied there (Aug. Conf. 2,3). Inscriptions: [1. 2031–2818, 4007–4009; 2. 625]; AE 1989, 882; 893; there are no Punic or Neo-Punic (→ Punic) inscriptions.

1 S. GESELL (ed.), Inscriptions latines de l'Algérie, vol. 1
2 J.-B. CHABOT (ed.), Recueil des inscriptions libyques, 1940/1.

H. DESSAU, s.v. M., RE 14, 201f.; C. LEPELLEY, Les cités de l'Afrique romaine ... vol. 2, 1981, 127–139; E. LIPIŃSKI, s.v. Madaure, DCPP, 267f.   W.HU.

Madrasha (*maḏrāšā*). Name for a Syrian poem form divided up into strophes that uses different patterns of isosyllabic metres (or *qālē*, literally 'melodies' according to which they were sung). Madrasha poetry, the greatest representative of which is considered to be → Ephraim the Syrian († in AD 373), could have influenced the development of the → Kontakion.

A. BAUMSTARK, Geschichte der syrischen Literatur, 1922, 39.   S.BR.

Maduateni Ethnicon for the place name → Madytus, often erroneously regarded as a small Thracian tribe, mentioned only in Liv. 38,40,7 in connection with the attack by Thracian tribes on Cn. Manlius Vulso in 188 BC.   I.v.B.

Madura see → Mathura

Madytus (Μάδυτος; *Mádytos*). City on the Thracian Chersonesus between Elaeus and Sestus, founded by Lesbos (6th cent. BC; Scyl. 67, Ps.-Scymn. 709; Str. 7, fr. 55). North of M., Xerxes had the pontoon bridge built over the → Hellespontus (Hdt. 7,33; 9,120). In 465 BC, M. was a member of the → Delian League (Plut. Cimon 4); a few tributes are recorded for 443/440 BC (ATL 1,336f.). In the → Peloponnesian War, M. was used as a harbour by the Athenian fleet (Xen. Hell. 1,1,3). Conquered in 200 BC by Philip V (Liv. 31,16,5), in 196 captured by Antiochus III, in 190 incorporated into Pergamum (Liv. 38,39,14) and in 133 BC handed over by will to the Romans, M. remained an important harbour. Episcopal see in the Byzantine period (Not. Episc. 2,70; 3,61).
→ Maduateni   I.v.B.

Maeander (Μαίανδρος; *Maíandros*).
[1] God of the homonymous river M. [2] that flows into the sea in the Bay of Miletus; son of → Oceanus and → Tethys (Hes. Theog. 339); furthermore, father of Samia and Cyane, who bears Miletus the twins → Byblis and → Caunus [1] (Ov. Met. 9,450ff.). The

sons of M. are, among others, → Calamus [1] (Nonnus, Dion. 11,464ff.) and → Marsyas [1].   AL.FR.
[2] Longest river in south-western Asia Minor (modern Menderes), has its origin near Celaenae and after a short course picks up the → Marsyas (Hdt. 5,118; Xen. An. 1,2,7f.). Additional tributaries: from the south the Morsynus, the → Harpasus [1] and an additional Marsyas (modern Çine Çayı). In a sharply winding course (hence the term 'meandering'), the M. flows between Priene and Miletus through a wide area made alluvial by it (→ *Maiándrou pedíon*) into the Icarian Sea. The M. was known from early times on (Hom. Il. 2,869, later Scyl. 98; Hdt. 2,29; Str. 13,4,12ff.; Ptol. 5,2,8; Plin. HN 5,106).

W. RUGE, s.v. M. (1), RE 14, 535–540; W. M. CALDER, J. M. COOK, s.v. Maeander, OCD³, 907.   W.BL.

Maeandrius (Μαιάνδριος; *Maiándrios*).
[1] **M. of Samos** Confidant of the tyrant → Polycrates, conducted negotiations with the Persian satrap → Oroetes (Hdt. 3,123; cf. Lucian. Charidemus 14) for him. After the death of Polycrates, M. himself managed to become tyrant in about 521 BC but soon had to give way to → Syloson, who was appointed by the Persians (Hdt. 3,142–6). He fled to Sparta but was expelled from the country by the ephors because of his wealth (Hdt. 3,148; Plut. Mor. 224a-b).

J. ROISMAN, M. of Samos, in: Historia 34, 1985, 275–7.   HA.BE.

[2] **M. of Miletus** Greek historian of the early Hellenistic period, author of *Historíai* and *Milesiaká*, if the name of Leandr(i)us that is cited on many occasions e.g. by → Callimachus [3] actually arose through a textual corruption of M. (see e.g. JACOBY). The definite fragments concern the history and customs of Miletus as well as Homeric questions. FGrH 491 and 492 with comm.   K.MEI.

Maeatae (Μαιάται; *Maiátai*, Lat. *Meatae*). Tribal group in southern Scotland, late 2nd or early 3rd cent. AD, south of the Caledonii, north of the Antonine Wall. The place names Dumyat and Myot Hill in the vicinity of Stirling could be derived from the M. M. may mean 'larger people' or 'inhabitants of the larger part'. The M. broke their treaty with Rome and revolted at the time of Septimius Severus in AD 210. Gradually fought down, they finally made peace in 212 with Caracalla (Xiphilinus 321; cf. Cass. Dio 76,12; Iord. Get. 2,14).
→ Limes (II. Britannia)

G. MAXWELL, The Romans in Scotland, 1989; I. A. RICHMOND, Roman and Native in North Britain, 1958.   M.TO.

Maecenas (Μαικήνας; *Maikḗnas*). Etruscan family name (cf. *mehnate*, *mehnati* and similar); the family is recorded in inscriptions for → Perusia (modern Perugia) and was probably originally settled there.

SCHULZE, 185; 529; M. PALLOTTINO, Etruskologie, 1988, 240.   K.-L.E.

[1] Father of M. [2], mentioned as early as 44 BC among the friends and counsellors of Octavian (→ Augustus) (Nicolaus of Damascus, Vita Caesaris 31,133).

[2] M., less often – with the family name of the mother – C. Cilnius M. (Tac. Ann. 6,11,2), friend of Augustus and patron of literature (see under C.).

A. LIFE B. WORKS C. THE MAECENAS CIRCLE

A. LIFE

Information about M. is found in the historical works of the Augustan era, especially in → Cassius [III 1] Dio and → Suetonius, in the poets of the Maecenas circle, especially in → Horatius' [7] poems and in both of the → Elegiae in Maecenatem passed down with the → Appendix Vergiliana. According to this source, M. descended on both the paternal and maternal sides from leading families (Hor. Carm. 1,1,1 et passim) of the Etruscan city of → Arretium; his father's family had been settled in Rome for several generations and had attained the equestrian class (→ equites) (Vell. 2,88,2), a rank which M. kept for his lifetime.

Born on 13 April (Hor. Carm. 4,11) around 70 BC, M. took part in the battle of Mutina in 43 (→ Mutina, war of), and (on the side of the triumvirate) in the battle of Philippi in 42. From 40, he was entrusted by Octavian (→ Augustus) with a series of important diplomatic missions, while he distinguished himself to a lesser degree militarily; from 36 he represented the princeps in Rome, when necessary, with unlimited authority. The fact of M.'s standing being not precisely defined under constitutional law fits the image of the early form of the → principate. Owing to M.'s marriage with → Terentia (before 23 BC, cf. Suet. Aug. 66,3; Hor. Carm. 2,12) and after the scandal about his brother-in-law Terentius, in which his wife was also involved, as well as the execution of the former, his relationship with the princeps cooled noticeably, the more so as Augustus paid attentions to the wife of his friend in a way that attracted attention. In the last years before M.'s death (8 BC), health reasons also forced him into a reclusive lifestyle.

M. understood how to enjoy the wealth gained through his powerful position. His splendid palace (with park) on the Esquiline was famous; some members of his circle also lived in its vicinity. He valued jewellery and fine clothing (Eleg. in M. 1,21ff.) and had, if we may believe the moralizing polemic of posterity (cf. Sen. Ep. 19,9; 101,10–12; especially 114,4–6 et passim), a weakness for beautiful women and boys.

B. WORKS

A clear individuality is also discernible in the c. 20 fragments of M's works. Individual titles of a collection of dialogues (at least partially in the form of the → prosimetrum, cf. fr. 7; 14 L.) are Prometheus (fr. 10), De cultu suo (fr. 11, autobiographical) and Symposium (fr. 12), in which Virgil, Horace and → Valerius Messalla appeared. The prose of the quotes, which is especially mannered in its rhythm, exposes M. as an Asianic poet (→ Asianism). As early as with his contemporaries (Augustus in Suet. Aug. 86,2), but also later (Sen. Ep.; Quint. Inst. 9,4,28), his deliberate obscurity, which expressed itself in neologisms (Eleg. in M. 1,67f.), bold transpositions and a strongly interlocked word order caused umbrage. In his poems (cf. [15]) – probably partially verse inserts from the Satires (cf. fr. 7) – M. reveals himself as a → Neoteric poet following → Catullus, in metre (Priapea fr. 1 = Catull. 17; Galliambics fr. 4 = Catull. 63; Phalaecean fr. 2; 3) as well as in subject matter (fr. 2 = Catull. 14; fr. 4 = Catull. 63) and in the honest openness of personal expression (fr. 1; 6). The classification of fr.15 is controversial (Elogium to Octavia, the sister of Octavian?) as well as of 17/18 and 21 (cf. test. 1–3), which point to an – autobiographical? – historical work. Direct knowledge of M.'s writings was, however, limited to the 1st cent. AD (cf. [1]).

C. THE MAECENAS CIRCLE

M.'s name is, however, remembered and has become a part of posterity's vocabulary, above all for his generous sponsorship of literature [16]. In the tradition of the nobility of the 2nd cent. BC, upheld by the Elder and Younger Scipio (→ Cornelius [I 71] resp. [I 70]) and → Fulvius [I 15] Nobilior, M. regarded it as his duty, after the break-up of the Republic, to encourage young poets in his circle of amici with recognition and also to sponsor them financially. → Vergilius ([9], cf. Verg. G. 1,1ff.; 2,39ff.; 3,40ff.), → Horatius [10; 11; 12; 14] and → Propertius are the best-known names. Others named in this context are: Varius, Plotius Tucca, Quintilius Varus, Aristius Fuscus, Valgius Rufus, Domitius Marsus and Aemilius Macer (cf. Hor. Sat. 1,5,1; 1,10,81ff.). Beyond this, the desire to see a precisely defined cultural politics directed by Augustus is clearly a modern misunderstanding. That does not preclude the fact that M. occasionally expressed the wishes of the princeps (cf. Verg. G. 3,41), perhaps for a national epic (cf. Hor. Carm. 2,12; Prop. 3,9), however the differing bias of the poets to this suggestion was determined as much by their poetological program (probably nearness to Callimachus [3], see Prop. 4,1,64) as by their temperament.

Horace, who was introduced into M.'s circle in 38 BC by Virgil and Varius (cf. Hor. Sat. 1,6), and received the → Sabinum in the late 30s (cf. Hor. Sat. 2,6), gives us a more exact picture of a friendship which combined closeness with inner independence (cf. especially Hor. Carm. 2,17; 3,29 and Epist. 1,7); in his work (the first three books of Odes, the Epodes, the first Satire book and the first Epistle book are dedicated to M.; in addition there is a series of individual poems addressed to him)

→ Circles, literary

FRAGMENTS: 1 P. LUNDERSTEDT, De C.M. fragmentis, 1911, 223–330 (with commentary), 1783–1787

2 COURTNEY, 276–281 3 FPL, 243–248.
BIBLIOGRAPHY: 4 E. NORDEN, Die antike Kunstprosa
1, ³1915, 292–294 5 W. WIMMEL, Kallimachos in Rom,
1960, 43–49; 250–265 6 R. AVALLONE, Mecenate, 1963
7 M. ANDRÉ, Mécène, 1967 8 Id., Mécène écrivain, in:
ANRW II 30.3, 1983, 1765–1787 9 A. LA PENNA, s.v.
M., EV 3, 1987, 410–414 10 Id., Enciclopedia Oraziana
1, 1996, 792–803 11 B. K. GOLD, Literary Patronage in
Greece and Rome, 1987, 115–141; 221–232 (M. and
Horace) 12 L. F. PIZZOLATO, L'amicizia con M. e l'evo-
luzione poetica di Orazio, in: Aevum antiquum 2, 1989,
145–182 13 W. EVENEPOEL, M.: A Survey of Recent Literature, in: AncSoc 21, 1990, 99–117 14 M. L. COLETTI,
M. e Orazio, in: M.L. Coletti (ed.), Musis amicus, 1995,
291–314 15 S. MATTIACI, L'attività poetica di Mecenate
tra neoterismo e novellismo, in: Prometheus 21, 1995,
67–86 (bibliogr. 85f.) 16 F. BALLANDI, L'immagine di
Mecenate protettore delle lettere nella poesia fra I e II sec.
D.C., in: A&R 40, 1995, 78–101.   P.L.S.

[3] Struck down by the sword two praetorians, who had
forced their way into the Senate chamber, together with
the consular Gallicanus, in AD 238 (Hdn. 7,11,1–4;
SHA Max. 20,6; SHA Gord. 22,8). PIR² M 36.   T.F.

[4] C. M. Melissus see → Melissus

Maecianus Avidius M., son of the usurper → Avidius
[1] Cassius, was *iuridicus Alexandriae* in AD 175; killed
towards the end of the revolt by the soldiers; his mother
was a Maecia (→ Maecius).

A. R. BIRLEY, Marcus Aurelius, ²1987, 192; PIR² A 1406;
R. SYME, Avidius Cassius – His Rank, Age and Quality, in:
Bonner Historia-Augusta-Colloquium 1984/85, 1987,
218.   W.E.

Maecilius Roman-Italian family name, etymologically
presumably from the praenomen *Maius* [1. 185]; light
defacement of the name in the MSS handed down, in
Livy (2,58,2): L. Mecilius as member of the first people's tribune council in 471 BC (presumably subsequently added to the list).

1 SCHULZE.

[1] M., Sp. According to Livy (4,48), M. proposed an
agricultural law as *tr. pl. IV* in 416 BC, which made
provisions for distributing the land conquered by Rome
and occupied by the nobility 'man for man' (*viritim*),
but it failed by a veto of six people's tribunes, won over
by the patricians to their side. The account shows itself
to be a reverse projection of the problems of the Gracchian period by the force of law implicitly accorded to
the → *plebiscita* (→ Hortensius [4]), which was, however, first actually granted beginning in 287.   C.MÜ.

Maecius Italian family name [1. 185; 469], with an
uncertain connection to the Roman *tribus Maecia*. M. is
encountered first among Rome's Latin neighbours (Liv.
10,41,5), from the 2nd cent. BC on, also in inscriptions
from Delos (ILS 9417; SEG 1,334) and Lucania (ILS
5665).

1 SCHULZE.

I. REPUBLICAN PERIOD   II. IMPERIAL PERIOD

I. REPUBLICAN PERIOD

[I 1] M. Geminus From Tusculum, challenged T. Manlius [I 12] Torquatus to a duel and fell during the Latin
War in 340 BC, according to legend (Liv. 8,7,2–12).

[I 2] M. Tarpa, Sp. Designed the plan for the dedication
celebrations of Pompey's new theatre in Rome in 55 BC
(about this, in comic despair Cic. Fam. 2,1,1). M. was
also an author (Donat. Vita Terentii 8, p. 9 W.). His
name is found in Horace, of whom M. seems to have
been a contemporary (Hor. Sat. 1,10,38; Hor. Ars P.
387), as a synonym for 'literary critic'.   JÖ.F.

II. IMPERIAL PERIOD

[II 1] M. M. Celer Senator, probably from Tarraconensis. C. AD 94 legate of a legion in the province of Syria,
where he had perhaps already served as *tribunus militum* (Stat. Silv. 3,2, 104ff.; 123ff.). In the year 101 *cos.
suff.* PIR² M 51.

[II 2] Q. M. Laetus Equestrian office holder. Procurator
of Arabia; *praefectus Aegypti* in AD 200–201 [1. 512].
Praetorian prefect as successor of → Fulvius [II 11]
Plautianus from 205. In 215 *cos. ord. II*, either because
of previous *ornamenta consularia* or because of an
adlectio inter consulares. He belonged to the quite large
group of equestrians in high posts, who crossed over
into senatorial status under the Severi and received a
second consulate. It is possible that CIL VI 1640 =
41185 applies to him (cf. G. ALFÖLDY in the comm. to
VI 41185). PIR² M 54.

1 G. BASTIANINI, Il prefetto d'Egitto, in: ANRW II 10.1,
1988, 503–517.

[II 3] M. Marullus Senator with the title *vir clarissimus*
(AE 1971,62). It must remain an open question whether
he has a connection to the alleged father of → Gordianus [1] named in SHA Gord. 2,1.

W. ECK, s.v. M. (15a), RE Suppl. 14, 273; PIR² M 56;
M.-TH. RAEPSAET-CHARLIER, Les femmes sénatoriales
des IIᵉ et IIIᵉ siècle dans l'Histoire Auguste, in: G. BONA-
MENTE et al. (ed.), Historia-AugustaColloquium Argen-
toratense, 1998, 277f.

[II 4] L. M. Postumus Senator, who is attested in AD 69
and 72 as *frater Arvalis* (PIR² M 57). He is the father of
the homonymous senator, who *i.a.* was *quaestor Augusti* in the year 79 and also later, probably legate of a
legion in Syria, *frater Arvalis. Cos. suff.* 98.

W. ECK, s.v. M. (19), RE Suppl. 14, 273; PIR² M 58.

[II 5] M. M. Probus Suffect consul under Septimius
Severus; *praefectus alimentorum* (as praetorian or consular); governor of Tarraconensis between AD 198 and
209; he also died there.

LEUNISSEN, Konsuln, 156; PIR² M 59.

[II 6] M. M. Rufus Proconsul of Pontus et Bithynia
under Vespasian; suffect consul in AD 81, probably

November and December (D. 3452; AE 1998,419). Proconsul of Asia under Domitian, probably in AD 94 [1].

1 W. WEISER, Q. Corellius Rufus und Marcus M. Rufus in Asia: Flavische Münzen aus Hierapolis und Ephesos, in: EA 20, 1992, 117–125. W.E.

[II 7] Poet, by whom 11 epigrams are extant from the 'Garland' of Philippus – erotic, anathematic and epideictic – (the funerary epigram Anth. Pal. 7,635 originates perhaps from → Antiphilus). For the Anth. Pal. 6,89, the *praenomen* Κοίντος (*Kоíntos*) is placed side by side with the *nomen* Μαίκιος (*Maíkios*; Μάκκιος according the *corrector* and the lemmatists J), whereby the poem Anth. Pal. 6,230 (ascribed without further information to a certain → Quintus) can be attributed to him. M. composes verses on an elevated level and is capable of witty and lively turns of phrase, with occasionally unusual ideas in an epigrammatic setting (Anth. Pal. 9,403: invitation to Dionysus to take part in the pressing of the grapes, cf. Verg. G. 2,7).

GA II 1, 278–285; 2, 310–317. M.G.A.

Maedi (Μαῖδοι, Μαίδοι; *Maîdoi, Maídoi, M(a)edi*). Thracian tribal league on the middle reaches of the Strymon, between Kresna and Rupel (modern Macedonia). According to the earliest witness (Thuc. 2,98), neighbours of the Sinti and Paeoni. In 429 BC, → Sitalces moved through their territory, which did not belong to the kingdom of the Odrysae, against the Macedons. After the withdrawal of Sitalces, the M. expanded their tribal territory to the north, probably subjugated the Dentheleti and established the fortified city of Iamphorynna (in the modern district of Kjustendil, Bulgaria). The Macedonians opposed this: in 340 BC, Alexander the Great founded Alexandroupolis in their territory. Until the end of the 4th cent. BC or even to the invasion of the Celts (280 BC), the M. were under Macedonian rulership. The Hellenistic strategia of *Maidiké* is named after them (Ptol. 3,11,6). Many military conflicts with the Macedonians are reported (e.g. Pol. 10,41,4). Philip V waged three campaigns against the M. (211, 209 and 181 BC; Liv. 26,25,6ff.; 40,22,1), who had conquered Petra on the northern slopes of the Olympus. In 172 BC, the M. allied with other Thracians in a league with Rome against the Macedonians (Liv. 42,19,6). In 117 BC, together with their dynast Tipas, they aided the Scordisci, who were invading Macedonia (Syll.³ 700). In 86 BC, Sulla moved through the M.'s territory (Plut. Sulla 23); in 29 BC, they were completely subjugated to Rome (Cass. Dio 51,23,2–27,2).

F. PAPAZOGLU, L'onomastique dardanien, in: Recueil de travaux de la faculté de philosophie Belgrad 8,1, 1964, 54; B. GEROV, Proučvanija vărhu zapadnotrakijskite zemi 1, 1959/1969, 159–165. I.v.B.

Maelius Rare Roman family name, attested in historical traditions only in the 5th and 4th cents. BC.

[1] **M., Q.** Jointly responsible for the Caudine treaty, M. gave up his office as *tr. pl.* 320 BC and was turned over to the Samnites (Liv. 9,8,13–10,2; Cic. Off. 3,109). C.MÜ.

[2] According to Liv. 4,12,6–16,1 and Dion. Hal. Ant. Rom. 12,1–4 M., a rich plebeian, gained a broad following in a famine 440/39 BC by buying grain and selling it cheaply; he relied on it when he aspired to the kingship. The Senate then made L. → Quinctius Cincinnatus dictator. His *mag. equitum* C. → Servilius Ahala killed M. when he refused the summons of the Senate (an older version, in Dion. Hal. Ant. Rom. 12,4,2–5, has Servilius by comparison act as *privatus*, but at the behest of the Senate, and gives a course of events similar to that of P. Cornelius [I 84] Scipio Nasica against Ti. → Sempronius Gracchus). It is debatable whether or not the tradition, which has M. a prominent example for the aspiration to the kingship (*adfectatio regni*), contains a historical core or is a simple *aition* (→ Aequimelium; → Monumental column: Columna Minucia). The agitation of a *tr. pl.* Sp. M. (MRR I 60) against Servilius and Minucius, which is handed down for 436, is presumably a 'doublet' of the earlier events, but it was also identified with M. and the historical core of the events of the years 440/39 were dated in 436.

T. J. CORNELL, The Value of the Literary Tradition, in: K. A. RAAFLAUB (ed.), Social Struggles in Archaic Rome, 1986, 58–61; GARNSEY, 70f.; P. M. MARTIN, L'idée de royauté à Rome, 1982, 339–360; A. MOMIGLIANO, Due punti di storia romana arcaica, in: Id., Quarto contributo alla storia degli studi classici e del mondo antico, 1969, 336–338; A. POLLERA, La caresia del 439 a.C., in: Bolletino dell'Istituto di Diritto romano 21, 1979, 141–168. C.MÜ.

Maelo (Greek Μέλωνος/*Mélōnos*; Μαίλος/*Maílos*). King of the → Sugambri with a Celtic name [1. 374], who is supposed to have started the war against the Romans according to Str. 7,1,4; this probably refers to the defeat of M. → Lollius [II 1] in 17/6 BC. After the forced relocation of the Sugambri to the left side of the Rhine (8 BC) he appears to have sought refuge with Augustus (R. Gest. div. Aug. 32). The son of his brother Baetorix, Deidorix, was carried along in the triumphal parade of Germanicus [2].

1 HOLDER, 2. W.SP.

M(a)enaca (Μαινάκη/*Mainákē*, Lat. Menace), city in southern Spain. The name is probably derived from μαίνη/*maínē* or Lat. *maena*, a salted fish (Avien. 426–431 confused M. with → Malaca [1. 80]; Scymn. 147; Steph. Byz. s.v. M., where M. is called Celtic). According to Str. 3,4,2 M. was a colony of → Phocaea, which no longer existed at that time. SCHULTEN [2. 35–38] assumed it was located west of the mouth of the Vélez on the hill Cerro del Peñón. This hypothesis is widely accepted among scholars, although probably unfounded. The excavations led by NIEMEYER on the grounds of → Toscanos on the west bank of the mouth of the Vélez (province of Málaga) showed that the assumed Greek *pólis* M. was a Phoenician settlement of unknown name ([3. 165ff.; 4. 11ff.]; → Colonization, with map). The beginning of the settlement of Toscanos can be traced back to the 8th cent. BC parallel to other comparable Phoenician settlements in southern Spain. Import finds from this time attest to the Phoenicians' close contact with the motherland, but also with cities in the Aegaean and the central Mediterranean area. In the middle of the 6th cent. BC the settlement was destroyed or abandoned and only revived in the Augustan-Early Iberian period. The Greek authors assumed a Greek origin from the regularity of the ruinous remains of the city [3. 179ff.].

1 A. SCHULTEN (ed.), Fontes Hispaniae Antiquae 1, 1955 2 Id., M., 1922 3 H. G. NIEMEYER, Auf der Suche nach M., in: Historia 29, 1980, 165–185 4 P. BARCELÓ, Aspekte der griechischen Präsenz im westlichen Mittelmeerraum, in: Tyche 3, 1988, 11–24.

SCHULTEN, Landeskunde 1², 321; TOVAR 2, 79f.   P.B.

Maenads (Μαινάς/*Mainás*, pl. Μαινάδες/*Mainádes*; Lat. *Maenas*, pl. *Maenades*). In modern research both the mythical companions (and antagonists) of → Dionysus and their historical admirers are mostly called Maenads. But in Greek cult terminology the women who honour the god with a dance ritual every three years are especially called *Bákchai* (singular *Bákchē*, Lat. *Bacchae*), while the substantivized adjective *Mainás* ('the mad one', from *maínesthai*: 'to be mad'), apart from four Hellenistic inscriptions with poetic tendencies [7. 52 with note 83], appears to be a purely literary designation.

Bákchai were probably women of the upper class and maybe organized in threefold *thíasoi* ('associations') with limited number of membership (presumably analogous to the mythical *thíasoi* of the three sisters of → Semele, who had contested the divinity of Dionysus; cf. Eur. Bacch. 680–682). A historical example are the *Thyiádes*, Attic women who went to Delphi every two years in order to climb Mount → Parnassus with the local *Bákchai* and to hold → *órgia* ('rites') in honour of Dionysus there (Paus. 10,4,3; 6,4; 32,7).

The ritual has been attested from the 3rd cent. BC on (above all in Boeotia with Thebes, in Delphi, in Ionian cities of Asia Minor and various regions of the Peloponnese [14. 137–146; 8; 9]; to what extent Maenadic ritual existed in Athens remains unclear because of the controversial interpretation of the so-called Lenaea vases [5; 6; 14. 146–150]), but it probably goes back to the archaic period; the decline took place in the 2nd cent. AD. Every second year (Diod. Sic. 4,3,3; Paus. 10,4,3) *bakcheía* (groups of *Bákchai*) went up a mountain in a winter night with *thýrsoi* (staffs made of

a fennel branch, *nárthēx*, with a bunch of ivy attached to the point) and with rhythmic cries of *eis óros, eis óros* ('up the mountain, up the mountain') in order to dance there (*oreibasía*, literally: 'mountain walk'). After they had untied their hair and put on the skin of a young buck deer (*nebrís*), they made sacrifices and danced barefooted with cries of *euhoí* or *euaí* by torch light to the sound of *týmpana* and *auloí*, special rhythmic and wind instruments, until they fell to the ground exhausted.

The term 'to be mad' (*mainás, maínomai, manía*; [7. 53–54 with n. 88]) refers to the characteristic running, jumping and rocking of the head back and forth during the dance as well as falling as the climax of the → ecstasy, which was understood to be a trance [3; 2; 4] or a condition of pleasant exhaustion ([7. 54; 8. 147]; cf. Eur. Bacch. 66f.). The women were probably looking for the special religious experience of being one with the god [11. 209].

Maenadism is clearly already assumed to be mythical in Hom. Il. 22,460 (cf. 6,389) and H. Hom. 2,386 and into late antiquity it is documented through rich literary and (from the early 6th cent. BC; from *c.* 540 BC in Etruria, → Fufluns; then also in Roman visual art) even richer iconographic [10] material. Thus the *Bassárai/Bassarídes* of Aeschylus (TrGF III T 68, F 23–25) probably had the tearing apart of → Orpheus by the homonymous Thracian Maenads as subject matter [15. 32–46]. While → Euripides (A. 12.) paid attention to some historical elements in the *Bákchai*, snake handling, the tearing apart (*sparagmós*) of animals and people (→ Pentheus) as well as eating raw meat (*ōmophagía*) are a part of the myth, which obviously exaggerates the ritual [3. 268–275].

In Attic tragedy the Maenads are often used as the Dionysiac image for the insanity of non-Dionysiac figures, even masculine ones like Hercules [12; 13].
→ Bacchus; → Dionysus; → Ecstasy

1 L'association dionysiaque dans les sociétés anciennes (Collection de l'école française de Rome 89), 1986 2 A. BÉLIS, Musique et transe dans le cortège dionysiaque, in: P. GHIRON-BISTAGNE (ed.), Transe et théâtre (Cahiers du GITA, 4), 1988, 9–29 3 J. BREMMER, Greek Maenadism Reconsidered, in: ZPE 55, 1984, 267–286 4 M.-H. DELAVAUD-ROUX, Danse et transe. La danse au service du culte de Dionysos dans l'Antiquité grecque, in: Transe et théâtre (s. [2]), 31–53 5 F. FRONTISI-DUCROUX, Le dieu-masque: Une figure du Dionysos d'Athènes, 1991 6 Id., Retour aux 'vases des Lénéennes', in: B. BRAVO, Pannychis e simposio. Feste private notturne di donne e uomini nei testi letterari e nel culto, 1997, 123–132 7 A. HENRICHS, Der rasende Gott: Zur Psychologie des Dionysos und des Dionysischen in Mythos und Lit., in: A&A 40, 1994, 31–58 8 Id., Changing Dionysiac Identities, in: B. F. MEYER, E. P. SANDERS (ed.), Jewish and Christian Self-Definition, vol. 3, 1982, 137–160, 213–236 9 Id., Greek Maenadism from Olympias to Messalina, in: HSPh 82, 1978, 121–160 10 I. KRAUSKOPF, E. SIMON, B. SIMON, s.v. Mainades, in: LIMC 8.1, 780–803; 8.2, 524–550 (Suppl.) 11 R. OSBORNE, The Ecstasy and the Tragedy: Varieties of Religious Experience in Art, Drama, and Society, in: CH.

Pelling (ed.), Greek Tragedy and the Historian, 1997, 187–211 12 R. Schlesier, Mixtures of Masks: Maenads as Tragic Models, in: Th. H. Carpenter, Ch. A. Faraone (ed.), Masks of Dionysus, 1993, 89–114 13 R. Seaford, Dionysus as Destroyer of the Household: Homer, Tragedy, and the Polis, in: [12], 115–146 14 H. S. Versnel, Inconsistencies in Greek and Roman Religion, vol. 1: Ter Unus: Isis, Dionysos, Hermes. Three Studies in Henotheism, 1990, 131–205 15 M. L. West, The Lycurgus Trilogy, in: Id., Studies in Aeschylus, 1991, 26–50 16 Sh. MacNally, The Maenad in Early Greek Art, in: J. Peradotto, J. P. Sullivan (ed.), Women in the Ancient World, 1984, 107–141 17 S. Moraw, Die Mänade in der attischen Vasenmalerei des 6. und 5. Jahrhunderts v. Chr. Rezeptionsästhetische Analyse eines antiken Weiblichkeitsentwurfs, 1998 18 L.-A. Touchette, The Dancing Maenad Reliefs. Continuity and Change in Roman Copies, 1995. T.H.

Maenalum (Μαίναλον, Μαίναλος, Μαινάλιον; *Maínalon, Maínalos, Mainálion*). Limestone mountain range about 30 km long between the eastern Arcadian plain and the Helisson valley, up to 1981 m high, with extended fir woods; in modern times without a standardized name; modern Tripolis is at its southern foot. Sacred to → Pan, who was called 'Maenalian' after it; in poets often in the genitive, hence it also means 'Arcadian'. The mountains also appear as the hunting grounds of → Atalante and → Artemis. M. is also the name of the chief city of the upper Helisson depression whose location is not known for certain, most likely near Apano-Davia on the upper Helisson river. Towards the end of the 5th cent. BC, the northern part of the region became dependent on → Mantinea (Thuc. 5,29,1; 67,2; 77,1, also 8,9,3f.), while the southern part remained with Sparta along with Oresthasium (Thuc. 4,1; 5,64,3; 67,1). When → Megale Polis was founded, the whole region was incorporated into the city (Paus. 8,27,3); in → Megale Polis there was a *phylè Mainalíōn* (φυλὴ Μαιναλίων, IG V 2,452). Games ἐμ Μαινάλωι (SEG 17,150) are also attested. Str. 8,8,2 mentioned M. among the Arcadian cities which had completely or almost disappeared in his time. The bronze-caster Nicodamus came from M. Literary evidence: Paus. 3,11,7; 6,7,9; 8,3,4; 36,5; 7f.; Steph. Byz. s.v. Μαίναλος; Syll.³ 183,15.

E. Meyer, s.v. M.(os), RE 14, 576f.; Id., s.v. Mainalos(on) (1), RE 14, 577f.
C.L. E.MEY.

Maenianum Gallery above the *tabernae* at the → Forum Romanum in Rome, named after the Roman censor M. → Maenius [I 3], from where spectators could follow the gladiatorial fights. The principle, attested here for the first time, of building the edge construction of a forum in two stories and constructing it as a bleacher, resp. viewing area on the upper floor, became widespread in the 2nd and 1st cents. BC in Roman architecture (→ Forum); thereafter, the tiers in the → amphitheatre were known as *maeniana* (→ Theatre).

W.-H. Gross, s.v. M., KlP 3, 864.
C.HÖ.

Maenius Name of a Roman plebeian family, perhaps of Etruscan origin [1. 185; 187]. The most important bearer of the name is M. [I 3]; the family is politically unimportant in the 1st cent. BC. *Lex Maenia* is the title of a Menippean satire of → Varro (Varro Men. 153–155). The law concerned the power of the paternal head of the house; content and dating are contested [3. 1085 – 1121]. A further *lex Maenia* probably passed before 290 BC directed that the 'agreement of the Senate' (*auctoritas patrum*) for elections be obtained before proclaiming the election results (Cic. Brut. 55).

1 Schulze   2 Walde/Hofmann, vol. 2   3 J.-P. Cèbe (ed.), Varron, Satires Ménippées, vol. 7, 1985.
K.-L.E.

I. Republican period   II. Imperial period

I. Republican period

[I 1] sold a plot of land to M. Porcius → Cato [1] in 184 BC for the construction of the Basilica Porcia in exchange for a reserved seat for himself for gladiatorial games (→ *munera*) above a column (presumably in the gallery of the Basilica). Ancient commentators (Ps.-Ascon. ad Cic. Div. Caec. 16,50; Porph. Hor. comm. ad sat. 1,3,21) designate the column the *columna Maenia* resp. *Maeni*, but it is not (as the commentators possibly did) to be confused with the identically named honorary column (*columna* [2] *Maenia*) for M.'s ancestor M. [I 3]. It is also possible that Lucilius (fr. 1203f. M) is referring to this column, which was known as a location for money-lending, at least in the late Republican period; the latter, in order to contrast M.'s questionable life with that of his forbear, has him seek out the *columna Maenia*.

F. Coarelli, Il Foro Romano 2, 1985, 39–53; E. Welin, Studien zur Topographie des Forum Romanum, 1953, 130–151.

[I 2] According to a presumably non-historical report, M. attempted as the first people's tribune in 483 BC to prevent troop conscriptions, in order to enforce an agrarian law (Dion. Hal. Ant. Rom. 8,87,3–5).

[I 3] M., C. As *cos.* in 338 BC (MRR I 138), M. triumphed over Antium, Lavinium and Velitrae. His victory over Antium is famous for the ships' prows captured as booty, which M. had brought to the speaker's platform at the Forum Romanum; this platform was named *rostra* (= 'ship's prow', → Rostrum), and [1. 318f.] after them. In addition, M. was honoured with two other memorials, the → *columna* [2] *Maenia* (cf. M. [I 1]) and an equestrian statue (Liv. 8,13,9; cf. Eutr. 2,7). Thus it is also possible that these are a single monument, i.e. an equestrian statue on a column [1. 338f.; 2. 39–53, esp. 43f.]. As dictator in 320, M. is supposed to have led an investigation too strictly (InscrIt 13,1,36f.; 416f.) and thus to have abdicated under pressure from his opponents (Liv. 9,34,14). However, this information – anyhow first woven into Livy's report of 310 – is possibly only a precursor to the events of his second dictatorship in 314 (MRR I 157; cf. [3. 194, n. 173]): at first employed against anti-Roman activities in Campania, M. also extended his investigation to Rome, whereby he offended leading circles. Himself threatened with accusations, he gave up his office, but was then acquitted in a trial (Liv. 9,26,5–22; cf. Diod. Sic. 19,76,4f.). As censor in 318 (MRR I 155), he was the first who had the so-called *maeniana* (→ *maenianum*) put up on the Forum Romanum (Fest. 120 L.).

1 T. HÖLSCHER, Die Anfänge römischer Repräsentationskunst, in: MDAI(R) 85, 1978, 315–357 2 F. COARELLI, Il Foro Romano, vol. 2, 1985 3 HÖLKESKAMP.   C.MÜ.

[I 4] M., C. He received the province of Sardinia as praetor in 180 BC. Beforehand he was supposed to investigate cases of persons providing poisons in Italy outside of Rome, which made such demands on him that he had to decide between this assignment and his province (Liv. 40,37,4; 43,2–3).

[I 5] M., Q. Son of M. [I 6], praetor in 170 BC. Directed business in Rome in the absence of the consuls, approved the Senate's decision concerning → Thisbe (Syll.³ 646) and regulated other questions concerning the East (MRR I, 420).   P.N.

[I 6] M., T. *Praetor urbanus* in 186 BC (MRR I, 371). Was legate of Q. Fulvius [I 12] Flaccus in Spain in 181 (Liv. 40,35,3).   P.N.

[I 7] M. Gemellus, C. Client of Cicero, went into exile to Patrae after a lost trial, became a citizen there and adopted Lyson [2]. Cause for the charge against M. was perhaps a scandal in 52 BC (Val. Max. 9,1,8).   JÖ.F.

II. IMPERIAL PERIOD
[II 1] M. M. Agrippa L. Tusidius Campester Equestrian from → Camerinum, who passed through the three equestrian *militiae*. He was thus sent to Britain into a war as *praef. cohortis II Brittonum* by Hadrian from Moesia inferior. Following the *militiae,* he became *praefectus classis* in Britain; also procurator there. He boasted that he had been *hospes* of Hadrian. He attained privileges for his fellow-citizens from Antoninus Pius. His son was the senator Tusidius Campester. PIR² M 67.   W.E.

Maeon (Μαίων; *Maíōn*, Latin Maeon).
[1] Son of a man named Haemon, leader of the 50 Thebans lying in wait for → Tydeus as he returns from a legation. Only M. is spared by the latter, who kills all the others. In gratitude, M. later buries him when he falls outside of Thebes (Hom. Il. 4,390–398; 14,114; Apollod. 3,67; Paus. 9,18,2; Stat. Theb. 2,690–703; 3,40–113). In Statius, M., who is sent back by Tydeus as a witness to the catastrophe, blames → Eteocles [1] for the disaster and takes his own life.

[2] Child of Creon's son → Haemon [5] and → Antigone [3] from a variously marital (Eur. Antigone; Hypothesis of Aristophanes of Byzantium on Soph. Ant.) or secret (Hyg. Fab. 72) relationship. According to Hyginus, who probably bases his text not on Euripides but rather on the 'Antigone' of Astydamas [2], the boy, having been raised by his mother among the shepherds, comes to the agon in Thebes, where a birthmark betrays his parentage and thus the disobedience of Haemon, who was supposed to kill Antigone because of the burial of Polynices (representation on Apulian vases [2. no. 14–16]).
→ Seven against Thebes; → Theban myths

1 D. VESSEY, Statius and the Thebaid, 1973, 110–116 2 I. KRAUSKOPF, s.v. Antigone, LIMC 1.1, 819, 823, 826.
                                                            CL.K.

Maeonia (Μαιονία; *Maionía*, Latin *Maeonia*).
[1] Area in Lydia around the → Gygaia Limne, at the foot of → Tmolus (Hom. Il. 3,401, cf. 2,864ff.; 10,431); primarily understood as the oldest country or tribal name (Μηίονες/*Mēíones*, Hdt. 1,7; 7,74; Diod. Sic. 4,31,5; Dion. Hal. 1,27,1; Plin. HN 5,110). Originally, M. comprised the → Catacecaumene [1] (Str. 12,8,13; 13,4,11) with the border region of Phrygia (Plin. HN 5,146; Ptol. 5,2,16), the valley of the Cogamus river (modern Alaşehir Çayı), the area around → Sardes (Plin. HN 5,110f.) with the Hermus valley right through to west of Sipylus (here once there was Tantalis, the capital of M., Plin. HN 5,117, cf. 2,205), the valley of the → Caystrus to → Larisa [7] (Str. 13,3,2) and finally the whole of Lydia. The Cabalians (Hdt. 7,77), whose capital → Cibyra [1] to the south-east on the border of Lycia and Pisidia was founded by the Lydians (Str. 13,4,17), were also regarded as Maeonians. In poetic language, M. was often used for Lydia (Verg. Aen. 10,141; Ov. Met. 6,5; 103; Ov. Fast. 2,310; Sil. 5,10). The equating of Maeonians and Lydians was not unanimously approved of in antiquity (Str. 12,8,3; 8,13; Dion Chrys. 78,31), but was considered to be a more plausible solution (Str. 13,4,5) to the problem, which remains unsolved even today (Maeonians as the older ethnic group?).
[2] City in the homonymous area of M. [1] in the → Catacecaumene [1]; belonged to the *conventus* of Sardes (Plin. HN 5,111), in the late antique period belonged to the *eparchia* of Lydia (Hierocles, Synekdemos 670,1). Settlement remains near Gökçeören in Merye.

BMC, Gr, Lydia LXVIf., 127f.; K. BURESCH, Aus Lydien, 1898, 194f.; F. IMHOOF-BLUMER, Lydische Stadt-Münzen, 1897 (repr. 1977), 92f.; J. KEIL, A. V. PREMERSTEIN, in: Denkschr. Akad. Wiss. Wien 53,2, 1908, no. 96, 165, 175; 54,2, 1911, no. 196; 57,1, 1914, no. 12f.; J. G. PEDLEY, Ancient Literary Sources on Sardis, 1972, Index s. Maeonia, Maeonians; W. M. RAMSAY, The Historical Geography of Asia Minor, 1890 (repr. 1972), 123, 168; W. RUGE, s.v. M. (1–2), RE 14, 582ff.; E. SCHWERTHEIM, Forschungen in Lydien, 1995; L. BORSAY, Lydia, Its Land and History, 1965.   H.KA.

Maeonius Murdered the Palmyrene prince → Odaenathus and his eldest son Herod in Emesa in AD 266/7 (SHA Tyr. Trig. 15,5; 17,1; SHA Gall. 13,1; different in Sync. I p. 717; Zon. 12,24 D.; Zos. 1,39,2). PIR² M 71.

T.F.

Maeotis (Μαιῶτις; *Maiôtis*, Latin *lacus* or *palus Maeotis*). The Asov Sea north-east of the Krim with an area of *c.* 38,000 km², with an outlet to the Black Sea (→ Pontus Euxinus) in the south through the Cimmerian → Bosporus [2], in the north-east confluence of the → Tanais in the M. The M. is exceptionally shallow (average depth 9 m) so that it easily freezes over. In spring, south-west winds drive the water of the Pontos Euxeinos into the M. Many rivers flow into the M., which has an abundance of fish (Str. 7,4,6). The size of the M. was vastly overestimated in antiquity (cf. for instance Hdt. 4,86: not much smaller than the Pontos Euxeinos). On the European coast lived → Scythians, on the Asian coast the → Maeotae.

CH. DANOV, s.v. Pontos Euxeinos, RE Suppl. 9, 879–881 (with bibliography).   I.v.B.

Maepha According to Ptol. 6,7,41 (Μαίφα μητρόπολις; *Maípha mētrópolis*), city in the interior of → Arabia Felix. Probably corresponds, with regard to the phonetic form, to epigraphically attested MYFʿT, once the capital of → Ḥadramaut, the ruins of which are now called Naqab al-Ḥaǧar. M. owed its importance – the city had solid fortifications – to its strategic position on the trading route from the harbour of → Cane to Inner Arabia.

H. V. WISSMANN, M. HÖFNER, Beitr. zur histor. Geogr. des vorislam. Südarabien (AAWM, Geistes- und Sozialwiss. Klasse), 1952, no. 4, 76, 82, 85f., 95, 104 and maps; H.v. WISSMANN, Zur Geschichte und Landeskunde von Altsüdarabien (SAWW, Phil. -histor. Klasse 246), 1964, 189, 416; A. H. AL-SHEIBA, Die Ortsnamen in den altsüdarab. Inschr. (Arch. Ber. aus dem Yemen 4), 1987, 56; S.-F. BRETON, Les fortifications D'Arabie Méridionale du 7ᵉ au 1ᵉʳ siècle avant notre ère (Arch. Ber. aus dem Yemen 8), 1994, 135–137, 51 (map) and passim   I.T.-N.

Maephath According to Ptol. 6,7,10 (Μαιφάθ κώμη; *Maipháth kṓmē*), town in the region of the Ἀδραμίται/ *Adramítai* (coastal dwellers of → Ḥadramaut) near the coast north-east of the harbour of → Cane. Was probably situated in Wādī Maifaʿ and should not be confused with → Maipha situated in Wādī Maifaʿa.   I.T.-N.

Maera (Μαῖρα; *Maîra*).
[1] According to the → *Nóstoi* (EpGF fr. 5), M. is the daughter of → Proetus, the son of Thersander (the son of → Sisyphus), and dies a virgin. In Hom. Od. 11,326 only her name is mentioned, together with Clymene and Eriphyle. In Pherecydes (FGrH 3 F 170 with JACOBY ad loc.), who names Antea as her mother (according to Hom. Il. 6,160, wife of Proetus of Argos), she is a com-

panion of → Artemis. She is shot dead by her when she gives birth to → Locrus [2] by Zeus.
[2] Arcadian heroine, daughter of → Atlas [2], wife of Tegeates in Tegea. The tombs of the royal couple are located there (Paus. 8,48,6). In Mantinea a tomb of M. was displayed and there was a dance-floor of M. (Paus. 8,8,1).
[3] The female dog who together with → Erigone [1] finds → Icarius [1] dead. According to Hyg. Fab. 130 and Astr. 2,4, she is turned into a star with the persons involved.
[4]
→ Nereids (Hom. Il. 18,48).

P. MÜLLER, s.v. M., LIMC 6.1, 341; W. OLDFATHER, M. VAN DER KOLF, s.v. M., RE 14, 604–605; SCHIRMER, s.v. M., ROSCHER 2, 2285–2286.   K.WA.

[5] Village in the area of → Mantinea on the border with Orchomenus, in ruins at the time of Pausanias (8,12,7). Position uncertain, presumably near modern Artemision (formerly Kakouri) in the north-eastern part of the plain of Mantinea.

S. and H. HODKINSON, Mantineia and the Mantinike, in: ABSA 76, 1981, 248–250; JOST, 139.   Y.L.

Maesades (Μαισάδης; *Maisádēs*). Odrysian prince who at the end of the 4th cent. BC, under the supreme rule of → Seuthes I, reigned over the regions of the Melandites, Thynians and Tranipsians, the so-called Thracian delta. After his death his son → Seuthes II was brought up by → Medocus (Xen. An. 7,2,32; 7,5,1).
→ Odrysae   U.P.

Maesaimanes (Μαισαμανεῖς/*Maisaimaneîs*, var. Μναισαμανεῖς/*Mnaisaimaneîs*, Ptol. 6,7,21). A people settling in north-western Arabia directly west of the Zamēs mountain range in the neighbouring area of the Thamydenians; definitely identifiable with the Batmizomaneis (var. *Banizomeneis*, Diod. Sic. 3,44,2) mentioned in Agatharchides (De mari Erythraeo 92) in the same region and with the Marsimani – named in the annals of Sargon II of Assyria from 715 BC after the Tamudi – who lived in the desert, owed tribute to no king and belonged to the faraway Arabs. The name of the Midianite tribe (→ Midian) that camped along the → Incense Road should therefore probably be reconstructed as *Banī/Bar Sīmān/Saimān*.

1 E. A. KNAUF, Midian, 1988, 85   2 H. VON WISSMANN, s.v. Madiama, RE Suppl. 12, 531–538.   W.W.M. A.D.

Maesesses Tribe of the → Bastetani (Liv. 28,3,3) in eastern Andalusia in a fertile region with silver mines. In 207 BC their region was conquered by P. → Cornelius [I 71] Scipio [1]. Orongis (probably identical with Aurgi, modern Jaén [2]) was situated here.

1 A. SCHULTEN (ed.), Fontes Hispaniae Antiquae 3, 1935, 131   2 SCHULTEN, Landeskunde 1, 84.   P.B.

Maesis (Μαῖσις; *Maîsis*). Son of Hyraeus, grandson of → Aegeus. With his brothers → Laeas [1] and Europas, he establishes in Sparta heroes' sanctuaries for his ancestors Aegeus (who is said to have been born there), Oeolycus, Cadmus and Amphilochus (Paus. 3,15,8).
→ Aegeidae   I.BAN.

Maesius
[1] **C.M. Aquillius Fabius Titianus** Consul in an unknown year; possibly identical with M. [3]. PIR² M 73.
[2] **C.M. Picatianus** Senator; perhaps from Brixia where he was honoured as a patron (CIL V 4338 = InscrIt X 5, 126). Praetorian legate of the *legio III Augusta* in AD 163–165 [1. 155f.]; suffect consul in 165 or 166. PIR² M 78.

1 THOMASSON, Fasti Africani, 1996.

[3] **C.M. Titianus** *Cos. ord.* in AD 245 together with Caesar Philippus; the family therefore held a high rank in senatorial society during this period (PIR² M 82; for the family [1. 139ff. = AE 1990, 129]).

1 M. G. GRANINO CECCERE, Iulii Apri e Maesii Titiani in un documento epigrafico dell'ager Tusculanus, in: MEFRA 102, 1990.   W.E.

Maesolia (Μαισωλία; *Maisōlía*, Ptol. 7,1,15; *Masalia*, Peripl. m.r. 62); the land of the Maesolians (Ptol. 7,1,79; 93) on the east coast of India. For the name and the position see → Maesolus. From an unnamed harbour there, the ships departed, according to Ptolemy, for → Chryse Chersonesus (Malacca).

1 B. CHATTERJEE, The Point of Departure for Ships Bound for 'Suvarnabhumi', in: Journ. of Ancient Indian History 11, 1977–1978, 49–52.   K.K.

Maesolus (Μαισῶλος; *Maisôlos*). Indian river, has its source in the Orudia mountain range (unclear according to [1]) and flows south to the Gulf of the Ganges (Ptol. 7,1,15; 37). Either modern Godavari or rather Kistna (Krishna) at whose delta the city of Masulipatam still lies today. DEY [2] also equates the name of the river M. with Old Indian *Mahāósāla*, a place of pilgrimage on the Godavari.

1 O. STEIN, s.v. Ὀρούδια, RE 18, 1526f. 2 N. L. DEY, The Geographical Dictionary of Ancient and Mediaeval India, 1927.   K.K.

Maeson (Μαίσων; *Maísōn*). In the catalogue of masks of → Iulius [IV 17] Pollux (4,148; 150), M. is listed among the slave characters of the New Comedy as a man with a red fringe of hair around his bald head [1]. Athenaeus (14,659a) specifies the mask type as a local cook (in contrast to → Tettix who comes from a foreign country) and names as his source Aristophanes of Byzantium (fr. 363 SLATER). The latter derives M. from

an actor of the same name from Megara (it has been debated since antiquity whether the Greek mother town or the Sicilian colony is meant) who invented this type of slave. People have sought to deduce from this a link with the Doric beginnings of the comic play, certainly incorrectly [2. 87–95]. In Epicharmus and in the Old Comedy there is certainly a great deal of talk about food, but people did not yet know of the M. type. The pictorial material also starts only in the 4th cent. BC [3]. Presumably numerous cooks appeared in → Menander [4] in the mask of M.
→ Comedy; → Masks

1 T. B. L. WEBSTER, J. R. GREEN, A. SEEBERG, Monuments Illustrating New Comedy, ³1995, vol. 1, 30–32 2 L. BREITHOLTZ, Die dorische Farce im griechischen Mutterland vor dem 5. Jahrhundert, 1960 3 R. GREEN, E. HANDLEY, Images of the Greek Theatre, 1995, 67, fig. 42.   H.BL.

Maevius Rare Italian proper name, variant of → *Mevius*.
[1] Accomplice of → Verres in Sicily (Cic. Verr. 2,3,175), perhaps the scribe who received gifts from Verres (2,3,176; 181; 185; 187).
[2] Centurio of Octavian, caught in 30 BC at Alexandria by Mark Antony, urged in vain to change sides and released out of respect (Val. Max. 3,8,8).
[3] **M., M.** Fell in battle in upper Italy in 203 BC as military tribune fighting against Hannibal's brother Mago (Liv. 30,18,15).   JÖ.F.

Maezaei (Μαιζαῖοι; *Maizaîoi*, Ptol. 2,16,5; Μαζαῖοι; *Mazaîoi*, Str. 7,5,3; Cass. Dio 55,32,4; *Mazaei*, Plin. HN 3,142; *Maezei* in inscriptions). Tribe to the north of Dalmatia near the Dalmatian-Pannonian border. According to Plin., Ptol. and Cass. Dio, it belonged to the Dalmatini, according to Str. to the Pannonii. The Pannonian origin of the M. is more probable although they were attached to the *conventus Salonitanus* ('legal district of Salona'). Their extensive area was subjugated by the Romans in 12 BC. They formed a peregrine tribal district that was administered by a *praefectus Maezeiorum* (CIL IX 2564). They were involved in the Pannonian uprising in AD 6–9 and were defeated in AD 7 by → Germanicus [2], who laid waste to their region (Cass. Dio l.c.). In the early Principate period, the M. were called up for military service and used in the *cohortes Dalmatarum* or in the Ravenna fleet (cf. ILS 2576; CIL XVI 14). The effects of Romanization were limited.

M. FLUSS, s.v. Maezei, RE 14, 283–286; G. ALFÖLDY Bevölkerung und Gesellschaft der römischen Provinz Dalmatien, 1965, 52; TIR L 34 Budapest, 1968, 75f.   J.BU

Magadis see → Musical instruments

Magalus (Greek Μάγιλος; *Mágilos*). Celtic name from *maglo-*, 'prince' [1. 234]. Chief of the → Boii who offered himself to → Hannibal [4] in 217 BC as an ally and leader for the crossing of the Alps (Pol. 3,44,5; Liv. 21,29,6).

1 SCHMIDT.   W.SP.

Magarsa (Μάγαρσα; *Mágarsa*). Settlement on the righthand bank of the Sarus in the region of → Mallus, 4 km south-west of the modern district capital of Karataş in → Cilicia Pedias on Cape Karataş in Dört Direkli where the sanctuary to Athena Magarsia was situated. After the end of Persian rule, M. first belonged to the empire of Alexander, then to the Seleucid kingdom. In the 2nd cent. BC, M. with Mallus was renamed Antioch on the Pyramus. From AD 72 finally in the Roman province of → Cilicia. Ancient remains: parts of the Hellenistic and Roman fortification walls, a stadium and the theatre cavea; priests of Zeus Olympios, Zeus Polieus and Athena Polias are known from inscriptions.

HILD/HELLENKEMPER, 335f., s.v. Magarsos.   M.H.S.

Magas (Μάγας; *Mágas*).
[1] Father of → Berenice [1].

GEYER, s.v. M., RE 14, 292f.

[2] M. was born no later than 320 BC as the son of Philippus and → Berenice [1], perhaps the brother of Theoxene (PP VI 14511), who married Agathocles [2] after 300 (there was no adoption by Ptolemy I: SEG 18, 743; on a house belonging to him in Alexandria cf. [1. 287]). M. reconquered the seceded → Cyrene for → Ptolemaeus I shortly after 301 and administered it. Given the geographical location, as well as for other reasons, his position must have been largely autonomous; after the death of Ptolemy I, M. revolted against Egypt (probably between 279 and 274), took the title of king and and married → Apama [3], a daughter of Antiochus [2] I. M. sought alliance with Cretan communities in order to oppose the Ptolemaic position on the island (Stv III 468; *koinón* of the Oreioi, Gortyn; cf. to Antiochus Stv III 486). The joint attack on Ptolemy II was not well co-ordinated: when the 1st → Syrian War began, M.'s campaign had already been called off. M. was 60 km from Alexandria (Taposiris), when he had to turn back on account of an uprising by the Libyan Marmarides (→ Marmarica)(Paus. 1, 7); he probably retained Paraetonium (Plut. Mor. 449e; 458a; perhaps turning up in SEG 17,817,4 (Cyrene) with *sképtra* (pl.!) a claim on the rulership in Egypt). Further disputes are not mentioned; there were no visible limitations in trade with either east or west.

Little is known of the administration of → Cyrenaea by M.; he was at least once an eponymous priest of the Cyrenaean Apollo (SEG 18, 743), received a cult in his lifetime (SEG 9, 112), minted coins according to the Ptolemaic model with the image of Ptolemy I, on whom he based his legitimacy; it is uncertain whether local coins continued to be minted. M. was one of the kings to whom → Aśoka sent Buddhist missionaries [2. XIII].

Shortly before his death in 250, M. betrothed his daughter → Berenice [3] II to Ptolemy III – a major change in policy, which was later not supported by Apama [3] (Iust. 26, 3; for the date of his death FGrH 86 F 7 is significant).

1 MITTEIS/WILCKEN   2 U. SCHNEIDER, Die großen Felsenedikte Aśokas, 1978.

BELOCH, GG IV² 2, 186ff.; F. CHAMOUX, Le Roi Magas, in: RH 216, 1956, 18–34; A. LARONDE, Cyrène et la Libye hellénistique, Paris 1987, 360ff.; O. MØRKHOLM, Cyrene and Ptolemy I. Some Numismatic Comments, in: Chiron 10, 1980, 145–159.

[3] Son of → Ptolemaeus III and → Berenice [3] II; sent to Asia in 223 or 222 BC by his father, after the death of Seleucus III, with command of the *prágmata* ('royal affairs') [1. 28ff.], perhaps in order to support → Attalus [4] I. The attempt was not successful, but was possibly one reason for the 4th → Syrian War. After the death of Ptolemy III, M. was killed in 221 by Sosibius with the assistance of the Spartan Cleomenes, because he had great influence with the army on account of his mother.

1 T. LARSEN (ed.), Pap. Graeci Haunienses 1, 1942, 6 (repr. 1974).

CHR. HABICHT, Athen in hellenistischer Zeit, 1994, 49f.; W. HUSS, Eine Expedition nach Kleinasien, in: AncSoc 8, 1977, 187–193; F. W. WALBANK, A Historical Commentary on Polybius 1, 564.   W.A.

Magdala

[1] (Greek Μαγδαλά; *Magdalá* < Hebrew *Migdal Numayyā*, 'Tower', Arabic *al-Maǧdal*). Harbour town on the north-western bank of Lake Genezareth, also known as *Taricheai* because of the production of saltwater fish there. Founded in the Hasmonean period (→ Hasmoneans), Hellenized M. developed into one of the largest cities of → Galilaea with a hippodrome and a stadium. Under emperor Nero, M. was annexed to the kingdom of Herod II Agrippa (→ Iulius [II 5]). During the First Jewish War, the city was a centre of resistance and was conquered in AD 67 by Titus after ferocious battles on water and land. A large part of the population was executed or enslaved. M. subsequently continued to exist as a town but lost its economic importance and after the death of Herod II Agrippa was passed to the province of Palestine. After the destruction of the Temple, the priests of the Ezechiel family settled there.

As the home town of Mary Magdalene (→ Maria [II 2]), M. became a destination for Christian pilgrims at the latest from the 6th cent. AD onwards. From the 8th cent. a church is attested on the site of the house of Mary Magdalene. The excavations conducted by the Franciscans in M. brought to light a rectangular building equipped in the interior on three sides with a series of pillars, which (*pace* CORBO [2]) appears not to have been a 'mini synagogue' but a well house. Roman villas and remains of a Byzantine monastery were also found.

1 M. Aviam, s.v. M., The Oxford Encyclopedia of Archaeology in the Near East 3, 399f. 2 V. Corbo, La mini-synagogue de Magdala, in: Le Monde de la Bible 57, 1989, 15–20 3 M. Nun, Ancient Anchorages and Harbours around the Sea of Galilee, 1988 4 D. Pringle, The Churches of the Crusader Kingdom of Jerusalem 2, 1998, 28. J.P.

[2] According to recently published Greek and Latin texts [1] in conjunction with texts from the excavation of → Dura Europos and Neo-Assyrian cuneiform tablets from Tall → Šēḫ Ḥamad, M. should very probably be identified with this town on the lower Ḫābūr [2]. In the latter as well as in Aramaic annotations on them, the town of Magdalu is mentioned. Tall Šēḫ Ḥamad is, however, undoubtedly also identical with the Middle and Neo-Assyrian provincial centre of Dūr-Katlimmu. Dual names for towns are attested on several occasions in ancient Oriental history; in this case, the second name probably goes back to the Aramaic-speaking population [3].

Through archaeology it is possible to demonstrate in M. a continuity of settlement from the Middle Assyrian (13th cent. BC) to the late Roman Imperial period (3rd cent. AD), however not at a single excavation site. In the Middle Assyrian and then again from the Hellenistic-Seleucid periods, the settlement covered an area of *c.* 25 to 30 ha. It now consisted of the citadel (the → tell) and the lower part of the city I; in the lower part of the city II that was abandoned, the cemetery of the Hellenistic and Parthian-Roman city [4] was located. In the Neo-Assyrian period and right through to the Achaemenid period, the settlement comprised an area of *c.* 60 ha and so had its largest intramural expansion.

1 D. Feissel, J. Gascou, Documents d'archive romains inédits du moyen Euphrate (IIIᵉ s. après J.-C.), I.: Les petitions, in: Journ. des Savants, 1995, 65–119 2 H. Kühne, A. Luther, Tall Šēḫ Ḥamad/Dūr-Katlimmu/Magdalu, in: Nouvelles Assyriologiques Brèves et Utilitaires, 1998, no. 117, 106–109 3 H. Kühne (ed.), Magdalu/Magdala. Tall Šēḫ Ḥamad von der postassyrischen Zeit bis zur römischen Kaiserzeit (Berichte der Ausgrabung Tall Šēḫ Ḥamad/Dūr-Katlimmu 2, Berlin 2004 4 M. Novák et al., Der parthisch-römische Friedhof von Tall Šēḫ Ḥamad/Magdala, Teil 1 (Berichte der Ausgrabung Tall Šēḫ Ḥamad/Dūr-Katlimmu 5), 2000. H.Kü.

Mageia see → Magic, Magi

Magi Fort in north-western Britannia (Not. Dign. Occ. 40,14; 40,49) with a *numerus Pacensium* as a garrison (4th cent. AD). Site contentious but an altar (CIL VII 1291) built by *vik(ani) Mag...* in Old Carlisle refers to it. It is, however, conceivable that M. was the fort in Burrow Walls and Maglona was the one in Old Carlisle (Not. Dign. Occ. 40,13; 40,29). Both forts were held right through to the 4th cent.

E. Birley, The Roman Fort and Settlement at Old Carlisle, in: Transactions of the Cumberland and Westmorland Archaeological and Antiquarian Society 51, 1951,

16–39; A. L. F. Rivet, C. Smith, The Place-Names of Roman Britain, 1979, 406. M.TO.

Magia Polla (also Maia). Mother of the poet → Vergilius, of lowly birth. Her dream of the birth of Virgil in Suetonius (Suet. De viris illustribus, Vergilius 1–3).

G. Brugnoli, Phocas, Vita di Vergilio, 1984; Id. (ed.), Vitae Vergilianae antiquae, 1997. ME.SCH.

Magic, Magi
I. Ancient Orient II. Judaism III. Greece and Rome IV. Christianity V. Islam

I. Ancient Orient
A. General B. Mesopotamia and Asia Minor C. Egypt

A. General
The magic of the ancient Orient and of Egypt is based on a view of the world that runs counter to that of religion. In the world-view of magic, men, gods and → demons are tied to each other and to the cosmos by sympathies and antipathies, whereas in the religious world view everything is created by the gods for their own purposes; the relations between men and the cosmos are the result of deliberate actions of the gods. In the practice of religion, however, both world views are integrated and complementary. The religious world-view manifests itself most clearly in the regular → cult, whereas magic is only employed to overcome public or private problems if the need arises. Usually, magic is used defensively; magic used offensively, against people – sorcery –, is feared as an antisocial activity and is punished. A particular instance of defensive magic is directed against diseases and the demons of diseases; it is complementary to medical science (→ Medicine) and is applied in cases of chronic and unidentifiable pains.

Every ceremonial act of magic comprises a manipulation of and with objects (→ Ritual) and an incantation often arranged in rhythmical speech, which gives form to the ritual's intent. The object of the magic ceremony is either to control or to deceive the natural or supernatural powers that are being opposed. This is usually achieved by means of preparing a model or by the introduction of a substitute. Natural materials (plants and minerals) can attract or divert (super)natural powers. The world-view of magic is identical with that of → divination. Both come increasingly under the influence of the dominant theistic system, i.e. their effects are regarded more and more as being directed and sanctioned by the gods. Magic rituals are consequently often accompanied by → prayers to gods.

B. Mesopotamia and Asia Minor
The most ancient sources of Mesopotamian magic (in the Sumerian language) originate from the 27th/26th cents.; they were passed on in the 2nd–

Amulet for the protection against the female demon Lamashtu

1 Head of the apotropaic demon Pazuzu. Pazuzu, who protects the carrier against the demon, is holding the amulet in his hand
2 Divine symbols
3 Seven demons with raised fists, with an apotropaic function against Lamashtu
4 Exorcist at the sick-bed
5 The demon Pasuzu
6 Lamashtu departing for the Underworld, standing on a donkey
7 Gifts and food for Lamashtu

1st millennium (provided with an Akkadian interlinear translation). By magical means, supernatural as well as natural, evil can be combated. The identity of natural evil is today often difficult to recognize because the incantations portray evil and the fight against it transferred onto a mythological plane. The supernatural opponents are demons or ghosts (i.e. the 'souls' of the dead). Demons, mostly only appearing in the Group of Seven (*Sebetti*), are beyond the control of divine order, lack cult support and plunder mankind wherever they can. Spells against demons often refer back to a mythical, primeval period, when Asalluhi, the son of the creator god Enki, was still walking the earth and was being taught about their struggle by his father. Apart from the Group of 'Seven' there are also individualized demons, hypostases of specific evils. Particularly feared is the child-stealing demoness Lamaštu (→ Lamia [1]), represented as a dog bitch, she-wolf or as a composite creature (see fig.). The counter-magic against her is well-at-tested and consists essentially in the making of a clay model of Lamaštu and her costumes together with a donkey, a ship and provisions for her journey back to the Underworld. The ritual can also be depicted on an amulet and then, apparently, has the same effect.

The spirits of the dead cause problems if they are not supplied with food and drink by members of their families who are still alive, because they then find no peace and haunt the living until their wishes are met; they attract attention to themselves by entering the heads of the living through the ears, causing headaches and mental illnesses. The magic remedy consists in a reburial using a clay model of the dead person. A special case is the 'whirlwind', the spirit of a girl who dies unmarried; she returns as *succuba* and is neutralized by marriage to a supernatural partner. Adversaries of natural origin are the dog, scorpion, snake and crop pests. Diseases are tackled together with a → physician; more often the correct treatment must be established by an interpreter of omens. Animals as well as diseases are at times portrayed as demons.

Vague and chronic pains are regarded as being caused by 'black magic'. The countermeasure is 'incineration' (*maqlû*): the witch and her method of magic are identified in spells, and models or symbolical representations of her are made and burnt. Similar rituals to those used against 'black magic' are used against human enemies and against the 'evil eye'. Witches and enemies are often portrayed as demons and opposed by gods on the cosmic level. Magic against humans is regarded as the forbidden ' black magic' and is consequently not represented in the official corpus of text. Exceptions are a love spell that brings a reluctant lover to his or her senses, and the collected sayings and instructions in the series 'On entering the Palace', which assisted the combating of an opposing party and of officials who oppress the people. Magic is sometimes employed where more usually 'confession of sins' and 'psalms of repentance' would be appropriate. Thus, there is a magic ritual against 'excommunication', i.e. the consequence of a crime against religious or social laws. In addition, there are spells and amulets for the calming of angry gods.

The future is predicted by the interpretation of signs (omens; → Omen); the consequences of a bad omen can be neutralized by using a 'ritual of dissolution' (*namburbi*; [5]). Usually, either a model of the bad omen is made and destroyed, or the predicted evil is diverted onto a substitute (figure). A special instance of the latter is the diversion of the consequences of an eclipse (→ Eclipses) onto a 'substitute king': the king whom the evil should actually affect then rules under the alias of 'farmer'. Individuals, buildings and the people can be protected by apotropaic figures of wood, clay or metal, which represent the frightful → monsters of primeval times. Magic protection against evil is offered by → amulets, their effects being based on cosmic sympathies and antipathies. During the 1st millennium, the cosmic relationships between plants, stones and the stars are systematized and documented.

Objects to be used in cult or magic ritual must be consecrated. There are special spells for this, which detach the object from its profane origin and imbue it with its new, sacral role. Special instances of this ritual of consecration are 'mouth-washing ' (mis pî) and 'mouth-opening' (pīt pî) in a cult image. The practitioners of magic are scholars, not priests. As with other practitioners, they serve the state, the temple or private individuals. The role of the 'old woman' is noteworthy as practitioner of Anatolian magic; in Mesopotamia, only women are recorded as being witches. The Anatolian magical texts of the 2nd half of the 2nd millennium are written in the Hattic, Hurrite, Luwian or Hittite languages. Apart from this, Mesopotamian texts were used.

C. EGYPT

Egyptian magic is directed against anonymous demonic spirits, spirits of the dead, specific demons or gods and against 'black magic'. Enemies of natural origin include snakes and scorpions, and diseases often portrayed as demons. The magical process can be represented as a battle between the healer and the disease or between the cosmic gods and their demonic adversaries (→ Seth and Apophis). Magic is a gift to mankind from the god of creation or a product of the early cosmos; it is personified in the deity Heka, 'Magic'. Even the gods employ magic; in addition, they have at their disposal 'brilliant light', a kind of creative energy, by means of which good is produced and evil destroyed. Egyptian magic is best evidenced in rituals for the dead (→ Dead, cult of the). It helps in the transformation of the deceased into a spirit and in the guaranteeing of its maintenance. A further well-attested application is the execration of absent enemies, of whom statuettes are prepared and then smashed and buried (→ Apotropaic texts). A ritual of consecration is used for making cult images come to life through 'opening of the mouth'. Amulets of various combinations of materials, form and colour help protect the wearer and are used during rituals for the dead. Stelae (cippi) show → Horus as a child conquering dangerous animals. Evidently, the presence of the representation transfers this attribute to the individual and helps, e.g. in the curing of snake bites or scorpion stings. Practitioners of magic are experts, but not necessarily scholars; they are often assisted by a 'wise woman'. There is no sharp distinction between practitioners of magic and medicine.

1 T. ABUSCH (ed.), Mesopotamian Magic: Textual, Historical, and Interpretative Perspectives, 1999 2 J. F. BORHOUTS, H. ALTENMÜLLER, L. KAKOSZY, s.v. M., mag. Lit., mag. Stelen, LÄ 3, 1138–1164 3 J. BOTTÉRO, V. HAAS, s.v. M., RLA 7, 200–255 4 P. ESCHWEILER, Bildzauber im alten Äg., 1994 5 S. M. MAUL, Zukunftsbewältigung. Eine Unt. altoriental. Denkens anhand der babylon.-assyr. Löserituale, 1994 6 G. PINCH, Magic in Ancient Egypt, 1994 7 E. REINER, Astral Magic in Babylonia, 1995 8 D. SCHWEMER, Akkad. Rituale aus Hattusa, 1998.   F.W.

II. JUDAISM

Magical practise and texts in → Judaism, both in antiquity as well as in the Middle Ages[17], were spread by various means, although all forms of magic are forbidden in the → Bible (Ex 22:17; Lv 19:26 and 31; 20:6 and 27; Dt 18:10f.) and similar bans feature in the Mishna (Mishna Sanhedrin 7,4 and 11) and the Talmud (Jerusalem Talmud Sanhedrin 7,19 [25d]; the Babylonian Talmud Sanhedrin 67a–68a). In addition to ancient reports of Jewish magic (e.g. the description of an exorcism by Jos. Ant. Iud. 8,2,5), there are numerous references to theoretical and practical magic such as treatises on the nature of magic or of demons [12; 10. vol. 1, vol. 3], manuals, medical magic formulae and amulet forms as well as amulets, curses and magic bowls [7; 8; 10]. An important source for the Jewish magic of late antiquity in an outlying area of the Egyptian-Graeco-Roman sphere of influence is represented by the Babylonian Talmud (→ Rabbinical literature) [2; 18]. The documents on applied magic can be dated in part to the period of late antiquity [7; 8; 1].

The situation regarding texts recorded in MSS on magic is more complicated. At least a proportion of these practices can also be dated to the period of late antiquity because of their language and content [1. 343f.]. To these belong, for example, the two manuals on magic 'The Book of Secrets' (Sefer ha-Rāzīm) [5; 6] and 'The Sword of Moses' (Ḥarbā dᵉ-Moše) [3], which contain, among other things, apart from a wealth of formulae and spells, a Greek prayer to Helius and magic names of Greek origin in Hebrew script, the Testamentum Salomonis [1. 372ff.] and theurgical instructions within the → Hekhalot literature [9].

References to Jewish magic in antiquity are also found in the Qumran literature (→ Qumran, the → Dead Sea (textual finds); → Astrology, chiromancy and → Physiognomy) [1. 364ff.] and in the Greek → magic papyri [4; 14]. The same is true of the Apocrypha (Book Tobit; → Apocryphal literature) and of pseudoepigraphic literature as well as the NT [15]. With all the examples quoted here strong influence can be detected from outside the Jewish world (Graeco-Egyptian or Babylonian), just as Jewish magic, for its part, influenced Greek texts on magic. Ancient Jewish magic, as with magic in general, is syncretistic and is, therefore, to be differentiated from the magic of other cultures mainly by language (Hebrew and Aramaic), then also by specific Jewish themes such as the rich angelology, the magic of names (secret names of God, angels and demons) and the use of Bible texts (šimmūš tōrā, šimmūš tᵉhillīm [10. vol. 3]).

1 P. S. ALEXANDER, Incantations and Books of Magic, in: SCHÜRER 3, 342–379 2 L. BLAU, Das altjüd. Zauberwesen, 1898 3 M. GASTER (ed.), The Sword of Moses, 1896 4 E. R. GOODENOUGH, Jewish Symbols in the Greco-Roman Period 2, 1953 5 M. MARGALIOTH (ed.), Sefer ha-Razim. A Newly Recovered Book of Magic from the Talmudic Period (Hebr.), 1966 6 M. A. MORGAN (transl.), Sepher ha-razim. The Book of the Mysteries, 1983 7 J. NAVEH, SH. SHAKED (ed.), Amulets and Magic

Bowls. Aramaic Incantations of Late Antiquity, 1985
8 Id., Magic Spells and Formulae. Aramaic Incantations
of Late Antiquity, 1993　9 P. SCHÄFER, Die Beschwörung
des sar ha-panim, in: Id., Hekhalot-Studien, 1988, 118–
153　10 Id., SH. SHAKED (ed.), Mag. Texte aus der Kairoer
Geniza 1, 1994; 2, 1997; 3, 1999　11 G. SCHOLEM, Major
Trends in Jewish Mysticism, ⁴1969　12 Id., Some Sources
of Jewish-Arabic Demonology, in: Journ. for Jewish
Studies 16, 1965, 1–13　13 Id., Kabbalah, 1974　14 M.
SMITH, The Jewish Elements in the Magical Papyri, in:
Soc. of Biblical Literature, Seminar Papers 25, 1986, 455–
462　15 M. SMITH, Jesus, the Magician, 1978　16 M. D.
SWARTZ, Scholastic Magic. Ritual and Revelation in Early
Jewish Mysticism, 1996　17 J. TRACHTENBERG, Jewish
Magic and Superstition. A Study in Folk Religion, 1939
18 G. VELTRI, M. und Halacha. Ansätze zu einem empi-
rischen Wissenschaftsbegriff im spätant. und frühma.
Judentum, 1997.　　　　　　　　　　　　　　　I.WA.

III. GREECE AND ROME
A. TERMINOLOGY　B. BASIC PRINCIPLES　C. DE-
VELOPMENT

A. TERMINOLOGY
1. GREEK　2. LATIN

1. GREEK

The modern term derived from Latin *magia* based on
the Greek term *mageía* (μαγεία) signifies that what a
mágos (μάγος, 'sorcerer') does and knows. The Greek
mágos/Lat. *magus* remains an ambiguous concept during the entire period of antiquity. On the one hand, the
mágoi are a certain caste of priests in Persia (or Persian
priests in general), who are closely connected to kingship: according to Hdt. 1,107f.; 1,120; 1,132; 7,19;
7,37; 7,43; 7,113f. they interpret dreams and *portenta*
(→ *prodigium*), carry out sacrifices to the river gods and
the dead, and recite → theogonies. Later writers (Xen.
Cyr. 8,3,11; [Pl.] Alcibiades maior 112 A) broaden their
meaning, and from the early Hellenistic period, they
become more and more stylized to the ideal of wise
men; thus the expression belongs in the field of ancient
ethnography.

On the other hand, in the Greek world the *mágoi* are
religious specialists beginning with Heracl. 22 B 14 DK,
whose responsibilities include a broad range of ritual
activities not linked to the polis (esp. initiation to the
mystery cults, → divination and → purification); this
becomes limited only during the 4th cent. BC to damaging magic and related matters. The genesis of the terminology in religious-philosophical (Heraclitus, Plato)
and in medical discussion (Hippoc. De morbo sacro,
late 5th cent. BC) indicates a part of ritual tradition
being dismissed as non-Greek (Persian) and, therefore,
to be polemically excluded (Heracl. B 14 is already
polemical). Magic was a polemical concept until beyond the end of antiquity, denoting whatever is to be
understood as not being a part of the particular religious tradition, though it is also idealized with typical
ambivalence (cf. Apul. Apol. 25–27).

The Latin borrowing of *magus* in the late Republi-
can-early Augustan period takes on both of its Greek
categories of meaning, clearly documented the ethnographical conceptual sphere being earlier (e.g. Cic. Leg.
2,26; Cic. Div. 1,46; 1,91; 2,26; Catull. 90); *magia* is
also a polemically pejorative term in Latin [1].

Another term for magician, often treated as a synonym in modern translations, is *góēs* (γόης), indicating a
derivation from *góos* ('lamentation for the dead') corresponding originally to a professional mourner, who
establishes for the dead the line between this world and
the hereafter [2. 82–123]. Yet already in the earliest references (Phoronis fr. 2 EpGF, Pherecydes FGrH 3 F 47)
góēs is used to signify → *daktyloi*, allowing important
later associations to be discerned. e.g. enchanting music
(the *daktyloi* are musicians) and, in Pherecydes, a binding magic, which brings the dead into action in further-
ance of the desires of the living, as is later recorded in
the defixion texts. Later *goetia*, after the classical period, is mostly associated with the world of the dead: the
góētes can (1) call up the dead (Pl. Leg. 909b 2; cf. 933a
2–b 3), (2) bring them under control when they are
harming the living (Plut. Mor. fr. 126 SANDBACH =
schol. Eur. Alc. 1128), and (3) initiate the living into the
mysteries, which guarantee their safety after death
(Diod. Sic. 5,64,4). Gradually, the meanings of *mágos*
and *góēs* grew closer, above all in the vernacular speech;
where *góēs* took on a more offensive meaning than
mágos [3]. In the period of late antiquity, the theurgists
(who practised → theurgy, a kind of religious magic)
firmly distanced themselves from the *goetai*.

The Greek texts, especially before the Imperial period, often use none of the general terms, but refer to
relevant rites, particularly that of binding (*katádesmos*,
Lat. → *defixio* or → *devotio*) or of spells (Homer. *epao-
idé*, later *epōidé* [4]). From Homer on the expression
phármakon is used to denote any powerful substance
effective for good or evil; from this is derived *pharmakeútriai* as a description of women (the mythological
prototype is → Medea, for example Soph. fr. 534 RADT;
cf. Theocritus' *Pharmakeútriai*, Theoc. 2), who utilize
their special knowledge in the field of effective substances especially for love magic, but also for harmful
magic.

2. LATIN

Earlier than the borrowing of the Latin loan-words
magus and *magia* in the late Republican / early Augustan period is *veneficus, –fica* ('poisoner'), which encompasses harm caused by chemical substances as well as
that caused as a result of magic rites (Plaut. Amph.
1043; Plaut. Pseud. 870; Cic. Brut. 217); Sulla's *lex
Cornelia de sicariis et veneficis* of 81 BC thus also becomes the legal basis of magic trials [1. 45f.; 5]. During
the Imperial period, the general term *maleficus, –fica*
('evildoer') increasingly appears instead of *veneficus*.
The earliest Latin expression for the word of ritual
power, which can also include magic, is *carmen*, occasionally specified as *carmen malum*; the Law of the
Twelve Tables (→ *Tabulae duodecim*) is already using

the derivations *incantare* and *excantare* to denote harmful magic (see under C. 4.).

B. Basic principles
1. Sources 2. Harmful magic and love magic
3. Magical healing 4. Magical divination
5. Theories in antiquity

1. Sources
Main sources for Graeco-Roman magic are, on the one hand, the spells inscribed onto thin lead tablets beginning with the late 6th cent. known as the *tabulae defixionum* [6; 7; 8] (→ *defixio*), and on the other, the papyrus books from Egypt dating mostly from the 3rd and 4th cents. AD, in which magic rites are recorded, in an often random way, as remedies [9; 10]; their sometimes extremely detailed ritual instructions allow a unique insight into the mechanisms of magic ritual, into its ideology and its diverse – Egyptian, Greek, Jewish, ancient Oriental – backgrounds [11]; in the discussion of these backgrounds after naive Hellenocentrism a complex discussion has developed, though sometimes one focussed mainly on Egypt [12]. Almost as important as the corpus of *defixiones* is that of the amulets (→ *phylaktērion*), of which admittedly only late examples survive; these were often inscribed with invocations and images of gods and demons [13; 14]. In addition, there are numerous literary texts, which sometimes perform their own literary stylization not indicated in the inscription; especially important in practice are the reports on magic trials that have been preserved especially in Tac. Ann (e.g. 2,27f.; 12,22) and as an independent trial oration in Apuleius' *Apologia*.

Ethnographical theory has not been able to fix on any standard term for magic since the influential constructions of J.G. Frazer [15; 16]. The definition of magic is, therefore, assumed to be affected by the domestic cultural perception, which is of course subject to historical changes; comparison with other cultures and religions adds depth and precision. In the Graeco-Roman world appropriately a not insignificant, though in its outlines indistinct, field of ritual behaviour becomes isolated, in which prior to the Imperial period binding magic (→ *defixio*) is central in the reality of society in the form of love magic and magic for causing harm; during the Imperial period (from the 1st cent. AD), private → divination becomes more and more important, and the field of so-called magic medicine is less clearly defined.

In modern discussion, in particular the evolutionary concept of magic originating with E.B. Tylor and J. G. Frazer has long been held, according to which magic is one method comparable to a technique but with false causality by which men attempt to master nature. Whilst Frazer attributed this attempt to the evolution of primitive cultures, B. Malinowski tried, by means of a synchronous explanatory model, to differentiate the closely existing areas of controllable and relatively risk-free activities that such techniques apply, from those difficult-to-control activities, which magic uses for support. Other theories promulgated, especially in Roman religious history, (e.g. by H. J. Rose) are orientated towards Tylor, and see magic as a mere ritual activity not, or only loosely, associated with a deity. Furthermore, there are approaches that regard magic or accusations of magic as attempts at solving social crises (M. Mauss, E.E. Evans-Pritchard); in more recent ethnological discussion, the term magic has (with justification) been fundamentally criticized as Eurocentric prejudice [1].

2. Harmful magic and love magic
Particular rites were current in the Greek world from the late archaic period (from the 6th cent. BC), especially that of binding magic, which was already developing in the domestic culture into the main fields of love magic (initially Pind. Pyth. 4,213–219) and of harmful magic (for example described in Pl. Resp. 2,364b). In practice, as documented by the inscribed defixion texts from the 5th cent. BC up to the end of the ancient period, classification into legal, erotic, agonistic and economic *defixiones* had been carried out since A. Audollent [6]. In erotic defixion, it is a matter of making submissive the reluctant object of erotic desire (the mythological aition is Aphrodite's gift of special rites to → Iason, in order to win the young Medea, Pind. Pyth. 4,193–196); in this, there is a preponderance in epigraphic material of rites carried out by men against women, admittedly with variations in distribution according to period and region, and at least during the Imperial period homo-erotic rites are also recorded. In contrast, the other three categories seek to influence an outcome by ritual in a confrontational or argumentative situation characterized by uncertainty [17]: legal *defixiones* (see below C.3.), which are recorded in Athens from the 5th cent. BC, attempt to hinder the adversary's evidence in a trial by causing voice loss and paralysis; agonistic *defixiones*, during the Imperial period and esp. in the sphere of horse-racing, seek to prevent victory of the opponent by interventions, and an economic defixion seeks to eliminate business competitors – its positive counterpart may be seen in the rites, preserved in the magic papyri, which seek to secure success for a new business.

The supernatural powers of intervention called upon in these texts comprise, in addition to the traditional Underworld deities of Greek myth (→ Persephone, → Hecate, → Hermes Chthonios; and extended in the → magic papyri to include Egyptian and western Oriental deities such as → Anubis or Ereškigal), also, at least during the Imperial period, all kinds of, often fanciful → demons.

3. Magical healing
Whilst in sections of modern research literature so-called magic → medicine is regarded as a significant special area, which is supported by prayer and incantation (*epōidḗ, carmen*) instead of scientific and rationally-based interventions, but which is not restricted to ritual treatments, such a special area is less clearly defined in the ancient world according to its own definition [18;

19]. However, the Hippocratic writer of the text *De morbo sacro* (late 5th cent. BC) established an unbridgeable gap between his own treatment of → epilepsy based on scientific aetiology and the cathartic, ritual treatment of the same disease proceeding from the idea of possession, and placed the ritual healers in the sphere of magic – the same contrast can be discerned in Apuleius (Apol. 43); in reality among ancient societies the contrast is less clearly defined. The temple medicine of → Asclepius based on → incubation exhibits no stark contrast to scientific medicine, for the therapies derived from the sick person's dream are often not different from those of the professional physicians. On the other hand, it is the trend that the area being dealt with by ritual means becomes less available to professional medicine. In Homer, haemorrhages are stopped by rituals (Hom. Od. 19,457f.) [20], and this is recorded in other cultures into the modern era; a ritual recorded by Cato the Elder (Agr. 160) with a long *carmen* concerns a dislocation of the thigh, and in the magic papyri certain toothaches and migraines are the object of healing rituals (only in this latter case does the entry in the papyrus books show the indigenous version of these rites). Amulets, too, have a great deal to do with the healing of diseases. To the field of magic belong all those medical aetiologies that argue for the concept of possession as a cause of illness and respond with → exorcisms or cathartic rites; in the wake of exorcisms by Jesus, corresponding stories have become very important particularly in the Christian lives of the saints [21; 22].

4. MAGICAL DIVINATION
According to the papyri as well as the decrees of the Christian emperors of the 4th cent., recorded in the Cod. Theod., and also to contemporary historians, private rites of divination played an increasingly important role in the magic of the Imperial period, whilst previously, with the exception of necromancy, it was not in evidence. As to forms, apart from the latter and the private transmission of dreams, a multitude of rites are represented, especially lecanomancy or hydromancy (the reading of signs in an oil film spreading on water) and lychnomancy (signs in the flame of a burning oil lamp) [23]. Also, the sorcerer of the Imperial period acquires knowledge of the future via his ritually-produced personal encounter with a deity (*sýstasis*), which mostly, though not exclusively, characterized → theurgy [24].

5. THEORIES IN ANTIQUITY
Theoretical reflection on magic took place mostly in the polemical debate on aspects of religious tradition that philosophy, medicine and later Christianity were engaged in [25; 26]. In his religious lawmaking in the *Nómoi*, Plato declared the well-attested harmful magic of his time (using → magic dolls) to be a sign of social disintegration, depending largely on the fear of those involved for the effectiveness of its rites (Pl. Leg. 11,933ab); this fear, for its part, is a consequence of men's mutual distrust: thus, magic becomes completely

left out of the religious realm, its reality declared to be purely psychological. On the other hand, later theories take the objective reality of magic as their starting-point. Returning to a concept widespread in his time, Apuleius (Apol. 25) declares magic to be a 'communion of speech between gods and men' (*communio loquendi cum dis*) and classifies it among current ritual practices, for which oral contact with the gods in prayer and hymn was central. Magic alone stands out from other rites because of its motive of self-interest. This same idea is the basis for Augustine's concept of magic, yet he suggests in connection with his semantic theories of speech, according to which speech occurs by arbitrary jointly-agreed signals, an overcoming of magic, whereby man agrees no more signals with the → demons as the bearers of magic, and thus interrupts communication (Aug. Doctr. christ. 36f.).

C. DEVELOPMENT
1. ARCHAIC GREECE 2. CLASSICAL AND HELLENISTIC GREECE 3. MAGIC IN GREEK LAW 4. REPUBLICAN ROME 5. IMPERIAL PERIOD UNTIL CONSTANTINE I

1. ARCHAIC GREECE
The development of terminology indicates that, in the self-view of the Greeks, magic was not excluded from religious tradition as a special field by philosophical and medical thought until the late 6th cent. BC. Thus, magic is, strictly speaking, non-existent in the archaic period. However, from Homer ritual details are found that elsewhere would be associated with the sphere designated as magic. That is true particularly for the field described by the term *pharmakeía*; → Helene's Egyptian *phármakon* (see above A. 1.), which is mixed in a drink in order to make Menelaus and Telemachus forget their troubles, or → Circe's *phármakon* that transforms men into swines, may be classified here – though in both cases the effective substance is associated with origins some distance from Greece (resp. Egypt and Aeaea, the island of Circe at the edge of the world). Even the incantation, with which Odysseus' uncle staunches the bleeding from his thigh wound (Hom. Od. 19,457f.), is to be ascribed to magic (or better: ritual) medicine and has counterparts among many cultures as late as the modern era. Gorgias [2] was by his own word present in person when his teacher Empedocles [1] was practicing magic (*goēteía*; Gorg. in Satyrus of Diog. Laert. 8,59), and Empedocles for his part maintained that he knew remedies against disease, the weakness of old age and death and was able to influence the weather (31 F 111 D-K) [27]; the approximately contemporary aetiological myth related by Pindar for the love spell with the help of the → iynx at last coincides with one of the central spheres of classical and post-classical *defixiones* [28; 29].

2. Classical and Hellenistic Greece

Defixio texts which are more commonly inscribed on strips of lead have been found from the late 6th cent. BC in various parts of Greece, from the mid 5th cent. BC in Attica, and – occasionally along with → magic dolls [30] – are found usually in graves, later also in wells and other places underground. From about the same time there are allusions in literature to binding rites, in which only partially with the assistance of the texts on lead strips and of magic dolls, but always through the manipulation of substances (Greek *ousía*), belonging to the victim, for instance hairs or scraps of clothing, individuals are 'bound' (*katadeín*) to the Underworld (Aesch. Eum. 306; 332f.; Pind. Pyth. 4,193–196; magic dolls: Pl. Leg. 11,933ab, later Theoc. 2). As to how far the phenomenon can be said to begin in this period, for instance as a result of renewed Mesopotamian influence [1. 169–174], is much disputed in research. The majority (see below C.3.) of the binding texts from Athens concern court cases; the prosopography shows that even the upper classes made use of these rites (cf. Pl. Resp. 364e). The texts are relatively simple, sometimes merely lists of names or short invocations to the gods of the Underworld. The inscription of a priest of Sarapis at Delos (mid 3rd cent. BC) represents, from the inner perspective, a successful curse in a trial [31].

Erotic *defixiones* also begin in the 5th cent., and are mostly utilized by a man in order to win over a woman or to win her back; the reverse, where a woman wants to win over a man or to keep him (though never by the use of spell tablets), is mentioned in the unsuccessful rite of → Deianira in Soph. Trach. [32], inscribed for instance in a very extensive *defixio* from Thessaly (mid 4th cent. BC) [33]. This then also becomes a theme of Theoc. 2, whose *Pharmakeútriai* capture literalized rites by a kind of ritual 'bricolage' in a Hellenistic genre picture. A further reflex on Hellenistic interest in this theme, this time Latin, is found in Laevius [2] fr. 27 Morel [34].

F.G. S.I.J.

3. Magic in Greek law

Magic was important and widespread in Greek law. This is true of the oath (→ Oath II.) and the curse (→ Curse II.), in which cases one is nowadays inclined to resolve the total dichotomy of 'religion' and 'magic' [17. 17–20]. In both cases, in the minds of the participants, supernatural powers were exerting an influence upon human lives. Whilst the oath, the conditional self-curse, faded in classical times to a formality in the introductions to court cases (Pl. Leg. 948b), or to an underhand tactical move in a trial (Aristot. Rh. 1377a) and replaced the missing legal means of sanction in international treaties only, the curse found plenty of uses by the population at all levels of society in love magic and harmful magic, as a means of 'magical self-help' (though rejected by enlightened spirits, Pl. Leg. 933a-e). Curses in the form of a → *defixio* also had legal aspects: an adversary (e.g. in a court case) could be rendered harmless in future by means of 'binding'; revenge for a murder victim could be brought down upon a (mostly unknown) culprit or a 'plea for justice' could be strengthened [45. 68–75]. The latter is also described as 'temple justice' and goes beyond 'magical self help': if someone had suffered a wrong, e.g. as a result of theft or offence to his honour, the known or unknown culprit could be required to render compensation under the sanction of a curse. Affected by divine punishment, the culprits confess, offer satisfaction and praise the deity by means of a 'confessional inscription' (recorded in Lycia during the Roman period [46]). The practice of magic was not a punishable offence in classical Athens, apart from possible prosecution on account of → *asébeia* or, in the event of a fatal outcome in love magic, involving → *pharmakeía*; around 470 BC in Teos, the application of magical means 'against the state or a private individual' was punished with the severest penalties (Syll.³ 38,1–5 [47]). For magic in the papyri [48. 199–202].

G.T.

4. Republican Rome

In Rome, a separate terminology develops from the loan-words *magia* and *magus* first in the early Augustan period, probably as a result of → Hellenization and of restorative of Augustan → religious policy. Magic is actually only seen previously as a criminal offence in other contexts. It is prohibited in the Law of the Twelve Tables to 'sing' (*ex-*, *incantare*) the praises of other crops on ones own land. This concerns a property offence, which the only trial report to such a case also indicates (case against the freedman C. Furius Cresimus, Plin. HN 18,41–43 = Piso, HRR fr. 33 [1. 58–61]); not until later is the rite associated with magical rites (Verg. Ecl. 8,99). The *lex Cornelia de sicariis et veneficis* of 81 BC then lays down the fundamentals for harmful magic to be classified under crimes of violence, which in actuality is rarely substantiated. A first case of court magic reported by Cic. Brut. in 216 is, in his own judgement, ambivalent; at least Cicero does not take such things seriously.

5. Imperial period until Constantine I

From Augustus new directions are set: now *magia* is excluded from religious tradition as negative. Agrippa [1] has 'astrologers and witches' (Cass. Dio 49,43,5) driven out of Rome in 33 BC, and Augustus banishes *Pythagoricus et magus* Anaxilaus [2] from Larissa (Jer. Chron., ad annum 28). Pliny the Elder then demonstrates how widespread magic rites are in the time of Nero (AD 54–68) and particularly the fear of *defixiones* [1. 48–54]. Tacitus' repeated reports on trials during the Julio-Claudian years (the period between Tiberius and Nero) show, however, that the accusation of → *devotio* is always at the root of a range of other charges, thus *per se* barely convincing [35]; the *SC de Pisone patre* also records that in the case of the death of Germanicus [2] the charge of *devotio* was actually taken up in advance and inside the family of Germanicus, but not by the Senate [36]. Magic, therefore, is shown to be an outwardly effective, but legally problematical charge. Consequently, how serious the position of Apuleius (→ Ap(p)uleius [III] of Madaura) was, accused by himself of magic in about AD 158, is not easy to determine; at any rate he was acquitted.

The Imperial period shows the tremendously rapid spread of *defixiones* to the entire empire. The chariot race (→ Circus) is a prominent area for the *defixio*, where the opposing party's driver is cursed in order to fail; this reflects the central social significance that chariot racing had in the mid and late Imperial period [37]. The texts are becoming technically much more detailed, especially the so-called 'Sethian curse tablets' (→ Sethianism), but some texts from the magic papyri also include explicit lists of → demons and detailed desires for destruction (the attribution of these texts to the Sethian → Gnosticism, which goes back to R. WÜNSCH [38], cannot be supported).

The origin of → theurgy as a ritual means of access to the divine occurs at the end of the 2nd cent.; it partially makes use of the same means as the sorcerer who seeks to achieve a *sýstasis*. It is important for → Plotinus, but especially for his successors → Porphyrius and → Iamblichus [2]; in reaction to Porphyry, Augustine rejects it completely as a false path to God (Aug. Civ. 10 *passim*) – even though it has a higher standing than the ordinary *goeteia*.

IV. CHRISTIANITY

The position of magic changes once more in the Christian imperium after emperor Constantine I (d. 337). Pagan magic, like astrology and haruspices, is prohibited; as a result of the Pauline re-evaluation of pagan gods as demons, every pagan ritual became a magical negotiation with demons; 'paganism' could be devalued as magic and condemned [39]. Magic was kept under close observation by imperial legislators, however, particularly because of its divination aspect: access by private individuals to knowledge of the future is ruthlessly suppressed by the emperor [40]. It is also clear, however, to what extent the accusation of magic could still be used, in order to dispose of unpopular personalities, as happened in the case of → Boethius [41]. The Christian theologians, for their part, reject magic in all its forms, including the philosophy of theurgy, as a false path to God; almost more important than the accusation that magic involves demons, which only applies to the pagan tradition, is that the human activity prescribed in the magic rite is an act of *superbia* ('arrogance'), which is completely contrary to Christian *humilitas* ('humility') (Aug. Civ. 10). In reality, this did not prevent Christian magic either in the Coptic, the Byzantine world or in western Christianity [42; 43]. Though it was now limited mainly to protective magic (amulets) and the overcoming of illness [44], the old connections were still entirely discernible.

→ Dead, cult of the; → Defixion; → Devotio; → Divination; → Healing god; → Hecate; → Iynx; → Magic; → Medicine; → Oracles; → Religion; → Rite; → Sacrifice; → Theurgy

1 F. GRAF, Gottesnähe und Schadenzauber. Die Magie in der griech.-röm. Ant., 1996   2 S. I. JOHNSTON, Restless Dead. Encounters between the Living and the Dead in Ancient Greece, 1999   3 R. BLOCH, Moses und die Scharlatane, in: F. SIEGERT, J. V. KALMS (ed.), Internationales Josephus-Kolloquium Brüssel 1997 (Münsteraner Josephus-Studien 4), 1999, 142–157   4 W. D. FURLEY, Besprechung und Behandlung. Zur Form und Funktion von ΕΠΩΙΔΑΙ in der griech. Zaubermedizin, in: G. W. MOST, H. PETERSMANN, A. M. RITTER (ed.), Philanthropia kai Eusebeia. FS A.Dihle, 1993, 80–104   5 R. GAROSI, Indagini sulla formazione del concetto di magia nella cultura romana, in: P. XELLA (ed.), Magia. Studi di storia delle religioni in memoria di R. Garosi, 1976, 13–93   6 A. AUDOLLENT, Defixionum Tabellae, 1904   7 D. R. JORDAN, A Survey of Greek Defixiones Not Included in the Special Corpora, in: GRBS 26, 1985, 151–197   8 J. G. GAGER (ed.), Curse Tablets and Binding Spells from the Ancient World, 1992   9 PGM   10 H. D. BETZ (ed.), The Greek Magical Papyri in Translation Including the Demotic Spells, 1986   11 W. M. BRASHEAR, The Greek Magical Papyri. An Introduction and Survey. Annotated Bibliography (1928–1994), in: ANRW II 18.5, 1995, 3380–3684   12 R. K. RITNER, Egyptian Magical Practice under the Roman Empire, in: ANRW II 18.5, 1995, 3333–3379   13 R. KOTANSKY, Incantations and Prayers for Salvation in Inscribed Greek Amulets, in: C. A. FARAONE, D. OBBINK (ed.), Magika Hiera. Ancient Greek Magic and Rel., 1991, 107–137   14 Id., Greek Magical Amulets. The Inscribed Gold, Silver, Copper and Bronze Lamellae, vol. 1, 1994   15 H. G. KIPPENBERG, B. LUCCHESI (ed.), M. Die sozialwiss. Kontroverse über das Verstehen fremden Denkens, 1978   16 H. S. VERSNEL, Some Reflections on the Relationship Magic-Rel., in: Numen 38, 1991, 177–197   17 C. A. FARAONE, The Agonistic Context of Early Greek Binding Spells, in: Id., s. [13], 3–32   18 G. LANATA, Medicina magica e religione popolare in Grecia fino all'età di Ippocrate, 1967   19 V. LANTERNARI, Medicina, magia, religione, valori, 1994   20 R. RENEHAN, The Staunching of Odysseus' Blood. The Healing-Powers of Magic, in: AJPh 113, 1992, 1–4   21 H. C. KEE, Medicine, Miracle and Magic in New Testament Times, 1986   22 P. CANIVET, A. ADNÈS, Guérisons miraculeuses et exorcismes dans l'Histoire Philotée, in: RHR 171, 1967, 53–82; 149–179   23 S. I. JOHNSTON, Charming Children. The Use of the Child in Late Antique Divination, in: Arethusa (2001)   24 Id., Rising to the Occasion. Theurgic Ascent in Its Cultural Milieu, in: P. SCHÄFER, H. G. KIPPENBERG (ed.), Envisioning Magic, 1997, 165–194   25 R. A. MARKUS, Augustine on Magic. A Neglected Semiotic Theory, in: Revue des Etudes Augustiniennes 40, 1994, 375–388   26 F. GRAF, Theories of Magic in Antiquity, in: M. MEYER, P. MIRECKI (ed.), Magic and Ritual in the Ancient World, 2002   27 P. KINGSLEY, Ancient Philosophy, Mystery, and Magic. Empedocles and Pythagorean Trad., 1995, 217–227   28 V. PIRENNE-DELFORGE, L'Iynge dans le discours mythique et les procédures magiques, in: Kernos 6, 1993, 277–289   29 S. I. JOHNSTON, The Song of the Iynx. Magic and Rhetoric in Pythian 4, in: TAPhA 125, 1995, 177–206   30 C. A. FARAONE, Binding and Burying the Forces of Evil, in: Classical Antiquity 10, 1991, 165–205   31 H. ENGELMANN, The Delian Aretalogy of Sarapis, 1975   32 C. A. FARAONE, Deianira's Mistake and the Demise of Herakles, in: Helios 21, 1994, 115–136   33 E. VOUTIRAS, Dionysophontos Gamoi. Marital Life and Erotic Magic in Fourth-Century Pella, 1998   34 A.-M.

TUPET, La m. dans la poésie latine, vol. 1, 1976, 212–219
35 D. LIEBS, Strafprozesse wegen Zauberei. M. und polit.
Kalkül in der röm. Geschichte, in: U. MANTHE, J. v.
UNGERN-STERNBERG (ed.), Große Prozesse der röm. Ant.,
1997, 146–158 36 W. ECK et al., Das Senatus Consultum
de Cn. Pisone patre, 1996 37 A. CAMERON, Circus Fac-
tions, 1976 38 R. WÜNSCH, Sethianische Verfluchungs-
tafeln aus Rom, 1981 39 F. E. SHLOSSER, Pagan Into
Magician, in: Byzantinoslavica 2, 1991, 49–53 40 M. TH.
FÖGEN, Die Enteignung der Wahrsager. Stud. zum kaiserl.
Wissensmonopol in der Spätant., 1993 41 PH. ROUS-
SEAU, The Death of Boethius. The Charge of Maleficium,
in: Studi Medievali 20, 1979, 871–889 42 M. MEYER, R.
SMITH (ed.), Ancient Christian Magic. Coptic Texts of
Ritual Power, 1994 43 H. MAGUIRE (ed.), Byzantine
Magic, 1995 44 TH. GELZER et al., Lamella Bernensis,
1999 45 H. S. VERSNEL, Beyond Cursing, in: [13], 60–106
46 A. CHANIOTIS, Tempeljustiz, in: G. THÜR, J. VÉLISSA-
ROPOULOS (ed.), Symposion 1995, 1997, 353ff. 47 R.
KOERNER, Inschr. Gesetzestexte der frühen griech. Polis,
1993, 294ff. no. 78 48 H.-A. RUPPRECHT, Einführung in
die Papyruskunde, 1994 49 K. LATTE, Heiliges Recht,
1920 (repr. 1990) 50 G. THÜR, IPArk 8: 'Gottesurteil'
oder 'Amnestiedekret', in: Dike 1, 1998, 13ff. F.G. S.I.J.

V. ISLAM
In the Arabic-Islamic cultural sphere, magic (siḥr)
played a great role and took on very varied forms in this
vast geographical area. Thus, the striving by religious
scholars to systematically comprehend the phenomenon of magic can be established quite early, resulting
in a distinction between 'allowed' and 'forbidden' magic. Arabic magic drew partly on indigenous Arabic tradition, in which many demons (ğinn), whose existence
even → Mohammed did not doubt, played a great role.
It experienced a decisive stimulus from the reception of
Hellenistic magic. The interest of the Arabs in Greek
arcane knowledge is recorded quite early: thus, emper-
or Leo IV (775–780) sent a book on Egyptian magic as
a gift to the ʿAbbāsid caliph at his request (Michael Syr.
478b CHABOT). Henceforth, countless magic texts were
written, which pretended to be translations of Indian,
Coptic, Nabataean and Greek authors, whose authenticity is very much in dispute. The most important compendium of this Hellenistic-influenced magic is the
Ġāyat al-ḥakīm of Pseudo-Maǧrīṭī (11th cent.), which
was translated into Latin quite early under the title of
Picatrix and had a great influence on the development
of magic in western Europe [1]. From the numerous
magic writings in the Islamic world, suffice it to cite
only the monumental Šams al-maʿārif of al-Būnī
(1225), a synthesis of magic knowledge in Islam.

EDITIONS: 1 D. PINGREE (ed.), 1986.

E. DOUTTÉ, M. et Religion dans l'Afrique du Nord, 1909;
T. FAHD, s.v. Siḥr, EI 9, 1997, 567b–571b; A. KOVA-
LENKO, M. et l'Islam. Les concepts de m. (siḥr) et de sci-
ences occultes (ʿilm al-ġaib) en Islam, 1991; G. RITTER
(ed.), Pseudo-Maǧrīṭī, Ġāyat al-ḥakīm, 1933 (transl.: Id.,
M. PLESSNER, 1962); M. ULLMANN, Die Natur- und
Geheimwiss. im Islam (HbdOr, 1.Abt., Ergbd. 6, 2.
Abschn.), 1972, 359–426. I.T.-N.

Magical papyri
I. GENERAL INFORMATION II. GENRES
III. AUTHORSHIP IV. RHETORIC

I. GENERAL INFORMATION
Loose term for the constantly increasing body of
Graeco-Egyptian magic texts (standard editions: [1; 2],
since then, newly published texts in [3]). The most
important distinction is to be made between the handbooks (until now more than 80 published copies) on
→ papyrus, which contain the instructions for acts of
magic, and directly used texts (at least 115 published
copies) on papyrus, metal (lead tablets), pottery shards,
wood, etc., corresponding to the extant instructions
only in the exception, but which are absolutely comparable with their content. A clear delineation cannot be
made between the procedures in these texts and the
Graeco-Egyptian magic tablets (cf. → defixio), and
phylakteria, resp. magic amulets (→ phylaktḗrion) [3].
The contents of the magical papyri (MP) vary greatly. With the exception of the papyrus 'Mimaut' (PGM
III), the first handbooks known in Europe (all marked
by pronounced erudition) were gathered in Egyptian
Thebes between 1816 and 1857 by an Armenian merchant and antiques dealer who called himself ANASTASI
or Jean D'ANASTASY (in part by order of the English
consul Henry SALT, 1815–1827) and sold on to muse-
ums, resp. private collectors [4]. Although the provenance and circumstances of the finds are unknown for
the most part, an important group of the papyri (PGM
IV, V, Va, XII, XIII) acquired by D'ANASTASY, the demotic papyri from London and Leiden (PLondinensis
10070 + PLeidensis J383 and two alchemist handbooks) were found in a tomb according to reports [5].
The only known complete handbook since 1857 (POs-
loensis 1 = PGM XXXVI), which primarily contains
recipes for love spells, was acquired in 1920 in the
→ Fajûm Oasis. All other books (or recipe pages) previously published, with a content of clearly lesser quality, are only extant in fragments, having been thrown
carelessly on the rubbish heap in antiquity like other
used books. Such differences indicate a correspondingly
differentiated level of expectation of the relevant
authors, resp. owners [6]. In spite of a plethora of single
editions and studies [7. 3506–3576] a comprehensive
monograph still does not exist.

II. GENRES
The MP are syncretistic late products of the magic
tradition of the Egyptian pr-ʿnḫ, 'House of Life' (temple). Their genres, which have little in common with
those of Old Egyptian magical practices [8], took on
new content as early as during the Late Period (535–332
BC) resp. in the Ptolemaic era, i.e. through the incorporation and adaptation of the Babylonian practice of
lecanomancy (divination by the inspection of water in a
basin). Also in cases where mixed forms are found, the
MP indicate an implicit hierarchy of values: (1) divina-
tory formulae, which make up c. 25 % of all spells,

among which the *ph-ntr* (demotic), the authentic self-manifestation of a deity (Greek *aútoptos* or *sýstasis*), represents the most complex form [9], followed by visions of the gods, who allowed themselves to be seen in the course of a lecanomancy, most often by a young boy acting as a medium [10] and finally appearances in dreams; (2) spells for requesting a → *páredros* (demonic factotum) [11]; (3) necromantic *práxeis* (activities) [12]; (4) magic for causing harm, above all spells concerning separation, sleeplessness and anger-abatement; (5) magic for relationships and attraction [13]; (6) directions for the preparation of amulets, resp. (exorcistic) phylakteria; (7) iatromagical recipes, above all for fever; (8) small miracles, i.e. to make oneself invisible, to open locked doors, to win at gambling.

Even when the complete handbooks contain all these genres without recognizable organizing principles, they contain, in harmony with their elevated language and their theological knowledge, principally recipes for more difficult *práxeis* [7. 3494–3506]. The texts directly used deal only with the categories (4)–(7).

III. AUTHORSHIP

The close connection between the authors of the MP and the 'House of Life' is proven most clearly by the repeated assertion that a certain recipe was copied from a model copy in a temple (i.e. PGM VII 862–865; cf. PGM IV 3125–3130). On the other hand, the recipes of the MP often presuppose that the carrying out of the *práxis* takes place in a private place [14]. As early as in the dynastic period, long before the 4th cent. BC, magical activities were not the exclusive property of the temple priests, but in part available to a wide circle of 'magi' (*hk3y*) and 'guardians' (*s3w*). Under the increasingly difficult socio- and religious-political circumstances of the Graeco-Roman period, many priests (who were less and less versed in the verbal and written tradition of the temple) were forced to put themselves as freelance 'magic services providers' into a situation, in which only the price determined the quality of the desired magic activity [15]. The discovery of competently composed magical tablets in North Africa, Asia Minor, Athens, Cyprus, Rhodes, Rome, etc. (cf. → *defixio*) indicates the readiness of such service providers to travel to foreign lands. The same tradition continues in the Coptic Christian practice of magic [16]. On the other hand, there were clearly still, in the 3rd to 4th cents. AD, some well-to-do priests who were able to devote themselves to higher magic in Egypt, above all the invoking of a deity and presumably also theurgic ascension practices (→ Theurgy; → Iamblichus [2] i.e. was a temple priest).

IV. RHETORIC

This situation caused the providers of magical services to call on 'interesting' foreign traditions and with these to develop the characteristics of the syncretistic MP as 'scribal magic' [17]. One of the oldest extant MP (late 1st cent. BC) [3. no. 72] indicates an early inclusion of Greek magical practices or charms, into the Egyptian temple magic [18]. The 'magical hymns' [1. vol. 2, 237–264] are likewise Greek compositions which – not firm in their textual form – were worked into various Egyptian contexts [19]. From the 2nd cent. AD at the latest, the attempt was made to incorporate many foreign (above all Jewish) gods' or angels' names into invocations [20] as well as to use ancient Egyptian techniques (e.g. → Magic spells and images) on a new scale, or to develop them further.

Even if the magical practice of some cheaper purveyors of magic gives a somewhat awkward impression, handbooks of D'ANASTASY (see above I.; above all the demotic ones) contain many excellent copies of the art of invocation from higher practices of magic. A rhetorically successful invocation implies long years of practice [21]; the chief requirement for it is the ability to compose a long erudite list, rich in variety, of the → epicleses and epithets of the chosen god(s) [22], to selectively insert appropriate, syllable-rich *lógoi* (→ *lógos* [2]) and magic spells, to formulate the request creatively and impressively.

→ Exorcism; → Logos [2]; → Magic III.; → Paredros B.; → Theurgy

1 PGM (standard edition) 2 H.-D. BETZ (ed.), The Greek Magical Papyri in Translation, 1986, ²1993 (transl. of [1]) 3 R. W. DANIEL, F. MALTOMINI, Supplementum Magicum (Pap. Colon. 16. 1-2), 2 vols., 1990–1992 4 W. DAWSON, E. UPHILL, Who Was Who in Egyptology, 1972, s. v. Anastasi, G. 5 K. PREISENDANZ, Pap.funde und Pap.forsch., 1933, 90–95 6 Id., Zur synkretistischen Magie im röm. Ägypten, in: H. GERSTINGER (ed.), Akten des VIII. Kongr. für Papyrologie, 1956, 111–125 7 W. BRASHEAR, The Greek Magical Papyri, in: ANRW II 18.5, 1995, 3380–3684 8 Y. KOENIG, Magie et magiciens dans l'Égypte ancienne, 1994 9 T. HOPFNER, Griech.-ägypt. Offenbarungszauber, vol. 2.1, 1924, ²1983, § 120–211 10 S. I. JOHNSTON, Charming Children, in: Arethusa 34, 2001, 97–117 11 L. J. CIRAOLO, Supernatural Assistants, in: M. MEYER, P. MIRECKI (ed.), Ancient Magic and Ritual Power, 1995, 279–295 12 D. OGDEN, Greek and Roman Necromancy, 2001, 191–216 13 C. A. FARAONE, Ancient Greek Love Magic, 1999 14 J. Z. SMITH, Trading Places, in: s. [10], 13–27 15 D. FRANKFURTER, Rel. in Roman Egypt, 1998, 198–264 16 M. MEYER, R. SMITH (ed.), Ancient Christian Magic, 1994 17 M. D. SWARTZ, Scribal Magic and Its Rhetoric, in: Harvard Theological Review 83, 1990, 163–180 18 C. A. FARAONE, Handbooks and Anthologies, in: Archiv für Religionsgesch. 2, 2000, 195–214 19 J. CALVO MARTÍNEZ, El tratamiento del material hímnico, in: MHNH 2, 2002, 71–95 20 N. JANOWITZ, Icons of Power, 2001 21 F. GRAF, The Magician's Initiation, in: Helios 21, 1994, 161–177 22 W. FAUTH, Helios Megistos, 1995, 34–120.

W. BRASHEAR, Magical Papyri: Magic in Book-Form, in: P. GANZ (ed.), Das Buch als magisches und als Repräsentationsobjekt, 1992, 35–57.   R.G.

Magical spells (ὀνόματα βάρβαρα/*onómata bárbara*, Lat. *nomina barbarica*).
I. GENERAL II. CATEGORIES III. ORIGINS
IV. POPULAR MEDICINE

I. GENERAL

Broad term for names, words and sounds used in ancient incantation practices of ritual magic and popular medicine. Their obscurity or indefiniteness was often understood by ancient observers as a synecdoche for the otherness of → magic, above all in poetical depictions of fictional witchcraft rituals (e.g. Lucan, 6,685–693; Lucian, Dialogi Meretricii 4,5). From the magician's perspective, such utterances underpinned his authority with divine/demonic powers; if spells were believed to contain authentic divine names, they contained a supposedly irresistible power (PGM I 36 f., XII 136 f., XIII 621–627; SEG 41, 1597, l. 11f.). From the point of view of speech act theory, such words characterize the special status of the implicit or explicit directives of the spell [1]. Seen from the standpoint of the theory of ritual behaviour, they contribute to a closer definition of the dynamics of the situational ideal evoked by a magical ritual (as a special form of religious activity). In contrast to ordinary contexts of communication, then, incomprehensibility dictated by context may be advantageous in magical practice.

II. CATEGORIES

Varying importance is attached to magical spells (MS), which occur in magical practices world-wide: they are unknown in the Babylonian spell book *Maqlû*, and are seldom found in Egyptian texts of the dynastic period. However, they often occur in Greek and Roman amulet practice (→ Phylakterion) and popular medicine, but the fullest accounts are in Graeco-Egyptian ritual magic of the Imperial period and related texts (e.g. in the → *Corpus Hermeticum* and the → Nag Hammadi corpus; cf. [2]), and in Jewish, Coptic, Syrian and Arabian magical texts.

Even where the tradition was highly developed, as in the Graeco-Egyptian papyri (→ Magical papyri), it is scarcely possible to define categories. However, a distinction can be made heuristically between a semantic and a phonetic plane. To the first category (in which the priority of the MS is to invoke a cultic or mythic figure) belong: recognized gods' and demons' names or epithets (e.g. Harpocrates, Iaō Sabaōth Adonai, Meliuchos; Damnameneus, Tabium; Nepheriēri, Pakerbēth); specialized gods such as the Egyptian decans and gods of the hours (e.g. Erō, Oumesthōth); angel names (e.g. Araga, but esp. names in -*ēl* and -*ōth*: e.g. Raphaēl, Thuriēl, Ab(r)aōth, Kentabaōth); more than 70 reasonably constant invocation formulae (→ Logos [2] B.), e.g. the *Bōrphōrphorba* logos (PGM IV 1256–1262) or the *Armiuth Lailam Chōouch Arsenophrē* logos (PGM VII 361f.), which were seen primarily as complex epithets or epicleses (e.g. PGM VII 1023–1025); also → palindromes, esp. the five best-known, which were often addressed as gods in ancient incantation practice (e.g. PGM VII 581–585; Lix 5–10).

The phonetic category includes vowel sequences (e.g. PGM IV 1222–1225; VII 307–309), which were often complex and purely invocatory, as well as the sparsely prescribed meaningless sounds or noises – roars, howls, claps, chirps, whistles and expressions in the language of birds and dog-headed apes (PGM XIII 79–89, 941–946) –, which aimed to highlight the infinity of expressive possibilities as a figurative expression of the effective potential of ritual activity [3. 104 f.]. Written counterparts of these phonetic MS, the *charakteres*, as well as geometric groupings (slopes, hearts, wings) developed in the course of the 2nd cent. AD. The intersection between the two categories is occupied by the true MS, which can neither be classified as names nor as pure sounds, but as individual words devoid of meaning, some of which were handed down by masters, but most of which were invented spontaneously in a ritual context for a single usage. In Graeco-Egyptian amulet practice, words from all of these categories were thought to possess an independent protective power.

III. ORIGINS

The origins of such MS were diverse. The root of the magical names and *lógoi* certainly lies in Egyptian terms (e.g. *ba, shai*), gods' names (or epithets) and → epicleses, as well as suitable words which are often difficult to recognize, partly owing to their obscurity, but also because of inconsistent habits of transcription probably caused by dialect (e.g. the Middle Egyptian word *kkw*/'darkness' is transmitted as χαχε/*chake*, καχε/*kache*, χωουχ/*chōuch* or χωωχ/*chōōch*; [4]). Deformations arose over the course of time, as knowledge of the language waned, and despite efforts at exact preservation. In the case of the ritual texts of Greek authorship, this process led to the transmutation of a highly specialized linguistic phenomenon into an increasingly incomprehensible process of repetition by rote, whose true function consisted in underpinning the self-conception of the participants in following the limitless might of the magi of the time of the Pharaohs. The priestly education clearly included the transmission of the ability to compose vowel sequences and actual MS at will. It is also conceivable that the production of such utterances presupposed a trancelike state, as with glossolalia.

The most important sources of non-Egyptian names, alongside the Greek gods of the 'Hymns', was the Jewish *Merkabā* tradition, which developed not only many new names (esp. Iaō, Adonai Sabaōth) and angel names (function + -*ēl*), but also techniques, such as *notarikon* and *temurah*, for the generation of new mystical names of God. On the other hand, the Babylonian-Syrian tradition is scarcely represented (esp. Baal, Baʿalšamīn, Ereškigal).

Rationalizations of MS developed, probably initially under Platonic influence, both in Egypt and Palestine.

According to one such tradition, such MS were literally untranslatable, because their effect depended solely upon the original phonetics (Orig. Contra Celsum 1,24; 4,43). By contrast, others understood MS as divine expressions with a double function of allowing mortals both a brief insight into the world of the gods, and a spiritual union (Iambl. Myst. 7,4f.; [5]).

IV. Popular medicine

The few preserved charms of popular medicine contain relatively simple, modest MS, whose invocatory, signifying or protecting functions are just as difficult to assess as those of ritual magic. Some MS (e.g. the → *Ephésia grámmata*) were clearly originally demons' names, others, such as perhaps the Catonian dislocation charm (Cato Agr. 160), were distorted phrases of some foreign or pre-Roman language (e.g. [6. no. 39; 7]); most, however, (e.g. *crissi crasi concrasi* [6. no. 191]) were spontaneous, meaningless inventions. It is likely that increasing literacy lent such meaningless formulae an increasingly important role in popular medicine, precisely because they sounded authentic [8].
→ Magic; → Magical papyri; → Medicine; → Phylakterion; → Ritual

1 T. TODOROV, Le discours de la magie, in: Id., Les genres du discours, 1978, 246–282 2 P. C. MILLER, In Praise of Nonsense, in: A. H. ARMSTRONG (ed.), Classical Mediterranean Spirituality, 1986, 481–505 3 S. CRIPPA, Entre vocalité et écriture, in: C. BATSCH et al. (ed.), Zwischen Krise und Alltag, 1999, 95–110 4 H.-J. THISSEN, Ägyptologische Beitr. zu den griech. magischen Papyri, in: U. VERHOEVEN, E. GRAEFE (ed.), Rel. und Philos. im alten Äg., 1991, 293–302 5 J. DILLON, The Magical Power of Names in Origen and Later Platonism, in: R. P. C. RICHARD (ed.), Origeniana tertia, 1985, 203–216 6 R. HEIM, Incantamenta magica Graeca Latina, in: Jb. für Class. Philol. Suppl. 19, 1892, 465–575 7 L. FLEURIOT, Deux formules de Marcellus de Bordeaux, in: Études celtiques 14, 1974, 57–66 8 H. S. VERSNEL, Die Poetik der Zaubersprüche, in: T. SCHABERT, R. BRAGUE (ed.), Die Macht des Wortes, 1996, 233–297.

W. BRASHEAR, The Greek Magical Papyri, in: ANRW II 18.5, 1995, 3576–3603.   R.G.

Magic doll

Loose term for an anthropomorphous statuette made from a variety of different materials for specific ritual purposes. The conceptual condition for such statuettes, which function as signs or images of a physical and social existence, is the context-contingent abolishment of the difference between living creatures and objects that are incapable of self-determination [1]. Such statuettes were used for beneficial as well as harmful purposes in the ancient Oriental empires, while in Mesopotamia and Egypt they served mainly as protective or deterrent charms. Efforts have been made to apply the same model to early Greek magic dolls [2].

Magical dolls seem to have come to the Greeks via Anatolia in the archaic period. Apart from Cyrene [3. 67–72], the only evidence for them exists in connection with private → magic. There is no agreement on

their use or interpretation. The limbs of some of the (metal) figures are mutilated; in the earliest literary record (Soph. fr. 536 SNELL) → Medea has a doll burned. In Plato (Leg. 933b) they are put up as an outward sign of a curse. In Rome, woollen images were produced as neutral substitutes of dead family members (Fest. 108,27 l.) during → Compitalia and therefore also used for harmful magic (Hor. Sat. 1,8,30–33). At the same time, there is first evidence for silent 'submission dramas' (ibid.) and the piercing of dolls (Ov. Am. 3,7,30) in love magic. In Roman Egypt, the traditional type of deterrent dolls was adopted for female love dolls [4]. In addition to that, instructions for the production of a completely different kind of doll, magical servant figures, show similarities with magic stories from ancient Egypt (cf. → *páredros* B.). The earliest literary example of such servants is Hor. Epod. 17,76 f.; cf. Lucian Philopseudes 14.
→ Compitalia C.; → Defixio; → Doll; → Magic B. 2.; → Phylakterion

1 A. GELL, Art and Agency, 1998, 96–154 2 C. FARAONE, Binding and Burying the Forces of Evil, in: Classical Antiquity 10, 1991, 165–205 3 W. BURKERT, Die orientalisierende Epoche, 1984 4 P. DU BOURGUET, Une ancêtre des figurines d'envoûtement percées d'aiguilles, in: Mélanges de l'Inst. français d'archéologie orientale du Caire 104, 1980, 225–238.

T. ABUSCH, Mesopotamian Witchcraft, 2002, 113–162; F. GRAF, Gottesnähe und Schadenzauber, 1996, 122–133; Y. KOENIG, Magie et magiciens dans l'Egypte ancienne, 1994, 131–185; D. OGDEN, Binding Spells: Curse Tablets and Voodoo Dolls, in: V. FLINT et al., Witchcraft and Magic in Europe: Ancient Greece and Rome, 1999, 1–90; M.-C. TRÉMOUILLE, Les rituels magiques hittites, in: A. MOREAU, J.-C. TURPIN (ed.), La Magie, 2000, vol. 1, 77–94.   R.G.

Magicians see → Entertainers

Magic Medicine see → Magic, Magi; → Medicine

Magister a memoria

Lat. *memoria* (Greek *mnémē*) refers to official issuing of documents in the sense of 'lasting testimonial' (cf. Aristot. Pol. 1321b 39: *mnémones*).

It is accepted that from the time of → Augustus an official sphere *a memoria* existed for the various official activities of the emperor to his court. Its head is, however, not mentioned until the 2nd cent. AD as *magister a memoria* or *magister memoriae*; this title survives until late antiquity (ILS 1672; Pan. Lat. 9,11 BAEHRENS; Cod. Iust. 1,23,7,1). The office head was initially a freedman, later a member of the equestrian class, and in late antiquity he even held the rank of a → *spectabilis*.

The title is a functional designation for a leading position in one of the later four offices of the imperial → chancellery (in late antiquity in the official sphere of the → *magister officiorum*, Not. Dign. Or. 11,13–16 and 11,19; Cod. Iust. 12,9, tit. de magistris scriniorum), but it is also a designation of status, to which, apart from the head of the *scrinium a memoria,* the heads of the other offices (*a → libellis, ab → epistulis, a dispositionibus*) are also entitled (Cod. Iust 10,48,11). Around 450, the *magister a memoria* was in charge of 62 officials (Cod. Iust. 12,19,10). The frequently changing business of his office in general was concerned, among other things, with the scheduling of matters of appointments and pardons, but it partly overlapped with those of other offices (*adnotationes et preces;* cf. Not. Dign. Or. 19, Not. Dign. Occ. 17).

MILLAR, Emperor, 265f.; HIRSCHFELD, 435; JONES, LRE, 367f.; 504f.; P. R. C. WEAVER, Familia Caesaris, 1972.
                                                                                                                     C.G.

Magister equitum The office of the *magister equitum* (ME) ('Master of the Cavalry') was an office assigned to the → *dictator,* and was never an independent office. Like the original designation of the dictator as *magister populi* (Master of the Infantry) (Cic. Rep. 1,40,63; Varro Ling. 5,82), it contains the word *magister* (root *mag-* = 'head, leader') and an indication of the original function as cavalry leader (→ *equites*).

The ME was appointed by the dictator as deputy (Liv. 8,32,1–8) for the period of his dictatorship. Appointment by a consul (Cass. Dio 42,21) or by election via the people's assembly (Liv. 22,8; Pol. 3,87) are exceptions. His period of office ended with the termination of the dictatorship (Liv. 4,34,5; 9,26,20); this, however, required his own → *abdicatio* (Liv. 4,34,5). He was subordinate to the → *coercitio* of the dictator, who could also ban him from official duties (cf. Liv. 8,36,1). The subordinate position of the office resulted from the nature of the dictatorship, and not primarily from the tactical requirements of the cavalry [1. 88–100].

His original function as cavalry commander gradually became less important. The ME was able to take on general military tasks and, as the dictator's representative, to carry out the same political tasks as he did, if necessary with the support of consuls or a *praefectus urbi* (Liv. 8,36,1). In rank, he stood after or alongside a praetor or a consular tribune (Cic. Leg. 3,3,8f.; Liv. 6,39,4; 23,11,10); in the time of → Caesar, he was entitled to the → *sella curulis,* the *toga praetexta* and six → *lictores.* Equipped with the powers of the magistrate, he could, if necessary, even summon the Senate independently (Plut. Antonius 8,3; Cic. Leg. 3,10; Cass. Dio 42,27,2).

The office survived until the end of the Republic, but lost its function with the beginning of the Empire – in the same way as the dictatorship; the Digests (1,2,2,19) equate the *praefectus praetorio* of the Imperial period with the ME of the Republic (see → *magister militum*).

1 M. STEMMLER, Eques Romanus – Reiter und Ritter, 1997.

W. KUNKEL, Staatsordnung und Staatspraxis der röm. Republik (HdbA 3,2,2), 1995, 717–719; U. v. LÜBTOW, Röm. Volk. Sein Staat und sein Recht, 1955, 168ff.; 198ff.; MOMMSEN, Staatsrecht 2,2, 173–180; H. SIBER, Röm. Verfassungsrecht, 1952, 108–110.   C.G.

Magister (ludi) see → School III. Rome

Magister militum Under Constantius [2] II (AD 337–361) the offices of the *magister peditum* and the *magister equitum* (for this office in the Roman Republic → *magister equitum*) were created and the military competencies of the *praefecti praetorio* were transferred to them (Zos. 2,33,3; Lydus, Mag. 2,10). This arrangement resulted from the separation of military and civilian functions in Roman offices that had started in the 3rd cent. At first, *magister peditum* and *magister equitum* were appointed as commanders of the relevant arms of service, although from the outset this principle was not followed strictly. Later, the office of the military commander-in-chief was called *magister utriusque militiae* or *magister militum* (MM). The MM had the supreme military command, the right to recruit and corrective control over the troops (both over → *comitatenses* and → *limitanei*) and over the *veterani,* whereas providing the *annona* and weapons remained in the purview of the → *praefectus praetorio* or the → *magister officiorum.* The regiments of the guards (*scholae*) were outside the command of the MM as well and were under the control of the *magister officiorum.* From the time of Constantius II there were three additional *magistri militum,* who had the supreme command over the troops of a region; the MM *praesentales* belonged to the immediate environment of the emperor, without any gradation by rank.

At first, the MM had the rank of *clarissimus* (→ *vir clarissimus*) and was *comes primi ordinis* (→ *comes*). Thereby, the *magistri militum* were at first below the *praefecti praetorio* who were *illustrissimi* (→ *illustris vir*); under Valentinian I they were elevated to the rank of *illustrissimus* as well. The first MM to hold the consulate was Flavius Bonosus in 344. Later on, the *magistri militum* were frequently consuls, in the 5th cent. they received the rank of *patricius* (at first Flavius Constantinus in 414). At the time the → *Notitia dignitatum* was compiled, there were two *magistri equitum et peditum in praesenti* or MM *praesentales* in the East, and the *magister peditum in praesenti* and the *magister equitum in praesenti* or *praesentalis* in the West. In addition, there were the regional *magistri equitum et peditum* or MM *per Orientem, per Thracias, per Illyricum* in the East and the *magister equitum per Gallias* in the West. Comitatensian cavalry and infantry units were assigned to the *magister peditum in praesenti* (Not. Dign. Occ. 5,144ff.) and the *magister equitum* (Not. Dign. Occ. 6,42ff) in the West (cf. *magister equitum per Gallias*: Not. Dign. Occ. 7,64ff.), but probably only in peace time.

The *officium* (office) of a MM consisted of *princeps, numerarius, commentariensis, primiscrinii, scriniarii, exceptores,* and *apparitores.* Although in the West, → Stilicho (*magister peditum in praesenti*) could hold the position of supreme commander because of a law regulating the appointment of associated *officia*, in the East the strong position of the *praefecti praetorio* and *magister officiorum* delayed a comparable development. In the West, the leading positions in the *officium* of the *duces* (→ *dux*) and *comites* were usually filled from the *officia* of the two *magistri militum praesentales* and rotated annually (see Not. Dign. Occ. 25,38); in the East they were filled with → *agentes in rebus* (cf. Not. Dign. Or. 28,48). In the East, there was no parallel development for the command of the western *magister peditum* over several *comites* and *duces limitum* (Not. Dign. Occ. 5,125f.; cf. Cod. Iust. 12,59,8: 467/70). The same is true for control over the fleets, the *laeti* and *gentiles* of the West (Not. Dign. Occ. 42,2ff. and 33ff.).

In the 4th cent., regular soldiers could advance to the rank of MM, but in the 5th cent. there was a fundamental change. From the late 4th cent. many Germans, esp. Franks, Goths, and Alans held the office of MM. This reflects the significance of these tribes for recruiting the army of late antiquity. Many of the German *magistri militum* descended from aristocratic or royal families (e.g. → Ricimer); during this time, several dynasties emerged who controlled this office for generations and established family alliances with the ruling families through marriage. As part of this development many *magistri militum* appointed their own bodyguards (*bucellarii*). However, there were hardly any family ties to the senatorial aristocracy of the time.

Of significance in the East was the Alanic-Gothic group with Ardabur [2] Aspar, his sons Ardabur [3] and Patricius, and the nephew of Aspar's wife, Theodoric Strabo. The political influence of this group is evident from the fact that they held consulates (Ardabur II, *cos.* 447; Patricius, *cos.* 459), yet when Aspar and part of his family (Ardabur II, Patricius) were murdered in 471 under emperor Leo [4] I, their reach for imperial powers was thwarted; they were replaced by an Isaurian-Roman group; the Isaurian MM *praesentalis* Zenosucceeded first in installing his underage son, emperor Leo [5] II. Finally, through a decree of the Senate, Zeno himself was declared Augustus.

In the West, the increasing disintegration of the imperial authority under Valentinian III – the murder of the powerful MM Aëtius [2] notwithstanding – strengthened the MM*praesentales* (esp. Ricimer) who dominated the weak emperors at will. In 475, the MM *praesentalis* Orestes declared his young son Romulus emperor. The Western Empire ended in 476 when Orestes was murdered and Romulus Augustulus disposed by Odoacer. In north-west Gallia the position of the MM increasingly became an independent political force (Aegidius, MM 457–464/5, and his son Syagrius) that survived the end of the Western Empire and was abolished only by Clovis, king of the Franks (486 victory near Soissons). In the 5th cent., the rule of German kings on the territory of the former Roman Empire was legitimized several times by appointing them as *magistri militum*; e.g. Alaric, king of the West Goths, was in-

stalled in the office of MM *per Thracias*, and under emperor Zeno the Ostrogothic federate leader Theodoric was appointed MM; the Burgundian kings Gundioc and Gundobad were *magistri equitum per Gallias*.

1 L. CRACCO RUGGINI, Les généraux francs aux IVᵉ-Vᵉ siècles et leurs groupes aristocratiques, in: M. ROUCHE (ed.), Clovis. Histoire et mémoire, vol. 2, 1997, 673–688 2 A. DEMANDT, s.v. m.m., RE Suppl. 12, 533–790 3 Id., Der spätröm. Militäradel, in: Chiron 10, 1980, 609–636 4 Id., Die Spätant., 1989 5 JONES, LRE 341–344, 608–610 6 J. M. O'FLYNN, Generalissimos of the Western Roman Empire, 1983 7 H. WOLFRAM, Das Reich und die Germanen – Zwischen Ant. und Mittelalter, 1990.   P.H.

Magister officiorum

A. ORIGIN OF THE OFFICE   B. RELATIONSHIP TO OTHER COURT OFFICES   C. JUDICIAL FUNCTIONS AND CHURCH POLITICS   D. CURSUS HONORUM E. DISSOLUTION OF THE OFFICE

A. ORIGIN OF THE OFFICE

An office of late antiquity created by → Constantinus [1] I, which was among the highest in the Roman empire (Not. Dign. Or. 11; Not. Dign. Occ. 9), attested for the first time in AD 320 (Cod. Theod. 16,10,1). The great imperial chancelleries (→ *scrinium*) of the *magister memoriae*, *magister epistularum* and *magister libellorum* and lesser palace officials, such as *admissionales*, *interpretes*, *mensores* (→ *mensor*), *decani* (→ *decanius*), *stratores*, *cursores*, → *lampadarii*, and *notarii* (→ *notarius*) were first of all probably mandated to the *magister officiorum* (MO), who was a standing member of the → *consistorium*. He was thus the head of the central administration (excluding finances) and chief of ceremonies at the court.

In the course of the following decades, the MO drew into his sphere many departments, which had previously been under the → *praefectus praetorio*. Especially his quality as superior of the → *agentes in rebus*, from whose ranks he drew, among others, the heads of office (*principes*) of higher posts from c. 340, allowed him soon to become the imperial organ of control of the entire imperial administration. The information from the *agentes* came together in the *schola*, which, together with the news from the *scrinia*, secured an advance in information for the MO, this became the basis for his advancement and his power. In as far as the *agentes* oversaw spy activities, as well as numerous other duties, the MO was at the same time chief of the state police as well. The MO was also commander of the palace guards (→ *scholae Palatinae*) as early as under Constantine I, and was therefore responsible for the security of the emperor. However, he did not command these troops in battle; this was the duty of the → *magister militum* instead.

B. Relationship to other court offices

Attempts to extend its influence to the military were unsuccessful in the West, however in the East, the *agentes in rebus* also gained access to the offices of the *duces* (→ *dux* [1]) and → *comites* as *principes officii*. There the *magistri officiorum* were also even entrusted with the supervision of border troops and fortifications in the 5th cent. From → Constantius [2] II, the MO also oversaw the → *cursus publicus* in competition with the *praef. praet*: prosecution in the event of misuse of the public post and the issuing of certificates of use (*evectiones*) was from now on the responsibility of both. Under Constantius II, an *agens in rebus* even received supervisory authority as *princeps officii* in the offices of the *praef. praet*. Around 390, the MO then received the overriding supervising authority over the weapons factories (→ *fabrica*), formerly under the *praef. praet*. All of this did not occur without interior struggles; they became especially obvious in the dispute between the MO→ Rufinus and the *praef. praet*. → Tatianus at the end of the 4th cent., resp. between the MO→ Tribonianus and → Iohannes [16] Cappadocius in the middle of the 6th cent. The latter was able to regain some powers for the prefecture.

There were contacts with other court offices only in so far as the *quaestor sacri palatii* took his personnel from the *scrinia*, which were subject to the MO, and a collaboration became necessary when the MO received judicial functions. There were, however, practically no contacts with the *comes sacrarum largitionum* and *comes rerum privatarum*. Finally, the MO, who was also in charge of the interpreters, was in charge of transacting emissary contacts as early as the 4th cent., domestically and abroad, and thus had a part in shaping foreign policy (Amm. Marc. 26,5,7; Lydus, Mag. 2,25). In 443 in the East, the MO was given the task of the annual inspection of the border troops (→ *limitanei*, Nov. Theod. 24).

C. Judicial functions and Church politics

The MO had jurisdiction over the employees (*officiales*) in the *scrinia* under his authority; however, he quickly managed to expand his competences, in that he extended jurisdictional authority over and above disciplinary jurisdiction and increased the circle of those who could demand a proceeding before their supervisor (*praescriptio fori*), i.e. about the large group of the *ministeriani* (→ *cubicularius* among others). From the 2nd half of the 4th cent., there was no longer the possibility of appeal against his judgements. In addition, the MO had special jurisdiction over the senators. → Leo [4] I placed the *duces* and officers of the border troops under the jurisdiction of the MO (Cod. Iust. 12,59,8), and in 529 the MO, together with the *quaestor sacri palatii*, became the court of appeal for judgements by military courts (Cod. Iust. 7,72,38).

A final area in which the MO, like many other officials, became active, was Church politics, since he had the personnel to organize synods and to enforce their decisions; at the same time, he frequently participated in the sittings himself. As a member of the *consistorium* and leader of the imperial audiences, he was also present at consultations with Church representatives and often led investigations against the latter as well. All this created frequent contacts with the emperor. Among the four court posts, the MO was approximately at the same rank as the *quaestor sacri palatii*. Still → *spectabilis* in 378, the MO was soon afterward → *illustris* (*vir*), in the 6th cent. → *gloriosus*.

D. Cursus honorum

A firm → *cursus honorum* for the *magistri officiorum* did not exist, though they previously held lower court appointments as a rule. Subsequent to the office of MO, they could become → *praefectus urbi* or → *praefectus praetorio*; in some cases, past *magistri officiorum* even became → *consul*. From the 5th cent., however, the *magisterium officiorum* was generally the high point and conclusion of a career.

The length of time in office varied widely: at first, long periods in office were usual; from approximately 370, these became noticeably shorter, until with → Zeno (474–5), a period of long incumbency set in. This corresponds to the development of the *cursus honorum* in so far as the post in the 5th cent. was a station, then the conclusion of the career. Most of the *magistri officiorum* originally came from the non-senatorial class and oriented themselves therefore as social climbers (→ *novus homo*) more toward the emperor than to the → *senatus*, though the office also became increasingly attractive for senators.

E. Dissolution of the office

In the western part of the empire, the office lost influence as early as the beginning of the 5th cent., since the power of the → *magister militum* was rising, due to the incursions of the Germanic tribes. In the east of the empire, the decrease in influence at the end of the 5th cent. is seen in the substitution of the *scholae palatinae* by the *excubitores*, whose command went to the *comes domesticorum* and not to the MO. From now on, the main area of activity of the MO was diplomacy. In the 7th cent., the *magisterium officiorum* in the east finally disintegrated into the subareas which had originally been united under the MO.

A. Boak, The Master of the Offices, 1924; M. Clauss, Der m.o. in der Spätant. (4.–6. Jh.), 1981 (with prosopography); R. Delmaire, Les institutions du Bas-Empire romain de Constantin à Justinien, vol. 1: Les institutions civiles palatines, 1995, 75–96; P. B. Weiss, Consistorium und comites consistoriani, 1975.   K.G.-A.

Magistratus

A. Term   B. Development   C. System of the magistrature   D. Decline of the magistrature

A. Term

Usually a certain bearer of state power elected by popular vote, however, at the same time it is also in concrete terms the office or in the plural the sum of individual offices of Roman or peregrine provenance. *Magistratus* is derived from *magister* (*magis*, 'more') (Varro Ling. 5,82; Dig. 50,16,57; Fest. p. 113 L.; CIL I² 401: *mac[i]steratus*). The concept is recorded in inscriptions from the 4th/3rd cents. BC, and in literature by Plautus (CIL I² 25: *macistr[a]tos*; I² 401; Plaut. Amph. 74; Plaut. Persa 76; Plaut. Rud. 477; Plaut. Truc. 761). The abstract expression 'magistrature' is not known in ancient sources. The common term for the office is occasionally associated in the surviving word pairs *magistratus potestasve, magistratus imperiumve* among others (CIL I² 593; 594; 582; 583) with the more specific powers of the office.

To the *magistratus* at the end of the Roman Republic (1st cent. BC.) belong the *consules* (→ *consul*), *praetores* (→ *praetor*), → *aediles, tribuni plebis* (→ *tribunus*), *quaestores* (→ *quaestor*), *vigintisexviri* or → *vigintiviri* as well as the special office of the → *censores* and the exceptional offices of the → *dictator* and *magister equitum* (→ *magister*) [1; 2]. Although the two last named extraordinary offices lacked the crucial criterion of election by the people, they were carried out under the *magistratus* on account of their unusual concentration of power (e.g. CIL I² 582). The → *interrex* as the deputy of the *magistratus* and the politically insignificant *tribunus militum* (→ *tribunus*) do not appear to have been *magistratus* in any real sense of the word [1. 283; 12f.].

B. Development

As the historiography of the annalists (→ Annalists) is less reliable in the early Roman period, the origin of the *magistratus* is disputed in research. Neither is it certain whether *magistratus* or earlier forms of it already existed during the period of the Monarchy, nor whether the highest office in the early Republic had one, two, or three posts [3. 281ff.; 4]. Since the principle of collegiality (→ *collega*) may have been seen as a product of the → struggle of the orders in the 5th and 4th cents. BC [5. vol. 1, 234ff.], the constitution of the consulate or a quite differently organized highest office with double or multiple posts can probably be excluded for the early period (otherwise [6; 7]). In all probability, after the disempowerment of the monarchy an annual official (*praetor maximus* or *magister populi*) was placed at the head of the government. Probably *praetores* or *tribuni militum* were assigned to the highest magistrature. Resulting from the class dispute over the highest office, it seems that finally the double consulate becomes established beyond the level of the consular tribune (→ Lici-

nius [I 43]). A patrician praetor as *minor collega* is now added to as a patrician and a plebeian consul. The creation of new *magistratus* (censor, aedility) or the increase in already existing offices (praetorship, quaestorship) takes account of growing internal and external political requirements. The people's tribunes are integrated, through the *lex Hortensia* 287 BC (→ Hortensius [4]), into the existing system of offices as regular magistrature of the whole community.

C. System of the magistrature

1. Categories of office   2. Laws and functions   3. Eligibility and administration of the office   4. The promagistrature

1. Categories of office

In the fully developed constitution of the classical Republic from the 3rd cent. BC, various categories of office are differentiated: the formerly revolutionary institutions of the → *plebs*, the plebeian aediles and the people's tribunes, are juxtaposed as *magistratus plebeii* to the offices formerly held only by patricians, the *magistratus patricii* (e.g. Gell. NA 13,15,4; Cic. Leg. agr. 2,26; Liv. 3,59,4). Curule *magistratus* are those which preside over the → *sella curulis* as official insignia according to their jurisdictional authority, i.e. the consuls and praetors as higher officials and both the formerly patrician aediles entrusted with market jurisdiction (e.g. Gell. NA 3,18,4; Cic. Att. 13,32,3; Fest. p. 43 L.; Liv. 23,23,5f.). There is also a further division into 'higher' and 'lower' offices: the *magistratus maiores* are the consuls, praetors and censors elected by the → *comitia centuriata*, the *magistratus minores* are the people's tribunes, aediles and quaestors elected by the *comitia tributa*; moreover the connection can also, however, be regarded as relative (e.g. Gell. NA 13,15; 13,16,1; Cic. Leg. 3,6; Liv. 3,55,9; 25,1,11; Dig. 47,10,32) [8].

2. Laws and functions

In Roman society, in which a high value is attached to *dignitas* (i.e. the socio-political status resulting from services to the state), the holding of a *magistratus* also conveys great honour. *Magistratus* is thus also referred to as *honos* ('honour', 'honorary office') (Liv. 6,35,3f.; Suet. Aug. 26; Gai. Inst. 1,96; Dig. 50,12,11). The chosen officials are *magistratus populi Romani* (e.g. Cic. Leg. Manil. 55; Vell. Pat. 2,42,1; Dig. 49,3,3) and thus are representatives of the sovereignty of the Roman people (→ *maiestas*), which they are there to maintain. The citizen who is not an official (→ *privatus*) has to treat the official, who embodies the will of the people, with the greatest respect. Places of honour are reserved for the *magistratus* at the games. Individual rights of honour are retained by the curule *magistratus* even after expiry of their period of office (thus they have the right, among others, to wear the *toga praetexta* again in certain circumstances, and can even demand a *magistratus'* funeral). With the exception of the quaestors and the plebeian officials, the *magistratus* wear the *toga praetexta* as a token of their official powers and sit on the *sella curulis* in their official capacity. The imperial power bearers preside over → *lictores*, who carry before them bundles of rods (*fasces*) to which axes are attached, as symbols of their punitive powers outside Rome (fundamental [9. 372ff.]; pictorial representation of the insignia of office [10; 11]).

Being honorary offices, the *magistratus* are naturally unsalaried. Expenses arising from the administration of the office are, however, if applicable, reimbursed through payment of a lump sum (→ *vasarium*) by the treasury. The *magistratus* is also authorized, in areas of Roman rule, to requisition or buy up at state expense everything necessary (e.g. accommodation, means of transport). He has a permanent staff (→ *apparitores*), paid by the state, at his disposal [9. 293ff., 320ff.; 1. 110ff.].

The powers of the office are designated – corresponding to the objective responsibilities of the *magistratus* – by → *imperium*, *auspicium* (→ *augures*) or → *potestas* [3]. This magistrative power is subject to various restrictions and limitations that curtail the individual and arbitrary powers of the office-holder and strengthen controls and co-operation: principle of annuity (exception: *dictator*, *censor*), principle of collegiality, prohibition of the *maior potestas* ('higher powers of office'), prohibition of continuation, of iteration and of cumulation. Moreover, common-law and legal regulations (*leges annales*) govern the official career (→ *cursus honorum*; *certus ordo*, interval and age stipulations) [12. 99ff.; 1. 6ff., 45ff.]. Apart from these principles and legal clauses, the *magistratus* is subject to a strict social screening through his membership of the aristocratic elite (→ *nobiles*) and thus he is held to virtual obedience to the Senate (→ *senatus*) [12; 13]. The → *consilium*, assigned to the *magistratus*, serves as a further means of scrutiny and also of communication, and in the sphere of the *militiae* there are also the *legati* (→ *legatus*) and senatorial legations.

The state power of the *magistratus* (with the exception of the plebeian and 'municipal' officials) extends to the official sectors of the *domi* and *militiae* (see → *domus*). The work of the *magistratus* is inseparably connected to religious matters. The 'patrician' *magistratus* for instance, practise interpretation of omens (*auspicium*), in order to discover the will of the gods. The higher officials are, like the people's tribunes, authorized to summon and lead the Senate and the people's assembly (*ius cum senatu/cum populo* or *plebe agendi*). The imperial power-bearers (→ *imperium*) have the right of → *iurisdictio*, → *coercitio* and command of the army. In the realm of the *militiae* they are free to take decisions; however, negotiated treaties or alliances require the approval of the Senate and the people [1; 12].

3. ELIGIBILITY AND ADMINISTRATION OF THE OFFICE

Access to a *magistratus* may be achieved by anyone who is a full Roman citizen, the son of a freeborn father,

whole in body and mind, honourable, prosperous and belonging to the upper class. Ultimately, however, the election official decides on the acceptance of the → *candidatus*, in which criteria such as observance of career directives or time limits (→ *cursus honorum*) also play a role. Unfair practices in the electoral campaign are countered by active but unsuccessful → *ambitus*-legislation from the 2nd cent. BC [14]. The taking up of office occurred on the 1st January from 153 BC (previously: 15 March) with the exception of people's tribunes and quaestors (10 or 5 December).

During the period of office the *magistratus* is traditionally not called to account; the former *magistratus* can, however, be prosecuted for any possible offences in office (→ *peculatus*, → *repetundarum crimen*, → *maiestas*). A general obligation of accountability does not exist. Early retirement from office (→ *abdicatio*) – voluntarily or forced – can proceed upon completion of work (dictatorship, censorship), for relevant reasons (technically defective election: *vitio creatus*) or as a result of very serious offences (e.g. *coniuratio*). Dismissals (→ *abrogatio*) also occurred (133 BC.: Plut. Ti. Gracchus 12; App. Civ. 1,51–54) [1. 252ff.].

4. THE PROMAGISTRATURE

The promagistrature, on the other hand, is not an office but the extension of official power. From 327/6 BC, the *magistratus* are given, on completion of a year in office, *pro magistratu*, i.e. 'in place of *magistratus*' (thus *pro consule*, *pro praetore*) powers of command (*imperium*) in the continuation of wars or the administration of a province. This → *prorogatio imperii* is a temporary measure to address adequately the problems of (world-)rule, without endangering the power of the aristocracy through new *magistratus*. The promagistrates, among them also *privati* after 211 BC, are subordinate to the proper officials. Prorogation happens by resolution of the Senate (and initially of the people also), who can take away from the deputies their *imperium* at any time [12. 116f.].

D. DECLINE OF THE MAGISTRATURE

In the late Republic, the magistrature becomes eroded by extraordinary commands (*imperia extraordinaria*), i.e. commands completely detached from the office and its principles. In the Imperial period, the ruler bolsters his rule with a range of official powers (*imperium (pro-)consulare*, *tribunicia potestas*), in addition to the bestowal of regular *magistratus*. The *magistratus* lose political significance through the omnipotence of the → *princeps*. The emperor seeks to counter the danger that still comes from these prestigious offices, by the regimentation of the *cursus honorum*, by changing and limiting competences. Particular scrutiny is given to the elections, which have degenerated into a mere formality as a result of imperial → *nominatio*, → *commendatio* and the → *destinatio* carried out in the time of Augustus (→ Tabula Hebana, → Tabula Siarensis [15. 507–547]). At the same time an imperial administration is set up, in which salaried departmental officials work as mandataries of the *princeps* and can be dismissed at any time [16]; these are not *magistratus*. In the period of late antiquity after the state and administration reforms of Diocletian (→ Diocletianus) the Republican *magistratus* no longer have any real official authority. The remaining quaestors, praetors and consuls now belong to the *dignitates* (→ Court title C.) [17; 18].

In the once independent cities of Italy, now ruled by Rome and its empire, are found *magistratus municipales* (Dig. 50,1,25), generally *duoviri iure dicundo* (→ *duoviri*), aediles and quaestors. They are the result of a standard order of *municipia* (→ *municipium*) and → *coloniae* at the time of → Caesar (→ Tabula Heracleiensis) and, as far as their position is concerned, they are to a certain extent the mirror image of the *magistratus* in Rome [15].

→ Cursus honorum

1 W. KUNKEL, Staatsordnung und Staatspraxis der röm. Republik, 2. Teil: Die Magistratur (HdbA 10,3,2,2), 1995 2 MRR 3 J. BLEICKEN, Zum Begriff der röm. Amtsgewalt, 1981 4 A. MOMIGLIANO, Roma arcaica, 1989, 131–163 5 F. DE MARTINO, Storia della costituzione romana, 6 vols., ²1972–1990 6 A. HEUSS, Gesammelte Schriften 2, 1995, 908–985 7 R. WERNER, Der Beginn der röm. Republik, 1963 8 G. LOBRANO, Plebei m., patricii m., m. populi Romani, in: SDHI 41, 1975, 245–277 9 MOMMSEN, Staatsrecht, vol. 1 10 TH. SCHÄFER, Imperii insignia, 1989 11 J. RONKE, Magistratische Repräsentation, 1987 12 J. BLEICKEN, Die Verfassung der röm. Republik, ⁷1995 13 W. KUNKEL, Magistratische Gewalt und Senatsherrschaft, in: ANRW I.2, 1972, 3–22 14 P. NADIG, Ardet ambitus, 1997 15 M. H. CRAWFORD, Roman Statutes, vol. 1, 1996 16 F. M. AUSBÜTTEL, Die Verwaltung des röm. Kaiserreiches, 1998 17 NOETHLICHS 18 A. DEMANDT, Die Spätantike, 1989.
L.d.L.

Magius Family name of Oscan origin. [I 184]. The family was prominent in Capua (M. [I 3], cf. Cic. Pis. 24) and M.'s [I 5] sons were the first to be admitted to the Senate in the 1st cent. BC.

SCHULZE.   K.-L.E.

I. REPUBLICAN PERIOD   II. IMPERIAL PERIOD

I. REPUBLICAN PERIOD

[I 1] Grandfather of the poet → Vergilius on his mother's side; was allegedly an official messenger (→ *viator*; Donat. Vita Vergilii 1).   W.K.
[I 2] **M., Cn.** From Larinum in Samnium, died about 88 BC; heir of his (half-?)brother N. Aurius. M.'s own heir was the son of his sister Magia, → Abbius Oppianicus (Cic. Clu. 21; 33).   JÖ.F.
[I 3] **M., Decius** Led the Roman faction in Capua in 216 BC. Sent by → Hannibal [4] to Carthage, but landed in Cyrene. Died in Egyptian exile (Liv. 23,7,4–8,3; 10,3–13; Vell. Pat. 2,16,2).   P.N.

[I 4] **M., L.** Praetor (?), officer in the army of C. Flavius [I 6] Fimbria, after whose death in battle against the supporters of Sulla in 85 BC, he defected to → Mithridates VI together with L. Fannius [I 3]. Both negotiated an alliance between Mithridates and Q. Sertorius in Spain in 76 or 75 (Cic. Verr. 1,87; Ps.-Ascon. 244 ST.; Sall. Hist. 2,79 M.), for which reason the Senate declared them enemies of the state. They later betrayed the king in order to return to Rome (App. Mithr. 308).

C. F. KONRAD, Plutarch's Sertorius, 1994, 191f.

[I 5] **M., Minatus** From → Aec(u)lanum, grandson of M. [I 3] (?). M. was a loyal supporter of Rome during the → Social War [3]; with T. Didius [I 4], he took Herculaneum in 89 BC and supported Sulla at his siege of Pompeii and the taking of Compsa (and Aec(u)lanum?), whereupon he received the citizenship of Rome as a reward (Vell. Pat. 2,16, 2f.; App. B Civ. 1,222f.). The great-grandfather of the historian C. → Velleius Paterculus.   K.-L.E.
[I 6] **M., N.** Praef. *fabrum* of Cn. → Pompeius from Cremona. Captured by Caesar in 49 BC and sent to Pompey with the offer of a conference with both leaders. Caesar denies (Caes. B Civ. 1,24,4f.) that M. came back with an answer, but seems to have confirmed this in private (Cic. Att. 9,13A,1; according to Cicero himself – Cic. Att. 9,13,8 – Caesar would no longer receive M.).   JÖ.F.
[I 7] **M. Atellanus, Cn.** Related to M. [I 3], but also his political opponent. Chief magistrate (*meddix tuticus*) in Capua in 214 BC (Liv. 24,19,1–2), attempted to hold on to an alliance with → Hannibal.   P.N.
[I 8] **M. Cilo, P.** Friend of M. Claudius [I 15] Marcellus and his comrade-in-arms in the civil war against Caesar. On the homeward journey to Rome, M. mortally wounded Marcellus in a quarrel at Piraeus on 23 May 45 BC and promptly stabbed himself to death (Val. Max. 9,11,4; Cic. Fam. 4,12). The motive was unclear; the involvement of Caesar, who had pardoned them both, was disputed by M. Iunius [I 10] Brutus (Cic. Att. 13,10,3).   JÖ.F.

II. IMPERIAL PERIOD

[II 1] **M. Caecilianus** Senator of praetorian status. In AD 21, he was falsely accused of 'lèse-majesté'; his accusers were punished. PIR² M 87.
[II 2] **M. Celer Velleianus** Brother of → Velleius Paterculus, adopted by one of the Magii. Originated from Capua. Admission to the Senate before AD 9; at that time legate of Tiberius in Dalmatia. In the entourage of Tiberius at the triumphal procession in AD 13; he received the praetorship as *candidatus* of the *princeps* in the year 15. PIR² M 88.
[II 3] **M.M. Maximus** Probably originating from Aeclanum, equestrian. *Praef. Aegypti* under Augustus, about AD 12–14/5. Whether he was in Egypt twice as praefect, is uncertain (cf. [1. 504; 2]).

1 G. BASTIANINI, Il prefetto d'Egitto, in: ANRW II 10.1, 1988, 503–517 2 PIR² M 89.

[II 4] **L. M. Valerianus** Senatorian. Commander of the *legio III Augusta*, governor of Numidia AD 256–258.

THOMASSON, Fasti Africani, 188f.   W.E.

Magnae (or *Magni*). Roman fort on Hadrian's Wall in northern England (Not. Dign. Occ. 40,43; Geogr. Rav. 107,11), probably dating to the Flavian period (AD 69–96), modern Carvoran, identified because of epigraphical evidence (*numerus Magn(c)es(ium)* [1. 1825]). In the early 2nd cent., before M. became part of the Hadrianic → Limes after AD 122, it may have been part of Trajan's border line [2. 192–196]. The fort was not integrated into the → *vallum* as was usually the case, but remained situated to the south. Under Hadrian and after him, the *cohors I Hamiorum* was stationed there until it was replaced by the *cohors II Delmatarum* in the 3rd cent. Rebuilt in stone in AD 136–138. Archaeological finds: a grain measure (*modius*) in bronze, dated to AD 90/1, a dedication for → Dea Syria [1. 1791].

1 R. G. COLLINGWOOD, R. P. WRIGHT, The Roman Inscriptions of Britain 1, 1965; 2 E. BIRLEY, Research on Hadrian's Wall, 1961.

D. BREEZE, The Northern Frontiers of Roman Britain, 1982.   M.TO.

Magna Graecia (Μεγάλη Ἑλλάς/*Megálē Hellás*, 'Great Greece').
I. GEOGRAPHY AND HISTORY II. RELIGION

I. GEOGRAPHY AND HISTORY
A. DEFINITION B. HISTORY UP TO THE ROMAN CONQUEST C. ROMAN PERIOD D. LATE ANTIQUITY

A. DEFINITION
From a geographical point of view, the concept of Magna Graecia (MG) is superimposed on *Italia* without being identical with it. In the 5th cent. BC, it referred to the outermost part of Italia, surrounded by the Tyrrhenian and Ionian Seas from → Laus [2] to → Metapontium. Later MG was used for the whole part of Southern Italy that had been settled by Greeks, from → Taras to → Cyme [2]. The term *Megálē Hellás* was already widespread around the middle of the 5th cent. BC. There seem to be two traditions: one of them (Athenaeus) linked MG to the fertility of the soil, the favourable climate and the wealth of the *póleis* in Southern Italy; the other tradition (Timaeus) connects it with the schools of philosophers, especially the → Pythagorean School, located in the towns of Southern Italy. In Roman times, MG referred to the 'wealthiest towns ' (*opulentissimae urbes*) of Southern Italy.

B. HISTORY UP TO THE ROMAN CONQUEST
As early as the middle Bronze Age, Southern Italy maintained intensive relations with the area of Aegaean culture (Mycenae, Crete, Cyprus); the mythological tradition of the → *Nóstoi* ('Epics of Return') bears witness thereof. Between the end of the Bronze Age and the early Iron Age, different ethnic and cultural groups emerged in Italy. From the end of the 9th cent. BC, relations with Greece resumed along the same Mycenaean trade routes ('precolonization'). The actual major → colonization began about 770 BC with the Chalcidic foundation of → Pithecussae on Ischia, a sort of 'proto-polis' which was followed in the middle of the 8th cent. by the foundation of Cyme on the → Campi Phlegraei. The purpose of the Euboean colonization was the control of the trade route through the Straits of Messina (→ Messana; → Rhegium). In the last third of the 8th cent. BC, a wave of colonization from Achaea followed (→ Croton, → Sybaris, → Caulonia, then → Metapontium in the 7th cent. BC.) The foundation of Taras, the only Spartan → *apoikía* in the West, is dated near the end of the 8th cent. BC. In the beginning of the 7th cent. BC there followed → Siris and → Locri [2] Epizephyrii. The new *póleis* rapidly developed into agricultural or maritime powers from which sub-colonies were founded.

Relations between the various *apoikíai* in Southern Italy were often characterized by rivalries: during the first decades of the 6th cent. BC, a coalition of Achaean *póleis* destroyed the Ionian Siris; little later, about the middle of the cent., Locri and Croton collided in the battle near → Sagra; in 510 BC, Sybaris was destroyed by Croton. An important aspect of colonization was the more or less conflict-laden contact with the original population which accelerated its social structuring and shaped the formation of an ethnic self-confidence. Following the Panhellenic foundation of → Thurii in 444 BC the political horizon of the towns in MG widened. From the beginning of the 4th cent. BC, the aggressiveness of the indigenous population grew, against which the Italiote League was soon created under the leadership of Taras. There was also the hegemonial pressure of Syracuse and the readiness of foreign powers to intervene (Sparta with Archidamus in 338 and Cleonymus in 303 BC; Alexander [6] in 331 and Pyrrhus of Epirus in 281 BC).

C. ROMAN PERIOD
The intervention of Rome in favour of local oligarchies lead to the gradual integration of the towns into the new Roman order. With the conquest of Taras in 272 and of Rhegium in 270 BC, the process was finally concluded. From then on Rome ruled MG with various treaties that assigned quite different rights to individual towns. However, these *foedera* (→ *foedus*) guaranteed a considerable degree of autonomy which allowed continuation of local traditions (magistrates, cults) up to the Imperial period. MG suffered seriously from the devastating conflicts of the 2nd → Punic War. To

counteract depopulation, Roman colonies (Luceria, Venosa, Paestum/Posidonia, Puteoli) were founded, which also furthered economic penetration by Rome and its control of the maritime trade routes. In the long run, the inequality of territorial infrastructure, the co-existence of Roman and local laws, and the growing trend to set up latifundia (→ Large estates) initiated a substantial decline, beginning with the Imperial period. Slowly, the Italiote towns became impoverished while, on the other hand, the culture of rich *villae rusticae* expanded.

→ Sicilia

Atti dei Convegni di Studi sulla Magna Grecia, 1961ff., especially Megale Hellas. Nome e immagine (1981), 1982; J. BOARDMAN, The Greeks Overseas, 1980; G. PUGLIESE CARRATELLI (ed.), Megale Hellas, 1983; E. LEPORE, Colonie greche dell'Occidente antico, 1989; G. PUGLIESE CARRATELLI (ed.), Italia Omnium Terrarum Parens, 1989; E. GRECO, Archeologia della Magna Grecia, 1992; M. AMERUOSO, Megale Hellas, 1996; E. M. DE JULIIS, Magna Grecia, 1996; G. PUGLIESE CARRATELLI (ed.), Magna Grecia, 4 vols., ²1996.   A.MU.

D. LATE ANTIQUITY

Even with the establishment of the Roman villa-civilization, MG was by no means fully Romanized; Lower Italy and Sicilia retained their Greek character, supported by the cents. of Byzantine rule.

After the settlement of the → Vandali in Northern Africa after AD 440, Lower Italy and Sicilia were continuously exposed to plundering raids which seriously endangered grain supplies for Rome. In 491, the Sicilian nobility joined → Theodoric, who at this time ruled Italy as the representative of the East Roman emperor, but the → Goti left self-administration of the island intact and only rarely intervened in its affairs. During the following periods, Sicilia played a part as an important Byzantine base in the battles against the Vandali (533) and then in the campaign against the Goti (535-555). When → Iustinianus [1] created the → Exarchate of Italia, Sicilia was given a separate civilian administration (under a praetor) in 536 and a military administration (under a *dux*), both in close contact with the central government in → Constantinople. The remaining Byzantine areas of Lower Italy, however, were directly dependent on the exarch in → Ravenna. The disputes of the → Langobardi with the Byzantine exarch of Ravenna barely affected Sicilia, even though the Langobardi invaded Italy in AD 568 and soon penetrated Lower Italy as well.

Expansion of the Muslim → Arabs turned Sicilia into the southeastern outpost of the Christian World after 652. The Arab threat to the island forced the Byzantine court to reorganize Sicilia as a separate → thema with more stringent controls around 700. During the first half of the 8th cent., all dioceses on the island were removed from the jurisdiction of the Pope in Rome and placed under the patriarchy of Constantinople. Following the conquest of Ravenna by the Langobardi, the

thema of Sikelia (including the Duchies of Calabria, Otranto and Naples) became responsible for the protection of Byzantine interests in Italy. From 827, the Arabs conquered Sicilia step by step; Byzantine resistance was able to hold on until 965 (fall of the fortress of Rametta). → Katepanate

L. C. RUGGINI, La Sicilia fra Roma e Bisanzio, in: Storia della Sicilia 3, 1980, 1-96; Q. CATAUDELLA, La cultura bizantina in Sicilia, in: Storia della Sicilia 4, 1980, 1-56.
                                                                    E.O.

II. RELIGION
A. GENERAL   B. MYCENAEAN AND PRE-COLONIAL TRADITIONS   C. THE NEEDS OF THE COLONISTS D. POPULAR RELIGION AND THE RELIGION OF THE UPPER CLASS   E. ROMAN PERIOD

A. GENERAL
MG does not have any religions that are fundamentally different from the rest of Greece. On the basis of current knowledge, the view that the cults of the Greeks in the West had a specific character because of a possible influence of local peoples cannot be supported. Without denying the existence and importance of Italic traditions, religious life of the Greeks in those regions was autonomous from indigenous surroundings. It is safe to assume that the colonists defended their cultural identity as Greeks *vis-à-vis* the local population by maintaining the religious traditions of their mother cities. Religious interactions are most frequently encountered where the indigenous population entered a process of → Hellenization, especially from the 4th cent. BC.

B. MYCENAEAN AND PRE-COLONIAL TRADITIONS
When the colonists left Aegaean Greece from around the middle of the 8th cent. BC (→ Colonization), the religious traditions of their home towns where still shaped by Mycenaean elements. When they arrived in Italy, they went ashore in areas where visitors since Mycenaean times had left traces of religious activities. Also, the major part of the myths connected with the foundation of colonies points to the Cretan world (legends surrounding → Minos and → Daedalus on Sicily, but also in → Iapygia), to the Trojan War and the epics of return, → *Nóstoi* (cult of Athena *Iliás* in → Siris, cf. Str. 6,1,14 or of Philoctetes in → Sybaris, cf. Ps.-Aristot. De mirabilibus ausculationibus 107). Hercules is most strongly connected with the movement of the Greeks towards the West (Hes. Theog. 287-292; Stesich. PMG fr. 181-186): His excursions (→ Geryoneus) coincide with the maritime routes to the West, where traces of Mycenaean seafarers can be found. Are these myths and cults a memory of the continuity with Mycenaean times? It is also possible that these myths were used by the historiographical traditions to legitimize the settlement of Greek colonists *a posteriori*. Thus, the claim of the Cretan origin of the → Iapyges (Hdt. 7,170) pro-

vides them with an older and even more illustrious lineage than that of the Spartans, who had settled in → Taras (Lat. Tarentum) in Iapygian territory. A similar discussion revolves around the sanctuaries located outside of the towns [5. 121f.]. The thesis that they constitute a reconstruction of remembered Mycenaean cults is contested by an obviously political argument: the political function of these sanctuaries may well be explained as that of territorial markers which also served as contact points with the indigenous populations.

At this point, we have no archaeological proof of continuity between the Mycenaean and the archaic epoch in MG. Where cults overlap in identical locations, the reason is a natural propensity for cultic activity. For this reason, current research stresses the importance of pre-colonial contacts between Greek traders and autochthonous populations (→ Commerce IV. A). The fact that these traders regularly landed on the coasts of Anatolia, Syro-Phoenicia and Crete may well explain the arrivals of two deities in Italy, even before the foundation of the colonies: deities which are absent from the Mycenaean pantheon, namely Apollo and Aphrodite. The latter is the goddess of seafaring and emporia *par excellence*. In → Locri [2], her sanctuary is in the part of town which is connected with the harbour and also linked with the U-shaped stoa (*centocamere*), which was outside of the city walls and where rites involving sacral prostitution took place (Ath. 12,515e; Iust. 21,3,2). On the promontory of Crimisa to the north of → Croton stands the sanctuary of Apollo *Alaíos* near a town named Calasarna. This name has been preserved by Strabo (6,1,3) and is reminiscent of Halasarna (the Mysian town, or also the deme of Cos), with its sanctuary of Apollo, famous for the rites in honour of Heracles. According to Pseudo-Aristoteles (De mirabilibus ausculationibus 107), Philoctetes dedicated the bow and arrows of Heracles in the temple of Apollo *Alaíos*; the settlers of Croton brought these reliquaries from the temple of Crimisa to their own temple when the city was founded. Apollo in MG was not the Delphic one, but rather an Aegaean one who, under the epiclesis → *Archēgétēs*, had his altar on the shores of → Naxus, the first Euboean settlement on Sicily (Thuc. 6,3,1).

C. THE NEEDS OF THE COLONISTS

The epiclesis *Archēgétēs* denotes the one who leads the colonial expedition and who provides the indispensable rulership (*archḗ*). Apollo *Archēgétēs* is the protector of those groups which are between two states of being, he is the god of the homeless and of the new citizens; thus he stands outside of the towns. Therefore, the view that the colonists limited themselves to importing the deities and cults of their home towns to their new lands is questionable. Thus, the Phocaeans did not import the city deities of → Phocaea, but rather the Ephesian Artemis and Delphic Apollo, who are common to all Ionians, to → Massalia (modern Marseilles) (Str. 4,1,4).

Similarly, we find Hera in Euboean colonies [1. 19–51]. She is not the main goddess of the Euboeans, but can also be encountered in Achaean foundations (at the mouth of the Sele near Posidonia (Latin: Paestum) or at the promontory of Lacinium. → Hera is the Samian protective goddess of shipping who on → Samos is venerated also as the goddess of the → *oíkos*, i.e. as the goddess of weddings and of the passing on of goods, both unifying elements of the new communities. Argive Hera finally has the sovereignty over a federated area. All these qualities correspond to needs of the colonists, and in this sense Hera complements Apollo *Archēgétēs*. Her importance can be seen from the fact that sanctuaries are found along the coast, as orientation points for shipping (Hera Lacinia near the promontory of Lacinium, → Lacinius; at the mouth of the river Sele, cf. Str. 6,1,1) but also in the interior (the temple known as *T avole Palatine* near Metapontium/Lat. Metapontum), where they were frequented by the original population. The archaic and polyvalent character of Hera is shown in numerous epicleses [3; 5]: *Prómachos* in Posidonia (martial function, normally reserved for Athena); *Eleuthería* at the promontory of Lacinium: protector of the freed (reserved for Demeter in Heraclea); *Eileíthyia*: protector of pregnant women (normally, → Eileithyia is a separate deity); → *Pótnia thḗrōn* (normally reserved for Artemis); oracle function in Cyme [2] (Latin Cumae), etc. The majority of the epicleses, the exact meaning of which is not always known, and archaizing tendencies appear to be the most original aspects of religion in MG [3; 5]: Zeus is called *Aglaiós* in Metapontium, *Kataibátēs* in Tarentum, *Keraunós* in Rhegium, *Meilíchios* in Croton and Pompeii, *Hórios* in Velia (Elea); Athene is called *Skylētría* in Iapygia, *Iliás* in Siris, *Eilenía* and *Myndía* in Metapontum. Many of these epicleses point to the Anatolian world and pre-colonial traditions.

During the classical period, the religion of the poleis in MG was not different from that of other Greek towns. The close connections between MG and the Panhellenic sanctuaries, especially in → Olympia (Paus. 6,19,1–15, *passim*; ML no. 10; 29; 57) indicate a feeling of belonging to the same culture. Also, the function of the → hero cult which preserves the memory of the *oikistes* does not differ from other hero cults in the Greek world which continued as local cults contributing to the identity of the various towns.

D. POPULAR RELIGION AND THE RELIGION OF THE UPPER CLASS

One special aspect is the contrast between popular religion with a propensity for chthonic cults – cult of the dead (→ Dead, cult of) or thesmophoric rites (→ Thesmophoria) – and a more elitist, more intellectual religion connected with Pythagoreanism. Beginning with the 4th cent. BC, especially in the country, small sanctuaries proliferated at the time when small estates began to flourish among Greeks as well as natives. They are dedicated to goddesses like Demeter, Persephone, Artemis or Aphrodite [4; 5]. The local work force employed for agrarian labour undoubtedly was receptive for rites based on the natural cycles of life and death, rites which were general enough to transcend ethnic boundaries. Cults of the dead take a special place in MG, in the form of the painted tombs in the Oscan area and Lucania, and in the extensive Tarentine or Daunian hypogaea (→ Hypogaeum). The terracotta tablets from → Locri [2] and → Medma point to a connection with the cults of Hades, of Persephone, of Hermes, of Aphrodite and of Dionysus. The last undoubtedly is the most typical figure of the religion of MG. Already in Sophocles (Ant. 1121) he appears as a protective deity; according to Plato (Leg. 1,637b), he was celebrated in Tarentum with exceptional enthusiasm. His iconography inspired the majority of imagery on Italian vases. The Roman → *senatus consultum de Bacchanalibus* of 186 BC shows the energy of his followers during that period.

A large number of Orphic gold leaves (→ Orphicae lamellae) was uncovered in MG. → Orphism might be the religious and mystic version of Pythagoreanism (→ Pythagoras). Far removed from the traditional religion of the polis, its existential dimension, with its promise of salvation based on communion with the divine, appealed to a society far more diverse and open than that of Greece. Pythagoreanism inspired → Parmenides, whose philosophy did not leave much room for the old deities. During the time of → Archytas [1], Pythagoreanism finally became the nucleus of political practice for the local upper classes, and it radiated from there to the non-Greek Italic elite [6] and even extended as far as Rome.

At this point the important role of MG and especially of Tarentum for the transmission of sacral architecture as well as of cults and myths to central Italy, Latium and Rome must be emphasised: the → Dioscuri, who were venerated in Tarentum and Locri [3. 38f.; 208–210], reached Lavinium in the 6th cent. BC and in 484 BC they were given a temple in Rome. Dispater and Proserpina were venerated in Rome at a place named T*arentum*. Tradition has it that Tarentine coroplasts (→ Damophilus [1] and Gorgasus) decorated the Roman temples of → Liber, → Libera and → Ceres (493 BC) [7]. Finally, Greeks from the Western colonies, e.g. → Stesichorus, brought → Aeneas [1] to Italy, and a Greek called Damastes from the vicinity of Troy turned the hero into the founder of Rome in the 5th cent. BC (Dion. Hal. Ant. Rom. 1,72,1).

E. ROMAN PERIOD

Religious continuity was not disrupted by Roman hegemony beginning in the 3rd cent. BC and with subsequent municipalization (→ *municipium*) of the poleis of MG in the 1st cent. BC. Intensified acculturation (→ Romanization) resulted in the expansion of the local → pantheon by new 'Roman' cults and deities (Capitoline Triad, later Mater Magna, Mithras, Isis, ruler cult). Aside from this, the traditional cults, their priestly offices and religious celebrations were continued to be observed, indeed given special attention by the local elites in the 1st and 2nd cents. AD – even though they were adapted to the changed political and cultural conditions [8.125–141].

→ Italia; → Colonization; → Latini, Latium

1 L. BREGLIA PULCI DORIA (ed.), Recherches sur les cultes grecs et l'Occident 1 (Cahiers du centre J. Bérard 5), 1979; 2 Id. (ed.), Recherches sur les cultes grecs et l'Occident 2 (Cahiers du centre J. Bérard 9), 1984; 3 G. GIANNELLI, Culti e miti della M.G., 1963; 4 F. GRAF, Culti e credenze nella M.G., in: Megale Hellas. Nome e immagine (Atti del Convegno di Studi sulla M.G. 21, 1981), 1982, 157–185; 5 G. MADDOLI, I culti delle 'poleis' italiote, in: M.G., vol. 3, 1988, 115–149; 6 A. MELE, Il pitagorismo e le popolazioni anelleniche d'Italia, in: AION 3, 1981, 61ff.; 7 M. CRISTOFANI, I santuari: tradizioni decorative, in: Etruria e Lazio arcaico (Quaderni di archeologia etrusco-italica 15), 1987, 116–118; 8 K. LOMAS, Rome and the Western Greeks 350 BC-AD 200, 1993.

I. MALKIN, Religion and Colonization in Ancient Greece, 1987.   J.-L.L.

Magna Mater see → Mater Magna

Magnates see → Archontes (III.)

Magnentius Flavius Magnus M., usurper, Roman emperor, AD 350–353. Born in Amiens *c.* 303, of non-Roman origin, not Christian. M. entered a military career and made it to the rank of → *comes*. The *comes rerum privatarum* → Marcellinus [5] incited him to conspire against → Constans [1]: On 18 January 350, M. revolted in Autun (Aur. Vict. 42; Zos. 2,42); Constans was killed. By the end of February, M. was recognized as emperor in northern Italy, and thereafter in the entire West and in Africa as well. In the Danube region, however, → Constantina, the sister of Constans, and Constantius [2] I persuaded → Vetranio to usurp the throne and incite resistance against M. In Rome → Nepotianus rose up, but was soon removed.

Initially, M. tried to become recognized by → Constantius [2] II. But after Vetranio's overthrow and the revolt of the Germans on the Rhine against M., he installed Decentius [1] as Caesar in 351 in order to strengthen his position. In his fight against Constantius I, M. had some early victories; but he was defeated in the battle of Mursa (28 September 351). His attempt to assemble a new army based in Aquileia failed and he had to flee to Gaul in the summer of 352 (Zos. 2,53), the only part left of his territory. In 353 M. was defeated again and withdrew to Lugdunum (Lyon) where he found himself in a hopeless situation and finally committed suicide on 10/11 August 353 (Socr. 2,32; Sozom. Hist. eccl. 4,7; Zon. 13,9).

M. favoured the followers of pagan religions (permission of night-time sacrifices, cf. Cod. Theod. 16,10,5), but he courted orthodox Christians as well and wanted to incite them against Constantius I, who was leaning towards Arianism; this is documented especially by surviving coins. Because of harsh taxation (income tax of 50%) M. became unpopular with the aristocracy. M. supposedly had considerable organisational and diplomatic talents. The sources portray him in a very negative light. PLRE 1, 532.

J. DIDU, Magno Magnenzio, in: Critica storica 14, 1977, 11–56; J. ZIEGLER, Zur religiösen Haltung der Gegenkaiser im 4. Jh.n.Chr., 1973, 53–74.   K.G.-A.

Magnes (Μάγνης; *Mágnēs*).

[1] Eponymous ruler of the central Greek region of Magnesia. His origins are variously described; the oldest reference (Hes. Cat. 7) calls him a son of Zeus and Thyia, daughter of Deucalion and a native of Pieria. Here Macedon, the mythical progenitor of the Macedonians, is referred to as his brother; according to Apollod. 1,16 he has a son named Pierus. These familial relationships indicate acquisition of land by the Magnesians from the north.

[2] Son of → Aeolus [1], eponym of the Aeolian tribe, father of → Dictys and → Polydectes (Hes. Cat. 8; Apollod. 1,88).   E.V.

[3] Apart from → Chionides the oldest poet of Attic Old Comedy [1. test. 2, 8, 9] known by name. In the list of Dionysiac victors [1. test. 4] he is found six places before → Cratinus [1]; he is said to have won eleven times altogether [1. test. 3, 4], and two of these victories are documented for the years 472 and 471 BC [1. test. 5, *6]. Decades later, → Aristophanes [2] still heralded him as an unusually successful poet and praised the multifaceted nature of his works [1. test. 7]. The total number of his writings is unknown. Already in the Alexandrian period none were extant anymore, yet a total of nine works were considered to be pseudepigrapha at the time [1. test. 3]. Coincidentally (or perhaps not?), a total of nine titles have been preserved (including a Διόνυσος α' and β'/'Dionysus 1 and 2', as well as two that anticipate titles by Aristophanes: Ὄρνιθες/'The Birds', Βάτραχοι/'The Frogs') and eight fragments from which nothing of the texts' content can be inferred.

1 PCG V, 1986, 626–631.   H.-G.NE.

Magnesia (Μαγνησία; *Magnēsía*).

[1] (Ethnicon Μάγνης, Μαγνῆτες/*Mágnēs, Magnêtes*; IG IX 2,1228 b16: dat. pl. Μαγνείτεσσι/*Magneítessi* 3rd cent. BC). The Thessalian coastal region of Peneius to the Gulf of → Pagasae with a narrow peninsula stretching far to the south, which encloses the Gulf of Pagasae in the east and south, filled up completely by the mountains → Ossa and → Pelion and their foothills. The east coast toward the open sea was without a harbour and feared by sailors; in 480 BC the fleet of Xerxes was shipwrecked here (Hdt. 7,188ff.). The southern part of this coast up to the homonymous cape in the south (Hagios Georgios) was called Σηπιάς/*Sēpiás*. The most important ancient settlements on the east coast of Ossa and Pelion were Homole, Eurymenae, Rhizous,

Meliboea and Casthanaea. The east side of the Magnesian Peninsula has no settlements; on the climatically favoured west side of Mount Pelion, → Laceria, → Boebe, → Iolcus at the location of the modern Kastro of Volo and Orminion are to be mentioned; on the west side of the Magnesian Peninsula are → Methone, Corope with the oracle sanctuary of Apollo Koropaios [1], Spalauthra and → Olizon.

The homonymous location M. on the Maeander [2] was founded by Magnesians according to tradition; in the catalogue of ships in the *Iliad*, M. is the kingdom of → Philoctetes (Hom. Il. 2,716ff.); the western slope of Pelion with Iolcus and Boebe is counted as belonging to the kingdom of Eumelus [1] (Hom. Il. 2,711ff.). The Magnesians appear in the catalogue of ships as a clearly belated insertion at the end of the entire list without any place name on the Peneius and Pelion (Hom. Il. 2,756ff.). The tribal name, which is related to the Macedonians, also points to a time of origin for the name after the immigration of the north-west Greeks in Thessalia. Pind. Pyth. 4,141ff. and Xen. Hell. 6,1,7 (= Ath. 1,15f.) mention archaic customs. The Magnesians are among the original members of the Pylaean-Delphian Amphiktyony (→ *amphiktyonía*) and are thus often mentioned in the Delphic inscriptions, but like the other Thessalian marginal tribes they were dependant on it (Aeschin. Or. 2,116; Paus. 10,8,2; Theopomp. FGrH 115 F 63; Aristot. Pol. 1269b 5ff.; Thuc. 2,101,2) and as subjects of the → Thessalians they shared their fate in general. With the rise of the tyrant dynasty of Pherae they became subject to them (Polyaenus, Strat. 6,2,1), but after → Pelopidas' intervention in 364 BC they were added to the Boeotian League (Diod. Sic. 15,80,6; Plut. Pel. 35,2). → Philippus II was able to keep the region for himself after his victory over the descendants of → Alexander [15] and to fortify it (Dem. Or. 1,13; 1,22; 2,11; 6,22; Isoc. Or. 5,21; Str. 9,5,16; Speusippus 1 [2]).

The most momentous event in the history of M. was the founding of Demetrias [1] by Demetrius [2] after 294 BC on the southern shore of the inner Gulf of Pagasae opposite modern Volo. Almost all of the region was added to the area of the new city and the settlements became *kômai* of Demetrias. There were, however, still independent *póleis* of the Magnesians, of which only Homole in the north can be named. The entire M. remained Macedonian, the Magnesians thus did not appear anymore in the lists of the Delphian Amphiktyony. In 196 BC, the Magnesians were declared independent by Rome (Pol. 18,46,5; 47,6; Liv. 33,32,5; Plut. Titus Flamininus 10,4). They constituted a separate → *koinón* under a *magnētárchēs* (Liv. 35,31,11; 43,5). The tension between Rome and the Aetolian League with events such as the occupation of Demetrias by the Aetolians and then Antiochus III in 192 BC and in the following years resulting from it, led to heavy agitation within the league and to M.'s temporary annexation to the Aetolians. M. had to return to Macedonian rulership. After the dissolution of the Macedonian kingdom the Magnesians were free again and able to reconstruct their *koinón* again, which continued into the Roman Imperial period. The league was a *sympoliteía* with a *strategos* at the head. Magnesians appear in Delphi again as *hieromnémones*. The complete dominance of Demetrias led to tension within the league in the 2nd cent. BC.

1 F. STÄHLIN, s.v. Κορόπη, RE 11, 1436f.; 2 E. BICKER-MANN, J. SYKUTRIS, Speusipps Brief an König Philipp, 1928, 3.

W. KENDRICK-PRITCHETT, Xerxes' Fleet at the Ovens, in: AJA 67, 1963, 1ff.; G. KIP, Thessalische Studien, 1910, 78ff.; PHILIPPSON/KIRSTEN, vol. 1, 127ff.; F. STÄHLIN, Das hellenische Thessalien, 1924, 39ff.; Id., s.v. M., RE 14, 459ff.; Id. et al., Pagasai und Demetrias, 1934, 178ff.; G. HOURMOUGIADIS, P. ASIMAKOPULOU-ATZAKA, K. A. MAKRIS, M., The Story of a Civilization, 1982. E.MEY.

[2] City in southwestern Asia Minor (3 km south of Ortaklar) on the right bank of the lower → Maeander [2] (Scyl. 98; Hdt. 1,161; Thuc. 1,138: Μαγνησία ἡ Ἀσιανή/*Magnesía hē Asianē*; later M. ἐπὶ Μαιάνδρου/ *M. epì Maiándrou* at Str. 14,1,39; Diod. Sic. 11,57,7; Ptol. 5,2,19; Plin. HN 5,114). Founded by the Thessalian M. [1], M. was destroyed in the 7th cent. BC by the → Cimmerii. In 465 BC a refuge for the banned Themistocles (Thuc. l.c.; Nep. Themistocles 10), it was founded anew in 400 BC at a nearby mountain (Diod. Sic. 14,36). Ruins of a temple of Artemis Leukophryene, inscriptions, coins.

O. KERN, Die Inschriften von M. am Mäander, 1900; K. HUMANN, M. am Mäander, 1904; L. BÜRCHNER, s.v. M. (2), RE 14, 1928, 471f.; W. M. CALDER, J. M. COOK, S. SHERWIN-WHITE, s.v. M. (1), OCD³, 912. W.BL.

[3] M. on Sipylus (M. ἡ ἐπὶ Σιπύλου/*M. hē epì Sipýlou*). Lydian city on the northern foot of the Sipylus (modern Manisa Dağı) on the left bank of the Hermus [2] (Hellanicus FGrH 4 F 191; Str. 12,8,2; 13,3,5), modern Manisa. In the 3rd cent. BC dominated by → *kátoikoi* and a garrison; after going over to Ptolemy III in the 3rd Syrian War shortly after 243 (?) incorporated by Smyrna, which had remained loyal to Seleucus II (Stv 492). In 216/213 BC, M. came under Antiochus [5] III, in 190 the battle (Liv. 37,38–44) against the Scipiones (Liv. 37,37,9f.; 38,58,9) took place near M. on the Hyrcanian plain to the north (→ Curupedion); in 189 under Eumenes [3] I (Liv. 37,56,3), from 133/129 in the Roman province Asia, in 84 declared *civitas libera* by Sulla (Str. l.c.; Paus. 1,20,5; App. Mith. 250); in the *conventus* of Smyrna (Plin. HN 5,120). In AD 17 damaged by an earthquake; reconstruction aid by Tiberius (Str. 12,8,18; Tac. Ann. 2,47). South-west of M. is the rock of the grieving → Niobe (Hom. Il. 24,602–617; Ov. Met. 6,149–312; Paus. 1,21,3), east near Akpınar the Hittite rock relief of the mother of the gods (Taş suret, Paus. 3,22,4).

E. AKURGAL, Ancient Civilizations and Ruins of Turkey, ⁷1990, 132f.; G. E. BEAN, Kleinasien 1, 1969, 55f. with pl.

2; TH. IHNKEN, Die Inschriften von M. am Sipylos (IK 8), 1978; MAGIE, vol. 1, 122f.; vol. 2, 976, 1102f.; W. RUGE, s.v. M. (3), RE 14, 472f. H.KA.

Magnets (Μαγνῆτις/*magnêtis* or Ἡρακλεία λίθος/ *Hērakleía líthos*; Lat. *magnes*). The name *magnes* supposedly comes from the homonymous discoverer, a shepherd on the mountain of Ida in the Troad (according to Nicander in Plin. HN 36,127) whom Isid. Orig. 16,4,1 holds to be a person from the Indus. The magnet is the well-known stone of iron oxide (Fe_3O_4) that attracts normal → iron and, as *ferrum vivum*, 'magnetizes' the iron in its turn (Plin. HN 34,147; Isid. ibid.; Lucr. 6,910–914). Plin. HN 36,128 differentiates, with the Greek stone expert Sotacus, five types of magnets from different regions, among which the Ethiopian one is the best. All of them can be used (Plin. HN 36,130) as eye remedies, above all to stem the flow of tears (*epiphorae*), and burnt and ground they cured burns. Dioscorides (5,130 WELLMANN = 5,147 BERENDES) knows only the internal use with honey mead to clear away thick mucus. For Thales (A 1, A 3 and A 22 = DIELS/ KRANZ vol. 2: 1985, vol. 3: 1993, 1, no. 11) magnets were endowed with a living soul. Empedocles [1] (A 89 = DIELS/KRANZ vol. 2: 1985, vol. 3: 1993, 1, no. 31) and atomists like Democritus [1] (A 165 = DIELS/ KRANZ vol. 2: 1985, vol. 3: 1993, 2, no. 68, from Alex. Aphr. 2,23 [1. 2,72,28], Greek text in [4. 222–224]) and Lucretius (6,998–1041) attempt an explanation of their functioning by way of pneumatics and atomistics. Theophr. De lapidibus 41 [2. 72] mentions that they can be worked on the lathe and despite a lack of affinity are similar to silver. As an amulet and in physiological explanations (e.g. respiration) they played a certain part in terms of sympathy.

1 I. BRUNS (ed.), Scripta minora, in: Supplementum Aristotelicum, vol. 2,2, 1892; 2 D. E. EICHHOLZ (ed.), Theophrastus, De lapidibus, 1965; 3 H. ROMMEL, s.v. M., RE 14, 474–486; 4 A. RADL, Der Magnetstein in der Antike. Quellen und Zusammenhänge (Boethius vol. 19), 1988. C.HÜ.

Magnia Urbica Wife of the emperor → Carinus (end of the 3rd cent. AD) from Colonia Iulia Gemella Accitana in Hispania (CIL II 3394). She bore the titles of *Augusta*, *mater castrorum* and *mater senatus ac patriae* (CIL VIII 2384; XI 6957). PIR² M 99.

H. COHEN, Description Historique des Monnaies frappées sous l'Empire Romain VI², 1886, 405–408. T.F.

Magnillus Belonged to the circle associated with → Symmachus, with whom he corresponded (Symmachus, Ep. 5,17–33). Governor of Liguria; in AD 391– 393 → *vicarius* in Africa, then indicted and acquitted; attested until 396 but no longer in an office, probably not a Christian. PLRE 1, 533. H.L.

Magnum Municipium Town (Tab. Peut. 5,2; Geogr. Rav. 4,16; CIL XIII 6538) that developed partly from a Dalmatian settlement near Balina Glavica (near Drniš, Bosnia-Herzegovina, probably identical with Sinotium/ Synodium: Str. 7,5,5; App. Ill. 78) and partly from a *vicus* close to the auxiliary camp near Umljanivići. *Beneficiarii* succeeded the auxiliary unit (cf. CIL III 9790; 14957ff.). Probably, MM was already a *municipium* under emperor M. Aurelius (cf. CIL III 9798).

> M. ZANINOVIĆ, Ilirsko pleme Delmati II [The Illyrian Tribe of Delmatae II], in: Godišnjak 5 (Centar za balka-nološka ispitivanja 3), 1967, 12f.; G. ALFÖLDY, s.v. Magnum, RE Suppl. 11, 931f. M.Š.K.

Magnus Roman *cognomen*, which originally designated bodily size or birth order ('the Elder'), as in the Republican PERIOD in the case of Sp. Postumius Albinus M. (*cos.* 148 BC) and T. Roscius M. (Cic. Rosc. Am. 17) [1. 275; 3. 47]. As an assumption of the epithet of Alexander [4] 'the Great' (ὁ μέγας/*ho mégas*, in the sense of great historical importance), first taken by Cn. Pompeius (*cos.* 70 and 55) in the 1st cent. BC, then inherited by his sons Cn. and Sex. Pompeius and their descendants. Sex. Pompeius used M. also as a *praenomen* resp. *nomen gentile* [4. 364f.]. In the Imperial period, more frequently an epithet.

> 1 KAJANTO, Cognomina; 2 J. REICHMUTH, Die lateinische Gentilicia, 1956; 3 P. P. SPRANGER, Der Große. Untersuchung zur Entstehung des historischen Beinamens in der Antike, in: Saeculum 9, 1958, 22–58; 4 SYME, RP 1, 1979. K.-L.E.

[1] M. of Emesa Author of works on prognostics, and of treatises about fevers and urines, possibly to be identified with M. [5] of Nisibis. His treatise on urines was translated into Arabic and is preserved in Greek in a variety of revisions and compilations (e.g. Gal. 19,574–601; Medici Graeci minores 1,307–316 IDELER). Although the document was later criticized by → Theophilus for its incompleteness and lack of practical use (De urinis, praef.), there are still all kinds of observations assembled in this, the first comprehensive and structured treatise on uroscopy, scattered throughout the entire Galenic Corpus. It probably contributed substantially to the development of the habit, first found in late antiquity, of treating urinoscopy as the prime method of medical diagnosis. V.N.

[2] Senator and consular, probably identical with C. Petronius Magnus of Canusium (CIL IX 338). He instigated a conspiracy against → Maximinus [2] Thrax in AD 235, in which senatorial circles and officers were involved, which was discovered. M. was probably executed with others (Hdn. 7,1,4–8; SHA Max. 10).

> PIR² M 100; PIR² P 286. K.G.-A.

[3] Flavius M. Was *vicarius* of a diocese (Cod. Theod. 8,5,6) in AD 354. Between 354 and 359, he was *proconsul Asiae* (ILS 733). In 359 he held a higher office in Constantinople (Lib. Ep. 84). He probably came from Antiochia [1] on the Orontes (Lib. Or. 40,12). PLRE 1,535 no. 9, cf. 534 no. 5.

[4] Vindaonius M. Pupil of → Libanius, orator and lawyer (Lib. Ep. 1271f.). Under → Iulianus [11], he had a church in Berytus burnt down, which he had to have rebuilt on orders from Jovian (Theod. Hist. eccl. 4,22,10). In AD 373 he had the duty as *comes sacrarum largitionum* of enforcing the installation of the Arian Lucius as bishop in Alexandria [1] after the death of Athanasius (Socr. 4,21,3). As *praefectus urbis Constantinopolitanae* (375–376), he inaugurated the Thermae Carosianae in Constantinople (Chron. min. 1,242). PLRE 1,536 no. 12. W.P.

[5] M. of Nisibis Physician and teacher in Alexandria around AD 370. A pupil of Zeno of Cyprus along with → Oribasius. He acquired great renown as orator and teacher of medicine, and was assigned a public teaching hall by the Alexandrians (Eunapius, Vitae Sophistarum 497f. BOISSONADE). Pupils came to him from all over the Eastern Mediterranean, including a distant relative, by the name of Chrysogonus, who had studied with Libanius in Antioch (Lib. Ep. 1208, 1358). Libanius also sought M.'s help, in bringing competitors to the games of 388 at Daphne (Ep. 843). An epigram to Galen can perhaps be counted among his writings (Anth. Pal. 16,270) (cf. M. [9]), and presumably some acrostic poems (→ Acrostich) in the 'Cyranides' [1]. A book by M. on urines, possibly the same as the one ascribed to M. [1] of Emesa, gained the praise of Theophilus for its structure and elegance (De urinis, praef.); at the same time he criticizes it, however, for being incomplete and of little practical use.

> 1 M. L. WEST, M. and Marcellinus: Unnoticed Acrostics in the Cyranides, in: CQ N.S. 32, 1982, 480f. V.N.

[6] Gaulish aristocrat from Narbo, relative of the emperor → Avitus [1]; under emperor → Maiorianus , *magister officiorum* in Spain, in 458 *praefectus praetorio Galliarum* and 460 *consul*, friend of → Sidonius Apollinaris (Sidon. Apoll. Epist. 1,11,10f.; Carm. 14,2; 23,455–63; 24,90–94; cf. 5,558–61; 15,150–57). PLRE 2, 700f.; 1318.

> J. HARRIES, Sidonius Apollinaris and the Fall of Rome, 1994.

[7] *Comes*, cavalry officer under → Belisarius in the Gothic War of emperor Justinian [1]; participated in the conquest of Naples in 536, was commander in Perusia in 537, occupied Tibur and was besieged by → Totila in Auximum in 544 (Procop. Goth. 1,5; 1,10; 2,4; 2,28; 3,11; Iord. Get. 60,312). PLRE 3B, 804f. K.P.J.

[8] M. of Carrhae (Ḥarran) composed a work of history about the Persian campaign of Iulianus [11], in which he had himself taken part. A longer excerpt from it is preserved in Iohannes Malalas (Chronographia, p. 328,20–332,9 DINDORF; FHG IV,4–6; FGrH 225). He is possibly identical with a homonymous *tribunus* who distinguished himself during the campaign for his bravery (Amm. Marc. 24, 4, 23f.; Zos. 3,22,4). PLRE 1,534 no. 3, cf. no. 2.   W.P.

[9] Author of a Greek epigram which praises the time in which the healing hand of → Galen made the mortal immortal (Anth. Pal. 16,270). The lemmatist affirms that M. was himself a physician; in this case it could be the M., who – in analogous and probably ironic exaggeration – is praised by → Palladas (Anth. Pal. 11,281: actually, one of the numerous physicians of this name, M. [5], lived in Alexandria at the end of the 4th cent. AD; cf. Eunap. VS 497 BOISSONADE).

A. CAMERON, The Greek Anthology from Meleager to Planudes, 1993, 67.   M.G.A.

Magnus Sinus (μέγας κόλπος/*mégas kólpos*, Ptol. 7,2,1; 7,3,1). A large ocean gulf in *India extra Gangem*, adjoining the Sinae, i.e. south-east Asia, with three rivers: Daonas, Dorias and Seros (Ptol. 7,2,7). Although the geography of south-east Asia seems hopelessly distorted in Ptolemy, and all interpretations of place names in that region must remain highly hypothetical, nonetheless the Magnus Sinus can be identified with the waters lying between the Malacca Peninsula and southern China.

H. TREIDLER, s.v. Μέγας κόλπος, RE Suppl. 10, 385ff.   K.K.

Mago (*Mgn* = '(god's) gift'; Greek Μάγων; *Mágōn*).
[1] Carthaginian, leading figure (king?) in the 2nd half of the 6th cent. BC; successor of → Malchus [1], efficient promoter of Carthaginian power (Iust. 18,7,19; 19,1,1; [1. 173f.; 2. 475f.]), to whom a great army reform with the goal of the deployment of mercenaries is erroneously attributed [3. 184–187]. As father (?) of → Hamilcar [1] and Hasdrubal (Iust. 19,1,2), M. is considered the ancestor of the Magonids (see stemma); since, however, according to Herodotus (7,165), Hamilcar was the son of a Hanno, and Iustinus (Prol. 19) refers to → Hanno [2] Sabellus rather than to M., the possibility of a misstatement by Iustinus is worth considering, so that M. would be identical with Hanno.

[2] Carthaginian commander from 397–375 BC against → Dionysius [1] I, who distinguished himself in 397–6 as victorious nauarch ('commander of the fleet') and also at Catana (Diod. 14,59–61). He also stayed in Sicily after the death of the chief commander → Himilkon [1], where he indeed had diplomatic successes with the Siculians, but after military defeats (among others at → Agyrium) had to conclude a peace which was unfavourable to Carthage (Diod. Sic. 14,90,2–4; 95f.). When M. fell in the next campaign (from 382) at Cabala in the year 375 (Diod. Sic. 15,15,2–16,2), his son Himilkon took command [1. 175–177; 2. 134f., 138].

[3] Carthaginian commander in Sicily, who as leader of an expeditionary force was called upon for aid in 344–3 BC by → Hicetas [1] against the rebellious Campanians in Entella against the intervention of → Timoleon, and appeared with an army and a fleet before Syracuse, but in light of the understanding among the local parties to the civil war, withdrew again into the western part of Sicily (epicracy), which was occupied by Carthage (Diod. Sic. 16,67–69; Plut. Timoleon 17–20; [1. 177–179; 4. 74f.]). M. is supposed to have committed suicide on the return to Carthage, his corpse is supposed to have been crucified as punishment for his failure (Plut. Timoleon 22,8).

[4] Carthaginian nauarch, whose offer to the Romans to aid them in their war against → Pyrrhus was refused in 279 BC and who subsequently sounded out the latter regarding his further intentions (Iust. 18,2,1–4; Val. Max. 3,7,11; [1. 180f.; 2. 211,36]).

[5] Youngest son of → Hamilcar [3] Barkas (born around 240 BC), who went with his brother → Hannibal [4] (→ Barcids, with stemma) to Italy in 218 and fought with him in 216 in the centre at → Cannae (Pol. 3,114,7; Liv. 22,46,7; [5. 193]), having already been entrusted with important duties earlier on (at Placentia, on the Trebia, in the forward march to Etruria) [cf. 1. 181f.; 5. 126, 128, 148] (2. → Punic War). In the autumn of 216, M. delineated the successes of Hannibal up to that point to the Carthaginian Senate and received the requested means for continuing to wage war, so that he could hire new contingents in the following months

The Magonids

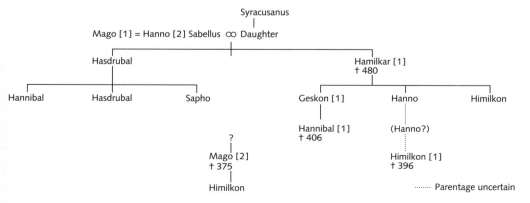

(Liv. 23,11,7–12; 12,5; 13,6–8; [1. 182; 5. 215f.]). In the spring of 215, M. was dispatched to Spain (Liv. 23,32), where he and his brother → Hasdrubal [3], whom M. supported in the changeable battles against Iberians and Romans (Liv. 23,49,5–12; 24,41–43; App. Hisp. 24,94–25,100), together with → Hasdrubal [5] did not attain any considerable successes over Cn. and P. → Cornelius [I 77; → I 68] Scipio until 211 (Liv. 25,32; 34–36; [1. 183; 5. 251, 266, 318–320]).

In the period following, M. operated in south-west Iberia [5. 351⁶²] and hired new mercenaries in Celtiberia, north-west Africa and on the Balearics (Liv. 27,20,3–8; 28,1–4; 16,13; 23,6–8; [1. 184; 5. 393, 406]). M., who had been *strategos* in Iberia since the Italian campaign of his brother Hasdrubal (208), retreated in 206 before the successful P. → Cornelius [I 71] Scipio to Gades (modern Cadiz), where he uncovered a pro-Roman plot (Liv. 28,30,1–5). Although M. again received monies from the Carthaginian Senate for Iberia, he had to leave Spain still in the autumn of 206, on instructions from Carthage, namely as a result of the defection by → Massinissa, in order to join Hannibal in Italy (Liv. 28,31; 36–37; [1. 185; 5. 407f.]). In 205, M. arrived in Liguria, where he strengthened his army; however, he did not follow the order to advance on Rome and ignored the opportunities to win Etruria, which was hostile to Rome (Liv. 28,46,7–11; 29,4,6; 5,3–9; 36,10–12; [1. 185f.; 5. 418, 422, 427f., 435]). In the year 203, M. obeyed the order to return to Carthage and is supposed to have died on the return trip near Sardinia from an injury (Liv. 30,18–19,5); another tradition reports on his continued waging of war in Italy (Zon. 9,13,10 D.), on his banishment from Carthage and his (violent?) death in 193 (Nep. Hann. 7,3f.; 8,1f.), which is, however, not very credible [1. 186f.; 5. 448⁶³; 463].

[6] Relative of the → Barcids, possibly son of → Hasdrubal [2]; together with → Hasdrubal [4], he came into Roman war captivity in Sardinia in 215 (Liv. 23,41,1f.; [1. 188f.]).

[7] Carthaginian envoy of → Hannibal [4] to → Philippus V together with → Bostar [3] and → Geskon [4]; allegedly intercepted by the Romans (Liv. 23,34; 38,1–9), possibly identical with → Magonus [1. 188; 5. 244–246].

[8] M., called 'the Samnite' (ὁ Σαμνίτης/*ho Samnítēs*; Pol. 9,25,4); Carthaginian, a (notoriously greedy?) friend of → Hannibal's [4] youth (Pol. 9,25), who fought successfully in Bruttium in the 2nd → Punic War as a high-ranking officer, won → Thurii in 212 BC, killed Ti. → Sempronius Gracchus in an ambush (Liv. 25,16,7–24; Diod. Sic. 26,16,1; [2. 364f.; 6. 61f.]) and in the year 208 defended → Locri [2] (Liv. 27,28,14–17; [1. 189f.; 6. 119f.]). M. is unlikely to be identical with an M. operating in Capua (Liv. 25,18,1; [1. 188, 1114]).

[9] Carthaginian city commandant from → Carthago Nova, which he lost in 209 BC, after a courageous four-day battle, to P. → Cornelius [I 71] Scipio (Pol. 10,12–15; Liv. 26,44–46; App. Hisp. 20,78–23,90; [5. 353–355]); M. was brought to Rome together with other distinguished prisoners of war by C. Laelius [I 1] (Pol. 10,18,1; Liv. 26,51,2; [1. 190f.]).

[10] Carthaginian envoy, who brought the Carthaginian dedication offer to Rome in 149 BC, with → Geskon [5] and → Hamilcar [5] (Pol. 36,3,7; [1. 191]).

[11] M., called 'the Bruttian' (ὁ Βρέττιος/*ho Bréttios*); Carthaginian senator, who pleaded for the acceptance of the Roman conditions in 149 BC, upon the return of the envoys from Rome (Pol. 36,5,1–5; [1. 191f.]).

1 GEUS ; 2 HUSS ; 3 W. AMELING, Karthago, 1993; 4 L. M. HANS, Karthago und Sizilien, 1983; 5 J. SEIBERT, Hannibal, 1993; 6 D. A. KUKOFKA, Süditalien im Zweiten Punischen Krieg, 1990. L.-M.G.

[12] The Carthaginian M., who is designated by Pliny as 'commander' (*dux*, Plin. HN 18,22), about whose life, however, no further information is available, was the author of a treatise composed in the Punic language about agriculture, which has not been handed down; on the basis of this source situation, some scholars considered M. to be the sponsor who had a compendium of agricultural knowledge compiled, or he has been considered a fictional author, to whom different writings have been attributed. The congruence of the topics handled by M. with the agrarian development in the area around Carthage, recognizable on the basis of archaeological finds, suggests a dating of the work to the 2nd half of the 3rd cent. or the 1st half of the 2nd cent. BC. After the Roman conquest of Carthage in 146 BC, M.'s work, which consisted of 28 books, was translated into Latin on the decision of the Senate, under the direction of Dec. Iunius Silanus; a motive for the translation may have been the desire to acquire information about agriculture in the arid areas of Africa. The Greek translation by → Cassius [III 2] Dionysius from Utica represents a very shortened editing into 20 books; a further version comes from Diophanes of Nicaea (after 63 BC.; cf. Plin. HN 18,22; Varro Rust. 1,1,8; 1,1,10f.; Columella 1,1,10).

As citings in Cicero and Varro show, M.'s treatise was a recognized manual on agriculture in the late Republic (Cic. De orat. 1,249; Varro Rust. 2,5,18; cf. Columella 1,1,6). The Roman → agrarian writers valued M. highly: Varro ends his list of the older authors with the remark that these have been completely surpassed by M., and Columella designates M. as the 'Father of Agriculture' (Varro Rust. 1,1,10; Columella 1,1,13). Pliny used the Greek translations by Cassius Dionysius and Diophanes for his discussion of agriculture (Plin. HN 8; 14; 15; 17; 18).

In the introduction of his work, M. stipulates programmatically that he who has acquired a land holding should sell his city house (Columella 1,1,18; Plin. HN 18,35); his expositions directed themselves accordingly to landowners who were prepared to look after their lands intensively, and are meant to offer the necessary

information for the successful running of an estate. M. treated → viticulture (Columella 3,12,5; 3,15,4; 4,10,1; 5,5,4), olive plantations (→ Oil, Olive tree; Plin. HN 17,93; 17,128), stock farming (Varro Rust. 2,1,27; Columella 6,1,2; 6,26; 6,37,3) and veterinary medicine (Varro Rust. 2,5,18), → apiculture (Columella 9,14,6), and the storage and conserving of fruit (Columella 12,4,2; 12,46,5). Because of the climatic differences, however, not all the recommendations of Punic agriculture were useable in Italy (Columella 1,1,6). Transmitted to the Roman upper classes by the Latin translation, M.'s systematic representation of agriculture exercised a strong influence on the development of Roman agronomy and thereby on the Italian estate economy.
→ Agriculture

EDITIONS: F. SPERANZA, Scriptorum Romanorum de re rustica reliquiae 1, 1974, 76–119.
BIBLIOGRAPHY: 1 W. AMELING, Karthago, 1993, 259f.; 2 ESAR 1, 285f.; 3 J. A. GREENE, D. P. KEHOE, M. the Carthaginian, in: Actes du IIIᵉ Congrès International des Études Phéniciennes et Puniques. Tunis 11–16 November 1991, vol. 2, 1995, 110–117; 4 J. HEURGON, L'agronome Carthaginois Magon et ses traducteurs en Latin et en Grec, in: CRAI 1976, 441–456; 5 W. RICHTER (ed.), L.J. Columella, 12 Bücher über Landwirtschaft, vol. 3, 1983, 576f., 622f.; 6 WHITE, Farming, 18; 7 K. D. WHITE, Roman Agricultural Writers 1: Varro and his Predecessors, in: ANRW I.4, 1973, 439–497, esp. 470–471.
K.RU.

[13] Commercial centre with excellent harbours on the Insula Minor (modern Menorca) of the → Baliares, modern Mahón, probably named after → M. [5], Hannibal's brother, who occupied the island in 206 BC after his flight from Gades (Liv. 28,37,8–10) and erected the *castellum* M. (Mela 2,124; Plin. HN 3,77; Ptol. 2,6,73; CIL II 3708–3710; 3712).

TOVAR 3, 277.   P.B.

Magodia see → Simodia

Magog In Ez 38:2 M. is the name of the country of the grand duke Gog, whom God has advance together with his armed forces against Israel to attack it; in doing so, however, he will die (for the text Ez 38:1–39:29 and its individual layers cf. [1]; see also Gn 10:2 where M. is counted among the sons of Japheth). Experts have raised the question whether Gog is to be associated with a historical figure, e.g. the Lydian king → Gyges, who appears in documents of Assurbanipal under the name *Gug(g)u*. M. would then be identifiable with Lydia.

The episode was diversely interpreted: Iosephus saw in Gog and M. the Scythes who invaded the Middle East around 630 BC (Jos. Ant. Iud. 1,123). Apc. 20:8f. refers to Gog and M. by the dual name for the mythical people's army that at the command of Satan attacks the people of God and ends the time of peace of the Thousand Year Empire. Rabbinic tradition also speaks, in the context of the apocalyptic events of the Messianic Age, of the war of Gog and M. (cf. the compilation of the extensive material in [3. 831–840]).

1 W. ZIMMERLI, Ezechiel. 2nd part, ²1979, 921–975; 2 L. GINZBERG, The Legends of the Jews, 7 vols., 1909–1938, s.v. Gog and M.; 3 H. L. STRACK, P. BILLERBECK, Kommentar zum Neuen Testament aus Talmud und Midrasch, vol. 3, ⁸1985, 831–840.   B.E.

Magonids see → Mago

Magonus (Μάγωνος; *Mágōnos*), more correctly: Mago [1. 188,1113], Carthaginian councillor in the army of → Hannibal [4]. In 215 BC he took the oath on the Carthaginian-Macedonian treaty (Pol. 7,9,1). M.'s identification with → Mago [7] is contentious [1. 14,53].

1 GEUS.   L.-M.G.

Magos see → Magic, Magi

Magpie Because in Greek the same name (κίσσα/*kíssa* or κίττα/*kítta*) is used for the magpie (*Pica candata*) and the → jay, and because these two corvids can be trained to talk, the respective context, as in Plin. HN 10,78 with the mention of the long tail, must ensure the designation. Plin. HN 10,98 reports on their removal of the eggs as a reaction to disruptive observation by humans. Actually, magpies build several nests to protect themselves. However, his description of how they hang two eggs stuck to a twig around their necks is sheer fabrication. The delight they take in imitating human language and their supposed death when failing with difficult words is mentioned by Plin. HN 10,118. Thomas of Cantimpré (5,104; [1. 223]) is the first to mention their black and white plumage, their spherical nest in thorns with a side entrance and their cunning behaviour when caught in a bird net. Albertus Magnus (De animalibus 23,135; [2. 1508]) even knows of the green iridescent tail. There are ancient representations on wall images and mosaics [3. 2,113]. In Medieval book illustration the magpie is a motif that is just as common as the jay [4].

1 H. BOESE (ed.), Thomas Cantimpratensis, Liber de natura rerum, 1973; 2 H. STADLER (ed.), Albertus Magnus, de animalibus, II, 1920; 3 KELLER; 4 B. YAPP, Birds in Medieval Manuscripts, 1981.   C.HÜ.

Magulaba According to Ptol. 6,7,37 (Μαγουλάβα/ *Magoulába*, also Μαγούλανα/*Magoúlaba*), town in → Arabia Felix between Silaeum and → Menambis. Probably the identical to modern al-Maḥǧar al-ʿAlā.

H. V. WISSMANN, Zur Geschichte und Landeskunde von Altsüdarabien (SAWW, Phil.-histor. Klasse 246), 1964, 417 (map); Id., M. HÖFNER, Beiträge zur historischen Geographie des vorislamischen Arabien (AAWM, Geistes- und sozialwiss. Klasse), 1952, no. 4, 37.   I.T.-N.

Magulnius Name of one of the leading families of Praeneste until 82 BC, only attested in inscriptions (CIL I² 188–191 et passim). The famous Ficoronian → Cista was given by a Dindia Magcolnia (= ' 'wife of M.' ') to her daughter (ILS 8562). K.-L.E.

Magusum One of the cities that according to Plin. HN 6,160 was destroyed by Aelius [II 11] Gallus in 24 BC. M. was then situated in modern Ǧauf (in modern Yemen) and is probably identical with modern Maǧzīr south of Yaṭill in Wādī 'l-Farḍa.

> H. v. WISSMANN, Zur Geschichte und Landeskunde von Altsüdarabien (SAWW, Phil.-histor. Klasse 246), 1964, 84 (map), 140; J. F. BRETON, Les fortifications d'Arabie Méridionale du 7e au 1er siècle avant nôtre ère (Arch. Ber. aus dem Yemen 8), 1994, 100 (map). I.T.-N.

Mahanajim (Hebrew *maḥⁿnayim*, literally 'double camp', cf. Ugarite *mḥnm* [3. 3,4] on the basis of the apparent dual form of *maḥⁿnæh*; Gn 32:8; 11; 1 Kgs 2:8; cf. also Jos. Ant. Iud. 7,10; Euseb. On. 130,4); already attested in the list of defeated 'Asians' of the Egyptian king Shoshenk I (ANET 263, no. 22) as *m-ḥ-n-m*. This town east of the Jordan appears as the boundary point between the territories of the tribes Gad and Manasse on the Israelite-Aramaic border between Penuel and the mountain range Gilead; according to Jos. Ant. Iud. 21,38, a Levite city. According to Biblical reports, M. served as a military base of Išbaal (2 Sam 2:8) and David (2 Sam 17: 24ff); according to 1 Kgs 4:14, M. was an Israelite administrative centre. As possible localizations, Tall Haǧǧāǧ, Tulūl aḍ-Ḍahab and Ḥirbat Rēšūnī are discussed.

> 1 D. V. EDELMAN, s.v. Mahanaim, Anchor Bible Dictionary 4, 1992, 472-473 (lit.); 2 E. A. KNAUF, s.v. M., Neues Bibel-Lex. 2, 1995, 687; 3 C. VIROLLEAUD (ed.), Palais Royal d'Ugarit 2, 1957. TH.PO.

Maharbal (*Mhrbᶜl* = 'servant of Bᶜl'; Greek Μαάρβας/ *Maárbas*).
[1] Carthaginian commander of dubious historicity, who is supposed to have outsmarted rebellious Libyans by means of doped wine and defeated them (Frontin. Str. 2,5,12; cf. Polyaenus, Strat. 5,10,1; [1. 193f.]).

[2] Carthaginian, son of a Himilkon, as → Hannibal's [4] commander in his absence he led the siege of → Saguntum in 219 BC (Liv. 21,12,1-3); identical with the outstanding officer of the first years of the 2nd → Punic War, who became famous for the saying *vincere scis, Hannibal, victoria uti nescis* ('you know how to win, Hannibal, you do not know how to use the victory', Liv. 22,51,1-4; Amm. Marc. 18,5,6; [2. 198-201]), when Hannibal after the victory at → Cannae (216) did not march on Rome; Florus (Flor. Epit. 1,22,19) incorrectly ascribes the dictum to a M., son of a Bomilcar (cf. [1. 194,1146; 195,1162]). M., who commanded the right flank cavalry at Cannae (Liv. 22,46,7; App. Hann. 20,91; 21,95; cf. Pol. 3,114,7), had attracted attention not only before and after the battle at Lake Trasimene (217) as a successful leader of cavalry especially when plundering (in the year 218: Liv. 21,45,2-4; in the year

217: Pol. 3,86,4f.; cf. App. Hann. 11,45-47; Liv. 22,13,9f.), but also by taking 6,000 Romans captive, with whom he had made an agreement which went beyond his authority and which was criticized by Hannibal (Pol. 3,84,14-85,3; [2. 154,82]). After the failed attack on Casilinum (216/5) M. is not mentioned anymore (Liv. 23,18,4; [1. 194-196]).

> 1 GEUS ; 2 J. SEIBERT, Hannibal, 1993. L.-M.G.

Maia
[1] (Μαῖα, Μαίας, Μαίη; *Maîa, Maías, Maíē*). Daughter of → Atlas [2] and Pleione, by → Zeus mother of → Hermes, who is called *Maiadeús* or *Maías hyiós* or *paîs* for this reason (e.g. H. Hom. 4,2f.,73; Aesch. Cho. 814). Nymph of the Arcadian Cyllene mountains. Homer only mentions her once as the mother of Hermes (Hom. Od. 14,435). Hesiod calls her the daughter of Atlas (Hes. Theog. 938) and counts her as one of the Pleiades (Hes. Cat. fr. 169; cf. also Simon. PMG fr. 555). The most detailed version of the story of the conception and birth of Hermes on the mountain Cyllene [1] is found in the Homeric Hymn to Hermes, while the event is only mentioned briefly in other sources (Hes. Cat. fr. 170; Apollod. 3,110-112). In Sophocles' satyr play *Ichneutaí* (TrGF 4, fr. 314, 272) it is said about a mountain nymph Cyllene that she was Hermes' wet-nurse when his mother was sick. According to Apollod. 3,101 M. is the foster mother of → Arcas because his mother → Callisto died. There is no evidence of cult worship of M. in the Greek world. Thus she is not mentioned by Pausanias in his report on his visit to the Hermes temple on the mountain Cyllene (Paus. 8,17,1).

Latin authors, however, report that M. was an important Roman goddess whose feast was celebrated every year in May together with that of → Mercurius in his temple in the Circus Maximus (CIL IX 421; InscrIt XIII 2, 458-459). There was a discussion on the apparent derivation of the name of the month (→ Months, names of the) from the goddess' name (Ov. Fast. 5,81-106; Macrob. Sat. 1,12,18-19; Auson. Eclogarum liber 10,9-10). Moreover M.'s connection with the god Volcanus (Gell. NA 13,23,2.; Macrob. Sat. 1,12,18) and the fact that the *flamen Volcanalis* sacrificed to the goddess on the calends of May is attested. According to Macrob. Sat. 1,12,20 M. received a pregnant pig as a sacrificial animal; ibid. 1,12,21 M. is identified with → Bona Dea. In Latin literature M. is the mother of Hermes beginning with Virgil (Verg. Aen. 8,138-141; 1,297; Hor. Carm. 1,2,43; Hor. Sat. 2,6,5; Ov. Met. 2,685f.; 11,303; Ov. Fast. 5,87f. et passim). At Verg. G. 1,225 she is called a star together with the Pleiades (→ Katasterismos).

> F. BÖMER, P. Ovidius Naso. Die Fasten, vol. 2, 1958, 295f.; H. CH. LINK, s.v. M., RE 14, 527ff.; R. PETER, s.v. M. (2), ROSCHER 2, 2235-2240; B. RAFN, s.v. M., LIMC 6.1, 333-334 (with bibliography); P. WEIZSÄCKER, s.v. M. (1), ROSCHER 2, 2234-2235. K.WA.

[2] see → Birth; → Gynaecology; → Iatromaia

Maiandrou pedion (Μαιάνδρου πεδίον; *Maiándrou pedíon*).
The plain which the → Maeander [2] (modern Menderes) washed up on its lower reaches (Hdt. 1,18; 161; Thuc. 3,19; Xen. Hell. 3,2,17; Str. 14,1,42); known for its fertility.

L. Bürchner, s.v. M.P., RE 14, 540.   W.BL.

Maidenhair see → Fern

Maiden sacrifice see → Human sacrifice

Maiesta According to Calpurnius Piso fr. 42 Peter = 10 Forsythe the wife of → Volcanus, no other references. Assumed Oscan origin [1] contributes little to clarification. It is possible that Piso, against a contemporary identification of → Maia as the wife of Volcanus and eponym of the month of May (conceivable with Gell. NA 13,23; Cincius fr. 8 GRF in Macrob. Sat. 1,12,18; Ov. Fast. 5,81–106), derives the name of the month from a goddess M., with M. for her part probably coming from Latin *maiestas* (Ov. Fast. 5,11–53 mentions the latter as a possible eponym of the name of the month). Further assumptions on the reality of M. [2] remain conjecture.

→ Annalists; → Months, names of the

1 G. Radke, Zur Entwicklung der Gottesvorstellung und der Gottesverehrung in Rom, 1987, 189; 2 G. Forsythe, The Historian L. Calpurnius Piso Frugi, 1994, 144–150.
AN.BE.

Maiestas
A. Definition   B. Religious and family sphere   C. Political sphere

A. Definition
As noun to the adjective *maius* ('increasing', 'bigger'), *maiestas* in general means an unusual, unquestionably superior power and dignity to be respected, notably 1. the sacredness of the gods or of a god (Cic. Div. 1,82; Christian: Cod. Iust. 1,1,1, pr.), 2. the → *patria potestas* of the *pater familias* towards the relatives and slaves subordinate to him (Liv. 4,45,8; Val. Max. 7,7,5; Cod. Iust. 6,20,12; see below B.) and especially 3. the majesty of the *populus Romanus* (Cic. Balb. 35; Cic. Part. or. 105; Dig. 48,4,1,1), the *res publica* (Cic. De orat. 2,164) and its highest offices (consul: Cic. Vatin. 22; praetor: Dig. 2,1,9) and decision-making organs (Senate: Val. Max. 1,8,1; 9,5,1), later of the emperor (Dig. 48,4,7,3; Cod. Iust. 9,8,6) (see C.). Traditionally a certain sacrality – often designated with the words *sacer*, *sacratus* – was common to all kinds of *maiestas*. Violating them was considered a serious breach of law – *maiestatis minutio* resp. *contemptio*, *crimen laesae maiestatis* or *contra maiestatem commissum* – and on occasion as → *sacrilegium*; because, in spite of historical changes, they remained fundamentals

of political-religious ideology and general civic loyalty during the Republic and in the Imperial period, and even in a Christian framework.

B. Religious and family sphere
1) The desecration of temples, resp. of churches, and the stealing or profanation of sacred objects could bring the heaviest penalties, i.e. work in the mines (*metallum*) or banishment (*deportatio*) (Dig. 48,13,7; Cod. Iust. 1,3,10; see → Religious law).

2) Patricide and generally the murder of relatives (→ *parricidium*) was avenged with an especially cruel death penalty (Cod. Iust. 9,17,1); lack of respect towards paternal authority could be punished by the father himself – in earlier times, according to his right to make decisions about the life and death of the members of his → family (IV. B.) (*ius vitae necisque*), in a family judicial procedure (Cic. Leg. 3,8,19) – or judicially like the murder of a relative (Cod. Iust. 9,15,1).

C. Political sphere
1. Crimen maiestatis   2. Contemptus maiestatis   3. Crimen laesae maiestatis   4. Reception in the Middle Ages and Modern Times

1. Crimen maiestatis
The death penalty or the heaviest other punishments were exacted for the *crimen maiestatis* directed 'against the Roman people and its safety' (*adversus populum Romanum vel securitatem eius*), which could be committed by Romans or subjected provincials, by the planned killing of a magistrate, by armed revolt or preparation for the same, by the liberation of prisoners or hostages, by the occupation of public and sacred buildings or by co-operation with an enemy power (*hostis*) (Dig. 48,4,1,1).

2. Contemptus maiestatis
The circumvention of the activity of an officeholder, or making his duties difficult, could be a *contemptus maiestatis* and usually resulted in high monetary fines (Dig. 2,1,2; 2,1,7 pr. and 2,1,9), not, on the other hand, simple disobedience. However, the latter was also punished, most often with penalties and – in legal processes – with procedural penalties (Dig. 2,3; 2,5,2).

3. Crimen laesae maiestatis
In the *crimen laesae maiestatis* towards the emperor, aspects of the following were combined: disobedience and resistance against the sovereignty of the state, offence against sovereign symbols and official traditions, endangering the state, high treason and simple treason. These formed the elements of an offence the extent of which was incalculable for the public. According to the individual case, this could lead to minor punishments or a pardon, on the one hand; on the other, it could result in the death penalty (Cod. Theod. 16,10,12; Dig. 48,4; Cod. Iust. 9,8: tit. ad legem Iuliam maiestatis). In strained domestic situations during the Imperial period (often, e.g., in the beginning decades of the Principate or

in the 3rd and 4th cents. AD), if the imperial exercise of power appeared to be, or was, in question, mere public statements critical of the emperor, gestures of disrespect and disloyalty, or *per se* minor misdemeanours, could be understood as *crimen laesae maiestatis* and be punished severely. The political character of the delator system, the corresponding trials and their intimidating effect is emphasized by contemporary writers (Sen. Ben. 3,26; Suet. Tib. 58; Tac. Ann. 6,18; Amm. Marc. 27,7 and 28,1; 29,2,4).

In these cases, the proceedings were occasionally taken over by the emperor, or led by specially formed courts. At the investigation, otherwise established trial norms could be disregarded, such as those which forbade the charging and questioning as witnesses e.g. slaves or *infami*, or excluded → torture for accused persons of free status (Cod. Theod. 9,6,2; Dig. 48,4,7; 48,4,8; Cod. Iust. 5,17,8,6; 9,1,20). The *constitutio Quisquis* of emperor → Arcadius in 397 (Cod. Theod. 9,14,3 = Cod. Iust. 9,8,5) made not only the preparation and attempt of a *crimen laesae maiestatis* liable for the death penalty, but its contemplation: *quisquis...vel... scelestam inierit factionem...vel...de nece... cogitarit (eadem enim severitate voluntatem sceleris qua effectum puniri iura voluerunt)... utpote maiestatis reus gladio feriatur*. Further, there was provision for confiscation of property and loss of office and honorary rights, under permanent and lasting inclusion of the children as well, and of close confidants; only daughters and wives are given a certain quarter.

However, a practice of sparing political opponents, or at least a sense of proportion regarding their punishment in tension-free times, existed in contrast to the sovereign's occasional reign of terror by criminal law (i.e. Plin. Pan. 42; SHA Pert. 8,6,8; Cod. Iust. 9,8,3).

4. RECEPTION IN THE MIDDLE AGES AND MODERN TIMES

With the medieval reception of Roman criminal law, the ancient legislation protective of the crown was adopted (e.g. in the Hohenstaufen constitution of Melfi) and in this respect affected later absolutist legislation protecting the crown, indeed until the totalitarian legal 'terror' measures of modern European history.

KASER, RPR 1, 60–65; 2, 202–206; LATTE, 50–63; U. v. LÜBTOW, Römisches Volk. Sein Staat und sein Recht, 1955, 21; E. MEYER, Römischer Staat und Staatsgedanke, ⁴1975, 175; 266; 320; 424; MOMMSEN, Strafrecht, 537–594; 612; P. G. STEIN, Römisches Recht und Europa, 1997, 110. C.G.

Maieutic method from the Greek μαιευτική (*maieutikḗ*, sc. *téchnē*), 'midwifery'. In Plato's dialogue *Theaetetus* (148e–151d) Socrates compares his ability to recognize whether or not hidden wisdom lies dormant in others, and to help them if necessary to bring it to light, with the craft of his mother, the midwife (*maía*) → Phaenarete, and of midwives in general, to recognize pregnancies and to help deliver the baby. It is contested whether or not the historical Socrates used this comparison but the stronger arguments speak against it. In → Middle Platonism the MM of Socrates was interpreted as his ability to bring others to activate their latent knowledge of ideas through → *anámnēsis* ('remembering') by asking pertinent questions (Plut. Platonicae quaestiones 1,1000e; Anon. in Pl. Tht. col. XLVII 24–XLVIII 7, CPF III 392). Nowadays the term M.M. refers generally to a didactic procedure in which the teacher, by asking astute questions, makes it possible for a student to attain new knowledge after reflection. K.D.

Maiistas (Μαΐϊστας; *Maïïstas*). Author (his name perhaps Egyptian) of the hexametric aretalogy of Sarapis. This forms the second part (l. 29–84) of an inscription (3rd cent. BC) on a column in the Serapeum of Delos, which tells the history of the cult of the god from its inception to the construction of the first temple [1]. The beginning of the inscription (l. 1–28) comprises the prose chronicle of the priest Apollonius II. M.'s text following may be a Greek aretalogy intended for Greeks, or an account of Egyptian religious life. M.'s use of language combines Homeric expressions, tragic (esp. Euripidean) vocabulary and contemporary words.

1 H. ENGELMANN, The Delian Aretalogy of Sarapis, 1975 (with older literature). S.FO.

Maiocariri Fortified location in the hills on the road from Mardin to → Amida (Diyarbakır). Amm. Marc. 18,6,6 describes the location of M. in a forested region with winegrowing and orchards. According to Amm. Marc. 18,10,1 Šābuhr moved before the siege of Amida in AD 359 from Horre (Horren) via M. to Carcha (Kerh). Not. Dign. Or. 36,36 names the *Cohors XIV Valeria Zabdenorum* as occupation force. The name M. means 'cold water' in Aramaic. M. can not be localized exactly yet, but should probably be searched for near modern Ceyhan.

L. DILLEMANN, Haute Mésopotamie Orientale et pays adjacents, 1962, 157–159; F. H. WEISSBACH, s.v. Maiocariri, RE 14, 578f. K.KE.

Maiorianus

[1] Iulius M. In AD 457–461 emperor in the West. He served under → Aetius [2] in Gaul, retired to his estates and probably served as *comes domesticorum* at least with → Valentinianus III. With → Ricimer he brought about the overthrow of → Avitus [1]. The East Roman emperor named him military commander and on 28 December 457 he was declared to be Augustus (on the date [1. 180–188]; against a step-by-step appointment [1. 185f.]). He emphasized the support for him in the Senate and military but the eastern emperor → Leo [4] I. did not recognize him. Most of the measures of his energetic politics to restore the old grandeur of Rome (like Nov. Maioriani 4) served to improve the system of taxation and public administration. Even though he was a Christian, he restricted the rights of the Church.

In Gaul and on the Iberian peninsula he tried to restore imperial authority and then felt himself to be strong enough to begin a military campaign against the Vandals (→ Vandali). But the loss of large parts of his fleets through treason forced him to negotiate a humiliating peace treaty with the Germanic tribes. This gave Ricimer, who was probably irritated by M.'s independent politics, the opportunity to overthrow him. On 7 July 461 or shortly before (on the date: [1. 186ff.]) he was executed near Dertona. M. was probably the last West Roman emperor who felt himself able to make his own politics (PLRE II 702f.). → Sidonius Apollinaris composed a panegyric on him (Carm. 4/5).

1 R. SCHARF, Zu einigen Daten der Kaiser Libius Severus und Maiorian, in: RhM 139, 1996, 180–188.

[2] In 379 AD *magister utriusque militiae* under → Theodosius II [2], grandfather of Maioranus [1]. PLRE I 537.   H.L.

Maiorina (Lat., in full *pecunia maiorina* or *nummus maior*). Ancient name for 'larger' bronze (Æ)/billon coins (→ Billon) of the 4th cent. AD. Some modern scholars avoid the ancient names because of the frequent changes in the coinage system. Maiorina was probably the name of the largest Æ nominal of the → coinage reform of AD 348 (*c.* $5^{1}/_{4}$ g, 2.8 % silver), only struck for a brief period, and of the somewhat smaller coins of 349–352 [2. 64f.]. The edict Cod. Theod. 9,21,6 of 349 AD forbad the elimination of silver from the maiorina, an edict of 356 (Cod. Theod. 9,23,1) the sale of the maiorina and of the → centenionalis from one province to another, probably in order to stop speculation [3. 292]. Whether the two nominals also belong to the coins put out of circulation in the edict is not clear [2. 67; 3. 294]. Maiorina was perhaps also the name for the large bronzes of 363–365 [1] that were probably demonetized in 371 (Cod. Theod. 11,21,1) [3. 472], likewise the large Æ coins minted after the reform of 379 or 381 (*c.* $5^{1}/_{4}$ g, low proportion of silver). Their minting ended in the West around 388, and in the East around 395 or 400. An edict of 395 prescribed that the centenionalis was the only valid coin after the *maior pecunia* had already for a long time no longer been struck. The *decargyrus nummus* – obviously the maiorina – was withdrawn from circulation (Cod. Theod. 9,23,2). Whether the edict only concerned the West or the entire empire is contentious [2. 91, 94; 3. 474f.].
→ Centenionalis

1 A. CHASTAGNOL, Un nouveau document sur la majorina, in: Bull. de la Soc. Française de Numismatique 30, 1975, 854–857;   2 G. DEPEYROT, Le système monétaire de Dioclétien à la fin de l'Empire Romain, in: RBN 138, 1992, 33–106;   3 M. F. HENDY, Stud. in the Byzantine Monetary Economy, 1985, 291–294, 451–453, 469–474; 4 J. P. C. KENT, The Family of Constantine I (The Roman Imperial Coinage, vol. 8), 1981, 34–36, 61, 64f.;   5 C. E.

KING, The Fourth Century Coinage, in: L'»inflazione« nel quarto secolo d.C., 1993, 1–87;   6 SCHRÖTTER, 492f.
           Dl.K.

Maiorinus *Praefectus praetorio Orientis* under Constantius II. Life and career are poorly attested. Coming from a curial family from the East, he had a meteoric rise in his career (Lib. Ep. 1510) which reached its peak with the praetorian prefecture. He presumably held this office between the summer of 344 and 28 July AD 346 (Cod. Theod. 11,22,1: first certain evidence for his supposed successor Flavius Philippus) with his headquarters in Antioch [1]. He died shortly before 357 (Lib. Ep. 560) and was buried in Buṣrā 'l-Ḥarīr (Syria) [1. 302–305]. He was probably a Christian (PLRE 1, 537f.).

1 L. ROBERT, Epigrammes de Syrie, in: Hellenica 11–12, 1960.   A.G.

Maiotae (Μαιῶται; *Maiôtai*). Greek collective name for the tribes on the east coast of the → Maeotis and in the lower and middle reaches of Kuban/north-west Caucasus (Hdt. 4,123; Str. 11,2,2–4; 11). These probably include Iranian and Caucasian tribes of the → Sindi, → Cercetae, Toretae, Dandarii and Psessii among others. Farming and fishing formed the primary basis of their livelihood (Str. 11,2,4). They traded actively with → Tanais in particular. The M. had to pay tributes to the → Regnum Bosporanum (Xen. Mem. 2,1,10; Polyaenus, Strat. 8,55). The city of → Theodosia especially had a policy of expansion on the Asian side of the Cimmerian → Bosporus [2]. From the 1st cent. BC a cultural and ethnic convergence with the → Sarmatae was observable.

V. F. GAIDUKEVIC, Das Bosporanische Reich, ²1971, 71f., 293; V. P. SILOV, O rasselenii meotskih plemen, in: Sovetskaja arheologija 14, 1950, 110ff.   I.v.B.

Maius Roman surname and cognomen [1. 61; 2. 13].

1 KAJANTO, Cognomina;   2 WALDE/HOFMANN 2.   K.-L.E.

Majuscule In contrast to → minuscules, majuscules are the scripts in which the letters of the alphabet are written between two often only imaginary horizontal lines.

A. GREEK SCRIPT   B. LATIN SCRIPT

A. GREEK SCRIPT

In Greek palaeography, majuscules are also called capitals and uncials, although the latter term is very controversial. Theoretically all Greek scripts before the emergence of the minuscules ought to be called majuscules (not only the actual and the stylized book hands, but also the half cursives, cursives and document hand [1. 132–133, 137], because there are no pertinent signs before that point in time of breaking out of the two-line grid. This only happened in the 4th cent. AD under the influence of the Latin minuscule with its four-line pattern.

The development of the Greek book majuscule happened rather slowly: the oldest extant scripts of the 4th cent. BC on papyrus still followed the pattern of inscriptions on stone (→ Inscription style); only in the following cent. did the letters become softer. An independent development of the book hand only began in the 1st cent. BC; later canonized scripts developed gradually out of calligraphic forms, like the Roman → uncial (middle of the 1st cent. until the 2nd/3rd cents. AD). Late antiquity and the Byzantine period knew of three to four canonized majuscules, the study of which is made extremely difficult by the lack of dated MSS from before 800 (Cod. Vatican. gr. 1666, only the Cod. Vindob. Med. gr. is datable to *c.* 512): the Bible majuscule (→ uncial; 2nd/3rd–8th/9th cents.), Alexandrian majuscule (earlier called Coptic-style uncials, 4th–10th cents.), ogival (pointed arch) majuscule where a variant slanted towards the right is differentiated from a vertical variant (2nd/3rd–10th cents. or 5th–11th cents.) and finally the liturgical majuscule (9th–11th cents.). The Alexandrian majuscule and the vertical ogival majuscule (also called Constantinopolitan majuscule) were also used as → display scripts. The development of canonical scripts from cent. to cent. is a sign of the crisis of the traditional book-hand writing technique, from which the history of the late-antique Greek majuscules takes its beginning [2. 5].
→ Capital scripts; → Display script; → Document hand; → Inscription style; → Minuscule; → Palaeography → Papyrus; → Uncial; → Writing, styles of

1 G. CAVALLO, Fenomenologia 'libraria' della maiuscola greca: stile, canone, mimesi grafica, in: BICS 19, 1972, 131–140; 2 Id., Scritture ma non solo libri, in: Id. et al. (ed.), Scrivere libri e documenti nel mondo antico (Papyrologica Florentina 30), 1998, 3–12; 3 E. G. TURNER, Greek Manuscripts of the Ancient World, ²1987 (ed. by P. J. PARSONS).

P. CANART, Paleografia e codicologia greca. Una rassegna bibliografica, 1991; M. NORSA, La scrittura letteraria greca dal secolo IV a.C. all' VIII d.C., 1939; R. SEIDER, Paläographie der griechischen Papyri, I. Tafeln, 1. Teil: Urkunden, 1967; II. Tafeln, 2. Teil: Literarische Papyri, 1970; III.1 Text, Urkundenschrift 1, 1990.

B. LATIN SCRIPT

The earliest evidence for Latin majuscule script goes back to the 7th to 4th cents. BC: the preserved texts, written in an archaic Latin → alphabet on imperishable material (stone, metal, ivory, terracotta), have solemn official and sacral character; a monumental script was used with 'slow' ductus and individually set letters. This majuscule with its imprecision in the drawing of lines and irregularities in letter-forming remained in place until the end of the 3rd cent. BC. At that time the so-called *capitalis quadrata* of Latin inscriptions developed under the influence of Greek epigraphic script,

whose line drawing and letter shape were more regular, until a more exact letter canon was fixed in the 2nd–1st cents. BC. Apart from this and the *scriptura actuaria*, which was applied with paint brushes in inscriptions, there are the *capitalis rustica* and the so-called *capitalis elegans* (→ Capital scripts) in book hand. But the latter refers only to an artificial imitation of epigraphic models. The older Roman cursive (also called majuscule or capital cursive) was also used as an everyday script (on wooden and wax tablets, graffiti and *tabellae defixionum* as well as papyrus). The last ancient book hand, which was influenced by the contemporary Greek script and was used especially for Christian texts, is the → uncial (4th–8th/9th cents.); it is included because it has the characteristic signs of the new four-line script of the minuscule (created between 2nd and 3rd cents. AD) into its two-line system.

The alphabet of the capital script was adopted as → display script also in later scripts and redesigned: in the → West Gothic script (under Arabic influence), in the insular script (maybe also under the influence of runes), in the Carolingian → minuscule (sometimes in connection with half uncial) and in the → Gothic script; the capital script was also imitated in Italian humanism.

B. BISCHOFF, Paläographie des römischen Altertums und des abendländischen Mittelalters, ²1986, esp. 76–98 English: Dáibhí ó Cróinin, David Ganz (tr.), Latin Palaeography: Antiquity and the Middle Ages, 1990.; L. E. BOYLE, Medieval Latin Palaeography: a Bibliographical Introduction, 1984 (cf. the Italian edition of 1999 as a supplement); E. A. LOWE, Codices latini antiquiores, I–XI and Supplementum, 1934–1971. P.E. G.M.

Makaron Nesoi (αἱ τῶν μακάρων νῆσοι; *hai tôn makárōn nêsoi*, Lat. *insulae fortunatae*, 'Islands of the blessed').
[1] Since Hes. Op. 167–173, the mythical country to which heroes are transported – instead of to dark, mouldy → Hades like 'normal people' – when their lives on earth are over. The concept of the *makaron nesoi* (MN) is closely linked with the idea of → Elysium (Hom. Od. 4,561ff.) as the place were the blessed reside after death (cf. Pind. Ol. 2,68–80; Hdt. 3,26; Aristoph. Vesp. 640; Eur. Hel. 1677; Aristot. Protrepticus fr. 43 R.; Pl. Symp. 179e 2; 180b 5; Pl. Grg. 523b 1; 8; 524a 3; Pl. Menex. 235c 4; Pl. Resp. 519c 5; 540b 7; Pl. Epin. 992b 8; Demosth. Epit. 34 etc.). On the mythology and religious concept of the MN, see also → Elysium. L.K.
[2] Originally the mythical land of the blessed transposed to the distant West by early Greek literature in the context of eschatological ideas (Hom. Od. 4,563ff.; Hes. Op. 167ff.; Pind. Ol. 2,68ff.). As that part of the world took on an ever clearer shape with the Phoenicians' and Carthaginians' exploratory voyages, the MN were at first identified with Madeira and Porto Santo (cf. Diod. Sic. 5,19f.; Plut. Sertorius 8) and later with the Islas Canarias (Canary Islands), which Juba II explored and described (FGrH 275 F 44; after that Plin. HN 6,202–205; Mela 3,102). Plutarch and Pliny l.c.

describe the MN as climatically particularly favoured (warm, little precipitation) and therefore as very fertile; Pliny l.c. knows eight of the islands (Ptol. 4,6,14 knows only six), of which Canaria (Gran Canaria), Capraria (Fuerteventura), Ninguaria (Tenerife), and Pluvialia/ Ombrios (Lanzarote) can be identified. Documentation: Ptol. 1,12,11; 14,9; 7,5,13; 8,15,10; 27,13; Plin. HN 6,202–205; Sall. Hist. 1,61; Mela 3,102; Solin. 212,3ff.; Mart. Cap. 6,702; Geogr. Rav. 443f.

C. TH. FISCHER, s.v. Fortunatae Insulae (1), RE 7, 42f.
E.O.

Make-up see → Cosmetics

Makra Kome (Μαχρὰ κώμη; *Makrà kṓmē*). Town in the upper valley of the Spercheius, in 198 BC conquered by the Aetolians during a plundering raid on Thessalia (Liv. 32,13,10). Makra Kome (MK) is localized near the ruins of the modern village of MK (formerly Varibopi) on the northern bank of the → Spercheius.

Y. BÉQUIGNON, La vallée du Spercheios, 1937, 316ff.; B. HELLY, Incursions chez les Dolopes, in: I. BLUM (ed.), Topographie antique et géographie historique en pays grec, 1992, 67; F. STÄHLIN, s.v. M.k., RE 14, 808f.
HE.KR.

Malaca (Μαλάκη; *Maláke*). City on the Spanish east coast, modern Málaga (name probably Semitic, not from Hebrew *malkah*, 'queen' but from Phoenician *mlkt*, 'place of work' [1. 574²]; in [2. 574; 4. 76] the possibility of a semantic reference to fish processing is mentioned); probably a settlement that was not established until the early 6th cent. BC as a substitute for the 200 years older Phoenician settlement on the Cerro del Villar on the western neighbouring river Guadalhorce that was abandoned because of sedimentation (Avien. 181; 426 confuses M. with → Maenace [3. 197]). For the pre-Roman period, little is known about M. [12. 66–69]. After the expulsion of the Carthaginians from Hispania (in 206 BC; → Punic Wars) M. came under Roman rule. M. was involved in 197 BC in the uprising of Culcha (Liv. 33,21,6). According to Plin. HN 3,8, M. was a *civitas foederata* (the Malacitani belonged to the *tribus Quirina*). According to Str. 3,4,3 it was an important trading centre for the African north coast. In AD 170 M. was destroyed by African pirates [4. 77] (cf. also Plut. Crassus 6; Bell. Alex. 64,2; Plin. HN 5,19; It. Ant. 404,2; Steph. Byz. s.v. M.).

The importance of M. is proven by coins and inscriptions, especially by the bronze tablet with the *lex municipii Malacitani* of AD 82–84 which was found together with the *lex municipii Salpensani* near M. [5. 175ff., 259ff.]; for the theatre cf. [4. 77]. M. had a significant tuna processing industry [2. 574] and an important export harbour for ores from the Sierra Morena. Inscriptions and finds attest to wide trading links (CIL II 251; VI 9677; XV 4203; [6; 12]). Christianity was introduced early. At the synod of Illiberis around AD 306 a bishop of M. is mentioned (*episcopus Malacita-*

nus [7; 10. 221, 234, 252, 288, 294, 305, 313, 348]). From about AD 555 to 570 M. was under Byzantine rule but was then annexed by → Leowigild and incorporated in the empire of the West Goths [8. 137f., 411, 150f.]. M. was a coin minting centre from the 2nd → Punic War onwards [9]. In 711–1487 M. was under Arab rule [11].

1 E. LITTMANN, in: SCHULTEN, Landeskunde 2; 2 SCHULTEN, Landeskunde 1²; 3 A. SCHULTEN (ed.), Fontes Hispaniae Antiquae 1, ²1955; 4 TOVAR 2; 5 J. L. LÓPEZ CASTRO, Hispania Poena, 1995; 6 A. SCHULTEN, Forschungen in Spanien, in: AA 1933, 3/4, 564f.; 7 Id. (ed.), Fontes Hispaniae Antiquae 8, 1958, 59f.; 8 Id. (ed.), Fontes Hispaniae Antiquae 9, 1947; 9 A. MATEU Y LLOPIS, La ceca visigoda de Málaga, in: Ampurias 7–8, 1945–1947, 243f.; 10 A. SCHULTEN (ed.), Fontes Hispaniae Antiquae 9, 1947; 11 A. SCHULTEN (ed.), Forschungen in Spanien, in: AA 1940, 1/2, 96; 12 J. A. MARTÍN RUIZ, Catálogo documental de los Fenicios en Andalucía, 1995.

SCHULTEN, Landeskunde 1², 322; TOVAR 2, 14f., 74, 76– 79; S. GIMÉNEZ REYNA, Memoria arqueológica de la provincia de Málaga (Informes y Memorias 12), 1946.
H.G.N. P.B.

Malachbelus (Aramaic *mlkbl*, 'messenger of Bel'). Palmyrene god, depicted or referred to in various forms and together with a changing array of other gods in → Palmyra and the Roman empire (Rome [3], Dacia [8], north Africa [4]).

In Palmyra M. was worshipped with Aglibol in the so-called 'sacred garden', a temple known through inscriptions (e.g. [6. no. 0197, 0314]), tesserae [7. 155– 161] and a relief [2. pl. 4,1]. The latter, the so-called Dexiosis relief of the 'sacred brothers' in which the two gods join hands, is also found in Rome and the northwestern surroundings of Palmyra [2. pl. 38f.]. On an altar with his name from the Baalšamīn temple in Palmyra (1st cent. AD) M. is pulled in a cart by two griffins and crowned with a wreath by the altar's donor [2. pl. 44; 6. no. 0181]. The hypothesis that M., as the → sun god, the moon god Aglibol and Baalšamīn formed a triad in Palmyra is not supported by the inscriptions. Both gods are mentioned in some texts along with the so-called Anonymous God, who is presumed to represent an aspect of Baalšamīn [6. no. 0327, 0347; 5. 2629–2631]. On tesserae, M. is associated with Gad Taimis [7. 135, 273–277, 279] and in inscriptions with Atargatis [6. no. 0273].

The Trastevere altar in Rome (early 2nd cent. AD) is well known, with four reliefs and a bilingual inscription [2. pl. 40–43; 6. no. 0248]. A god in a griffin quadriga is depicted on the side with the Aramaic inscription 'consecrated to M. and the Palmyrene gods'. The other sides show a bust with a sun wreath, eagle and the Latin inscription *Soli sanctissimo sacrum*, a bearded bust with a veil and sickle, and a cypress from which a child is emerging with a goat. The four sides may refer to the development of the character of M. from a vegetation god, to the messenger of the primary god, and then to the sun god [5. 2635], although it is not clear whether every side represents M. The characterization of M. as the sun god, which is found among Palmyrene soldiers outside Palmyra, is of secondary importance and may be explained by the influence of religious ideas regarding the role of the sun god in the Roman army [1].

→ Baal; → Palmyrene religion

1 L. DIRVEN, The Palmyrenes of Dura-Europos, 1999; 2 H. DRIJVERS, The Religion of Palmyra, 1976; 3 E. EQUINI SCHNEIDER, Il santuario di Bel e delle divinità di Palmira. Comunità e tradizioni religiose dei Palmireni a Roma, in: Dialoghi di Archeologia 5, 1987, 69–85; 4 Id., Palmireni in Africa, in: L'Africa romana 5, 1988, 394f.; 5 M. GAWLIKOWSKI, Les dieux de Palmyre, in: ANRW II 18.4, 1990, 2605–2658; 6 D. HILLERS, E. CUSSINI, Palmyrene Aramaic Texts, 1996; 7 H. INGHOLT et al., Recueil des tessères de Palmyre, 1955; 8 S. SANIE, Die syrischen und palmyrenischen Kulte im römischen Dakien, in: ANRW II 18.2, 1989, 1233ff. T.KAI.

Malangitae (Μαλαγγῖται; *Malangîtai*). According to Ptol. 6,7,23, a people in central Arabia who lived on the *Máreitha órē* (Μάρειθα Ὄρη), i.e. on the ʿĀriḍ. Probably corresponds to the tribe of the Maḏḥiǧ which was expelled by Imruʾ al-Qais, the king of the → Lakhmids in *c*. AD 300.

H. v. WISSMANN, Zur Geschichte und Landeskunde von Altsüdarabien (SAWW, Phil.-histor. Klasse 246), 1964, 175, 195f., 404–406. I.T.-N.

Malaria The term malaria covers a polymorphous complex of feverous diseases whose origin can be traced back to the parasite *plasmodium* carried by the anopheles mosquito. In antiquity, malaria could be distinguished by some of its symptoms: recurrent attacks of fever, particularly of three and four-day duration, swelling of the spleen (splenomegalia) or black urine. Aetiologialy the feverous diseases were related to swampy regions, especially within the framework of climatic medicine. Treatment was symptom-based and primarily covered attacks of fever (antipyretic active agents) and the spleen (diuretic agents).

Malaria is probably a zoonosis that has its origin in the forests of tropical Africa from where it is said to have spread to Mesopotamia (possibly the Nile Valley was the corridor to the Mediterranean). Its history during antiquity remains unclear: undoubtedly already present in Greece from time immemorial, malaria remained at a very low level until the 5th cent. BC. In around 430 BC it is said to have appeared again because of the reintroduction of the parasite *plasmodium falciparum*, with the focuses of the disease initially limited; then it appears in the Hippocratic 'Epidemics' 1 (around 410 [?]) and 2 (end of the 5th/beginning of the 4th cent. BC) in a malignant form. In the Hellenistic period it is said to have spread so that in the Roman epoch and by the time of Galen it reached the stage of

hyperendemia. After that it is said to have gone back to a low level that was maintained during the Byzantine age.

Malaria has been regarded as a direct cause of the decline of ancient culture and the death of countless famous men, among them also Alexander the Great [1]. Its spread appears indeed to be connected with the decline of state administration in late antiquity as well as with impoverishment, a fall in births and hence economic, social and political weakness, although it cannot be represented necessarily as the first cause of such trends.

1 D. ENGELS, A Note on Alexander's Death, in: CPh 73, 1978, 224–228.

L. J. BRUCE-CHWATT, J. DE ZULUETA, The Rise and Fall of Malaria in Europe, 1980; M. D. GRMEK, Les maladies à l'aube de la civilisation occidentale, 1983, 355–407; Id., La malaria dans la Méditerranée orientale préhistorique et antique, in: Parasitologia 36, 1994, 1–6; Id., Bibliographie chronologique des études originales sur la malaria ... , in: Lettre d'information du Centre Jean Palerne 24, 1994, 1–7; F. E. KIND, s.v. Malaria, RE 27, 1928, 830–846. A.TO.

Malaric Frank, defended in AD 355 as *tribunus gentilium* of the → scholae Palatinae the *magister peditum* Silvanus who was accused of planning to usurp power (see → Mallobaudes). In 363 M. declined appointment as *magister equitum per Gallias* (Amm. Marc. 15,5,6; 25,8,11; 10,6). PLRE 1, 538. P.KE.

Malatha (Μάλαθα; *Málatha*, Jos. Ant. Iud. 18,147; *Moleatha*, Not. Dign. Or. 34,45), modern Arabic Tall al-Milḥ ('salt hill') or Hebrew Tel Malḥatā; settlement situated in the centre of the Beerševa Basin in northeastern Negev at the confluence of two Wadis. Because of the wealth of wells in the erea, a major fortified settlement was already established in the Middle Bronze Age, part of a southern defence line. Destroyed by the Egyptians and obviously restored in the 10th cent. BC under → Solomon, M. remained uninhabited until Roman times after it was destroyed again in the 6th cent. BC as a result of Babylonian conquest. As the seat of the *cohors prima Flavia*, M. was then expanded into a fortress. Recent excavations of Byzantine M. uncovered major private and public buildings as well as an extensive necropolis, indicating the importance of M. as a junction of communications as well as a religious and agricultural centre.

Y. BAUMGARTEN, I. ELDAR, M. KOCHAVI, s.v. Tel Malhata, The New Encyclopedia of Archaeological Excavations in the Holy Land 3, 1993, 934–939; O. KEEL, M. KÜCHLER, Orte und Landschaften der Bibel 2, 1982, 351–354. J.P.

Malatya see → Asia Minor

Malchus (* *Mlk* ='king'; Greek Μάλχος, *Málkos*; Latin *Malchus, Maleus, Mazeus*).
[1] Carthaginian, father of → Carthalo [1]. Historicity and interpretation of the only source text concerning M. as first historically tangible personality of → Carthage in Iustin (18,7; cf. Oros. 4,6,6–9) are frequently and vehemently contested to the present day, beginning with the titular character of his name and his place in the chronology of the (early?) 6th cent. BC. M. is supposed to have fought successfully as commander in Libya and Sicily, but unsuccessfully in Sardinia. The latter led to the banishment of M. and his citizen troops and, in reaction, to M.'s siege of Carthage. M. is supposed to have executed his son and priest striving for mediation, as well as ten 'senators' after the capture of the city. M. justified himself successfully before the people's assembly, and left the constitution unchanged. Later, he was indicted and executed due to his alleged efforts to become the tyrant [1. 196–198; 2. 59f., 62f., 459]. Most probably these events mirror a power struggle between an ambitious M. as king with limited powers and ambitious aristocrats, among them M.'s successor → Mago [1] [3. 73–80].

    1 Geus ;   2 Huss ;   3 W. Ameling, Karthago, 1993.
                                                    L.-M.G.

[2] M., in Nabataean *Maliku* [*mlkw*], king of the Nabataeans (→ Nabataei, Nabataeans), *c.* 57–29 BC, was attacked in 55 by A. → Gabinius [I 2], the governor of Syria (Jos. Ant. Iud. 14,103), sent auxiliary forces to Caesar in 47 to Alexandria (Bell. Alex. 1; Jos. Ant. Iud. 14,128), refused in 40 to take in → Herodes [1] the Great during his flight from the Parthians (Jos. Ant. Iud. 14,370–373) and was fined in 39 by P. → Ventidius due to his support of the Parthians (Cass. Dio 48,41,5). In the year 34, M. → Antonius [I 9] gifted → Cleopatra [II 12] with Nabataean territory on the Gulf of ʿAqaba, which M. leased back; Herod had to guarantee the payment of the lease (Jos. Ant. Iud. 15,96 with 132). M. sent Antonius auxiliary troops for the war at Actium (→ Actium; Plut. Antonius 61f.), however, Herod attacked him in 32, instigated by Antonius, because he was behind in his lease payments, and defeated him in 31 (Jos. Ant. Iud. 15, 107–160). In 30, M. had the ships burned which Cleopatra had had dragged over the strait to the Gulf of Suez (Plut. Antonius 69,3; Cass. Dio 51,7,1), and thus secured the goodwill of the triumphal Octavian (→ Augustus [1]).
[3] **M. II.** Son and successor of → Aretas [4] IV, AD 40/1–70, known from coins until the 23th year of his reign and by inscriptions dated after him until the 25th year. In 67, M. sent Vespasian 1,000 horsemens and 5,000 foot soldiers, mostly archers, to Ptolemais for the Jewish War (Jos. BI 3,68). The Peripl. m.r. 19 mentions him when speaking of a trade route from → Leuke Kome [2] to Petra.

    G. W. Bowersock, Roman Arabia, 1983, 35–43; Schürer, vol. 1; J. Starcky, Pétra et la Nabatène (DB Suppl. 7), 1966, col. 909–911, 916–919.   K.BR.

[4] Byzantine historian of the late 5th cent. AD, came from → Philadelphia in Syria and lived later as teacher of rhetoric in Constantinople. In his *Byzantiaká* (Βυζαντιακά, 'Byzantine History') he describes, following the historian Priscus, the period from 473 until the death of the Western Roman emperor Iulius → Nepos in 480. Only fragments of his work – which stylistically belongs to the tradition of Atticism (→ Second Sophistic) – are preserved: in → Constantinus [9] VII Porphyrogenetus and in the → Suda, where they are in part ascribed to the Isaurian historian Candidus,.

    Editions: R. C. Blockley, The Fragmentary Classicising Historians of the Later Roman Empire, vol. 1, 1981, 71–83, 124–127; vol. 2, 1983, 402–462; L. R. Cresci (ed.), Malco di Filadelfia, Frammenti, 1982.
    Bibliography: B. Baldwin, Malchus of Philadelphia, in: Dumbarton Oaks Papers 31, 1977, 89–107.   AL.B.

Maldras Son of Massilia, was elevated to king of the Suebi by the king of the West Goths → Theodericus II in AD 456 after the murder of → Rechiarius, although he had to defend himself against other pretenders [1. 124]. In 457 he plundered Olisipo (Lisbon) and laid waste to Gallaecia, in 459 to Lusitania and Portumcale Castrum (Oporto). In the same year, he murdered his brother, was then killed himself in 460 (Chron. min. 2,29–31 Mommsen). PLRE 2, 704.

    1 D. Claude, Geschichte der Westgoten, 1970.   M.MEI.

Malea
[1] (Μαλέα ἄκρα/*Maléa ákra*, Μάλεια/*Máleia*, Μαλέαι/*Maléai*, ἀκρωτήριον Μαλέας/*akrōtérion Maléas*, Μαλειάων ὄρος/*Maleiáōn óros*, cf. Hom. Od. 3,287; 19,187; modern Κάβο Μαλιάς, Ἅγιος Ἄγγελος). The south-east cape of the Peloponnese, feared in antiquity and in modern times, southern foothill of the → Parnon (cf. the proverb passed on by Str. 8,6,20 'if you sail around M. forget those at home' [1. 262ff.]). The main difficulty for ancient navigation lay in the gusty, often stormy headwinds that frequently lasted for days or weeks; they blew predominantly from the west in the summer, from north to east in the winter, while the passage between M. and Cythera is otherwise free of obstacles. The cape itself is the end of an about 500 m high chalk plateau which runs from west to east and plunges in steep cliffs especially towards the south. The dark, bare high cliff walls on the cape contributed to its reputation for being dangerous, as did the fact that there was no harbour near the cape in which to take refuge. Traffic around the cape was nevertheless lively and in favourable circumstances not difficult; a trader in imperial times from Asia Minor boasts that he passed M. 72 times (Syll.³ 1229). Ships with rudders generally did not have to fear the wind conditions. M. was also the name for the broader region around the cape, in which the cult of Apollo Lithesios is attested [2. 863f.], maybe even the whole Parnon peninsula. M. counted as the birthplace of → Silenus (Paus. 3,25,2 [2. 864]; cf. Str. 8,5,2; 6,20; Paus. 3,23,2).

1 R. BALADIÉ, Le Péloponnèse de Strabon, 1980; 2 F. BÖLTE, s.v. Malea (1), RE 14, 859–865. C.L. E.MEY.

[2] Name of various places, especially on the Peloponnese, the originally independent god → Maleatas was named after it, who was later identified with Apollo, with main cultic centres on the mountain Cynortium above the Asclepius sanctuary of Epidaurus and on the east coast of the Parnon peninsula, probably near Tyrus (Laconia) north of Leonidi. Inscriptions: IG V 1, 927; 929; 929c.

> K. A. RHOMAIOS, Ἱερὸν Ἀπόλλωνος Τυρίτου, in: Praktika 1911, 1912, 254–276; H. WATERHOUSE, R. HOPE SIMPSON, Prehistoric Laconia: Part 2, in: ABSA 56, 1961, 131. Y.L.

Maleatas (Μαλεάτας; *Maleátas*). The epiclesis M. for → Apollo is derived from the place-name → Malea [1], the cape in the south-east of the Peloponnese (of the Mani) feared for its storms (Hom. Od. 3,287 et passim). → Poseidon had a cult there (Eur. Cyc. 293; Paus. 3,23,2). Typically, however, it is Apollo rather than Poseidon who bears this epiclesis in the eastern Peloponnese and radiating outward from there, for example in Piraeus (IG II² 4962); here M., as well as Apollo, receives his own preliminary sacrifices before → Asclepius. Another link with → healing cults is found in Tricca (Paus. 2,27,7), which as early as Homer (Il. 2,729) is considered the home of Asclepius. The most important shrine of Apollo M. is the one located high above → Epidaurus, which was built on the site of a Mycenaean shrine and also precedes the healing god Asclepius in its function [1].

→ Malus

> 1 V. LAMBRINUDAKIS, Remains of the Mycenaean Period in the Sanctuary of Apollon Maleatas, in: R. HÄGG, N. MARINATOS (ed.), Sanctuaries and Cults in the Aegean Bronze Age, 1981, 59–65. C.A.

Malecidas (Μαλεκίδας/*Malekídas*, also Μαλκίτης/*Malkítēs*). Theban, → Boeotarch during the Theban hegemony (IG VII 2408), who, after the death of → Pelopidas in 364 BC, led an army of 7,000 hoplites and 700 cavalry, together with Diogeiton, against → Alexander [15] of Pherae. Alexander was forced to relinquish his control over the Thessalian cities and obliged to supply troops (Plut. Pel. 35). M. is apparently identical with the Boeotarch Malgis, mentioned by Pausanias (9,13,6) in connection with the Battle of Leuctra.

> J. BUCKLER, The Theban Hegemony, 1980, 137. HA.BE.

Maleficium see → Magic; Magi

Maleus (Μάλεως, Μάλεος; *Máleōs, Máleos*). The mythography of late antiquity mixed together several persons of this name [1].
[1] A cliff protecting the harbour of Phaestus on Crete was said to have been dedicated by a M. to → Poseidon

(schol. Hom. Od. 3,296; Suda s.v. M.); the link to Cape → Malea [1], which is established as early as the Odyssee, can be found also in the grave epigram Anth. Pal. 7,275 of the Imperial period.
[2] Named as one of the Tyrrhenian robbers (also known as Μαλεώτης/*Maleótēs*) and as the father of Aletis (Hsch. s.v.) alias → Erigone [1], who is otherwise referred to as the daughter of → Icarius and is part of the rural component of the festival of the → Anthesteria (→ Aiora).
[3] Also to be regarded as mythological is king M. (also Lat. *Maleus*) of the pre-Greek Pelasgians in Italy (Str. 5,2,8; schol. Stat. Theb. 4,224 and 6,382). M. is also named there as the inventor of the trumpet (*salpinx*), who is called M*elas* in the schol. Hom. Il. 18,219.

> 1 A. BURCKHARDT, s.v. Maleos, RE 14, 875–881. C.A.

Malia, Mallia Minoan palace on Crete, on the northern coast *c.* 40 km east of Heraklion, with two harbour bays. The relatively low level of ancient building on top of the site and of later reconstruction makes genuine insight into Minoan palace architecture possible. Like the palaces of → Knossos, → Phaestus and → Zakros, the buildings are grouped around a large central court. The history of the palace with its individual building phases also corresponds to the development of the other palaces. The first palace was built at the beginning of the 2nd millennium BC. Destruction around 1700 BC was presumably caused by an earthquake. The definitive destruction which led to the abandonment of the palace (around 1450 BC) cannot have been caused by the volcanic eruption on Thera (Santorini) with subsequent tidal wave, which occurred earlier. The residential area surrounding the palace has been well researched. At the seafront, there are necropoleis with rich discoveries, such as gold finds (Chrysolakkos). West of the palace, finds from the Roman period indicate a large *villa*, also a basilica and a bath.

→ Minoan culture and archaeology

> H. VON EFFENTERRE, Le palais de Mallia et la cité minoenne, 2 vols., 1980; J. W. MYERS et al., Aerial Atlas of Ancient Crete, 1992, 175–185; O. PELON, Guide de Malia. Le palais et la nécropole de Chrysolakkos, École française d'Athènes. Sites et monuments 9, 1992; J.-C. POURSAT, Guide de Malia au temps des premiers palais. Le quartier Mu, École française d'Athènes. Sites et monuments 8, 1992; I. F. SANDERS, Roman Crete, 1982, 147. H.SO.

Malichae (Μαλῖχαι; *Malîchai*). According to Ptol. 6,7,23, a people of → Arabia felix, in the hinterland of the Red Sea. The M. probably correspond to the Banū Malik in ʿAsīr in modern Saudi Arabia (cf. *Baramalacum*, Plin. HN 6,157). I.T.-N.

Malichu insula (Plin. HN 6,175 after Juba). Island off the west coast of → Arabia Felix in the southern Red Sea. It served as the next point of orientation for seafarers after passing Exusta (→ Catacecaumene [2]). M. can probably be identified with the island of Ḥanīš al-kubrā (13° 43' N, 42° 45' E); it rises to a height of 407 m. When Ptol. 6,7,44 mentions Malichou (Μαλίχου /Malíchou, Var. Μαλιάχου δύο /Maliáchou dýo, i.e. the two islands of Malichus), this may refer to the two Ḥanīš Islands, i.e. the main island and its smaller, northern neighbour, Ḥanīš aṣṣuḡrā.   W.W.M. A.D.

Malichus (Μάλιχος; *Málichos*, variant form: Malchus, Μάλχος; *Málchos*). Confidant and secret rival of → Antipater [4], whom he served in 57 BC as a unit commander against the Hasmonaean prince Alexander (Jos. BI 1,162; Jos. Ant. Iud. 14,84), and in 43 during the levy of the tribute demanded by C. → Cassius [I 10], murderer of Caesar (Jos. BI 1,220; Jos. Ant. Iud. 14,273–276). In the same year, he had Antipater poisoned (Jos. BI 1,226; Jos. Ant. Iud. 14,281), but fell prey to the vengeance of his victim's son, → Herodes [1] the Great (Jos. BI 1,234; Jos. Ant. Iud. 14,288–293).

P. RICHARDSON, Herod. King of the Jews and Friend of the Romans, 1996, 115–117.   K.BR.

Malieis (Μαλιεῖς; *Malieîs*). Tribe of the estuary plain of the → Spercheius, whose territory bordered on the gulf named after them, and in the west, in the Spercheius Valley, on that of the Aenianes. Homer makes no mention of them. They were among the original members of the Pylaeic-Delphic amphictyony (→ amphiktyonía), whose first centre, the sanctuary of Demeter at Anthele, lay in their territory (Aeschin. or. 2,116; Paus. 10,8,2; Theopomp. FGrH 115 F 63). Their archaic customs are often mentioned (Aristot. Pol. 1297b 14ff., fr. 512 USENER 1870). According to older reports, they provided mostly light infantry (Paus. 1,23,4; Thuc. 4,100,1), but for the army of Alexander also sent cavalry (Diod. Sic. 17,57,3).

Herodotus (see below) has their territory encompassing the southern part of the Spercheius plain as far as the mountains, with their capital at → Trachis. Thuc. 3,92,1 correspondingly divides the tribe into the Paralioi, Hiereis and Trachinioi. Like the other tribes of northern Greece, they were forced in 480 BC to attach themselves to the army of Xerxes (→ Persian Wars). Pressed by their neighbours the Oetaei, they turned to the Spartans for help in 426 BC, who founded Heraclea [1] nearby to replace Trachis (Thuc. 3,92), but this led to difficulties with the other M. and neighbouring tribes (Thuc. 5,51). In the 4th cent., until the outbreak of the → Corinthian War (Xen. Hell. 4,2,17), they were dependent on Sparta (Xen. Hell. 3,5,6; 4,3,9). The war against Sparta led to their losing the territory south of the Spercheius; Heraclea [1] fell to the Oetaei (Scyl. 62; Paus. 10,23,13). The new centre of their lands became Lamia [2] north of the Spercheius (possibly on territory that was originally Achaean); from now on, almost without exception, it provided the → *hieromnémones* in the → *amphiktyonía*. The M. were now on the side of

Thebes (Xen. Hell. 6,5,23; Diod. Sic. 15,85,2). They are included with the Oetaei and Aenianes in the list of the Corinthian League of Philippus II (Syll.³ 260b 9) and belonged to the Aetolian League from c. 235 BC (→ Aetolians, map). Their lands were united with Thessalia in 189 BC, more precisely with the territory of Achaea Phthiotis, and in the Imperial Period they remained with it, so that geographers of the Imperial Period considered the M. as part of Thessalia.

G. DAUX, Delphes au IIᵉ et au Iᵉʳ siècle, 1936, 309f., 673; R. FLACELIÈRE, Les Aitoliens à Delphes, 1937, 36, 40, 247, 358; G. KIP, Thessal. Stud., 1910, 42ff.; F. STÄHLIN, Das hellenische Thessalien, 1924, 212ff.; Id., s.v. Malieis, RE 14, 900ff.   HE.KR. E.MEY.

Malleolus
[1] see → Arrow
[2] Cognomen (from *malleus*, hammer) in the family of the Publicii in the Republican period.

1 KAJANTO, Cognomina, 342.   K.-L.E.

Malli (Μαλλοί; *Malloí*). Indian people at the confluence of the Punjab rivers → Hydaspes, → Acesines [2] and → Hydraotes, with several fortified cities. In league with the → Oxydracae, they violently resisted Alexander the Great. They are probably the ancient Indian Mālava who later emigrated to the east and are attested numismatically and epigraphically in Rājasthān (2nd cent. BC) and in Madhya Pradesh. Their name there is still preserved as Mālwā.

K. K. DAS GUPTA, The Mālava, 1966.   K.K.

Mallius Roman gens name (in manuscripts commonly confused with Manlius and Manilius).
[1] **M. Maximus, Cn.** *Homo novus* (Cic. Planc. 12), praetor at the latest in 108 BC, consul in 105 together with P. → Rutilius Rufus. The war against the Cimbrians (→ Cimbri) in the Rhone area was assigned to him. Because his predecessor, proconsul Q. → Servilius Caepio, did not want to obey his supreme command and provoked the Cimbrians to attack, their two armies were severely beaten at Arausio; M. lastly on 5 October 105. Among the 70,000 dead were his two sons and the legate M. Aurelius [I 18] Scaurus (Liv. Per. 67; Granius Licinianus p. 10f. CRINITI; Cass. Dio 27, fr. 91; Oros. 5,16,1–7; MRR 1,555). M. and Caepio were indicted in 103 BC and despite being defended by the orator M. Antonius [I 7], M. was condemned and went into exile (Cic. De orat 2,125; Liv. Per. 67; Granius p. 12).
[2] **M. Pantolabus** (nickname 'Money grabber'). Poor and miserable jester (*scurra*) in several grand houses of Rome in the 1st cent. BC. Mocked by Horace (Hor. Sat. 1,8,11 with Porphyrio ad loc.; 2,1,22).   K.-L.E.

Mallobaudes As *comes domesticorum et rex Francorum* M. defeated the Alemanni at Argentaria (Horburg/Alsace) in AD 378. He probably took part in

→ Gratianus' [2] expedition on the right bank of the Rhine [1. 600] in order to subjugate them (Amm. Marc. 31,10,6–17). In Franken he later killed the invading king of the Alemanni → Macrianus [1] (Amm. Marc. 30,3,7). Identification with the Frankish *tribunus armaturarum* who in 354 AD interrogated → Constantius [5] Gallus (Amm. Marc. 14,11,21) and who, together with → Malaric, spoke in defence of → Silvanus in 355 AD (Amm. Marc. 15,5,6) is contentious [2].

1 P. KEHNE, s.v. Gratian, RGA 12, 598–601; 2 M. WAAS, Germanen im römischen Dienst, ²1971, 91f.; 3 PLRE 1, 539. P.KE.

Mal(l)oea City in the Thessalian country of Perrhaebia (→ Perrhaebi) in the valley of the Titaresius, identified with the ruin Paliokastro near Sykia. It is mentioned as the neighbouring town of Chyretiae only during the wars at the beginning of the 2nd cent. BC and only by Livy: in 199 and 191 M. went over to the Aetolian side and was won back by Philip V (Liv. 31,41,5; 36,10,5; 13,4) who had to give it back to Perrhaebia in 185 (Liv. 39,25,16). In 171 BC M. surrendered to king Perseus (Liv. 42,53,8) and soon afterwards was conquered by the Roman army and plundered (Liv. 42,67,7).

J.-CL. DECOURT, La vallée de l'Enipeus en Thessalie, 1990, 117ff.; F. STÄHLIN, s.v. Mal(l)oia, RE 14, 913ff. HE.KR.

Mal(l)orix Celtic name compound with *mall-*, 'slow' [1. 236]. Together with Verritus, M. asked in Rome in AD 58 as king (?) of the → Frisii for permission to resettle the tribe in Roman territory, took a seat in the theatre of Pompey among the senators and was given presents by Nero along with citizenship (Tac. Ann. 13,54; Suet. Claud. 25).

1 SCHMIDT. W.SP.

Mallovendus Celtic name (cf. → Mal(l)orix). Prince of the → Marsi who had subjugated himself to the Romans and who betrayed to → Germanicus [2] in AD 15 the hiding place of the eagle standard of one of the fallen legions of → Quinctilius Varus (Tac. Ann. 2,25). W.SP.

Mallow (μαλάχη/*maláchē*, μολόχη/*molóchē* in Dioscorides, Lat. *malva*). In antiquity there were various species (cf. Plin. HN 20,222) from the family of the *Malvaceae* with rose-like flowers as well as the marshmallow (→ *althaea* [2], *Althaea officinalis*, ἀλθαία/*althaía*, ἐβίσκος/*ebískos*, Lat. *hibiscus*, *althaea malva agrestis*, Isid. Orig. 17,9,75) with white or pink flowers. Being harsh on the stomach (Dioscorides 2,118 WELLMANN = 2,144 BERENDES), the garden mallow was not much in use, but it was (since Hes. Op. 41) used as a remedy until the modern era. Along with mucilage that forms a kind of gelatine in water (Theophr. Hist. pl. 9,18,1;

Plin. HN 20,230) the root contains starch and some asparagine. Apart from this, the seeds and leaves were recommended internally (e.g. for coughs: Plin. HN 20,225) and externally for inflammation, and wounds of all kinds (Theophr. Hist. pl. 9,18,1; Dioscorides 3,146 WELLMANN = 3,153 BERENDES: marshmallow [1. fig. 225]; *hibiscus*: Plin. HN 20,29; *malva*: Plin. HN 20,222–230 with application for insect bites, as an aphrodisiac and abortifacient drug).

1 H. BAUMANN, Die griechische Pflanzenwelt, 1982.

P. WAGLER, s.v. Althaia (3), RE 1, 1694–1696. C.HÜ.

Mallus (Μαλλός; *Mallós*). One of the oldest cities of → Cilicia Pedias (Ptol. 5,8,4; 8,17,44; Scyl. 102; Stadiasmus maris magni 162f.; Plin. HN 5,22). The exact localization is still unknown; it is thought, on the basis of inscriptions, to lie near modern Kızıltahta and on the west bank of the → Pyramus [1. 665], where remains of an imperial-period building can be detected. North of it are the ruins of a Roman bridge [2. 337]. Here Alexander the Great crossed the Pyramus in 333 (Arr. Anab. 2,5). M. was probably renamed Antioch on the Pyramus in the 2nd cent. BC [3. 547], together with Magarsa. Pompey settled pirates in M. (era of M. from 67/6 BC). As a station for lines of communication in the Sassanid campaigns in the 3rd cent. AD under Severus Alexander, the city became a Roman *colonia* [4. 183]. Conquered and pillaged in 260 by Šapur I [5. 312f.]. From the beginning of the 5th cent. part of *Cilicia I* (Hierocles, Synekdemos 704,8). Bishops from M. are attested at the synods of Ephesus. → Crates [5], → Zenodotus and → Moschion came from M.

1 H. TH. BOSSERT, Vorberatung über die archäologische Untersuchung von Karataş, in: Belleten 14, 1950, 664–666; 2 HILD/HELLENKEMPER, 337, s.v. M.; 3 M. GOUGH, s.v. M., PE, 547; 4 R. ZIEGLER, Wann wurde M. zur römischen Kolonie, in: E. SCHWERTHEIM (ed.), Studien zum antiken Kleinasien 2, 1992, 181–183; 5 A. MARICQ, Classica et Orientalia. 5. Res Gestae Divi Saporis, in: Syria 35, 1958, 295–360.

L. ROBERT, Contribution à la topographie de villes de l'Asie Mineure Méridionale, in: CRAI 1951, 256–258. M.H.S.

Malnutrition, Famine
I. TERMINOLOGY AND CAUSES II. MEASURES AGAINST FAMINE AND MALNUTRITION III. LAWS AND INSTITUTIONS SECURING THE FOOD SUPPLY IV. MALNUTRITION AND FAMINE IN TOWN AND COUNTRY V. MALNUTRITION AND INFECTIOUS DISEASES VI. ARCHAEOLOGICAL EVIDENCE

I. TERMINOLOGY AND CAUSES
Although they refer to similar situations, the terms famine, food supply problems, starvation and malnutrition are not identical. Famine is a modern term and difficult to translate into Greek and Latin. λιμός (*limós*) and *fames* are terms for hunger, but they can also refer

to food shortages that cause people to starve. Commenting on the situation of September 57 BC, Cicero distinguishes between *inopia*, *fames* and *caritas* ('privation', 'starvation', 'price increases'; Cic. Dom. 11f.); famine is not identical with either temporary starvation caused by a food shortage or chronic starvation, i.e. chronic malnutrition caused by long-term insufficient food supply. Famine is not identical with privation. Both refer to supply problems; their impact, however, varies. Historians tend to equate famine with privation or with similar terms like price increases, shortage or starvation. The vagueness of the terminology makes a comparative historical analysis of famine difficult. It is no coincidence that many historians think famine was a frequent phenomenon in pre-industrial societies – as is true for food shortage. But if the term famine is reserved for a particularly acute supply problem that, because of starvation, results in a significant increase in the mortality rate in a town or region and in turn leads to the collapse of the social, political and moral structures, famine was a comparatively rare event in antiquity.

The frequent food shortages were caused by geographical factors such as climate, surface conditions and soil quality in the Mediterranean as well as a low productivity level of ancient → agriculture, a transportation system of rather limited capacities and the limited scope of the local and supra-regional administration. Therefore, → grain, the most important staple, remained relatively scarce in the Mediterranean. In addition, droughts led to crop failures; and grasshoppers could destroy entire crops. Given these circumstances, the food supply often broke down; however, these breakdowns were only temporary. Before the crisis could turn into a catastrophe, the officials of the local or supra-regional administration usually intervened as did the clergy in Late Antiquity.

II. Measures against famine and malnutrition

Capacities for managing supply problems varied greatly from region to region. The prospects for receiving aid supply was worse for towns of the interior than for coastal towns, as Gregory Nazianzen noted when he commented on supply problems in Caesarea in Cappadocia (Greg. Naz. Or. 43,34–35). Admittedly, in times of rising prices the expenses for → land transport affected the price of wheat only minimally; furthermore the ruling elite in the interior, usually wealthy land owners, were aware of their responsibility to use their own resources in averting famine.

Where local resources turned out to be insufficient or the local elite incapable, the central powers intervened as a last resort, at least in the Roman Empire: e.g. under Domitian (AD 81–96) a provincial governor tried to secure the grain supply for Antioch [5] in Pisidia by making the hoarding of grain a punishable offence (AE 1925, 126), and in the 2nd cent. Hadrian permitted the shipment of grain from Egypt to Ephesus (Syll.³ 839; cf. AE 1968, 478). However, another instance

reveals that the presence of the emperor could possibly cause a famine: the prosperous town of Antioch [1] was frequently visited by emperors since it was the capital of the province of Syria and a military base for wars against the Persians. In 361/2, when Julian stayed in the town, the army and the entourage of the emperor caused supply problems, but tensions between him and the *curiales* prevented a quick resolution of the crisis. Julian, who only had a limited understanding of economic processes, attempted to end the shortage by providing for Antioch grain from the imperial stockpiles at a fixed price and far below market value. Since his cheap grain was not rationed, it was quickly bought up by speculators and resold at a high price in the surrounding areas or even in remote regions (Amm. Marc. 22,14,1–2; Lib. or. 1,126; 15,8ff.; Julian. Mis. 368c). However neither in this instance nor in any others was there any danger that the suffering of the people would reach the extent of the people of Edessa, where a terrible famine raged between 499 and 502. Although emperor Anastasius had money and grain sent to the unfortunate inhabitants of the town, it was too little and too late to actually alleviate the famine.

III. Laws and institutions securing the food supply

In antiquity the cities of the Mediterranean were forced to develop processes or create institutions that would avert or overcome food shortages. These included donations of the local elite and the rulers (→ Euergetism), funds for purchasing grain, appointing officers for buying and distributing grain and sometimes even building granaries and establishing price controls.

In the 5th cent. BC, Athens initially had no institutions to secure the grain supply. The strength of its fleet along with control over strategically important points in the Aegaean, especially on the Hellespont, ensured that enough grain was imported to Attica; in addition, the grain market in Athens was very attractive for merchants, because of the great number of consumers. However, when Athens lost its hegemony in the 4th cent. BC, supply problems ensued. For the first time the Athenians took special measures so that merchants would land in the harbour of Piraeus, to control their routes and to protect the still large population from the profiteering of small merchants and bakers (Lys. 22; Dem. Or. 34,37; 35,51; Aristot. Ath. Pol. 51,3).

Rome was the only city with a comprehensive administrative system for supplying and distributing grain and it used resources from all over the Mediterranean; in Late Antiquity this system was transferred to Constantinople as the new imperial residence. The Roman system of providing grain (*annona*; → *cura annonae*) resulted from the conflicts of the Late Republic; originally, the distribution of cheap grain to the urban population of Rome was regulated through the popular → grain laws (Lex Sempronia 123/122 BC: Cic. Off. 2,72; Cic. Tusc. 3,48; Cic. Sest. 103); from 58 BC, grain was free for the *plebs*. Under Augustus the grain supply was organised as *curatio annonae* (R. Gest. div. Aug. 5). Several times in the Late Republic shortage of grain and rising prices caused unrest (on the year 57 BC, cf. Cic. Dom. 10ff.); even in the early Principate Rome experienced difficulties in its grain supply because of crop failures and weather-related disruption of the shipping routes (Suet. Claud. 18,2).

IV. MALNUTRITION AND FAMINE IN TOWN AND COUNTRY

Famine and malnutrition were not limited to urban areas; they were part of the harsh realities of an agrarian society. Already Hesiod mentions hard work as a way of avoiding starvation (Hes. Op. 299–307; 391–395), but it was also necessary to use the scarce supplies wisely if they were to last to the next harvest (Hes. Op. 361–369).

Although the urban population ultimately depended on the rural population for their food supply (Lib. Or. 50,33f.), they had some decisive advantages: privileged access to the grain donated by wealthy individuals or rulers since classical euergetism focussed mostly on the cities (as did Christian charity in Late Antiquity). → Galen of Pergamum, a city dweller himself, was very well aware of the structural disadvantages of the rural population. He makes the interesting comment that 'the city dwellers had the habit of collecting and storing enough grain for the entire year immediately after the harvest, leaving the rural population with whatever was left, i.e. various kinds of legumes of which they also took a lot into the city' (Gal. 6,749 KÜHN). Galen considered this practice a widespread phenomenon 'among many peoples subject to Rome'. Naturally, as soon as a food shortage loomed, the rural population activated a complex system of survival strategies: they relied on social networks within the peasantry, including kinship, neighbourhood and friendship, as well as on relationships of patronage and dependancy they had entered with the owners of large estates. In addition, they resorted to wild plants more than usual and to less nutritious food or even to fruits that were only consumed during a famine. From Galen's work 'On the Powers of Food' an impressive list of field produce (vetches, tubers, thistles, etc.), usually fodder for livestock and used for human consumption only in an emergency, can be compiled (e.g. Gal. 6,522–523; 546; 551; cf. also Columella 2,10,1).

Galen who was especially interested in the effects of malnutrition from a medical point of view, describes the diet of farmers in winter, consisting mostly of legumes, and their transition in spring towards a diet of various 'unhealthy' foods: 'They ate twigs and buds from trees and shrubs, as well as tubers and roots of indigestible plants; they filled up on wild herbs and cooked fresh grass.' (Gal. 6,749). Elsewhere, in the context of a food shortage in the Thracian town of Aenus, he mentions the consumption of poisonous vetches (Comm. in Hippoc. Epid. II = CMG V 126,4–6L). The symptoms outlined in the text, namely weakness of the muscles and paralysis, indicate lathyrism (poisoning). Toxins in the food and the diseases they caused were a consequence of food shortages since farmers and bakers tried to save flour by not removing harmful seeds (darnel, αἰγίλωψ/*aigílōps*) and other foreign substances (Gal. 7,285). As a last resort the rural population moved into the towns in great numbers, such as the farmers around Edessa (Chron. Iosua Stylites 40; 43).

In order to understand the seriousness of these supply shortages, however, the dichotomy of town and country needs to be transcended. In both areas certain groups were at risk: the unemployed or underemployed poor in the towns, the day labourers in the country as well as women and young children in cities and country alike.

V. MALNUTRITION AND INFECTIOUS DISEASES

Compared to the research on temporary food shortages not much scholarly attention has been devoted to chronic malnutrition, although there is reason to believe it was a common phenomenon in ancient societies. Malnutrition was a pathological condition, caused by a deficiency of certain nutrients, vitamins or minerals; e.g. the eye diseases mentioned in many texts suggest a deficiency of vitamin A (→ Disease). Food shortages were often followed by outbreaks of epidemics (→ Epidemic diseases), since the immune system was weakened by malnutrition and starvation. Thus, in the sources epidemics and famine are often mentioned together (*pestilentia fameque*: Obseq. 13, 165 BC; cf. 22, 142 BC). Nutrient deficiencies, in turn, could be caused or worsened by infectious diseases. Rich and poor alike were susceptible to deficiencies caused by diseases because an adequate diet did not protect from infections. However, the rich upper class faced fewer diseases that were caused by malnutrition. Throughout ancient society young children of all social classes were extremely susceptible to infections when they went through the difficult transition to an adult diet.

VI. ARCHAEOLOGICAL EVIDENCE

The archaeological evidence for malnutrition is mostly based on the analysis of human skeletons. However to date, the material has not yet been systematically assembled. Scientific analysis of human bones is a relatively new procedure; the methods and interpretations are still being refined, and the data are continuously increasing.

→ Nutrition; → Grain trade, Grain imports

1 T. GALLANT, Risk and Survival in Ancient Greece, 1991; 2 P. GARNSEY, Famine and Food Supply in the Graeco-Roman World, 1988; 3 Id., Cities, Peasants and Food in Classical Antiquity, 1998; 4 Id., Food and Society in Classical Antiquity, 1999; 5 Id., C. R. WHITTAKER (ed.), Trade and Famine in Classical Antiquity, 1983; 6 P. GAUTHIER, De Lysias à Aristote (Ath. pol. 51,4): le commerce du grain à Athènes et les fonctions des sitophylaques, in: Revue historique de droit français et étranger 59, 1981, 5–28; 7 P. HERZ, Studien zur römischen Wirtschaftsgesetzgebung: Die Lebensmittelversorgung, 1988; 8 H. P.

KOHNS, Versorgungskrisen und Hungerrevolten im spätantiken Rom, 1961; 9 Id., Hungersnot und Hungerbewältigung in der Antike, in: H. KLOFT (ed.), Sozialmaßnahmen und Fürsorge: Zur Eigenart antiker Sozialpolitik, 1988, 103–121; 10 L. MIGEOTTE, Le pain quotidien dans les cités hellénistiques: à propos des fonds permanents pour l'approvisionnement en grain, in: Cahiers du Centre G. Glotz 2, 1991, 19–41; 11 I. MORRIS, Death-Ritual and Social Structure in Classical Antiquity, 1992; 12 R. STROUD, The Athenian Grain-Tax Law of 374/3 BC (Hesperia Suppl. 29), 1988; 13 C. VIRLOUVET, Famines et émeutes à Rome des origines de la République à la mort de Néron, 1985. P.GA.

Malophoros (Μαλοφόρος; *Malophóros*). Doric 'Apple bearer' or 'Sheep bearer', epithet for → Demeter in → Megara, where her temple lay in the port district (Paus. 1,44,3). In the Megarian colony of → Selinus on Sicily, she had a sanctuary outside the city [1]. According to the foundation myth, Demeter received the name from the first sheep breeders of Megara (Paus. 1,44,3). Scholarship has applied the epithet M. either to sheep [2] or to the mysteries' symbol of the → pomegranate [1]. However, the word is possibly consciously ambiguous and points to the apples that people dedicated to the goddess at her harvest festival at the time of the → Opora (cf. Theocr. 7,144; Paus. 9,19,5). These, as in the Boeotian cult of Hercules, were stylized to represent sheep by inserting small sticks (Hesych. s.v. Μήλων Ἡρακλῆς; Poll. 1,30f.).

1 M. DEWAILLY, Les statuettes aux parures du sanctuaire de la Malophoros à Sélinonte, 1992; 2 E. MANTZOULINOU-RICHARDS, Demeter Malophoros: the Divine Sheep-Bringer, in: Ancient World 13, 1986, 15–22. G.B.

Malta see → Melite [7]

Maluginensis Cognomen in the family of the Cornelii (→ Cornelius [I 57/58], [II 30]).

KAJANTO, Cognomina, 210. K.-L.E.

Malum Punicum see → Pomegranate

Malus
[1] (Μᾶλος; *Mâlos*). Son of Amphictyon, eponym of the → Malieis and of their city Malieus (Androtion in Steph. Byz. s.v. Μαλιεύς; *Malieús*). In the poems of → Isyllus of Epidaurus (CollAlex 132–135 = [1. 380–383 no. 40]) M. is an Epidaurian king who introduces the cult of Apollo → Maleatas. Therefore, M. is probably an Epidaurian etymology to explain the name Maleatas. In Isyllus, M. – through the mediation of Zeus – marries the Muse Erato and becomes the father of Cleophema, hence the grandfather of → Aegle [5] and the great-grandfather of → Asclepius.

1 L. KÄPPEL, Paian, 1992.

U. v. WILAMOWITZ-MOELLENDORFF, Isyllos von Epidauros, 1886 (repr. 1967), 188. K.v.S.

[2] (Μάλος; *Málos*). Village in Galatia, modern Kalecik, in the Kalmizene area (inscription b, AD 251 [1. 205]); significant wine production; home to a Montanist community (→ Montanism), Jewish synagogue [1. 209B], nearby martyrium of St. Theodotus of Ancyra (died in 312 AD); *c.* 13 km north-west, sanctuary of Zeus Bussurigios ([1. 201, 203f.], modern Karahüyük).

1 S. MITCHELL, Regional Epigraphic Catalogues of Asia Minor. 2: The Ankara District. The Inscriptions of North Galatia, 1982.

S. MITCHELL, The Life of Saint Theodotos of Ancyra, in: AS 32, 1982, 93–113; MITCHELL, vol. 2, 18, 49, 93; BELKE, 201f. K.ST.

[3] (Μαλούς; *Maloús*). Arcadian river south-west of → Megale polis (Paus. 8,35,1) that first takes up the Syrus before it flows on the lefthand side into the → Alpheius [1]; today probably the stream at Neohori ([1]; different previously [2]).

1 F. GEYER, s.v. Syros (1), RE 3 A, 690; 2 F. BÖLTE, s.v. Malus (1), RE 14, 942–947. E.O.

Mamala According to Ptol. 6,7,6 (Μάμαλα κώμη; *Mámala kṓm[e]*), settlement of the → Cassanitae on the west coast of Arabia. Probably the same as Ṣalīf or Lōḥiyya. Not to be confused with → Mamali.

H. v. WISSMANN, De mari Erythraeo (Stuttgarter Geogr. Stud. 69), 1957, 300, 42b. I.T.-N.

Mamali Region in southern Arabia mentioned in a partly extant naval report of 323 BC in Theophr. Hist. pl. 9,4,2 (Μαμάλι/*Mamáli*), probably Maʿmal near modern ʿAsīr in Saudi Arabia on the coast.

H. v. WISSMANN, De mari Erythraeo (Stuttgarter Geogr. Stud. 69), 1957, 300 n. 42b; Id., M. HÖFNER, Beiträge zur historischen Geographie des vorislamischen Südarabien (AAWM, Geistes- und sozialwiss. Klasse), 1952 no. 4, 76, 82, 85f., 95, 104, with maps; Id., Zur Geschichte und Landeskunde von Altsüdarabien (SAWW, Philos.-histor. Klasse 246), 1964, 189, 416. I.T.-N.

Mamercinus Cognomen in the Republican period in the families of the Aemilii (→ Aemilius [I 18–26]) and Pinarii.

KAJANTO, Cognomina, 176. K.-L.E.

Mamercus
[1] (Μάμερκος/*Mámerkos*). Tragedian of the 4th cent. BC mentioned in Plut. Timoleon 31,1 (TrGF I 87). B.Z.
[2]
→ Praenomen exclusively used by the Patrician *gens* of the → Aemilii (also used there as a → cognomen, but never for freedmen); shortened to *Mam.*; Greek Μάμερκος/*Mámerkos*. First attested for the father of Aemilius [I 25], traced back to M., son of → Numa Pompilius (Plut. Numa 8,18f.). The name also occurs in

Oscan (Μαμερεκς/*Mamereks*) and in Etruscan (*Mamarce, Mamerce, Mamurke*, 7th–5th cent. BC) as a praenomen and is derived from the Italian name of the god that is attested in Oscan (dat. Μαμερτει/*Mamertei*) and now also in Lat. (*Mamartei* on the → Lapis Satricanus). Like → Marcus, it was probably used primarily for children born in March (Oscan *Mamerttio-*).

KAJANTO, Cognomina 176; SALOMIES, 34f., 240.   H.R.

Mamers According to Festus (116,2; 150,34), the Oscan form of → Mars. The appearance of M. in Oscan dedicatory inscriptions (VETTER 196; [1. no. 177, 179]: 3rd/2nd cents. BC) and the Oscan roots of the → Mamertini, important since the 4th cent. BC, seemed to support Festus [2. 155, 167, 172]; this led to the marginalization of Varro's postulate of the Sabine origin of M. (Varro, Ling. 5,73). The so-called → Lapis Satricanus (AE 1979, 136), found in Satricum 50 km southeast of Rome, a dedicatory inscription *Mamartei* ('for Mamars'), is proof of the existence of a Latinized form at *c.* 500 BC. It remains doubtful, however, whether this means that Oscan and Sabine M. are derived from a Latin-Roman Mars [3. 293–295] and that the confusing variety of other dialect forms originated here. It may be, instead, that Mamars in Satricum is the result of linguistic influence from the Sabine [4. 85–87].

1 P. POCCETTI, Nuovi documenti italici, 1979;   2 E. T. SALMON, Samnium and the Samnites, 1967;   3 G. RADKE, Zur Entwicklung der Gottesvorstellung und Gottesverehrung in Rom, 1987, 293–295;   4 C. DE SIMONE, L'aspetto linguistico, in: C. M. STIBBE et al., Lapis Satricanus, 1980, 71–94.

U. W. SCHOLZ, Studien zum altitalischen und altrömischen Marskult und Marsmythos, 1970, 46–79; WALDE/HOFMANN 2, 43–45.   C.R.P.

Mamertina see → Messana

Mamertini Former Oscan mercenaries, predominantly from → Campania, hired by → Agathocles [2] of Syracuse. After his death (289 BC), they conquered the town of Messana between 288 and 283 BC. They called themselves M. after the war god → Mamers, the Oscan form of Mars (Diod. Sic. 21,18,1; Cass. Dio fr. 40,8; Fest. 150,30–35), plundering a wide area and enforcing tributes (Pol. 1,7,2–5; 8,1; Plut. Pyrrhus 23,1). After the M. had conquered wide areas of Northern Sicily (Diod. Sic. 22,13,1–2), they concluded a treaty with Carthage in 279/8 against the militarily superior → Pyrrhus (Diod. Sic 22,7,4; Plut. Pyrrhus 23,1).

After joining with several Greek towns in Sicily [1. 109f.], they were able to defeat Pyrrhus decisively in 275 in lower Italy (Plut. Pyrrhus 23,5; 24,2) and to add deserting Roman auxiliary forces from Campania to their ranks as their allies in Rhegium (Pol. 1,7,6–8; Diod. Sic. 22,1,2–3; Dion. Hal. Ant. Rom. 20,4–5; Liv. Per. 15; Cass. Dio fr. 40,7–12). Following a Roman punitive action against the deserters and the partial loss

of their area to → Hieron [2] II of Syracuse (Pol. 1,8,2) who decisively defeated them in 269 near the Longanus river (Pol. 1,9,7–8), only a Carthaginian force in Messana could save the M. from being destroyed altogether (Diod. Sic. 22,13,7–8).

According to Polybius (1,10,1–11,3) one part of the M. asked the Carthaginians for help against Hieron after the battle at the Longanus river, another one offered dedition to the Romans (→ *deditio*), but it appears that these requests for help are not connected in any way, nor did they occur at the same time. The M. probably forced the Carthaginian garrison, in place since 269, into retreat in 264, with the support of a Roman advance party under the military tribune C. Claudius, or expelled a recently arrived Carthaginian 'protective force', thus enabling the landing of a consular army under App. Claudius [I 3] in Sicily (Cass. Dio fr. 43,5–10; Zon. 8,8,8–9). All these events constitute the beginning of the First → Punic War. After concluding peace with Hieron (263), the Romans apparently granted federation status to the M. (*foedus*: [2. 57f.]; Cic. Verr. 5,50–51) thereby giving them preferential treatment over Sicilian communities which were granted the status of *societas sine foedere* [3. 352f.].

1 P. GAROUFALIAS, Pyrrhus, King of Epirus, 1979;   2 W. DAHLHEIM, Struktur und Entwicklung des römischen Völkerrechts im dritten und zweiten Jahrhundert v.Chr., 1968;   3 D. KIENAST, Entstehung und Aufbau des römischen Reiches, in: ZRG 85, 1968.

W. HOFFMANN, Das Hilfegesuch der Mamertiner am Vorabend des Ersten Punischen Krieges, in: Historia 18, 1969, 153–180; B. D. HOYOS, Unplanned Wars. The Origins of the First and Second Punic Wars, 1998, 11–115; E. SANTAGATI RUGGIERI, Un re tra Cartagine ei mamertini: Pirro e la Sicilia, 1998.   K.-W.W.

Mamilius Latin name of an ancient dynasty from → Tusculum (in manuscripts frequently confused with *Manilius* and *Manlius*). Because the city was considered a foundation of → Telegonus, the son of Odysseus and Circe, the Mamilii, from the early 2nd cent. BC at the latest, traced their lineage to Odysseus, via Mamilia, the daughter of Telegonus (coins: RRC 149; 362; in literature, from the Augustan period: Fest. 116f. L; Liv. 1,49,9; Dion. Hal. Ant. Rom. 4,45,1). In the 5th cent. BC, with M. [I 1] the family was accepted in Rome, some members repeatedly reached the consulate (M. [5–7]); probably died out in the 1st cent. BC.

MÜNZER, 65–68; SCHULZE, 442; T. P. WISEMAN, Roman Studies, 1987, 209.

[1] **M., L.** Son of M. [2]; in 460 BC, when he was dictator of Tusculum, he supported the Romans in their fight against Appius Herdonius [1] without having been asked. For this reason he was awarded Roman citizenship in 458 (Liv. 3,18,2–4; 29,6; Dion. Hal. Ant. Rom. 10,16,4).   K.-L.E.

[2] **M., Octav(i)us** Predominantly, tradition has M.'s praenomen as Octavius but it probably was Octavus

[1. 119]. He was ruler of Tusculum and son-in-law of L. → Tarquinius Superbus [12] who joined him after his expulsion and abortive repatriation at the hands of → Porsenna. M. also attempted to repatriate the Tarquinians, agitated against Rome among the Latins and was killed as their military leader in the battle at the → Lacus Regillus (499 or 496 BC) (Liv. 1,49,9; 2,15,2; 18,3;19, 7–10; 20,8f.; Dion. Hal. Ant. 5,50,1; 51,2; 61,1–3; 6,2,1; 5,3–5; 11,3–12,4). In spite of all embellishments (cf. Dion. Hal. Ant. Rom. 6,4,1: possibly his son rather than M. himself was the Latin warlord), there probably was a historical person behind the literary figure of M.

1 SALOMIES.   C.MÜ.

[3] M. Atellus, C. In 209 BC, he was the first plebeian to become → curio [2] maximus, he died in 174 (MRR 1,289). The office required an age of 50 and could not be combined with any magistrature outside of Italy. For this reason M. Atellus must be distinguished from another C. Mamilius, plebeian aedile in 208, praetor in 207 (Sicilia) and member of a legation to Philippus V of Macedonia in 203.

R. FEIG VISHNIA, State, Society and Popular Leaders in Mid-Republican Rome 241–167 B.C., 1996, 229 n. 182.
                                                        TA.S.

[4] M. Limetanus, C. As people's tribune, he organized a special court in 109 BC (quaestio Mamiliana) which sentenced five Roman politicians because of alleged preferential treatment of the Numidian King → Jugurtha (Sall. Iug. 40,1f.; Cic. Brut. 127; MRR 1,546).
                                                        K.-L.E.

[5] M. Turrinus, C. Consul in 239 BC (MRR 1,221). He or his father was co-opted into the College of Augurs between 260 and 254. In 207, a Q. Mamelius Turrinus, probably the consul's son, was plebeian aedile and praetor in 206, allegedly at first peregrinus, then in command as a protector against Hasdrubal [5]. The last information belongs to the rather implausible sources that relate a permanent ongoing presence of Roman troops in the Po Valley. In both career steps, he closely followed – his brother? – C. M.

J. SEIBERT, Forschungen zu Hannibal, 1993, 246–252.

[6] M. Vitulus, L. (?) Name of one of the consuls of 265 BC, reconstructed from corrupted sources (MRR 1,201).

[7] Q. Vitulus, M. Consul in 262 BC, he conquered → Acragas in Sicily together with his colleague L. Postumius (MRR 1,204), after an extended siege.

D. HOYOS, Unplanned Wars, 1998, 108–110.   TA.S.

Mammius L.M. Pollio. Senator. During his tenure as consul designatus in AD 49, and at the urging of → Agrippina [3], he proposed to the Senate that Claudius [III 1] should marry his daughter to the son of Agrippina [3], the future emperor Nero (Tac. Ann. 12,9). He is attested as consul in May of the same year. PIR² M 126.   W.E.

Mamre Mentioned in the Bible (probably from the Hebrew root mr', 'become fat, fatten', as 'place that is fat/fattens'; Greek Μάμβρη/Mámbrē; Latin Mambre) as an oak grove where → Abraham [1] built an altar (Gn 13:18), and where, as he played host to three men, interpreted as a divine apparition, the birth of his son → Isaac [1] was announced to him (Gn 18). According to Biblical indications, the place is identical with → Hebron (thus Gn 23:17 etc.; but cf. Gn 13:18: 'in' or 'near Hebron'). M. has been located in the vicinity of Hebron from the 2nd cent. BC (cf. e.g. Book of Jubilees 14,10; Jos. BI 4,533). M.'s beginnings are obscure; however, it was in all probability an old tree sanctuary. Excavating in 1926–1928, A. E. MADER found a rectangular temenos of the Herodian period on the site of the modern Ramet al-Ḥalīl (c. 3 km north of modern Hebron) near a hoard of bronze vessels (Early Bronze Age I) and Iron Age wall and ceramic remains (Iron Age II); the temenos had been destroyed during the 1st Jewish Revolt (AD 66–70). The temenos that was erected on its ruins by emperor Hadrian (117–138) was consecrated to Hermes. From at least the time of Hadrian, M. was also an important market place, where a communal festival was celebrated by Jews, Christians and those of other faiths (Sozom. Hist. eccl. 2,4,2ff; GCS 50,54f.). During the Bar-Kochba revolt (AD 132–135, → Bar Kochba), M. served as a commercial centre for the slave trade (Hier. comm. in Zachariam 11,4f; CCL 76A, 851). Under Constantine the Great, a basilica was built in the eastern section of this district (cf. Euseb. vita Const. 3,51–53); it was destroyed in AD 614 during an assault by the Persians. The place is marked on the Madaba Map (→ Cartography) with a tree and a church building. In Christian iconography, the motif of the hospitality towards the three men became dominant.

1 O. KEEL, M. KÜCHLER, Orte und Landschaften der Bibel. vol. 2: Der Süden, 1982, 697–713; 2 A. E. MADER, Mambre. Die Ergebnisse der Ausgrabungen im heiligen Bezirk Ramet el-Halil in Südpalästina 1926–28, 1957; 3 Y. MAGEN, Elonei M. – Herodian Cult Site, in: Qadmoniot 24, 1991, 46–55; 4 A. NEGEV, s.v. M., Arch. Bibellex. 1991, 288; 5 P. WELTEN, s.v. M., TRE 22, 11–13.   B.E.

Mamucium Roman fort near Manchester, on the road from Deva to Eboracum, first occupied in the Flavian period (AD 69–96), probably under Cn. Iulius [II 3] Agricola. Renovated in the early 2nd cent. [1]. An inscription on a Severan building suggests a further extension in the 3rd cent. [2. 581]. In the 4th cent., M. gained considerable strategic importance, before being abandoned after AD 370. A large vicus surrounded the fort.

1 G. D. B. JONES, S. GREALEY, Roman Manchester, 1974; 2 R. G. COLLINGWOOD, R. P. WIGHT, The Roman Inscriptions of Britain 1, 1965.   M.TO.

Mamurius Veturius Blacksmith under king → Numa Pompilius who produced eleven copies of a bronze shield that has dropped from the sky during an epidemic in order to protect the shield from theft. M. was rewarded by being mentioned in the → Carmen Saliare; the priesthood of the → Salii kept the shields and used them in their dances (Dion. Hal. Ant. Rom. 2,71; Ov. Fast. 3,383–392; Plut. Numa 13; Min. Fel. 24,11; Paul Fest. 117,13 l.). M. is also believed to have created a bronze statue of the god → Vertumnus (Prop. 4,2,61). As there is no mention of M. in Livy (1,20,3f.), Varro or Vergil, it is suspected that M. is a construct from the Augustan period [2. 160–165]. [4. 98f.] regards M. as a fabrication based on the *Mamuri Veturi* in the → Carmen Saliare (Varro, Ling. 6,49), the interpretation of which is subject to dispute, as well as an aetiology of the shield dances of an old, widespread priesthood.

Traditional stories of M. may contain some historical truth: Veturii can be found as far back as the 7th cent. BC [3. 306, 458 n. 34]; there was a consul from the ranks of the Roman *gens Veturia* in 499 BC (Liv. 2,19,1, if authentic: [4. 284; 5. 294–296]) and the *gens Veturia* may have maintained its own family tradition about M. Because Livy relies on the tradition of the *gens Valeria* via → Valerius Antias [4. 12–16], the fact that there is no mention of M. in Livy may reflect that tradition. Ennius (Ann. 114) contains different information: Numa received the shields from the nymph → Egeria. These variants may indicate an early mythological tradition [1]; however, the existence of such a tradition is questionable.

The festival of the Mamuralia (14 March in later calendars, instead of the Equirria) later included the expulsion from the city of a man dressed in animal hide (Lydus, Mens. 4,49; [2. 162]); this continued into the Byzantine era.

1 M. BEARD, Acca Larentia Gains a Son. Myths and Priesthood at Rome, in: M. M. MACKENZIE, CH. ROUECHÉ, Images of Authority, 1989, 41–61;   2 J. N. BREMMER, Three Roman Aetiological Myths, in: F. GRAF (ed.), Mythos in mythenloser Geschichte, 1993, 158–174;   3 T. P. CORNELL, The Beginnings of Rome, 1995;   4 R. M. OGILVIE, A Historical Commentary on Livy 1–4, 1965;   5 R. E. A. PALMER, The Archaic Community of the Romans, 1970.   C.R.P.

Mamurra Unusual Italic personal name, known through M., a Roman equestrian from Formiae (Catull. 43,5 etc.; Hor. Sat. 1,5,37), who was an associate of Pompey in *c.* 66 BC, was in Spain with Caesar in 61, and served as the latter's *praefectus fabrum* in Gaul from 58 (Catull. 29,18–24). Around 55/4, M. was periodically at Rome, where his luxurious house caused a furore (Plin. HN 36,48). His rival *in eroticis*, → Catullus [1], depicts him as a scandalous war profiteer and a philanderer (Catull. 41) (allegedly in cahoots with Caesar, Catull. 57). Caesar's association with M. was criticized (Suet. Iul. 73; probably also Cic. Att. 13,52,1, often

seen as evidence that M.'s death occurred at the end of 45). M.'s assets later went to the Imperial house (ILS 1586). Evidence of a *cognomen* M. among the Vitruvii, of whom there were many at Formiae, (ILS 5566), suggests that he may have been related to the architect → Vitruvius.

W. C. McDERMOTT, Mamurra, eques Formianus, in: RhM 126, 1983, 292–307.   JÖ.F.

Man, concept of see→ Anthropology

Manaechmus Platonic philosopher from Alopeconnesus or Proconnesus, known only from a note from the Suda (2,317,22ff. = [1. 44; 2. 118, fr. 2]). He wrote, in addition to other philosophical works, three books on Plato's 'Republic'.

Identification with the mathematician Menaechmus [2. 546f.] can be excluded [1. 203], and it is doubtful that he is identical to Manaechmus named by Photius (Bibl. cod. 167 p. 114b 8) [3. 699f.].

1 DÖRRIE/BALTES 3, 1993;   2 F. LASSERRE, De Léodamas de Thasos à Philippe d'Oponte. Témoignages et fragments, 1987;   3 K. FIEHN, s.v. Menaichmos, RE 15, 699–700.   M.BA. M.-L.L.

Manaemus (Μανάημος; *Manáēmos*). Greek form of the Hebrew proper name Menahem ('the comforter'), attested in the Old Testament (2 Kgs 15:14ff.) and in other Semitic languages.
[1] Essenian (→ Essenes) (1st cent. BC), who foretold Herod (→ Herodes [1]) the Great that he would become king and that he would turn his back on godliness and and justice, and who predicted, in a second prophecy, the duration of his reign (Jos. Ant. Iud. 15,10,5). Like M. [3], the son of Judas Galilaeus, he is identified with the scribe M. [1; 2].
[2] In his youth, a companion of →·Herodes [4] Antipas, described as one of the five prophets and teachers who had the leadership of the Jewish-Hellenistic community in → Antioch [1] (Acts 13:1) [3].

1 P. RICHARDSON, Herod. King of the Jews and Friend of the Romans, 1999, 256ff.;   2 SCHÜRER 2, 574, 587;   3 N. KOKKINOS, The Herodian Dynasty. Origins, Role in Society and Eclipse, 1998, 270.   I.WA.
[3] see → Menahem ben Yehuda

Mana genita see → Genita Mana

Manalis lapis The object and function were already obsolete in the 1st cent. BC, and therefore required explanation. Paul Fest. 115 l. knows of two explanations: (1) the *manalis lapis* (ML) was an entrance to the underworld through which the souls of the subterraneans, alias → Di Manes, 'streamed' (*manāre*) into the upper world; (2) the ML was a stone (or a water jug: Varro in Non. 547 with dubious rationalization) located at the temple of Mars outside the Porta Capena in Rome which the pontifices (→ Pontifex) pulled into the city in times of drought (cf. Paul Fest. 2 l., associating ML with → *aquaelicium*). Owing to the secondary etymological link between Di Manes and *manāre*, (1) is hardly tenable, despite [1. 275–281]. Thus, most explanations from ancient sources derive *manalis lapis* from the intransitive (Serv. Aen. 3,175) or transitive (Paul Fest. 115 L.) form of *manāre* and link it to a ritual pleading for rain.

The models of comparative theology of the late 19th cent. held that ML belonged to an early stage of development in Roman religion, linked with the 'rain god ' → Jupiter Elicius [5] and used as a 'fetish' for 'rain magic' [2. 65ff.; 4. 78f.], in particular 'imitation magic', in which water was poured over a stone [3. 970f.]. In this case the fictitious contrast between religion and magic led to unverified hypotheses, which, moreover, were based on a late tradition, established in the 1st cent. BC [1. 270–273].

→ Magic, Magi; → Procession; → Religion

1 F. BÖMER, Der sogenannte lapis manalis, in: ARW 33, 1936, 270–281;   2 W. FIEDLER, Antiker Wetterzauber (Würzburger Stud. zur Altertumswiss. 1), 1931;   3 W. KROLL, s.v. manalis lapis, RE 27, 969–971;   4 LATTE ;   5 G. WISSOWA, s.v. manalis lapis, ROSCHER 2.2, 2308f.
AN.BE.

Manasse (Hebrew *Menašše*; Greek Μανασσῆ(ς)/ *Manassê(s)*).
[1] Israelite tribe in Middle Palestine, east of the Jordan (→ Judah and Israel).
[2] King of Judah. During his unusually long reign (*c.* 696–642 BC), Judah was restricted to Jerusalem and its environs after the Assyrian conquests of 701 BC (→ Judah and Israel), but progressively regenerated politically and economically [2. 169–181]. M. (in cuneiform script *Me-na-se-e/si-i* or *Mi-in-se-e*) as a loyal vassal of the Assyrians was obliged to provide them with regular tribute and military aid. According to an inscription of Asarhaddon (680–669 BC), M. supplied building material to → Nineveh [5. 397], and according to an inscription of Assurbanipal (668–627 BC), he took part in an Assyrian campaign against Egypt (ANET 294). The OT depiction is tendentious [1. 31–44]; it represents M. as a counterpart to the 'reformer' Josiah (2 Kgs 22f.), with hindsight makes him alone responsible for the fall of → Jerusalem in 597 BC (2 Kgs 21:10–15; 23:26f.; 24:3f., Jer 15:4), and in a kind of catalogue of vices – in part in adoption of older tradition – accuses him of perversions of the cult, magical/mantic practices and rule by terror (2 Kgs 21:1–18). This historical interpretation is taken up some centuries later in the text of 2 Chr 33:11–17, where the consequences of the 'sin of M.' (2 Kgs 24:3, cf. 17:21f.) and theological explanations for the long reign are recounted in the form of legend, with deportation (to Babylon!), conversion, return to Jerusalem and reform. The traditions are clearer in apocryphal texts, which present the martyrdom of the prophet Isaiah under M. (martyrdom of Isaiah 1:1; 6–13, cf. also Jos. Ant. Iud. 10,98) and a prayer for forgiveness by M. (OrMan 13) as a paraphrase of 2 Kgs 21:16 and 2 Chr 33:13; 18f.

E. BEN-ZVI, Prelude to a Reconstruction of the Historical Manassic Judah, in: Biblische Notizen 81, 1996, 31–44; I. FINKELSTEIN, The Archaeology of the Days of Manasseh, in: M. COOGAN et al. (ed.), Scripture and Other Artifacts. FS Ph.J. King, 1994, 169–187; A. SCHOORS, Die Königreiche Israel und Juda im 8. und 7. Jh.v.Chr., 1998; H. SPIECKERMANN, Juda unter Assur in der Sargonidenzeit, 1982; TUAT, vol. 1.   R.L.

[3] Brother of Jaddua the High Priest of Jerusalem, and, as the latter had no children, his presumptive successor. The fact that M. was married to Nikaso, the daughter of Sanballat, the governor installed in Samaria by Darius [3] III, led to his flight to → Samaria, where Sanballat promised him the construction of a temple to Yahweh on Mount Garizim in competition with Jerusalem (Jos. Ant. Iud. 11,302f.; 306ff.). The date of construction (during the 4th cent. BC) of this temple (destroyed in 128 BC by Iohannes → Hyrcanus [2]) is uncertain.

H. H. ROWLEY, Men of God, 1963, 246–276; B. PORTEN, s.v. History. Kingdoms of Juda and Israel, Encyclopaedia Judaica 8, 1971, 624.   J.RE. ER.K.

Manates Archaic people of Latium, possibly identical with the Sanates Tiburtes, who were neighbours of the Forcti Gabini, and who, according to Plin. HN 3,69, as one of the 30 *pagi* of the *populi Albenses*, gathered for sacrificial rites on Mons Albanus.

NISSEN 2, 555–557; M. PALLOTTINO, Le origini di Roma, in: ArchCl 12, 1960, 27; A. ALFÖLDI, Early Rome and the Latins, 1963, 13.   G.U.

Manaua (Μάναυα; *Mánaua*). Settlement in western Cilicia near the mouth of the Melas (→ Pamphylia), with a river port for Side as well [1. 17–20], the modern Manavgat. In Late Antiquity also the name of a mountainous region in Isauria (*klíma*; Georgius of Cyprus, 855). Diocese of *Pamphylia I* [2].

1 J. NOLLÉ, Side im Altertum 1, 1993;   2 J. DARROUZÈS, Notitiae episcopatuum Ecclesiae Constantinopolitanae, 1981.   F.H.

Manceps The term *manceps* (formed from *manus* and *capere*) denotes a person who lays his hand on something in order to acquire it, as well as one who takes something on by means of a → lease or acquires something by public auction.

The term could also apply to entrepreneurs who undertook private contracts. Thus Suetonius refers to the great grandfather of Vespasian, the father of T. Flavius Petro, as *manceps operarum*, recruiting entire teams of agricultural workers in Umbria and hiring them out to the great estates in the Sabine territories (Suet. Vesp. 1,4; cf. Plaut. Curc. 515; Plin. Ep. 2,14,4;

→ Paid labour). The term also refers to the buyers of property sold for instance by the republic in the course of the → proscriptions (Cic. Rosc. Am. 21).

In most cases, however, *mancipes* were people who entered into contracts with the city or the state to undertake public tasks, the *publica* (tax collection, especially in the province of Asia; supplies to the army; public works; the management of public enterprises such as mines and salinas). By signing the contract, the *manceps* acquired the title of *redemptor*, *emptor* or *conductor*, depending on the context: *Manceps dicitur qui quid a populo emit conducitve, quia manu sublata significat se auctorem emptionis esse* (Fest. 137). There might be one or several contractors; in the awarding of a contract for the upkeep of the temple of Castor in 75 BC a certain P. Iunius was the sole *manceps* (Cic. Verr. 2,1,141).

The *manceps* or *mancipes* had to provide guarantors (*praedes*). The *lex parieti faciendo* from Puteoli (105 BC), an index of works put out to tender by the city, ends with a list of five names; the first is that of the contractor, C. Blossius (*qui redemerit*); the other four names are those of the guarantors (*praedes*) named by the *manceps*: Q. Fuficius, Cn. Tetteius, C. Granius, Ti. Crassicius (CIL X 1781 = ILS 5317).

Some *publica* were the subject of several contracts to individual *mancipes*, who each undertook a particular part of the total project. An inscription of the 1st cent. BC, for example, tells us that repairs to the *via Caecilia* were carried out by four *mancipes* who had concluded separate contracts. Each *manceps* was responsible for a length of 20,000 paces, and received the sum of 150,000 sesterces for his services (CIL I² 808 = ILS 5799 = ILLRP 465). In other cases the *mancipes* were entrusted with the entire project in common; they formed themselves by contract into a *societas* (leaseholder company). The *manceps* or *mancipes* might also have other partners (*socii*), who need not necessarily themselves be contractors.

However, the word *manceps* is not used in association with the great companies of *publicani* of the late Republic. Thus Cicero speaks of *auctores*, not *mancipes*; he refers to the father of Cn. Plancius as *maximarum societatum auctor* (Cic. Planc. 32). It cannot be ascertained whether the *auctores* had a different function from the *mancipes*, or whether it is merely the case of a distinct term for those who signed the contract. Also, *manceps* is by no means identical with the word *publicanus* (→ *publicani*); it is rather the case that the term was reserved for the actual contractors. During the Principate, *mancipes* were responsible for the upkeep of individual roads (Tac. Ann. 3,31,5; CIL VI 8468 = ILS 1471: *manceps viae Appiae*); an inscription attests a *manceps aedis per annos XIII* for Praeneste (CIL XIV 2864 = ILS 3688a).

In late antiquity, *mancipes* supervised various public facilities; they managed the *stationes* of the → *cursus publicus* (Cod. Theod. 8,5,36: duty of presence; period of service), were responsible for supplying the baths of the city of Rome with wood (Cod. Theod. 14,5,1; cf.

11,20,3), and had oversight of bread supplies for Rome (Socr. 5,18; Cod. Theod. 14,3,18).

→ Logistics; → Leasehold; → Taxes

1 C. NICOLET, Deux remarques sur l'organisation des sociétés de publicains à la fin de la république romaine, in: H. VAN EFFENTERRE, (ed.), Points de vue sur la fiscalité antique, 1979, 69–95; 2 Id., 'Frumentum mancipale', en Sicilie et ailleurs, in: A. GIOVANNINI, (ed.), Nourrir la plèbe, 1991, 119–141. J.A

Manching
A. GENERAL B. EXPLORATION C. HISTORY
D. BUILDINGS E. FINDS

A. GENERAL
Large Celtic settlement (→ Oppidum) south of Ingolstadt (Upper Bavaria) in a strategically favourable position on a dry gravel ridge between the Danube and areas of wetland (Donaumoos) extending from west to east, near a river crossing and formerly accessed by branches of the Danube (harbour?). The level settlement area is almost circular, with a diameter of 2.5 km, comprising 380 ha.; it is traversed by an ancient arterial road, here following the south bank of the Danube (→ Ister [2]), (cf. location plan).

B. EXPLORATION
The outer wall of M. has been known since the Middle Ages as the *Pfahl* ('the stake'). C. 1900 an Early to Middle La Tène period burial ground (*Steinbichel*) was discovered in the area of the village (c. 4th/3rd cents. BC). First excavations were carried out prior to the 2nd World War, and then on a large scale since the 1950s. In 1937 a second burial ground was discovered east of M. (*Hundsrucken*). Up to the present, some 13.5 ha. (3.5% of the total area) have been investigated archaeologically; this makes M. one of the most thoroughly investigated Celtic *oppida*. M. corresponds in many respects to → Caesar's information with regard to the Gaulish *oppida*, and is also described as the capital of the → Vindelici; however, there are no traditions on the location.

C. HISTORY
The Celtic settlement lasted some 200 years; it began in the Middle → La Tène period (mid 3rd cent. BC) on the ancient junction, at first as a large, unfortified settlement with indications of large-scale farmsteads and commercial facilities; the more recent burials in both necropoleis also belong to this settlement.

M. was largely extended, remodelled and first fortified at the transition to the Late La Tène period (c 130/120 BC), after what seems to have been phases of unrest and destruction. An outer wall of approx 7.2 km was built, at first using the *murus gallicus* technique, with four gates (east and south gate extant) orientated on the arterial roads. As early as around the end of the 2nd cent. BC the wall was entirely renewed using the native *Pfostenschlitz* (Preist construction) technique

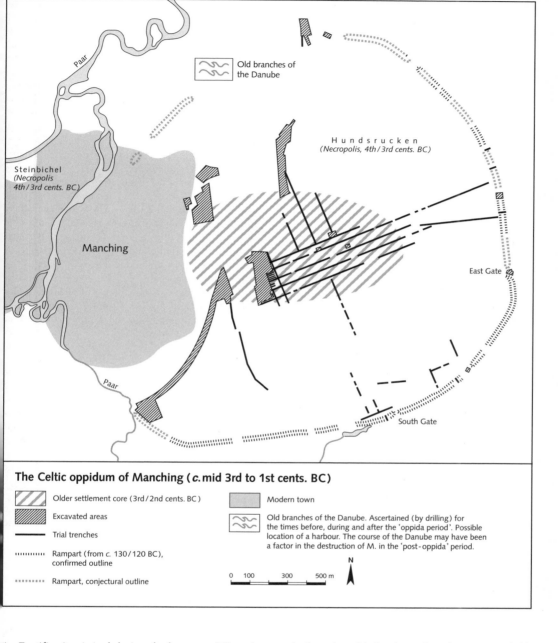

The Celtic oppidum of Manching (*c.* mid 3rd to 1st cents. BC)

Older settlement core (3rd/2nd cents. BC)	Modern town
Excavated areas	Old branches of the Danube. Ascertained (by drilling) for the times before, during and after the 'oppida period'. Possible location of a harbour. The course of the Danube may have been a factor in the destruction of M. in the 'post-oppida' period.
Trial trenches	
Rampart (from *c.* 130/120 BC), confirmed outline	
Rampart, conjectural outline	0 100 300 500 m N

(→ Fortifications), and during the last cent. BC again replaced using the same technique. The three phases of fortification are also evident at the east gate, which has been completely excavated. Enormous achievements with regard to the transportation of raw materials and the organization can be calculated for the fortification only.

D. BUILDINGS

Constuction is on a large scale, and uniformly orientated on the east-west arterial road, in part with large plots segregated by sideways and fences. On these plots are built various kinds of post-based structures (half-timbered), variously arranged according to function. The settlement shows several areas of utilization; in part these include agricultural farmsteads, but also clusters of storehouses (on the old arm of the Danube), whitesmiths' and blacksmiths' forges, potteries, glassworks, minting works, etc. Agriculture and animal husbandry were also at least partly carried out in the settlement area. Iron smelting itself is presumed to have taken place outside the *oppidum* in the *Feilenmoos* to the south (outside the area of the plan shown). Smaller, clearly segregated 'temple-like' structures are distributed over the settlement as cult sites; in addition, the → viereckschanze (rectangular ditched enclosure) c. 2 km south of M. can be considered as an associated cult site.

E. FINDS

The rich finds provide detailed insights into late Celtic everyday life in a large settlement organized on a quasi-urban basis, with a population of probably several thousand. The food supply (meat, grain, etc.), household equipment of ceramics and utensils, the raw materials and tools for crafts, a monetary economy and other areas of life can be reconstructed by interdisciplinary investigation. Extensive trade relations to the Germanic area but especially to the Mediterranean, are attested by Roman → amphorae, Campanian pottery Italian glassware, etc.

So far, no graves of the numerous population are known – as is the case for other *oppida*. In the course of renewed unrest (final destruction of the east gate by fire) M. came to an end around the middle of the last cent. BC: thus definitely prior to the Roman conquest of the region in 15 BC. It was only after a lengthy interruption of settlement that the location was used again as the Roman road station → Vallatum (!) in the 1st–3rd cents. AD.

→ Celtic archaeology; → Coinage, standards of; → Glass; → Pottery, production of

> R. GEBHARD, Ergebnisse der Ausgrabungen in M., in: H. DANNHEIMER, R. GEBHARD (ed.), Das keltische Jahrtausend, 1993, 113–119; W. KRÄMER, Zwanzig Jahre Ausgrabungen in M., 1955 bis 1974, in: Ausgrabungen in Deutschland, vol. 1, 1975, 287–297; Id., F. MAIER (ed.), Die Ausgrabungen in M., vol. 1–15, 1970–1992; S. SIEVERS, Vorberatung über die Ausgrabungen 1996–1997 im Oppidum von M., in: Germania 76, 1998, 619–672.   V.P.

Mancinus Cognomen in the family of the Hostilii (Hostilius [7–9]).   K.-L.E.

Mancipatio first occurs in Pliny (HN 9,35,117 *mancupatio*) in place of → *mancipium* (*mancupium*), to describe an ancient Roman civil law action establishing power over persons (→ *mancipium*) or objects (→ *dominium*).

The *mancipatio* procedure for the 2nd cent. AD is depicted as follows (Gai. Inst. 1,119): in the presence of five witnesses and a bearer of the scales (*libripens*), all of them Roman citizens of full age (→ *quirites*), the person receiving the object declares as follows: a) that he is the owner under Quiritary law, and: b) that he has purchased the object with this copper and these copper scales; whereupon he strikes a copper coin against the scales and gives it to the person from whom he is receiving the *mancipium*, as if it were the purchase price. *Mancipatio nummo uno* (for one coin), as depicted here, is *mancipatio* in a developed form; from the perspective of the 2nd cent. AD it appears as *imaginaria quaedam venditio* (symbolic sale). It concerns slaves,

freedmen (→ *emancipatio*), animals and Italic land (Gai. Inst. 1,120). *Mancipatio* leads to (civil) rightful ownership on the part of the buyer. However, if the seller did not own the object in the first place, he (and not the buyer) is liable to any claims. Also, he must pay back the amount of double the purchase price.

The active rol of the acquirer and the more passive role of the seller deserve attention. Equally mysterious is the formula of the *mancipatio*, with the acquirer's declaration of ownership and 'order of purchase'. In modern literature, the *mancipatio* is often held to be a unilateral act of seizure on the part of the acquirer, with the seller's tacit acquiescence. However, rather than being an expression of the justification of ownership, the form of the *mancipatio* states that it already exists. The ritual of *mancipatio* as it were 'outwits' the law, which holds that the objects in question – persons belonging to the *familia* and working animals belonging to the agricultural economy (Italic land does not enter into consideration until later) – are inalienable; *mancipatio* is 'alienation of the inalienable' [3]. The acquirer's declaration of ownership conceals the act of alienation. His 'order of purchase' justifies the seller's receipt of the purchase price presupposing the acquirer's ownership. Variations of the *mancipatio* formula are found in the → *coemptio* (transfer of the power of *manus*, Gai. Inst. 1,113), and further in the *testamentum per aes et libram* (Gai. Inst. 2,104, → Testament). The *mancipatio* may embrace additions (*lex in mancipio dicta*).

→ *Emancipatio* and → *adoptio* later arose as new compound transactions using *mancipatio*. *Mancipatio* disappears from practical legal affairs in the course of the 2nd/3rd cents. AD. Justinian expunged it from the classical sources, as he did the → *in iure cessio*.

→ Lex, leges II

> 1 KASER, RPR I 43–48, 131–134, 403f., 413–415, 438f.; RPR II 274f.; 2 WIEACKER, RRG 1, 332–340; 3 J. G. WOLF, Funktion und Struktur der ancipatio., in: M. HUMBERT (ed.), Mél. A. Magdelain, 1998, 501–524.   D.SCH.

Mancipium (originally *mancupium*) initially denotes the Roman legal transaction later called → *mancipatio*. *Mancipium* is one of those 'ancient Roman legal terms of transparent clarity' [2]; it appears to denote an act of taking something by hand. It is thus interpreted in ancient etymology (Varro, Ling. 6,85; Gai. Inst. 1,121). But another interpretation is more probable: just as *aucupium* (bird-trapping) derives from *auceps*, so *mancupium* derives from *manceps*; *auceps* denotes the bird-trapper (*avem capiens*), *manceps* one who grasps domestic power (*manum capiens*) rather than one who grasps with the hand (*manu capiens*). *Mancipium* is accordingly that legal transaction by which domestic power (→ *manus*) is obtained; power over the wife *in manu mancipioque* Gell. NA 4,3,3; 18,6,9. The dependent child, who stands *in potestate* of the father (→ *patria potestas*), but who has been mancipated to somebody, for instance because of caused damage, is *in* *mancipium* and *servorum loco* (on the position of a slave, Gai. Inst. 1,123; 4,79). The *praetor* compels release when the child has repaid his debt (Papinianus, Coll. 2,3,1). *Manus, mancipium* and *potestas* are various forms of the power of the → *pater familias* (Gai. Inst. 1,49). Slaves are termed *mancipium* because they are frequently acquired by *mancipatio*; Florentinus Dig. 1,5,4,3 gives another interpretation: *mancipia vero dicta, quod ab hostibus manu capiuntur* ('they are termed *mancipium* because they have been captured with the hand from enemies'). *Mancipium* disappears in the West after the 3rd cent. AD, and is expunged from the sources by Justinian.

1 KASER, RPR I 43f., 56f., 69.; RPR II 131, 142; 2 MOMMSEN, Schriften, vol. 3, 145–149; 3 J. G. WOLF, Funktion und Struktur der Mancipatio, in: M. HUMBERT (ed.), Mél. A. Magdelain, 1998, 501–524.   D.SCH.

Mandaeans ('those who know', from the Aramaic *manda*, 'knowledge, gnosis'). Term describing an ancient Middle Eastern religious community, still extant today, which had already settled in southern Iraq (Mesene) and south-western Iran (Ḥuzistān) in pre-Islamic times; today as a consequence of the Gulf Wars (1980/1986, 1990/1991) they also live in the USA, Australia and Europe. In Arabic they are known as 'Ṣābians' (*ṣābiʿūn*, 'baptist') or *Muġtasila* ('who wash themselves'), in older European literature as 'Disciples of John the Baptist' or 'John's Christians'. The old names the community used to refer to itself are: 'Naṣoraeans' ('observers' of rites and teachings), 'the chosen of justice' or 'tribe of life'. 'Mandaeans' refers to the lay members as opposed to the priests (*tarmidi*, 'disciples, pupils').

Their transmitted literature in its own Eastern Aramaic dialect and distinctive script, includes various works and genres: the extensive collection of theological/mythological and poetic texts called the 'Treasure' (*ginza*) or 'Great Book' (*sidra rba*); the complementary 'Teachings of the Kings (Angels)' (*drašia dmalkia*) or 'Teachings of John (the Baptist)' (*dYahya*); the book of rituals for baptism and the mass of souls (*qolasta*); the '1012 questions' (*alf trisar šuialia*) for the instruction of priests, as well as numerous scrolls, often illustrated and some of them still unedited. In addition, there are magical texts on clay vessels, lead tablets or paper, the oldest of which can be dated to the 4th–7th cents. AD. The core literature is undoubtedly pre-Islamic and presumably goes back to the 1st–2nd cents. AD; ideologically it belongs to the context of oriental → Gnosticism. The cult practice (repeated baptisms and ablutions) can be anchored in the baptist milieu of Early Jewish groups. During the 3rd cent. AD at the latest, the Mandaeans. gradually migrated out of the Syrian-Palestinian Jordan region via → Harran to Mesopotamia.

Although the central teachings presuppose a strict dualism between light and darkness, the good god of 'life' (*haiji*), and the 'spirit' (*ruha*) and lord of darkness,

earth (*tibil*) and humanity (*adam*) were created by a fallen demiurge, and the liberation of the 'soul' (*nišimta*) is the only object of redemption, the Mandaeans. have not developed an ascetic lifestyle; thus, they have maintained their independent status alongside → Judaism, → Christianity and → Islam to the present day. 40,000 to 50,000 adherents are estimated to live worldwide.

W. FOERSTER (ed.), Die Gnosis. 2: Koptische und mandäische Quellen (introduction and translation by M. Krause and K. Rudolph), ²1995; E. S. DROWER, The Mandaeans of Iraq and Iran, 1937, ²1962; E. LUPIERI, I Mandei. Gli ultimi gnostici, 1993; K. RUDOLPH, Die Mandäer, 2 vols., 1960/1; Id., Theogonie, Kosmogonie und Anthropogonie in den mandäischen Schriften, 1965; Id., Mandaeism (Iconography of Religions 21), 1978; Id., Gnosis und spätantike Religionsgeschichte, 1996, 301–626; S. A. PALLIS, Mandaean Bibliography 1560–1930, 1933 (repr. 1974); G. WIDENGREN (ed.), Der Mandäismus, 1982.   KU.R.

Mandane (Μανδάνη; *Mandánē*).
[1] According to Hdt. 1,107, Xen. Cyr. 1,2,1 and Iust. 1,4,4, daughter of the Medean king → Astyages, wife of the Persian Cambyses [1] and mother of Cyrus [2]. It seems that the dynastic link thus transmitted was meant to lend retrospective legitimation to the claims of Cyrus to the Medean (and, if M.'s mother was the Lydian princess Aryenis (Hdt. 1,74), also the Lydian) throne.

[2] According to the court story surviving in Diod. Sic. 11,57,1–5, the daughter of Darius [1] I and sister of Xerxes I.

BRIANT, 34f., 907, 929.   J.W.

[3] Town on the coast of Cilicia Tracheia (Stadiasmus Maris Magni 192–194; → Cilices, Cilicia), 18 km west of Celenderis, modern Akyaka.

HILD/HELLENKEMPER, 340f.   F.H.

Mandatum
A. CONCEPT   B. RIGHTS AND DUTIES   C. SPECIAL FORMS

A. CONCEPT
In Roman law, the *mandatum* is a contract to perform a task. The contractor (the mandatary) undertakes to the client (the mandator) to perform a service for the latter free of charge (Dig. 17,1; Cod. Iust. 4,35; Gai. Inst. 3,155–162; Inst. Iust. 3,26); if, on the other hand, a wage (*merces*) is agreed for the service, then an ordinary contract for a task or service (→ *locatio conductio operis* or *operarum*) arises.

The *mandatum* is a consensual contract (→ *consensus*), and thus arises by means of an informal agreement between the parties. The task to be accomplished may be legal (e.g. the assumption of a surety for the mandator) or practical (e.g. the care of a garden) in nature, but must not offend against accepted moral standards and must (at least in part) be in the interest of the mandator. A 'task' that is in the exclusive interest of the contractor (the so-called *mandatum tua gratia*, Gai. Inst. 3,156; Dig. 17,1,2,6), is held to be merely a non-binding suggestion (*consilium*).

As regards motivation for carrying out the unpaid *mandatum*, the Roman sources mention → *amicitia* ('friendship'; Dig. 17,1,1,4); the uncharged assumption of tasks customary amongst the Roman elite, such as services in the context of the → *artes liberales* (e.g. instruction in rhetoric), are conceived of as *mandatum* [5. 13–37]; acceptance of a gift offered in consideration (*salarium*, *honorarium*) does not prevent such an agreement from being seen as a *mandatum*.

During the Principate, in particular circumstances the emperor provides for the possibility of a legal claim for promised *salaria* by way of the procedure of *cognitio* (→ *cognitio*, cf. Cod. Iust. 4,35,1) [5. 319–338].

B. RIGHTS AND DUTIES

Actions arising from *mandatum* tend to be based on the consideration of good faith (*bonae fidei iudicia*; → *fides*). By an *actio mandati directa* the mandator requires execution of the *mandatum* as per contract, and provision of the service in question. The mandatary is in any case liable for → *dolus* (wicked intent), and probably also for the similar liability of gross negligence; modern scholarship overwhelmingly rejects a sweeping liability of → *culpa* for any negligence in the classical period, owing to the character of *mandatum* as an unpaid transaction based on friendship [2. 339]. The legal consequences of exceeding the agreed limits of the *mandatum* were controversial (Gai. Inst. 3,161; Dig. 17,1,4). Condemnation arising from the *actio mandati directa* leads to → *infamia* (Gai. Inst. 4,182). If the mandatary incurs expenses or damages arising specifically in the course of proper execution of the *mandatum*, he may demand restitution from the mandator by an *actio mandati contraria*.

The *mandatum* implies no power of representation with regard to third parties, acting merely as a medium of indirect representation; the mandatary is obliged to transfer the effects of any transaction concluded between himself and the third party to the mandator by a further legal act.

The *mandatum* ceases by termination or by the death of one of the parties to the agreement. Termination (*revocatio*, → *renuntiatio*) is possible so long as *res integra* pertains, i.e. execution of the *mandatum* has not yet begun or its cessation does not lead to a breach of trust between the parties. Untimely termination incurs liability for damages. *Mandatum morte solvitur* ('*mandatum* is dissolved by death'): owing to the highly personal character of the Roman *mandatum*, there is no question of transference of rights and obligations to descendants; if execution of the *mandatum* had already begun, the heir of the mandator has to reimburse expenses incurred up to the time of death, just as the mandatary has to produce the proceeds arising from the *mandatum* up to that moment.

Variations that had arisen since the 3rd cent. (lapse of requirement that there should be no charge, thus stricter binding of the parties as regards termination of the *mandatum* and increased liability of the mandatary) are largely removed by Justinian (Inst. Iust. 3,26,13). The distinction, already vague in classical terminology, as against externally authorized → *iussum* – especially as regards contracts with legal content, which were often delivered in parallel – appears to have become entirely blurred in late antiquity.

C. SPECIAL FORMS

The credit mandate (termed in post-antiquity *mandatumqualificatum*) is the contract to grant a sum in credit to a third person in the name and account of the mandatary; the mandatary undertakes only to make good any deficiency in the course of repayment, giving rise to a relationship similar to a surety. The effect of a transfer (→ *cessio*) is obtained by means of a *mandatum ad agendum in rem suam* (a legal mandate in one's own cause). The *mandata principis*, internal directives to officials, represent a form of imperial → *constitutiones*. → Fides; → Revocare

1 HONSELL/MAYER-MALY/SELB, 335ff. 2 KASER, RPR I, 577ff.; II, 415ff. 3 H. T. KLAMI, Teneor mandati, 1976 4 V. MAROTTA, Mandata principum, 1991 5 D. NÖRR, S. NISHIMURA (ed.), M. und Verwandtes, 1993 6 A. WATSON, Contract of Mandate in Roman Law, 1961 7 R. ZIMMERMANN, The Law of Obligations, 1990, 413ff.
V.T.H.

Mandela *Pagus* ('district') in the land of the Sabini (Hor. Epist. 1,18,105) at the confluence of Digentia and Anio, later Massa Mandelana (CIL XIV 3482), modern Mandela near Vicovaro. Near M. Chalcolithic tomb chambers and a Roman *villa*.

G. LUGLI, La villa sabina di Orazio, in: Monumenti antichi, pubblicati dall' Accademia dei Lincei 31, 1926, 457–598; C. F. GIULIANI, in: Tibur 2, 1966, 67–77. G.U.

Mandonius Iberian. Like his brother → Indibilis, together with whom he is mostly mentioned, he was a prince of the → Ilergetes; in the 2nd → Punic War he changed sides several times as an ally initially of the Carthaginians and then of the Romans: he joined P. → Cornelius [I 71] Scipio in 208 BC, because of the good treatment the latter had given to M.'s wife and relatives who had been taken hostage (Pol. 10,18,7–15; 35,6–8; Liv. 26,49,11–16; 27,17,3). Later he was received back into the alliance with Rome, despite his defecion in 206 (Liv. 28,31,3–7; 34,3–11); he had to pay for breaking it in 205 with his execution, after the victory of L. → Cornelius [I 36] Lentulus and L. → Manlius Acidinus over the rebellious Ausetanians and Sedetanians (Liv. 29,3,1–5). L.-M.G.

Mandrobulus (Μανδρόβουλος; *Mandróboulos*). The theophoric name is derived from 'Mandrus', a – deduced – god of Asia Minor. A drama by → Cleophon and a dialogue by → Speusippus are named after M. The proverb ἐπὶ τὰ Μανδροβούλου χωρεῖ τὸ πρᾶγμα was already no longer understood in antiquity; the ancient → Paroimiographoi offered conjectures with regard to its explanation – as in Suda ε 2659, 2716 – presuming that it related to turns for the worse.

W. KROLL, s.v. Mandroboulos, RE 14, 1039f.　　H.A.G.

Mandrocleidas (Μανδροκλείδας; *Mandrokleídas*).
[1] Spartiate (Μανδρικλείδας/*Mandrikleídas* in good MSS). Plutarch (Plut. Pyrrhus 26,24) passes down a memorable statement by M. who is said to have attempted in 272 BC to convince → Pyrrhus of the Spartan will to resist him so as to prevent further plundering raids in Laconia by his troops [1. 128f.].
[2] Spartiate (probably not identical to M. [1]), talented follower of → Agis [4] IV. whose reform plans he energetically supported before the Spartan people's assembly in 243/242 BC. He was indicted by the new ephores of the year of office 242/241 (Plut. Agis 6; 9; 12). His fate after the death of Agis IV is unknown.

1 P. GAROUFALIAS, Pyrrhus, King of Epirus, 1979.
　　　　　　　　　　　　　　　　　　K.-W.W.

Mandrocles Architect of Samos. For a considerable fee he built the pontoon bridge over the Bosporus (Hdt. 4,87,1ff.) for → Darius [1] I in 513/2 BC in the context of the campaign against the Scythians. M. attained fame through a votive offering in the Heraeum of → Samos: a panel painting described in detail by Herodotus (4,88,1–89,2), which depicted the (pontoon) bridge and praised the architect in an epigram.

H. SVENSON-EVERS, Die griechische Architekten archaischer und klassischer Zeit, 1996, 59–66 (with additional literature).　　C.HÖ.

Mandubii Gaulish people who are only mentioned in Caes. B Gall. 7,68,1 and Str. 4,2,3. Capital → Alesia (*oppidum Mandubiorum*). Their territory is probably identical to the modern region of Auxois (*pagus Alisiensis* in the Middle Ages). In Roman times the M. appear to have merged with the → Haedui people.

P.-M. DUVAL, Chronique gallo-romaine, in: REA 61, 1959, 368–370.　　Y.L.

Mandubracius King of the → Trinobantes in southeastern Britannia, who on the occasion of the murder of his father by → Cassivellaunus had fled to Caesar on the mainland. When Caesar invaded Britannia for the second time in 54 BC, M. was able to return to his tribe by providing hostages and grain (Caes. B Gall. 5,20; 22,5; Oros. 6,9,8).

EVANS, 100ff.　　W.SP.

Manducus Roman mask figure with an etymologically transparent name (derived from the verb *mandere/manducare*, meaning 'chewer', 'eater'); its origin, however, is uncertain. According to Paul. Fest. 115 M. was brought along in the celebratory procession at the circus games (*pompa circensis*; cf. [1]) as a tooth-gnashing monster to elicit laughter and fright. If we follow Varro (Ling. 7,95), this M. seems to have found his way into the improvisational → Atellana fabula, where he was identified with the character of → Dossennus [1] (whose name has been reconstructed through conjecture). If true, the originally frightening figure would have turned into a gluttonous clown (cf. Hor. Epist. 2,1,173). In the titles and fragments of the literary *Atellana*, however, M. does not appear.
→ Masks

1 LATTE, 248–251.

J.-G. PRÉVAUX, Manducus, in: M. RENARD (ed.), FS A. Grenier, 1962, 1282–1292 (= Coll. Latomus 58 III); J. B. LOWE, Plautus' Parasites and the Atellana, in: G. VOGT-SPIRA (ed.), Studien zur vorliterarischen Periode im frühen Rom, 1989, 161–169.　　H.BL.

Mandulis Local deity of Kalabsha (Talmis), attested in several temples at → Dodekaschoinos and on Philae. Clearly of non-Egyptian origin, presumably a god of the Blemmyes (→ Blem(m)yes). The name, in Egyptian rendering, *mrwl*, *mnrwl*, *mntwl*, in Greek M., might be → Meroitic and has been attested from the Ptolemaic period. The important temple at Kalabsha was built under Augustus for the → Sun God and Lord of the Heavens. M. was represented in human form as an adult or a child, but also as a falcon with a human head (*Ba*). The Greeks identified him with → Apollo, who comes from Olympus to Nubia at the right hand of → Isis. According to Greek inscriptions in Kalabsha, M. and an otherwise unknown Breith form a divine pair of brothers (sun-moon).

C. DESROCHES-NOBLECOURT, Les zélateurs de Mandoulis et les maîtres de Ballana et de Qustul, in: P. POSENER-KRIÉGER (ed.), Mélanges G.E. Mokhtar, 1985, 199–218; E. KORMYSHEVA, Götterglaube in Meroe, in: Meroitica 18 (in print).　　A.I.O.

Manduria City of the Messapii and the Sallentini south-east of → Taras (Tab. Peut. 7,1; Steph. Byz. s.v. Μανδύριον; *Manduris*, Geogr. Rav. 4,31; 5,1; *Amandrinum*, Guido 72), with source (Plin. HN 2,226; [2; 5]). After siding with Carthage in 209 BC, it was reconquered by the Romans (Liv. 27,15,4: 3,000 prisoners and huge booty). The Spartan king → Archidamus [2] fell at M. in 338 BC (Plut. Agis 3,2); modern Manduria. Finds of Messapian inscriptions [3; 5]; important archaeological remains: triple ring of walls (5th, 4th and 3rd cents. BC), large necropolis (mostly 4th–3rd cents. BC) [1; 4].

1 A. ALESSIO, Manduria, in: F. D'ANDRIA (ed.), Archeologia dei Messapi, 1990, 307-321; 2 BTCGI 9, 1991, 327-330; 3 C. SANTORO, Manduria nell'ambito della civiltà messapica, in: Studi Linguistici Salentini 20, 1993, 157-186; 4 A. ALESSIO (ed.), Oltre le mura, 1997; 5 J.-L. LAMBOLEY, Recherches sur les Messapiens, 1996, 141-151.   M.L.

Maneros (Μανερῶς; *Manerôs* Hdt. 2,79; Μανέρως; *Manérōs* Plut. Is. 17,367 etc.). According to Hdt. l.c. M. is the only son of the first king of Egypt who, after his early death, is honoured by a dirge 'M.', which is said to correspond to the Greek → Linus song. M. means either Egyptian *mniw-rȝ* 'gooseherd' (CERNY) or *r jmntt r jmntt* 'westward! westward!' (LLOYD), a cry heard at funerals. It is not clear which Egyptian name or which sequence of Egyptian words was garbled to form Greek M. [1. 338].

1 A. B. LLOYD, Herodotus, Book 2. Commentary 1-98, 1976.   L.K.

Manes, Di. Roman spirits of the dead, particularly the *animae* ('souls') of deceased individuals. They are part of the Underworld and also referred to as *di* → *inferi* (e.g. CIL X 2936; VI 13388) and contrasted with the gods above ground (*di superi*); in metonymy, they may stand for the Underworld itself. Literature of antiquity explains *di manes* euphemistically as 'the good' (Paul Fest. 132 l.; Serv. Aen. 1,143) and links them with Lat. *mane*, 'the morning', with → *mania* or with → Mater Matuta (Paul Fest. 109 l.). The salutation frequently found on gravestones and in memorial inscriptions, *dis manibus* in the dative plural followed by the name of a person in the genitive singular, refers to the deceased individual to whom the monument is dedicated. The term *manes* is always used in the plural, even when it refers to a single person; this shows that *di manes* is considered to be a collective noun.

With the rituals of the funeral procession (*funus*) and burial, the deceased was received among the *di manes* [1. 392-395]. Accordingly, the unburied dead (*insepulti*) did not belong this group [2. 137]. Varro reports the idea that the deceased was regarded as a god by his descendants (Antiquitates rerum divinarum fr. 211 CARDAUNS in Plut. Quaest. Rom. 14; Plin. HN 7,56). However, this idea was not expressed in the cult [3. 193-198]. Public and private commemorations were held for the *di manes* (→ Parentalia). They were offered animal sacrifices but also simple sacrificial gifts ([1. 193ff.]; Ov. Fast. 2,535).

There is no clear difference between the *di manes* and the *di parentes* [4. 17-26]; the latter term emphasizes the connection to the descendants. The *manes* were identified with other spirits who were considered to be the souls of the deceased. Apuleius (De deo Socratis 15,152) describes all spirits as → lemures: of these, the *di manes* were those who had become gods because they had led a good life. The → genius, the embodiment

of the active force of the living, was also associated with the *di manes* (Serv. Aen. 6,743). It was commonly believed that the *manes* appeared to the living as ghosts (Sen. Herc. f. 187, 648, 765; Herc. O. 1062, 1525) or in dreams (Tib. 2,6,37) and frightened them.

→ Afterlife, concepts of; → Burial; → Dead, cult of the; → Deification; → Lemures, Lemuria

1 F. CUMONT, Lux perpetua, 1949; 2 M. DUCOS, Le tombeau, locus religiosus, in: F. HINARD (ed.), La mort au quotidien, 1995, 135-144; 3 J. SCHEID, Die Parentalien für die verstorbenen Caesaren als Modell für den römischen Totenkult, in: Klio 75, 1993, 188-201; 4 F. BÖMER, Ahnenkult und Ahnenglaube im alten Rom, 1943.

H. LAVAGNE, Le tombeau, mémoire du mort, in: F. HINARD (ed.), La mort, les morts et l'au-delà dans le monde romain, 1987, 159-165; C. PASCAL, Le credenze dell'oltretomba nelle opere letterarie dell'antichità, 1912.
                                          FR.P.

Manetho

[1] According to uncertain sources, M. (see [1]) was a priest from Sebennytus, who lived under Ptolemy I and II and played a part in the introduction of the cult of Sarapis (→ Sarapis) [2]. As a Hellenized Egyptian, he wrote in Greek about Egyptian topics. A number of isolated quotations have survived from a maximum of eight works, among them a work regarding the preparation of *kyphi* (incense), further a *hierá bíblos* about Egyptian religion, as well as a book about rituals. The question of the works' authenticity remains unsettled; demonstrably pseudo-epigraphic are an astrological didactic poem and the list of kings (→ Kings' lists) from the Book of Sothis [8]. Today, M.'s history of Egypt (*Aigyptiaká*) is considered his most important work, yet it attracted no interest from the Greek and Romans. Only the Jewish historian Josephus [4] and Christian chronographs used M.'s *Aigyptiaká* for the sake of biblical apologetic and chronology and thus documented it in excerpts. The original work has been lost.

The *Eklogé Chronographías* of → Syncellus Georgius (late 8th cent. AD) contain excerpts from the complete work *Aigyptiaká* (FGrH 609; English translation [8]), in the form of a list of kings with names of rulers and the duration of reigns. The lists are distributed in three bks.: 1) dynasties of gods until the 11th dynasty (until 1992 BC); 2) 12th to 18th dynasties (1991-1305); 3) 19th to 30th dynasties (1305-342); the 31st (Persian) dynasty (342-332) is considered a non-Manethonian addendum. Syncellus drew upon excerpts from the Christian chronographs → Sextus Iulius Africanus and → Eusebius [7], who changed and glossed the text. These excerpts, the original versions of which have largely been lost, were probably in turn based on an excerpt (epitome) from the *Aigyptiaká* penned by an unknown author, who confined himself to the list of kings [1].

Remains of a historical narrative next to the Kings' list have presumably survived in preserved excerpts of Flavius Josephus' *Contra Apionem* (1,26-33), which only refer to the 15th to 19th dynasties (1650–1197). These fabulous, deliberately biased narratives report with anti-Semitic tendencies on the alliance between the Asian → Hyksos and Egyptian lepers, led by a priest named Osarseph who is identified with the biblical Moses. Even if these accounts do not represent examples of original Manethonian historiography [6], they are chiefly pseudo-Manethonian fables from the 1st cent. AD [5]. This unsettled issue is linked to the question whether an annalistic representation of history was part of M.'s sources or whether he merely had of a list of kings at his disposal. While the tradition of the kings' list is well documented in Egypt [3], there are numerous indications of the existence of an annalistic tradition, but no remaining texts [4]. Therefore the question of the form and content of the Egyptian annals remains open. No definite statements can therefore be made regarding the nature of M.'s annalistic sources.

→ Historiography

1 J. VON BECKERATH, Untersuchungen zur politischen Geschichte der Zweiten Zwischenzeit in Ägypten., 1964, 11–13;   2 P. M. FRASER, Ptolemaic Alexandria 1, 1972, 505f.;   3 W. HELCK, Untersuchung zu M. und den ägyptischen Königslisten, 1956;   4 Id., s.v. Annalen, LÄ 1, 278–280;   5 R. KRAUSS, Das Ende der Amarnazeit, 1978, 204–231;   6 P. SCHÄFER, Die M.-Fragmente bei Josephus und die Anfänge des antiken 'Antisemitismus', in: G. MOST (ed.), Aporemata 1, 1997, 186–206;   7 H. J. THISSEN, Der Name M., in: Enchoria 15, 1987, 93–96;   8 W. G. WADDELL, M., 1956, XIVf.   R.K.

[2] Author of an astrological hexametric didactic poem Ἀποτελεσματικά (Apotelesmatiká) in 6 bks., born on 28 May AD 80 according to his own horoscope in the → sphragis (6,738–750). The work, addressed to a certain Ptolemaeus in Egypt, is composed of heterogeneous parts and the sequence of the bks., which may originate from different authors, is out of order. Part of the oldest core are the bks. 2 (fixed stars), 3 (planetary constellations), 6 (nativities), later added are bks. 4, 1 and 5 (ὅρια/hória, planetary constellations in irregular succession). Some pentameters appear at the end of bk. 6. M. draws from the → Anubion (cf. pentameter) and is quoted by → Hephaestion [3].

EDITIONS: A. KÖCHLY, Manetho, 1851 (ed. maior), fr. PSI no. 157; W. and H. G. GUNDEL, Astrologumena, 1966, 159–164; O. NEUGEBAUER, H. B. VAN HOESEN, Greek Horoscopes, 1959, 92 no. L 80.   W.H.

Mani, Manichaeans

A. SOURCES   B. BEGINNINGS (MANI) AND HISTORY   C. BASIC IDEAS AND AFTERLIFE

A. SOURCES

Until the beginning of the 20th cent., knowledge of Manichaeism was based primarily on anti-Manichaeist literature, be it the edicts of the Roman Imperial era (from → Diocletianus), the Christian (e.g. → Ephrem of Edessa, → Epiphanius [1] of Salamis, → Augustinus,

Theodor bar Konai) and Islamic heresiologists (Muḥammad ibn an-Nadīm, al-Bīrūnī, Šahrastānī) or the influential novel Acta Archelai by → Hegemonius (4th cent.). An early source is the polemic of the Neoplatonist Alexander of Lycopolis (pròs tàs Manichaîou dóxas, c. 300). Two Greek recantation formulas are from the 6th cent.

The excavations in Turkestan (Turfan, Bezeklik, Khocho) between 1902 and 1914 first brought to light original Manichaeist texts in Iranian dialects, Old Turkish (Uigur) and Chinese, some of which were illustrated (6th–12th cents.); they are still in the editing process. Since 1918 we have been in possession of a fragment of a Latin text of Manichaeist origin (so-called Tebessa Codex, 4th cent.). Around 1930/31, the Manichaica in Coptic (4th cent.), originating in the → Fayum oasis, was acquired. The only original Greek text found so far, the so-called Cologne Mani Codex, also comes from Egypt. Since then there have been other finds in the Egyptian Dakhleh oasis (ancient Kellis). These sources have provided a solid basis for research and fundamentally altered our conception of Manichaeism.

B. BEGINNINGS (MANI) AND HISTORY

Manichaeism is the only ancient religion that was consciously established by its founder M. as a supraregional religion. 'M. the Living' (Greek Manichaîos, Aramaic mani haija, 'vessel/spirit of life') was born on 14 April AD 216 near → Seleucia/Ctesiphon on the Tigris, grew up in a baptist community which he left in c. 240 in a dispute after experiencing his first revelation. He was soon able to establish a community and undertake missionary journeys to the East (Media, Kushan, India, Turan). In 242 he was active at the court of king Šābuhr I (→ Sapor), which proved useful to him later on. He sent some of his capable apostles to Egypt, Syria and Parthia, where communities were established. His success ended in Persia under king Bahrām I (273–276); he was imprisoned and died in prison on 14 (or 28) February 276, a fact which his followers interpreted as his 'crucifixion' (his body was probably displayed on a cross).

The subsequent persecution of the Manichaeist 'church' in Iran led to its migration to regions of Central Asia, but also to the West. From 763 to 840, Manichaeism was the state religion in the Uigur kingdom. In the 7th cent. Manichaeism also reached China and competed with Buddhism and Nestorian Christianity (→ Nestorius, Nestorianism). Persecution put an end to this in 843/44, although Manichaeism did not completely disappear from China until the 17th cent. (last remaining temple in Fukien). The Roman Empire as well witnessed a great deal of success in the beginning: Egypt, northern Africa, Italy, Spain. The imperial edicts (AD 297, 372, 379) and their implementation, particularly by the Christian emperors, supported by the polemics of the former Manichaeist → Augustinus (from 388), led to the end of Manichaeism in the West. However, its name remained present in the catalogues of heretics for its dualistic successors (Bogomils, Cathars or Albigensians), also in the Islamic East.

C. BASIC IDEAS AND AFTERLIFE

Manichaeism had a Gnostic foundation (→ Gnosticism), but it more strongly integrated Iranian-Zoroastrian (→ Zoroaster, Zoroastrianism) and Christian characteristics, and in the East also Buddhist. This manifests itself in its typical adjustment to the religious concepts of the respective missionary areas and the adoption of their terminology. This method apparently dates back to M., who, in contrast to his predecessors → Zoroaster, Buddha and → Jesus, emphasized that he created both a canon of texts and a solid community structure ('church').

Of his works, which are not preserved or only as fragments in translations, five are considered canonical: the 'Great (or Living) Gospel', the 'Treasure of Life', the 'Book of Mysteries', the *Pragmateîa* and the 'Book of Giants'. In addition, there are 'The Book Dedicated to Šābuhr' (*Šābuhragan*), a collection of M.'s epistles, a liturgical collection of prayers and hymns and a so-called 'Picture Book' (*Eikón, Ardhang*).

The fragmentary nature of these works makes it impossible even today to reconstruct more closely the original teachings of M., but based on the literary-critical and tradition-critical analysis of the extant literature, it is possible to identify as a basic structure the teachings of the 'two principles and the three periods': i.e. the contrast of spirit and body, light and darkness, good and evil, as well as the three-part salvation history, i.e., the period of separateness of light and darkness, the period of mingling and the period of separation or re-establishment of the original condition. His cosmology, which is quite mythical in character, is solely in the interest of soteriology: in the interest of freeing the (five-part) 'soul' of primeval man, sent by the 'Father of Greatness', which has gone into darkness, a redemptive process is set in motion, parallel to cosmogony, in which the 'light-*noûs*' or the 'shining-Jesus' and human beings play a central role. 'Reason', awakened by the 'Apostle of Light' (Greek *noûs*) (ultimately by M.), leads to the successive liberation of the 'suffering soul' (of God), until, at the end of time, the powers of light themselves defeat darkness and finally destroy it. M.'s 'church' was the redemptive institution created for this purpose; in the form of the strictly ascetic *electi* ('the chosen') or *perfecti*, from whom the hierarchy was recruited, and the laypersons who supported them (*auditores, katechoúmenoi*), they carried out on earth the work of their master, through preaching, singing and copying or illustrating their books, thus providing for an afterlife (if only in literary terms) – with regard to art history also in neo-Persian miniature painting.

→ Gnosticism; → Heresiology; → Heresy; → Mandaeans; → Religion; → Syncretism; → Zoroaster, Zoroastrianism

BIBLIOGRAPHY AND TEXTS IN TRANSL.: G. B. MIKKEL-SEN, Bibliographia Manichaica (Corpus Fontium Manichaeorum. Subsidia, vol. 1), 1997; A. ADAM, Texte zum Manichäismus., ²1969; J. P. ASMUSSEN, A. BÖHLIG, Die Gnosis, vol. 3. Der Manichäismus, 1980, ²1995 (bibliography); H. J. KLIMKEIT, Hymnen und Gebete der Religion des Lichts (Abh. der Rheinisch-Westfälischen Akad. der Wiss. 79), 1989; Id., Gnosis on the Silk Road, 1993. BIBLIOGRAPHY: A. Böhlig, Gnosis und Synkretismus, 2 parts, 1989; P. BRYDER (ed.), Manichaean Studies, 1988; F. DECRET, L'Afrique manichéenne, 2 vols., 1978; I. M. F. GARDNER, S. N. C. LIEU, Manichaean Documents from Roman Egypt, in: JRS 86, 1996, 146–169; M. HEUSER, H. J. KLIMKEIT, Studies in Manichaean Literature and Art, 1998; O. KLIMA, Manis Zeit und Leben, 1962; P. MIRECKI, J. BEDUHN (ed.), Emerging from Darkness, 1997; C. RÖMER, M., 1993; S. N. C. LIEU, Manichaeism in the Later Roman Empire and Medieval China, ²1992 (bibliography); Id., Manichaeism in Mesopotamia and the Roman East, 1994, ²1999; The Oasis Papers: Proc. of the 1ˢᵗ International Symposium of the Dakhleh Oasis Project, 1999; H. J. POLOTSKY, Abriß des manichäischen Systems, 1935 (= RE Suppl. 6, 241–272); H. J. PUECH, Le Manichéisme, 1949; A. VAN TONGERLOO, S. GIVERSEN (ed.), Manichaica Selecta. FS J.Ries, 1991; G. WIDENGREN (ed.), Der Manichäismus (Wege der Forsch. 168), 1977; G. WIESSNER, H. J. KLIMKEIT (ed.), Studia Manichaica, 1992.   KU.R.

Mania (Μανία; *Manía*).

[1] Greek personification of madness. Cultic worship as *Maníai* (plural!) in the place of that name near Megalopolis. According to Paus. 8,34,1–3, → Orestes went mad there (identification with Erinyes/Eumenides? → Erinys). In the singular M. is found only in Quint. Smyrn. 5,451ff. for the rage of → Ajax [1]. M. appears with an annotation of the name on a Lower Italian vase by → Asteas depicting Hercules's infanticide (→ Lyssa, → Oestrus).   L.K.

[2] Another name for the Roman goddess → Larunda or Mater Larum (Varro, Ling. 9,61; Arnob. 3,41). The two earliest pieces of epigraphical evidence of the name are controversial: a graffito from the 6th cent. BC may refer to the identical feminine praenomen [1]. The entry from 11 May in the Late-Republican → Fasti Antiates Maiores is incomplete, the addition MA[niae] being conjectural (InscrIt 13,2 p. 456). In the literature M. is referred to as the mother or grandmother of the → Larvae and the → Manes (Fest. 114 L.). A dog was sacrificed to → Genita Mana, who can be indentified with M. (Plin. HN 29,58). She was considered the goddess of birth and death (Plut. Quaest. Rom. 52; [2]).

The Maniae are either terrible spectres grandmothers frighten their grandchildren with or people whose ugly appearance caused terror (Paul Fest. 128,20 l.; schol. Pers. 6,56). In addition, Maniae was the term used for the dolls made of flour (Fest. 114 l.) or wool (Paul Fest. 273 l.) that were suspended at crossroads during the → Compitalia for M. and the → Lares (Macrob. Sat. 1,7,35).

the ; 1 C. DE SIMONE, Graffiti e iscrizioni provenienti dall'Acqua Acetosa Laurentina, in: PdP 36, 1981, 141f. no. 6;   2 E. TABELING, Mater Larum, 1932, 89–102.
FR.P.

[3] Satrap from Aeolis (north west Asia Minor), installed and supported by → Pharnabazus. Her family came from Dardanus. Together with Greek mercenaries, who she used to accompany in a chariot, she attacked the Troad and added some coastal towns to her satrapy. She was murdered by her son-in-law Meidias of Scepsis. Her satrapy was conquered in 399 BC by the Spartan → Dercylidas, who also took hold of the treasures kept in Scepsis and Gergis (Xen. Hell. 3,1,10–15).

D. M. LEWIS, Sparta and Persia, 1977.   P.HÖ.

[4] Mentioned along with two other women by Polyaenus (8,50) as a friend of → Berenice [2] I, who were believed to have concealed Berenice's death to make possible the military campaign of Ptolemy III. Probably not historical, since the story appears to be based on Seleucid propaganda.

B. BEYER-ROTTHOFF, Untersuchungen zur Außenpolitik Ptolemaios' III., 1993, 22 A. 25; M. HOLLEAUX, Études, vol. 3, 1968, 306.   W.A.

[5] M., whose real name was Melitta or Demo, was an Athenian hetaera known for amusing comments and sometime lover of → Demetrius [2] Poliorcetes (Machon at Ath. 13,578b–579d; Plut. Demetrius 27,9).
A.ME.

Manicae (χειρίς; *cheirís*).
A. SLEEVE B. ARM PROTECTION   C. GLOVE
D. MANACLES

A. SLEEVE
→ Clothing from as early as the Minoan-Mycenaean period had sleeves down to the wrist, shorter ones to the elbow or just to the upper arm. In the archaic and classical periods the → chiton with sleeves was the usual dress for 'barbarians' (Persians, Scythians et al.), but it was also worn by Greeks. In Roman dress *manicae* were initially a sign of effeminacy (→ Tunic) – → Commodus could still be censured because he wore a tunic with sleeves (Cass. Dio 72,17, cf. SHA Heliogab. 26,3). From the 3rd cent. AD, the adoption of the Iranian sleeved coat as part of semi-official and official dress marked a change, so that beginning in the 4th cent. *manicae* on garments were more or less the norm (→ Dalmatica, → Clothing).

B. ARM PROTECTION
Leather upper arm protection, part of a soldier's armor, often fitted with metal. → Gladiators (*retiarii*) wore *manicae* as well, not only of metal but also of woven leather straps.

C. GLOVE
The Greeks and the Romans only exceptionally wore gloves (Plin. Ep. 3,5,15); physicians did, for example, and sometimes workers in the fields (Hom. Od. 24,230).

D. MANACLES
Worn by slaves and prisoners of war. In myth, → Andromeda is chained to a rock. Various types of manacles have been preserved.

AD A.: E. KNAUER, Ex oriente vestimenta. Trachtgeschichtliche Beobachtungen zu Ärmelmantel und Ärmeljacke, in: ANRW II 12.3, 1985, 578–741; A. PEKRIDOU-GORECKI, Mode im antiken Griechenland, 1989, 77f.; A. STAUFFER, Textilien aus Ägypten, Ausstellung Fribourg 1991–1992, 1991.; ad C.: ; SP. MARINATOS, Kleidung, Haar- und Barttracht (ArchHom I H), 1967, 14.
AD D.: E. KÜNZL, Schlösser und Fesseln (J 25–30), in: Id., Die Alamannenbeute aus dem Rhein bei Neupotz. Plünderungsgut aus dem römischen Gallien, 1993, 365–378.
R.H.

Manichaeism see → Gnosticism

Manilius Roman *gens* name, probably taken from the forename → Manius, which in mss is frequently confused with Mallius, Manilius, Manlius. The family was significant in the 2nd cent. BC through M. [I 3] and [I 4].

J. REICHMUTH, Die lateinischen Gentilicia, thesis Zurich 1956, 116; SCHULZE, 166; 442.   K.-L.E.

I. REPUBLICAN PERIOD   II. IMPERIAL PERIOD
III. POET

I. REPUBLICAN PERIOD

[I 1] M. (or Manlius?), L. Senator in 97 BC, wrote about the → Phoenix (as first in Lat.: Plin. HN 10,4f.), about natural wonders and sacred law.

SCHANZ/HOSIUS 1, 605f.

[I 2] M., C. People's tribune in 66 BC, popular politician (MRR 2,153). His first law, which provided in equal measure for the registration of freedmen into all → *tribus*, secured for M. a large following and was passed by the people's assembly on 31 December 67, but was annulled by the Senate after formal objections (Cass. Dio 36,42,2f.). In the street battles that followed against gangs loyal to the Senate, under L. Domitius [I 8] Ahenobarbus, many of M.'s followers lost their lives (Ascon. 45; 65 C.). On the other hand, the well-known *lex Manilia* was successful. It gave Pompey supreme command against → Mithridates VI in addition to command in his campaign against the pirates (Cic. Leg. Man. passim). After M.'s time in office, he was accused of embezzlement, an accusation which Cicero, as the official in charge, delayed, allegedly in M.'s interests (Plut. Cicero 9,5–7; Q. Cicero, Commentariolum petitionis 51). Organized disturbances in January 65 and the 'First Catiline Conspiracy', put paid to the trial (Cass. Dio 36,44,1–4). A second accusation of → *maiestas* (Schol. Bobiensia p. 119 STANGL) under the protection of Ahenobarbus's gangs, led to M.'s sentencing *in absentia* and his exile (Ascon. 60 C.; Schol. Gronoviana p. 322 ST.; [1]).

1 J. T. RAMSAY, The Prosecution of C.M. in 66 B.C. and Cicero's Pro Manilio, in: Phoenix 34, 1980, 323–336.
JÖ.F.

[I 3] M., M' (especially in the Livian tradition, instead of his forename M.). Senator and important jurist of the 2nd cent. BC. Although M., as praetor in Hispania ulterior, had to accept a defeat with heavy losses against the Lusitanians in 155 (or 154) BC (App. Hisp. 234), he became consul in 149, perhaps because of his status as a jurist,(MRR 1,458) and began the 3rd → Punic War as leader of the land forces, together with his colleague L. Marcius [I 7] Censorinus (App. Lib. 349). When the Carthaginians, who had at first declared their submission, reacted with bitter resistance to the ultimatum of the Roman commanders (in detail differing Diod. Sic. 32,6,3 and App. Lib. 377) to leave Carthage, M., who was inexperienced in war, had no decisive success at the siege of the city and later in battle against the Punic army under → Hasdrubal [7]. It even took the stout-hearted intervention of the tr. *mil.* P. Cornelius [I 70] Scipio Aemilianus (Liv. Per. 49; App. Lib. 469; 484–492: cf. [1. 444–6]) to save him from impending defeat. After his consulship, M. apparently did not appear again politically. The consul Μάλλιος/*Mállios*, who is supposed to have warned Ti. → Sempronius Gracchus in 133 of violent activity (Plut. Gracchi 11,2–3), could hardly have been M. [2. 348]. Since Cicero has him participate in the conversation in *De re publica* (Cic. Rep. 1,18), he may have lived at least until 129. In 108, Cic. Brut. compares M. as orator with P. → Mucius Scaevola, whom he is said to have outdone in the abundance of his sayings (*copia*). His significance as a jurist was rated even more highly. Pomponius (Dig. 1,2,2,39) counts him, with P. Mucius and M. Iunius [III 1] Brutus, among the founders of the → *ius civile*. He regularly gave legal advice (Cic. De orat. 3,133) and he left behind several juristical writings, among them the *Actiones* (Varro Rust. 2,5,11; 2,7,6), evidently a collection of sales forms (Cic. De orat. 1,246 *venalium vendendorum leges*), and the *Monumenta*, whose content is completely unclear (= *commentarii*? [3. 542]).

1 HUSS, 440–447; 2 A. E. ASTIN, Scipio Aemilianus, 1967 (index); 3 WIEACKER, RRG, 541f.   W.K.

[I 4] M., A. *Cos.* in 120 BC (InscrIt 13,1,163; MRR I, 523). He was probably a son of P. Manilius, who went to Illyria with a senatorial commission in 167 (MRR I, 435), and brother of M. [I 3].   P.N.

[I 5] M., Sex. In 449 BC, with M. Oppius leader of the Roman army in the dispute with the → *decemviri* [1]

(Liv. 3,51,2–10; Dion. Hal. Ant. Rom. 11,43,5).
K.-L.E.

II. IMPERIAL PERIOD

[II 1] M. Presumably a senator, entrusted with τῶν τροφῶν διάδοσις (*tôn trophôn díadosis*, 'the distribution of foodstuffs') in Rome by → Caracalla, allegedly because he was active as a → *delator* (Cass. Dio 78,22,1). He may have been charged with the supervision of the water supply and, in part, grain delivery (*curator aquarum et miniciae*) [1. 185, n. 175]. Relegated to an island by Macrinus. PIR² M 128.

1 W. ECK, Die staatliche Organisation Italiens in der hohen Kaiserzeit, 1979.

[II 2] Ti. M. Fuscus Senator. In AD 191–193, legate of a legion in Dacia (→ Daci). Joined → Septimius Severus, who in 194 named him as praetorian governor of the new province of Syria Phoenice. Suffect consul in 195 or 196, presumably in that province. As *magister* of the → *quindecimviri sacris faciundis* he promulgated the secular games in 203 (CIL VI 32326, I. 6; → *Saeculum*). *Cos. II* in 225. PIR² M 137.

[II 3] M. M. Vopiscus Suffect consul in AD 60, one of the early senators from the Iberian peninsula. M. [II 4] was his descendant. PIR² M 140.

[II 4] P. (?) M. Vopiscus Probably son of M. [II 3]. It is unknown whether he became a senator. According to Statius (Silv. 1 prooem. and Silv. 1,3) he was an *amicus* of → Domitianus and wrote poems. Statius described his villa at Tusculum.

SYME, RP 6, 465f.; PIR² M 141.

[II 5] P. M. Vopiscus Vicinillianus L. Elufrius Severus Iulius Quadratus Bassus Patrician. *Triumvir monetalis*, military tribune of the *legio IV Scythica* around AD 100, when A. Iulius [II 119] Quadratus was governor of Syria [1. 99]. Quaestor of → Traianus, praetor, *cos. ord.* in AD 114. Probably from Spain [1. 465f.]. PIR² M 142.

1 SYME, RP 4.   W.E.

III. POET

[III 1] Roman didactic poet
A. LIFE B. WORK C. INFLUENCE ON LATER AUTHORS

A. LIFE
About the life of the author we know as good as nothing. Among the various names data in the manuscripts, M. Manilius is the most probable. His creative period falls at the end of Augustus's reign and at the beginning of Tiberius's. The *terminus post quem* is the battle of the Teutoburg Forest in AD 9 (Manil. 1,899f.). Augustus is at first the living addressee (1,384f.; 2,507–509), but is then replaced by Tiberius (4,764–766).

B. Work

The *Astronomica* are the oldest representation of the system of Hellenistic → astrology intended as a cohesive unity. The unwarlike universal poem (2,24 *pacis opus*) combines astrological theory as a kind of 'anti-Lucretius' [2. 136, n. 3] with the Stoic world view, which is the basis of this teaching and was standard for → Aratus [4]. For some individual teachings, M. offers the oldest, if not indeed the only source [7. 144–149]. His models were Greek texts, both poetic – Hesiod (Manil. 2,12), Aratus (Manil. 1) – and prose – → Nechepso Petosiris (Manil. 1,41; 1,47), → Teucer of Babylon (Manil. 5). Some details are from Egyptian culture. While recent scholars practically no longer see Posidonius as a possible source [1; 12. 13–21, 159–161], more and more elements of hermetic writing have come to light (→ Corpus Hermeticum), cf. Manil. 1,30 *Cyllenie* ([7. 134, n. 30], too negative [12. 21–26]).

Book 1 describes the beginning of the world, → constellations, celestial orbits (→ kykloi) and comets, book 2, the signs of the zodiac and their relations to other things as well as the doctrine of the 12 'houses' (sectors of the daily rotation), book 3 the 12 *áthla*, a system similar to the houses-doctrine, which appears to be more strongly directed to the beginning of certain actions (*katarchaí*), the *locus fortunae*, the tricky determination of the ascendant, the chronocrators which rule time periods, and deals with the time of the rising of the signs of the zodiac, as well as life expectancy and seasons, book 4, the effects of the signs of the zodiac and zodiacal geography, expanding on non-astrological and ethnographic sources, book 5, the effects of the → paranatellonta (constellations outside the zodiac) and the six classes of stars. M. probably ignored, as did Aratus, the planets out of poetic considerations. Much of what other astrologers define in planetary terms is designated by M. as zodiacal. According to Manil. 5,709, he dealt probably as little with the planets in the (somewhat overestimated) lacunae SCALIGER discovered as with the descents of the paranatellonta. A book 6 mentioned in mss probably did not exist (finally [3]). Instead of passing through the planetary spheres, M. descends from the fixed star sphere to earth three times in other ways: in book 1 to comets, plague and civil wars, in books 2–4 to geography and ethnography, in book 5 to the colourful everyday world [7. 245–268]. The philosophical parts of the work are particularly valuable: the preamble to book 4 concerning fate (*fatum*) links the celestial part (books 1–3) to the terrestrial (books 4–5), the preamble to book 2 concerning cosmic sympathy and the close of book 4 about the idea of the microcosmos frame the second 'descent' (*descensus*) and lay the philosophical foundation for the theoretical construction.

The style is less argumentative than that of → Lucretius. Like Aratus, M. proceeds in an ecphrasis-like, descriptive manner (4,438): *tantum monstranda figura* ('the form is only to be shown'). For the most part M. had Greek prose to transform into Latin hexameter. Greek compound nouns, in particular, created difficulties. The metre is pure; it has been affected by the hexametrist Catullus, the authors of the *Culex* and *Ciris*, Tibullus and Ovid, perhaps also Horace and Propertius but primarily Lucretius and Virgil, whose *Georgica* are also a model of composition. M.'s figures of style border on Ovid's formulation and may have astrological relevance [7. 214–227]. Along with the Greek expressions there are also a number of archaisms and elements of Latin vulgar speech, especially in the everyday world described with a realism *avant la lettre* [4. 36, cf. 91] in books 4–5, when the astrologically based mirror motif of the comedies of Menander serves as their model (5,470–476) [7. 189–191, 267].

C. Influence on later authors

Individual verses of M. were used by → Germanicus [2] (who is the adopter according to the judgment of most scholars), the *Aetna* poet, Lucan, Seneca Tragicus, Valerius Maximus, Juvenal, Nemesian, Dracontius and perhaps also Claudian. → Firmicus Maternus draws objectively from M.'s book 5 and must also have used the source available to M. [7. 139–144]. Columbanus knows M. only from florilegia.

M. was rediscovered, together with Lucretius, by POGGIO in 1417. His work immediately enjoyed great success: it was edited in 1471 by REGIOMONTANUS and in 1484 by L. BONINCONTRI, who added more verses of his own and interpreted the poet publicly in Florence. In the spirit of M., the latter composed two cosmological '*world poems*', and his famous friend PONTANO wrote his *Urania*. Both expanded among other things the planets and descents of the paranatellonta omitted by M. J. J. SCALIGER's commentaries on M. ([1]1579, [3]1655) were long considered a manual of astrology. GOETHE also occupied himself with M. in the course of his nature poetry [12. 145f.; 7. 265[441]]. An investigation of the poem from the viewpoint of the history of astrology began hesitantly at the end of the 19th cent. with F. BOLL, philological research only in the 1970s, particularly in Italy.

→ Astrology; → Didactic poetry; → didactic poetry

1 R. BLUM, M.' Quelle im ersten Buch der Astronomica, 1934;   2 F. BOLL, Studdien über Claudius Ptolemäus, in: Jb. für class. Philol., Suppl. 21, 1894, 49–243;   3 S. COSTANZA, Ci fu un sesto libro degli Astronomica di Manilio?, in: S. BOLDRINI (ed.), Filologia e forme letterarie, FS F. Della Corte, vol. 3, 1987, 223–263;   4 E. FLORES, Contributi di filologia Maniliana, 1966;   5 W. HÜBNER, Die Rezeption des astrologischen Lehrgedichts des M. in der italienischen Renaissance, in: R. SCHMITZ, F. KRAFT (ed.), Humanismus und Naturwissenschaft, 1980, 39–67;   6 Id., Die Eigenschaften der Tierkreiszeichen in der Antike, 1982;   7 Id., M. als Astrologe und Dichter, in: ANRW II 32.1, 1984, 126–320;   8 F.-F. LÜHR, Ratio und Fatum, Dichtung und Lehre bei M., 1969;   9 A. MARANINI, Filologia fantastica, 1994;   10 M. PAUER, Zur Frage der Datierung des astrologischen Lehrgedichtes des M., 1951;   11 E. ROMANO, Struttura degli Astronomica di Manilio, 1979;   12 C. SALEMME, Introduzione agli Astro-

nomica di Manilio, 1983; 13 B. SOLDATI, La poesia astrologica nel Quattrocento, 1906; 14 E. ZINN, Die Dichter des alten Rom und die Anfänge des Weltgedichts, in: A&A 5, 1956, 7–26.   W.H.

Maniolai nesoi (Μανιόλαι νῆσοι; *Manióloi nêsoi*). An archipelago off the coast of India, beyond the Ganges (Ptol. 7,2,31). Otherwise attested in Greek literature only in Pseudo-→ Palladius (*Perí tōn tēs Indíēs ethnōn* 1,5), but located by him in the vicinity of Ceylon (perhaps the Maldives or in the dangerous waters around the southern tip of India). Later often mentioned by Arabs, Persians and others. From the time of Ptolemy it was believed that these islands were so magnetic that they pulled the iron nails out of ships.

> A. HERRMANN, s.v. Μανιόλαι νῆσοι, RE 14, 1145f.; W. BERGHOFF (ed.), Palladius. De Gentibus Indiae et Bragmanibus (Beitr. zur klass. Philol. 24), 1967.   K.K.

Manipulus The *manipulus* (maniple) was a tactical unit of the Roman legion introduced in the 4th cent. BC (Liv. 8,8,3: *et quod antea phalanges similes Macedonicis, hoc postea manipulatim structa acies coepit esse*). It enabled troops to be more flexibly deployed for battle than with the → phalanx. Soldiers armed with the → *pilum* (throwing spear) were given more room. The legion was deployed for battle in three ranks (*hastati, principes*, → *triarii*), each of the first two ranks comprising ten *manipuli*, each of 120 men, while the rank of the *triarii* comprised ten *manipuli*, each of 60 men. Lightly armed soldiers (→ *velites*) also formed part of the *manipulus*. Each *manipulus* contained two → *centuriae*, and the longest-serving → *centurio* commanded the whole unit. In deploying for battle, an interval was left between the *manipuli*, which was closed during the battle. It was thus possible to absorb a retreating battle-rank into the rearmost rank (Liv. 8,8,9f.). During Caesar's period the *manipulus* had been replaced by a larger tactical unit, the cohort, which consisted of three *manipuli*. The titles of a legion's centurions, however, continued to refer to the original deployment in *manipuli*. During the Principate the word *manipulus* was also used figuratively to refer to any group of soldiers.
→ Cohors; → Legio

> 1 A. K. GOLDWORTHY, The Roman Army at War, 100 BC – AD 200, 1996; 2 L. KEPPIE, The Making of the Roman Army, ²1998.   J.CA.

Manius Rare Roman → *praenomen*, principally used by the patrician families Aemilii, Sergii and Valerii and by the plebeian Acilii, most often in Upper Italy (rarely *nomen gentile*: ILS 6230 and M. [I 2] below), acronym: a five-stroked M (ꟽ, ꟽ, in print M'.). Two alternatives for the name's origin have been proposed since antiquity: derivation from *mane* 'in the morning' (Varro, Ling. 6,60; Fest. 135 L.; Liber de Praenominibus 5: 'one

born in the morning') or from *manus* 'good' i.e. from the *di* → *manes*, euphemistically the 'good gods' (Zos. 2,3,2). Neither of the two has yet been convincingly argued.

> SALOMIES, 36f.   H.R.

[I 1] (Old Latin *Manios*). Maker or commissioner of the famous 6th cent. BC brooch of Praeneste (Fibula Praenestina) (CIL I² 3; → Needle).

> A. E. GORDON, The Inscribed Fibula Praenestina, 1975, 17.   K.-L.E.

[I 2] Contact of M. Antonius in Italy who, with Fulvia [2] and L. Antonius [I 4], unleashed the Perusine War against Octavian in 41/40 BC (App. B Civ. 5,75; 112) and served as their messenger (App. B Civ. 5,128–133). M. was executed as a scapegoat in 40 or 39 as part of the *Triumviri*'s settlement (App. B Civ. 5,278).   JÖ.F.

Manliana Name of two road stations in Italy: one on the *Via Aemilia Scauri* near Populonia (Tab. Peut. 4,2; Geogr. Rav. 4,32; It. Ant. 292,4) and the other on the road from Siena to Chiusi (Tab. Peut. 4,4; Geogr. Rav. 4,36; Ptol. 3,1,49).   H.SO.

Manlia Scantilla Wife of Didius [II 6] Iulianus, who after his acclamation as emperor (AD 193) conferred on her the title *Augusta*. According to the Historia Augusta (HA Did. 8,9f.) she outlived her husband. PIR² M 166.   W.E.

Manlius (in Greek usually Μάλλιος/*Mállios*, often confused in MSS with Mallius and Manilius). Name of a Roman patrician family, probably of Etruscan origin [1. 227]. It attained an early political zenith in the 5th and 4th cents. BC with the Vulsones and Capitolini branches (continued by the Torquati). Sources connect the family's history primarily with the repelling of the Celts (→ M. [I 8] and [I 12]. Stemmata, details of which are uncertain: [2. 1157f., 1166]). A period of decline ended in about 260 BC with the emergence of the younger Vulsones line and the new Acidini, who, however, died out in the 2nd cent. BC. The Torquati produced one of the foremost politicians of the Second → Punic War in M. [I 19], but after that their prominence declined. Even in the 1st cent. BC it could not be regained, despite M. [I 17] (stemma: [2. 1182]). The patrician Manlii died out in the early Imperial period, but the name had already been passed on to plebeian bearers.

> 1 SOMMER ; 2 F. MÜNZER, s.v. M., RE 14, 1149–52.   K.-L.E.

I. REPUBLICAN PERIOD   II. IMPERIAL PERIOD

I. REPUBLICAN PERIOD

[I 1] M., C. Centurion under P. Cornelius [I 90] Sulla. After a ruinous civilian life (Cic. Cat. 2,14; 20), M. rallied several thousand armed men in support of → Catilina at Faesulae in the autumn of 63 BC (Sall. Catil. 56,1f.), beginning the rising on 27 October (Cic. Cat. 1,7), whereupon he was proscribed (Sall. Catil. 36,2). In January 62, M. commanded Catilina's right flank at Pistoria and fell (Sall. Catil. 59,3; 60,6).   JÖ.F.

[I 2] M., Cn. M. was the first of his family to attain the consulship, doing so in 480 BC. During his tenure, he fell in battle against Veii (Liv. 2,43,11; 47,1–7; Dion. Hal. Ant. Rom. 9,5,1; 9,11,1–12,2). Where a *cognomen* occurs in the sources, it is *Cincinnatus*, a name otherwise found only in the *gens Quinctia* (InscrIt 13,1,89; 356f.).   C.MÜ.

[I 3] M., C. Landowner and olive farmer, friend of Cato [1]'s (Cato Agr. 144f.). He may have accompanied him on campaign to Greece in 191 (Plut. Cato 13,2).

[I 4] M., L. Governor of Gallia Transalpina in 78 BC, who went to war against → Sertorius, but was defeated by L. → Hirtuleius (Caes. B Gall. 3,20,1; Liv. p. 90).

[I 5] M. (Vulso?), P. *Triumvir epulo* (→ Septemviri) from 196 BC. Fought in Spain as praetor under the consul M. Porcius → Cato [1] in 195 (MRR 1, 340). Expelled from the Senate by Cato in 184 (Plut. Cato 17,7), M. was elected praetor again in 182, and took reinforcements to Hispania Ulterior (MRR 1,382). After a lengthy command in 181, he died in an epidemic at Rome in 180 (Liv. 40,42,7).

[I 6] M. Acidinus, L. *Praetor urbanus* in 210 BC, he was an emissary to Greece in 208, secured the Umbrian passes against Hasdrubal [5] in 207 and went to Spain in late 206 with proconsular imperium as the successor to P. Cornelius [I 71] Scipio, remaining there until 199 (MRR 1,293; 296; 300).

[I 7] M. Acidinus Fulvianus, L. Natural son of Q. Fulvius [I 10] Flaccus and Sulpicia, adoption by M. [I 6] made him probably the first plebeian to become a patrician. He was praetor in Hispania Citerior in 188 BC, remaining there with proconsular imperium until 185 (*ovatio de Celtiberis* on his return). In 183 he was sent as an emissary to the Celts beyond the Alps, and went with P. Cornelius [I 81] Scipio Nasica and C. Flaminius [2] as triumvir to found the colony of → Aquileia [1] (ILLRP 324; MRR 1,380). He was consul in 179 BC alongside his natural brother Q. Fulvius [I 12] Flaccus (MRR 1,391f.).   K.-L.E.

[I 8] M. Capitolinus, M. Consul in 392 BC (→ *ovatio* for a victory over the Aequians; MRR 1,92) and → interrex in 387 (Liv. 6,5,5f.). M. is, however, best known for two reasons. Firstly, as a defender of the Capitol (→ Capitolium), he was said to have prevented its capture in a surprise night attack during the sack of Rome by the Gauls in 387 (otherwise dated to 390) by throwing the first attackers from the rock, forewarned by the honking of the geese. Secondly, however (along with Sp. → Cassius [I 19] and Sp. → Maelius [2]; cf. Cic. Phil. 2,87; 114) he was cited as an example of aspiration to royal power (*adfectatio regni*): M. was allegedly condemned and executed in 384 for attempting to use the offer of help to plebeians in financial distress to amass a following whose support he aimed to exploit for an ascent to kingship. M.'s house is said then to have been demolished by order of a popular vote, and the *gens Manlia* to have decided never again to use the *praenomen* Marcus (Liv. 5,47; 6,11; 6,14–20; Dion. Hal. Ant. Rom. 13,7,3–8,2; 14,4; Plut. Camillus 27; 36; Cass. Dio fr. 25,10; 26,1–3; Vir. ill. 24; Diod. Sic. 14, 116, 5–7, according to whose version in 15,35,3 However, M. was not condemned to death, but was forcibly removed.)

M. K. JAEGER, Custodia Fidelis Memoriae: Livy's Story of M. Manlius Capitolinus, in: Latomus 52, 1993, 350–363; P. M. MARTIN, L'idée de royauté à Rome 1, 1982, 351–354; T. P. WISEMAN, Topography and Rhetoric: The Trial of Manlius, in: Historia 28, 1979, 32–50.

[I 9] M. Capitolinus, P. As consular tribune in 379 BC, M. suffered a defeat at the hands of the Volscians (Liv. 6,30,2–6). Named *dictator* in 368 during the internal disputes surrounding the *leges Liciniae Sextiae* (→ Licinius [I 43]), he chose for his *magister equitum* one C. Licinius, the first plebeian to hold the office (MRR 1,112) – a clear indication that M. favoured political balance, which was probably also the reason for his election in 367 at the last college of consular tribunes (Liv. 6,42,3; Fast. Capitolini).

[I 10] M. Capitolinus Imperiosus, Cn. Cos. 359 and 357 BC (InscrIt 13,1,402f.; identity of the two consuls not confirmed, however, owing to missing iteration numbers). → Interrex in 356 (Liv. 7,17,11; probably unhistorical). In 351, M. was censor with C. Marcius Rutilus, M.'s colleague in his second consulship (MRR 1,127). In 345 he was *magister equitum* of the *dictator* L. Furius Camillus (Liv. 7,28,2–6).

[I 11] M. (Capitolinus) Imperiosus, L. While *dictator clavi figendi causa* ('for driving in the nail' in the Temple of Jupiter for marking the year; MRR 1,117) in 363, M. is said to have drawn criticism for not abdicating immediately afterwards. The accusation of mistreating his son (→ M. [I 12]) made against M. by the *tr. pl.* M. Pomponius, which the historical sources connect with these events, and the entanglements spun out of the allegations (Cic. Off. 3,112; Liv. 7,3,9–5,9; Val. Max. 5,4,3; 6,9,1; Sen. Ben. 3,37,4), are hardly credible.

S. P. OAKLEY, A Commentary on Livy Books VI–X, vol. 2, 1998, 72–95.

[I 12] M. Imperiosus Torquatus, T. The most famous member of his *gens* (cf. Cic. Sull. 32). *Dictator* in 353, 349 and 320 BC (MRR 1,125, 129, 153; the first two dictatorships at least are questioned with good reason in [1. 65]) and *cos.* in 347, 344 and 340 (InscrIt

13,1,106f.; 406–409). During his third consulship, M. obtained a decisive victory and triumph over the Latins and Campanians (Liv. 8,11,11–14; Diod. Sic. 16,90,2; cf. InscrIt 13,1,69). M. was quickly associated with legendary traits: at first, he is said to have responded to the accusations of the *tr. pl.* M. Pomponius against his father M. [I 11] by threatening Pomponius with death, which the sources to some extent treat not as an offence against the inviolability of a *tr. pl.*, but as an expression of his filial piety (*pietas*) (!) (Cic. Off. 3,112; Liv. 7,5; Val. Max. 5,4,3; App. Sam. 2; Sen. Ben. 3,37,4; Vir. ill. 28,1f.). As *tr. mil.* in 361 (discrepancies in the ancient dating; cf. Liv. 6,42,5f.) M. is said to have fought his famous single combat with a Gaul, which brought him his torque (*torquis*) and the *cognomen* Torquatus (which was passed down to his descendants) as the spoils of victory (Claudius Quadr. fr. 10b HRR [= Gell. NA 9,13]; Liv. 7,9,8–10,14; Vir. ill. 28,3; MRR 1,119f. and other sources; cf. [2. 113–48]). Finally, legend ascribes to M. the famous story that, while *cos. III* in 340, he had his own son executed for fighting a single combat although he was victorious, because it was against his father's explicit orders (Liv. 8,6,14–7,22; Zon. 7,26,3–5; Cic. Fin. 1,23; 34f.; Val. Max. 2,7,6; cf. [2. 436–51]).

1 BELOCH, RG   2 S. P. OAKLEY, A Commentary on Livy Books VI–X, vol. 2, 1998.   C.MÜ.

[I 13] M. Mancinus, T. As people's tribune in 109 BC, he obtained for C. Marius [I 1] the supreme command in the war against → Jugurtha (Sall. Iug. 73,7), launching a fierce attack on Marius' predecessor, Q. Caecilius [I 30] Metellus (Gell. NA 7,11,2f.).   K.-L.E.

[I 14] M. Torquatus Scion of an old patrician family, probably without political office, but a skilled forensic orator (Hor. Epist. 1,5,9 in connexion with Sen. Controv. 2,5,13), a friend of Horace's, who addressed his Epist. 1,5 and Carm. 4,7 to him.

SYME, AA, 395f.   W.K.

[I 15] M. Torquatus, A. Did not take up his praetorial posting to the province of Sardinia in 167 BC, the Senate having instead entrusted him with the investigation of capital offences (Liv. 45,16,4). *Cos.* in 164, succeeding his brother M. [I 20]. He is probably the document witness mentioned in the Senate decree on Tibur (ILS 19) as well as the consul whose sudden death is referred to in Plin. HN 7,183.   P.N.

[I 16] M. Torquatus, A. Praetor around 70 BC, but afterwards politically unsuccessful. As Pompey's legate in 67, he fought the pirates near the Balearics (Flor. Epit. 1,41,9). In 52, M. conducted the trial against T. Annius [I 14] Milo (Ascon. 39; 54C), before leaving Rome in 49 together with Pompey. M. was still in Athens in 46/5, waiting for Caesar's pardon (Cic. Fam. 6,1–4). He appears in 42 as a follower of Caesar's assassins on Samothrace (Nep. Att. 11,2).

[I 17] M. Torquatus, L. (C. 108 – before 50 BC) Sulla's proquaestor in Greece and Italy (MRR 2,61), praetor in

68 (?), then governor of Asia. Despite losing the election, M. ousted P. Cornelius [I 89] Sulla as *cos.* in 65, thanks to the legal action by his son M. [I 18]. M. escaped the alleged murder plot of the First Catilinarian Conspiracy (Cic. Sull. 11) and earned the title of *imperator* in 64/63 as *procos.* of Macedonia (Cic. Pis. 44). In 58 he campaigned in vain for Cicero (Cic. Pis. 77f.). In 54 he failed in his prosecution of A. Gabinius [I 2] (Cic. Ad Q. Fr. 3,3,2). Cic. Fin. 1,39; 2,62 presupposes M.'s death.

[I 18] M. Torquatus, L. (C. 90–46 BC) son of [I 17], on whose behalf in 66 BC he successfully accused the *cos. des.* for 65, P. Cornelius [I 89] Sulla. Soon afterwards M. was Master of the Mint (MRR 2,445) and attained priestly office (MRR 2,485). His second accusation against Sulla was defeated in 62 by Cicero's defence (Cic. Sulla *passim*). M., praetor not before 49 (Cic. Fin. 2,74), contributed much to Pompey's near-victory against Caesar's forces at Dyrrhachium in 48 (Caes. B Civ. 3,66,1–70,2). While fleeing to Spain in 46, M.'s ship was boarded by the Caesarians at Hippo Regius and he was killed (Oros. 6,16,5 against Bell. Afr. 96,1). M., probably the subject of Catullus's epithalamion (Catull. 61), and himself an amateur poet (Plin. Ep. 5,3,5), appears in Cicero (Fin. 1 and 2; cf. Brut. 265) as a determined advocate of Epicurus.   JÖ.F.

[I 19] M. Torquatus, T. Triumphed over Sardinia as consul in 235 BC (MRR 1,223). In 231, he was forced to resign, along with Q. Fulvius [I 10] Flaccus, because of a technical error in the election to the censorship. As consuls in 224, the two won a decisive victory over the Boii. He successfully put down a revolt on Sardinia in 215, on behalf of the indisposed praetor, once more under the auspices of Flaccus, who was then urban praetor. In 212, both were defeated in the election of the pontifex maximus by P. Licinius [I 18] Crassus. In 211, after his election by the *centuria praerogativa*, M. refused, apparently voluntarily, his third consulship. He was the first to cast his vote in the Senate in 210, yet when the new *princeps senatus* was chosen in 209, he took second place again, apparently voluntarily, to Fabius [I 30] Maximus. In 208, as dictator, he conducted elections after the deaths of the consuls, arranged games and promised more for 203. He died in 202. The historical tradition depicts him as an example of a strictness that was no longer in accord with the times, who proposed refusing to buy the freedom of Romans captured in 216 in the battle against → Hannibal [4] at → Cannae, and also opposed the idea of replacing with Latins the senators who had fallen in the war (Liv. 22,60f.; 23,22,7). He is also linked with the sole instance in Republican times of the closing of the Temple of → Janus in 235 (Varro, Ling. 1,165; Liv. 1,19,3), an early confusion with M. [I 21] in the annalistic tradition, as the ceremony was simultaneously, and correctly, associated with the peace of the year 241. TA.S.

[I 20] M. Torquatus, T. Was probably the grandson of M. [I 19] and brother of M. [I 15]. Pontifex from 170, *cos.* in 165 (MRR 1,438). In 162 he accompanied Cn.

Cornelius Merula to Egypt, to reconcile the brothers Ptolemy VI, Philometor and Ptolemy VIII (Pol. 31,10,9–10; 17–19). In 140 he pronounced his own son, who had been adopted by D. Iunius [I 28] Silanus, guilty of abuse of office in Macedonia.

[I 21] M. Torquatus Atticus, A. Censor in 247 BC and *cos.* in 244 and 241. During his second consulship he put down the Faliscan revolt and celebrated a triumph (MRR 1,219). For the first and only time in the Republican period, he had the Temple of → Janus closed (→ M. [I 19]).   P.N.

[I 22] M. Vulso, A. As *cos.* in 474 BC, M. is said to have celebrated an → *ovatio* and concluded a forty-year peace with → Veii (MRR 1,28). Allegedly accused of failing to put through the agrarian law of Sp. Cassius [I 19] in 473 by the *tr. pl.* Cn. Genucius [2], he is said to have escaped trial only by the tribune's deposition (Liv. 2,54,2–55,2; Dion. Hal. Ant. Rom. 9,37,3–38,3). In 454, M. was a member of a three-man delegation sent to Greece to study the laws there (Liv. 3,33,3; 33,5; Dion. Hal. Ant. Rom. 10,56,2), which is quite consistent with his being one of the → *decemviri* [4] *legibus scribundis* in 451 (InscrIt 13,1,27; 364f.).   C.MÜ.

[I 23] M. Vulso, A. Triumvir from 194 to 192 BC for the settlement of Ager Thurinus (MRR 1,345). Probably *praetor suffectus* in 189 (MRR 3,137). Although he was assigned the province of Gallia for his consulship of 178, he marched against the Histri (→ Histria, Histri) on the northern Adriatic, but they defeated him, and his colleague D. Iunius Brutus had to relieve him (Liv. 41,1–7). In 177, both marched once more against the Histri, until the consul C. Claudius [I 27] Pulcher succeeded them.   P.N.

[I 24] M. Vulso, Cn.. As curule aedile in 197 BC, he arranged → *ludi Romani* that were more lavish than ever. He served as praetor on Sicily in 195 and, after several unsuccessful attempts, he became consul in 189. To demonstrate Roman power in the former sphere of influence of → Antiochus [5] III, he conducted a campaign through south west Asia Minor and against the Galates, which was as successful as it was brutal. It was depicted in literary form by a participant as an 'Anábasis', finding its way into the tradition through Polybius (21,33–39) (Liv. 38,12–27 etc.; MRR 1,360). Hannibal wrote a polemic, now lost, against the undertaking [4]. Traces of the controversy surrounding his activities even among his contemporaries, Greek as well as Roman, can be found in the form of alleged oracles, the opposition to his triumph and dating to 189 BC of the incipient Roman moral decline by L. Calpurnius [III 1] Piso. As *procos.* in 188, M. took an oath at the peace of Apamea, regulating the fulfilment of its conditions and their consequences together with → Antiochus [5] III and a ten-man senatorial delegation (Pol. 21,40–45; Liv. 38,37–39; MRR 1,366). Laden with spoils, the troops were attacked on the homeward march in Thrace. M. was allowed a triumph in 187 after all, but nothing is known of his further career: his candidacy for the censorship in 184 failed.

J. GRAINGER, The Campaign of Cn. M. Vulso in Asia Minor, in: AS 45, 1995, 33–42; GRUEN, Rome, Index s.v. M.   TA.S.

[I 25] M. Vulso, L. As *praetor peregrinus* in 218 BC, he was besieged by the Boii in Cannetum (Pol. 3,40,11–14). He probably died at the Battle of Cannae in 216.

[I 26] M. Vulso, L. Praetor in 197 BC (Sicilia). In 189, he was his brother M.'s [I 24] legate in the war on the Galates (MRR 1,364). He was sent to Antiochus [5] III in 188 to accept the latter's oath (Liv. 38,39,1f.).   P.N.

[I 27] M. Vulso Longus, L. Consul in 256 and 250 BC, respectively with the brothers M. and C. Atilius [I 21 and 17] Regulus, always acting in concert with them (Pol. 1,25–29). He celebrated a naval triumph in 256 after the victory over the Carthaginians at → Eknomon, and after the withdrawal from the invasion of Africa ordered by the Senate, while his colleague remained with some forces in enemy territory (MRR 1,208). In 250, despite bitter struggles, it proved impossible to dislodge the Carthaginians from → Lilybaeum (MRR 1,213).

→ Punic Wars   TA.S.

II. IMPERIAL PERIOD

[II 1] M. Probably from a prominent family. He was condemned to exile in AD 17 following an adulterous relationship with Appuleia Varilla, who was related to the imperial family. PIR² M 151.

[II 2] Q.M. Ancharius Tarquitius Saturninus Suffect consul in AD 62 [1. 20; 34; 2. 227ff.]. Proconsul of Africa in 72/3 [3. 300]. PIR² M 153.

1 H. ENGELMANN, D. KNIBBE, Das Zollgesetz der Provinz Asia. Eine neue Inschrift aus Ephesos, in: EA 14, 1989, 1–206 2 W. ECK, Miscellanea Prosopographica, in: ZPE 42, 1981, 227–256 3 J. REYNOLDS et al. (ed.), The Inscriptions of Roman Tripolitania, 1952.

THOMASSON, Fasti Africani, 43.

[II 3] L. M. Patruinus. Senator, who was attacked by the local population in AD 70 in the *colonia Seniensis*. Suffect consul in 74. PIR² M 156.

[II 3a] M. Severus *Procurator ad Mercurium* in Alexandria [1] in July AD 161 (POxy. 4060, l. 123).

[II 4] C.M. Valens Senator, born in about AD 6. He suffered defeat against the Silures as legionary legate in Britain in 51/2. By then he was already somewhat old for legionary legate, and his career was delayed further. He was legionary legate again in the revolutionary year AD 69, when he took the side of → Vitellius, who did not, however, admit him to the consulship owing to the defamations of Fabius [II 21] Valens. At the age of 90, he was admitted to the ordinary consulship by Domitian in AD 96. Shortly after the end of his consulship he died (Cass. Dio 67,14,5). PIR² M 163.   W.E.

Mannerism Pan-Europian term for the epoch of the transition from the Renaissance to the Baroque (1530–1630). Aesthetics: anti-naturalistic emotion, irrationalism. Stylistic principle: *discordia concors* (union of the incompatible). Linguistic obscuration by means of tropes, metaphors, *concetti* and hypertrophying of Asianistic stylistic devices involving short sentences that combine the bizarre and monstrous with pathos and elements of contemporary language to achieve surprise effects. In 1948, E. R. Curtius adopted the term mannerism for the study of comparative literature as the 'complementary phenomenon of the Classicism of all periods', which is still contentious today. → Asianism is consequently the first European mannerism and → Atticism the first European → Classicism. Accordingly [2] sees mannerism in Hellenism, the Latin Silver Age, in the late Middle Ages, in the 'conscious' mannerism of Romanticism and in modernity from 1880 to 1950.

1 E. R. Curtius, Europäische Literatur und lateinisches Mittelalter, ⁸1973 (English translation: European Literature and the Latin Middle Ages); 2 G. R. Hocke, Manierismus in der Literatur, 1967.   G.F.S.

Mannerists The M. are a large group of 15 or more attic red-figure vase-painters whose affected style retains aspects of the Archaic. Active from c. 480 BC until near the end of the century, they favoured decorating *column-kraters*, *hydriai*, and *pelikai* (see → Pottery, shapes and types of)in an old-fashioned manner: elongated figures with small heads whose drapery has groups of stacked folds, picture frames with black ornament, and antiquated subject matter, such as Ajax and Achilles playing a board game.Their figures often gesture to exaggeration, giving a theatrical air to the action, and they can be stiff and somewhat awkwardly posed.

Dyonisian, *komoi*, (see → Komos)and symposia scenes are the subjects they preferred to paint, and they have a related interest in scenes of dance and music. In the second generation domestic scenes became popular, due to the influence of contemporary artists. On occasion the M. also painted rare myths, including the only known vase-painting of the madness of → Salmoneus.

The earliest M. (c. 480–450 BC) derive from the workshops of Myson. The most important was the → Pan Painter.; others include the Pig Painter, Leningrad Painter, and Agrigento Painter. The leaders of the next generation (c. 450–425 BC) are the Nausicaa Painter and Hephaestus Painter, the two after whom the seven member 'Nausicaa-Painter Group' is named. The Academy Painter and the Painter of Athens 1183 represent the last glimmer of the tradition near the end of the 5th cent.

Beazley, ARV², 562–588, 1106–1125, 1659–1660, 1683–1684, 1701, 1703; J. Boardman, Athenian Red Figure Vases. The Archaic Period, 1975, 179–193; T. Mannack, s.v. Mannerist Workshop, The Dictionary of Art 32, 1996, 56; M. Robertson, The Art of Vase-Painting in Classical Athens, 1992, 126f., 143–152, 216f.   J.O.

Mannus (*mannulus*) or *buricus* (according to Porph. Hor. comm. epod. 4,14; Veg. Mulomedicina 3,2,2; for the name [1. 2, 29]) was the name given to the small horse or pony imported from Gaul (for the origin [2. 289]) in the 1st cent. BC to Rome as a luxury animal (Lucr. 3,1063; Plin. Ep. 4,2,3: *mannulus*; Jer. Ep. 66,8), particularly for ostentatious ladies (Hor. Carm. 3,27,7; Prop. 4,8,15; Ov. Am. 2,16,49f.). People would harness the small, fast and temperamental animal to a two-wheeled coach ('gig', *parva esseda, carpentum, covinnus*; [3. 416, 464]: Mart. 12,24,8) or ride it (Sen. Ep. 87,9; Auson. Epist. 8,7). Open wounds were treated by applying its dung (Q. Serenus, Liber medicinalis 804f.). → Horse

1 Walde/Hofmann; 2 O. Antonius, Grundzüge einer Stammesgeschichte der Haustiere, 1922; 3 Blümner, PrAlt.   C.HÜ.

Manoeuvres Military exercises (*exercitium, exercitatio militaris, decursio*), for a long time little studied by historians, contributed considerably to the military success of the Roman army and appear to have been conducted on the Field of Mars (→ Campus Martius) in early times. From the late 3rd cent. BC, military exercises were developed further in both practice and theory. Cornelius [I 71] Scipio Africanus organized manoeuvres systematically in Spain in 210 BC (Pol. 10,20; Liv. 26,51,3–7) and then in Sicily (Diod. Sic. 27,4,6; Zon. 9,11,7). While Cato the Elder [1] tended rather to be a theoretician of military matters, commanders such as P. Cornelius [I 70] Scipio Aemilianus or C. Marius [I 1] foregrounded practice: Scipio Aemilianus increased the fighting power of his troops at → Numantia through tough military exercises (App. Hisp. 86), and in a similar manner Marius prepared his soldiers for battles against the → Cimbri and → Teutoni (Plut. Marius 13,1; 14,1–3; 16,3; Frontin. Str. 4,1,7). → Augustus, → Traianus [1] and → Hadrianus formulated and then as *principes* expanded the catalogue of regulations that were valid for the military (Veg. Mil. 1,8,11; cf. Suet. Aug. 24; Plin. Pan. 18; SHA Hadr. 10). The significance of the *exercitatio* was generally acknowledged: Flavius Josephus [4] considered the constant military exercises that were at times conducted under war conditions to be a significant cause of the military strength of the Roman army (Jos. BI 3,72–75). During his military career, Trajan concerned himself intensively with exercises for his soldiers (Plin. Pan. 13,1–3), and in a speech, when visiting the *legio III Augusta* in Lambaesis, Hadrian praised the *exercitationes* which lasted several days (CIL VIII 2532; 18042 = ILS 2487; 9133–9135).

In each army encampment there was an exercise area or *campus* (AE 1931,113; 1933,214; 1972,636) as well as a training hall or *basilica exercitoria* ([4. no. 978, 1091]; AE 1971,364). For the → cavalry, a riding track was constructed. The organization of the manoeuvres was assigned to soldiers of the bottom military ranks, e.g. the *discentes* (→ *discens*; ILS 2393; 9070), the *campidoctor* (ILS 2088; 2416; 2803), *doctor cohortis* (ILS 2088), *optio campi*, *armatura* (ILS 2362; 2363; 4729), *exercitator* (ILS 2182; 2187; 2453) and the *magister campi*, but was usually under the control of the higher ranks, the → *centuriones*, *tribuni* and *legati*. The military was regarded as a *disciplina* that had rules and could be learnt (Liv. 9,17,10). In exercise areas, altars were set up for the → personification of this *disciplina* (ILS 3809; 3810).

In late antiquity, Vegetius reckoned *armorum exercitio* with *disciplina castrorum* and *usus militiae* as the most important prerequisites for the military success of the Romans (Veg. Mil. 1,1; cf. 2,23).

→ Armies; → Disciplina militaris; → Recruits, training of

1 LE BOHEC, 111–125; 2 Y. LE BOHEC, Les discentes de la IIIᵉ légion Auguste, in: L'Africa romana 4, 1987, 235–252; 3 Id., Le pseudo camp des auxiliaires à Lambèse, in: Cahiers du groupe de recherches sur l'armée romaine et les provinces 1, 1977, 71–85; 4 R. G. COLLINGWOOD, R. P. WRIGHT, The Roman Inscriptions of Britain, 2 vols., 1965–1990; 5 G. HORSMANN, Untersuchung zur militärischen Ausbildung im republikanischen und kaiserzeitlichen Rom, 1991.   Y.L.B.

Mansio Derived from *manēre* ('to stay'), *mansio* is the term for a sojourn or stopover (Cic. Att. 8,15,2; 9,5,1) as well as the station on a Roman road where one stops for rest and food (Plin. HN 6,96; 6,102). It is also used in the sense of accommodation (SEG 26, 1392 l. 23; Suet. Tit. 10,1). Consequently *mansio* also represents the stretch between two such places (Plin. HN 12,52; Lactant. De mort. pers. 45) or the travelling time taken, a day's journey (Plin. HN 12,64; CIL V 2108 = ILS 8453). Furthermore *mansio* came to mean a building (CIL VI 30745 = ILS 4353; CIL VI 2158 = ILS 4944). From the 3rd cent, *mansio* as a technical term stands for an inn with accommodation, particularly on the → *cursus publicus* (It. Ant.; Dig. 50,4,18,10; Cod. Theod. 8,5,1; 8,5,35). Besides rest, these public facilities served mainly for changing draught animals. The *mansiones* were situated on the main roads at a distance of about 37 km from each other, and in between there were several simple changeover stations, *mutationes*.

1 H.-C. SCHNEIDER, Altstraßenforschung, 1982, 95–101; 2 P. STOFFEL, Über die Staatspost, die Ochsengespanne und die requirierten Ochsengespanne, 1994, 16–17; 3 E. W. BLACK, Cursus Publicus, 1995.   A.K.

Mansuanius C. M. Severus. Legate of the *legio I Italica*; not identical with → Cossonius Gallus (see addenda), as has been suggested (AE 1998, 1131).   W.E.

Mantellum (*mantellum*, *mantelium*, χειρόμακτρον; *cheirómaktron*). A rectangular linen cloth with braiding and fringes; in cult activity it served as a hand towel carried by the servants of the sacrifice, at meals is served

for cleaning hands (e.g. Xen. Cyr. 1,3,5) and as a tablecloth (Mart. 12,28). In Sappho (99 DIEHL) the *cheirómaktron* is mentioned as a head adornment. In its main functions as a tablecloth and towel the *mantellum* corresponds with the *mappa* that was also a popular gift at Saturnalia (Mart. 5,18,1). There is evidence that from the time of Nero (Suet. Nero 22) a *mappa* (flag) was used to signal the beginning of the games in the Circus. A *mappa* (cf. Mart. 7,72; 10,87; 12,29,11f.) was smaller than a *mantellum* and so was brought as a cloth for eating at table (napkin; cf. Mart. 12,28). In contrast to the *mantellum* it had no cult use.

→ Table utensils

F. FLESS, Opferdiener und Kultmusiker auf stadtrömischen historischen Reliefs, 1995, 17.   R.H.

Mantennius

[1] L. M. Sabinus Senator. In AD 214 known as *m agister tertium* of the → *sodales Augustales Claudiales* (CIL XIV 2391). He must therefore already have been a senior member of the sodality. After a suffect consulship he became legate of Moesia inferior, where he is attested from 227 to 229 (AE 1972, 526 = [1. 13]). PIR² M 172.

1 V. BOŽILOA, J. KOLENDO, L. MROZEWICZ, Inscriptions latines de Novae, 1992.

[2] L. M. Sabinus Equestrian. Father of M. [1] and M. [3]. Praetorian tribune. Under → Commodus sent as praefect of Egypt where he is attested until 194 (PIR² M 173). Married to the daughter of the procurator T. Flavius Germanus.

[3] L. M. Severus Senator. Son of M. [2]. He was buried by his maternal grandfather T. Flavius Germanus in Praeneste (CIL XIV 2955). PIR² M 174.   W.E.

Manthurea (Μανθ(ο)υρέα; *Manthouréa/Manthyréa*). The name given both to the south western part of the eastern Arcadian plain near → Tegea and to a deme of Tegea (Μανθυρεῖς; *Manthureîs*). In M. there was originally a cult of Athena Hippia which Tegea adopted at the time of Augustus along with the cult image. Evidence: Paus. 8,44,7; 45,1; 47,1; Steph. Byz. s.v. M.

F. BÖLTE, s.v. M., RE 14, 1255f.   E.O. C.L.

Mantias (Μαντίας; *Mantías*).
[1] Son of Mantitheus of Thoricus In 377/76 BC → *tamias* of the shipyards (IG II² 1622,435f). In 360/359 BC Athenian strategos of a naval division and auxiliary troops sent to assist the Macedonian claimant Argaeus against → Philip II. By delaying in Methone, he was co-responsible for Argaeus's defeat (Diod. Sic. 16,2,6 and 16,3,5; in c. 358/7). Details about his family are distorted by *diabolē* ('slander, calumny') in Demosthenes (Or. 39 and 40). For his trierarchies cf. IG II² 1604,10 and 46 as well as 1609,61f.

DAVIES, 364–368; DEVELIN, no. 1907; PA 9667; TRAILL, PAA 632545.
J.E.

[2] Greek pharmacologist, a follower of → Herophilus [1], lived in the 2nd half of the 2nd cent. BC, teacher of → Heraclides [27] of Tarentum. Galen (De temperamentis medicamentorum simplicium et facultate 6, prooem. = 11,794–795 K.) refers to him as the first major writer on compound drugs. His portrait appears in the pantheon of great pharmacologists in the Vienna Dioscorides Codex (Cod. med. gr. 1, fol. 2). His 'On drug remedies' was widely cited by later pharmacologists [1]. In a second treatise, 'The drug-seller or in the surgery', he commented on wider aspects of medicine, including bandaging and perhaps bloodletting, which he strongly favoured (Gal. De venae sectione adversus Erasistratum 5 = 11,163 K.). He also wrote about regimen and gynaecology and supported the use of flutes and drums to avert an imminent attack of 'hysterical suffocation' (Sor. 3,4; → Hysteria).
→ Pharmacology

1 STADEN, 515–518. V.N.

Mantica A Roman sack made of leather for transporting goods of all kinds including food (Apul. Met. 1,18). The *mantica* was carried on the shoulder so that it lay over the back and chest (Pers. 4,24; Hor. Sat. 1,6,106), or when travelling on horseback over its hindquarters. A *manticula*, a small leather sack, was carried by poorer people. *manticulari* also means 'steal' or 'cheat', and the thief ('cutpurse') was called a *manticulator* (*-arius*).
R.H.

Mantichoras (μαντιχώρας; *mantichóras*, also *martichoras*, μαρτιχώρας; *martichóras*). According to Ctesias (in Aristot. Hist. an. 2,1, 501a 24ff.), an Indian animal with the body of a lion and the face of a human, with three rows of teeth. The fur was vermilion and the tail was shaped like a scorpion's so that the *mantichoras* could shoot deadly spines like arrows. The voice sounded like a mixture of a shepherd's pipe and trumpet. The *mantichoras* is described as fast, wild and man-eating (the meaning of the name, which is of Persian origin; cf. Ael. NA 4,21). According to Aelianus, Ctesias claims to have seen one in Persia. Paus. 9,21,4 identifies the mythical creature as the tiger and rejects its extraordinary attributes as rumours. J.STE.

Manticlus (Μάντικλος; *Mántiklos*). The sanctuary of → Heracles Mantiklos in → Messana was founded by M. according to Pausanias (4,23,10; 26,3). M. may be a fictitious person reconstructed from an epiclesis, as the history of the First → Messenian (Aristomenes) War (about 500/489 BC), with which M. is connected, contains fictitious elemants [1. 169–181]: as a son of a → mantis (seer) Theoclus, M. was allegedly chosen by → Aristomenes [1] beside his son to be a colonist of the Messenians during their flight to Sicily
→ Colonization; → Messenian Wars

1 F. JACOBY, FGrH IIIa, ²1954, 100–195.

F. KIECHLE, Messenische Studien, 1959; I. MALKIN, Religion and Colonization in Ancient Greece, 1987, 92–113.
C.A.

Mantinea (Μαντίνεια; *Mantíneia*).
I. NAME AND LANDSCAPE   II. TOPOGRAPHY   III. HISTORY

I. NAME AND LANDSCAPE
Older form of the name Μαντινέα, Attic and later literary form Μαντίνεια, the tribe was οἱ Μαντινεῖς; *hoi Mantineîs*. The tribal name is primary, with the town name derived from it. The town lies in the northern part of the large eastern Arcadian plateau, some 12 km north of → Tripolis (630 m elevation). The land of the great plain of M. is, like the entire plateau, almost entirely flat, primarily loamy soil and therefore very fertile, but owing to the altitude the climate is harsh and has high precipitation, so that typical Mediterranean vegetation no longer thrives and tree growth is even today extremely sparse [1]. The entire plateau is devoid of surface outflows, and is drained only by swallow-holes (katabothra). The north-west of the plain in particular is therefore swampy, and today lies under water in winter. The northern part of the plain, including M., lies lower than the southern part (13 × 4–7 km), including Tegea and modern Tripolis. In antiquity, bogginess was counteracted by digging drainage ditches and maintaining the katabothra. In ancient times the most southerly part of the plain was covered by a great oak forest, the Pelagos.

II. TOPOGRAPHY
The city site visible today, almost exactly in the middle of the region, is probably that founded in 368/7 BC, the city of the 5th cent. apparently occupying the same location. Apart from the city walls, only sparse remains survive, mostly Roman. The well-preserved walls, enclosing an elliptical space [2. 176], stretch for 3942 m, with 10 gates and around 105 towers, stone plinths 4·2–4·7 m in diameter and 1–1·8 m in height, clay brick superstructure. Especially noteworthy among the buildings is the 4th-cent. BC theatre, on the west side of the agora (c. 85 × 150 m), the others excavated here have not been certainly identified with those mentioned by Pausanias (8,71–12,1).

III. HISTORY
A. ARCHAIC AND CLASSICAL PERIODS   B. HELLENISTIC AND ROMAN PERIODS

A. ARCHAIC AND CLASSICAL PERIODS
The original tribal confederacy consisted of five *démoi* (→ Demos [2]), corresponding to the natural dictates of the landscape, with a focal point, called *Ptólis* (Paus. 8,12,7), on a limestone knoll, possibly the modern Gurtzuli hill about 1 km north of the later city

[3. 47–56; 4]. M. is mentioned as 'delightful' in Hom. Il. 2,607. In about 550 BC, Cyrene appointed → Demonax [1] of M. as its lawgiver (Hdt. 4,161f.; Diod. Sic. 8,30,2; Ath. 4,154d-e). 500 hoplites from M. fought alongside Sparta at Thermopylae in 480 BC (Hdt. 7,202). Late arrival at the battle of Plataeae in 479 (Hdt. 9,77) meant that they were left off the Serpent Column (Syll.³ 31) (→ Persian Wars). M. also sided with Sparta on other occasions (Hdt. 9,35,2; Paus. 8,8,6; Thuc. 3,107–113; Xen. Hell. 5,2,3). The date of a victory for which M. consecrated a Nike at Olympia cannot be established (Paus. 5,26,6). The *synoikismós* of five *démoi* mentioned by Str. 8,3,2 probably belongs in the period 478–473 BC [5. 140–151]. In the 420s BC → Nicodorus's constitutional reform (Ael. VH 2,23) was basically democratic (Thuc. 5,29,1; Xen. Hell. 5,2,6f.; Aristot. Pol. 1318b 23ff.). The Mantineis were regarded as being served 'by very good laws' (εὐνομώτατοι; *eunomótatoi*, Ael. VH 2,22), hence the role of → Diotima from M. in Plato's *Sympósion* (Symp. 201d; 211d).

The reform was probably connected with the expansion of dominion over neighbouring regions to the west, which brought M. into conflict with Sparta. M. responded by forming the anti-Spartan confederacy in 420 BC (Thuc. 5,29; IG I³ 83). After a war, a treaty was concluded by which M. was compelled to surrender the conquered territory (Thuc. 5,64–81; Xen. Hell. 5,2,2; IG V 1, 1124?). Relations with Sparta remained tense, and in 385 Sparta forced the abandonment of the city and resettlement in the villages, imposing a change to an aristocratic constitution (Xen. Hell. 5,2,1–7; 6,4,18; Isocr. 4,126; 8,100; Diod. Sic. 15,5; 12; Pl. Symp. 193a). After the Spartan defeat at Leuctra, the city was founded again in 371/0 BC (Xen. Hell. 6,5,3–5; 8f.; 10ff.; Paus. 8,8,10) [5. 251–256]. The democratic constitution was restored, the citizenry was divided into five *phýlai* named after gods (IG V 2,271 [6. 133–135; 7]) and new coinage was minted. Under the leadership of → Lycomedes [4], M. was the chief advocate of Arcadian unification, in this as throughout its history in opposition to → Tegea (Xen. Hell. 7,1,23ff.; 4,2f.; 4,33ff.; Diod. Sic. 15,59; 62ff.; 82,2ff.; Paus. 8,27,2). When the collapse of the Arcadian League (→ Arcadia with map) led to the battle of M. (362 BC) [8. 63–66], M. allied itself with Sparta (Xen. Hell. 7,5,1ff.; Diod. Sic. 15,82ff.).

B. HELLENISTIC AND ROMAN PERIODS

In 303 BC resistance to → Demetrius [2] was successful (Plut. Demetrius 25,1). In about 270 a confederation was formed with Areus [1] of Sparta (IG II², 686f.; Syll.3 434,24; 38; Stv 3, 476). M.'s later fate can only be vaguely discerned, owing to the confused state of the sources: in about 230 BC, M. was a member of the Achaean League (Pol. 2,57,1; coins), then it joined the Aetolian League (Pol. l.c.; 2,46,2). Cleomenes [6] III conquered the city in 229/8, but by 227 it had been retaken by Aratus [2] (Plut. Aratus 36,2; Plut. Cleo-

menes 5,1; Paus. 2,8,6; Pol. 2,57,2ff.). M. acquired an Achaean garrison (Pol. 2,57,3; Plut. Aratus 36,2). In 226 BC, there was yet another upheaval in favour of Cleomenes, when the Achaean colonists were murdered (Pol. 2,58,4ff.; Plut. Aratus 39,1; Plut. Cleomenes 14,1). This led to the city's greatest catastrophe: → Antigonus [3] conquered it in 223 BC and in retribution for the murders its citizens were executed, deported to Macedonia or sold into slavery (Pol. 2,54,11f.; 58,12; 62,11f.; Plut. Aratus 45,4f.).

M. was settled again under the name of Antigonea (Plut. Aratus 45,6; Paus. 8,8,11; IG V 2, 299). As such the city was a member of the Achaean Confederacy, but the old name continued to be used. Machanidas suffered a defeat at M. against Philopoemen in 207 BC (Pol. 11,11ff.; Plut. Philopoemen 10) [8. 66–68]. M. took part in the battle of → Actium (31 BC) on the side of the future Augustus (Paus. 8,8,12; 9,6).

Str. 8,8,2 mentioned M. as one of the cities which had entirely vanished, or of which only traces remained. This is refuted by Pausanias's description of the 2nd cent. AD (l.c.), the surviving remains and epigraphical evidence until the 3rd cent. AD, including honorific inscriptions (1st cent. AD) for priestesses (IG V 2, 265f.) [9] and for L. Verus (IG V 2,303). The emperor Hadrian's visit in AD 125 afforded the city not only special support but also the restoration of its old name (Paus. 8,8,12; 10,2; 11,8). Antinous [2] had a temple and a cult at M. (Paus. 8,9,7f.), as did Hadrian (IG V 2,302; SEG 11, 1090; questionable whether this refers to the same temple). There were Roman merchants in M. in the 1st cent. AD (IG V 2, 307), and there is evidence of a synagogue in AD 212 (IG V 2, 295). New coins were minted during the Severan dynasty (193–235). Reference is also made to M. in Hierocles, Synekdemos 647,7 (Μαντίνα) and in the late place-name list IG IV 619,8 (= SEG 16,254, Μαντίνια, also IG XIV 1102,35). The Slav invasion drove part of the population to Messene, where two villages south-east of Kalamata still bear the name of Mandinia today. Ruins of several Byzantine churches prove that a settlement survived. Epigraphical evidence: IG V 2, 261–342a; [10. 660–663]. Coins: HN² 418; 449f.

1 PHILIPPSON/KIRSTEN 3,1, 245–259;   2 J.-P. ADAM, L'architecture militaire grecque, 1982;   3 M. MOGGI, Processi di urbanizzazione nel libro di Pausania sull'Arcadia, in: RFIC 119, 1991, 46–62;   4 T. KARAGHIORGA-STATHAKOPOULOU, in: Πελοποννησιακά, Suppl. 19, 1992/3, 97–115 (excavation report);   5 M. MOGGI, I sinecismi interstatali greci 1, 1976;   6 N. F. JONES, Public Organization in Ancient Greece, 1987;   7 J. ROY, Polis and Tribe in Classical Arkadia, in: M. H. HANSEN, K. RAAFLAUB (ed.), More Studies in the Ancient Greek Polis, 1996, 107–112;   8 PRITCHETT 2, 1969;   9 M. JOST, Évergétisme et tradition religieuse à M. au Ier siècle av. J.-C., in: A. CHASTAGNOL et al. (ed.), Splendidissima civitas, 1996, 193–200;   10 SCHWYZER, Dial.

F. CARINCI, s.v. Arcadia, EAA², 1994, 334f.; S. and H. HODKINSON, M. and the Mantinike, in: ABSA 76, 1981, 239–296; R. HOWELL, A Survey of Eastern Arcadia in

Prehistory, in: ABSA 65, 1970, 85–88; JOST, 124–142; W. F. WYATT, s.v. M., PE, 549f. Y.L. E.MEY.

Mantis (μάντις; *mántis*), the commonest Greek word for 'seer', 'soothsayer', occurs from Homer onwards throughout antiquity. A *mantis* was usually a person. However, in sanctuaries with prophetic functions, the deity itself was regularly referred to as *mantis* (e.g. Aesch. Cho. 559), mortals in these cases serving the deity only as a mouthpiece. This relation between deity and inspired human is expressed by Pindar in his invocation of the Muse: 'Prophesy, Muse, but I will be your mouthpiece' (fr. 150 SNELL). Since the μαντική τέχνη (*mantikè téchnē*, 'art of prophecy') was potentially a divine attribute, it was to be expected that mortals could only demonstrate it in so far as they had access by inspiration to the superior knowledge of the gods [1]: hence the Greeks derived *mantis* from *maínesthai*, 'to rage', evoking the association of prophetic madness with prophetic, and by extrapolation also poetic, inspiration (Eur. Bacch. 299; Pl. Phdr. 244c). Plato often speaks of the prophecies of a 'true' or 'divinely inspired' *mantis* as an example of insight not gained by rational processes (Pl. Ap. 22a; Pl. Men. 99f.; Pl. Ti. 71e; [2]). However, while special, divinely inspired insight was occasionally ascribed to the *mantis* in myth and literature, the *mánteis* in historical times (prosopography: [6]) did not work as inspired → prophets, but operated through the interpretation of signs (Paus. 1,34,4). Their most important technique was haruspicy, the interpretation of the viscera of sacrificial animals (→ Sacrifice), but they also made pronouncements based on spontaneously arising signs, such as the flight of birds, dreams (→ Dream interpretation) and omens (→ Divination). *Chrēsmológoi*, 'interpreters of oracles' (→ Oracles), seem to have carried out activities which, though related, were clearly distinct, although later sources often conflate them with *manteis*.

Families of *mánteis* such as the Melampodidae (→ Melampus [1]) and the Iamidae (→ Iamus), in which the art of prophecy was inherited, were familiar in myth. It was said there were still families practising in the 5th cent. BC (the Iamidae and the → Telliadae: Hdt. 9,37, possibly also the → Clytiadae). The connexion between the Iamidae and the 'prophetic altar' of Zeus at Olympia (Pind. Ol. 6,5; 64–72; [3]) was hereditary. However, *mánteis* were not usually associated with specific sanctuaries, but worked independently, giving advice to those who approached them in exchange for payment (Hdt. 9,38,1; 9,95). It might be thought that the relationship between *manteis* and the army was more strongly institutionalized, since the armies of all Greek states had to be accompanied by at least one *mantis* [4], but there was, for instance, no official '*m antis* of the Athenians'. It was probably a matter for the commander to secure himself the services of a *m.* for a particular campaign. Naturally, it was possible for individuals and states to make a regular claim on the services of a particular *mantis*, who could in that way

attain prestige and influence. Famous examples include → Tisamenus of Elis, whose advice Herodotus (9,33) says helped the Spartans to five victories in war, leading to his becoming the only non-Spartan to be granted citizenship, → Lampon [2] in Periclean Athens, who was closely associated with the foundation of → Thurii [5. 131–139] and → Aristander [1] of Telmessus, the famous seer of Alexander [4] the Great.

In the 'Odyssey' (Hom. Od. 17,382–384), a *mantis* is a specialist summoned in from outside. Teisamenus and Aristander are historical examples of such imported religious experts. We still hear of itinerant *mánteis* even in the 4th cent. BC (Isocr. 19,6). However, the widely-held view that *mánteis* typically came from remote backward regions of the Greek world is not tenable [4. 52f.; 6]: Athenian *mánteis* were generally Athenian citizens and often educated people, e.g. Miltas, a member of Plato's Academy (Plut. Dion 22,6), and the Atthidographer → Philochorus.

Mánteis (and *chrēsmológoi*) made their living as religious specialists from religion, which was otherwise unusual. As a result, they were attacked in comedies for their mercenariness, unlike e.g. → priests [7]. In tragedies, on the other hand, the archetypal *mantis* → Teiresias supports the cause of religion in a way priests hardly ever did (Soph. Ant., OT; Eur. Bacch.; [8; 9]). According to Cicero (Div. 1,95), the Athenians sought the advice of *mánteis* whenever a public decision was required; the despatch of colonists and the waging of war were areas in which they were particularly involved [5; 10]. Yet we do not hear of a single historical *mantis* who pursued a personal religious agenda, or who opposed the decisions of a city in the name of the gods. → Prophets; → Vates

1 L. ZIEHEN, s.v. M., RE 14, 1345–1355; 2 E. R. DODDS, The Greeks and the Irrational, 1951, 64–101; 3 L. WENIGER, Die Seher von Olympia, in: ARW 18, 1915, 53–115; 4 W. K. PRITCHETT, The Greek State at War, vol. 3, 1979, 47–90; 5 W. LESCHHORN, Gründer der Stadt, 1984; 6 P. KETTS, Prosopographie der histor. griech. Manteis bis auf die Zeit Alexanders des Großen, 1966; 7 N. D. SMITH, Diviners and Divination in Aristophanic Comedy, in: Classical Antiquity 8, 1989, 140–158; 8 R. STAEHLIN, Das Motiv der Mantik im antiken Drama, 1912/13; 9 J. JOUANNA, Oracles et devins chez Sophocle, in: J.-G. HEINTZ (ed.), Oracles et prophéties dans l'antiquité (Actes du Colloque de Strasbourg 15–17 juin 1995), 1997, 283–320; 10 M. H. JAMESON, Sacrifice before Battle, in: V. D. HANSON (ed.), Hoplites, 1991, 197–227. R.PA.

Mantitheus (Μαντίθεος; *Mantítheos*).

[1] Athenian, involved in the mutilation of the Herms (→ Herms, mutilation of the) while a councillor in 415 BC (And. 1,43,4), fled to Sparta and then, like → Alcibiades [3], to Asia Minor, where they were arrested at Sardes. They escaped to Clazomenae in 411 (Xen. Hell. 1,1,10). In 409, M. was named as one of a delegation to the Persian King (Xen. Hell. 1,3,13), and in 408 he was entrusted with the supervision (see → Epimeletai) of the Athenian conquests on the Hellespont, while Alcibiades returned to Athens.

M. Ostwald, From Popular Sovereignty to the Sovereignty of Law, 1986, 548.

[2] Athenian, of a family without wealth, whose career is known through the speech in his defence by Lysias [1] (Lys. 16). He stayed away from Athens until shortly before the end of the rule of 'the Thirty' (→ Triakonta), and proved himself as a hoplite in 395/4 (Lys. 16,13; 15f.). Between 391 and 389 he was forced to defend himself against the accusation, made during the scrutiny for admission (→ Dokimasia) to the office of councillor, that he had supported the 'Thirty' as a cavalryman. Perhaps grandfather of M. [3] ([1. 364f.] is sceptical).

1 Davies ; 2 PA 9674; 3 Traill, PAA 632630.

[3] Athenian, son of → Mantias [1], probably from the latter's second marriage to a daughter of Polyaratus from Thoricus. His lengthy disputes over name and inheritance rights with his half-brother Boeotus, who also called himself M., are known from two speeches of Demosthenes (Or. 39 and 40). In the matter of the name dispute, he evidently failed (see IG II² 1622, 435).

Davies, 364–368; PA 9675, 9676; Schäfer 3, 211ff.; Traill, PAA 632700, 632705; cf. 267790.　　　　BO.D.

Mantius (Μάντιος; *Mántios*).

Son of the seer → Melampus, brother of → Antiphates, father of → Cleitus [1] and of the seer → Polypheides (Hom. Od. 15,242ff.), according to Paus. 6,17,6 also of → Oïcles (who in Hom. ibid. is his nephew), grandfather of → Theoclymenus.　　　　L.K.

Manto (Μαντώ; *Mantó*). Daughter of → Teiresias, from Thebes, like her father gifted as a seer, priestess of Apollo Ismenios (Eur. Phoen. 834ff.). When the → Epigoni [2] conquer Thebes, M. is consecrated to Apollo at Delphi (Apollod. 3,85; Paus. 9,33,2; schol. Apoll. Rhod. 1,308). Diod. Sic. 4,66,5f. calls her Daphne [2], and describes her as an excellent poet, from whom even Homer took some verses. Later, M. participates in the founding of the colony of → Colophon [1] in Asia Minor (with the oracular sanctuary of Apollo at → Clarus [1]). There she marries Rhacius (Mela 1,88) and gives birth (by Apollo) to → Mopsus, who also becomes a seer (Paus. 7,31; Apollod. Epit. 6,3; Str. 14,5,16). During her stay at Delphi she is said to have had two children by → Alcmaeon [1]: → Amphilochus [2] and → Teisiphone. Alcmaeon gives the children to → Creon [2] of Corinth (Apollod. 3,94 after Eur. Alcmaeon in Corinth).　　　　L.K.

Mantua (Μάντουα; *Mántoua*). Small (Str. 5,1,6) fortified (Plin. HN 3,130; Serv. Aen. 10,198) city in the 10th region between the swamps on the river → Mincius, modern Mantova (an Etruscan origin for the name cannot be sustained; possible association with local names of watercourses, cf. the names *Abdua*, *Padua*,

Meduacus). For Plin. in HN 3,130 M. was an Etruscan foundation. In fact, during the Etruscan expansion in the plain of the Padus [2. 18–35] M. was a trading settlement, linked to the → Padus by a waterway and to the plain and the Alps by several roads. Until the 1st cent. BC it was not Celticized. Since the → Punic Wars the city had enjoyed good relations with Rome. In the mid 1st cent. BC M. was a *civitas*, and under Augustus adopted in the *tribus Sabatina*. During the civil war following Caesar's death its territory, although already small (less than 1000 km²; [3. 53f.]), was affected by the confiscations of agricultural areas of Cremona, which were insufficient to satisfy the veterans: hence Virgil's complaints (Ecl. 9,28; G. 2,198). M. was located on second-rank lines of communication [4. 286], such as that from → Verona to → Hostilia (Tab. Peut. 4,4; Geogr. Rav. 4,30; Guido 15). It is mentioned as a centre for the production of armaments (Not. Dign. Occ. 9,26). A *collegium nautarum* is attested (CIL V Suppl. 669). Sparse archaeological remains: traces of a wall [5. 535f.]. M. was the birthplace of Virgil (→ Vergilius[4], cf. Ov. Am. 3,15,7; Mart. 1,61; 2,14; 195,2; Sil. Pun. 8,535).

1 Nissen 2, 202–204; 2 R. De Marinis, in: R. Bussi (ed.), Misurare la terra. 4: Il caso mantovano, 1984; 3 P. Tozzi, Storia padana antica, 1972; 4 Miller ; 5 A. M. Tamassia, s.v. M., in: EAA Suppl., 1995.　　　　A.SA.

Manturanum (modern San Giuliano). Etruscan settlement near Barbarano Romano (south of Viterbo) on a tuff plateau at the confluence of two streams. Apart from an inscription of an Estruscan sherd, mediaeval geographers pass down the name of M. (or Marturanum). This agrarian centre, which existed from the 8th to the 3rd cent. BC, flourished during the 6th cent. Its second blooming came in the Hellenistic period. The precipices opposite the town of San Giuliano contain rock graves with chambers lying, as in → Blera (Bieda), behind mostly cube-shaped façades. On the surrounding plateaus there are → tumuli with chamber tombs showing similarities to the tombs at Cerveteri (→ Caere) and Orvieto. In front of the monumental tumulus Tomba Cima there is a monument with 18 → cippi cut from the tuff outcrops, probably serving the cult of the dead.

→ Castel d'Asso; → Funerary architecture (C.1); → Norchia; → Volsinii

A. Gargana, La necropoli rupestre di San Guliano, in: Monumenti antichi 33, 1929, 297–467; G. Ravera, La nécropole rupestre de San Giuliano, in: Archeologia 170, 1982, 77–78; S. Steingräber, Etruskische Monumentalcippi, in: ArchCl 43, 1991, 1079–1102.　　　　M.M.

Manturna A divinity mentioned by Varro, Antiquitates Rerum Divinarum fr. 149 Cardauns (in Aug. Civ. 6,9), probably taken from the → *Indigitamenta* of the *pontifices* (→ *Pontifex*), classified there as a 'goddess of marriage'. She was invoked to keep a wife with her husband. M. is not attested elsewhere, but according to [1] should be linked to the Etruscan god → Mantus, with a suffixation characteristic of Etruscan.

→ Etruscan; → Sondergötter

1 RADKE, 198. K.v.S.

Mantus Etruscan god, eponym of → Mantua, but not attested under this name in Etruscan sources. According to Servius and Schol. Veronense (on Verg. Aen. 10,198–200) M. is the Etruscan name of the Rom. god of the underworld → Dis Pater, corresponding to the Greek → Hades. Tarchon is said to have consecrated the Etruscan city of Mantua to him, and named it after him. As with Hades, there was no cult attached to M. Perhaps M.was regarded as god of the Underworld in Etruria too, if he is to be identified with the Etruscan *Aita* (< Hades), who appears with Φ*ersipnai* (→ Persephone) in Etruscan tomb paintings [1].

1 S. STEINGRÄBER, Etruskische Wandmalerei, 1985, 337f. no. 93–95 fig. 251 and 286–294 no. 32 fig. 43.

PFIFFIG, 320–322. L.A.-F.

Mantzikert see → Turks

Manuale Portable wooden reading desk. *Manuale* was probably originally an adjectival attribute of *lectorium*. Substanticised it then took on the meaning of (reading) desk [1]. The sole written reference is found in Mart. 14,84. A *manuale* is illustrated on two reliefs from Neumagen [1. fig. 15–16] and in Vergil's Codex Romanus (Cod. Vaticanus Latinus 3867, VI). Two kinds of reading desk are attested: one with a base and one without. Only the latter can be defined as a *manuale* as such. This is a wooden board with ends so bent as to hold in depressions both rolled-up ends of the scroll. By this means the scroll did not have to be held in both hands and was protected from wear.

1 E. PUGLIA, La cura del libro nel mondo antico, 1998, 70–74. T.D.

Manubiae see → War booty

Manumissio The Latin term for → Manumission (C.), the freeing of slaves. G.S.

Manumission

A. EARLY LEGAL SYSTEMS   B. GREECE   C. ROME

A. EARLY LEGAL SYSTEMS

The manumission of slaves is not attested for all ancient legal systems. Thus the Mesopotamian statutes of Eshnunna and Hammurabi make no such stipulations [1. 161]. In Hittite law too, nothing is known of manumission. The existence of manumission is, however, assumed for Egypt, although categorisation of the unfree (or rather, not entirely free) 'bondsmen' as slaves as such is disputed [2. 147]. This circumstance suggests

that the legal systems of Greece and Rome also did not know of manumission from their beginnings.

B. GREECE

Several forms of manumission existed in Greece from the 5th cent. BC at the latest. The most ancient option open to the slave-owner to implement his wishes is usually held to be *hierodouleia* (→ Hierodouloi; cf. [3. 93f.]). This was a means by which the slave was dedicated to a divinity. It is, however, questionable whether the effect of this sacral act was to free the slave at all. A counter-indication is that the slave became the property not 'of himself', but of the divinity. So the purpose of the act of dedication was not manumission as such, but secondary considerations: the publicising of the manumission and the securing of recompense in the form of the services to be carried out by the freed slave (→ *paramonē*). Accordingly, informal, non-sacral manumission may have been the original form of the act in Greece. Support for this surmise is provided by the chronological sequence of datable extant references [4. 108–153].

Apart from sacral dedication, other forms of manumission existed in Greek law; these probably also served the purpose of publicity, their intention being to document the status of the freedman in public and in the eyes of all. A fictitious trial of status may apply here, where the slave-owner sued the freedman for the latter's freedom (δίκη ἀποστασίου, *díkē apostasíou*) and lost the lawsuit according to prior plan. For other forms of manumission on the other hand, observance of form was a necessary prerequisite for the act to take effect, as in manumission ἐν ἐννόμῳ ἐκκλησία (*en ennómōi ekklesía*, by resolution of the popular assembly at the request of the slave-owner). But in the case of manumission διὰ κήρυκος (*dià kḗrykos*, by herald) the publicizing function was to the fore. From the Hellenistic period we have numerous documents in which manumission is effected by bequest, or declared by a notary solemnly invoking the gods [5. 96f.].

Manumission in the form of purchase was particularly widespread. In many cases the slave was able to pay the price from savings he may have accumulated during his servitude, or he took out a loan for the purpose, paying it off by his labour. While fulfilling this obligation of *paramone* the former slave is only half free: if he fails to fulfil it, the freedman reverts to slavery, or the slave does not achieve manumission at all [4. 189–200]. Finally, the legal status of the freedman remains inferior: he does not obtain citizenship, but only a status comparable to that of settled foreigners (→ metoikos).

C. ROME

Manumission (*manumissio*) in Roman law is scarcely less diverse in form than it was in Greece. The ancient law applying only to Roman citizens (*ius civile*) already contained three forms of manumission: manumission by bequest (*manumissio testamento*) was evidently an early development. It either followed immediately upon the death of the testator, or might depend on the slave's paying a price to the heirs: such a *statuliber* is already provided for in the Twelve Tables (*c.* 450 BC, → *tabulae duodecim*). In striking similarity to the case in Greek law, a fictitious legal action was possible during the lifetime of the slave-owner, with a trustee as the slave's spokesman making the declaration of freedom (→ *adsertor libertatis*) and laying the staff on him (thus *manumissio vindicta*). The former owner as respondent remained silent. Finally, the former slave could, with the approval of his master, be entered on the citizenship list by public authority (→ *census: manumissio censu*). Not only by this formal means, however, but also by the other forms of manumission mentioned, the freedman became a Roman citizen. He was nevertheless largely excluded from political office.

In the course of time these forms of manumission were simplified and amended: in place of the formal *manumissio vindicta* the more or less informal declaration of the spokesman to the magistrate was now sufficient. Manumission by bequest could also take the form of an entailed commission (→ *fideicommissum*), so that the heir or another beneficiary was simply obliged for his part to implement the manumission. In this way the heir or beneficiary concerned acquired the legal status of patron, and thus had a claim to the services of the freedman (→ *operae libertorum*). A type of manumission equivalent to the ancient forms during the Christian period was manumission before the priest and parish (*manumissio in ecclesia*).

But even manumissions without the benefit of the forms of *ius civile* were in time recognized: if the master declared the manumission before witnesses (*inter amicos*) or in a letter of manumission (*per epistulam*), the *praetor* protected the freedman from any legal challenge to his liberty (→ *vindicatio in libertatem*) on the part of his master or the latter's heirs. In such cases of 'praetorial manumission', freedmen did not become Roman citizens, although they did receive the rights of the Latin law.

Under Augustus, laws were enacted restricting manumission: the *lex Fufia Caninia* (2 BC) provided that only a defined proportion of slaves could be freed by bequest, e.g. of 30 slaves only 10. The *lex Aelia Sentia* (AD 4) made manumissions for the purpose of disadvantaging creditors null and void. The same applied as a rule to manumissions carried out by the master under 20 in respect of slaves. If the slave to be freed was not at least 30 years old, he acquired only the rights of the Latin law.

With manumission, the former slave-owner assumed the status of → *patronus*. Besides the services probably promised as a matter of course, according to objective law he enjoyed the following prerogatives: if the freedman left no will, as a rule the patron became his heir; as regards freedwomen and the children of freedpersons, he was their guardian. Even the master's right over life and death with regard to the slave (*ius vitae*

necisque) persisted as the right of the patron until the Imperial period.

1 R. Yaron, The Laws of Eshnunna, ²1988; 2 W. Helck, Wirtschaftsgeschichte des alten Ägypten im 3. und 2. Jahrtausend v.Chr., 1975; 3 A. Biscardi, Diritto greco antico, 1982; 4 K. D. Albrecht, Rechtsprobleme in den Freilassungen der Böotier, Phoker, Dorier, Ost- und Westlokrer, 1978; 5 R. Taubenschlag, The Law of Greco-Roman Egypt in the Light of the Papyri 332 B.C. – 640 A.D., ²1955.

A. Calderini, La manomissione e la condizione dei liberti in Grecia, 1908; F. Bömer, Untersuchungen über die Religion der Sklaven in Griechenland und Rom, Teil 2: Die sogenannte sakrale Freilassung in Griechenland ..., in: Abh. der Akad. Wiss. und Lit. Mainz, Geistes- und Sozialwiss. Klasse, 1960, no. 1; H. Rädle, Untersuchungen zum griechischen Freilassungswesen, thesis 1969; A. Kränzlein, Bemerkungen zu den griechischen Freilassungsinschriften, in: Symposion 1979, 237–247; Kaser, RPR I, 115–119; 293–301; II, 132–142; Honsell/ Mayer-Maly/Selb, 70–74; W. Waldstein, Operae libertorum, 1986; A. Ankum, Die manumissio fideicommissaria der Arescusa, des Stichus und des Pamphilus, in: Ars Boni et Aequi, FS W. Waldstein, 1993, 1–18; C. Masi Doria, Zum Bürgerrecht der Freigelassenen, in: ibid., 231–260; J. G. Wolf, Die manumissio vindicta und der Freiheitsprozeß. Ein Rekonstruktionsversuch, in: Libertas. Symposion aus Anlaß des 80. Geburtstags von F. Wieacker, 1991, 61–96; T. Giménez-Candela, Bemerkungen über Freilassungen in consilio, in: ZRG 116, 1996, 64–87.					G.S.

Manus *Manus* is used in Roman law in the sense of the 'controlling and protecting hand', expressing the family law concept of a relationship based on domination. Originally, *manus* may have described the hegemony of the head of the family (→ *pater familias*) not merely over his children (→ *patria potestas*) but also over his wife. Already in the Law of the Twelve Tables (5th cent. BC), however, paternal power is treated separately. The meaning of *manus* is accordingly restricted to the husband's relationship of power over his wife. Our best source for *manus* are the 'Institutions' of → Gaius (2nd cent. AD). In the → 'Digesta' of Justinian and therefore in the prime source of common law since the High Middle Ages, *manus* was expunged from the classical texts. At that time (6th cent. AD) it had long fallen out of use. In the 5th cent. BC on the other hand, the husband's *manus* over his wife may have been the rule. But already at that time there was evidently marriage without *manus* (cf. Gai. Inst. 1,111 presumably on 6,3 *lex XII tab.*).

Manus over the wife was based i.a. on the formal transactions of → *coemptio* ('bride purchase') or → *confarreatio* (shared 'bread sacrifice'). As there was no particular legal form for the solemnising of marriage itself (→ Marriage III. C.), formality and social attention as regards the setting up of a household were concentrated on the ritual acts for the establishment of *manus* (→ Wedding customs). In the absence of any such act, the husband acquired manus by *usus* ('practice' of the marriage) after one year of cohabitation with a woman. The woman, however, could prevent this by means of a *trinoctium* (separation from the man for three successive nights) before the elapse of one year. The three ways of establishing *manus* were referred to in combination as *conventio in manum* ('transfer' – that is, from paternal power in the family of origin – into the *manus* of the husband; Gai. Inst. 1,110). Mere *deductio in domum mariti* (probably the solemn 'escorting (of the woman) into the man's house'), on the other hand, did not confer *manus*.

As by the time of Gaius (Inst. 1,111 end) *manus* by *usus* had already been in part revoked, in part had fallen out of use, it must be assumed that marriage in the Roman Imperial period was as a rule free of *manus*. This did not of course mean that the woman became legally autonomous (*sui iuris*). As a rule she remained under the *patria potestas* of her father. If she was released from his power too (→ *emancipatio*), by convention she required a guardian (→ Family B.2.; → *tutela*), but by the marriage laws of Augustus (1st cent. BC) she was released from this requirement if she had three (as a freedwoman: four) legitimate children (→ *ius* E.2.).

The jurist Gaius uses the presumably ancient legal term *filiae loco* ('bearing the legal status of daughter') to describe the effects of *manus* on the wife. As regards personal rights, this means that the wife was subject to her husband without legal restriction. The power of the husband originally embraced the *ius vitae necisque* (power over life and death), not to speak of the right to administer corporal punishment and to expel the wife from the nuptial home. Cases of flagrant abuse, however, were subject to the sanctions of → ecclesiastical / religious law, and later the moral supervision (*regimen morum*) of the censor (→ *censores*). As regards inheritance law, the status of the woman married *in manu* was equivalent after her husband's death to that of a daughter. As regards property law, she was in the same position as a dependent child, and incapable of earning anything on her own account. If she was independent before marriage and had her own property, this passed to her 'married lord'. For wives there is no record of a → *peculium* (personal fortune), such as was frequently left to dependent sons, and in view of the sharing of the household with the husband such a provision is unlikely. If the husband himself (still) stood under the tutelage of his father, the father's power extended to cover the daughter-in-law too.

→ Family (IV.B.3); → Marriage; → Mater familias → ; → Matrimonium; Woman II.

Honsell/Mayer-Maly/Selb, 396ff.; Kaser, RPR I 56f., 72ff., 76ff., 323f., 330f.; Treggiari, 16–32.   G.S.

Manuscript fragments Pages or fragments of codices (→ Codex; mainly made of → parchment) or printed books which were used particularly during the 15th–17th cents. in the whole of Europe as casings, pastedowns, flyleaves or reinforcing strips for individual folios, fascicules or the spine. These MS-fragments of mainly liturgical, biblical and legal content, but also fragments from private documents, are important in terms of palaeography, history and textual criticism: classical authors are rare in this context (e.g. fragments of Juvenal in a MS from Orleans, 9th cent. AD; Horace fragments from Einsiedeln, 10th cent.). Today these fragments have often been separated from the MSS and are being kept separately, sometimes forming special collections (e.g. the Philip Bliss Collection in the Green Library, Stanford). The object of the study of these MF (practiced in a systematic way, particularly in Germany, since the 19th cent.) is their detection, identification and cataloguing: the aim is amongst other things the reconstruction of the original MS whose pages were frequently used for several MSS kept in the same library.

R. G. Babcock, Reconstructing a Medieval Library. Fragments from Lambach, 1993; A. Petrucci, La descrizione del manoscritto, ²2001, 132–134.   M. P. M.

Manuscripts
A. Definition B. Character C. Dissemination

A. Definition
1. Term 2. Significance for the history of transmission

1. Term
The handwritten book is the source of our knowledge of almost all ancient literature. The very few exceptions to this rule are provided by inscriptions, i.e. the *Res Gestae Divi Augusti* (→ Augustus) on a temple wall in Ankara, or the philosophical manifesto of → Diogenes [18] of Oenoanda [14. 199–202]. A distinction is usually made, though not entirely correctly, between those books written in the ancient world, generically but not quite accurately known as papyri (→ papyrus), and those produced later, when the papyrus scroll (→ Scroll) had given way to the → codex as the standard format of a book.

2. Significance for the history of transmission
Manuscripts are of interest for the editor of a classical text in so far as they are helpful in reconstructing the precise words of an ancient author. It is quite common to find that a text has been transmitted to us in a great number of copies, of which only one or a mere handful are of value to the editor. Thus for a long time relatively recent manuscripts were disregarded or underestimated if textual witnesses from the early Middle Ages were available. But some editors were able to show that the more recent manuscripts in a few cases provided valuable readings which appeared to derive from ancient tradition. It has also become apparent that some recent manuscripts incorporate necessary emendations to the text proposed by medieval or Renais

sance scholars. However, besides their interest for the constitution of the text manuscripts also have significance for the history of literary or intellectual culture: the effort necessary for the production of a handwritten book implies a need for exploiting its contents. Advances made in Greek and above all in Latin palaeography allow scholars to identify in a growing number of cases the original owner or the cultural environment for which a book was made.

B. Character

1. Variants 2. Marginal notes 3. Division markings 4. Dating and determination of provenance 5. Text content

1. Variants

Readers have always been aware that handwritten texts are prone to error, and manuscripts regularly show the the results of their checking one against another, especially against the exemplar itself. The ancient subscriptions (→ Subscriptio) draw attention to this process, which is, however, seldom mentioned in the Middle Ages [3. 66]. Sometimes the original text has been changed, whether by overwriting or after erasure (a good sheet of membrane has enough thickness to bear the cutting away of a patch from the surface). Variants were also written in the margin or in the space between the lines, sometimes accompanied by an indication that they emanate from a particular source (rarely specified as clearly as one would wish), e.g. *u.c.* for *uetus codex*, more often simply by *al(iter)* or *uel* or γϱ(άφεται). But at times it looks as though such markings accompany readings that have been conjectured by their originator himself, and some scribes clearly tried to correct the text while copying it (→ Interpolation) – not out of 'dishonesty' or 'insincerity' on the part of the scribe, but rather as an attempt to understand the existing text. Scribes and scholars were not to know that the inventions of printing and photography and the stability of modern civilisation would allow the detailed investigation of manuscript traditions, and elevate sincerity over readability as the prime virtue of a manuscript.

2. Marginal notes

Most texts are written with sizeable margins. This may have been partly for the sake of appearance, but it certainly provides room not only for correction but also for annotation. This can include, for example, comments on the difficulty of reading the exemplar. The oldest manuscript of → Propertius (Wolfenbüttel, Cod. Gud. lat. 224) has a number of letters in the margin drawing attention to sententious and other lines, perhaps those thought worthy of excerption: in some places these markings are nonsensical (i.e. *uuta*, for *nota*?) and must have been copied from an exemplar. In other places the glosses indicate a greater involvement with content (i.e. *uere ais poeta* and *modeste* beside Prop. 4,1,54 and 58 respectively in Florentinus Laurentianus S. Marco 690, a manuscript copied in *c.* 1400–

1405 for Niccolò Niccoli and later palimpsested). Comments can also help to clarify difficulties in the text, with glosses on personal names especially frequent. Words over the line or in the margin were often not clearly recognizable as a gloss or variant: this has often led to corruption in a copy. In some cases the commentary is thorough, and there may well be far more words of scholia written on a page than of text (i.e. in the great Iliad, Venice, Marcianus Graecus 454 or the page of the Virgil manuscript, Bern 165 [4. fig. no. LXVIII]. Scribes frequently used a different script for marginalia, with ligatures and abbreviations employed more freely to save space.

3. Division markings

As aids to the reader, divisions between and within works were marked off in a variety of ways (→ Poems, division of), and titles were recorded (and often invented) to give some idea of content (i.e. in the Oblongus of → Lucretius). In numerous MSS of → Ovidius' *Metamorphoses* the titles are accompanied by synopses of the myth about to be narrated; manuscripts of the *Fasti* have a calendar in tabular form appended at the end of the text. In its earliest period of transmission Greek drama seems not to have consistent attribution of speakers, but this is increasingly added as time goes by; the occasional → stage directions transmitted with the text of → Aristophanes [1] (i.e. Aristoph. Thesm. 277) are almost certainly later additions.

4. Dating and determination of provenance

Manuscripts also contain various characteristics that are of interest to the codicologist, and so to the historian of textual traditions. Physical attributes such as the → ink, → parchment or paper (often dateable by watermarks) and the binding can give essential information about dating and provenance, as can aspects of production like the number of gatherings (*Lagenzählung*), the → ruling and of course the → script itself, also → punctuation (including details like the use of supralineals on the 'o' (ó), to indicate vocatives in Latin mss) and decoration, which may range from a brief flourish to fill a gap to the most ornate work of art that we see in 'illuminated manuscripts'. Already the ancient Virgil manuscripts contain pictures illustrating the adjacent text (see [3. 244ff] with illustrations). Flyleaves before and after the text pages were often used to try out the scribe's pen (*probationes pennae*), and as these are independent of the the the text contained within, they can also be very helpful in reconstructing a manuscript's history.

5. Text content

The contents of a single codex can be straightforward (e.g. the collected works of a single author), but some manuscripts are extremely diverse: a classic example is Bern 363 (s. ix 3/4), which contains texts by Disocorides, half of → Servius' commentary on → Vergilius [4], various rhetorical works, extracts from → Horatius and (somewhat shorter) from Ovid's *Metamorphoses*, Bede's *Ecclesiastical History,* and various medieval poems (facsimile [10]), and for most of these it is a manuscript of importance to editors. On the Greek side, a codex of extraordinary significance is Flor. Laur. 32,9, which contains the seven extant plays of both → Aeschylus and → Sophocles, as well as the *Argonautica* of → Apollonius [2] Rhodius.

C. Dissemination
1. Collections 2. Manuscripts in ancient libraries 3. Middle Ages and Renaissance

1. Collections

Manuscripts of Greek and Latin texts continued to be written until the second half of the 16th cent., and the total number surviving is considerable: estimates suggest there may be as many as 45,000 Greek manuscripts, and the figure for Latin manuscripts must be several times as large. The vast majority now belong to public and institutional libraries of Europe and North America. No ancient library has survived into the modern era, but some monasteries and early secular libraries still possess medieval books originally written specifically for their collections. Yet such volumes form no more than a very tiny proportion of the total; even if losses through theft or unreturned loans are left out of account, books have always travelled easily with their owners.

2. Manuscripts in ancient libraries

In the Roman empire, there were numerous private and public → libraries; some of the latter were very well stocked. Practically none of them survived so as to be discovered *in situ* in modern times. The few exceptions are worth listing: the Coptic Codices found in 1945 in Nag Hammadi, and the large collection of nearly 600 scrolls found in cave 4 at → Qumran; it is, however, not certain that the cave was intended to serve as a library [9. 192-193]. A better case can be made for the so-called Dišnā papers to be treated as an ancient library (cf. [9. 172-174] for the discovery in 1952; cf. also [15]). This was a collection, partly of Greek, partly of Coptic texts, built up at Pachomius' Monastery (in Upper Egypt) from the 4th cent. onwards and eventually buried in the 7th cent. A further example of an ancient library partially recovered *in situ* is the find of papyri made at Tura in 1941; this yielded eight codices with works of → Origenes and → Didymus [5] the Blind. But the prime example of an ancient library is the collection of carbonized rolls found in 1752 in the villa belonging to the Piso family in Herculaneum (→ Herculanean papyri). This library was mainly Greek and consisted primarily of titles on Epicurean philosophy. It is quite different from the literary papyri found in Egypt, which are essentially texts discarded from a very large number of private libraries that cannot be individually identified.

3. Middle Ages and Renaissance
a) The transition from ancient to medieval book production

In late antiquity and in the succeeding 'Dark Ages', libraries in all the territories of the Roman empire were either destroyed or greatly decimated, and the means at the disposal of the secular and ecclesiastical authorities only partially offset the losses. → Cassiodorus' foundation at Vivarium did not survive, but the monastery of Bobbio preserved some of its old stock. In western Europe as well as in Byzantium, a revival can be traced from *c.* 800 (→ Macedonian Renaissance). In both regions this is connected with the adoption of a new → minuscule script. For the last two or three cents., production had been hindered somewhat by the decline in the supply of papyrus (the standard writing material of antiquity). → Parchment as an alternative, though more durable, was also more expensive. The new minuscule script permitted a more economical use of writing material. In the Byzantine area a small additional stimulus to production came from the establishment of paper factories in various Arab lands; certainly by the 11th cent. the Byzantines were regularly taking advantage of this new invention.

Most of western Europe had to wait longer before enjoying the same benefit, and although paper production is attested *c.* 1147 under Arab influence [17. 133f] at Xátiva, south of Valencia, it is not until the 13th cent. or later that production on a substantial scale spread to other countries. Even in Byzantium shortage of writing material was problematic at times: parchment was a seasonal product, dependent on the consumption of meat [18. 1-15]. As a result, palimpsests obliterating the original text to make way for something deemed to be more important were created (examples in [14. 192-195]).

Books copied in the new scripts make their exemplars obsolete and a huge quantity of old volumes, some of them dating back to late antiquity, were discarded; it has been calculated that today there are still extant more than 6,700 Latin manuscripts in the new Carolingian → minuscule, whereas the number of Latin manuscripts, whether complete or in fragmentary state, surviving from earlier than *c.* 800, is about 1,865 [16; 47].

b) Libraries and manuscript collections

Book production was often undertaken, as in antiquity, by the individual, either acting on his own account or as a professional copyist. Many monasteries, both in the West and Byzantium, were centres of book production. From the 9th cent. onwards one can trace the existence of a number of private and institutional libraries. The most important one in the West was that assembled for Charlemagne in his palace; it was probably matched by one in the palace of the Byzantine emperor, but much less is known of libraries in the Byzantine empire. The stock of books was gradually enlarged, especially in the West in the 12th cent. Some universities developed the so-called → pecia system, whereby master copies of basic texts were divided into smaller sections to be rented out by booksellers to students [6; 2]. There is no trace of this system in Byzantium, and there, probably much more than in the West, many texts continued to be extant in one copy only. And there were also setbacks, as when in 1204–5 the Fourth Crusade created havoc in the Byzantine empire.

Some inventory lists of the larger libraries survive [5]. The best example from the Byzantine world is from the monastery of St. John on Patmos; a catalogue from the year 1200 lists a little over 300 volumes (an exact calculation is difficult); one fifth of these were of paper, the remainder of parchment (up-to-date edition in [1. 15–30 with 6 fig.]). More catalogues survive from the West, and in the 13th cent. the organization of one monastic order reached an unusual level of sophistication: the English Franciscans put together a union catalogue of the holdings of their various houses across the country (preserved in MSS Bodleian Library, Tanner 165 and Cambridge, Peterhouse 169). Occasionally a private collection could rival that of an institution: Richard of Fournival (fl. c. 1250), assembled at Amiens a library of around 300 volumes, which soon after his death formed the basis of a library for the Sorbonne.

The popes also had a rich and important collection. After their early Lateran library disappeared, a new one was established in the 13th cent. (there is a catalogue of it dating from 1295), and a third had to formed at Avignon where the curia was in exile during the years 1309–77; only a small part of this found its way back to Rome [13].

The number of important collections slowly increased during the Renaissance. The great private collectors included Petrarch, Coluccio, Salutati and Niccolò Niccoli; the papal library took a great step forward under Nicolas V (1447–1455), and the Medici ensured that their library was worthy of the cultural aspirations of Florence.

As far as Greek was concerned, from c. 1400 the new awareness of the benefits to be gained by studying the other classical language stimulated a search for MSS in all accessible regions of the former Byzantine empire; the outstanding collections were those formed by the Medici, Nicolas V and Cardinal Bessarion, who in 1468 left his books to Venice, where they still form the core of the Biblioteca Marciana (for these libraries see [8; 7; 11]). Great quantities of Latin MSS were also rescued from neglected monastic libraries by humanists who realized that the stock of Latin literature could be increased. Notable finds had been made by Petrarch (1304–1374), while Boccaccio (1313–1375) unearthed treasures in Montecassino, and a generation later, Poggio, who searched in Germany and Switzerland, was even more successful. The search for Greek books continued long after the Renaissance, and even in the 18th and 19th cents. substantial quantities were being brought to western Europe. The movement of Greek

MSS written before c. 1600 has been such as to leave only a rather small proportion of them in the countries where they were produced, whereas Latin MSS, though by no means exempt from displacement, have perhaps suffered a trifle less. ;

Movement of MSS from one country to another was common; but movement within the same country from one library to another has also been frequent, chiefly as a result of the confiscation of church property, in the 16th cent. in England, in the Napoleonic era in France and other European states. The process of loss and renewal and the movement of books have meant that few libraries have maintained collections intact over the long term. For instance, the library at Patmos now owns only a little more than 100 of the 300 volumes listed in 1200. But some of the large libraries put together in the Renaissance have survived to the present day and have been successful in varying degrees in maintaining their holdings (for information on the history of some of the larger collections of Greek MSS see [12. 1–13]).

→ Codicology; → Palaeography; → Papyri; → Codex

1 C. Astruc, Travaux et mémoires 8, 1981; 2 I. J. Bataillon, R. H. Rouse (ed.) La production du livre universitaire au moyen âge: exemplar et pecia, 1988; 3 B. Bischoff, Paläographie des römichen Altertums und des abendländischen Mittelalters, 1979; Engl. transl. Latin Palaeography: Antiquity and the Middle Ages, 1990.; 4 É. Chatelain, Paléographie des classiques latins (2 vols.), 1884–92; 5 A. Derolez, Les catalogues de bibliothèques, 1979; 6 J. Destrez, La pecia dans les manuscrits universitaires du xiiie et du xive siècle, 1935; 7 R. Devreese, Le fonds grec de la Bibliothèque Vaticane des origines à Paul V (Studi e Testi 244), 1965; 8 E. B. Fryde, Greek manuscripts in the private library of the Medici 1469–1510, 1996; 9 H. Y. Gamble, Books and Readers in the Early Church, 1995; 10 H. Hagen, Augustinus Beda Horatius Ovidius Servius alii: Cod. Bernensis 363 phototypice editus, 1897; 11 L. Labowsky, Bessarion's library and the Bibliotheca Marciana, 1979; 12 G. Laurion, Les principales collections de manuscrits grecs, in: Phoenix 15, 1961, 1–13; 13 F. Milkau, G. Leyh, Handbuch der Bibliothekswissenschaft 3/1, ²1955; 14 L. D. Reynolds, N. G. Wilson, Scribes and Scholars, ³1991; 15 J. M. Robinson, The Pachomian monastic library at the Chester Beatty Library and the Bibliothèque Bodmer, 1990.; 16 R. H. Rouse, in: R. Jenkyns, The Legacy of Rome: A New Appraisal, 1992; 17 O. Valls i Subirà, The History of Paper-Making in Spain I, 1978; 18 N. G. Wilson, in: (no ed.), Byzantine Books and Bookmen (Dumbarton Oaks Colloquium), 1975.

P. Ganz (ed.), The role of the book in medieval culture, Bibliologia 3–4, 1986; M. B. Parkes, Pause & effect: an introduction to the history of punctuation in the West, 1992; C. Questa, R. Raffaelli (ed.), Il libro e il testo, 1984; L. D. Reynolds (ed.), Texts and transmission, 1983, xiii-xliii; E. G. Turner, Greek manuscripts of the Ancient World, ²1987.   S.H. N.W.

Manus ferrea see → Navigation

Manus iniectio 'Laying on hand' occurs twice in connection with the most ancient type of Roman trial, the → *legis actio*: first, anyone wishing to accuse another may, if the defendant refuses to attend, force him to appear before the → praetor by *manus iniectio*, i.e. the use of force. The defendant may escape only by means of a → *vindex* (a person who guarantees the appearance of the defendant at a fixed later date; see *lex XII tab.* 1–4).

The second context for this a measure of compulsion – also involving a *vindex* – was that of the enforcement of a confirmed debt (*legis actio per manus iniectionem, lex XII tab.* 3,1–6). For this condition to obtain, the debtor's obligation to pay a sum of money had to be confirmed by an order of the court or in some other way be incontestable, e.g. by → *confessio* (confession, acknowledgement) or in the case of obvious theft. If the debtor did not pay within 30 days, the creditor could lay his hand on him before the praetor, and upon uttering a particular formula (Gai. Inst. 4,21) was granted custody of him (→ *addicere*). To be released from this arrest, the debtor required either here again a *vindex* who successfully challenged the creditor's right of seizure (*manum depellere*), or the intervention of a third party to pay in his place. To enable him to fulfil these requirements, the creditor had to bring the debtor, whom he held under private arrest subject to detailed stipulations (→ *addictus*; → Prison sentence), to the office of the praetor on three successive market days and there proclaim the amount of the sum owed. If nobody paid, the creditor was thereupon allowed to sell the debtor *trans Tiberim*, kill him (in the case of several creditors, they could cut him in pieces, *lex XII tab.* 3,6), or keep him as a bond-slave until he had worked off the sum (relevant terms contained in a *lex Poetelia,* probably from 326 BC).

→ Obligatio; → Debt

M. KASER, K. HACKL, Das röische. Zivilprozeßrecht, ²1996, 66, 131ff.; W. WALDSTEIN, Haftung und dare oportere, in: Festschrift G. Wesener, 1992, 519ff.   C.PA.

Maon

[1] (Hebrew *ma'on* '(hidden) camp, home'). Town 13 km south of → Hebron on the Ḫirbet Ma'īn at the edge of the Judaean Desert (1 Sam 23:24f.; 25,1f.; LXX Μαων/Μααν), also mentioned in the → Arad Ostraka . [1. no. 25]. Euseb. On. 130,12 mentions M. as a settlement east of Daroma. The Roman road from Hebron to Mampsis and Elath ran along here. In the excavation campaigns in 1987–88, a synagogue from the 4th–7th cent. built on the north-south axis was uncovered, as well as coins from the era of Valentinian I (AD 364–365) and fragments of several menorahs, the stems of which are flanked by lions.

[2] (Greek Μαών; *Maón*, Euseb. On. 134,16; identifiable with Hebrew *bêt ba'al me'ôn* in Jos 13:17), corresponds to modern Mā'īn, about 8 km south west of → Medaba. According to an inscription of the Moabite king Meša (→ Moab) (KAI 181, l. 30 et passim) *ba'al me'ôn*; cf. Nm 32:38; Ez 25:9; 1 Chr 5:8 (LXX and Euseb. On. 44,21 Βεελμεών/Βεελμαών/οικος Βεελμων/ οικος Μαων). Fortified in the 9th cent. BC by King Meša. A mosaic from the 6th/7th cents. represents among other things probably the church of the town.

1 Y. AHARONI, Arad Inscriptions, 1981.

Z. ILAN, D. AMIT, s.v. M., NEAEHL 3, 942–944; L. F. DE VRIES, s.v. M., Anchor Bible Dictionary 4, 1992, 512–513 (bibliography).   TH.PO.

Mapalia At the latest since Sall. Iug. 18,8 and Verg. G. 3,340, *mapalia* was the common expression, for the Romans as well, for the straw huts of the Numidians. Some North African areas were also called mapalia: 1) an imperial domain between → Hippo [6] Regius and → Calama (Aug. Epist. 66); 2) a domain that was probably also imperial in the Bagradas Valley (CIL VIII Suppl. 4, 25902; 3) a *dioecesis Mappaliensis* as a district within a Numidian diocese (PL 67,198).

H. DESSAU, s.v. M., RE 14, 1403; M. M. MAGALHÃES, C. A. SERTÁ, M., Lo spazio urbano e il nomadismo, in: A. MASTINO, P. RUGGERI (eds.), L'Africa romana. Atti del X convegno di studio 1, 1994, 499–502.   W.HU.

Mapharitis (Μαφαρῖτις/*Mapharîtis*, Peripl. m.r. 22). A region in the interior of south western Arabia Felix. In its capital Saye (Σαυή), three travel days from the port of → Muza, resided a prince by the name of Cholaebus (Χόλαιβος), in the middle of the 1st cent. AD. Compare the contemporary Sabaean inscription Shar'abi-as-Sawā 1 (squeeze of inscription in [1] and [2]), according to which Kulayb Yuha'min, the tribal leader of Ma'āfirum, had a temple built below the city of Šawām. At the time, parts of eastern African Azania were under the administration of the prince of M. (Peripl. m.r. 16; 31).

The earliest evidence of M. comes from the beginning of the 7th cent. BC in the report of the deeds of the Sabaean king Karib'il Watar who burnt down all the towns of Ma'āfirān (Répertoire d'Épigraphie Sémitique 3945,3). The inhabitants of that region were the Mapharitae (Μαφαρῖται/*Mapaharitai*; Ptol. 6,7,25) or Amphryaei (Plin. HN 6,158) who lived close to the Homerites. In the Sabaean inscription Jamme 631,33, for the period of king Ša'irum Awtar in the first quarter of the 3rd cent. AD, archers from Ma'āfirum are mentioned who fought on the side of the Abassinians against the Ḥimyar. The tribe Ḏū-Ma'āfirim is also mentioned in the inscription Mi'sāl 3,9 (middle of the 3rd cent.), and members of the Ma'āfir are listed in the Sabaean text Fakhry 74,5 from the year 499 and in the late Sabaean Christian inscription Istanbul 7608bis, 10 from the period around 530. The Yemenite scholar al-Hamdānī (10th cent.) could still describe in detail the borders and settlements of the tribal region of Ma'āfir [2]. It is that area south of the modern city of Ta'izz that since the 14th cent. AD has been known by the name al-Ḥuǧariya.

→ Arabia

1 Y. M. ABDALLAH, The City of Sawā in the Periplus of the Erythraean Sea, in: Arabian Archaeology and Epigraphy 6/4, 1995, 259–269; 2 D. H. MÜLLER (ed.), Ṣifat ǧazīrat al-ʿArab, 1884, 99f. W.W.M. A.D.

Maple (*acer*). Depending on how one classifies them, there are 100–200 species of the hardwood genus *Acer* L., the names for which in most European languages, including Greek ἄκαστος (ákastos) and Latin *acer* and *ornus,* are derived from an Indo-European tree name beginning with an a – not from the adjective *acer (*with an *ā).* Apart from the Central European A*cer pseudo-platanus* L. (sycamore maple), *platanoides* L. (Norway maple) and *campestre* L. (field or common maple), in southern Europe one finds, among other species, *Acer opalus Mill., monspessulanum* L. and *orientale* L. As deciduous trees of other genera were also counted among the maples, it remains unclear what the Greek names ἄκαστος (already in Hesiod), σφένδαμνος (sphéndamnos) and γλῖνος (glînos) or the Latin *acer* (in Ovid, Pliny, etc.) refer to. C.HÜ.

Mappa see → Mantellum; → Table utensils

Mara
[1] see → Mariaba
[2] According to Ptol. 6,7,37 (Μάρα μητρόπολις; *Mára mētrópolis*), city in the interior of → Arabia Felix, mostly identified with the Sabaean capital Mārib (→ Mariaba).

City i ; H. v. WISSMANN, Zur Geschichte und Landeskunde von Altsüdarabien (SAWW, Philos.-histor. Klasse 246), 1964, 417 (map). I.T.-N.

Mar Aba (*Mār Ābā,* Μὰρ ᾿Αβᾶ; *Màr Abâ*). → Katholikos of → Seleucea/→ Ctesiphon [2] in AD 540–552. Converted from → Zoroastrianism to Christianity, M. studied in → Nisibis and then undertook extensive journeys in the Roman empire. In Alexandria [1] he impressed → Cosmas [2] Indicopleustes with his erudition (the latter names him, in the Hellenized form of his name, *Patríkios,* cf. Topographia Christiana 2,2). Although he spent much of his period in office in exile or, as a confessor, in prison, he nonetheless remained extremely active in church administration and in pushing forward reforms that are passed down to us in detail in the *Synodikon Orientale* of the Eastern Church (→ Nestorianism) (synods of 544).

O. BRAUN, Ausgewählte Akten persischer Märtyrer, 1915, 188–220; J. B. CHABOT, Synodicon Orientale, 1902, 318–351, 540–561; W. WOLSKA, La topographie chrétienne de Cosmas Indicopleuste, 1962, 63–73. S.BR.

Maracanda (Μαράκανδα, ἡ Μαρακάνδα; *Marákanda, hē Marakánda*), modern Afrasiab/Samarkand, founded as an oasis city at the end of the 14th cent. BC in the fertile plain of the → Polytimetus (modern Serafšān), old capital of → Sogdiana (Arr. Anab. 3,30,6), the size of 60 *stadia* (Curt. 7,6,10). Trading centre for trade to the north and east (finds from the Tang period). There is hardly any information about the period before Alexander [4] the Great. After being conquered by Alexander the Great in 329 BC, for 2 years M. was his base of operations against the Transoxanians. At a banquet in their castle, → Cleitus [6] was murdered. Nevertheless M. was not the capital of the new satrapy of Sogdiana-Bactria. Later M. was probably an important town in the kingdom of Euthydemus (→ Euthydemus [2]), but by 150 BC it belonged to the Yuezhi (→ Indo-Scythians) and disappears beyond the horizon of the Graeco-Roman world. In the 5th cent. AD the city was the centre of a developing Hephthalite empire (→ Hephthalitae). In about the middle of the 6th cent. the West Turkish Khan took possession of it, and in 711 it was finally brought under Islamic rule by Kutaiba ben Muslim. Testimonials regarding the development of the city are provided almost exclusively by Arabic sources (Dinawarî, Tabarî).

Excavations in front of the citadel uncovered the Qarakhanid (10th–13th cent.) Friday Mosque, beneath which a solid brick building was discovered, presumably the Sogdian central temple. In the city area there were rooms belonging to Umayyad palaces (?), several rings of city walls and gates. A further Sogdian temple may lie below the cult and burial district of the Timurid period (15th cent. AD; Shah-i Zinda), which had been extended in the Qarakhanid era as a sanctuary. The Alexandrian and Graeco-Bactrian layers had not yet been reached in 1990. The most valuable stock of art works to date was in the ruins of a Sogdian city palace: among other things found in a large room (10 × 10 m) from the 7th cent. AD were historicizing wall paintings depicting Turks, Chinese, mountain dwellers, Koreans and others. In addition there is the sole representation of → Yazdgird III.
→ Graeco-Bactria (with maps)

L. I. AL'BAUM, Živopis' Afrasiaba, 1975; F. ALTHEIM, Geschichte der Hunnen, esp. vol. 2, 1960 (repr. 1969); M. MODE, Sogdien und die Herrscher der Welt: Türken, Sasaniden und Chinesen in Historiengemälden des 7. Jahrhunderts n.Chr. aus Alt-Samarkand, 1993; I. M. MUMINOV (ed.), Istorya Samarkanda, 2 vols., 1969; G. A. PUGACENKOVA, Samarkand, Buchara, 1975. B.B. G.WI.

Maranitae (Μαρανῖται; *Maranîtai*). According to Agatharchides (De Mari Erythraeo 88 GGM 1,177), Arab tribe that settled in the coastal strip of the Red Sea. Sources tell of their conflict with the *Garindaneîs* (Γαρινδανεῖς), who took advantage of the absence of the M. to seize for themselves, in an underhand manner, their possessions and estates. I.T.-N.

Marathesium (Μαραθήσιον; *Marathḗsion*). Town on the west coast of Asia Minor (ruins at the Ambar Tepe [1]); after an exchange with Samos, it belonged to the territory of Ephesus (Scyl. 98; Steph. Byz. s.v. M.; Plin. HN. 5,114). From 478/7 BC it was a member of the → Delian League (ATL 1,336f.; 515; 2,80; 3,204; 307).

R. Meriç et al (Ed.) IK 17,1, 1981, 111 (with inscriptions 3112–3114), 100 (map).

Magie 2, 886.   H.SO.

Marathon (Μαραθών; *Marathṓn*). Large Attic paralia deme of the Aeantis phyle, 10 (?) → *bouleutai*, in a flat coastal area in the east of Attica, capital of the Attic Tetrapolis (M., Oenoe, Probalinthus, Tricorynthus), not identical with modern Marathonas. The name is pre-Greek. There are important prehistoric, ancient and early Christian remains at various sites on the plain (map [10. 223 fig. 271]): Neolithic and Early Helladic settlement near Nea Makri (Probalinthus?) [8; 9; 10. 219], Early Helladic settlement near Kato Souli (Tricorynthus). The upper ring wall is not prehistoric [5. 37ff.] but medieval, fortified Early Helladic settlement near Plasi [10. 216 fig. 272], Early Helladic and Mycenaean necropolis near Tsepi [10. 216f. fig. 273– 280], important Middle Helladic and Mycenaean necropolis of a local dynasty in Vrana [10. 217 fig. 281– 288], the princely seat belonging to it has not been located. For Pan's cave (Paus. 1,32,2) see → Oenoe. The position of the ancient deme centre of M. is contentious [10. 219], and on the basis of the settlement structure of Attica we can expect more than one village settlement. Sanctuaries: Gymnasium and Temenos of Hercules near Valaria [10. 219 fig. 311], Temenos of Athena [10. fig. 314], summit sanctuary (statue platform?) on Stavrokoraki [4. 152f.], Imperial sanctuary of Isis and baths near Vrexisa [1; 2; 10. 218f. fig. 306–312]. In the Imperial period Latifundium of → Herodes [15] Atticus of M. who died here (Mandra tis Graias [10. 218 fig. 304, 305]).

In the north east of the bay of M. is the Cynosura [2] headland, on which the Persian fleet landed in 490 BC before the famous Battle of M. in which Athenians and Plataeans under Miltiades defeated the numerically superior Persians [3; 10. 216, 219f.] (→ Persian Wars). For the tomb of Miltiades and the Tropaion (Paus. 1,32,4f.) cf. [10. 254 fig. 315f.; 11]. The battle painting in the Stoa Poikile in Athens (Paus. 1,15,3) also depicted among others the hero M. The burial mound of the fallen Athenians (τύμβος, Paus. 1,32,3, modern Soros) lies in the middle of the plain where the battle was decided (Hdt. 6,107ff. [10. 216 fig. 270]). It was 9 m high and had stelae with the names of the fallen. The identification of the burial mound of the Plataeans at Vrana is contentious [6]. The philosopher → Boethus [3] was from M.

→ Attica (with map); → Macaria; → Marathon runner; → Marathon; → Battle sites

1 S. Albersmeier, Ägyptisierende Statuen aus M., in: M. Minas (ed.), Aspekte spätägyptischer Kultur. Festschrift E.Winter, 1994, 9–21;   2 X. Arapogianni, Το ρωμαϊκό βαλανείο στην Βρεξίζα του Μαραθώνος, in: ArchE 132, 1993, 133–186;   3 J. A. S. Evans, Herodotus and the Battle of M., in: Historia 42, 1993, 279–307;   4 H. Lauter, Der Kultplatz auf dem Turkovuni, 1985;   5 J. R. McCredie, Fortified Military Camps in Attica (Hesperia

Suppl. 11), 1966;   6 A. Mersch, Archäologischer Kommentar zu den 'Gräbern der Athener und Plataier' in der Marathonia, in: Klio 77, 1995, 55–64;   7 A. Onasoglou, Τα ιερά της τετραπόλεως του Μαραθώνα, in: Archaiología 39, 1991, 62–66;   8 M. Pantelidou Gofa, Η νεολιθική Νέα Μάκρη. Η κεραμεική, 1995;   9 D. Theocharis, Ἀνασκαφή νεολιθικοῦ συνοικισμοῦ ἐν Νέᾳ Μάκρῃ (Ἀττικῆς), in: MDAI(A) 71, 1956, 1–29;   10 Travlos, Attika (with bibliography up to 1982);   11 E. Vanderpool, A Monument to the Battle of M., in: Hesperia 35, 1966, 93–106.

B. Ch. Petrakos, M., 1998; Traill, Attica, 22, 53, 62, 67, 111 no. 87, table 9; Whitehead, Index s.v. M.   H.LO.

Marathon running The marathon as an agonistic discipline is an invention of the modern age. Longer → foot races than the → *dólichos* (max. 24 stadia = *c.* 4·6 km) were not known to antiquity. Just as the *dólichos* was originally run in the context of the training of messengers (*hēmerodrómoi*; *dromokérykes*), the marathon was ultimately part of (military) communication.

The ancient tradition regarding the narration of the unique marathon after the Persian battle (490 BC) is scant: according to Plutarch (Mor. 347c) an Athenian hoplite in armour (→ *hoplitai*) ran from the battlefield at → Marathon to Athens, announced the victory to the Prytaneion, collapsed and died. According to 'most' the messenger was called Eucle(e)s and only Heraclides Ponticus (the Elder) (fr. 156 Wehrli) mentions a Thersippus from the deme of Erchia. In Lucian (Pro Lapsu inter Salutandum 3) on the other hand, a dying *hēmerodrómos* by the name of Philippides appears.

The origin of the patriotic episode has not been fully clarified. The narrative pattern appears in origin legends of local weapon runs (Philostr. De Gymnastica 7) and in the report on Euchidas of Plataeae who after the battle there (in 479 BC) ran to Delphi and back (about 180 km) and died (Plut. Aristides 20,4–6). Within the context of the battle of Marathon, sources mention exceptional achievements of runners, such as the 'running step' of the hoplites (Hdt. 6,112; 116), and particularly the run by → Phidippides, with a request for help, to Sparta *before* the battle (Hdt. 6,105f.). The widespread variant, Philippides, has then slipped into the passage by Lucianus.

The legend of the heroic runner proved to be longlived. At the first Olympic Games of the modern age (in Athens in 1896), at the instigation of the classical philologist M. Bréal, a marathon was included in the programme on the supposed original course of about 40 km. In London in 1908 (4th Games) a distance of 42·195 km was run for the first time and in 1921 this was confirmed as the official length for the modern marathon.

→ Sports

W. Decker, Sport in der griechischen Antike, 1995, 73; F. J. Frost, The Dubious Origins of the 'Marathon', in: AJAH 4, 1979, 159–163; Y. Kempen, Krieger, Boten und Athleten, 1992, 96ff.; I. Kertész, Schlacht und 'Lauf' bei

Marathon, in: Nikephoros 4, 1991, 155–160; P. Siewert, Die Namen der antiken Marathonläufer, in: Nikephoros 3, 1990, 121–126.   T.FR.

Marathus Modern ʿAmrīt, important town in northern Phoenicia south of → Aradus [1], which controlled it in 333/2 BC (Arr. Anab. 2,13,8; 14,1; 15,6; Curt. 4,1,6) and in 218 (Pol. 5,68,7). Around the middle of the 2nd cent. M. was independent and was able to defend itself against the Aradians (Diod. Sic. 33,5f.). According to Str. 16,2,12, M. was destroyed and its land divided among settlers from Aradus, but the city must have continued to exist (Mela 1,67; Plin. HN 5,78; 12,124; Ptol. 5,15,16; Dionys. Per. 914). Excavations by M. Dunand uncovered remains (Hellenistic burial complexes etc., a spring sanctuary) from the 6th–2nd cent. BC.

R. Dussaud, Topographie historique de la Syrie antique et médiévale, 1927, 123ff.; E. Honigmann, s.v. M. (2), RE 14, 1431–1435; G. Lehmann, Untersuchungen zur späten Eisenzeit in Syrien und Libanon, 1996, 105f.; TAVO B IV 9.1, 9.2, 1991.   H.J.N.

Marathus(s)a (Μαραθοῦσσα; *Marathoûssa*, 'fennel island'). The most southerly of the islands off → Clazomenae in the south west of the Gulf of Smyrna, modern Hekim or Çiçek Islands. Few remains. Evidence: Thuc. 8,31,3; Str. 14,1,36; Plin. HN 5,137; Steph. Byz. s.v. Μαράθουσα.

G. Winkler, R. König (ed.), C. Plinius Secundus der Ältere, Naturkunde, B. 5, 1993, 262f. (commentary).   H.KA.

Marble
I. Terminology, properties, identification
II. Occurrence III. Ownership and administration of quarries IV. Quarrying and
transportation V. Storage, distribution,
prices VI. Techniques of working
VII. Marmorarii VIII. Use

I. Terminology, properties, identification
Geologically speaking, marble is a metamorphic rock of crystalline structure (average crystal size 0.3 to 1.0 mm) and variable translucency, derived by medium- or high-level metamorphosis from limestone and dolomite [21. 17–20]. The ancient terms μάρμαρον/ *mármaron* (originally masc. μάρμαρος/*mármaros* = 'gleaming stone'; later attested in all three genders) and Latin *marmor*, however, mean all white and coloured rocks capable of being polished, including hard rocks such as → granite, greywacke and porphyry, and it is in this sense that marble is used here. As a natural material for working with, marble was useful like no other type of rock. It was widely and abundantly available, in various qualities and colours. It was possible to work it well and extremely precisely, to polish it highly and to sculpt

in large dimensions. Depending on variety and application, it could take sufficient pressure and load (compared to other stones, metamorphic marble was almost elastic), and it was relatively durable. On aesthetic and ideological grounds it was highly prized. Marble is extremely heavy, weighing some 2.75 tonnes or more per cubic metre.

Owing to their distinctive colours and patterns, polychrome marbles can often be definitely ascribed to a particular place of origin, and therefore they constitute readily accessible historical evidence. Monochrome marbles, esp. the many white marbles, are harder to attribute. Advances in their identification have been attained by a combination of archaeological and scientific methods (such as isotope analysis, the investigation of trace elements and the use of cathode luminescence) [21. 32–45; 34. 19–25]. Pliny (Plin. HN 36,1–74) gives a comprehensive description of the occurrence and properties of various marbles, as well as their use in sculpture and architecture.   H.SCHN.

II. Occurrence
The Mediterranean world possesses rich deposits of marble [14. 153–159]. The most important quarries for white export marble were in Greece, Asia Minor and Italy (accompanied below by either the ancient or the modern name and core periods of working):

Greece: Athens: (*marmor*) *Pentelicum*, the celebrated Pentelic marble (Cic. Att. 1,8,2; cf. Plut. Poplicola 15), and *marmor Hymettium* (Plin. HN 17,6; 36,7), both 5th cent. BC to late Roman period; Paros: Παρία λίθος/*Paría líthos* (Str. 10,5,7; cf. Plin. HN 4,67), *marmor a Paro*, the celebrated Parian marble (Vitr. De arch. 10,2,15), *lychnites* (Plin. HN 36,14;), 6th cent. BC to Roman period; Naxos: 7th cent. BC to Roman period; Delos: Greek and Roman period; Lesbos: μάρμαρον Λέσβου/*mármaron Lésbou* (Edictum Diocletiani (= ED) 33,16), dating uncertain; Thasos: *marmor a/e Thas(i)o* (Vitr. De arch. 10,2,15; Plin. HN 36, 44), *Thasius lapis* (Sen. Ep. 86,6), μάρμαρον Θάσιον/ *mármaron Thásion* (ED 33,17), 6th cent. BC – 6th cent. AD.

Asia Minor: Proconnesus: *marmor Proconnesium* (Vitr. De arch. 2,8,10; 10,2,15; Plin. HN 36,47), μάρμαρον Προκοννήσιον/ *mármaron Prokonnésion* (ED 33,7), 6th cent. BC – 6th cent. AD; Heraclea on the Latmus and Ephesus: both 6th(?)/5th cent. BC – 6th cent. AD; Dokimeion: 4th(?) cent. BC – 6th cent. AD; Aphrodisias: Hellenistic to late Roman period.

Italy: Luna: *marmor Lun(i)ense* (Plin. HN 36,14; 36,48), *c.* 50 BC – 3rd cent. AD.

Under Augustus the Romans began to exploit coloured marble systematically. The most important quarries were in Greece: Carystus: (μάρμαρον) Καρύστιον/(*mármaron*) *Karýstion* (Str. 9,5,16; 10,1,6), *marmor Carystium* (Plin. HN 36,48), 1st cent. BC to late Roman period; Chalcis: *fior di pesco*, late 1st cent. BC to late Roman period; Laris(s)a: λίθος Θετταλή/*líthos Thettalé* (Poll. 7,100), (μάρμαρον) Θεσσα-

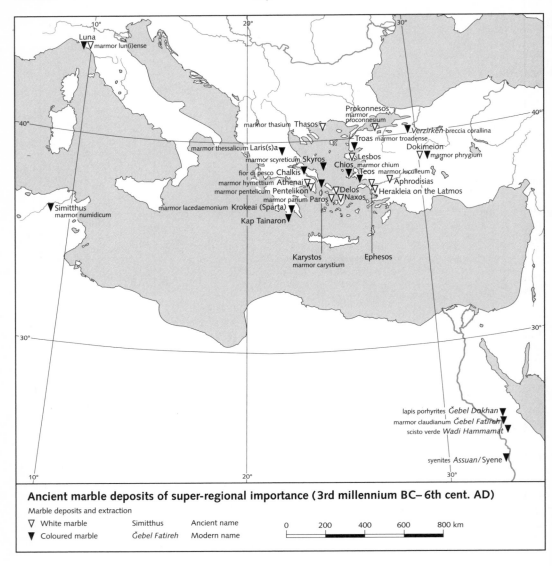

Ancient marble deposits of super-regional importance (3rd millennium BC– 6th cent. AD)

Marble deposits and extraction

▽ White marble   Simitthus   Ancient name   0   200   400   600   800 km

▼ Coloured marble   *Ğebel Fatireh*   Modern name

λικόν/(*mármaron*) *Thessalikón* (Paulus Silentiarius, Hagia Sophia 388), early 2nd cent. – 6th cent. AD; Chios: *marmor Chium* (Plin. HN 5,136), late 1st cent. BC to (late?) Roman period; Scyros: λίθος Σκυρία/*líthos Skyría* (Str. 9,5,16), *(marmor) Scyreticum* (Plin. HN 31,29), 1st cent. BC to late Roman period; Croceae: *marmor Lacedaemonium* (Plin. HN 36,55), μάρμαρον Λακεδαιμόνιον/*mármaron Lakedaimónion* (ED 33,2), late 1st cent. BC to late Roman period; Cape Tainaron: *(marmor) Taenarium* (Prop. 3,2,11), 1st cent. BC to (late?) Roman period.

Asia Minor: Troas: *marmor Troadense* [43. 467, l. 5], 2nd cent. BC – 6th cent. AD; Teos: (probably) λίθος λευκολλεία/*líthos leukolleía* (Str. 9,5,16; cf. ED 33,4), *marmor Luculleum* (Plin. HN 36,49–50), 1st cent. BC to late Roman period; Dokimeion: λίθος Δοκιμαίος/*líthos Dokimaíos* or Συνναδικός/*Synnadikós* (Str.

9,5,16; 12,8, 14), *(marmor) Phrygium* (Tib. 3,3,13), 1st cent. BC – 6th cent. AD; Vezirhan (and other Mediterranean locations): *breccia corallina*, 1st cent. BC to late Roman period.

North Africa: Simitthus: *marmor Numidicum* (Plin. HN 5,22; 36,49), 2nd cent. BC – end of 3rd cent. AD.

Egypt: Ğebel Dokhan: *(lapis) porphyrites* or *leptopsephos* (Plin. HN 36,57), 1st cent. AD to late Roman period; Ğebel Fatireh: μάρμαρον Κλαυδιανόν/*mármaron Klaudianón* (ED 33,6), 1st cent. BC to late Roman period; Wādī Ḥammāmāt: *scisto verde* (greywacke), 3rd millennium BC to late Roman period; Assuan: *lapis Thebaicus*, also called *syenites* and *pyrrhopoecilus* (Plin. HN 36,63), 3rd millennium BC to late Roman period.

In addition there is a rich spectrum of other coloured stones, notably various kinds of alabaster, lacustrine limestone and breccia, which were often widespread during the Roman Imperial period [33. 37–52]. Just as important, but little researched, are the countless smaller marble deposits (more than 40 near Ephesus alone) of local significance [34. 304], which contributed greatly to the development of the urban infrastructure of the Mediterranean world.

III. OWNERSHIP AND ADMINISTRATION OF QUARRIES

In the Greek period, marble quarries were either the property of the polis or in private hands; exploitation, for the most part concentrated on particular projects and particular times, was undertaken by operatives appointed by contract. Similar forms of organization probably applied to most of the smaller deposits of local significance during the Roman Imperial period. There is some evidence that the most important quarries for white and coloured export marble formed part of the *patrimonium Caesaris* probably from the Julian-Claudian period, (on this and on the following cf. [31. 17–25]). During the Roman Imperial period extracted blocks of marble might be inscribed according to complex criteria (with considerable local differences and frequently associated with the internal organization of the → quarries and/or the accountability of the operators to the imperial administration), often naming the consul (64 such names are attested up to AD 236). Such evidence indicates that imperial slaves and freedmen often served as contractors and administrators, some of them responsible for several quarries in widely separated locations.

IV. QUARRYING AND TRANSPORTATION

The technology of marble-quarrying went through various stages [32. 47–72]. In Egypt, from around 3000 BC, the softer sandstones and limestones were for the first time separated from the surrounding rock by working channels and split from the base rock by wedges (often wooden wedges; the early copper wedges were later replaced by ones of bronze, then of iron; at the same time, the splitting technique was further developed by means of differentiated sequences of wedge holes); extremely hard rocks were extracted by the excavation of grooves that might be the width of a man, probably with the aid of sharp-edged stone hammers made of dolorite. After the introduction of iron wedges during the 1st millennium BC, splitting by wedge hole became increasingly widespread (in Greek marble quarries from the period c. 600 BC, in Egyptian hard-rock quarries from the beginning of the Principate at the latest). During late antiquity quarrying was also occasionally carried out by saws [44. 31]. Usually raw blocks were either supplied in a form determined by conditions at the quarry or dimensioned in accordance with their envisaged use, or prepared and also sometimes finished at the quarry by specialist stonemasons, to save on weight for transportation, among other reasons. The quantities of marble quarried in antiquity were enormous: exploitation of Pentelic marble is estimated at some 400,000 m³ [52. 861], with a weight of c. 1.1 million tonnes, that of the very expensive Numidian marble at at least 250,000 m³ with a weight of c. 700,000 tonnes.

From the later 7th cent. BC, enormous blocks and great quantities of marble were transported in Greece over long distances, in the archaic period already blocks of over 70 tonnes in weight. Often lengthy → land transport (e.g. some 120 km from the *marmor Claudianum* quarry to the Nile) was effected using sometimes purpose-built roads, levers, wooden sledges, carts, draught animals; loading onto ships by specialized cranes [21. 97–142; 29]. On account of the high specific gravity of marble and the high demand for imported marble, it must be assumed that many cargo ships (average cargo capacity some 100 to 450 tonnes) were used per year. Transportation to Rome of the large obelisks made from *syenites*, of which the largest, today standing in front of the Lateran, was over 32 m tall and weighed more than 455 tonnes, required specialised methods, including the building of gigantic specialised ships (Plin. HN 36, 70–71).

V. STORAGE, DISTRIBUTION, PRICES

While small quantities of coloured imported marble were stored in the Late Minoan palace at → Knossos [53. 290–292], for the later Greek period indications for the storage of marble appear to be absent. This constitutes a fundamental difference from the situation in Rome: whereas in the Greek period marble was normally probably ordered, quarried and paid for only with a specific project in mind (for the unfinished proto-Parthenon up to the second/third drums of the pillars more than 15,000 tonnes of Pentelic marble [28. 8]), under the Romans marble became a mass product. Rich stores of select marbles did not exist until the Principate, probably from the time of Augustus. The most important and largest – each associated with marble workshops – were at Ostia (Portus) and Rome; there they constituted a unique imperial treasure. The quantity, quality and diversity of the marble stored suggest a differentiated production model: rough blocks, perhaps for smaller structures and sculptures as well as floor and wall → incrustation and column shafts in standard sizes (length: some 9–18 Roman feet?) were extracted and prepared on a production-line basis, while more lavish architectural elements and larger column shafts (length: more than 30 Roman feet?) were usually probably ordered for specific building projects, but not always used in that context [31. 24–25, 157–159].

The storage, sale and use of imported marble in Ostia and Rome were evidently not subject to drastic imperial restrictions. On the contrary, the many instances of imported marble from the great (imperial) quarries on Roman Crete alone encourage us here too (and therefore at the same time in other Roman provinces) to assume the storage of marble, and indicate more or less flexible mechanisms of marble distribution

[37]. The intensive, empire-wide transportation and trading of heavy loads of marble and marble items was one of Rome's greatest technical (and ideological) achievements (cf. Str. 12,8,14; Plin. HN 36,1-3) – one that was never again to be realized to the same extent.

The highest prices for the most important coloured (and some white) marbles are known for the early 4th cent. from the *Edictum Diocletiani* issued in AD 301; the maximum price for one foot of *marmor porphyreticum* or *marmor Lacedaemonium* was 250 denarii, for *marmor Numidicum* and *marmor Phrygium* 200 denarii, for *marmor Luculleum* and *marmor Thessalicum* 150 denarii, for *marmor Claudianum* 100 denarii, *marmor Carystium* 50 denarii, *marmor Proconnesium* and *marmor Scyreticum* 40 denarii (ED 33,1-18). The unit on which these prices are based was probably one cubic foot of sawn marble slab, corresponding to the most common use for coloured marble at that time; other terms evidently applied to large sculptural blocks, architectural elements and column shafts of coloured marble. Demand and prices for marble probably increased during the 4th cent., so that Julian [11] expressly encouraged the quarrying of marble (Cod. Theod. 10,19,2).

VI. Techniques of working

The mastering of iron technology in the Greek world from the last years of the 2nd millennium BC onwards was a prerequisite for the gradual introduction during the 7th cent. BC of tip-hardened tools that were later to become standard in marble working, such as the (pointed) hammer, the point, the tooth chisel, the flat chisel, the drill and the rasp [7; 21. 177-194]. The different characteristics of the various kinds of marble determine their workability: Parian *lychnites* and white marble from Aphrodisias are, for example, relatively soft; Pentelic marble is somewhat harder; coloured marbles are more frequently hard; white Thasian marble is almost as hard as the extremely hard-to-work varieties of granite, porphyry and greywacke [46. 17-24].

The fluting of → columns was expensive, and the fluting of monolithic shafts of coloured marble such as those of Numidian marble in the → Pantheon unusual. It was still more labour-intensive to grind and polish marble surfaces to different degrees of fineness [43. 227f.]; the polishing materials employed were corundum, → pumice and fine sand of various grades. The *politores* of the Principate, esp. in the 2nd cent. AD, developed the subtlest of polishing techniques, producing effects from matt to high gloss [7. 313-315]. In the planing of marble surfaces, extreme precision was sometimes achieved, down to $^1/_{1000}$ mm in the connecting surfaces of individual drums of the Pantheon columns. The thin marble floor slabs (c. 30 mm), internal walls (c. 10 mm) and figurative incrustations (only c. 4-5 mm) were cut to size directly on site with the aid of iron saws and a special sand (Plin. HN 36,51-53). The technique of piecemeal assembly, important for repairs and shared-labour production (e.g. of head and

body) is demonstrated in Graeco-Roman sculpture from the 6th cent. BC onwards [32. 135-162].

VII. Marmorarii

While Greek marble workers were usually called λιθουργός/ *lithourgós* and λιθοξόος/*lithoxóos*, more rarely μαρμαροποιός/ *marmaropoiós*, for Roman marble workers the new term *marmorarius* was coined (evidently adopted into Greek as μαρμαράριος/*marmarários*), and is attested in a great number of Latin and Greek inscriptions (e.g. ILS 4681; 5442; 6331; 7539; 7678). *Marmorarii* (frequently freedmen), supported by other specialist workers in the quarry [8], in the stone masons' workshop and on the building site, executed all kinds of marble work, even the carving of inscriptions (ILS 7679). Together with the *pictores* (painters) and *statuarii* (sculptural casters) they were craft-workers of luxury goods (Sen. Ep. 88,18). In the *Edictum Diocletiani* the maximum daily wage of a *marmarários/marmorarius* is set at 60 denarii, that of the 'simpler' *lithourgós techneítēs* or *lapidarius structor* on the other hand restricted to 50 denarii (ED 7,2; 7,5). Until the 4th cent. AD, *marmorarii* frequently travelled with the marble they were to work. Later they were more strictly bound by law to a particular location, to fulfil urgent restoration work in their local area [19. 322]. In late antiquity marble workers were freed from the *munera* (→ *munus*) at the same time as other highly qualified craftsmen (Cod. Theod. 13,4,2).

VIII. Use

During the early Bronze Age (3rd millennium BC), the Cyclades formed the centre of widespread and highly specialized marble production, primarily of small vessels and sculptures. During the Minoan-Mycenaean period, seals, vessels, furniture, architectural panelling and column bases were manufactured from coloured marble, such as *marmor Taenarium* and *marmor Lacedaemonium* [53. 287-295]; there is no evidence here of marble as a building material and for sculpture. From the 7th cent. BC, white marble came into use in areas influenced by Greek culture, at first in sculpture (at least 60,000 statues of archaic Kurai/Korai [49. 21]), and from the early 6th cent. BC also in architecture. From the classical period onwards public buildings and their relief decoration were increasingly executed in white marble, sculpture in the round on the other hand more frequently in bronze.

In Rome there is evidence of white Greek marbles from 146 BC onwards (Temple of Jupiter Stator; Vell. Pat. 1,11,5) and of coloured marbles in particularly lavish contexts from the 1st cent. BC onwards [47. 144-148]. Rome underwent a marble revolution under Augustus (cf. Suet. Aug. 28,3) and from the 1st cent. AD onwards this spread to the entire empire. The public and to some extent also the domestic space in Rome and later in the provinces was fundamentally transformed by the systematic use of large quantities of not only Italian *marmor Lunense* but also white and coloured export marbles (buildings, sculptures, ceremonial kraters, candelabra, puteals, etc.) [23; 47. 148f.; 54. 319–328]. New aesthetic and ideological horizons were opened up, esp. by the many coloured marbles, which, from the time of Augustus, were for the first time used deliberately in architecture – in the building of temples, forums, baths, theatres, nymphaea, administrative buildings, houses – and for almost all themes in sculpture (with an emphasis on larger than life-size statues of orientals and Dacians) as well as for large ceremonial basins (→ Roma). At the same time, the first Egyptian → obelisks made from *syenites* were brought to Rome and erected at central locations (Plin. HN 36,70–74: *Mausoleum Augusti, Solarium Augusti, Circus maximus*). This practice persisted, with varying intensity and emphasis, at least to the 3rd cent. The central objects for the reconstruction of workshops and the production and trade of marble are capitals, → sarcophagi and imperial portraits. There is also evidence of lavish use of white and coloured (frequently imperial) export marbles during this period in the Roman provinces, to the extent of imitating coloured marbles in wall-painting and on mosaics [11. 271f.; 40. 155–170].

In the late antique and early Byzantine periods *marmor Proconnesium*, white marbles from Docimeum, *lapis porphyrites*, *marmor Thessalicum*, *marmor Carystium* and *marmor Troadense* were preferred from among the traditional, frequently re-used white and coloured marbles in architecture and sculpture. The monolithic columns favoured during the Roman Imperial period are evidence for the use of specific rock types: while marbles and breccias could barely support shaft lengths of more than 30 Roman feet (*c.* 9 m), granite (*syenites*/*marmor Claudianum*) ones could extend to at least 60 Roman feet (*c.* 18 m) [31. 143–147]. Other rocks, such as *marmor Lacedaemonium*, provided only small blocks, with a maximum size of some 0.5 × 0.5 × 1.0 m [48. 245].

IX. IDEOLOGICAL ASPECTS

Complementary to the always high prestige value of marble various ideological aspects came into play, depending on the cultural context and period setting; these may best be seen in the Roman Imperial period. On the one hand, the use of marble for private houses was expressly criticised by Pliny (Plin. HN 36,2–8) and characterized by Juvenal as an expression of profligacy (→ Luxury) on the part of members of the elite class (Juv. 14,86–95). On the other hand, esp. the precious and exotic marbles, which were transported at great expense from the edges of the Roman world and modelled and polished to high perfection according to requirement, were a tangible symbol of Rome's superior culture, its presence ever growing and setting its mark ever more clearly on the principal living spaces of the Roman empire, thus at the same time relating them more strongly to one another.

From the time of Hadrian onwards this ideological context acquired a further dimension: monolithic columns of coloured marble (for imperial connotations Str. 12,8,14; Stat. Silv. 4,2,18–29) began to play a decisive role in an imperial gift economy, evidently with the intention of visibly deepening the political loyalty of provincial elites to the emperor in Rome [37]. Furthermore, in the sculptures worked from coloured marble there was a direct relationship between the colour of the marble and the theme represented, in the sense of a heightened interpretation of reality [47. 139–160].

1 A. M. ABRALDES, Pentelethen: The Export of Pentelic Marble and Its Use in Architectural and Epigraphical Monuments, 1997;   2 ADAM, 23–60;   3 A. AMBROGI, Vasche di età romana in marmi bianchi e colorati, 1995;   4 N. ASGARI, The Proconnesian Production of Architectural Elements in Late Antiquity, Based on Evidence from the Marble Quarries, in: C. MANGO (ed.), Constantinople and Its Hinterland. Papers from the Twenty-Seventh Spring Symposium of Byzantine Studies in Oxford, 1995, 263–288;   5 R. BELLI PASQUA, Sculture di età romana in basalto, 1994;   6 G. BORGHINI (ed.), Marmi antichi, 1989;   7 M. L. BRUTO, C. VANNICOLA, Strumenti e tecniche di lavorazione dei marmi antichi, in: ArchCl 42, 1990, 287–324;   8 A. BÜLOW-JACOBSEN, On Smiths and Quarries, in: B. KRAMER et al., Akten des 21. Internationalen Papyrologenkongresses 1, 1997, 139–145;   9 I. CALABI LIMENTANI, s.v. Marmorarius, EAA 4, 870–875;   10 A. CLARIDGE, Roman Methods of Fluting Corinthian Columns and Pilasters, in: Città e architettura nella Roma imperiale (Analecta Romana Instituti Danici, Suppl. 10), 1983, 119–128;   11 S. CORCORAN, J. DELAINE, The Unit of Measurement of Marble in Diocletian's Prices Edict, in: Journal of Roman Archaeology 7, 1994, 263–273;   12 J. J. COULTON, Lifting in Early Greek Architecture, in: JHS 94, 1974, 1–19;   13 H. CUVIGNY, The Amount of Wages to the Quarry-Workers at Mons Claudianus, in: JRS 86, 1996, 139–145;   14 H. DODGE (ed.), Marble in Antiquity. Collected Papers of J.B. Ward-Perkins, 1992;   15 E. DOLCI, Carrara. Cave antiche, 1980;   16 Id. (ed.), Il marmo nella civiltà romana, 1989;   17 A. DWORAKOWSKA, Quarries in Ancient Greece, 1975;   18 Id., Quarries in Roman Provinces, 1983;   19 M. L. FISCHER, Marble, Marble Trade and *marmorarii*, in: R. KATZOFF (ed.), Classical Studies in Honor of D. Sohlberg, 1996, 319–336;   20 Id., Marble Studies: Roman Palestine and the Marble Trade, 1999;   21 R. FRANCOVICH (ed.), Archeologia delle attività estrattive e metallurgiche, 1993;   22 R. GNOLI, Marmora Romana, 1971, ²1988;   23 T. M. GOLDA, Puteale und verwandte Monumente, 1997;   24 G. GRUBEN, Anfänge des Monumentalbaus auf Naxos, in: A. HOFFMANN et al. (ed.), Bautechnik der Antike, 1991, 63–71;   25 W. V. HARRIS (ed.), The Inscribed Economy. Production and Distribution in the Roman Empire in the Light of *instrumentum domesticum* (Journal of Roman Archaeology, Suppl. 6), 1993;   26 N. HERZ, E. G. GARRISON, Geological Methods for Archaeology, 1998;   27 M. J. KLEIN, Unersuchungen zu den kaiserlichen Steinbrüchen am Mons Porphyrites und Mons Claudianus in der östlichen Wüste Ägyptens, 1988;   28 M. KORRES, Vom Penteli zum Parthenon. Werdegang eines Kapitells zwischen Steinbruch und Tempel, 1992;   29 V. LAMBRINOUDAKIS, The Sanctuary of Iria on Naxos and the Birth of Monumental Greek Architecture, in: D. BUITRON-OLIVER

(ed.), New Perspectives in Early Greek Art, 1991, 173–188; 30 Y. LINTZ, D. DECROUEZ, J. CHAMAY, Les marbres blancs dans l'antiquité, 1991; 31 M. MAISCHBERGER, Marmor in Rom. Anlieferung, Lager- und Werkplätze in der Kaiserzeit, 1997; 32 Marble. Art, Historical and Scientific Perspectives on Ancient Sculpture (Symposion ... J. Paul Getty Museum, 1988), 1990; 33 H. MIELSCH, Buntmarmore aus Rom im Antikenmuseum Berlin, 1985; 34 M. MOLTESEN, The Lepsius Marble Samples, 1994; 35 S. MROZEK, Einige wirtschaftliche Aspekte der Herstellung von Inschriften in der frühen römischen Kaiserzeit, in: H. SOLIN et al. (ed.), Acta Colloquii Epigraphici Latini Helsingiae, 1995, 303–312; 36 C. NAPOLEONE, s.v. Marmo, EAA suppl. secondo, vol. 3, 547–553; 37 S. PATON, R. M. SCHNEIDER, Imperial Splendour in the Province: Imported Marble on Roman Crete, in: A. CHANIOTIS (ed.), From Minoan Farmers to Roman Traders. Sidelights on the Economy of Crete, 1999, 279–304; 38 D. P. S. PEACOCK, Roman Stones, in: Journal of Roman Archaeology 7, 1994, 361–363; 39 Id., V. A. MAXFIELD, Survey and Excavations: Mons Claudianus 1987–1993, vol. 1. Topography and Quarries, 1997; 40 P. PENSABENE (ed.), Marmi Antichi. Problemi d'impiego, di restauro e d'identificazione, 1985; 41 Id., Le vie del marmo. I blocchi di cava di Roma e di Ostia: Il fenomeno del marmo nella Roma antica, 1995; 42 Id., Marmi antichi II, 1998; 43 M. PFANNER, Über das Herstellen von Porträts, in: JDAI 104, 1989, 157–257; 44 F. RAKOB (ed.), Simitthus I. Die Steinbrüche und die antike Stadt, 1993; 45 J. M. REYNOLDS, J. B. WARD PERKINS, The Inscriptions of Roman Tripolitania, 1952; 46 P. ROCKWELL, The Art of Stoneworking. A Reference Guide, 1993; 47 R. M. SCHNEIDER, Bunte Barbaren. Orientalenstatuen aus farbigem Marmor in der römischen Repräsentationskunst, 1986; 48 Id., Kolossale Dakerstatuen aus grünem Porphyr, in: MDAI(R) 97, 1990, 235–260; 49 A. M. SNODGRASS, Heavy Freight in Archaic Greece, in: P. GARNSEY et al. (ed.), Trade in the Ancient Economy, 1983, 16–26; 50 D. VANHOVE, Roman Marble Quarries in Southern Euboea and the Associated Road Networks, 1996; 51 M. WAELKENS, s.v. Cave di marmo, EAA suppl. secondo, vol. 2, 71–88; 52 J. B. WARD PERKINS, s.v. Marmo, EAA 4, 1961, 860–870; 53 P. WARREN, Lapis Lacedaemonius, in: J. A. SANDERS (ed.), ΦΙΛΟΛΑΚΩΝ. Lakonian Stud. in Honour of H. Catling, 1992, 285–296; 54 P. ZANKER, Augustus und die Macht der Bilder, 1987.

MAP: R. GNOLI, Marmora Romana, 1971; N. HERZ, M. WAELKENS (ed.), Classical Marble: Geochemistry, Technology, Trade, 1988; M. MAISCHBERGER, Marmor in Rom, 1997, esp. 14; G. BORGHINI (ed.), Marmi antichi, 1989. R.M.S.

Marble, paintings on

In Greek and Roman → painting, stone, and especially → marble, was a popular surface for paintings, as it lent itself to representations with varied functions. Images for the funerary cult, which are mostly badly preserved, existed on marble tombstones in many regions of the Mediterranean area from archaic times into the Hellenistic period. Like the relief stelae which were also painted with colours (→ Polychromy), they were erected in necropoleis. → Reliefs and painting were also combined either by painting details and attributes on sculpted and smoothed surfaces, or by adding a small painted 'predella picture' under a relief. Although the topics of → grave paintings were dictated by the genre and they were therefore often only of craftsmanly level, even famous painters, such as e.g. → Nicias of Athens, are historically attested (Paus. 7,22,6; Plin. HN 35,132). A similar practice can be inferred for votive images and votive reliefs in Greek sanctuaries. Painted marble metopes in architectural contexts are known from a variety of epochs. Tools and furniture, like e.g. the back of a marble throne from a grave in Vergina, or sarcophagi were also used as surfaces for paintings.

The ancient painting techniques and substances used for painting on marble have recently been verified and reconstructed with the help of special photographic techniques (UVR, infrared) and chemical analyses. Research was based on what were hitherto believed to be encaustically painted (→ Encaustic (painting)) Hellenistic funerary stelae from → Demetrias [1], now proven to have been produced with an egg tempera technique, and the Roman marble paintings from Herculaneum, which were modelled on Greek tablet paintings and gave the genre its name. The tablets found there were signed by the Athenian painter Alexander and depicted subjects from the myths, everyday life and plays. Because of their faded state of preservation they had formerly been believed to be → monochrome paintings. However, microscopically various pigments can be identified that stem from multicoloured representations. The individual steps of the painting process are also discernible: contours and structural details were sketched in dark colours without the use of foundation. This was covered with a medium colour, already giving it a slightly plastic effect, before finally differentiating colours, shadows and light were added. Even today it is unclear whether the signature refers to the copyist or whether he copied it from the late 5th-cent. original. The most famous picture of the series, the 'Knucklebone players', was still used by CANOVA as a model for his works.

V. V. GRAEVE, Marmorbilder aus Herculaneum und Pompeji, in: Dialoghi di Archeologia 2, 1984, 89–113; Id., F. PREUSSER, C. WOLTERS, Marmorbilder auf griechischen Grabsteinen, in: Restauro 1, 1981, 11–34; Id., F. PREUSSER, Zur Technik griechischer Marmorbilder auf Marmor, in: JDAI 96, 1981, 120–156; I. SCHEIBLER, Griechische Malerei der Antike, 1994, 2ff., 132ff.; C. SCHWANZAR, Ein Bild des Athener Malers Alexandros, in: W. ALZINGER (ed.), Pro Arte Antiqua, FS H.Kenner, vol. 2, 1985, 312–318; K. SISMANIDIS, Klines ke klinoïdisis kataskeves ton makedonikon taphon, 1997. N.H.

Marble sculptures

Crystalline limestone marble was the preferred stone material in Graeco-Roman → sculpture. Marble was partially painted or gilded, otherwise impregnated with a coating of wax and oil (gánōsis). Coloured marble was used to match the colour of clothing and hair; painted effects were achieved by adding metals to jewellery, weapons, hairpieces and eyes. The term → akrolithon is used for elaborate mixed techniques. Stucco was often added to economize with material or time. The proportions of the blocks often called for techniques involving dowels and glue and assembly from several pieces. Ancient praise of works having been made 'from a single stone' (ex *uno lapide*) turns out to be mostly unwarranted where it can be verified. The statues were built with a plinth at their feet, which was set into the base using lead casting.

Small-scale marble sculptures already existed in Cycladic culture (3rd millennium). With the beginning of Greek sculpture in the 7th cent., starting from the island of Naxos, large formats are immediately attempted. In archaic times, marble – decorated with elaborate paintings and mixed techniques – is the preferred material. From the 5th cent., marble colossal statues are produced mainly in the form of acroliths. From that time on, bronze rather than marble is used in the round sculpture; in architectural sculpture, however, marble continues to be used almost exclusively. In Italy, marble appears as material for sculpture from the middle of the 2nd cent. BC; from the mid–1st cent. BC, the quarries in Luna [3] supply most of the material for statues and ornamental reliefs (→ Marble) in addition to imported marble from Paros and the Pentelicon. The fact that the majority of works are purchased privately leads to a specialization in → copies and repairs and to mobile workshops in the Mediterranean region. Export-oriented workshops emerge at the quarries of → Aphrodisias [1] and near Proconnesus and Docimum/Asia Minor for the production of sarcophagi. After the 3rd cent. AD, the marble used for new works is obtained by reworking and recycling due to the decreasing demand.

A. MORETTI, J. B. WARD-PERKINS, s.v. Marmo, EAA 4, 1961, 860–870; P. PENSABENE (ed.), Marmi antichi. Problemi d'impiego, di restauro e d'identificazione, 1985; R. GNOLI, Marmora romana, 1988; N. HERZ (ed.), Classical Marble: Geochemistry, Technology, Trade, 1988; Marble. Art Historical and Scientific Perspectives on Ancient Sculpture (Symposium ... J. Paul Getty Museum 1988), 1990; Y. LINTZ (ed.), Les marbres blancs dans l'antiquité, 1991; J. B. WARD-PERKINS, Marble in Antiquity. Collected Papers, 1992.   R.N.

Marbod see → Maroboduus

Marcella

[1] Roman aristocrat, Christian, *c.* 335 to 410/1. As a young widow she founded a monastic women's community on the Aventine and brought in → Hieronymus as a teacher from 383 to 385; he wrote letters 23–29, 32, 34, 37, 38, 40–44, 46 (in the name of Paula and Eustochium) and 59, 97 (to M. and Pammachius) to her; important Roman participant in the controversy about Origen (cf. Jer. Ep. 97, Rufin. Apologia contra Hieronymum 2,20f., Jer. Apologia contra Rufinum). Further mention in Jerome's Comm. to the Gal. and Eph., Ep. 47,3; 48,4; 54,18; 65,2; 107,3, Comm. to Jon,

Dan and Ez. Obituary: Jer. Ep. 127.
→ Woman (IV. Christianity); → Monasticism; → Origenes; → Paula; → Rufinus

S. LETSCH-BRUNNER, Marcella Discipula et Magistra, 1998.

[2] Wife of → Porphyrius.   S.L.-B.

Marcellianus Son of the *praefectus praetorio Galliarum* → Maximinus [3], through whose influence he was appointed *dux Valeriae c.* AD 373. He promoted the construction of a fortification ordered by → Valentinianus I on the territory of the → Quadi. He had their king Gabinius [II 5] treacherously murdered in 374 AD (Amm. Marc. 29,6,3–5; in Zos. 4,16,4 he is called Celestius). PLRE 1, 543f. no. 2 and 190 (Celestius).   W.P.

Marcellina Sister of → Ambrosius, bishop of Milan; lived with her widowed mother in her parents' home in Rome even after she was consecrated as a nun by pope → Liberius [1] (352–66) on the sixth of January in an unknown year. Ambrose dedicated his treatise *De Virginibus* ('On Virgins'; begun on 21 January 376) to M.; his letters 20 (April 386), 22 (June 386) and 41 (end of 388) are addressed to her (and through her to the Christians in Rome). M. was an important informant for Ambrose's biographer → Paulinus. M. died soon after Ambrose (died 397). She is presumably identical with the M. mentioned in Jer. Ep. 45,7.

S. LETSCH-BRUNNER, Marcella. Discipula et Magistra, 1998, 58–63.   S.L.-B.

Marcellinus
I. GREEK   II. ROMAN

I. GREEK
(Μαρκελλῖνος; *Markellînos*).
[1] Greek author of a treatise on pulses. His reference to followers of → Archigenes suggests the late 1st or 2nd cent. AD as the earliest date of its composition. A more precise dating would be possible if he were the author of a recipe quoted by Galen (De compositione medicamentorum secundum locos 7,5 = 13,90 K.) from → Andromachus [5] the Younger, but the identification is uncertain. M.'s stylized preface refers to the great names in sphygmology from the past, esp. → Aegimius [3], → Hippocrates [6], → Herophilus [1] and → Erasistratus; however, M. follows his own eclectic approach. He defines the pulse, explains the taking of the pulse and diagnosing different pulses (in his time the Herophilean waterclock was no longer in use; ch. 11) and then lists briefly the different pulses according to the condition of the patient. The work ends with short descriptions of the pulse types and the diagnoses to be drawn from them.

H. SCHÖNE, M.' Pulslehre. Ein griechisches Anekdoton, in: FS zur 49. Versammlung deutscher Philologen und Schulmänner in Basel im Jahre 1907, 448–472; H. VON

STADEN, Les Manuscrits du De Pulsibus de Marcellinus, in: J. JOUANNA, A. GARZYA (ed.), Storia e ecdotica dei testi medici greci, 1996, 406–425.   V.N.

[2] Author or editor of a comprehensive biography of → Thucydides (cf. Cod. E, Palatina Heidelberg. 252; 10th/11th cents.), which has been ascribed to him since the 10th cent. AD (cf. Suda s.v. ἀπήλαυσε, ἀπολαύειν and μέτριος); possibly identical with the Hermogenes scholiast → M. [3] [2. 539]. Inconsistency with regard to content, style and disposition of the work (which probably dates from the 5th/6th cents. AD), however, suggests that the *vita* is a contamination of several texts sharing an interest in the style and biography of Thucydides and coming from different authors, partly mediated by the grammarian → Didymus [1] Chalkenteros [3. 1453–1486]. Beside the introduction (ch. 1), the biography contains three main parts, which can only tentatively be ascribed to specific authors [4. 557]. The first section (chs. 2–44/45?), the most important and comprehensive part of the *vita,* may be a revision of a 'Life of Thucydides' from → Proclus' 'Chrestomathia' [3. 1472]. The second section (chs. 45–53) deals mostly with Thucydides' style; an ascription to → Caecilius [III 5] of Cale Acte cannot be excluded. It is debatable whether the third section (chs. 54–58) was written by → Zosimus of Ascalon or by Caecilius.

> EDITIONS: 1 O. LUSCHNAT (ed.), Thukydides, 1, 1954, ²1960; 2 L. PICCIRILLI (ed.), Storie dello storico Tucidide, 1985.
> BIBLIOGRAPHY: 3 E. BUX, s.v. Marcellinus (49), RE 14, 1450–1487; 4 J. MAITLAND, Marcellinus' Life of Thucydides: Criticism and Criteria in the Biographical Tradition, in: CQ 46, 1996, 538–558.   GR.DA.

[3] Author of a commentary on → Hermogenes' treatise 'On Stasis' (Περὶ τῶν στάσεων). The work, which probably dates from the 5th cent. AD, is preserved, along with the commentaries of the Neoplatonist → Sopater and of → Syranus, in a → catena [1]. The 'prolegomena' of the commentary, with their general introduction to rhetoric, can also largely be traced back to M. [2].

> 1 WALZ 4, 1833; 2 H. RABE, Aus Rhetoren-Handschriften., in: RhM 64, 1909, 539–590, 584ff.
>
> G. A. KENNEDY, Greek Rhetoric under Christian Emperors, 1983, 112–115.   M.B.

II. ROMAN

[1] Roman bishop from AD 296, according to the Liber Pontificalis 1,61 a native of the city of Rome; according to Euseb. Hist. eccl. 7,32, he was executed during the persecutions under → Diocletianus on 24 October 304. However, his behaviour during the time of the persecutions is disputed. His name is missing from the → Chronographer of 354 (MGH AA 9,1,70). Augustine defended M. against the → Donatists, who accused him of treachery (Contra litteras Petiliani 2,92,102; De unico baptismo 16,27), but in his bishops' list (epist. 53,4) he includes the unknown Marcellus in place of M.

A. DI BERARDINO, s.v. M., Papst, LThK³ 6, 1300 (bibliography); M. CHRISTOL, s.v. Marcellin, Dictionnaire Historique de la Papauté, 1994, 1086f.   O.WER.

[2] **Antonius M.** *Praeses Lugdunensis primae* in AD 313 (Cod. Theod. 11,3,1); *praefectus praetorio* of → Constans [1] 340–342 (Cod. Theod. 6,22,3; 11,12,1), initially alone, then together with Fabius Titianus (CIL III 12330); *consul ordinarius* in 341. PLRE 1, 548f.,16; cf. 1,545,5.   B.BL.

[3] **M. Aurelius M.** Of equestrian descent, *vir perfectissimus*; had the city walls of Verona built in AD 265 (CIL V 3329 = ILS 544). He may be identical to the governor of Mesopotamia and *rector Orientis* mentioned by Zosimus (1,60,1), whom the Palmyrenes wanted to proclaim emperor, but who refused. In 275, M. was *consul ordinarius* together with emperor → Aurelianus [3] (CIL VI 10060; 30976; VIII 5515 = 18845; questionable AE 1934,183).

> A. STEIN, Der römische Ritterstand, 1927, 244; PIR² M 178; PLRE I 544,1; 545,2; 549,17.   T.F.

[4] During the stay of → Constantius [2] II in Antioch, between AD 340 and 350, he attained the position of *praeses Phoenices* and of *comes Orientis.* He was a member of the commission of high officials charged with investigating the heresy of Photinus at Sirmium in 351 (Epiphanios, Haereses 71,1). PLRE 1, 545f., 6 and 7.

[5] As *comes rei privatae* of Constans [1], he played a decisive role in the uprising of → Magnentius (Zos. 2,42, 2–3). The latter promoted him to → *magister officiorum* and he remained his most important advisor (Zos. 2, 46,3; Julian Or. 2,57d–59b). He was entrusted with the suppression of the revolt of → Nepotianus and probably fell in AD 351 in the battle of Mursa. PLRE 1, 546, 8.

[6] According to Petrus Patricius (FHG 4, 190 fr. 16), he participated as *stratēlátēs,* i.e. *magister militum* in a delegation of→ Magnentius and → Vetranio to Constantius [2] II (AD 350). Petrus probably misunderstood the official title *magister* in his Latin source, so that M. can be assumed to be identical with M. [5] (different PLRE 1, 546, 9).

> B. BLECKMANN, Constantina, Vetranio und Gallus Caesar, in: Chiron 24, 1994, 55.   B.BL.

[7] *Praeses* of the province of Lugdunensis I in AD 313; *Praef. praet. Italiae* in 340/1; *consul ordinarius* in 341; grandfather of St. → Melania (the Elder). PLRE 1, 548f., 16.

[8] *Comes rerum privatarum* of emperor → Constans [1] in AD 349/50; instigated the conspiracy against him and proclaimed → Magnentius emperor on 18 January 350, becoming his *magister officiorum.* M. then fought against → Nepotianus, whom he had executed after the capture of Rome on 30 June 350. M. disappeared at the battle of Mursa (28 September 351); he was probably killed, but his body was never found.

> CLAUSS, 168–169; PLRE 1, 546, 8.

[9] *Magister militum* of → Magnentius; participant in a joint delegation of Magnentius and → Vetranio to Constantius [2] II, who had almost all its members taken prisoner. PLRE 1, 546, 9.

[10] Brother and *comes* of the usurper Magnus → Maximus [I 7]; he was in Italy during his brother's uprising and fell into the hands of → Valentinianus II, who freed him in the context of the second legation of → Ambrosius. As his brother's commander, M. lost the battle of Poetovio to → Theodosius I in AD 388. PLRE 1, 547, 12.

[11] *Praeses* of Cyrenaica in AD 405/6; praised in Synes. Epist. 62 for his justice and because he protected the population from encroachments by the army.

                                         K.G.-A.

[12] Flavius M. *Tribunus et notarius.* In AD 410, M. was sent to Africa by the emperor Honorius [3] to arbitrate in the Donatist controversy (→ Donatus [1]). He led a theological debate between Catholics and Donatists. The latter were eventually denounced, as expected, and thereafter persecuted with fervour. An appeal of the Donatists to the emperor was fruitless. He seems to have become embroiled in the revolt of → Heraclitanus and in spite of the intervention of → Augustinus in 413 to have been executed by → Marinus [1], later rehabilitated. M. was baptized, personally pious and lived an austere life. He was also interested in theology: he corresponded with → Hieronymus (Jer. Ep. 126 = Aug. Epist. 165) and Augustine (from M. Epist. 136, to M. Epist. 128f.; 133; 138f.; 143). Several writings of Augustine, e.g. *De civitate Dei*, are dedicated to M. PLRE II 711f.

[13] Prominent Roman who broke with → Valentinianus III in AD 454, creating a virtually independent dominion in Dalmatia. He refused the imperial rank offered to him, fighting instead as *magister utriusque militiae*, later also as *patricius*, in the service of → Maiorianus and Anthemius (→ Anthemios [2]), and was successful above all against the Vandals (→ Vandali); M. was on good terms with Leo [4] I. He was murdered in 467, possibly at the instigation of → Ricimer. He was a pagan. PLRE II 708–710.   H.L.

[14] M. Comes *Cancellarius* of emperor Justinian I. At Constantinople, he wrote a Latin world chronicle, which Cassiodorus recommended in his chapter entitled *De historicis christianis* (Cassiod. Inst. 1,17). M.C. continued the chronicle of → Hieronymus up to AD 518 and was in turn supplemented by an anonymous successor up to 548. The increasing emphasis placed on contemporary history, which was beginning to prevail generally at this time in Latin annals, is evident [1]. M.C. was of limited importance. Only → Beda Venerabilis referred to him, among others, for his own world chronicle.

1 S. MUHLBERGER, The Fifth Century Chroniclers. Prosper, Hydatius and the Gallic Chronicler of 452 (= ARCA 27), 1990.

EDITIONS: TH. MOMMSEN, Chronica minora saec. IV. V. VI. VII. (= MGH AA 11), vol. 2, 37–109.   U.E.

Marcellus

I. GREEK   II. ROMAN

I. GREEK

(Μαρκέλλος; *Markéllos*).

[1] Rhetor from Pergamum known solely from a brief reference in the Suda; he is said to have written a book (or several books) entitled Ἀδριανὸς ἢ περὶ βασιλείας/ *Adrianòs è perì basileías* ('Hadrian, or On Monarchy'). He would thus have lived in the first half of the 2nd cent.; whether Dio's [I 3] speeches *perì basileías*, addressed to Trajan, served as a model is uncertain.   M.W.

[2] M. from Side. Famous physician and poet of the 2nd cent. AD, author of 42 bks. of *Iatriká* in hexameters concerning remedies; three fragments about fishes are extant, which partly correspond to the so-called *Koiranídes* of the → *Corpus Hermeticum* ; one section deals with lycanthropy (werewolves). The funerary epigram Anth. Pal. 7,158 ascribes to the work 40 vls. entitled *Chironides*, which Hadrian and Antoninus Pius had set up in the libraries of Rome. In 160, → Herodes [16] Atticus engaged M. to compose two poems (59 and 39 hexameters respectively, of good poetical quality) in memory of his wife Regilla, which were to be chiselled into his Triopium [2; 5].

1 E. HEITSCH, Die griechen Dichterfragmente der römischen Kaiserzeit, vol. 2, 1964, 16–22; 2 W. AMELING, Herodes Atticus, vol. 2, 1983, no. 146 (with bibliography and commentary); 3 E. L. BOWIE, The Greek Renaissance in the Roman Empire, in: BICS Suppl. 55, 1989, 201–202; 4 M. WELLMANN, Marcellus von Side als Arzt und die Koiranides des Hermes Trismegistos (Philologus Suppl. 27,2), 1934, 1–50; 5 U. v. WILAMOWITZ-MOELLENDORFF, Marcellus von Side (1928), in: Id., KS, 2, 1941, 192–228.   S.FO.

[3] Author of *Aithiopiká*, of which two records on Atlantis are extant in Proclus (in Pl. Ti. 1,177; 181) (FGrH 671).   P.L.S.

[4] Bishop of Ancyra (died 374). Born around 280 and first mentioned as bishop in 314. At the council of → Nicaea in 325, M. opposed both → Arius (→ Arianism) and the followers of → Eusebius [8] of Nicomedia and → Eusebius [7] of Caesarea. Later, a document given personally to emperor Constantine (CPG 2800; fr. in [4. 2–121]) sharply attacked the Sophist → Asterius [2] and both Eusebii (rebuttal from Eusebius of Caesarea [1. 13–61]). After the denunciation of his work and two banishments, M. went to Rome (341 rehabilitation by the Roman Synod; also by the western regional Synod at Serdica in 342). A letter written in 340/1 to the Roman bishop Iulius [III 1] (*Epistula ad Iulium*: [4. 124–129]) contains the oldest evidence of the ancient Roman creed (possibly written by M., thus [3. 407]). Increasingly isolated following his return to the East, M. was once again denounced several times (e.g. in 344 together with his student Photinus of Sirmium, posthumously in 381 in Constantinople). In his theology, he emphasized the oneness of God in a hypostatic union (*monás*), which is not annulled by creation or incarnation. Various writings (CPG 2800–2806) – some disputed – are ascribed to M.

1 G. FEIGE, Die Lehre Markells von Ankyra in der Darstellung seiner Gegner, 1991; 2 K. SEIBT, Die Theologie des Markell von Ankyra, 1994; 3 M. VINZENT, Die Entstehung des 'Römischen Glaubensbekenntnisses', in: W. KINZIG et al., Tauffragen und Bekenntnis, 1999, 185–409; 4 Id. (ed.), Markell von Ancyra: Die Fragmente. Der Brief an Julius von Rom (Suppl. to Vigiliae Christianae 39), 1997 (Bibliography: CIII–CXI). J.RI.

[5] Bishop of → Apamea [3] on the Orontes at the time of → Theodosius I; at his instigation the local temple of Zeus Belos was destroyed (according to Theod. Hist. eccl. 5,21,5–15 this was preceded by unsuccesful attempts by the praetorian prefect; cf. also Lib. Ep. 1351 = 9, 400,10–12 FOERSTER]). An exchange of letters with Persian (?) martyrs (Theod. Hist. eccl. 5,21,16; cf. also 5,27,3) is lost. When M. also wanted to destroy the temple of Aulon (El Gub), he himself died a martyr's death (Sozom. Hist. eccl. 7,15,12–15; Theod. Hist. eccl. 5,21,16; Theophanes, Chron. ad annum 5883, p. 71,31–33 DE BOOR).

J. GEFFCKEN, Der Ausgang des griechisch-römischen Heidentums (Religionswiss. Bibl. 6), 1963 (repr. of the 1929 edn.), 154, 158. C.M.

II. ROMAN

Diminutive form of the Roman given name Marcus, a *cognomen* in the family of the Claudii (→ Claudius [I 7–15; II 42–44]); the most famous bearer of the name was the nephew of Augustus, C. Claudius [II 42] M. Greek bearers of the name, → Marcellus I.

KAJANTO, Cognomina, 39, 173. K.-L.E.

[1] A M. is mentioned as *proconsul* in two inscriptions from Africa: ILAlg 591 and [1. 304]. Since ILAlg probably mentions C. Iulius [II 48] Cornutus Tertullus as a predecessor (AD 116/7?), this proconsulship belongs to the time thereafter; the senator may be identical with M. Vitorius M., *cos. suff.* 105, or M. Asinius [II 10] M., *cos. ord.* 104. PIR² M 190.

1 J. REYNOLDS et al. (ed.), The Inscriptions of Roman Tripolitania, 1952.

THOMASSON, Fasti Africani, 53f.

[2] **M.** He was sent to Judaea by Vitellius, the legate of Syria, in AD 36 or early 37, to replace → Pontius Pilatus. Since Josephus (Ant. Iud. 18,89) describes him as *epimelētḗs* (→ Epimeletai), it is not certain whether he should be regarded as the *praefectus Iudaeae* in the legal sense. However, he certainly fulfilled the function of the post until the arrival of Marullus in 37. PIR² M 193. W.E.

[3] From → Serdica, he was *magister equitum per Gallias* under Constantius [2] II in AD 356/357 and was entrusted with the task of supervising the Caesar → Iulianus [11]. When Julian was surrounded by Franks at Sens, he refused him aid. Constantius replaced him with

Severus. Thereafter, M. tried in vain to intrigue against Julian at the court (Amm. Marc. 16,4,3; 7,1–3; Zos. 3,2,2; Julian. Ep. Ad Athen. 278B). His son took part in a conspiracy against the emperor Julian and was executed (Amm. Marc. 22,11,2). PLRE 1, 550f. no. 3.

[4] Relative of the usurper → Procopius, who appointed him *protector* (AD 365–366). He conquered Cyzicus and eliminated Serenianus, the *comes domesticorum* of → Valens. After Procopius' death, he had himself proclaimed emperor at Calchedon, but was soon taken prisoner and executed by the *magister militum* Equitius [2] (Amm. Marc. 26,10,1–5; Zos. 4,6,4; 4,8,3–4). PLRE 1, 551 no. 5. W.P.

[5] High-ranking eastern Roman officer; under → Belisarius he led the cavalry against the Persians in AD 530, and in 533 a division of barbarian allies against the Vandals. After the victory over the Vandals, he remained in Africa and became *dux Numidiae* in 536 (PLRE 3B, 814 no. 2).

[6] Initially a magistrate, he was *comes excubitorum* (chief of the palace guard) at Constantinople from AD 541–552. On the orders of → Iustinianus [1] I, he summoned → Belisarius back from Italy. In 549, he thwarted an attempt on the lives of the emperor and of Belisarius (PLRE 3B, 814–816 no. 3).

[7] Eastern Roman general, son of → Vigilantia, the sister of → Iustinianus [1] I, and brother of → Iustinus [4] II; from AD 544, he fought in the Persian War as *magister militum*, and in 562 against the Huns in Thrace; he became *patricius* in 565 (PLRE 3B, 816f. no. 5). F.T.

[8] **M. Empiricus** Author of a treatise *De medicamentis*, who is described in its title as → *magister officiorum Theodosii senioris*. M.E. is said to have lived in Burdigala (modern Bordeaux) and to have been a Christian, although these details cannot be proved. He is identified with the M. in the Cod. Theod. 16,5,29, who was entrusted by Arcadius with the battle against the pagans in AD 395 (cf. also 6,29,8), and with the M. mentioned in the Suda (μ 203), who carried out administrative tasks in the Orient. The designation *empiricus* dates from the Renaissance and refers to the term *expertum* ('proven'), which relates to the medicines mentioned by M. M.E. was not a follower of the Empiricist school, all the less so since he seems not to have been a physician.

The treatise De medicamentis, which was dedicated to M.E.'s sons and was completed after 408, is presented in its preface as a compilation resulting from the author's reading, and aiming at the codification of the inventory and composition of medicines in use at the time. The recipes were arranged 'from head to foot', more according to the principle of accumulation than of selection. Prefixed to it are a treatise *De mensuris et ponderibus* ('On Weights and Measures') and a corpus of genuine or fictitious letters from physicians.

Sources: 1. the → Medicina Plinii, Ps.-Apuleius (*Herbarium* by the so-called Apuleius Platonicus, 6th cent. AD) and several works of Late Antiquity; whether they were used directly or in the material previously compiled is unknown; 2. Roman popular medicine, with its entire arsenal of especially symbolic interpretations; it has earned the work the reputation of being a collection of 'superstitious' ideas, belonging in the context of the degeneration of classical medicine.

The treatise was perhaps already known to → Sextus Placitus, but certainly to → Theodorus Priscianus, and it was cited as a source in other works of Late Antiquity. There is textual evidence in one MS of the 9th cent. and in two MSS of the 9th/10th cents.; the *editio princeps* was published by Janus CORNARIUS in 1536.

E. LIECHTENHAN et al., M., De medicamentis (ed. M. NIE-DERMANN), 2 vols. (CML 5,1–2), ²1968; M. NIEDERMANN (ed.), M., De medicamentis liber, 1916, V–XXXV; C. OPSOMER, R. HALLEUX, M. ou le mythe empirique, in: PH. MUDRY (ed.), Les écoles médicales à Rome, 1991, 159–178; SCHANZ/HOSIUS 4,2, 1920, § 608, 2.   A.TO.

[9] see → Ulpius [7–8] Marcellus

Marcia

[1] Possibly daughter of Q. Marcius [I 16] Philippus (*cos.* 281 BC), wife of M. Atilius [I 21] Regulus, mother of two sons (Sil. Pun. 6,403–409; 576). As a widow she allegedly took revenge on two Carthaginians who had promised to protect her husband (Diod. Sic. 24,12; HRR I 144f. fr. 5).

[2] According to Suet. Iul. 6,1 from the royal family of the Marcii Reges, grandmother of Caesar.

[3] Probably daughter of Q. Marcius [I 21] Rex, Vestal priestess, in 114 BC sentenced to death for incest along with → Aemilia [2] and → Licinia [4] (Cass. Dio 26 fr. 87,1–5).

[4] Daughter of L. Marcius [I 14] Philippus (*cos.* 56 BC), wife of M. → Porcius Cato Uticensis, who ceded her to the orator Hortensius [7] on his request (App. B Civ. 2,99; Plut. Cato minor 25; on the wedding between 55 and 52 BC, cf. [1. 201³⁴]) and married her again in 50 BC after Hortensius' death (Plut. Cato minor 52,5f.; Luc. 2,326–330; Str. 11,9,1; cf. Plut. Cato minor 52,7). They had one son and two daughters (Luc. 2,331; App. B Civ. 2,99).

1 R. FEHRLE, Cato Uticensis, 1983.

[5] Daughter of L. Marcius [I 15] Philippus (*cos. suff.* 38 BC) and Atia [2] (sister of Augustus' mother, Ov. Pont. 1,2,140; on her person, see Ov. Fast. 6,802–810). From 15 BC M. was the wife of Paullus Fabius [II 14] Maximus, whose death she allegedly caused through indiscretion (reporting Augustus' visit to Agrippa [2] Postumus in Planasia to Livia) (Tac. Ann. 1,5,1f., according to [1. 336⁹⁷⁸] implausible). Their children were Paullus Fabius [II 16] Persicus and Fabia [5] Numantina (her married name).

1 VOGEL-WEIDEMANN ; 2 PIR² M 257.

[6] Secretly kept the books of her father A. → Cremutius Cordus (Cass. Dio 57,24,4; Sen. Dial. 6,1,2) that were

to be burned (→ Censorship) and with Caligula's consent made them accessible to the public (Suet. Cal. 16,1; Sen. Dial. 6,1,3). From her marriage to a certain Metilius she had two sons, both of whom she outlived, and two daughters, Metilia Marcia and Metilia Rufina. On the occasion of the death of one of her sons (AD 38 or not before 47) → Seneca the Younger addressed to her a consolatory treatise (Sen. Dial. 6: *Ad Marciam de consolatione*). PIR² M 256, cf. PIR² M 535.

[7] M. Aurelia Ceionia Demetrias (ILS 406), daughter of M. Aurelius Sabinianus, freedwoman ([Aur. Vict.] Epit. Caes. 17,5). M. was first a *concubina* of M. Ummidius Quadratus and after his death in AD 182 of → Commodus (Cass. Dio 72,4,6; SHA Comm. 8,6; 17,1; Hdn. 1,16,4); perhaps a Christian herself (Cass. Dio 72,4,7), she convinced Commodus to allow exiled Christians to return (Hippolytus, Refutatio omnium haeresium 9,12,12). Probably M., rather than his sister, informed him of an uprising against him (in Cass. Dio 72,13,5; for a different view, see Hdn. 1,13,1). When Commodus wanted to get rid of M., her future husband → Eclectus and Aemilius [II 6] Laetus, instead they succeeded in having him murdered (Hdn. 1,16,4–17,11; 2,1,3; Cass. Dio 72,22,1 and 4; SHA Comm. 17,1f.). In 193, after → Didius [II 6] Iulianus had just been declared emperor, M. had him killed (Cass. Dio 73,16,4; SHA Did. 6,2). PIR² M 261.   ME.SCH.

[8] M. was possibly the name of the wife of the older M. Ulpius Traianus and the mother of the future emperor → Traianus. She might have been a sister of M. [9] Furnilla, Titus' second wife. She owned land at the confluence of the Tiber and the Nar [1. 257–264; 2. 13; 308]. A monumental portrait, apparently found on the Forum Traiani in Rome, should possibly be attributed to her [3. 473–81].

1 E. CHAMPLIN, Figlinae Marcianae, in: Athenaeum 61, 1983, 257–263   2 A. BIRLEY, Hadrian, 1997   3 D. BOSCHUNG, W. ECK, Ein Bildnis der Mutter Traians?, in: AA 3, 1998, 473–481   W.E.

[9] M. Furnilla Daughter of Q. Marcius [II 3] Barea Sura and Antonia Furnilla (CIL VI 31766), second wife of → Titus (from AD 65), who repudiated her (Suet. Tit. 4,2). From this marriage she had a daughter named Iulia.

E. CHAMPLIN, Figlinae Marcianae, in: Athenaeum 61, 1983, 257–263, esp. 260–263; KIENAST, ²1996, 112f.; PIR² M 265; RAEPSAET-CHARLIER, 525; VOGEL-WEIDEMANN, 133 n. 738; 137; 431f.; 435.

[10] M. Otacilia Severa Augusta (on the form of the name, cf. [1]), wife of emperor M. → Philippus Arabs, mother of M. → Iulius [II 107] Severus Philippus (AE 1944, 40; 54), from AD 244 *Augusta, mater Caesaris, mater castrorum et senatus et patriae* (ILS 507; 513; AE 1954, 110, cf. also MAMA 8,331; IGR 1,695; 757; AE 1969/70, 496; 497; AE 1978, 721–723; ILS 509). M. had the right to mint (CIL III 12270; base of an honorary monument: CIL VIII 20139). Eusebius mentions a letter of Origen to the couple (Euseb. Hist. eccl. 6,36,3). M. probably perished together with her family in AD 249.

1 RIC, vol. 4.3, 72–81 no. 30, 39, 43, 64, 109–111; 82–86; 92–95.

KIENAST, ²1996, 200f.; PIR² M 266; M. WEGNER, Das römische Herrscherbild, vol. 3, 1979, 57ff.   ME.SCH.

[11] M. Volusia [Egn]atia Quieta *Clarissima femina*, honoured in Elaioussa Sebaste in Cilicia, from where she probably came.

W. ECK, Eine Senatorenfrau aus Elaiussa Sebaste, in: EA 33, 2001, 105 ff.   W.E.

Marciana Ulpia M., born in the second half of August (cf. Feriale Duranum) *c.* AD 50, daughter of M. → Ulpius Traianus (*pater*), sister of the emperor M. Ulpius → Traianus, married to the senator C. Salonius → Matidius Patruinus, widowed around 78; lived in Trajan's house with her only daughter Salonia → Matidia [1]. Praised by Pliny (Pan. Lat. 84) in 100; from *c.* 102 elevated to *Augusta*. Coins were not minted until 112; these describe M.'s daughter Matidia as *Augustae filia* on the reverse (RIC 2,299). The cities of Marcianapolis and Colonia Marciana Traiana → Thamugadi (Timgad) are named after her. M. died on 29 August 112, was consecrated (→ *consecratio*) and received a *funus censorium* (→ Fasti Ostienses) on 3 September; consecration coins for M. were issued [4. 256f.]; later her father was consecrated too. All these honours contributed to the charismatic elevation of the Ulpius side of Trajan's family and were significant for the candidacy of Hadrian, the husband of M's. granddaughter Vibia → Sabina, as Trajan's successor.

1 W. ECK, s.v. Ulpius (56a), RE Suppl. 15, 932–934; 2 KIENAST, 125f.; 3 RAEPSAET-CHARLIER, no. 824; 4 H. TEMPORINI, Die Frauen am Hofe Trajans, 1978, 184–261.
          H.T.-V.

Marcianopolis City founded by Trajan and named after his sister Marcia (cf. Zos.1,42,1; 4,10,3; Greek authors call it Μαρκιανούπολις; *Markianoúpolis*. M., modern Reka Devnia in north east Bulgaria, about 20 km west of Odessos, today's Warna, was the administrative centre of *Moesia inferior*. M. was a junction of strategically important roads: from Constantinople to Durostorum, from Odessus to Nicopolis (modern Nikiup) and from M. to Noviodunum (Amm. Marc. 27,5,6, modern Babadag).

Under Commodus M. was given the right to issue its own coin. This autonomous minting was particularly developed in Severan times and is an important source of knowledge about local cults (of Zeus, Sarapis, Asclepius, Concordia, et al.) and about the administration of the province. From AD 238 the citizens had to resist attacks from the Goths and other tribes from *Scythia minor* and neighbouring areas. The governor Tullius Menophilus (AD 238–40) was especially successful in

fighting the → Carpi. M. regained importance in the 4th cent. AD as the capital of the province of *Moesia II*; it was considered the largest city in Thracia (Zos. 4,10,3). Constantine I (the Great) was in M. in AD 332 (Cod. Theod. 3,5,4f.). From 366 to 370 Valens resided in the city, which was to serve him as a military build-up point against the Goths. Here he celebrated his *quinquennalia* in 368 (Them. Or. 8; ILS 770). In 377, the *comes* Lupicinus [2] was defeated near M. in a battle against the Goths (Amm. Marc. 31,5,9). There is evidence of a weapons factory in M. at the end of the 4th cent. or the beginning of the 5th cent. (Not. Dign. Or. 11,34). Justinian restored M. after destructions and fortified the city (Procop. Aed. 4,11). M. was an episcopal see.

M. FLUSS, s.v. Markianupolis, RE 14,2, 1505–1511; V. VELKOV, Roman Cities in Bulgaria, 1980.   J.BU.

Marcianus

[1] (Μαρκιανός; *Markianós*). Geographer from → Heraclea [7] between AD 200 (he used the geographer Protagoras) and 530 (he is often quoted by Steph. Byz.), possibly after 400 (GGM 1, CXXX; [2. 272; 3. 997; 6. 156f.]) or even closer to Steph. Byz. [1. 46]. Personal information about him is not available.

Only 21 quotes from his *Epitome* of the eleven books of the *Geōgraphía* by → Artemidorus [3] of Ephesus have been handed down by Steph. Byz. and one as Schol. Apoll. Rhod. 3,859 (GGM 1, 574–576), more detailed excerpts, on the other hand, from his 'Periplous of the outer sea' (= Per.; 2 B., GGM 1, 515–562) and smaller extracts from the 'Epitome of the Periplous of the inner sea, written by Menippus of Pergamum in three books' (= Epit. Per. Menipp.; 3 B., GGM 1, 563–573; title conjectured by MÜLLER).

M. used the *Geographoumena*, the geographical study by Artemidorus, as a basis for his *Epitome* which served his description of the inner sea – i.e. the Mediterranean and the Black Sea (→ Mare Nostrum, → Pontus Euxinus) – because of its exceptional exactness (Epit. Per. Menipp. 1,3f.). From the 'Periplous of the outer sea', of which M. was particularly proud (Epit. Per. Menipp. 4), the following are preserved: a) references to M.'s authorities → Artemidorus [3], Claudius → Ptolemaeus [5. 772–789] as well as the geographer → Protagoras [7. 22]; b) the structure of the study in bk. 1: east (and south), bk. 2: west (and north) Oceanus (Per. 1,1); c) an excursus on the reasons for the different distances given by his sources (Per. 1,2; cf. Epit. Per. Menipp. 5: in order to find a mean value M. – just like Protagoras – cites in each case the longest and shortest distance); d) subsequently, (Per. 1,3) M. takes the Mediterranean as starting-point, presents (1,4ff.) the measurement of the circumference of the earth according to → Eratosthenes [2] and Ptolemy, the measurement of the mainlands, the size of the Oikoumene (1,6), and finally the most significant islands. This is followed (from 1,11) by the *periplous* along the east African coast in one direction and (from 1,15), in the other direction, by the *periplous* of the Arabian peninsula, the Persian Gulf and the Indian Ocean to China. Bk. 2 covers, starting from the 'Columns of Hercules' (Per. 2,3), in one direction the *periplous* of the Atlantic Ocean from the Spanish west coast up to the Vistula and Sarmatia (Baltic) (2,37–40), including the British Isles (2,41–45). The *periplous* in the other direction around western Africa (2,46) has been lost almost entirely [6. 169]. M.'s systematic approach is demonstrable also elsewhere: each time, a description of an entire region (περιγραφή) is followed by a detailed description (τὰ κατὰ μέρη) [6. 171].

M. takes his bearings from a map of the earth; he knows (Per. 1,4) the cartographic survey of the earth by Claudius Ptolemy (→ Cartography). His → Periplous is not based on personally experienced sea journeys; it is determined by the perspective of the theoretician [4. 81–87, esp. 85; 6. 162–164]; the genus, which was widely expanded in Hellenistic literature, is reduced to the most precise information possible about distances; more detailed geographical data can only occasionally be found [3. 997; 6. 174; 7. 19–24].

M.'s plan is recognizable: to provide, in a uniform style, through these three works extensive and precise information about the Oikoumene, starting from the coasts. It is interesting to note that at the end of Per. 2 Rome, as the centre of the → Roman Empire, which was not identical with the → Oikoumene, is particularly taken into consideration. Certainly, M. only drew from his sources; however, in view of the shattering of the scholarly tradition in Late Antiquity, M.'s plan is worthy of respect.

→ Geography; → Oceanus; → Periplous; → Ptolemaeus (Claudius); → Stephanus of Byzantium

1 A. DILLER, The Tradition of the Minor Greek Geographers, 1952; 2 F. GISINGER, s.v. Marcianus (27a), RE Suppl. 6, 271–281; 3 F. LASSERRE, s.v. Marcianus (9), KlP 3, 996f.; 4 E. OLSHAUSEN, Einführung in die historische Geographie der alten Welt, 1991; 5 E. POLASCHEK, s.v. Klaudios Ptolemaios, RE Suppl. 10, 680–833; 6 G. HARTINGER, Die Periplusliteratur, thesis Salzburg 1992; 7 E. A. WAGNER, Die Erdbeschreibung des Timosthenes von Rhodos, thesis Leipzig 1888.   H.A.G.

[2] see → Icelus

[3] Proconsul of Baetica around AD 22, whose full name was probably M. Granius M. (CIL IX 2335 = ILS 961 = AE 1990, 222).   W.E.

[4] As → Gallienus' general M. repeatedly defeated the Goths in Achaea around AD 262/3 and took part in the conspiracy against the emperor at Mediolanum in 268 (Zos. 1,1,40,1f.; SHA Gall. 6,1; 13,10; 14,1; 14,7; 15,2; SHA Clod. 6,1; 18,1; AE 1965, 114 = 1975, 770c). PIR² M 204.   T.F.

[5] A Novatian who, as tutor of emperor Valens' daughters, was active on behalf of his fellow-believers; AD 384–95 Novatian bishop in Constantinople (→ Novatianus). His son Chrysanthus was also made a bishop. Whether he is identical with the M. mentioned in Libanius (Ep. 54) is questionable. PLRE I 554.

[6] Belonged to the circle around → Symmachus (Symmachus, Ep. 8,9; 23; 54; 58; 73 are addressed to him); in AD 384 *vicarius* in the West, 393/4 *proconsul Africae*, supposedly after converting to 'paganism' under Eugenius [1]; in 409/10 prefect of the city of Rome under Attalus [11]. Whether he is identical with Iulius Agrius Tarrutenius M. on CIL VI 1735 is uncertain. PLRE I 555f.   H.L.

[7] Emperor of East Rome (AD 450–457), born *c.* 392, son of a Thracian soldier, died in Constantinople 1 January 457. His career began in military service in the Balkans, and he fought against the Persians in 421, probably already as a *tribunus*. From *c.* 430 he was successively *domesticus* (personal adjutant) of the *magistri militum* father and son Ardaburius the Elder and Aspar (→ Ardabur [1] and [2]). During the war against the Vandals (431–434) he was temporarily a prisoner of Geiseric (→ Geisericus). He owed his throne to Aspar and the pious Augusta → Pulcheria, the elder sister of Theodosius II, who after her brother's death lived in an unconsummated marriage with him. Thus legitimated, he was proclaimed emperor by the Senate, army and people on 25 August 450.

His bold decision to refuse to pay the extremely powerful → Attila his annual tribute of *c.*150,000 gold *solidi*, thereby relieving the budget of a considerable burden, went unpunished because the Hun army concentrated its attacks on the western part of the Empire until the tyrant's death in 453. To secure the borders, M. organized smaller military operations in Egypt against the Blemmyes, in Syria and Palestine against the Arabs and in the eastern Black Sea region against the kingdom of Lazica under → Gobazes, which he made a client state of East Rome. Peaceful diplomacy marked the relations with Persia and the Vandals. The Ostrogoths and Gepides in Pannonia were obligated to the Empire as *foederati*. When the Theodosian dynasty in the western part of the Empire died out with the murder of → Valentinianus III in 455, M. considered himself ruler over the whole Empire in the dynasty's name and refused to recognize the emperors → Petronius Maximus and → Avitus [1], who had no legitimacy by virtue of dynasty, but he did nothing about the Vandal invasion of Italy in 455.

M. was prudent in financial politics. By saving the tribute to the Huns he was able to free the senatorial aristocracy from taxes imposed during his predecessor's time. He took firm steps against tax evasion by the owners of large estate and against corrupt officials, who had caused considerable harm to the state and the municipalities, and he ordered the consuls to reserve for the water conduits in Constantinople the money that used to be given to the people when they assumed office. There were over seven million gold *solidi* in the state treasury at his death.

Under Pulcheria's influence M. attempted to break the power of the Monophysite (→ Monophysitism) patriarch → Dioscorus [1] of Alexandria, who, since coming into office in 444, had caused considerable unrest in the Empire. He convened a council at Nicaea in 451 which was opened in October of that year, but in Chalcedon (→ Chalcedonense); pope → Leo [3] I, who had initially opposed the council, also sent a legation. On 25 October 451, the council, prompted by the imperial couple, passed the creed on the two natures of Jesus Christ that pope Leo I had drafted; all this earned M. the reputation as a protector of orthodoxy.

A monumental column from his time is preserved in Constantinople, which, according to the inscription, once stood in the centre of a forum. A statue of an emperor is preserved, the so-called 'Colossus of Barletta', but it probably depicts Leo [4] I rather than M.

> ODB 2, 1296f.; PLRE 2, 714f. no. 8; F. A. BAUER, Stadt, Platz und Denkmal in der Spätantike, 1996, 213–216 (on the column and the forum of M. as well as the 'Colossus of Barletta'); A. DEMANDT, Die Krise im Ostreich (450–518), in: HdbA III/6, 183f.; STEIN, Spätröm. R. 1, 465–471, 495, 520–523.

[8] M., Flavius Son of emperor → Anthemius [2] and of Aelia Marcia Euphemia, daughter of emperor M. [6]; consul in AD 469 and 472, magister militum praesentalis and patricius c. 471–474. He rebelled against emperor → Zeno in 475/6 as a supporter of → Basiliscus, was unsuccessful in his own cause in 479 (referring to his marriage to Leontia, a daughter of → Leo [4] I, who – unlike her elder sister Ariadne, Zeno's wife – was born to Leo after he had become emperor) and once again with → Illus and → Leontius in 484. (PLRE 2, 717f. no. 17).

[9] Son of a sister of → Iustinianus [1] I, East Roman general under → Iustinus [4] II; very wealthy, in AD 572 patricius and magister militum per Orientem in the war against the Persians, recalled by Imperial order in 573. PLRE 3B, 821–823 no. 7. F.T.

[10] see → Marcianus I

Marcias Goth, commander of the troops in the Gothic part of Gaul which → Vitigis abandoned in AD 536/7 (Procop. Goth. 1,13,15–16; 29). From there, M. was called to the siege of Rome (Procop. Goth. 1,19,12; PLRE 3B, 823f.) WE.LÜ.

Marcina Etruscan town in the ager Picentinus (cf. Plin. HN 3,70), later inhabited by Samnites, at a distance of 120 stadia from Pompeii (Str. 5,4,13); therefore probably to be identified with Vietri sul Mare (Salerno) (archaic graves).

> B. D'AGOSTINO, Marcina?, in: Dialoghi d'Archeologia 2, 1968, 139–151; M. FREDERIKSEN, Campania, 1984, 33. G.U.

Marcion Christian heretic, born about 85, died about 160. M. came from Sinope in Pontus, was a wealthy nauclerus (ship owner/overseas trader, Tert. De praescriptione haereticorum 30,1; → naukleros, → Navigation). About 140, he joined the Roman congregation,

but broke with it in 144 (ibid. 30,2). M. then founded a counter-church (Tert. Adversus Marcionem 4,5,3) which spread rapidly in spite of immediate counteractions. The dispute with M. forced reflections on the basic concepts and contents of the Christian faith. Even though the main Church prevailed, M.'s church lasted into the 4th cent. in the West, even into the 5th cent. in the East. There is no direct documentation by M. himself; our knowledge is based exclusively upon the literature directed against him and his church, primarily → Tertullianus. HARNACK [3] reconstructed M.'s teachings on the basis of source material, but his representation of M. as a theologian whose thoughts do not fit the framework of antiquity needs revision.

The conflict between the main Church and M. was based on the evaluation of the Christian tradition. M. considered the tradition fundamentally distorted: the OT does not say anything about the transcendental good God of the Gospel, but speaks only of a just creator of the world (Tert. Adversus Marcionem 2,29,1). The OT is irrelevant for Christian faith and should not be interpreted allegorically (ibid. 5,18,10). Only a canon compiled from the Gospel according to Luke and 10 Pauline letters, which M. purged from references to the OT God [2] with the methods of textual criticism of antiquity, is said to provide information on the Christian God. M. defended his hermeneutics with 'Antitheses' (thus the title of his work; the term is only found in Tertullian). A juxtaposition of law and Gospel shows the differing natures of both Gods (ibid. 1,19,4f.); the Creator manifests himself in the deficient world and in the law, which seduces humans to sin because they want to please God out of fear of punishment (ibid.1,27,3). Without posing any demands (ibid. 1,27,1), the good God liberates the soul through Christ from the bondage to the creator. Whoever believes, and is baptized, expresses his distance to the world by radical asceticism (ibid. 1,29,1).

The difference between the two Gods, the devaluation of the world and his criticism of the OT show M.'s closeness to → Gnostiscism, but there is no mythological-cosmological speculation on his part. It appears that the tension between the philosophical concept of God (God has nothing to do with evil, Pl. Resp. 379c) and the image of God in the OT lead to M.'s distinction between the two Gods (against [3]).

→ Canon; → Heresy; → Heresiology

> 1 B. ALAND, s.v. M./Marcioniten, TRE 22, 89–101 (bibliography); 2 R. M. GRANT, Heresy and Criticism. The Search for Authenticity in Early Christian Literature, 1993, 33–47; 3 A. v. HARNACK, M. Das Evangelium vom fremden Gott, ²1924; 4 G. MAY, Marcione nel suo tempo, in: Cristianesimo nella Storia 14, 1993, 205–220; 5 U. SCHMID, M. und sein Apostolos, 1995; 6 M. VINZENT, Christ's Resurrection: the Pauline Basis of M.'s Teaching, in: Studia Patristica 31, 1997, 225–233. K.GRE.

Marcius Old Roman *nomen gentile*, derived from the prename → Marcus. Tradition knows of a patrician branch with the (mythical) king Ancus M. [I 3] and Cn. M. → Coriolanus as its most important members. The younger members of the family (from the 3rd cent.) were plebeian without a link to the patrician Marcii being evident. Important families included the Rutili, later also the Censorini, Tremuli, Reges and Rallae. In the Late Republic the family claimed descent from the kings Ancus M. and Numa Pompilius (therefore the cognomen *Rex*, see M. [I 5]; RRC 346; 425; Suet. Iul. 6,1; [4. 154]) as well as perhaps kinship with the mythical Italic king Marsyas (Solin. 1,7; Plin. HN 3,108; [1. 113–119]).

1 F. COARELLI, Il Foro Romano. Periodo repubblicano ed augusteo, 1985; 2 J. REICHMUTH, Die lateinische Gentilica, 1956, 94; 3 SCHULZE, 188, 466; 4 T. P. WISEMAN, Legendary Genealogies in the Late Republic, in: G&R 21, 1974, 153–164.   K.-L.E.

I. REPUBLICAN PERIOD   II. IMPERIAL PERIOD

I. REPUBLICAN PERIOD

[I 1] Marcii According to Roman tradition (Liv. 1,40f.; Dion. Hal. Ant. Rom. 3,73; 4,4f.), the two sons of king Ancus → Marcius [I 3] and instigators of the murder of his successor → Tarquinius Priscus with the objective of preventing the succession of Tarquinius' confidant Servius → Tullius. The Marcii are absent from the Etruscan tradition (→ Mastarna); there the Roman leader *Cneve Tarchunies Rumach* ('Cn. Tarquinius of Rome'), who is probably identical with Tarquinius Priscus, is killed in the conflict with Mastarna alias Servius Tullius of Vulci, his later successor as ruler of Rome, and other Vulcians. The appearance of the Marcii in Roman tradition is explained with the historiographical attempt of harmonizing the tradition of a consensual and internally regulated succession in Rome's early period with the violent death of Tarquinius Priscus and the succession of the outsider Servius Tullius (who, according to Roman tradition, was born of a slave woman).

T. P. CORNELL, The Beginnings of Rome, 1995, 119–150; R. THOMSEN, King Servius Tullius, 1980, 57–114.
AN.BE.

[I 2] Allegedly one or several seers (→ *vates*) whose predictions (*carmina Marciana*) in 212 BC caused the establishment of the *ludi Apollinares* (→ *ludi*) to be established (Cic. Div. 1,89; 113; Liv. 25,12; Serv. Aen. 6,70).
K.-L.E.

[I 3] Ancus M. According to Roman tradition the fourth of the seven mythical kings of Rome and the grandson of → Numa Pompilius (Liv. 1,32,1; Cic. Rep. 2,33). The Roman annals contrast him with his predecessor Tullus → Hostilius [4]: while the later died by not properly performing the rites recorded by Numa, M.'s restoration of Rome's sacred order included, among others, the instructions to the *pontifex* for making Numa's regulations publicly accessible (Liv. 1,32,2).

The following, among others, are attributed to him (cf. [2]): expansion of Roman citizenship to the Latin communities conquered during war and settling their inhabitants on the Aventine and the Palatine; territorial expansion of Rome including the founding of → Ostia; introduction of the ritual declaration of war by the → *fetiales* [3].

1 D. BRIQUEL, Le règne d'Ancus M. Un problème de comparaison indo-européenne, in: MEFRA 107, 1995, 183–195;   2 R. M. OGILVIE, A Commentary on Livy I–V, 1965, 125–145;   3 J. RÜPKE, Domi militiae, 1990, 105–108.   C.F.

[I 4] M., Cn. According to Livy (6,1,6), M. as *tr. pl.* in 389 BC accused Q. → Fabius [I 11] Ambustus because as a delegate to the Gauls in 391 he became embroiled in a fight with them contrary to international law and, consequently, participated in causing the Gauls' attack against Rome in 390 (→ Allia).

[I 5] M., Numa According to the legendary tradition, M. was the father of king Ancus M. [I 3], who originated from M.'s liaison with Pompilia, the daughter of → Numa Pompilius. M. was already linked to him through his father M. (?) Marcius, the progenitor of the *gens Marcia*, who, according to Plutarch, was a relative and confidant of Numa Pompilius (and after the latter's death a candidate for the royal office). Also, M. was allegedly appointed by Numa Pompilius as *pontifex* and by Tullus → Hostilius [4] as *praef. urbi* (Plut. Numa 5,4; 6,1; 21,4–6; Liv. 1,20,5; 32,1; Tac. Ann. 6,11,1).
C.MÜ.

[I 6] M. Censorinus, C. Supporter of C. Marius [I 1]. Mint master in 88 BC (RRC 346); he had the consul Cn. → Octavius murdered (App. B Civ. 1,327f.); in 82 defeated by Cn. → Pompeius at Sena Gallica, after the battle he was captured at the Porta Collina by P. Cornelius [I 90] Sulla and killed (App. B Civ. 1,401; 414; 433; Cic. Brut. 311; cf. 237).   K.-L.E.

[I 7] M. Censorinus, L. Probably as the curule aedile at the *ludi Romani*, he had the *Hecyra* of → Terentius performed in 160 BC (Didascaliae ad Ter. Hec.), he was praetor no later than 152 and in 149 became consul (MRR 1,458). During the 3rd → Punic War, he received the naval command and his colleague M. Manilius [I 3] the command of the land army (App. Lib. 349). In the camp outside Utica he participated in the perfidious tactic of first disarming the Carthaginians and then forcing them to leave their town (differing in detail, App. Lib. 377 and Diod. Sic. 32,6,3). When the Carthaginians desperately defended their city, M. besieged it without significant impact from the south. After several lesser naval operations in the summer (Zon. 9,27), he returned to Rome in the autumn to hold elections (App. Lib. 468). In 147 M. was censor (MRR 1,463); details are unknown. M. was apparently open to Greek culture since the Academic philosopher → Cleitomachus [1] dedicated one of his works to him (Cic. Acad. 2,102).   W.K.

[I 8] M. Censorinus, L. Nephew of M. [I 6]; attempted in vain to protect Caesar on 15 March 44 (FGrH 90 F 130, p. 410). As *praetor urbanus* in 43, he followed M. Antonius [I 9] into the *bellum Mutinense* and was ostracized by the Senate (Cic. Phil. 11,36 *et passim*). M. bought the town house of Cicero (Vell. Pat. 2,14,3), who was proscribed, and in 42–40 was propraetor of Achaia and Macedonia (IG II/III² 4113). His consulate (MRR 2,386; PIR² M 223) began on 1 January 39 with a triumph *ex Macedonia*. M. is probably attested in 17 BC at the *ludi saeculares* (CIL VI 32323, l. 44) and survived Mark Antony's demise.

[I 9] M. Coriolanus, Cn. see → Coriolanus

[I 10] M. Crispus, Q. Legate of L. Calpurnius [I 19] Piso in Macedonia in 57–55 BC, praetor in about 54 (?) (MRR 3,138); in 46 he commanded three of Caesar's cohorts at Thapsus (Bell. Afr. 77,2). In 45, M. received Bithynia (Cic. Phil. 11,30) as *procos.*, in 44/43 he besieged Q. Caecilius [I 5] in Apamea and in 43 he lost his army to one of Caesar's murderers C. Cassius [I 10].
JÖ.F.

[I 11] M. Figulus, C. In 169 BC he unsuccessfully fought at sea against → Perseus; *cos.* in 162 together with P. Cornelius [I 83] Scipio Nasica Corculum; when the election was declared invalid, both consuls abdicated (MRR 1,441f.). In 156, M. was again consul and fought against the Dalmatians who had invaded Illyria (MRR 1,447).
K.-L.E.

[I 12] M. Figulus (Thermus?), C. *Cos.* in 64 BC, possibly identical with Minucius Thermus and a M. by adoption (MRR 3,138). M. helped Cicero in 63 against → Catilina (Cic. Phil. 2,12). Regarding his tomb, Cic. Leg. 2,62. A L. Figulus, probably M.'s son, gathered a fleet in 43 for L. Cornelius [I 29] Dolabella (App. B Civ. 4,60,258; cf. Cic. Fam. 12,13,3).
JÖ.F.

[I 13] M. Philippus, L. Mint master in 113 or 112 BC (RRC 293). About 104, as people's tribune, he introduced an agrarian law but withdrew it due to the Senate's resistance (Cic. Off. 2,73). Probably after skipping offices (Cic. Off. 2,59), M. became praetor no later than in 96 and after two electoral defeats he became consul together with Sex. Iulius [I 9] Caesar in 91. He was a decided opponent of the reform laws of the people's tribune M. Livius [I 7] Drusus (Cic. De or. 1,24; 3,2), which were supported by the conservative faction in the Senate, and (using his office as augur) after the death of Drusus' sponsor, L. Licinius [I 10] Crassus, he was able to have these laws abrogated (Cic. Leg. 2,31; Ascon. 61 C.). His outlook was confirmed after the murder of Drusus by the outbreak of the → Social War [3]. In the subsequent Civil War between → Marius [I 1] and → Cornelius [I 90] Sulla, he probably came to an arrangement with Marius because of his populist leanings and in 86 became censor together with M. Perperna. In 86 he defended the young Cn. → Pompeius, in 82 he sided with Sulla and gained Sardinia for him. After Sulla's death he became the most important Roman politician. In 78 he fought the attempt by M. Aemilius [I 11] Lepidus to abolish Sulla's constitution (Sall. Hist.

1,77M) and applied for a special command for Pompey to fight → Sertorius. He probably died soon after. As a major extempore speaker (who, therefore, published nothing), M. was later known for his puns (Cic. Brut. 173).
K.-L.E.

[I 14] M. Philippus, L. Born about 102 BC, died after 43, son of M. [I 13], stepfather of Augustus and father-in-law of M. → Porcius Cato. M. was praetor in 62 and administered Syria in 61–60 for → Pompeius; in 58 he married Atia [1] in his second marriage. Although related to Caesar, M., a master in double-crossing, still showed some distance to him as *cos.* in 56 (Cic. Prov. cons. 39; Cass. Dio 39,25,2). During the Civil War, M. did not openly take sides despite some gestures of distrust by the Senate (Caes. B Civ. 1,6,5), possibly with Caesar's approval as a 'good example' for others (Cic. Att. 10,4,10). In 44 M., now one of the *principes civitatis* (Cic. Phil. 8,28), advised his stepson publicly to disclaim Caesar's inheritance. However, he immediately supported Octavian's (→ Augustus) decision to accept it, using disinformation (Cic. Att. 15,12,2), intrigues and his great wealth (cf. Macrob. Sat. 3,15,6), by gathering powerful followers of Caesar and introducing the heir e.g. to Cicero (Cic. Att. 14,12,2). M. broke very late with M. Antonius [I 9], allegedly for the sake of a possible consulate for his son M. [I 15] (Cic. Fam. 12,2,2). He was a member of the Senate delegation that failed to reconcile with Mark Antony in 43 and thus incurred Cicero's anger (Cic. Phil. 9,1; Cic. Fam. 12,4,1). In the summer of 43, M. withdrew from politics (Cic. Epist. fr. 23B [15] SH. B.) but not without casting a long shadow as Octavian's teacher in craftiness. His younger son is perhaps Q. M. L. f., *cos. suff.* in 36 (AE 1991, 894 with InscrIt 13,1,58f.).

[I 15] M. Philippus, L. Son of M. [I 14] from his first marriage, c. 80 – after 33 BC, perhaps *III vir monetalis* in c. 56 (MRR 2,445). As people's tribune, M. cautiously supported Caesar in 49 (Caes. B Civ. 1,6,4), in 44 as praetor he contradicted the plans of Mark Antony of distributing provinces (Cic. Phil. 3,25). M. sided with Octavian (→ Augustus) afterwards; in 38 *cos. suff.* (InscrIt 13,1,342f.) and in 34–33 *procos.* in Spain, he triumphed on 27 April 33 *ex Hispania* (InscrIt 13,1,282; 291) and built the *porticus Philippi* with the booty (Tac. Ann. 3,72; Ov. Fast. 6,796; 801; [1. 146–148]). M. was married to his step-aunt Atia [2]. PIR² M 241a.

1 A. VICOGLIOSI, s.v. Porticus Philippi, LTUR 4, 1999.
JÖ.F.

[I 16] M. Philippus, Q. Triumphed over the Etruscans as consul in 281 BC (MRR 1,190) and was the first to employ *proletarii* in the army. Censor in 269; in 263 the *magister equitum* of the dictator Cn. Fulvius [I 14] Maximus Centumalus (InscrIt 13,1,73) for the centenary of the *clavus annalis* (the annual driving-in of a nail). As the most important representative of his *gens*, he bore the epithet *Philippus*.

MÜNZER, 64.
P.N.

[I 17] **M. Philippus, Q.** Probably the grandson of M. [I 16], in 188 BC praetor (Sicilia), already in 186 consul together with Sp. Postumius Albinus. Both investigated the notorious Bacchanalia scandal (→ Bacchanal(ia)). M. then suffered a severe defeat in the territory of the Apuani in Liguria (MRR 1,370). In 183 – probably because of earlier family contacts to the Macedonian royal family – he became delegate to Macedonia and the Peloponnese. From 180 → *decemvir* [4] *sacris faciundis*, in 174 he made solemn vows for the extinction of the plague. In 172 he led a delegation of five to Greece and together with A. Atilius [I 24] Serranus negotiated a truce (only under pretence and, therefore, disputed in Rome) with king → Perseus, so that Rome would be able to complete the preparations for war with Macedonia (Liv. 38,38–42). In 169 he became *cos. II* and received the command against Perseus. His risky offensive towards South Macedonia (in the company of the historian → Polybius) was unsuccessful (Pol. 28,13; Liv. 44,1–9 *et passim*; Syll.³ 649; dedication in Delos: IDélos 3,1429 A 31f.), so that M. was replaced by M. Aemilius [I 32] Paullus in 168. In 164 censor together with him.

→ Macedonian Wars

GRUEN, Rome, Index s.v. M.   K.-L.E.

[I 18] **M. Philippus, Q.** *Procos.* of Cilicia in 47 BC [1] and recipient of Cic. Fam. 13,73f. His identity with the companion of Cn. Pompeius Strabo in 89 is uncertain (MRR 3,139).

1 SYME, RP 1, 120–148.   JÖ.F.

[I 19] **M. Ralla, M.** Was *praetor urbanus* in 214 BC. In 203 he protected the Italian coasts with a fleet of forty ships (Liv. 30,2,5). Fought in 202 under Cornelius [I 71] Scipio in Africa and, after the victory at Zama, he accompanied the Carthaginian peace delegation to Rome (Liv. 30,38,4).

[I 20] **M. Ralla, Q.** As people's tribune in 194 BC, he achieved the ratification of the peace with Philip V of Macedonia (Liv. 33,25,6–7). In 194 he dedicated a temple to Fortuna Primigenia on the Quirinal and in 192 supposedly two, but probably only one temple to Jupiter on the Capitol (MRR 1,346; 353).

[I 21] **M. Rex, Q.** As *praetor urbanus* in 144 BC, he repaired the Aqua Appia and Anio Vetus aquaducts (Frontin. Aq. 1,7). He also built the → Aqua Marcia, which was renowned for the quality of its water. Its origins were attributed to the mythical king Ancus → Marcius [I 3] (Plin. HN 31,41–42). The attempt to undermine construction through reference to the Sibylline Books failed (Liv. Per. Oxyrhynchia 54). As *propraetor* he continued the work in 143.

[I 22] **M. Rex, Q.** Consul in 118 BC. He took the death of his only son with composure and even on the day of the funeral he held a legally required Senate session (Val. Max. 5,10,3). He campaigned against the Stoeni in Liguria and triumphed over them in 117 (MRR 1,527; 529). Later he was probably accused and successfully defended by M. Antonius [I 7].

ALEXANDER, 33f.; MÜNZER, 386–389.   P.N.

[I 23] **M. Rex, Q.** Lived *c.* 114 – *c.* 61 BC, *praetor* in 71, as *cos.* in 68 mostly in office without colleagues (Cass. Dio 36,4,1), married to Clodia [3]. As *procos.* of Cilicia in 67, M. refused help for L. Licinius [I 26] Lucullus against Mithridates VI of Pontus and received his brother-in-law Clodius [I 4], who had intrigued against Lucullus. M., who perhaps was supposed to initiate a new Roman policy in Syria [1], was prematurely replaced by → Pompeius in 66 (→ Manilius [I 2]) and waited in vain for many years for a much hoped-for triumph. In 63 the Senate employed him against the Catilinarians surrounding C. Manlius [I 1] (Sall. Catil. 32,3–34,1). M. died soon after (cf. Cic. Att. 1,16,10 of May 61).

1 G. DOWNEY, The Occupation of Syria by the Romans, in: TAPhA 82, 1951, 149–163.

[I 24] **M. Rufus** Quaestor in 49 BC; he secured the passage of the army of C. Scribonius Curio to Utica (Caes. B Civ. 2,23,5; 24,1) and attempted to save the remains of that army from destruction (ibid. 2,43,1–4).   JÖ.F.

[I 25] **M. Rutilus, C.** Rose as the first of the plebeian Marcii to become consul and held the office in 357, 352, 344 and 342 BC (MRR 1,122, 125, 132–134). As *cos. I* he defeated and triumphed over → Privernum (Liv. 7,16,3–6; InscrIt 13,1,69), as *cos. II* he possibly was the originator of a *lex Marcia* regarding usury mentioned by Gaius (Inst. 4,23), as *cos. IV* he supposedly prevented a mutiny in Campania through skilful action (Liv. 7,38,8–39,7; Dion. Hal. Ant. Rom. 15,3,10–12). In 356, M. was the first plebeian → dictator (MRR 1,123) and gained a great victory over the Etruscans (Liv. 7,17,6–9; Eutr. 2,5,3) for which, according to Livy (7,17,9; 10,37,10), he was granted a triumph 'without the Senate's approval at the command of the people' (cf. [1. 720f.]) – but this is disputed in the written sources [2. 89, n. 96]. Likewise, as the first plebeian, M. together with Cn. Manlius [I 10] Capitolinus, his colleague during the first consulate, was censor in 351 (InscrIt 13,1,405).

1 S. P. OAKLEY, A Commentary on Livy Books VI–X, vol. 1, 1997; 2 HÖLKESKAMP.

[I 26] **M. Rutilus Censorinus, C.** Son of M. [I 25]. As *tr. pl.* in 311 BC, he and his colleague L. Atilius [I 3] passed a law according to which the people would no longer elect 6 but 16 military tribunes (Liv. 9,30,3 [1. 152]). As *cos.* in 310 (MRR 1,161f.), he conquered → Allifae (Diod. Sic. 20,35,1f.; Liv. 9,38,1). After opening the great priestly colleges to plebeians in 300 (*lex Ogulnia*), M. simultaneously became pontifex and augur (Liv. 10,9,2) – a clear indicator of his high standing. This is also evident in the fact that he became censor twice, in 294 and 265, which earned him (and his heirs) the *cognomen* Censorinus (InscrIt 13,1,426f.; 432).

1 HÖLKESKAMP.   C.MÜ.

[I 27] M. Septimus, L. Military tribune in 211 BC. After the death of the brothers P. and Cn. Cornelius [I 68 and 77] Scipio in Spain, he assumed the command of the leaderless army together with the legate Ti. Fonteius [I 4] and passed it on to the *propraetor* C. Claudius [I 17] Nero (Liv. 25,37–39 with great exaggeration of the achievements of M.). In 206 deputy general under P. Cornelius [I 71] Scipio (participated in the battle of Ilipa; concluded a treaty with Gades; Cic. Balb. 34).

K.-L.E.

[I 28] M., Tremulus Q. Consul in 306 and 288 BC (MRR 1,165f., 185). During his first consulate he defeated the Hernicii, who under the leadership of → Anagnia had declared war against Rome, and together with his colleague P. Cornelius [I 5] Arvina he gained an important victory over the Samnites. He celebrated a triumph over the Hernicii and was also honoured with an equestrian statue (Liv. 9,42,10–43,22; Diod. Sic. 20,80,1–4; InscrIt 13,1,69); on M.'s equestrian statue [1. 19, 57f.; 2. 57–60]).

1 G. LAHUSEN, Untersuchungen zur Ehrenstatue in Rom. Literarische und epigraphische Zeugnisse, 1983;   2 M. SEHLMEYER, Stadtrömische Ehrenstatuen der republikanischen Zeit, 1999.

C.MÜ.

II. IMPERIAL PERIOD

[II 1] Q. M. Barea Soranus Senator. Related to Artorius Geminus. Suffect consul in AD 34, proconsul in Africa 41–43; member of the → *quindecimviri sacris faciundis* and *fetialis* (→ *fetiales*); father of M. [II 2] and M. [II 3]. PIR² M 218 (with stemma).

VOGEL-WEIDEMANN, 135–138.

[II 2] Q. M. Barea Soranus Son of M. [II 1]. Suffect consul in AD 52 [1. 266]. As designated consul he applied to have the imperial freedman → Pallas honoured with the *ornamenta praetoria* and 15 million sesterces (Tac. Ann. 12,53). Proconsul of Asia, probably in 61/2. In 66 accused in the Senate; he and his daughter Servilia were sentenced; the choice of the manner of death was left to them; regarding the political implications of the trial [2. 429–438]. PIR² B 55.

1 G. CAMODECA, L'archivio puteolano dei Sulpicii, 1992; 2 VOGEL-WEIDEMANN.

[II 3] Q. M. Barea Sura Son of M. [II 1], brother of M. [II 2]. Marcia [9] Furnilla was his daughter; obviously there was a political connection to the Flavii family. PIR² M 219.

[II 4] L. M. Celer M. Calpurnius Longus (PIR² M 221) see → Calpurnius [II 10].

[II 5] C. M. Censorinus Son of the consul of 39 BC. *Triumvir monetalis* about 18/7 BC; as legate in Asia probably under → Agrippa [1], he passed an edict regarding Jewish cultic practice (Jos. Ant. Iud. 16,165). Suffect consul in 8 BC. Proconsul of Asia in AD 2/3 where he died in office. He is the last known senator in whose honour games were established (SEG 2, 549). He is not known to have had a son because CIL VI 877a does not

refer to the secular games of Claudius (AE 1988, 20). PIR² M 222.

[II 6] M. Claudius Agrippa M. allegedly rose from being a former slave to equestrian status. He was exiled to an island for offences committed as an *advocatus fisci* but was recalled by → Caracalla and entrusted with the duties of an *a cognitionibus* and *ab* → *epistulis*. Because he sold military service positions, he was transferred to the Praetorians 'as a penalty'. He participated in the conspiracy against Caracalla and, as a result, was given the *ornamenta consularia* by → Macrinus and made governor of Pannonia inferior, Dacia and Moesia inferior. It is disputed whether he accumulated these governorships: he is attested in Moesia by coins, but all other information depends on Cassius Dio (79,13,2–4) and the Historia Augusta (HA Carac. 6,7). Therefore, especially the evaluations should be viewed with scepticism.

D. BOTEVA, Legati Augusti pro praetore Moesiae Inferioris, in: ZPE 110, 1996, 246f.; ECK, Statthalter, 204f.; PISO, FDP 1, 1993, 182–86; PIR² M 224.

[II 7] Q. M. Dioga Equestrian from → Leptis Magna, who according to [1], began his career under Marcus [2] Aurelius and then rose through a series of procuratorial offices to the prefecture of the *annonae* (see → cura annonae II.) at the beginning of → Caracalla's rule. His last known position was the *praefectura vigilum* before AD 215–217; cf. [2]. PIR² M 231.

1 M. CHRISTOL, Un fidèle de Caracalla: Q. M. Dioga, in: Cahiers du Centre G. Glotz 2, 1991, 165–188.

R. SABLAYROLLES, Libertinus miles, 1996.

[II 8] M. Festus According to InscrIt IV 1, 180 an equestrian, [*a cubiculo* ?] *et a memoria* of Caracalla, who was honoured by the council and people of → Tibur. He is most likely identical with the Festus whom Herodian (4,8,4f.) called a freedman of → Caracalla. He supposedly accompanied the emperor to the East but died at Troy, where Caracalla prepared a splendid funeral for him. His model were the funerary games that → Achilles held for Patroclus. If this identification is correct, he must have been retroactively elevated to the status of a freeborn person (*restitutio natalium*) through an imperial act of mercy. Consequently, Festus could not have been a *libertus* of the emperor; perhaps he was a slave of Marcia [7], the concubine of Commodus. PIR² M 234.

[II 9] M. M. Hortalus Senator whose name is recorded in Tacitus (Ann. 2,37,1) as Marcus Hortalus. However, because of AE 1987, 163 his name is Marcius, not Hortensius, as was noted, e.g. in PIR² H 210. M. was a grandson of the orator Hortensius [7] but bore the *nomen gentile* of his grandmother to emphasize his relationship to Augustus. In AD 16, in the Senate, he asked Tiberius for financial support, which he had received from Augustus before – after all, he argued, he had raised four sons at his request (cf. → Hortensius [6]; Tac. Ann. 2,37f.). Tiberius granted him the money albeit under humiliating circumstances. Regarding the genealogical problems ([1. 655–701; 2. 249f.; 3. 251–260] = AE 1991, 1568–1571; 1994, 1757–1759).

1 M. Corbier, La descendance d'Hortensius et de Marcia, in: MEFRA 103, 1992;   2 J. Briscoe, The Grandson of Hortensius, in: ZPE 95, 1993;   3 W. Eck, M. Hortalus, nobilis iuvenis und seine Söhne, in: ZPE 95, 1993.

[II 10] M. Hortalus Praetor peregrinus in AD 25 (AE 1987, 163). He could theoretically be identical with the homonymous senator M. [II 9] (cf. AE 1991, 1568ff.; 1994, 1757). However, he is more likely to be one of his four sons who in 16 supported their father's pleading in the Senate [1. 251–260].

1 W. Eck, M. Hortalus, nobilis iuvenis und seine Söhne, in: ZPE 95, 1993.

[II 11] M. [Hor]tensinus Proconsul of → Cyprus under → Tiberius. In a dedication of a statue for Tiberius, he refers to his ancestor, the orator Hortensius [7] (SEG 30, 1635 = AE 1991, 1568 = [1. 251–60]; cf. AE 1994, 1759). He was either a son or brother of M. [II 9] and, therefore, a brother or uncle of M. [II 10] (AE 1994, 1575–1759; PIR² H 206 is outdated).

1 W. Eck, M. Hortalus, nobilis iuvenis und seine Söhne, in: ZPE 95, 1993.

[II 12] Sex. M. Priscus Governor of the province of → Lycia from Nero to the early reign of Vespasian [1. 65–75]. Suffect consul with Cn. Pinarius Aemilius Cicatricula in December of AD 71 or 72. PIR² M 242.

1 W. Eck, Die Legaten von Lykien und Pamphylien unter Vespasian, in: ZPE 6, 1970.   w.e.

[II 13] M. Salutaris A high state official (vir perfectissimus, according to Iulius [IV 19] Romanus' description in Char. p. 297,8 B), who was active in the financial administration of Egypt about the mid–3rd cent. AD. The same Iulius Romanus recorded two interpretations of Virgil by M. (ibid. and p. 262,10 B.). His work seems to have been a grammar compilation for schools rather than a commentary on Virgil.

Schanz/Hosius, vol. 3, 175; A. Stein, P. Wessner, s.v. M. (99), RE 14, 1590f.   p.g.

[II 14] Q. M. Turbo Fronto Publicius Severus Equestrian from → Epidaurum in Dalmatia (AE 1955, 225). M. began as a centurio in the legio II adiutrix in Aquincum, where he possibly became acquainted with Hadrian. Praefectus vehiculorum under → Traianus; tribunus equitum singularium; primus pilus. As the procurator ludi magni, he embarked on a procuratorial career, became prefect of the fleet of Misenum, participated in the → Parthian War and was honoured with the dona militaria. Trajan ordered him to go to Egypt to fight rebellious Jews in Alexandria [1]; he was possibly given the rank of a praefectus Aegypti, though not the office itself. Afterwards, Hadrian assigned him to suppress an uprising in Mauretania. Probably still in AD 117 or early 118, he was given a special command in

Pannonia inferior and Dacia [1. 21], possibly already as the praef. praet. ([2. 247ff.] = AE 1993, 1361) – the differences in the historical records are difficult to reconcile ([3. 91f.] with bibliography). Honoured as praetorian prefect in → Sarmizegetusa and → Tibiscum (after 128), also in Utica. M. was very closely linked to Hadrian, who possibly let him hold the office of praef. praet. alone for a long period after 121. M. was only replaced about 136/7 because he apparently was linked to the 'opposition' against appointing Aelius Caesar (→ Ceionius [3]). PIR² M 249.

Flavius [II 29] and T. Flavius Priscus Gallonius Fronto Q. M. Turbo, who pursued an equestrian career to the governorship of Mauretania Caesariensis [4. 201f.; 5. 238ff.] may have been his adoptive sons.

1 RMD 1;   2 W. Eck, in: K. Dietz, D. Hennig, H. Kaletsch (ed.), Klassisches Altertum, Spätantike und frühes Christentum. FS A. Lippold, 1993;   3 A. Birley, Hadrian, 1997;   4 Thomasson, Fasti Africani;   5 W. Eck, Zu Inschriften von Prokuratoren, in: ZPE 124, 1999, 228–241.

[II 15] Q. M. Victor Felix Maximilianus Legionary legate under Septimius Severus and Caracalla in Dacia; M. [II 16] is his son. PIR² M 253.
[II 16] P. M. Victor Maximillianus Son of M. [II 15]. In the → album [2] of Canusium probably mentioned as a praetorian (CIL IX 338, l. 29). He is probably identical to M. Maximillianus who was the consular legate of Pannonia superior in AD 240 [1. 100ff.]; perhaps he is also identical with the proconsul of Asia in 253/4, [– –]us Maximillianus (IGR IV 1381 = TAM V 230). PIR² M 254 and 390.

1 W. Eck, M. M. Roxan, Zwei Entlassungsurkunden – tabulae honestae missionis – für Soldaten der römischen Auxilien, in: Arch. Korrespondenzblatt 28, 1998.   w.e.

Marcodurum Settlement in the western territory of the → Ubii, possibly modern Düren or, more probably, Merken near Düren, where the cohortes Ubiorum were destroyed during the uprising of Iulius [II 43] Civilis in AD 69 (Tac. Hist. 4,28,2).

A. Franke, s.v. M., RE 14, 1680f.; C. B. Rüger, Germania Inferior, 1968, 82.   ra.wi.

Marcomagus Station (It. Ant. 373,2; Tab. Peut. 3,1) on the Roman road from Augusta [6] Treverorum to Colonia Agrippinensis, modern Nettersheim-Marmagen, district of Euskirchen. It was possibly associated with a vicus located in the Urft valley south of Nettersheim, which was probably abandoned in the 2nd half of the 3rd cent. AD (cf. [1; 2]; CIL XVII 2, 554 of AD 350–353).

1 A.-B. Follmann-Schulz, Die römischen Tempelanlagen in der Provinz Germania inferior, in: ANRW II 18.1, 1986, 750–753;   2 J. Hagen, Römerstraßen der Rheinprov., ²1931, 124–131.

H. G. Wackernagel, s.v. Marcomagus vicus, RE 14,
1609; O. Kleemann, Zur älteren Geschichte des Dorfes
Nettersheim in der Eifel, in: BJ 163, 1963, 212–220; H. G.
Horn, Nettersheim, in: Id. (ed.), Die Römer in Nord-
rhein-Westfalen, 1987, 571–575.   RA.WI.

Marcomanni A Germanic tribe belonging to the
→ Suebi (border people [26. 161f.]) that was probably
forced from the middle Elbe region into the upper and
middle Main region by the migrations of the → Cimbri
and → Teutoni. The M. supplied mercenaries: from 72
BC for the → Sequani in their war against the Haedui, in
60 BC for the → Dacians during the destruction of the
→ Boii kingdom in Bohemia, in 58 for → Ariovistus
against Caesar (Caes. B Gall. 1,51,2). Severely defeated
by Claudius [II 24] Drusus probably in 9 BC (Oros.
6,21,15; Flor. 2,30,23; cf. Cass. Dio 55,1,2), under
their king Marbod (→ Maroboduus) they moved to
Bohemia (Vell. Pat. 2,108,2), where they perhaps defeated remains of the Boii (Tac. Germ. 42,1), and they
left their previous settlement territory to the → Hermunduri (Cass. Dio 55,10a,2 [1. 314–316]); another
part of the M. was probably settled in Flanders (Suet.
Aug. 21,1; R. Gest. div. Aug. 32). The → Lugii, → Semnones, → Langobardi and others were allied with Marbod's kingdom.

'Since there was no one else left to defeat in Germa-
nia other than the Marcomanni ' (Vell. Pat. 2,108,1),
Tiberius advanced in AD 6 from → Carnuntum possibly via Mušov [2; 3], and C. Sentius Saturninus from
→ Mogontiacum possibly via Marktbreit [1; 4], to
Bohemia. Because of the Pannonian-Dalmatian revolt,
Rome made peace (Vell. Pat. 2,109,5; 110,1f.; Tac.
Ann. 2,46; Cass. Dio 55,28). Marbod's neutrality in the
Roman conflict with → Arminius in AD 17 led, after the
defection of the Semnones and Langobardi (Tac. Ann.
2,45,1; 46,3), to the indecisive battle between Arminius
and Marbod, resulting in the latter withdrawing 'into
the hills'. Shortly afterwards Marbod was driven out by
→ Catualda, who in turn was driven out by the Hermunduri (Tac. Ann. 2,62f.); whereupon → Drusus [II 1]
the Younger settled the followings of the two leaders
between the rivers March and → Cusus (Waag?; Tac.
Ann. 2,63,6 [5]) and appointed the Quadian → Vannius as their king (Tac. Ann. 12,29,1). The *Vannianum
regnum* was supported by Rome (Plin. HN 4,81) and
included the remaining Marcomanni in Bohemia and
the → Quadi in Moravia [6; 7; 8. 40–42; 9. 270–277].
The M. were required to supply Rome with auxiliary
troops (Cass. Dio 67,7,1; on the issue of client states in
general [10]). After 30 years, Vannius was driven out by
the Lugii and the Hermunduri and his sister's sons
→ Vangio and → Sido shared the rule (Tac. Ann.
12,29,2–30,2). The Romans kept them compliant with
money (Tac. Germ. 42,2; cf. Tac. Hist. 3,5,1; 21,2).

In 89 and 92–93 there were armed conflicts between
Domitianus [1] and the M., → Quadi and → Iazyges, in
which the Romans suffered bitter defeats; the Suebi
were only defeated by Nerva in 97 after another inva-

sion into Pannonia [11. 84f.]. However, Pannonia superior was not spared invasions by its northern neighbours in the period following, e.g. in 118 and 136–
140/4 [11. 87]. The trade of the M. with the Roman
Empire was particularly important [8. 41f.; 12; 13;
14. 123f.], bringing with it intensive Roman influence
[15; 16. 695ff.]. The three Germanic wars of the
Roman emperors Marcus [2] Aurelius and Commodus
([17; 18] cf. [11. 133–198]) between c. 167 and 182
(→ Burii), in which the M. played a leading role, put
Rome on the defensive (e.g. SHA Aur. 12,13; 13,1;
17,2; SHA Avid. Cass. 3,6; Eutr. 8,12,2). However,
Marcus Aurelius forced the M. to accept peace in 173
and 174 [11. 158ff.]. A renewed breach of treaty resulted again in a war (AD 177–180; [19]) and in the emper-
or's oath to force the M. and Quadi to a → *deditio*
(Cass. Dio 72,18), possibly with the intention of establishing a province of Marcomannia (SHA Aur. 27,10;
cf. also the archaeological evidence [20; 21]). When he
died there were more than 20,000 Roman soldiers in
the land of the M. and Quadi; Commodus ended the
war on the terms of the peace of 174/5 [22], which again
resulted in an armed conflict with the Buri(i). Scenes
from the M. wars are depicted on the Column of
Marcus Aurelius in Rome [23; 24]. M. who were taken
prisoners were settled near Ravenna, but after unrest
they were relocated into the provinces, especially Gaul
(Cass. Dio 71,11,4f.).

Septimius Severus, who was proclaimed emperor in
Carnuntum, attempted to calm the 'peoples subjected
by Rome in the north' with promises (Hdn. 2,9,12).
Caracalla incited the M. against the → Vandals (Cass.
Dio 77,20,3). Elagabalus' plan of campaigning against
the M. was abandoned (SHA Heliogab. 9,1f.). Together
with the → Scythians, the M. devastated Roman territory in 253 (Zos. 1,29,2). Gallienus felt compelled to
settle them in Pannonia superior under king Attalus
(Epit. de Caes. 33,1). Diocletian was able to defeat the
M. in 299 (Aur. Vict. 39,43; Fasti Hydatiani a. 299
MGH AA 9,1,230). When Valentinian I fought against
the Quadi in 374/5, their neighbours were also affected
(Amm. Marc. 29,6,1). The M. continued their invasions into the Empire even in the late 4th cent. (Claud.
Carm. 5,26ff.), but in 396 bishop Ambrosius was able
to persuade the M. through their already Christian
queen Fritigil to conclude a treaty with → Stilicho (Paulinus of Milan, Vita Ambrosii 36). The *Notitia* mentions a *tribunus gentis Marcomannorum* (Not. Dign.
Occ. 34,24), but M. served as Roman mercenaries also
in Italia (ibid. 5,198f. = 7,38) and Africa (Synesius of
Cyrene, Epist. 110, Epistolographi Graeci Hercher for
405; PLRE 2 s.v. Chilas p. 284). In 451, the M. fought
against Attila on the → Campi Catalauni (Paul. Diaconus, Historia Romana 14,2, MGH AA 2,201). In the
5th and 6th cents., Bohemia was increasingly depopulated by a migration in groups to the south (cf. [25]). To
what extent the M. contributed to the ethnogenesis of
the → Baiovarii is uncertain.

1 M. PIETSCH et al., Das augusteische Truppenlager Marktbreit, in: BRGK 72, 1991, 263–324; 2 T. KOLNÍK, Zu den ersten Römern und Germanen an der mittleren Donau, in: R. ASSKAMP, S. BERKE (ed.), Die römischen Okkupation nördlich der Alpen zur Zeit des Augustus, 1990, 71–84; 3 M. BÁLEK, O. ŠEDO, Das frühkaiserzeitliche Lager bei Mušov, in: Germania 74, 1996, 399–414; 4 F. X. HERRMANN, Das Römerlager bei Marktbreit, in: Gymnasium 99, 1992, 546–564; 5 J. TEJRAL, Die älteste Phase der germanische Besiedlung zwischen Donau und March, in: Ausklang der Latène-Zivilsation und Anfang der germanischen Besiedlung im mittleren Donauraum, 1977, 307–342; 6 T. KOLNÍK, Anfang der germanischen Besiedlung in der Südwestslowakei und das Regnum Vannianum, in: Ausklang ... (s. [5]), 1977, 143–171; 7 A. LEUBE, Das Regnum Vannianum im Spiegel neuer Forschungsergebnisse, in: A. SCHEEL (ed.), Rom und Germanien. FS W. Hartke, 1982, 52–55; 8 R. WOLTERS, Der Waren- und Dienstleistungsaustausch zwischen dem römischen Reich und dem Freien Germanien, in: MBAH 9/1, 1990, 14–44; 9 Id., Römische Eroberung und Herrschaftsorganisation in Gallien und Germanien, 1990; 10 P. KEHNE, Die Eroberung Galliens ... , in: Germania 75, 1997, 265–284; 11 M. T. SCHMID, Die römische Außenpolitik des 2. Jahrhunderts n.Chr., 1997; 12 U.-B. DITTRICH, Die Wirtschaftsstruktur der Quaden, Markomannen und Sarmaten im mittleren Donauraum und ihre Handelsbeziehungen mit Rom, in: MBAH 6/1, 1987, 9–30; 13 A. STUPPNER, Terra Sigillata im nördlichen Niederösterreich, in: MBAH 13/2, 1994, 70–94; 14 K. TAUSEND, Bemerkungen zum Wandaleneinfall des Jahres 271, in: Historia 48, 1999, 119–127; 15 T. KOLNÍK, Q. Atilius Primus, in: Acta Archaeologica Academiae Scientiarum Hungaricae 30, 1978, 61–75; 16 K. GENSER, Der österreichische Donaulimes in der Römerzeit, 1986; 17 H. FRIESINGER et al. (ed.), Markomannenkriege, 1995; 18 G. DOBESCH, Aus der Vor- und Nachgeschichte der Markomannenkriege, in: AAWW 131, 1994, 67–125; 19 C. M. HÜSSEN, J. RAITÁR, Zur Frage archäologischer Zeugnisse der Markomannenkriege in der Slowakei, in: [17], 217–232; 20 J. TEJRAL, New Contributions to the Research on Roman Military Disposition North of the Middle Danube, in: Eirene 30, 1994, 123–154; 21 Id. et al., The Fortification of the Roman Military Station at Mušov near Mikulov, in: Archeologia (Warsaw) 45, 1994, 57–68; 22 M. STAHL, Zwischen Abgrenzung und Integration, in: Chiron 19, 1989, 289–317; 23 M. JORDAN-RUWE, Zur Rekonstruktion und Datierung der Marcussäule, in: Boreas 13, 1990, 53–69; 24 H. WOLFF, Welchen Zeitraum stellt der Bilderfries der Marcus-Säule dar?, in: Ostbairische Grenzmarken 32, 1990, 9–29; 25 H. CASTRITIUS, Barbari – antiqui barbari. Zur Besiedlungsgeschichte Südostnorikums und Südpannoniens in der Spätantike, in: FMS 29, 1995, 72–85; 26 SCHÖNFELD.

TIR M 33,55–58; U.-B. DITTRICH, Die Beziehungen Roms zu den Sarmaten und Quaden im 4. Jahrhundert, 1984, 26–47.   K.DI.

Marcomannus Author of a commentary – based, among others, on → Hermagoras [1] (of Temnus) – on Cicero's rhetorical works, from which → Marius [II 21] Victorinus quotes, in part polemically [1. 173, l. 25ff.; 299, l.13ff.]. It is also used in the rhetoric of → Consultus Fortunatianus [1. p. 98,26f.] and → Sulpicius Victor

[1. p. 339,2ff.; 340,14–341,28], as well as (according to title and subscription) of → Iulius [IV 24] Victor, works which in part still belong to the 4th cent. Since Victorinus seems to deal with M. as his direct predecessor, dating M. to the 4th cent. AD seems appropriate; the Germanic name also fits this theory.

1 C. HALM, Rhetores Latini Minores, 1863.

D. MATTHES, Hermagoras, in: Lustrum 3, 1958, 78 n. 2; 122 n. 6; P. L. SCHMIDT, in: HLL, vol. 5, § 522.8.   P.L.S.

Marcomer Frankish *dux*, later *rex*, broke through the Limes in AD 388 and probably destroyed the punitive expedition army led by → Quintinus. In 389 he negotiated with → Valentinianus II and provided hostages. In 391/2, M. avoided an attack by → Arbogastes and in 392 entered into a → *foedus* with Eugenius [1] (Greg. Tur. Franc. 2,9). In 395 he presumably fled to → Stilicho or was arrested by him and was interned in Etruria (Claud. Carm. 8; 18; 21). PLRE 1, 557.   P.KE.

Marculus Donatist (→ Donatus [1]) bishop in Numidia, maltreated with a delegation of bishops in Vegesela (Numidia) by → Macarius. M. was taken prisoner and – probably on 29 Nov. 347 AD – executed, according to the Donatist Acts [1] by being pushed off a high cliff. He was buried as a martyr in Nova Petra and revered by the Donatists. There is archaeological evidence for a *memoria domni Marchuli* in Vegesela (Ksar el Kelb in Algeria).

1 J.-L. MAIER, Le dossier du donatisme, Bd. 1: Des origines à la mort de Constance II (303–361), 1987, 275–291; 2 A. MANDOUZE, Prosopographie chrétienne du Bas-Empire, Bd. 1: Afrique, 1982, 696f.   AL.SCHI.

Marcus (Μάρκος; *Márkos*).
I. GREEK II. ROMAN

I. GREEK
[1] (Lat. Marcus). The author of the second → Gospel (Mk) could be a missionary (Iohannes) M. who is often mentioned in the NT especially in close association with → Paulus (Acts 12:12:25; Phm 24 among others) (for example, for the first time → Papias around AD 130, see Euseb. Hist. eccl. 3,39,15). The fact that evidence of a closeness to Paul's theology can barely be found [3] is an argument against this identification, while the straightforwardness of this assumption supports it, as the biographical details and the accepted period when the work was written coincide [1]. The author, who wrote in Greek, appears to have a command of Aramaic as well as of Latin. Whilst the Latin words (e.g. Mk 6:27; 15:15) could indicate that Rome was the place where the work was written, the Aramaic terms (e.g. 5:41; 7:34; 15:34) as well as the explanations of Jewish customs (e.g. 7:3f.; 14:12) demonstrate that the author is acquainted with Palestinian → Judaism. Presumably M. writes as a Jewish follower of → Jesus for addressees who are primarily non-Jewish but believe in Christ. Mk

is dated around AD 70 by most scholars although suggestions for an earlier dating around AD 40 have never been completely silenced [6]. Since the 19th/20th cents. Mk is mostly regarded as the earliest Gospel. The conclusion, which is missing from notable textual evidence (16:9–20), does not appear to have belonged to its original scope.

Mk is divided up into two parts (1:14–8:26; 9:14–16:8; cf. [2]) whose preludes are developed in a strictly parallel manner (1:1–1:13; 8:27–9:13): the title of Christ (1:1; 8:27–30), the Baptist and the fulfillment of prophesies (1:2–8; 9:9–13), the confirmation that Jesus is the son of God (1:9–11; 9:2–8), the temptation by → Satan (1:12f.; 8:31–9:1). The first part of Mk poses the question: Who is this Jesus? (4:41; 8:27). The second part begins with the answer: the 'Christ' (8:28f.; → Messiah), in order from then until the end to interpret this answer by the fact that Christ must suffer. A healing of a blind man in two phases at the transition from the first to the second part (8:22–26) shows that anyone who sees Jesus as the Christ first recognizes him vaguely; no one can see clearly until he recognizes Christ in suffering as the son of God (thus, as the first one to do so, a Roman [!] captain in 15:39). The second healing of the blind (10:46–52) occurs immediately and totally for it is directly before the start of the Passion.

The 'Messianic secret' [5] structures Mk theologically: the gradual revelation of the Messiahship of Jesus through word and deed is contrasted with lack of understanding (e.g. 4:13; 7:18), strategies for disguise (4:11f.) and commands to keep silent (e.g. 1:44; 3:12) in order at the same time to reveal Christ as the suffering one. The addressees of Mk are also integrated into this concept through the call to imitation of Christ (in suffering). This theology of succession [3] contains a social aspect (community) and leads to correct action (ethics; cf. [4]).

→ Bible; → Gospel; → John [1]; → Luke; → Matthew

1 M. Hengel, Probleme des Markusevangeliums, in: P. Stuhlmacher (ed.), Das Evangelium und die Evangelien (WUNT 28), 1983, 221–265; 2 P. Lamarche, Evangile de Marc, 1996; 3 L. Schenke, Das Markusevangelium, 1988; 4 T. Söding (ed.), Der Evangelist als Theologe (Stuttgarter Bibelstudien 163), 1995, 167–195; 5 W. Wrede, Das Messiasgeheimnis in den Evangelien, ³1963; 6 G. Zuntz, Wann wurde das Evangelium Marci geschrieben?, in: H. Cancik (ed.), Markus-Philologie (WUNT 33), 1984, 47–71.

H. Cancik (ed.), Markus-Philologie (WUNT 33), 1984.
P.WI.

[2] Rich Sophist of Byzantium who traced his origin back to Byzas, the founder of the city; probably that Memmius M. through whose magistratures Byzantine coins representing Byzas can be dated to the time of Antoninus Pius, Marcus Aurelius and Commodus ([1], on a sarcophagus of his son – or slave? – [2]); possibly the rhetoric teacher of Marcus Aurelius (SHA Aur. 2,4, cf. [3]). The rhetorical ability of M., a student of Isaeus of Assyria, was admired (despite his unkempt appear-

ance) not only by → Polemon but also by Hadrian when M. visited him as an envoy on behalf of the city of Byzantium (Philostr. VS 1,24,529–530).
→ Philostratus; → Second Sophistic

1 I. N. Sworonos, Νομισματικὰ Ἀνάλεκτα, in: Ἐφεμερίς Ἀρχαιολογικὴ 3, 1889, 114–115; 2 BE 1968, Nr. 342; 3 A. R. Birley, Marcus Aurelius, ²1987, 66; 4 PIR M 465.
E.BO.

[3] Bishop of Arethusa (Syria), one of the leading Eastern bishops, participated in the synods of Antioch (341), Serdica (342/3), Sirmium (351) and Seleucia (359). In summer 341 he travelled as a member of the delegation of four to Trier (Augusta [6] Treverorum) in order to hand to Emperor Constanine the so-called fourth Creed of the church consecration synod of Antioch (Athan. De synodis 25,1; Socr. 2,18,1; Sozom. Hist. eccl. 3,10,4). In Serdica 342/3, he sided with the Eastern synod participants against the Western pro-Athanasian synod (→ Athanasius). In Seleucia (359) he supported the positions of the Homoean → Acacius [2] (Epiphanius, Panarion 73,20,1); he is considered to be the editor of the fourth Creed of Sirmium of 22.05.359 negotiated between the Homoeans and Homoeousians (→ Arianism) (Socr. 2,37,17; Hil. Collectanea antiariana bk. 6,3). Under Iulianus [11] Apostata he was persecuted (Lib. Ep. 819; Greg. Naz. or. 4,88–91), and he was cited in the Greek calendar of saints on 28.03. as a confessor (Propylaeum ad Acta Sanctorum Novembris 565ff.).

H. C. Brennecke, Studien zur Geschichte der Homöer (Beiträge zur Historischen Theologie 63), 1988. O.WER.

[4] M. Eremites J. Kunze [6] proved in 1895 that a series of ascetic treatises (CPG III, 6090–6100 = PG 65, 905–1140) and a Lógos dogmatikós directed against → Nestorius (CPG 6101: [6. 6–30]) were written by a monk in the 1st half of the 5th cent. who according to late information in Georgius [5] Monachos (Chronicon p. 599,5 de Boor = PG 110, 734 B) was a student of → Iohannes [4] Chrysostom and initially lived near the ascetic → Neilus of Ancyra in Ancyra/ Galatia but then settled in another desert region (Palestine or Syria) as an ascetic (→ Asceticism). M. was a respected monastic teacher and, despite being close to them in certain respects from the point of view of doctrine, he fought energetically against the ascetic Eastern monastic movement of the Messalians [1] and supported a 'pre-Nestorian (Cappadocian?) Christology with an Alexandrian orientation' [4. 97]; the fourth treatise, De baptismo (CPG 6093 = PG 65, 985–1028), is directed, according to the Nestorian theologian Babai († 628), against Macarius/Symeon and his adherents [2. 253]. The first two logoi belong together, which contain 412 maxims about the 'spiritual law' of Romans 7:14; the tenth treatise is directed against the Melchisedechians (a haeresiological collective term for groups in which Melchisedek [cf. Ps 109,4; Hebr 7,3] was especially revered and accorded particular theological honour; see

especially Epiphanius, Adversus haereses 55,1,1–55,9,18).

LIT.: 1 K. FITSCHEN, Messalianismus und Antimessalianismus, 1998; 2 W. FRANKENBERG (ed.), Euagrius Ponticus (= AAWG 13/2), 1912; 3 O. HESSE, M.E. und Symeon von Mesopotamien, 1973; 4 Id., Erwägungen zur Christologie des M.E., in: Paul de Lagarde und die syrische Kirchengeschichte, 1968, 90–99; 5 Id., s.v. M.E., in: TRE 22, 1992, 101–104; 6 J. KUNZE, M.E., 1895.; Translation.: ;   7 O. HESSE, Marcus Eremita, Bibliothek der Griechischen Literatur 19, 1985.   C.M.

II. ROMAN

One of the most common Roman first names, probably also used in Umbrian (abbreviation *Ma.*) and occasionally in Etruscan (*Marce*); acronym: *M.*; in Greek in the Republican time it was Μααρκος (*Ma arkos*), later Μάρκος (*Márkos*). The name is derived from the name of the god *Mars* (gen. *Martis*) and people probably liked to use it for children born in March. For the Evangelist → Marcus.
→ Mamercus

SALOMIES, 37f.   H.R.

[1] The Evangelist → Marcus [1].
[2] **Marcus Aurelius** Roman emperor AD 161–180

A. UNDER HADRIAN B. UNDER ANTONINUS PIUS C. JOINT RULE WITH LUCIUS VERUS D. FROM THE DEATH OF VERUS TO THE UPRISING OF AVIDIUS CASSIUS E. FROM THE UPRISING OF AVIDIUS CASSIUS TO MARCUS' DEATH IN AD 180 F. RELATIONSHIP WITH THE CHRISTIANS G. THE 'MEDITATIONS'

A. UNDER HADRIAN

M. was born in Rome on 26.04.121, the son of Annius [II 16] Verus and Domitia [8] Lucilla; his original name was M. Annius Verus. According to Galen (7,478), he is also said to have initially borne the name of his maternal great-grandfather, Catilius Severus. After the premature death of his father, M. was adopted by his great-grandfather of the same name, Annius [II 15]; the latter, *cos. III* in 126 and *praef. urbi*, held very high office under Hadrian. In this way Hadrian's attention was soon also drawn to the senator's young son; in jest he is said to have called him *Verissimus* (Cass. Dio 69,21,1f.). He gave him prominence in the public arena by providing him with an *equus publicus* (→ *equites*; this is possibly a misunderstanding on the part of the author of HA Aur. 4,1) and admitting him to the priesthood of the → Salii.

After his elementary education, M. was introduced to grammar and to the Latin and Greek languages and literature. Diognetus who taught him painting was the first person to steer him in the direction of philosophy. At about the age of twelve, M. therefore also changed his outward lifestyle and lived very modestly. At the age of 14, he was given the *toga virilis*; probably in 136, at

the instigation of Hadrian, he was betrothed to Ceionia [1] Fabia, the daughter of → Ceionius [3] Commodus whom the emperor also adopted in the same year. Presumably the scheduled marriage was one of Hadrian's dynastic plans. When Hadrian after Aelius Caesar's (= Ceionius [3]) death in February 138, adopted T. Aurelius → Antoninus [1] Pius, the latter also had to adopt M. and the son of the late Aelius Caesar, Lucius → Verus; Antoninus war M.'s uncle on his mother's side.

B. UNDER ANTONINUS PIUS

After Hadrian's death the engagement was broken off and M. was betrothed to the daughter of his adoptive father, Annia Galeria → Faustina [3], who had previously been engaged to be married to Lucius Verus. This was a clear declaration of who was to be Pius' heir. In 139, M. became quaestor, in 140 consul for the first time, and in 145 for the second time. Also in 139, he became *princeps iuventutis* (→ *princeps*) and a member of all the priestly colleges. This was followed in 145 by his marriage to Faustina. When his first child was born in November 147, M. was given the *tribunicia potestas* on 1 Dec. and perhaps also an *imperium proconsulare*; Faustina was given the cognomen *Augusta* (Fasti Ostienses for the year 147).

Although M. therefore clearly took up the position immediately after Antoninus Pius, his education was continued. Cornelius → Fronto [6], *cos. suff.* in 143, and Claudius → Herodes [16] Atticus, *cos. ord.* in 143, became his teachers in Latin and Greek rhetoric. Of significance is the way in which he completely turned to philosophy, influenced by Iunius [II 28] Rusticus and → Epictetus [2]. The exchange of letters with Fronto especially – which also provides us with knowledge of many details of his family life (for instance M.'s closeness to his mother, his care for his numerous children, several of whom died very young) – gives us insight into his rhetorical, spiritual and moral development. The relationship with Pius must have been warm and trusting (M. Aur. 1,16).

C. JOINT RULE WITH LUCIUS VERUS

Antoninus Pius had obviously envisaged that M. would be the sole ruler. When he died on 07.03.161, M. succeeded him as ruler. His name was now M. Aurelius Antoninus Augustus. He alone adopted the *cognomen* Antoninus from his adoptive father, while Verus did not. Nevertheless, M. immediately conferred upon Lucius Verus the *tribunicia potestas* and the *imperium proconsulare*, as Hadrian had also viewed him as the future Augustus. Only the office of *pontifex maximus* was bestowed solely upon M.; after Verus returned from the east in 166, he became *pater patriae*. M. also betrothed his eldest daughter → Lucilla to Verus. Formally there were therefore two Augusti; however, M.'s leading rank was undisputed. This was further emphasized when in August 161 Faustina gave birth to two sons, of whom → Commodus ultimately became M.'s successor.

M.' s relationship with the leading senatorial families and the Senate as a whole was extremely harmonious so that there were no internal problems at all at the beginning of his rule. However from the outset, M. who had never stayed in the provinces and with the army before 161, had to deal with fierce battles over many years with enemies outside the empire. Even under Pius there had been tensions with the Parthians in the east; in 161 the latter penetrated into Armenia and presumably destroyed the *legio IX Hispana* under the leadership of the governor of Cappadocia, Sedatius Severianus. The expedition corps that assembled in 162 in the east was nominally led by Lucius Verus but was actually under the leadership of experienced senatorial commanders like the governor of Cappadocia, Statius Priscus, and Pontius Laelianus as *comes* of Verus; M. however also retained supreme command for the campaigns in the east (Fronto Epist. ad M. Antoninum 2,2,2). After the victories of his generals, Verus quickly adopted the victor's names Armeniacus, Medicus, Parthicus Maximus that M. added to his titles only hesitantly and not until later. Although Verus lived a very permissive life even after his marriage to Lucilla, M. did not make any changes to Verus' official position. When an epidemic broke out in the east and tensions mounted on the Danube front, Verus was recalled. On 12.10.166 he celebrated together with M. a triumph over the Parthians. M. also conferred upon him the title of *pater patriae* and this increased even more the official equality of rank between the two rulers. According to HA Verus 8,6–9,1, tensions did however arise, as Verus simply no longer wanted to recognize the self-evident superior rank of M.

During the → Parthian War, pressure had already been mounting on the Danube front. At the same time, the whole of Italy and Rome had been enveloped in the epidemic and there had been heavy human casualties. Probably in order to lessen the consequences, M. appointed *iuridici* (→ *iuridicus*) in Italy, whose role was to facilitate jurisdiction over non-contentious matters, among these being the appointment of tutors for orphaned children; immediately before this he appointed his own *praetor tutelaris* (ILS 1118) in Rome for this purpose.

M. had two legions established, the *II and III Italica*, for the war against the Germans who had invaded, and perhaps already as preparation for the setting up of new provinces north of the Danube. After incursions by Germanic peoples in Dacia and Pannonia, M. moved north together with Verus where his own defence line, the *praetentura Italiae et Alpium*, was developed (ILS 8977). In the winter of 168/9 M. led the military campaign from Aquileia [1] where the epidemic was taking its highest toll of victims. Verus, who was seeking to return to Rome, died on the return journey in February 169. M. had the deceased deified (→ Deification).

D. FROM THE DEATH OF VERUS TO THE UPRISING OF AVIDIUS CASSIUS

After further preparations, M. returned to the north in order to repulse the Germans. The first offensive failed as the → Marcomanni and → Quadi bypassed the Roman armies, among other things plundering Raetia, breaking through to upper Italy and laying siege to Aquileia. At that time one legion each was sent to Raetia and Noricum to strengthen the defences; the result was a change from a praesidial procurator to a senatorial *legatus Augusti pro praetore* as governor. Separate army groups liberated the provinces from the invading Germans; the later emperor Pertinax and one of M.'s sons-in-law, Claudius [II 54] Pompeianus, had decisive roles.

At the same time, however, the entire Balkans were overrun by the → Costoboci whose campaign of pillaging advanced as far as Greece. M. initially moved his main headquarters to → Carnuntum, facing the territories of the Marcomanni and Quadi, and in 174 to Sirmium when he was fighting especially against the → Iazyges. This was then also the political-administrative centre of the empire where above all important legal cases were brought before the imperial court, e.g. the one against Herodes Atticus. Victories and defeats alternated. From 172, the Romans advanced across the Danube into the land of the Marcomanni. In Dacia however, a Roman army was encircled by the Quadi and at risk of dying of thirst; their rescue by 'miraculous rain' was claimed by pagans and Christians alike as a sign of the power of their religion. From 173 onwards the Germans were slowly forced back and final victory appeared possible; however, the rebellion of → Avidius [1] Cassius in the east forced M. into an overly hasty peace.

E. FROM THE UPRISING OF AVIDIUS CASSIUS TO MARCUS' DEATH IN AD 180

The uprising in April 175, probably provoked by the false rumour of the death of M. and an arrangement between Faustina and Avidius Cassius, was quickly suppressed. Nevertheless, M. moved with his son Commodus – who became *princeps iuventutis* – and with Faustina to the east; Faustina died in Asia Minor. M. elevated the place where she died to the status of a city: → Faustinupolis. After a visit to Alexandria [1], M. returned via Athens to Rome where together with Commodus, he celebrated a triumph over the Germans on 23 Dec. 176. In mid–177 he elevated his son to the rank of Augustus, thus making him his successor, although M. knew the latter's personality defects. However, dynastic thinking was all too natural and self-evident; the idea of the 'adoption of the best' (see → Adoptive emperor) stood no real chance against it.

As the Danube border did not remain calm, the campaigns were resumed. M. stayed in Viminacium and Sirmium, where he died on 17.03.180 after entrusting his son to his senatorial friends and army commanders. M. was deified by the Senate and then laid to rest in the→ Mausoleum Hadriani. For Cassius Dio (71,36,4), who during this period was already a member of the Senate, an era came to an end with M.; this, in any case, is his judgement when he looks back on M.'s death and the transfer of rule to Commodus.

F. Relationship with the Christians

In later Christian historiography, M. was not considered an enemy of the Christians. M. had a knowledge of this new religion, but he did not have a high regard for its adherents, not even because of their willingness to die, as he regarded this as ill-considered and not to be taken seriously (M. Aur. 11,3). It is a matter of contention whether M. enacted special decrees against Christians (cf. Meliton of Sardes in Euseb. Hist. eccl. 4,26,5f.). However, the regulations of the *SC de pretiis gladiatorum minuendis* (FIRA I² no. 49) could have been applied against Christians. This would perhaps also explain the persecution measures implemented in Lyons (Lugdunum) in 177 (or later), in the course of which M. also intervened with a letter (Euseb. Hist. eccl. 5,1; [1. 320ff.]; → Martyrdom, literature of). The Apology by Meliton [3] of Sarde was also especially addressed to M. 178 is the probable date of the writing of → Celsus against the Christians in which the hostile agitation of groups in the empire against the young religion can be seen all too clearly as well as the reproach of civic irresponsibility that was made against it. This could have suited M.

G. The 'Meditations'

Among the Roman emperors, M.'s' personality was exceptional. He was very deeply influenced by the philosophy of the Stoa (→ Stoicism; → Epictetus [2]). His path to this viewpoint is discernible in his exchange of letters with Fronto [6]. Iunius [II 28] Rusticus, whose views were shaped by his family tradition of Stoic opposition to various emperors of the 1st cent., became his actual philosophy teacher. The Stoa with its orientation towards rationality and the fulfilment of duty had developed at this time particularly into a philosophy of practical politics to which M. felt himself obligated. His dealings with his brother Lucius Verus, with the senatorial ruling class as well as with the cities of the empire, was moulded by it although this did not lead him to disregard the traditional rules. The obligation to act rightly and the possibility of realizing this was the basic insight that guided him in all things – despite a pessimism discernible in his 'Meditations' that did however not lead him to despise the world but to recognize the lack of perfection, especially his own. This prevented M. from overvaluing external things; only 'virtue' (*areté*) had unchanging value.

M. set down his self-reflections in his 'Meditations' written in Greek and passed down to us without a title (*Eis heautón* in one of the MSS is not original), which in the modern version are divided up into 12 bks. They are captured in a concise, aphoristic style. He probably to a large extent wrote them when he was quite old, espe-

cially during his long stays on the Danube from 170. With the exception of bk. 1 that describes the people who moulded his character and with whom he lived, these are aphorisms of Stoic origin concerning correct moral decisions, duties towards the gods, the individual and the community. All of this is rendered in a generalized form so that for the most part M.'s personality is within reach only indirectly. In statements like 'Take care that you are not "Caesarified"' (6,30), it does however become clear that his statements contain references to himself. PIR² A 697.

→ Epictetus [2]; → Parthian Wars; → Monumental column (Column of M. Aurelius); → Stoicism; → Stoicism

1 J. H. Oliver, R. E. A. Palmer, Minutes of an Act of the Roman Senate, in: Hesperia 24, 1955.

G. Alföldy, Konsulat und Senatorenstand unter den Antoninen, 1977; W. Ameling, Die Kinder des Marc Aurel und die Bildnistypen der Faustina Minor, in: ZPE 90, 1992, 147–166; E. Asmis, The Stoicism of M. Aurelius, in: ANRW II 36.3, 1989, 2228–2252; A. R. Birley, M. Aurelius. A Biography, ²1987; P. A. Brunt, M. Aurelius and the Christians, in: C. Deroux (ed.), Stud. in Latin Literature and Roman History, Bd. 1, 1979, 483ff.; E. Champlin, Fronto and Antonine Rome, 1980; R. P. Duncan-Jones, The Impact of the Antonine Plague, in: Journal of Roman Archeology 9, 1996, 108–136; R. Klein (ed.), Marc Aurel, 1979; F. Pirson, Style and Message on the Column of M. Aurelius, in: PBSR 64, 1996, 139–179; K. Rosen, Die angebliche Samtherrschaft von Marc Aurel und Lucius Verus, in: Historia-Augusta-Colloquium, Colloquium Parisinum 1990, 1991, 271ff.; Ibid., Marc Aurel, 1997; G. R. Stanton, M. Aurelius, Lucius Verus, and Commodus: 1962–1972, in: ANRW II 2, 1975, 478–549; W. Szaivert, Die Münzprägung der Kaiser M. Aurelius, Lucius Verus und Commodus, 161–192, 1986.; On the letters: ; M. P. J. van den Hout, M.Cornelius Fronto, Epistulae, ²1988.; On the ; 'Meditations' Ed.: J. Dalfen, ²1987; R. Michel, ²1992 (Greek-German). Lit.: P. A. Brunt, M. Aurelius and His Meditations, in: JRS 64, 1974, 1–20; P. Hadot, La citadelle intérieure. Introduction aux Pensées de Marc Aurèle, 1992 (English tr. by M. Chase, The Inner Citadel, 1998); R. B. Rutherford, The Meditations of M. Aurelius: A Study, 1989 (review: P. A. Brunt, in: JRS 80, 1990, 218f.). W.E.

[3] Proclaimed emperor by soldiers in Britain in AD 406 in a mutiny against → Honorius [3], eliminated in 407. PLRE II 719f.

[4] Son of the usurper → Basiliscus and of → Zenonis. As a child he was made the Caesar of his father in AD 475, and soon he was also proclaimed Augustus. After the return of the emperor → Zeno in 476, he was expelled with his father to Cappadocia and killed there. PLRE II 720. H.L.

Marde (Μάρδη/*Márdē*, Μάρδις/*Márdis*, Lat. *Maride*). Fortress on the southern edge of the → Izala mountain range (Ṭūr 'Abdīn), modern Mardin. Apart from a dubious identification with the ancient Oriental settlement of Mardaman, there are no indications that M. was of major significance prior to late antiquity. In

Amm. Marc. 19,9,4, M. is one of the *castella praesidiaria* against the Persians. Under Iustinianus (AD 527–565) M. was refortified (Procop. Aed. 2,4,14) and according to Byzantine, Syrian and Armenian sources, it continued to be an important military base against the Persians.

→ Syria

L. DILLEMANN, Haute Mésopotamie Orientale et pays adjacents, 1962, 214,216; F. H. WEISSBACH, s.v. M., RE 14, 1648.   K.KE.

Mardi (Μάρδοι; *Márdoi*). Near Eastern tribes in Armenia (Ptol. Geog. 5,12,9), Media and Hyrcania south of the Caspian Sea in the modern Elburz Mountains/ northern Iran (Str. 11,13,3), called Amardi here (Str. 11,6,1; 7,1; Plin. HN 6,36; Steph. Byz. s.v. Ἀμαρδοί/ *Amardoí*, s.v. M.), in Margiane (Str. 11,8,8; Plin. HN 6,47); also one of the four Persian nomadic tribes (Hdt. 1,125,4) living above the Elymaïs region (Str. 11,13,6; Plin. HN 6,134; Arr. Ind. 40,6) in modern Anşan. Persian M. served in the Achaemenid army (Hdt. 1,84,2; Aesch. Pers. 994) and Armenian M. as mercenaries of Orontas (Xen. An. 4,3,4). The Median M. were subjugated by Alexander the Great (Arr. Anab. 3,24,1–3; 4,18,2). The Armenian M. were subjugated in 176/171 by → Phraates I (Just. Epit. 41,5,9). M. appear as opponents of the Romans in 68 BC (Plut. Lucullus 31,9) and 36 BC (Str. 11,13,3), as well as in AD 59/60. (Tac. Ann. 14,23,3). It is somewhat improbable that all the M. were originally related to each other and that the different places where they lived were only the result of their nomadic lifestyle.

A. B. BOSWORTH, A Historical Commentary on Arrian's History of Alexander, vol. 1, 1980, 299, 351ff.; R. N. FRYE, The History of Ancient Iran, 1984, 89f., 210; O. LENDLE, Komm. zu Xenophons Anabasis, 1995, 209; J. SEIBERT, Die Eroberung des Perserreiches (Beih. TAVO Nr. 68), 1985, 107, 117f., 141; G. WIRTH, O. VON HINÜBER, Arrian, Greek-German, 1985, 879f.   H.KA.

Mardion (Μαρδίων; *Mardíōn*). Slave or statesman of Cleopatra VII. The propaganda of Octavian declared him, a eunuch, to be responsible for leading the Egyptian state (PP VI 14615).   W.A.

Mardonius (Μαρδόνιος/*Mardónios* < old Persian *Marduniya*).
[1] Aristocratic Persian, son of the Gobryas [3] who plotted with → Darius [1] I against Gaumāta (Gaubaruva; Hdt. 6,43,1 et passim) and a sister of Darius (Hdt. 7,5,1), grandson of M. [3. DB IV 84], husband of the daughter of Darius, Artazostra (Hdt. 6,43,1; [2. PFa 5,1f., 110, 118]) and father of Artontes (Hdt. 9,84,1). As a young man M. reorganized the political affairs of the Ionian cities on behalf of the Great King (Hdt. 6,43,1) after the defeat of the → Ionian Revolt in 494 BC (Hdt. 6,43,3: δημοκρατίας κατίστα), subjugated Thrace (wounded in an attack by the Brygians: Hdt. 6,45,1) and Thasos again and made Macedonia into a

vassal state for the second time. A large part of his fleet was wrecked (during the return journey) at Mount Athos (Hdt. 6,44,2–3). As cousin and brother-in-law of → Xerxes I, he is said to have had a great influence on him (Hdt. 7,5,1; Ctesias FGrH 688 F 13) and to have advised him to wage war on Greece for selfish motives (Hdt. 7,6,1). Originally one of the six *stratēgoí* (Hdt. 7,82) in the campaign, he assumed supreme command of the Persian troops that remained in Greece (Hdt. 8,107,1) after the Battle of Salamis (in 480). He spent the winter in Thessaly, negotiated in vain with the Athenians, destroyed their city for the second time (Hdt. 8,130–9,14; Plut. Aristides 10–19) and finally assembled his men at Plataeae (497 BC) for the battle against the allied Greeks under Pausanias (Hdt. 9,31–89) at which he was killed by the Spartan Arimnestus (Hdt. 9,64,2; Plut. Aristides 19,1). M. is said to have been depicted on a marble column of the so-called 'Pers. Hall' in Sparta (Paus. 3,11,3).

→ Persian Wars

1 BRIANT, s.v.; 2 R. T. HALLOCK, Selected Fortification Texts, in: Cahiers de la Délégation archéologique française en Iran 8, 1978, 109–136; 3 R. KENT, Old Persian, 1953.   J.W.

[2] Scythian eunuch, teacher of Basilina, the mother of Emperor → Iulianus [11], and from AD 338 also teacher of the latter himself. PLRE 1,558, 1.

[3] Eunuch, *primicerius sacri cubiculi* under → Valens; in AD 388 probably *praepositus sacri cubiculi* under → Arcadius; the addressee of several letters from → Libanius; owner of the estate of Kosilaukome near Chalcedon, to which Valens had the alleged head of John the Baptist brought. PLRE 1, 558, 2.   K.G.-A.

Marduk The city god and chief god of → Babylon was only a local god of lowly importance prior to the rise of the city to political prominence under → Ḥammurapi (18th cent. BC). The name 'M.' (better perhaps: Maruduk) probably derives from an unknown Mesopotamian substrate language although Babylonian scholars interpreted it to mean 'bull-calf of the sun', based on the logographic writing of M. in the Sumerian language. Early in time M. was already equated with the Sumerian god of healing and incantation Asalluḫi and was then considered like the latter to be the son of the god of wisdom, Enki/Ea. M.'s original nature can no longer be determined with confidence. His emblem, a spade with a triangular blade, may be considered to be an indication that M. originally had traits of a god of irrigation and vegetation.

With the rise of Babylon from a city state to the capital city of the Babylonian empire, M. became the supreme god of Babylonia. His temple → Esagil, in which the cult image of M. and that of his wife Zarpanitum was worshipped, became the most important sanctuary in the empire. M. was now equated with the Sumerian king of the gods → Enlil, who was worshipped in Nippur. This elevation of a god was unprecedented in Mesopotamian religious history. It was based on the theological 'insight' that M. had been chosen by the gods of the city states which had been subjugated by Ḥammurapi as their ruler.

The most important source for the theology of M. is the epic → Enūma ēliš . Making use of ancient mythemes originally assigned to other deities, it describes M. as the creator of the world who saved the gods who were threatened by the powers of chaos in a heroic battle, gave order to the cosmos and created man. The most important assertion of Enūma ēliš and other theological texts is that all divinity can be traced back to M. and that all the gods are ultimately manifestations of M. M.'s accomplishment in giving order to the cosmos as described in the Enūma ēliš was the paradigm which governed the actions of the Babylonian kings. They regarded themselves as the guardians of the order created by M. from which their claim to rule the world derived. The world order created by M. was renewed annually through a ritual at the Babylonian New Year's celebration. Babylonian henotheism strongly influenced Assyrian and possibly also Jewish theology. In the 1st millennium BC the name M. increasingly became a taboo and was to a large extent replaced by the honorary title Bēl ('Lord').

→ Akitu Festival

W. SOMMERFELD, Der Aufstieg M.s (AOAT 213), 1982; id., s.v. M., RLA 7, 360–370; W. G. LAMBERT, Studies in M., in: BSOAS 47, 1984, 1–9; W. VON SODEN, Monotheistische Tendenzen und Traditionalismus im Kult in Babylonien im 1. Jahrtausend v.Chr. (Studi e materiali di Storia delle Religioni 51), 1985, 5–19.   S.M.

Marduk-apla-iddin(a) Name of two Babylonian kings.
[1] M. I. Antepenultimate king of the dynasty of the Kassites (1171–1159 BC; → Cossaei).
[2] M. II. (721–710 BC and 703) from the Chaldaean tribe (→ Chaldaei) of the Bīt Jakīn; the Merodachbaladan of the OT (in Ptolemy: Μαρδοκέμπαδος/Mardokémpados). As King of the Sealand he paid a tribute to the Assyrian → Tiglatpilesar III in 729, and subsequently in 721 he succeeded as the leader of an anti-Assyrian coalition in Babylon (in the confusion caused by the coming into power of → Sargon II) in having himself installed as king. He retained this power until 710. After a military defeat he had to retreat. In 703 he was able to eliminate Marduk-zākir-šumi, who had been appointed by → Sennacherib in Babylon. After a second reign of nine months, he fled to the south of Mesopotamia after another defeat. From there he was finally (in 700: campaign of Sennacherib to the Sealand) expelled to → Elam where he died, probably before 694. The message to Heziekiah of Judah passed down to us in the OT (2 Kg 20:12–19; Is. 39:1ff.) is part of his anti-Assyrian activities. Several of his descendants later became leaders of the anti-Assyrian resistance in Babylonia. According to a cuneiform tablet, he established a garden with exotic trees.

J. A. BRINKMAN, s.v. M., RLA 7, 374f.   J.OE.

Mardus see → Gaumata

Marea Town west of Alexandria [1], situated on the southern bank of Lake Mareotis in a famous winegrowing area (Str. 17,799); Egyptian mrt, modern Kaum al-Idrís, regarded in the Egyptian temple lists as in the 3rd district of lower Egypt, in Roman times however itself the capital of the Mareotis. M. is first attested in Hdt. 2,18, where it is stated that the inhabitants felt that they were Libyans. From the beginning of the 26th dynasty to the Persian period, the border garrison against Libya was situated in M. From here came the revolt of the Libyan prince → Inarus against Artaxerxes I (463–454 BC; Thuc. 1,1104ff.; Diod. Sic. 11,71ff.). According to Diod. Sic. 1,68, the decisive battle between Apries and Amasis took place at M., but this is doubtful (→ Momemphis). In the early Christian period the region was considered especially dangerous because of constant attacks from robbers and bedouins. In the late Roman period a special legal position of the Mareoteans in relation to the Egyptians is attested, and under Justinian I (527–565) the region was partitioned from Egypt and allocated to Libya. Shortly after the Arab conquest, however, it again belonged to Egypt.

1 H. KEES, s.v. M. Mareotis, RE 14, 1676–1678;   2 S. TIMM, Das christlich-koptische Ägypten in arabischer Zeit, vol. 4, 1988, 1593–1603, s.v. Maryūṭ.   K.J.-W.

Mare Germanicum (North Sea). This shelf sea, a marginal sea of the Atlantic (→ Oceanus), assumed its present form in the Jura. In the west, it is separated from the Atlantic by the Straits of Dover, in the north-west, by the line of the Orkney and Shetland Islands. In the east, the Skagerrak separates it from the Baltic Sea (→ Mare Suebicum). There are few bordering archipelagos north-west and south-east.

The Mare Germanicum (MG) extends over an area of 0.58 million km², it contains 0.054 km³ of water, its medium depth is around 94 m, its greatest depth is 725 m near Arendal in the Norwegian Trench. It is located within the West Wind Drift, and therefore storms are frequent in winter and there is often fog in autumn. The MG has a moderate, humid climate; the median air temperatures are up to 6°C in winter in the north-west, up to 2°C in the north-east, and around 17°C in summer in the south-east and 14°C in the north. Through the Straits of Dover (35.5 km) and its 475–km-wide opening in the north-west it has an intensive exchange of water with the Atlantic. In the north, the salt content of its water can be above 35 ‰, in the south it is around 32–24 ‰ (effect of freshwater rivers). The tide is partly caused by the moon, but mostly by the flow from the Atlantic and thus the tide is stronger in the north. On the coast of England the tidal range is between 3 and 6 m (spring tidal range up to 6.5 m). On the European coast between 2 and 4 m (spring tidal range up to 4 m), but on Jutland's north coast it is only 0.5 m. Onshore storms cause storm tides. Tidal currents along the coasts have speeds up to 2,5 nautical miles/hour and between Scotland and the Orkney Islands they can reach up to 10 nautical miles/hour. Because of vertical circulation and the intensive exchange of water with the Atlantic the MG is especially rich in fish.

In antiquity, the coastline from the Channel to Jutland was closer to the Friesian Islands (Plin. HN 4,97, e.g. *Burcana*, modern Borkum); it ran in a straight line and was interrupted by the lagoons of the → Rhenus (Rhine), lacus Flevo (IJsselmeer, → Flevum), → Amisia (Ems), → Visurgis (Weser) and → Albis (Elbe). The earliest reports of the MG come from → Pytheas of Massalia, who at the end of the 4th cent. BC sailed along the British east coast, the Norwegian west coast and the German north coast (Str. 1,4,2; cf. → Thule). Caesar's fleet landed in 55 BC on the British coast of the MG and in 54 when attempting another landing, it drifted into the MG (Caes. B Gall. 5,8,2). In several campaigns (56 and 53 BC) against the Germanic → Menapii Caesar advanced by land to the mouth of the Rhine (Caes. B Gall. 3,28f.; 6,5f.). The earliest mention of the MG is probably the *septentrionalis Oceanus* in Plin. HN 2,167, who also has the term MG (HN 4,103). With the British and the Germanic coast to the left of the Rhine the Roman empire was bordering on the MG until the 5th cent. AD.

G. Dietrich, Allgemeine Meereskunde, 1965; Westermann Lexikon der Geographie 3, 1970, 588–590, s.v. Nordsee; A. Franke, s.v. Nordsee, RE 17, 935–963; A. R. Lewis, Shipping and Commerce in Northern Europe A.D. 300–1100, 1958.   E.O.

Mare Nostrum (μεγάλη θάλασσα/*megálē thálassa*, Mediterranean). Because of various earth movements that are still ongoing (rising, sinking; formation of numerous islands, e.g. the archipelago between Greece and Anatolia and Cyprus, Crete, Sicily, Sardinia, Corsica, the Balearic Islands; still active volcanoes and earthquakes) the appearance of the Mare Nostrum (MN) changed constantly (connections to the various adjoining seas, e.g. the Atlantic, the Miocene seas in the northern foothills of the Alps and south Asia). Only in the early Tertiary Era (Miocene period, over 7 to 23 million years ago) and after the folding of the south Apennines and the formation of the Aegean and Marmara basin did the MN take the shape it has today, with its various divisions, e.g. the → Tyrrhenian Sea, the Pamphylian Sea (→ mare Pamphylium) and smaller seas like the Ionian Sea (→ *Iónios kólpos*), the Aegean (→ *Aigaíon pélagos*) including the → Icarian Sea (*Ikários póntos*) and the → Myrtoan Sea (*Myrtōon pélagos*), the Sea of Marmara (→ *Propontis*), and the Black Sea (→ *póntos eúxeinos*). The MN is part of the Eurasian-African Ridge and includes numerous basins that drop steeply from its coasts; there are only a few wide and shallow shelves (Gulfs of Lyons and Valencia, Small and Great Syrte, and in front of the Nile Delta with a growth of 33 m each year). On the ancient coastline and on the effect of eustatic changes in sea level, see → coastline, changes in.

Today the MN occupies an area of 2.97 million km² and holds 4.24 million km³ of water. Its median depth is around 1429 m, its greatest depth is (to the west of the Peloponnese) around 5121 m. There is a western and an eastern basin (along the line Rā's aṭ-Ṭib/Tunesia – Capo Boeo/Sicily – Punta di Faro/northern opening of the Strait of Messina).

The climate in the Greek and Roman world until the 8th cent. AD was essentially the same as it is today: mild, wet winters and hot, dry summers (median air temperatures in winter up to 16 °C in the east, up to 11 °C in the west, and in the summer 26 °C in the east and 23 °C in the west); the precipitation increases from east to west. A very settled weather situation is typical of the eastern basin. The western MN is located in the West Wind Drift and therefore heavy northwest storms occur in the Gulf of Lyons during the winter and in the *Iónios kólpos*. In winter navigation was especially difficult; the term *mare clausum* ('closed sea') referred to the time between 11 November and 10 March according to a theory in Veg. Mil. 4,39 (cf. [1]). In the Aegean, northern winds (summer → Etesians, today called *Meltemia*) prevail between Azores high and Asiatic low. At the surface the water temperature is usually higher than the air temperature. The salt content of the water is around 38/39 ‰. The tides are insignificant (spring tide lift of 0.5 m in the Small Syrte and in the *Iónios kólpos*). Noticeable tidal currents occur only near some straits (Euripus, Messina). In general, there is a current towards the east along the south coast and towards the west along the north coast; ancient open-sea seafaring took advantage of these currents by navigating parallel to the coast. The weak vertical circulation (lack of nutrients) and low inflow from the Atlantic was unfavourable for fishing.

Ancient authors made various statements about the origins of the MN. The formation of islands, straits and bays and the sinking of entire regions was explained by effects that could be periodically observed, such as the work of rivers, currents, earthquakes, volcanoes and catastrophic storms. Saltwater lakes, sea shells and petrified imprints of fishes and sea plants found in the interior indicated former sea levels (for references, see [2; 3]).

The only self-contained geographical treatment of the MN is the anonymous *Stadiasmòs étoi períplous tês megálēs thalássēs* ('Survey or Circumnavigation of the Great Sea', GGM 1,427–514), a sound description of the coasts of the Mediterranean from the Hellenistic period in a Byzantine edition. The *Stadiasmos* reveals the intensity of coastal shipping in the MN was practised; there was also deep-sea navigation – e.g. on the routes Alexandria – Puteoli or Brundisium – Dyrrhachium. Because of seafaring, the sea was seen less as a separation than as a bridge between the countries bordering on the MN; and thus the demarcation line between the two large administrative units of the Roman empire ran north-south through Scodra, rather than east-west, and at various times Italia and Africa were regarded as a single administrative unit. In Greek literature the MN is first mentioned in Hecat. FGrH 1 F 26 where it is called 'the great sea' (μεγάλη θάλασσα/ *megálē thálassa*). In the Hellenistic period, because of advances in geographical knowledge, it is called ἡ εἴσω θάλασσα/*hē eísō thálassa* or ἡ ἐντὸς θ./ *hē entòs th.* ('the interior sea'; Aristot. Mete. 354a 11), from which the terms *mare internum* and *mare intestinum* (Plin. HN 2,173 and Flor. 2,13,293) were derived. As a term of Roman imperialism MN first occurs in Caes. B Gall. 5,1,2, whereas *mare mediterraneum* is a medieval word formation (cf. Isid. Orig. 13,6,1).

1 E. DE SAINT-DENIS, Mare clausum, in: REL 25, 1947, 196–214; 2 A. FORBIGER, Handbuch der alten Geographie 1, 1842, 644ff.; 3 H. BERGER, Geschichte der wissenschaftliche Erdkunde der Griechen, 1903, 284ff.

G. DIETRICH, Allgemeine Meereskunde, 1965; V. BURR, Nostrum Mare, 1932; Westermann Lexikon der Geographie 3, 1970, 1000–1002, s.v. Mittelmeer; E. OLSHAUSEN, Einführung in die Historische Geographie der Alten Welt, 1991, 17, 156f. (bibl.); J. ROUGÉ, M.N., 1986.   E.O.

Mare Pamphylium Sea bay that carves in deeply on the south coast of Asia Minor on the Lycian, Pamphylian and Cilician coastal fringe between the promontories of Hiera Akra (modern Gelidonya Burun) and → Anemurium (cf. Plin. HN 5,96; 102; 129), modern Gulf of Antalya. Occasionally, the Gulf of Iskenderun (→ Alexandria [3]) was included in the Mare Pamphylium (MP) as well (Dionys. Per. 508 = GGM 2,135), or it was even equated with the *Aigýption pélagos* (Αἰγύπτιον πέλαγος, App. proemium 6f.). Shipwrecks near Ulu Burun and Gelidonya Burnu document the stormy nature of MP that is also passed down to us in ancient sources [1].

1 J. NOLLÉ, Pamphylische Studien 1–5, in: Chiron 16, 1986, 209–212.   W.MA.

Mares

[1] (Μάρες; *Máres*). One of the five tribes which formed the 19th tax district under → Darius [1], probably west of → Colchis. Mentioned only by Hecataeus (FGrH 1 F 205) and Hdt. 3,94,2; 7,79 where they are described together with the Moschi, Tibareni, Macrones and Mossynoeci as lightly armed soldiers with small leather shields and javelins.   I.v.B.

[2] (Μάρης; *Márēs*). Progenitor of the → Ausones. Because his Centaur-like figure appears too fabulous, he is made into the inventor of riding (Ael. VH 9,16). M. could also be the same as the Etruscan god → Maris, who is identified with → Mars.

RADKE, 199.   I.BAN.

Mare Suebicum (Baltic Sea). Shallow marginal sea of the Atlantic or the North Sea (→ *mare Germanicum*); since about 8000 BC the connection with the North Sea has been broken in various ways. Subdivisions are the shallow Kattegat and the shallow Bælt Sea, the actual Baltic Sea with various basins and depths up to 50 m (west of Bornholm), 100 m (east of Bornholm), 249 m (east of Gotland), 459 m (east of Landort, maximum depth of the Mare Suebicum (MS)) and larger islands (Fyn and Sjælland in the west, Bornholm, Öland, Gotland, Åland, Saaremaa and Hirumaa), the Gulfs of Riga, Finland and Bothnia; the average depth is 55 m.

The MS today has an area of 0.42 million km², and its volume is about 0.023 million km³. It lies in the region of the wWest Wind Drift, is not as stormy as the North Sea but instead the waves are often shorter and steeper (in the western MS rarely up to 3 m, in the central MS up to 5 m); in autumn and winter there is frequently a fog that only disperses slowly (obstacle for navigation) in areas close to land, in spring also on the high seas. As only a little exchange of water occurs with the North Sea because of the shallow and narrow Bælt and because about 250 rivers flow into the MS, the salt content is only 6–8 ‰. Stormy weather conditions stir up the sea from the bottom up (strong vertical circulation, hence an abundance of fish). The surface temperatures in summer are 17/18°C on the coasts, and on the open sea 15/16°C, and sections of the MS (Bottnic and Finnish Gulfs) freeze over in winter. Low tidal ranges (in the Kattegat no more than 0.5 m, further east only a few cm). Air pressure fluctuations and wind-related water accumulation build the sea up to a height of 1 m, and storm tides up to over 3 m. The speed of the current in the direction of the North Sea is 2 to 4 nautical miles/hour.

The trade with → amber from the MS that reached the Graeco-Roman world without exception over land, provided the Romans with the initial information about this sea (Plin. HN 37,45). Further information about the MS reached Rome through the lfuture emperor Tiberius, who went past it in AD 5 with a fleet travelling east to Jutland (R. Gest. div. Aug. 26; Vell. Pat. 2,106; Plin. HN 2,167). Thus, the geographer → Philemon in his Periplus, and also later Pliny the Elder (FHG 4,474 and Plin. HN 2,167; cf. Tac. Germ. 45), were able to report in greater detail about the MS. In Tac. Germ. 45 we encounter the sea for the first time as the MS.

G. DIETRICH, Allgemeine Meereskunde, 1965; S. G. SEGERSTRÅLE, The Baltic Sea, 1957; Westermann Lexikon der Geographie 3, 1970, 710–712, s.v. Ostsee; O. KUNKEL, s.v. Ostsee, RE 18, 1689–1854.   E.O.

Mare superum see → Ionios kolpos

Mare Tyrrhenum The Tyrrhenian Sea, the western part of the Mediterranean Sea (→ Mare Nostrum), bordered by the Italian west coast, the Sicilian north coast and by Corsica and Sardinia. The name goes back to the Greek name of the Etruscans (Τυρσανοί/ *Tyrsanoí*; Τυρσηνικὸν πέλαγος/*Tyrsēnikòn pélagos* in Thuc. 4,24). The Romans spoke of the *Tuscum mare* (Varro, Rust. 3,9,17; Cic. Orat. 3,19,69; Liv. 5,33,8) or, in contrast to the *mare superum* (Adriatic), of the *mare inferum* (Cic. Att. 9,5,1). Before Roman rule was established in the → Punic Wars, the Mare Tyrrhenum was frequently the site of disputes between rival trading powers (Etruscans, Greeks, Carthaginians; e.g. in the naval battle of Alalia/→ Aleria in 545 BC: Hdt. 1,166). The Etruscans built numerous harbours on the Campanian coast.

V. BURR, Nostrum Mare, 1932; H. M. DENHAM, Das Tyrrhenische Meer, ⁴1984; M. PALLOTTINO, Italien vor der Römerzeit, 1987. H.SO.

Marganeis (Μαργανεῖς/*Marganeîs*). Small community west of → Olympia in the plain north of the Alpheius between the modern villages of Phloka and Strephi, dependent on Elis as → *períoikoi*. Exact location unknown. In the war of the Spartans against Elis in 401 BC on the Spartan side (Xen. Hell. 3,2,25; Diod. Sic. 15,77,4, Μάργανα/*Márgana*), in the peace of 400 BC autonomous (Xen. Hell. 3,2,30), in 294 in the battle at Nemea again on the side of the Spartans (Xen. Hell. 4,2,16), but claimed by Elis (Xen. Hell. 6,5,2). Last mentioned in 364 BC as an ally of the Arcades in the occupation of Olympia (Xen. Hell. 7,4,14). Other mentions in Steph. Byz. s.v. Μάργανα and Str. 8,3,24 (Μαργάλαι, Μαργάλα/*Margálai, Margála*). Y.L.

Margarita see → Pearl

Margiana (Μαργιανή/*Margianḗ* < Ancient Persian *Marguš* > New Persian *Marv*). Fertile eastern Iranian country through which the Murġāb flows (Ptol. 6,10,1; Plin. HN 6,16; Str. 2,1,14; 11,10,1; in the Avesta M. is regarded as one of the most beautiful of countries created by → Ahura Mazdā) in modern Turkmenistan. Ptol. 6,10 names the Derbicci, Massageti, → Parni, → Daae and Topuri as inhabitants of M. and also mentions individual cities, among which Antioch [7] Margiane (Giaur-Qalᶜa with the original Achaemenid citadel and later Parthian fortifications 30 km east of modern Marv/→ Merw), founded or re-established by → Antiochus [2] I, was the most important. The revolt led by the Margianian Frāda against Darius [1] I was put down in a bloody manner on 28 December 521 BC by his Bactrian satrap Dādaršiš [1. DB III 12–19]. The administrative classification of M. remains uncertain in the Achaemenid time and it probably became Parthian under Mithridates. After the battle of Carrhae (53 BC; → Ḥarran) Orodes II is said to have deported 10,000 Roman prisoners of war (Plin. HN 6,16) to M.

1 R. KENT, Old Persian, 1953; 2 R. SCHMITT, s.v. M., RLA 7, 380–381; 3 Ausgrabungsberichte in der Zeitschrift IRAN seit 1963. J.W.

Margidunum On the great Roman road of the *Fosse Way* between Lincoln and Leicester lay various Roman settlements; one of the largest was M., near East Bridgeford, Nottinghamshire. Originally a Roman fort (late Claudian/early Neronian period), abandoned in around AD 70 [1; 2]. M. probably served as a military supply base, since the local iron ore was intensively smelted. After the end of the military occupation, the civilian settlement continued on both sides of the *Fosse Way*, possibly in conjunction with a → *mansio* (or *mutatio*). Residential and other buildings were modest. The centre of the settlement was equipped in the late 2nd cent. with earthen fortifications, and in the middle/at the end of the 3rd cent. a stone rampart was added [3]. The settlement lasted until the early 5th cent. and then ended abruptly; no subsequent settlement. → Britannia (with maps)

1 F. OSWALD, The Commandant's House at M., 1948; 2 Id., Excavation of a Traverse at M., 1952; 3 M. TODD, The Roman Settlement at M., in: Transactions of the Thoroton Society 73, 1969.

M. TODD, The Coritani, ²1991. M.TO.

Marginalized groups
A. DEFINITION   B. HISTORY OF SCHOLARSHIP
C. INDIVIDUAL MARGINALIZED GROUPS

A. DEFINITION
Since the 1920s sociologists (Chicago School) have studied the phenomenon of marginalized groups (MG). In the German-speaking countries scholars have used the term (*Randgruppen*) since the 60s. MG are defined as minorities 'who are seen by the majority as outside of the social norm, and who therefore have the status of social outsiders ... groups who are socially declassed and/or are socially despised. A significant percentage of them live in poverty' [3. 666]. Population groups whose values, norms, behaviour and/or external appearance differ from the majority of the population are subject to prejudice and stigmatization [33. 236]. This means that belonging to a marginalized group generally is not based on gender or age; to this end, women, children and old people are not affected, and neither are the lower social classes. Members of the upper classes have always tended to dissociate themselves from them; working people, especially wage earners, were despised and individual professions even pushed to the social margins. However, we should not assume that in antiquity all → artists and craftsmen (→ Crafts V.G.) were marginalized [42]. Because the term lacks precision and specificity, some sociologists, especially those interested in practically oriented social work, view it very critically [6] or distance themselves from it [22. 459]

Sociologists increasingly focus on the relationship between the social majority and MG, on the process of excluding various MG, and on the strategies of the ruling groups or the majority for protecting the current system of values. It should be mentioned that many supposed MG are rather disorganized and disintegrated aggregations. Since exclusion, marginalization and stigmatization can be regarded as a universal phenomenon in the history of mankind – taking different forms depending on concrete historical and social circumstances and with various consequences for various groups and individuals [6. 17] – the MG of various cultures and time periods have to be studied individually.

B. History of scholarship

Influenced by sociology and a comparable area of Medieval Studies and Early Modern Studies [8; 14; 15; 18], scholars of antiquity came late to a more intensive study of MG, although various issues such as the discrimination of certain groups of persons (prostitutes, vagrants) had been discussed previously. Since social history, legal history, history of medicine, archaeology and other disciplines are involved in studying the issues related to MG, an interdisciplinary approach is called for. After sporadic preliminary studies an initial survey was published in 1988 [43; 44]. A similar publication exists for the Ancient Orient [12]. The most recent study examined the issue in late antiquity in the West and includes outlooks on a range of time periods [26]. In the field of historical scholarship, research on MG has proven a valid approach and has been made popular especially for the Roman world [41. 31–35].

C. Individual marginalized groups

In the following paragraphs various MG will be discussed individually, in keeping with the ancient tendency for classification as well as with modern scholarly practice. In antiquity, the concept of MG was not yet fully developed. When we enumerate various groups of persons, it does not necessarily imply that every single individual who was a member of that group *eo ipso* had marginalized status or was perceived as marginalized. Furthermore, for many members of MG the barriers to mainstream society were permeable and we need to distinguish between permanent marginalization (e.g. persons with physical disabilities) and marginalization that was of limited duration or existed only in certain geographical areas (e.g. foreigners and ethnic minorities).

In antiquity the following characteristics led to marginalization: 1) not being part of the legal and cult community of the state, 2) not being part of the normative family, 3) practising infamous professions and activities that nevertheless were needed and tolerated by the society and thus not prohibited, 4) criminal activities, especially those directed against property and subject to prosecution, 5) not practising a settled and agrarian lifestyle and economy, 6) deviant and somewhat provocative behaviour with regard to existing norms and mainstream society, 7) begging, 8) disability and disease. Often several of these factors coincided increasing the marginalization; individual poverty had the same effect. Society and state reacted with contempt and social exclusion, legal discrimination and criminalization.

Specifically, certain groups of persons met these characteristics: 1) strangers should be mentioned first, provided they were not socially integrated into their environment [47; bibliography in: 21. 565–573]. Migrants from the east met a wave of rejection in Rome (cf. Juv. 3,61–125), but integration and socio-economic ad-

vancement in the foreign society was possible for them as well [36]. Among these groups were also the exiled and fugitives, including slaves and serfs (→ *colonatus*); and here also belongs the *anachoresis* (→ Rural exodus) in Egypt [25. 16–33; 26. 151–162]. Among the religious minorities are Christians in pagan environments and Jews in the Diaspora [27; 32; 49]. 2) Children from marriages that were not legal (→ *nóthos*) were marginalized in classical Athens. Along with Cynic philosophers (→ Cynicism), buffoons, slaves, the poor and the sick, they were confined to the Cynosarges Gymnasium outside of the area of the city proper [28. 199–208]. In the Roman territory the → *spurius* is subject to numerous similar restrictions (no entry into the official register of birth, setbacks in the admission for → *decurio*), yet he could gain acceptance by the society. In general widows and orphans [19], although often in dire socioeconomic circumstances, should not be counted among MG because they remained integrated into their family unit and the state took protective measures on their behalf.

3) → Prostitution by men and women was reason for social exclusion especially when it was practised to make a living [5; 23; 38. 296–341; 26. 200–233]. At least in Athens of the 5th/4th cents. BC the male homosexual prostitute was subject to → *atimía* ('loss of civil rights') which meant exclusion from secular and religious offices and prohibition from appearing as a public speaker, becoming a herald or lawyer or to even setting foot in the Agora (Aeschin. In Tim. 19 ff.). This applies to pimps (Lat. *lenones*) as well. Professions whose existence was based on violent or natural death had certain restrictions as well: executioners (Lat. *carnifices*) had to live apart from the rest of the population. Undertakers (Lat. *vespillones*, *libitinarii*) practised a dirty business, yet, interestingly a freedman like Trimalchio in → Petronius' [5] novel assesses the *libitinarius* very differently (Petron. Sat. 38,14: *honesta negotiatio*). It says a lot when Juvenal lumps into one group murderers, sailors, thieves, runaway slaves, executioners and makers of biers (Juv. 8,173–175). In the Roman world, *turpitudo* ('dishonour') is also attached to performing artists such as musicians and actors [4; 24; 26. 233–250], → entertainers (buffoons, clowns, acrobats), → gladiators [26. 250–258; 29; 48] and beast-fighters (*bestiarii*). Professional athletes [16] and chariot drivers [17] may be counted among them as well although they were able to acquire professional and social prestige and the legal regulations gave them a certain leeway. Soldiers dishonourably discharged with *missio ignominiosa* were subject to discrimination as well.

4) Thieves and cattle thieves typically were individual perpetrators [26. 289–365], whereas brigands (*latrones*, cf. [11; 25. 101–141; 26. 367–417; 35; 39. 190–202]) usually worked in larger groups that sometimes even required military intervention by the state. Because of their military and economic potential, pirates [1; 37] cannot be regarded as socially declassed and they always found access to legality (→ Piracy).

Fortune-telling, witchcraft and → magic were often punishable offences [26. 259–286]. Prisoners had their rights drastically restricted [20; 26. 419–474]. 5) Shepherds [26. 143–151; 40. 276, 280] and mountain dwellers [9] had their separate living space at the margin of the urban-agrarian society where the transition towards robbery was fluid. Migrant workers [25. 142–177; 26. 138–151] and pedlars (circitores) both had to deal with society's aversion to lowly work and dealers of small wares.

6) In Athens some philosophers were seen as outsiders [34. 68–71] and even faced persecution. In their appearance, dress and language the Cynics [13. 172–181] stood out as counterparts to the dominant social structures (→ Cynicism, → Diogenes [14]). 7) A special group among the poor are beggars who had to depend solely on the generosity of others for their survival and who could be found in cities as well as travelling through the countryside [30. 68–74; 26. 33–132]. 8) The physically disabled faced many exclusions [7], but if they were working, they secured themselves social recognition [10]. → Dwarves as well as deformed buffoons were often a source of amusement [45; 46]. Pathological alcoholism could also result in marginalization [2; 50] (→ Intoxicating substances).

→ Poverty; → Begging; → Freedmen; → Prostitution; → Brigands, bands of; → Slavery

1 L. Casson, Piracy, in: M. Grant, R. Kitzinger (ed.), Civilisation of the Ancient Mediterranean, vol. 2, 1988, 837–844; 2 J. H. D'Arms, Heavy Drinking and Drunkenness in the Roman World, in: O. Murray, M. Tecusan (ed.), In vino veritas, 1995, 304–317; 3 H. Drechsler, W. Hilligen, F. Neumann (ed.), Gesellschaft und Staat. Lexikon der Politik, ⁹1995; 4 M. Ducos, La condition des acteurs à Rome, données juridiques et sociales, in: J. Blänsdorf (ed.), Theater und Gesellschaft im Imperium Romanum, 1990, 19–33; 5 C. Edwards, Unspeakable Professions: Public Performance and Prostitution in Ancient Rome, in: J. P. Hallett, M. B. Skinner (ed.), Roman Sexualities, 1997, 66–95; 6 K. Gahleitner, Leben am Rand. Zur subjektiven Verarbeitung benachteiligter Lebenslagen, 1996; 7 R. Garland, The Eye of the Beholder. Deformity and Disability in the Graeco-Roman World, 1995; 8 B. Geremek, Der Außenseiter, in: J. Le Goff (ed.), Der Mensch des Mittelalters, 1990, 374–401; 9 H. Grassl, Bergbewohner im Spannungsfeld von Theorie und Erfahrung der Ant., in: E. Olshausen, Stuttgarter Kolloquium zur historischen Geographie des Altertums 5, 1996, 189–196; 10 Id., Behinderung und Arbeit, in: Eirene 26, 1989, 49–57; 11 Th. Grünewald, Räuber, Rebellen, Rivalen, Rächer: Studien zu Latrones im römischen Reich, 1999; 12 V. Haas (ed.), Außenseiter und Randgruppen. Beiträge zu einer Sozialgeschichte des Alten Orients, 1992; 13 J. Hahn, Der Philosoph und die Gesellschaft, 1989; 14 B.-U. Hergemöller et al., s. v. R., LMA 7, 433–438; 15 Id. (ed.), Randgruppen der spätmittelalterlichen Gesellschaft, ²1994; 16 G. Horsmann, Die Bescholtenheit der Berufssportler im römischen Recht, in: Nikephoros 7, 1994, 207–227; 17 Id., Die Wagenlenker der römischen Kaiserzeit. Untersuchung zu ihrer sozialen Stellung, 1998; 18 B. Kirchgässner, F. Reuter (ed.), Städtische Randgruppen und Minderheiten, 1986; 19 J. U. Krause, Witwen und Waisen im römi-

schen Reich, vols. 1–4, 1994/95; 20 Id., Gefängnisse im römischen Reich, 1996; 21 Id. et al., Bibliographie zur römischen Sozialgeschichte, vol. 2, Schichten, Konflikte, religiöse Gruppen, materielle Kultur, 1998; 22 D. Kreft, I. Mielenz, Wörterbuch Soziale Arbeit, ⁴1996; 23 W. A. Krenkel, Prostitution, in: s. [1], 1291–1297; 24 H. Leppin, Histrionen. Untersuchung zur sozialen Stellung von Bühnenkünstlern im Westen des römischen Reiches zur Zeit der Republik und des Prinzipats, 1992; 25 P. McKechnie, Outsiders in the Greek Cities in the Fourth Century BC, 1989; 26 V. Neri, I marginali nell'occidente tardoantico, 1998; 27 K. L. Noethlichs, Das Judentum und der römische Staat: Minderheitenpolitik im antiken Rom, 1996; 28 D. Ogden, Greek Bastardy in the Classical and Hellenistic Periods, 1996; 29 W. Pietsch, Gladiatoren – Stars oder Geächtete?, in: P. Scherrer, Steine und Wege, FS D. Knibbe, 1999, 373–378; 30 M. Prell, Sozialökonomische Untersuchung zur Armut im antiken Rom, 1997; 31 J. M. Rainer, Zum Problem der Atimie als Verlust der bürgerlichen Rechte insbesondere bei männlichen homosexuellen Prostituierten, in: RIDA, 3ᵉ Série 33, 1986, 89–114; 32 P. Schäfer, Judeophobia. Attitudes Towards the Jews in the Ancient World, 1997; 33 B. Schäfers (ed.), Grundbegriffe der Soziologie, ⁵1998; 34 P. Scholz, Der Philosoph und die Politik, 1998; 35 B. D. Shaw, Der Bandit, in: A. Giardina (ed.), Der Mensch der römischen Antike, 1991, 337–381; 36 H. Sonnabend, Zur sozialen und rechtlichen Situation von Migranten aus dem Osten im Rom der späten Republik und frühen Kaiserzeit, in: A. Gestrich, Historische Wanderungsbewegungen. Migration in Antike, Mittelalter und Neuzeit, 1991, 37–49; 37 P. de Souza, Piracy in the Graeco-Roman World, 1999; 38 B. E. Stumpp, Prostitution in der römischen Antike, ²1998; 39 J. Sünskes Thompson, Aufstände und Protestaktionen im Imperium Romanum, 1990; 40 G. Volpe, Contadini, pastori e mercanti nell'Apulia tardoantica, 1996; 41 K. W. Weeber, s. v. Außenseiter, in: Id., Alltag im Alten Rom: ein Lexikon, 1995, 31–35; 42 I. Weiler, »'Künstler-Handwerker'« im Altertum – Randseiter der antiken Gesellschaft?, in: G. Erath, Komos. FS Th. Lorenz, 1997, 149–154; 43 Id., Zur Geschichte sozialer Randgruppen in der Alten Welt, in: E. Weber, Römische Geschichte, Altertumskunde und Epigraphik. FS A. Betz, 1985, 659–672; 44 Id. (ed.), Soziale Randgruppen und Außenseiter im Altertum, 1988; 45 Id., Überlegungen zu Zwergen und Behinderten in der antiken Unterhaltungskultur, in: Grazer Beiträge 21, 1995, 121–145; 46 Id., Physiognomik und Kulturanthropologie. Überlegungen zu behinderten Gauklern, in: G. Dreser, G. Rathmayr (ed.), Mensch – Gesellschaft – Wissenschaft, 1999, 191–210; 47 Id., Fremde als stigmatisierte Randgruppen in Gesellschafts-Systemen der Alten Welt, in: Klio 71, 1989, 51–59; 48 Th. Wiedemann, Emperors and Gladiators, 1992; 49 Z. Yavetz, Judenfeindschaft in der Antike, 1997; 50 P. Zanker, Die Trunkene Alte, 1989.   H.GR.

Margites (Μαργίτης/Margítēs < μάργος/márgos, 'mad'). Greek mock epic. First attributed it to → Homerus [1] by Aristotle (Poet. 1448b 30ff.; Eth. Nic. 1141a 14) on the basis of literary-historical considerations. Probably to be dated in the 6th cent. BC at the earliest (the note of the Byzantine commentator Eustratios CAG 20 p. 320,36 that Archilochus and Cratinus had already testified to the Homeric origins is without significance; the quote in Ps.-Pl. Alc. 2, 147c is not by Aristotle). The *Margites* is written in hexametres combined with (occasional?) iambic lines (cf. the inscription on Nestor's cup and Xenophanes B 14 DK) and deals with a carefree and inexperienced (fr. 6) anti-hero (the antipode of the much-suffering and experienced Odysseus), who is skilled in no trade (fr. 2–3) and can be seen as the prototype of the good-natured chump (contamination with other fools: fr. 4a). The poem purports to be the work of an old epic singer (i.e. not an early work of Homer's, as the fiction of the vitae has it) that was performed in Colophon (fr. 1), thus excluding the (exiled) Xenophanes [4. 39ff.] as its author. The core, or at least the highlight, of the plot is the description of the wedding night, during which M. has to receive hands-on instruction from the bride on what to do (fr. 4). If the irregular hexametric-iambic fragment POxy. 2309 (fr. 7) can be attributed to the *Margites*., the description contained graphic and downright obscene elements. Two more fragments (POxy 3963–3964 = fr. 8–9) also seem to make reference to the wedding night, the second one with its description of a jolly celebration possibly constituting the poem's ending. We can thus assume that it was a coherent plot (rather than an episodic sequence of 'adventures'), which led Aristotle to raise the status of the *Margites* to that of a 'prototypical comedy' by no lesser author than Homer himself.

TESTIMONIES, FRAGMENTS: 1 IEG 2, 69–77.
BIBLIOGRAPHY: 2 H. LANGERBECK, M., in: HSPh 63, 1958, 33–63; 3 M. FORDERER, Zum homerischen M., 1960; 4 F. BOSSI, Studi sul Margite, 1986; 5 D. J. JAKOB, Die Stellung des M. in der Entwicklung der Komödie, in: Hellenika 43, 1993, 275–279.   R.GL.

Margus (Μάργος; *Márgos*).
[1] M. from Carynea, probably serving as nauarch of the Achaean fleet contingent during the Illyrian War, was killed in 229 BC near Paxos 'after faithfully serving the koinon of the → Achaeans '(Pol. 2,10). During the reformation of the league, he killed the tyrant of Bura in 275, thus forcing Iseas, the tyrant of Carynea, to resign and to have his town join the league (Pol. 2,41). Before → Aratus [2] he played a prominent part and in 255 he was the first to be elected sole *strategos* (Pol. 2,43).
                                                                    J.CO.

[2] M. was in office as Ptolemaic *strategos* in Caria in 273 BC

J. AND L. ROBERT, Fouilles d'Amyzon, vol. 1, 1983, 118ff.
                                                                    W.A.

[3] The most important river (today Morava) in Moesia superior which flows from the south into the Danubius (Danube) to the west of Viminacium. From Horrea Margi the river is open for shipping (*Margus*, Iord. Get. 300; Geogr. Rav. 4,16; 212,4; Plin. HN 3,149; Μάργος, Βάργιος, Str. 7,5,12).

[4] Fortress, port, trade- and customs station (CIL III 8140) in Moesia superior near Viminacium, modern Orašje in Serbia, Požarevac District. *Municipium* in the 2nd half of the 2nd cent. AD (CIL III 8111; 8223, cf. 8113). Near M., Carinus was defeated by Diocletianus (AD 285). As late as around AD 400 M. was an important fleet station (*Margus/Margum*, Eutr. 9,20,2; SHA Car. 18,2; Not. Dign. Or. 41,33; Aur. Vict. 39,11; *Margo*, It. Ant. 132,4; Not. Dign. Or. 41,24,39; Iord. Get. 58,300).

M. FLUSS, s.v. M., RE 14, 1709–1710; TIR L 34 Budapest, 1968, 77f.   J.BU.

Mari (Syrian town, modern Tall Ḥarīrī, on the Euphrates, 15 km from the border to Iraq). French excavations since 1933 document three periods: the pre-Sargonic period (24th cent. BC) with an enormous palace (from it about 40 administrative documents were recovered which are similar to those from the archives at → Ebla) and several temples (containing numerous statuettes of praying persons, some of them with inscriptions). The second, poorly documented, period is synchronous with the 3rd dynasty of Ur in southern Mesopotamia (21st cent. BC), during which M. was the seat of an independent dynasty. The last 50 years of the history of M. (1st half of the 18th cent. BC) are best documented, thanks to an extensive palace archive of about 2,000 clay tablets and tablet fragments (excavated between 1934 and 1937).

The texts permit the reconstruction not only of the history of M. but also that of → Syria in considerable and accurate detail: Jaḥdun-Lim, of nomadic origin, took over rulership in M.; a successor, Sumu-Jamam, was driven out after a two-year rule (in about 1796) by Šamši-Adad, a ruler of nomadic origin. From Ekallatum (on the Tigris river north of Assur) the latter founded the 'Kingdom of Upper Mesopotamia', which extended along the Tigris as far as M. on the middle Euphrates. His younger son Jasmaḥ-Adad, installed in M., was driven out after 8 years of rule by Zimrilim, a nephew of Sumu-Jamam; the 14 years of his reign are extensively documented. In 1761 → Ḥammurapi of Babylon terminated Zimrilim's rulership and ordered the destruction of the palace, after everything of interest to him had been taken away. Unintentionally, he thus contributed to the preservation of the numerous archives. Two types of texts are found in the archives: first, letters, some of them in an unusually lively language (containing many drafts of → international treaties), second, administrative documents. They document political life of the Near East – from Hazor in Palestine to as far as Bahrein, from Ḥattusa in Anatolia to Anšan in Iran – the daily life in the palace (with 25.000 m² one of the largest in the Near East), religion and economy. The dossiers illuminating the phenomena of prophecy (→ Prophets) and nomadism (→ Nomads) found special attention because of their relation with the OT.

J.-M. DURAND, Les documents épistolaires du palais de M., vol. 1, 1997; vol. 2, 1998; vol. 3 2000; J.-G. HEINTZ, Bibliographie de MARI [1933–1988], 1990 (annual supp-

lements since 1992 in the journal Akkadica); J.-R. KUP-
PER, A. SPYCKET, s.v. M., RLA 7, 382–418; MARI, Anna-
les de Recherches Interdisciplinaires, 8 vols. since 1982.
D.CH.

Maria
I. ROMAN WOMEN   II. BIBLICAL FIGURES

I. ROMAN WOMEN
[I 1] Name of two sisters of C. Marius [I 1]; one was the
wife of M. Gratidius [2] and mother of C. Marius [I 7]
Gratidianus, the other one was the mother of C. Lusius
[I 1].   K.-L.E.

[I 2] Mentioned by Claudianus (Laus Serenae 69), possibly wife of → Honorius [2], the brother of → Theodosius I, therefore the mother of → Serena and → Thermantia.

> J. R. MARTINDALE, Notes on the Consuls of 381 and 382,
> in: Historia 16, 1967, 254–256; PLRE 1, 558.

[I 3] Born about AD 385, daughter of → Stilicho and
→ Serena; married to → Honorius [3] in 398 (Claud.
Epithalamium [Carm. 10] 118f.); died childless in
407/8. Her sister → Thermantia succeeded her as the
wife of the emperor. PLRE 2, 720, 1.   K.G.-A.

II. BIBLICAL FIGURES
[II 1] Mother of Jesus. Already in the NT writings
growing interest in the person of M. can be detected.
→ Paulus only mentions that → Jesus was born by a
woman (ek gynaikós Gal 4:4); two Gospels with
accounts on her virginity at Jesus' conception (Mt 1:18–
25; Lk 1:26–38) provide the basis for the later expansion of her veneration. M.'s song of praise (Lk 1:46–55),
based on models in the OT, points to the influence of
prophetic traditions in the shaping of her image. Only
Jo 19:25–27 mentions her presence at the crucifixion of
Jesus. According to Acts 1:14 she is a member of the
post-Easter community but does not play a prominent
role. Aside from these positive references, the NT also
contains a rejection of the mother of Jesus, since Jesus
downgrades family bonds in favour of the community
of followers (Mk 3:31–35; Mt 12:46–50; Lk 8:19–21).

Apocryphal writings, such as the so-called Protogospel of James (→ New Testament apocrypha) from the
mid–2nd cent. as well as accounts of the so-called tran-
situs Mariae (M.'s death and assumption), which are
attested in various traditions from the 4th cent., describe M.'s life and death in detail and document growing interest in her person. The Protogospel of James
attributes the birth of M., too, to a direct intervention of
God. After a long period of childlessness, an angel
announces the desired child to her parents Joachim and
Anna. Whereas the NT does not describe the exact circumstances of the virgin birth of Jesus, the Protogospel
describes an examination of M. after the birth by a midwife, confirming her physical intactness. The creeds of
the Early Church, the Apostolicum and the → Nicaeno-
Constantinopolitanum, maintain, within the context of

their Christological statements, that Christ was born by
the virgin (parthénos) M.

Above all, hymnic and poetic texts of the → Church
Fathers expand the praise of M. with an abundance of
images and symbols without aiming at a dogmatic fixa-
tion. → Iustinus [6] Martyr and Irenaeus of Lyons
(→ Irenaeus [2]) develop an Eve-M. typology as a parallel to the Adam-Christ typology. Irenaeus writes that
'the son of God became man through the virgin so that
disobedience, which originated with the snake, would
come to an end along the same path upon which it had
begun' (Iren. Adversus haereses 3,22,4).

The designation of M. as 'the bearer of God' (theo-
tókos) can first be found at the beginning of the 4th
cent. in Alexander of Alexandria, and consequently
gained increasingly greater importance. The esteem of
M.'s virginity and the stress on her perpetual virginity is
linked to the growing ascetic movement. The epithet
Aeí Parthénos ('Ever-Virgin') for M., which can be
found, among others, in → Athanasius, Didymus [5] the
Blind and → Epiphanius [1] of Salamis, is a prevalent
characteristic of the veneration of M. in the Eastern
Churches, next to the title of 'Mother of God'. However, a certain reticence regarding the circumstances of
her perpetual virginity characterises the statements of
the Church Fathers (cf. → Basilius [1] of Caesarea,
Homilia in Sanctam Christi Generationem 5). In the
incipient → monasticism of the late 3rd and 4th cents.,
M. is considered, next to other women, as a paragon of
virtue and virginity, then slowly rising to the prevalent
type of virginity (cf. Athanasius, Letter to the Virgins
[Syrian/Coptic]).

The definition of M. as 'the bearer of God' (theotó-
kos) established at the Council of Ephesus in AD 431
(Anathema 1) stands in the context of the Christological conflicts of the Early Church and serves the maintenance of Christ's divinity. Even though some of the
Church Fathers criticized this title of M. as they perceived the danger of super-elevating her as a goddess,
the epithet gained acceptance especially in the Eastern
Churches. Although the veneration of M. flourished
from about the middle of the 5th cent., the decision of
the Council of 431 must not be overestimated. The
church of Santa Maria Maggiore in Rome, dedicated
under pope Sixtus III (432–440), is the first documented
church in the West dedicated to M.

While in the NT M. still is considered a member of
the post-Easter community, she increasingly became
the prototype of the faithful and a symbol of the
Church. This line of interpretation is developed mainly
in the West; Aug. De sancta virginitate 6,6, writes:
Christ as the head of the Church was born by a virgin as
an indication that Christians, as members of the
Church, are born by a virgin, i.e. the Church. Feasts
have been celebrated in the East since the 5h cent., and
since the 7th also in the West.

Images of M. in Christological scenes are documented since the 3rd cent., but the scope was expanded in the
5th/6th cents. by covering the apocryphal narratives,

thus departing from the strict orientation on Christ. The further development of the veneration of M. shows an increasing adaptation to her divine son. The dogma of M.'s Immaculate Conception by her mother Anna, as proclaimed in 1854 by the Roman-Catholic Church, can be viewed as an expression of this tendency. Even though the Early Church already advocated M.'s impeccability, it was not a matter of freedom from original sin. Rather, the discussion was marked by the veneration of Christ's divinity, whose mother could not be contaminated by sin.

Attempts of feminist reconstruction regard the flourishing of the veneration of M. as a continuation of cults of ancient goddesses that had been suppressed by Christianity. While there are obvious parallels, especially in the imagery (→ Isis; → Mother goddesses), direct links can not be proved.

W. BEINERT, H. PETRI (ed.), Handbuch der Marienkunde 1–2, ²1996–1997; S. BENKO, The Virgin Goddess. Studies in the Pagan and Christian Roots of Mariology, 1993; R. BROWN et al. (ed.), M. im NT. Eine Gemeinschaftsstudie von protestantischen und römisch-katholischen Gelehrten, 1981; L. HEISER, M. in der Christus-Verkündigung des orthodoxen Kirchenjahres, 1981; T. KLAUSER, s.v. Gottesgebärerin, RAC 11, 1071–1103; L. LANGENER, Isis lactans – M. lactans: Untersuchungen zur koptischen Ikonographie, 1996; C. MULACK, M.: die geheime Göttin im Christentum, ⁴1991; J. PELIKAN, Mary Through the Centuries. Her Place in the History of Culture, 1996; K. RUHL, Isis lactans – M. lactans: das Bild der stillenden Gottesmutter im Ägypten der Pharaonen, in der koptischen Kunst und in den Darstellungen des späten Mittelalters, 1998; M. WARNER, M. Alone of All Her Sex, 1976; J. ZMIJEWSKI, M. im Neuen Testament, in: ANRW II 26.1, 1992, 596–716.   R.A.

[II 2] M. Magdalene Disciple of Jesus from → Magdala on Lake Genezareth. In the NT, M. Magdalene is primarily connected with the traditions of the Crucifixion (Mk 15:40f.; Mt 27:55f.; Lk 23:49; John 19:25), burial (Mk 15:47; Mt 27:61; Lk 23:55f.), discovery of the empty tomb (Mk 16:1–8; Mt 28:1–10; Lk 24:1–11; John 20:1f.) and the appearance of the Resurrected (Mt 28:9f.; John 20:11–18: here she is the first witness of the Resurrection; Mk 16:9–11); the Synoptic Gospels always mention her first in a group of women, John mentions her alone. In the Pauline sense she is an apostle (compare John 20:18 with 1 Cor 9:1). Lk 8:1ff. reports that she followed Jesus with other women and that she was cured by him. Christian-Gnostic texts of the 2nd/3rd cents. (the Gospels according to Mary, Thomas and Philippus; the Dialogue of the Saviour; the → Pistis Sophia and others; see → Gnosticism, → New Testament apocrypha) emphasize M. Magdalene as the recipient of secret revelations, as a dialogue partner and Jesus' favourite disciple. From the 4th cent., M. Magdalene is increasingly identified with the sinner in Lk 7:36–50 and with Mary of Bethany (John 12:1–8), she thus changes in the general view from a witness of the Crucifixion and Resurrection to a repentant prostitute.
→ Gnosis; → Jesus; → New Testament

R. ATWOOD, Mary Magdalene in the New Testament Gospels and Early Tradition, 1993; D. BADER (ed.), M.M. Zu einem Bild der Frau in der christlichen Verkündigung, 1990; I. MAISCH, Between Contempt and Veneration. M.M., the Image of a Woman through the Centuries, 1998 (German orig. 1996); A. MARJANEN, The Woman Jesus Loved. Mary Magdalene in the Nag Hammadi Library and Related Documents, 1996; S. PETERSEN, 'Zerstört die Werke der Weiblichkeit!' M.M., Salome und andere Jüngerinnen Jesu in christlich-gnostischen Schriften, 1999.
                                                                            S.P.

Mariaba (Μαριαβα; *Maríaba*). Capital of the Sabaean kingdom in the south-west of → Arabia Felix, today the town of Mārib (15° 26′ N, 45° 16′ O). M. is mentioned as the metropolis of the Sabaeans in Str. 16,768, according to Eratosthenes, and in Str. 16,778, according to Artemidorus. It can be found as *Mariba* in Plin. HN 6,160 as well as in R. Gest. div. Aug. 26; Ptol. 6,7,37 lists the metropolis Μαράβα/*Marába* (variant Μάρα/*Mára*, Βάραβα/*Báraba*). The name form → Marsyaba (Str. 16,782) is surely a contamination of Mariaba and Saba. Sabaean inscriptions also render the name in two different ways; the form *mryb*, Maryab or Marīb is documented until the 2nd cent. AD, later exclusively the form *mrb*, Marīb or Mārib.

The ancient city of M. lies on a plain rising 1,160–1,200 m above sea level in the dry delta of the Wādī Adhana. Before the river oasis of M., this Wadi breaks through a bottleneck in the mountains; the building of a dam permitted full cultivation. Recent research has found that the beginnings of irrigation in the oasis go back to the end of the third millennium. After the erection of the great dam, 16 m high and 620 m in length, was completed in the 6th cent. BC, the irrigated area measured about 9,600 hectares. The favourable location predestined M. to be the metropolis of the Sabaean kingdom being the largest city of ancient South Arabia with a walled area of about 110 hectares. The often-mentioned and renowned royal castle Salḥīn [2] was also situated within the city. Further, M. was an important stop on the caravan route that connected the incense region with the Mediterranean (→ Incense Road). The oldest Sabaean inscriptions, which can be dated to the 8th cent. BC, also originate from M. and its surroundings. In 24 BC, M. withstood the siege of a Roman army under → Aelius [II 11] Gallus that had reached the gates of the city.

M. was also of importance in religious regards, since, with its large temple Awām, nowadays Maḥram Bilqīs, of the god Almaqah in the southern half of the oasis it owned the central cult site of the kingdom where numerous votive inscriptions were placed. After the dam had burst several times between the 4th and 6th cents. AD, the repairs being documented by the long dam building inscriptions CIS IV, 540 of the year 450 and CIS IV, 541 of the year 542, the final disaster appears to have occurred in the early 7th cent., mentioned in the Koran (34,16) as the flood of the dike, resulting in the desolation of the oasis and M.'s sinking into insignificance.
→ Saba, Sabaei

1 A. Jamme, Sabaean Inscriptions from Maḥram Bilqîs, Mârib, 1962; 2 W. W. Müller, s.v. M., EI 6, 559–567; 3 J. Schmidt (ed.), Antike Technologie – Die sabäische Wasserwirtschaft von Mārib, 1991/1995; 4 H. von Wissmann, Die Geschichte von Saba'. vol. 2: Das Großreich der Sabäer bis zu seinem Ende im frühen 4. Jahrhundert v.Chr., 1982.   W.W.M. A.D.

Mariades (Μαριάδης; *Mariádes*). Citizen and councillor of Antioch on the Orontes. M. was excluded from the → *boulé* for embezzlement of public funds. He fled to the Persian Empire and betrayed the city when it was invaded by → Sapor *c*. AD 260. Sapor had him executed shortly afterwards. Or. Sib. 13, 89–102; SHA Tyr. Trig. 2,2–3; Amm. Marc. 23,5,3; Zos. 1,27; 3,32,5; Ioh. Mal. 12,295–296. PIR² M 273.   K.G.-A.

Mariamme

[1] (Hebrew *Mirjam*; the form *Mariamne* in Fr. Hebbel's drama is a corruption from later MSS). Granddaughter of → Aristobulus [2] II. and Iohannes → Hyrcanus [3] II. Born *c*. 53/52 BC, M. was a celebrated beauty. Married to Herod (→ Herodes [1]) the Great, she became involved in the intrigues and conflicts between → Hasmoneans and Herodeans. In 29 Herod had her executed on suspicion of unfaithfulness based on the calumnies of his sister → Salome (Jos. Ant. Iud. 15,218–236).

A. Schalit, König Herodes, 1969, 566ff.   K.BR.

[2] (or Mariamne). One of the three towers (Hippikos, → Phasaelis, M.) of the palace of Herod (Herodes [1]) the Great at → Jerusalem, named after Herod's wife M. [1] (Jos. Ant. Iud. 15,9,3; Jos. BI 5,4,4). At the time of the complete destruction of Jerusalem by Roman troops (AD 70) only these towers and a part of the western city wall were spared to serve as a reminder of the strength of the city's defences (Jos. BI 6,9,1; 7,1,1). The precise location is uncertain, but all three towers were on the site referred to today as the 'Citadel' and the 'Tower of David' near the Jaffa Gate.

R. Amiran, A. Eitan, Excavations in the Courtyard of the Citadel, Jerusalem, in: Israel Exploration Journal 20, 1970, 9–17; M. Broshi, Excavations along the Western and Southern Wall of the Old City of Jerusalem, in: H. Geva, Ancient Jerusalem Revealed, 1994; C. N. Johns, The Citadel, Jerusalem – A Summary of Works since 1934, in: Quarterly of the Department of Antiquities in Palestine 14, 1950, 121–190; Schürer 1, 304f.; G. A. Smith, Jerusalem. The Topography, Economics and History from the Earliest Times to A.D. 70, Bd. 2, 1908, 492ff.   I.WA.

[3] (Μαριάμμη/ *Mariámmē*; also Mariamne). Of the several towns of this name in Syria and Phoenicia, the modern Marġamīn in Syria, south of Rafanīya between Ḥimṣ and the Mediterranean, is the most important. Its foundation on the river Eleutherus possibly goes back to Alexander the Great (Arr. Anab. 2,13). Its name and strategic position indicate development under Herod

the Great. The presence of bishops and a church is documented between AD 451 and 536.

Jones, Cities, 267, 543, table 2.   T.L.

Mariana City on La Marana plateau on the Tyrrhenian coast in the north-east of → Corsica, on the left bank of the Guola (modern Golo), 2 miles to the east of its mouth (Ptol. 3,2,5). Descended from a colony of veterans under Marius [I 1] around 100 BC (Plin. HN 3,12,1; Mela 2,122; Sen. Dial. 7,9; Solin. 3,2,5). Topography: near the *insula episcopalis* of La Canonica the *decumanus* with *porticus* is situated, surrounded by shops and houses from the high Imperial period. Necropoleis from the Imperial period in the west and east of the city centre; so far, no graves have been found that can be ascribed to the Republican settlement (attested by black varnished pottery and coins).

G. Moracchini-Mazel, Les monuments paléochrétiens de la Corse, 1967, 7–88, 99–102; Fouilles de Mariana I–VIII, in: Cahiers Corsica, 4–7; 9–12 (1971); 17 (1972); 25–26, 32 (1973); 37–39 (1974); 92 (1981); Ph. Pergola, La Corse, in: N. Gauthier (ed.), Topographie chrétienne des cités de la Gaule 2,1, 1986, 99–102.   R.Z.

Mariandyni (Μαριανδυνοί; *Mariandynoí*). Originally a Plāïc-speaking (Paphlagonian) population in northern Anatolia, overlayered by groups of Thracian descent. Area of settlement: to the east of the watershed between the lower Sangarius and Hypius [1], to the south of the coastal area Thyni(a)s (up to Kales), to the west of the Caucones in the area of the lower Billaeus and the Paphlagonian area on the middle Ladon, to the north of Abant and Köroğlu Dağları (Str. 8,3,17; 12,3,4). Subjugated by → Croesus, subsequently part of the Persian satrapy Katpatuka (cf. Hdt. 1,28; 3,90,2) [1. 41ff., 60; 2. 192ff., 203f.]. The area of the Caucones is often counted as being part of Mariandynia (Ptol. 5,1,3). Parts of the Mariandyni had to submit to Heraclea [7] Pontica and were integrated into the territory of Heraclea (or Cierus) as dependent → *períoikoi* or as an agricultural population with the status of → Helots or → *penestaí*, [3]. The free M. lived to the south of the Akçakoca Dağları and the northern part of the Düzce basin (from 281 BC gradually incorporated into Bithynia).
→ Claudioupolis [1]

1 K. Strobel, Galatien und seine Grenzregionen, in: E. Schwertheim (ed.), Forschungen in Galatien (Asia Minor Studien 12), 1994, 29–65; 2 Id., Die Galater 1, 1996; 3 A. Bittner, Eine Polis zwischen Tyrannis und Selbstverwaltung, 1998.

D. Asheri, Über die Frühgeschichte von Herakleia, in: Forschungen an der Nord-Küste Kleinasiens 1 (ETAM 5), 1972, 9–34; A. Avram, Bemerkungen zu den M., in: Studii Clasice 22, 1984, 19–28; K. Belke, Paphlagonien und Honorias, 1996, 251; W. Ruge, s.v. M., RE 14, 1747–1749.   K.ST.

Mariandynus (Μαριανδυνός; *Mariandynós*). Aeolian (Steph. Byz. s.v. Μαριανδυνία), son of Phineus and Idaea [3] (daughter of Dardanus) or of a Scythian woman; also identified as the son of Cimmerius or of Phrixus (schol. Apollo. Rhod. 1,1126; 2,140. 723. 780). As a son of Titias he has two brothers: Priolas and → Bormus. Following the latter's death, M. turned to aulody (song with flute accompaniment), in which he instructed → Hyagnis (schol. Aesch. Pers. 940). M. reigned over a part of Paphlagonia, then over the land of the Bebryces in Bithynia, which was named after him (Str. 12,3,4; Theopomp. FGrH 115 F 388).

PRELLER/ROBERT II⁴ 816.   I.BAN.

Marianus
[1] Early Byzantine poet, contemporary of emperor Anastasius I (AD 491–518). According to Suda s.v. M., he originally was a descendent of a Roman family of senators, emigrated to Eleutheropolis in Palestine with his father and was a *patríkios* under Anastasius, composed iambic paraphrases of the works of Hellenistic authors (→ Theocritus; → Apollonius [2] Rhodius' 'Argonautica'; → Callimachus' 'Hecale', 'Hymns', 'Epigrams'; → Aratus [4]; → Nicander's 'Theriaka'). Possibly identical with M. [2].

1 J. GEFFCKEN, s.v. M., RE 14, 1750.   GR.DA.

[2] M. Scholasticus Epigrammatist of the 'Kyklos' of Agathias. Six rhetorical poems of epideictic character are extant: the aetiological genesis of a spa called 'Eros' (Anth. Pal. 9,626f.), the glorification of a palace that was erected for the empress Sophia (ibid. 9,657: to be dated 566/7, erroneously attributed to Agathias by Zon. 14,10), the description, applying Neoplatonic symbolism, of a park (Anth. Pal. 9,668f.) and of a statue of Eros (ibid. 16,201). The traditional equation with → M. [1] of Eleutheropolis is unlikely.

Av. and A. CAMERON, The Cycle of Agathias, in: JHS 86, 1966, 17, 21; Av. CAMERON, Notes on the Sophiae, the Sophianae and the Harbour of Sophia, in: Byzantion 37, 1967, 11–20.   M.G.A.

[3] Philagrius cites five corrupt iambic dimetres under M.'s name in connection with Verg. Ecl. 1,19. The MSS describe the author as *poeta Lupercorum* or *Lupercanorum*; it is usually assumed that the actual title was *Lupercalia*. The lines claim that Rome's name was derived from the name of its founder, Roma, the daughter of Aesculapius. Nothing is known about the author, but the similarities with → Alfius [4] Avitus regarding metre and the use of *topoi* suggest a time in the 1st half of the 3rd cent. AD.

COURTNEY, 405.   ED.C.

Mārib see → Mariaba

Marica Goddess who was worshipped in a → grove between the estuary of the → Liris and → Minturnae (modern Minturno), probably as early as the beginning of the 7th cent. BC. A temple which was still frequented in the late Republican period can be dated to the late 6th cent. According to Plutarch (Marius 39), once something had been carried into the temple it was not allowed to remove it. Archaeological findings – anatomical votive offerings (→ Consecratio) and representations of babies (→ Kourotrophos) among others – as well as the location of the sanctuary outside the city near the coast suggest that her sphere of influence was wide-ranging. The grove was struck by lightning in 207 BC, which was reported to Rome as a prodigium (Liv. 27,37,2f.). Votive inscriptions for M. are found in Minturnae (CIL I² 2438 = ILLRP 216; AE 1908, 83) and in → Pisaurum (CIL I² 374 = ILLRP 19: probably 3rd cent. BC). In the antiquarian tradition M. was equated to Venus (Serv. Aen. 7,47), Diana (schol. Aug. Civ. 2,23 BOLL) or, as a supposed spring nymph, to Circe (Serv. Aen. 12,164; Lactant. Div. inst. 1,21,23) and the mother of Latinus [1] (Verg. Aen. 7,47).

J. W. BOUMA, Religio votiva, vol. 3, 1996, 54f.; P. MINGAZZINI, Il santuario della dea M. alle foci del Garigliano, in: Monumenti Antichi Reale Accademia dei Lincei 37, 1938, 693–981; RADKE, 199; F. TROTTA, Minturnae preromana e il culto di M., in: F. COARELLI (ed.), Minturnae, 1989, 11–28.   K.v.S.

Mariccus A Boian; in AD 69, as 'self-styled saviour and divine protector' of Gaul, he instigated an uprising in the territory of the Haedui; this was put down by → Vitellius. M. was executed (Tac. Hist. 2,61).
→ Haedui; → Boii   W.SP.

Marina
[1] M. Severa First wife of → Valentinianus I, mother of the emperor → Gratianus [2], whose elevation to Augustus she helped effect; removed from the court and divorced before AD 370 because of some fraud, in 375 called back to the court by Gratianus. PLRE I, 828, 2.

[2] Youngest daughter of → Arcadius and → Eudoxia [1], born 403, died AD 449; built a palace in Constantinople; following the example of her sister → Pulcheria she dedicated herself to a chaste life.→ Cyrillus [2] of Alexandria dedicated a work about the true faith to her and her sisters. PLRE 2, 723,1.   K.G.-A.

Marine Style see → Pottery

Marinianus
[1] Jurist from Galatia in Asia Minor, belonging to the group around → Symmachus. M was a teacher of law in Rome (Symmachus, Ep. 3,23,2) and in AD 383 *vicarius Hispaniae* (Cod. Theod. 9,1,14). PLRE I, 559f.

D. LIEBS, Die Jurisprudenz im spätantiken Italien, 1987, 64, 98.   T.G.

[2] **Flavius Avitus M.** Attested in AD 422 as praetorian prefect of Italia, Illyria and Africa, and in 423 as *consul*, perhaps *patricius*. Along with his wife he contributed to the renovation of St. Peter's Basilica under Pope → Leo [4] I (ILS 8989). PLRE 2, 723f.   H.L.

[3] **(Licinius Egnatius) M.**

A close relative if not son of → Gallienus, probably killed along with the emperor in AD 268 at the instigation of the Senate (Zon. 12,26 D.). It is doubtful whether he is to be identified with the *cos. ord.* of 268 (CIL III 3525 = 10492 = ILS 2457 = AE 1944,85; VIII 18842).

> A. ALFÖLDI, Studien zur Weltkrise des 3. Jahrhunderts n.Chr., 1967, 109f.; KIENAST, 222; I. KÖNIG, Die gallischen Usurpatoren, 1981, 127f.; PIR² L 198; PLRE I, 559,1.   T.F.

Marinus
I. GREEK   II. ROMAN

I. GREEK
(Μαρῖνος; *Marînos*).

[I 1] **M. of Tyre** Greek geographer, known only through his immediate successor Claudius → Ptolemaeus, who mentions M. as a source in his 'Introduction to the Representation of the Earth' (γεωγραφικὴ ὑφήγησις/ *geōgraphikḗ hyphḗgēsis*, = 'G.'). Arabic texts which mention M. all trace back to the 'G.' [8. 189].

Place names used by M. allow his work to be dated to between AD 107 and 114/5; cities are mentioned with the name of Trajan refering to his Dacian Wars (ended AD 107), but not names of cities which trace back to Trajan's Parthian Wars (114–116 AD) [2. 1767 f.; 5. 95]. In his 'G.', which caused the works of M. to be forgotten, Ptolemy dealt with M. in detail (e.g. G. 1,6 ff., especially G. 1,18 f.; [7. 695–710, 753–757]). He maintained the scientific objectives (γνώμη/*gnṓmē*) structuring the work of M.(G. 1,19,1), but corrected M.'s cartography (on the basis of astronomy) as well as his distance information ([7. 806–811]. He strongly emphasizes the achievement of M. [6]). Ptolemy describes the scientific work of M. with his 'Correction of the Geographic Atlas' (ἡ τοῦ γεωγραφικοῦ πίνακος διόρθωσις, G. 1,6,1; [7. 806], *pace* [6. 795]), to which he devotes several treatises or editions (συντάξεις/*syntáxeis* or ἐκδόσεις/*ekdóseis*). Using many individual data (G. 1,6,1), M. compiled information for creating a map (→ Cartography). It is disputed whether a map was added to every treatise; Ptolemy may not have known any ([7. 806], *pace* [6. 795]). The last treatise in any case did not have one (G. 1,17,1). M. probably placed greater value on distance and direction information and on their use for determining every location than on the execution of the map itself. His procedure can be visualised as the creation of various lists of place names, grouped by province and country, with each individual place name accompanied by a topothetic note [3. 1027]; however, most of them were incomplete and had to be supplemented from other lists (G. 1,18,4).

Nevertheless, HONIGMANN [2. 1785 f.] was able to draw a square flat map of the → *oikoumene* using M's information (extracted from Ptolemy's G.). On this map, the *oikoumene* extended as a rectangle to both sides of the northern latitude of Rhodes (= 36°), which runs through the centre of the Mediterranean; for M., – not the equator – was the line of orientation [2. 1771–1789; 8. 162, 164]. His zero meridian ran in the west through the → Makaron Nesoi (Madeira – Porto Santo [4. 37,1]). On the latitude of Rhodes, M. then counted 15 hour intervals (ὡριαῖα διαστήματα) to the east, each of which is bounded by the meridians, under which the rising and setting of the sun differs by one hour (= 15°). Thus for him the west-east extent of the *oikoumene* as far as China (→ Cattigara, → Sera, → Sinai) is 225°; that would be (1° on the latitude of Rhodes = *c.* 400 stadia, G. 1,11,2) 90,000 stadia (Ptolemaeus himself, G. 1,14,8, reduced this to 180° = 72,000 stadia). Arranged parallel to the Rhodian latitude are seven parallel bands/zones (κλίμακα/*klímaka*), each of which differs in the length of the day by 30 minutes [8. 164]; thus, for example, the 4th *klíma* is bounded by the latitudes which run through the Hellespont and Rhodes [2. 1780]. For the north-south extent of the *oikoumene*, M. assumed 87° (= 43,500 stadia) (G. 1,7,2), marked by the locations → Thule and → Agisymba or Cape → Prason, i.e. a stronger extension of the *oikoumene* to the south than to the north. All this produces a map with a rectangular grid of parallels and meridians, although the latter converge toward the pole, for, unlike earlier projections, M. adhered to the cylindrical projection. With good reason, Ptolemy (G. 1,20,3–7) reproaches him for making a cartographic error here; the intervals on the various circles of latitude represent completely different distances [2. 1779 f.].

M.'s achievement consists primarily of the compilation of individual information on the position of places. He based this particularly on travel reports and thus determined the distances of towns more by means of path measurements and days of march or sail than through astronomical observations; that fits in with his cartographic system, in which designation by degrees forms only an outer framework [3. 1028]. Of course, the assignment of geographic information to M. is known only through the direct criticism of Ptolemaeus (in G. 1). Thus, we know that M.'s sources were Diodorus of Samos for the sea route to India; an Alexander for the journey to Cattigara; Septimius Flaccus and Iulius Maternus (in the time of Claudius) for inner Libya as far as Agisymba near Lake Chad; Diogenes, Theophilus and Dioscorus for the east coast of Libya to Zanzibar; the Macedonian merchant Maēs for the Seric trade route; the geographer Philemon and his informants for Ireland's north-western longitude. Furthermore, M. adopted the twelve-armed wind rose from Timosthenes ([4. 32]; (→ Winds) and astronomical approaches from → Hipparchus [6] [2. 1790 f.; 3. 1028].

→ Geography II; → Cartography; → Oikoumene

1 O. A. W. DILKE, Greek and Roman Maps, 1985, 72–86; 2 E. HONIGMANN, s.v. Marinos, RE 14, 1767–1796; 3 F. LASSERRE, s.v. Marinos, KlP 3, 1026–1029; 4 H.v. MŽIK, Des Klaudios Ptolemaios Einführung in die darstellende Erdkunde. Theorie und Grundlagen (I en II preface), 1938 (tr. and comm.); 5 E. OLSHAUSEN, Einführung in die historische Geographie der Alten Welt, 1991; 6 N. G. PHOTINOS, s.v. Marinos, RE Suppl. 12, 791–838; 7 E. POLASCHEK, s.v. Klaudios Ptolemaios. Das geographische Werk, RE Suppl. 10, 680–833; 8 R. WIEBER, Marinos von Tyros in der arabischen Überlieferung, in: M. WEIN-MANN-WALSER (ed.), Historische Interpretationen, 1995, 161–190.   H.A.G.

[I 2] M. of Alexandria Anatomist and teacher, fl. AD 120., credited by → Galen with the renaissance of → anatomy after centuries of neglect. His major work on anatomy was in 20 books, epitomized by Galen into four; only the general section headings of Galen's epitome have survived (Gal. De libriis propriis 3 = 19,25–30 K.). This treatise is probably identical with the work describing his own practical anatomical procedures, praised by Galen (Administrationes anatomicae 1 = 2,290,283 K.). Galen's references to his work on muscles and nerves may also derive from the same major work. Galen also mentions M.'s exposition of sections in → Hippocrates' [6] ' Aphorisms' (Gal. 18A 113, 123 K.), probably from a commentary by M., and in *Epidemiae* II (CMG 5,10,1,312), where M. had shown Hippocrates' anatomy to be fundamentally correct.

M. was the teacher of → Quintus, Galen (Gal. (?) 15, 136 K.) and Antigenes, whom Galen met in Rome, c. AD 163 (Gal. (?) 14,613 K.). If M. really is the author of the work on blood vessels (*Artēriaká*) mentioned by → Andromachus [5] the Younger (Gal. De compositione medicorum secundum locos 7,2 = 13,25 K.), his medical activities would have begun in the 90s of the 1st cent. AD at he latest; however, this identification is not certain.   V.N.

[I 3] Arian bishop in Constantinople. After the death of Demophilus (AD 386), the Thracian M. succeeded him as bishop of the Arians (→ Arianism) in the capital. According to the descriptions by Socrates (5,12,5–8; 23,1–11) and Sozomenus (7,14,4; 17,9–14), his ouster by Dorotheus, who had come from → Antioch [1], and dogmatic conflicts later led to a schism among the Arians. M. taught that the first divine person should be called 'Father' even before the existence of the Son. Dorotheus at the other hand only wanted to speak of a 'Father' afterwards. As a result, the followers of M. built their own places of worship. Because of the profession of one of their most zealous partisans, the Syrian pastry seller (*psathyropólēs*) Theoctistus, they were called *psathyrianoí*. The term 'Goths', says Sozomenus (7,17,11, τῶν Γότθων), was also applied to them, because Selinas, bishop of the Goths, approved of their views. Later, there was a conflict within this group between M. and Agapius, the Arian bishop of Ephesus whom M. had appointed, and whom the Goths supported.
→ Arianism

M. SIMONETTI, s.v. Marino di Costantinopoli, in: A. DI BERARDINO (ed.), Dizionario patristico e di antichità cristiane 2, 2119f.   J.RI.

[I 4] Neoplatonist philosopher from Neapolis in Samaria, end of the 5th cent. AD. According to Damascius (Vita Isidori 141), M. had abandoned the Jewish faith and turned to Hellenism. This may indicate that M. recognized Abraham's worship of the one God in the theology of the One, the highest god of the Neoplatonists, and may explain his move to Athens. It is unknown when and how M. became a student of → Proclus in the Neoplatonist school. Proclus dedicated his important commentary on the myth of Er in Plato's 'Republic' (Procl. in Plat. Resp. 2, p. 96,2) to M. Proclus also mentions a statement by M. on the comparison of the moving spheres of heaven with triremes (ibid. p. 200,30). M. must have been one of the most loyal students of Proclus, because he wanted M. to succeed him.

When Proclus died in AD 485, M. did succeed him, but probably only for a few years; his successor was Isidorus [7]. On the first anniversary of his teacher's death, M. held his eulogy, which has been preserved under the title 'Proclus or On Happiness'. This speech is the most important document on the history of philosophical teaching in Athens in the 5th cent. AD. Isidorus rejected M.s' exegesis on the Platonic 'Philebus' so strongly that he burned his copy (Damascius, Vita Isidori 1–42); Isidorus also criticized M.s' view that the objects of the Platonic 'Parmenides' are not the gods as Syrianus and Proclus had stated, but the Forms (Vita Isidori fr. 245). M. wrote a commentary on Euclid's 'Data', of which only the preface has been preserved, and expressed the wish that philosophy be as accurate as mathematics (Elias, Prolegomena philosophiae 10, p. 28,29 BUSSE). His greatest merited was to have been one of the teachers of Isidorus and → Damascius on logic and natural science. Some of his views were cited by Damascius in Pl. Prm., p. 294,14 RUELLE and Stephanus of Alexandria, in Aristot. An., p. 535,31, where he sees the acting intellect as an angel between the first cause and human beings. This teaching was restated in the Arabic philosophy by Al-Farabi and Ibn Sina.
→ Neoplatonism

EDITIONS: J. FR. BOISSONADE (ed.), Marini Vita Procli, 1814; R. MASULLO (ed.), Marino, Vita di Proclo, 1985; H. D. SAFFREY, A. PH. SEGONDS (ed.), Marinus, Proclus ou Sur le bonheur (Coll. des Univ. de France), 2001
TRANSLATION: CH. FARAGGIANA DI SARZANA (ed.), Marino di Neapoli, Vita di Proclo, in: Proclo... (I Classici del pensiero), 1985, 257–322 (it.)
BIBLIOGRAPHY: GGPh¹, 631–632; H. J. BLUMENTHAL, Marinus' Life of Proclus, Neoplatonist Biography, in: Byzantion 54, 1984, 469–494; Id., Neoplatonic Elements in the 'de anima' Commentaries, in: R. SORABJI (ed.), Aristotle Transformed, 1990, 319–320; K. HULT, Marinus the Samaritan, in CeM 43, 1992, 163–178.; J. MANSFELD, Prolegomena Mathematica from Apollonius of Perga to the Late Neoplatonists (Philosophia Antiqua 80), 1998, 61–65; M. MICHAUX, Le commentaire de Marinus

aux 'Data' d'Euclide, 1947; J. MOGENET, Holstenius et l'horoscope de Proclus, in: Collectanea Vaticana in honorem ... Albareda (Studi e Testi 220), 1962, 281–308; O. NEUGEBAUER, H. B. VAN HOESEN, Greek Horoscopes, 1959, 135–136; SH. SAMBURSKY, Proklos und sein Nachfolger M. (SHAW, Mathematisch-naturwiss. Klasse 2, 1985), 1985; O. SCHISSEL VON FLESCHENBERG, Marinos von Neapolis und die neuplatonischen Tugendgrade, 1928 (review by W. THEILER, in: Gnomon 5, 1929, 307–317); R. WALZER, Lost Neoplatonic Thought in the Arabic Tradition, in: Le Néoplatonisme, 1971, 319–328.

H.SA.

II. ROMAN

[II 1] In AD 413, M., as *comes (Africae?)*, defeated → Heraclianus, carried out the death sentence against him and proceeded against his followers with great severity, one of those executed being → Marcellinus [12]. He was probably relieved of his post in the same year of 413. Christian. His identity with the Maurianus mentioned in Cod. Theod. 15,11,1 (PLRE 2, 737) is questionable. PLRE 2, 724.

H.L.

[II 2] M. from Apamea (Syria). Eastern Roman official, follower of monophysite christology (→ Monophysitism); attested from *c.* AD 498, initially as overseer of taxes in Antioch [1] but soon thereafter as adviser to → Anastasius [1] I in matters of finance and religious politics. Under his influence the emperor transferred responsibility for state revenues from the curials to franchised tax-collectors (*vindices*), and in 512 wrote a monophysite addendum to the invocation of God in the *Trishagion* hymn. In 512–515/17 M. attained high office as a → *praefectus praetorio*. In 515 he used flame-throwers containing sulphur to destroy the fleet of the usurper → Vitalianus, who was threatening Constantinople. Attested again as *praefectus praetorio* under → Justinus [1] I in 519, because of his monophysite convictions he fell into disfavour with the latter (by 521 at the latest) and lost his post. His death should be set not later than 539.

PLRE 2, 726–728 Nr. 7; STEIN, Spätröm. R. 2, 177, 184, 194, 204, 210f., 213, 224, 244f., 783.

F.T.

Marion M. was installed by → Cassius [I 10] Longinus as ruler (' *tyrannos* ') of the city of Tyre in 43/2 BC. M. supported the Hasmonean → Antigonus [5], who had returned from exile, in his attempt to regain ground in Galilee and Judea against Herod (→ Herodes [1]). Herod drove M. out of Galilee, but gave gifts to some of the captured Tyrian soldiers and sent them home (Jos. BI. 1,238f.; Ant. Iud. 14,297f.).

SCHÜRER, Bd. 1, 277f.

A.ME.

Maris (Μάρις). Son of king Amisodarus. Fights under Sarpedon on the side of Troy with his brother → Atymnius [1]. When he tries to avenge his brother, who has been killed by Nestor's son → Antilochus, he is killed by the latter's brother → Thrasymedes (Hom. Il. 16,317ff.).

I.BAN.

Marissa (Hebrew *Mārē'šā*, *Mārešā*, 'settlement on the heights'; Gr. Μάρισ(σ)α; *Máris(s)a*). City in the southwest of Judea (→ *Palaestina*). M. became Edomite (Edom) after the Exile and was probably an important administrative centre. It is known to us from frequent OT references (Jos 15:44; 2 Chr 14:8f.; 20:37 inter al.), non-biblical sources (e.g. Flavius Josephus) and numerous archaeological finds from *Tell Sandahanna* ('Hill of St. Anna'; also known as *Tell Mārēšā*) located *c.* 2 km south of the modern Bet-Guvrin. Trade relations and political contacts with Ptolemaic Egypt (Zeno archive) as well as Phoenicia (Sidonian burial caves) and Idumaea are documented. In the post-biblical era, Euseb. On. 130,10f. refers to the site of the former M. as ἔρημος/*érēmos*, two miles from Eleutheriopolis, the Roman successor to M.

G. HÖLSCHER, s.v. Maris(s)a, RE 14, 1808f.; O. KEEL, M. KÜCHLER, Orte und Landschaften der Bibel 2, 1982, 854–880; A. KLONER, s.v. Mareshah (Marisa), in: NEAEHL 3, 948–957.

J.RI.

Maritima (*M. Avaticorum*, Mela 2,78; *oppidum M.*, Plin. HN 3,34; Μαρίτιμα κολωνία, Ptol. 2,10,5; *colonia M.*, Geogr. Rav. 5,3; 4,28). Capital of the Avatici (Gallia Narbonensis). It was preceded as a settlement by a pre-Roman *oppidum*, whose name is unknown. It is possible that M. was a *colonia* founded under Caesar or Augustus. The site is not precisely known: on the *Étang de la Valduc* or the *Étang de Berre* near Miramas, or, more probably, near Martigues. Important staging-post on the trade route from → Massalia to → Arelate via Saint-Blaise and La Crau.

G. BARRUOL, Les peuples préromains du Sud-Est de la Gaule, 1969, 195f.; J. CHAUSSERIE-LAPRÉE, Martigues, 1995.

Y.L.

Maritime Law see → Fenus nauticum; → Iactus; → Nautikon daneion; → Nomos nautikos; → Maritime Loans

Maritime loans In ancient Greek, a maritime loan (ML) was called ναυτικά/*nautiká*, ναυτικὸς τόκος/*nautikòs tókos* or ναυτικὸν δάνεισμα/*nautikòn dáneisma* (cf. → *nautikòn dáneion*) and in Latin it was called *traiectitia* or *pecunia nautica*; the expression → *fenus nauticum* cannot be found before Diocletian. The first mention of a ML occurs in Babylonian texts; ML are documented in Greece from the 5th cent. BC on and continued into the Roman period and the Middle Ages. Although there are fewer sources available for the Roman period than for the 4th cent. BC, we can assume that MLs were common in the Roman period as well.

A ML contract was concluded between the lender and a merchant or a ship owner, and a banker or another businessman kept a copy of the contract; most of the time the contract covered one shipping season, usually one trip or a round trip. The object of the agreement was a sum of money for which the ship, the cargo, other merchandise or the real estate of the debtor served as security. Sometimes the cargo was purchased with the borrowed money which had to be paid back with interest only after the ship had returned safely. If the ship or the cargo was lost, the debtor was released from his obligation to pay back the money owed unless he was responsible for the loss; thus the risk of the mercantile trip was borne solely by the lender, justifying the high interest (*pretium periculi*).

The text of a ML contract has survived in Demosthenes' [2] speech in court against Lacritus (*c.* 340 BC): The loan amounts to 3,000 drachmai for a voyage from Athens to the Bosporus and maybe even to the Borysthenes (modern Dnjepr), and for the return voyage; the interest is 22.5 %. 3,000 amphorae of wine from Mendes were to serve as security. Furthermore it was agreed to bring the goods purchased in the Pontus to Athens and that the debtors would pay back the loan and the interest within 20 days of their return (Dem. Or. 35,10–13). MLs were in dispute in other trials as well; the following speeches of Demosthenes feature references to ML: Phormion was granted a loan of 2,000 drachmai for a voyage to the Pontus (Dem. Or. 34,6); Dionysodorus violated a contract for a maritime loan by not returning to Athens with his ship but sailing to Rhodes instead without paying back his loan (Dem. Or. 56,3). There are also two contracts for MLs on papyrus (1st half of the 2nd cent. BC; middle of the 2nd cent. AD [3]).

According to the lenders a prerequisite for extending MLs was the general validity of any voluntarily entered agreement and that the debtor must always comport himself honourably (Dem. Or. 56,2). In an appeal to the judges at the end of a speech, Demosthenes, however, notes the economic significance of MLs and pointedly remarks that the lenders made available the money required to do commerce and that without MLs no shipowner and no passenger could go to sea (Dem. Or. 34,51).

The financial backers were usually land owners as well as businessmen and merchants with financial interests; to make money with MLs an investor had to be familiar with trade in the Mediterranean. A lender mentioned in the speech against Apaturius had for a long time been active in international trade and himself knew many merchants and ports; he had retired from commerce seven years ago and now specialized in granting loans for international commerce (Dem. Or. 33,4–5). At his death, Demosthenes' father had lent 7,000 drachmai in MLs (Dem. Or. 27,11). Bankers (→ *trapezítēs*; → *argentarius* [2]) were also involved in extending MLs; in many cases the contract was deposited with them. The written text of the contract could become important evidence in case of a lawsuit involving MLs. Working through middlemen from the financial world who were familiar with maritime trade, members of the upper class were probably active in these financial dealings as well.

In the literature, MLs were often criticized because of their inherent risk; e.g. Philostratus reports that Apollonius of Tyana felt sorry for merchants and ship owners because they had to borrow money at exorbitant rates of interest (Philostr. VA 4,32). Surprisingly most of the Church Fathers did not condemn MLs.

Recent scholarly work has demonstrated that MLs in the Roman period corresponded in their structure to Greek MLs and that there was continuity rather than change. MLs did not lose their important function when, from the 2nd cent. BC on, Roman merchants formed *societates* (→ *societas*). Cato may serve as an example of this theory provided the contracts he concluded through his freedman were a special type of ML (Plut. Cato maior 21,6). Papyri point to contracts with several debtors as well, although it is not clear whether the debtors formed a *societas*.

→ Loan;   → Commerce;   → Nauclerus;   → Nautikon daneion; → Navigation; → Interest

1 A. BISCARDI, Actio pecuniae traiecticiae. Contributo alla dottrina delle clausole penali, 1974; 2 R. BOGAERT, Banques et banquiers dans les cités grecques, 1968; 3 Id., Banquiers, courtiers et prêts maritimes à Athènes et à Alexandrie, in: Chronique d'Égypte 40, 1965, 140–156; 4 L. CASSON, New Light on Maritime Loans, P. Vindob. G. 40822, in: ZPE 84, 1990, 195–206; 5 P. MILLETT, Maritime Loans in the Structure of Credit in Fourth-Century Athens, in: GARNSEY/HOPKINS/WHITTAKER, 36–52; 6 J. ROUGÉ, Prêt et société maritimes dans le monde romain, in: D'ARMS/KOPFF, 291–303; 7 Id., Recherches sur l'organisation du commerce maritime en Méditerranée sous l'Empire romain, 1966; 8 G. E. M. DE SAINTE-CROIX, Ancient Greek and Roman Maritime Loans, in: H. EDEY, B. S. YAMEY (ed.), Debits, Credits, Finance and Profits. FS W. T. Baxter, 1974, 41–59; 9 A. TCHERNIA, Moussons et monnaies: les voies du commerce entre le monde gréco-romain et l'Inde, in: Annales 50, 1995, 991–1009; 10 J. VELISSAROPOULOS, Les nauclères grecs, 1980.

J.A.

Maritime Transport see → Navigation

Marius Oscan *praenomen* (→ Egnatius [I 3]). Attested as a Roman *nomen gentile* from the 2nd cent. BC. The most important holder is the seven-time consul M. [I 1]; the prominent Imperial-period Spanish bearer of the name, M. [II 3], is probably a descendant of family members of that Marius.

SALOMIES, 76; J. REICHMUTH, Die lateinischen Gentilicia, 1956, 99; SCHULZE 189, 360.

I. Republican Period   II. Imperial period

I. Republican Period

[I 1] M., C. The seven-time consul; victor over Jugurtha and over the Cimbri and Teutoni.

A. The rise to political prominence   B. The war against Jugurtha and the victories over the Cimbri and Teutoni   C. The return to Roman internal politics   D. The civil war between Marius and Sulla   E. Personality and political heritage

A. The rise to political prominence

Born *c.* 157 BC near Arpinum, from an equestrian (but by no means 'peasant', as claimed by tradition) family with ties to Rome. He acquired early military experience: in 134 he served with particular distinction under P. Cornelius [I 70] Scipio at Numantia in Spain (acquaintance with → Jugurtha), became military tribune and possibly fought under M'. Aquillius [I 3] or his successors in Asia [6. 30f.]. C. 123 *quaestor*. In 119 he rose to become people's tribune (probably with the support of the Caecilii Metelli), but against the strong resistance of consul L. Caecilius [I 24] Metellus Delmaticus promulgated a law directed at preventing the direct influencing of voters in the balloting procedure (Cic. Leg. 3,38f.; → *comitia*). It was probably because of this that his 117 campaign for aedileship failed. However, a year later M. was able to obtain election as *praetor urbanus* for 115, although himself barely securing acquittal on a charge of seeking office by devious means (→ *ambitus*). As *propr.* in 114 he was successful in keeping the peace in Hispania citerior; his relatives probably succeeded in acquiring the mines in the province [5. 23], thus laying the foundation of their descendants' wealth (→ M. [II 3]). In 110 he married Iulia [1], from the patrician family of the Iulii Caesares (later to be the aunt of Caesar), who in 109 bore him a son, C.M. [I 2]. In 109 Q. Caecilius [I 30] Metellus Numidicus chose him as his legate and representative for the war against Jugurtha in Africa, where M. again distinguished himself.

B. The war against Jugurtha and the victories over the Cimbri and Teutoni

When in 108 M. wanted to stand for the consulate, Metellus at first refused to release him, and this led to a serious rift between the two men (Sall. Iug. 63–65). When M. was finally able to stand, he sharply attacked Metellus (for his supposed failures in the waging of the war) and the nobles supporting him, thus by the support of the people and the equestrians (who saw their economic interests harmed by the war; → *equites Romani*) securing the consulate for 107. He obtained supreme command against Jugurtha by plebiscite, although the Senate had already extended the period of Metellus' command. M. built up the army in Africa anew, resorting to the recruitment of propertyless volunteers (Sall. Iug. 86,2). The 107–105 campaigns, however, were indecisive until M.' *quaestor*, P. → Cornelius [I 90] Sulla, succeeded in persuading king Bocchus [1] I of Mauretania to deliver up Jugurtha (for this reason Sulla later claimed credit for success in the war for himself).

The severe Roman defeats in Gaul at the hands of the Cimbri and Teutoni(→ Cimbri) then led to M.' election *in absentia* as *cos. II* for 104, against the rules of the → *cursus honorum*. After his triumph over Jugurtha on 1 Jan. 104, M. took over the remnants of the Roman army in Upper Italy, which had already been re-organised by P. → Rutilius Rufus, and – continually elected consul until 100 BC- improved the training and equipment of the troops, thereby and by the admission of volunteers becoming the founder of the professional Roman army ('Marian reform' of the army; [8], → Armies). It was not until 102 that he defeated the Teutoni and Ambrones at Aquae Sextiae (Aix-en-Provence), then in 101 together with Q. Lutatius [I 3] Catulus the Cimbri at Vercellae (near Rovigo in Upper Italy) after the latter had crossed the Alps; the two men shared a triumph.

C. The return to Roman internal politics

Upon his return to Rome, M. was to a large extent isolated in the Senate, as he lacked sufficient allies for his internal political aims, while the people and the equestrians continued to support him. Already in 103 this had led to his using the help of the people's tribune L. Appuleius [I 11] Saturninus to obtain land for the veterans of the Africa campaign; in 100, with the express support of M. (and against the resistance of Metellus Numidicus, who consequently had to go into exile), Appuleius again proceeded with the establishment of colonies. Then, however, with his ally the *praetor* C. → Servilius Glaucia, who had ambitions for the consulate for 99, he sought to further his own political goals by force, whereupon M. put down the uprising and Saturninus, Glaucia and their supporters were killed. But M.' relationship with the Senate did not improve, as he obstinately prevented the return of Metellus. His hopes for the censorship coming to nothing, M. went to Asia Minor, negotiated with → Mithradates VI and became *augur* in his absence. After his return in 97, M. appears scarcely to have taken any open part in internal politics; we have evidence only for his intervention in court on behalf of some of his supporters. He seems to have supported both the desire of the Italians for citizenship and the political claims of the equestrians, and probably for that reason opposed the conservative reform programme of the people's tribune M. Livius [I 7] Drusus [1] in 91. When, however, in that year the Senate allowed king Bocchus I to dedicate a group of statues on the Capitol showing the surrender of Jugurtha to Sulla, only the sudden outbreak of the → Social War [3] prevented M. from opposing it by force. In that war he fought with success against the Marsi, but – unlike Sulla – appears not to have put himself forward for further military command (partly on account of his advanced age).

D. The civil war between Marius and Sulla

As the Social War was nearing its end, the war in the east against Mithridates VI was already looming. The military command was set to give new impetus to M.' career, but his younger rival Sulla became consul in 88 and was given supreme command. When Sulla was already with the army, a plebiscite forcibly carried through by the people's tribune P. → Sulpicius, who enjoyed the support of M., took the command away from Sulla and transferred it to M. To everyone's surprise, Sulla ignored the people's decision, led his army against Rome and had his opponents killed. In dramatic flight, M. escaped his pursuers, narrowly avoiding execution at Minturnae (Cic. Planc. 26; Cic. Sest. 50; Cic. Pis. 43 *et passim*), and finally joined his veterans in Africa together with his son. When in 87 the consul and Sulla's opponent L. Cornelius [I 18] Cinna was driven from Rome, M. used the opportunity to return with his own followers. With Cinna he organised the taking of Rome, the two men exacting cruel revenge on their political opponents, either actual or supposed. Appointed consul for 86 (together with Cinna), M. died on 13 Jan. the same year at the age of 70 (Posidonius' eyewitness account of the ailing M. in Plut. Marius 45).

E. Personality and political heritage

Being a → *novus homo*, in spite of his significant military successes M. was always destined to failure when it came to Roman internal politics, as he never succeeded in finding long-term allies among the nobility. The rift with his former supporters, the Caecilii Metelli, was momentous, as they henceforth patronised M.' opponent Sulla. In internal politics, M. never carried through ideas of reform. Generous though he was in granting Roman citizenship as a commander on the battlefield (Cic. Balb. 46; Val. Max. 5,2,46), his attitude towards the Italians in their demand for citizenship was determined by tactical considerations (App. B Civ. 1,306). In the end, his personal ambition and error of judgement regarding Sulla's character triggered Rome's first great civil war, preparing the way for Sulla's (and later Caesar's) use of the army in internal politics (his so-called reform of the army probably represented only the culmination of the tendency towards a professional volunteer army). The late Republic (Cicero) and early Empire (*elogium*: InscrIt 13,3 no. 83), while not glossing over the discontinuities in his career, nevertheless regarded him as the 'second saviour of Rome' and a leading member of Rome's ruling elite. Main sources: numerous mentions by Cicero (in part from personal recollection: poem *Marius*); Sall. Iug. Liv. Per. 66–80; *elogium* (InscIt 13,3, no. 83: *cursus honorum*); App. B Civ. 1,130–346; Plut. Marius; Collection of sources: [7].

1 Badian, Clientelae, 192–225; 2 E. Badian, Studies in Greek and Roman History, 1963; 3 Id., Marius and the Nobles, in: Durham University Journal 25, 1963/64, 141–154; 4 CAH 9, ²1995, Index s.v. M.; 5 T. F. Carney, A Biography of C. M., 1961; 6 R. J. Evans, Gaius M., 1994 (lit.); 7 A. H. J. Greenidge, A. M. Clay, Sources for

Roman History 133–70 B.C., ²1960; 8 E. Gabba, Republican Rome, the Army and the Allies, 1976, 1–19; 9 J. van Oothegem, Gaius M., 1964; 10 V. Werner, Quantum bello optimus, tantum pace pessimus. Studien zum M.-Bild in der antiken Geschichtsschreibung, 1995; 11 R. Weynand, s.v. M. (14), RE Suppl. 6, 1363–1425 (sources).

[I 2] M., C. Son of M. [I 1], born 109 BC; in 93 married to Licinia [6], daughter of M. Licinius [I 10] Crassus. In 90 and 89 he served in the → Social War [3]. When L. → Cornelius [I 90] Sulla marched on Rome in 88, he fled the city with his father and reached Africa. Detained there by the Numidian king → Hiempsal [2], he was able to elude capture, and in 87 returned to Rome with his father (Nep. Att. 2; Plut. Marius 35,8–12; Liv. Per. 77). When in 82 the return of Sulla was imminent, M. (only 27 years old) became consul. He fortified Praeneste, and even before the final battle ordered the assassination of the leading members of the aristocracy in Rome. Defeated by Sulla at Sacriportus, he fled to Praeneste and was besieged there by Sulla's legate Q. Lucretius [I 6] Afella. An attempt by the Samnites to free him failed, and M. was killed while fleeing Praeneste (Sall. Hist. 1,35f. M.; Liv. Per. 86–88; Vell. Pat. 2,26,1; App. B Civ. 1,8–94; MRR 2,65f.).   K.-L.E.

[I 3] M., C. The 'fake M.' (for his legitimacy, however, see [1] with sources) appeared in Rome in 45 BC claiming to be the grandson of M. [I 2]. In the autumn, Caesar banished him from Italy; in March 44 M. returned, sacrificed to the dead Caesar and gathered followers, whereupon in April M. Antonius had his rival seized amidst great bloodshed and killed without trial.

1 F. J. Meijer, M.' Grandson, in: Mnemosyne 39, 1986, 112–121.

[I 4] M., L. *Tribunus plebis* 62 BC, in collaboration with M. → Porcius Cato he introduced a law against exaggerated reports of victory; 61 legate to C. Pomptinus in Gallia Narbonensis (Val. Max. 2,8,1; Cass. Dio 37, 48,1f.). The co-prosecutor against M. Aemilius [I 38] Scaurus could be M.' son (Ascon. 22; 29c).   Jö.F.

[I 5] M., M. Quaestor probably 82 BC at the latest. By 76 at the latest an officer under Q.→ Sertorius in Spain; in 75 sent by Sertorius to king → Mithridates VI in Asia, on whose side he fought, but in 72 defeated by L. Licinius [I 26] Lucullus near Lemnos (Plut. Sertorius 24,2; Plut. Lucullus 12,5; App. Mith. 332–338).

C. F. Konrad, Plutarch's Sertorius, 1994, 200–202.
                                                                          K.-L.E.

[I 6] M., M. Cultured close friend, possibly even a relation of → Cicero, who wrote Fam. 7,1–4 to him; resident in Campania, and owing to his gout an infrequent traveller (Cic. Ad Q. Fr. 2,8,2f.).   Jö.F.

[I 7] M. Gratidianus, M. Natural son of M. Gratidius [2] from *Arpinum* and Maria [1], sister of C. Marius [I 1], and adopted by her brother M. M. (praetor 102 BC [?] in *Hispania*, MRR 1,568); thus a relative of

Cicero. Originally a businessman from the equestrian order, as a gifted speaker (Cic. Brut. 223) M. became people's tribune under the regime of L. Cornelius [I 18] Cinna in 87; he was regarded as responsible for the suicide of Q. Lutatius [I 3] Catulus (Liv. Per. 79; Schol. Bernensia Lucan. 2,173 p. 61 U.; MRR 2,27; 52). As praetor in 85 he promulgated an edict withdrawing the devalued *denarius* that had been issued since 91 (→ Livy [I 7]) and introducing penalties for abuse of the highly fluctuating value of gold [1]. This made him so popular that the people of the city of Rome set up statues of M. in their districts and sacrificed in front of them (Cic. Off. 3,80; Plin. HN 33,132; 34,27), and in 84 he was re-elected praetor. Upon the capture of Rome by the Sullani (→ Cornelius [I 90] Sulla) in Nov. 82 M. was taken prisoner and cruelly put to death at the tomb of Catulus, with the decisive participation of L. Sergius → Catilina (Q. Cicero, Commentariolum petitionis10; Sall. Hist. 1,44; 55,14 M.; Liv. Per. 88; Ascon. 87; 90 C., etc.).

1 M. H. CRAWFORD, The Edict of M.M.Gratidianus, in: PCPhS N.S. 14, 1969, 1–4. K.-L.E.

II. IMPERIAL PERIOD

[II 1] Imperator Caesar M. Aurelius Marius Augustus Proclaimed Augustus in Gaul in succession to → Postumus, probably in May or June AD 269; murdered after a few months (PIR² A 1555; PLRE 1, 562).

RIC 5,2, 374–378; A. CHASTAGNOL, L'empereur gaulois M. dans l'Histoire Auguste, in: A. ALFÖLDI (ed.), Historia-Augusta Colloquium 1971, 1974, 51–58; KIENAST, ²1996, 245. A.B.

[II 2] P. M. *Consul ordinarius* in AD 62; *curator aquarum* 64–66. He never bore the cognomen *Celsus*, long ascribed to him [1. 334]. PIR² M 294.

1 W. ECK, Ergänzungen zu den Fasti Consulares des 1. und 2. Jahrhunderts n.Chr., in: Historia 24, 1975.

[II 3] S. M. A rich citizen from Corduba in Hispania Baetica, his wealth came mostly from the gold-mines and silver-mines in the *montes Mariani* (Sierra Morena). *Amicus* of → Tiberius. In AD 25 he was accused by a compatriot but protected by Tiberius. When in 33 he supposedly failed to relinquish his daughter to Tiberius, he was accused by the latter, and, upon being condemned, thrown from the Tarpeian Rock (→ Tarpeium saxum); his wealth was seized for the *fiscus* (Tac. Ann. 6,19,1). Whether he is to be identified with a S. M. in a *hospitium* agreement ([1. 217–222] = AE 1991, 1017) must remain uncertain. PIR² M 295.

1 W. ECK, F. FERNÁNDEZ, Sex. Marius in einem Hospitiumvertrag aus der Baetica, in: ZPE 85, 1991.

[II 4] A. M.Celsus Legate to *legio XV Apollinaris,* in AD 63 he led it into war against the Parthians (→ Parthian Wars). → Galba called upon him as an adviser, and sought through him to put down the revolts of the Prae-

torians in Jan. 69, but without success. → Otho protected M. against the anger of the soldiers rebelling against Galba, and made him one of his *amici*. One of the leaders of Otho's army against Vitellius, during the battle of Bedriacum he advised the soldiers to give up the fight. It was probably for this reason that → Vitellius did not punish him; in July/ August 69 he was even allowed to retain his suffect consulate, to which he had already been appointed by Nero. M. succeeded in gaining the trust of → Vespasianus, who named him commander of the army in Lower Germany probably in the spring of 71. Under M.' leadership, in the spring of 73 the *legio VI Victrix* erected a victory monument at Xanten ([1. 195ff.] = AE 1979, 413). Immediately thereafter he was transferred as consular legate to Syria, where in the same year or at the beginning of 74 he was replaced by Ulpius → Traianus; perhaps M. had died in Syria. M. was probably the son of M. [II 5]. PIR² M 296.

1 C. B. RÜGER, Ein Siegesdenkmal der legio VI victrix, in: BJ 179, 1979; 2 ECK, Statthalter, 137f.

[II 5] Q. M.Celsus *Praetor peregrinus* in AD 31; perhaps the father of M. [II 4]. PIR² M 297.

ECK, Statthalter, 137f.

[II 6] M. Cordus M. may have held office in the province of Asia at the beginning of Nero's reign; there he possibly replaced Iunius [II 38] Silanus, who had been murdered by Agrippina [3] or Nero.

PIR² M 299; G. R. STUMPF, Numismatische Studien, 1986, 171–173; VOGEL-WEIDEMANN, 400–405; W. WEISER, Namen römischer Statthalter auf Münzen Kleinasiens. Corrigenda et Addenda zu Gerd Stumpfs Münzcorpus, in: ZPE 123, 1998, 278f.

[II 7] C. M. Etruscus Galianus Senator; military tribune with the *legio II Adiutrix* in *Pannonia*, and at that time appointed quaestor.

L. KOCSIS, in: Budapest Regisegei 28, 1992, 120.

[II 8] M. Maturus Presidial procurator of → *Alpes maritimae* in AD 69, he tried to prevent the followers of → Otho from taking over his province. He was loyal to → Vitellius until the late autumn of 69, but then made his troops swear an oath to → Vespasianus. The latter promoted him to procurator in Hispania Tarraconensis, where together with the governor Aurelius [II 14] Fulvus he took part in a legal dispute (AE 1952, 122). PIR² M 306.

[II 9] L. M. Maximus Cos. ord. in AD 232; probably the son of M. [II 10]. PIR² M 307.

[II 10] L. M. Maximus Perpetuus Aurelianus Son of M. [II 12], brother of M. [II 13]. Senator. M.' career, which began under Commodus, comes down to us in its entirety in CIL VI 1450 = ILS 2935. In AD 193 legionary legate in Moesia inferior; there he joined → Septimius Severus, who employed him in the civil wars as a military commander, at Byzantium against → Pescennius Niger as well as at Lugdunum against → Clodius [II 1]

Albinus. Subsequently praetorian governor of Belgica, then suffect consul in 198 or 199; consular legate of Germania inferior, then (attested in 208) in Syria Coele(→ Coele Syria), where he is frequently mentioned in the papyri of Dura-Europus. He was finally proconsul in Africa, likewise in Asia, for two years; the periods of office are under → Caracalla, but the sequence is disputed (see [1. 84f.]). Appointed *praefectus urbi* by Macrinus; *cos. ord. II* in 223.

Various people honoured M. with statues at his house on the *m ons Caelius* in Rome. He was active as a writer, especially as a historian, his works still being widely available in → Ammianus' time. The extent to which his biographies of the Roman emperors since Trajan formed part of the → *Historia Augusta* is disputed (cf. e.g. [2. 30–45], who regards M. only as a subsidiary source; on the other hand, for M. as the basis of the HA [3. 2679–2757]). PIR² M 308.

1 THOMASSON, Fasti Africani; 2 R. SYME, Historia Augusta Papers, 1983; 3 A. R. BIRLEY, Marius Maximus: The Consular Biographer, in: ANRW II 34.3, 1997.

[II 11] Q. M. Nepos Senator who asked → Tiberius for financial support; the emperor complied with his request, but exposed him publicly; later expelled from the Senate (Sen. Ben. 2,7,1f.; Tac. Ann. 2,48,3). PIR² M 309.

[II 12] L. M. Perpetuus Equestrian procurator, perhaps from Africa; son of the *scriba librarius* of the same name (ILAlg 592); father of M. [II 10] and M. [II 13]. Among others, M. probably had the praetorian prefect Gavius [II 6] Maximus to thank for his rise [1. 157ff.]. He was *procurator monetae, procur. vicesimae hereditatium, procur. stationis hereditatium, procur. provinciae Lugdunensis et Aquitaniae.* PIR² M 313.

1 W. ECK, in: Picus 8, 1988, 157–162.

[II 13] L. M. Perpetuus Son of M. [II 12], brother of M. [II 10]. M.' senatorial career began under Commodus. Military tribune in Syria, then *quaestor Augusti*, uncertain whether already under → Septimius Severus. Legionary legate in *Syria Coele* (→ Coele Syria), governor of Arabia under Septimius Severus; the period is disputed. Suffect consul, consular legate of *Moesia inferior*, governor of the *tres Daciae*, attested in AD 214; later proconsul of Asia or Africa (AE 1987, 69 = CIL VI 41188; cf. also 41187; PISO, FPD I 169–77). PIR² M 311.

[II 14] L. M. Perpetuus Son of M. [II 13]. *Cos. ord.* 237. PIR² M 312.

[II 15] M. Priscus From the province of Hispania Baetica; admitted to the Senate under Nero (or Galba or Vespasian). Suffect consul under → Domitianus *c.* AD 85; proconsul of Africa, probably 97/8. While there he allowed himself to be bribed to a massive extent, and was prosecuted by the Senate. Pliny (Ep. 2,11,17–24; 2,12,1; 3,9,3; 6,29,9) reports on the trial at the end of 99/beginning of 100, he and Tacitus having represented the prosecution. The bribery money was assigned to the

→ *aerarium*; M. himself lost his senatorial rank and had to go into exile outside Italy. PIR² M 315.

THOMASSON, Fasti Africani, 49.

[II 16] M. Pudens Procurator, either in Gallia Narbonensis or of the *patrimonium* in Rome under Marcus [2] Aurelius. His successor in office was Domitius Marsianus (AE 1962, 183 = [1. 349–366]). Possibly brother to M. [II 12]. PIR² M 316.

1 H.-G. PFLAUM, Une lettre de promotion de l'empereur Marc Aurèle pour un procurateur ducénaire de Gaule Narbonnaise, in: BJ 171, 1971.

W. ECK, in: Picus 8, 1988, 157ff.

[II 17] M. Secundus Presumably of equestrian rank, held an office in Egypt in AD 217, when Macrinus came to power. Macrinus took him into the Senate and made him praetorian governor of *Syria Phoenice*, where he died in the uprising against Macrinus (Cass. Dio 79,35,1ff.). PIR² M 318.

[II 18] M. Siculus From Urvinum Mataurense, where he held various municipal offices. Subsequently *tribunus militum legionis XII, praefectus duorum principum* (uncertain in which connection) and *praefectus* in the fleet of Cn. Lentulus in Sicily (CIL XI 6058); identified with the T. Marius in Valerius Maximus (7,8,6), who throughout his life maintained that he would make Augustus his heir, having achieved the highest military offices and great wealth through him. In the event, he did not even mention him in his will. PIR² M 319.

DEMOUGIN, 38ff. Nr. 25.

[II 19] L. M. Vegetinus Marcianus Minicianus Myrtilianus Senator, perhaps from Hispania Baetica. After a not very distinguished career, during which his highest office appears to have been the *praefectura frumenti dandi*, he became suffect consul, not before the 3rd cent. AD.

CABALLOS, Senadores 1, 208ff.; PIR² M 323.   W.E.

[II 20] Claudius M. Victor (or Victorius) Teacher of rhetoric in Marseille (active during the 420s/430s AD), author of the *Alethia*, an OT epic in 3 bks. He begins with the Creation and ends with the destruction of Sodom and Gomorrah. If Gennadius' note (Vir. ill. 61) is correct, a 4th bk. taking the biblical story up to the death of Abraham has been lost. The author's comprehensive use of Christian exegesis gives the poem the character of a comm. in verse. On the other hand, his familiarity with philosophical terminology and his anthropological digressions suggest the influence of → Lucretius [III 1]: A prayer (*precatio*) prefacing the poem defines the work as a didactic poem aimed at young people. The *Alethia* is extant only in one MS from the 9th cent. M.V. may have influenced the biblical epic of Alcimus Ecdicius → Avitus [2], but was himself only seldom read in the Middle Ages.

→ Biblical poetry

EDITIONS: C. SCHENKL, CSEL 16, 1888, 335–498; P. F. HOVINGH, CCL 128, 1960, 115–193, 269–299.
LITERATURE: H. H. HOMEY, Studien zur Alethia des C.M.V., 1972.   M.RO.

[II 21] C. M. Victorinus
A. BIOGRAPHY   B. WORKS   C. PHILOSOPHY AND THEOLOGY

A. BIOGRAPHY

M.V. was probably born towards the end of the 3rd cent. AD in Africa (*Afer*), and from about 340 taught rhetoric in Rome. Under emperor Constantius [2] II (337–361) he held the chair of rhetoric in Rome and bore the title *vir clarissimus*; in advanced age this prominent scholar converted to Christianity (perhaps in 355/6; Aug. Conf. 8,2,1–3,5), which evidently aroused great public interest. M.V. contributed to the formation of a specialist Latin terminology for philosophy; he is at the same time the first Latin Christian whose works show Neoplatonic influences, and the first Latin commentator on → Paulus. He died a while before 386 (Aug. Conf. 8,2,3), after having ceased his teaching activities in 362 owing to the anti-Christian measures of → Iulianus [11].

B. WORKS

M.V.' output comprises in particular treatises on grammar, rhetoric, dialectic, and after his conversion theology (cf. Cassiod. Inst. p. 128,14–129,12 MYNORS; Jer. Contra Rufinum 1,16; Aug. Conf. 8,2,3). The first category includes an *Ars grammatica*, which became merged with the grammar of → Asmonius (CPL 1543). Of the second group of works we have a comm. on Cicero's *De inventione* under the title *Explanatio in Rhetoricam Ciceronis*, in which individual terms and sentences are explained (CPL 1544). The third group of writings is to a large extent lost; they comprised (for another view [10. 187–190]) translations and commentaries with regard to Aristotle's work on categories and Porphyry's introduction to Aristotle, Cicero's Dialogues and 'Platonic books'. He produced his theological works after his conversion; they include commentaries on St. Paul's letters to the Galatians, Philippians and Ephesians (CPL 98), relying not on Greek Christian models (→ Origenes) but on the methods of philosophical commentaries. Nine tracts on the Trinity must also be mentioned, including four books against → Arianism *Ad Candidum Arrianum* (CPL 95; [5. 95–173]); the treatise *De generatione divini verbi ad Candidum* [5. 15–48] and three hymns *De trinitate* [5. 285–305]. The Arian Candidus in these works is an invention of M.V.; his second letter (CPL 681) contains in addition two translations of Greek sources on the Arian dispute (CPG 2, 2025a/2045a).

C. PHILOSOPHY AND THEOLOGY

M.V. adopted fundamental principles of (Porphyrian) → Neoplatonism, but inseparably linked them to his specific project of a Christian theology of the Trinity and to his personal conception of God [10]. In this connection he took up some of → Porphyry's specifics, e.g. his triad of the One/Being, Life and Thought (*esse, vita, sapientia*: Mar. Vict. *A dversus Arium* 1,26 and 4,7) and his distinction of pure, unqualified Being (*esse*) from determined, intelligible Being (*sic esse*: ibid. 1,29) as an interpretation of the two 'hypostases' of → Plotinus. The spirit is a bond between Father and Son (*patris et filii copula*: Hymnus 1,4). M.V. uses Porphyrian Neoplatonism to explain the ὁμοούσιος/homoûsios ('essential equivalence') between father and son of the Nicene creed; thus he lends the Christian Trinity the structure of the Porphyrian triad. In his commentaries on Paul, M.V. lays stress on Paul's dismissal of works: *ipsa enim fides sola iustificationem dat* ('justification is provided solely by faith itself', ad Gal. 2,15), because he understands this against the Platonic backdrop of the opposition between the *vita contemplativa* of the intellect and *vita activa* ('theoretical' and practical life). Through his friend Simplicianus, M.V. probably played an indirect but important role in the emergence of a Milan circle of Christian Neoplatonists, which in turn provided → Ambrosius and → Augustinus with vital stimulation.

EDITIONS: 1 A. LOCHER, 2 vols., 1972/1976 (critical review by P. HADOT, in: Latomus 35, 1976, 133–142); 2 I. MARIOTTI, Marii Victorini ars grammatica, 1967, 65–96; 3 C. HALM, Rhetores Latini Minores, 1863, 155–304 Explanatio; 4 F. GORI, CSEL 83/2, 1986 (Comm. Gal., Phil., Eph.); 5 P. HENRY, P. HADOT, CSEL 83/1, 1971, 54–277 (theology).
LITERATURE: 6 K. BERGNER, Der Sapientia-Begriff im Kommentar des M.V. zu Ciceros Jugendwerk De inventione, 1994; 7 E. BENZ, M.V. und die Entwicklung der abendländischen Willensmetaphysik (= Forschungen zur Kirchen- und Geistesgesch. 1), 1932; 8 ST. A. COOPER, Metaphysics and Morals in M.V.' Commentary on the Letter to the Ephesians, 1995; 9 W. ERDT, M.V. Afer, der erste lateinische Pauluskommentator, 1980; 10 P. HADOT, M.V., 1971; 11 G. MADEC, P. L. SCHMIDT, in: HLL, vol. 5, § 564; 12 W. STEINMANN, Die Seelenmetaphysik des M.V., 1990; 13 A. ZIEGENAUS, Die trinitarische Ausprägung der göttlichen Seinsfülle nach M.V., 1972.   C.M.

[II 22] Bishop of Aventicum(Avenches; the episcopal see was later transferred to Lausanne) from 574 to 594; born 530/1, probably in Autun of a distinguished Roman family. M. wrote a world chronicle of the world, continuing that of → Prosper Tiro of Aquitaine from 455 to 581. Sources: consular lists; *Annales Gallici*; *Annales Ravennates* for 455–467; a source from Lombardy for 532–579; a Burgundian-Frankish source for 500–581; for 571–581 his own first-hand experience. M. reports on events in Italy, with particular attention to the → Lombards; of especial value are his comments on current home events and on the Burgundians. His work, which linguistically speaking bears witness to the dissolution of the case system, remained without influence during the Middle Ages.

EDITIONS: PL 72, 791–802; TH. MOMMSEN, MGH AA 11, 1894, 225–239; J. FAVROD, La chronique de M. d'Avenches (455–581), 1991.

BIBLIOGRAPHY: W. ARNDT, Bischof M. v. Aventicum, 1875; C. SANTSCHI, La chronique de l'évêque M., in: Rev. Historique Vaudoise 76 (1968), 17–34; J. FAVROD, Les sources et la chronologie de M. d'Avenches, in: Francia 17,1, 1990, 1–21; S. TEILLET, Des Goths à la nation gothique, 1984, 406f.   J.M.A.-N.

[II 23] M. Mercator Opponent of the Pelagians in the 5th cent. AD; little is known of his life (sources: Aug. Epist. 193; Jer. Ep. 154,3.). He probably came from Campania. Before 418, on a journey to Africa, he made the acquaintance of → Augustinus and wrote two lost works against → Pelagius and Caelestius. Together with Jerome and others he prepared the proclamations, *Tractoria* (CPL 1645), of Pope Zosimus (417/8). In the writings and translation of a dossier from 429/430 directed against Nestorius, collected or written by M. shortly after the Council of Ephesus (431), extant only in the *Collectio Palatina* (Pal.), we encounter him as a monk in the vicinity of Constantinople. He largely follows Augustine in the dispute against Pelagianism (CPL 780; 781), and → Cyrillus [2] of Alexandria in that against Nestorius, but against the Pelagians relies on Nestorius (Pal. 30–35). The compiler of Pal., which was directed (*c.* 543/550) against Antiochene Christology in the dispute concerning → Origenes, took M. up, as M. traced Pelagianism back to the teaching of → Theodorus of Mopsuestia (cf. Pal. 51: CPG 3860), supposedly brought to Rome by → Rufinus the Syrian (CPL 200; Pal. 3; 15). As regards Pelagius (CPL 754), M. attests (CPL 781; Pal. 36: 69,17–29) that the controversy also rests on the fact that the concept of the Church had changed since the 4th cent. The reply to the so-called Counter-Anathematisms of Nestorius (CPG 5761) in Pal. 37 with a translation of the anathematisms of Cyrillus [2] (CPG 5317) probably is by M., while the subsequent critical remarks in Pal. 37 may be ascribed to the compiler of Pal. (CPL 664b), who, unlike M. (Pal. 18), links Nestorius not to Paulus of Samosata but to Photeinus of Sirmium (81,39–83,8).

P. CHIESA, Ad verbum o ad sensum?, in: Medioevo & Rinascimento 1, 1987, 1–51; A. LEPSKA, L'originalité des répliques de M.M. à Julien d'Eclane, in: Revue d'Histoire Ecclésiastique 27, 1931, 572–579; B. NISTERS, Die Collectio Palatina, in: Theologische Quartalschrift 113, 1932, 119–137; S. PRETE, Mario Mercatore polemista antipelagiano, in: Scrinium Theologicum 11, 1958; Id., Il 'Commonitorium' nella letteratura christiana antica, 1962; J. SPEIGL, Der Pelagianismus auf dem Konzil von Ephesus, in: Annuarium historiae conciliorum 1, 1969, 1–14; O. WERMELINGER, Rom und Pelagius, thesis 1975; Id., M.M. Denkschrift in der Angelegenheit des Caelestius, in: Adversus tempus. Mélanges W. Rordorf, 1983, 62–71.   K.U.

Market

I. ANCIENT ORIENT AND EGYPT   II. CLASSICAL ANTIQUITY   III. EARLY MIDDLE AGES

I. ANCIENT ORIENT AND EGYPT

The concept of the market is the subject of controversial discussions in classical Middle Eastern studies and Egyptology, since there was no term, neither in the Mesopotamian area nor in Egypt, that clearly designated the market as a place and a *modus operandi*. Background of the discussion are, on the one hand, the studies regarding pre-modern societies inspired by K. POLANYI (among others by M. FINLEY for the classical world), according to which a market did not exist as a system of supply and demand with the result of price formation. On the other hand, there are scholars who impose, in some cases rather without reflection, modern concepts coined by neo-classical economical theory upon the economies of the Ancient Orient (of Mesopotamia and Egypt).

The question of the existence of market mechanisms or market development in Ancient Oriental societies needs to be dealt with against the background of the predominant economic structures. The economies of Mesopotamia as well as of Egypt, both being agrarian economies, were regulated by institutional households (temple, palace), which integrated more or less completely the entire population (→ Oikos economy), i.e. almost all the needs of the individual were satisfied by the *oikos*. Even in those cases where parts of the population individually practised agriculture for their self-supply (→ Subsistence farming), hardly any room remained for market exchange, since everything that was produced was also self-consumed. There is no evidence for individual production of cash crops (i.e. production with the purpose of market exchange). Insofar, only basic beginnings of markets existed, in terms of what became manifest, for instance, in the Athenian → Agora.

→ Money, money economy; → Commerce; → Oikos economy; → Economy

1 M. FINLEY, The Ancient Economy, ²1985; 2 J. RENGER, Formen des Zugangs zu den lebensnotwendigen Gütern: Die Austauschverhältnisse in der altbabylonischen Zeit, in: Altorientalische Forschungen 20, 1993, 87–114 (with extensive bibliography); 3 Id., On Economic Structures in Ancient Mesopotamia, in: Orientalia NS 63, 1994, 157–208 (with bibliography); 4 P. VARGYAS, The Problem of Private Economy in the Ancient Near East, in: Bibliotheca Orientalis 44, 1987, 376–385.   J.RE.

II. CLASSICAL ANTIQUITY

The word market can be understood either as a place serving essentially the exchange of goods, or as a system of exchange, in which supply and demand meet. It is controversial as to what extent a market in the latter sense emerged during Graeco-Roman antiquity. Markets in pre-archaic times are suspected only in power centres, particularly in the vicinity of the palace (ἀγορή/

agorē: Hom. Il. 8,489–99; 11,807–8), but in the course of the formation of the → polis during the 8th cent. BC they took root near the coast (ἐμπόριον, → *empórion*) and within urban centres (Greek ἀγορά/→ *agorá*; Lat. → *forum* ; → *macellum*). Periodic markets and fairs are documented from the beginning of the Classical period until Late Antiquity in rural areas and on the occasion of religious festivals (Greek πανήγυρις/*panḗgyris*; Lat. *nundinae, conventus, mercatus*). Markets could also be established spontaneously, e.g. to supply soldiers on military campaigns (cf. e.g. Thuc. 6,44,2f., 415 BC; Xen. An. 2,3,24ff.; 3,2,20f.; 4,8,23f.). A special Roman development were private markets on large estates; a neighbouring city had the right to object to the establishing of such → *nundinae*, which were subject to the control of a great land owner (Plin. Ep. 5,4). Private houses, workshops and stores (*tabernae*) that were not tied to a market further served as places of exchange.

A. GREECE B. ROME

A. GREECE

In Greece, permanent markets formed on the urban *agoraí*, but they remained subordinate to the political function of these public meeting places. Since purchase, exchange and banking transactions were largely settled in booths (σκηναί/*skēnaí*) and on tables (τράπεζαι/ *trápezai*, 'banks'), the development of the commercial aspect of the *agorá* is difficult to determine archaeologically. However, some stores, workshops and the public mint are attested for the Athenian *Agorá* from the late 6th/early 5th cents. BC based on material remains and finds of coins. The construction of permanent buildings, in particular market halls with colonnades (*mákelloi*) only began during the 3rd cent. BC. Trading on the market was, with the exemption of special regulations, subject to a tax (τέλος/*télos*) that represented a considerable source of income for the cities or rulers. Supervisors (→ *agoranómoi/ metronómoi*) were in charge of keeping order and ensuring the validity of measures and weights. Greek markets do not seem to have been controlled beyond this, apart from the grain markets, which were supervised by → *sitophýlakes* or *agoranómoi*.

Periodic markets and fairs took place in rural areas (Dem. Or. 23,39) and on the occasion of regional and supraregional gatherings. Again, it is difficult to verify the latter in detail, but they are assumed as a self-explanatory event during larger festivals in Hellenistic and Roman times (Men. Fr. 416 KÖRTE = fr. 481 KOCK); Polybius mentions an annual *agorá* and *panḗgyris* of the Aetolian League, which has sometimes been understood as an indication of a commercial market on the occasion of the federal elections (Pol. 5,8,4ff; cf. Cic. Tusc. 5,3; Str. 10,5,4: Delos). Markets held on the occasion of festivals are furthermore detectable indirectly through documented epigraphical provisions regarding market supervision. Thus, *hieromnémones* (ἱερομνήμονες, 'temple supervisors') are at-

tested for Tegea, who had to arrange 'everything pertaining to the goods' at the festival of Athena Alea in Tegea (early 4th cent. BC, LSCG 67,26–27). An *agoranómos*, elected for the → Panathenaea, who kept the grain prices low and supervised 'the other goods', is mentioned in an inscription from Ilium (3rd cent. BC, I. Ilion 3, cf. LSCG 65,99; Andania, 92–91 BC). From the 2nd cent. BC, the office of *panēgyriárchēs* (πανηγυρι-άρχης, 'head of the *panḗgyris*') is attested epigraphically [4. 1522], but it remains uncertain whether this office served alone or only partially the supervision of the market. Nevertheless, an inscription from Lycian Oenoanda (SEG 38, 1462, AD 124/5) determines that at the *panēgyris* taking place every four years, three *panēgyriárchai* were to keep order on the *agorá*, see to the supply of food for the visitors, the supervision of the prices, the examination of the goods and the punishment of offenders. Finally, the provisions for tax exemption (ἀτέλεια/*atéleia*) for participants of a *panḗgyris* also suggest its function as a market (LSCG 65,101; Andania, 92–91 BC). Yet it remains unclear as to what extent the markets of the *panēgýreis* functioned as general fairs or confined themselves to accommodating the visitors of the festival.

B. ROME

The development in Rome differs insofar from the Greek cities as that the oldest *fora* (→ *forum*) appear to have been food markets (*Forum Boarium*: cattle market; *Forum Holitorium*: vegetable market). Only the later → *Forum Romanum* united commercial, religious, political and judicial functions. However, food and livestock were yet again driven out onto special markets (*macella* or specialized *fora*; cf. Varro, Ling. 5,145–146), at the latest in the 1st cent. BC. The *mercati Traianei* (Trajan's markets), that were constructed above the → *Forum Traiani*, but separate from the latter, hosted temporary booths and tables as well as permanent shops and a market hall. Under Roman rule, the supervision of markets was the responsibility of the Roman rulership of the aediles (→ *aediles*), who, like the *agoranómoi*, controlled measures, weights, prices of rare goods, as well as compliance with regulations or payment of shop rentals.

Of particular significance for the economic connection of city and hinterland were the *nundinae*, which must at first be understood as market days taking place at regular intervals ('every ninth day' = every eight days). From the 2nd cent., however, less frequent fairs or permanent markets were also referred to as *nundinae*. Since *nundinae* have furthermore been verified for cities with a *macellum*, *macellum* and *nundinae* are presumed to have had different functions (→ *macellum* with fig.). *Nundinae* primarily served the rural population, offering an opportunity to come into contact with city dwellers, merchants and public affairs. A series of market calendars (*indices nundinarii*) from South Latium, Campania and Samnium, dating back to the 1st cent. AD, provide particularly good insight into the practice of the *nundinae*. These calendars suggest a supraregional connection or even a co-ordinated network of markets; markets were thus more than mere local supply centres within a subsistence economy. Furthermore, the inclusion of city Roman *nundinae* in the market calendars indicates the likelihood that the hinterland was economically connected to Rome by the *nundinae*. The 25 towns appearing in the calendars are also known, to a large extent, as judicial and administration centres (*praefecturae*), suggesting a link between market days and court days as well as the considerable continuity of individual *nundinae*.

→ Forum; → Commerce; → Economy

1 J. M. CAMP, The Athenian Agora, 1986; 2 J. M. FRAYN, Markets and Fairs in Roman Italy, 1993; 3 L. DE LIGT, Fairs and Markets in the Roman Empire, 1993; 4 L. DE LIGT, P. W. DE NEEVE, Ancient Periodic Markets. Festivals and Fairs, in: Athenaeum 66, 1988, 391–416; 5 R. MACMULLEN, Market-Days in the Roman Empire, in: Phoenix 24, 1970, 333–341; 6 R. MARTIN, Recherches sur l'agora grecque, 1951; 7 J. NOLLÉ, Nundinas instituere et habere, 1982.   S.v.R.

III. EARLY MIDDLE AGES
A. DEFINITION AND STATE OF RESEARCH B. BASIC FEATURES OF THE DEVELOPMENT

A. DEFINITION AND STATE OF RESEARCH
The traces of written records from the centuries of transition between Late Antiquity and the Early Middle Ages indicating market places or market development (*forum, nundinae, mercatus*; *cambio, emptio, venundatio*) have always been disputed in research. Yet today, chances to arrive at new market-historical conclusions are clearly better, thanks to productive excavations of settlements and trading places, numismatics geared toward the history of money, refinements in regards to the history of law and constitution, regional-historical profiling, the historical semantics of leading terms as well as economic-geographical and anthropological theory reception.

Analytically, this means primarily distancing oneself from anachronisms such as the abstract model of supply and demand, or the theory of value or price formation based on production costs. 'Markets' were places visited at appointed times for a controlled, direct exchange of goods and varied considerably according to purpose, participation, duration and type of control. A valid typology of the early medieval market places remains a desideratum; this also applies to market-specific exchange activity, due to a lack of contemporary reflections on the matter (except for traces in legal texts pertaining to sales law).

B. BASIC FEATURES OF THE DEVELOPMENT
Starting-point must be the continuation, but also the diminution of the traditional combination of partially very old fairs at crossroads, scheduled market dates in the *villae rusticae*, weekly *nundinae* in the *vici* and day markets in the *civitates*; the maritime trade was not punctual enough for fixed supraregional market places and dates. In addition there were the border markets. This thinning and weakening structure was significantly modified by innovations, beginning in the 7th cent. With the long-distance trade shifting north, dozens of long-distance trade places/shore markets (Dorestad, Hamwih, Haitabu, Birka and others) emerged along the coast of the North Sea and the Baltic Sea, but also on river courses, and developed rapidly between the 8th and 10th cents. without consolidating into pre-urban permanent settlements; some places later disappeared completely. Alongside, distribution or collection markets under the land-owners' control developed in many places, as well as monasterial consumer markets, which were gradually equipped by the Franconian rulers with licenses for minting as well as for customs clearance or customs imposition. The markets were control sites for the transfer of goods and manifold sources of dues. All this reveals the interrelation between rulership and market development. In association with the 'old' market places, these new market places formed a novel conglomerate, which then discontinuously grew into the city-country-pattern typical for the Middle Ages.

→ Money, money economy; → Commerce; → Price

1 H. ADAM, Das Zollwesen im fränkischen Reich und das spätkarolingische Wirtschaftsleben, 1966; 2 P. CONTAMINE et al., L'économie médiévale, 1997; 3 R. HODGES, Primitive and Peasant Markets, 1988; 4 L. DE LIGT, Fairs and Markets in the Roman Empire, 1993; 5 Mercati e mercanti nell' alto medioevo: l'area euroasiatica e l'area mediterranea, 1993; 6 M. MITTERAUER, Markt und Stadt im MA, 1980; 7 K. POLANYI, C. M. ARENSBERG, H. W. PEARSON (ed.), Trade and Market in Early Empires. Economies in History and Theory, 1957; 8 H. SIEMS, Handel und Wucher im Spiegel frühmittelalterlicher Rechtsquellen, 1992; 9 K. DÜWEL, C. DIETRICH et al. (ed.), Untersuchungen zu Handel und Verkehr der vor- und frühgeschichtlichen Zeit in Mittel- und Nordeuropa, vols. 1–6 (AAWG), 1985–1989.   LU.KU.

Market inspection see → Aedilees; → Agoranomoi; → Market; → Metronomoi

Markets see → Agora; → Forum; → Macellum; → Market

Marmarica (Μαρμαρική; *Marmariké*). Region on the north coast of Africa between Egypt and the → Cyrenaica. The borders of M. varied over time: during the time of the 30th dynasty (380–342 BC), the region of the Marmaridae stretched from the border of the Libyan district (near Apis) to the west (Ps.-Scyl. 108 [GGM 1,82–84]). According to Ptol. 4,5,2–4, however, the eastern border of the district of M. (*sic!*) only began near *Pétras Mégas Limén* (west of → *Catabathmus Mégas*), i.e. at the westernmost point of Egypt. Ptol. (4,4,2; 5f.) puts the western border of M. to the east of Darnis, the author of the It. Ant. to the west of Limniade and Darnis (70,7–9).

From the time of Ps.-Scyl. 108 (GGM 1,82), the inhabitants of this region were generally referred to as Marmaridae [1. 164f.]. Subsequently, they extended their settlements as far as (Eu-)Hesperides; according to later authors, they only occupied the eastern and southeastern Cyrenaica (cf. also Diod. Sic. 3,49,1; Str. 2,5,33; 17,1,13; 3,1; 3,23; Plin. HN 5,39; differently in 5,33).

M., which was often regarded as an uncertain possession of the rulers of Egypt or the Cyrenaica, occasionally appeared in power politics. According to Hdt. 3,13,3f., 'the neighbouring Libyes' (προσεχέες Λίβυες), who most likely are the Marmaridae, submitted themselves to → Cambyses [2]. During his foray into Egypt (274 BC), → Magas of Cyrene was threatened from the rear by the Marmaridae and forced to retreat (Polyaenus, Strat. 2,28,2). According to Flor. Epit. 2,31, P. Sulpicius Quirinius, probably as governor of → Creta et Cyrenae, subjugated the Marmaridae at the same time as the → Garamantes (probably in the year AD 2; cf. also OGIS 2,767. Luc. 4,680 referred to them not inappropriately as *Marmaridae volucres*, 'winged Marmaridae'). Probus, presumably the *praef. Aegypti* and not the later emperor, also fought successfully against the Marmaridae around the year AD 269 and restored Claudiopolis (= Cyrene?) (SHA Probus 9,1; 12,3; SEG IX 9).

During the restructuring of Egypt by Diocletian (AD 297), M. seems to have initially merged with the newly established province of Libya, but was later separated from → Pentapolis as Libya Sicca (Amm. Marc. 22,16,1; also Liber generationis 2 anni 334, Chron. min. 1,102,83f.). According to Philostorgius 1,9 and Theod. Hist. eccl. 1,7,14, M. constituted a Christian diocese. At the turn of the 4th to the 5th cent., Libyan tribes initially invaded the territory of Libya superior, but then also that of Libya inferior. Justinian managed once more to calm the situation. He restored the old fortifications and built new ones (Procop. Aed. 6,2).
→ Libyes, Libye

1 J. DESANGES, Catalogue des tribus africaines de l'antiquité classique à l'ouest du Nil, Dakar: University of Dakar, Faculté des letters et des sciences humaines, Publications de la Section d'histoire, No. 4, 1962.

H. KEES, s.v. M., RE 14, 1881–1883.   W.HU.

Marmarium (Μαρμάριον/*Marmárion*). Harbour on the SW coast of → Euboea, which probably had the purpose of handling the marble from the quarries of Carystus [1]; today's Marmara where, near the chapel of St. Nikolaos, the building elements of a sanctuary of Apollo Marmarios are located. References: Str. 10,1,6; Steph. Byz. s.v. M.; Nonn. Dion. 13,164; Eust. Ilia 281,4.

F. GEYER, Topographie und Geschichte der Insel Euboia, 1, 1903, 106.   H.KAL.

Marmax (Μάρμαξ; *Mármax*). Suitor of → Hippodamia [1], and the first to be killed by → Oenomaus (Hes. fr. 259a). His horses Parthenia and Eripha are buried together with M. M. was also called Mermnes (schol. Pind. O. 1,127b) or Mermnon.   AL.FR.

Marmorarius see → Marble

Marmor Parium Hellenistic chronicle on marble from → Paros; two extensive parts have survived: In the year 1627, fragment A (lines 1–93) from Smyrna came into the possession of Earl Thomas Howard of Arundel, but lines 1–45 were lost during the turmoil under Charles I. and are only known from the *editio princeps* by J. SELDEN [1]. Lines 46–93 have been in Oxford since 1667. In 1897, fragment B (lines 101–132, FHG 1, 542–555) was discovered on Paros; today, it is kept at the local museum there.

The Marmor Parium represents a Greek universal chronicle with the purpose of educating and entertaining a large public. The inscription was set up in 264/3 BC and makes brief references to the events of Greek (predominantly Athenian) history, starting with → Cecrops in 1581/0, and ending with the Athenian archon Diognetus in 264/3. The surviving parts end abruptly with the year 299/8.

All sections are arranged according to the same template by giving the time span from the respective occurrence up to the year 264/3. Apart from political events, there are strikingly many references of a cultural-historical nature, most of all about the large Greek festivals (with the exception of the Olympic Games) and about literary history. Examples: A 59 (referring to 456/5): 'Since the poet Aeschylus, who lived for 69 years, died in Gela, 193 years [had passed] when the elder Callias was archon in Athens.'; B 8 (referring to 324/3): 'Since the passing of Alexander and Ptolemy seizing power, 60 years [had passed] when Hegesias was archon in Athens.'

Due to the introductory sentence being corrupt in the record, the author of the chronicle is unknown, but he is likely to be a Greek from the islands, possibly even a Parian. The basis are various works on history, especially atthidographic (→ Atthis) literature.

1 J. SELDEN (ed.), Marmora Arundelliana, 1628, 1ff.

IG XIII 5, Nr. 444 (1903) and IG XII Suppl. (1939), p. 110; FGrH 239 (with comm.); F. JACOBY, Das Marmor Parium, 1904 (repr. 1980); TOD, 205; R. M. ERRINGTON, Diodorus Siculus and the Chronology of the Early Diadochoi, 320–311 B.C., in: Hermes 105, 1977, 478–504; O. LENDLE, Einführung in die griechische Geschichtsschreibung, 1992, 280f.   K.MEI.

Marmot Plin. HN 8,132 refers to the *Marmota marmota* as 'Alpine mouse' (*mus Alpinus*) and stresses its size (like a badger, *meles*) and its hibernation (*conduntur hieme*) thought to be based on its collection of food [1. 175]. The fact that its pelt is scrubbed off on the back he explains by saying that both sexes, lying on their back and holding food with their front legs, pulled themselves by their tails backwards into their den. The story of their supposed locomotion on two legs (ibid. 10,186) is, of course, not true. Timotheus of Gaza 56 [2. 49] reports of the steppe marmot (bobac; ἀϱϰτόμυς/ arktómys) that these animals feed the guard of the pack, but that they kill him if he neglects his watch duties.

1 LEITNER ; 2 F. S. BODENHEIMER, A. RABINOWITZ, Timotheus of Gaza On Animals, n.d. (1950).   C.HÜ.

Marne culture Celtic cultural group in the early La Tène period (5th cent. BC) in the catchment area of the rivers Marne, Seine and Aisne (Champagne). French scholars also call it 'Aisne-Marne culture'; already in the 19th cent., it was called 'Marnia' on the basis of numerous grave finds (over a hundred necropoleis with several thousand graves), being an independent group at the northwest edge of the early → La Tène culture. Typical are especially the full body burials in shallow grave necropoleis, the weapons (sword, lance), especially jewellery (neck rings; → torques) as grave goods and food (parts of animal skeletons), the typical ceramics with their hard-edged wall profiles, with their geometrical scratched or painted patterns etc. Rich graves (→ Princes' tombs) stand out because of two-wheeled → war chariots, splendid horse harnesses, Mediterranean bronze vessels and → helmets given as grave goods.

Sometimes, late → Hallstatt and early La Tène culture (6th–4th cent BC) are also included under the Marne culture. Around 400 BC, a significant decrease in the number of burials can be observed (start of the Celtic migrations?), and only in the 2nd half of the 4th cent. the number of graves increases again. However, there are also the beginnings of new burial customs as is indicated by newly emerging cremation burials and enclosed burials etc. So far, settlements are hardly known for the Marne culture.

→ Funerary architecture; → Hallstatt culture; → Celtic archaeology; → La Tène culture

J.-P. DEMOULE, Chronologie et société dans les nécropoles celtiques de la culture Aisne-M., du VIᵉ au IIIᵉ siècle avant notre ère, 1999; M. GREEN (ed.), The Celtic World, 1995, esp. 555–557; H. LORENZ, Totenbrauchtum und Tracht. Untersuchungen zur regionalen Gliederung in der frühen Latènezeit, in: BRGK 59, 1978, esp. 220–224; S. MOSCATI (ed.), I Celti, 1991, 147–154; 243–250.   V.P.

Maroboduus King of the → Marcomanni of a noble family (*genere nobilis*, Vell. Pat. 2,108,2). In Rome, Maroboduus received the 'favours' of Augustus (Str. 7,1,3) early on – more is not known. After returning to his people, M. made himself king (Vell. Pat. 2,108,2) and after 9 BC, he went with the Marcomanni and other Suebian groups – probably with Roman approval – from the Main region into Bohemia which had become sparsely populated after the → Boii had moved away (→ Boiohaemum, Str. 7,1,3; Tac. Germ. 42,1). By sub-

jugation and treaties with the → Lugii, Zumi, Butones, Sibini and → Semnones, M. enlarged his tightly organised kingdom (Str. 7,1,3; Vell. Pat. 2,108,2,). In this endeavour, he could count on a very skilled army of 70.000 foot soldiers and 4.000 horsemen with an almost Roman discipline (Vell. Pat. 2,109,1f.).

The relations with Rome, which also included an active two-way trade (Tac. Ann. 2,62,3), were good initially. Without directly provoking Rome, M. demonstrated a self-confident strength. His emissaries acted as petitioners, but also with the claim of equality of rank (*pro pari*). Even some tribes and persons no longer loyal to Rome sought refuge in M.'s domain (Vell. Pat. 2,109,1–2). Whether his considerable increase in power, described by Velleius Paterculus, actually posed a threat to Italy or the neighbouring regions of Noricum, Pannonia and Germania, is doubtful. Velleius is apparently more interested in justifying a preventive war against the potential leader of an anti-Roman coalition [1. 158f.; 2. 193]. For in a large-scale pincer attack in AD 6, both C. → Sentius Saturninus starting in Mogontiacum (Mainz) and proceeding through the region of the Chatti, and Tiberius starting in Carnuntum, targeted the core of M.'s power (Vell. Pat. 2,109,5). Before the armies could join, the Illyrian-Pannonian uprising forced the breaking-off of the offensive by the twelve legions and a rapprochement with M. The peace [2. 270], possibly secured by treaty, initially ensured for M. autonomy and equality of rank (Tac. Ann. 2,26; 46), but in the retrospective view of → Arminius, it earned him the reputation of a 'traitor' to the Germanic cause (Tac. ann. 2,45). In subsequent times, too, M. remained with his wait-and-see neutral policies: The severed head of P. → Quinctilius Varus, sent to him in AD 9 as an invitation to an alliance, he forwarded to Rome for burial (Vell. Pat. 2,119,5). However, it appears that M., after AD 9, did not support the Roman side either during the campaigns led by Tiberius and Germanicus (Tac. Ann. 2,46,5).

In the battles following the recall of → Germanicus [2], M. and Arminius, in AD 17, become adversaries – cf. the impressive *mise en scène* in Tacitus (Tac. Ann. 2,45; 46). In this context, M.'s image, viewed from the perspective of a supposedly Germanic national consciousness, compares unfavourably with that of Arminius. After the secession of the Semnones and Lombards from M., the power relationships appeared to be in balance because → Inguiomerus, the uncle of Arminius, went over to M. (Tac. Ann. 2,45,1) and was celebrated by him as the true victor over Varus (Tac. Ann. 2,46,1). Forced to retreat during battle, M. appealed to Tiberius who reminded M. of his earlier vacillating stance and rejected the call for help (ibid. 2,46,5). The *princeps* sent his son Drusus [II 1] to the Danube in order to initiate the complete destruction of M.'s power (ibid. 2,62,1).

Marcomanni competitors, in particular → Catualda who had once been persecuted by M., staged an uprising against him in AD 18 and forced him into the

Roman empire after conquering his royal castle (ibid. 2,62). Tiberius again declined to support M. and granted him Ravenna as a place of residence where he lived for another 18 years. The followers of M. and the later expelled Catualda were settled in the *regnum Vannianum* (→ Vannius) north of the Danube in the region of the March (Tac. Ann. 2,63).

In one of Tiberius' speeches, also intended to improve his own image, M. appears in a list of great rulers of antiquity – more dangerous than Philip II., Pyrrhus and Antiochus [5] III. (ibid. 2,63). This assessment certainly does justice to M.'s independent position, demonstrated several times, the size of the kingdom he created and of his material resources as well as the consistent and remarkable organisation of his kingdom [2. 273]. These aspects deserve to be emphasised *vis-à-vis* the juxtaposition of the 'traitor' M. and the 'liberator' Arminius found in earlier German research shaped by nationalist-historical sentiments.

1 J. DOBIÁŠ, King M. as a Politician, in: Klio 38, 1960, 155–166; 2 R. WOLTERS, Römische Eroberung und Herrschaftsorganisation in Gallien und Germanien, 1990.
V.L.

Maron (Μάρων; *Márōn*). Priest of Apollo in the Thracian city of → Ismarus; first mentioned in the Cicones episode in the Odyssey: For being spared during a plundering raid by Odysseus' warriors, M. gives Odysseus amongst other things a heavy wine as a present, with which Odysseus can later stun the → Cyclops (Hom. Od. 9,39–61; 196–211). M.'s name appears to be derived from the name of the Thracian city of Maronea [1] whose environs were known for good wine (Hom. Od. 9,45; Archil. fr. 2); a numismatically documented M. cult also existed here. Because of this passage from the Odyssey, M. is later associated with the sphere of Dionysus and is given an appropriate family tree (in Hes. Cat. 238, he is the grandson of → Oenopion and great grandson of Dionysus). In Nonnus' *Dionysiaká*, he is mentioned several times as Dionysus' charioteer and stands out in a dancing competition with Silenus (19, 159–224; 295–348).

B. GR. KRUSE, s.v. M., RE 14, 1911–1912.   E.V.

Maronea (Μαρώνεια; *Marṓneia*).
[1] North Aegean city on the southwest slopes of the Ismarus, today's Maronia. Founded by Chios (1st half of the 7th cent. BC; Scyl. 678) in the tribal lands of the → Cicones. Mythography associates M. with the Homeric *Márōn* (Hom. Od. 9,197); first mentioned by Hecat. FGrH 1 F 159. The most important occupations were viticulture and sheep breeding. As of 529 BC, M. minted silver coins when the exploitation of the silver mine south of present-day Agios Georgios began. The Athenian tribute lists of 454 to 424 BC and 418/17 BC show the economic upswing of M.: Originally, the city had to pay 1 talent and 3.000 drachmas; in 437 BC, it was already 3 talents (ATL 1, 116; 157; 207 fr. 38). The

source of this wealth was, most of all, the close economic relations to the → Odrysae and to the Thracian hinterland in general where M. made use of quite a few emporia. The number of citizens at that time must have come to about 1.200. Just like Abdera and Neapolis (today's Kauala), M. became part of the domain of king Amadocus II. of the Odrysae, but it remained autonomous as long as M. paid tribute to the Odrysae as well as to the → Delian League (IG II 2, 126; Syll.³ of the year 358). A Thracian fortress was situated not far from the city (today's Agios Georgios). The mint of the Odrysaean rulers Medocus, Amadocus II. and Teres II. was located at M. The most important gods of the city were Apollo, Dionysus, Zeus and → Maron. In the 4th BC, the port was constructed/extended. In 376, M. suffered under the invasion of the → Triballi (Diod. Sic. 15,36). In Hellenistic times, a large-scale theatre was built in M., which was extended even further in Roman times.

In the 2nd half of the 3rd cent. BC, M. became a Ptolemaic possession; conquered by Philip V in 200 BC. Shortly before 196 BC, M. (together with Aenus) was transferred to Antiochus III by Rome. Thus, this coastal strip became a bone of contention between Philippus V and Eumenes [3] (Liv. 39,27f.). In 184 BC, Thracians raided the city (Pol. 22,13). After 167 BC, M. was incorporated into the first district of the Macedonian *merídes* (μερίδες, Diod. Sic. 31,8,8). From the Romans, M. received the status of a *civitas libera* (Liv. 37,60,7). In Roman times, its importance declined, but it held quite a few privileges under Hadrianus (IGR 1, 830). M. enjoyed a new upswing again in early Christian and Byzantine times. Archaeological investigations have been carried out since 1960.

E. SCHÖNERT-GEISS, Griech. Münzwerk. Die Münzprägung von M., 1987; CH. KARADIMA-MATSA, Η ανασκαφική έρευνα στη M., in: Archaia Thrake 2, 1997, 557–565.
I.v.B.

[2] Mining area in → Laurium, probably belonging to the deme of Thoricus [2. 102ff.], whose development in 483 BC – according to a supposition by [1. 313] due to ore deposits being reached in the 3rd contact zone of marble and slate (because of the re-introduction of pit mining) – made the shipbuilding programme of Themistocles (Aristot. Ath. Pol. 22,7; Hdt. 7,144; Plut. Themistocles 4; Nep. Themistocles 2) possible [3. 277ff.]. During the 4th cent. BC, the importance of M. declined considerably [2. 103].

1 R. J. HOPPER, The Laurion Mines, in: ABSA 63, 1968, 293–326; 2 H. LOHMANN, Atene, 1993; 3 P. RHODES, A Commentary on the Aristotelian Athenaion Politeia, 1981.
H.LO.

Maronites Christian religious community going back to the Syrian hermit Maro(n) (Μάρω(ν)/ *Márō(n)*, Syriac *Morun*; 4th/5th cent. AD), the patron saint of a monastery on the → Orontes near → Apamea [3] in Syria, which became the centre of the resistance against the → Monophysitism. After the death of the patriarch Anastasius II (died 609), the Antiochene (→ Antioch

[1]) patriarchal see remained vacant (Persian invasions); in 636, the region came under Arab rule. Its isolation in terms of geography and Church politics led to a disconnection from the development of Church dogma. Under emperor → Heraclius [7], the Maronites became followers of → Monotheletism, referring to documents of the 5th ecumenical synod of Constantinople, which were regarded as fake by the 6th synod.

M. BREYDY, Geschichte der der syro-arabischen Literatur der M. vom VII. bis XVI. Jh., 1985. K.SA.

Marpessa (Μάρπησσα; *Márpēssa*, 'the robbed one').
[1] Daughter of the Aetolian river god→ Evenus [3]. She is kidnapped by → Idas, who escapes the persecuting Evenus with the help of his father Poseidon. M.'s father plunges into the river, which is named after him. M. is then taken from Idas by Apollo, and a fight ensues between him and the god, during the course of which Idas disarms the god of his bow (Hom. Il. 9,555ff.). Zeus settles the dispute by leaving the choice to M., who elects Idas, to avoid Apollo leave her when she is old (Simon. fr. 58, PMG 563 PAGE). Idas and M. name their daughter Alcyone, in memory of M.'s abduction (Hom. l.c.). The name M. is associated with Greek *márptein*, 'to rob', 'to grab'. AL.FR.
[2] Name of the dominant massif on the island of Paros, famous for its marble (Steph. Byz. s.v. M.).

H. KALETSCH, s.v. Marpissa, in: LAUFFER, Griechenland, 409. H.KAL.

Marpessus (Μάρπεσσος/ *Márpessos*; *Marmessos, Marmi(y)ssos*). Town in the Troad, regarded as the home of the Hellespontine → Sibyl (Paus. 10,12,3). Its location is derived from Paus. ibid. ('240 stadia from → Alexandria [2] Troas ') and Lactant. Div. inst. 1,6 (*circa oppidum Gergithum*). After LEAF [1. 106] calculated this to be in the area of Ballı Dağı, a definite location seems now to have been established by COOK [2. 281–283] at Dam Kale near Zerdalli, approx. 8 km north of Gergis.

1 W. LEAF, Strabo on the Troad, 1923; 2 J. M. COOK, The Troad, 1973, 280–283.

W. RUGE, s.v. M., RE 14, 1918. E.SCH.

Marriage
I. ANCIENT ORIENT II. GREECE III. ROME
IV. JUDAISM V. CHRISTIAN

I. ANCIENT ORIENT
Marriage in the Ancient Orient was always potentially polygamous, but in most cases it was monogamous in practice. Only kings had more than two wives. Marriage to members of inferior social groups was just as valid as marriage between them. Marriage between close relatives was basically forbidden, except between half-brothers and half-sisters who shared a father. A

marriage could be concluded in any of four ways: 1) by a contract between the groom or his parents and the parents of the bride; 2) by giving a bridal gift, by means of which the bride attained the public status of a wife; 3) by means of a 'symbolic abduction of the bride' by the bridegroom; 4) by agreement either by consummation, by *verba solemnia* (solemn utterances) or by *in domum deductio* (leading the woman into the house of the man). The family usually provided the bride with a dowry which might contain the original bridal gift. Divorce was possible, unilaterally or by mutual consent, through uttering forms of words such as 'You are not my spouse'. In the event of divorce or of a violation of the contract, the marriage contract could provide for financial penalties for the husband, or enslavement or death for the wife; see → Family.

P. PESTMAN, Marriage and Matrimonial Property in Ancient Egypt, 1961; M. ROTH, Babylonian Marriage Agreements, 1989; R. WESTBROOK, Old Babylonian Marriage Law, 1988. RA.WE.

II. GREECE
Marriage was referred to in ancient Greece using the general terms for a relationship (φιλότης, *philótēs* and φιλία, *philía*) or for association (κοινωνία, *koinōnía*) (Aristot. Eth. Nic. 8,12,1162a; Xen. Oec. 3,15), to any of which could be added the element γαμική (*gamikḗ*, from γάμος, *gámos*: 'wedlock', 'marriage'). Its symbolic place was the marriage-bed (εὐνή/*eunḗ*, λέκτρον/ *léktron*, λέχος/*léchos*), which was lavishly arrayed with cloths. The wedding procession often depicted in vase painting (lekythos of the Amasis Painter, New York MMA [2. 66]; Attic black-figured krater [3. Fig.135]; red-figured pyxis, London BM [1. 1277,23; 1282,1]; red-figured kylix, Berlin SM F 2530) led to the marriage-bed, and it was also used in tragedy as a synonym for marriage (Eur. Med. 206; 265; 436). Both *koinōnía* and *philótēs* denote besides their abstract meaning also the sexual union taking place on this bed (Hom. Od. 8,271; 10,334; Aristot. Pol. 7,16,1334b; Eur. Bacch.1276). 'Bed companion' (ἄλοχος, *álochos* or ἄκοιτις, *ákoitis*) is thus also a term for wife.

Poets, philosophers and orators agreed in citing the securing of issue as the absolute and predominant motive for entering into a marriage. This was supposed to safeguard the continuity of family property and cults and to secure provision for one's own old age as well as an appropriate funeral (Hes. Theog. 603–607; Aristot. Eth. Nic. 8,12,1162a; Pl. Leg. 773e; Lys. 13,45; Isaeus 2,10; Dem. Or. 59,122; Xen. Oec. 7,11; 7,18–19). Therefore, the husband's or wife's infertility was a significant reason for divorce. Because of the agrarian structure of the Greek household, marriage was also understood as a working association of husband and wife, who worked as the 'team' in the joint yoke (ζεῦγος, *zeûgos*) of the household (Xen. Oec. 7,18). A transfer of possessions was always included in the contract of marriage, which rendered marriage a financial matter (Plut. Solon 20; Pl. Leg. 774c). Thus a wedding gift (ἕδνα, *hédna*) was paid and → presents (δῶρα; *dôra*) or a dowry (φερνή, → *pherné*) as well as a marriage-portion (προίξ, → *proíx*) were given.

Because of the association of citizenship with descent or landownership, and the use of marriage alliances for the accumulation of power, there was also a political dimension to marriage. Marriage strategies depended on the preferred form of inheritance transfer and the political system, both of which varied in the individual poleis and epochs. According to the conditions of the marriage by exchange of goods as described by Homer and Hesiod, which earlier scholarship often mistook for marriage by purchase, goods (often livestock, but also gifts of jewellery and clothing) were transferred to the bride and her father by the groom in expectation of services in return. The transfer of bridal goods was accompanied by exogamous marriage practices, which served to create wide-ranging alliances between individual houses. Tyrants of the 6th cent. BC (cf. Theognis 891–894) preferred such exogamous marriages, as they acquired allies in the struggle for supremacy in their home polis as well as outside resources for the establishment of a retinue (Peisistratus: Hdt. 5,94; Miltiades: Plut. Cimon 4; Hdt. 6,39; Periander: Hdt. 3,50; 5,92; Diog. Laert. 1,94) by means of marriage. The struggle for power advanced the tendency towards polygamy, as it is shown by Peisistratus and some tyrants of Lower Italy. The connubial residence was predominantly patrilocal. However, it also happened that the groom married into the family of the bride and thereafter participated in their privileges. Prestigious weddings and competitions among suitors characterized this type of marriage (Sicyon: Hdt. 6,126–131).

The dowry marriage of classical times, which was connected with divergent forms of transfer, was characterized by the tendency towards endogamous marriages within a locality or a kinship or status group. The Periclean citizenship law of 451 BC decreed that only children both of whose parents were Athenian citizens obtained citizenship (Plut. Pericles 37; Aristot. Ath. Pol. 42; Dem. Or. 59,16–17; 59,52; 57,30; Isaeus 8,43). For Athenian aristocrats, the possibility of a marriage alliance with families of other poleis was thus excluded: the polis had become an endogamous unit. The law distinguished strictly between legitimate wife and concubine (παλλακή, *pallaké*). In this way it limited the number of citizens and lawful heirs of an → *oíkos*. While the legal speeches and New Comedy were about conflicts of inheritance law which evolved from this regulation, tragedy broached the issue of conflicts which arose from the concubinate (Soph. Trach.) and the loss of status of a foreign wife (Eur. Med.).

At Athens, the → *engýesis* (ἐγγύησις), the verbal promise of marriage uttered before witnesses which accompanied the agreement of the dowry, and the → *ékdosis* (ἔκδοσις), the giving away of the bride on the wedding day, constituted the formal elements of the legitimate conclusion of a marriage from which legitimate children (γνήσιοι, *gnésioi*) issued. The children of a union with a foreigner were called *nóthoi* (νόθοι) and did not come into the line of inheritance, even if there were no legitimate sons. In this case, at Athens, the inheriting daughter (ἐπίκληρος, → *epíkleros*) was married to the nearest male relative (Plut. Solon 20).

1 Beazley, ARV; 2 Beazley, Paralipomena; 3 C. Bérard, J.-P. Vernant, La cité des images, 1984 (Engl. tr. by D. Lyons, A City of Images, 1989); 4 R. Just, Women in Athenian Law and Life, 1989; 5 W. K. Lacey, The Family in Classical Greece, 1968; 6 C. Reinsberg, Ehe, Hetärentum und Knabenliebe im antiken Griechenland, 1989; 7 J. P. Vernant, Mythe et société en Grèce ancienne, 1979, 57–81; 8 B. Wagner-Hasel, Geschlecht und Gabe, in: ZRG 105, 1988, 32–73; 9 H. J. Wolff, Marriage Law and Family Organization in Ancient Athens, in: Traditio 2, 1944, 43–95.

III. Rome

A. Marriage and Matrimonium B. Age at Marriage and Wedding C. Marriage and Manus D. Concubinatus and Contubernium

A. Marriage and Matrimonium

In the Roman Empire, different cultures and thus different wedding customs and rituals, and individual ideas of marriage, co-existed. The genuine Roman traditions concerning marriage and matrimony derived from those of the Latins. After fixed rules for marriage and matrimony had developed, a fully valid marriage under Roman law was available to Roman citizens, Latins and anyone to whom the right of *conubium* had been granted. The *conubium* meant the ability of two people of different gender to marry one another. This did not exist between progenitors and descendants, between other close relatives, between minors, or with slaves or foreigners. Because of the *matrimonium*, an institution which regulated motherhood, a man married a woman in order for her to provide him with legitimate children who received his own legal status. In legal theory, marriage was only discussed when it had already been practised for a long time during which more and more exact legal regulations had developed. In the Digests, the following basic definition by Modestinus (early 3rd cent. AD) is given at the beginning of the section on marriage: 'Marriage is the union of man and woman, communion of life, and participation together in the divine and human law' (23,2,1). It was assumed that this 'association of man and woman which we call *matrimonium*' derived from natural law and the behaviour of animals (Ulpian; Dig. 1,1,1,3; cf. Cic. Off. 1,54). The phrase *liberorum creandorum causa* ('for the procreation of children') is used in connection with marriage and wives throughout Latin literature.

In Roman marriage (*iustum matrimonium*), a woman became *uxor* (spouse) of her husband, *materfamilias* (the female head of the household) and *matrona* (a married woman); the man became *vir* (husband) of his wife and her *maritus* (spouse); each of the two became *coniunx*. Children of the marriage were recognized as the children of the husband. Common law, the laws and edicts of praetors or principes had an influence on the development of marriage, particularly on the regulations concerning dowries, the law of succession, the *conubium*, on the legal assessment of adultery and extra-marital sexual relationships. The marriage laws of Augustus, the *lex Iulia de maritandis ordinibus* (18 BC) and the *lex Papia Poppaea* (AD 9), refused to recognize those relationships as fully valid marriage which arose between senators, their descendants and freedwomen, actors or actresses or their children, and between freeborn citizens and prostitutes, procuresses, actresses, adulteresses or women who had been convicted in a public trial. From the early Principate to the reign of Septimius Severus, soldiers below a certain rank were not granted fully valid legal marriage. The *lex Iulia de adulteriis et de stupro* (approx. AD 18) provided penalties for adultery.

B. Age at Marriage and Wedding

Little testimony exists concerning age at marriage in the Roman Empire, and they all concern only the small group of people of whom records exist in funerary inscriptions. At the time of their first marriage, which was permitted for girls from the age of 12 and for young men from the age of 14, women were generally around 20 and men around 30 years of age. In the leading political class, the age at marriage was often lower, particularly from the early Principate onwards, when the minimum age for assuming political offices was dropping and the marriage laws allowed candidates to reduce the required age by one year for each child they had. At the same time, the right of receiving inheritances was limited for unmarried and childless people, with the age limit for women being 20 years and for men 25 years. Betrothal preceded marriage; it could not be enforced and the agreement of both parties and both *patresfamilias* was required; in classical law this also applied to marriage. At the wedding (*nuptiae*), usually religious and social ceremonies were performed and financial agreements concluded. The noun *nuptiae,* like the verb *nubere*, which described the entry of a woman into a marriage, referred to the wearing of a veil, while the corresponding verb for the groom (*in matrimonium ducere*) referred to the symbolic act of leading the procession to his house, with the bride following him.

The ideal was an enduring and harmonious bond. Marriage ended with the death of a *coniunx*, with divorce or dissolution of the *conubium*. The continuance of the marriage required the constant consent of both spouses, specifically in that they regarded one another as *coniunx* (*affectio maritalis*).

C. Marriage and Manus

Marriage could be connected with the *manus*, the legal power of the husband over his wife. The rituals upon which this relationship was founded were closely

connected with the conclusion of marriage (*confarreatio, coemptio*). The *coemptio* could also be held later, as could the procedures for the annulment of the *manus*. In the 5th cent. BC, the *manus* was established by a one-year cohabitation and was stopped by the absence of the wife for three nights per year. By the time of Cicero, it seems to have become unusual for women to give themselves into the *manus* of the man. A woman *in manu mariti* was a member of her husband's family, and she was subject to his legal power and that of his *paterfamilias*. All of her possessions, and all possessions she subsequently acquired, became the property of her husband. She was regarded as a blood relative of her children, and in the absence of a will, she had the same status in regard to inheritance as a daughter.

A wife who was not subject to the *manus* of her husband remained in legal association with the family of her birth. In the absence of a will, husband and wife were subordinate to blood relatives in the order of inheritance. In the absence of a will, inheritance from mothers to children was strictly limited until the 2nd cent. AD. The husband had the dowry at his disposal as long as the marriage endured. In principle, the entire remaining property of a husband and wife not *in manu* was strictly separated: common law, confirmed by jurists, prescribed that substantial gifts between *coniuges* were null and void if these had not been confirmed by testament or expressly affirmed following a divorce. From AD 206, gifts were regarded as effective unless it could be proved that the giver had changed his/her mind.

Both parents felt strongly obliged to leave property to their children. The will could order the usufruct of property or other gratuities in order to secure the living of a widow. A legacy to the surviving *coniunx* was a sign of conjugal affection. The Augustan marriage laws limited the opportunities for childless or unmarried citizens to inherit by will, unless the heirs were close relatives. The existence of a child entitled a *coniunx* to inherit by the will of a deceased spouse.

The honouring of a *coniunx* at the funeral and praise in funerary inscriptions corresponded to conventional ideas. Most of the virtues and abilities praised in funerary inscriptions and in literary texts applied to either sex. *Pudicitia*, unconditional love and faithfulness, was ascribed primarily to women. Mutual affection was often emphasized. Lifelong celibacy and chastity among adult Roman women is attested primarily for the Vestals. Men were forced to remain single in some cases, e.g. soldiers. Although the renunciation of marriage was occasionally voluntary, monogamous marriage and remarriage were normal phenomena in Roman society.

D. Concubinatus and Contubernium

Legally not fully valid marriages (*matrimonia iniusta*) were partially admitted. The *concubinatus*, a stable sexual relationship with a woman of a different legal status (the issue of which were not regarded as legitimate children), increasingly offered an alternative to marriage. Marriage arose from the *concubinatus*, if both partners were marriageable and regarded one another with *affectio maritalis*.

The *contubernium*, a relationship in which one or both partners were slaves, was designed in imitation of marriage, but the children were illegitimate, and the continuance of the *contubernium* was always uncertain. If both partners became Roman citizens and wished to do so it could be transformed into a marriage. → Marriage

1 J. Evans Grubbs, 'Pagan' and 'Christian' Marriage: The State of the Question, in: Journal of Early Christian Studies 2/4, 1994, 361–412; 2 M. Kaser, RPR I, 63–74 (pre-classical), 266–290 (classical); II, 107–141 (post-classical.); 3 B. Rawson (ed.), The Family in Ancient Rome, 1986; 4 Ibid. (ed.), Marriage, Divorce and Children in Ancient Rome, 1991; 5 S. Treggiari, Roman marriage. Iusti coniuges from the time of Cicero to the time of Ulpian, 1991. SU.T.

IV. Judaism

The biblical idea, according to which the sexual, economic and social bond between man and woman is to be regarded as an anthropological constant (cf. Gn 2:23f), was absorbed and developed in rabbinical Judaism. Thus, the conclusion of a marriage was regarded as a duty which should be fulfilled by the age of 20; a celibate life, on the other hand, was regarded as a sin (bKid 29b). The corresponding Halakhic regulations were developed in the Mishna, Tosefta and Talmud treatises Kǝtūbbot ('Marriage contracts'), Qiddūšīm ('Betrothals') and Šōṭāh ('Those suspected of adultery'). They make clear that the actual marriage ceremony in Talmudic times consisted of two parts: the betrothal (Hebrew ʾerūsīn), in which the groom recited the relevant blessing to the bride before two witnesses and gave her the marriage certificate or an object of value (mQid 1,1), which was followed by the actual wedding ceremony (Hebrew qiddūšīm). The latter took place on a later occasion and it was followed by the consummation of the marriage. The regulation of the conjugal finances, which served to protect primarily the wife in case of divorce or widowhood, were stipulated in a marriage contract (Hebrew kǝtūbbah). Where a husband died childless, his brother was obliged to wed the widow, his sister-in-law (Levirat). The children of this relationship were then regarded as the legal issue of the deceased (cf. here the remarks in the treatise Yǝbāmōt, 'Sisters-in-law'). According to Jewish understanding, the dissolution of a marriage by divorce was possible (cf. here the Mishna treatise Gittīn, 'letters of divorce' with the corresponding interpretation in the Talmuds); it could generally only happen on the initiative of the husband. Legitimate grounds for divorce were the subject of extremely controversial discussion in the Halakhah.

Z. W. Falk, s.v. Ehe/Eherecht/Ehescheidung III. Judentum, TRE 9, 312–318; T. Ilan, Jewish Women in Greco-Roman Palestine. An Inquiry into Image and Status, Texte und Studien zum Antiken Judentum 44, 1995, 57–96 (both include further literature). B.E.

V. Christian

In the OT, marriage was a ceremony of civil law between the marrying couple and between their families. The husband had sole claim to his wife, but not vice versa. Nonetheless, polygyny (1 Kgs 11:3; Gen 29:15–30:24) was unusual, often arising in circumstances such as childlessness (Gen 16:1–6). The NT and Christianity also took (strictly monogamous) marriage as an institution, tailored to local customs and laws, for granted.

A. Asceticism, Marriage, Divorce
B. Wedding ceremonies and the status of spouses

A. Asceticism, Marriage, Divorce

Jesus assigned a higher priority to the *imitatio dei* and the rule of God than to marriage (Lk 14:26; cf. also Mk 12:18–27). Nonetheless he valued the latter as a God-given order of creation, and thus as indissoluble (Mk 10:1–12). According to Paul (→ Paulus [2]), sex was only permitted within marriage. In his view, the married couple should only temporarily abstain from their mutual connubial duties (1 Cor 7:1–6). Paul himself, however, preferred voluntary celibacy (7:7). Compared to more extreme ascetic trends (→ Gnosis; → Marcion) or libertine movements (e.g. → Carpocratians), Christianity always adhered to marriage (1 Tim 4:3; 3:2; 12) while valuing traditions of ascetic living highly. Nevertheless, → Asceticism continued to gain in importance (celibacy as a higher way of life). An important influence in this regard was → Augustine (Confessions 8,12,29: conversion exemplified as liberation from sexual desire).

Marriage, regarded as indissoluble (see above), could only be dissolved in cases of adultery (Mt 5:32; Herm. Mand. 4,1,29; Iust. Mart. 2 Apol. 2,4) or religious differences (1 Cor 7:12–16), possibly when entering a closed religious community. Controversy surrounded remarriage, for instance in cases of widowhood (Tert. De monogamia).

B. Wedding ceremonies and the status of spouses

The traditional Jewish role of the father of the bride in blessing the bridal couple was taken over by clerics. The first evidence supporting the blessing of the couple by the church can be found from the 2nd cent. onwards (Ignatius to Polycarpus 5,2; Tert. Ad uxorem 2,8,6). From the 4th cent., this blessing could be performed as a Bridal Mass (*Missa pro sponsis*). Church wedding ceremonies only became the customary practice in the West in the 11th cent.

Paul emphasizes the equality of status and duty within a marriage (1 Cor 7:3 f.). However, Eph 5:21–33 points out the supremacy of the husband, and interprets marriage as a likeness of the community of Christ and His Church (cf. also Col 3:18 f.). An insight into the 'community of the heart' of a married Christian couple is found in → Tertullian's ' two books To His Wife'. → Univira; → Widows; → Woman IV.

H. BALTENSWEILER, Die Ehe im Neuen Testament, 1967; C. MUNIER, Ehe und Ehelosigkeit in der Alten Kirche, 1987; A. NEHRING i. a., s. v. Ehe, in: RGG⁴ 2, 1999, 1069–1090 (Lit.).   M.HE.

Marriage, Age at
I. OBJECT OF RESEARCH AND METHOD   II. AGE AT MARRIAGE IN ANCIENT GREECE   III. AGE AT MARRIAGE IN THE ROMAN EMPIRE

I. OBJECT OF RESEARCH AND METHOD
In pre-industrial societies, the age of husband and wife at first marriage – alongside mortality and the menopause – determined the time-span available for procreation. An extension of this period usually caused a proportional rise in fertility. At the same time, the age of the husband influenced the size of the generation gap and the social and legal relations within the → *oíkos* and *familia*. Ancient historians have developed various methodological approaches to establish this age, which differ in the choice of the sources and their assessment.

All efforts to determine age at marriage in the ancient world begin by evaluating social expectations in relation to an appropriate age margin. The methodological problems and the necessary differentiations of time, location and social rank to be made in the study are the same issues and results as those found in comparative demography for other epochs.

II. AGE AT MARRIAGE IN ANCIENT GREECE
Most studies of the age at marriage in ancient Greece have focused on the literary evidence (legal speeches as well as medical, philosophical and historiographic texts), and to a lesser extent on epigraphic and anthropological sources. Generally, a first-marriage age of 14–15 years for girls and of just under 30 years for men can be assumed. However, there is substantial variation according to polis, region, date and social status. Recommendations on marriage age in poetry and political theory offer an approximate indication; thus, according to Hesiod, a man should marry at the age of around 30, and a woman should be five years an adult (Hes. Op. 695–698). Plato, who addresses this question several times, asserts 25–35 years for a man, 16–20 years for a woman (Pl. Leg. 721b; 772d; 785b). The age difference between the father and his children, and the health of children and women were decisive arguments for Aristotle in this regard: the father should not be too young, because he would then lack authority; the woman likewise, because early births threatened her life; an age of 37 for the man and 18 for the woman was, according to Aristotle, suitable for marriage (Aristot. Pol. 1334b 29–1335a 35).

III. AGE AT MARRIAGE IN THE ROMAN EMPIRE
According to Roman law, the legal minimum age for a legitimate marriage was 12 for girls and 14 for boys (cf. Cod. Iust. 5,4,24). However, comparative cultural studies have revealed that considerable differences between a legal lower limit and the time of actual marriage were possible; moreover, the aforementioned law is a *lex imperfecta*, a breach of which did not lead to punishment, but only to the loss of the benefits connected with the regulation. The Augustan laws set a *terminus ante quem* with the decree that women and men should have a child by the ages of 20 and 25 respectively (Ulp. 16,1; FIRA 2,278), and the legislation of Hadrian concerning child allowance may have set a corresponding *terminus post quem*, stipulating the expiry of support after the 14th year (for girls) and the 18th year (for boys) (Dig. 34,1,14,1). Literary evidence suggests a similar range (approx. 12–18 years for girls, 20–30 for men). However, these numerical statements should not be accepted uncritically; it is unknown to what extent these testimonies were indeed representative. Medical writings do not provide unanimous information on the onset of sexual maturity, which usually anteceded marriage; for girls, an age of 14 is most often cited (e.g. in Soranus). This indicates a fertile period from 15 to 40 years for women (Sor. 1,20; 1,33f.).

However, it is by no means certain that such individual statements can be extrapolated, and the factors affecting menarche in antiquity are also questionable. Although it is not possible to exclude pre-pubertal marriages, child marriages seem to have been uncommon. An evaluation of Roman inscriptions (primarily funerary inscriptions), which allow the calculation of age at marriage, produced an average age of 15 for girls and 23–24 for men [7]. In more recent research, this study has been criticized for the small number of inscriptions that were examined and the strong predominance of urban Roman evidence. Accordingly a slightly higher age for both women and men (slightly below 20 and late 20s respectively) for those of lower social rank was suggested. The late marriage of men and their high mortality once over 50 years of age has also led to a re-evaluation of the → *patria potestas* and the father-son relationship in the *familia* [11]. However, the value of epigraphic materials as sources is questioned in principle by the observation that funerary inscriptions always derive from the context of death, not that of life or marriage [13].

Age at marriage can also be deduced from Egyptian contracts and domestic declarations from the period of the Principate. Here, a median derived from census declarations is 17.5 years (women) and over 25 years (men); from contracts, a usual female age at marriage of 17–19 years can be assumed; however, there may have been considerable deviations from these patterns.
→ Family; Marriage; → Women

1 R. S. BAGNALL, B. W. FRIER, The Demography of Roman Egypt, 1994; 2 M. DURRY, Le mariage des filles impubères, in: CRAI 1955, 84–90; 3 Id., Le mariage des

filles impubères dans la Rome antique, in: RIDA 2, 1955, 263–273; 4 Id., Sur le mariage romain, in: RIDA 3, 1956, 227–243; 5 E. EYBEN, Geschlechtsreife und Ehe im griechisch-römischen Altertum und im frühen Christentum, in: E. W. MÜLLER (ed.), Geschlechtsreife und Legitimation zur Zeugung, 1985, 403–478; 6 D. GOUREVITCH, Le mal d'être femme, 1984; 7 K. HOPKINS, The Age of Roman Girls at Marriage, in: Population Studies 18, 1965, 309–327; 8 J.-U. KRAUSE, Witwen und Waisen im römischen Reich I: Verwitwung und Wiederverheiratung, 1994; 9 S. B. POMEROY, Families in Classical and Hellenistic Greece, 1997; 10 R. P. SALLER, Men's Age at Marriage and Its Consequences in the Roman Family, in: CPh 82, 1987, 21–34; 11 Id., Patriarchy, Property and Death in the Roman Family, 1994; 12 Id., D. I. KERTZER (ed.), The Family in Italy from Antiquity to the Present, 1991; 13 B. D. SHAW, The Age of Roman Girls at Marriage. Some Reconsiderations, in: JRS 77, 1987, 30–46.   J.W.

Marriage contracts A number of marriage contracts [MCs] are found among the Greek papyrus documents from Ptolemaic and Roman Egypt; they regulated both the moral obligations of the marriage partners and conjugal property law. They date from the period between the 4th cent. BC and the 6th cent. AD, and are (in contrast to the verbal agreements on dowries attested from Classical Athens) not to be understood as agreements between two families – as represented by the bride's father and the groom – but as an arrangement between the marrying couple themselves. Not only the bride's father and the groom took part, but also the mother of the bride and the bride (POxy. 372; 496; 1273), occasionally also the brother of the bride. The ἔκδοσις (*ékdosis*), the transfer of the bride to the groom, was a formal element of the MC. The bride could undertake the *ékdosis* herself without thereby becoming a concubine. The agreements regarding the goods brought to the marriage by the bride did not concern the classical dowry, or προίξ (*proíx*), which secured a share of the mother's family property for the children, but the traditional trousseau, the φερνή (*phernḗ*), which consisted in Greece (Plut. Solon 20,6) as also in Ptolemaic Egypt of clothing, jewellery and household equipment, whose value was often expressed in money. The oldest papyrus with a MC comes from Elephantine (311/310 BC), where there was a Greek garrison. The MC concluded between Demetrias from Cos and Heraclides from Temnus gave the *phernḗ*, which consisted of clothing and jewellery, a value of 1,000 drachmas (PElephantine 1).

As well as the value of the *phernḗ*, its return in the event of divorce, the extent of fines in the event of delayed return and the obligations of the husband to maintain the wife and uphold monogamy, were regulated in the MC. Duties demanded of the wife in the MC concerned domestic obligations and the guarding of the husband's honour. A MC from Tebtynis from the year 92 BC, for example, forbade the husband from taking another woman into the house and fathering children with her; in return, the wife was forbidden to leave the

house by day or night without the permission of the husband, and to enter a relationship with another man (PTebtunis I 104; cf. BGU 1052, 13 BC).

In Roman times, the term *proíx* was increasingly used alongside the word *phernḗ* because of assimilation with the → *dos*; further obligations were also agreed along with the dowry, such as the παράφερνα (*parápherna*) and προσφορά (*prosphorá*). In the MC between Chaeremon and Sisois, the father of Thaisarion, from the year AD 66 (PRylands 154) the distinction is clearly drawn between *phernḗ* and *parápherna*; the *parápherna* concerned jewellery and clothing, but also vessels for domestic use, objects which were precisely listed and generally did not pass into the possession of the husband. As *prosphorá*, the father of the bride gave the husband several estates; the husband for his part undertook actually to farm these lands and to pay all the taxes pursuant to them. In the event of divorce, it was stipulated that these estates would revert to Sisois, if still alive, otherwise to the wife; jewellery and clothing should, if the husband demanded divorce, be returned immediately or within 30 days. This MC was concluded in writing only when the *parápherna* and the estates were exchanged; prior to this, Chaeremon and Thaisarion had lived together in the form of γάμος ἄγραφος (*gámos ágraphos*), which probably constituted a full marriage, but was not contractually regulated.

1 T. GERGEN, Die Ehe in der Antike, 1995; 2 G. HÄGE, Ehegüterrechtliche Verhältnisse in den griechischen Papyri Ägyptens bis Diokletian, 1968; 3 J. M. MODRZEJEWSKI, Zum hellenistischen Ehegüterrecht, in: ZRG 87, 1970, 50–84; 4 S. B. POMEROY, Women in Hellenistic Egypt, 1990, 83–124; 5 H.-A. RUPPRECHT, Kleine Einführung in die Papyruskunde, 1994, 108–110; 6 Id., Zum Ehegattenrecht nach den Papyri, in: Bulletin of the American Society of Papyrologists 22, 1985, 291–295; 7 H. J. WOLFF, Grundlagen des griechischen Eherechts, in: TRG 20, 1952, 1–29, 157–181.   B.W.-H.

Marrucini Sabellian tribe of the Adriatic coast on the lower course of the → Aternus (Ptol. 3,1,20), with the main settlement at Teate (Plin. HN 3,106; also *Teate Marrucinorum*, CIL VI 2379, and *Teate Marrucino*, Itin. Anton. 310), modern Chieti; neighbours of the → Vestini, → Paeligni and → Frentani (Str. 5,4,2). In 304 BC, they concluded a peace treaty with Rome and an alliance (Liv. 9,45,18), which they upheld until the outbreak of the → Social War [3] (91 BC) (App. B Civ. 1,39). Together with the Vestini, Marsi and Frentani, the M. belonged to one of the seven units into which the allies of Rome were divided in 225 BC (Pol. 2,24,12). A reference to the descent of the *gens Asinia* (→ Asinius) from the M. is found in the poem Catull. 12, dedicated to Asinius Marrucinus.

J. PERIN, s.v. M., in: E. FORCELLINI, Onomasticon totius latinitatis, 1920; G. TAGLIAMONTE, I Sanniti, Caudini, Irpini, Pentri, Carricini, Frentani, 1996, 145, 150.   A.BO.

Marruvium (Μαρούιον; *Maroúion*). *Vicus*, later *municipium*, in Central Italy on the → lacus Fucinus with a harbour settlement on the Aternus, modern S. Benedetto dei Marsi. Inhabited by Sabellian Marrubii or → Marsi [2. 76], it was, from the 2nd cent. BC, dominant among its surrounding settlements (Str. 5,4,2; Sil. Pun. 8,510), and wealthy (Plin. HN 3,106). Various etymologies are cited for the place name [8]: the sea (Serv. Aen. 7,750), an eponymous commander (Cato in Prisc. 2,487,10; Serv. Aen. 7,750; 10,388; Sil. Pun. 8,505), the tribal ancestor Marsia, who was said to have founded the institution of augury (→ *augures*) [2. 25–46] for which the Marsi were well known (Plin. HN 3,108; Isid. Orig. 9,2,88). The citizens of M. were said to have magical skills, a gift from → Circe or Medea-Angitia (Serv. Aen. 7,750). Archaeological remains: urban site with rectangular street grid, public buildings (amphitheatre, *capitolium*, two monumental tombs [9]). The presence of a theatre is attested only by finds of statuary. Contrary to [1; 3] no fortification sites have been found; reused wall fragments [9] have to be attributed to the terracing of the town. Epigraphic records for the *municipium* in [2. 94], for urban institutions [2. *passim*], for cults of → Venus [2. 35], → Minerva, the → Penates [2. 72], → Vertumnus [2. 104; 5. 38f.] and → Bona Dea [2. 92] and for the social structure of the town [2; 4; 5; 6; 7].

1 C. LETTA, I Marsi e il Fucino nell'antichità, 1972; 2 C. Letta, S. D'AMATO, Epigrafia della regione dei Marsi, 1975, 20–130; 3 A. LA REGINA, s.v. M., in: PE, 553; 4 I. VALDISERRI PAOLETTI, Cippi funerari cilindrici dal territorio di M., in: RAL 35, 1980, 193–216; 5 G. PANI (ed.), Inscriptiones Christianae Italiae, septimo saeculo anteriores (Regio IV), 1986, 38f.; 6 S. SEGENNI, I liberti a M., in: Studi Classici e Orientali 37, 1987, 439–494; 7 S. Segenni, Iscrizioni inedite della IV regio, in: Epigraphica 51, 1989, 141–160; 8 R. MALTBY, A Lexicon of Ancient Latin Etymologies, 1991, 369; 9 P. SOMMELLA, s.v. M., in: EAA, Suppl. 2 (1971–1994), 1996, 555.   M.I.G.

Mars
I. CULT AND MYTH   II. ICONOGRAPHY

I. CULT AND MYTH
Mars is one of the oldest Italic-Roman deities. His original functions have been superimposed to such an extent that it proves difficult, maybe even impossible, to determine today the concepts that the Italic-Roman people had of him. The limitation of his function to the aspect of war corresponded to the interest of the Roman aristocracy to control the social significance and use of warfare.
A. NAME   B. FUNCTIONS   C. MARS ULTOR
D. IDENTIFICATIONS

A. NAME
Of the different forms of the name, *Mārs* was probably the earliest, since it spread in Italy so early and so widely that it cannot even have been influenced by Latin

(e.g. Tabulae Iguvinae Ia 11; VIb 1). The Arval hymn (→ Carmen Arvale; CIL 1² 2 = ILLRP 4) contains *Marma(r)*, *Mar(s)*, *Ma(r)mor*; the so-called → Lapis Satricanus (CIL 1² 2832a: *c.* 500 BC), presumably composed in Roman Latin, has *Mamartei*, nom. **Mamars*. According to Varro (Ling. 5,73), → *Mamers* is the Sabinian, according to Verrius Flaccus, the Oscan form (Paul. Fest. 116,2; Paul. Fest. 117,3; 23). In South Etruria and Campania, the related forms *Mamarc-*, *Mamerc-* occur as personal names. At an earlier time, these reduplicated forms were possibly preferred as particularly expressive for formal occasions such as prayers and votives [1. 378–381]. The form *Mavors* (CIL 1² 991 = ILLRP 217; Enn. Ann. 104) may be an analogous coining based on popular etymology (cf. *magna vertere*, 'to roll over something great', i.e. 'to destroy': Cic. Nat. D. 3,62). Like the related **Maurs* (dat. *Maurte*) in CIL 1² 49 = ILLRP 221 (Tusculum), *Mavors* can only be found in Latium ([2. 209f.] erroneously identifies *Maurte* as feminine). The forms *Marspiter*, *Maspiter* are apparently based on → Jupiter (CIL VI 487 = ILLRP 220; Varro, Ling. 10,65).

The Roman antiquarian etymology was *quod maribus in bello praeest*, 'because he commanded men in war' (Varro, Ling. 5,73). There is no generally accepted modern etymology; the name may not even be Indo-European [3].

B. FUNCTIONS
In historical times, M. is almost exclusively known as god of war and associated especially with the organized → phalanx and the fortunes of war. This function, which must originate from earliest times, reduces an originally larger lexical field, the exact area of which has been widely discussed and which probably had to do with the establishing and the control of borders, literally as well as figuratively.
1. WAR   2. 'ITALIC' MARS   3. MARS AND OTHER GODS

1. WAR
There is evidence for the fact that M. already played a significant role in the ritual determination of warfare in the early Roman Republic. A sequence of ancient festivals connected with M. marked the beginning of the fighting season in March, where the → Salii performed their dance (Dion. Hal. Ant. Rom. 2,70,2; [4. 144f.]). The → *suovetaurilia* at the censorial → *lustrum* (ibid. 4,22,1) and the → *lustratio exercitus*, *lustratio classis* (Cic. Div. 1,102; App. B Civ. 5,96) took place in honour of M. The temple of M. outside the Porta Capena in Rome (dedicated in 388 BC) was the starting point of the annual → *transvectio equitum* (Dion. Hal. Ant. Rom. 6,13,4).

Until Augustan times, the only place closely connected to M. within the → *pomerium* was a room in the → *regia*, where the *hastae Martis* ('the spears of M.') were kept, the 'spontaneous' movements of which communicated prodigies in the 2nd cent. BC (Liv. 40, 19,2;

Gell. 4,6,2). In this room, a special link between commanders and M. was created with a ritual of unknown age, during which the leader of an army, before leaving the city, touched one of the spears and spoke the words *Mars vigila*, 'Mars, awake!' (Serv. Aen. 8,3; Plut. Romulus 29,1; [5. 133–135]). A series of deifications from the Middle Republic (CIL 1² 609: M. Claudius Marcellus, *cos. III* 214; temple for M. Gradivus in the Campus Martius of D. Iunius Brutus, *cos.* 138: Plin. HN 36,26; Prop. 4,3,71) as well as stories of M.'s intervention in battles (C. Fabricius Luscinus, *cos.* 282: Val. Max. 1,8,6) suggest the same link. The mythology of M. as father of → Romulus (Liv. 1,4,2; Dion. Hal. Ant. Rom. 1,76,1f.; 2,2,3; Hor. Carm. 3,3,16) gave the expansionist ambitions of the epoch a touch of predestination. Q. Fabius [I 24] Maximus Allobrogicus, *cos.* 121 BC, appears to have been the first general to dedicate a sanctuary to M. on a battlefield outside of Italy (Str. 4,1,11).

The informal identification of M. and the Greek → Ares must have preceded the first → *lectisternium* of the → Twelve (Olympian) gods in 217 BC, where M. formed a pair with → Venus (Liv. 22,10,9). This identification resulted in a view of the war as an ideal-typical male undertaking (cf. Plaut. Mil. 11f.), which continued to dominate the iconographical and literary representations and which is also the basis for the antonomasia M. = war (Quint. Inst. 8,6,24) and its result (e.g. M. *communis*, the lot/fate shared by everyone during war: Liv. 10,28,1).

Epigraphical testimonies indicate changes in the votive practice (→ Votive offerings) in context with a general continuity between the Late Republic and the Principate. Like the great Republican generals (Sulla in Sicyon: CIL 1² 2828 = ILLRP 224; Caesar: App. B Civ. 2,68; Octavian in Actium/Nicopolis: AE 1992, 1534; cf. Plut. Marius 46, 433e; Prop. 2,34b,56), the emperors regularly invoked M., after a victory and increasingly in light of an impending victory (e.g. Trajan in Parthia, BMCRE 3,262 no. 258). At the public celebration of 1 January, he was invoked as *Pater* ('father') and *Victor* ('victor'). He thus was given an important part in the imperial theology of victory (M. Augustus: e.g. AE 1992, 1770; 1994, 589). On the other hand, M. was institutionalized as a kind of god of the army. At military deifications, he was often mentioned immediately following the Capitoline Trias (cf. CIL VII 1114; VIII 2465; ILS 2181; AE 1994, 1446); on 7 January, when the troops were released, he received sacrifices; the → Feriale Duranum further lists for 1 March (*feriae Martis*: 1.20; cf. CIL II 4083) a sacrifice for M. in camp. Despite the literary tradition (e.g. Dion. Hal. Ant. Rom. 4,70,5), there are hardly any indications for votive offerings of individual soldiers for M. alone (CIL III 3470).

2. 'ITALIC' MARS

Only few Roman deities have experienced as many re-evaluations in the past 150 years as M. [6. 1–18].

There are three main reasons for the assumption that M. was not exclusively a god of war in early times: 1) Some of his areas of activity do not have a typical military character. M. was, for instance, invoked in a → *lustratio agri* from the 2nd cent. BC as god of protection for the fields and animals of an agrarian estate (Cato Agr. 141). The Arval hymn (*Carmen Arvale*) also seems to associate M. with the protection of borders from contamination. Moreover, there is no reason to interpret the numerous local and gentilic Italic *Martes* as predominantly military (e.g. CIL 1² 33 = ILLRP 248; ibid. 1513 = 573; CIL XI 5805; AE 1995, 248). 2) The → *ver sacrum*, where in an emergency the entire human, animal as well as vegetable yield of a year would be dedicated to the gods, was tied closely to M.: the animals holy to him (e.g. *picus*, 'woodpecker'; *hirpus*, 'wolf') were often the ones that showed the exiled individuals affected by the rite of the *ver sacrum* their way (→ Hirpini; → Picentes: Str. 5,4,2; 12; cf. Dion. Hal. Ant. Rom. 1,16). 3) Archaic iconographic testimonies suggest that M. was associated with the taking in of children by families [7]. The Lapis Satricanus (see above), probably an act of deification to M. by the *sodales*, 'companions' of a P. Valerius, possibly implies a special relationship with the young warriors ('ephebes'). According to a more recent trend in research, in pre- and protohistoric epochs M. may have been a deity who, analogous to → Apollo, embodied the border between order (on the inside) and disorder (outside) and controlled the cycle of regeneration [8]. This, however, remains speculation.

3. MARS AND OTHER GODS

In historical times, M.'s relationship with → Venus superposed earlier associations with → Nerio (Gell. NA 13,23) and → Bellona (Liv. 8,9,6). The assimilation of → Quirinus with Romulus led, in the later Republic, to speculations that Quirinus may be a form of M. *tranquillus* ('calm', 'peaceable'; Serv. Aen. 1,292) or even of the Sabine M. Enyalius (Dion. Hal. Ant. Rom. 2,48,2) [9. 246–271]. These reflections linked two gods whose ancient priesthood (→ *flamines*) had become incomprehensible. By identifying him with Ares, M. was considered to be the son of → Juno/Hera (Ov. Fast. 5,229–260).

C. MARS ULTOR

C. Iulius Caesar's intention to dedicate a temple to M. (Suet. Iul. 44,1) was taken up by his heir Octavian (→ Augustus) probably in 42 BC (Ov. Fast. 5,573; RRC 494/7–9), but not carried out until 19 BC the Parthians returned the legion standards lost near Carrhae (= → Ḥarran). The temple was originally planned for the Capitolium (Cass. Dio 54,8,3), but finally integrated into the Forum [III 1] Augustum (consecrated on 12 May, 2 BC; Suet. Aug. 29,2) [10. 83–95]. Its program, with the temple of M. in the centre, translated the new political reality as well as Augustus' religious and culture political practice into a figurative form [11]; it was imitated by a series of provincial towns (e.g. Emerita,

Tarracona). The new temple of M. replaced the → regia as the symbolic centre of Rome's military power (Cass. Dio 55,10,2–5). However, the cult was not exclusively of official nature: some votives of private individuals are also known (CIL IX 4108).

D. IDENTIFICATIONS

Apart from the assimilation with Ares, M. was identified with a large number of local deities, primarily in Roman Gallia and Germania. In deifications, M. appears alone, with indigenous epithet or in association with local gods [12]. Only the names of these deities are known in the majority of cases, but the Celtic god of war was, like the early M., also the protector of natural fertility. M. thus represents an important link in the transfer between the Roman and the indigenous pantheа (→ Pantheon) [13. 94–111].

1 WACHTER ; 2 RADKE ; 3 A. G. RAMAT, Studi intorno ai nomi del dio Marte, in: Archivio Glottologico Italiano 47, 1962, 112–142; 4 G. WISSOWA, Religion und Kultus der Römer, ²1912; 5 J. RÜPKE, Domi militiae, 1990; 6 U. W. SCHOLZ, Studien zum altitalischen und altrömischen Marskult und Marsmythos, 1970; 7 L. ARCELLA, L'iscrizione di Satricum e il mito di P. Valerio, in: SMSR 58, 1992, 219–247; 8 H. S. VERSNEL, Apollo and M. One Hundred Years after Roscher, in: VisRel 4–5, 1985–1986, 134–172 (= Id., Inconsistencies in Greek and Roman Religion, vol. 2, 1993, 289–334; 9 DUMÉZIL; 10 J. W. RICH, Augustus' Parthian Honours, in: PBSR n.s. 53, 1998, 71–128; 11 E. LA ROCCA, Il programma figurativo del Foro di Augusto, in: Id. et al. (ed.), I luoghi del consenso imperiale: il Foro di Augusto, il Foro di Traiano, 1995, 74–87; 12 H. MERTEN, Der Kult des M. im Trevererraum, in: TZ 48, 1985, 7–113; 13 T. DERKS, Gods, Temples and Ritual Practices, 1998.

J. H. CROON, Die Ideologie des Marskultes unter dem Prinzipat und ihre Vorgeschichte, in: ANRW II 17.1, 1981, 246–275; SIMON, GR, 135–145; J. H. VANGAARD, The October Horse, in: Temenos 15, 1979, 81–95.   R.G.

II. ICONOGRAPHY

Italic bronze statuettes from the 6th to 4th cents. BC document M. as a lance-wielding warrior with shield and lance, naked but helmeted, or fully armed, with helmet, greaves and (adorned) armour, mostly without beard; approximately in the mid 5th cent. BC, the version of the calmly standing figure with positioned lance and patera was added. The only large sculpture documented from Republican times is the similarly armed 'Todi M.', also with the sacrificial cup in his right hand (Etruscan bronze statue, Rome, MV, around 400 BC, identification with M. likely); earliest verified epigraphical representation of the armed god on the Praenestine Cista (Berlin, SM, last third of the 4th cent. BC; → Praenestine cistae). Among the numerous bronze statuettes from the provinces (1st cent. BC to 2nd/3rd cents. AD), there is one type predominantly known through coins and gems: M., beardless, the cloth in motion around his hips, in dance-like position, with helmet, lance or sword and → tropaion (trophy) or signum (standard) – possibly in allusion to the cultic dance of the → Salii, cf. Hellenistic representations of armed dancers (Pyrrhicists). This type is considered the patron of the praetorian camp; the same M. iconography can be found on coins of the signis-receptis- demissions coined in 19–16/15 BC after the recovery of the Roman standards lost to the Parthians.

The lost cult statue of the temple of M. Ultor on the → Forum Augustum in Rome, consecrated in 2 BC, can be deduced from later records. These are, next to coin images, gems and bronze statuettes, especially the colossal statue of the Forum of Nerva (Rome, MC, Domitian copy, around AD 90), the Algiers marble relief (NM, early Imperial period) and the Sorrento marble base (Mus. Correale; early 1st cent. AD). Characteristic are the full, curled beard, armour, shield and lance. On the Ara Pacis Augustae, M. appears with Romulus and Remus, bearded and armed, as father of the state founder and thus as ancestor of Rome (relief on the entrance steps in the west, 13–9 BC). On further state reliefs, he must be understood as war and protection deity of the emperors and their undertakings: Cancelleria reliefs, frieze A (Rome, MV, AD 94/96), Arch of Trajan at Beneventum (townside and outside, AD 114), Arch of Constantine in Rome (panels of the Arch of Marcus Aurelius, AD 176).

Representations of M. with other deities and especially with → Venus as one of the central themes of national and private Roman visual arts were wide-spread on votive and sarcophagus reliefs, mosaics, coins, gems, medallions and especially in Pompeian → wall paintings.

Inscriptions from the north-west provinces of the Roman empire document the great worship of M. with native epithet; numerous representations exist that show him primarily as god of war in arms (for Roman copies/transformations of Ares statues see → Ares, iconography).

H. J. MARTIN, Zur Kultbildgruppe im M.-Ultor-Tempel, Wiss. Zschr. der Wilhelm-Pieck-Univ. Rostock, Ges. und sprachwiss. Reihe 37, 1988, 55–64; M. SIEBLER, Studien zum augusteischen M. Ultor, 1988; E. SIMON, G. BAUCHHENSS, s.v. Ares/M., LIMC II, 505–580 (with additional literature); H. S. VERSNEL, Apollo and M. One Hundred Years after Roscher, in: Visible Rel. 4–5, 1985–86, 134–172 (= Id., Inconsistencies in Greek and Roman Rel., vol. 2, 1993, 289–334).   A.L.

Marsanes Title of a very fragmentarily preserved Gnostic text from → Nag Hammadi (Codex X,1) in the Coptic language (Subakhmimic). The name Marsanes is also attested in the Anonymum Brucianum, in which M. appears alongside Nikotheus as a prophet of the highest truth [1. 235], and in Epiphanius (Adversus haereses 40,7,6) in the context of the description of the Archontes (here in the form Marsianes; → Archontes [II]): he was translated to heaven and returned after three days. NHCod X,1 also describes an ascension into the divine spheres. The author distinguishes between thirteen levels of cognition/gnosis, which are symbolically described as seals. They are headed by the non-being, silent Father, the invisible Spirit endowed with three powers, Barbelo (a female hypostatis of God) and the unbegotten Spirit. The central part of the text contains speculations about the connections between letters, the soul and the heavenly powers. The final part is badly damaged.

The text may be part of the Sethian Gnostic writings (→ Sethianism); it was possibly known by the Gnostics with whom → Plotinus argued (see Porph. Vita Plotini 16: 'Apocalypses of Zoroastres, Zostrianus and others'). The terminology shows clear references to Neoplatonic writings [2; 3]. There is also a possibility of underlying theurgic practices (→ Theurgy).

→ Gnosis, Gnostics, Gnosticism

1 C. SCHMIDT, V. MACDERMOT, The Books of Jeu and the Untitled Text in the Bruce Codex (NHS 13), 1978; 2 B. A. PEARSON, The Tractate Marsanes and the Platonic Tradition, in: B. ALAND (ed.), Gnosis. FS H. Jonas, 1978, 373–384; 3 Id., Gnosticism, Judaism and Egyptian Christianity, 1990, 148–164.

TEXT AND TRANSLATION B. A. PEARSON, Nag Hammadi Codices IX and X (NHS 15), 1981, 211–352; J. M. ROBINSON, R. SMITH, The Nag Hammadi Library in English, ³1988, 460–471; G. LÜDEMANN, M. JANSSEN, Bibel der Häretiker, 1997, 535–550. J.HO.

Marsi

[1] Tribe in the Central Italian Appenninus near → Lacus Fucinus (Str. 5,2,1; Ptol. 3,1,57), regarded as brave and warlike (Str. 5,4,2; Plin. HN 3,106; Liv. 8,29,4; Verg. G. 2,167; cf. the etymological derivation from 'Mars'). As descendants of a son of → Circe they allegedly were immune to snake poison (Plin. HN 7,15; 21,78; 25,11; 28,30; Gell. NA 16,11,1; cf. Cic. Div. 1,132; 2,70; Hor. Epod. 17,29; Hor. Carm. 2,20,18). Characteristic of the M. was the cultivation of vegetables and herbs on their land (cf. Plin. HN 25,48; Columella 2,9,8; 6,5,3; 12,10,1). The area of the M. was bisected by the *via Valeria* (Str. 5,3,11). The following towns of the M. are known: Anxa (modern Gallipoli), → Antinum, Lucus Fucens (modern Luco), → Marruvium (San Benedetto; Plin. HN 3,106), and Archippe (Plin. HN 3,108). Early on the M. entered into friendly relations with Rome: In 308/7 BC the consuls supported them against the → Samnites (Diod. Sic. 20,44,8); in 304/3 BC a treaty with Rome was concluded (Diod. Sic. 20,101,5; Liv. 9,45,18). The → Social War [3] (91–89 BC) was called *bellum Marsicum* after its instigators (see Diod. Sic. 37,1; Str. 5,4,2; Diod. Sic. 37,2; Liv. per. 72–76; Vell. Pat. 2,15).

NISSEN 2, 454; R. SCLOCCHI, Storia dei M. 1–3, 1911; G. DEVOTO, Gli antichi Italici, 1931, 335ff.; C. LETTA, I M. e il Fucino nell'antichità, 1972; Ders., S. D'AMATO, Epigrafia della regione dei M., 1975. S.D.V.

[2] German tribe that first settled on the Rhine but by 8 BC had retreated 'into the interior' (Str. 7,1,3). Later the M. lived between the rivers Ruhr and Lippe. They were thought to be descended from one of the eponymous sons of the god Mannus (Tac. Germ. 2,2). In the battle against Varus they apparently fought on the German side. In AD 14, → Germanicus [2] devastated their land in a surprise attack and destroyed the famous sanctuary of Tamfana (Tac. Ann. 1,50f.). The following spring Caecina [II 8] was able to thwart an attack by the M. (Tac. Ann. 1,56,5). In AD 16, Germanicus mounted another campaign against the M. whose leader → Mallovendus had recently surrendered. On that occasion the second eagle standard of Varus' legions, lost to the M. in AD 9, was won back (Tac. Ann. 2,25,1f.. cf. 1,60,3). According to a controversial remark in Cass. Dio 60,8,7, Gabinius [II 3] supposedly seized the third lost eagle standard from the *Marúsioi* in AD 41; it is rather unlikely that the M. are meant (cf. Suet. Claud. 24,3; Str. 7,1,4).

M. SCHÖNFELD, s.v. M. (2), RE 14, 1979f.; 2 D. TIMPE, Die Söhne des Mannus, in: Chiron 21, 1991, 69–125, bes. 104–106. RA.WI.

Marsigni German tribe settling 'in the back of', i.e. to the north or north-east of the Marcomanni and Quadi (Tac. Germ. 43,1).

E. SCHWARZ, Germanische Stammeskunde, 1956, 164; G. PERL, Tacitus, Germania, in: J. HERRMANN (Ed.), Griechische und lateinische Quellen zur Frühgeschichte Mitteleuropas bis zur Mitte des 1. Jahrtausends unserer Zeitrechnung, part 2, 1990, 245. RA.WI.

Marsiliana d'Albegna Of the Etruscan settlement (possibly Caletra in antiquity) on the confluence of Albegna and Elsa in the Maremma/south Etruria only the necropoleis are known, and they provide evidence for a significant agrarian centre in the late 8th to 6th cents. BC. Earliest phase: pozzetto graves dating from the late Villanovan period for cremations and fossa graves for inhumations. Later fossa graves were placed within a stone circle made of travertine slabs, before they are replaced by chamber tombs. The sample alphabet on an ivory writing tablet from the richly furnished Circolo degli Avori (2nd half of the 7th cent.) includes the letters b and d that are not used in Etruscan. This reflects the adoption of the western Greek alphabet by the Etruscans.

→ Ager Caletranus; → Italy, alphabetical scripts (with fig.)

M. MICHELUCCI, s.v. M., EAA Suppl. 2, 1971–1994, vol. 3, 1995, 558–559; A. MINTO, M. d'A., 1921. M.M.

Marsonia Fort and settlement in → Pannonia inferior on the river Savus and on the road from Siscia to Sirmium, modern Slavonski Brod in Croatia. The road starting at Siscia bifurcated north of Marsonia; the northern branch led to Sirmium via Cibalae, the southern branch via Marsonia and Saldis. In late antiquity, *auxilia ascarii* are mentioned as the garrison of Marsonia (Not. Dign. Occ. 32,43).

M. FLUSS, s.v. M., RE 14, 1981; TIR L 34, Budapest, 1968, 78.   J.BU.

Marsup(p)ium see → Purse

Marsus Isaurian, East Roman general, honorary consul AD 484; fought against the Vandals in 468; he followed → Illus to Antioch in 481, and died in 484 having taken part in Illus' uprising against Emperor → Zeno.

PLRE 2, 728f. Nr. 2; STEIN, Spätröm. R. 1, 577f.   F.T.

Marsyaba (Μαρσύαβα/ *Marsýaba*, var. Μαρσίαβα/ *Marsíaba*, Μαρσυαβαί/ *Marsyabaí* Str. 16,782). A town of the tribe of the Rhammanitae (Ῥαμμανῖται; *Rhammanîtai*) in → Arabia Felix, subject to Ilasarus (Ἰλασάρος; *Ilasáros*). In 24 BC, M. was unsuccessfully besieged for six days by the Roman army (→ Aelius [II 11] Gallus); cf. the contemporary Sabaean inscription Répertoire d'Épigraphie Sémitique 4085, according to which the leader of the tribe of the Rhammanitae built an irrigation system for his master Ilšaraḥ. In other campaign reports (R. Gest. div. Aug. 26; Plin. HN 6,160) the town is named Mariba, and in two further passages by Strabo (16,768 and 778) it is referred to as → Mariaba (cf. this passage for the form of the name).

1 H. VON WISSMANN, Die Geschichte des Sabäerreiches und der Feldzug des Aelius Gallus, in: ANRW II 9.1, 1976, 396–400.   W.W.M. A.D.

Marsyas (Μαρσύας; *Marsýas*).

[1] Phrygian river god and → Celaenae's god of protection, represented as → satyr or → silenus. The name is derived from a toponym that can be found repeatedly throughout Asia Minor and Syria; the river, at the source of which Celaenae lies, also carries this name (M. [5]). M. was considered the discoverer of flute playing (*aulós*), the inventor of the bandage used for flute playing (*phorbeiá*) and of songs for the worship of the goddess → Cybele. According to the myth, the possibility to play music with the flute was discovered by Athena, but she dismisses her discovery when she realizes that it disfigures her face. M. takes over the flute and then, relying on his musical talents, challenges → Apollo to a contest, which, however, he loses; he is hung on a tree and maltreated as a punishment for challenging the god.

The earliest literary records for this myth stem from the 5th cent. BC (Melanippides of Melos, PMG 758; Hdt. 7,26; presumably also a satyr play by Euripides); → Myron's sculpture group with M. and Athena also dates from this time; the popularity of the motif stands

in the context of the growing significance of flute playing and Phrygian music for the education of this period. After these primarily aetiologically oriented versions of the myth, from the 4th cent. BC, M.'s hubris toward Apollo is emphasized more strongly (Pl. Symp. 215b; Diod. Sic. 3,59,2ff.); in the Hellenistic and Roman literature, the representation of the punishment became more strongly the focus of attention (Anth. Pal. 7,696; 9,266; 16,6; Alexander Polyhistor FGrH 273 F 76; Ov. Met. 6,382–400; Apul. Flor. 3); this is also intensely received in the Hellenistic visual arts.

O. JESSEN, s.v. M., ML 2, 2439–2460; I. WEILER, Der Agon im Mythos, 1974, 37–59; P. RAWSON, The Myth of M. in the Roman Visual Arts: An Iconographic Study, 1987; A. WEISS, s.v. M., LIMC 6.1, 367–378; J. P. SMALL, Cacus and M. in Etrusco-Roman Legend, 1982, 68–92; 127–142; F. FÜHMANN, M. Mythos und Traum, 1993.   E.V.

[2] The Suda (s.v. M., no. 227–229 ADLER) names three men designated as historians called M.: the son of Periander from Pella and brother (on the mother's side) of → Antigonus [1] (cf. Plut. Mor. 182c), the son of Critophemus from Philippi (referred to as 'the Younger') and the son of Marsus from Tabae.

(a) The first, a *sýntrophos* of → Alexander [4] the Great (i.e. he grew up with him), wrote a history of Macedonia (*Makedoniká*) in 10 bks. (until Alexander's return from Egypt to Syria), a work about Alexander's *agōgḗ* (title presumably *Alexándrou agōgḗ*), that possibly dealt with the his education and upbringing, and a history of Athens (*Attiká*) in 12 bks. (never quoted). (b) Nothing is attributed to the second M.: the loss of a list must be assumed. (c) The third M. wrote an 'Ancient History' (*Archaiología*) in 12 bks., a 'Mythology' (*Mythikḗ*) in 6 bks. and several works about his native city → Tabae.

The fact that the second M. (b) also wrote a Macedonian history (this is why he is sometimes distinguished from the first as 'the Younger') is evident from four fragments (FGrH 135–136 F 4–7) (F 8 may also come from it). The third, M. from Tabae (c), to whom no quotation is attributed by name, is often discarded by scholars as a mere mistake (see [1. 450]), but for no apparent reason. The history of Phaon and Aphrodite (Ath. 2,69d), attributed to M. the Younger (b), would be more suitable for the historian from Tabae (c) (also F 19, naming a M. without further specification). The work of M. of Tabae appears to have no longer been read in Late Antiquity; only quotations from later works were known (often – as far as they are available to us – only marked as *by M.*).

We do not know which M. served as the priest of Hercules (Ath. 11,467c); the fragment describes a royal ritual. Two quotations (FGrH 135–136 F 2–3), precisely attributed to a 'History of Alexander bk. 5', appear to originate from a second work of M. the Younger (b) lost in the Suda. They do not match the *Agōgḗ* (JACOBY FGrH 135–136 before F 2 and comm.). Most fragments, however, cannot be attributed with certainty to any of the three.

1 W. HECKEL, M. of Pella, Historian of Macedon, in: Hermes 108, 1980, 444–462 (primarily on (a); with bibliography).

EDITIONS: FGrH 135–136 F 1–25 with commentary (FGrH II D).   E.B.

[3] Μαρσύας/*Marsýas*, according to Pol. 5,45,8ff.; 61,7, Μαρσσύας/*Marssýas*, according to Str. 16,753; 755; 756 is the name of the fertile plain of the Orontes between Laodicea [2] and Chalcis, otherwise mostly referred to as → Coele Syria.   H.J.N. K.Z.

[4] Left tributary of the → Maeander in south-west Asia Minor, has its source in the Carian landscape → Idrias (Hdt. 5,118); modern Çine Çayı.

[5] Another tributary of the Maeander; together with the Obrimas and Obras it flows around the city of Apamea [2] (Plin. HN 5,106); modern Dinar Suyu. Xen. An. 1,2,8 a castle of the Persian Great King has been attested near → Celaenae on the sources of this M.

[6] Eastern tributary of the → Orontes, border between Apamea [3] and the tetrarchy of the Nazerini (Plin. HN 5,81), modern Nahr Marzbān.

[7] Western tributary of the Euphrates, between Samosata and Zeugma (Plin. HN 5,86); modern Merzumen Dere.   H.SO.

Marsyas Painter (MP) One of the most significant Attic red-figure vase painters of the 4th cent. BC from the group of the painters of → Kertsch ware. He received his name from a representation of → Marsyas on the pelike St. Petersburg St. 1795. Approximately 13 of his works have so far been preserved, primarily large vessels (lebetes gamikoi, pelikes, hydrias, lekanides, among others); P. VALAVANIS recently added 10 → Panathenaic prize amphorae from Eretria, contributing greatly to the clarification of chronological problems of this epoch. The MP's themes derive from the world of women, gods and mortals (Dionysus, Ariadne, Demeter and Kore, Thetis and Peleus, among others). His figures are harmonic and monumental at the same time and rendered with confident, single brush strokes. Contractions and shortenings contribute to the spatial rendition of the figures, but also to their statue-like characterisation. The naked parts of the figures are rendered with accuracy, while rich detail and particular volume distinguish the fabrics of the garments. The lebes gamikos St. Petersburg, ER 15592, stands out from his work, with its representation of the *epaúlia*, the feast of the newly-wed wife. P. VALAVANIS argues that the work stretches over the decades between 370 BC and 340–330 BC and that the MP is identical with the Eleusinian Painter; however, this question remains unsettled.

BEAZLEY, ARV², 1474f.; BEAZLEY, Paralipomena, 495ff.; BEAZLEY, Addenda², 381; P. VALAVANIS, Panathenaikoi amphoreis apo ten Eretria, 1991.   S.DR.

Marten Since there are no descriptions, we can not know whether the two species, beech marten (*Martes foina*, with white throat patch) and pine marten (*Martes martes*, with yellow throat patch), were known in antiquity. Hom. Il. 10,335 and 458 κτιδέην κυνέην/ *ktidéēn kynéēn* could be translated as 'helmet of marten fur' [1. 1,160].ἴκτις/*íktis* (Aristot. Hist. an. 2,1,500b 24; cf. Plin. HN 29,60: *mustelarum genus silvestre*) may be a → weasel. Aristoph. Ach. 880 mentions *íktis* pelts on the market in Athens; Nik. Ther. 196 speaks of them killing poultry, which suggests martens. Aristot. Hist. an. 8(9),6,612b 10–17 apparently describes a beech marten ([2. 903; according to [1. 1,162] a weasel, *Mustela nivalis boccamela*), the size of a Pomeranian (→ Dog [1]), which not only chases birds but loves honey as well.

→ Ferret; → Polecat

1 KELLER ;   2 A. STEIER, s.v. Mustela, RE 16,903–908.
                                                         C.HÜ.

Martha Syrian prophetess who came to Rome in 105 BC. Although M. had been banned from practising her art by the Senate, she gained access to members of the high nobility by correctly predicting the outcome of gladiatorial fights. In 102, Iulia [1] sent her to her husband C. Marius [I 1] in Gallia where she helped to lift the morale of the Roman troops who were fighting the Teutons (Plut. Marius 17,2–5 after Posidonius).   K.-L.E.

Martialis
[1] **M. Valerius M.** the Roman poet Martial.
A. BIOGRAPHY B. WORK C. HISTORY OF RECEPTION

A. BIOGRAPHY
The epigrammatist M. was born between AD 38 and 41 (cf. Mart. 10,24: 57th birthday) in Bilbilis in the province of Hispania Tarraconensis. Around 64, he came to Rome (10,103), where he was probably at first promoted in the circle of → Seneca. His poetic production does not become tangible for us until much later, when he celebrated the inauguration of the *amphitheatrum Flavianum* (→ Colosseum) in 80 with a book of epigrams (*De spectaculis* or *Epigrammaton liber*), preserved only in excerpts. The books *Xenia* and *Apophoreta*, counted as bks. 13 and 14, follow later (c. 83–85). The 12-bk. *Epigrammata* took shape gradually in the years 86 to c. 102. Bk. 12 was composed in Spain, where M. returned to in 98, living on an estate that he owed to a benefactor named Marcella. In his letter 3,21, Pliny the Younger writes an obituary to M., revealing his date of death to be no later than AD 104. M. was awarded the Roman equestrian rank on the basis of a titular tribunate awarded to him (3,95,9; 5,13); he owned an estate north-east of Rome near Nomentum, and later also a house in Rome. His self-representation as 'beggar poet' should not be viewed strictly autobiographically. He received from Titus the

ius trium liberorum, the privileges of a father of three children, later renewed by Domitian; he was most likely unmarried.

B. Work

M. was looking back at an already enduring history of the genre of Greek and Latin → epigram, but it was he who emphatically raised the term *epigramma* to a generic term designating a literary genre. While the epigram was seen in contemporary Roman society as amateur poetry practiced on the side, and on the lowest rank within the hierarchy of literary genres (12, 94, 9), M., for whom the epigram is the centre of his life's work, claims literary prestige for the genre because of its aesthetic quality. Among his Latin predecessors, he names in particular → Catullus [1], → Domitius [III 2] Marsus and → Albinovanus [5] Pedo. From the history of the Greek epigram, he primarily uses the authors of the directly preceding decades, mainly → Lucillius, who was the first to assign a decisive role to the satirical epigram. The topics and form of M.' work, however, are overall largely independent.

In his early epigram bks., M. cultivates the variation of one topic per book. In *De spectaculis,* he describes and comments on the individual shows at the amphitheatre; the *Xenia* and *Apophoreta,* in which the length of two verses per epigram remains constant, offer brief, inscription-like characterizations of objects. The later 12 bks. are characterized by a great variety of topics and in poem size as well as of metre. Variation also determines the composition of the individual bks. The satirical epigram plays a significant role overall, but does not dominate as one-sidedly as late antique and post-classical reception may suggest. Other sub-genres of the epigram tradition, as well as many additional themes, appear repeatedly in M.'s work: among others, funerary epigrams, epigrams on objects, works of art and villas, homages to the emperor, praise of various friends and benefactors, historical exempla, bizarre events, reflections on life, poetological concepts. Overall, M. paints a picture of daily life in the Rome of his day (cf. 8,3,20; 10,4,10: *hominem pagina nostra sapit*; 'my text has the flavour of man'). He contrasts the closeness to life of his epigram with the distance from life of mythological poetry (9,50; 10,4). The great genres enjoy more prestige, but he refers to the popularity of his poems among their audience (4,49). Obscenity, according to M.' statements, is an essential, genre-specific element of his poems (1 praef.); it is, however, missing from bks. 5 and 8.

The mockery is directed not so much at known contemporaries, as is the case in Catullus for instance, but at human behaviour patterns, described by using fictitious names (1 praef.; 10,33,10: *parcere personis, dicere de vitiis*: 'to spare persons, to speak of mistakes'). Compared to the clear-cut types and professional groups mocked by Lucillius, M.' people are more differentiated, more concrete and multifaceted. M. names his friends and benefactors by their real names. The thesis

that critical undertones can be read into M.'s panegyric epigram of the emperor Domitian, although repeatedly put forward in newer research, remains controversial. After the death of Domitian (AD 96), M. programmatically disclaims the personified flatteries (*blanditiae*) (10,72, to Nerva) – which of course is in itself another form of homage to the emperor, now adapted to the new regime.

M.' preferred metres are the elegiac distich and the Catullus-inspired hendecasyllables; other metres used occasionally such as choliambs as well as, sporadically, iambs or even hexameters (6,64) contribute to the metric diversity (→ Metre). According to the content's closeness to life, many elements of colloquial speech can be found. M.' greatest accomplishment lies in his skill for form, in which tendencies of the genre tradition coalesce with the contemporary predilection for emphasis into an apogee of the ancient epigram. The division of individual epigrams into a first, descriptive part, outlining the circumstances, and a briefly focussed, commented final part, oftentimes with a surprise effect, is characteristic. Against Lessing's designations of these parts as 'expectation' and 'revelation', it is to be noted in accordance with more recent research, that the first part does not only serve the preparation of a solely important final punch line, but also represents, as a richly detailed, vivid description, an essential element of M.' concept of the epigram.

C. History of reception

M. frequently mentions the success of his epigrams with his contemporaries. Yet Pliny the Younger remains rather reserved in his obituary with regard to M.' possible posthumous fame (Ep. 3,21,6). → Iuvenalis, who knew M. in person, used motifs from his epigrams in his satires. In Late Antiquity, M. is known and occasionally quoted; M. is also used by epigrammatists such as → Ausonius and → Luxurius, but overall the genre takes a rather different direction in this epoch. The fact that M. was primarily considered a representative of the satirical epigram is revealed by the expression *mordax sine fine Martialis* ('the ceaselessly acid-tongued Martial') in → Sidonius Apollinaris (Carm. 9,268) as well as by the designation as *satyricus* in → Theodorus Priscianus (*Libri de physicis fragmentum* p. 251 ROSE), which is based on the late antique expansion of this term beyond the borders of the genre → satire. M. himself considered epigram and satire as two different literary genres (12,94,7–9).

One of the three recensions in which M.' text is preserved in the Middle Ages goes back, according to the *subscriptio,* to an edition of Torquatus Gennadius from AD 401. From the 11th cent. onwards, M. receives the epithet Cocus. In the high Middle Ages, M. is read as a moralistic-satirical poet. Godefrid of Winchester's (*c.* 1050–1107) *Liber proverbiorum,* inspired by M. in this respect, is sometimes even transmitted under M.' name and added to his real work as a 15th bk.

Humanism led to a new preoccupation with M. and his work, which at first included imitations of the obscenity (ANTONIUS PANORMITA, 15th cent.). M. formed an important basis for Neo-Latin and vernacular composition of epigrams from the 15th to the 18th cent. and for the theory of the epigram. In this context, however, he has to compete with Catullus and the Greek Anthology. ANDREA NAVAGERO (1483–1529) is said to have burnt one copy of M.' work each year. Some editions from the 16th cent. onwards, especially those of the Jesuits, leave out the obscene poems. M.'s way of exaggerating and highlighting certain points finds favour particularly with those epochs that themselves attribute great significance to this trait, as for instance the Baroque era. The Neo-Latin epigrammatist John OWEN (1564–1622) is considered the English M.; LESSING's epigram theory is essentially based on M., while HERDER turns towards the Greek epigram. GOETHE and SCHILLER draw the title of their *Xenien* from M.

Besides the one-sidedly antiquarian-oriented commentary by FRIEDLÄNDER, the older commentaries such as those by COLLESSO or Matthaeus RADER retain their significance; modern commentaries are only available for some individual books. A proper literary appraisal has gained new momentum over the last years.
→ Epigram;   → Satire;   → #Epigrammatic   poetry#;
→ Satire

EDITIONS: W. M. LINDSAY, ²1929; W. HERAEUS, I. BOROVSKIJ, 1976; D. R. SHACKLETON BAILEY, 1990 (with Eng. transl.).
TRANSLATIONS: W. HOFMANN, M., Epigramme, 1997; P. BARIÉ, W. SCHINDLER, M.V.M., Epigramme, 1999.
COMMENTARIES: M. RADER, 1602; V. COLLESSO, 1680; L. FRIEDLÄNDER, 1886; U. WALTER, 1996 (selection).
ON SINGLE BOOKS: Bk. 1: M. CITRONI, 1975; P. HOWELL, 1980; Bk. 2: CRAIG. A. WILLIAMS, 2004; Bk. 5: P. HOWELL, 1995; Bk. 6: F. GREWING, 1997; Bk. 7: GUILLERMO GALÁN VIOQUE, 2002; Bk. 8: CHRISTIAN SCHÖFFEL, 2002; Bk. 10: GREGOR DAMSCHEN and ANDREAS HEIL, 2004; Bk. 11: N. M. KAY, 1985; Bk. 13: T. J. LEARY, 2001; Bk. 14: Id., 1996.
BIBLIOGRAPHY: K. BARWICK, M. und die zeitgenössische Rhetorik, 1959; W. BURNIKEL, Untersuchungen zur Struktur des Witz-Epigramms bei Lukillios und M., 1980; C. J. CLASSEN, M., in: Gymnasium 92, 1985, 329–349 (repr. in: Id., Die Welt der Römer, 1993, 207–224); F. GREWING (ed.), Toto notus in orbe. Perspektiven der M.-Interpretation, 1998; N. HOLZBERG, Neuansatz zu einer M.-Interpretation, in: WJA 12, 1986, 197–215; Id., M., 1988; P. LAURENS, L'abeille dans l'ambre. Célébration de l'épigramme de l'époque alexandrine à la fin de la Renaissance, 1989; M. LAUSBERG, M.: Epigramme, in: H. V. GEPPERT (ed.), Große Werke der Literatur, vol. 2, 1992, 41–62; H. P. OBERMAYER, M. und der Diskurs über männliche 'Homosexualität' in der Literatur der frühen Kaiserzeit, 1998; M. PUELMA, Dichter und Gönner bei M., in: Labor et Lima, 1995, 415–466; Id., Epigramma: osservazioni sulla storia di un termine greco-latino, in: Maia N.S. 49, 1997, 189–213; E. SIEDSCHLAG, Zur Form von M.s Epigrammen., 1977; J. P. SULLIVAN, M. the Unexpected Classic, 1991; B. W. SWANN, M.'s Catullus, 1994.
ON RECEPTION: M. CITRONI, La teoria lessinghiana dell'epigramma e le interpretazioni moderne di Marziale,

in: Maia 21, 1969, 215–243; R. E. COLTON, Juvenal's Use of M.'s Epigrams, 1991; F.-R. HAUSMANN, M. in It., in: Studi medievali 17, 1976, 173–248; Id., M., in: F. E. CRANZ, P. O. KRISTELLER (ed.), Catalogus Translationum et Commentariorum 4, 1980, 249–296; W. MAAZ, Lateinische Epigrammatik im hohen Mittelalter, 1992; J. P. SULLIVAN (ed.), M., 1993.   MA.L.

[2] Flavius Areobindus M. East Roman official, was → *magister officiorum* in AD 449 and perhaps also in 457. The sources mention him in the context of the politics against → Attila and as participant at the council of Calchedon in 451. PLRE 2, 729.   F.T.

Martianus Capella Martianus Minneus Felix Capella, author of a Latin encyclopaedic work in 9 bks. called *De nuptiis Philologiae et Mercurii* ('Philologia's wedding with Mercury'), which he dedicated to his son [11. 1], originated from Carthage, according to the subscriptions of the MSS. Several remarks in the work (Mart. Cap. §§ 577, 999) suggest he may have been a lawyer. Today, the period of composition is thought to lie in the 420s [3. 98–111] or (rather) around AD 470 [2. 309f.; 11. 21–28; cf. also 14. 165], written perhaps in Rome rather than in Carthage [3]. The text, the title of which is not original but appears for the first time in Fulgentius [1] (*Expositio sermonum antiquorum* p. 123,4f. HELM), takes the form of a Menippean → satire and offers a mixture of prose and verse with no less than 15 different metres. The space accorded to the latter in the individual bks. is distributed completely unevenly: in bks. 1 and 3–8, lyrical parts are rather rare, in bk. 2 each of the nine muses sings in another metre. Martianus Capella (MC) uses classical prosody with great skill (among others hexametres, pentametres, iambic dimetres and the senarius, trochaeic tetrametres, asklepiads and hendecasyllables; see → Metre).

In terms of content, the work seems to be intended as a textbook of the → artes liberales, which is introduced by the allegoric setting of a holy wedding. Bks. 1 and 2 portray Mercury's looking for a wife. In vain he wooed Sophia (Wisdom), striving for virginity, Mantice (Divination), engaged to Apollo, and prudish Psyche (Soul), who has taken a liking to Cupido (Desire). On the advice of Virtus (Virtue), he turns to Apollo for help, who warmly recommends him the elegant and educated, but mortal virgin Philologia (→ Philology). The wedding wish must first be approved by an assembly of the gods. They agree under the condition that the bride rid herself before the marriage from her flaw of earthly existence. Philologia is thus heightened to divine honours and receives as her wedding gift the female servants of Mercury, namely the personifications of the seven liberal art. Each of the ladies, carefully described in clothing and appearance, pays Philologia homage with a self-portrayal, in which she explains in abbreviated form – and on a very low technical level – the science that she represents. Thus speak Grammar, Dialectic, Rhetoric, Geometry, Arithmetic, Astronomy and Music; seen as too earthly and too close to the mortal humanity, both architecture and medicine are eliminated (§ 891). Neo-platonic elements, the recognition of the Chaldaean Oracle (→ *oracula Chaldaica*) and → Theurgy, as well as a strong leaning towards demonology (§§ 7, 22, 80, 82), led to the impression that *De nuptiis* was anti-Christian propaganda in disguise [11. 17–24, 172f.; cf., however, 3. 107]. The religious orientation, however, cannot be determined with certainty.

As regards the form, MC has indeed something new to offer, although predecessors and role models are apparent throughout. Among his literary ancestors, M. Terentius → Varro, as master of the Menippean satire, must be named first, to whom MC seems to be paying his respects several times (§§ 335, 578, 817). The composition of the material, however, shows little influence of the Varronian *Disciplinarum libri*. The presentations of the personified *artes* draw, among others, from the *De figuris* of Aquila [5] Romanus (rhetoric), Euclides [3] and Nicomachus (arithmetic), Pliny the Elder and Solinus (geometry); also from → Aristides [7] Quintilianus and possibly the → Anonymi Bellermann (music). The description of the assembly of the gods discussing the marriage wishes of their colleague borrows from Seneca's *Apocolocyntosis* and Apuleius' *Metamorphoses* (→ Ap(p)uleius [III]), the influence of Lucianus' [1] *Concilium deorum* and Iulianus' [11] *Caesares* is also imaginable. The influence of → Symposium literature in the style of Athenaeus [3] and Macrobius [1] has been rightfully pointed out [2. 311]. It is exceedingly controversial if and to what extent MC was able to speak and understand Greek [11. 5f.].

The literary appeal of the work, disavowed in all respects, has recently found advocacy [7]. The multiple layers in form and content, and the difficult literary and historical categorization of the mixture of textbook, → encyclopaedia and philosophical treatise were exactly the factors that had been harmful to MC's fame as a poet [8. 211–213]; but despite all the magniloquence (accumulation of attributes, predilection for abstracts), lack of sense of form and style (monstrous sentences such as §§ 3, 69, 200–204, 436) and the evident factual deficits in the different disciplines: the treasure of knowledge of the *artes liberales* is presented in a clear and entertaining manner, in comparison to similar works of antiquity [5. 55–58], the effect on the occidental education system of the Middle Ages and early modern times and the influence on later authors were, due to the lack of similar programmatically encompassing works, huge. JOHANNES SCOTUS [10. esp. 35–48] wrote a commentary on the work, a commentary of REMIGIUS OF AUXERRE became itself an important text [6; 9; 13]; MARTIN OF LAON and ALANUS OF LILLE were influenced by the work. NOTKER THE GERMAN translated bks. 1 and 2 into Old High German [1]. From the High Middle Ages, interest in the work continuously declined, but no less a person than HUGO GROTIUS edited the text as a 16-year-old in 1599.

→ Artes liberales; → Encyclopaedia; → Technical literature; → ENCYCLOPAEDIA

1 H. BACKES, Die Hochzeit Merkurs und der Philologia. Studie zur Notkers Martianübersetzung, 1982; 2 B. BALDWIN, Rezension zu [11] (SHANZER), in: MLatJb 23, 1988, 309–312; 3 I. B. BARNISH, Martianus Capella and Rome in the Late Fifth Century, in: Hermes 114, 1986, 98–111; 4 A. CAMERON, Martianus and His First Editor, in: CPh 81, 1986, 320–328; 5 B. ENGLISCH, Die Artes liberales im frühen Mittelalter, 1994; 6 M. L. W. LAISTNER, Martianus Capella and His 9th Cent. Commentators, in: Bull. of the John Rylands Library (Manchester) 9, 1925, 130–138; 7 F. LEMOINE, Martianus Capella, 1972; 8 Id., Judging the Beauty of Diversity, in: CJ 67, 1971/2, 209–215; 9 C. E. LUTZ, The Commentary of Remigius of Auxerre on Martianus Capella, in: Mediaeval Stud. 19, 1957, 137–156; 10 G. SCHRIMPF, Das Werk des Johannes Scottus Eriugena im Rahmen des Wissenschaftsverständnisses seiner Zeit, 1982; 11 D. SHANZER, A Philosophical and Literary Commentary on Martianus Capella's De Nuptiis Philologiae et Mercurii Book 1, 1986; 12 H. J. WESTRA, The Juxtaposition of the Ridiculous and the Sublime in Martianus Capella, in: Florilegium 3, 1981, 198–214; 13 Id. (ed.), The Berlin Commentary on Martianus Capella's De nuptiis Philologiae et Mercurii 1, 1994; 14 J. A. WILLIS, Martianus Capella und die mittelalterliche. Schulbildung, in: Altertum 19, 1973, 164–174; 15 C. E. LUTZ, Martianus Capella, in: P. O. KRISTELLER, Catalogus translationum et commentariorum, vol. 2, 1971, 367–381; 16 Id., Martianus Capella. Addenda et Corrigenda, in: F. E. CRANZ, P. O. KRISTELLER, Catalogus translationum et commentariorum, vol. 3, 1976, 449–452; 17 J. MITTELSTRASS, s.v. Martianus Capella, Enzyklopädie der Philosophie und Wissenschaftstheorie 2, 1995, 773f.

EDITIONS: J. WILLIS, 1983.
TRANSLATION: W. H. STAHL, R. JOHNSON, E. L. BURGE, Martianus Capella and the Seven Liberal Arts, 2 vols., 1971–77.
COMMENTARY: B. 1: SHANZER (see above [11]); B. 2: L. LENAZ, Martiani Capellae De nuptiis Philologiae et Mercurii liber secundus, 1975; B. 6: G. GASPAROTTO, Martiani Capellae De nuptiis Philologiae et Mercurii liber sextus, 1983; B. 7: L. SCARPA, Martiani Capellae De nuptiis Philologiae et Mercurii liber VII, 1988; B. 9: L. CRISTANTE, Martiani Capellae De nuptiis Philologiae et Mercurii liber IX, 1987.   G.K.

Martina In the context of → Germanicus' [2] sudden death in Syria in AD 19, Martina was said to have prepared the poison that killed him. Allegedly she was a friend of → Munatia Plancina, the wife of Cn. → Calpurnius [II 16] Piso, Germanicus's adversary. Cn. Sentius, Calpurnius Piso's successor in Syria, sent her to Rome, but she died suddenly in Brundisium during the journey (Tac. Ann. 2,74,2; 3,7,2). Since the poisoning of Germanicus is a fabrication, the allegations against Martina are also without foundation (cf. [1. 153; 154f.]).

1 W. ECK, A. CABALLOS, F. FERNÁNDEZ, Das Senatus consultum de Cn. Pisone patre, 1996.   W.E.

Martinianus *Magister officiorum* of → Licinius [II 4]; after the fall of Hadrianopolis [3] (3 July AD 324), Licinius made him Augustus (incorrectly Caesar in the literary sources). After Licinius's capitulation, Martianus was banished to Cappadocia, where he was executed in 325.

PLRE 1, 563; M. CLAUSS, Der magister officiorum in der Spätantike (4.–6. Jh.), 1980, 171.   B.BL.

Martinus

[1] Bishop of Tours (Caesarodunum (Turonum)), Christian monk and miracle worker (→ *Miracles; Miracle workers*, born in 316/7 in Sabaria/ Pannonia; died on 8 November 397 in Candes/Loire. According to → Sulpicius Severus' *Vita Martini* (composed in 396/7, complemented by 3 letters and 2 (3) dialogues), M. was the son of a Roman tribune and performed his military service under the emperors → Constantius [2] II and → Iulianus [11] Apostata. During this time he converted to Christianity ('Sharing of the cloak' in Amiens, Vita 3), parting from the military (356 ?). M. then lived in ascetic seclusion in the entourage of bishop → Hilarius [1] of Poitiers. In 370/1, surprising election to bishop of Tours, foundation of the monastery of Marmoutier (Vita 9–10). M.'s activities as bishop were primarily determined by mission and organization of the Church. In the conflict regarding the Spaniard → Priscillianus (heretic convicted by the Church) M. resisted the national persecution and execution by the usurper → Maximus [7] (Sulp. Sev. Dialogi 3,11–13).

The texts on M. by Sulpicius Severus, composed in the classical tradition, stand at the beginning of Christian Latin hagiography. Their historical value is contested. The scholarly discussion pertains to the chronology and the apologetic-polemic tendencies that turn the ascetic M. into a model bishop, the defender of the faith and the exemplary monk, who by far surpasses all the heroes of Eastern monasticism (e.g. Antonius [5]). The tomb of the bishop, worshipped as a → saint, in Tours became the destination of numerous pilgrims (→ Pilgrimage). Besides the tomb the *cappa* ('cloak'; the terms chapel and chaplain are derived from it) of the saint became a much revered relic; under the Merovingians, it became the relic of the empire, M. himself became the patron of the Frankish kings and the Frankish kingdom → Monasticism

EDITIONS: (Sulp. Sev., Vita Martini): K. HALM, CSEL 1, 1866; J. FONTAINE, SChr 133–135, 1967–1969.
BIBLIOGRAPHY: T. D. BARNES, The Military Career of Martin of Tours, in: Analecta Bollandiana 114, 1996, 23–33; V. BURRUS, The Making of a Heretic. Gender, Authority and the Priscillianist Controversy, 1995; R. VAN-DAM, Saints and Their Miracles in Late Antique Gaul, 1993; C. STANCLIFFE, St. Martin and His Hagiographer. History and Miracle in Sulpicius Severus, 1983; L. PIETRI, La ville de Tours du IVe au VIe siècle, 1983; F. PRINZ, Frühes Mönchtum im Frankenreich, 1965 (^{2}1988).   K.-S.F.

[2] Thracian, East Roman officer under → Iustinianus [1] I. First mentioned as officer in the Persian War in AD 531. In 533, he commanded a division of the federates in the Vandalic War (→ Vandali) and, after the victory at Tricamarum, remained in Africa until 536. As *magister militum*, from 537 he assisted the general → Belisarius besieged by the Gothic king → Vitigis, until the end of the siege (March 538). After the fall of Ravenna, he followed the recalled Belisarius to Constantinople in 540 to then be sent again to the Persian front, where he superseded Belisarius as *magister militum per Orientem* in 543. Upon imperial order, he invaded Persarmenia, where he was crushingly defeated in the battle at Anglon. In 544, he liberated Edessa from Persian siege by paying a sum of 500 Roman pounds (160 kg) of gold. From 551–554, he fought in → Lazica under the command of → Bessas, whom he superseded as *magister militum per Armeniam* in 555. In 556, he liberated Phasis from its Persian besiegers, but failed with an expedition into the heartland of Lazica. Therefore, and because of his participation in the murder of the Lazian king → Gobazes (555), emperor Justinian I relieved him from his office in 556. PLRE 3, 839–848 no. 2.
                                                              F.T.

[3] M. of Bracara (M. Dumiensis), born in Pannonia, *c.* 515–580. As a monk he came to Gallaecia in the Suebi kingdom in 550. In Dumio near Bracara Augusta (modern Braga), he founded a monastery, became its abbot and in 556 bishop, then archbishop of Braga. He was a participant of the first council of Braga (561) and headed the second (572). M. converted the Arian (→ Arianism) Suebi to Catholicism. Moral-philosophical works: *De ira* ('On anger'), to bishop Vitimer of Aurea (the model is Seneca) and the *Formulae vitae honestae*, to the Suebian king Miro. Ascetic works: *Pro repellenda iactantia, De superbia* and *Exhortatio humilitatis*. The pastoral instruction *De correctione rusticorum*, composed at the suggestion of bishop Polemius of Astorga, castigates remains of old religion among the newly converted Suebi. *Sententia patrum Aegyptiorum* (revision of the → *Apophthegmata patrum*); *De pascha; De trina mersione* (defence of his practice of baptism). Further: *Acta* of the two councils; the *Canones Martini*; three verse inscriptions. His works were of considerable influence in Europe, affecting for instance → Gregorius [4] of Tours, → Venantius Fortunatus and → Isidorus [9] of Seville.

EDITIONS: PL 72, 17–52; 74, 381–394; 84, 569–586; C. W. BARLOW, 1950.
BIBLIOGRAPHY: S. BODELÓN, M. of Braga and John of Biclaro in Recent Scholarship, in: MLatJb 31, 1996, 199–204.
BIBLIOGRAPHY: J. FONTÁN, M.B., Un testigo de la tradición clásica y cristiana, in: Anuario de Estudios Medievales 9, 1974–1979, 331–341; Id., San Martín de Braga una luz en la penumbra, in: Cuadernos de filología clásica 20, 1986f., 185–199; J. ORLANDIS, D. RAMOS-LISSÓN, Die Synoden auf der Iberischen Halbinsel, 1981, 78, 86–89.   J.M.A.-N.

Martis, ad Various stations derived their names from a cult site of Mars *ad (fanum) Martis.*

[1] Station on the road through the → Alpes Cottiae above Segusio at the confluence of the Bardonecchia and the Dora Riparia, modern Oulx.

[2] Station in Etruria near Pescia on the *Via Cassia* between Pistoriae and Luca.

[3] Station in Umbria on the *Via Flaminia,* 74 miles from Rome, between Narnia and Mevania (*Vicus Martis Tudertium*, CIL XI 4744–4751), modern Santa Maria in Pantano near Massa Martana.

    MILLER, 229, 289, 304.   G.U.

Martius

[1] **L. M. Macer** Senator, probably from Arretium. M.'s career began under Tiberius; between AD 41 and 44 he was governor of Moesia under the command of Memmius [II 4] Regulus. Finally he became proconsul of Achaia by direct appointment. PIR² M 343.

    M. TORELLI, in: EOS 2, 289.

[2] **L. M. Macer** M.'s career included three offices of the *vigintiviri* and culminated in the praetorship. Since he was also *Salius Palatinus* (→ *Salii*), he must have been a patrician; but it is uncertain whether he was the first in his family to be a patrician (CIL XI 1837). It is not clear whether he or M. [1] is identical with Marcius Macer who fought on Otho's side in the battle of Bedriacum. PIR² M 344.

[3] **P. M. Sergius Saturninus** Son of M. [4]. Patrician; in AD 180 admitted to the → Salii. *Cos. ord.* 198. PIR² M 346.

[4] **P. M. Verus** Senator. M. took part in the → Parthian War of Lucius → Verus as a legionary legate. He wrote → *commentarii* which Verus was supposed to pass on to Cornelius → Fronto [6], who wanted to write a history of the campaign. In AD 166 suffect consul; between 172 and 175 legate of Cappadocia. From there he informed Marcus [2] Aurelius of the defection of Avidius [1] Cassius and immediately started moving his own troops against him. M. succeeded Cassius in Syria in 175 and kept this position until 178; on January 1st 179 he began his second consulship. He may have been admitted to the ranks of the patricians; he probably died AD 190. PIR² M 348.

    E. DĄBROWA, The Governors of Roman Syria, 1998, 117ff.   W.E.

Martyrdom, literature of Apart from the stories of the Passion of Christ in the Gospels, the Christian literature of martyrdom begins around the middle of the second century with two Greek missives by persecuted communities in Asia Minor and Gaul, the 'Martyrdom of → Polycarpus ' and the letter of the communities of Vienne and Lyons. Both letters describe the events from arrest to execution. Because of several parallels with Christ's Way of the Cross, the *Martyrium Polycarpi* ele-

vates the death by burning of the bishop of Smyrna (AD 167/8?) to a perfect end in accordance with the Gospels. In the letter from Vienne and Lyons (AD 177; Euseb. Hist. eccl. 5,1,3–5,2,8) the 'afflictions' of the Gaulish martyrs are seen as a fatal feud with Satan, whom, in imitation of Christ, the martyrs finally overcome.

Other martyrdom texts read like trial transcripts with sometimes dramatic dialogues, culminating in confession and death sentence; examples are the Greek Acts of → Iustinus [6] (*c.* AD 165) or the oldest preserved Latin martyrology, the Acts of the Scillitan Martyrs (AD 180). Especially this type exists in mixed forms (e.g Acta Cypriani, AD 258). A third variation can be found in the → *Passio Perpetuae et Felicitatis* , the most significant Latin martyr texts (AD 203; → Perpetua), which influenced the entire northern African literature of martyrdom.

Even when describing historical events none of these early texts – with the exception of a few autobiographic notes by martyrs – can be regarded as authentic documents in the modern sense (nearly all the post-Constantine texts are fiction). Almost always revision, literarization, and interpretation (also for polemic purposes within the Church) come into play. From the very beginning these were not historiographic documents. They were literary creations to be used in the liturgy of the communities, especially on the anniversary of the martyrdom. They celebrated the memory of the dead, they sought to strengthen the persecuted community, and they edified their audience by reminding them of a great period of the early Church (→ Saints, veneration of saints).

→ Acta Sanctorum; → Martyrs

EDITIONS: A. A. R. BASTIAENSEN et al., Atti e passioni dei martiri, 1987.
BIBLIOGRAPHY: TH. BAUMEISTER, M. VAN UYTFANGHE, s.v. Heiligenverehrung, RAC 14, 96–150; 150–183; W. BERSCHIN, Biographie und Epochenstil im lateinischen Mittelalter, vol. 1, 1986; G. W. BOWERSOCK, Martyrdom and Rome, 1995; H. DELEHAYE, Les Passions des martyrs et les genres littéraires, 1921 (²1966); G. LANATA, Gli atti dei martiri come documenti processuali, 1973; V. SAXER, Bible et Hagiographie. Texte et thèmes bibliques dans les Actes des martyrs authentiques des premiers siècles, 1986.
                      PE.HA.

Martyria (μαρτυρία, *martyría*). In Greek law, the deposition in court of a testimony, its content or a document drawn up for this purpose. Witnesses (μάρτυρες, *mártyres*; synonyms [2. 2032f.]) were formally invited to be present at business transactions, and witnesses to wrongful acts were called by the injured or avenging party. At the time of the Attic orators (5th/4th centuries BC) they were not sworn in but affirmed that they were 'acquainted with' a formulaic phrase drawn up by the person presenting the case or 'present' at an event. Only in cases of → homicide did the witnesses join the principals in swearing to the guilt or innocence of the defendant (→ *diōmosía*), putting them on a par with those who swore a personal oath for the defendant [2. 2034–37]. Nevertheless, Athenian courts were not formally bound by a *martyria*; any juror could decide against it in a secret vote. Officials who were personally accountable for their decision (→ *diamartyría*) were bound by it. In → Gortyn (III) too there were binding *martyriai* determining the trial, with the number and qualifications of the witnesses precisely specified. In Athens adult free men who were not disenfranchised were competent to give a *martyria*; women could give a *martyria* through their → *kýrios* ('head of family') or swear an oath outside court. Slaves were not allowed to give a *martyria*; they were interrogated under → torture on a topic relating to the *martyria*, outside court and in the presence of the party they were testifying against.

Anybody requested by a party to appear as a witness had the option, without any legal consequences, to either swear outside court that he 'did not know' (→ *exōmosía*) about the case in question or confirm the case before the court. Only in the latter case was the witness liable to a charge of false testimony (→ *pseudomartyríôn díkē*). However, a witness who did not appear in court without being exempted could be charged with → *lipomartyríou díkē*. A *martyria* based on hearsay was forbidden, yet the *martyria* of someone who was sick or out of town could be submitted in writing through an *ekmartyría* (affidavit of another witness). The transition from 'oral' to 'written' *martyria* (c. 370 BC) did not bring about a change in the formulation of the oath or in the procedure; the litigants were allowed to use a *martyria* in court only if it had been presented in the preliminary hearing (→ *diaitētaí* [2]).

1 A. R. W. HARRISON, The Law of Athens, vol. 2: Procedure, 1971; 2 K. LATTE, s.v. Martyria, RE 14, 2032–2039; 3 G. THÜR, Beweisführung vor den Schwurgerichtshöfen Athens, 1977, 315ff.; 4 .Id, in: IPArk, 238–243 (no. 17). G.T.

Martyrius Latin grammarian, assumed to have lived before → Cassiodorus, probably in the first half of the 6th cent. AD. M. was the son of a certain Adamantius, whom he owed his education and who is thus named in the MSS *Adamanti(i) sive Martyrii* and in Cassiodorus *Adamantius Martyrius*. In a manuscript *subscriptio* the designation *Sardianus grammaticus* appears, perhaps named after Sardes (Lydia). He is the author of a treatise *De B muta et V vocali* in 4 parts, documented in 5 MSS from the humanistic period, which go back to two lost codices (one from Bobbio, the other one from Venice). The text was almost completely adopted by Cassiodorus in *De orthographia* (GL 7,167–199), but this version departs slightly from the directly documented version. The work seeks to establish rules for the use of the consonants *B* and *V* and, although of minor theoretical interest, it is interesting from a linguistic-historical point of view. It is certain that M. used bilingual Greek-Latin glossaries (or vice versa).

EDITIONS: GL 7,165–199 (lower part of the page; the upper part of pages 167–199 comprises the *excerpta* of Cassiodorus); SCHANZ/HOSIUS 4.2, 219–221; P. WESSNER, s.v. Martyrios (23), RE 14,2041–2043. P.G.

Martyrologium Edessenum Early calendar of martyrs (Syrian), preserved in a MS copied in → Edessa [2] in November AD 411. The main part of the text is translated from a Greek calendar showing links with → Nicomedia. It is supplemented, however, by the names of Persian martyrs.

F. NAU, Les ménologes des Évangeliaires coptes-arabes (Patrologia Orientalis 10,2), 1923, 5–26 (repr. 1973). S.BR.

Martyrs
A. HISTORY OF THE CONCEPT   B. CULT

A. HISTORY OF THE CONCEPT
Around the mid–2nd cent. AD, Christian reflection in regards to the fate of persecution (Jewish theological tradition from the religious persecution under → Antiochus [6] IV Epiphanes; Early Christian characteristics: following and imitating of Jesus as well as the experience of the rejection of missionary preaching; influences of the Graeco-Roman environment regarding the perception of heroic death, in part mediated through → Diaspora Judaism) had reached a point, in reaction to extreme experiences, where the search for clear concepts became necessary. The terminology of the Roman work *Pastor Hermae* (→ Hermas; differentiation between those who suffered and whose death is remembered: *pathóntes*, and those otherwise inflicted: *thlibéntes*, indicating reasons for both) did not take hold, but the terminology from Asia Minor, appearing for the first time around AD 160 in the *Martyrium Polycarpi*, did: the individual executed for his beliefs is a 'witness' (*mártys*), his death is a 'testimonial' (*martýrion* or *martyría*) that can also be expressed verbally as 'witnessing' (*martyreín*). The differentiation of the *Pastor Hermae* survived insofar as that from the end of the 2nd cent. AD the martyr was distinguished from the 'confessor' (*homologētés*, Lat. *confessor*), although the boundaries were fleeting at first. The Greek technical term *mártys* became, as a loan-word, part of the Christian Latin vocabulary (*martyr*) and of numerous European languages (e.g. German 'Marter'); in the East, the term was frequently translated into the languages of the Christian Orient.

The original meaning is probably rooted in the thought complex of the congruence of word and deed and its witnessing word character (→ Ignatius [1] of Antioch with influences of the Diaspora Judaism and of popular philosophy). Older scholarship assumed a continuous shift of meaning of the witness terminology in the NT and even already in the OT, or all too direct influences from the Stoa.

B. CULT

The *Martyrium Polycarpi* also contains the earliest statements on the veneration of martyrs, which can best be understood with regard to the beginnings as an enhancement of the cult of the dead (→ Dead, cult of the). The Christian community (not a family) assembles at the tomb of → Polycarpus, in order to commemorate in joy, on the anniversary of his death, all martyrs named in the account of the martyrdom. The custom of distinguishing between martyrs and other deceased spread throughout the entire Church, while the individual forms could vary. In Carthage, a calendar with the days of the deaths of martyrs was established during the time of bishop → Cyprianus [2] (mid–3rd cent. AD); Carthage also knew the practice of reading accounts of martyrdom during the inner-city church service.

All apostles were considered martyrs, sometimes with the exception of John; from the end of the 2nd cent. AD, they were commemorated in the form of the veneration of the martyrs (emphasizing the tomb, memorial day). Later, their veneration surpassed that of the other martyrs, partly because referring to them resulted in significance for the reputation of the communities within church politics. Early testimonies for the burial *ad sanctum* ('near a saint', i.e. in the vicinity of a tomb of a martyr) come from Carthage and Salona. For → Origenes, martyrs were friends of God with the privilege of free speech (*parrhēsía*), who rendered a service to the earthly Church. Invocations of the apostles Peter and Paul as graffiti were found under S. Sebastiano outside Rome (Constaninian foundation as *basilica apostolorum*) during excavations at a place where the funerary banquet (*refrigerium*) was celebrated in their honour, e.g.: *Paule Petre petite pro Erote rogate* ('Paul, Peter, plead, pray for Eros').

In post-Constantinian times, bishops made an effort to repress the widespread practice of a private funerary banquet at the martyrs' tombs, in favour of the common celebration of the Eucharist. The martyrs increasingly became Christian heroes, who were to outbid the old heroes. Individual practices of the → hero cult and worship of the gods were received (e.g. *incubatio*).

For the martyrs in Islam see → Shiites; → Sunnites.
→ Acta Sanctorum; → Dead, cult of the; → Hero cult; → Lapsi; → Martyrdom, literature of; → Saints, Veneration of saints; → Shiites; → Sunnites; → Tolerance

TH. BAUMEISTER, Genese und Entfaltung der altkirchlichen Theologie des Martyriums, 1991 (bibliography); Id., s.v. Heiligenverehrung I, RAC 14, 96–150; N. BROX, Zeuge und Märtyrer Untersuchungen zur frühchristlichen Zeugnis-Terminologie, 1961; P. GERLITZ et al., s.v. Martyrium, TRE 22, 196–220.   TH.BA.

Martys see → Märtyrs

Marullus

[1] 1st-century BC Roman teacher of rhetoric from Cordoba, teacher of → Seneca the Elder (Sen. Controv. 1, praef. 22–24) and his friend M. → Porcius Latro (ibid., praef. 24; 2,2,7; 7,2,11). His method of instruction consisted of isolated practice in individual areas of *inventio* and *elocutio* (see ibid. praef. 23; → *partes orationis*). While Latro esteemed M.'s *sententiae* (ibid. 1,2,17), Seneca, citing a range of *sententiae* and *colores*, characterises him as a 'dry fellow, who offers little that is attractive but does not use a common form of language either' (*non vulgato genere dicens*, ibid. praef. 22). Also criticised was his strictly functional use of figures of speech (ibid. praef. 23).

H. BORNECQUE, Les déclamations et les déclamateurs, 1902, 179f.; L. A. SUSSMAN, The Elder Seneca, 1978, 20f.; J. FAIRWEATHER, Seneca the Elder, 1981, 256f. *et passim*.

[2] Literary mimographer from the time of → Marcus [2] Aurelius (SHA Aur. 8,1). A pun of his is quoted in Aen. 7,499 and Serv. Ecl. 7,26 (cf. also SHA Aur. 29,1f.). His fame was kept alive (through Donatus?) in Hier. Adversus Rufinum 2,20.

FRAGMENTS: M. BONARIA, Romani Mimi, 1965, 81f., cf. 136.
BIBLIOGRAPHY: Id., Marullo, in: Dioniso 35, 1961, 3f., 16–27; P. L. SCHMIDT, in: HLL, vol. 4, § 496.   P.L.S.

Marus Northern tributary of the → Ister (Danube), the modern Morava in Moravia (Tac. Ann. 2,63; Plin. HN 4,81). The name means 'slow'. It should not be confused with the *Máris* in Hdt.4,48 or the *Márisos* in Str. 7,3,13. An important trade route northwards to the Mare Balticum. After the surrender of → Maroboduus in AD 19, the Romans settled the → Marcomanni between the M. and the → Cusus under the rule of the Quadian king Vannius (Tac. 2,63). According to Plin. HN 4,81, the M. separated the Suebi and Vannius's kingdom from the Bastarnae and other Germanic tribes.

M. FLUSS, s.v. M., RE 14, 2054.   PL.CA.

Maruthas (Μαρουθᾶς, *Marouthâs*; Syrian *Mārūṯā*).
[1] Bishop of Maiperqaṭ (Martyropolis [Martyr City], in the south-east of modern Turkey], was an Imperial envoy to the Sāsānid court on at least two occasions. In AD 410 he took part in the Synod of → Seleucea/→ Ctesiphon, at which the 'Church of the East' adopted the canons of the Council of → Nicaea. It is thanks to him that news of the Persian martyrs under Šābuhr II (→ Sapor) reached the Roman Empire. Of the numerous works ascribed to him, a homily to the 'Low Sunday' may be genuine; the 'Canons of Mārūṯā' are certainly of a later date [1; 2; 3].
[2] Syrian Orthodox Metropolitan of Taḡrīṯ/Mesopotamia (died AD 649). Appointed at the time of Emperor → Heraclius' [7] invasion of the Sāsānid empire (628/9), he introduced a great number of reforms and developed vigorous building activity. His extant works are liturgical in content. A detailed biography, written by his successor Denḥā, has also survived [4].

1 M. Ensslin, s.v. M., RE 14, 2054–2056; 2 J. M. Fiey, M. d'après Ibn al-Azraq, in: Analecta Bollandiana 94, 1976, 35–45; 3 A. Vööbus, The Canons ascribed to M., 1982; 4 F. Nau, Histoire d'Ahoudemmeh et de Marouta (Patrologia Orientalis 3,1), 1905, 61–96 (repr. 1982).

S.BR.

Mary see → Maria

Marzabotto An Etruscan city lying *c.* 30 km south of modern Bologna on the Pian di Misano plateau above the River Reno in the northern foothills of the Emilian Apennines. Italian excavations since the 19th cent. have uncovered large parts of the city and an acropolis on the hill Misanello to the west. The city, which was constructed in the last quarter of the 6th cent. BC in an orthogonal compass-aligned layout (cf. site map), was in its earlier mid–6th century settlement only a small collection of huts. After flourishing in the 5th century, the city was conquered by the Celts in the middle of the 4th cent., which led to the end of the city at the beginning of the 3rd cent.

On the acropolis there were sacred buildings facing south. Of these, building B, a platform with a central sacrificial pit, was probably dedicated to the cult of → Dis Pater, who according to the *libri rituales* (Cic. Div. 1,72; cf. 2,49; → Divination) is linked to the founding rites of a city. Building C is a large, very broadly based, three-*cella* temple, with a pronaos (→ Temple) in front. Above the temple there is an open area, probably an *auguraculum*. The city is divided up by a main *cardo*, several secondary *cardines*, and three broad *decumani* (→ *decumanus*), each 15 m wide. Floorplans within the *insulae* (→ *insula*) vary. The basic outline is a long corridor leading to a courtyard around which the rooms are grouped. The beginnings of an atrium house with a

Marzabotto: Map of the Etruscan town (*c.* late 6th to *c.* mid 4th cents. BC)

Public space   Sanctuary   Votive depository   Craftsmen's workshops

0   100 m

central *tablinum,* and similarities with houses in → Olynthus, are recognisable here (→ House).

The earlier theory of colonization by → Clusium or → Volsinii (Orvieto) is probably incorrect, as the numerous instances of *nomina gentilia* in -*alu* point to a population originating in the Po valley, → Bononia (Felsina) in particular. M.'s importance probably lay in the trade of raw metals from → Populonia, as well as its own bronze products, in the Po valley and further north.

→ House II. C. (Etruscan)

G. A. MANSUELLI, G. SASSATELLI, s.v. M., EAA Suppl. 2, 1971–1994, vol. 3, 1995, 559–562; G. SASSATELLI, Bologna e M. Storia di un problema, in: Studi sulla città antica. L'Emilia Romagna, 1983, 104–127.
CARTOGRAPHICAL BIBLIOGRAPHY: L. BANTI, Die Welt der Etrusker, 1960, esp. 27, fig.; G. PUGLIESE CARRATELLI (ed.), Rasenna, Storia e civiltà degli Etruschi, 1986, table after p. 306.   M.M.

Masada (Greek Μασάδα, *Masáda*; Hebrew *mṣdh,* Arabic *Tall al-Sabʿ*). The name, which is recorded only in Greek and Latin, is probably derived from the Aramaic *mʿṣādā* ('fortress'). It stands in isolation on a rocky plateau on the western shore of the Dead Sea, a rhomboid 600 m north-south and 300 m east-west; 50 m above sea-level with steep cliffs *c.* 350 m above ground level in the east and *c.* 150 m in the west. Jos. BI 7,280–294 offers a detailed description, and it is mentioned in Plin. HN 5,73 and Str. 16,2,44. In 1838, M. was identified by E. ROBINSON and E. SMITH, subsequently investigated several times and eventually excavated in 1963–1965 under the direction of Yigael YADIN.

Built as a fortress by either Jonathan (Jos. BI 7,285) or → Alexander [16] Iannaeus (BI 4,399), M. was reconstructed in grand style by → Herod [1] the Great: surrounded by a casemate wall, with two gates to the east and west, large underground cisterns, several palace complexes with bath-houses and storerooms. Occupied by insurgents in AD 66 and besieged and captured by the Romans under → Flavius [II 44] Silva in 73/4 (BI 7,275–407). M. then became the base for a Roman garrison. In the Byzantine period there was a small colony of monks.

Modern archaeological and historical research has deflated the mythical exaggeration of the defence, and the description by → Iosephus [4] Flavius of the collective suicide of the defenders, placing them in a literary context [3; 4; 5].

EXCAVATION REPORTS: 1 M.: The Yigael Yadin Excavations 1963–1965. Final Reports 1–6, 1989–1999.
BIBLIOGRAPHY: 2 E. NETZER, s.v. M., The New Encyclopedia of Excavations in the Holy Land 3, 1993, 973–985; 3 SH. J. D. COHEN, M.: Literary Tradition, Archaeological Remains, and the Credibility of Josephus, in: Journal of Jewish Studies 33, 1982, 385–405; 4 N. BEN-YEHUDA, The M. Myth. Collective Memory and Mythmaking in Israel, 1995; 5 M. HADAS-LEBEL, Massada. Der Untergang des jüdischen Königreichs oder die andere Geschichte von Herodes, ²1997.   H.BL.

Masaesylii (Μασαισύλιοι; *Masaisýlioi*). West Numidian tribe in → Mauretania Caesariensis (between the River Mulucha and Cape Bougaroun): Pol. 3,33,15; Liv. 28,17,5; Str. 17,3,9; Plin. HN 5,19; 52; 21,77. For its localization in Mauretania Tingitana: Plin. HN 5,17; Ptol. 4,2,17. Among the kings of the M. were → Syphax (Punic *Spq*), Vermina (Punic *Wrmnd*) and Arcobarzanes.

→ Libyes, Libye

J. DESANGES, Catalogue des tribus africaines ... , 1962, 62.   W.HU.

Mascas (Μάσκας; *Máskas*). Xen. An. 1,5,4 locates the River M. south of the confluence of the Chabora (→ Ḫabur) and the Euphrates and describes it as encircling the city of → Corsote in the desert. It may well have been only a canal. Etymologically, it is perhaps connected with the Akkadian *mašqû*, 'watering hole/place'. There was a Neo-Assyrian town called Mašqite in the north of Anatolia.

R. D. BARNETT, Xenophon and the Wall of Media, in: JHS 73, 1963, 4f.; F. H. WEISSBACH, s.v. M., RE 14, 2069f.   K.KE.

Mascezel Christian son of the Moorish king Nubel; in AD 374 he supported the unsuccessful attempt at usurpation by his brother → Firmus [3] against → Valentinian I. In 397 he fled to Italy to escape his other brother → Gildo, who had tried to kill him and had had his sons killed. In 398, under → Stilicho's command, he fought against Gildo and won (allegedly through a miracle) despite numerical inferiority. He is said to have been drowned by Stilicho shortly afterwards.PLRE 1, 566.
                                                 K.G.-A.

Mascula Town in Numidia on the road from Thamugadi to Theveste in the middle of the fertile land of the Musulamii, modern Khenchela (It. Ant. 33,6). M. was under Punic influence [1. 163–177]. In the Severian period (AD 193–235) M. was a *municipium* CIL VIII 1, 2248. Bishops are attested from 256: Cypr. Sententiae episcoporum 79. Inscriptions: CIL VIII 1, 2228–2274; 2, 10184–10188; Suppl. 2, 17668–17719; 3, 22281; 22282; AE 1989, 882.

1 M. LEGLAY, Saturne africain. Monuments 2, 1966.

H. DESSAU, s.v. M. (1), RE 14, 2064.   W.HU.

Mases (Μάσης; *Másēs*). Location and harbour on the southwestern coast of the Argolid peninsula on the eastern shore of the bay of Koilada, north west of the modern village of Kampo, with few ancient remains. Mentioned in Hom. Il. 2,562; in the historical period it was the port of → Hermion(e). References: Str. 8,6,17; Paus. 2,35,11; 36,1f.; Steph. Byz. s.v. M.; Eust. in Hom. Il. 288,11.

R. Baladié, Le Péloponnèse de Strabon, 1980, 240f.; M. Jameson, Inscriptions of the Peloponnesos, in: Hesperia 22, 1953, 167f.; C. N. Runnels, T. H. van Andel, The Evolution of Settlement in the Southern Argolid, in: Hesperia 56, 1987, 303–334. Y.L.

Masices (Μάσικες; *Másikes*, Μάζικες; *Mázikes*). Name of several North African peoples (Anon. Cosmographia 1,39 = GLM 88). It corresponds roughly to the modern term 'Berber'. The M. have been localized in → Mauretania Tingitana (south of the territory of the Metagonitae: Ptol. 4,1,10), in Mauretania Caesariensis (CIL VIII 1, 2786; 2, 9613; Ptol. 4,2,19; Provinciarum omnium laterculus Veronensis 14,3 = GLM 129; Amm. Marc. 29,5,17; 21; 25f.; 51; Iulius Honorius, Cosmographia A 48) and south of the province of Africa (Liber generationis, Chron. min. 1,107,197: between *Afri qui et Barbares* [= *Bavares*] and *Garamantes qui et Marmaridae*; Expositio totius mundi 62). In late antiquity the M. made raids into Tripolitania and the Egyptian oases (Philostorgius 11,8). In Veg. Mil. 3,23, these M. are described as camel drivers.

J. Desanges, Catalogue des tribus africaines... , 1962, 34, 63, 112f.; J. Desanges, S. Lancel, L'apport des nouvelles Lettres... , in: Les lettres de saint Augustin découvertes par Johannes Divjak, 1983, 87–98 and 99, here 90f.; Ph. Leveau, L'aile des Thraces, la tribu des Mazices et les praefecti gentis en Afrique du Nord, in: Antiquités africaines 7, 1973, 153–191. W.HU.

Masintha Young noble Numidian, who fled to Rome to escape the demands for tribute exacted by King → Hiempsal [2] II. Caesar represented him in court against Hiempsal's son → Juba [1], later hid him and in 61 BC took him to Spain with him. His motives were probably assumed to be of a sexual nature. (Suet. Iul. 71). According to an interpretation of Vitr. De arch. 8,3,25 [1. 31–33], M. owned the territory around Ismuc, not far from Zama, and in 46 he and his son C. Iulius fought on Caesar's side against Juba.

1 K. Jeppesen, Vitruvius in Africa, in: H. Geertman, J. J. de Jong (ed.), Munus non ingratum (BABesch Suppl. 2), 1989, 31–33. JÖ.F.

Masistes (Μασίστης; *Masistēs*). According to Hdt.7,82 son of Darius [1] I and Atossa [1], satrap of Bactria (Hdt. 9,113) and Persian commander-in-chief (Hdt. 7,82). After the cruel death of his wife, M. is said to have been killed by the king's troops in 479/8 BC, together with his sons, while on his way to Bactria bent on insurrection (Hdt. 9,107–113). The name M. probably derives from the Old Persian *ma θ iišta-* (Greek μέγιστος/*mégistos*, 'the greatest'). Iust. 2,10,1–11 and Plut. Mor. 173b-c; 488d-f recount how, in exchange for recognising his kingship, Xerxes I was said to have conferred on his elder brother Ariamenes the title of παρ' αὐτῷ μέγιστος (*par' autôi mégistos*, 'the greatest at his [= Xerxes's] court') or τὴν δευτέραν μεθ' ἑαυτόν (*tền deutéran meth' heautón*, 'a rank second only to his [= Xerxes's] own').

1 Briant, 540f.; 2 H. Sancisi-Weerdenburg, Yaunā en Persai, 1980, 48–83. J.W.

Masistius (Μασίστιος; *Masístios*). According to Hdt. 7,79, son of Siromitres, a Persian cavalry commander killed at Plataeae in 479 BC (Hdt. 9,20–22; Plut. Aristides 14; Diod. Sic. 11,30,4). The Athenians dedicated the armour of the 'Persian most highly regarded after → Mardonius by king and people' (Hdt. 9,24) to Athena Polias (Paus. 1,27,1).
→ Persian Wars J.W.

Maskelli Maskello (Μασκελλι Μασκελλω). The two first 'names' in one of the most common *lógoi* (→ *lógos* II. 2) in Graeco-Egyptian magic texts (→ Magic). The *lógos* appears mainly in so-called *agṓgima* (coercive love spells; for example PGM IV 2755–2757, XIXa 10f.), but it also appears in other genres (albeit not with protective amulets) and is often identified expressly as a formula of 'necessity' (e.g. *katà tês pikrâs Anánkēs*, 'according to bitter *Anánkē*', PGM VII 302; cf. XII 290f.). The suggestion that M.M. is derived from the Hebrew *mśkel*, 'psalm of praise', and represents a type of 'recitative annotation' [1] is doubtful: M.M. does not appear, for example, in the Aramaic magic bowls. The *lógos* is important for two reasons: It is one of only a few formulae which incorporate Greek words and words similar to Greek; and the variety of formal variations show that ideally the *lógoi* were fixed, but in practice were subject to the expressive needs of the context.
→ Magic

1 H. J. Thissen, Ägyptologische Beiträge zu den griechischen magischen Papyri, in: Religion und Philosophie im alten Ägypten. Festschrift für Ph.Derchain (Orientalia Lovaniensia Analecta 39), 1991, 298f.

Z. Ritoók, Ein neuer griechische Zauberpapyrus, in: Acta Antiqua Academiae Scientiarum Hungaricae 26, 1978, 433–456, here 437–442. R.G.

Masks
I. Phoenicia II. Greece and Rome

I. Phoenicia
Facial masks and head protomes (also shortened human representations including the neck and shoulder part) are a common type of monument since the 9th/8th cent. BC in the Phoenician-Punic world. They spread from the Levant (here going back to the 2nd millennium, e.g. in Tell Qāsila, also from Tyrus, 'Amrīt, Akhzib, Hazor, Sarepta etc.) via Cyprus, Carthage, Sicily (Motya), Sardinia and Ibiza into the far west (Cadiz). The masks (with openings for eyes and mouth) mostly show a grimace, probably with demonic meaning. Among the protomes attested in the west (with closed

Tragedy

a) Classical period

b) Hellenism

Satyr plays

Satyr

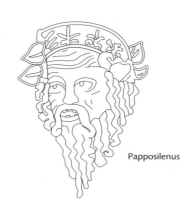

Papposilenus

Middle and New Comedy

Old men

Young woman

Youth

Hetaeras

Slaves

(types → Maison)

Greek theatre masks

back and a face without openings), idealized women's faces in Greek form language predominate, particularly since the 5th cent. BC. The masks are found at graves and sanctuaries, pointing to a cultic and apotropaic function.

→ Colonization III (with map)

W. CULICAN, Some Phoenician Masks and Other Terracottas, in: Berytus 24, 1975–76, 47–87 (ibid., Opera Selecta, 1986, 391–431); E. GUBEL, s.v. Masque, DCPP, 277–279.   H.G.N.

II. GREECE AND ROME
A. TERM B. EFFECT AND DISSEMINATION C. DEVELOPMENT OF THE THEATRE MASK D. THEATRE IN PRACTICE

A. TERM
Greek πρόσωπον (*prósōpon*, 'that which one looks at'): face, façade, mask; then, metaphorically, stage figure, person (besides προσωπεῖον/*prosōpeîon*, 'belonging to the face': mask); Latin *persona* (Etruscan origin; not from *personare*, 'to sound through', e.g. → Gavius [I 2] Bassus by Gell. NA 5,7).

B. EFFECT AND DISSEMINATION
A mask allows someone to step out of his personality (→ Ecstasy) and by being transformed – possibly into a god or an animal – to attain supernatural powers; but it also effects a transformation into the ridiculous and aggressively obscene [1] or serves to create panic (e.g. in initiation rites). The wearing of masks has been attested in various Greek cults, e.g. that of Artemis Orthia in Sparta ([2. 161, 489]; [3]) or the Arcadian Demeter Kidaria [2. 477f.]. But → Dionysus [4; 5] is the mask god par excellence. The mask is a symbol of his presence and at the same time a cultic image [6. 276–279]: On the so called Lenaea vases Maenads dance around him and worship him in the form of a mask attached to a tree or a pillar [7]. Masks in graves and on sarcophaguses carry an eschatological meaning, pointing to Dionysian → Mysteries [8].

While the singers of the Dionysian cultic songs (→ dithyrambus) performed unmasked, the dramatic genres of Satyr plays, tragedy and comedy all presupposed masks for the choir and actors. Either these were 'invented' for purposes of dramatic effect or absorbed from cult. The origins of → tragedy point to dancers dressed as goats; roosters or piggy-back riders on black-figured Attic vases from the early 5th cent. BC are probably connected to → comedy when it was not yet part of the urban *agones* [9]. The so called Pronomos krater (→ Pronomos painter) shows how the singers or actors change under the influence of masks: all the people taking part in a → satyr play are arranged around a centrally positioned Dionysus, and while several choreutes still chat with their masks in hand, a masked person already breaks into an ecstatic dance [10]. In the 'Bacchae' → Euripides praises the power of the god and plays an ambivalent game with appearance and reality,

with divine presence and dramatic fiction. Dionysus appears in the form and mask of a stranger (Eur. Bacch. 4; 53–54) and persuades his opponent Pentheus to go into the mountains with him. Disguised as a Maenad, with a different mask (ibid. 831–833), Pentheus plunges into the catastrophe which is unveiled in the end by the → epiphany of Dionysus.

C. DEVELOPMENT OF THE THEATRE MASK
→ Thespis, who was the first to face the tragic choir as speaker, is said to have performed wearing white lead makeup at first and later a mask. Vase figures attest that until the end of the 5th cent. BC few characteristics were sufficient to differentiate a tragic mask typologically according to gender, age and class. Even features and a barely opened mouth showed no signs of passion. It is difficult to say what was Dionysian about such a neutral mask [11]. In the 4th cent. BC a development began towards greater realism and emotional expression, which blossomed fully in the Hellenistic period and was decisive for the usual image of the mask from then on. Above the forehead, the hair was now high and arched (ὄγκος, *ónkos*), and the crests of hair falling over the sides gave the mask a stiff, strange dignity. The myths portrayed must have seemed horrifying and unreal to the audience.

The actors in a Satyr play held on the tragic masks and were thus in stark contrast to the choir of satyrs, the animal-like followers of the deity. Their masks were characterized by a pug nose and pointed animal ears, as many vase pictures attest.

The masks of the Old Comedy are easier to reconcile with Dionysian ecstasy. They show crude, often almost grotesque facial features and wide open mouths; the contrast with the tragic mask is shown in para-tragedic scenes like the kidnapping of → Telephus [12. fig. 1,102 and 11,4]. It seems technically impossible that masks appeared on the comic stage portraying contemporaries, as Aristoph. Equ. 230–233 jokingly suggests [13]. Only later did comedy masks become more restrained in expression, fitting to the character of the budding New Comedy. From now on, fixed types of masks develop, differing in hair and beard style, facial colour and mimic expression of the brows and the mouth (→ Facial expression). The grammarian → Iulius [IV 17] Pollux (4,133–154) lists 28 masks for tragedy and 44 for the New Comedy in a catalogue based on Hellenistic material, the latter ordered according to old men, youths, slaves, old and young women [14; 15]. However, rich terracotta finds (masks and statuettes of actors of the 4th and 3rd cents. BC) from the necropolis of Lipari [16] and the texts of Menander [4] surpass Pollux's typology in variety and complexity [17].

Greek tragic dramas have been performed in Syracuse since Aeschylus; in southern Italy the 4th cent. farces called → *phlýakes* combined elements of the Attic Old Comedy with those native impromptu plays [12]. This is where the Romans were introduced to masked plays. At first they adopted the masks only for the crude

→ *Atellana fabula*. Here, these did not serve to change but to hide the person behind it, because the actors, as free Roman citizens, had to remain anonymous. This was different in tragedy and comedy (imported since 240 BC); these were religious festivals, but not associated with any specific mask cult, and since freedmen and slaves performed in these no masks were necessary. Perhaps they were added by → Cincius [4] Faliscus or→ Q. Roscius [I 4] Gallus. Masks was indispensable for the pantomime dancer of the Imperial period, who portrayed all of the characters of a myth by himself (Lucian Salt. 66). Unlike the frightening masks of tragedy, those of pantomime were splendid [18].

D. THEATRE IN PRACTICE

The mask was seen as a theatrical prop; hence the maker was given the general name of σκευοποιός (*skeuopoiós*: 'prop maker'). Masks were made of linen and plaster, then painted. They were placed on top of the head like a visor helmet; a quick change of mask was imperative in comedy because of the maximum of three actors (→ hypokrites). Since some rolls had to played by different speakers in different scenes, the masks could be identified with a certain character but not with a certain actor and his voice. In certain situations characters returned to the stage with changed masks: blinded (Oedipus; Polymestor) or in mourning with shaved head (Admetus). References in the text to facial mimic or expression appeal to the imagination of the spectator [19]. Much had to be clarified through → gestures; pain or shame for instance were expressed by covering the head (Hippolytus).

Victorious → choregoi or protagonists hung masks as offerings in the temple of Dionysus [20]. This may have lead to the custom of using masks as a decorative element of construction (not only on theatres) [21; 22]. Numerous portrayals of masks in frescos and mosaics convey an impression of the lost originals.

1 BURKERT, 171 2 NILSSON, GGR, Vol. 1 3 J. B. CARTER, The Masks of Ortheia, in: AJA 91, 1987, 355–383 4 W. WREDE, Der Maskengott, in: MDAI(A) 53, 1928, 66–95 5 F. FRONTISI-DUCROUX, Le dieu-masque: Une figure du Dionysos d'Athènes, 1991 6 SIMON, GG, 1969 (³1985) 7 DEUBNER, 127–134 8 R. MERKELBACH, Die Hirten des Dionysos, 1988 9 G. M. SIFAKIS, Parabasis and Animal Choruses, 1971 10 P. E. ARIAS, B. B. SHEFTON, M. HIRMER, A History of Greek Vase Painting, 1962, Taf. 218f. 11 S. HALLIWELL, The Function and Aesthetics of Greek Tragic Masks, in: Drama 2, 1993, 195–211 12 O. TAPLIN, Comic Angels, 1993 13 K. J. DOVER, Portrait-Masks in Aristophanes, in: R. E. H. WESTENDORP Boerma (ed.), Komoidotragemata, Studia Aristophanea (FS W.J.W. Koster), 1967, 16–28 14 C. ROBERT, Die Masken der neueren attischen Komödie, 1911 15 T. B. L. WEBSTER, J. R. GREEN, A. SEEBERG, Monuments Illustrating New Comedy, Vol. 1, ³1995, 6–51 16 L. BERNABÒ-BREA, Menandro e il teatro greco nelle terracotte liparesi, 1981 17 P. G. McC. BROWN, Masks, Names and Characters in New Comedy, in: Hermes 115, 1987, 181–202 18 M. KOKOLAKIS, Pantomimus and the Treatise περὶ ὀρχήσεως, in: Platon 11,

1959, 3–56 19 R. LÖHRER, Mienenspiel und Maske in der griechischen Tragödie, 1927 20 J. R. GREEN, Dedication of Masks, in: RA 1982, 237–248 21 J.-C. MORETTI, Des masques et des théâtres en Grèce et en Asie Mineure, in: REA 95, 1993, 207–223 22 H.-U. CAIN, Chronologie, Ikonographie und Bedeutung der römischen Maskenreliefs, in: BJ 188, 1988, 107–221.

L. BERNABÒ-BREA, Le maschere ellenistiche della tragedia greca (Cahiers du Centre J. Bérard 19), 1998; M. BIEBER, s.v. Maske, RE 14, 2070–2120; H.-D. BLUME, Einführung in das antike Theaterwesen, ³1991, 88–95; C. CALAME, Le récit en Grèce ancienne, 1986, Ch. 4; F. FRONTISI-DUCROUX, Du masque au visage. Aspects de l'identité en Grèce ancienne, 1995; K. MEULI, Altrömischer Maskenbrauch, in: MH 12, 1955, 206–235 = Gesammelte Schriften, Vol. 1, 251–282; PICKARD-CAMBRIDGE/ GOULD/ LEWIS ; D. WILES, The Masks of Menander, 1991.   H.BL.

Masonitae According to Ptol. 6,7,25 (Μασονῖται; *Masonîtai*) a tribe southwest of the *K límax óros* (Κλῖμαξ ὄρος, today Ǧabal Išbīl) in → Arabia Felix. Probably connected to *maṣanī* ('fortresses').

H. v. WISSMANN, Zur Geschichte und Landeskunde von Altsüdarabien (SAWW, Philos.-histor. Klasse 246), 1964, 415.   I.T.-N.

Masonry
A. DEFINITION   B. GREECE   C. ROME

A. DEFINITION

In this article, masonry will be understood as the various construction and design techniques of the structure of the walls of buildings, terraces, and defensive architecture (city walls, etc.) in ancient stonework, but not the various areas of application of woodworking; cf. → construction technique; → materiatio; on Roman cement construction cf. also → opus caementicium.

B. GREECE
1. SIMPLE MASONRY 2. FULL BLOCK AND HOLLOW MASONRY 3. ASHLAR MASONRY 4. AESTHETIC EFFECT

1. SIMPLE MASONRY

The walls of simple early Greek buildings were first made of wood or wattle work. From the 8th century BC, a combination of air-dried mud bricks and vertical or horizontal wooden supports was increasingly used (Lefkandi, Eretria, Sparta); real half-timbered walls, although they have not been attested to date, were probably also common, as is shown by the transformation of this construction principle into stone in Lycian graves (Xanthus). Massive walls made of mud bricks, long known and attested in the advanced civilisations of the Orient, were common in Greek architecture into the 3rd century BC, but they have rarely been preserved. Mud-brick masonry was found in practically every area of construction (residence, temple, city walls, etc.); in residential and utilitarian buildings this technique was predominant into the Hellenistic period. Mud-brick

Examples of ancient masonry techniques

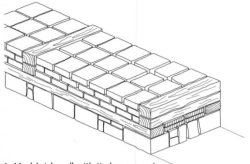

1. Mud-brick wall with timber supports

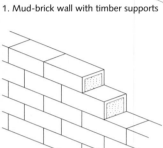

2. Single-course isodomic ashlar masonry

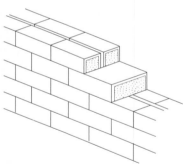

3. Isodomic ashlar masonry with alternate courses of stretchers and headers

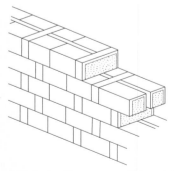

4. Isodomic ashlar masonry with irregularly spaced headers

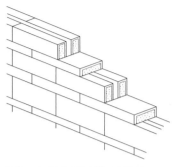

5. Pseudo-isodomic ashlar masonry

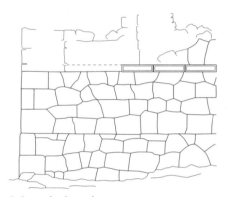

6. Coursed polygonal masonry (Larisa on the Hermus)

7. Composite construction (Byzantine land wall of Constantinople)

walls could, depending on their use, be up to 9 m thick, and displayed a correspondingly considerable stability. The bricks were laid in the usual overlapping order, and fixed with clay mortar as a binding medium; they were plastered to keep them dry; and were further protected from moisture by a broadly overhanging roof. For additional protection from dampness/backwater, mud-brick masonry was usually built on a base of quarry- or dressed stone at least c. 0,5 m high (compare the classical city wall of Athens in the area of the → Kerameikos).

2. FULL BLOCK AND HOLLOW MASONRY

Various forms of full block masonry as well as of double-shelled masonry are found already in the Mycenaean period, but here, as down to the 3rd century BC, it is found mostly on defensive and protective structures (city or fortress walls) as well as representative architecture. Polygonal 'Cyclopean' masonry dominates the Bronze Age citadels of → Tiryns and → Mycenae; the masonry was either laid in massive courses (Tiryns) or double-shelled and filled with quarry-stone (Mycenae, protective wall before the shaft graves). In historical Greece, the technique of irregularly layered, massive or double-shelled quarry-stone walls endured in fortification structures into the Hellenistic period (numerous examples of city walls from the 4th–2nd centuries BC). It was important in construction to lay the quarry-stones as tightly and seamlessly as possible, to ensure maximal stability on the one hand, and on the other to make it as difficult as possible to remove individual stones, thus making it hard to dismantle the wall, for instance in the case of a siege. For this reason small stones were hammered into the remaining gaps until maximal smoothing was achieved ('filling-in'). An alternative to 'Cyclopean' quarry-stone masonry was coursed walls made of flat quarry stones with large individual ashlars in between, as is attested at Miletus.

Polygonal masonry is a skillful variation on rough quarry-stone and Mycenaean Cyclopean masonry. Here, many-sided stones are stacked on top of one another and against one another in such a way that maximal flush jointing is achieved, and hence maximal durability and invulnerability of the interlocked stones, which were smoothed on the outside. Polygonal masonry could be either completely polygonal, that is, with only one horizontal edge along the top of the wall, or in several courses on top of one another, with repeated horizontal adjustment (e.g. Larisa on the Hermus). Genuine polygonal masonry is to be found frequently from the late 7th to the early 5th centuries BC, then again in the late 4th/3rd centuries BC. In the Late Classical and Hellenistic periods, it often forms part of a decorative-retrospective understanding of architectural forms, which are seen as time-honoured and ennobling, but are no longer used in the sense of their former function as fortifications (cf. various temenos walls; polygonal supporting walls as bearers of inscriptions in the Apollo sanctuary of Delphi; polygonal masonry in civil use as well in the 4th/3rd centuries BC in northwest Greece, e.g. Cassope).

3. ASHLAR MASONRY

Common to the various forms of ashlar masonry in Greek architecture is the fact that it is laid without mortar, and, unlike in defensive structures, the ashlars are connected by metal clamps, at least in building construction (on laying stones and caulking joints → anathyrosis; → construction technique). Ashlar masonry could be arranged as isodomic in single courses (where overlapping of the joints is absolutely essential) or isodomic in two courses (where isodomic = perfectly horizontal layering consisting in tiers of the same height). In the latter type, the stretchers, which are laid in the direction of the wall's alignment, and the headers, which are laid perpendicular to the alignment for stability, can be combined in different ways. Along with perfectly right-angled joints, there are often trapezoidal or slanted joints; also current was a pseudo-isodomic design, in which individual courses of ashlars were separated by flat, plate-shaped layers (pseudo-isodomic = layering consisting of tiers of unequal height, e.g. Pergamum). However, it is generally not possible to retrace a 'genetic' line of development from polygonal masonry via masonry consisting of horizontal courses with angled butt joints to 'genuine' ashlar masonry as the 'ideal form'.

4. AESTHETIC EFFECT

The exterior surfaces of polygonal masonry, both isodomic and pseudo-isodomic, often became the object of particularly intricate, largely visible (that is, demonstrative) elaboration. These include merely apparently 'unfinished elements', as well as cleverly formed cushion-shaped convexities in ashlar walls (Magnesia on the Maeander), bossed ashlars (Priene), or smooth ashlars (Selinunte), which are just as much the sign of aesthetic considerations above and beyond all functional aspects as are, for instance, the chisel marks on the fortification walls at Eleusis. Because of its henceforth hair-thin, almost imperceptible joins, isodomic masonry with optimal fitting accuracy was able, when viewed at a distance, to transmit the impression of a monolithic, highly artificially constructed wall. This, too, displayed the competence and aesthetic impulse of the builder (→ Könnensbewußtsein). In the Hellenistic period, decorative masonry increasingly became the background for elaborate façades (→ Gables; → Windows).

C. ROME

Roman masonry initially used traditional Greek forms and procedures, but combined these with technical innovations. In its development, fired and therefore weather-resistant mud brick, developed in Greece in the late 4th cent. BC (→ Bricks; Brick stamps; early uses include the so-called 'Necromanteion' at Ephyra and the so-called 'Katagogeion/marketplace building'), in Cassope, but also to → *opus caementicium* or poured cement, first attested in Campania were of great importance. Beyond Greek-influenced ashlar or massive stone masonry, which became increasingly rare in the Roman empire and was reserved for sacral and representative purposes, Roman masonry was used for revetting a cement core, which it was used to decorate or to 'make invisible'. The goal of Roman revetment masonry was to suggest a structure consisting of small parts, which in reality did not exist from the viewpoint of construction. The camouflaging and simultaneously ennobling significance of masonry in Roman architecture is shown by Vitruvius' comprehensive description of the possibilities and techniques used in masonry design, as well as of the respective advantages and disadvantages of each procedure once chosen (Vitr. De Arch. 2,8). [2]1994

The masonry-simulating materials used for revetting a cement core were various kinds of tufa, limestone and a wide variety of bricks; for the equally current facing of cement walls with large-surfaced plates of marble or travertine, see → Incrustation. Tufa blocks or bricks were prepared in a wedge or pyramid shape and attached to the cement core with mortar (cf. → Construction technique, with fig.: Roman construction technique); horizontal courses of brick could alternate with tufa block revetment in reticulate, diamond- or rhomb-shaped patterns. The adequacy of a 'developmental model' for the formal configuration of cement revetments by means of tufa stones (for instance, *opus incertum* = irregular arrangement = early; *opus quasi-reticulatum* = approximately reticular arrangement = evidence of progress; *opus reticulatum* = precise reticular arrangement = the ideal form) is as debated as it is revelant for dating individual stages of Roman architecture, with its often tortuous and highly ramified construction history.

Massive brick masonry became increasingly important from the 1st cent. AD on, achieving a quite specific decorative character (e.g. the city walls of Constantinople) in late antiquity, by means of variations on courses of runners and stretchers or layers of bricks and mortar and the decorative elements connected therewith. It reached its high point in the brick 'decorativism' of Byzantine church architecture.

→ Construction technique

J. P. ADAM, La construction romaine. Matériaux et techniques, 1984; M. E. BLAKE, Roman Construction in Italy from Tiberius through the Flavians, 1959; Id., Roman Construction in Italy from Nerva through the Antonines, 1973; A. C. BROOKES, Stoneworking in the Geometric Period at Corinth, in: Hesperia 50, 1981, 285–302; R. GINOUVÈS, R. MARTIN, Dictionnaire méthodique de l'architecture grecque et romaine, vol. 1, Matériaux, techniques, 1985; T. L. HERES, Paries. A Proposal for a Dating System of Late-Antique Masonry Structures in Rome and Ostia, 1982; W. HOEPFNER, E. L. SCHWANDNER, Haus und Stadt im klassischen Griechenland, [2]1994, s.v. Mauerwerk; s.v. Mauertechnik, 354; T. E. KALPAXIS, Hemiteles. Akzidentelle Unfertigkeit und 'Bossen-Stil' in der griechischen Baukunst, 1986; H. LAUTER, Die Architektur des Hellenismus, 1986, 48–49, 253–257; C. MANGO, Byzantine Architecture, 1986, 8–19; R. MARTIN, Manuel d'architecture greque, vol. 1: Matériaux et techniques, 1965, 371–385; M. MILLER, Befestigungsanlagen in Italien vom 8. bis 3. Jahrhundert v.Chr., 1994; W. MÜLLER-

WIENER, Griechisches Bauwesen in der Antike, 1988, 64–80; A. K. ORLANDOS, Les matériaux de construction et la technique architecturale des anciens Grecs, vol. 1, 1966, Vol. 2, 1968; F. RAKOB, Hellenismus in Mittelitalien: Bautypen und Bautechnik, in: P. ZANKER (ed.), Hellenismus in Mittelitalien, 1976, 366–376; C. J. RATTÉ, Lydian Masonry and Monumental Architecture at Sardis, 1989; R. C. VANN, A Study of Roman Construction in Asia Minor. The Lingering Role of a Hellenistic Tradition in Ashlar Masonry, 1982; V. A. WALSH, W. A. MCDONALD, Greek Late Bronze Age Domestic Architecture. Toward a Typology of Stone Masonry, in: Journal of Field Archaeology 13, 1986, 493–499.; R.L. Scranton, Greek Walls, 1941   C.HÖ.

Masorah, Masoretes Since the Hebrew alphabet is a consonantal alphabet and thus does not write any vowels, written words can often be pronounced and interpreted in various ways. In order to solve this problem, individual consonant letters were used also as vowel letters (*matres lectionis*) from early on (so called plene writing; cf. Aramaic documents from as early as the 9th century BC or the Shiloah inscription from the 7th century BC). Furthermore, in order to secure the pronunciation of the holy text definitively, the so-called Masorah ('tradition', from Hebrew *msr*, 'to pass down') was developed, which contains both the vowel signs and accents of the Bible text as well as various marginal comments on the text. From about the 6th century AD, Jewish scholars called Masoretes used diacritical signs modelled on the older Syrian vocalization to designate the vowels and the quality of individual consonants. In the beginning, relatively simple systems were created, which marked the vowel above the corresponding consonant ('supralinear pointing'). Here, the signs used in Babylon differed from the ones used in Palestine. From the end of the 8th to the beginning of the 10th century AD, → Tiberias was the center of Masoretic activity. The so-called Tiberian pointing was created here, which generally placed the vowel underneath the consonant and which, because it recognizes long and short vowels, is much more differentiated than the earlier systems. The Ben Asher family was the most important within the Tiberian school; their system of pointing can be found in the Biblia Hebraica Stuttgartensia, which is based on the Codex Firkovich (earlier Codex Leningradensis) from the year 1008.

The comments of the Masoretes, which are printed next to the Bible text, are the Masorah in the narrower sense of the word. They are divided into the Marginal Masorah with *Masorah Magna* and *Masorah Parva* as well as the Final Masorah. The *Masorah Parva*, which can be found on the right- or left-hand side of the Bible text respectively, note when a term should be read differently from the way the traditional text has determined (so called K^{e}tīḇ-Q^{e}rē); they also note how often certain words and forms occur in the text and where exegetically noteworthy terms occur. The *Masorah Magna* – originally in the upper and lower margin (Publication [1]) – lists the occurrences in question. The final

Masorah – at the end of each book – gives the number of words and letters used in the book. In this way the Bible text is to be protected from changes of any kind as they may occur, above all, when copying a text.

→ Bible

> 1 A. DOTAN, s.v. Masorah, Encyclopaedia Judaica 16, 1971, 1402–1482; 2 E. Tov, Der Text der Hebräischen Bibel. Handbuch der Textkritik, 1997, Index s.v. M.; 3 G. E. WEIL (ed.), Massorah Gedolah iuxta codicem Lenigradensem B19a, vol. 1: Catalogi, 1971; 4 E. WÜRTHWEIN, Der Text des Alten Testaments. Einführung in die Biblia Hebraica, ⁵1988, 13–37.   B.E.

Mass see → Missa

Massa (Lat. for 'lump'); a formless mass especially of crude metal (such as *massa auri, obryzae, argenti, ferri,* etc.) in contrast to *ramentum* (small piece) and *regula* (bar). The bullion gold that went into the Imperial Roman treasury was entrusted to an authority called the *scrinium aureae massae,* with a *primicerius sacrae massae,* under the supervision of the *comes sacrarum largitionum* (→ Comes A.; Cod. Iust. 12,23,7,7; 12,23,7,16 from 384; Not. Dign. Occ. 11,92; 11,95; Not. Dign. Or. 13,26; 13,29); and bullion silver to the *scrinium ab argento.*

> 1 W. ENSSLIN, s.v. Massa (3), RE 14, 2122; 2 SCHRÖTTER, 376.   DI.K.

Massabatae (Μασσαβάται/*Massabátai,* Μεσσαβάται/ *Messabátai,* Latin *Messabatae*). Inhabitants of the region of Massabatice (Μασσαβατική/*Massabatikḗ,* Μεσ(σ)αβατική/*Mes(s)abatikḗ*), which was named after them, in southern → Media or northern Elymaeis (Str. 11,13,6; 16,1,18; Plin. HN 6,134), or – less likely – south of the Elymaeis region in the northernmost part of → Persis (Ptol. 6,4,3; cf. Plin. HN 6,135).

> R. N. FRYE, The History of Ancient Iran, 1984, 89.   H.KA.

Massaga (Massaka). Capitol city of the Assaceni in modern Swat west of the Indus, Old Indian Maósakā-vatī; conquered by Alexander the Great. Hellenistic wall remains were found in excavations of neighbouring sites.

> P. CALLIERI et al., Bir-Kot-Ghwandai 1990–1992 (Annali. Istituto Universitario Orientale 52, Supplemento 73), 1994.   K.K.

Massalia (Μασσαλία/*Massalía,* Latin *Massilia*), modern Marseilles.
A. FOUNDING   B. DEVELOPMENT UP TO AND DURING THE THIRD CENTURY BC   C. MASSALIA AND ROME

A. FOUNDING
Around 600 BC the Phocaeans founded M. (→ Colonization IV.), attracted by the potential resulting from the proximity of the Rhône and the rocky bay of Lacydon for the establishment and securing of a harbour (founding legends in Aristot. fr. 549 ROSE = Ath. 13,576a; Iust. 43,3,4–13). M.'s early topography is difficult to determine; there were probably no permanent structures before the arrival of the Greek settlers. The first Phocaean settlers apparently only made use of part of the later city area (Fort Saint-Jean, cf. map, no. 1, and Butte Saint-Laurent, cf. map, nos. 2–4); but the city quickly expanded to the neighbouring Butte des Moulins, and from the end of the 6th century BC to the Butte des Carmes (cf. map, no. 28) and to where the modern stock exchange is now located (cf. map, no. 33): traces of an archaic fortress (*c.* 510–500 BC) were found there [1. 186–190]. The status of the first settlement – → *empórion* or colony – is a matter of debate, as is the role of the Phocaeans, who came to M. after the conquest of → Phocaea by the Persians (between 545 and 540 BC) [2; 3]. The production of amphorae [4] and the minting of coins [5. 245–260] began in these years. M. rapidly evolved into an economic power; its rise was facilitated by the lack of larger neighbouring towns (Greek, Etruscan or Phoenician) and by the fertile hinterland (vine, olives, grain). Little can be said about how far the city controlled its surroundings. Its geopolitical situation allowed it to control trade between the Iberian world and the Greek settlements as well as the access routes into the centre of Celtic Europe. After the battle of Alalia (→ Aleria; 537 BC), M. had to cede its Iberian outposts to → Carthage. A dedication (Apollo statue, Paus. 10,18,6) to the sanctuary of Delphi in 525 BC still reveals the city's wealth at the time.

B. DEVELOPMENT UP TO AND DURING THE THIRD CENTURY BC
After a time of economic and political stagnation in the 5th century BC, which was caused by the expansion of Carthage, M. developed significantly. The city's topography may remain obscure for the most part, but we know that the area of M. was c. 50 ha – it was thus one of the largest cities in the western Mediterranean region. M. expanded further to the north around 300 BC (*rue Leca*) and so reached the size that it kept until the end of antiquity and beyond. In the 3rd and 2nd centuries BC, M. was surrounded by a large city wall; walls also divided the city into three sections. According to Str. 4,1,4, there were sanctuaries of Artemis of Ephesus and Apollo of Delphi in M., probably where Fort Saint-Jean stands today [1. 193]. The calendars of Lampsacus and Phocaea list the names of other deities: Dionysus, Apollo Thargelios, Leucothea, Cybele [5. 141–150]. M. was governed by an oligarchy of merchants with a council of 600 *timoûchoi,* which in turn was headed by a committee of fifteen men (Str. 4,1,5). In the 4th century BC, → Pytheas [4] set out from M. to explore the Gallic coast of the Atlantic and sailed along the Breton coast. In the 3rd century BC, M. controlled the entire Rhône delta. Moreover, M. had established outposts along the coast and in the interior since the 6th

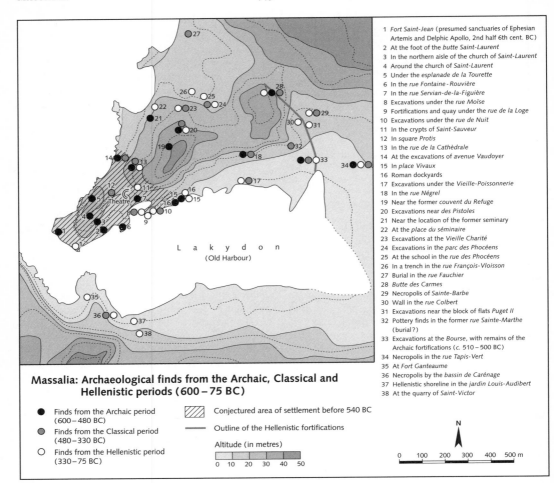

Massalia: Archaeological finds from the Archaic, Classical and Hellenistic periods (600–75 BC)

● Finds from the Archaic period (600–480 BC)

◐ Finds from the Classical period (480–330 BC)

○ Finds from the Hellenistic period (330–75 BC)

▨ Conjectured area of settlement before 540 BC

— Outline of the Hellenistic fortifications

Altitude (in metres)
0 10 20 30 40 50

1 Fort Saint-Jean (presumed sanctuaries of Ephesian Artemis and Delphic Apollo, 2nd half 6th cent. BC)
2 At the foot of the butte Saint-Laurent
3 In the northern aisle of the church of Saint-Laurent
4 Around the church of Saint-Laurent
5 Under the esplanade de la Tourette
6 In the rue Fontaine - Rouvière
7 In the rue Servian-de-la-Figuière
8 Excavations under the rue Moïse
9 Fortifications and quay under the rue de la Loge
10 Excavations under the rue de Nuit
11 In the crypts of Saint-Sauveur
12 In square Protis
13 In the rue de la Cathèdrale
14 At the excavations of avenue Vaudoyer
15 In place Vivaux
16 Roman dockyards
17 Excavations under the Vieille-Poissonnerie
18 In the rue Négrel
19 Near the former couvent du Refuge
20 Excavations near des Pistoles
21 Near the location of the former seminary
22 At the place du séminaire
23 Excavations at the Vieille Charité
24 Excavations in the parc des Phocéens
25 At the school in the rue des Phocéens
26 In a trench in the rue François-Vloisson
27 Burial in the rue Fauchier
28 Butte des Carmes
29 Necropolis of Sainte-Barbe
30 Wall in the rue Colbert
31 Excavations near the block of flats Puget II
32 Pottery finds in the former rue Sainte-Marthe (burial?)
33 Excavations at the Bourse, with remains of the Archaic fortifications (c. 510 – 500 BC)
34 Necropolis in the rue Tapis-Vert
35 At Fort Ganteaume
36 Necropolis by the bassin de Carénage
37 Hellenistic shoreline in the jardin Louis-Audibert
38 At the quarry of Saint-Victor

N

0 100 200 300 400 500 m

century BC, e.g. Emporion (→ Emporia) on the Iberian coast, → Agatha, Tauroeis/Tauroention (modern Le Brusc-Six-Fours), Olbia, → Antipolis (Antibes) and Nicaea (Nice) on the Gallic coast and Theline (→ Arelate), Rhodanousia (Espeyran?), Avennion (modern Avignon) and Kaballion (Cavaillon) in the interior. In founding these cities, M. was involved to a considerable extent in connecting south and central Gaul with the economic region and cultural centres on the Mediterranean.

C. Massalia and Rome

The history of the relations between. M. and Rome was marked strongly by M.'s geo-strategic position between Italy and Spain, further by its proximity to certain peoples (→ Ligures, → Vocontii, → Salluvii), who threatened M. To these threats M. responded with the construction of new fortifications in the 2nd century BC [1. 194ff.]. The relationship between M. and Rome was very positive over a long period: M. supported Rome against → Hannibal (by contributing to the Roman victory on the Ebro in 217 BC [5. 58–61]; → Punic Wars) and supported Rome's diplomatic efforts in the region.

From the beginning of the 2nd century BC, M. appealed to Rome several times for help (in 181 for dealing with the Ligurian pirates; in 154 against the Oxybii and the → Deciates, who were holding Nicaea and Antipolis under siege). The interventions in favour of M. were also in Rome's own interest, as she sought to secure the passage from Italy to Spain for herself. In 125 BC, M. asked for help against the Salluvii, who had devastated the city's territory. Massiliot contingents probably took part in Rome's subsequent campaign, which led to the subjugation of the entire region and its degradation to the status of a Roman province (Gallia Transalpina). M.'s position was undiminished but Rome was now able to control two main trade routes: the Rhône corridor and the old tin route (the axis Aude – Garonne – Gironde). In 49 BC, Caesar laid siege to the city, as it had allied itself with Pompey (Caes. B. Civ. 1,34–36; 56–58; 2,1–16; 22). It lost significant portions of its territory, but retained its autonomy and proved its vitality again and again during the Imperial period, even when it was overshadowed by Narbo Martius (Narbonne) and Arelate (Arles).

Ancient structures: water structures (baths, wells, cisterns, aqueducts, sewerage), a Roman theatre, harbour (from archaic times to the Roman period) [1. 196; 5. 109–121; 6], burial sites from all periods. Sources: Str. 4,1,4f.; Aristot. Pol. 1305b; 1321a; Plin. HN 3,34.

1 H. Tréziny, Marseille grecque, in: RA 1997, 185–200; 2 J. Brunel, Marseille et les fugitifs de Phocée, in: REA 50, 1948, 5–26; 3 M. Gras, L'arrivée d'immigrés à Marseille au milieu du VIe siècle av. J.-C., in: P. Arcelin (ed.), Sur les pas des Grecs en Occident (Études Massaliètes 4), 1995, 363–366; 4 M. Bats (ed.), Les amphores de Marseille grecque (Études Massaliètes 2), 1990; 5 Id. et al. (eds.), Marseille grecque et la Gaule (Études Massaliètes 3), 1992; 6 A. Hesnard, Les ports antiques de Marseille, Place Jules-Verne, in: Journal of Roman Archaeology 8, 1995, 65–78.

M. Bats, Commerce et politique massaliètes aux IVe et IIIe siècles av. J.-C., in: PdP 37, 1982, 256–268; A. Brugnone, In margine alle tradizioni ecistiche di Massalia, in: PdP 50, 1995, 46–66; M. Clavel-Lévêque, Marseille grecque, 1977; D. Roman, Y. Roman, Histoire de la Gaule, 1997; F. Salviat, s.v. Massalia, in: PE, 557f.

Maps M. Bats et al. (eds.), Marseille grecque et la Gaule (Études Massaliètes 3), 1992, passim, esp. 73, 78, 84; R. Chevallier, Gallia Narbonensis, in: ANRW II.3, 686–828, esp. 713, fig. 9; 747, fig. 35.   Y.L.

Massa Veternensis City in Etruria, birthplace of Constantius [5] (Amm. Marc. 14,11,27), possibly the ancient settlement on the territory of Vetulonia with necropoleis on Lago dell'Accesa in the mining area of the Colline Metallifere, in which copper, iron, lead and silver were mined. There is little evidence from the Neolithic period, more from the Aeneolithic and Bronze periods, but remains are especially numerous from the Iron Age to the Imperial Roman period. The settlement around Lago dell'Accesa was probably abandoned, as were others in the hinterland of Vetulonia, in the 6th/5th cents. BC, at the time of the demise of → Vetulonia. But life in MV flourished again on the Poggio Castiglione: in the 4th/3rd cents. BC, an area of about 1 ha. was claimed for urban development (city wall, buildings on perpendicular streets). The archeological finds (terra sigillata, oil lamps, glass ware) in both the areas of Accesa and Poggio Castiglione go into the late Imperial period.

D. Levi, La necropoli etrusca del Lago dell'Accesa, in: Monumenti Antichi 35, 1933, 11ff.; G. Camporeale (ed.), L'Etruria mineraria, 1985; Id. (ed.), Massa Marittima. Museo Archeologico, 1993; Id. (ed.), L'abitato etrusco dell'Accesa. Il quartiere B, 1997.   Gl.C.

Massieni (Mastieni). Iberian tribe on the southeast coast of Spain (Avien. 422; 425; 450), with dwelling places from the Chrysus (modern Guadiaro) River to → Carthago Nova [1. 52, 197, 186f.]. The principal town was Mastia (cf. Pol. 3,24,2; 4, here called Ταρσήιον/*Tarséion*, indicating that it probably belonged to → Tartessus' sphere of influence). → Hasdrubal

[2] may have founded Carthago Nova on the site of Mastia around 221 BC. The → Bastetani, which may possibly be identified with the M., later appeared in their place [2].

1 A. Schulten (ed.), Fontes Hispaniae Antiquae 12, 1955; 2 Tovar 2, 26

Tovar 2, 27f.   P.B.

Massinissa (Lat. M. or Masinissa, Greek Μασανάσσης/ *Masanássēs* (Pol.), Μασαννάσας/*Masannásas* (inscriptions), Numidian form of the name Massanassa). M. lived c. 230–148 BC (Pol. 36,16); son of Gaia, the eastern Numidian prince of the → Massyli (IG XI 4, 1116; 1115 = Syll.³ 652: Delos shortly before 167 BC; IDélos 1577; Liv. 24,49,1); brought up in Carthage (App. Lib. 10,37). From 212 BC he was commander of a Numidian cavalry corps in Spain in the service of → Hasdrubal [3]. Here he defeated Roman troops at → Castulo in 211 BC (App. Lib. 10,37; Liv. 25,32–36). In 208 he operated at → Carthago Nova (Liv. 27,20).

The battle of → Ilipa (206 BC) ended Carthaginian hegemony in Spain; M.'s nephew → Massiva [1] negotiated with Rome; M. promised Scipio military support for his African campaign (Liv. 28,35; App. Hisp. 37,149f.) [1. 285ff.]. It was M.'s intention, after his return from Spain in 206, to claim by force his inheritance as Gaia's son against a group led by his own brother, Oezalces, and the latter's son, Capussa, who had taken over the rule of the Massyli. However, as these two groups engaged in their rivalries, → Syphax, prince of the western Numidian → Masaesyli, won control over the Massyla as well. M. was driven out of the country [4. 46–51; 5. 2156]. In 203, together with Laelius [I 1], he attacked the encampment of Syphax. After the victory at the 'Great Plains' over Syphax and the Carthaginian troops, they both maintained contact with the enemy (Pol. 14,1–10; 15,4; Liv. 30,3–9; Diod. Sic. 27,6); Syphax was defeated and taken prisoner at → Cirta (Liv. 30,9–12).

M. was now in control of both Numidian tribal areas, and after the battle of → Zama (202 BC.) was confirmed by Rome as their ruler (Liv. 30,44,12). With the occupation of Cirta, Syphax's wife → Sophoniba, daughter of Hasdrubal [5] and granddaughter of Geskon [3], fell into in M.'s hands. Before her marriage to Syphax in 205 she is said to have been betrothed to M., and after her marriage to have ensured her husband's loyalty to Carthage. When the Romans demanded that she be handed over, M. is said to have murdered her. The traditional story of Sophoniba is rich in fictional elements (Liv. 30,12–15; Diod. Sic. 27,7).

M.'s Numidian cavalry were decisive for Roman victory in the battle of Zama (Pol. 15,14). At the end of the Second → Punic War, M. was able to establish himself as Roman client king over all of Numidia. His relationship with Cornelius [I 71] Scipio ensured the continuity of his dynasty (Pol. 36,16) [4. 51–53]. It is unclear to what extent M. ruled after 203 as a sovereign ruler [7; 8. 231;

9] or as a dependent client king [6. 24–84]. Restricted as it was in its freedom to make political or military decisions, → Carthage (Pol. 15,18) saw its predominance in the region challenged by M.'s dominion over Cirta and Siga after 201. Challenged, no less, by a rival who secured and expanded his own kingdom at the expense of Carthage, supported by the recognition of the rights of possession of his family granted to him by the peace treaty of 201 between Rome and Carthage. In 195–161 BC, M. gained control over the *empória* (→ Emporion) on the Minor Syrtis, previously dependencies of Carthage, and took possession of the hinterland as well. These actions were based on Roman arbitrations acknowledging his rights of possession (Pol. 31,21; Liv. 33,47,7; 34,62; 40,17,1–6; 42,23–24; Str. 17,3). M. thus brought about the Third → Punic War between Rome and Carthage, which in 150 BC had begun to take military action against M.'s encroachments without authorisation from Rome. M. died before the outbreak of this war (App. Lib. 105,496ff.); Diod. Sic. 32,16; Pol. 36,16).

M. changed the political and social conditions in the territories over which he ruled, furthered urbanisation and trade, as well as more intensive farming, probably through the adoption of Carthaginian techniques, and he arranged for the settlement of formerly nomadic herdsmen. (Pol. 36,16; Str. 17,3,15; App. Lib. 106,499; → Nomads). As a Hellenic king, M. supported Delos in 179 BC with donations of corn. The influence of Greek and Roman civilisation on the table-manners and musical tastes of the king is attested by Ptolemy VIII. Euergetes II, who probably knew the king from personal contact (FGrH 234 F 7–8). → Polybius [2] became acquainted with M. in Scipio's environment: his literary obituary of the king established the image of M. as a cultivated and civilising founder of the Numidian nation (Pol. 36,16).

→ Carthage; → Cornelius [I 71] Scipio; → Numidae, Numidia; → Punic wars; → Sophoniba; → Syphax

1 C. LEIDL, Appians Darstellung des 2. Punischen Krieges in Spanien, 1996; 2 P. G. WALSH, Massinissa, in: JRS 55, 1965, 149–160; 3 T. KOTULA, Masynissa, 1976; 4 M.-R. ALFÖLDI, Die Geschichte des numidischen Königreiches und seiner Nachfolger, in: H. G. HORN, C. B. RÜGER (ed.), Die Numider, 1979, 43–74; 5 W. SCHUR, s.v. Massinissa, in: RE 14, 2154–2165; 6 H. W. RITTER, Rom und Numidien. Untersuchungen zur rechtlichen Stellung abhängiger Könige, 1987; 7 D. TIMPE, Herrschaftsidee und Klientelstaatenpolitik in Sallusts Bellum Jugurthinum, in: Hermes 90, 1962, 334–375; 8 W. DAHLHEIM, Struktur und Entwicklung des römischen Völkerrechts im 3. und 2. Jahrhunders v. Chr., 1968; 9 C. SAUMAGNE, La Numidie et Rome. Massinissa et Jugurtha, 1966.

A. BERTHIER, La Numidie. Rome et le Maghreb, 1981; S. GSELL, Histoire ancienne de l'Afrique du Nord, vol. 3, 31928; C. A. JULIEN, Histoire de l'Afrique du Nord, 21956; F. RAKOB, Architecture royale numide. Architecture et société de l'archaïsme grec à la fin de la république romaine (Collection de l'École française de Rome 66), 1983, 325–348. B.M.

Massiva

[1] Nephew of → Massinissa, grandson of Gaia. M. was taken prisoner by the Romans in 209 BC in the second → Punic War as a cavalry commander in the service of Carthage. In order to initiate contact with Massinissa, Cornelius [I 71] Scipio freed him (Liv. 27,19,8–12; 28,35,8–13).

→ Numidae, Numidia

M.-R. ALFÖLDI, Die Geschichte des numidischen Königreiches und seiner Nachfolger, in: H. G. HORN, C. B. RÜGER (ed.), Die Numider, 1979, 43–74; C. SAUMAGNE, La Numidie et Rome. Masinissa et Jugurtha, 1966.

2] Grandson of → Massinissa, son of → Gulussa. M. went to Rome in 112 BC, following the murder of → Adherbal [4], where he laid claim to → Iugurtha's Numidian empire. Sp. Postumius Albinus supported M.'s claim against Jugurtha before the Senate with the intention of provoking a war. Jugurtha had M. murdered by his right-hand man Bomilcar; the conspiracy was made public (Sall. Iug. 35; Liv. Periochae 64; Flor. Epit. 1,36,8 (3,1,8); App. Num. fr. 1).

M.-R. ALFÖLDI, Die Geschichte des numidischen Königreiches und seiner Nachfolger, in: H. G. HORN, C. B. RÜGER (ed.), Die Numider, 1979, 43–74. B.M.

Massylii (Μασσύλιοι/*Massýlioi*, etc.). An Eastern Numidian tribe, from the east of Cape Bougaroun. References: Hesianax FGrH 763 F 1; Pol. 3,33,15; Strab. 17,3,9; Plin. HN 5,30; Sil. 16,170–172 (who confuses the M. with the → Masaesyli); App. Lib. 10,37; 27,110; 46,195. In the second century BC, the territory of the M. sometimes reached from the Mulucha river as far as the Gulf of Sidra (except for the province of Africa). Apart from the 'suffete' Zilalsan (Numidian *Zllsn*), the Massylian kings included Gaia (Numidian *Gjj*), his son → Massinissa (Punic *Msnsn*), his sons → Micipsa (Punic *Mkwsn*), → Gulussa (Punic *Glsn*) and → Mastanabal (Punic *Mstnʿbʾ*), their successors → Adherbal [4] (Punic *ʾdrbʿl*), → Hiempsal [1] I. and → Jugurtha, and their successor → Gauda. After the death of Gauda (before 88 BC), the throne and the kingdom seems to have been shared between Masteabar (eastern Masaisylia and western Massylia) and → Hiempsal [2] II (eastern Massylia and Emporia). The last western Massylian king was Arabion (44–41/40 BC), the last (ruling) eastern Massylian king → Juba [1] I (before 50 to 46 BC). Altogether, the Massylian dominion seems to have been divided five times: in 118 BC (?), after 118 BC, 105 BC, 88 BC and 46 BC.

→ Libyes, Libye

G. CAMPS, Origines du royaume massyle, in: Revue d'histoire et de civilisation du Maghreb 3, 1967, 29–38; F. DECRET, M. FANTAR, L'Afrique du Nord dans l'Antiquité, 1981, 99–115; J. DESANGES, Catalogue des tribus africaines ..., 1962, 109f.; W. HUSS, Die westmassylische Könige, in: AncSoc 20, 1989, 209–220. W.HU.

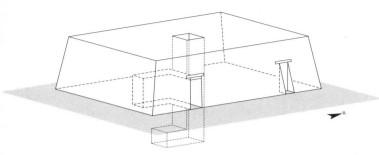

Isometric schematic drawing of a mastaba tomb (4th Dynasty). Subsidiary cult niche in the eastern façade of the overground structure; the cult chapel is on the south side. The grave shaft leads from the roof of the overground stucture to the underground burial chamber.

Mastaba (Arabic: 'bench'). Basic form for ancient Egyptian non-royal graves in the Old Kingdom. The emergence of the mastaba form can be traced to the beginning of the first dynasty (3000–2870 BC) in the region of Memphis. It consists of long, rectangular, north-south oriented, high and solidly filled-in structures with sloping side walls, which reproduce the basic shape of a house in an elementary stylised manner. Originally, the structure covered the grave chamber, which was situated in a cavity beneath it, definitively, but already in the course of the first dynasty the chamber was made accessible by steps leading down from the east, then from the north, and from the fourth dynasty (2570–2450 BC) by vertical shafts. In the most monumental constructions, the block itself was initially structured on the outside by a complex pattern of niches, adapted from the decorative architecture of palaces and sacred buildings. Later on, the walls are generally smooth, except for the east side, where cult sites are marked by two niches ('false doors'), which were the focus for pictorial and written decoration. By the third Dynasty (2635–2570 BC), these cult places, in some cases protected by front chapels and corridors, were preferentially included in small chambers, sometimes decorated on all sides, within the building. Except for the decorated stone parts of the cult sites, the tombs were originally made of mud bricks; from the fourth dynasty, massive stone structures became the norm in the royal cemeteries.

In the later Old Kingdom, the desire to extend the wall surfaces available for decoration by adding more and more rooms to the body of the mastaba, plus the wish to provide a number of grave shafts for family members, led to a gradual loss of the compact form. The block-like structures subsequently became chapels, which enclosed the cult site alone, and the grave shafts might be arranged in loose contact with them. The mastaba form also became obsolete through competition from rock graves, especially fashionable in Upper Egypt. In the Middle Kingdom, various clearly archaic mastaba structures were erected, while the further development of the private grave was determined by an orientation toward the forms of temple architecture.
→ Funerary architecture; → Burial; → Dead, cult of the

1 G. A. REISNER, The Development of the Egyptian Tomb, 1936;   2 J. VANDIER, Manuel d'archéologie égyptienne 2,1, 1954, 251–292.   S.S.

Mastanabal Youngest of the sons and heirs of → Massinissa; co-regent with → Micipsa and Gulussa after the death of Massinissa in 148 BC, supreme judicial authority. M.'s sons were → Iugurtha and → Gauda (Sall. Iug. 5; Liv. Periochae 50; App. Lib. 106; Zon. 9,27 D.).
→ Numidae, Numidia

M.-R. ALFÖLDI, Die Geschichte des numidischen Königreiches und seiner Nachfolger, in: H. G. HORN, C. B. RÜGER (ed.), Die Numider, 1979, 43–74; H. W. RITTER, Rom und Numidien. Untersuchungen zur rechtlichen Stellung abhängiger Könige, 1987; C. SAUMAGNE, La Numidie et Rome. Masinissa et Jugurtha, 1966.   B.M.

Mastarna (Variants: Maxtarna, Macstrna). Mythical or historical Etruscan of unknown origin. Friend of and fellow-warrior to the relatives or legendary ancestors of the *gens Vipina/Vibenna* in Vulci. He came to Rome and became king under the new name of Servius → Tullius. The Etruscan word m*acstrna* is supposed to be the equivalent of the Latin → *magister*, a designation for officials [1. 199–231], but it could equally be a noun with the meaning 'commander' (ET Ager Tarquiniensis 1,1). An Etruscan and a Roman tradition exist about M. On a wall-painting in the grave of the *gens Saties* in Vulci (the so-called Tomba François, ca. 330 BC [2]) M. cuts through the bonds of his friend Caile Vipinas (Etruscan tradition in Emperor → Claudius [III 1], CIL XIII 1668 l. 19, in his speech to the Lugdunensi), an Etruscan leader (Dion. Hal. Ant. 2,36,2; Varro Ling. 5,46; Tac. Ann. 4,65,1f.) from Vulci (Fest. 486,15f. L., emended and expanded by R. GARRUCCI and K.O. MÜLLER), while the latter's brother Avle Vipina and other Vulci heroes are slaughtering the generals of other Etruscan towns (Velzna/→ Volsinii, Sveam/Suana) and of Rome. The expulsion of M. from Etruria mentioned by Claudius (CIL XIII 1668 l. 20–27), as well as his arrival in Rome, the naming of Mons Caelius after his friend, and his further successes, plus the many variations in the tradition, betray the origin of the tradition in a Roman milieu. One basis of genuine tradition is available, however, telling of the deeds of a *gens Vipina*, whose heroic exploits were represented in Etruria from the sixth to as late as the third century [3. 234f.].

1 A. ALFÖLDI, Early Rome and the Latins, 1963, 176–235; 2 S. STEINGRÄBER, Etruskische Wandmalerei, 1985, 385 Nr. 178 Fig. 184; 3 F. BURANELLI etc., La Tomba François di Vulci, 1987, 234f.   L.A.-F.

Mastaura (Μάσταυρα; *Mástaura*). Town in Lydia on the southern slopes of the → Mes(s)ogis (Str. 14,1,47; Plin. HN 5,120; Steph. Byz. s.v. M.; Anth. Pal. 11,230, with a pun on the place-name), ruins to the north of Nazilli. From the Roman period, municipal institutions and cults are known from inscriptions and coins. In Christian times an episcopal see, it was represented at the councils of Ephesus (431) and Calchedon (451) (Hierocles, Synekdemos 659,8; Not. episc. 1,101; 3,21; 7,91; 8,108; 9,15; 10,156).

K. BURESCH, Aus Lydien, 1898; JONES, Cities, 78; LIEBENAM, 561; W. M. RAMSAY, A Historical Geography of Asia Minor, 1890, 104. H.KA.

Mastic (μαστίχη; *mastíchē*, Lat. *mastiche, mastix*). Aromatic resin of the mastic tree (*schínos*; pistacia lentiscus L.) and the oil from its berries. The name is presumably derived from *masásthai*, 'to chew', since the resin was popular for chewing, because of its pleasant taste and hardness, for dental care and against bad breath, just as small pieces of mastic wood were used as toothpicks. The small, evergreen mastic tree (and bush) was planted and cultivated all over the Mediterranean, although its resin was not of the same quality everywhere. The best mastic resin came from the island of → Chios, of which the colourless variety was most highly prized (Plin. HN 12,72) and the yellowish-green variety seen as inferior. The oil derived from the resin was used against disorders of the gut and the stomach, helped against coughs and colds, and could dye the hair red (Plin. HN 32,67). The wood of the mastic tree and its berries were boiled to make a medicinal wine (Plin. HN 14,112), and the oil was made into an ointment. Equally useful against digestive disorders were extracts from the bark, seeds and leaves of the mastic tree. Beside this, branches were used indoors as air-fresheners, berries were used to feed birds, and young shoots as fodder for goats. Mastic played only a small part in religion and in myths; → Pentheus, for example, hid in the branches of a mastic tree (Theocr. 26,11), and in Callim. (H. 3,201) the nymphs of Artemis deck themselves with mastic branches.

A. STEIER, s.v. Mastix, RE 14, 1930, 2168-2175. R.H.

Mastigophoroi (μαστιγοφόροι; *mastigophóroi*, 'whip-carriers'). In Sparta, young men (ἡβῶντες/*hēbóntes*), who assisted the → *paidonómoi* in the → *agōgē* of boys (Xen. Lac. 2,2). In Athens in 404 BC they were the infamous 300 policemen under the Thirty (→ *triákonta*; Aristot. Ath. Pol. 35,1). In Corcyra they were 425 guards in charge of prisoners (Thuc. 4,47,3). In Hellenistic Egypt they were servants to higher dignitaries, e.g. the *oikonómos*, the representative of the king in the *nomoí* (PTebtunis 121,58; cf. P CZ 80,4). K.-W.W.

Mastos see → Pottery, shapes and types of

Mastramela Town of the Salluvii (Gallia Narbonensis) beside a lagoon of the same name (now Étang de Berre) or on an elevation rising above it between Rhodanus (Rhône) and Massalia. The identification with Saint-Blaise is uncertain. It is possible that → Maritima Avaticorum was founded by the inhabitants of M. References: Artemidorus, in Steph. Byz. s.v. Μαστραμέλη (πόλις καὶ λίμνη τῆς Κελτικῆς); Plin. HN 3,34 (*stagnum* M.); Avien. Ora maritima 701 (*oppidum Mastrabalae priscum*).

G. BARRUOL, Les peuples préromains du sud-est de la Gaule, 1969, 196f.; F. GATEAU et al., Carte archéologique de la Gaule (13/1: Étang de Berre), 1996. Y.L.

Mastroi (μαστροί/*mastroí*, 'searchers', 'trackers') is the name given in some Greek towns to official accountants with functions similar to those of the *eúthynoi* (→ *eúthynai*) or → *logistaí* (e.g. Delphi: Syll.³ 672; Pallene: Aristot. fr. 657 ROSE). The accounting process is called *mastráa/mastreía*, e.g. in Elis (IvOl 2 = BUCK 61) and Messenia (IG V 1, 1433,15-16), the person liable to account, *hypómastros*, e.g. in Messenia (IG V 1, 1390 = Syll.³ 736,51,58). After the → synoikismos of Rhodes, the councils of the three original towns of Ialysus, Camirus and Lindus continued under the designation *mastroí*. It is possible that the function of the Roman quaestor can be traced back to the model of the *mastroí* in the Greek settlements of Lower Italy [1].

1 Busolt/Swoboda 1, 487-488; 2 K. LATTE, The Origin of the Roman Quaestorship, in: TAPhA 67, 1936, 24-33. P.J.R.

Mastruca (also *mastruga*). Sardian word (Quint. Inst. 1,5) for a close-fitting garment made of (sheep)skin, sleeveless and reaching down to the upper thighs. The Romans considered those who wore it to be uncivilised (Cic. Scaur. 45d; Cic. Prov. cons. 15), thus Alaricus in: Prud. in Symm. 1,659f. In Plaut. Poen. 1310-1313 it is also used as a term of abuse. R.H.

Mastusia (Μαστουσία/*Mastousía*, Μαζουσία/*Mazousía*). Unidentified location on the southern tip of the Thracian Chersonnesus [1] (Str. 7, fr. 52; Ptol. 3,2,9; 12,1; Mela 2,2,25). I.v.B.

Matalum (Μάταλον; *Mátalon*). Town on the Southern coast of Crete (Strab. 10,4,11; Stadiasmus maris magni 323), originally the harbour for → Phaestus (Pol. 4,55,6), later for → Gortyn; now called Matala. According to one myth, this is where Zeus made landfall after abducting Europa. Only a few classical remains from the Roman period. Some early Christian cliff graves on the northern side of the bay, now partly below sea-level.

H. BUHMANN, s.v. Matala, in: Lauffer, Griechenland, 410; I. F. SANDERS, Roman Crete, 1982, 161. H.SO.

Matasuntha Granddaughter of → Theoderic [3] the Great; having been forced into marriage in 536 AD by → Vitigis, she tried to betray Ravenna to the Byzantines in 538, supposedly in order to marry → Belisarius (?) (Procop. Goth. 2,10,11). In 540 she and Vitigis (d. 542) were brought to Constantinople, and in 549/50 she married → Germanus [1] (d. 550). Birth of a son, Germanus, in 550/1. M. bore the unusual title of a *patricia* (Iord. Get. 81).

> PLRE 3B, 851f.; H. WOLFRAM, Die Goten, 1990, 343, 347, 357.   WE.LÜ.

Mataurus (Μέταυρος; *Métauros*). River (Plin. HN 3,73), modern Petrace, and town (*Taurianum*, Mela 2,68; Geogr. Rav. 4,36) in Bruttium (→ Bruttii) on the Tyrrhenian Sea, founded by Zancle (Solin. 2,11) or Locri (Steph. Byz., s.v. M.). Home of the poet → Stesichorus (Steph. Byz.; Suda s.v. Στησίχορος) [2], modern Gioia Tauro. Archaeological remains of a necropolis (archaic and Imperial periods) in Contrada Pietra [1; 4]; architectural terracotta finds from the archaic period [4].

> 1 A. DE FRANCISCIS, Μέταυρος, in: Atti e memorie della Società Magna Grecia N.S. 3, 1960, 21–67; 2 D. MUSTI, Problemi della storia di Locri Epizefirii, in: A. STAZIO (ed.), Atti XVI Convegno sulla Magna Grecia, 1977, 23–145; 3 CL. SABBIONE, M., in: E. LATTANZI (ed.), Il Museo Nazionale di Reggio Calabria, 1987, 108–114; 4 BTCGI 8, s.v. Gioia Tauro, 1990, 142–152.   M.L.

Matchmaking s. → Brothels; → Lenocinium

Matella see → Chamber pot

Mater familias While the word → *pater familias* indicates a clearly defined legal status, the designation of the Roman mother of a family is a social rather than a legal one. Originally, MF was the honorary title for a married woman living in the →*manus* (marital control) of her husband, with whom she had children. Her social position was, in contrast with (and in compensation for) her legal status (→ Manus), a high one. She had precedence over all other members of the household apart from her husband. By the time the *manus* marriage had fallen into disuse, the term MF – literally the mother of the family – had apparently lost value as a means of social distinction. Thus Ulp. Dig. 50,16,46,1 (early third century AD) states that MF refers to any woman who leads a moral life, regardless of whether she is married, widowed, free-born or a freedwoman.

> → Marriage; → Woman   G.S.

Materialism The concept of materialism does not appear until the first half of the eighteenth century, and is first used polemically in the context of the criticism of materialist thought in Enlightenment philosophy, as antithesis of idealism or spiritualism (KANT). Here, only those teachings will be designated as materialism which

(a) represent a monism which holds that all being can be reduced to one or more material principles, while (b) that which appears to be non-material is either an epiphenomenon of the material or consists of very fine matter, and (c) the separate existence of any non-material (incorporeal) essence is systematically denied.

This definition does not apply to the early Ionian → natural philosophy (→ Milesian school; → Anaximenes [1]; → Thales). Although they assumed a material principle to explain the visible (material) world (water, air etc.), this is neither an explicit antithesis, nor is it ruled out that nature (φύσις, *phýsis*), the knowledge of which is at issue, or its constitutive, elementary principles, has souls. Nor is the above definition of materialism fully applicable to the Stoa (→ stoicism). The Stoics did teach a monism, but not one of matter, but of corporality. They postulated a prime matter without qualities (as did Aristotle), but they assumed nevertheless an active principle, immanent in the body but separate from matter, which qualifies matter (→ matter).

The first definite and consistent philosophy of materialism begins with → atomism, developed by → Leucippus [5] and his pupil → Democritus [1], and given its classical form by → Epicurus. Greek atomism is (a) monistic, since being as fullness (πλῆρες, *plêres*) consists exclusively of very small and indivisible corporeal particles, the 'atoms' (ἄτομα/*átoma*, ἀδιαίρετα/*adihaíreta*). These have no qualities and are distinguishable only by size, form and perhaps (after Epicurus, definitely) mass. The void (κενόν, *kenón*) required for their motion is non-being. Cosmogenesis and ontogenesis are explained in reductionist manner solely by the movement of the atoms in the void, and by their shape; similar atoms combine through mechanical necessity and thus form macroscopic conglomerates.

The epistemology of the Greek monists is strictly materialistic-sensualistic as well. All things continually produce images (εἴδωλα, *eídōla*), made out of of the most fine matter; these affect the senses. Genuine knowledge (γνώμη γνησίη, *gnómē gnēsíē*) is made possible only by the *nous*-soul, which, itself consisting of the smallest atoms (b), pervades the entire organism. A materialist ethic will have to (c) abandon all transcendental foundations (the gods, the immortal soul), or, speaking positively, will be firmly orientated towards the here and now. This cannot yet be said of Democritus, unless the warnings against the great movement of souls and against the too much and the too little (fr. 191) are interpreted literally. However, the interpretation of happiness as cheerfulness (εὐθυμία/*euthymía*) and freedom from fear or passion (ἀθαμβία/*athambía*) already prefigures Epicurus's hedonistic ethics. Epicurus explicitly denies that gods and death have any meaning for human life. Man must guide his actions by the constitution of his body-soul instead, which is nothing more than the mingling of atoms. In later polemical reception, hedonism was quite wrongly denounced as an ethic of (sensual) pleasure. Epicurean ἡδονή (*hēdoné*, → Pleasure) is characterised primarily by the avoidance of pain (λύπη/*lýpē*) ('negative hedonism': H. MARCUSE); the joys are, as in Democritus, rather of a modest kind. Epicurus evaluates occasional feelings of euphoria (χαρά/*chará*, εὐφροσύνη/*euphrosýnē*) far below the continuous state of (catastematic) composure (ἀταραξία/*ataraxía*), in which is the goals, happiness, is to be found (a clear distinction to the hedonism of Aristippus [3] of Cyrene).

Aristotle gives a differentiated judgment on early atomism; he often praises natural philosophy because it has scientific method and principles in accordance with nature (cf. Aristot. Gen. corr. 325b 35ff.). He seems to have no problem with materialism, but takes issue with the atomistic concept of a continuum (συνεχές/*synechés*) and the assertion of the void. What appeared to the atomists to be a (mechanistic) natural necessity was for Aristotle, for want of a final cause, pure chance (τύχη/*týchē*).

The Peripatetics criticized – probably justifiably – the atomist thought on sense perception and knowledge. In the Hellenic period, atomism lived on as Epicureanism through the founding of numerous schools. It was preserved in the great didactic poem *De rerum natura* of → Lucretius [III 1] and extensive mention in → Cicero (e.g., *De finibus* and *De natura deorum*), which, after a long period of opposition, led to its renewal by some of the Renaissance humanists: L. VALLA, B. TELESIO, and, above all, PETRUS GASSENDI. In classical times, materialism itself was hardly ever attacked (the exception is in Plot. *Enneades* 6,9,5); but the Peripatetics objected to its violation of fundamental ontological suppositions, and the Christian tradition to its anti-metaphyiscal, worldy ethics. If the ethics of Epicurus largely fell prey to the (unjustified) verdict of orientation towards pleasure and philosophical justification of man's lower urges (KANT is an exception), his ontology and epistemology blossomed anew, if momentarily, in the age of the Enlightenment (esp. HELVÉTIUS, D'HOLBACH, DELAMETTRIE), and later through K. MARX and historical-dialectical materialism.

→ Epicurus; → Ethics; → Matter; → Principle; → Space; → Atomism

C. BAILEY, The Greek Atomists and Epicurus, 1928; E. BIGNONE, Epicuro, 1920; J. BOLLACK, A. LAKS (eds.), Études sur l'épicureisme antique, 1976; D. CLAY, Lucretius and Epicurus, 1983; M. FORSCHNER, Die stoische Ethik. Über den Zusammenhang von Natur-, Sprach- und Moralphilosophie im altstoischen System, 1981; M. HOSSENFELDER, Epikur, 1991; H. A. K. HUNT, Physical Interpretation of the Universe. The Doctrines of Zeno the Stoic, 1976; F. A. LANGE, Geschichte des Materialismus, 1866 (repr. 1974); D. LEMKE, Die Theologie Epikurs, 1973; H. LUDWIG, Materialismus und Metaphysik. Studien zur epikureischen Philosophie bei T. Lucretius Carus, 1976; PH. MERLAN, Studies in Epicurus and Aristotle, 1960; J. SCHMIDT, Lukrez und die Stoiker. Quellenuntersuchungen zu De rerum Natura, 1975. H.SCHN.

Materiarius see → Wood

Materiatio
A. CONCEPT B. GREECE C. ROME

A. CONCEPT
Collective term used in Vitruvius (4,2,1) for all kinds of timber construction and the carpentry trades necessary in building. *Materiatio* thus comprises the field of constructional wood building, including the construction of framework structures, roof-trusses (→ Roofing), galleries and inserted ceilings but also the manufacturing of the necessary tools and implements (dowels, wooden nails, wedges, rafters, pegs) as well as, finally, the provision of temporary scaffolding for moving stone in building work and the auxiliary wood constructions used by the Greeks to transport material and by the Romans in cast concrete construction (→ Opus caementicium; → Construction techniques), e.g. formwork and falsework scaffolding.

B. GREECE
In addition to the widespread use of wood in ancient Greece in the construction of wattle-and-daub walls and as an anchoring material for → masonry, a specialised woodworking craft of joinery became necessary in the late 8th and 7th cents. BC for the building of wooden → temples and later, when building in stone became more widespread, primarily for the construction of roof-trusses and scaffolding. There is ample evidence for the use of → wood in → roofing, esp. in buildings based on column and ashlar constructions, as well as inserted ceilings, in the form of beam holes, traces of mountings and dowel holes, as well as occasionally in the shape of surviving → architectural inscriptions. Solid archaeological evidence, however, exists only in a few exceptional cases. Wood was used extensively in the construction of Greek temples, and this may explain the destruction by fire of many prominent buildings of this type described in ancient literature. Spans of up to a good 11 m (cella of the → Parthenon) required rafters with a considerable cross-section. Sizes of 29 × 26 cm are attested for a floor spanning 7 m in a house in Ammotopus. Cross-sections of more than 30 × 30, indeed, over 40 × 40 cm (Delphi; Brauron), were not infrequent. The stockpiling and working of wood (usually with axes, less often with saws) was a significant cost and labour factor in the construction of public buildings.

Similarly, our knowledge of the wooden scaffolding used for moving stone blocks and column sections, for smoothing and, where necessary, for painting the surfaces of buildings, is derived only indirectly from traces of the mountings (e.g. the Propylaea at Athens) or from literary descriptions. The same is true for the numerous technical implements needed in Greek construction (cranes, pulleys, equipment for the transport of building materials from the quarry to the building site; → Lifting devices). Sophisticated wooden structures supported the temporary buildings of Hellenistic ceremonial architecture, including, for instance, various magnificent tent constructions under Ptolemy II (Ath. 5,196a–197c), as well as 'floating' or 'moving' buildings such as Ptolemy IV's Nile ship (Ath. 5,203e–206a), Hieron II's luxurious grain ship, and Alexander the Great's hearse.

C. ROME

It is safe to assume that by the Republican period, Rome already had a highly specialised *materiatio*. The erection of temporary wooden structures, e.g. for theatrical performances and gladiatorial games, complete with matching scenery, is widely attested in ancient literature and by the excavation of what are believed to be post holes (e.g. for speakers' platforms in the → Forum [III 8] Romanum in Rome). Axes, saws, planes and chisels as well as various materials for hardening and impregnating the wood were applied with equal routine. Wood also played an important role in Roman Campanian house building, both for the outer framework architecture and the internal division of buildings. On account of the special circumstances of their burial, the remains of ancient wooden structures have been preserved to a considerable extent in the houses at → Herculaneum, which were covered by the lava of Vesuvius in AD 79. The specific characteristics of Roman → construction techniques (→ opus caementicium; → Bricks) would have been impossible without a highly specialised joinery trade and well-developed woodworking techniques, e.g. for formworking walls, vaults and domes (→ Vaults and arches, construction of; → Dome, Construction of Domes) and for formwork and falsework structures in the bridging of valleys and rivers with roads and aqueducts (→ Roads and bridges, construction of; → Water pipes). Among the few surviving examples of ancient woodworking that are significant in architectural as well as in decorative and artistic terms are the doors of St Sabina in Rome and St Barbara (Sitt Barbara) in Cairo, both from the 5th century AD.

For the artistic use of wood cf. → wood (C. Wood in painting and sculpture). See also → shipbuilding.

L. HASELBERGER, Dächer griechischer Wehrtürme, in: MDAI(A) 94, 1979, 93–112; H. VON HESBERG, Temporäre Bilder oder die Grenzen der Kunst, in: JDAI 104, 1989, 61–82; A. T. HODGE, The Woodwork of Greek Roofs, 1960; M. HÜLSEMANN, Theater, Kult und bürgerlicher Widerstand im antiken Rom, 1987; R. KROES, Woodwork in the Foundations of Stone-Built Roman Bridges, in: BABesch 65, 1990, 97–105; H. LAUTER, Die Architektur des Hellenismus, 1986, 48–63; J. LIVERSIDGE, Woodwork, in: D. STRONG (ed.), Roman Crafts, exhibition catalogue, London 1976, 155–165; R. MARTIN, Manuel d'architecture grecque I: Matériaux et techniques, 1965; R. MEIGGS, Trees and Timber in the Ancient Mediterranean World, 1982; W. MÜLLER-WIENER, Griechisches Bauwesen in der Antike, 1988, 216, s.v. Holz; A. K. ORLANDOS, Les matériaux de construction et la technique architecturale des anciens Grecs, vol. 1, 1966; vol. 2, 1968; J. V. THIRGOOD, Man and the Mediterranean Forest. A History of Resource Depletion, 1981.   C.HÖ.

Mater Larum see → Larunda; → Mania

Mater Magna

[1] More fully *Mater Deum Magna Idaea* (see [1] on the name), the goddess *Métēr*/→ Cybele, who was brought from Pergamum to Rome in 204/5 BC as demanded by the → *Sibyllini libri* and with the help of → Attalos [4] I. Even in antiquity the precise place of origin was disputed: → Pessinus (Liv. 29, 10,5; 11,7), Pergamum (Varro ling. 6, 15), or the mountain chain → Ida [2] in the Troad (Ov. fast. 4,263f.). The cult of *Métēr*/Kybele is attested at all three places. Research favours an origin on Ida [2.16–20] or from Pessinus [3.318] – in each case through the mediation of Pergamum. The MM, whose cult image was, according to tradition, a sacred stone, was located until the completion of her own shrine in the south-western area of the Palatine in the temple of → Victoria (Liv. 39, 27,2) and transferred to her own temple (*aedes*) on 11 April 191 (Liv. 36, 36, 3f.;[4]). To the feast of the MM, the *ludi Megalenses*, which was held from the 4th to the 10th of April (InscrIt 13,2 p. 435–438) performances were added in 194 (Liv.34,54,3; Val. Max. 2,4,3) or 191 BC (Liv. 36,36,4 following Valerius Antias). The steps of the temple and the open area in front of them were used for performances during the *ludi scaenici* (Cic. har. resp. 24; Liv. 36,36,4f.;[5. 206;6].

Augustus showed a particular interest in the goddess from the Troad, who was connected with → Aeneas [1], the Trojan ancestor of the Romans, and with the *gens Iulia*, which claimed to descend from → Venus, the divine mother of Aeneas (→ Iulius) [7]: the goddess who crowns Augustus on the so-called *gemma Augustea* is iconographically the MM wearing the crenellated civic crown (*dea turrigera*). The topographical description in Virgil (Aen. 776–795) of the route from the Roman Forum Boarium via the Lupercal (→ Lupercalia), the *clivus Victoriae* and the archaic wall ('of Romulus') of the *caput imperii* to the Palatine temple of the MM and the house of Augustus (→ Roma) can be read (as [8] suggests) as a programmatic sequence: Romulus the founder (Aen. 776–780), the imperium and the walls of the citadel (ib. 781–783), the MM and her descendants (ib. 784–787), Rome and the Iulii (ib. 788–790), and finally Caesar Augustus as the new founder of the imperium (ib. 791–795). This programmatic sequence is given visual expression in the topographical connexion of the temple of the MM and the *domus Augusti* (linked with the temple of the Palatine Apollo) in the south-western area of the Palatine.

The temple of the MM is depicted on a relief of the so-called *ara pietatis* (43 AD) [9. vol. 3, nr. 2]: a temple in Corinthian hexagonal style is shown, the goddess herself is depicted only as a civic crown on a throne (*sella*), flanked, one of each to a side, by corybantes (→ Curetes) and lions. The original temple, destroyed by fire in 111 BC, was in the following years renewed by a certain Metellus (Ov. fast. 4, 347f.); his precise identity is disputed (Q. Caecilius [1 30] Metellus Numidicus or Q. Caecelius [1 21] Metellus Caprarium; cf. [10]). After a further fire (Ov. fast. 4,347f.; Val. Max 1,8,1; Obsequens 39) Augustus had the temple rebuilt (R. Gest. div. Aug. 19). The extensive excavations in the temple area ([5] with bibliography) have brought to light among other things terra-cotta figures of → Attis, which possibly date from as early as the second century BC ([11]; on the dating [12]). Medallions from the time of Antoninus Pius [13. plate 15f.] show a shrine of the MM. This has been identified with a *tholus Cybelis* mentioned by Martial ('Rotunda' of Cybele; Mart. 1, 70,9f.) and localised as near the Arch of Titus on the → via Sacra. However, the identification is questionable, now that Martial's *tholus* has recently been associated with the temple on the Palatine ([5. 207f.] with bibliography). A statue of the MM also stood in the Circus Maximus ([9. vol. 3, nr. 252]; Tert. de spectaculis 8).

Representations on coins [13] show that the iconography of the MM was essentially that of Cybele. In Lucretius the two goddesses are finally merged; this indicates that they were not necessarily distinguished by the Romans. Inscriptions [5] are mostly kept generalised; toponymic appellations such as *Idaea*, *Phrygia* or *Palatina* do however appear more frequently in some provinces, and seem to point to a deliberate differentiation (→ polytheism). On the cult of the MM, see → Cybele C2.

1 K. ZIEGLER, Mater Magna oder Magna Mater?, in: J. BIBAUW (ed.), Hommages à M. Renard (Coll. Latomus 102), 1969, 845–855; 2 E. S. GRUEN, Studies in Greek Culture and Roman Policy, 1990, 5–33; 3 G. WISSOWA, Religion und Kultus der Römer, 2nd ed. 1912; 4 J. RÜPKE, Fehler und Fehlinterpretationen in der Datier. des dies natalis des stadtrömischen MM-Tempels, in: ZPE 102, 1994, 237–240; 5 P. PENSABENE, s.v. Magna Mater, aedes, LIMC 3, 208–208, 456–458; 6 S. M. GOLDBERG, Plautus on the Palatine, in: JRS 88, 1998, 1–20; 7 R. M. WILHELM, Cybele: the Great Mother of Augustan Order, in: Vergilius 34, 1988, 77–101; 8 T. P. WISEMAN, Cybele, Vergil and Augustus, in: T. WOODMAN, D. WEST (edd.), Poetry and Politics in the Age of Augustus, 1984, 117–128; 9 M. J. VERMASEREN, Corpus cultus Cybelae Attidisque, 7 vols. (EPRO 50.1–7), 1977–1989; 10 M. G. MORGAN, Villa publica and MM, in: Klio 55, 1973, 231–245; 11 P. ROMANELLI, MM e Attis sul Palatino, in: M. RENARD (ed.), Hommages à J. Bayet, 1964, 619–626; 12 F. COARELLI, Public Building in Rome between the Second Punic War and Sulla, in: PBSR 45, 1977, 1–23; 13 R. TURCAN, Numismatique romaine du culte métroaque, 1983.

L. E. ROLLER, In Search of God the Mother, 1999, 261–343; S. A. TACACS, Mater Deum Magna Idaea, Cybele, and Catullus' Attis, in: E. LANE (ed.), Cybele, Attis, and related Cults, 1996, 367–386. For further titles, see Cybele. S.TA.

[2] Staging-post on the *via Herculia* in Hirpinia, named after a shrine of the MM. [1] (Itin. Anton. 103)

Miller, 377. G.U.

Mater Matuta Goddess of dawn, worshipped in Italy and Rome (Lucr. 5,655f.), whose name, in the form of an adjective, like Lat. *maturus*, 'at the proper moment', goes back, by way of the stem **mātū-*, to √*mā*, 'good' [1]. Statuettes portraying the goddess with the sun's disc around her head and a child in her arms (→ kourotrophos), and the temple dedicated to her in Satricum (now Le Ferriere) in Latium (with anatomical votive offerings: [5. Vol. 1–2]), go back to the seventh century BC [2; 3; 4]. Her temple near the Forum Boarium (S. Omobono) in Rome (Votives, see [5. Vol. 3, 84–86; 6. 45–60]) may be dated to the second quarter of the sixth century BC. Historiographical tradition ascribes its foundation to Servius→ Tullius (Liv. 5,19,6), and its restoration to M. → Furius [I 13] Camillus (396 BC: Liv. 5,23,7; Plut. Camillus 5,1). The temple was part of a sacral complex which also contained the twin temple of → Fortuna [7. 205–244]. The → natalis templi of both shrines fell on the 11th of June, on which day the festival of MM, the → Matralia, was celebrated [8. 341–388]. The rite, carried out by the *matrones*, emphasised the attributes of the goddess as Aurora and as protectress of children.; DUMÉZIL has compared the cult of MM with the Vedic myth of Aurora [9]. The → *interpretatio Graeca* equates MM with Ino-Leukothea (e.g. Ov. Fast. 6,545).

→ Matralia; → mother goddesses; → votive practice

1 WALDE/HOFMANN 2, 54; 2 SIMON, GR, 152–157; 3 R. R. KNOOP, Antefixa Satricana, 1987; 4 P. S. LULOF, The Ridge-Pole Statues from the Late Archaic Temple at Satricum, 1996; 5 J. W. BOUMA, Religio votiva, Vol. 1–3, 1996; 6 Il viver quotidiano in Roma arcaica, 1989; 7 F. COARELLI, Il foro boario, 1988; 8 N. BÖELS-JANSSEN, La vie religieuse des matrones dans la Rome archaïque, 1993; 9 G. DUMÉZIL, Déesses latines et mythes védiques, in: Coll. Latomus 25, 1956, 9–43.

M. HALBERSTADT, Mater Matuta, 1934. FR.P.

Maternum Way station in Etruria on the *via Clodia*, 12 miles from Tuscana and 18 miles from Saturnia (Tab. Peut. 5,1). Its exact location is unknown.

Miller, 296. G.U.

Maternus

[1] At first a soldier, then ringleader of a group of rebels, with whom he exercised considerable influence through raids in Gaul and Hispania. If the *bellum desertorum* (War of the Deserters) can be connected with him, the *legio VIII Augusta*, which was stationed in Argentorate, fought against him. When M. tried to kill → Commodus himself, he is said to have been betrayed by other members of his movement and was executed (HA Comm. 16,2; Hdn. 1,10; 11,5; [1. 178ff.]; cf. also [2. 69f.]). PIR² M 363.

1 TH. GRÜNEWALD, Räuber, Rebellen, Rivalen, Rächer, 1999; 2 J. C. WILMANNS, Die Doppelurkunde von Rottweil und ihr Beitrag zum Städtewesen in Obergermanien (Epigraphische Studien 12), 1981, 69f.

[2] An acquaintance of the poet → Martialis [1], from Bilbilis in Spain, who was active as a → *iuris consultus* in Rome (PIR² M 362). He is not connected with M. Cornelius Nigrinus Curiatus Maternus, since the latter's principal cognomen was Nigrinus.

[2a] Bishop of the Christian community in → Colonia Agrippinensis (now Cologne). → Constantinus [1] may have become acquainted with him during visits to the city before AD 312. Since he obviously held him in high regard, Constantine appointed M. a member of the college of judges which, under the leadership of the Roman bishop Miltiades [5], was to pass judgment on → Donatus [1] and his followers in Rome in 313. He had already dispatched the necessary documents in advance (Eus. HE 10,5,19 f.). M. also attended the Council of Arles (Arelates) in 314 (CCL 148,4; 15; 18; 20; 21), and perhaps before 312 was one of the leading Christian figures who introduced Constantine to the new religion. In the Middle Ages it was claimed that M. had formerly been bishop of Augusta [6] Treverorum (modern Trier), but this is extremely unlikely.

O. ENGELS, ST. WEINFURTER, Series episcoporum Ecclesiae Catholicae Orientalis, vol. 5.1, 1982, 7.   W.E.

[3] see → Firmicus Maternus

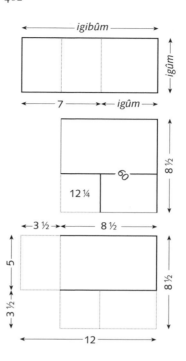

Mathematics Almost all we know about the mathematics of the pre-Greek cultures of the Ancient Near East, essentially Mesopotamian and Egyptian mathematics, originates from written sources. These are mainly from the scribal traditions, even though some sources give a glimpse of the mathematics of 'lay' practitioners.

When scribes were concerned with the properties of mathematical objects, the purpose was always to calculate something. That is always true in professional practice, but it also holds for school texts, even when these deal with situations that would never occur in practice or when they determine quantities of no practical value. The same is true concerning practitioners like merchants and surveyors, but not always for architects and other artists. However, it is almost always impossible to extract with any certainty from buildings and other works of art the mathematical knowledge that underlies their symmetries. One can say that almost all pre-Greek mathematics that we understand as such was aimed at calculation. Even their geometries always work with measurable distances, surfaces, etc.

I. ANCIENT ORIENT   II. CLASSICAL ANTIQUITY

A. MESOPOTAMIA   B. EGYPT   C. MESOPOTAMIAN AND EGYPTIAN INFLUENCES ON GREEK MATHEMATICS

A. MESOPOTAMIA
Mesopotamian writing and mathematics appear to have been created at the same time, as part of a single process. During the 4th millennium BC, administrators

of temples in → Uruk developed procedures for the administration of a new complex society. In this process, they apparently united several older techniques of a mathematical character and thus created a number notation system with the base of 60, a new area metrology based on the metrology for lengths, and some methods of calculation which fitted the metrological structures. During the 3rd millennium, these techniques were further developed, and the number system and metrology were extended and refined. In the Fara period, we find a scribal profession which did not coincide with the temple administration, and there are documents indicating the attempt to explore the possibilities of scribal tools: writing and mathematics. Apart from the first literary texts, there are also examples of 'supra-utilitarian mathematical' problems, i.e. calculations beyond practical applications, like divisions of very large round numbers or quantities by divisors that are awkward with respect to the structure of the number system and metrology. (Until then, apparently all mathematical teaching was based on 'model documents' emulating real administrative documents.)

Supra-utilitarian problems are also attested from the Akkad period, while the evidence from the Ur III period includes only model documents. However, during the Ur III period (based on experiments of previous centuries) the sexagesimal place-value number system was created, which was intended to be used in the huge number of calculations required by the Ur III administration. The system could only be useful when multiplication and reciprocal tables (division by n was performed as multiplication by $1/n$) and tables of technical constants and metrological conversions had been made available; probably its development only became possible in the context of a centralised administration. Since the notation was not equipped with the equivalent of a zero or a decimal point, ⟪⟪⟪𒀹𒀹𒀹⟪⟪ 𒁹 (30+3 − 20+1) could mean $33;21 = 33 + {}^{21}/_{60}$ as well as $33,60 = 33×60 + 21$ (or $33,0;21 = 33×60 + {}^{21}/_{60}$, etc.). Consequently, it could only be used for intermediate calculations and school exercises, when the order of magnitude was known in advance.

At the new start of the school after the collapse of Ur III, supra-utilitarian mathematics returned. Its core was now a second-degree 'algebra' based on geometry, for which the following problem can serve as an example. The product of two numbers from the table of reciprocals, *igûm* and *igibûm* ('the reciprocal' and 'its reciprocal') is taken as $60 = 1,0$. The *igibûm* is given to exceed the *igûm* by 7. The product of the two is presented as a rectangle with an area of 60 (see fig.), and the outer half of the excess of the rectangle over the square on the *igûm* is 'broken off' and moved in such a way that a gnomon is created (still with the area of 60). The small square $3^1/_2 × 3^1/_2 = 12^1/_4$ is then added to the gnomon – a step which produces a square with an area of $72^1/_4$ (and therefore with sides of $8^1/_2$). The relocated part $3^1/_2$ is 'torn out' from one of the sides, so that the *igûm* remains as $8^1/_2 − 3^1/_2 = 5$, then it is 'joined' to the other side, and the *igibûm* is found as $8^1/_2 + 3^1/_2 = 12$.

The numerical steps are exactly those of the solution of a modern system of equations, and the 'analytical' method is also similar: the unknown quantity is represented and treated as 'known'. The only difference is that here the representation consists of 'lengths', 'widths', 'sides of squares' and 'areas', rather than letters standing for numbers. The lines were used, however, just like the abstract numbers of today, to represent other quantities, whether numbers, prices, working days or geometrical quantities. There was no formal proof of the correctness of the procedure, but as in modern equational algebra it could immediately and 'naively' be 'seen' that it was correct.

There are hundreds of problems of this kind (most of them directly expressed within the geometric representation) from the Old Babylonian Period. Further, the representation of *areas* by lines allowed the formulation of certain higher-degree problems that could be solved biquadratically. Some mixed third-degree problems were solved by factorisation. Since the more extensive mathematical texts distinguish in their structure between algebraic and non-algebraic problems about (e.g.) squares, we can characterize this 'algebra' as a true mathematical discipline.

The origin of this discipline was presumably a small group of geometrical problems that circulated among non-scribal, Akkadian speaking land-surveyors around 2000 BC: to find the side of a square from the sum of 'its four sides and its area'; to determine the length and width of a rectangle from its area and the sum of its sides; and so on. The number of these problems (which persisted until the late Middle Ages in the context of

land surveying), was closely restricted, and they were never used in algebraic representation of entities of other kinds. Only the Old Babylonian school made an algebra and a discipline out of them. The aim was hardly mathematical research, rather it was connected with the ideal of 'scribal humanism': virtuoso execution of professional activity far beyond everyday necessity. A scribe proved himself a 'real scribe' by his ability to read and write Sumerian and not only Akkadian which everybody spoke, and also by his ability to solve complicated mathematical problems – and not only calculations of everyday administrative accounting.

Apart from algebra of this kind and other less conspicuous types of supra-utilitarian mathematics, there was obviously a body of mathematical knowledge that could serve daily administration. (Practically) rectangular areas were determined as the product of length and width, and, likewise, the areas of (practically) right-angled triangles and trapeziums. To determine the area of a not quite rectangular quadrilateral the 'surveyors' formula' was used (average length × average width); more irregular shapes were divided into practically rectangular parts. The diameter of a circle was determined as $^1/_3$ of its circumference, its area as $^1/_{12}$ of the square on the circumference (the area of a semicircle in contrast as $^1/_4$ of the product of diameter and arc).

Volumes were measured in area units, under the tacit assumption that areas had a thickness of 1 cubit. Prismatic volumes were then calculated by 'raising' the virtual thickness of the base to the true height. This process was so fundamental that 'raising' became the general term for all multiplication based on proportionality. Truncated cones and pyramids were occasionally (and not very accurately) approximated by middle cross sectional area × height, in one case correctly (whether by accident is uncertain).

The slope of a slanting surface was specified by the setback per cubit of increased height. There was no general measure of the inclination of two lines to one another (a quantified concept of angle), but there was certainly a distinction of practically right angles from those that are not right angles.

After the end of the Old Babylonian period (about 1600 BC) we have no more traces of the scribal school; and along with the school, almost all traces of mathematical activity disappear for about 1,000 years. Only from the 4th–6th cents. BC a handful of mathematical texts are extant, which were written in the environment of omen- and exorcist-scholars (by contrast, earlier Mesopotamian mathematics is completely detached from religion, magic and even numerology). Apart from multiple-figure reciprocal tables (presumably meant for astronomical calculations) there are hardly any fundamental changes in the scanty material. Algebra still occurs. Apart from some reciprocal/*igûm-igibûm* problems, however, it seems (on terminological grounds among others) that it represents a new borrowing from the surveyors and is not a continuation of an old scribal tradition. Since the technique did not serve representation beyond that of *igûm-igibûm* pairs, one might object to calling it 'algebra'. Two tables from the Seleucid period contain certain characteristic innovations in method and problem formulation, which also appear elsewhere.

B. EGYPT

The first record of Pharaonic-Egyptian mathematics is the Early Dynastic or Late Predynastic 'Macehead of King Narmer' (*c.* 3500 BC), on which a tribute to the king of 400,000 bulls, 1,422,000 goats and 120,000 prisoners is represented numerically. This illustrates well that the legitimacy of the Pharaonic state was derived from conquest (and the promise of cosmic stability), unlike that of the early Mesopotamian state, which was based on mathematical justice. None the less, the development of Egyptian mathematics in the 3rd millennium was (with one exception, see below) closely linked to government: beginning with the First Dynasty the height of the Nile was observed yearly, doubtless in order to estimate from it the potential harvest and tax. Every second year, the 'wealth of the country' was assessed.

Little is known about 3rd-millennium mathematical techniques. The system of whole numbers was already fully developed on the Narmer Macehead. There were special symbols for certain simple fractions, i.e. for $^2/_3$, $^1/_2$, $^1/_3$ and $^1/_4$; otherwise metrological subdivisions were used. The first evidence of later *ro*-reciprocals (namely $^1/_4$, $^1/_5$ and $^1/_6$, see below) are from the 24th century BC. From their application it is clear that the later characteristic *system* of Egyptian fractions did not yet exist.

The geometry of temple and pyramid construction and the 'canonical system' that was used for the proportioning of the human body in art was also based on metrological units and their subdivisions. Their development began no later than in Early Dynastic times (end of the 4th millennium). Land surveying and the planning of temples were achieved using measuring ropes. (Already on the Narmer Macehead, the symbol for 100 is seen to be the measuring rope, which was 100 cubits long.) The 'canonical system' was used within a net of squares.

What is normally referred to as 'Egyptian mathematics' only emerges in the Middle Kingdom (beginning of the 2nd millennium), presumably as a consequence of the institution of the scribal school (3rd-millennium scribal education appears to have been apprenticeship-based). The main sources for our knowledge of it are two large papyri, the 'Rhind Mathematical Papyrus' (RMP) and the 'Moscow Mathematical Papyrus' (MMP). RMP is a kind of teacher handbook, while MMP is probably the work of a pupil, corrected by a teacher.

The core of RMP/MMP mathematics was a system of whole numbers and reciprocals, arithmetical techniques linked to them, and an approach based on additivity and proportionality (the latter in the sense that every quantity is understood as a 'number' and every

number could count or be measured by every other number). Whole numbers were written by repeating the symbols for 1, 10, 100, ..., 100,000. For $^2/_3$, $^1/_2$ and $^1/_3$ there were special symbols (reproduced here as 3″, 2′ and 3′). Other reciprocals were written with the symbol *ro*, 'part', above the corresponding number (here *n̄*). In any number, a particular reciprocal could occur no more than once: $\overline{5}\,\overline{5}$ was therefore not a number (in the 24th cent. BC, however, it had been used to mean $^2/_5$). Instead, it was a problem whose solution was $3′\,\overline{15}$.

As a first example we can look at the multiplication of $8\,3″\,\overline{6}\,\overline{18} = 8^8/_9$ by itself (RMP 42):

1	$8\ 3″\ \overline{6}\ \overline{18}$
2	$17\ 3″\ \overline{9}$
4	$35\ 2′\ \overline{18}$
/8	$71\ \overline{9}$
/3″	$5\ 3″\ \overline{6}\ \overline{18}\ \overline{27}$
3′	$2\ 3″\ \overline{6}\ \overline{12}\ \overline{36}\ \overline{54}$
/6	$1\ 3′\ \overline{12}\ \overline{24}\ \overline{72}\ \overline{108}$
/18	$3′\ \overline{9}\ \overline{27}\ \overline{108}\ \overline{324}$
Sum	$79\ \overline{108}\ \overline{324}$

The meaning is as follows: '1 time '8 $3″\,\overline{6}\,\overline{18}$ is 8 $3″\,\overline{6}$ $\overline{18}$; '2', '4' and '8 times' the same are found by repeated doubling. The first doubling presents no problem, but by the second the main problem of the Egyptian number representation becomes apparent: since $\overline{9}$ cannot be doubled as $\overline{9}\,\overline{9}$, but only as $\overline{6}\,\overline{18}$, the whole doubling results in 35 $3′\,\overline{6}\,\overline{18}$, where $3′\,\overline{6}$ is then changed to 2′.

The choice of finding '3‴', '$\overline{6}$' and '$\overline{18}$' of 8 $3″\,\overline{6}\,\overline{18}$ illustrates the calculators' preference for the main fractions 3″ and 2′ and for the expression of smaller parts by successive halving (which evidently was not always possible). In order to add the resulting fractions $\overline{9}$, $3″\,\overline{6}\,\overline{18}$ $\overline{27}$, $3′\,\overline{12}\,\overline{24}\,\overline{72}\,\overline{108}$, and $3′\,\overline{9}\,\overline{27}\,\overline{108}\,\overline{324}$, all fractions were taken of a suitable reference quantity (functionally similar to a common denominator), e.g. 108. 3″ of it is 72, $\overline{6}$ is 18, ..., $\overline{24}$ is $4^1/_2$, ... Altogether the result is $217^1/_3 = 216+1^1/_3$. 216 is 2 of 108, $1^1/_3$ is $\overline{108}\,\overline{324}$ of it.

The scheme for division was similar to that for multiplication, only here the dividend was 'emptied' by successive doubling and fractioning of the divisor. RMP begins with a 'table' of 2/*n*, *n* = 3, 5, ..., 101, to be used for such multiplications and divisions. Since not only the results but also the calculations are given, this table is the most extensive known coherent piece of Egyptian mathematics.

For practical purposes this system was hardly better than the use of metrological subdivisions. We sometimes also come across very coarse approximations in administrative documents. The advantages of this system appear only within a school context:

it allows a) exactness, and hence the determination of whether the pupil 'has found correctly', as formulated in the teacher's annotation to the MMP, and b) a theoretical integration of all techniques. It is clear that this integration was aimed at: after the 2/*n* tables the first 34 problems are all formulated abstractly, in numbers, reciprocals and indefinite 'quantities'. Its application permits the display of calculatory virtuosity. What the Old Babylonian schools aimed at with algebra, the Egyptians achieved with their reciprocals.

The practical-arithmetical problems that are solved with these arithmetical techniques in RMP and MMP often correspond to the partnership and alligation problems of modern times (except that their proportional shares are not among business partners, and mixtures are concerned with the grain content of bread and beer, and not with the metal content of coins). The principle used in the solution is often a variant of the 'simple false position'.

In geometrical calculations the area of a rectangle was found as the product of its length and width, that of an isosceles triangle as mid-line (i.e. height) × half the base line, with the explicit justification that in this way the triangle was transformed into its rectangle. These calculations were followed by metrological conversions (area units differing from the square cubit were used). The area of a circle was determined as the square of $^8/_9$ the diameter. The interesting parameter was thus not the ratio between circumference and diameter (π), but the ratio of area to diameter ($\sqrt{\pi}/_4$), which was approximated (with fair accuracy) as $^8/_9$. (For this reason it is mistaken to search for π in the pyramids and elsewhere.) It cannot be decided whether a problem in MMP finds the surface of a hemisphere or the equally great curved surface of a semi-cylinder correctly.

Prismatic volumes were found as the product of base area and height (after further multiplication with a metrological correction factor). One problem in MMP (correctly) calculates the volume of a truncated pyramid.

Hollow measure had its own metrologies, even though these were linked to the metrologies for length and volume (probably by a secondary normalization). Of particular interest is a subdivision of the *hekat* by continued halving (until 1/64). Already in the 3rd millennium, each of these parts possesses a hieratic symbol; after 1500 BC, corresponding hieroglyphs were invented which can be put together to form the (apparently still later) 'healing eye of Horus'. The chronology shows that this sacral underpinning is a secondary accretion.

As in Mesopotamia, slopes were measured as the relation of the horizontal displacement of the sloping side and the vertical rise of 1 cubit. There were no calculations with quantified angles.

Further documents of the RMP and MMP kind exist only from the Demotic (actually only from the Graeco-Roman) period. Fundamentally not much has changed, although there are terminological innovations and there is evidence of a certain slackening of the strict rules of arithmetic (e.g. there are tables of m/n in which m can be up to 10). It is interesting, however, that there is presumably a transmission of several formulas and problems from Mesopotamia: e.g., the 'surveyors' formula'; the calculation of the area of a circle as $^1/_4$ product of circumference and diameter and the assump-

tion that the former is three times the latter; the determination of the volume of a truncated cone as *mean cross sectional area* × *height*, and of problems showing the characteristic innovations of the Seleucid period. Rule by the Assyrians and Achaemenids and the activities of their military scribes and officials thus appear to have influenced Egyptian mathematics.

Neither in the 2nd-millennium texts nor in the Demotic sources are there any formal proofs. However, as in Mesopotamia, it is obvious that the often quite complicated calculations are based on insight and not only on accidental experience.

C. Mesopotamian and Egyptian influences on Greek mathematics

Without doubt the Greeks adopted the reciprocals of the Egyptians, and the sexagesimal fractions of Hellenistic astronomy originate in Babylonian astronomy. In contrast the claim by → Herodotus [1] and other Greek authors that Greek geometry was based on Egyptian surveying seems less credible.

After the first decoding of Babylonian algebra at a moment when it was still understood as a purely arithmetical technique, Neugebauer proposed around 1935 that the geometry of Book II of Euclid's 'Elements' (→ Euclides [3]) should be understood as a geometrical translation of Babylonian results which had become necessary through the discovery of irrationality. This thesis was generally accepted. Since 1970, however, there have been objections that the conceptualisation of Greek geometry is quite different from that of an arithmetic algebra; that all the Babylonian texts solve problems and find numbers, whereas 'Elements' II proves theorems which at best can be understood as algebraic identities; and that the Greeks were unable to read the clay tablets.

The geometrical interpretation of Babylonian algebra and the discovery of the survival of the Near Eastern surveyors' tradition (which undoubtedly left traces in the pseudo-Heronic *Geometrica*; → Hero [1]) puts the whole question in a new perspective. The Greeks did not need to make a geometrical translation: the diagram which was the basis for the solution of the *igûm-igibûm* problem (see fig.) is practically identical to that of 'Elements' II,6. Absent from the Babylonian version is only a diagonal, which Euclid uses to prove that the diagram is correctly constructed instead of having its parts 'naively' moved around. Rather than a translation, 'Elements' II,1–10 constitute a 'critique' (in a quasi-Kantian sense) of the old but still surviving surveyors' solutions – namely an investigation into why and under what conditions they hold. To this end the 'Elements' must (e.g.) *define* a right angle (Definition 10), and then *postulate* (Postulate 4) that all right angles are equal, since this does not follow from the definition.

Fundamentally, therefore, the Neugebauer hypothesis is confirmed: the geometry of 'Elements' II is a recasting of a technique which is first known from the Old Babylonian clay tablets. However, the Greek geometers were certainly familiar with it from a living tradition (as NEUGEBAUER later claimed) and not from the clay tablets. Since this tradition also reached Egypt in the classical era, it can not be excluded that Herodotus was also right.

→ Astronomy; → Science

1 J. HØYRUP, Algebra and Naive Geometry. An Investigation of Some Basic Aspects of Old Babylonian Mathematical Thought, in: Altorientalische Forschungen 17, 1990, 27–69, 262–354 (with references to sources and secondary literature); 2 P. DAMEROW, R. K. ENGLUND, H. J. NISSEN, Frühe Schrift und Techniken der Wirtschaftsverwaltung im Alten Orient, 1990 (English edn.: Archaic Bookkeeping, 1993); 3 R. K. ENGLUND, Organisation und Verwaltung der Ur III-Fischerei, 1990; 4 J. FRIBERG, s.v. Mathematik, RLA 7, 531–85; 5 O. NEUGEBAUER, Mathematische Keilschrifttexte, 3 vols 1935/7; 6 W. F. REINECKE, s.v. Mathematik, LÄ 3, 1237–45 (with bibliography); 7 B. L. VAN DER WAERDEN, Erwachende Wissenschaft, 2 vols, ²1966/1980 (English title: Science Awakening); 8 O. NEUGEBAUER, Vorlesungen über Geschichte der antiken mathematischen Wissenschaften, vol. 1: Vorgriechische Mathematik, ²1969; 9 Id., The Exact Sciences in Antiquity, ²1969; 10 K. VOGEL, Vorgriechische Mathematik, 2 vols, 1958–1959; 11 R. J. GILLINGS, Mathematics in the Time of the Pharaohs.

J. HØYRUP, Lengths, Widths, Surfaces. A Portrait of Old Babylonian Algebra and its Kin. 2002; E. ROBSON, Mesopotamian Mathematics 2100–1600 BC. Technical Constants in Bureaucracy and Education. 1999; J. RITTER, Closing the Eye of Horus, in: J. Steele and A. Imhausen, Under One Sky: Astronomy and Mathematics in the Ancient Near East, 2002, 297–323   JE.HØ.

II. CLASSICAL ANTIQUITY
A. GREECE   B. ROME AND THE MIDDLE AGES
B. ORIGIN

A. GREECE
Proceeding from the Pythagoreans (→ Pythagoras, → Pythagorean School), in Greek antiquity μαθήματα/ *mathémata* or μαθηματικὴ τέχνη/*mathēmatikè téchnē* is understood to comprise the four disciplines of arithmetic, geometry, astronomy and (the theory of) music. The specialization of the term toward its modern meaning begins with Aristotle [6]. In Latin, mathematics means (according to Gell. 1,9,6) those sciences which need arithmetical and geometrical operations.

Although the Greeks used the mathematical knowledge of the Babylonians and the Egyptians (see above I.-II.), they developed mathematics in a specific way. In contrast to pre-Greek mathematics their knowledge contained a new type of logical and systematic approach. The Greeks recognised the necessity to prove mathematical assertions, and created the necessary *instruments*. The early Greek mathematical development is closely related to philosophy. Logical conclusion and indirect proof (→ Eleatic School) were applied to mathematics. The Greeks recognised that proofs must be derived from definitions and axioms. In this way Greek

mathematics became the model for modern mathematics.

Greek mathematics can be divided into three periods: an early period (before → Euclides [3], *c.* 300 BC) from which works are known only by later citation or compilations, the classical period, characterised by the great works of Euclid, → Archimedes [1] and → Apollonius [13], and a late period (1st–6th cents. AD), in which e.g. → Pappus of Alexandria, → Theon of Alexandria, → Diophantus [4] and → Proclus worked. Theon transformed classical mathematical texts into a standard form, in which they spread in the Byzantine period. Some Greek texts survived only through translations or adaptations in Arabic.

In addition to the scholarly mathematics of the Greeks, naturally there were also applied arithmetic and geometry, but this is less well documented.

The following categorisation into subdisciplines is oriented according to modern concepts.

1. THEORETICAL ARITHMETIC   2. ARITHMETIC
3. ALGEBRA   4. GEOMETRY   5. SPHERICS AND
TRIGONOMETRY

1. THEORETICAL ARITHMETIC
For the Greeks, arithmetic (ἀριθμητικὴ τέχνη/*arithmētikè téchnē*) was the theory of whole numbers and their relations to one another. Proceeding from the idea that the world is built on numbers, the Pythagoreans attained significant knowledge about the theory of numbers. They composed diagrams in the form of triangles, squares, other polygons and rectangles (figured numbers, polygonal numbers) with pebbles (*pséphoi*) and linked them to arithmetical investigations which resulted e.g. in the summation formulas for natural numbers, square numbers and cube numbers. The Pythagoreans were interested especially in primes, perfect numbers (equal to the sum of their aliquot parts) and amicable numbers (mutually equal to the sum of their aliquot parts). Pythagorean arithmetic is represented mainly in bks 7–9 of Euclid's 'Elements'. The Pythagoreans proved that there are infinitely many primes (Eucl. Elem. 9,20), and indicated a procedure for finding perfect numbers (*ibid.* 9,36).

The theory of → music led to work on proportions and to the procedure of 'reciprocal subtraction' (ἀνθυφαίρεσις/*anthyphaíresis*), by which the greatest common divisor of two numbers can be found. By application of reciprocal subtraction to quantities in general (esp. the diagonal and side of squares and pentagons) in the 5th century BC, → Hippasus [5] presumably discovered that there are quantities which have no common measure (in modern terms: there exist irrational numbers, such as $\sqrt{2}$ and $\sqrt{5}$). This led to the replacement of the old Theory of Proportions, which applied only to natural numbers (set out in Eucl. Elem. bk. 7), by a new theory of proportions for arbitrary quantities (→ Eudoxus [1], adopted from Eucl. Elem. bk. 5). An axiom of measurability (formulated in Eucl.

Elem. 5, def. 4) is fundamental to it. Another form of this axiom (*ibid*. bk. 10,1) is the basis of the 'method of exhaustion'. This was used by Greek mathematicians, above all by → Archimedes [1], to solve infinitesimal problems. → Theaetetus classified the various types of irrationality (taken from Eucl. Elem. bk. 10) and showed their relationship with the five regular poly-hedrons (see Eucl. Elem. bk. 13, cf. below 4. Geometry). The Pythagorean number theory (primarily its results on prime, amicable, perfect and figured numbers) and their Theory of Proportions were compiled by → Nico-machus of Gerasa. In the adaptation by → Boethius, they were also known in the West throughout the Middle Ages.

2. ARITHMETIC

The counterpart of the scholarly arithmetic of the Greeks was practical calculation, 'logistics' (λογιστικὴ τέχνη/*logistikè téchnē*). Our knowledge in this area is based almost exclusively on Byzantine sources (see [7]). To write numbers, Greek mathematicians used an al-phabetical system in which the 24 letters of the Greek alphabet and three other, obsolete, symbols were used for the 9 units, 9 tens and 9 hundreds (→ Numerical systems). This system did permit a concise representa-tion of numbers, but it was ill suited to performing cal-culations. Multiplication and division were especially obscure. They were made easier by the use of multipli-cation tables. In fractions (as for the Egyptians) reci-procals ($1/n$) played a special role, however, general fractions were also known. Astronomers used sexagesi-mal fractions for their calculations, which can be traced back to the Babylonians. These fractions were based on the positional principle, and consequently even compli-cated calculations could be carried out easily.

More suitable for practical calculations than the letter numbers of the Greeks was the → *abacus* (ἀβάκιον/*abákion*). A calculation board, found on the island Salamis, has survived, as well as a pictorial rep-resentation on a vase [2. 104–111] of carrying out a calculation. The calculation board was divided by lines into columns in which calculating stones were put. Each column had a particular value which was indicated by numerical symbols. There were columns for the powers of ten (1, 10, 100, 1000) as well as columns for the fives (5, 50, 500) and for fractions. The value of a stone (*psêphos*) depended on the column in which it was placed. Calculating with an abacus was easy to learn, as stones had only to be added or taken away. When more than four stones were placed in a tens column (or more than one stone in a fives column), it had to be replaced by one stone in the next higher column. For subtraction, if necessary a stone was replaced by several stones in the next lower unit.

Likewise, the Romans performed practical calcula-tions with abaci, which were based on the same princi-ples as the Greek abaci (→ *Abacus*). Moreover, for cal-culating in writing there were auxiliary tables. The mid–5th century *calculus* of Victorius, which states the mul-tiples of numbers (including fractions) written in Roman numerals, is still extant.

3. ALGEBRA

For the Greeks, algebra (the name derives from a 9th-century Arabic text by al-Ḥwārizmī) was not an independent mathematical subdiscipline. Presumably influenced by the Babylonians (see above III), algebraic content was expressed in the form of geometrical terms ('geometrical algebra'): transformations of areas were the equivalent of algebraic conversions (Eucl. Elem. bk. 2). The three types of quadratic equations were solved by means of two-dimensional constructions (see Eucl. Elem. Book 6). There was no general theory for equa-tions of the third and higher degrees. Problems which led to cubic or biquadratic equations (e.g. doubling the cube, trisecting an angle, cutting a sphere, constructing a heptagon) were solved individually by means of neusis constructions (νεῦσις/*neûsis*), conic sections or curves of higher degrees. Calculations were expressed in words (without mathematical symbols). One exception was Diophantus [4], who used algebraic symbols to solve definite and indefinite equations of the first, second and higher degrees. In contrast to his predecessors, Dio-phantus's algebra is separated completely from geom-etry.

4. GEOMETRY

The term 'geometry' (γεωμετρία; *geōmetría*), which in Greek originally meant land surveying, was already used by Aristotle to denote an exact, axiomatically con-structed science which, in contrast to geodesy, dealt with shapes which are not perceivable by the senses (Aristot. Metaph. 2,997b 26). 'Elements' of geometry, i.e. an organised compilation of what was known in the field of elementary geometry, were written by → Hip-pocrates [5] of Chios and → Leon [6]. The fundamental geometrical work, which was used until modern times, was Euclid's 'Elements' [3].

Greek geometry began with → Thales of Miletus, who devised propositions mostly about circles and their symmetries. He used different kinds of angles and rec-ognised the necessity of proving geometrical proposi-tions. The so-called 'Theorem of Pythagoras' was prob-ably adopted by the Greeks from the Babylonians. The Pythagoreans worked intensively on geometry. In about 440 BC the foundations were laid and confirmed with proofs for the complete elementary geometry, in-cluding the theory of the circle. Euclid's planimetric books 1–4 essentially originated from the Pythago-reans. It was known that there could be no more than five regular solids (regular polyhedrons, Platonic solids). Three of them (tetrahedron, hexahedron = cube, dodecahedron) were already familiar to the Py-thagoreans, the others (octahedron, icosahedron) were presumably discovered by Theaetetus. The relation-ships between the individual polyhedrons and the proof that there are only five such solids, can be found in bk. 13 of Euclid's 'Elements'.

Work on regular polygons, especially squares and pentagons, led to the discovery of irrational quantities (see above 1. Theoretical Arithmetic) in the 5th century BC. The division in mean and extreme ratio (later called the 'golden section'), which was needed for the construction of a regular pentagon, requires the solution of the quadratic equation $x^2 + ax = a^2$, which is geometrically a special case of the 'application of areas'. This is an old Pythagorean procedure, which is closely related to the Babylonian solution of quadratic equations (see above 3. Algebra). The discovery of irrational quantities led to a systematic formulation of a 'geometrical algebra' (linear and quadratic).

In around the year 300 BC, Euclid compiled the knowledge of his predecessors and contemporaries and brought it into systematic organisation. Proceeding from definitions, postulates and axioms, he built in his 'Elements' a structure of theorems and constructions which are founded logically on each other. The 'Elements' do not only deal with questions of geometry, but also (mainly in bks. 5 and 7–9) arithmetic and the theory of proportions and (in bk. 2) 'geometrical algebra'. They are not a comprehensive presentation of Greek mathematics: conic sections are missing from it, as are the curves of higher degrees and practical mathematics.

By the 5th century BC, the Greeks were also working on higher geometrical problems, particularly the three 'classical problems': squaring the circle, doubling the cube, and trisecting an angle. They can not be solved by elementary geometry with ruler and compass, as the first is connected with the transcendental number π and the other two lead to cubic equations. → Hippocrates [5] of Chios showed that special crescents, i.e. shapes delimited by two arcs, can be transformed into squares of the same area (see fig. under → Hippocrates [5]). He reduced the problem of the doubling of a given cube (the 'Delian Problem') to the interpolation of two geometric means between two given line segments. This idea was successful: for the determination of these geometric means later scholars used mechanical devices (→ Mesolabium), interpolation, transcendental curves (e.g. the quadratrix, → Hippias [5]) and conic sections (→ Menaechmus [3]). The theory of conic sections was also developed further independently of the 'classical problems'. The culmination of this development was the *Kōniká* by → Apollonius [13], in which the theory of conic sections was treated comprehensively and systematically.

The area of a circle had been approximated ('exhausted') by → Antiphon [4] by means of inscribed polygons of increasing numbers of sides, whereas → Bryson sandwiched the circle between inscribed and circumscribed polygons. In doing so he used a kind of principle of continuity. This procedure was perfected by Archimedes [1], who showed by means of inscribed and circumscribed regular 96–gons that the number π lay between $3\,{}^{10}/_{71}$ and $3\,{}^{1}/_{7}$. Using an axiom of measurability (see above 1. Theoretical Arithmetic), → Eudoxus [1] had developed a procedure for handling infinitesimal processes. Archimedes brought this procedure (the 'Method of Exhaustion') to a level of virtuosity and used it to calculate areas, volumes, arcs and

centres of gravity of curvilinearly bounded surfaces and solids. For the heuristic derivation of his formulas he used the → mechanical method, then confirming its results with exact infinitesimal procedures.

In addition to scholarly geometry, there were also practical procedures which we know primarily from the writings of → Heron. Some of them (e.g. the determination of the areas of triangles and quadrangles) were derived from Egyptian and Babylonian methods (see I.) and were, particularly through the works of the Roman surveyors, also influential in the Western Middle Ages and until the 16th century.

5. SPHERICS AND TRIGONOMETRY

Geometry on a sphere, which was important for astronomical purposes, was developed by → Autolycus [3], → Theodosius [1] and → Menelaus [6]. Theodosius and Menelaus presented it in an all-geometrical form. In order to perform calculations on a sphere, straight lines were assigned to angles and arcs, and calculations were performed with the straight lines. Greek mathematicians chose for this the chord which spans an arc. Sine trigonometry, which is used today and which works with half-chords, was first developed by the Indians and the Arabs. Unlike arithmetic and geometry, Greek trigonometry developed fully only in the first cents. AD, primarily through Menelaus and Claudius → Ptolemaeus.

By the 4th century BC, estimations of the values of trigonometric functions were being used. For the foundation of a practically useful science, the construction of a numerical table of trigonometric functions was required, for which lemmas were needed. Among these was a theorem, ascribed in Arab sources to Archimedes, and the 'Theorem of Ptolemaeus', which was formulated in 'Almagest' 1,10. This also contains a chord table which proceeds in steps of 30 minutes (1,11). By means of this chord trigonometry the Greeks were able to solve all astronomical problems on the sphere of the heavens.

B. ROME AND THE MIDDLE AGES

Greek mathematical knowledge was not developed further by the Romans. Only few of the mathematical works of the Greeks were translated into Latin. Only (parts of) translations of → Boethius have survived. The practical applications of mathematics had greater significance, particularly in surveying (→ Surveyors, → Limitatio). In the tradition of → Heron there are treatises on surveying, which in late antiquity were compiled in the *Corpus Agrimensorum* (→ Surveyors). The most important mathematical writings in this collection originate from → Frontinus (1st century AD), Balbus (*c.* 100), Epaphroditus and → Vitruvius Rufus (2nd century?). Extracts in → Columella (bk. 5) and the *Fragmentum Censorini* (→ Censorinus) also belong to this tradition. The writings of the *agrimensores* were intended to be guides for practitioners. They indicate rules without proof and are not comparable in level with the works of the great Greek mathematicians. They form,

Two-dimensional geometrical figures and the terms for them according to Euclid's definitions

			Greek term		Latin term
CIRCLE		Circle	κύκλος	kýklos	*circulus*
	○	Circumference	περιφέρεια	periphéreia	*circumferentia*
	⊘	Diameter	διάμετρος	diámetros	*diametrus*
	⊘	Radius	ἡ ἀπὸ του κέντρου πρὸς τὴν περιφέρειαν	hē apò toû kéntrou pròs tền periphéreian	*radius*
	⊖	Semicircle	ἡμικύκλιον	hēmikýklion	*semicirculus*
	◐	Sector	τομεύς	tomeús	*sector*
TRIANGLE		Triangle	τρίγωνον	trígōnon	*triangulum*
	△	Equilateral	ἰσόπλευρον	isópleuron	*aequilaterum*
	△	Isosceles	ἰσοσκελές	isoskelés	*isosceles; aequicrurium*
	△	Scalene	σκαληνόν	skalēnón	*scalenum*
	◺	Right-angled	ὀρϑογώνιον	orthogónion	*orthogonium; rectangulum*
	◿	Obtuse-angled	ἀμβλυγώνιον	amblygónion	*amblygonium; obtusangulum*
	▷	Acute-angled	ὀξυγώνιον	oxygónion	*oxygonium; acutangulum*
QUADRANGLE		Quadrangle	τετράγωνον	tetrágōnon	*tetragonum*
	▢	Square	ἰσόπλευρον	isópleuron	*quadratum*
	▭	Rectangle	ἑτερόμηκες; ὀρϑογώνιον	heterómēkes; orthogónion	*parte altera longior; rectangulus*
	▱	Rhomb	ῥόμβος	rhómbos	*rhombus*
	▱	Parallelogram	ῥομβοειδές	rhomboeidés	*rhomboides*
	▱	Irregular quadrangle	τραπέζιον	trapézion	*trapezium*

On the circle, cf. Euclid, bk. 1, definitions 15–19, on the triangle, 20f., and on the quadrangle, 22. M. Haa.

however, the beginning of mediaeval Western geometry. The geometry of Gerbert (died 1003) and the writings on *Geometria Practica* in the late Middle Ages (e.g. by Hugo von St. Victor and Dominicus de Clavasio) are based on them.

Through Marcus Terentius → Varro's *De disciplinis* geometry and arithmetic also found their way into the encyclopaedic writings of the Romans (→ Encyclopaedia). Some geometric fragments, which have been transmitted in the MSS of the *agrimensores*, may derive from Varro's encyclopaedia. Arithmetic and geometry are also found in later writings of the same kind (→ Martianus Capella, → Macrobius, → Cassiodorus). Together with astronomy and the theory of music they had been combined under the name *quadrivium* since Boethius, and from late antiquity they formed together with the *trivium* (grammar, rhetoric, logic) the Liberal Arts (→ *artes liberales*). Boethius translated Nicomachus's 'Arithmetic' and Euclid's 'Elements'. In the syllabus for instruction in the monasteries, drafted by Cassiodorus, the Liberal Arts, and thus also mathematics, were well established, and from the 12th century arithmetic and geometry were also taught in the universities in the context of the Liberal Arts.

The scholarly mathematics of the Greeks was passed on in Byzantium and from the 9th century was also known to the Arabs through translation. In the 12th century most of the originally Greek mathematical writings were translated from Arabic into Latin and were able to continue their influence in the West from then on. Apart from certain exceptions (individual translations from Greek in the 12th century in Sicily, Wilhelm von Moerbeke, *c.* 1269), the original Greek texts of the mathematical writings became available again in the West only from the 15th century.
→ Mathematics

1 O. Becker, Das mathematische Denken der Antike, 1957; 2 G. Friedlein, Die Zahlzeichen und das elemen-

tare Rechnen der Griechen und Römer und des christlichen Abendlandes vom 7. bis 13. Jahrhundert, 1869; 3 H. GERICKE, Mathematik in Antike und Orient, 1984; 4 T. L. HEATH, History of Greek Mathematics, 1921, 2 vol.; 5 J. L. HEIBERG, Geschichte der Mathematik und Naturwissenschaften im Altertum, 1925 (reprint 1960); 6 K. MENNINGER, Zahlwort und Ziffer, vol. 2, 1958 (Engl. tr.: Number words and number symbols); 7 K. VOGEL, Beiträge zur griechischen Logistik. Erster Teil (SBAW), 1936; 8 B. L. VAN DER WAERDEN, Erwachende Wissenschaft, 1956 (English title: Science Awakening); 9 H. G. ZEUTHEN, Geschichte der Mathematik im Altertum und Mittelalter, 1896.

S. CUOMO, Ancient Mathematics. 2001   M.F.

Mathia (Μαθία). Chain of mountains above → Corone in Messenia (Paus. 4,34,4), modern Likodimo.

F. BÖLTE, s.v. M., RE 14, 2195.   C.L.

Mathos (Μάθως/*Máthōs*). Libyan, Carthaginian officer in the First → Punic War in Sicily, 241–238/7 BC. With → Spendius leader of the 70,000(?) insurgents in the → Mercenaries' War, which M. propagandised among the Libyans and Numidians as a freedom fight against Carthage. M. besieged and conquered → Hippo [5], besieged Carthage and for a long time defended himself in his operational base at → Tunes until, after vicissitudinous battles, the joined forces of Hamilcar [3] and Hanno [6] were finally able to end the Libyan War. Captured, M. was tortured to death (Pol. 1,69–88; Diod. 25,5; [1. 255–266; 2]). The symbol in the shape of the Punic letter *mem* frequently occurring on the ΛΙΒΥΩΝ coins of the insurgents stands for M. and emphasises his eminent role [2. 97–112; 3. 30f.]. M. was given a powerful literary characterisation in G. FLAUBERT's (1862) novel 'Salammbô'.

1 HUSS ; 2 L. LORETO, La grande insurrezione Libica contro Cartagine del 241–237 a.C., 1995; 3 W. HUSS, Die Libyer Mathos und Zarzas und der Kelte Autaritos als Prägeherrn, in: SM 38, 1988, 30–33.   L.-M.G.

Mathurā The Old Indian name M. designates two towns.

[1] The northern M. (also *Méthōra*/Μέθωρα in Megasthenes fr. 13a apud Arr. Ind. 8,5) in the land of Śūrasena, at the confluence of the Yamuna and the Ganges. It was an old and important centre of the cult of Kṛṣṇa, but also of that of the Indian Heracles; the latter may not, however, be simply identified with Kṛṣṇa. Ptol. 7,1,50 knew the town as Modura in the land of the Caspiraei (→ Caspeira).

[2] The southern M., capital of the Pāṇḍya kingdom (Pandion) in the south of Tamil Nadu. Also known to Ptol. (7,1,89) as Modura.

1 K. KARTTUNEN, India in Early Greek Literature, 1989, 210ff.; 2 G. WIRTH, O. VON HINÜBER (ed. and tr.), Arrian, Der Alexanderzug – Indische Geschichte, 1985, 1107ff.   K.K.

Matiane In Ionian Greek Matiene (Ματιανή/*Matiané*, Ματιηνή/*Matiēné*), its inhabitants are Matieni (Ματιηνοί; *Matiēnoí*). According to Hdt. 5,49; 52 a region east of Armenia and the sources of the Little Zab river (Zabatus), according to Hdt. 1,202 also of the → Gyndes and the → Araxes [2] (contra: Strab. 11, 14, 13). M. was part of → Media according to Strab. 2,1,14; 11,7,2; 11,8,8 and Steph. Byz. s.v. M., while according to Strab. 11,13,2; 7 it may have extended from the southern shore of Lake Urmia to the sources of the Little Zab and the Gyndes (on distances along the Royal Road, cf. Hdt. 5,52 with comm.). In Herodotus' tribute-list (3,94) the Matieni, who are also supposed to have taken part in Xerxes' campaign (Hdt. 7,72), together with the → Saspeires and the Alarodians, belong to the 18th nome of the Achaemenid kingdom.   J.W.

Matidia

[1] **Salonia Matidia** Born on 4 July (see the Feriale Duranum) before AD 69, daughter of Ulpia → Marciana and the senator C. Salonius → Matidius Patruinus from Vicetia. On 29 August 112, after the death and consecration of Marciana, she was elevated to *Augusta* (see the Fasti Ostienses). She was married at least twice, to a certain Mindius and to L. → Vibius Sabinus, and lived for a long time as a widow in the house of Trajan. Her daughters were (Mindia) M. [2] and Vibia → Sabina, wife of Hadrian. She was honoured on coins as *Matidia Augusta Divae Marcianae Filia* (RIC II, 300f.). M. accompanied Trajan and → Plotina on the Parthian campaign (113–117). She died in December 119: there was a funeral oration by Hadrian (CIL XIV 3579), and a consecration and other posthumous honours (including a large temple in Rome) because of her dynastic significance.

Kienast, 126f.; Raepsaet-Charlier, No 681.

[2] **(Mindia) Matidia** Granddaughter of → Marciana, daughter of the older Matidia [1] and probably of a certain Mindius, sister of → Sabina, and hence sister-in-law of Hadrian and aunt *(matertera)* of → Antoninus [1] Pius. Apparently unmarried and childless, she possessed enormous wealth, which enabled her to make various endowments (*summo genere, summis opibus nobilissima femina*, Fronto Ad M. Caesarem 2, 16; Ad amicos 1, 14 = HAINES 2,94ff.). M. was still alive under Antoninus Pius.

W. ECK, s.v. Matidia, RE Suppl. 15, 131–134; S. MRATSCHEK-HALFMANN, Divites et praepotentes (Historia Einzelschriften 70), 1993, 70f.; 377 no. 326; Raepsaet-Charlier, no. 533; A. M. ANDERMAHR, Totus in praediis (Antiquitas 3,37), 1998, 332–336 no. 331.   H.T.-V.

Matidianus see → Mindius

Matidius C. Salonius M. Patruinus. Senator from Vicetia in Upper Italy. He was praetor before 78 AD, when he acted as *magister* of the → Arvales fratres. He died the same year (CIL VI 2056). An inscription from Vicetia refers to another senator who was elevated to the Senate by Claudius; whether he became a patrician at the same time is disputed [1; 2. 324ff.]. He is either M. or his father. M. was married to Trajan's sister, Ulpia → Marciana. Their daughter was → Matidia [1] the Elder. PIR² M 365; 366.

1 G. ALFÖLDY, Ein Senator aus Vicetia, in: ZPE 39, 1980, 255–266; 2 Scheid, Collège. W.E.

Matisco Town in the Provincia → Lugdunensis on the Arar River (Saône) in the territory of the → Haedui, 70 km north of Lugudunum, modern Mâcon (Saône-et-Loire). There are Celtic remains in the environs as well, e.g. in Varennes-lès-Mâcon. In 52 BC M. was a staging station (Caes. Gall. 7,90,7; 8,4), in the Roman Imperial period it was the starting-point of the road to Augustodunum. A *castrum* was built in the 4th century AD. Necropolis. Sources: Itin. Anton. 359; Tab. Peut. 2,5 (*Matiscone*); Notitia Galliarum 1,5; Geogr. Rav. 4,26 (*Matiscum*). Inscriptions: CIL XIII 2581–2595.

A. BARTHÉLÉMY, L'oppidum de M., in: Rev. Archéologique de l'Est 24, 1973, 307–318; A. REBOURG, Carte archéologique de la Gaule (71/3–4: Saône-et-Loire), 1994; C. ROLLEY, s.v. M., PE, 559. Y.L.

Matius
[1] **Matius, C.** Contemporary and friend of Cicero (Cic. Fam. 11,27f.) and Caesar, who played a kind of mediating role between the two. In 53 BC he was in Gaul (Cic. Fam. 7,15,2) with Caesar, for whom M. remained a useful assistant even after the outbreak of the Civil War, although he tended to operate behind the scenes. In the summer of 47, M. was the addressee of the message announcing Caesar's victory at Zela, which became proverbial ('I came, I saw, I conquered': *veni, vidi, vici*, Plut. Caesar 50,3: the name is corrupted to Amantius). Filled with gloomy forebodings after the Ides of March in 44 (Cic. Att. 14,1,1), M. soon sided with Octavian (→ Augustus), whom he supported in the establishment of the *ludi Victoriae Caesaris* (Cic. Att. 15,2,3; Cic. Fam. 11,27,7; 28,6).

C. CICHORIUS, Römische Studien, 1922, 245ff.; A. HEUSS, Cicero und Matius, in: Historia 5, 1956, 53–73; Id., Matius als Zeuge von Caesars staatsmännischer Größe, in: Historia 11, 1962, 118–122; B. KYTZLER, Matius und Cicero, in: Historia 9, 1960, 96–121; Id., Beobachtungen zu den Matius-Briefen, in: Philologus 104, 1960, 48ff.; J. T. RAMSEY, A. LEWIS LICHT, The Comet of 44 BC and Caesar's Funeral Games, 1997, 5; 20; 24; 170f.

[2] **M., C.** Son of Matius [1]. He was the author of textbooks on economics (*Cocus, Cellarius, Salgamarius*: Colum. 12,4,2), which were highly prized by Augustus (Plin. HN 12,13; Tac. Ann. 12,60). He was also known for practical achievements, such as refining types of apples (*m ala Matiana*: Plin. HN 15,49; Colum. 5,10,19; 12,47,5) and creating a pork fricassee (Apicius 4,3,4).

Schanz/Hosius 1,604f. T.FR.

[3] **M., Cn.** Early 1st-century BC poet. Fragments of his translation of the 'Iliad', as well as of mimiambs (in choliambs) survive. Matius is one of the few Latin representatives of this genre, invented by the Hellenistic poet → Herodas. The few fragments (frr. 14–17 are set in a rural environment, while fr. 11 is a comedic motif), with their love of linguistic experiments (such as neologisms as *albicasco, columbulatim,* etc.) and their charming imagery (frr. 12/13) make the loss of this work particularly regrettable. The fact that on the one hand, M. looks backwards with his 'Iliad' translation, while on the other he anticipates features of the → Neoteric Poets in his metrics, links him with his contemporary → Laevius [2]. He is cited by Varro ('Iliad', fr. 1f.) and above all by Gellius (frr. 3, 7–13), who continually praises him for his verbal creativity (cf. also Ter. Maur. 2416ff. = GL 6,397).

FRAGMENTS: A. TRAGLIA, Poetae Novi, 1974², 1–4, 35–40, 115–119; Courtney, 99–106; FPL, 111–117.
BIBLIOGRAPHY: A. TRAINA, Poeti latini 1, 1986², 47–68 (fr. 6/7); G. COLOMBO, Cneo Mazio e la sua versione dell'Iliade, in: RIL 115, 1981, 141–159. P.L.S.

Matralia Roman festival of → Mater Matuta celebrated on 11 June (Paul. Fest. 113,2 L.; InscrIt 13,2 p. 468ff.). The fact that the → *Fasti Antiates Maiores* (InscrIt 13,2, p. 12) have the addition 'of Mater Matuta and → Fortuna ' is evidently related to the jointly celebrated birthday (→ *Natalis Templi*) of the Roman double temple to the two goddesses in the → Forum Boarium. The festival was widespread in Italy [2. 308]. The most detailed description is found in Ovid (Ov. Fast. 6,473–562) [1. 371–376].

Participants in the festival were exclusively married women. According to Tertullian (De Monogamia 17) only *matronae univirae* ('who had married only once') could dedicate wreaths. The exclusion of slaves was ritually staged by the beating and driving out of a maid (Ov. Fast. 6,481f.; 551–558; Plut. Quaest. Rom. 16; Plut. Camillus 5,2). Each woman baked a cake (*testuacium*: Varro Ling. 5,106) as a festive gift in an ancient earthen vessel. Her prayer was primarily for her sisters' children (Ov. Fast. 6,559; Plut. Qu.R. 17; Plut. Camillus 5,2). At the festival, she therefore acted as a *matertera* (maternal aunt), i.e. in a role which formed an important social network, similar to e.g. godparenthood.

The divine model for the celebrating aunt was Mater Matuta herself, who was identified with the Greek Ino → Leucothea (Ov. Fast. *passim*; Plut. Camillus 5,2; for archaeological evidence [3. 152ff.]). The latter had, according to myth, brought up the boy → Dionysos after the death of his mother (→ Kourotrophos). For the other known ritual elements as well, intercultural comparison helps with interpretation. Punishing a slave in the role of an adulteress emphasizes the status of a legitimate wife as part of a ritual staging of the Mater Matuta / Leucothea myth. The baking of a cake, with which the women, following the goddess, demonstrate their responsibility for the preparation of grain for consumption, refers (esp. in calendrical connection with the Vestalia, → Vesta) to the incorporation of the Matralia into a cycle of festivals of agrarian significance [4. 165ff.]. Furthermore, the mythological background, linguistic associations and archaeological finds point to a relationship between the ritual and initiation of the young [4. 173ff.].

1 F. BÖMER, P. Ovidius Naso. Die Fasten, vol. 2: comm., 1958; 2 J. CHAMPEAUX, Fortuna: Recherches sur le culte de la Fortune à Rome et dans le monde romain des origines à la mort de César, vol. 1: Fortuna dans la religion archaïque, 1982, 308ff.; 3 Simon, GR; 4 M. TORELLI, Il culto romano di Mater Matuta, in: Mededelingen van het Nederlands Instituut te Rome, Antiquity 56, 1997, 165–176.   G.B.

Matres/Matronae Celtic goddesses of maternal fertility, canonically represented in three. The two Latin appellations are identical in content. Evidence of the Matres, scattered over a wide area in Gaul, northern Spain, Italy, and in the northwestern and northeastern provinces of the Roman Empire, began in southern Gaul no earlier than the middle of the 1st century AD. Evidence of the Matronae can be divided into two groups: Matronae without epithet are concentrated in Cisalpine Gaul from the 1st third of the 1st century AD, Matronae with multiple names have over 800 dedications in Lower Germany in Ubian territory to the left of the Rhine after the middle of the 2nd century AD. Whereas the Ubian Matronae were distinguished by their own costume with large coat fastenings, crescent-shaped lockets or neck torques and large hoods, the other triads follow in dress and type of image the Hellenistic-Roman tradition of *mētēr* representations (→ Cybele). The blessing and protecting functions of the Matres/Matronae triads are shown by their attributes: horns of plenty, fruit and nuts, items of toilet, animals, anthropomorphic associates, water dispensing vessels and shells. A child-nursing function with corresponding attributes (→ Kourotrophos) is found only in the case of the Matres. Representations of trees on altars of the Rhine Matronae point to an original local tree cult. The male partner of the Matronae is → Mercurius.

The abundance of Latin, Celtic and Germanic epithets for the Matres/Matronae are derived from topological descriptions, river, lake and tribal names or formulate characteristics of the goddesses. Some epithets of the Ubian Matronae have been traced back to the curiae, whose basilical cult buildings have been demonstrated in M. sanctuaries. Other epithets point to family associations. With some 70 votives the *Matronae Aufaniae*, whose place of origin is in Bonn, are the strongest group of the Ubian M. and altogether the most significant of the triads by virtue of their high-ranking dedicators. The other Matres/Matronae were worshiped predominantly by lower class groups. The threeness of the Matres/Matronae is probably not a matter of a true

pluralisation; it should rather be understood as a symbol of the universality of the godhead being worshipped.

see → Mother Goddesses

F. HEICHELHEIM, s.v. M., RE 14, 2213–2250; G. BAUCHHENSS, G. NEUMANN, Matronen und verwandte Gottheiten (Suppl. BJ 44), 1987; T. DERKS, Gods, Temples and Ritual Practices: the Transformation of Religious Ideas and Values in Roman Gaul, 1998, 119–130.   M.E.

Matriarchy see → Gynaecocracy; MATRIARCHY

Matrica Auxiliary fort on the right bank of the Danube on the road from Aquincum to Intercisa in → Pannonia inferior; the modern Százhalombatta in Hungary. The camp was built in approximately the 2nd century (Itin. Anton. 245,5; *Matrice*, Not. dign. occ. 33,36). Under Commodus, *burgi* (→ *burgus*) were built in the vicinity, which were intended to prevent 'the clandestine crossing of brigands' (CIL III 3385). Remains of *canabae* and baths (partially restored) are extant.

TIR L 34 Budapest, 1968, 78–79; Zs. VISY, Der pannonische Limes in Ungarn, 1988, 91–93.   J.BU.

Matrimi see → Amphithaleis Paides

Matrimonium Besides → *nuptiae* the Roman term for → marriage. *Matrimonium* ('motherhood') was associated with the root *mater* ('mother'), from which the word is derived. Linguistically, a woman was led or given into *matrimonium*, and a man had a woman *in matrimonio*. In law, too, *matrimonium* was primarily significant because of motherhood: *iustum* (recognised by law) or *legitimum* (lawful) *matrimonium* is a marriage between Roman citizens or between a Roman and a woman who was entitled to → *conubium*. The children of such a marriage were Roman citizens, and their status followed the → *ius civile*, i.e. the legal principles applying to Roman citizens (see → *patria potestas*). The opposite of this is *matrimonium non legitimum* or *matrimonium iuris gentium* ('according to the common law of the peoples') between non-Romans or with a woman without *conubium*. Such marriages were not affected by Roman law, but were recognised as marriages in the sense of lawful cohabitation.   G.S.

Matron (Μάτρων; *Mátrōn*) of Pitane. Greek parodist and poet (→ Gastronomical Poetry), end of the 4th cent. BC. Aside from six short fragments (SH 535–540) the *Deípnon Attikón* survives due to Athenaeus (SH 534). It is a poem in 122 hexameters, describing a sumptuous banquet: an endless list of dishes (above all fish), enlivened effectively by interweaving epic military images, which the poet skillfully borrows from Homer in a manner reminiscent of the cento technique (cf. Eust. 1665,33). As in the cento there is no lack of contradictions and obscure passages; this does not appear to have diminished M.'s esteem in antiquity (cf. Ath. 4,134d).

The dependence of → Lucilius' [I 6] *Cena rustica* on M. (so [1]) remains pure hypothesis.

1 L. R. SHERO, Lucilius's *Cena rustica*, in: AJPh 50, 1929, 64–70

EDITION AND COMMENTARY: P. BRANDT, Corpusculum poesis epicae Graecae ludibundae, 1, 1888.
BIBLIOGRAPHY: E. DEGANI, La poesia gastronomica greca (II), in: Alma Mater Studiorum 4/1, 1991, 147–155; Id., On M.'s Atticon Deipnon, in: J. WILKINS *et al.* (ed.), Food in Antiquity, 1995, 413–438; Id., in: H.-G. NESSEL-RATH (ed.), Einleitung in die griechische Philologie, 1997, 245. O.M.

Matrona

[1] Under Roman law of the Republican period, there was a difference between the *matrona* as the legal wife and the *mater familias*, the wife who was in the → *manus* of her husband and thus belonged to his family (Gellius 18,6,8–9). This difference disappeared along with the marriage with manus (→ Marriage), and since Augustus the terms *matrona* and *mater familias* are interchangeable in legal texts.

In social terms, the word *matrona* expresses the public function of an honourably wed wife, which in early times possibly corresponded to the functions of the → *patronus*. This fact alone shows that the *matronae* were members of the wealthy upper class. In the early Republic the *matronae* were rewarded by the senate with honors for donations of gold. For instance, according to Livy, they were given the privilege in 395 BC of travelling to sacrificial ceremonies and games in a four-wheeled wagon (*pilentum*) and on festival days as well as on other days of using the *carpentum*, a two-wheeled wagon (Liv. 5,25,9). Furthermore, in 390 BC, it was ordered 'that after their death a solemn eulogy was to be held for them as for men' (Liv. 5,50,7). The *matrona* was the head of her husband's house and took part in all of its activities.

In the Republic, it seems, the *matronae* were united in an → *ordo* (Val. Max. 5,2,1). Several public demonstrations by the *matronae* indicate this: in 195 BC, for instance, prompted by the initiative of the tribunes to repeal the *lex Oppia* (Liv. 34,1,5), and in 42 BC, against the measures of the *triumviri* (App. B. civ. 4,32–34), although ancient authors denounced such public behaviour as inappropriate for women. Resolutions of the senate also mention the *matronae* as a group (Liv. 5,25,8–9; 27,37,7–10; cf. Plin. HN 7,120: *matronarum sententia*). In the Imperial period a *conventus matronalis* is mentioned (Suet. Galba 5,1; SHA Heliogab. 4,3–4), which examined and regulated the morals and etiquette of Roman upper class women.

The marks of the *matrona* status were → clothing: the → *stola* (Festus 112L: *matronas appellabant eas fere, quibus stolas habendi ius est*) and *vittae* (hairbands) braided into the hair, which *matronae* were obligated to wear in the Imperial period (→ hair-style). Since Vespasian, the *stola* as well as the *palla* (coat) seamed with purple were reserved for wives of senators and marked the highest social rank.

Matronae had important duties in Roman religion, e.g. in the → Matralia, → Matronalia, Cerialia (→ *ludi*), Vestalia and all cults of → Iuno. In the Republican period the *matronae* were repeatedly ordered to hold festivals of prayer and thanksgiving for the city. During the Principate, they participated in the *ludi saeculares*. Since the beginning of the Republic, there was a *luctus matronarum*, a one year period of state mourning for men who had served their city well. The *matronae* also initiated the establishment of several cults: the cult of → *Fortuna muliebris* established after the reconciliation with Coriolanus was separately dedicated by *matronae*; the cult of the *Pudicitia Plebeia* was also founded by them.
→ Family; → Woman; → Gender roles

1 J. GAGÉ, Matronalia. Essai sur les dévotions et les organisations cultuelles des femmes dans l'ancienne Rome, 1963; 2 P. GRIMAL, Matrona (les lois, les mœurs et le langage), in: R. BRAUN (ed.), Hommage à J. Granarolo, 1985, 195–203; 3 B. HOLTHEIDE, Matrona stolata – femina stolata, in: ZPE 38, 1980, 127–134; 4 KASER, RPR; 5 B. I. SCHOLZ, Untersuchungen zur Tracht der römischen Matrona, 1992; 6 J. L. SEBESTA, L. BONFANTE (ed.), The World of Roman Costume, 1994; 7 S. TREGGIARI, Roman Marriage. Iusti Coniuges from the Time of Cicero to the Time of Ulpian, 1991; 8 G. WISSOWA, Religion und Kultus der Römer, 1902. M.DI.M.

[2] Tributary of the Sequana (Seine), today Marne. In Caesar's time it was the border between Belgae and Celtae (Caes. B Gall. 1,1,2; Amm. Marc. 15,11,3; Auson. Mos. 462; Sidon. Panegyricus maior 208; Geogr. Rav 4,26, *Maderna*). A dedication to M. was found by Belasmes (6 km south of Langres) near the source of the M. (CIL XIII 5674). Y.L.
[3] Pass on the road Segusio – Brigantium (Itin. Burd. 556; Amm. Marc. 15,10,6), today Mont Genèvre in the French Alps. F.SCH.

Matronae see → Matres

Matronalia

A. THE MAIN TESTIMONIES   B. SIGNIFICANCE OF THE FESTIVAL

A. THE MAIN TESTIMONIES

The Ps.-Acronian commentary on Hor. Carm. 3,8,1 notes that the calends of March were called M. and that this referred to a special festival for the Roman wives and mothers (*matronae*, see B.) (*Kalendis Martiis Matronalia dicebantur, ... , et erat dies proprie festus matronis*). Ovid places the origins of the festival in the period of the wars between the Romans and the Sabines (→ Sabini). He attributes the report on its origins to the god Mars, who himself explains the first day of the month dedicated to him: most of the Sabine women who were kidnapped by Romulus and his companions were, according to the poet, already mothers, and the war continued for a long time; they therefore gathered in the sanctuary of Iuno and decided to stand between the two armies. Mars comments on the success of the measure as follows: 'According to proper custom the mothers celebrate my ceremonies and my festival' (*rite colunt matres sacra diemque meum* ...); 'the mothers of Latium are right in honouring this time of fertility, as their service and their wishes are to give birth' (*tempora iure colunt Latiae fecunda parentes/quaque militiam votaque partus habet*, Ov. Fast. 3,234 und 243–244). He adds that on that day a temple to Iuno was officially built by the young Latin women on the place where Romulus kept watch, that is on the Esquilin, (Ov. Fast. 3,247); the temple of the goddess of birth Iuno → Lucina is meant here.

Plutarch writes that the festival was one of those established immediately after the Romans and Sabines were united (Plut. Romulus 21,1, 30f.). Festus confirms the calendar date of the festival and its connection with Iuno Lucina (Fest. 131 L.).

B. SIGNIFICANCE OF THE FESTIVAL

The first of March is an important date, as it is the beginning of the year in the so-called calendar of Romulus (Macrob. Sat. 1,12,3). Moreover in the eyes of the Romans 'the calends of March belonged to the women' (*Martias Kalendas esse feminarum* ... , Serv. Aen. 8,638), and indeed the information available shows that at that time the *matronae* were honoured in two qualities:

a) The → *matrona* as mother: The Roman woman is *per definitionem* called to be a mother; the word *matrona* itself is derived from *mater* (*matrona ... dicta a matris nomine*, Gell. NA 18,6,8). Ovid correctly emphasises the context of fertility given by this date: The trees bud again, the buds grow, the seed becomes a fertile sprout (Ov. Fast. 3,237–240; cf. 3,253–258 on Iuno → Lucina).

b) The *matrona* as wife of the *pater familias*: The mother of the family had an important social status in Rome. Being a mother, she was entitled to respect and received valuable gifts on the M. We know that daughters gave gifts to their mothers (Plaut. Mil. 691) and that husbands especially gave gifts to their wives – as on their birthdays – (Suet. Vesp. 19; Tert. De idololatria 14,4; Pomp. Dig. 24,1,31,8; cf. Juv. 9,53). The men prayed that the marriage would hold (*pro conservatione coniugii*, Ps.-Acro on Hor. Carm. 3,8,1). The women themselves waited on their slaves at table in order – according to Macrobius – 'to spur them on to zeal' (Macrob. Sat. 1,12,7). This remark shows the role granted to the matrons in running their household.

R. SCHILLING, Janus, le dieu introducteur, le dieu des passages, in: MEFRA 72, 1960 = Id., Rites, cultes, dieux de Rome, 1979, 233–239; ST. WEINSTOCK, s.v. M., RE 14, 2306–2309; DUMÉZIL, 1966, 291–292.   G.F.

Matta (ψίαθος/*psíathos*). Mat or coarse cover made of rushes and straw, in Egypt also of papyrus (cf. Theophr. Hist. pl. 4,8,4). It served as bedding on the floor for farmers, travellers and the poor; in an Attic inscription it is also listed as part of the furnishings of a house [1]. According to Augustine (Contra Faustum 5,5) he who sleeps on a *matta* is the follower of a doctrine that preaches a frugal life (*mattarius*). A sleeping-mat could also be called χαμεύνη/*chameúnē* (Poll. 6,11).

1 Hesperia 5, 1936, 382 no. 6 A.   R.H.

Mattathias (Hebr. *mattityah*), from Modeïn, a member of the Jewish Joarib class of priests, clan father of the → Hasmoneans. M. resisted the religious edict of → Antiochus [6] IV. Joined by the pious ones (Greek Ἀσιδαῖοι/*Asidaîoi*, Hebr. *Ḥᵃsīdīm*), who had also fled into the Judaean desert, he began a guerilla war against the Jewish loyalists. After his death (167/166 BC) his son → Judas [1] Maccabeus became the leader of the Jewish rebellion (1 Macc 2,1–70).

SCHÜRER, vol. 1.   K.BR.

Matter (Greek ὕλη/*hýlē*, Lat. *materia*).
A. DEFINITION OF THE TERM   B. HISTORY OF THE TERM   C. LATER RECEPTION

A. DEFINITION OF THE TERM

Cicero translates *hýlē* (ὕλη), used by Aristotle and the Stoics, as *materia*. Aristotle uses *hýlē* for his own material cause (→ Principle) as well as for the principles (ἀρχαί/*archaí*) of the → Presocratics and for Plato's concept of 'space' (χώρα/*chóra*). *Hýlē* and *materia* originally denote timber, the 'material' from which something can be constructed (thus still in Plato). The concept does not become a technical term until Aristotle; it is fully developed in the 'Physics' where the opposition matter-form (ὕλη-εἶδος/*hýlē-eídos*, Lat. *materia-forma*) corresponds to that of possibility-reality (δύναμις- ἐνέργεια/*dýnamis-enérgeia*, Lat. *potentia-actus*). The Aristotelian definition of *hýlē* as 'that from which' (τὸ ἐξ οὗ, Aristot. Ph. 7,3 and elsewhere) has a decisive influence on the further history of the term and is in clear contrast with the Platonic *chóra* as 'that in which it becomes' (τὸ ἐν ᾧ γίγνεται, Plat. Ti. 50d 1).

B. HISTORY OF THE TERM

Matter is the subject of discussion whenever philosophical knowledge of the visible and changeable world is sought. Early Ionian → Natural philosophy (see also → Milesian School) with an interest in cosmogony searched for the → 'principle' (ἀρχή/*archḗ*); to use the term 'matter' here means to follow Aristotle's anachronistic doxography (cf. Aristot. Metaph. 1,3–10), even if material principles are established that despite all differences are always described as everlasting, alive and very capable of transformation. Later speculations were greatly influenced by → Parmenides and the → Eleatic School, with the principles of immutability and the impossibility of the Many originating from the One taken into account in various ways. Dual conceptions explaining processes in the visible physical world make further contributions; → Empedocles for instance adds Strife and Love (νεῖκος καὶ φιλία/neíkos kaì philía) as actively separating and combining powers to the four elements; → Anaxagoras [2] thinks mind (νοῦς/noûs) is the moving cause of cosmic matter.

In spite of all the difference, the Atomists are the most consistently Eleatic in their thought. → Leucippus [5] and → Democritus [1] (→ Atomism) regard the ultimate indivisible bodies (ἄτομα, átoma) as having the essential attributes of Parmenidean Being: eternality, indivisibility, homogeneity and immutability. The problem of processuality, which occurs when a formal, active principle is dispensed with, can however not yet be solved by this early materialistic monism. In the 'Timaeus', Plato takes Eleatism further: he makes space (χώρα/chṓra; τόπος/tópos) assume the role of the material substrate. This space is neither empty nor material but should rather be regarded as analogous to a continuous field in mathematics (which is why modern physics likes to tie up with this concept). The chṓra is affected by the → Ideas (immutable Being) in such a manner that it is able to receive their copies whilst itself being without qualities, imperishable and imperceptible. Through the definitions of matter developed later in the tradition (passivity, affectability and receptivity), space becomes the realm of becoming in the sensual world; it is saved from absolute non-being through participation in the Ideas (μέθεξις/méthexis) – a different concept from that of Parmenides. The perceptible bodies themselves are constructed of geometrically conceived elementary bodies that are no longer divisible into bodies, but only into more basic mathematical structures (surfaces; cf. Pl. Ti. 48e–68d).

Aristotle authoritatively developed the notion of matter within the context of his natural philosophy as a concept of reflection introduced in relation to certain substances or processes; from there it is transferred to other fields like → logic, psychology, etc. Physics aims at knowledge of the first principles and causes of its subject area, processual being; therefore, the principles of this being and its processuality must be determined. Change takes place within a range from a condition of relative beginning to an end state, called 'form' and 'deprivation' respectively (εἶδος and στέρησις/eídos and stérēsis, Lat. forma and privatio) by Aristotle. Because these are qualifications, a qualifiable substratum (ὑποκείμενον/hypokeímenon; literally: that which lies underneath) is required. The ultimate basis of all change is the first or ultimate matter (πρώτη, ἐσχάτη ὕλη/prôtē, eschátē hýlē), which can only be attained by abstraction and is free of any form and therefore completely without qualification. Nevertheless, it is not simply non-being; its ontological status is that of potential being (δυνάμει ὄν/dynámei ón). The structure of the physical world is the result of a successive re-shaping of matter, in which, at each level of being, that which must be qualified is called 'matter'. Thus, a continuous scale arises of natural spheres of being and objects; in each case the entities of the lower sphere constitute the matter for those of the higher sphere, since new forms are added at each level. Matter is first formed through the forms of elementary qualities (hot-cold, wet-dry); through their combination elementary bodies (στοιχεία/→ stoicheía) are formed, which interact through relations of continuity and opposition. The above applies only to the sublunar sphere; the supralunar heavenly bodies do not originate or pass away but consist of their own element, ether.

Alongside the Aristotelian tradition monistic stances can be found as well. → Epicurus takes Democritus further. He solves the problem of processuality by attributing to the atoms not just size and form but a third property, gravity (βάρος/báros). His ideas of simple atomic bonding and of space as an absolute referential system for atomic movements are pioneering. For → Stoicism, being is characterized by its capacity to act and to be acted upon, a capacity unique to bodies alone. Thus, Being is completely physical or material; yet, this is not a strictly materialistic stance because the matterform dualism is immanent in matter. In matter, an active and a passive (matter in the strict sense, hýlē) principle was distinguished; the latter was understood as a quality-less body (ἄποιον σῶμα, ápoion sôma), also described as sluggish and unmoving. → Pneuma (πνεῦμα/pneûma, also λόγος/lógos, θεός/theós) takes on the function of form, which can penetrate matter because of its fine material nature.

In → Plotinus, matter is not a principle but proceeds through → emanation from the highest cause of Being, the One and the Good. Emanated matter is found at every level of being, e.g. at the level of nous it is intelligible matter (ὕλη νοητή/hýlē noētḗ). The sensible matter of the lowest level is in strict opposition to the highest principle and is therefore Non-being, Many and Evil (πρῶτον κακόν/prôton kakón; Plot. Enneades 2,4).

Cicero (De natura deorum) passes down to us elements both of Epicurean and of Stoic natural philosophy. Both are subjected to Academic Sceptic criticism; he, like the early Middle Ages, had little interest in the natural philosophy; it is only mentioned in passing in other contexts. Neoplatonic ideas, primarily those of Proclus, were passed down to the early Christian Middle Ages by Ps.-Dionysius Areopagita (De coelesti hierarchia), and later by Augustine (especially De genesi ad litteram). The first great synthesis is achieved in JOHANNES SCOTUS ERIUGENA (De divinitate naturae), who presents a thoroughly Neoplatonic but nonetheless autonomous and comprehensive philosophy of nature. The Neoplatonic idea of the emanatively produced, continuously graded world, in which matter assumes the lowest position, is reshaped through the later encounter with Peripatetic philosophy (late Middle Ages).

C. LATER RECEPTION

These different concepts of matter are developed further in the respective schools, with Platonism dominating in the early Middle Ages because the 'Timaeus 'was known form an early date, whilst after the reception of Aristotelian natural philosophy, the Peripatetic concept became predominant. The commentaries of Avicenna (Ibn Sînâ) and Averroes (Ibn Rušd) were also highly influential. In the High Middle Ages, two schools can be roughly distinguished: one, influenced by Dominican thought (ALBERTUS MAGNUS, THOMAS AQUINAS), understood matter primarily as the material substrate that imbues being with transience and indeterminacy, which is why e.g. the heavenly bodies and the immortal souls can only be material in an analogous sense (under the influence of → Neoplatonism, the anti-Thomist DIETRICH VON FREIBERG later taught the purely immaterial nature of heaven). On the other hand, the Franciscan school (BONAVENTURA, DUNS SCOTUS) under the influence of Avicebron (Ibn Gebirol) put forward a hylemorphistic argument and stressed the coherence of the entire created world (Augustine), a coherence guaranteed by a universal materiality. Numerous distinctions, like those between *materia corporalis* and *spiritualis* (physical and spiritual matter), safeguard the special position of the supralunar spheres. The basis of modern science is laid at the beginning of the 14th cent. by the Franciscan Franciscus DE MARCHIA, who was the first to postulate a uniform and quantitatively determined matter for the whole of creation.

→ Materialism; → Principle

C. BAEUMKER, Das Problem der Materie in der griechischen Philosophie, 1890 (repr. 1963); H. BENZ, Materie und Wahrnehmung in der Philosophie Plotins, 1990; L. BLOOS, Probleme der stoischen Physik, 1973; I. CRAEMER-RUEGENBERG, Die Naturphilosophie des Aristoteles, 1980; H. HAPP, Hyle. Studien zum aristotelischen Materiebegriff, 1971; E. A. MOODY, Studies in Medieval Philosophy, Science and Logic, 1975; E. McMULLIN, The Concept of Matter in Greek and Medieval Philosophy, 1965; S. SAMBURSKY, Physics of the Stoics, 1959; N. SCHNEIDER, Die Kosmologie des Franciscus de Marcia. Texte, Quellen und Untersuchungen zur Naturphilosophie des 14. Jahrhunderts, 1991; D. J. SCHULZ, Das Problem der Materie in Platons Timaios, 1966. NO.SCH.

Matthaeus (Gr. Ματθαῖος/*Matthaîos* or Μαθθαῖος/*Maththaîos*), the Evangelist.

According to church tradition – probably based on Mt 9,9 (tax collector M. instead of Levi in Mk 2,13) – M. was the author of the anonymously passed down first gospel (= Mt), by and large the most influential book in the history of European thought. The author's name M. follows the principle that Christian canonical writings (→ Canon V.) must have an apostle as author.

A. COMPOSITION AND CONTENTS B. ORIGIN
C. BASIC THEOLOGICAL PRINCIPLES

A. COMPOSITION AND CONTENTS

Mt begins with a programmatic introduction (1,1–4,22) as well as the teachings and healings of → Jesus, the Son of David and → Messiah of Israel, among his people (4,23–25; 8,1–9,35). Then it recounts the increasing tension with the leaders of the people (12,1–16,20) and Jesus' 'withdrawal' from them (for example 12,15; 14,13). Then follows a narrative section on the community of disciples that has been formed in Israel in the meantime (16,21–17,27; 19–20). This is followed by the parting of Jesus and the leaders of Israel, his leaving the temple (21,1–24,2) and the Passion and Easter Narratives (26–28). The course of the narrative is structured by five of Jesus' discourses (compare five books of Moses): Sermon on the Mount (5–7), Missionary Sermons (10), Parables of the Kingdom (13), Sermon on Community Relation (18), Eschatological Sermon (24f.). Like, for instance, Dt and unlike the discourses of Greek historians, they are directed at the community of contemporary readers.

B. ORIGIN

It is commonly accepted that Mt originated between AD 80 and 90 in Syria. It was written by an unknown Christian Jew for Christian Jewish communities who followed the Jewish law (compare 5,17–19) and who had to find a new direction after the destruction of the temple (AD 70) and the separation from the synagogue (compare especially 23,1–24,2). They became integrated in the greater Gentile Christian church. They already undertook missionary activities, also among the pagan population (24,9–14), to which the Resurrected Lord opens the way (28,19). The author most likely used the gospel of Mark (→ Marcus I [1]) and the lost 'source of sayings' Q (a collection of Jesus' sayings) as his main sources, along with shorter collections of both written (5,21f.; 27f.; 33–37; 6,2–6; 16–18) and orally transmitted material. The language of Mt is a Greek strongly influenced by the → Septuagint.

C. BASIC THEOLOGICAL PRINCIPLES

The break with the mother religion, Judaism, is reflected in the vehement, probably still inner-Jewish polemic (Mt 23; 27,24f.: presumably referring to the destruction of the temple in Jerusalem) as well as in the so-called 'fulfillment quotations' (for example 1,23; 2,15; 18; 23; fulfillment of Biblical prophecies in the life of Jesus). M. also emphasises Jesus' observance of the law (5,17–19), but a Jesus who interprets the Torah from the point of view of the Commandment to Love as the most important commandment (22,34–40). Mt places a strong emphasis on 'ethics': The laws which prepare for entry into the Kingdom of Heaven are to be kept by all people (28,20; compare 5–7: Sermon on the Mount). Jesus is not only a figure of the past, but 'Immanuel', 'God-with-us' (1,23), that is the presence of God, which will accompany the community and help it in its 'little faith' (14,28–31) until the end of the world (28,20). At the same time Jesus is the model for the 'better righteousness' demanded of the community (5,20) and for obedience to the father (3,13; 4,1–11).

→ Bible; → Gospel; → Iohannes [1]; → Lucas [1]; → Marcus I [1]

W. Davies, D. Allison, A Critical and Exegetical Commentary on Matthew, 3 vols., 1988, 1991, 1997; U. Luz, Das Evangelium nach Matthäus, 4 vols., 1985–2002; G. Stanton, A Gospel for a New People, 1992; G. Strekker, Der Weg der Gerechtigkeit, 1962; W. E. Mills, The Gospel of Matthew, Bibliographies for Biblical Research (New Testament Series 1), 1993. U.L.

Matthew see → Matthaeus

Matthias (Ματθίας/Matthías); variant of the proper name Mattathias, Hebr. *Mattityah*, 'gift of God'). Father of the historian → Iosephus [4] Flavius, of whom little is known apart from his son's statements in his *vita* (Jos. Vit. 1). He lived from AD 6 until after AD 70, since Iosephus reports on the fate of his parents during the Jewish War (Vit. 41; Jos. BI 5,13,1). M. was a member of the priestly clan of Yehoyarib (1 Chr 24,7) and his great-grandmother was presumably a daughter of → Alexander [16] Iannaeus and therefore a Hasmonean (Vit. 1,4; critical [3], affirmative [2]).

1 M. Radin, The Pedigree of Josephus, in: CPh 24, 1929, 193–196; 2 T. Rajak, Josephus. The Historian and His Society, 1983, 11–45, esp. 15f.; 3 Schürer I, 45f. I.WA.

Mattiaci A tribe that settled in Wetterau and Taunus during the Imperial period. The Celtic name is associated with *Mattium*, the main city of the → Chatti (cf. Ptol. 2,11,14: Ματτικόν; *Mattikón*). It is debated whether the M. were a sub-tribe of the Germanic Chatti which had already separated from them during the Augustan period, and settled in the above-mentioned area with Roman permission (for earlier research, cf. [1; 2. 52–57; 3]), or whether the M. are those mentioned as having defected because of the destruction of Mattium in AD 15 (Tac. Ann. 1,56,4; not very convincing, cf. [4. 20–22]), or, finally, whether the Chatti merely kept the original place-name Mattium when the M. withdrew from their territory to the Rhine before the advancing Germans [3. 198–200, 241–248]. This would make their Germanic ethnicity questionable. It is all the less certain whether finds of Germanic ceramics in the Wetterau are to be directly associated with the M.

Roman attempts around AD 47 to exploit veins of silver in the land of the M. – presumably north of the Taunus in the area of the Lahn – were not very productive (Tac. Ann. 11,20,3). During the rebellion of Iulius [II 43] Civilis in AD 69, a group of Chatti, Usipetes and M. laid siege to → Mogontiacum, but were forced to retreat with losses (Tac. Hist. 4,37,3). Relations between Rome and the M. were generally good, so that the latter were exempted from taxes and required only to serve in the military (Tac. Germ. 29,1f.). A *cohors Mattiacorum* is attested as early as AD 78 in Moesia (CIL XVI 22), and the *cohors II Mattiacorum* from AD 99 in Moesia inferior (CIL XVI 44). With the founding of the *civitas U(lpia) Mattiacorum* (so far the appellation is only attested in CIL XIII 7061, where it is a

conjectural restoration), probably under Trajan, the M. were incorporated into the Roman administrative system. → Aquae [III 4] Mattiacae (the modern Wiesbaden) and Castellum Mattiacorum (the modern → Kastel) were named after them. *Pilae Mattiacae*, little balls of soap used to dye one's hair, are mentioned by Mart. 14,27,2. In later sources (inscriptions and Not. Dign. Occ.), *numeri Mattiacorum seniorum* or *iuniorum* are mentioned in Italy and Gaul [1].

1 M. Schönfeld, s.v. M., RE 14, 2320–2322; 2 H.-G. Simon, in: D. Baatz, F.-R. Herrmann (ed.), Die Römer in Hessen, 1989², 38–65; 3 A. Becker, Rom und die Chatten, 1992; 4 W. Czysz, Wiesbaden in der Römerzeit, 1994. RA.WI.

Mattiarii The *mattiarii* were Roman soldiers armed with short-shafted weighted darts (*plumbatae, mattiobarbuli*) (Veg. Mil. 1,17; 2,16; 3,14; 4,29). The *legiones palatinae mattiarii seniores* (Not. Dign. Or. 6,42) or *mattiarii iuniores* (ibid. 5,47) which are attested in the → *Notitia dignitatum* appear to have come from two tetrarchian *legiones* in Illyricum (Veg. Mil. 1,17). Further, *legiones comitatenses* of *mattiarii constantes* (Not. Dign. Or. 9,31) and *mattiarii iuniores* (ibid. 5,232) as well as of *mattiarii Honoriani Gallicani* (Not. Dign. Occ. 5,220) have been attested. The *mattiarii* were sent to the West by Constantius II in A.D. 361 along with the → *lancearii*; in 378 they fought in the Battle of Adrianople (Amm. Marc. 21,13,16; 31,13,8).

1 D. Hoffmann, Das spätrömische Bewegungsheer und die Notitia Dignitatum, 1969; 2 P. Southern, K. R. Dixon, The Late Roman Army, 1996; 3 M. C. Bishop, J. C. N. Coulston, Roman Military Equipment from the Punic Wars to the Fall of Rome, 1993. P.H.

Mattress (τύλη/*týlē*; Latin *culcita, torus*). Mattresses were laid on the Greek and Roman → kline (lying on the supporting straps of the *kline*, Petron. Sat. 97,4) or were spread out directly on the floor (Ath. 15,675a; Alci. 4,13,14; χαμεύνη/*chameúnē*: Theoc. 7,133; 13, 33). Mattresses were filled with wool, straw, reeds, sea grass, hay, hair, feathers; the feathers of Germanic geese being especially valued (Plin. HN 10,54, compare Ov. Met. 8,655 on rushes). There also was the κνέφαλλον/*knéphallon* (Poll. 10,42) and the τυλεῖον/*tyleíon*, the fine underbed made of wool cut away by fullers when cropping cloth. In Greek and Roman art matresses on *klinai* are especially shown in symposium or wedding scenes. R.H.

Matuccius L. Matuccius Fuscinus. Praetorian legate of the *legio III Augusta* in the year AD 158; he was already designated to be consul at that time. On 21 June 159 he is attested as being consul along with M. Pisibanius Lepidus. PIR² M 374.

B. E. Thomasson, Fasti Africani, 1997, 151f.; P. Weiss, in: Chiron 29, 1999. W.E.

Matunas Etruscan family name of an important gens from → Caere (today Cerveteri; 4th/3rd century BC), known from the inscriptions of two chamber tombs in that place, the Tomba dei Tarquini and the Tomba dei Rilievi. The latter is the most elaborately furnished Etruscan chamber grave in the form of an → Atrium with thirteen niches which represent cubicula. The names ascribed to the dead compose a genealogy of four generations, the name of the grave's donor Vel Matunas, son of Lars, being inscribed on a → Cippus at the entrance to the grave.

→ Funerary architecture (III. C. 1.)

J. Heurgon, Die Etrusker, 1971, 230–234; M. Cristofani, Le iscrizioni della tomba dei Rilievi di Cerveteri, in: SE 34, 1966, 221–238.   F.PR.

Matusia Apellation (possibly from √mātu-; *mā-, 'good': [1. 206]) of → Minerva in Sentinum (Ancona) in Umbria (CIL XI 5740), who because of the ending -usia has been regarded as a family goddess [2], which is questionable [1. 16f.].

1 Radke ; 2 Schulze, 200.   W.-A.M.

Matuta see → Mater Matuta

Mauretania (Μαυρουσία/Maurousía).
I. Name II. Geography III. History IV. Archaeology

I. Name

In the second century BC, M. comprised approximately the area of Morocco and western Algeria and was probably called by its Greek name of Maurusia (cf. Coelius Antipater, HRR 1,175 fr. 55). The formation of names in M. (Ἑρπεδιτανοί/Herpeditanoî), which follows the same pattern as those found in Iberia (e.g. Turdetani, Cassetani), and the existence of the Nektíbēres (Νεκτίβηρες) in M. speak for the fact that Libyans and Iberians are related.

II. Geography

In geological terms, M. is characterized largely by the mountain ranges of the Rif Atlas, the Middle Atlas and the High Atlas, which enclose the region of the Meseta. In antiquity corn of good quality was harvested along the fertile Mediterranean coast, in the Mulucha valley and on the plains of Volubilis and Sala (Str. 17,3,11; Mela 3,104). Grapes for wine and vegetables were also bountiful, as were olives (Str. 17,3,4; Plin. HN 5,3; 13; Paus. 1,33,5). The elephants that lived in the Atlas and in the mountains of Septem (modern Ceuta) were used for military and economic purposes (Str. 17,3,4; 6; Mela 3,104; Plin. HN 5,18; 8,15; 32; Juv. 11,122–125). Many lions and panthers were exported to Rome (for the circus games; Str. 17,3,4; Plin. HN 8,53). The horses of this region were used by the famous Moorish cavalrymen (Str. 17,3,7; Paus.

8,43,3). Cattle and sheep, fish, murex snails, citrus wood, salts and mineral resources (copper, marble and gemstones) were important for the economy of the region (Vitr. De arch. 8,2,6f.; Mela 3,104; Plin. HN 5,12; 6,201; 13,91–95; Ptol. 4,2,17; CIL VIII Suppl. 3, 21848).

III. History
A. Pre-Roman history   B. In the Roman Empire

A. Pre-Roman history

M.'s history was strongly influenced by Phoenicians and Carthaginians [1. 31–33, 70f.]. → Lix [1] and → Tingis (modern Tangier) were ancient Phoenician trading posts, and Phoenician traders visited → Mogador from at least the second half of the 7th century BC. Perhaps Phoenicians – and not Carthaginians – first established an outpost on Kerne that was important for the trade in gold from Guinea. In 406 BC Mauritanian formations fought on the Carthaginian side (Diod. Sic. 13,80,3). In the middle of the 4th century BC, the rebel leader Hanno was supported by Mauritanian troops (Iust. 21,4,7). Hamilcar [3] Barcas punished Mauritanian soldiers who had supported M. Atilius [I 21] Regulus in 256 BC (Oros. 4,9,9). In the Second → Punic War Mauritanian cavalry and infantry fought on the Carthaginian side (Pol. 3,33,15; 15,11,1). In 204 BC, however, King Baga placed 4,000 cavalrymen at the disposal of → Massinissa, the enemy of Carthage (Liv. 29,30,1f.). In the Jugurthine War (111–105 BC) the eastern Mauritanian king → Bocchus [1] I first supported his father-in-law → Jugurtha, only to turn him over to the Romans later on. In reward, he received the former western Masaesylian (→ Masaesyli) territories between the Mulucha River and the city of Saldae (Sall. Iug. 80,3; 111,1).

In 81 BC, Bogudes [1] I, the son of Bocchus I, joined Pompey who was fighting against the Numidian pretender to the throne → Hiarbas [2], the rival of the eastern Massylian (→ Massylii) king → Hiempsal [2] II (Oros. 5,21,14). M. was drawn ever deeper into the maelstrom of Rome's internal partisan battles. In 81 BC, Q. Sertorius crossed over from Spain to M., liberated Tingis – the western Mauritanian king Ascalis who was supported by Sulla had retreated there – and returned to Spain at the request of the Lusitani with 700 Mauritanian cavalrymen (Plut. Sertorius 9–12). The Catilinarian P. Sittius fled to M. in 63 BC and led the mercenary soldiers of the eastern Mauritanian king → Bocchus [2] II against the eastern Massylian king → Juba [1] I. While Juba I joined Pompey, the eastern Mauritanian king Bocchus II and the western Mauritanian king Bogudes [2] II remained loyal to Caesar from 49 BC. In 46 BC, Bocchus II received the former eastern Masaesylian territories between Saldae and the mouth of the Ampsaga and the western Massylian territories between the mouth of the Ampsaga and the city of → Chullu. By this time at the latest, Bogudes II had gained possession of M. to the mouth of the Mulucha. The region around → Cirta fell – perhaps a little later – to P. Sittius.

When Bogudes II supported M. Antonius [I 9] in 38 BC, Bocchus II occupied M. west of the Mulucha with the consent of Octavian (the later Augustus) and united both 'Mauritanian' kingdoms. M. now extended from the Atlantic to Chullu. But Bocchus II died in 33, leaving no heir. Octavian founded twelve *coloniae* in the region in the following years (33–25 BC): along the coast Igilgili, Saldae, Rusazus, Rusguniae, Gunugu, Cartennae and Zulil, in the interior Tubusuctu, Aquae Calidae, Zucchabar, Babba and Banasa [2. 332–358]. In 25 he 'enfeoffed' the eastern Massylian prince → Juba [2] II, the son of Jubas I with M. (Plin. HN 5,16; Cass. Dio 53,26,2). Juba II, who married → Cleopatra [II 13] Selene around 20 BC, built → Caesarea [1] (modern Cherchel) into one of the most important cities of North Africa. In AD 24, Ptolemy (23–40 AD), the son of Jubas II, put down a rebellion by the Numidian → Tacfarinas (Tac. Ann. 4,23–26).

B. IN THE ROMAN EMPIRE

In AD 40, however, Caligula, the great-grandson of Mark Antony, had Ptolemy, a grandson of Mark Antony, murdered [3. 467–487]. Still in the same year, M. became a province and received its own provincial era [4. 843–861]. Two years later Claudius divided the province into M. *Tingitana* (with its capital at Tingis) and M. *Caesariensis* (with its capital at Caesarea). Both provinces were placed in the control of a *procurator Augusti* with the rank of *ducenarius*. Both provinces only had auxiliary troops, which around 70 AD amounted to 19 *cohortes* and 5 *alae*, about 15,000 men (Tac. Hist. 2,58,1). A → limes was built to protect the southern border. There was often unrest, under Domitian, Hadrian, M. Aurelius and Commodus (cf. [5]). Mauretanian sheikhs rose to the highest positions, e.g. Lusius Quietus (118 executed as the real or presumed opponent of Hadrian), M. Opellius Macrinus (the first emperor from the equestrian class, 217–218) and M. Aemilius Aemilianus (emperor, 253–254). The province of M. *Sitifensis* (Sitifis) was created before AD 288. In the time between AD 295 and 303 the two provinces of M. *Caesariensis* and M. *Sitifensis* were attached to the diocese of Africa. The province of M. *Tingitana*, however, was attached to the diocese of Hispaniae.

During the Constantinian and post-Constantinian eras, the Christian Donatist movement (→ Donatus [1]) played a large role in M. Thus in 372 the sheikh Firmus received support from the Donatists in his revolt against the government until the *magister equitum* Theodosius brought him down in 374 or 375 (Amm. 29,5,2–56 [6. 148–150]). From 429 on, the Moors operated alongside the Vandal Geiseric (→ Geisericus) and in 533 they still supported the Vandal → Gelimer against the Eastern Roman general → Belisarius. By the end of the 6th century, only the former M. *Sitifensis*, several cities of M. *Caesariensis* and the fortress of → Septem were still

part of the Mauritanian kingdom. In the years from 708 to 711, M. came under Arabian control. Inscriptions: CIL VIII 2; [7; 8].

→ Masaesyli; → Massyli

1 HUSS ; 2 N. K. MACKIE, Augustan Colonies in Mauretania, in: Historia 32, 1983; 3 D. FISHWICK, The Annexation of Mauretania, in: Historia 20, 1971; 4 G. DI VITA-EVRARD, La dédicace des horrea de Tubusuctu et l'ère de la province dans les Maurétanies, in: A. MASTINO (ed.), L'Africa romana. Atti del IX convegno di studio 2, 1992; 5 M. RACHET, Rome et les Berbères (Collection Latomus 110), 1970; 6 E. L. GRASMÜCK, Coercitio (Bonner Historische Forschungen 22), 1964; 7 L. GALAND, J. GASCOU (ed.), Inscriptions antiques du Maroc, 2 vols., 1966/1982; 8 L. CHATELAIN (ed.), Inscriptions latines du Maroc, 1942.

P. LEVEAU, S. LANCEL, M. PONSICH, M. P. SPEIDEL, in: ANRW II 10.2, 1982, 683–738, 739–786, 787–816, 817–849, 850–860; G. CAMPS, Remarques sur la toponymie de la Maurétanie césarienne occidentale, in: Y. LE BOHEC (ed.), L'Afrique, la Gaule, la religion à l'époque romaine. Mélanges à la mémoire de Marcel Le Glay (Collection Latomus 226), 1994, 81–94; J. CARCOPINO, Le Maroc antique, ²1947; S. GSELL, Histoire ancienne de l'Afrique du Nord 7, ²1930; 8, 1928; F. LÓPEZ PARDO, Mauritania Tingitana, 1987; J. MAZARD, Corpus nummorum Numidiae Mauretaniaeque, 1955; P. ROMANELLI, Storia delle province romane dell'Africa, 1959; B. THOMAE, Praesides provinciarum ..., in: OpRom 7, 1969, 163–211, especially 191–202; B. E. THOMASSON, s.v. M., RE Suppl. 13, 307–316; ST. WEINSTOCK, s.v. M., RE 14, 2344–2386.   W.HU.

IV. ARCHAEOLOGY

The tribes that lived as nomads in M. until well into the Imperial period first came into contact with the developed Mediterranean cultures through Phoenician settlements along the Atlantic and the Mediterranean coast. From the sources we know that → Lix(us) [1], which according to tradition was already founded around 1100 BC but for which archaeological evidence only dates back to the 8th century BC, played a pioneering role in this process. However, extensive acculturation did not take place, and only the immediate hinterland of the few Phoenician and Carthaginian trading posts – e.g. on the island of Mogador (ancient Kerne?), at Tangier (Tingis) and east of the Straits of Gibraltar on Rachgoun Island (off the mouth of the Oued Tafna) [1] as well as Tipasa – were affected. The perhaps corrupt → Periplus by the Carthaginian → Hanno [1], dating from the early 5th century BC, records a new settlement of 'Libyo-Phoenices'; a move that was apparently intended to strengthen the urban population. Individual urban centres developed in the interior, e.g. → Banasa, with → Volubilis apparently following later on. Barter trade with the indigenous population remained difficult (the report in Hdt. 4,196 is enlightening).

The cultural profile of the time is marked by the close proximity of the Phoenicians and Carthaginians in the south of the Iberian Peninsula (→ Hispania, with map), which was considerably more powerful in economic

terms because of its rich deposits of ore. M. was basically dependent on viticulture and the production of
fish sauces (garum, → liquamen) [3], for which there is
evidence in Lix from about the 5th century BC.

The originally Carthaginian Iol, which was renamed
→ Caesarea [1] in the Augustean period and built into a
magnificent royal residence and metropolis under the
short-lived dynasty of → Juba [2] II, remained the
exception as far as public buildings and sculptures in
the Roman style were concerned [4]. After M. was incorporated into the Roman Empire, increasing urbanization in the plains also helped spread a more or less
standardized provincial culture.

→ Colonization III. (with map)

> 1 G. VUILLEMOT, Reconnaissances aux échelles puniques
> d'Oranie, 1965, 55–130; 2 J. DESANGES, Recherches sur
> l'activité des Méditerranéens aux confins de l'Afrique,
> 1978, 39–85; 3 M. PONSICH, M. TARRADELL, Garum et
> industries antiques de salaison dans la Méditerranée occi-
> dentale, 1965; 4 K. FITTSCHEN, Juba II. und seine Resi-
> denz Jol-Caesarea (Cherchel), in: Die Numider. Exhibi-
> tion catalogue Bonn 1979, 227–242.
>
> M. C. SIGMAN, The Romans and the Indigenous Tribes of
> M. Tingitana, in: Historia 26, 1977, 415–439; J. SPAUL,
> The Roman Frontier in Morocco, in: Bulletin of the Insti-
> tute of Archaeology, University College London 30, 1993,
> 105–119; P. ROUILLARD, Maroc; S. LANCEL, Algérie, in:
> V. KRINGS (ed.), La civilisation phénicienne et punique.
> Manuel de recherche (HbdOr I 20), 776–785, 786–795.
>   H.G.N.

Mauricius (Μαυρίκιος; *Maurίkios*). Flavius M. Tiberius, East Roman emperor (A.D. 582–602), born in 539
in Arabissus (Cappadocia), died on 27th Nov. 602 in
Calchedon. M. replaced the caesar and later emperor
→ Tiberius II in 574 as chief of the guard and was given
the command in 577 as *magister militum per Orientem*
to continue the Persian war. After victories near Calli-
nicus in 580 and near Constantina in 581, he was given
a triumphal reception in 582 in Constantinople. Tiberius, emperor since 578, affianced him to his daughter
Constantina and gave him the title of caesar; after his
death in August of 582 M. became emperor and married Constantina in a splendid ceremony.

At this time the territory of the Eastern Empire was
mostly intact; in the West only parts of the territory that
→ Iustinianus [1] I reconquered in Italy and North
Africa remained. M. organised them as → Exarchates
with the centres in Ravenna and Carthage and planned
to divide the empire into an eastern and western part
under the rule of his two oldest sons despite the reduced
territory.

But the empire was threatened by foreign powers
both in the East and the West. The Persian War continued under → Chosroes [5] I's son and successor
Hormisdas [6] IV (since 579). Only when the latter's
son → Chosroes [6] II, king from 590 on, defeated the
usurper → Wahram in 591 with Byzantine help, could
peace be made and under M. the relationships remained

friendly from then on. But the war in the East prevented
the defense of the border along the Danube for too long.
Already before M.'s time, Avars (→ Avares) and Slavs
raided this part of the empire several times. In 584
Slavic invaders threatened Constantinople, in 586 the
Avars threatened Thessalonica. Only after long battles
was a treaty made with the Avars in 598 and in 602 a
decisive victory was achieved against the Slavs. But the
population was no longer willing to bear the constant
wars and consequent financial limitations. A revolt
resulted in → Phocas, an officer of middle rank, being
declared emperor, who soon had M. and his six sons,
later also his wife and three daughters beheaded with
the sword.

It is uncertain whether the emperor was actually the
author of a strategic handbook (→ *Stratēgikón* of Pseu-
do-M.).

> P. SCHREINER (translation and comm.), Theophylaktos
> Simokates, Geschichte, 1985 (main source); ODB 2, 1318
> and 3, 1962f.; PLRE 855–860 Nr. 4; M. WHITBY, The
> Emperor Maurice and His Historian, 1988; P. SCHREI-
> NER, s.v. Maurikios, LMA 6, 411.   F.T.

Mauropous, Iohannes Byzantine scholar and bishop,
born around 990 in→ Paphlagonia, died around 1092
(?). M. composed epigrams, letters and speeches, and as
the founder of a school of law and editor of Konstantinos IX's novellae he had great influence at the court of
Constantinople until the middle of the 11th century.
His promotion to metropolitan of Euchaïta was however an exile in disguise. He is important as the teacher
and predecessor of → Psellos.

> A. KARPOZILOS, s.v. M., LMA 4, 414f.   J.N.

Mauryas Members of an Indian dynasty founded at the
end of the 4th century BC by Chandragupta Maurya
(→ Sandracottus), whose territory soon included all of
North India (see map). A military campaign by → Seleu-
cus I, who wanted to reconquer Alexander [4] the
Great's Indian conquests, failed; in a treaty Chandragupta was granted all southeastern satrapies (including
Arachosia) and Seleucus received 500 war elephants in
exchange. Seleucus's emissary to Chandragupta was
→ Megasthenes, whose *Indiká* (FGrH 715), preserved
in countless fragments, became the standard work on
India. Little is known about Chandragupta's son and
successor, Bindusāra-Amitrochates. At his court
→ Daimachus [2] of Plataeae (FGrH 716) was the emissary of → Antiochus [2].

→ Aśoka (269/8–233/2 BC), at the other hand, the
son of Bindusāra, is famous for his so-called edicts,
monumental inscriptions on rocks and pillars, which
served to spread Buddhist moral teachings. These inscriptions can be found everywhere in his empire, which
reached from Afghanistan (→ Arachosia) to Karnataka
and Andhra Pradesh, but not to the southern point of
India. They are mostly in Middle Indian dialects, in the
northwest also in Aramaic and Greek.

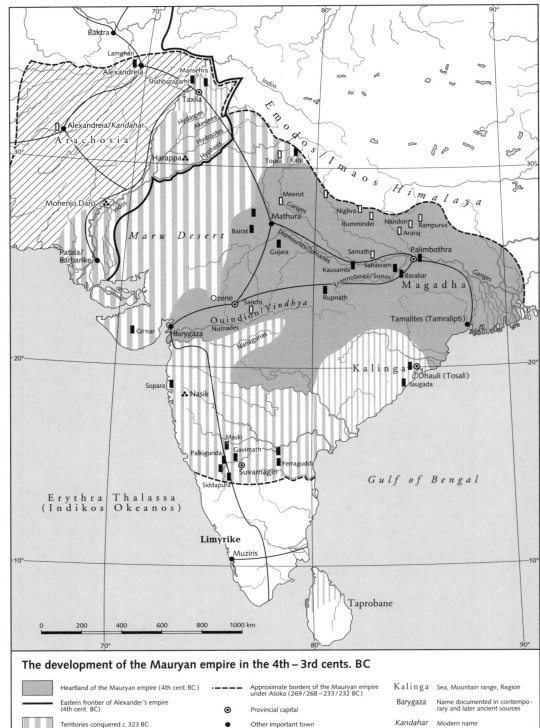

The development of the Mauryan empire in the 4th – 3rd cents. BC

Heartland of the Mauryan empire (4th cent. BC)	▪▪▪ Approximate borders of the Mauryan empire under Aśoka (269/268–233/232 BC)	**Kalinga**	Sea, Mountain range, Region
Eastern frontier of Alexander's empire (4th cent. BC)	◉ Provincial capital	**Barygaza**	Name documented in contemporary and later ancient sources
Territories conquered c. 323 BC	● Other important town	*Kandahar*	Modern name
Territory conquered from Seleucus Nikator c. 305 BC	▮ ▯ Find spots of Aśoka inscriptions (rock edicts / pillar edicts)		
Territories conquered c. 300–268 BC	⁂ Important archaeological site		
Territories conquered by / under the influence of Aśoka, c. 261 BC	— Important trade route (confirmed)		

After Aśoka's death the empire soon fell apart and the later Mauryas, who also appear to be insignificant in Indian sources, are rarely mentioned in Graeco-Roman sources (e.g. Sophagasenus in Pol. 11,34,11). There were probably close relations between the Mauryas and the early Hellenistic kingdoms (trade must have flourished as well), but they are attested only sparsely in the sources.

→ India

K. KARTTUNEN, India and the Hellenistic World, 1997, 253ff.; F. F. SCHWARZ, Die Griechen und die Maurya-Dynastie, in: F. Altheim, R. Stiehl (eds.), Geschichte Mittelasiens im Altertum, 1970, 267–316; F. F. SCHWARZ, Herrschaftslöwe und Kriegselefant. Literaturvergleichende Beobachtungen zu Pompeius Trogus, in: M.B. de Boer, T.A. Edridge (eds.), Hommages à M.J. Vermaseren 3, 1978, 1116–1142; R. THAPAR, Aśoka and the Decline of the Mauryas, 1963.

MAP LITERATURE: J. SEIBERT, Vorderer Orient. Das Alexanderreich (336–323 v.Chr.), TAVO B V 1, 1985; H. WALDMANN, Vorderer Orient. Die hellenistische Staatenwelt im 3. Jh.v.Chr., TAVO B V 3, 1983.   K.K.

Mausoleum (Μαυσ(σ)ωλεῖον; *Maus(s)ōleîon*; Lat. *mausoleum*). Monumental tomb for the satrap → Maussollos of Caria (died 353 BC) and his wife Artemisia [2] (died 351 BC) near the city of → Halicarnassus in Lycia, probably only completed during the time of Alexander. It was counted as one of the → Wonders of the World and became eponymous for a standard type of representative → funerary architecture.

Modern archaeology has focused much on the monument, which was frequently discussed and described in ancient literature (Str. 14,656 ff.; Diod. Sic. 16,45; Plin. HN 36, 30–31 and *passim*). Scant archaeological evidence in combination with contradictory descriptions of details in ancient accounts inspired a great number of sometimes highly divergent reconstructions. The tomb, attributed to the famous architects → Pytheus and → Satyrus (Vitr. De arch. 7 praef. 12–13), was nearly 50 m high and situated within a large peribolos on a base made of three steps. It was distinctly rectangular in shape (c.32×26 m), unlike later adaptations (e.g. the mausoleum of Belevi, fig. s.v. → funerary architecture, vol. 4, 1175 f.) that were square in plan. The building followed the general type of earlier Lycian tombs, e.g. at → Xanthus (cf. esp. the 'Nereid' monument of the Lycian prince Pericles, dating to *c.* 400 BC, now in London, BM), but it elevated this type to previously unknown dimensions and sumptuousness.

The elevated main storey consisted of an Ionian peristyle with 11×9 columns surrounding a pseudeo-cella; above it was a pyramid roof with 24 steps. Danish excavations in the 1960s revealed that the actual chamber was not in the pseudo-cella but off centre in the base of the building. The building was lavishly decorated with

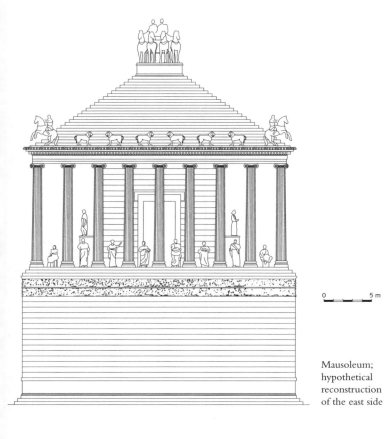

0 ___ 5 m

Mausoleum;
hypothetical
reconstruction
of the east side

sculptures: relief friezes ran along its sides, there were free-standing sculptures between the columns and on the roof (lions and horses as → acroteria, a quadriga with statues of Maussollus and Artemisia on the ridge of the roof). The four famous sculptors → Bryaxis, → Leochares, → Scopas and → Timotheus are attested to have worked there, but so far none of the extant panels of the relief frieze or any free-standing statues have been convincingly attributed to any individual sculptors.

The Mausoleum was probably destroyed by an earthquake in the early Middle Ages; in the 15th and 16th cents. large sections were used as building material for the crusader castle at Bodrum. From the early 19th cent., Stratford CANNING brought various fragments of the Mausoleum to the BM in London. Inspired by this, an expedition directed by Charles NEWTON undertook deep and large-scale excavations from 1856 to 1865. He was able to recover substantial parts of the architectural sculpture (numerous frieze panels, quadriga with Maussollus and Artemisia) and also brought them to London. The activity of these treasure hunters largely destroyed the archaeological evidence and with it any chance of a well-founded reconstruction of the building complex.
→ Mausoleum

W. EKSCHMITT, Die sieben Weltwunder, 1984; A. VON GERKAN, Grundlagen für die Herstellung des M. von Halikarnassos, in: MDAI(R) 72, 1965, 217–225; W. HOEFNER, Zum M. von Halikarnass, in: AA 1996, 95–114; K. JEPPESEN et al. (ed.): The M. at Halikarnassos: Reports of the Danish Archaeological Expedition to Bodrum, vol. 1ff., 1981ff.; K. Jeppesen, Tot operum opus. Ergebnisse der dänischen Forschungen zum M. von Harlikanass seit 1966, in: JDAI 107, 1992, 59–102; F. KRISCHEN, Weltwunder der Baukunst in Babylonien und Jordanien, 1956, passim; L. E. ROLLER, s.v. M. of Halikarnassos, in: N. THOMSON DE GRUMMOND (ed.), An Encyclopedia of the History of Classical Archaeology, 1996, 736–737; R. W. H. STÜCKLE, Halikarnassos und das M. Zwei übersehene Abbildungen des 16. Jh., in: MDAI(Ist) 39, 1989, 561–568. C.HÖ. H.KA.

Mausoleum Augusti According to Suetonius (Augustus 100,4; cf. Str. 5,3,8) one of the earliest buildings built under Augustus on the → *Campus Martius* in Rome. It was probably begun in 28 BC, inspired in form and content by the → Maussoleum and the tomb of Alexander [4] the Great, and completed around 23 BC. A circular building with a total diameter of 87 m, it consisted of an indeterminate number of concentrical walls made of tuff, that had been several stories high and were connected by radial walls. The entire building formed an elaborately constructed → tumulus. While it had been intended as → Augustus' tomb from the outset, it was initially integrated into a public park which was lavishly landscaped. The actual tomb was at the centre of the MA, accessible through an entrance at the south side of the ground floor. This entrance was flanked by two Egyptian → obelisks, which are now in the

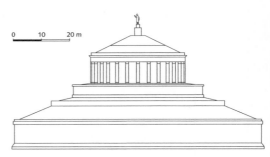

Rome, Mausoleum Augusti (schematic front elevation)

Piazza del Quirinale and Piazza Esquilino in Rome. Bronze tablets attached to nearby pillars displayed the official autobiography of the emperor – the *Res gestae divi Augusti* – for the people of the city of Rome to read. As *Monumentum Ancyranum* it is preserved in its most complete form on the walls of the entrance to the temple of Roma and Augustus in Ancyra.

The MA served as the family tomb of the *gens* Iulia; in 23 BC, Claudius [II 42] Marcellus was the first to be buried there, followed by Agrippa [1], Nero Claudius [II 24] Drusus, L. Iulius [II 33] and C. Iulius [II 32] Caesar, until in AD 14 Augustus himself was interred. Then came Drusus [II 1] Minor, Livia [2] and Tiberius. Iulia [6], Augustus' daughter, and Nero were excluded for political reasons; Caligula, however, ignored objections and added the ashes of his mother Agrippina [2] and of his brothers Nero and Drusus [II 2] Caesar (for the problem of a dynastic plan behind the various Augustan buildings on the Campus Martius see → Horologium Augusti).

The MA was a topographical benchmark for ancient Rome and was continuously known from the time of its construction through to the modern period. The reconstruction drawn by Étienne DUPÉRAC, published in *Speculum romanae magnificentiae* by Alfonse LAFRÉRY (1575), continues to inform our idea of the original building. Excavated since the 18th cent., extensively under MUSSOLINI from 1927 to 1938 (→ Fascism).
→ Ara Pacis; → Ustrinum; → Mausoleum

RICHARDSON, s.v. M.A., 247–249 (with bibliography); G. DAVIES, s.v. Mausoleum of Augustus, in: N. THOMSON DE GRUMMOND (ed.), An Encyclopedia of the History of Classical Archaeology 2, 1996, 733–736. C.HÖ.

Mausoleum Hadriani A funerary monument on the west bank of the Tiber; construction began around AD 130 under → Hadrianus and was completed in AD 139 by Antoninus Pius. In a solemn dedication ceremony Hadrian's remains were transferred from Puteoli where he had been buried provisionally. Although the MH was located in the *horti Domitiae* it directly was connected with the → Campus Martius through the newly constructed *pons Aelius* (dedicated AD 134). The two-storied circular building (diameter: *c.* 64 m; original height: c. 21 m) stood on a square base with massive

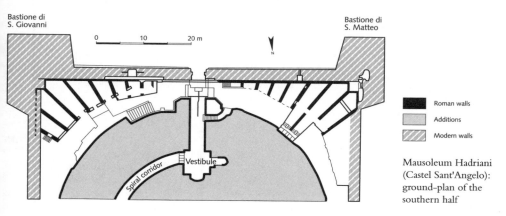

Bastione di S. Giovanni

Bastione di S. Matteo

N

0   10   20 m

Spiral corridor   Vestibule

Roman walls

Additions

Modern walls

Mausoleum Hadriani (Castel Sant'Angelo): ground-plan of the southern half

projecting corners (distance from edge to edge: c. 87 m; height: *c.* 10 m). The brick base was covered with marble slabs to which tablets with funerary inscriptions were attached. The circular mausoleum itself was accessible through a vestibule and an upward-spiralling corridor. A square central chamber of 8×8 m, entirely covered in marble, housed the mortal remains of the Roman emperors from Hadrian to the Severans.

The post-classical history of the MH is complex; many alterations to the ancient building have made it very difficult to distinguish between the ancient and post-classical phases and to reconstruct the ancient structure. In the 4th cent. the MH was integrated into the Aurelian city wall as an outwork; it served as a fort (Procop. BG 1,22,12–25) and from Theodosius' time already as a prison. For this purpose, the building was significantly modified in the 10th cent. From 1277, under Pope Nicholas III, the compound became part of the fortifications of the Vatican. It was now named 'Castel Sant'Angelo' after a small chapel. A drawing from c. 1500, preserved in the Codex Escurialensis, captures the fortress-like character of the building with its monumental post-classical and medieval alterations.

RICHARDSON, s.v. M.H., 249–251 (with further bibliography); N. THOMSON DE GRUMMOND (ed.), s.v. Castel Sant'Angelo, in: N. THOMPSON DE GRUMMOND (ed.), An Encyclopedia of the History of Classical Archaeology 1, 1996, 253–255.   C.HÖ.

Maussolus (Μαύσσωλος; *Maússōlos*, in inscriptions also Μαύσσωλλος; *Maússōllos*). → Satrap of Caria (377–353 BC), son of → Hecatomnus. The name M. is → Carian, the word formation points to Indo-European and Ancient Anatolian origins, although the etymology is not clear. M. is to be considered a preserver and supporter of ancient Anatolian and Carian culture, esp. in the area of religion (cf. [1. 57–64; 591–644]; there is little evidence for affinity with Greek cults. Nevertheless he opened himself to Greek influence and became, along with → Pericles of Limyra, a founder of Hellenism in Anatolia. He moved his royal seat from Mylasa to → Halicarnassus on the coast. He enlarged Halicarnassus, a city of Carian as well as Ionian and Dorian

tradition, through → synoikismos (Callisthenes FGrH 124 F 25) and beautified it with buildings. The → sibling marriage to his sister → Artemisia [2], which remained childless, points to Hellenistic customs as well.

Although M. participated in the satrap revolt of the 60s, he submitted to the Persian suzerainty when greater sacrifices were called for. He changed his course and pursued Persian interests in the Aegaean, along with his own. In the → Social War [1] of 357–355 between Athens and members of the → Athenian League he supported Chios, Rhodes and Cos – islands he would later control (Demosth. 15; Diod. Sic. 16,7). On the mainland he annexed Heraclea [5] on the Latmus as well as Iasus [5] and possibly re-founded Priene. Since he probably left the urban institutions intact (in Iasos → *bolḗ* and → *dḗmos* continued to exist), he was well-liked: Conspiracies against him (in Iasus) were punished by exile (Syll.3 169 = [2. no. 1]); in Caunus [2] statues of M. and his father graced the main sanctuary of the city. M.'s political influence reached far beyond his territory to Erythrae in the north, Crete in the west and Phaselis in the east. Famous Greek artists worked on his tomb, the → Maussolleum (with fig.).

→ Caria C.; → Asia Minor IV. E.

1 A. LAUMONIER, Les cultes indigènes en Carie, 1958; 2 W. BLÜMEL (ed.), Die Inschriften von Iasos, 1985.

P. BRIANT, Histoire de l'Empire Perse, 1996, 686–689; P. FREI, Zentralgewalt und Lokalautonomie, in: Transeuphratène 3, 1990, 157–171; S. HORNBLOWER, Mausolus, 1982.   P.HÖ.

Mavia Arabic princess who undertook raids in Palestine and Phoenicia c. AD 372. In 378 she made peace with → Valens and requested the hermit Moses as bishop for her people (Socr. 4,36,1–12; Sozom. Hist. eccl. 6,38,1–9; Theod. Hist. eccl. 4,23). After the battle of Hadrianopolis [3] she supported the Romans with troops (Amm. Marc. 31,16,5; Sozom. Hist. eccl. 7,1,1). She married her daughter to the *magister equitum* Victor (Socr. 4,36,12). According to Theophanes (annus mundi 5869 = 1,64,12 DEBOOR) she was a Roman by birth who had been captured by the Saracens. PLRE 1, 569.   W.P.

Mavors s. → Mars

Mavortius

Consul AD 527. M. lived in the Ostrogoth kingdom and played an important role for the transmission of literary texts. He is attested as an editor of Horace and Prudentius. He probably wrote the *Iudicium Paridis* (Anth. Lat. 1,10), perhaps also the *Cento de ecclesiis* (Anth. Lat. 1,16).

PLRE 2, 736f.   H.L.

[2] see → Lollianus [7]

Maxentius From 28 October 306 to 28 October 312, Valerius Maxentius ruled over Italy and Africa as emperor but was not recognised by his co-rulers of the 3rd → tetrarchy. As the son of the western Augustus, → Maximianus [1], and Eutropia [1] he could be seen as successor (Pan. Lat. 10,14,1), especially since – through his marriage (certainly later than 293) to Valeria → Maximilla [1], the daughter of → Galerius [5] and (through Valeria) granddaughter of → Diocletianus – he was also connected to the Iovians (→ Tetrarchy) who ruled in the East (Lactant. De mort. pers. 18,9). When the throne changed hands in 305, instead of the natural dynastic principle the tetrarchy system was applied and thereby the biological sons of co-rulers in the tetrarchy were precluded from succeeding to the throne.

Like → Constantinus [1] I M. rejected this principle; in October 306, several months after Constantine's claim to the throne, M. had himself proclaimed emperor in his villa, 16 km outside the gates of Rome, by both the Praetorian Guard, threatened in their existence by Galerius and Severus, and by the people of the city of Rome who worried about planned taxes ([Aur. Vict.] Epit. Caes. 40,2; Eutr. 10,2,3; ILS 666; 667) (cf. Lactant. De mort. pers. 26,1–3; Zos. 2,9,2–3; Aur. Vict. Caes. 40,5; Eutr. 102,3). Because M. hoped the Tetrarchic Collegium would acknowledge him later, he refrained from using the title of Augustus and instead called himself *princeps*. Yet Galerius [4] refused to acknowledge him and ordered → Severus, who had become the western Augustus, to take military action against M. (Zos. 2,10,1; Lactant. De mort. pers. 26,5). Under these circumstances, M. attempted to legitimise his rule by persuading his father Maximianus, who was in Campania, to resume the imperial office (Lactant. De mort. pers. 26,7). Severus' troops had almost reached Rome when Maximianus succeeded in inducing them to defect. He persuaded Severus, who had fled to Ravenna, to give up resistance and accept confinement near Rome. Not long thereafter Galerius marched into Italy and attempted to free Severus; however, the rescue mission failed and Severus was murdered (Anon. Vales. 10; for a different version, see Lactant. De mort. pers. 26,10–27,1). Refusing to negotiate an agreement (Anon. Vales. 7), M. fought back Galerius' advance on his own while his father stayed with Constantine. The success gave M. confidence to claim superiority over his father when the latter returned from Gaul, claiming that he had bestowed the imperial office on him (Lactant. De mort. pers. 28,1). In an assembly of soldiers and members of the urban Roman population Maximianus tried to settle the contentious issue of imperial power by tearing the purple cloak off M.'s shoulders (Lactant. De mort. pers. 28,3–4; Eutr. 10,3,1). The deposition failed and Maximianus had to leave Italy. He then (November 308) met with Diocletian and Galerius in Carnuntum (near Vienna) and → Licinius [II 4], who had been made Augustus, was ordered to fight M. (Zos. 2,11,1; Anon. Vales. 13), yet his limited resources precluded him from carrying out the order.

M.'s position was threatened as well when he temporarily lost the African provinces after → Domitius [II 4] Alexander's usurpation. In Carthage the usurpation was soon (probably in the autumn of 310) brutally suppressed by the expeditionary corps of the praetorian prefect → Ceionius [8] (Aur. Vict. Caes. 40,17–19; Zos. 2,12,1–3; 2,14,2–4) and M. celebrated a triumph (Zos. 2,14,4) in Rome. It is disputed whether Constantine was allied with Domitius Alexander against M. However, propaganda had fostered the conflict between the two rulers since 310 when M. demonstratively consecrated his father Maximianus who had been killed by Constantine (CIL IX 4516; VIII 20989; RIC 6, 382; → *consecratio*). Maximianus apparently undertook military measures in Raetia and planned an incursion into Illyricum to prepare for a conflict with Licinius (Zos. 2,14,1).

Galerius' death prompted a series of conflicts between the co-rulers, among them Constantine's offensive war (Eutr. 10,4,3; Euseb. Hist. eccl. 9,9,1) against M. In spring 312 Constantine crossed the Alps with a small elite army. M. left the defence of northern Italy to his generals, especially to the praetorian prefect Ruricius Pompeianus. M. delayed any military engagement with Constantine, who had won battles near Susa, Turin and Verona, until Constantine was in the immediate vicinity of Rome. Drawing from his experience of battles with Severus and Galerius, M. intended to stop Constantine's attack at the fortress of Rome in order to demoralise the rival's troops. Based on this reasoning, the Milvian bridge (→ Pons Milvius) across the Tiber had been destroyed. But when Constantine was a day's march away from Rome, M. changed his plans and marched out his troops over a pontoon-bridge. Constantine beat them near Saxa Rubra and in a hasty flight over the bridge the troops were annihilated. M. himself met his fate in the Tiber (Lactant. De mort. pers. 44,9; Aur. Vict.] Epit. Caes. 40,7; Zos. 2,16,4; Anon. Vales. 12). His head was impaled on a pole and paraded around Rome (Zos. 2,17,1; FGrH 219 Praxagoras T 1,4).

The victorious Constantine denied his family connection with M. by insisting that M.'s' birth was illegitimate (Pan. Lat. 9,4,3; Anon. Vales. 12; Aur. Vict.] Epit. Caes. 40,13), and denounced the defeated rival as a tyrant (cf. e.g. ILS 694; Pan. Lat. 9,4,4; 14,5; 10,8,3;

9,4); this precluded any appreciation of M.'s domestic policy.

Since M. was not part of the tetrarchy, he did not feel bound by its religious policy and stopped persecuting Christians in his part of the empire (Euseb. Hist. eccl. 8,14,1; Optatus Milevitanus 1,18); he again permitted the election of a bishop in Rome and gave back Church property (→ Tolerance). Along with M.'s alleged refusal of → *proskýnēsis* to his father and father-in-law (Lactant. De mort. pers. 18,9), his religious policy has been seen as an expression of his Christian creed; however, his consultation of ancient Roman rites immediately prior to the battle at the Milvian bridge invalidates this assumption. The consultation fits with his general imperial ideology that is informed by his idea of Rome and manifested in naming his son (born after 305 (?), appointed consul in 308 and deceased and elevated to a god in 309) Valerius Romulus, in his forceful building program (Aur. Vict. Caes. 40,26), preserved especially in the ruins of the M. Basilica, and in his coin propaganda. By focussing his propaganda on the city of Rome he hoped his hold of the capital would legitimise him in the conflict with his imperial rivals. His relationship with the people of Rome, who suffered a grain shortage during the usurpation of Domitius Alexander, appears to have been a difficult one, especially because the presence of the army in Rome was unusually high. In a bloody conflict with the military 6,000 Romans lost their lives (Chron. Min. I, p. 148,28–29; Zos. 2,13; Euseb. Hist. eccl. 8,14,3.6).

B. BLECKMANN, Konstantin der Große, 1996; M. CULLHED, Conservator urbis suae. Studies in the Politics and Propaganda of the Emperor M., 1994; D. DE DECKER, La politique religieuse de Maxence, in: Byzantion 38, 1968, 472–562; TH. GRÜNEWALD, Constantinus Maximus Augustus, 1990; KIENAST, 291–292; H. LEPPIN, M., in: M. CLAUSS (ed.), Die römischen Kaiser, 1997, 302–305.
B.BL.

Maxim see → Aphorism

Maximianus

[1] M. Aurelius Valerius M. Herculius Roman emperor, AD 286–305 or 310; on 13 December 285 (?) proclaimed Caesar by → Diocletianus and employed in the fight against the → Bagaudae (Eutr. 9,22,1; Pan. Lat. 7,8,3); after proving himself he was proclaimed Augustus on 1 April (Chron. Min. I, p. 229 f.) or 1 May 286 (cf. [1. 22]). Diocletian received him as a brother in his family, with M. acquiring the epithet Herculius while Diocletian became Iovius (→ Tetrarchy).

As Augustus, M. continued military operations in the western part of the empire, e.g. he warded off an incursion of Burgundians, Alamanni, Chaibones and Herulians into Gallia (Pan. Lat. 10,5; 11,7,2) and led campaigns into the region to the right bank of the Rhine as well as against Frankish pirates (Pan. Lat. 11,7,2). However, → Carausius had become emperor in 286 or 287 [2. 39–45] and ruled over Britain and parts of the Gaulish coast of the North Sea. His usurpation presented a problem for M. In 289, Diocletian and M. met in Raetia (Pan. Lat. 10,9,1) and planned sea operations against Carausius (Pan. Lat. 10,12,8 and 13,5); although they prepared for these by building a fleet (Pan. 10,12), they never put their plan into action. In an effort to finally settle the struggle against Carausius, Diocletian at last decided to send → Constantius [1] as Caesar to M.'s side (Aur. Vict. Caes. 39,20–24; Eutr. 9,22,1; → Tetrarchy). The new Caesar, appointed on 1 March 293, joined the family of the Herculians as M.'s adoptive son and was married (possibly already prior to his appointment) to Theodora, M.'s daughter or stepdaughter.

After 293, M. spent most of his time in Raetia or in northern Italy (on 31 March 296 in Aquileia, Fragmenta Vaticana 313). In 296, during the operations of Constantius and Asclepiodotus against → Allectus, Carausius' successor, M. rushed to the Rhine border (Pan. Lat. 8,13,2). M. fought several battles in Africa, and probably before 1 March 297 (Pan. Lat. 9,21,1–3) in the part of Mauretania that belonged to the diocese of Hispania (PArgentoratensis 480). The emperor's sojourn in Spain could explain the construction of a tetrarchic residence in Corduba [3]. In 297 [cf. 4], M. acted against the → Quinquegentanei in Mauretania Sitifensis (Aur. Vict. Caes. 39,22f.; Eutr. 9,22–23; Pan. Lat. 7,8,6; AE 1949,258). He probably visited Carthage for the first time on 10 March 298 (Fragmenta Vaticana 41); from there he fought the Ilaguas (Coripp. Johannis 1,478f.; 7,530f.) in 298. Late in 298/9 – and probably for the first time – he came to Rome (CIL VI 1130 [restored]) from Africa (Pan. Lat. 7,8,7). In November 303 he visited Rome again for a joint triumph with Diocletian on the occasion of the Vicennalia (Pan. Lat. 7,8,8; Lactant. De mort. pers. 17,1; Eutr. 9,27,2). Both emperors agreed to retire from active politics on 1 May 305. M. became Senior Augustus and retired to Lucania.

The elevation of his son → Maxentius in October 306 brought M. back to active politics; in particular, he helped capture Severus (Anonyma Valesiana 10). At the time when → Galerius [5] attacked Maxentius (307), M. visited Constantine, who was M.'s adoptive grandson through Constantius (Pan. Lat. 7,3,3). He strengthened the ties within the Herculian family by marrying his daughter → Fausta to Constantine. Constantine took advantage of this affiliation after 307 by claiming the title of Augustus that the head of the Herculians bestowed, yet he did not do much for M. in return. By late 307, M. returned to Italy where Maxentius meanwhile had single-handedly repelled Galerius' attack. His attempt to oust his son from the imperial position failed and M. had to flee back to Constantine (Lactant. De mort. pers. 29,1). In the meeting at Carnuntum (November 308) M. could not convince Diocletian to assume the joint position of senior emperor and M. had to return to Constantine once again (Lactant. De mort. pers. 29; Zos. 2,10,4–5). The Senior Augustus was given → Arelate as a residence. M. took advantage of the absence of his son-in-law who was leading a campaign against the Franks, to seize power again by handing out *donativa* (→ *donativum*) to the remnants of the troops that had remained in Arelate (Lactant. De mort. pers. 29,3–5). Constantine returned quickly and besieged M. in Massilia. M. was soon handed over by his soldiers (Lactant. De mort. pers. 29,6–8). When an alleged plan to assassinate Constantine was quickly discovered, M. was forced to commit suicide (Lactant. De mort. pers. 30,1–5). Constantine imposed → *damnatio memoriae* over him (Lactant. De mort. pers. 42,1); although Maxentius had banished his father, he nevertheless had him consecrated (Lactant. De mort. pers. 43,4 f.; Zos. 2,14 f.; RIC 6, 382) for reasons of propaganda. As Fausta's father, M. later regained significance in the propaganda of the Constantinian house. Especially in the struggle against Magnentius,→ Constantius [2] II emphasised his descent from M. and other emperors (ILS 730; 732).

1 F. KOLB, Chronologie und Ideologie der Tetrarchie, in: Antiquité Tardive 3, 1995, 21–31;   2 P. J. CASEY, Carausius and Allectus: The British Usurpers, 1994;   3 R. HIDALGO, A. VENTURA VILLANUEVA, Sobre la cronología e interpretación del palacio de Cercadilla en Córduba, in: Chiron 24, 1994, 221–237;   4 R. REBUFFAT, Maximien en Afrique, in: Klio 74, 1992, 171–179.

J. ARCE, Un relieve triunfal de Maximiano Herculeo en Augusta Emerita y el Pap. Argent. Inv. 480, in: Madrider Mitteilungen 23, 1982, 359–371; T. D. BARNES, The New Empire of Diocletian and Constantine, 1982; F. KOLB, Diokletian und die Erste Tetrarchie, 1987; A. PASQUALINI, Massimiano Herculius. Per un' interpretazione della figura e dell' opera, 1979; KIENAST, 272–275.   B.BL.

[2] see → Galerius [5] Maximianus
[3] **Maximianus of Pola** Bishop of Ravenna after AD 546. In the Three-Chapter Controversy (controversy surrounding the major representatives of the Antiochene Christology [Theodorus of Mopsuestia, Theodoretus of Cyrrhus, Ibas of Edessa] in the Fifth Ecumenical Council of Constantinople in 553), M. sided with the Emperor Justinian. He built numerous churches, consecrated San Vitale and S. Apollinare in Classe, donated liturgical implements and encouraged the veneration of relics; an ivory throne (cathedra of M.) carries his monogram. Through the *Liber Pontificalis* (book of the bishops of Ravenna; similar to the → *Liber Pontificalis* of the city of Rome) of Agnellus (early 9th cent.) he also became known as an author of exegetic and liturgical books and of a chronicle (on M., 1136–146; vol. 2. 1, 300–337]). M. is surrounded by legends, especially concerning his relationship to the Emperor Justinian.

1 D. MAUSKOPF-DELIYANNIS (ed.), The Liber Pontificalis ecclesiae Ravennatis, 1994; 2 C. NAUERTH, Agnellus von Ravenna, Liber Pontificalis, Bischofsbuch, Fontes Christiani 21/1.2 (transl. and introduction), 1996.   CL.NA.

[4] Roman elegiac poet of the 6th cent. AD. From the 15th to the 18th cent., M.'s six chiastically arranged elegies ([15. 365]; cf. [4. 65 ff.]) of various length, for the first time preserved completely in MSS of the 11th/12th cents., [12] and in part with an appendix of shorter poems (the so-called *Appendix Maximiani*) (4,26 M.), were attributed to Cornelius [II 18] Gallus, although M. was named explicitly [3. 15 ff.; 8. 277 f.]. At the outset M. reveals himself as an old man (1,1 ff.) (hardly justifiable doubts on the biographical content: [2; 11]): An 'Etruscan' by birth (5,5; 5,40), he claims to have been a poet and world-renowned orator (1,37; 1,63) in Rome (1,9–14). A peace mission (of uncertain date) into the Eastern Roman Empire (5,1–3) and a former friendship with → Boethius (died 524) (3,47) are mentioned. His poems are original, although not always as far as impeccable prosody is concerned; their language is mostly inspired by → Ovid [14; 9]; topics of the uniquely Roman love elegy [6; 10] are combined with the tone of lament – in antiquity first associated with → elegy [3. 84 f.]. The lament is usually about the afflictions of old age, described in detail (1; 6); M. specifically finds himself deserted by his companion of many years (2) and in a love affair with a Greek woman his virility fails him (5). The curious culmination of the cycle, whose hero once was able but unwilling (see esp. 1,73 ff.) and who now is willing but unable, is an obscene hymn to the *mentula* (penis), elevated by the disappointed Greek woman to a cosmic power comparable to *amor* in Boethius [14. 112 f.] (5,87 ff.).

The overall interpretation of the last Roman elegiac poet (satire [13], allegorical instruction [3], or even 'protreptics for the monastic ideal' [11]) is extremely controversial. Because he warns against the foolish desire for a long life, M. was considered an *ethicus* in the Middle Ages and was read in schools [7. 25]. Even [15], a father of modern gerontology, cites him extensively as an authority. A modern English translation and an adequate critical edition remains to be desired (cf. [5]).
→ Elegy

EDITIONS.: 1 PLM, vol. 5, 1883, 313–348; 2 R. WEBSTER, 1900 (with comm.); 3 T. AGOZZINO, 1970 (comm.; text acc. to PLM); 4 F. SPALTENSTEIN, 1983 (comm.; text acc. to PLM).
BIBLIOGRAPHY: 5 CH. SEQUI, Appendice bibliografica, in: P. MASTANDREA et al. (ed.), Concordantia in Maximianum, 1995, 177–196.
LITERATURE: 6 A. FO, Significato, tecniche e valore della racolta elegiaca di M., in: Hermes 115, 1987, 348–371; 7 R. B. C. HUYGENS (ed.), Accessus ad auctores, 1970; 8 U. JAITNER-HAHNER, M. und der Fucus Italicus, in: M. BORGOLTE (ed.), Litterae medii aevi, FS J.Autenrieth, 1988, 277–292; 9 P. MASTANDREA, Loci similes, in: Concordantia, s. [5], 125–176; 10 P. PINOTTI, M. elegiaco, in: G. CATANZARO (ed.), Tredici secoli di elegia latina, 1989, 183–203; 11 CH. RATKOWITSCH, Maximianus amat, 1986 (in: WS 103, 1990, 207–239); 12 W. SCHETTER, Studien zur Überlieferung und Kritik des Elegikers M., 1970; 13 J. SZÖVÉRFFY, M. a Satirist?, in: HSPh 72, 1967, 351–367; 14 F. WILHELM, M. und Boethius, in: RhM 62, 1907, 601–614; 15 GABRIELE ZERBI, Gerontocomia, 1489.   W.STR.

Maximilla

[1] **Valeria Maximilla** Daughter of → Galerius [5] and wife of → Maxentius. The marriage produced two sons, Valerius Romulus (died 309?) and another son who is mentioned along with her as late as 312 (Pan. Lat. 12,16,5).

PLRE 1, 576   B.BL.

[2] In the middle of the 2nd. cent. AD she founded, together with Montanus and → Priscilla, the Christian revivalist movement of → Montanism. She was also a writer (Hippolytus, *Refutatio omnium haeresium* 8,19,1), but only a few of her prophetic sayings have survived (collected in [1. 145 f.]). M. saw herself as the last prophet before the end of the world (Epiphanius [1] of Salamis, Panarion 48,2,4).

> 1 K. ALAND, Bemerkungen zum Montanismus und zur frühchristlichen Eschatologie, in: Id., Kirchengeschichtliche Entwürfe, 1960, 105–148.   M.HE.

Maximinus

[1] **M. Daia** Roman emperor, AD 305–313. The son of → Galerius' [5] sister and like Galerius born in Dacia ripensis, possibly in Šarkamen (modern Serbia), he rose from *protector* to *tribunus* (Lactant. De mort. pers. 19,6); as Galerius' adoptive son he became Caesar in the change of rulers of 305 (thereafter: Galerius Valerius Maximinus). As co-ruler over the diocese Oriens he continued the persecutions of Christians (Euseb. Hist. eccl. 8,14,9). Like → Constantinus [1] not content with the title of Caesar, M. proclaimed himself Augustus in 310, since the title *filius Augustorum* offered to him by Galerius as a compromise was not enough for him (Lactant. De mort. pers. 32,5).

After Galerius' death (May 311) M. seized Asia Minor and advanced to the Bosporus. A military confrontation between → Licinius [II 4] and M. was only just avoided (Lactant. De mort. pers. 36,1–2). As the longest-serving emperor, M. at first held the highest rank in the new joint rule (MAMA I 19; VII 8) and as head of the Iovians (see → Diocletianus B.) he intended to continue the tetrarchic heritage (→ Tetrarchy). Thus he attempted to marry Valeria, the widow of Galerius and daughter Diocletian, and betrothed his daughter to Canidianus, Valeria's adoptive son (Lactant. De mort. pers. 50,6); he also tried to continue the tetrarchic religious policy: He organised the communities to petition against Galerius' Edict of Toleration that he himself had temporarily accepted (Euseb. Hist. eccl. 9,7; CIL III 12132; [1]); he used the forged Acts of Pilate as anti-Christian propaganda (Euseb. Hist. eccl. 9,5,9; → Tolerance); imitating the Christian episcopal system, he appointed pagan high-priests on the polis and provincial level (Lactant. De mort. pers. 36, 4–5). These measures recall the religious policy of Iulianus [11] and explain the favourable assessment of M. in pagan literature ([Aur. Vict.] Caes. 40,18–19), whereas the other sources paint a rather negative portrait of an emperor prone to excesses (Lactant. De mort. pers. 37–38; Euseb. Hist. eccl. 8,14,8–18).

Shortly after the conclusion of the marital alliance between Licinius and Constantine (see → Constantia [1]) when, with the consent of the Senate, M. was ousted from the highest position in the joint rule, civil war broke out between Licinius and M. in spring 313. In July 313, M. fled and died from an illness in Tarsus (Aur. Vict. Caes. 41,1; Eutr. 10,4,4; Zos. 2,17,3; for a different version, see Lactant. De mort. pers. 49,2–7). Immediately after his military defeat at the Thracian Campus Ergenus (Lactant. De mort. pers. 46,10), he had adopted the religious policy agreed upon by Constantine and Licinius near Milan, so as to win the loyalty of the Christians in his part of the empire. Licinius killed M.'s family and his most important followers (Euseb. Hist. eccl. 9,10,3–11,8).

> 1 S. MITCHELL, M. and the Christians in A.D. 312. A New Latin Inscription, in: JRS 78, 1988, 105–124.

H. CASTRITIUS, Studien zu M. Daia, 1969; I. POPOVIĆ, M. TOMOVIĆ, Golden Jewellery from the Imperial Mausoleum at Sarkamen (Eastern Serbia), in: Antiquité tardive 6, 1998, 287–312.   B.BL.

[2] **M. Thrax** Imperator Caesar C. Iulius Verus M. Roman emperor, AD 235–238, born 172 or 173 (Zon. 12,16; Chron. pasch. I, p. 501 D.) in → Thracia, of humble origin (Hdn. 6,8,1; fictional: SHA Maximini duo (= Max.) 1,5 and Iord. Get. 15,83); the epithet *Thrax* ('the Thracian') is documented only for the late 4th cent.

Under → Septimius Severus, M. completed the *militae equestris*, including service in the cavalry; the various offices are not known. Around 215, M. married Caecilia Paulina (Hdn. 6,8,1; SHA Max. 2,2 ff.; Iord. Get. 15,84–87; [1. 86 f.]).

From 231 to 233, during the Persian Wars, M. successfully commanded troops in Mesopotamia (Hdn. 7,8,4; Iord. Get. 15,88); in 234, Severus Alexander ordered him to the Rhine as *praefectus tironibus* to prepare the army for the campaign against the Germans [1. 86 f.]. In February/March 235 the soldiers proclaimed him emperor although he had not yet reached senatorial rank and killed Severus Alexander (Hdn. 6,8,4–5; 9,6; SHA Max. 8,1; Aur. Vict. Caes. 25,1; Eutrop. 9,1; CIL VI 2001; 2009; IGR 3, 1213). M. led the army against the Germans, laid waste their homes (Hdn. 7,2; Aur. Vict. Caes. 26,1; SHA Max. 11,7–12,6) and as victor he took the title *Germanicus Maximus*. He elevated his son Iulius [II 145] to the rank of Caesar; in 236 he held the regular consulship (CIL XIII 8954; RIC 4,2,143 f.; Aur. Vict. Caes. 25,2). Later he fought Sarmatians and Dacians near the Danube, apparently successfully (epithet *Dacicus* and *Sarmaticus Maximus*: CIL II 4757; 4826; 4853; 4870). As early as 235 M. persecuted the Christian clergy for political reasons, with only localised repercussions (Euseb. Hist. eccl. 6,28).

Because of the high financial needs, esp. for the army, M. soon faced wide opposition (Hdn. 7,3), resulting in the uprising of the Gordiani (→ Gordianus [1–2]) in Africa in 238; the uprising spread to Italy through the initiative of the majority in the Senate that was hostile towards M. [2. 197]. In the middle of January 238, the Senate majority declared M. and his son *hostes publici* ('public enemies') and encouraged the governors to defect (Hdn. 7,7,2; 7,7,4–6; SHA Max. 15,2). From the Danube, M. marched to Northern Italy and unsuccessfully besieged well-defended Aquileia. Around the middle of 238 the soldiers finally mutineered and killed M. and his son. M.'s name was subject to *damnatio memoriae* (Hdn. 7,8; 7,12,8; 8,1–5; SHA Max. 21–23; SHA Max. Balb. 11,2; Zos. 1,15).

1 A. LIPPOLD, Der Kaiser M. Thrax und der römische Senat, in: Bonner Historia Augusta Colloquium 1966/7, 1968; 2 T. KOTULA, L'insurrection des Gordiens et l'Afrique romaine, in: EOS 50, 1959/1960.

A. BELLEZZA, Massimo il Trace, 1964; DIETZ; KIENAST, 138ff.; X. LORIOT, Les premières années de la grande crise du IIIe siècle ... , in: ANRW II.2, 1975, 657–787; M. PEACHIN, Roman Imperial Titulature, 26f.; PIR² M 619.

T.F.

[3] High-ranking official during the rule of → Valentinianus I; a lawyer from Sopianae in the province of Valeria. Between *c*. AD 364 and 368 he successively controlled the provinces of Corsica, Sardinia and Tuscia. 368/370 he was *praefectus annonae*, 370–371 *vicarius urbis*, 371–376 *praefectus praetorio Galliarum*. Several laws addressed to him have been preserved (Cod. Theod. 9,24,3; 9,6,1 f.; 9,19,4 etc.). In Rome he brought against the senatorial aristocracy numerous cases for witchcraft, poisoning and adultery (Amm. Marc. 28,1,5–57; Symmachus, Or. 4,11, Symmachus, Ep. 10,2). → Gratianus [2] had him decapitated (Amm. Marc. 28,1,57). PLRE 1, 577 f. no. 7. W.P.

[4] East Roman official from a respected family, AD 449 envoy of → Theodosius II to → Attila, fought in Isauria in 450 and in 453, probably as *comes rei militaris*, in the Egyptian Thebaid. He negotiated a '100-year' peace with the Nobadii and Blemmyes; however it never went into effect since he died soon afterwards. PLRE 2, 743 no. 11. F.T.

[5] Bishop of Trier (Augusta [6] Treverorum), died after 346, advisor of Emperor Constans, supporter of → Athanasius, whom he knew from his first exile (336/7; Jer. Chron. ad annum 343). Together with → Iulius [III 1] of Rome and → Ossius of Corduba he called in the Council of Serdica in 342/3. He could not personally attend it and the eastern bishops imposed a ban on him (Hil. Collectanea antiariana A 4,1,27; Socr. 3,11,7). He ratified the decrees of Serdica belatedly in Gallia, probably only on 5 December 346, but not at the fictitious Synod of Cologne.
→ Arianism

G. ISSELSTEIN, E. SAUSER, s.v. M., LThK³ 7, 8 (Lit.).

[6] Arian bishop of Gothic origin (probably Illyria); his dates are controversial (between 365/70–450). In the first half of the 5th cent. he wrote a comm. on the acts of the Council of Aquileia (381) and on the letter of bishop Auxentius of Milan (Ambrosius' predecessor); in addition to an Arian confession of faith, it contains biographical data for the Gothic bishop → Ulfila. He is credited with a *Dissertatio contra Ambrosium* and various homiletic treatises. As a Gothic military bishop he may have debated in 427/8 with Augustine (Aug. Contra Maximinum Arrianum PL 42,743–814; Aug. Contra Sermonem Arrianorum PL 42,683–708).

WORKS: SChr 267, 1980; CCL 87, 1982.
BIBLIOGRAPHY: R. KANY, s.v. M., Gotenbischof, in: S. DÖPP, W. GEERLINGS (ed.), Lexikon der antiken christlichen Literatur, 1998, 432f. O.WER.

Maximius Attianus Senator; quaestor in the province of Asia in AD 209 at the earliest (AE 1998, 1361 f.); positively identical to the consular governor of Germania superior in 229 AD.

ECK, Statthalter, 91 f. W.E.

Maximus (Μάξιμος; *Máximos*).
I. GREEK II. ROMAN

I. GREEK

[1] **Maximus of Tyre** AD 2nd cent.; author of 41 short *dialéxeis* (lectures), according to the most important MS (Cod. Parisinus graecus 1962) delivered in Rome (the Suda dates a visit to the reign of Commodus, AD 180–191). His concepts are simple yet rhetorically sophisticated (frequent use of comparisons, quotations from poetry, mythological and historical examples); his main topic is ethics, but he also touches on physics, theology and epistemology, e.g. pleasure (*hēdonḗ*, 29–33), Socratic love (18–21), Platonic theology (11), *daímones* (8–9), prayer (5), prophecy and free will (13), evil (41), and recovery of memory (10). Noteworthy is his assessment of the various forms of discourse (poetry, oratory, historiography) in relation to philosophy (1, 4, 17, 22, 25, 26). Although M. avoids any explicit affinity to Plato (he only despises Epicurus), he actually is a (Middle-)Platonist with a special interest in Plato's Socrates. As a philosophical orator he may be compared to Dio Chrysostom, Favorinus and Apuleius. M. was read by the Humanists of the 15th cent. and by their teachers and students (LANDINO, FICINO, POLIZIANO; BESSARION, LASCARIS; REUCHLIN) as well, but has not been studied much since then.
→ Middle Platonism; → Second Sophistic

EDNS.: M. TRAPP, 1994; G. KONIARIS, 1995.; Comm.: ; A. F. SCOGNAMILLO, 1997 (18 only).; Transl.: ; M. TRAPP, 1997.
LIT.: G. SOURY, Aperçus de philososophie religieuse, 1942; G. KONIARIS, On M. of Tyre: Zetemata 1, in: Classical Antiquity 1, 1982, 87–121; Id., On M. of Tyre: Zetemata 2, in: Classical Antiquity 2, 1983, 212–250; J. PUIGGALI, Étude sur les Dialexeis de M. de Tyre, 1983.

M.T.

[2] Author of an astrological didactic poem of which a total of *c.* 615 verses in hexameter and a paraphrase in prose have been preserved. Not before the 2nd cent. AD, highly unlikely to be identical with the Neoplatonist → M. [4] of Byzantium. In 12 sections, of which the first 3 ¹/₂ are lost, the poem Περὶ καταρχῶν ('On Choosing the Right Moment') discusses: 1. Birth, 2. purchase of slaves, 3. seafaring and commerce, 4. travels, 5. marriage, 6. disease, 7. surgical interventions, 8. runaway slaves, 9. instruction of children, 10. farming, 11. captivity, 12. theft. The four cardinal points of the daily rotation are not crucial as they are elsewhere, but the position of the moon in the zodiac is and so are the planets and some → paranatellonta. M. uses → Dorotheus [5] of Sidon and is in turn used by → Nonnus.
→ Astrology; → Didactic poetry

EDN.: A. LUDWICH, 1877; a new edn. was planned by D. PINGREE (†).
LIT.: W. and H. G. GUNDEL, Astrologumena, 1966, 234f.
W.H.

[3] **M. of Lycia** (Lib. Ep. 1384). We know of the Neoplatonist who taught in Athens only through Libanius. Severus of Lycia, a relative and friend of Libanius, was one of his students (Lib. Ep. 309; 659; 665; 1384; 1451). M. died before AD 361. (Lib. Ep. 665. 1451).

[4] Born in Byzantium; according to Socr. 3,1,16,327a, father of one Euclides. The Suda (s.v. Μάξιμος, 3, 322.1–4 EAGLE) is uncertain whether the place of origin was Epirus or Byzantium, probably by confusing him with M. [5] of Ephesus (a fellow student of Priscus) and the rhetor M. [1] (probably the author of Περὶ τῶν ἀληθῶν ἀντιθέσεως). M. may be identical with the Christian M., the addressee of a letter from Basil (Basil. Epist. 9) before AD 361/2. Several of the writings attributed to M. by the Suda (Περὶ καταρχῶν cf. M. [2]; Περὶ ἀριθμῶν; Ὑπόμνημα εἰς Ἀριστοτέλην) might actually be his.

[5] **M. of Ephesus** Neoplatonist of the 4th cent. AD. The most important information about M. comes from Eunapius (Eun. Vit. soph. 7,1–8,1), who claims to have met him in his youth (probably AD 369). This detailed, rhetorically exaggerated testimony, presented in novelistic style, as was typical for Eunapius, fashions M. into a martyr for → theurgy while accusing him of a too provocative stance towards Christians.

M. was a student of → Aedesius [1] (this provides a date) and followed the lead of the Neoplatonist → Iamblichus [2], who made theurgy the predominant element in his philosophy. M. introduced emperor → Iulianus [11] to this philosophical outlook. By predicting misfortune for Greece and its traditional religion, he inspired Julian to renew the pagan religion with Platonic inspiration.

Called to Constantinople by Julian in 362, M. gained great influence at court although he also had numerous enemies. In 363 he accompanied the emperor on his campaign against the Persians and (along with Priscus) he was with the fatally wounded Julian in the

last moments of his life (Amm. Marc. 25,3,23). Under Jovian, M. was still an imperial favourite; his problems began under Valentinian and Valens: He was arrested together with Priscus, but was released in 367 through the intervention of Clearchus, the *vicarius Asiae*. He returned to Constantinople where his declamations were met with moderate success while his philosophical instruction was very successful. In 371, when M. predicted to Valens 'death without burial', he was arrested and sent to Antioch [1] for trial. Found guilty, he was transported back to Ephesus and executed under the proconsul Festus in 372.

Julian. Ep. 26, 190 and 191, as well as Lib. Ep. 694 are addressed to M.. Simplicius' statement in his commentary on Categories – that M. wrote a similar work agreeing in almost every point with Alexander [26] of Aphrodisias – is probably accurate (Simpl. in Aristot. Cat. CAG VIII, p. 1,14–16 VEAL). Iamblichus, a passionate theurgist, also wrote a commentary on Categories, Simplicius' declared model. Suda s.v. Μάξιμος, 3, 322,1–4 EAGLE seems to confuse M. with M. [4].
→ Neoplatonism; → Theurgy

J. BOUFFARTIGUE, L'empereur Julien et la culture de son temps (Collection des Études augustiniennes, Série antiquité 133), 1992; R. GOULET, Sur la chronologie de la vie et des Œuvres d'Eunape de Sardes, in: JHS 100, 1980, 60–72.
L.BR.

[6] Christian Cynic from Alexandria. In 379 he supported → Gregorius [3] of Nazianzus in establishing the orthodox community in Constantinople; on the urging of Petrus, the bishop of Alexandria, M. was installed there as bishop in 380. The choice was supported in the West, but it found neither the approval of → Theodosius the Great nor of the Council of Constantinople, which declared it invalid in 381.
H.L.

[7] **Maximus Homologetes** (Maximus Ὁμολογητής/ *Homologētḗs*, 'the Confessor').
A. LIFE   B. WRITINGS/THEOLOGY

A. LIFE
The historicity of the Greek *vita* of M. with its encomiastic traits was put in perspective when it was shown to have been compiled only later [2], as well as by the Syrian *vita* [3] that gives a reliable account, its Monophysite polemics (→ Monophysitism) notwithstanding. According to it, M. was born around AD 580 in Hesfin (Palestine) as the son of a Samaritan merchant and a Persian slave woman and given the name Moschion (Μοσχίων). As an orphan he was placed at the Laura monastery of St. Chariton near Tekoa. There he was named M. and educated by abbot Pantaleon. During the Persian siege of Constantinople (626) he went to North Africa. There he opposed the Monenergetic and Monotheletic positions (→ Monotheletism) of the patriarchs → Sergius and Pyrrhus. He rejected the Pro-monotheletic efforts of the decree (ψῆφος) of 634 and of the edict (ἔκθεσις) of → Heraclius [7] of 638. In 649, under Pope Martin I, he attended the Lateran Synode in Rome that condemned Monotheletism and assisted in

compiling the acts. In 653 he was exiled to → Bizye in Thrace. In 662, after the re-opening of his case had failed, he was tortured and mutilated (he lost his tongue and hand) in Constantinople and exiled to → Lazica where he died on 13 August of the same year. In 680, the 3rd Ecumenical Synode of Constantinople rehabilitated him and canonised his teaching of two wills in Christ. He received the epithet 'Confessor' (*Confessor* or *Homologētḗs*).

B. Writings/Theology

M. is the most important and discerning theological writer of the 7th cent. In his writings he developed a mystical theology that has at its core the deification of man and that emphasises the absolute pre-eminence of God in the unity. His thought synthesises ancient and patristic traditions (→ Gregorius [3] of Nazianzus and (Ps.-)→ Dionysius [54] Areopagita). His fight against → Monotheletism was a struggle for apophatic theology, preserving the opposition of God and man. In the Occident, M. gained influence through the translations of Iohannes Scotus Eriugena and → Anastasius [3] Apokrisiarios.

1 CPG 3, no. 7688–7711, 7715–7721; 2 W. LACKNER, Zu Quellen und Datierung der Maximusvita (BHG3 1234), in: Analecta Bollandiana 85, 1967, 285–316; 3 S. BROCK, An Early Syriac Life of Maximus the Confessor, in: Analecta Bollandiana 91, 1973, 299–346; 4 K. SAVVIDIS, Die Lehre von der Vergöttlichung des Menschen bei M. dem Bekenner und ihre Rezeption durch Gregor Palamas, 1997. K.SA.

II. Roman

Roman *cognomen*, originally probably indicating special merits (e.g. Plut. Pompey 13,11) or birth order (*maximus natus*). In the Republic it was passed down in the patrician families of the Valerii and (after the → Samnite Wars) of the Fabii (Fabius [I 21–30; II 13–14]), later in other *gentes* as well (→ Carvilius [3–4]; list of the names [1. 2539]). See also → Maximus I.

1 F. MÜNZER, M. FLUSS, s.v. M., RE 14, 1930; 2 KAJANTO, Cognomina, 71–74, 275f.; 3 J. REICHMUTH, Die lateinische Gentilicia, 1956, 47. K.-L.E.

[1] Senator, according to Pliny (Epist. 8,24,7) → Traianus sent him to Achaia to set in order the political status of the free cities (*ad ordinandum statum liberarum civitatum*). Probably identical with S. Quintilius Valerius Maximus (PIR² Q s.v. Quintilius).
[2] Consular officer in Trajan's → Parthian War; defeated by the Parthian king Arsaces and killed in AD 116 (Cass. Dio 68,30,1f.). In that context Fronto mentions a certain Appius Santra. It is controversial whether both of them are identical and whether the name in Fronto (p. 212, 20 ff. VAN DEN HOUT) is read correctly (PIR² A 950); possibly identical with T. Iulius [II 97] Maximus (cf. [1]).

1 SYME, RP 1, 249; 5, 567ff.

[3] Freedman of → Traianus and *procurator* in Pontus-Bithynia under Virdius Gemellinus (Plin. Ep. 10,27; 28; 85). Since Virdius Gemellinus probably was a patrimonial rather than a general fiscal procurator, Maximus probably only worked for the → *patrimonium*.
[4] Freedman of → Parthenius, Domitian's *a cubiculo* (chamberlain). Following orders of his patron, he and the *cornicularius* Clodianus killed Domitian in AD 96. PIR² M 429.
[5] Numerous addressees by this name in → Plinius's collection of letters. It is largely controversial how to identify the persons and to figure out to whom precisely the information applies (cf. most recently [1. 708]).

1 SYME, RP 2.

[6] Defended Marcianupolis in Thrace against the Goths in AD 248. PIR² M 427.

CHR. HABICHT, Beiträge zur Prosopographie der altgriechischen Welt, in: Chiron 2, 1972, 129ff. W.E.

[7] **Magnus Maximus** Usurper, AD 383–388. Spaniard; his date of birth is unknown. Maximus served his way up under the emperor's father, Theodosius, and in 369 took part in his campaign to Britain. Later he became *comes Britanniarum*, and in spring 383 the troops proclaimed him emperor against → Gratianus [2] (Pan. Lat. 2,23; 38). M. quickly crossed over to Gallia where Gratianus' army joined him, thereby expanding his territory to Britain, Gallia, and Spain. Gratianus was ambushed and killed by his own troops.

From his residence in Trier (Augusta [6] Treverorum), M. initiated negotiations with → Valentinianus II and → Theodosius I. He tried to persuade the young emperor of the West to come to Trier to him; in a first legation (Ambr. Epist. 30,3–7) to M., → Ambrosius managed to delay until he had Italy secured against an invasion. Nevertheless, Valentinian and Theodosius had no other choice but to *de facto* recognise the usurper. In spring 387, Ambrosius undertook a second legation to Trier to ask for the corpse of Gratianus, but M. refused (Ambr. Epist. 30). In summer 387, M. invaded Italy without warning; encountering only negligible resistance, he occupied it and took reside in → Aquileia [1] (Zos. 4,42–43; Socr. 5,11–12). Valentinian II fled to the East. In spring 388, Theodosius undertook a counter-campaign and defeated M. in one naval and several land battles (Poetovio, Siscia; cf. Pan. Lat. 2,34–35, the naval battle under Valentinian's command near Sicily). Although Theodosius wanted to spare M., angry soldiers killed him on 28 August. His family and supporters were treated with clemency.

As a Christian, M. had adopted the Nicene Creed, a circumstance he used repeatedly to interfere with Valentinian's politics (Avell. 39). Gaulish-Spanish bishops persuaded him to proceed rigorously against the Priscillianists (→ Priscillianus), and a trial in 384/5 resulted in several death sentences (Pan. Lat. 2,29; Sulp. Sev. 2,49–50).

H. R. BALDUS, Theodosius der Große und die Revolte des Magnus Maximus – das Zeugnis der Münzen, in: Chiron 14, 1984, 175–192; K. GROSS-ALBENHAUSEN, Imperator christianissimus, 1999, 94–99.   K.G.-A.

[8] **Flavius Petronius M.** Member of a rich senatorial family. Born AD 396, he had a brilliant career: *c.* 415–417 *comes sacrarum largitionum*, 420/421 and again later (433?) *praefectus urbi*, 433 and 443 consul; he must have been *praef. praet.* before 439, 439/441 documented as *praef. praet. II*, *patricius*. M. allegedly was behind the murders of → Aetius [2] in 454 and of → Valentinianus III in 455. On 17 March 455, M. was acknowledged as emperor. By marrying → Eudoxia [2] and by marrying his son and Caesar Palladius to a daughter of Valentinian he attempted to establish a dynastic legitimisation. When the Vandal → Geiseric attacked Rome in 455, he tried to flee but was killed by a mob on 31 May 455. The soldiers apparently never held M. in high regard. Christian.

PLRE II 749–751; DELMAIRE, 190–194.

[9] Legate of the Roman senate to → Constantius [2] II in AD 361. After his stay in Antioch, he met → Iulianus [11] I near Naissus (modern Niš); on the recommendation of Vulcacius → Rufinus, the latter appointed him to the office of Roman city prefect (Symmachus, Relat. 34,5). Pagan. PLRE I 582.
[10] M. of Raphia in Palaestina; AD 359/62 *p raeses Armeniae*, 362/3 governor in Galatia, supported Ancyra through building activity; in 364 *praefectus Aegypti*; friend of → Libanius; not a Christian. PLRE I 583.
[11] In AD 409, → Gerontius [3] proclaimed him emperor against → Constantinus [3] III; he fled to Spain in 411. Probably identical with the usurper, proclaimed in Spain in 418 and soon thereafter captured by imperial troops and executed in Ravenna in 422. PLRE II 744 f.

[12] **Flavius Maximus** Consul AD 523, *primicerius domesticus* 535, *patricius*, married an Ostrogoth princess. As one of the suspicious senators, he was removed from Rome by → Belisarius. The Goths murdered M. in 552 in Campania. PLRE II 748 f.   H.L.
[13] **M. of Madaura.** Correspondent of → Augustinus and *grammaticus* in Madaura in the 2nd half of the 4th cent. One of his letters, written around 390, has been preserved (Aug. Epist. 16) together with Augustine's answer (Epist. 17). M., who very likely was the teacher of the adolescent Augustine, addresses his former, now famous, pupil. While defending Roman polytheism, he points out contrasts with the Christian cult. M. requests explanations about the Christian God and asks Augustine for a conciliatory attitude and mutual understanding. Augustine's answer is decidedly cool and written in an apologetic tone.

A. GOLDBACHER (ed.), CSEL 34,1895; C. WENDEL s.v. M. (42), RE 14, 2571; P. MASTANDREA, Massimo di Madauros, Padua 1985 (with edn.).   P.G.

[14] **M. Taurinensis** M. was bishop of Turin at least from 398 and died between 408 and 423 (Gennadius, Vir. ill. 40); apparently he was not originally from Turin (sermo 33,1). 111 *sermones* (homilies) by him, for the most part authentic, have been preserved (CPL 221; PL 57, 221–760 contains sermons by bishop M. II of Turin, c. 451–465, as well along with fakes after [Ps.-]Augustine and Leo I of Rome; for criticism regarding the authenticity of [1] cf. [4; 7; 8; 9]). The brevity of M.'s authentic sermons has repeatedly led to the assumption that only excerpts of the originals have been preserved [10. 290; 5]. Since M.'s sermons are topical rather than exegetic, many of them deal with contemporary topics, such as the holidays of the Church year, biblical figures and saints, but also with the remnants of pagan religion in Northern Italy, e.g. on country estates (sermo 30 f., 98, 107 f.). M. also is also familar with → Ambrosius (sermo 95 f.), whom he probably did not meet in person. In his sermons M. is primarily the pastor of his community; he wants to save it from theological confusion and ethical errors.

EDN.: 1 A. MUTZENBECHER, CCL 23, 1962.
LITERATURE: 2 G. BANTERLE, Massimo di Torino, I sermoni, 1992; 3 D. DEVOTI, Massimo di Torino e il suo pubblico, in: Augustinianum 21, 1981, 153–167; 4 H. J. FREDE, Kirchenschriftsteller, 1995, 636–640; 5 O. HEGGELBACHER, Das Gesetz im Dienste des Evangeliums, 1961; 6 M. MODEMANN, Die Taufe in den Predigten des heiligen M. von Turin (Europäische Hochschulschriften. Theologie 537) 1995; 7 A. MUTZENBECHER, Zur Überlieferung des M.T., in: Sacris erudiri 6, 1954, 343–372; 8 Ead., Bestimmung der echten Sermones des M.T., in: ibid. 1,2 1961, 197–293; Ead., Der Festinhalt von Weihnachten und Epiphanie in den echten Sermones des M.T. (Studia Patristica 95 = TU 80), 1962, 109–116; 10 H. G. OPITZ, s.v. M. (26), RE Suppl. 6, 289f.   C.M.

Maxula (Μαξοῦλα/*Maxoûla*). City in the province of Africa proconsularis (→ Africa [3]), to the east of Tynes, modern Radès. Sources: Ptol. 4,3,7 (Μαξοῦλα/*Maxoûla*); 4,3,34 (Μαξοῦλα παλαιά/*Maxoûla palaiá*); It. Ant. 57,3 (*M. Prates*); 58,1 (*M. Civitas*); Tab. Peut. 6,1; Stadiasmus Maris Magni 122f. (GGM 1,471); Geogr. Rav. 88,38. Since it was located by the sea, it is possible that at times the Greeks (also) called it *Leukòs Týnes* (Λευκὸς Τύνης, Diod. Sic. 20,8,7) [1. 66–68]. Traces of Punic influence have been found [2. 292–295]. In Pliny (Plin. HN 5,24) and in inscriptions (CIL VIII Suppl. 112253; 4, 24328; AE 1949, 175), M. is -probably by mistake – described as a *colonia*. Inscriptions: CIL VIII Suppl. 1, 12458–12461; 4, 24328–24330.

1 W. HUSS, Neues zur Zeit des Agathokles, in: ZPE 39, 1980, 63–71; 2 C. G. PICARD, Cat. du Musée Alaoui. Nouvelle série, Bd. 1,1, n.d. (= Cb 1072–1074); 3 L. TEUTSCH, Das Städtewesen in Nordafrika... , 1962.

AATun 050, Bl. 21, Nr. 2; M. SCHWABE, s.v. M., RE 14, 2576.   W.HU.

Mazaeus (Μαζαῖος; *Mazaîos*). Persian nobleman, highly respected at the Achaemenid court (Curt. 5,1,18; Plut. Alexander 39), father of Antibelus, Artiboles and Hydarnes. Under → Artaxerxes [3] III, M. was satrap of Cilicia and Persian commander in the war against the rebellious Phoenicians (Diod. Sic. 16,42,1f.). Under → Darius [3] III, he administered → Coele Syria and 'Syria between the rivers'. In 331 BC, he withdrew from his position near Thapsacus, enabling Alexander [4] the Great to cross the Euphrates (Arr. Anab. 3,7,1–2; Curt. 4,9,7–8,12; Diod. Sic. 17,55,1). He then commanded the Persian right wing at → Gaugamela (Arr. Anab. 3,14,6ff.; Curt. 4,16,1ff.; Diod. Sic. 17,58,2; 17,60,5ff.) with great commitment and initially with success, but later fled to Babylon (his wife appears to have been Babylonian). Together with the municipal authorities, he surrendered the city to the Macedonians according to Babylonian ceremony (Curt. 5,1,17). Alexander showed him mercy, and M. soon was appointed satrap of Babylonia (Arr. Anab. 3,16,4; Curt. 5,1,44), which he administered to his death in 328 (Arr. Anab. 4,18,3; Curt. 8,3,17). Some coins of M. are extant [3. 850–854; 4].

1 H. BERVE, Das Alexanderreich auf prosopographischer Grundlage, 1926, 243–245; 2 BRIANT, s.v. M.; 3 G. LE RIDER, Histoire économique et monétaire de l'Orient hellénistique, in: Annuaire du Collège de France 1995–1996, 1996, 829–860; 4 A. LEMAIRE, Remarques sur certaines légendes des monnaies ciliciennes, in: O. CASABONNE (ed.), Mécanismes et innovations monétaires dans l'Anatolie achéménide. Numismatique et histoire, 1998.   J.W.

Mazara Town on the Sicilian south coast 20 km southeast of Marsala at the mouth of the river of the same name, modern Mazara del Vallo, probably a Phoenician foundation. After the foundation of Selinus, the Mazara river was the border to Motya (later Lilybaeum) and Segesta and was therefore much disputed. In 409 BC, the town was conquered by → Hannibal [1] on the march to Selinus (Diod. Sic. 13,54,6), and early in the First → Punic War it was destroyed by the Romans (23,9,4) but continued to exist as a small port. In AD 827 the Arabs destroyed it but the Normans rebuilt it. Archaeological and epigraphic evidence begins in the Roman period.

BTCGI 9, 502–508.   GI.F. K.Z.

Mazarus (Μάζαρος; *Mázaros*). *Hetaîros* (→ *hetaîroi*) of → Alexander [4] the Great. According to Arrian (Arr. Anab. 3,16,9), he was appointed fortress commander in Susa in 331/30 BC. Curtius (5,2,16) names Xenophilus instead. Since the name M. is Iranian, Arrian probably confused him with the Persian predecessor.

A. B. BOSWORTH, A Historical Commentary on Arrian's History, vol. 1, 1980, 319.   E.B.

Mazdaism see → Zoroastrianism

Mazdak Leader of a religious revolutionary movement in Sassanid → Iran under King Cavades [1] (AD 488–496, 498/9–531). The fundamental characteristic is a strong social egalitarianism.

A basic difficulty in researching Mazdakism is that almost all information originates from sources that are hostile to it. The only contemporary report is found in the Syriac chronicle of Joshua → Stylites. Byzantine (Procop. BP 1,5–11; 2,9; Agathias, Historiae 4,27–30; Ioh. Mal. 465, 633 and 653 MIGNE) and Arabic sources from a later period are particularly important because they partially preserve the Iranian tradition (al-Šahrastānī, *Kitāb al-milal wa-l-niḥal*; Ibn al-Nadīm, *Fihrist*).

The classification of Mazdakism in the history of religion is disputed, because it exhibits Gnostic traits (dualism, → Gnosticism) but is essentially closer to → Zoroastrianism than to → Manichaeism. Against the background of a deep political and social crisis in late 5th-cent. Iran, it can be described as a kind of 'reformed egalitarian Zoroastrianism' that attempted to popularize this elitist religion. The doctrines of M. were initially supported by King Cavades [1], who was looking for allies in his conflict with the influential nobility. However, in the second phase of his reign, Cavades [1] turned away from M. His successor Chosroes [5] I decisively fought Mazdakism. Its remnants survived in small groups in Iran into the Islamic period and influenced Gnostic sects of Islam.

→ Gnosticism; → Manis; → Sassanids; → Zoroastrianism

A. CHRISTENSEN, Le règne du roi Kawādh I. et le communisme mazdakite, 1925; O. KLIMA, Mazdak: Geschichte einer sozialen Bewegung im sassanidischen Persien, 1957; Id., Beiträge zur Geschichte des Mazdakismus, 1977; E. YARSHATER, Mazdakism, in: Cambridge History of Iran 3, 1983, 991–1024.   I.T.-N.

Mazippa s. → Tacfarinas

Mazonomon (μαζονόμον/*mazonómon*, μαζονόμιον/*mazonómion*, Latin *mazonomus*), from μάζα/*máza* ('barley bread') and νέμω/*némō* ('to issue'). Originally, a wooden plate, to pass barley bread (cf. Ath. 5,202c); a carrying bowl made of bronze and gold is also mentioned (Ath. 4,149a; 5,197f). Later a serving plate for poultry (Hor. Sat. 2,8,86; Varro, Rust. 3,4,3), which the scholiasts equated with the Roman → *lanx* (Porph. Hor. Sat. 2,8,86). The *mazonomon* has not been identified in art with certainty.   R.H.

Mazyes (Μάζυες/ *Mázyes*, Μάξυες/ *Máxyes*). The M. are first mentioned in → Hecataeus [3] of Miletus (FGrH 1 F 334) as 'those roaming about Libya' (Λιβύης νομάδες). Stephanus s.v. M., who records this comment, continues: εἰσὶ δὲ καὶ ἕτεροι Μάξυες καὶ ἕτεροι Μάχλυες ('the M. and the Machlyes are different tribes'). According to Hdt. 4,191,1, the *Máxyes* (Μάξυες, *sic!*), who are described as 'the Lybians ... who plough' (ἀροτῆρες ... Λίβυες), lived to the west of the

Triton river. The root *maz* or *max* is of Libyan origin ('noble'). Cf. the word *amazigh* (Tuareg), which is still in use.

→ Libyes, Libye

J. DESANGES, Catalogue des tribus africaines de l'Antiquité à l'Ouest du Nil, 1962, 111, 113; H. KEES, s.v. Maxyes, RE 14, 2576–2580.   W.HU.

Mead (Greek ὑδρόμελ/*hydrómeli*, Latin [*aqua*] *mulsa*). A beverage usually made of one part → honey and two parts water (Columella 12,12; Dioscorides, De materia medica 5,9 WELLMANN) that was usually consumed fermented with an alcohol content of 15% but occasionally also unfermented. Apart from → beer, mead was the oldest intoxicating drink in the Mediterranean. When wine arrived in the historical period, mead was supplanted first in Greece and then largely in Italy, especially because grapes were produced in larger quantities and at a lower cost than honey. In colder regions of the ancient world that were not suited for viticulture (among the Scythians, Celts, Germans and Slavs), mead continued to be a popular drink (Plut. Symp. 4,6,2,672b) and even found favour in wine-growing regions (Plin. HN 14,113; Ath. 11,468a). Mead only played a cultic role as a sacrifice and in the cult of the dead during the Greek archaic period. However, it had a fixed place in medicine during the entire ancient period, especially as a light diet in times of illness, a laxative and an emetic (Plin. HN 22,110–112; Gal. De alimentorum facultatibus 1,1,23).

J. ANDRÉ, L'alimentation et la cuisine à Rome, 1961, 1981; A. DALBY, Siren Feasts: A History of Food and Gastronomy in Greece, 1997; M. SCHUSTER, s.v. Met, RE 15, 1297–1310.   A.G.

Meals Meals, i.e. drink and food taken at particular hours, are at the centre of ancient → table culture. The type and sequence of meals and their position in the larger order and that of the overarching rhythm of life are so complex that they cannot be discussed here in their entire structural, spatial and temporal differentiation.

In the Greek and Roman world, daily meals were subject to a fixed order that was at first primarily guided by the natural environment, especially sunrise and sunset (cf. the names of the meals: ἄριστον/*áriston*, morpheme: 'early' and *vesperna*, morpheme: 'evening'). Later on they also had to follow the dictates of the working world. Three meals a day were usual in Homeric society: the light breakfast (*áriston*) at daybreak, the midday meal (δεῖπνον/*deîpnon*) and the evening meal at sunset (δόρπον/*dórpon*), with the time of the main meal varying. The Greeks also took three daily meals in the Classical and Hellenistic periods, the light breakfast (ἀκράτισμα/*akrátisma*), the modest, usually hot midday meal (*áriston*) and a multiple-course meal in the early evening (*deîpnon*). The latter two meals evolved from the breakfast and lunch of the Ho-

meric period, with the *deîpnon* at the end of the day now constituting the main meal.

The arrangement of daily meals in Rome underwent a similar development (cf. Plut. Symp. 8,6,5,726e-f). In the early Republic, people took three meals a day, the modest breakfast (*ientaculum* or *ieientaculum* in Plaut. Curc. 72–73) after sunrise, the midday main meal (*cena*) and a light meal in the evening (*vesperna*). In the later afternoon, there was (especially in the countryside) a kind of early supper, *merenda* (cf. Plaut. Vid. 52). Beginning in the late Republic, the light breakfast (*ientaculum*) was followed towards noon by a somewhat richer cold or hot meal (*prandium*), a sort of second breakfast without courses. The old *vesperna* was replaced by the → *cena*, the main meal of the day routinely consisting of multiple courses (Fest. 54). It began late in the afternoon and could last late into the night. Until the end of antiquity and beyond, this arrangement of daily meals remained in effect. The rich favoured four or more meals over three (Suet. Nero 27,2; Suet. Vit. 13,1), while the poor often only had the means for one meal or went hungry (→ Nutrition, → Dietetics, → Malnutrition, Famine).

The organisation of meals was not restricted to the daily meals that were taken in the family circle but it also included public meals that were either taken at home with guests or in what were often large social groups gathering at public locations (temple, market place, gathering rooms). Many of these public meals resulted from the superordinate rhythm of life that was determined by custom, religion and social forces. Thus, the annual rhythm of numerous public meals arose from the municipal festive calendar. Almost all religious feasts, such as the → Panathenaea and the → Saturnalia, were associated with a feast (ἑστίασις/*hestíasis*, δημοθοινία/*dēmothoinía*; Latin *epulum*) in which the meat of sacrificial animals was distributed among the urban population. The men of some Greek communities (especially Sparta and Crete) regularly gathered for a communal meal (συσσιτία/*syssitía*), and professional colleges and cult associations usually had a communal table every month. Other meals were associated with childbirth, naming celebrations, birthdays, marriages and the cult of the dead (περίδειπνον/*perídeipnon*, cena feralis, silicernium). A meal could also be arranged to mark the arrival or departure of strangers (*cena viatica*) or simply the master of the house's desire to celebrate a feast with his friends.

Determining the internal structure of individual private and public meals is almost impossible in many cases because of the source situation. This applies in particular to daily meals but also to most public meals. We are only relatively well informed with respect to the private → banquet (σύνδειπνον/*sýndeipnon*, συμπόσιον/*sympósion*; Latin *convivium*).

Even though the banquet may have ranked highest in the hierarchy of meals, it did not occur nearly as often as one might suppose given its frequent mention in the sources. More than other meals, its purpose was not merely to quench the participants' hunger. Its ancient names with the prefixes συν- and con- ('with', 'together') indicate its critical function, namely that of forging a community. In terms of the time of day, the banquet took the place of the principal meal of the day but it was much more opulent: the meal took longer and the dishes and wines were more carefully selected. It also frequently included a drinking party (symposium, → comissatio) where music, dance and other presentations provided entertainment for the guests (cena recta, 'formal meal'; Mart. 2,69,7). The enormous social significance of the banquet was reflected in the high degree of ritualization, with formal invitations, predetermined seating arrangements and specific conversation topics. → Banquet; Nutrition; → Table culture

H. BLÜMNER, Die römischen Privataltertümer, 1911; G. BRUNS, Küchenwesen und Mahlzeiten (ArchHom Q), 1970; A. DALBY, Siren Feasts: A History of Food and Gastronomy in Greece, 1997; J. N. DAVIDSON, Courtesans & Fishcakes. The Consuming Passions of Classical Athens, 1997; K. F. HERMANN, H. BLÜMNER, Lehrbuch der Griechischen Privalterthümer, Freiburg ³1882; A. MAU, s.v. Cena (2), RE 3, 1895–1897; Id, s.v. Convivium, RE 4, 1201–1208; C. MOREL, E. SAGLIO, s.v. Coena, DS 1, 1269–1282; I. NIELSEN, H. S. NIELSEN (ed.), Meals in a Social Context. Aspects of the Communal Meal in the Hellenistic and Roman World, 1998; P. SCHMITT-PANTEL, La cité au banquet. Histoire des repas publics dans les cités grecques, 1992. A.G.

Meander

[1] Among ancient → ornaments the meander has the longest continuous tradition, spanning from its first appearance in prehistoric cultures to Christian Late Antiquity. In the Neolithic and Bronze Age the meander appears in linear pottery cultures, on the Balkan and in Italy as a running ornament [1] and in Helladic and Mycenaean decorations occasionally as a crenellated meander [3. 24]. There is, however, no continuity to the Proto-Geometric und Geometric Periods where the meander is the prevailing ornament. In addition to its basic form (running to the left and to the right) there are numerous variations such as double, triple, multiple, stepped and hooked meander. Crenellation and swastika patterns are related [5. 42–84]. The geometric meander probably represents vegetative tendrils [4. 328–340]. In representations of the 5th cent. BC. the meander sometimes takes on the function of a → 'labyrinth' [4. 262–269]. From the late 4th cent. on the meander is associated with the river → Maeander [2] as documented by coins from the cities on the Maeander [2. 152 f., pls. 1–3]; the coins provide also the earliest known instance of the Greek term for the ornament.

In the Hellenistic and Roman Periods the meander is of undiminished importance in the ornamentation of architectural sculpture (e.g. the reliefs of the → Ara Pacis) and as a frame for → mosaic panels in all the regions of the Empire (e.g. [6. 249, s.v. M.]). There has been little interpretative research of the meander in representations of the Roman Empire and early Christianity [7].

1 O. KUNKEL, Der M. in den vor- und frühgeschichtlichen Kulturen Europas, 1925 2 K. REGLING, Die Münzen von Priene, 1927 3 N. HIMMELMANN-WILDSCHÜTZ, Der M. auf geometrischen Gefäßen, in: MarbWPr 1962, 10–43 4 Ders., Über einige Bedeutungs-Möglichkeiten des frühgriechischen Ornaments, in: AAWM 1968, Nr. 7, 259–346, Taf. 1–8 5 N. KUNISCH, Ornamente geometrischer Vasen. Ein Kompendium, 1998 6 M. DONDERER, Die Chronologie der römischen Mosaiken in Venetien und Istrien, 1986 7 H. MAGUIRE, Magic and Geometry in Early Christian Floor Mosaics and Textiles, in: Jb. der Öst. Byzantinistik 44, 1994, 265–274. DI.WI.

[2] **river** see → Maeander   DI.WI.

Measure of volume

I. ANCIENT ORIENT   II. EGYPT   III. GREECE   IV. ROME

I. ANCIENT ORIENT

Measures of volume were used to measure liquids and especially grain and other bulk solids (dates, etc.). Therefore, they were employed in the administration of grain, including the issuing of rations. According to cuneiform sources, ordinary measuring vessels (especially the *sea*) were made of wood. Special measures for liquids can only be identified locally with a standard 'vessel' usually containing 20 or 30 litres. Despite all temporal and local differences, a relatively constant absolute size of the small unit (Sumerian SÌLA, Akkadian *qû* = c. 0.8–1.0 litres) may be assumed in Mesopotamia. Beginning with the earliest sources (about 3000 BC), the relationship between measures in Babylonia is generally based on the factors of 5 or 10 but also 6, which allow easy division. The ratio of 6 BAN/*sutu*, 'sea' = 1 BARIGA/*parsiktu*, 'bushel', which is the basic measure of every system, is fixed. Depending on the period, 1 *sea* = 10 or 6 litres. The large measure of volume is the *kor* of 4 bushels (in the 3rd millennium 144 or 240 l) or 5 'bushels' (300 l in the late 3rd and 1st half of the 2nd millennium, 180 l in the 1st millennium).

A relationship (based on barley) between measures of volume and the *mina* (→ Weights) appears to have existed (TUAT vol. 1, 19:144–6; 21st century BC). In North Mesopotamia (Syrian Ḡazīra, Assyria) 10 *sea* = 1 *imēru* or 'donkey load'; with 1 *sea* = 10 litres, but also 8 or 9 litres (a decimal system is already documented for the 3rd millennium in Syria). In late Bronze Age NW-Syria (→ Ugarit, Alalaḫ) and in Hittite texts, the *parīsu* was used as the ordinary measure of volume and is equivalent to the Babylonian *parsiktu*. In cuneiform texts from Ugarit the use of *dd* ('sack'?) is documented as the measure of volume. The measures of volume in Hittite texts are based on the ratios of 2, 4 and 6 with the *parīsu* being the largest unit [1. 522ff.]. In Palestine, the OT is the only source available in the 1st millennium. It indicates a decimal ('Assyrian') (1 *chomer* or 'donkey load' = 10 *'epah* = 100 *'omer*) and a 'Babylonian' system (1 *kor* = 30 *se'ah* = 180 *qab*) [2nd vol. 1,320–26].

1 M. A. POWELL, TH. VAN DEN HOUT, s.v. Maße und Gewichte, RLA 7, 492–530   2 R. DE VAUX, Das Alte Testament und seine Lebensordnungen, ²1964.   WA.SA.

II. EGYPT

From the Old Kingdom [2] on, the most common Egyptian measure of volume was based on the unit *heqat* (c. 4.8 l). Originally ten *heqat* were called a 'sack' (*khar*; c. 48 l). Double and quadruple *heqat* (as a 'large measure'), of which 10 or 5 make for a (double) 'sack' of c. 96 l, are also attested. In the New Kingdom, a sack contained 4 *oipe*, i.e., 4 fourfold *heqat* (c. 76.8 l) with the ratios being based on a factor 4. These units were mostly used to measure grain, but also fruit, minerals and pigments. One *heqat* consisted of 10 → *hin*, which was also used for measuring fluids. Beginning in the 5th cent. BC, the → *artabe* (documented in varying sizes but mostly c. 32 l), a Persian measure originally, was used instead of the 'sack' as the largest unit for dry substances. Several other vessels are also documented as measures of volume for liquid and dry substances but their standard size cannot be determined with certainty.

1 W. HELCK, S. VLEEMING, s.v. Maße und Gewichte, LÄ 3, 1201–1205 und 1210–1211   2 P. POSENER-KRIÉGER, Les mesures de grain, in: C. EYRE et al. (ed.), The Unbroken Reed, Gedenkschrift A.F. Shore, 1994, 269–271.

III. GREECE

The Greeks differentiated measures for dry (grain, fruits – μέτρα ξηρά) and liquid substances (wine, oil – μέτρα ὑγρά). These had different names according to their derivation from common sizes (jug, pitcher and basket, sack, etc.) as well as the form and material of the vessels used. They only coincided for the smallest sizes and became standardized during Solon's reform (about 600 BC). Depending on the region, place and time as well as their derivation from particular weight systems, the measures of volume varied in size. Some of their absolute sizes are disputed. Measures for dry goods [1. 104–107] are the → medimnos (*c.* 52.53 l) = 6 → hekteis (*c.* 8.75 l) = 48 *choinikes* (→ choinix, *c.* 1.09 l) = 96 *xestai* (→ xestes, *c.* 0.54 l) = 192 *kotylai* (→ kotyle, *c.* 0.27 l). Measures for liquids are [1. 101–104] the → metretes (*c.* 39.39 l) = 12 *choes* (→ chous, *c.* 3.28 l) = 72 *xestai* (→ xestes, *c.* 0.54 l) = 144 *kotylai* (→ kotyle, *c.* 0.27 l) = 576 → oxybaphon (*c.* 0.07 l) = 866 kyathoi (→ kyathos, *c.* 0.04 l). The conversions are based on the widespread Attic standard [1. 505, 703 table X] but special regional forms (→ Cyprus) or local and temporal deviations [1. 102] are not taken into account. The Aeginetan standard assumed by HULTSCH [1. 501–505], which deviates up to 40 % from the norm, has not yet been documented archaeologically [4. 28 n. 84].

Larger quantities of measuring containers have been found especially in Athens [2. 39–45] and Olympia [4. 28 n. 84]. An Argive vase of the late 8th or early 7th cent. BC [3. 465] is considered to be the earliest evidence. Cylindrical vessels inscribed with μέτρον

(*métron*) or δημόσιον (*dēmósion*) predominate among dry measures. In Athens these bore a seal with the head of Athena and an owl as state guarantees [3. 467f. and fig. 111–112]. Liquid measures (→ Calibration) are usually the *olpe,* the *oinochoe* or the amphora, which also received inscriptions and seals [3. 467]. Finds of numerous measuring containers from the Hellenistic period in the area of the Tholos in the Athenian Agora suggest a measuring table with sample measures (σηκώματα/*sēkṓmata*) there [3. 469]. This type of stone table with cavities of varying sizes to take up metal sample measures is also known from Chios, Delos and Thasos [3. 471 and fig. 113]. A measuring table of the 2nd cent. AD from Gythium in Laconia contains five hollows for the measures *modios, chous, kotyle* and *hemihekteus* as well as another illegible measure [3. 472].   H.-J.S.

IV. ROME

Roman measures of volume are closely related in name, quantity and grading to those of the Greek system. The standard measure for dry goods is the → modius (*c.* 8.75 l) = 2 *semodii* (*c.* 4.37 l) = 16 *sextarii* (→ sextarius, *c.* 0.54 l) = 32 *heminae* (→ hemina, *c.* 0.27 l) = 64 *quartarii* (→ quartarius, *c.* 0.13 l) = 128 *acetabula* (→ acetabulum, *c.* 0.06 l). Plaut. Men. Prologue 14 mentions the *trimodium* (*c.* 26.26 l), which is equivalent to an → amphora, as a large measure. The primary measure for liquids is the amphora (*c.* 26.26 l) or the → quadrantal = 2 *urnae* (→ urna, *c.* 13.13 l) = 8 *congii* (→ congius, *c.* 3.28 l) = 48 *sextarii* (*c.* 0.54 l) = 96 *heminae* (*c.* 0.27 l) = 192 *quartarii* (*c.* 0.13 l) = 384 *acetabula* (*c.* 0.06 l) = 576 *cyathi* (→ cyathus, *c.* 0.04 l). The smallest unit is the → cochlear (*c.* 0.011 l) = $^1/_4$ *cyathus* = $^1/_{48}$ *sextarius* [1. 112–126, 704 table XI], which was also used as a measure in medicine (cf. table regarding the → cochlear). The large measure was the → culleus (*c.* 525.2 l) = 20 amphorae, which was mainly used for wine barrels. Conversions to absolute sizes slightly vary among metrologists. Thus, [1] calculated the *modius* at 8.754 l and the amphora at 26.26 l [1. 703 table XI], [5] at 8.733 l and 26.196 l [5. 844 table XII] and [6. 94 Suppl. I] at 8.697 and 26.092 l. The special measures for oil derived by [6] are disputed.

Similar to Greek culture, measuring containers with and without inscriptions (ILS 8627–8628) are known, with the cylindrical *modius* being an especially common motif on imperial coins against the background of the city of Rome's grain supply (→ cura annonae). Images of *modii* are also found on gravestones of bakers and persons involved in the grain trade [7. 24]. The calibration tables with cavities for holding sample measures (→ Calibration, → Ponderarium) are equivalent to the forms known from Greece. An example of a measuring table of this kind is located at the edge of the Pompeii forum (CIL X 793). Primarily in late Antiquity, special forms (*modius castrensis*) are encountered whose standards are heavily disputed.

→ Measures of volume and length

1 F. Hultsch, Griechische und römische Metrologie, ²1882   2 M. Lang, M. Crosby, The Athenian Agora 10. Weights, Measures and Tokens, 1964   3 M. Guarducchi, Epigrafia Greca 2, 1969   4 H. Büsing, Metrologische Beiträge, in: JDAI 97, 1982, 1–45   5 H. Nissen, Griechische und römische Metrologie, HbdA I²   6 A. Oxé, in: BJ 147, 1942   7 G. Zimmer, Römische Berufsdarstellungen, 1982   8 H. Chantraine s.v. Hohlmaße, KlP 2, 1198f.   9 LAW, s.v. Maße und Gewichte, 3422–3426   10 D. P. S. Peacock, D. F. Williams, Amphorae and the Roman Economy, 1986   11 R. F. Docter, Amphorae Capacities and Archaic Levantine Trade, Hamburger Beiträge zur Archäologie. 15/17, 1988/1990, 143–188   12 N. Spichtig, P. Kamber, Zur Berechnung und Interpretation von Gefäßvolumina, Jahrbuch der Schweizerischen Gesellschaft für Urgeschichte 74, 1991, 226–228.   H.-J.S.

Measures

I. Ancient Orient   II. Classical Antiquity

I. Ancient Orient

Although the different basic measurement systems (length, → measures of volume and → weights) were created and defined independently of each other, at least in Mesopotamia relationships between them were established.

In the Ancient Orient as elsewhere, the terms for measures of length were based on body parts (cubit, palm and finger widths), however, the foot was not used as a basic measure of length. Regional and temporal differences must be considered.

The Babylonian 'cubit' (Sumerian *kùš*, Akkadian *ammatu*, normally *c.* 50 cm; in the 1st millennium BC also the 'large cubit' of 75 cm) is subdivided into 30 'fingers', in the 1st millennium also into 24 fingers (of 2.083 cm each) known from the system of length measures found in the Old Testament (= 2 spans = 6 palms). 'Spans' and 'palms' are only rarely encountered in Mesopotamian texts. Similarly, the basic Egyptian unit, the 'cubit' (*mḥ*) of *c.* 52.5 cm, which is attested since the 3rd dynasty (2635–2570 BC), consists of 7 palms of 4 fingers each (1.87 cm each).

Larger Egyptian measures of length were derived from the cubit (100- and 1,000-fold). The largest measure, the *jtrw*, consists of about 20,000 cubits = 10.5 km. Like other measures of length, the exact definition of the *nbj* measure used by craftsmen is still debated. In Mesopotamia, the entire system of measures of length referred to the cubit, for example: 1 'reed' = 6 cubits (3 m) in early Babylonia (3rd–2nd millennia), 7 cubits (3.5 m) in North Mesopotamia and in the 1st millennium; 2 reeds = 1 'rod'; 1 'chain' = 120 cubits (60 m); one 'mile' (*bēru* = 1,800 rods = 21,600 cubits, 10.8 km) was the largest measure of length.

Among Hittite measures of length, only the 'finger' (*kalulupa*) as the smallest unit can be interpreted reliably; the *gipeššar* is probably equivalent to the cubit (therefore *c.* 50 cm), larger measures of length are 30 and 3,000 times the *gipeššar*. The Old Testament only

records daily-life values like a 'day's journey' and an 'arrow shot' for longer distances.

Lengths were measured with cubit rods, of which some have been preserved in Babylonia (early 3rd millennium) and especially in Egypt. Larger distances were measured with ropes.

In Mesopotamia, two systems of length measurements were incorporated into astronomy: 1 cubit is equivalent to 5 sun diameters (2.5°); and 1 'mile' = 30° = 2 hours (identical to the distance covered by the sun in that time). But time could also be measured by weight (water clock).

In Mesopotamia, Egypt and among the Hittites, → square measures were derived from measures of length, and from these measures of volume, which are rarely attested. Capacity measures constitute a separate system that was originally derived from (standardized) containers. The standard system of Mesopotamia probably linked measures of volume and capacity, and in addition, a relationship between capacity measures and weights also seems to have existed. There was also a close association between capacity measures and area units in order to determine the necessary amount of seeds.

→ Mathematics

D. Ahrens, R. C. A. Rottländer (ed.), Ordo et Mensura IV–V, 1998; H. Büsing, Metrologische Beiträge, in: JDAI 97, 1982, 1–45; W. Helck, S. Vleeming, s.v. Maße und Gewichte, LÄ 3, 1199–1214; M. A. Powell, s.v. Weights and Measures, Anchor Bible Dictionary 6, 1992, 897–908; id., Th. van den Hout, s.v. Maße und Gewichte, RLA 7, 458–530; E. Roik, Das Längenmaßsystem im alten Ägypten, 1993.

A. D. H. Bivar, Achaemenid Coins, Weights and Measures, in: Cambridge History of Iran 2, 1985, 625–630.
                                                                J.RE. WA.SA.

II. Classical Antiquity

As in the Ancient Orient and in Egypt, the different measuring systems of Classical Antiquity were based on units that initially largely used body parts and other natural parameters. This is particularly the case with linear measures and → square measures, which are derived from the former. It is controversial in research if and to what extent → weights and → measures of volume also correlated with linear measures in the sense of modern consistent metrological systems.   C.HÖ.

A. Linear measures   B. Linear measures in Ancient Architecture

A. Linear measures

Linear measures (or measures of length) are the first among all metrological systems, even before humans weighed objects or measured fluids. While measures of fingers, arms or feet were used to express smaller units, larger dimensions were determined by human requirements and expressed in steps or day journeys. Metrological reliefs show parts of a male figure with arms extended, beside which a lower arm, a foot and a spread hand with fingers as well as a measuring rod from which the units for span, foot and cubit can be determined.

The basic unit of linear measures is the cubit (πῆχυς/ → pê chys, Latin → cubitus), which comprises the lower arm to the tip of the middle finger and according to HULTSCH measured 46.2 cm [6. 697 table II B] but according to NISSEN 44.4 cm [7. 836 table II]. It is divided into 2 spans (σπιθαμή/→ spithamé; the measure of the spread hand from the tip of the thumb to the tip of the little finger of c. 23 cm), equalling 6 palms (παλαιστή/→ palaisté, Latin palmus) of c. 7.5 cm and also 24 fingers (δάκτυλος/ → dáktylos, Latin digitus) of c. 1.9 cm.

The other basic unit apart from the cubit is the foot (πούς/→ poús, Latin → pes), which the Greeks and Romans fixed at $^2/_3$ of the cubit. According to HULTSCH, it measured 30.7 cm [6. 697 table II B] in Greece and 29.5 cm [6. 700 table II B] in Rome, but according to NISSEN 29.6 cm [7. 836 table II] and was equivalent to 4 palms or 16 fingers. The common multiples of the foot (usually as measures of distance) are the → passus (βῆμα διπλοῦν/bêma diploûn) of 5 feet (1.48 m), → decempeda (ἄκαινα/→ ákaina, κάλαμος/ kálamos) of 10 feet (2.96 m) and the milia (μίλιον, mílion) of 5,000 feet (1481.5 m) [6. 701 table VII; 7. 838 table III A-C]. In addition, the following units existed in Greece: the πλέθρον (→ pléthron) of 100 feet (HULTSCH 30.8 m/NISSEN 29.6 m), the στάδιον (→ stádion) of 600 feet (HULTSCH 185 m/NISSEN 177 m) and the ἱππικόν (hippikón) of 2,400 feet (HULTSCH 740 m/NISSEN 708 m) [6. 697–698 table II B, III A; 7. 836 Tab. II]. Distances were also indicated by the time required for a certain distance, e.g., a two-minute walk (στάδιον/stádion) or an hour's walk (σχοῖνος/→ schoînos, c. 6,300 m). Roman measures of distance are the mile (mille passus, Pl. milia passuum, abbrev. MP) of 1481.5 m and the → leuga (abbrev. L) of 2,200 m, equivalent to 1$^1/_2$ miles, which was widespread in Gaul and Germany.

Instruments for measuring length in the Roman period included folding brass measuring sticks ('bronze'), less frequently made of wood or bone, which were equivalent in length to the Roman foot of 29.6 cm and had scaled divisions of 16 digiti or were divided according to the uncial system into 12 unciae. The latter divided the Roman foot according to the duodecimal system into 12 sections of 2.47 cm each [1. 35–36]. A foot measure in stone that was also divided into 16 digiti, was found in Gortyn [5. 473 and fig. 115].

→ Measures and Weights; → Metrology; → Square measures

1 K. W. BEINHAUER (ed.), Die Sache mit Hand und Fuß – 8000 Jahre Messen und Wiegen, 1994   2 H. BÜSING, Metrologische Beiträge, in: JDAI 97, 1982, 1–45   3 H. CHANTRAINE, H.-J. SCHULZKI, Bemerkungen zur kritischen Neuaufnahme aniker Maße und Gewichte, in: Saalburg-Jahrbuch 48, 1995, 129–138   4 I. DEKOULAKOU-SIDERIS, A Metrological Relief from Salamis, in: AJA 94, 1990, 445–451   5 M. GUARDUCCI, Epigrafia Greca 2,

1969   6 F. HULTSCH, Griechische und römische Metrologie, ^{2}1882 reprint 1972)   7 H. NISSEN, Griechische und römische Metrologie, in: Handbuch der klassischen Altertumswissenschaften 1, ^{2}1892;   8 R. C. A. ROTTLÄNDER, Antike Längenmaße – Untersuchung über ihre Zusammenhänge, 1979   9 Id., Die Standardfehler der Methoden der überkommenen Historischen Metrologie, in: D. AHRENS, R. C. A. ROTTLÄNDER (eds.), Ordo et Mensura V. (5. Internationaler Interdisziplinärer Kongreß für Historische Metrologie München 1996), 1998   10 H. WITTHÖFT, Zur Feststellung der Maße seit der Antike, in: D. AHRENS, R. C. A. ROTTLÄNDER (eds.), Ordo et Mensura III. (3. Internationaler Interdisziplinärer Kongreß für Historische Metrologie Trier 1993), 1995.   H.-J.S.

B. LINEAR MEASURES IN ANCIENT ARCHITECTURE

Various Greek building inscriptions document the considerable significance of linear measures, especially the unit of the foot (→ pous), in the context of planning and construction of building projects (e.g., the building inscriptions of Eleusis [1] and Epidaurus as well as the syngraphé of the arsenal of → Philo in Piraeus; cf. also → building trade). These inscriptions, some of which are fragmentary, others quite well preserved, have been much debated in recent research. So far, only the Erechtheion construction documents (IG I^2 372ff., → Athens [1]) constitute a case documented with sufficient precision, in which the combination of a preserved inscription and a preserved building provides clarity regarding the measure of the foot, which was used. The 'Erechtheion foot' on average measures (measured with the frequently used standard blocks of the building walls that are recorded as 4×2×1.5 feet) c. 32.7 cm with a maximum variation of 2 cm.

In the course of modern measuring of ancient architecture, which usually cannot be transferred conclusively to an ancient system of measurements or proportions (→ Proportion), it could be confirmed that at least in the context of Greek architecture of columns and blocks of the 6th–4th cent. BC variant foot measures were used. Consequently, the world of the Greek poleis must have had incompatible measuring systems (as well as → weights), similar to the small German states of the 18th and early 19th cents. There remains fundamental dissent among scholars regarding the number and precise definition of these measures. Likewise, to some extent well founded considerations have been discussed that buildings of this period were not exclusively designed and built according to foot measures but also according to modular measures (embatés) as described by Vitruvius for the Roman building industry (→ Vitruvius). Thus, the highly complex system of measures of the → Parthenon on the Athenian Acropolis, which was often inexactly executed during its construction, can be described with far fewer contradictions by means of a modulus of 28.627 cm than has been possible so far with any directly or indirectly contemplated, supposedly authentic ancient Greek foot measure – a basic measure that is equivalent to precisely $^{14}/_{16}$ (= 14 dáktyloi,

→ *dáktylos*) of the Erechteion foot of *c.* 32.7 cm, which is definitely documented on the Acropolis (→ Parthenon).

Unlike in ancient Greece, ancient Rome with its centralistic, command-oriented organization used a foot measure of *c.* 29.5 cm, which was largely binding as the basic measure in architecture and building project planning.

→ Measures of volume; → Metrology; → Square measures; → Weights; → Weights and measures

H. Bankel, Zum Fußmaß attischer Bauten des 5. Jh.v.Chr., in: MDAI(A) 98, 1983, 65–99; Id., Moduli an den Tempeln von Tegea und Stratos? Grenzen der Fußmaßbestimmung, in: AA 1984, 413–430; Id., Akropolis-Fußmaße, in: AA 1991, 151–163; H. Büsing, Metrologische Beiträge, in: JDAI 97, 1982, 1–45; Id., Zur Bauplanung attisch-ionischer Säulenfronten, in: MDAI(A) 100, 1985, 159–202; Ch. Höcker, Planung und Konzeption der klassischen Ringhallentempel von Agrigent, 1993, 36–59; W. Koenigs, Maße und Proportionen in der griechischen Baukunst, in: H. Beck (ed.), Polyklet. Der Bildhauer der griechischen Klassik, exhibition catalogue. Frankfurt/Main 1990, 121–134; D. Mertens, Entgegnungen zu den Entwurfshypothesen von J. de Waele, in: AA 1981, 426–430; Id., Der Tempel von Segesta und die dorische Tempelbaukunst des griechischen Westens in klassischer Zeit, 1984, 43–45; 175–186; L. Schneider, Ch. Höcker, Die Akropolis von Athen, 1990, 129–137; J. de Waele, Der Entwurf der dorischen Tempel von Akragas, in: AA 1980, 180–241; B. Wesenberg, Zum metrologischen Relief in Oxford, in: MarbWPr 1975/76, 15–22; Id., Beiträge zur Rekonstruktion griechischer Architektur nach literarischen Quellen, 9. Beihefte MDAI(A), 1983.   C.Hö.

Meat, consumption of
I. Greece   II. Rome

I. Greece
The diet of the Greeks in Antiquity was largely vegetarian and, as in most pre-modern agrarian societies, consisted of grains, pulses, vegetables and fruit. Olives (pickled or as oil), cheese, fish and meat supplemented the diet and provided animal and plant fats. For most people, only a small part of their diet consisted of meat. Literary sources can be misleading in this regard: The heroes of the Homeric epics appear to have lived on meat and owned large herds, while the preparation of particular animal parts is described in detail by the comedy writers of Athens, which Athenaeus cites in copious number in the 3rd cent. AD (Ath. 94c–96f). Although the heroes in Homer owned large herds, civilized humanity is described as σιτοφάγος ('corn-eating', Hom. Od. 9,191; cf. Hdt. 4,109,1). The interest of comedy writers in feasts shows how scarce meat normally was.

Nevertheless, meat played an important role in social life. Animal sacrifices offered to gods and heroes were one of the most important Greek cultic actions and constituted significant social events for the entire citizenry of a polis. The great majority of domestic animal bones is found in sanctuaries. Almost every slaugh-

tering event was a gift to the gods, though most edible parts of the sacrificed animals were eaten by the people who attended the cult act. Sometimes, it was demanded that this should happen in the sanctuary itself, but sometimes the meat could be eaten at home. Occasionally, the meat was sold, as was demanded, for example, in Thoricus (Attica) (SEG 33,147, about 430 BC). Animals with deformities or injuries as well as plough and draft oxen were not permitted to be sacrificed and, therefore, were slaughtered and eaten in the individual households.

For sacrifices, mainly domestic animals were used: pigs, goats, sheep and cattle. In most regions of Greece, it was only possible to keep goats and sheep, which, as a result, were more frequently sacrificed than cattle. In the classical period young pigs were mainly used for this purpose. In later centuries, the meat of grown pigs was increasingly eaten.

Undoubtedly, the share of meat in the diet was dependent on the population's purchasing power and local circumstances. In mountainous regions such as Epirus and Illyria, which leaned towards animal husbandry rather than field cultivation, more meat was produced and consumed. By contrast, heavily populated regions such as Attica hardly had sufficient pasture for livestock. However, since many festivals, particularly in Athens, required numerous sacrificial animals, they probably had to be imported, but there is little information on that kind of import trade.

1 A. Burford, Land and Labour in the Greek World, 1993, 146–156   2 Isager/Skydsgaard, 89–93   3 M. Jameson, Sacrifice and Animal Husbandry in Classical Greece, in: Whittaker, 87–119   4 W. Richter, s.v. Ziege, RE 10A, 415–418   5 V. Rosivach, The System of Public Sacrifice in Fourth-Century Athens, 1994.   Mi.Ja.

II. Rome
In principle, many types of meat were available in the Roman empire, but a large part of the population ate meat only sporadically. Mostly, pigs, cattle, sheep and goats were slaughtered, with the pig being the only animal raised exclusively for meat production (Varro, Rust. 2,4; Columella 7,9–11; Plin. HN 8,205–213). The udder, liver and other parts of the pig are specifically mentioned in the → Edictum [3] Diocletiani among foodstuffs (4,4ff.). There was a supra-regional livestock and meat trade with large markets in Italy (such as the Campi Macri in Gallia Cisalpina; Varro, Rust. 2 praef. 6) and also in Rome (Forum boarium, suarium). The *censor* Ti. Sempronius Gracchus already had butcher stalls built in Rome in 169 BC (Liv. 44,16,10f.). In the vicinity of the larger cities, systematic rearing of poultry and small animals for the demand of wealthy families may be presumed (*pastio villatica*; Varro, Rust. 3). There probably were markets for young animals as well (Columella 7,9,4). Many animals, such as hares and poultry, were sold alive in the markets. Since there were no means to cool it, fresh meat was mostly eaten in the fall and winter. Salting, smoking and air-drying were

used for preservation (Cato Agr. 162; Columella 12,55). The meat of sacrificial animals was important in provisioning the population with fresh meat. For Christians, eating sacrificial meat was problematic, especially if its origin was known, and, therefore, they were largely excluded from the meat markets (1 Cor 8; 10,14–33; cf. Plin. Ep. 10,96,10).

Under the Principate the population of the city of Rome was provisioned with meat by free market trade. In Late Antiquity, meat became part of the public supply of foodstuffs for the administration, the army and the population of the capitals (Rome, Constantinople). In Rome, the meat supply was organized by the administration from the early 4th cent. AD on (*tribunus fori suarii*; cf. Zos. 2,9,3). Since the early 5th cent. AD, the *plebs frumentaria* received meat (monthly 5 Roman pounds, that is about 8 kg annually) during the months from November to March. Overall, it seems, 4,000 rations were issued every day. Therefore, a figure of about 120,000 recipients may be deduced (Cod. Theod. 14,4,10,3; 14,4,10,5 of July 29, 419 AD). The *suarii*, who were responsible for supplying pigs, formed a *corpus* (the edicts relating to the *suarii*: Cod. Theod. 9,30,3; 14,4; Nov. Val. 36). The inclusion of meat in the public supplies of foodstuffs probably indicates a change in Rome's dietary habits in late Antiquity. Depictions of butchers and the sale of sales are found in numerous grave reliefs in Italy.

→ Nutrition; → Meat dishes

1 J. ANDRÉ, L'alimentation et la cuisine à Rome, ²1981 2 S. J. B. BARNISH, Pigs, plebeians and potentes, Rome's economic hinterland c. 350–600 AD., in: PBSR 55, 1987, 157–185   3 M. CORBIER, The ambiguous status of meat in ancient Rome, in: Food & Foodways 3, 1989, 223–264 4 J. FRAYN, The Roman meat trade, in: J. WILKINS, D. HARVEY, M. DOBSON (eds.), Food in antiquity, 1995, 107–114   5 P. HERZ, Studien zur römischen Wirtschaftsgesetzgebung. Die Lebensmittelversorgung, 1988, 277ff. 6 M. ISENBERG, The sale of sacrificial meat, in: CPh 70, 1975, 271–273   7 JONES, LRE, 702ff.;   8 W. RINKEWITZ, Pastio Villatica, 1984;   9 I. SCHWARZ, Diaita. Ernährung der Griechen und Römer im klassischen Altertum, 1995 10 B. SIRKS, Food for Rome, 1991, 361–387. 11 ZIMMER, 1–17; 180.   P.H.

Meat dishes A collective term for dishes made from the muscle tissue and innards of mammals and birds. In Antiquity, a minor number of meat dishes was made using birds (e.g., → blackbird, → thrush, → duck, → goose, → chicken, → pigeon, → quail) and game (especially → rabbit, red deer (→ Deer), wild boar (→ Pig); in the Roman period also rabbit and dormouse). However, most meat dishes were prepared from domestic animals – → sheep, → pig, → cattle and → goat. The pig must be particularly emphasized in this group because it was the only domestic animal exclusively raised for slaughter and provided quantitatively the most and qualitatively the best meat since the classical Greek period and the late Roman Republic (Varro, Rust. 2,4,10; Plin. HN 8,209). The latter aspect was reflected in the

price: Early in the 4th cent. AD, pork cost fifty percent more than the meat of other animals for slaughter (CIL III 2, p. 827 4,1–3).

In the absence of modern cooling methods, meat had to be consumed immediately or preserved by salting, smoking, drying or sausage making. Preserved meats such as ham, bacon and sausage were comparatively expensive (CIL III 2, p. 827 4,7–16).

Meat used in the kitchen was generally tough and lean, except for pork. Therefore, it was routinely boiled until tender and then grilled or roasted in an oven or a pan. This form of preparation was fashionable: it is also encountered in the fine cuisine of the upper class (Apicius 6,9,1; 7,10; 8,8,1), which in principle preferred the tender meat of young animals (Juv. 11,66–67). The lower classes ate meat – if at all – only as a side dish to the main dish – bread or gruel made of pulses. Dishes other than bacon or cheap innards such as tripe were rarely served. In wealthy households, it was popular to start meals with appetizers made from birds or high quality innards (Apicius 4,5,1–2). In particular, the uterus (→ uterus), udder and liver of the pig were considered → delicacies. The main dish was often a whole roasted animal (e.g., a pheasant or piglet) accompanied by a lavish sauce.

Regular consumption of meat was mainly dependent on income. While a vegetarian diet originally prevailed in Antiquity, the demand for meat increased with growing wealth in Greece and later also in Italy (Ath. 10,419–420; Plaut. Pseud. 810–825). The supply improved until finally during the Roman Imperial period all classes ate meat from slaughtered animals (Juv. 11,78–85). However, consumption remained very limited, especially among the urban lower classes, while the wealthy enjoyed meat as a daily luxury.

→ Nutrition; → Meat, consumption of

J. ANDRÉ, L'alimentation et la cuisine à Rome, ²1981, 114–148; L. BODSON (ed.), L'animal dans l'alimentation humaine: les critères de choix, 1988; A. DALBY, Siren Feasts. A History of Food and Gastronomy in Greece, 1996; E. FOURNIER, s.v. Cibaria, DS 1,2, 1157–1162; J. HAUSSLEITER, s.v. Fleisch II (als Nahrung), RAC 7, 1105–1110; F. ORTH, s.v. Kochkunst, RE 11, 944–982.   A.G.

Mecca (*Makka*; Μαχόραβα; *Makóraba*, Ptol. 6,7,32). The most important of the holy cities of → Islam only accessible to Muslims, located in modern Saudi Arabia. Mecca is the place where the prophet → Muhammad was born and worked until he emigrated (→ Hejira) to Medina (→ Yaṯrib). It is the direction of prayer and the destination of pilgrimage (→ Kaaba). Mecca was already an important centre of trade in the pre-Islamic period. The first Koranic revelations (→ Qur'an) are primarily a critique of the materialism and lack of faith of Meccan merchants.

→ Macoraba

W. M. WATT et al., s.v. Makka, EI 6, 142a–170b.   H.SCHÖ.

Mechane The Greeks called any mechanical device μηχανή but in the narrow sense it referred to the Greek theatre machinery: a crane installed behind the stage as a flying apparatus that can be swung into the scene to take the characters in a drama to a remote location or cause gods to appear up high. The *mechane* is referred to in drama texts and later sources under many names: κρεμάθρα (*kremáthra*, 'suspension device', Aristoph. Nub. 218), γέρανος (*géranos*, 'crane' [in both senses], Poll. 4,130), αἰώρημα (*aiórēma*, 'swing', schol. Aristoph. Pax 80), κράδη (*krádē*, 'fig branch', Aristoph. fr. 160 K.-A.: comical depiction?). The *mechane* were invented and silently employed in → Tragedy but evidence of their use comes from → Comedy because it included the reality of theatre in the play and employed it for comical effects. In Euripides, Bellerophontes charges up to the gods on Pegasus and Aristophanes parodied this in 'Peace' with his comical hero's flight on a dung beetle. In the process, he lets his hero fearfully call to the machine operator to be careful (μηχανοποιός, *mēchanopoiós*, Aristoph. Pax 174; cf. fr. 160; 192 K.-A.). Presumably, the experiment-happy Aeschylus introduced the *mechane* together with the solid stage building (SOMMERSTEIN on Aesch. Eum. 404f., not so [1]). In the post-Aeschylean 'Prometheus', Oceanus arrives flying on a griffin (284–287). Sophocles declined to use the *mechane*, but Euripides frequently employed it [2], especially for the appearances of the gods at the end of the drama: → Deus ex machina.
→ Ekkyklema

1 O. TAPLIN, The Stagecraft of Aeschylus, 1977, 443–447 2 N. C. HOURMOUZIADES, Production and Imagination in Euripides, 1965, 146–169.

H.-D. BLUME, Einführung in das antike Theaterwesen, ³1991, 66–72; D. J. MASTRONARDE, Actors on High: The Skene Roof, the Crane and the Gods in Attic Drama, in: Classical Antiquity 9, 1990, 247–294; H.-J. NEWIGER, Ekkyklema und M. in der Inszenierung des griechischen Dramas, in: WJA 16, 1990, 33–42.   H.BL.

Mechanical method The 'Method' (Ἔφοδος; *Éphodos*) of → Archimedes [1] is our source for his mechanical method from which he derived geometric formulas. To compare the surfaces of two figures, he disassembled each into an infinite number of parallel lines and balanced them on a scale. On one side of the scale, one surface is hung up at one point, i.e., as a whole. On the other side, the surface is hung up along the entire arm, i.e., each layer remains where it is and acts with a different leverage. When each pair of infinitely thin layers (lines) is in balance, this also applies to the surface as a whole, which is conceived as the sum of the infinite number of parallel lines. Archimedes determined the volume of bodies in the same manner, by dividing them into infinitely thin surfaces. In this way, he obtained, for example, the formulas for the surface of a parabola segment and the volume of a sphere. Archimedes explicitly notes that the mechanical method is no more than a heuristic procedure that does not suffice as a proof. The formulas derived in this manner are proved elsewhere with the help of exact infinitesimal methods. Archimedes' mechanical method is similar to the method of indivisibles with the help of which B. CAVALIERI and other mathematicians of the 17th cent. determined areas and volumes.
→ Archimedes [1]; → Mathematics

1 O. BECKER, Das mathematische Denken der Antike, 1957, 109–110 2 B. L. VAN DER WAERDEN, Erwachende Wissenschaft, 1956, 354–361.   M.F.

Mechanics
I. TERM AND DEFINITION, CONTENT AND SCOPE
II. THE BEGINNINGS OF THEORETICAL MECHANICS III. INDIVIDUAL DISCIPLINES OF MECHANICS

I. TERM AND DEFINITION, CONTENT AND SCOPE
Mechanics (μηχανικὴ τέχνη, *mēchanikḕ téchnē*) in ancient and medieval thought was a discipline that dealt with the use of artificial technical devices and instruments (*machinae*; in the early modern period: 'arts') as well as procedures for artificially creating motion that would not have occurred on their own or spontaneously ('naturally') in nature. Mechanics also includes the theoretical analysis of these instruments and their effect. In Antiquity, mechanics was *not* the description and explanation of naturally caused motion and, therefore, not a discipline of the 'natural sciences' (φυσική *physikḗ*, physics) – it only became one in the late 16th cent. (G. GALILEI, J. KEPLER). Rather, in our modern understanding, ancient mechanics was a technical science. Contrary to → physics, which is concerned with the natural, and, therefore, always identical, performance of bodies, mechanics considered motions that are not intrinsically performed by the body based on its natural properties, but are effected artificially and only through external force, by humans for their own ends. It always relates to movements that humans cannot directly effect with their own diminutive powers, but those which they induce by cleverness or an instrument (μηχανή/*mēchanḗ*) (Aristot. Problemata mechanica 847a-b).
→ Geminus [1] (1st cent.BC; quotes in Procl. In primum Euclidis librum commentarius p. 41,3–18) and in greater detail → Pappus of Alexandria (about 300; Collectio 8,2; cf. also Vitr. De arch. 10,1) divide mechanics into disciplines of construction (→ Construction technique, with fig.), technology of lifting devices, catapult building, irrigation and drainage devices, marvels and automata, water clocks and sun dials, and finally 'spheres' (armillary spheres, astrolabes (→ astrolabium), globes, planetaria). Pappos explicitly also included geometric construction effected by instruments other than compasses and rulers in mechanics. For Pappus, in c. AD 300, mechanics proper consist of the construction of irrigation and drainage devices (→ Irrigation), which the Greeks first observed in Egypt during the Hellenistic

period and refined further with a number of technical inventions (cf. Vitr. De arch. 10,4–5).

II. The Beginnings of Theoretical Mechanics

The term *mēchanē* originally exclusively meant 'means' and 'ruse', regardless if this means was of intellectual or instrumental nature. A more specific meaning developed parallel to this in the 2nd half of the 5th cent. BC when, beyond the skillfull use of tools (Aischyl. Pers. 722; Hdt. 1,94,6) and the products of such skillful use (Aeschyl. Pers. 114: ship, bridge), *mēchanē* also came to mean the tools themselves and their combination (Hdt. 2,125,2: a lifting device; cf. Aristoph. Pax 174, for theatres). As early as the 5th century, doctors already used mechanical instruments such as the winch, lever and wedge, whose effects were mostly described verbally (cf., e.g., Hippoc. De Fracturis 31).

The earliest preserved text on mechanics is the *Problemata mechanika* of Aristotle [6]. Unlike later works on mechanics, it is not yet axiomatically structured, but proceeds, like earlier mathematical writings, by the *problemata* method. The starting-point of the treatise is the phenomenon of associated concentric circles of unequal sizes that are fixed, for example, as wheels on a shaft and of which the outer (larger) wheel is turned faster by the same force than each inner (smaller) wheel. In a geometric analysis, the movements of the circles are shown to be composed of a natural component (heaviness) and a forced, unnatural component, so that the resulting movement is overall (for the heavy body) unnatural and artificial. The circle in itself, which actually comprises the opposites, is considered the causal principle of the effect of associated concentric circles. The action of numerous other devices and instruments is explained by reducing them to this initial problem. For example, → scales and the lever are interpreted by equating the lever and scale arms with the radiuses of circles of different sizes; the wedge, roller, winch (shaft-mounted wheel), catapult and sail are explained in similar ways.

As early as around 350 BC, Plato mentioned fixed circles with radiuses of differing size (Pl. Leg. 893cd). According to Diogenes Laertius, the Pythagorean Archytas [1] of Tarentum (4 Jh. v.Chr.) wrote a treatise entitled *Perì mēchanês* (Περὶ μηχανῆς) and 'first treated mechanical instruments (τὰ μηχανικά/*tà mēchaniká*) methodically using mathematical principles'. Therefore, Archytas probably wrote the first theoretical work on mechanics. He, too, began with an analysis of fixed circles. Mechanical inventions are also attributed to him (Gell. 10,12,9f.), in which case the distinction between the Pythagorean Archytas and an architect of the same name in Diogenes Laertius would become pointless.

III. Individual Disciplines of Mechanics A. Mechanical Technology B. Pneumatics C. Construction of Catapults and Siege Engines

A. Mechanical Technology

Using a new approach in the analysis of fixed circles (ropes with weights running over rollers), → Archimedes [1] replaced the dynamic approach of Aristotelian mechanics by static observation of the object in a balanced state. In the *Elementa mechanica*, which has largely been reconstructed from excerpts in the Arabic translation of → Hero of Alexandria's *Mēchaniká*, foundations are gradually created in a strictly axiomatic order, starting with a definition of the centre of gravity and its determination in various bodies and surfaces. The discourse begins with the static theory of a rigid beam, which is resting on different arrangements of vertical posts ('On Supports'). In the following treatise 'On Scales' this rigid beam functions as a balance arm supported at its centre with different suspension point arrangements for the scales, and eventually is used to explain a fixed pulley. The various simple machines are analytically derived and their effectiveness is explained statically: lever and scales, pulley and shaft (→ Winch), wedge and → screw (as a threaded wedge) as well as the hoist (Vitr. De arch. 10,3). On this theoretical foundation, Archimedes probably invented screws and the hoist while the gear wheel was invented by Ctesibius. Hero of Alexandria combined these simple machines, which were supplemented by the sloped surface, into complex machines with the objective of lifting a load with a lesser force. Composite machines of this type are mainly hoisting devices (→ Lifting devices, with fig.), cranes (Hero, Mechanica 3; Vitr. De arch. 10,2), engines using cog wheel transmission toothed wheels between several axles (Heron, Mechanica 1,1), different kinds of water- and animal-powered → mills, water-lifting devices including the Archimedean screw (Vitr. De arch. 10,4–6), and finally standing and moving → automata (wonder works), especially when they are powered by the weight of solid bodies. According to Hero, Pappus wrote a summary of Mechanics around 300 (collectio 8).

B. Pneumatics

According to Arabic authors, to whom the entire corpus of Greek works was still available, → pneumatics is the science of instruments involving compressed air. The construction of these instruments is based on the assumption that nature avoids empty spaces. Pneumatic devices move liquids against their nature within closed vessels. The definition and foundations of pneumatics originate from → Ctesibius [1], who discovered the power of air based on its physicality. This he used as the starting-point for the construction of pneumatic devices, like the simple pipette, Tantalus' cup and drinking vessels, but also complex inventions such as the fire pump (*Ctesibii machina*: Vitr. De arch. 10,7).

C. Construction of Catapults and Siege Engines

The construction of → catapults began with Dionysius [1] I (405–367 BC), who called many technicians (τεχνῖται *technîtai*), among them Pythagoreans from Lower Italy, to Syracuse (Diod. Sic. 14,41ff.) for this purpose. Catapults rapidly advanced from simple to very efficient weapons that hurled long arrows and stones of several pounds over long distances. Their construction was mainly based on the multiplication of a basic ratio. By order of the first two Ptolemies in Alexandria, catapult dimensions were optimized (Philo of Byzantium, Belopoiika; Vitr. 10,10f.) after costly experiments by technicians (including Ctesibius). The duties of technicians and mechanics also included the construction of siege engines and siege towers (→ Siegecraft), which were first employed successfully during the campaigns of Alexander and the Wars of the Diadochi (Vitr. 10,13ff.).

→ Mechanical method; → Mechanics

1 F. De Gandt, Force et science des machines, in: J. Barnes et al (ed.), Science and Speculation, Studies in Hellenistic Theory and Practice, 1982, 96–127   2 A. G. Drachmann, Ktesibios, Philon and Heron. A Study in Ancient Pneumatics, 1948   3 Id., Fragments from Archimedes in Heron's Mechanics, in: Centaurus 8, 1963, 91–146;   4 Id., The Mechanical Technology of Greek and Roman Antiquity, 1963   5 B. Gille, Les mécaniciens grecs, 1980   6 G. H. Knutzen, Technologie in den hippokratischen Schriften περὶ διαίτης ὀξέων, περὶ ἀγμῶν, περὶ ἄρθρων ἐμβολῆς (AAWM 1963, 14), 1964   7 F. Krafft, Die Anfänge einer theoretischen Mechanik und die Wandlung ihrer Stellung zur Wissenschaft von der Natur, in: W. Baron (ed.), Beiträge zur Methodik der Wissenschaftsgeschichte, 1967, 12–33   8 Id., Heron von Alexandria, in: K. Fassmann (ed.), Die Großen der Weltgeschichte 2, 1972, 333–379   9 Id., Dynamische und statische Betrachtungsweise in der antiken Mechanik, 1970;   10 E. W. Marsden, Greek and Roman Artillery: Historical Development, 1969   11 Id., Greek and Roman Artillery: Technical Treatises, 1971   12 H. Schneider, Das griechische Technikverständnis, 1989   13 I. Schneider, Archimedes, 1979   14 A. Schürmann, Griechische Mechanik und antike Gesellschaft, 1991.

F.KR.

Mecisteus (Μηκιστεύς; *Mēkisteús*). Son of the mythical king → Talaus of Argos, brother of → Adrastus [1]. In the 'Iliad' he is only mentioned as the victor in boxing at Oedipus' funeral games (Hom. Il. 23,678–680; likewise in Paus. 1,28,7). A passage in Herodotus (Hdt. 5,67), according to which he was killed by → Melanippus together with → Tydeus, indicates that his name was among the → 'Seven against Thebes'. However, Aischyl. Sept. 488 names → Hippomedon [1], another son of Talaus (as does Apollod. 3,63) in his stead. M.' son → Euryalus [1] participated in the Trojan War as leader of the Argives and belongs to the → Epigoni [2] who later conquered Thebes.

J. Tamborino, s.v. Mekisteus, RE 15, 363.   E.V.

Meclodunum Town of the → Senones on an island in the Sequana river (Seine). Caesar (Caes. B Gall. 7,58,2; 6; 60,1; 61,5) uses two forms: Meclodunum ('fortress of Metlos') and Metlosedum ('residence of Metlos' = 'reaper'); modern Melun. Metlosedum is probably the Celtic form and Meclodunum the Latin form. At M. a bridge crossed the Sequana (Caes. B Gall. 7,58,5). Sources: It. Ant. 383; Tab. Peut. 2,4. Inscriptions: CIL XIII 3010.   Y.L.

Mecyberna (Μηκύβερνα/*Mēkýberna*). M., which is located about 20 stadia east of → Olynthus on the northern coast of the Gulf of Torone, is first mentioned in Hecat. FGrH 1 F 150 and in the context of Xerxes' campaign (Hdt. 7,122). After 446 BC it is recorded in the Athenian tribute lists. In 432, M. revolted against Athens, was dissolved as a *pólis* and lost its population to Olynthus, but was reconquered before 425. In the 'Peace of Nicias' (→ Peloponnesian War), its independence from Olynthus was established but Olynthus seized it in the following winter. Until its conquest by Philip II in 349, M. functioned as the port of that city. According to excavations, M. was not destroyed but it was the foundation of Cassandria (→ Potidaea) which brought about its demise: the town was abandoned, its people relocated to the new settlement.

F. Papazoglou, Les villes de Macedoine à l'époque romaine, 1988, 427; M. Zahrnt, Olynth und die Chalkidier, 1971, 203f.   M.Z.

Meda (Μήδα; *Méda*).
[1] The wife of → Idomeneus [1], whom she deceived with Leucus [3] during his absence, and by whom she and her daughter Cleisithyra were later murdered (Apollod. Epit. 6,9; Tzetz. schol. Lycoph. 384; 1093; 1218).

Th. Gantz, Early Greek Myth: A Guide to Literary and Artistic Sources, 1993, 607, 697–698.

[2] Daughter of → Icarius [2] and sister of Penelope (schol. Hom. Od. 4,797).
[3] Daughter of Phylas, with Hercules the mother of Antiochus, the hero of the 10th Attic phyle → Antiochis [1] (Paus. 1,5,2; 10,10,1).   I.BAN.

Medaba (Hebrew *mêd'bā*, Moabitic *mhdb'*, Arab. *Mādebā*, Greek Μήδαβα; *Médaba*,' gently flowing water'). Settlement in the East Jordanian hill country on the → King's Highway, 33 km south of Amman. Evidence of settlement dates back to the Middle Bronze Age II. From the early Iron Age only graves have been found. In the 9th cent. BC, M. was in the possession of the Israelites, but was then conquered and expanded by the Moabite king Meša (→ Moab) (Jos 13,9; Nm 21,30; KAI 181, 7ff., 30). In the 2nd cent. BC, it was in the possession of the B'nê 'Amrat (1 Macc 9,36ff.) or Arameans (Ios. Ant. Iud. 13,1,2ff.) and, subsequently, first came under Hasmonean (Hyrcanus I.; Ios. Ant. Iud. 13,9,1; 15,4; 14,1,4; Ios. Bl. 1,2,6) and then after 69 BC under Nabataean rule. Beginning in AD 106, a Jewish community (mMiq 13,9,16) is attested, and the affiliation with the Roman province of Arabia (Eus. On. 128,19f; 104,11) with its own polis constitution and right to mint. In the 5th cent. AD, M. was an episcopal see and developed its Christian Byzantine culture, especially in mosaic art, until its conquest by the Arabs in the 7th cent. Resettlement occurred only in the late 19th cent. The excavations have revealed a colonnade, forum, city wall, inscriptions, several churches and numerous mosaic floors. A famous artefact of M.'s time of prosperity is the mosaic map of M. from the 2nd half of the 6th cent, which was discovered in 1884. It depicts the geography of Palestine and the eastern Nile delta on an area of over 50 m².

H. DONNER, H. CÜPPERS, Die Mosaikkarte von Madeba I, 1977; M. PICCIRILLO, s.v. Medeba, Anchor Bible Dictionary 4, 1992, 656–658; Id., Chiese e Mosaici di Madaba, 1989; W. ZWICKEL, s.v. Madeba, Neues Bibel-Lexikon 2, 1995, 683–684.   TH.PO.

Medallion Modern technical term for describing particularly heavy and large coins or coin-like items of high artistic quality made of gold, silver or bronze. In the Greek sphere, medallions are only encountered in the Roman imperial period, the term medallion for → *dekádrachmon* is archaic. Medallions like coins were minted as part of the state's monopoly over coinage but were not intended for circulation. Gold medallions are based on the standards for coinage (→ Coinage, standards of) and are multiples of the → aureus and the → solidus. Silver medallions are only partially based on the standards for coinage and the bronze ones never. Therefore, precious metal medallions may well have entered circulation. Medallions served as gifts commemorating special occasions, religious festivals, on New Year and festive events in the imperial household such as births, marriages (Lucilla and Lucius Verus, Salonina and Gallienus) and also deaths (Faustina I, wife of Antoninus Pius). Other representations refer to *profectio*, *fortuna redux* (→ Fortuna) and the emperor's → *adventus*, as well as his virtues and victories (*victoria Augusti*). Medallion recipients were ranked official circles as suggested by differing sizes and metals. The rare bimetallic medallions, which usually consisted of a copper core and an outer layer of brass, belong to the period from Antoninus [1] Pius to Diocletian. Gold and silver medallions are still rare in the 1st and 2nd cents. but increase in frequency during the 3rd with most originating in the 4th and 5th cents. The 2nd and 3rd cent. gold medallions from the hoards of Tarsus and Abukir, which were handed out as victory prizes at festival games, constitute a separate group. Some show images of Alexander the Great. In a wider sense, → contorniati are also medallions.

→ Aureus; → Dekadrachmon; → Contorniati; → Coinage, standards of; → Solidus; → Medals

F. GNECCHI, I medaglioni romani, 1912; J. M. C. TOYNBEE, Roman Medallions, 1944; SCHRÖTTER, 382f.; K. CHRIST, Antike Numismatik, 1972, 86ff.; GÖBL, vol 1, 30f.   GE.S.

Meddix (Oscan *medìss*). Oscan (→ Osci) and Volscian (→ Volsci) term for an official (Fest. 123), which is etymologically equivalent to the Latin *iudex*. If the term refers to the supreme magistrate of a *touta*, an '(entire) people', occasionally (for example, among the Campanians, Liv. 24,19,2) *tuticus* is added (analogous to *magistratus populi* or *publicus*). In → Ennius [1] (Enn. Ann. 298) there is an *alter meddix* in addition to the *summus meddix* (= *m. tuticus*), possibly the *meddix* of a → *pagus* as well. There also seem to have been other *meddices* whose particular responsibilities were specified through epithets (cf. [1] s.v.).

It appears that normally the office would have been held by a single person. In contrast to the Roman dictatorship with which it was compared because of the title, it was a regular and in some places (e.g., Capua) also eponymous annual office. Apart from wielding supreme judicial and military powers, the *meddix* was also according to inscriptions responsible for buildings. In later inscriptions, such as the municipal law of → Bantia, the terminology was clearly influenced by that of Rome [2. 24].

1 J. UNTERMANN, Wörterbuch des Oskisch-Umbrischen, 2000 2 M. CRAWFORD (ed.), Roman Statutes, 1996, vol. I.

ST. WEINSTOCK, s.v. *meddix*, RE 15, 26–29; Id., Zur oskischen Magistratur, in: Klio 24, 1931, 235–246; E. T. SALMON, Samnium and the Samnites, 1967, 84–101.   H.GA.

Medea (Μήδεια/*Mḗdeia*, Lat. Medea). Born in → Aea/Colchis (M. Αἰαίη: Apoll. Rhod. 3,1136) as the daughter of → Aeetes, who was the son of Helios and the brother of Circe, and the Oceanid → Idyia (Hes. Theog. 956ff., 992ff., Apollod. 1,129) or → Hecate (Diod. Sic. 4,45,3). Sister of → Chalciope [2] and → Apsyrtus [1] (Apollod. 1,83.132), betrothed to Styrus (Val. Fl. 5,257f.), wife of → Jason [1] and by him the mother of Medeius (Hes. Theog. 1001) or → Mermerus and Pheres (Apollod. 1,146). Subsequently she is the wife of → Aegeus and mother of Medus (Apollod. 1,147). On the Isles of the Blessed she became the spouse of → Achilles [1] (Apollod. Epit. 5,5; Ibycus fr. 291; Sim. fr. 558 PMG; Lycoph. 174; Apoll. Rhod. 4,811ff.) [1].

M. is closely connected with the myth of the Argonauts. Made to fall in love with Jason by Hera with Aphrodite's help (Pind. P. 4,213ff.; schol. Eur. Med. 527; Apoll. Rhod. 3,7ff. 275ff.; Val. Fl. 6,455ff.). In return for a promise of marriage, M. supports him in performing the tasks given to him by Aeetes in order to obtain the Golden Fleece (Apollod. 1,129–131; → Iason) and flees with him from Colchis. To hold up their pursuers, M. cuts up her brother Apsyrtus (Pherecydes FGrH 3 F 32; Apollod. 1,133 [2. 83ff.]; in Apoll. Rhod. 4,421ff. she lures him into a fatal trap). Because of Zeus' anger, M. and Jason must be absolved of the murder by → Circe (Apollod. 1,134; Apoll. Rhod. 4,557ff.). M. is saved from being turned over to her pursuers by a ruse of → Arete [1], the queen of the Phaiaces: the immediate marriage of M. to Jason (Apollod. 1,137f.; Apoll. Rhod. 4,1004ff.). M. overcomes the bronze giant → Talos (Apollod. 1,140f.; Apoll. Rhod. 4,1638ff.).

After the return to Jason's home in → Iolcus, M. avenges Hera (by convincing Pelias' daughters to commit patricide) (Apollod. 1,144; Soph. Rizotomoi fr. 534ff. TrGF 4; Eur. Peliades fr. 601ff. TGF) and Jason (whose parents and brothers had been driven to death by → Pelias) (according to Nostoi fr. 7 PEG I; Ov. Met. 7,162ff., M. rejuvenates → Aeson [1], in Pherecydes FGrH3 F 113, Sim. fr. 548 PMG Jason). Thereupon, → Acastus banishes M. and Jason from Iolcus (Apollod. 1,14f.; Diod. Sic. 4,50ff.). Both go into exile in Corinth. M. bears Jason two sons.

This is where the early epics that still entered the mythographic collection of Pherecydes/Apollodonius attach: already Creophilus (PEG I 161: 7th cent. BC) fr. 9 knows of M. as the murderess of the Corinthian king → Creon [2], her flight without her children and Jason to Athens (cf. Hdt. 7,62,1: pre-Euripidean [3. 114 n. 1]), pointing at her falling out with Jason presumably because of his liaison with the king's daughter, the slaying of the children by the Corinthians and the rumour of M.'s infanticide (cf. Apollod. 1,145f.). The Corinthian epic poet → Eumelus [5] (PEG I 108: 8th cent. BC) even made Aeetes a Corinthian by birth (fr. 3; Pind. O. 13,53f.), so that M. as the heiress to the throne could go with Jason from Iolcus to Corinth (fr. 5; Sim. fr. 545 PMG; Apollod. 1,145f.). However, since no Corinthian descendants of Jason and M. other than Mermerus and Pheres are documented, the epic had to eliminate the two brothers from Corinth: Thus, the children perish during M.'s attempt (or Hera's, out of gratitude for M. rejecting Zeus' advances, schol. Pind. O. 13,74g) to make them immortal in the temple of Hera → Acraea [2] (Eumelus fr. 5 PEG). Another version claims that the Corinthians killed the children, who were left by M. in the temple when she fled (Apollod. 1,146; Parmeniscus schol. Eur. Med. 264; cf. Eur. Med. 1379ff.). M. flees from Corinth on the snake-drawn chariot of her grandfather Helios (Apollod. 1,147). In Athens she becomes the wife of → Aegeus and mother of Medos (Apollod. 1,147; cf. Eur. Med. 663ff.; in Diod. 4,54,7 M. flees to Hercules in Thebes). After the failed attempt to murder → Theseus, the son of Aegeus (Eur. Aegeus fr. 1ff. TGF), M. returns with Medos to her homeland, where she reinstalls Aeetes as ruler after killing → Perses (Apollod. 1,147) and names the Medians after herself (Hdt. 7,62,1). After her earthly existence, M. as a goddess becomes the wife of Achilles in the Islands of the Blessed (Apollod. Epit. 5,5).

M. is a creation for the Thessalian Argonaut myth [4. 18ff.]. Her nature is explained by her origin in Colchis, the land of sorcery *par excellence*, and by the fact that descent from Helios is generally associated with → magic. Homer fashioned his Circe after M. (Str. 1,2,40). The fairy tale of the king's daughter who helps the foreign youth against her own father [2. 149ff.; 5. 167; 6. 325ff.] underlies even the earliest version only to a limited extent because M. merely serves as a tool of Hera's revenge on Pelias there (there is no animosity between the latter as the legitimate ruler and Jason: Pherecydes FGrH 3 F 105; Apollod. 1,109; Pind. P. 4,250; Apoll. Rhod. 3,66ff. 1134ff.; schol. Eur. Med. 527 [4. 12ff.]) and because M. is a goddess herself (Hes. Theog. 956ff., fr. 376; Alcm. fr. 163 PMG; Apollod. 1,129; Musaeus 455 F 2 [7. 234f.]), whose relationship with a mortal is evident in the son Medeius named after her [4. 25ff.] and who lives in → Elysium after her earthly existence. Neither can a 'M. *initiatrix*' [2. 39ff.] and a founding heroine [2. 71ff.] or prophetess/muse M. [2. 103ff.] be documented, because in Pind. P. 4 M. only foretells the founding of Cyrene in Delphi's stead [4.262f.].

There is no literary evidence for splitting the M. character into a Thessalian (or Aeaeian-Colchian) and a Corinthian heroine [1. 48ff.], whose place was then taken by an infanticidal Hera as a '*reproductive demon*' and it is also superfluous [2. 57ff.]. The relocation of M., who was associated with Hera from the beginning, to Corinth was favoured by the cult of Hera Acraea and her temple legend of the graves of two times seven heroes there [2. 46ff.; 5. 173ff.; 7. 230f., 240ff., 322f.] as well as by the Helios cult [8. 64].

The infanticide was introduced to the Attic stage by Neophron (TrGF 1 no. 15) and (according to Dicaearchus fr. 63 WEHRLI; Aristot. fr. 635) after him especially by → Euripides (Med. 1271ff.), from where it entered inseparable from M.'s name into Roman (Sen. Med. 969ff.; Val. Fl. 5,442ff.; but cf. Ov. Met. 7,1–424; Ov. Epist. 12) and world literature [2. 297ff.; 6; 9], including Christa WOLF's novel [10]. On M. in art, see [1. 56–64; 2. 253ff.; 10. 127ff.; 11; 12. 91–100; 13; 14].

→ Argonauts; → Euripides [1] (B. 2.; → D. 2.)

1 A. LESKY, s.v. M./Medeios, RE 15, 29–65   2 J. J. CLAUSS, S. I. JOHNSTON (eds.), Medea: Essays on Medea in Myth, Literature, Philosophy, and Art, 1997   3 U. v. WILAMOWITZ-MOELLENDORFF, Die griechische Heldensage, (SPrAW 1925), in: KS 5.2, 85–126   4 P. DRÄGER, Argo pasimelousa, Vol. 1, 1993;   5 U. v. WILAMOWITZ-MOELLENDORFF, Griechische Tragödie, III, ⁷1926   6 K.v. FRITZ, Die Entwicklung der Iason-Medea-Sage und die Medea des Euripides, in: Antike und moderne Tragödie, 1962, 322–429   7 U.v. WILAMOWITZ-MOELLENDORFF, Hellenistische Dichtung, Vol. 2, ²1962   8 O. JESSEN, s.v. Helios, RE 8, 58–93   9 W.-H. FRIEDRICH, Medeas Rache, in: E.-R. SCHWINGE (ed.), Euripides, 1968, 177–237   10 M. HOCHGESCHURZ (Ed.), Christa Wolfs Medea, 1998   11 H. MEYER, Medea und die Peliaden, 1980   12 M. VOJATZI, Frühe Argonautenbilder, 1982   13 M. SCHMIDT, s.v. M., LIMC 6.1, 386–398   14 E. KEPETZIS, Medea in der Bildenden Kunst vom Mittelalter zur Neuzeit, 1997.

A. LESKY, s.v. M./Medeios, RE 15, 29–65; J. J. CLAUSS, S. I. JOHNSTON (Eds.), Medea: Essays on Medea in Myth, Literature, Philosophy, and Art, 1997. P.D.

Medeon

[1] (Μεδεών/*Medeón*; ethnicon Μεδεώνιος). Phocian town in the eastern part of the bay of Anticyra [2] (Str. 9,2,26; Paus. 10,36,6; Hdt. 1,38,21; Steph. Byz. s.v. M.), localized in the fortified centre of which the considerable remains can be found on the hill-top of the modern Hagioi Theodoroi (the acropolis of M.) and in the surrounding area. These remains include a section of the surrounding wall, with three towers; outside the wall, on the north-eastern slope of the hill, a necropolis with about 100 graves. Their dating allows an analysis of its habitation from the Early Helladic period to the 2nd cent. AD: interruption during the Bronze Age; between the 9th and 8th cent. BC, the town underwent a period of expansion; from the 7th cent. BC onwards, steady decline (surely connected with the concurrent rise of → Delphi; cf. the sparse sources for the 5th cent. BC, see also the assessment in Paus. 10,3,2). In addition, a Mycenaean tholos grave has been found, used as a place of worship from the 8th to the 6th cent. BC [1. 29f.; 2. 219–221; 3]. United in a → *sympoliteía* with → Stiris in the 2nd cent. BC (IG IX,1,32; Syll.³ 647). From the 1st cent. BC, M. was deserted; Pausanias saw its ruins (10,36,6). Remains of thermal baths were also found (3rd cent. AD); they were most likely part of the Roman villa (with floor mosaics), destroyed at the end of the 6th cent. AD, located on the plain below the acropolis. During the 9th cent., a monastery was built on the area once occupied by M.

1 C. VATIN, Médéon de Phocide, 1969 2 P. G. THEMELIS, in: ASAA 61, 1983, 213–255 3 C. MORGAN, Athletes and Oracles, 1990, 118–126, esp. 123f.

F. SCHOBER, Phokis, 1924, 36f.; W. KROLL, s.v. Medeon, in: RE 15, 65f.; C. VATIN e.a.., Médéon de Phocide, 1976; N. D. PAPACHATZIS, Παυσανίου Ἑλλάδος Περιήγησις 5, 1981, 444–446; J. M. FOSSEY, The Ancient Topography of Eastern Phokis, 1986, 11, 26–29; K. BRAUN, s.v. Medeon, in: LAUFFER, Griechenland, 410f. G.D.R.

[2] (Μεδεών). Boeotian city mentioned already in Hom. Il. 2,501 (Plin. HN 4,26; Dionysius son of Calliphon 99, GGM 1; Stat. Theb. 7,260; Nonn. Dion. 13,66; Steph. Byz. s.v. M.); for a time, it took its name from Mt. Phoenicis (modern Mt. Phagas or Sphingion), on whose northern flanks M. has been situated, near Onchestus in the border region between Thebes and Haliartus, on a hill-top now called Kastraki, close to the modern settlement of Davlosis (Str. 9,2,26; 3,13); remains of houses of the fortifications are still visible.

FOSSEY, 312–314; E. KIRSTEN, s.v. Phoinikis, RE 20, 1308f.; S. LAUFFER, M., in: MDAI(A) 63/4, 1938/9, 177–185; P. W. WALLACE, Strabo's Description of Boiotia, 1979, 109. P.F.

[3] see → Medion

Medes

Medes (Μῆδοι, *Mêdoi*, Old Persian *Māda*, Lat. *Medi*). Ethnolinguistically, the population is defined as western Iranian, and their north-west Iranian language is only indirectly documented in loan words and names in secondary transmission (Achaemenid royal inscriptions, Neo-Babylonian and Neo-Assyrian cuneiform texts) from the 9th cent. BC onwards. The Medes were first mentioned in 835 BC in the annals of → Salmanassar III as enemies of the Assyrians. The Median tribes were apparently only linked by a fairly loose political union. They – or their rulers – were a constant source of trouble for their Mesopotamian neighbours, and only those in the west of Media were temporarily conquered. Under their 'king'→ Cyaxares [1], they (together with the Babylonians) even dealt the fatal blow to the Assyrian empire at the end of the 7th cent. In military campaigns against the Lydians, the M. managed by 585 BC to extend their territory up to the → Halys (Hdt. 1,79). However, when Astyages was defeated by the Persian Cyrus [2] a few decades later, the M. became Persian (→ Persia) subjects.

In view of the limited information provided by Mesopotamian sources about the 'distant M.' – as opposed to Herodotus' comprehensive report on the formation of the Median empire (1,95–106) – and the equally insufficient archaeological record (Godīntappe, Tappe Nūš-e Ğān, Bāb Ğān from the 7th cent.), there is a lively debate amongst scholars regarding the political order of the M. (tribal federation or formation of an empire) and the extent of the legacy and influence of Median institutions in the Persian empire [1; 2; 5. 60–62; 7; 8]. There is also controversy as to why Greek literature used the term M. to refer to the Persians (cf. τὰ Μηδικά, Μηδισμός) [5; 9]. Furthermore, there are differences in the methodology and content of the definition of 'Median art' [4; 6. 62–64]. Median dress (trousers; close fitting, almost knee-length long-sleeved top; *akinakes*; soft tiara, slightly tilted towards the front with tied-up ear flaps) was also worn by non-M. as well as by the Persian great king (possibly as a war dress, although his tiara was 'upright') [3].
→ Media

1 S. BROWN, The Medikos Logos of Herodotus and the Evolution of the Median State, in: AchHist 3, 1988, 71–86 2 Id., Media and Secondary State Formation in the Neo-Assyrian Zagros, in: JCS 38, 1986, 107–119 3 P. CALMEYER, s.v. M., Tracht der, RLA 7, 615–617 4 Id., s.v. M., Kunst, RLA 7, 618–619 5 D. F. GRAF, Medism, in: JHS 104, 1984, 15–30 6 O. W. MUSCARELLA, Miscellaneous Median Matters, in: AchHist 8, 1994, 57–64 7 H. SANCISI-WEERDENBURG, Was There Ever a Median Empire?, in: AchHist 3, 1988, 197–212 8 Id., The Orality of Herodotus' *Medikos Logos* or: the Median Empire Revisited, in: AchHist 8, 1994, 39–55 9 CH. TUPLIN, Persians as Medes, in: AchHist 8, 1994, 235–256. J.W.

Medesicaste

Medesicaste (Μηδεσικάστη/*Mēdesikástē*).
[1] Daughter of the Trojan king → Priamus by one of his concubines (Apollod. 3,153), wife of Imbrius of Peda-

eum (Hom. Il. 18,171ff.). M. is depicted amongst the captured Trojan women on the Cnidian → lesche at Delphi (Paus. 10,25,9f.).

[2] Daughter of → Laomedon [1] and sister of Priam. Together with her sisters Aethylla and Astyoche, she sets fire to the ships transporting them to Greece as prisoners of war (Apollod. Epit. 6,15c; Tzetz. Schol. Lycoph. 921; 1075).

TH. GANTZ, Early Greek Myth: A Guide to Literary and Artistic Sources, 1993, 701.   I.BAN.

Medeus see → Medea

Medi see → Medes

Media Region in north-western Iran, in Neo-Assyrian records referred to as KUR *Ma-da-a-a*. The borders of M. changed in the course of history and cannot be defined exactly in geographical terms; its political centre was → Ecbatana. In historical times, the ethnolinguistic classification of M.'s predominant inhabitants was Iranian (→ Medes). More or less neglected by classical Greek records, the geography of M. gained importance in the Western mind from the Alexandrian period. Polybius praised the strategically advantageous location, and also the size, natural resources, dense population, as well as the industriousness of the inhabitants of this 'most important province within Asia'. He also referred to the breeding of the famous Nisaean horses (→ Nisa; Pol. 5,44f.; 10,27; cf. Diod.Sic. 17,110,6; Arr. Anab. 7,13,1; Str. 11,13,7). The people are described as both city and country dwellers, living in hundreds of villages by means of arable farming and cattle breeding (Diod. Sic. 19,32,1–3; 37,2; 39,1; 44,4; Str. 11,9,1). According to Str. 11,13,8, the annual contributions to the Great King of M. Atropatene (in north-western M., during his time separated from 'Greater M.') alone amounted to 4,000 mules, 3,000 horses, and 100,000 sheep, in addition to silver tributes. The military resources of M. Atropatene were recorded as 10,000 horsemen and 40,000 foot soldiers (Str. 11,13,2).

Even if M.'s administrative structure during the Achaemenid period remains unclear (Satrap Miturna/ Hydarnes [1] under Darius I: [3. PFa 18]; Oxydates (Arr. Anab. 3,20,3), and Atropates (Arr. Anab. 4,18,3) under Alexander the Great), evidence corroborates the assumption that M. Atropatene (and Rhagae?: Diod. Sic. 19,44,4) were at that time ruled by satraps. *These were parádeisoi* (→ parádeisos) or respectively *stathmoì basilikoí* (Plut. Artaxerxes 25,1; → Royal Road) not only in the vicinity of Ectabana, but also in → Bīsutūn (in the district of Kampanda: [3. DB II 27]) and other locations along the great military roads. The most important *via militaris* (Curt. 5,8,5) towards the east went from Ectabana via Rhagae, the 'Caspian Gates', and Hecatompylus to Bactria and Central Asia (Arr. Anab. 3,19,1–2; 20,2 and elsewhere); but from its main settlement, there were also links to Babylonia, Armenia,

and Cappadocia (Plut. Eumenes 16,1–2), into Persis (through the Gabiene region, as well as to northern Mesopotamia (Arr. Anab. 3,16,1). M., or more precisely Greater M., was one of the core territories of both the → Seleucid and the → Parthian Kingdom (Seleucid and Parthian monuments in → Bīsutūn). M. Atropatene (the modern Azerbaijan) with its main city of Gazaka, which had been mainly independent since 323 (Atropates), became an Asarcid 'vassal' probably around 120 BC. In the Sassanid period, the region of Mād was divided into several provinces. Mād (with the districts/ dioceses of Vastān [= Bīsutūn]/Bēṯ Madāyē and Nēmāvand [Nehāvand]/Nehāvand), as well as Hamadān (with the eponymous district/ diocese and also the district of Abhar) provide the most evidence. M. Atropatene was home to Ādur ī Gušnasp, one of the three main Sassanid sanctuaries (under a separate administration from that of the province of Adurbadagan).

1 BRIANT, 757–761   2 R. GYSELEN, La géographie administrative de l'empire sassanide, 1989, s.v. Mād   3 R. KENT, Old Persian, 1953   4 M. SCHOTTKY, M. Atropatene und Gross-Armenien in hellenistischer Zeit, 1989   5 Id., Quellen zur Geschichte von M. Atropatene und Hyrkanien in parthischer Zeit, in: J. WIESEHÖFER (ed.), Das Partherreich und seine Zeugnisse, 1998, 435–472.
                                                                    J.W.

Media, Wall of The wall of Media (Μηδίας τεῖχος, *Mēdías teîchos*) is only mentioned with this designation by Xenophon in his *Anábasis*, initially just in passing in connection with a defensive ditch at the Euphrates, built at the order of Artaxerxes [2] II (Xen. An. 1,7,15). Xenophon gives a comprehensive description of the wall in his report of the events following the battle of → Cunaxa in 401BC (An. 2,4,12): it was supposedly 20 feet (*c.* 6 m) wide, 100 feet (*c.* 30 m) high, and 20 parasangs (*c.* 80 km) long, built from fired bricks placed in asphalt. According to Xenophon (An. 2,14,13), the closest major city on the Tigris was → Sittace, and a further 80 parasangs along supposedly the town of → Opis on the river Physcon (An. 2,4,25). This fortification is probably identical with the structure described by Strabo as the 'Wall of Semiramis' (Σεμιράμιδος διατείχισμα; *Semirámidos diateíchisma*) near the village of Opis (Str. 2,1,26; 11,14,8). Ammianus Marcellinus also mentions the remains of a wall, seen by Julian's [11] army in AD 363 close to the village of Macepracta (Amm. 24,2,6).

The identification of the Wall of Media and the locations mentioned above remained controversial; in particular, Xenophon seems to have confused the names of Sittace and Opis. At present, the wall is identified as the still partially visible Ḥabl aṣ-Ṣaḥr ('stone line') about 20 km south-west of Baghdad. Archaeological findings at Ḥabl aṣ-Ṣaḥr indicate a wall of about 5.5 m, in height, 1.75 to 1,40 m wide, made from clay bricks mortared with asphalt, with a total length of 15 km; initially, it ran parallel to the Euphrates in a south-eastern direction, turning north-east after 8 km, and towards the east after a further 2.4 km. It was probably built by → Nebuchadnezzar (605–562) as part of a fortification system to protect Babylon (mainly against the Medes), which ran between the ancient Sippar (the modern Abū Ḥabba) and Upe (Greek Opis, the modern Tulūl al-Muğailiꜥ), where the Euphrates and Tigris run closest to each other; it had already fallen to ruins at the time of Xenophon.

1 R. D. BARNETT, Xenophon and the Wall of Media, in: JHS 83, 1963, 1–26   2 O. LENDLE, Kommentar zu Xenophons Anabasis, 1995, 112–115.   L.B.

Media Atropatene see → Atropates; → Media

Medical ethics

A. INTRODUCTION   B. ETHICS IN HIPPOCRATIC MEDICINE   C. ETHICS IN ROMAN MEDICINE   D. ETHICS IN CHRISTIAN MEDICINE

A. INTRODUCTION

Medical ethics can be defined as the attitude of those schooled in the art of healing towards those whom they want to heal. How this appears in detail, depends on the healer's social group and standing and also the society in which he or she works. Furthermore, healers and those seeking healing may well have completely divergent views on medical ethics. It is possible to regulate for any desired attitude in the sense of the earlier definition by laws or professional codes of conduct, or even outside of the law through the sanctioning power of public opinion or the opinion of certain groups.

B. ETHICS IN HIPPOCRATIC MEDICINE

In Greek antiquity, medical ethics was directed at two major areas: On the one hand, it was concerned with establishing those schooled in the art of healing as a cohesive group, particularly by defining healing as a sacred and secret art (e.g. Hippocrates, *Iusiurandum*, *Lex*) [1] which must only be disclosed to fellow healers. On the other hand, regarding the success of a particular treatment, it was concerned with establishing patient trust [2]. The pragmatic treatises *De decenti ornatu* and *Praeceptiones* in the *Corpus Hippocraticum*, both dating to the Hellenistic period, provided physicians with instruction on adequate professional conduct, regimenting their language, attire, and demeanour when demanding payments, with the overall aim of raising their reputation and boost the healing process. The Hippocratic Oath (→ Hippocrates [6]) emphasized the obligation to one's teacher and to the patient, e.g. keeping silence and not indulging in sexual relations, but these obligations are part of the overall religious context of personal holiness. The references in the oath to euthanasia and termination of pregnancies (→ Abortion) are contradicted by statements and practices described elsewhere within the collection of Hippocratic works. The legends surrounding Hippocrates depict him as an example of moral uprightness, not least due to his refusal to treat the Persian king Artaxerxes I, because he was the enemy of Greece [3].

C. ETHICS IN ROMAN MEDICINE

Discussions among the Stoics about professional ethos, e.g. amongst judges, may have sharpened the self-perception of physicians as a professional group [4]. Similarly, the proliferation of medical collegia may have also led to the development of local regulations, e.g. over medical fees (inscription Ephesus 385). However, because of the Roman tradition of self-sufficiency in medical care and a popular medical ethics as embodied by Cato in his *De agri cultura* and by Pliny the Elder, the potential evil arising from Greek physicians was frequently conjured up, and emphasis placed on the need for each family to look after its own members itself [5]. → Scribonius Largus (*Compositiones*, praef.) develops the Hippocratic Oath in a Roman, military context, in which the decision to act as a physician brings with it certain obligations equivalent to those of the Hippocratic Oath [6]. Epigraphical records also confirm that the Oath was well known as a manifesto of medical ethics, even if its heavily pietistic tone was not always accepted [7].

However, most works on medical ethics equate good medicine with successful practice; in that way, moral conduct became a kind of professional etiquette for physicians, as e.g. in Galen's detailed explanation of appropriate behaviour by a physician in his commentary on Epidemics 4,4,7 (CMG 5,10,2,2, pp. 197–217). In his *Quod optimus medicus*, Galen recommended what amounts to a philosophy of medicine as an integral component of a successful healing concept; however, successful healing was also conceivable without the conscious adoption of such philosophy. Galen's own appreciation of the moral physician is best evident in his description of a statue of Asclepius, in whom he saw an amalgamation of ethics, sound judgement, and philanthropy [8]. From the Hellenistic period onwards, honorary decrees for physicians also emphasize the moral and charitable conduct of the healer in question.

Roman legal regulations (Dig. 27,1,6,2; 50,9,1; Cod. Theod. 10,53,9) for civilian physicians prescribed that candidates be examined for their medical qualification and their moral conduct, even if the precise definition of the latter was left to each examining body itself. In the 6th cent. AD Cassiodorus (Var. 6,19) assumed that the census of *archiatri* (→ *archiatrós*) would place a check on such incidents as, e.g., the very public way in which physicians debated their patients and cases. Roman law provided for the punishment of certain transgressions, such as poisoning or the administration of love potions, but did not otherwise intervene in the doctor-patient relationship [9]. Public displeasure about failing physicians, whether justified or not, could also have contributed somewhat towards a quality assurance within medical practice (Gal. In Hippoc. Epid. II: CMG 5,10,2,1, p. 401). Questions regarding both the propriety of therapy and an apropriate response from the patient were also debated publicly, albeit without reaching a consensual conclusion (e.g. Lucian, Bis accusatus; Libanius, Progymnasma 8).

D. ETHICS IN CHRISTIAN MEDICINE

Christian medicine adopted a range of Jewish attitudes towards health and sickness, not least the communal philanthropic obligation to help the poor and the sick [10]. In this context, the Hippocratic Oath played a major part, not least as a symbol; its pagan introductory phrase was modified in the Christian sense. The rejection of abortion of the original Oath was retained, even further endorsed by Christian moral theology (→ Abortion). Later ethical oaths and declarations alluded to individual statements within the Hippocratic Oath or rephrased the Oath in view of the respective religious context, as shown for example by the as yet undated Hebrew Oath of Asaph; however, their common trait is a general concern for a greater efficiency in medical practice. The Hippocratic complaint that the misfortune of others filled a physician with grief (Corpus Hippocraticum, De flatibus 1) became a description of the good physician who took upon himself the suffering of others [11]. The ethics of Christian charity and Christian compassion for all human life resulted in extending the Hippocratic notion of service to the patients in one's care and to one's medical group to encompass all of humanity. Nevertheless, Christian theologians occasionally questioned whether the activities of the physician could be reconciled with the life of a clergyman. The religious obligation to save the immortal soul occasionally clashed with the medical efforts to care for the sick body. Pseudonymous texts such as the *Testamentum Hippocratis* and similar works written in Greek or in Oriental languages provide a systematic record of useful advise from older works in an easily accessible manner [12; 13].

→ Ethics; → Hippocrates; → Medicine; → Hippocratic Oath; → Hippocratism; → Medicine

1 J. JOUANNA, Un témoin inconnu de la tradition hippocratique, in: A. GARZYA (ed.), Storia e ecdotica dei testi medici greci, 1996, 253–272 2 H. FLASHAR, J. JOUANNA (ed.), Médecine et morale dans l'Antiquité (Entretiens de la Fondation Hardt 43), 1997 3 J. RUBIN PINAULT, Hippocratic Lives and Legends, 1992 4 L. EDELSTEIN, Ancient Medicine, 1969, 319–368 5 F. KUDLIEN, Medical Ethics and Popular Ethics, in: Clio Medica 5, 1970, 91–121 6 K. DEICHGRÄBER, Professio medici. Zum Vorwort des Scribonius Largus, in: AAWM 9, 1950, 855–879 7 H. VON STADEN, Character and Competence, in: [2], 158–195 8 F. ROSENTHAL, Science and Medicine in Islam, 1990, Ch. 3, 52–87 9 K. H. BELOW, Der Arzt im römischen Recht, 1953, 122–134 10 D. W. AMUNDSEN, Medicine, Society and Faith in the Ancient and Medieval Worlds, 1996 11 O. TEMKIN, Hippocrates in a World of Pagans and Christians, 1991 12 K. DEICHGRÄBER, Medicus gratiosus, in: AAWM 29, 1970, 194–309 13 L. C. MACKINNEY, Medical Ethics and Etiquette in the Early Middle Ages: the Persistence of Hippocratic Ideals, in: BHM 26, 1952, 1–31 14 D. GOUREVITCH, Le triangle hippocratique dans le monde gréco-romain, 1984 15 H. KOELBING, Arzt und Patient in der antiken Welt, 1977 16 F. KUDLIEN, s.v. Gesundheit, RAC 10, 902–945 17 C. LICHTENTHAELER, Der Eid des Hippokrates, 1984 18 E. WENKEBACH, Der hippokratische Arzt als das Ideal Galens, in: Quellen und Studien zur Geschichte der Naturwissenschaft und der Medizin 3, 1933, 169–175.; V. NUTTON, Ancient Medicine, 2004 V.N.

Medical services (military)
I. GREECE II. ROME

I. GREECE

No organized medical service developed in the context of Greek warfare. Alongside regular assistance to fellow soldiers, including that from warriors knowledgeable in the art of healing (an early reference in Hom. Il. 4,190–219 and 11,828–848, → Machaon and → Podalirius), there are sporadic references from the 5th cent. BC onwards to physicians treating the wounded, but this treatment was mainly improvised (cf. Xen. An. 3,4,30). It was rarely administered on the battlefield, but in nearby settlements, and was restricted to wound treatment. It was possible for physicians to number amongst the military contingents from cities (Sparta: Xen. Lac. 13,7); however, because the actual fighting was generally restricted to a small geographical area, it was more probable that the wounded were transported to their own or an allied city to receive treatment. The emergence of mercenary troops in the 4th cent. BC and the geographically more wide-ranging conduct of war in the Hellenistic period favoured a permanent presence of physicians and a specialization in military medicine. However, documentary evidence and more detailed information remains elusive. The responsibility lay with the commander in the field or respectively the ruler (Diod. Sic. 17,103,7 f.); his physicians (e.g. Diod. Sic. 15,87,5; Arr. Anab. 6,11,1) – at the same time status symbol of his position – most likely treated his officers and occasionally also the ordinary soldiers.

II. ROME

For the Republican period, there are no indications of an organized medical service within the military. Documentary evidence is sparse and rarely significant (Liv. 2,47,12; Dion. Hal. Ant. Rom. 5,36,3; Cic. Tusc. 2,38), and at best point to a rather improvised consultation of physicians. A fundamental change – together with the enormous expansion of the empire and its theatres of war – was only brought about by the establishment of the military monarchy of → Augustus. The particular care of the *princeps* for the welfare of his soldiers, regularly demonstrated in visits to the sick (Vell. Pat. 2,114,2; SHA Hadr. 10,6), was reflected in the establishment of high standards of hygiene (e.g. baths), in diet and training, and also in the supply with drinking water (Veg. Mil. 3,2). A regular military medical service was established, also deployed on the battle field, as depicted in one of the scenes on Trajan's column. Legionary camps (an early example: Haltern; exemplary Vetera/ Xanten as well as Housestead) were equipped with infirmaries (*valetudinaria;* basic principles in Hyg. Liber de munitionibus castrorum 4), placed under the supervision of the *praefectus castrorum* and the medical direction of an *optio valetudinarii* (CIL IX 1617 = ILS 2117). The medical staff – mainly *immunes* (Dig. 50,6,7) – comprised *capsarii* (medical orderlies), *seplasiarius, marsus, librarius,* as well as vets (*veterinarii, pecuarii*), and even *discentes capsario[rum]* (CIL VIII 2553 and AE 1906,9 = ILS 2438, for *legio III Aug.*). In contrast with modern armies, the medical staff were completely integrated into their respective units (legion, *auxilia,* warship etc.).

An insight into everyday life in the military medical service is provided by the Tabula Vindolandensis (→ Vindolanda Tablets) I 154: of the 752 men of the *cohors I Tungrorum,* 15 were sick, 6 wounded, and 10 suffering from eye infections. The best epigraphical evidence is for military physicians: there was a military service structure for physicians with numerous ranks and grades, the significance and ranking of which is at times controversial. Records confirm the positions of *medicus* (= *m.*) *miles, m. ordinarius* (in the rank of a *centurio*; ILS 2432), also *m. castrensis* (ILS 2126; *m. castrorum*: ILS 2193a), *m. legionis, m. cohortis* (ILS 2601; 2602), and *m. alae* (ILS 2542), but also *m. clinicus* (CIL VI 2532 = ILS 2093), *m. chirurgus,* and *m. ocularius,* in addition to naval physicians (*m. duplicarius;* CIL X 3442–3444 = ILS 2898–2900). The physicians, often of Greek origin, were probably generally recruited after they had completed their training, but there is also some indication of medical training within the army. That some of them achieved a high degree of professionalism is evident in their medical and pharmacological handbooks (Cels. De medicina 5,26; 7,5); → Pedanius Dioscorides was a military physician. There are no records to illustrate the exact historical development of the military medical service during the Principate. The level of institutionalized medical care achieved by the Roman army was only matched in modern times by the armies of the 18th or even 19th cent.

1 A. K. BOWMAN, Life and Letters on the Roman Frontier. Vindolanda and Its Peoples, 1994, 60; 104 f.   2 R. W. DAVIES, The Roman Military Medical Service, in: Saalburg Jb. 27, 1970, 84–104   3 A. KRUG, Heilkunst und Heilkult. Medizin in der Antike, 1985, 204–208   4 V. NUTTON, Medicine and the Roman Army: a Further Reconsideration, in: Medical History 13, 1969, 260–270   5 Id., The Doctors of the Roman Navy, in: Epigraphica 32, 1970, 66–71   6 C. F. SALAZAR, Die Verwundetenfürsorge in Heeren des griechischen Altertums, in: AGM 82, 1998, 92–97   7 Ead., The Treatment of War Wounds in Graeco-Roman Antiquity, 2000, 68–83   8 J. C. WILMANNS, Ärzte und Sanitätsdienst im römischen Germanien, in: Wehrmedizinische Monatsschrift 1990, H. 10, 491–499   9 Ead., Der Sanitätsdienst im Römischen Reich. (Medizin der Antike. 2), 1995.   J.H.

Medicinal plants
I. SOURCES   II. NUMBER AND FREQUENCY OF MEDICINAL PLANTS USED   III. THERAPEUTIC APPLICATIONS

I. SOURCES
The main sources for our knowledge of ancient medicinal plants are the *Corpus Hippocraticum* (= *CH*; cf. → Hippocrates [6]); → Theophrastus (H. plant. 9); → Scribonius [II 3] Largus; → Pedanius Dioscorides (*De materia medica*); → Pliny [1] (*Naturalis historia*); → Galen (*De simplicium medicamentorum temperamentis et facultatibus*) as well as the *Corpus toxicologorum* (→ Nicander' [4] *Thēriaká* and *Alexiphármaka*; the two anonymous toxicological treatises that used to be taken as volumes 6 and 7 of Dioscorides; → Philumenus), augmented by papyri. In their works, → Oribasius, → Aetius [3], and → Paulus [5] of Aegina assimilated the knowledge of earlier periods.

In Pedanius Dioscorides, about 60 % of therapeutically used substances are plants (637 of 1,066 chapters). The Greek healers → Podalirius, → Machaon, and → Melampus [1] were seen as the mythological pioneers of using medicinal plants in the treatment of diseases (in external and internal applications). → Diocles [6] of Carystus (4th cent. BC) was regarded as the author of the first ever herbarium (*Rhizotomikón*), but the knowledge of medicinal plants is much older and is based on their widespread use. The first pictorial representations of medicinal plants were ascribed to Crateuas, but it is likely that other such illustrations already existed earlier.

II. NUMBER AND FREQUENCY OF MEDICINAL PLANTS USED
Amongst the 380 plant names listed in the *CH* (equivalent to about 350 different botanical species and divisible into two groups), the first group of about 44 plants accounts for 1,500 (i.e. almost 50 %) of the total of 3,100 references; these 44 medicinal plants – with the exception of a small number of exotic plants and substances – consist of commonly found species (cf. table below).

Local products (plant breeding and cultivation, e.g. in the Mycenaean world [1]) were at an unspecified time (perhaps during the 'Oriental century', i.e. 750–650 BC [2]) joined by imports from Arabia and North Africa (→ Myrrh, → Caraway, → Incense, → Silphion; cf. table). Greek plants (from Asia Minor, the Aegean, Greece) were used as medicinal plants from very early on; the number of plant substances used in this way increased in later periods, as did diversification and specialization; the second group of 335 plants in the *CH* accounts for the about 1,600 references not covered by the previously mentioned 44 plants, with 255 plants (i.e. *c.* 67 % of 380) accounting for 500 references (i.e. *c.* 16 % of 3,100). While imports from the Orient increased as a consequence of the military campaigns of Alexander [4] the Great, between the 4th and 1st cents.

(*1)	CH (*2)	Greek name	Latin name (*3)	Main areas of use in antiquity (selection) (*4)	Modern medical properties (*5)	Identification (*6)	Common name	Diosc. (*7)	Plin. HN (*8)
1	87	smýrna	balsamum, myrrha	69 + 18 (ophthalmology, wound treatment)	?	Commiphora abyssinica Engl.	Myrrh	1,64	12,66–71
2	72	kýminon	cuminum	51 + 21 (stomach complaints, fever)	adstringent, peptogenic, emmenagogic, lactogenic, stomachic	Cuminum cyminum L.	Cumin	3,59	20,159–162
3	63	helléboros	elleborum, elleborus	16 + 47 (consumption, purification, hydropsy, rheumatism)	Veratrum album: antirheumatic, H. cyclophyllus: diuretic	Helleborus cyclophyllus Boiss. Veratrum album L.	Hellebore	4,162 4,148	25,47–61
4	49	skórodon	alium	34 + 15 (purulent inflammations, disorders of the rectum and the respiratory tract, fever, ophthalmology)	antiseptic, mucolytic, analgetic, cholagogue, antibiotic	Allium sativum L.	Garlic	2,149	20,50–57
5	47	linózôstis	mercurialis	39 + 8 (fever)			Mercury	4,189	25,38–41
6	46	sélinon	apium	29 + 17 (jaundice, angina, diseases of the brain)	emmenagogic, diuretic, blood-cleansing	Apium graveolens L.	Celery	3,64	19,124 20,112–118
7	46	práson	porrum	38 + 8 (choléra, diarrhoea, jaundice)	diuretic, laxative	Allium porrum L.	Leek	2,149–150	20,44–49
8	45	linon	linum	38 + 7 (wound treatment, pleurisy, rectal disorders, coughs in children, 'tumours': phŷma/oídēma)	adstringent, diuretic, anti-inflammatory, mucolytic, promotes wound healing; treatment of skin disorders, sexual organs, respiratory organs	Linum ustiatissimum L.*	Linseed	19,2–25	
9	45	libanôtós	balsamum, myrrha	36 + 9 (wound treatment, burns, dispnoea in children, pneumonia, tenesmus, 'head ulcers': kephalês hélkē)	adstringent, antiflatulent, diuretic, mucolytic, sedative, anti-dysentery; treatment of sexual organs, bronchitis	Boswellia spp. (int.al. B. carteri Birdw.)	Frankincense	1,68	12,51–65
10	45	silphion	silphium	25 + 20 (fever, gall bladder complaints, hydropsy, týphos)	?		Silphion (not identified)	3,80	19,38–45 22,100–106
11	43	ánnēson	anesum, anisum	39 + 4 (complaints of the diaphragm and the loins region, dispnoea in children, jaundice)	?	Pimpinella anisum L.	Aniseed	3,56	20,185–195
12	43	teûtlon	beta	8 + 35 (angina, purulent inflammations, consumption)	?	Beta vulgaris L.*	Beet	2,123	20,69–73
13	41	krámbē	brassica, caulis	38 + 3 (diseases of the brain, consumption)	?	Brassica oleracea L.	Cabbage	2,120	20,78–95
14	40	origanon, origanos	origanum	15 + 25 (angina, consumption, lung diseases, pneumonia, 'tumours': phŷma/oídēma)	antispasmodic	Oregano		3,27	20,175–180

15	37	rhoé, sídion	punica arbor, punicum	25 + 12 (choléra, wound treatment, diarrhoea, dysentery, fever, ophthalmology)	astringent	Punica granatum L.	Pomegranate	1,110	23,106–114
16	35	akté	sambucus	30 + 5 (diseases of the brain, diarrhoea, blood composition disorders, disorders caused by phlegm, cf. → Humoral theory)	diuretic, mildly laxative, emetic	Sambucus spp.	Elder	4,173	24,51–53
17	35	myrrhínē, myrsínē	myrtus, myrta	34 + 1 (anal prolapse)	adstringent, antiseptic, disinfectant	Myrtus communis L.*	Myrtle	1,112	23,159–166
18	33	elatérion	elaterium	24 + 9 (gall bladder complaints, day blindness)	for weak eye-sight, purifying	Ecballium elaterium (L.) A. Rich.	Squirting cucumber	4,150	20,3–10
19	31	elelísphakon, elelísphakos	salvia	26 + 5 ('pulmonary apoplexy': pyretós, lyngódēs, choléra, diarrhoea, pneumonia)	for leucorrhoea and inflammations of the respiratory tract, for menopausal complaints, peptogenic, strengthening	Salvia spp.*	Sage	3,33	22,145
20	31	kypárittos, kypárissos	cupressus, cyparissos	30 + 1 ('head ulcers': kephalēs hélkē)	antiseptic, adstringent, vasoconstrictive, for wound treatment	Cupressus sempervirens L.	Cypress	1,74	24,15
21	30	krithé	hordeum	23 + 7 (pains in hips and sides, fever, acute disorders, pleurisy, rectal disorders)	abortifacient, antigalactic, for fever and bronchitis, inflammations, for the treatment of sexual organs, stimulating peripheral circulation	Hordeum vulgare L.* subspp.	Barley	2,86	22,134–136
22	30	péganon	ruta	20 + 10 (consumption, angina, pneumonia, disorders of the spleen, 'tumours': phýma/oidēma, wound treatment)	emmenagogic, emetic, anticarcinogenic	Ruta graveolens L.	Ruewort	3,45–46	20,131–143
23	29	dáphnē	laurus	29 + –	emmenagogic	Laurus nobilis L.	Bay Tree	1,78	23,152–158
24	29	sýkon	ficus	18 + 11 (excessive eating, angina, gall bladder complaints, choléra, diarrhoea, haemostasis, 'tumours': phýma/oidēma, wound treatment)	peptogenic disinfectant, diuretic, anti-inflammatory, mildly laxative, stomachic, treatment of sexual organs and tumours	Ficus spp.	Fig	1,127	23,117–131
25	26	elaía	olea	22 + 4 (diarrhoea, inflammations, 'tumours': phýma/oidēma)	anticarcinogenic, antiseptic, adstringent, cholagogue, diuretic, mildly laxative	Olea europaea L.*	Olive tree	1,105	23,69–79
26	26	glykysídē	paeonia	25 + 1 (typhos)	emetic and laxative, liver protection	Paeonia officinalis L.	Peony	3,140	27,84–87
27	26	márathon, márathros	feniculum	24 + 2 (jaundice, respiratory tract disorders)	abortifacient, diaphoretic, diuretic, emmenagogic, lactogenic	Foeniculum vulgare Miller*	Fennel	3,70	20,254–258
28	26	pyrós	frumentum	19 + 7 (throat complaints, problems with bowel movements, contusion of the nose, hydropsy)	anti-inflammatory, mildly laxative, treatment of wounds and bleeding	Triticum spp.	Wheat	2,85	18,61–70
29	25	phakós	lens, lenticula	11 + 14 (choléra, wound treatment)	stomach protection, skin disorders	Ervum lens L.	Lentil	2,107	18,198 22,142–147

30	25	*knidios kókkos*	*cneorum*	6 + 19 (coxalgia, hydropsy, purulent inflammations, consumption, spleen disorders, *typhos*)	diaphoretic	*Daphne gnidium* L.		4,172	21,55
31	25	*lōtós*	*lotos*	19 + 6 (wound treatment)	astringent (tannin), protecting mucous membranes	-	Clover	4,110	21,34,99,103
32	25	*sikýa*	*cucurbita*	20 + 5 (gall bladder complaints, coxalgia, liver diseases, stranguria)	purifying	*Lagenaria siceraria (Molina)* Standl.	Bottle Gourd	4,176	19,69–74
33	24	*glḗchōn*	*puleium*	19 + 5 (diarrhoea, blood composition disorders fever, purification)	blood-cleansing, for digestive disorders	*Mentha pulegium* L.	Pennyroyal	3,31	20,152–157
34	23	*kykláminos*	*cyclaminos, cyclaminum*	20 + 3 (gall bladder complaints, pneumonia)	laxative, emmenagogic	*Cyclamen* *spp.	Cyclamen	2,164–165	25,114–116
35	22	*kýpeiros, kýpeiron*	*cyperus, cypirus*	22 + –	?	*Cyperus esculentus* L.	Tigernut	1,4	21,115–116
36	21	*melánthion*	*melanthion, git*	21 + –	emmenagogic, lactogenic	*Nigella sativa* L.*	Black cumin/ Black caraway	3,79	20,182–184
37	19	*astaphís*	*staphis*	18 + 1 (rectal diseases)	?	*Delphinium staphisagria* L.	Stavesacre	4,152	23,17–18
38	19	*bátos*	*morum, morus, rubus*	17 + 2 (*choléra*, diarrhoea)	antidiarrhoeal, anti-inflammatory	*Rubus* spp., *Morus nigra* L.	Blackberry bush	4,38	24,117–124
39	19	*kénchros*	*milium*	– + 19 (fever, pleurisy, diseases of the brain)	cough medicine, cooling, for the treatment of the sexual organs	*Panicum miliaceum* L.*	Millet	2,97	22,130–131
40	19	*skammōnía*	*scammonia*	11 + 8 (kidney complaints, coxalgia, fever, inflammation of the liver, lung diseases, rheumatic diseases, *typhos*)	diuretic, laxative, antirheumatic	*Convolvulus scammonia* L.*	Scammony Bindweed	4,170	26,59–61
41	18	*ágnos*	*vitex*	11 + 7	antispasmodic in digestive disorders	*Vitex agnus-castus* L.	Chaste Tree/ Monks' Pepper Tree	1,103	24,59–63
42	18	*sḗsamon*	*sesamum*	7 + 11 (bronchitis, expectoration of blood, jaundice rheumatism, coughs in children)	emmenagogic, mildly laxative	*Sesamum orientale* L. (*S. indicum* L.)	Sesame	1,34	22,132–133
43	17	*krómmyon*	*cepa*	10 + 7 (purification, gall bladder complaints, diseases of the brain, jaundice, purulent inflammations)	?	*Allium cepa* L.	Onion	2,149	20,39–43
44	14	*koríannon*	*coriandrum*	7 + 7 (jaundice, consumption, diarrhoea, tenesmus)	antiflatulent and for digestive disorders, stomachic, antispasmodic, antidiarrhoeal	*Coriandrum sativum* L.*	Coriander	3,63	20,216–218

(*1) Ordered according to how frequently they are mentioned. Cf. the alphabetical index of plant names (see below).

(*2) *Corpus Hippocraticum* (*CH*) quoted from the edition by E. LITTRÉ, 10 vols., 1839–1861 (with French translation). The numbers refer to the total number of times that a plant is mentioned.

(*3) Latin plant name according to J. ANDRÉ, Les noms de plantes dans la Rome antique, 1985.

(*4) First figure: number of gynaecological indications; second figure: other indications (the most important of which listed in brackets). Square brackets: number of times that a plant is mentioned. No figure: one reference. Disease name in italics: ancient terminology (if different from the modern term). Gynaecological indications in *CH* (in alphabetic order of English terms): Abortion: 17; Amenorrhoea: 18; Childbirth: 3; Fertility tests: 2; Genital organs (injuries, inflammations): 14; Gynaecology (without further specification): 174; Haemorrhages: 76; 'Hysteria': 68; Infertility: 14; Lactation (increase): 8; Lactation (termination): 5; Leucorrhoea: 16; Menstruation (stimulation): 11; Metrorrhagia: 5; Miscarriages (prevention): 17; Placenta removal: 24; Postpartum haemorrhage: 77; Pregnancy (minor complaints): 15; Pregnancy test: 2; Proconceptive agents: 67; Uterus (displacement, swelling, hydropsy): 350.

(*5) Cf. G. ALIOTTA et al., Le piante medicinali del Corpus Hippocraticum, 2002. Question mark (?): ancient applications as yet unconfirmed in scientific pharmacological literature.

(*6) Identifications according to BNP or (*) according to G. ALIOTTA et al. respectively (see above *5).

(*7) Pedanius Dioscorides: references according to M. WELLMANN, 3 vols., 1906–14; reprint 1958.

(*8) Plinius , Naturalis historia: references according to J. C. MAYHOFF, 5 vols., 1892–1909; reprint 1967.

Alphabetical index of plant names. The figure refers to the number within the table.

1. **Greek names:** *ágnos* 41 – *akté* 16 – *ánnēson* 11 – *astaphís* 37 – *bátos* 38 – *dáphnē* 23 – *elaía* 25 – *elatérion* 18 – *elelísphakon* 19 – *glēchōn* 33 – *glykysídē* 26 – *helléboros* 3 – *kénchros* 39 – *knídios kókkos* 30 – *koríannon* 44 – *krámbē* 13 – *krithḗ* 21 – *krómmyon* 43 – *kykláminos* 34 – *kýminon* 2 – *kypárissos, kypárittos* 20 – *kýpeiros, kýpeiron* 35 – *libanōtós* 9 – *línon* 8 – *linózōstis* 31 – *márathon, márathos* 27 – *melánthion* 36 – *myrrhínē, myrsínē* 17 – *oríganon* 14 – *pēganon* 22 – *phakós* 29 – *práson* 7 – *pyrós* 28 – *rhoễ* 15 – *sélinon* 6 – *sésamon* 42 – *sídion* 15 – *síkyā* 32 – *sílphion* 10 – *skammōnía* 40 – *skórodon* 4 – *smýrna* 1 – *sýkon* 24 – *teûtlon* 12.

2. **Latin names:** *alium* 4 – *anesum* 11 – *anisum* 11 – *apium* 6 – *balsamum* 9 – *beta* 12 – *brassica* 13 – *caulis* 13 – *cepa* 43 – *cneorum* 30 – *coriandrum* 44 – *cucurbita* 32 – *cuminum* 2 – *cupressus* 20 – *cyclaminos* 34 – *cyclaminum* 34 – *cyparissos* 20 – *cyperus* 35 – *cyprus* 35 – *elaterium* 18 – *elleborus* 3 – *elleborum* 3 – *faeniculum* 27 – *ficus* 24 – *frumentum* 28 – *git* 36 – *hordeum* 21 – *laurus* 23 – *lens* 29 – *lenticula* 29 – *linum* 8 – *lotos* 31 – *melanthion* 36 – *mercurialis* 5 – *milium* 39 – *morus* 38 – *morum* 38 – *murtus* 17 – *myrrha* 1 & 9 – *olea* 25 – *origanum* 14 – *paeonia* 26 – *porrum* 7 – *puleium* 33 – *punica arbor* 15 – *punicum* 15 – *rubus* 38 – *ruta* 22 – *salvia* 19 – *sambucus* 16 – *scammonia* 40 – *sesamum* 42 – *silphium* 10 – *staphis* 37 – *vitex* 41.

BC the range of medicinal herbs was also expanded by the flora of the western Mediterranean (Italy, southern France, Sicily, Corsica, Sardinia), with a further expansion in the 1st cents. BC and AD. (→ Commerce with → Spices in the Roman Empire). The encyclopaedias of the 1st cent. AD (Pedanius Dioscorides and Pliny) show very clearly the extent to which both the requirements and the opportunities of traditional medical school had grown. Between the 4th and 6th cents. AD, the number of medicinal herbs in use sank again to about 400, a more manageable quantity (the alphabetical recension of Dioscorides is the direct result of this reduction and not at all an indication for an increasing tendency in late-antique science to order items alphabetically). Late-antique western handbooks as well as Byzantine therapeutic manuals (*iatrosóphia*; cf. → *iatrosophistés*; → Pharmacology VII.) largely stick with this quantity.

III. THERAPEUTIC APPLICATIONS

The terminology to describe the therapeutic effect of plants has its roots in the *Problémata* of the Aristotelian School, e.g. in Theophrastus (cf. [3]). In Dioscorides, it was expressed in the term *dýnamis* (literally 'power', 'effective properties'). Galen introduced a materialistic system by defining a relationship between the properties of medicinal herbs on the one hand, and the bodily fluids (→ Humoral theory) and elements of the world on the other, and by making these properties measurable [4]. However, this system, combined by early Byzantine authors with that of Dioscorides, could not prevail, but it was taken up in the Arab world and subsequently became known again in the West through the translations of medical texts (made in Salerno from the 11th cent. onwards) from Arabic into Latin.

Dioscorides classified medicinal herbs systematically on two levels: firstly in groups based on their properties (i.e. analgetic, toxic, or psychotropic medicinal herbs, whose effects were well known), and secondly in groups according to a *scala naturae*, i.e. a hierarchy of all natural elements.

The general therapeutic principle of Greek medicine is that of allopathy (*contraria contrariis*). Initially, any pathogenic fluid (→ Humoral theory) was to be eliminated from the body with the aid of purifying agents (mainly hellebore/→ *helleborus*, cf. table below); as a second therapeutic step, this was later followed by treating the external symptoms of a disease (symptomatic treatment), which explains the comprehensive range of medicinal herbs to ensure a diversification of effects.

Medicinal herbs were collected by specialists (*rhizotómoi*) [5] and traded by various professional groups [6]. Pliny provides a list of precisely defined prices [7], and the *Edictum* [3] *Diocletiani* set the legal basis for such definition [7]. Medicinal herbs were used as a whole or in parts (roots, leaves, fruits, seeds, secretions, etc.), both fresh and dried. In case of the latter, they were preserved in particular containers depending on

their nature (Dioscorides, De materia medica, praef. 9). For simple drugs and prescriptions, depending on their method of administration, medicinal herbs were combined with a binding agent (e.g. water, wine, vinegar, resin, or gum); in composite remedies, they were combined with several other products (including mineral and animal products), and were mixed with one or more binding agents. The form in which they were administered varied according to the application (external or internal), the organ in question, and the type of illness: e.g. external application, bath, or steambath, drink, poultice, clyster, cream, diet, blistering plaster, embrocation, fumigation, gargling, infusion, inhalation, irrigation, enema, liniment, ointment, powder, suppository, swab.

→ Disease; → Medicine; → Pharmacology; → Intoxicating substances; → Pharmacology

1 P. FAURE, Parfums et aromates de l'Antiquité, 1987, 99–145   2 W. BURKERT, The Orientalizing Revolution, 1995, 41–87   3 A. TOUWAIDE, Die aristotelische Schule und die Entstehung der theoretischen Pharmakologie, in: Die Apotheke 1996, 11–22   4 Id., La thérapeutique médicamenteuse de Dioscoride à Galien, in: A. DEBRU (ed.), Galen on Pharmacology, 1997, 255–282   5 G. E. R. LLOYD, Science, Folklore and Ideology, 1983, 119–135   6 J. KORPELA, Aromatarii, pharmacopolae, thurarii et ceteri. Zur Sozialgeschichte Roms, in: PH. J. VAN DER EIJK (ed.), Ancient Medicine in Its Socio-Cultural Context, 1995, Bd. 1, 101–118   7 A. SCHMIDT, Drogen und Drogenhandel im Altertum, 1924, 103–107.

G. ALIOTTA, D. PIOMELLI, A. POLLIO, A. TOUWAIDE, Le piante medicinali del Corpus Hippocraticum, 2003; I. ANDORLINI, L'apporto dei papiri alla conoscenza della scienza medica antica, in: ANRW II 37.1, 1993, 458–562; J. ANDRÉ, Les noms de plantes dans la Rome antique, 1985; M. AUFMESSER, Etymologie und wortgeschichte Erläuterungen zu De materia medica des Pedanius Dioscurides Anazarbeus, 2000; R. J. DURLING, A Dictionary of Medical Terms in Galen, 1993; K. KARTTUNEN, India and the Hellenistic World, 1997, 129–252; M. G. RASCHKE, New Studies in Roman Commerce with the East, in: ANRW II 9.2, 1978, 604–1361; J. RIDDLE, Dioscorides on Pharmacy and Medicine, 1985; Id., Quid pro quo. Studies in the History of Drugs, 1992; J. SCARBOROUGH, Theophrastus on Herbals and Herbal Remedies, in: Journ. of the History of Biology 11, 1978, 353–385; J. STANNARD, Pristina medicamenta, 1999; A. TOUWAIDE, Le strategie terapeutiche: i farmaci, in: M. GRMEK (ed.), Storia del pensiero medico occidentale, vol. 1, 1993, 353–373; Id., Bibliographie historique de la botanique: les identifications de plantes médicinales, in: Lettre J. Palerne 30, 1997–1998, 2–22; 31, 1998, 2–65; Id., Le médicament en Alexandrie, in: G. ARGOUD (ed.), Sciences exactes et sciences appliquées à Alexandrie, 1998, 189–206; Id., De la pratique populaire au savoir codifié, in: A. ROUSSELLE (ed.), Monde rural et histoire des sciences en Méditerranée, 1998, 81–105.   A.TO.

Medicina Plinii Compilation of medical texts written in Latin and attributed in the MSS to an otherwise unknown Plinius Secundus Iunior. Mentioned by → Marcellus [8] Empiricus, it is generally accepted to date back to the early 4th cent. AD or even slightly before that.

The compilation starts with the author's declaration of his intention to prevent the counterfeiting of medicinal products whose ingredients he then lists together with the relevant composition. The work consists of three books. Bk. 1–2: medicinal preparations, ordered according to the organ to which they applied (listed 'from head to toe'), without describing the pathological findings for which the drugs/medical products are to be applied. Bk. 3: medicinal preparations for diseases affecting the entire organism.

Its main source is the *Historia naturalis* of → Pliny the Younger (esp. bks. 20–33), whose material is augmented with personal comments by the author and other additions. The compilation stands out because of its openness towards popular medicine, which thus became codified in line with the general trend at that time. It also takes into account magical formulas and other forms of therapy which are not strictly pharmacological in nature.

The compilation was used as reference by Marcellus Empiricus, probably also by Ps.-Apuleius, as well as for the *Additamenta* to → Theodorus Priscianus. An expanded version is the *Physica Plinii*, of which several versions are extant, the oldest probably dating to the early 6th cent. AD.

H. Gertler, Über den medizinisch-pharmazeutischen Gehalt der Medicina Plinii Secundi Junioris, in: Beitr. der Univ. Erfurt 14, 1968/9, 49–53; A. Önnerfors, Plinii Secundi Iunioris qui feruntur De medicina libri tres, 1964; Id., In Medicinam Plinii studia philologica, 1963.   A.TO.

Medicine
I. Mesopotamia II. Egypt III. Jewish Medicine IV. Classical Antiquity

I. Mesopotamia
Magic formulae – such as spells, apotropaea, and prophylacterics – and rational elements, i.e. empirically derived treatment methods with plant, mineral, or animal substances, characterize the image of medicine in a Mesopotamia. The treatment of diseases – seen as either caused by demons, or as a punishment sent by the gods, or as the result of being bewitched, as well as the result of natural causes – was the domain of two different experts, the *asû*, more versed in herbal lore, evident from as early as the mid–3rd millennium BC, and the spell expert/ magical healer (*w*)*ašipu* (for both see [3]).

A. Available sources, their age and transmission B. Nature and content of the texts

A. Available sources, their age and transmission
The oldest evidence of medical-therapeutic literature is provided by two clay tablets with prescriptions in Sumerian (end of the 3rd millennium; [4]). Further-

more, also known are some Sumerian spells against scorpion and snake bites from the middle of the 3rd millennium BC [12]. A comparatively small corpus of medical texts comprising more than 100 clay tablets is written in Old Babylonian (early 2nd millennium BC). However, the majority of texts (more than a thousand clay tablets, *i. a.* from Assur, Ninive, Sippar, Babylon, and Uruk) dates from the 9th–4th cents. BC, reflecting, though, a much older practice. Some of these are library copies (library of → Assurbanipal), some texts belonging to individuals, who – according to → Colophon [2] – often copied prescriptions for one particular case only. Very little is known about the training of → physicians. It is generally assumed that one of the training centres for physicians was in the Gula temple in Isin.

B. Nature and content of the texts
The medical literature can be divided into two categories: medical-therapeutic and prognostic-diagnostic. The first group concerns a substantial collection of prescriptions against illnesses of the head, eyes, ears, teeth, as well as internal diseases and those afflicting the feet or joints. In the 1st millennium BC, this collection was compiled in a handbook of 44 tablets, entitled 'If the head of a person burns with fever' [10]. Alongside purely medical-therapeutic instructions, this corpus also contains many elements of a magical nature. The texts are all structured in the same way: 'If a person shows ... symptoms, you should ...'. Noteworthy is the absence of magical practices as a healing method in texts dating from the Old Babylonian period (18th/17th cent. BC).

The texts of the second group are steeped in the tradition of Babylonian → divination. The description of the symptoms is followed by the diagnosis of the outcome of the disease (e.g. the sufferer will be healed/ will die), or the diagnosis is 'the hand of the deity X' [14] as an indication for a specific disease. These texts are compiled in a forty-tablet handbook, entitled 'When the exorcist comes to the house of a sick person' [13]. Late cuneiform tablets with medical contents show that attempts had been made to combine both of these handbooks [8]. A late text from Uruk is notable because it traces the location of a disease to the bodily organs [10].

A further important source of medical knowledge is extant in the form of herbaria. One of these pharmacopoeias boasts more than 1,200 entries. According to this handbook, disgusting substances (e.g. human excrements) can be seen as cover names for pharmaca in order to maintain professional secrecy. It is no longer tenable to describe this as a form of *Dreckapotheke* ('filth medicine') [11]. That surgical operations were also undertaken can de deduced from § 215–220 of the law book of → Ḥammurapi, according to which an *asû* was faced with a potential penalty or punishment if the operation failed. It is conceivable that comparatively simple operations were carried out, e.g. as part of the treatment of battlefield wounds or the treatment of injuries caused by animals – however, the extant texts contain no such information. Letters from the 18th, 14th/13th or respectively 7th cents. BC document contemporary cases of illness at the courts of *i. a.* Mari [3], Hattusa [6], Ugarit [3], Babylon [14] and Assyria [15].

There is no documentary evidence of any relations with Classical Greek medicine, cf. Hdt. 1,197.

→ Amulet; → Demons; → Healing deities, healing cults; → Disease; → Magic

1 R. D. BIGGS, Medicine, Surgery, and Public Health in Ancient Mesopotamia, in: J. M. SASSON (ed.), Civilizations of the Ancient Near East, vol. 3, 1995, 1911–1924   2 Id., G. BECKMANN, s.v. M., RLA 7, 623–631   3 A. L. OPPENHEIM et al.. (ed.), Chicago Assyrian Dictionary, vol. 1/2, 1968, s.v. *asû, āšipu*; vol. 10, 1977, s.v. *marāṣu, murṣu*   4 M. CIVIL, Préscriptions médicales sumériennes, in: RA 54, 1960, 57–72   5 E. DION, Medical Personnel in the Ancient Near East in Aramaic Garb, in: ARAM 1, 1989, 206–216   6 E. EDEL, Ägyptische Ärzte und ägyptische Medizin am hethitischen Königshof, 1976; 7 I. FINKEL, On TDP Tablets XXIX and XXXI, in: JCS 46, 1994, 87f.   8 F. KÖCHER, Die babylonisch-assyrische Medizin, vols. 1–6, 1963–1980   9 Id., Spätbabylonische medizinische Texte aus Uruk, in: C. HABRICH et al. (ed.), Medizinische Diagnostik in Geschichte und Gegenwart, 1978, 17–39   10 Id., Ein Text medizinischen Inhalts aus dem neubabylonischen Grab 405, in: R. M. BOEHMER et al. (ed.), Uruk: Die Gräber, 1995, 203–217   11 M. KREBERNIK, Die Beschwörungen aus Fara und Ebla, 1984   12 R. LABAT, Traité akkadien de diagnostics et prognostics médicaux, 1953   13 S. PARPOLA, Letters from Assyrian Scholars (AOAT 5/2), 1983;   14 M. STOL, Epilepsy in Babylonia, 1993   15 H. WASCHOW, Babylonische Briefe aus der Kassitenzeit, 1936.

II. EGYPT

Egyptian medicine, too, combines magical-religious and empirical-rational elements. Disease, generally seen as a disturbance in the natural order, was traced back to supernatural as well as natural causes. Experts responsible for healing were physicians, priests, and magicians, with the likelihood of the boundaries between them being blurred.

A. AVAILABLE SOURCES, THEIR AGE AND TRANSMISSION   B. NATURE AND CONTENT OF THE TEXTS

A. AVAILABLE SOURCES, THEIR AGE AND TRANSMISSION

More than a dozen medical texts of different lengths and quality are known. The actual medical literature dates back to the Middle and the New Kingdom (between 2000–1200 BC), but the composition of some papyri dates back to the Old Kingdom. The copying of medical texts was done in the 'House of Life', which was also the place, where physicians were trained. In contrast with Mesopotamia, specialist physicians existed (from the Old Kingdom); we know of a 'physician of the belly', a 'guardian of the anus' as well as eye and dental surgeons. Egyptian medicine was so highly regarded that physicians were sent to neighbouring

countries, or foreign rulers came to Egypt to seek medical treatment. Both Hom. Od. 4,229ff. and Hdt. 2,84 praise Egyptian medicine.

B. NATURE AND CONTENT OF THE TEXTS

According to Clement of Alexandria (Clem. Al. Strom. 6, 35–37; around AD 200), the Egyptians had six books of medical knowledge (on the structure of the body, diseases, tools of the physician, remedies, diseases of the eye, and female diseases). However, this information does not correspond with the extant texts. Alongside specialists books such as PSmith (surgical textbook, Old Kingdom), PKahun (gynaecological textbook, Middle Kingdom), PRamesseum V (remedies for muscle and joint diseases, Middle Kingdom) and PChester Beatty IV (remedies for internal complaints), we find collective MSS. The largest of these is PEbers (more than 100 columns on a length of 20 m), other collective MSS are PHearst, the Berlin Medical Papyrus, and the London Medical Papyrus. The language of the texts is Middle Egyptian, the script is Hieratic. The prescriptions generally follow the pattern 'If you investigate ... and you find ... , then you should ...'.

Interaction between Egyptian and Greek medicine is known on the level of drugs [2], but it is unclear whether the doctrine of putrefaction or the anatomic practices of the mummifiers influenced Greek practitioners. Several remedies from ancient Egyptian texts continued to be used in Coptic medicine in the 4th century AD, and even later in Greek medical prescriptions.

1 W. WESTENDORF, Handbuch der altägyptischen Medizin, 1998   2 M. H. MARGANNE, Links between Egyptian and Greek Medicine, in: Forum 3,4, 1993, 35–43   3 T. BARDINET, Les Papyrus médicaux de l'Egypte pharaonique, 1995   4 H. GRAPOW, Grundriß der Medizin der alten Ägypter, 9 vols., 1954–1973; 5 J. NUNN, Ancient Egyptian Medicine, 1996.   BA.BÖ.

III. JEWISH MEDICINE

Although the notion of Yahwe as the healer of his people is common in the Old Testament, stories of physical healing are relatively rare [7]. Physicians (*rofʾīm*) are denounced as ineffective and leading to a lack of trust in God's mercy (e.g. 2 Chr 16:11–13). By Hellenistic times, there is a shift to a more positive evaluation of medicine (Sir 38:1–15). King Solomon is held up as a model of medical learning (Jos. Ant. Iud. 8,44), and groups such as the → Essenes (ibid. 8,136) or the → *Therapeutai* displayed a great interest in medicine. Herbs form the basis of most medical treatment [8], but many diseases are, at least from Hellenistic times on, ascribed to the intervention of demons, to be cured by → exorcism and religious means. Charismatic prophets and healers, among whom some have placed Christ, also healed the sick [9].

IV. Classical Antiquity

A. Sources of Classical Medicine B. Pre-Hip-
pocratic Medicine C. Hippocratic Medicine
D. Religion and Medicine E. Hellenism
F. Greek Medicine in Republican Rome
G. Imperial period H. Late antiquity
J. Christianity K. Summary

A. Sources of Classical Medicine

Literary texts of Greek and Latin medicine show a
very unequal chronological distribution. Between the
Corpus Hippocraticum (*c.* 430–370 BC, → Hippocrates [6]) and the 1st cent. AD, the only extant original
works are those of → Nicander of Colophon and
→ Apollonius [16] of Citium. The 1st cent. AD saw the
writing of the major Latin syntheses of → Celsus [7] and
Pliny the Elder (→ Plinius), along with the works of the
pharmacologist → Scribonius Largus and those of the
Greek authors → Pedanius Dioscorides, → *Anonymus
Parisinus*, → Rufus of Ephesus, and → Soranus. From
the 2nd cent. AD come → Aretaeus, the → *Anonymus
Londinensis*, and, most importantly, → Galen, whose
later authority helped to drive out alternative views and
to impose the Hippocratic tradition as the only true
form of medicine. From the 4th cent. onwards, important treatises in Latin are extant, particularly → Caelius
[II 11] Aurelianus, alongside some shorter practical
instructions and prescription collections. Similar short
texts including *problémata physiká* ('anthologies of
problems') are found in Greek alongside more comprehensive overviews as those by → Alexander [29] of
Tralles and → Paulus of Aegina. The learned tradition
of commentaries on Hippocratic texts was extended to
Galen, whose works were also to dominate the Greek
encyclopaedias of → Oribasius and Aetius. A consequence of this chronological distribution of sources is
that for a large part of Antiquity, historians are dependent on fragments and → doxographies, often written
many centuries later and, in Galen's case, often compiled with polemic intent [10]. Because these texts are
largely prescriptive in nature, it is necessary to gather
confirmation on actual medical practices from literary
reports about treatments on papyri, or from archaeological evidence, and also with the aid of palaeopatho-
logy (→ Disease) [11]. Epigraphical records regarding
the career, family, and, occasionally, medical practice
of physicians are considerable, but much needs to be
added to the traditional epigraphical collections by
Oehler and Gummerus [12; 13]. Visual information
on medical practice is also comparatively sparse [14].

B. Pre-Hippocratic Medicine

Archaeological finds confirm reports in the Homeric
epics of a sound knowledge in wound surgery (→ Surgery), and Mycenaean tablets also show the existence of
drugs (→ Pharmacology; [15]). → Machaon, physician
and son of Asclepius, is praised for his services ('a physician is a man worth many others': Hom. Il. 11,514;

the following verse then explains this praise), which included healing herbs and bandages. Ideas on illness –
regarding its origins as well as its cure – were regularly
linked to deities. Many healers (*iatroí*) came from families who claimed to be descended from the gods, particularly from → Asclepius; some of their treatment
methods show parallels with those of shamans in other
cultures [16]. A similar tradition within pharmacology
traced curative competence back to → Chiron the centaur. Several → Pre-socratics such as → Alcmaeon [4]
discussed medicine and the structure of the human body
within the context of explaining the cosmos, or they
were themselves medical practitioners such as e.g
→ Empedocles [1]. They developed their theories,
which were partially based on earlier ideas of opposites
[17], within the framework of an open debate and by
speculation; religious explanations of the healing process were frequently complemented or even replaced by
non-religious appeals to the workings of nature.

C. Hippocratic Medicine

By around 450 BC healing by *iatroí* was common in
Greece; some of these physicians travelled from town to
town, others belonged to well-established families.
Some towns, especially Cos and Cnidus, were famous
for their doctors, but it would be an exaggeration to
talk of a sharp distinction between Coan and Cnidian
medicine [18; 19]. *Iatroí* faced strong competition from
others offering healing, including exorcists, *rizotomoi*
(root-cutters), surgeons (although *iatroí* themselves
could carry out surgical intervention), and also → midwives (*maîai*). → Hippocrates [6] of Cos, who taught
medicine in Athens in around 420 BC and, according to
a later legend, worked there during the great 'plague of
Athens' (→ Epidemic diseases), was the most famous
physician of his age, even if none of the works compiled
in the *Corpus Hippocraticum* (=*CH*; see → Hippocrates
[6] with bibliography) can be firmly identified as being
written by him.

This corpus of texts, particularly if the doxographi-
cal information in the → *Anonymus Londinensis* is also
considered, shows a multitude of medical theories in a
wide range of genres [20; 21]. There is no official medical line, even though there are general similarities in the
way in which authors discussed a particular case, rejected supernatural causes, and with the aid of logic and
dialectic often arrived at very shrewd observations, e.g.
the portents of death in the 'Hippocratic face' (pinched
nose, sunken eyes, hollow temples, cold ears, dry facial
skin, etc.), or the relationship between a blow on one
side of the head and damage to the opposite side of the
body. Some authors of the *CH* according to Anonymus
Londinensis 4,3 believed in residues as the causes of
disease, with undigested food as the source of these
harmful substances (e.g. Hippoc. *De flatibus*). The majority of the authors of the *CH* saw health as a kind of
balance, particularly of bodily fluids. Although the
theory of the four humours – blood, yellow bile, black
bile, and phlegm – whose balance was subject to con-

stant change, dominated the later Hippocratic tradition, it was not represented by the majority of the authors of the *CH*; they preferred other combinations of fluids or emphasized yellow bile and phlegm as the causes of illness. Other authors, notably the one of *De locis in homine*, thought in terms of harmful secretions moving around the body. Bodily imbalances were to be rectified first by careful observation of the patient, the environment, and, where possible, antecedents, which would allow a prognosis to be made that both identified the cause and predicted the future course of the disease if uncorrected. Allopathic remedies, predominantly dietary measures (→ Dietetics) and herbal medicines, were used to restore the balance [22].

Attacks of malarial fever (→ Malaria) with their recurrent course offered a model for the understanding of acute diseases, which could only be diagnosed on the basis of external manifestations, since anatomical or pathological examinations of the human body were not as yet carried out. Complaints developed, until a crisis was reached that was resolved either by death, recovery, or remission. The resolution could either take the shape of coction in the body or occur as evacuation. Crises could happen so regularly as to be expressed mathematically, as two-day or three-day fevers. Both the *Epidēmíai* and the *Prognōstikón* take the length of the time interval between crises as an indication of the severity of the disease [23].

→ Mental illness, esp. in *De morbo sacro*, was not explained as the result of divine intervention, but as that of physical changes within the body, and was included among the symptoms taken into account when investigating illness. Chronic complaints appear less frequently in the *CH*, although the author of *De aëre, aquis, locis* gave attention to long-term environmental factors. In the 'constitutions', some of the authors of the *Epidēmíai* collated an array of information on individual patients, in order to provide an insight into the diseases from which a whole community suffered in the course of a year. These are frequently traced back to climatic factors affecting the air breathed in.

Patients, where such information is provided, come from all strata of society. Women were treated on the same basis as men, albeit based on a more flawed physiology (→ Gynaecology). Physicians gathered information on women's diseases also from female sources, and women could always look for help from other women with a specific knowledge in female problems, including → midwives. Throughout antiquity, though, medical texts on gynaecology were written by men for men. Plato's division of physicians into slaves who only treat slaves, and free citizens who treat other free citizens (Leg. 720a-e), owes more to his ideas on politics and true knowledge than to reality.

The *CH* shows how physicians worked alone or in groups, giving occasional public talks or taking part in debates (*De arte*), and sometimes by writing in an almost oracular prose for a specialist audience (*Aphorismi, De dentitione*). There was a general awareness that medicine is practiced in the public sphere, with not only the patient and his or her immediate family listening or looking on, but also an interested public. The 'therapy of the word', the establishment of a trust-based relationship with the patient, was also a kind of insurance policy and a warning of a possible lethal outcome – or, in cases with a favourable outcome, an advertisement [25]. 'Physician's (*iatroí*) also distinguish themselves from other healers by their appeal to ethical standards, in which ethical medicine is equated with effective treatment, and in which all that contributes to the recovery of health is acceptable (→ Medical ethics). The → Hippocratic Oath is unusual in its strong religious flavour, reflecting also the transition from keeping medical knowledge within a family to passing it on to a group of pupils who are being trained.

Alongside the treatment of individuals, physicians also ensured the medical care of the Athenian armed forces, and from the late 6th cent. BC on, 'public physicians' (→ Democedes) are attested. They were paid a lump-sum fee for setting up practice in a community, but the precise details of their other commitments could vary from place to place. Some treated citizens free of charge or appeared as expert witnesses in cases of homicide or bodily harm [26].

D. RELIGION AND MEDICINE

→ Healing deities (esp. → Apollo) and healing cults had a long tradition in Greece even prior to the spread of the cult of → Asclepius in the late 5th cent. BC, perhaps as a result of the great 'Plague of Athens' (Thuc. 2, 47–54,58; 3,87). Religious healing was an alternative to secular healing, esp. in cases of chronic complaints or mental disorders, and seems to have increased in popularity with the building of major temples in Athens and Epidaurus in the time Hippocrates (himself an Asclepiad) was active. Those who, like Aelius → Aristides [3] relied only on divine intervention for physical healing, were always a minority, and the recourse to such methods – like healings by magi and witch-doctors – always has to be seen as complimentary to the consultation of physicians [27; 28]. The explicit rejection of any possibility of religious healing by the *iatroí* is restricted to the much later → Methodists. The question of greater efficiency of religious or non-religious cures of certain ailments may well have been the subject of debate. However, many doctors participated in the cult of Asclepius, and some of them we know to have been lavish benefactors to healing shrines. By Roman times at the latest, some healing cults, notably those of Asclepius, Hercules, and → Sarapis, had spread across the entire empire, whereas others retained a more local reputation (→ Nodens; Deae Matronae, → Matres). The size and wealth of sanctuaries such as those of → Pergamum or → Aegeae show that they retained their reputation until well into the late Imperial age [29].

E. HELLENISM

Medical theories from the period after Hippocrates have to be reconstructed entirely from later reports. Some physicians, referred to as → Dogmatists [2], continued to speculate about the causes of disease, favouring some kind of imbalance in order to attempt treatment by eliminating the root cause of a disease. Others, particularly the → Empiricists – who constituted a more clearly defined school – rejected any emphasis on the causes in favour of a detailed comparison of actual cases, enabling them to base any therapy on interventions that had proved successful in similar cases. Even though Hippocrates retained his reputation and the *CH* was compiled and studied in Alexandria, the Hippocratic four humour theory was far from being dominant.

The conquests of Alexander brought Greek physicians into closer contact to healers and remedies from a much wider world. New plants and mineral remedies from Asia and eastern Africa became available; however, it remains doubtful whether Greek physicians also adopted non-Greek theories, with the possible exception of a belief in → demons. The broad spectrum of healers remained, but the wide spread of the Hellenistic polis also implied a certain homogenization. There are many indications pointing to a comparable role of physicians in the public life of cities across the entire eastern Mediterranean: in many places, there are reports from that period regarding, for example, public medical lectures, the presence of physicians at public festivals, the existence of municipal doctors, the training in 'medical schools' or the 'apprenticeship' in a medical household, as well as particular privileges enjoyed by physicians, especially tax exemption [30].

The centre of medical learning moved from Greece to the courts of Hellenistic monarchs, particularly to → Alexandria [1]. The Mouseion, the library, and the interest of the ruling monarchs in sciences, offered exciting opportunities for physicians who flocked there from all over the Greek world [31]. The understanding of the human body was much advanced by the anatomical research of → Herophilus [1] and → Erasistratus in around 280 BC (→ Anatomy), with human dissection and arguably vivisection being introduced for the first time [32]. There were significant improvements in surgery with new instruments and new techniques, particularly in the treatment of potentially chronic ailments (→ Surgery), as well as in → Pharmacology [33]. Erasistratus developed a rather mechanistic approach to his understanding of the human body, with reference to a number of concepts taken from contemporary science; he rejected any humoral theories.

F. GREEK MEDICINE IN REPUBLICAN ROME

Evidence for medical practice among the Etruscans is confined to a few names of physicians from this region dating to the 1st cent. BC. Elsewhere in Italy, the → Marsi had a reputation as herbalists and snake charmers, while in Greek colonies, esp. in Elea (→ Velia) and Tarentum, *iatroí* could be found – sometimes in large numbers, as in Metapontum (SEG 30,1175) with about one *iatrós* per 6,000–7,000 inhabitants. In his work *De agricultura*, → Cato [1] preserved several incantations and medical prescriptions that were typical for a rural community. Self-help, personal knowledge of locally available remedies and a repertoire of remedies that did not require the involvement of a specialized healer, are the features of a tradition whose outstanding representative was Plin. HN 29,6,12–21 – contrasting the practically-minded Roman → *pater familias* with the theorizing, treacherous, and dangerous Greek physician. The polemic against Greek medicine, originating with Cato, was a mixture of truth, politics, and literary stereotypes (the lecherous, incompetent quack was already familiar to Aristophanes), but exerted a lasting influence, particularly in view of the implication that in Roman times Greek medicine was second-rate [34]. Medicine in Latin also became part of the encyclopaedical tradition of *artes*, e.g. by → Varro, → Celsus [7], and up to → Isidorus [9] (cf. → *artes liberales*; → Encyclopaedia).

Whether the surgeon → Archagathus [3] was the first Greek physician (*medicus*) in Rome in 219 BC, as claimed in Cassius Hemina, fr. 26 PETER, is uncertain, but his arrival, with the grant of citizenship rights and a consulting room at public expense shows clearly that in the appointment of a physician the Roman Senate acted in the same way as a Greek *boulé*. How many other physicians followed him, is not known – references to physicians in Roman comedies constitute a rather doubtful evidence. Polybius' hostility towards 'theoretical' physicians unable to help the sick (12,25d 2–7) may reflect a Greek rather than a Roman situation [35]. During the Republican period and in Rome itself into the 3rd cent. AD, most of the *medici* bore Greek names and frequently were slaves or freedmen, which must have had an inevitable effect on the status of the art of medicine, even after Julius Caesar had granted citizenship to all physicians in Rome (Suet. Iul. 42) [36]. Cicero's praise of medicine as an 'honourable art' (Off. 1,42,151) is significantly modified by the addition 'honourable for those whose rank it befits'.

Two medical theories can be associated with Greeks working during the late Republican and early Imperial age: The school of the → Pneumatists, founded by → Athenaeus [6] of Attaleia, took up the Hippocratic humoral theory and imposed on it the concept of → *pneûma* as the controlling and organizing power. Much more is known about the → Methodists, some of whose teachings can be traced via → Thessalus of Tralles and → Themison of Laodicea to → Asclepiades [6] of Bithynia in the early years of the 1st cent. BC. Asclepiades enjoyed a tremendous reputation almost as a miracle healer, and treated many Roman senators. His theory, a combination of → Atomism and the mechanistic teachings of Eristratus, enjoyed considerable success, particularly in Thessalus' simplified reformulation, and continued to be recognized far into the 5th cent. AD. It emphasized the causation of diseases and the need not only to treat symptoms, but root causes. Because the Methodists only considered a narrow spectrum of 'common conditions' within an atomistic universe, they perceived a simple correlation between observable symptoms and their causes, and also between causes and their allopathic treatment. They also modified the treatment of chronic disorders, in order to take into account changes as manifested in the respective symptoms (whereas Dogmatist physicians – → Dogmatists [2] – continued with the same treatment until the initial cause was eliminated).

G. IMPERIAL PERIOD

Greek medicine, whether practised by Greeks, by bearers of Greek names, or supporters of Greek theories, can be found all over the Roman empire, from Hadrian's Wall in northern England to southern Egypt. Physicians competed on the very same medical marketplace as specialists (→ Ophthalmology), peddlers of medicinal products, surgeons, female healers, and medical prophets such as → Alexander [27] of Abonutichus. Their status differed from place to place and largely depended on their patients: physicians treating the imperial family or senators enjoyed a certain prestige and probably earned more money than a simple local physician (some of whom were women) [37]. Some, particularly in Asia Minor (e.g. → Statilius Criton), belonged to families prominent in their locality. In Rome, slave families were often treated by physicians who were themselves slaves. In Italy, many physicians, such as → Galen were immigrants intent on making substantial money in the empire's capital, but flourishing medical professions could also be found in Greek centres such as Ephesus and Alexandria.

Medicine was a matter of the individual with little involvement by the state. → Hospitals only existed for slaves or in larger military camps and forts, the army having a complex system of medical organization [38]. Roman emperors continued with the Hellenistic tradition of exemption from municipal tax for all medical professions, but the restriction of those eligible introduced by Antoninus Pius (mid–2nd cent. AD) resulted in a legal framework which contained a partial definition of the required competence, but left the selection of such physicians (→ archiatrós) to the local council [39].

The writings of Pliny the Elder (→ Plinius), → Rufus, → Soranus, and esp. → Galen, contain references to a great number of physicians whose treatments and practices in some cases bordered on → magic and fraud (even though the boundary between these categories was never fixed or legally defined) [40]. Galen reported on a renaissance of anatomy under → Marinus [2] in around AD 110, as well as of a tradition of an exegesis of the works of Hippocrates developed in Alexandria by his teachers and others. Hippocratic medicine remained a minority concern, nor was Galen's ideal of the philosopher-physician as common as later generations assumed. Egyptian papyri show physicians practicing

healing alongside other activities, esp. farming – a connection that can be observed in Europe well into the 20th cent. At the same time, medical colleges or groups of physicians existed in cities such as Tarsus or Benventum, who undoubtedly had access to copies of at least part of the abundant medical literature that was in circulation in the 2nd cent. AD [41]. In Ephesus, annual competitions were held for physicians, the results of which were epigraphically recorded for public reference (IK Ephesus 1161–1167).

H. LATE ANTIQUITY

From the 4th cent. AD onwards, Galenism was the dominant medical theory in the Greek world, even though it was less influential on Latin medicine than the → Methodist school (→ Caelius [II 11] Aurelianus). Medicine was increasingly defined as written knowledge, whether in form of an excerpt (→ Oribasius) or a handbook, often explicitly targeted at those who would have problems consulting a *medicus*, or in form of comprehensive editions of complete works, particularly of Galen and Hippocrates [42].

A similar rigidity can be observed in the legal regulations for physicians, used in the *Codex Theodosianus* (13,3) to define the privileges of various groups of physicians; at the tip of a prescribed number of physicians were the court physicians, who by the 6th cent. at the latest were also charged – at least in theory – with the supervision of the entire medical profession (Cassiod. Var. 6,19). *Medici* continued to be found throughout the empire, even though they were increasingly restricted to the bigger cities. Beyond them, self-help and the rural medicine of Cato and Pliny prevailed. In the Latin West, medical books and even compendia of remedies become rarer in around AD 600. North Africa's intensive network of medical intelligence was replaced by short compendia of practical knowledge, as defined in Cassiod. Inst. 1,31. By contrast, a critical, theory-oriented approach to medicine, expressed in both Greek and Syrian, flourished in the East until the Arab conquests and beyond.

J. CHRISTIANITY

With the rise of Christianity, medicine changed in a various respects [43]. The emphasis on universal charity resulted in an increase of → hospitals to nurse the needy, and occasionally in the proliferation of medical care. Some theologians associated disease with sin, and rejected human remedies in favour of Christian healing through prayer, confession, faith, and the laying-on of hands (Jac 5,14–16). However, like those who denied the needs of the body in favour of those of the soul, they were always in a minority. The majority of Christians followed → Basilius [1] in reasoning that a providential God had ensured the availability of remedies on earth for man to use them. Occasionally, the suspicion that outstanding physicians could be sympathizers of 'paganism' (→ Gesius) resulted in hostilities towards them, and → Augustinus worried that his congregation might adopt the magic religious practices of the pagans [44]. Healings by saints (→ Cosmas and Damianus), particularly with the expulsion of → demons, offered an alternative to secular treatment, but generally there was co-operation rather than conflict. The teleological emphasis on God's purposeful creation of an ordered world, a characteristic feature of Galenism, undoubtedly contributed towards its predominance.

K. SUMMARY

Many essential questions on ancient medicine have to remain unanswered. Even though in the 2nd cent. AD, physicians can be found everywhere in the Roman world, it is impossible to estimate the extent of medicalization. The solution of public health-care problems, even if they were discussed and debated by physicians, was left to others. Furthermore, no certainty can be assumed as to the extent and importance of professionalization within the health-care system. However, the most important question is that regarding the effectiveness of ancient medicine. There is palaeopathological evidence of patients recovering after major surgery, and complex operations such as lithotomies and herniotomies are frequently mentioned [45]. Herb-based remedies may have shown an effect in more than 10% of all cases in which they were used, but they were seldom administered in toxic doses, and mineral-based remedies were not applied internally, but externally only. It is likely that the majority of medicinal preparations only had little direct effect, but the placebo effect can not be ruled out [46]. Ancient remedies may not have had a curative effect, but in the hands of a competent physician they were unlikely to have worsened a patient's condition. An ancient master of diagnosis such as Rufus or Galen with his intellectual and practical powers will have been at least as effective as a physician in the first half of the 20th cent.

→ Aristides [3], P. Aelius; → Anatomy; → Antidotarium; → Archiatros; → Asclepius; → Ophthalmology; → Training, medical; → Surgery; → Dietetics; → Dogmatists [2]; → Empiricists; → Epidemic diseases; → Erasistratus; → Galen; → Mental illness; → Gynaecology; → Midwife; → Hippocrates [6]; → Hospital; → Disease; → Malaria; → Medical ethics; → Surgical instruments (with illustr.); → Methodists; → Pedanius Dioscorides; → Pharmacology; → Pneumatists; → Sarapis; → Scribonius Largus; → Soranus; → Statilius Criton; → Medicine

1 A. H. GARDINER, The House of Life, in: JEA 24, 1938, 157–179 2 M. H. MARGANNE, Links between Egyptian and Greek Medicine, in: Forum 3,5, 1993, 35–43 3 E. REINER, Astral Magic in Babylonia, 1995 4 M. STOL, Epilepsy in Babylonia, 1993 5 F. KÖCHER, Die babylonisch-assyrische Medizin, 1–6, 1963–1980 6 R. LABAT, Traité akkadien de diagnostics et prognostics médicaux, 1951 7 H. C. KEE, Medicine, Miracle and Magic in New Testament Times, 1988 8 I. and W. JACOB, The Healing Past, 1993 9 G. VERMES, Jesus the Jew, 1973 10 P. J. VAN DER EIJK (ed.), Ancient Histories of Medicine. Essays in Medical Doxography and Historiography in Classical Antiquity, 1999 11 A. KRUG, Heilkunst und Heilkult, 1985 12 J. OEHLER, Epigraphische Beiträge zur Geschichte des Ärztestandes, in: Janus 14, 1909, 111–123 13 H. GUMMERUS, Der Ärztestand im römischen Reiche, 1932 14 A. HILLERT, Antike Ärztedarstellungen, 1990 15 S. LASER, Medizin und Körperpflege (ArchHom 3,2), 1983 16 F. KUDLIEN, Der Beginn des medizinischen Denkens bei den Griechen, 1967 17 G. E. R. LLOYD, Polarity and Analogy, 1971 18 W. D. SMITH, Galen on Coans versus Cnidians, in: BHM 47, 1973, 569–578; 19 J. JOUANNA, Hippocrate. Pour une archéologie de l'école de Cnide, 1974 20 Id., Hippocrate, 1992 21 G. E. R. LLOYD, The Revolutions of Wisdom, 1987 22 EDELSTEIN, AM, 65–111 23 V. LANGHOLF, Medical Theories in Hippocrates, 1990 24 A. W. NIGHTINGALE, Plato's Lawcode in Context, in: CQ 49, 1999, 100–122; 25 P. LAIN ENTRALGO, The Therapy of the Word in Classical Antiquity, 1970 26 L. COHN-HAFT, The Public Physicians of Ancient Greece, 1956 27 G. E. R. LLOYD, Magic, Reason, and Experience, 1979 28 Id., Science, Folklore, and Ideology, 1983 29 EDELSTEIN, Asclepius 30 F. KUDLIEN, Der griechische Arzt im Zeitalter des Hellenismus, in: AAWM, 6, 1979 31 P. M. FRASER, Ptolemaic Alexandria, 1972 32 STADEN 33 M. MICHLER, Die hellenistische Chirurgie, 1, 1968; 34 NUTTON, vii, 30–58 35 E. D. RAWSON, Intellectual Life in the Late Roman Republic, 1985, 171–184 36 J. KORPELA, Das Medizinalpersonal im antiken Rom, 1987 37 F. KUDLIEN, Die Stellung des Arztes in der römischen Gesellschaft, 1986 38 J. C. WILMANNS, Der Sanitätsdienst im römischen Reich, 1995 39 NUTTON, V, 191–226 40 V. NUTTON, From Medical Certainty to Medical Amulets, in: Clio Medica 22, 1991, 13–22 41 O. M. VAN NIJF, The Civic World of Professional Associations in the Roman East, 1997 42 J. SCARBOROUGH (ed.), Symposium on Byzantine Medicine, in: Dumbarton Oaks Papers 38, 1984 43 O. TEMKIN, Hippocrates in a World of Pagans and Christians, 1991 44 R. MACMULLEN, Christianity and Paganism in the Fourth to Eighth Centuries, 1997; 45 R. JACKSON, Doctors and Diseases in the Roman Empire, 1988 46 J. M. RIDDLE, Quid pro quo. Studies in the History of Drugs, 1992.

T. BARDINET, Les Papyrus médicaux de l'Egypte pharaonique, 1995; L. I. CONRAD, M. NEVE, V. NUTTON, R. PORTER, A. WEAR, The Western Medical Tradition, 800BC–AD 1800, 1995; EDELSTEIN, AM; V. J. FLINT, The Rise of Magic in Early Medieval Europe, 1993; D. GOUREVITCH, Le Triangle hippocratique dans le monde gréco-romain: Le malade, sa maladie, et son médecin, 1984; H. GRAPOW, Grundriß der Medizin der alten Ägypter, 9 vols., 1954–1973; M. D. GRMEK (ed.), Western Medical Thought from Antiquity to the Middle Ages, 1998; ANRW vol. 37,1–3, 1993–1996; J. NUNN, Ancient Egyptian Medicine, 1996; V. NUTTON, Healers in the Medical Marketplace, in: A. WEAR (ed.), Medicine in Society, 1992, 15–58; Id., Ancient Medicine, 2004; J. PREUSS, Biblisch-Talmudische Medizin, 1911; P. J. VAN DER EIJK, H. F. J. HORSTMANSHOFF, P. H. SCHRIJVERS (ed.), Ancient Medicine in its Socio-Cultural Context, 1995; W. WESTENDORF, Handbuch der altägyptische Medizin, 1999. V.N.

Medicus

[1] Victory title (victory over the Medes = Persians), first awarded to → Marcus [II 6] Aurelius and Lucius

→ Verus, evidently as the result of a victorious campaign against → Media Atropatene in AD 165/6. This title next appears as an epithet for Probus, Diocletian, and his co-rulers, then for Constantine, in each case with the addition *maximus*. The title has been erroneously ascribed to other rulers.

P. KNEISSL, Die Siegestitulatur der römischen Kaiser, 1969, 99ff.; 211; 247.   W.E.

[2] see → Medicine

Medimnos (μέδιμνος; *médimnos*) is the largest Greek unit of measurement for dry substances, with a volume of 6 *hekteis* (→ Hekteus), equivalent to 48 *choinikes* (→ Choinix) and 192 *kotylai* (→ Kotyle [2]). According to HULTSCH, it equals *c*. 52.5 l, according to NISSEN *c*. 51.8 l with considerable regional differences.
→ Measures of volume

1 F. HULTSCH, Griechische und römische Metrologie, ²1882, 108, 703 tab. X   2 M. LANG, M. CROSBY, Weights, Measures and Tokens (The Athenian Agora 10), 1964, 41ff.   3 H. NISSEN, Griechische und römische Metrologie, in: HdbA I², 834–890, esp. 842 tab. X.
H.-J.S.

Medina see → Ya_tr_īb

Mediolan(i)um (Μεδιολάν[ι]ον/*Mediolán[i]on*).
[1] The modern city of Milan. It was founded in the early 4th cent. BC by the Insubres (Liv. 5,34,9) at the juncture of several Alpine valleys in the Padus/Po plain (Pol. 2,34,10); in 222 BC, it was captured by Cn. Scipio; it was later to become the most important city of that region (Pol. 2,34,15). Following an uprising in the Second → Punic War, M. came under Roman rule in 194 BC. In 89 BC, it was granted Latin law, in 49 BC Roman citizenship. Since the Augustan period, the city had become an important junction, but also a significant centre of learning (Plin. Ep. 4,13,3). Tac. Hist. 1,70,1 lists M. among the strongly fortified *municipia* of that region. Later it became a *colonia* (epigraphical evidence: CIL V 634). Under the tetrarchy of → Diocletianus, M. rose in status by becoming a mint and also, because of its advantageous strategic location, a temporary imperial residence. It was in M. in 313 that Constantinus [1] the Great and Licinius [II 4] agreed to tolerate Christianity and all other religions (Lactant. De mort. pers. 48,2ff.; 'Edict of Milan', → Christianity). The work of bishop Ambrosius (374–397) is a further indication of the importance of the city in church politics; Ausonius ranked it seventh in his *ordo urbium nobilium*, and praised its architecture. In 402, the imperial residence was moved to Ravenna, and in 452, M. fell to the Huns. After that, M. experienced a further short period of bloom before it was completely destroyed under Gothic rule (Procop. Goth 2,21,1ff.). Ancient remains: town walls, circus, horreum, mausoleum, theatre, amphitheatre, baths, various basilicas.

A. CALDERINI, Storia di Milano 1, 1953; Atti del convegno 'Milano Capitale dell'Impero Romano', Milano 8–11 Marzo 1990, 1992; M. MIRABELLA ROBERTI, s.v. Milan, PE 561.   C.HEU.

[2] Settlement of the Bituriges Cubi (Tab. Peut. 2,3; CIL XIII 8922) in Aquitania I, the modern Châteaumeillant (Cher) between Argentomagus (Argenton-sur-Creuse) and Aquae Neri (Néris-les-Bains). Late Latène *oppidum*, Imperial age *vicus*.

J.-F. CHEVROT, J. TROADEC, Carte Archéologique de la Gaule 18 (Cher), 1992, 190–199.   MI.PO.

[3] Settlement near Geldern/North Rhine-Westfalia on the road from Colonia Traiana to Atuatuca (It. Ant. 375,3), the modern Mylen.   F.SCH.

[4] **M. Santonum** (Str. 4,2,1; Ptol. 2,7,6; It. Ant. 459,3; Geogr. Rav. 4,40; CIL XIII 8899; 8901), main settlement of the Santoni in Aquitania II, modern Saintes (Charente-Maritime).

CHR. VERNO, J.-F. BUISSON, Saintes-Mediolanum, Civitas Santonum, in: L. MAURIN (ed.), Villes et agglomérations urbaines antiques du Sud-Ouest de la Gaule (= 6ᵉ suppl. à Aquitania), 1992, 154–162.   MI.PO.

[5] (Μεδιολάνιον/*Mediolánion*, Lat. *Mediolanum*). Probably Whitchurch in Shropshire, where a 1st cent. AD Roman fort was replaced by a civilian settlement; however, cf. Ptol. 2,3,11 localizing M. as a settlement of the Ordovices in Wales.

G. D. B. JONES, P. V. WEBSTER, Mediolanum: Excavations at Whitchurch, 1965–66, in: AJ 125, 1968, 193–254.
M.TO.

[6] Fort in Moesia Superior dating from Late Antiquity (Cod. Theod. 10,1,8), its garrison described as *milites Dacisci* (Not. Dign. Or. 40,21).   J.BU.
[7] **M. Aulercorum** (Μεδιολάνιον, Ptol. 2,8,9; It. Ant. 384,4; Tab. Peut. 2,2; Amm. Marc. 15,11,12). Chief place of the → Aulerci Eburovices, modern Evreux (Eure). In later periods, M. is referred to as *civitas Ebroicorum* (Notitia Galliarum 2,4). Ruins of a Roman theatre (CIL XIII 3200); ring-wall, smithy, potter's workshop, graves. Le Vieil-Evreux (6 km south-east of Evreux) was the location of a cult-place.

J. MATHIÈRE, La civitas des Aulerci Eburovices, 1925.
Y.L.

Mediomatrici Tribe in Gallia → Belgica; capital of their *civitas* was → Divodurum (modern Metz). Their territory in modern Lorraine comprised the upper basins of the rivers Maas, Moselle and Saar (Str. 4,3,4; Ptol. 2,9,7), and originally extended eastwards as far as the Rhine (Caes. B Gall. 4,10,3; Str. l.c.). It is unlikely they participated in the Gallic War (→ Caesar). In 52 BC they sent 5000 men to support Vercingetorix who was besieged in → Alesia (Caes. B Gall. 7,75,3); they had to cede their territories west of the Rhine in the lower Alsace between the Vosges and the Rhine to the Germanic tribe of the Triboci. Their southern neighbours were the Leuci, in the west, they bordered on the Remi, and in the north on the Treveri (Ptol. 2,9,7). It seems as if the M. only provided few soldiers to the Roman army, and no complete units. They were well known for their production of salt (in Saulnois) and iron.

Trade and commerce flourished because of the convenient location of the territory, particularly main junction of Divodurum. It lay along major trading routes, within a comparatively close-meshed network of roads, and had connections to the administrative centres of → Durocortorum and → Augusta [6] Treverorum and to the navigable river Moselle (*nautae Moselici*: CIL XIII 4335; Ven. Fort. 10,9,1). Particular mention should be made of the production of cloth (CIL V 5929; XIII 4564; Not. Dign. Occ. 11,59; 12,27), the trade in chalk (CIL III 4336; 4481), and the brewing of beer (CIL XIII 597). There were trading colonies in Augusta Treverorum (Trier), Burdigala (Bordeaux), Lugdunum (Lyon), Autessiodurum (Auxerre), in Britannia, in Germania Superior, and on the Great St. Bernard. From the Claudian period onwards, more and more *vici* developed (e.g. Bodatius, *Marosallum/ Marsal, Savarus, Pons Savari/Saarburg, Bliesbruck, Le Hérapel) as well as *villae rusticae* (e.g. Nilvange, Grémecey, Eply), some even as large as 'latifundia' (St. Ulrich, Rouhling). However, the circular or longish dug-out houses (French *mardelles*) characteristic for the area of the M. prove that the majority of the largely rural population remained faithful to ancient Celtic tradition well into the 4th cent. AD. A Celtic sanctuary of supraregional character was located on Mt. Donon (CIL XIII 4548; ESPÉRIANDIEU, Rec. 6,4569–4603). Apart from the customary Roman and Celtic deities, grave steles in the shape of houses are a typical feature of the M.
→ Divodurum

B. BEAUJARD, Les vici des Médiomatriques au Bas-Empire, in: Caesarodunum 11, 1976 (extra volume), 296–306; Y. BURNAND, Histoire de la Lorraine 1, 1990; G. COLLOT, La civilisation gallo-romaine dans la cité des Médiomatriques 1, ¹1964 (²1981); 2, ¹1974; J.-M. DEMAROLLE, Les importations de produits céramiques en pays médiomatrique en 1ᵉʳ siècle après J.-C., in: Ktema 13, 1988, 109–120; F. PETRY, Vici, villas et village, in: Caesarodunum 17, 1982, 211–227.   F.SCH.

Medion (Μεδιών/*Mediṓn*; Μεδεών/*Medeṓn*, Thuc. 3,106). City in central → Acarnania, south of the modern village of Katouna, on the important route from the Gulf of Ambracia to the central plain between Aetolia and Acarnania. In 231 BC, the city was unsuccessfully besieged by the Aetolians (Pol. 2,2f.), in 191 it supported Antiochus III (Liv. 36,11,10–12,12). Mentioned repeatedly in lists of *theōrodokoi*. (IG IV 1², 95 l. 13; [1. 157 Z. 2]; SEG 36, 331 l. 44–46). Inscriptions: IG IX 1²,2, 387f.; SEG 25, 633; [2. 229]. Coins: [3].

1 BCH 90, 1966   2 BE 1973   3 BMC, Gr, vol. 7: Thessaly to Aetolia, 188.

PRITCHETT 7, 83–90; D. STRAUCH, Römische Politik und griechische Tradition, 1996, 303.   D.S.

Medismos (μηδισμός/*mēdismós*). The term *medismos* was used to describe the voluntary collaboration of individual Greeks or whole cities with the Persians, whom the Greeks often referred to as 'Medes'. Apart from active political-military collaboration with the → Great King, the verb *mēdízein* also refers to the adoption of Persian customs and practices together with a luxurious way of life. *Medismos* was perceived as a graver offence than the betrayal of the home town to another Greek town, because it affected pan-Greek interests as well as the interests of individual poleis. Spectacular cases of *medismos* included the collaboration of the Thessalian → Aleuadae dynasty with → Xerxes, providing him with an army contingent for the battle of Plataeae (479 BC) (Hdt. 9,1; 31; 58), and also the behaviour of the Spartan regent → Pausanias, who not only wore Persian clothes and travelled with a Persian bodyguard, but who allegedly offered the rulership over all of Greece to the Great King, if the latter gave him his daughter in marriage (Thuc. 1,128,5ff.; Diod. Sic. 11,44,3). The accusation of *medismos* also played a part in the internal politics of the Athenian democracy; this is demonstrated by four ostraca (→ Ostrakismos) from the Kerameikos, describing Callias [4] as *ho Mḗdos* ('the Mede').
→ Barbarians; → Persian War

D. F. GRAF, Medism: The Origin and Significance of the Term, in: JHS 104, 1984, 15–30.   E.S.-H.

Mediterranean see → Mare Nostrum

Mediterranean languages Mediterranean languages are defined as those spoken in the Mediterranean region prior to the immigration of Indo-European and Semitic tribes, and of which we only have indirect evidence, i.e. traces which they (as substrate languages) have left in languages that are attested. A number of lexical equivalences between Greek and Latin that cannot be traced to either the Indo-European root language nor to any other known sources, can be explained as borrowings from unknown Mediterranean languages: cf. Greek σῦκον, Lat. *ficus* 'fig'; Greek (ϝ)οῖνος, Lat. *vīnum* 'wine'; Greek κυπάρισσος, Lat. *cupressus* 'cypress'; Greek ὄνος, Lat. *asinus* 'donkey '(?). A number of these lexical equivalents are very common in the Mediterranean region and comprise several Indo-European languages (e.g. → Albanian, → Hittite) as well as Semitic ones (→ Semitic languages). The Mediterranean words have survived particularly well in specific lexical areas, such as names of plants, animals (see examples above), or places. The research into the toponymy not only of the Mediterranean coast, but also in the Alpine and

Pyrenean regions (→ Pre-Romance languages) has identified – albeit not always with the necessary reservation – a number of Mediterranean stems and suffixes, e.g. the Aegean-Anatolian –σ(σ)– and –νθ- suffixes (such as Παρνασσός, Κόρινθος etc., equally in common nouns such as ἀσάμινθος 'bath tub', or κυπάρισσος).

The possibility of reconstructing small fragments of lost Mediterranean languages thanks to their survival in later language strata has inspired the interest (and imagination) of Indo-Europeanists and Romance linguists from the end of the 19th cent. on; attempts have been made to establish certain linguistic features of these languages (e.g. in respect of vocalism, consonantism, word structure), and also to establish different Mediterranean language families (Aegean-Anatolian, Afro-Iberian-Sardinian, Tyrrhenian). However, many questions remain unanswered; the study of the Mediterranean languages shares both the uncertainties and the attraction of any research into the prehistory of language.

→ Greece, languages; → Hispania II. languages; → Italy, languages; → Pre-Greek languages; → Pre-Romance languages

V. BERTOLDI, Colonizzazioni nell'antico Mediterraneo occidentale alla luce degli aspetti linguistici, 1950; G. DEVOTO, Storia della lingua di Roma, 1940; J. HUBSCHMID, Mediterrane Substrate, 1960; A. MEILLET, Aperçu d'une histoire de la langue grecque, [4]1935; L. R. PALMER, The Latin Language, [2]1961; D. SILVESTRI, La teoria del sostrato, 3 vols, 1977–1982; B. TERRACINI, L'héritage indo-européen et les substrats méditerranéens, in: Actes du Ier congrès de la Fédération internationale des Associations d'ét. classiques (ACEC 1), 1951, 31–41.
M.B.C.

Meditrinalia The Roman festival of Meditrinalia was celebrated on 11 October (InscrIt 13,2, p. 519) with the tasting and → libation of the fresh must. To that end, it was mixed with the boiled down must of the previous year; this was seen as a way of preserving it (Columella 12; Pall. Agric. 11, 14 and 17–19; [1. 916–919]). The name Meditrinalia was derived from the Latin *mederi*, 'to heal'. In the same way as the mixing of the wine was to preserve its qualities, the tasting and libation of a mixture of new wine with that of the previous year was seen as a preventative measure against old and new illnesses (Varro, Ling. 6,21; Paul Fest. 110 L.; [3. 98–105]). It is likely that the name of the festival gave rise to the creation of the goddess Meditrina in antiquarian literature. At the time of the grape harvest, must was sacrificed to → Liber (Paul Fest. 423 L.; Columella 12,18,4). However, the addition of *feriae Iovi* to 11 October in the → Fasti Amiternini and the Fasti fratrum Arvalium has led to the interpretation of the Meditrinalia as a festival in honour of → Jupiter ([2; 3. 105–107]; disagreeing: [4. 75]).

→ Vinalia; → Wine

1 W. ABEL, s.v. Mustum, RE 16, 912–926   2 F. BÖMER, Iuppiter und die römische Weinfeste, in: RhM 90, 1941, 30ff.   3 G. DUMÉZIL, Fêtes d'été et d'automne, 1975 ([2]1986), 98–107   4 LATTE, 74–76.
A.MAS.

Medius

[1] (Μήδιος/*Médios* in MSS; better Μήδειος/*Médeios*, in epigraphy).

Dynast of Larisa [3], of the → Aleuadae family, successor of Aristippus; in 395 BC he joined the newly formed anti-Spartan alliance in the fight against the tyrant → Lycophron [2] of Pherae and captured Pharsalus, which housed a Spartan garrison (Diod. Sic. 14,82,5f.; cf. Aristot. Hist. an. 618b).

H.-J. GEHRKE, Stasis, 1985, 191.   HA.BE.

[2] Son of Oxythemis of Larisa, probably a grandson of M. [1], *hetairos* (→ Hetairoi) of → Alexander [4] the Great.; M. took part in Alexander's Asian campaign, but not as a member of the army. He is first mentioned in 326 BC as one of the *triérarchoi* of the → Hydaspes fleet (Arr. Ind. 18,7). On the 18th of the month of Daisios (May-June) 323, M. invited Alexander to a banquet, the main description of which is found in the → Alexander Romance. Alexander's excessive drinking at that banquet caused his death (it is impossible to say whether or not poison also played a part). The *ephemerides* (→ ephemeris) used by → Arrianus (but not those used by Plutarch) have M. interact frequently with Alexander during the last days of the latter's life. After Alexander's death, M. fought initially under → Perdiccas, then very successfully as fleet commander under → Antigonus [1] (Diod. Sic. 19,69,3; 75; 77,2–5; 20,50,3: battle off → Salamis in Cyprus, 307 BC). He was honoured in Athens (Syll.[3] 342). He wrote about Alexander, but the nature of his work is unclear (fragment in FGrH 129).

BERVE 2, no. 521.   E.B.

[3] Stoic philosopher of the 3rd cent. AD, an older contemporary of the Neoplatonist → Longinus [1] (Porph. Vita Plotini 20), against whom he defended the traditional Stoic division of the soul into eight parts (Procl. in Pl. Resp. 1,233,29–234,30 KROLL).   B.I.

Medlar (μεσπίλη/*mespílē*, μέσπιλον/*méspilon*, ἀρωνία/ *arōnía*: Dioscorides; Lat. *mespilus* or *-a*, the fruit *mespilum*). *Mespilus germanica* L. (family *Rosaceae*), a bush or tree probably native to southern Europe, was cultivated in Greece as a wild apple tree at least since about 370 BC on account of its small, three-cored, sweet fruits (Middle Comedy, → Eubulus [2] in Ath. 14,640c). Theophrastus (Hist. pl. 3,12,5f. = Plin. HN. 15,84) describes three thorn-bushes under this name, of which only μεσπίλη ἡ σατάνειος/*mespílē hē satáneios* is recognized as medlar. Dioscorides (1,118 WELLMANN = 1,169f. BERENDES) distinguishes between a tree similar to hawthorn with its characteristic fruits and a species in Italy more similar to an apple tree (also known as ἐπιμηλίς/*epimēlís* or σητάνιον/*sētánion*). The edible fruits of both trees, as well as the wine produced from them (Dioscorides 5,24 WELLMANN = 5,32 BERENDES; Plin. HN 14,103), were said to be well digestible and have an astringent effect. Old medlar trees are infested with certain worms (Plin. HN 17,221 according to Theophr. l.c.). Palladius (agric. 4,10,19–22) provides expert information on cultivation, treatment in case of diseases, grafting, and storage of the fruits.

→ Mespila [2]

H. GOSSEN, s.v. Mispel, RE Suppl. 8, 358ff.   C.HÜ.

Medma (Μέδμα; *Médma*). Locrian colony (Thuc. 5,5,3; Scymn. 308; Str. 6,1,5; EM 581,15) founded at the beginning of the 6th cent. BC and located on the west coast of Italy (Hecat. FGrH 1 F 81; Μέσμα/ *Mésma*, Scyl. 12; Plin. HN 3,73), near the eponymous spring and south of the eponymous river (the modern Mesima) [1; 4. 114ff.], with its own emporium, the modern Rosarno. At the turn of the 6th/5th cents., it was victoriously allied with Hipponium and Locri against Croton, and in 422 with Hipponium against Locri (Thuc. 5,5,3). In 396 BC, Dionysius I resettled 4,000 of M.'s citizens to → Messana (Diod. Sic. 14,78,5) and handed their land to Locri. M. was the home town of Philippus of Opus, a Socratic and a student of Plato. Bronze coins of the 4th–3rd cents. with the legend ΜΕΔΜΑ or ΜΕΣΜΑ [3]. Rectangular town layout dating from the 5th–4th cents. BC; rich production of roof and votive terracottas (statuettes, *pínakes*) for the Persephone cult [2; 4; 5] (→ Persephone).

1 H. RIX, M., Ort und Fluß in Bruttium, in: Beiträge zur Namenforschung 3, 1951, 243–251   2 M. PAOLETTI, S. SETTIS (ed.), M. e il suo territorio, 1981   3 G. GORINI, Per uno studio della monetazione di M., in: Numismatica e antichità classiche 14, 1985, 127ff.   4 S. SETTIS, Archeologia in Calabria, 1987   5 Id., s.v. M., EAA Suppl. 2, 1995, 580–582.   M.L.

Medobriga (or *Medubriga*; Celtic [1. 526] 'Castle of Medus'). Town in Lusitania (→ Lusitani), captured in 48 BC by Q. → Cassius [I 16] Longinus, together with the *Herminius mons* (the modern Sierra de la Estrella), to which the inhabitants had fled (Bell. Alex. 48,2). According to CIL II 760, the *Meidobrigenses* were involved in the building of the Tagus bridge in Alcántara during the reign of Trajan. According to Pliny, the inhabitants of M. were also known as *Plumbari* (*qui et Plumbari*, HN 4,118) – apparently, there was a lead-mine associated with M. [2. 254f.].

1 HOLDER 2; 2 TOVAR 2.

F. RUSSEL CORTEZ, A localização dos Meidobrigenses, in: Zephyrus 4, 1953, 503–506.   P.B.

Medocus (Μήδοκος/*Médokos*). Appearing as Μήτοκος/*Métokos* on silver and bronze coins, in ancient and modern literature also known as Ἀμά- or respectively Ἀμήδοκος (*Amá-* or *Amédokos,* I or the Elder, Isoc. Or. 5,6; Harpocr. s.v. Ἀμάδοκος). Odrysian king (Xen. An. 7,2,32; 7,3; 7,11) *c.* 410/05 to *c.* 387 BC (Diod. Sic. 14,94,2), successor to → Seuthes I. His resi-

dence was presumably located on the upper course of the Hebrus (Xen. An. 7,3,16–17). He was a friend of → Alcibiades [3] (Diod. Sic. 13,105,3). M. supported his co-ruler → Seuthes II (Xen. An. 7,2,32–34), who later rose against him (Aristot. Pol. 1312a). Both were reconciled in 389 by → Thrasybulus, and entered into an alliance with Athens (Xen. Hell. 4,8,26; Diod. Sic. 14,94,2; IG II/III² 21 and 22; StV II 238).

→ Odrysae

Z. H. ARCHIBALD, The Odrysian Kingdom of Thrace, 1998, 122–125; U. PETER, Die Münzen der thrakischen Dynasten (5.–3. Jahrhundert v.Chr.), 1997, 89–99.   U.P.

Medon (Μέδων/*Médōn*).
[1] Illegitimate son of Oileus and Rhene, who led → Philoctetes' men to Troy after the latter had to be left on Lemnos (Hom. Il. 2,726ff.). He had killed a member of his stepmother Eriopis' family and thus had to leave his home and flee to Phylace (Thessaly; ibid. 13,695ff.). He is killed by Aeneas (ibid. 15,332).

W. KULLMANN, Die Quellen der Ilias (Hermes ES 14), 1960, 113; 122f.; 162f.; F. PRINZ, Gründungsmythen und Sagenchronologie (Zetemata 72), 1979, 59f.

[2] Herald in the palace of → Odysseus, who told → Penelope about the suitors' plan of attacking → Telemachus (Hom. Od. 4,696ff.). On the latter's intervention, Odysseus spared M. when killing the suitors (ibid. 22,356ff.). In Hom. Od. 24,439, M. tries to dissuade the Ithacans from their anger against Odysseus. Both Apollod. Epit. 7,27 and Ov. Epist. 1,91 mention M. as one of Penelope's suitors.
[3] One of the Tyrrhenian pirates who kidnapped → Dionysus on his journey to Naxos, but were turned into dolphins by the latter (Ov. Met. 3,671; Hyg. Fab. 134).
[4] Son of → Pylades and → Electra [4]; together with his brother Strophius, he is supposed to have killed Aristodemus (Paus. 2,16,7; 3,1,6). He is identical with Medeon who gave his name to a Boeotian (or Phocian) town (Steph. Byz. s.v. Μεδεών).
[5] Son of → Codrus, who was in dispute with his brother Neileus regarding the rulership of Athens until the Delphian oracle decided in M.'s favour (Paus. 7,2,1; Hellanicus FGrH 4 F 125).   J.STE.
[6] A Spartan sculptor whose name is also mentioned as → Dontas by Pausanias in his description of the votive offerings in the treasury (→ thesauros) of the Megarians in Olympia. It is assumed that this was a spelling mistake (μεδον[τας/*me Dontas*).   R.N.
[7] (Μήδων/*Médōn*). Macedonian from Beroea, high-ranking friend and supporter of → Perseus and a military commander in the 3rd → Macedonian War (cf. Liv. 42,58,7); he surrendered to L. → Aemilius [I 32] Paullus in 168 BC and together with → Pantauchus persuaded → Pydna to capitulate (Liv. 44,45,2;7); in 171, both Pantauchus and M. were sent as Macedonian emissaries to P. → Licinius [I 14] Crassus (Pol. 27,8,5). Iden-

tical [1. 159f.; 2. 114f.] with the commander of the mountain fortresses of Pythium and Petra, besieged by P. → Cornelius [I 83] Scipio Nasica in 168 BC (Liv. 44,32,9: Midon; Pol. 29,15; Plut. Aem. Paullus 16,2–3: Μίλων).

1 E. Olshausen, Prosopographie der hellenistischen Königsgesandten, 1974   2 S. Le Bohec, Les 'philoi' des rois Antigonides, in: REG 98, 1985, 93–124.   L.-M.G.

Medontidae (Μεδοντίδαι; *Medontídai*). Aristocratic Athenian family, whose ancestor → Medon [5] renounced the royal title in 1069 BC, and was supposedly the first to hold the archonship (→ árchontes) for life. The office was then said to have become hereditary within his family, until the term of office was limited to ten years in 753. The ten-year archonship was also said to have been held exclusively by the M. down to 713 (Aristot. Ath. Pol. 3,3; Paus. 4,5,10). However, there is no authentic evidence for this position of power sustained over centuries, which is likely to be a construct of the 5th cent.

Rhodes, 98ff.; K.-W. Welwei, Athen, 1992, 53f., 67f., 101f.   E.S.-H.

Meduacus Name of two rivers within the problematic hydrographic network of the central course of the Veneto. According to Tab. Peut. 4,4 and 4,5, the M. maior is the modern Brenta, which flows into the Adriatic, and the M. minor is the modern Bacchiglione, which bifurcated at → Patavium (Plin. HN 3,121), where it formed a harbour (Liv. 10,2,6).

Nissen 2, 219.   A.SA.

Medulli Alpine tribe, subjugated by Augustus (CIL V 7817 = Plin. HN 3,137); they lived east of the Vocontii and south of the Allobroges (Str. 4,1,11; 4,6,5; Ptol. 2,10,7) along the upper course of the Arc near modern Modane, and, according to Vitr. De arch. 8,3,20, were particularly prone to suffer from goitre. They belonged to the tribes governed by → Cottius [1] (CIL V 7231) and later to the *prov. Alpes Cottiae*.

TIR L 32,92; G. Barruol, Les peuples préromains du sud-est de la Gaule, 1975, 334–337.   K.DI.

Medullia Town of the *prisci Latini*, founded by Alba Longa north of the → Anio (Liv. 1,33,4; 38,4; *Medullum*, Plin. HN 3,68). The town was captured by the Romans in the war against the Latini (340–338 BC). Deserted by the end of the Roman Republic; its exact location is unknown.

Nissen 2, 563.   G.U.

Medus see → Medea

Medusa (Μέδουσα; *Médousa*). Mythological monster, one of the three Gorgons (see → Gorgo [1]): M. is mortal, whereas her two sisters Sthenno and Euryale are immortal.   L.K.

Mefitis The name of the goddess M. is derived from Oscan *mefitis*, 'suffocating, sulphurous exhalation' (cf. Verg. Aen. 7,83f.; Serv. Aen. 7,84). Hence the first evidence of a cult of M. is found on Oscan territory: Aeclanum (Vetter 162), Pompeii (Vetter 32) and Rossano di Vaglio. There had been a temple since the 4th century BC in which M. was worshipped beside → Juppiter and → Mars [1; 2]. In the 1st century BC, M. was also worshipped in the nearby Roman town of Potentia (CIL X 130–133 and p. 961; cf. ibid. 3811, from Capua). Her most prominent temple was at the *lacus Ampsanctus* (Valle d'Ansanto, Rocca San Felice: [3; 4]), with a spring and a lake that gave off sulphurous vapours which nobody could breathe in safely. The animals to be sacrificed were killed by the suffocating gas. The *umbilicus Italiae* was located there (Serv. Aen. 7,563). M. was also worshipped in Grumentum (CIL X 203: M. Fisica; cf. Venus Fisica, CIL IV 1520; X 928), in Atina (CIL X 5047; [5]) and in Aequum Tuticum (CIL IX 1421). There were a temple and a grove dedicated to M. on the Esquiline in Rome (Varro Ling. 5,49; Paul. Fest. 476 L.), and also a temple at Cremona (Tac. Hist. 3,33; cf. CIL V 6353, from Lodi).

M. was identified with → Venus (Vetter 182). Servius (Aen. 7,84) mentions an identification with → Juno. The existence of a god M. connected with → Leucothea or Albunea is doubtful (Serv. Aen. 7,84). → Italia

1 D. Adamesteanu, M. Lejeune, Il santuario lucano di Macchia di Rossano di Vaglio, 1971   2 M. Lejeune, M. d'après les dédicaces lucaniennes de Rossano di Vaglio, 1990   3 A. Bottini et al., Valle d'Ansanto, in: NSA 30, 1976, 359–524   4 I. Rainini, Il santuario di Mefite in Valle d'Ansanto, 1985; 5 W.v. Sydow, Archäologische Funde und Grabungen im Bereich der Soprintendenzen Latium und Ostia 1957–1975, in: AA 1976, 372.

R. Mambella, s.v. M., LIMC 6.1, 400–402; P. Poccetti, M., in: AION 4, 1982, 237–260.   A.MAS.

Megabates (Μεγαβάτης; *Megabátēs*). Name of several distinguished Persians, including:
[1] Father of Megabazus [2] (Hdt. 7,97), cousin of Darius [1] I and of the satrap Artaphernes [2]. He commanded the unsuccessful assault on Naxos (500 BC; Hdt. 5,30–35). He may be identical with the M. who was replaced by Xerxes as satrap of Hellespontian Phrygia in 477 (Thuc. 1,129,1), or the M. who is described as an 'admiral' in [1. 8,5–7].

1 G. G. Cameron, Persepolis Treasury Tablets, 1948.

[2] The beautiful son of Spithridates, who was the lover of Agesilaus [2]. He and his father surrendered to the king of Sparta in 396/5 (Xen. Hell. 3,4,10; 4,1,6; 4,28;

Xen. Ag. 5,4–5; Hell. Oxyrh. 21,4; Plut. Agesilaus 11; Plut. Mor. 31C; 81A; 209D; Max. Tyr. 19,5).   J.W.

Megabazus (Μεγαβάζος; *Megabázos*). Name of several distinguished Persians.
[1] Commander under Darius [1] I, father of Oebares (Hdt. 6,33) and of Bubares (7,22). After his Scythian campaign in 513, the king left him in Europe to conquer Thrace (Hdt. 5,2). M. subjugated all the inhabitants of the Hellespont, Perinthus (5,2), and Thrace (ibid.) who were not already subjected to the Persians (Hdt. 4,144), as well as the Paeonians (5,15). He accomplished the subjugation of the Macedonian king → Amyntas [1] through envoys (Hdt. 5,17f.; Iust. 7,3,7).
[2] Naval commander under Xerxes I, son of → Megabates [1] (Hdt. 7,97).
[3] Persian envoy who tried in vain to stir up the Spartans against Athens in 458 BC (Thuc. 1,109,2–3).   J.W.

Megabyzus (also Μεγάβυξος/*Megábyxos*, Hdt. Μεγάβυζος/*Megábyzos* < Old Persian *Bagabuxša*, Elamite *Ba-ka-bu-uk-šá*).
[1] Distinguished Persian, son of Dātūvahya (according to Hdt. 3,153 father of → Zopyrus), He conspired with Darius [1] I against → Gaumāta/Smerdis ([2. DB IV 85], Hdt. 3,70 *passim*).
[2] According to Hdt. son of → Zopyrus (and hence grandson of M. [1]). Commander under → Xerxes in his Greek campaign (Hdt. 7,82; 121). Later he was the opponent of the Athenians in Egypt (Thuc. 1,109,3; Diod. 11,74,6 *passim*) and in the battle for Cyprus (Diod. 12,3,2–4). Ctesias (FGrH 688 F 14,34ff.) describes the close relationships of M.'s family to the dynasty in a novelistic style.

1 BRIANT, Index s.v. Megabyzos   2 R. KENT, Old Persian, 1953.   J.W.

Megaclea (Μεγάκλεια; *Megákleia*). According to the *Vita Ambrosiana* (1,3,3–4 DRACHMANN), wife of Pindar (→ Pindarus), daughter of Lysitheus and Calline. In Eustathius's verse biography, which is preserved in the proem of his lost Pindarus commentary, Timoxeine is given as the name of Pindar's wife (Τιμοξείνη, 3,302,1 DRACHMANN). In both sources the children are called Protomache, Eumetis and Daephantus. Pindar composed a → Daphnephorikon for him (fr. 94c SNELL-MAEHLER).   E.R.

Megacles (Μεγακλῆς; *Megaklês*). A name that was increasingly common in the Athenian house of the → Alcmaeonids in the 7th–5th cents. BC.
[1] The first historical M. Plutarch (Solon 12,1) designates him by name as the *árchōn* (632/1?), allegedly responsible for the defeat of the Cylonian revolution (→ Cylon [1]) and the subsequent curse of the Alcmaeonids (Hdt. 5,71; Thuc. 1,126).
→ Peisistratids

DEVELIN, 30f.; PA 9688; TRAILL, PAA 636340.

[2] Grandson of M. [1], son of Alcmaeon [3], the most prominent (despite the importance of → Cleisthenes [2]) of the → Alcmaeonids. For decades in 6th-century BC Athens, he was a leading politician and man of power, against whom others, particularly → Peisistratus, had difficulty holding their own. Of the three 'parties' mentioned by Herodotus (Hdt. 1,59,3; Aristot. Ath. pol. 13,4), M. led the 'Coastlanders' (παράλιοι/ *parálioi*). M.'s power base probably stretched from Athens to the south and southeast (modern Glifada and around the southern peak of Mount Mavrovouni as far as Hagios Dimitrios), but hardly as far as Anavissos (cf. [1. 5–8]; contra, [2. 372]). Either in 575 or not until 555 (thus [3. 40^18] despite Hdt. 1,61,2), he contracted a dynastic marriage to Agariste [1], the daughter of Cleisthenes [1] of Sicyon, in competition with → Hippocleides (Hdt. 6,126–130). Dominant until his brief [3. 33f.; 4. 11–13] exile after the violent return of the → Peisistratids in 546, he then participated in the aristocratic regime of Peisistratus' 'third tyranny'. The year of his death is unknown, but he was succeeded by his eldest son Cleisthenes [2] (archon in 525/4). Owing to the wealth and power of his family, M. was more active in building and cultural activities than is usually assumed.

u   1 K. H. KINZL, Regionalism in Classical Athens?, in: The Ancient History Bull. 3, 1989   2 DAVIES   3 K. H. KINZL, Betrachtungen zur älteren griechischen Tyrannis, in: AJAH 4, 1979, 23–45   4 Id., Note on the Exiles of the Alkmeonidai, in: RhM 119, 1976, 311–314   5 PA 9692; 6 TRAILL, PAA 636345.

[3] Son of M. [2]. His granddaughter Isodice was the wife of Cimon (Plut. Cimon 4,10; 16,1).

DAVIES, 9688; PA 9693; TRAILL, PAA 636450.

[4] Son of Hippocrates [2], grandson of M. [2], brother of Pericles' mother Agariste [2], from Alopece. Exiled by → ostrakismos (more than 4,000 ostraca from the Kerameikos [1. 153]) in 487/6 BC (Aristot. Ath. pol. 22,5). He was victorious in the Pythian four-horse chariot race in 486 (Pind. P. 7). His return to Athens in 480 is not attested. A second ostracism in the 480s ([2. 137–145]; cf. Lys. 14,39) remains hypothetical.

1 F. WILLEMSEN, S. BRENNE, Verzeichnis der Kerameikos-Ostraka, in: MDAI(A) 106, 1991, 147–156   2 Id., Ostraka einer Meisterschale, in: MDAI(A) 106, 1991, 137–145.

DAVIES, 9688; PA 9695; TRAILL, PAA 636455.

[5] Son of M. [4], winner of the Olympic four-horse chariot race in 436 BC. He is last mentioned in 425 (Aristoph. Ach. 614f.). He was insignificant politically.

DAVIES, 9688; PA 9697; TRAILL, PAA 636460.

[6] Syracusan, brother of → Dion [I 1].   K.KI.
[7] An architect mentioned in Pausanias (6,19,7), who together with one Pothaeus and one Antiphilus was said to have built a *de facto* non-existent Carthaginian treasury in → Olympia. The structure in question was prob-

ably the Syracusan treasury, built in the years after 480 BC.

> H. SVENSON-EVERS, Die griechischen Architekten archai- scher und klassischer Zeit, 1996, 363–368 (with further bibliography).   C.HÖ.

Megaclides (Μεγακλείδης; *Megakleídēs*). Peripatetic exegete of Homer, contemporary of → Ephorus, → Phi- lochorus and → Chamaeleon (cf. Tatian, Oratio ad Graecos 31,2; Eus. Pr. Ev. 10,11,3). He must therefore have lived in the second half of the 4th cent. BC. M.'s interpretations of Homer, which in addition to criticism (cf. schol. Hom. Il. 22,36) and questions of composition (cf. ibid. 16,140) are primarily concerned with factual issues, are preserved only in fragments. They probably stem from a work 'On Homer' (Περὶ Ὁμήρου; cf. Suda s.v. Ἀθηναίας) which commented on the 'Iliad' and the 'Odyssey', in at least two volumes (cf. schol. Hom. Il. 16,140(A)). M.'s texts, as well as second-hand infor- mation on his work, are transmitted in several places, of which the confirmed ones (unconfirmed: Aristot. Poet. 24,1460a 1ff. [2. 410]; Ael. Var. 4,26; in hypothesis A on Hes. Sc. [3. 442]) can be divided into four groups: 1. Some of M.'s interpretations of passages are preserved in the Homeric scholia: a. Scholia on the 'Iliad' (10,275(B); 16,140 (AT); 21,195(G); 22,36(B); 22,205(BT); uncertain: 5,640(B)), b. Scholia on the 'Odyssey' (6,106; uncertain: 9,5f.). 2. According to Athen. 12,512e ff., M. attacked the Cynics' 'philo- sophical' representation of Odysseus (→ Antisthenes) and the contemporary portrayal of Heracles. 3. The Suda (s.v. Ἀθηναίας) and Hesychius (s.v. Ἀθηναία) report a note by M. on the names of Athenian women (cf. Eust. in Hom. Il. 1,84,18); there are also passages on M. in Pausanias, Photius and Aelius Dionysius. 4. In the Ammonius Papyrus (POxy. 221, col. 9,3).
→ Philologyí

> , wch   1 E. BUX, s.v. Megakleides, RE 15, 124–125   2 A. GUDEMAN (ed.), Aristoteles, Περὶ ποιητικῆς, 1934   3 M. VAN DER VALK, Researches on the Text and Scholia of the Iliad, 2 vols, 1963 and 1964.   GR.DA.

Megaclo (Μεγακλώ; *Megaklṓ*). Daughter of the Les- bian king → Macar. In a rationalistic interpretation, the Lesbian local historian → Myrsilus of Methymna repre- sents her (FGrH 477 F 7, cf. Arnob. 3,37) as the founder of the seven Lesbian → Muses: she taught seven slave women to celebrate the deeds of ancient times with lyres, thus softening the grudge the king held against his wife. In gratitude, M. erected bronze statues in their honour in a sanctuary and instituted cult worship.
                                                          H.A.G.

Megaera (Μέγαιρα/Mégaira, 'the envious one', Lat. Megaera). Name of one of the Erinyes (→ Erinys; Apol- lod. 1,3f.; Cornutus 10; Verg. Aen. 12,845–847; Lucan. 1,572–577, 6,730; Stat. Theb. 1,712; more in [1. 123]), perhaps also a name for the destructive power of per-

sonified envy in general and the evil eye in particular (Orph. Lithika 224f., cf. Orph. Lithika kerygmata 2,4). A 3rd century AD altar with a votive inscription to M. has been found in Pergamum. Votive offerings may have been made with the aim of warding off envy [2].

> 1 E. WÜST, s.v. Erinys, RE Suppl. 8, 82–166   2 W. RADT, Ein Altärchen aus Pergamon für die Erinys, in: R.M. Boehmer, H. Hauptmann (ed.), Beiträge zur Altertums- kunde Kleinasiens. Festschrift K.Bittel, 1983, vol. 1, 449– 453.   S.I.J.

Megaleas (Μεγαλέας;*Megaléas*). A Macedonian, ap- pointed by → Antigonus [3] Doson in his will as head of the chancery (*epì toû grammateíou*) of → Philippus V in 222 BC (Pol. 4,87,8). Together with → Apelles [1] and → Leontius [2] M. opposed the anti-Aetolian western policy of the young king and in the year 218 physically attacked → Aratus [2], for which he was condemned by court martial. Released on Leontius's bail, M. fled to Thebes, where he took his life before being extradited (Pol. 5,2,8; 15f.; 25,1f.; 26–28) [1. 170].

> 1 ERRINGTON.   L.-M.G.

Megale polis see → Megalopolis

Megalesia see → Kybele; → Mater Magna

Megaloi/-ai Theoi/-ai see → Theoi Megaloi, → Theai Megalai

Megalophanes (Μεγαλοφάνης/*Megalophánēs*; proper- ly: Demophanes, Δημοφάνης/*Dēmophánēs* [1. 228– 233]), from Megalopolis. A pupil of → Arcesilaus [5] like his friend → Ecdemus. Together they established a liberal constitution in → Cyrene in *c*. 250 BC [2. 431] and later became → Philopoemen's teachers. M.'s and Ecdemus' reputation for remorseless enmity towards tyranny was not merely academic: it resulted from their participation in the assassination of → Aristodemus [6] (*c*. 253) and in the overthrow of → Nicocles [4] of Sicyon in league with → Aratus [2] (Pol. 10,22,2f.; Plut. Philopoimen 1,3–5) [2. 395f., 401].

> 1 K. ZIEGLER, Plutarchstudien, in: RhM 83, 1934, 211– 250   2 H. BERVE, Die Tyrannis bei den Griechen, 1967.
>   L.-M.G.

Megalopolis (Μεγάλη πόλις/*Megálē pólis*, Lat. *Mega- lopolis*).
A. LOCATION AND ARCHITECTURAL REMAINS
B. HISTORY

A. LOCATION AND ARCHITECTURAL REMAINS
The ancient city lies in the middle of the western Arcadian plateau (22 km × 10 km, 427 m elevation), which is criss-crossed by a multitude of small streams, north of modern Megalopolis (formerly Sinanou), on both sides of the lower reaches of River Helisson [1],

some 4 km above the confluence with the Alpheius River, where the most important roads to Arcadia, Messenia and Laconia cross. The city wall, now difficult to distinguish, consisted of clay bricks on stone foundations and has a circumference of about 8.4 km, corresponding to the 50 stadia (8.85 km) mentioned in Pol. 9,26a. The wall follows the line of hills surrounding the city. Pol. 2,55,2 says that it was much too big for the number of inhabitants. South of the Helisson is the large theatre, described by Pausanias (8,32,1) as the biggest in Greece. Immediately to the north, adjacent to its *skēnē,* is the Thersilion, the 52 × 66 m column-supported chamber of the 10,000 strong assembly of the Arcadian League. Structures on the northern bank of the Helisson were grouped around the large agora, the southern part of which was occupied by the sanctuary of Zeus Soter [1. 225f.], on its eastern side stood the Stoa Myropolis built by the tyrant → Aristodemus [6] (Paus. 8,30,7), and its northern side bordered on the 156 m long, three-winged portico of Philippus II [2. 122–126].

B. HISTORY

The founding of the 'Great City', combining the largest part of western Arcadia with support from Thebes, probably took place in 368/7 BC (Diod. Sic. 15,72,4) [3; 4; 5; 6]. The number of incorporated towns, which nevertheless remained partly independent or as villages, is given by Pausanias (8,27,3f. also 27,5ff.; Str. 8,8,1) as forty. A collection of money for its founding is documented in inscriptions (IMagn. 38 = Syll.³ 559,28f.). Resettlement proceeded partly by force (cf. Diod. Sic. 15,94). As a city M. first appears in Xen. Hell. 7,5,5 in the battle of → Mantinea on the side of Tegea and thus of Thebes in 362. Sparta repeatedly tried to destroy the new foundation, e.g. in 352. As a result M. sought the support in particular of Philip II and received through him the Belmantis border region.

Further important dates: in 331 besieged by Agis [3], victory of Antipater [1] over Agis [3], who fell in the battle, later on the side of Cassander. In 318 besieged by Polyperchon. After that under the suzerainty of Antigonus [2]. In *c.* 270 under the rule of Antigonus' supporter Aristodemus. Victorious defence against a Spartan attack led by Acrotatus [2]. Tyranny of → Lydiadas [1]. In perhaps 249/8 another failed Spartan attack. Lydiadas then took M. into the Achaean Confederacy (→ Achaeans, with map), in which he held the office of *strategos* several times (235/4). Under Cleomenes III there were new tensions and open war with Sparta, in which the city suffered much and Lydiadas died. In 223 Cleomenes conquered the city and plundered it. After that it was rebuilt and was given a new constitution. On a nomothetic commission of the Achaean Confederacy M. was represented by three members (IG IV 1², 13,24ff.). More Spartan and Aetolian attacks. Donations for the construction of fortifications are documented in inscriptions (IG V 2, 434; 440f.), contributions even came from Antiochus [6] in 174 (Liv. 41,20,6). As

a result of → Philopoemen's reforms formerly dependent towns became full members of the Confederacy (Plut. Philopoemen 13,5). Border agreements with Thuria (IvOl 46) and Sparta (IvOl 47 = Syll.³ 665).

The poetic description of M. as the 'great solitude' (μεγάλη ἐϱημία/*megálē erēmía,* Str. 8,8,1; 16,1,5) is exaggerated, inscriptions show continued, if modest, survival in the Imperial period [7], in addition to ruins and abandoned buildings, excavations have also brought to light repair work and new buildings from the Roman period. Under Augustus a bridge was built, a hall under Domitianus (IG V 2, 456f.). Neither does Pausanias's description give too bad a picture. Coins were minted again in the Severian period (193–235). A fragment of Diocletian's Price Edict (CIL III p. 1920f.) was found in M. → Philopoemen, the historian → Polybius [2] and the poet → Cercidas [3] were from M. Evidence: Paus. 8,27,1–16; 30–33; Plin. HN 4,20; Ptol. 3,16,19; Steph. Byz. s.v. Μεγάλη πόλις; Geogr. Rav 5,22. Inscriptions: IG V 2, 431–494. Coins: HN² 418; 444; 450f.. Archaeology: [8].

1 JOST, 220–233   2 T. SPYROPULOS et al., Megalopolis. Vorbericht. 1991–1993, in: AA 110, 1995, 119–128   3 M. MOGGI, Il sinecismo di Megalopoli, in: ASNP, third series, 4, 1974, 71–107   4 Id., I sinecismi interstatali greci 1, 1976, 293–325   5 S. HORNBLOWER, When Was Megalopolis Founded?, in: ABSA 85, 1990, 71–77   6 N. H. DEMAND, Urban Relocation in Archaic and Classical Greece, 1990, 111–118   7 J. ROY et al., Megalopolis under the Roman Empire, in: S. WALKER, A. CAMERON (eds.), The Greek Renaissance in the Roman Empire (BICS Supplement 55), 1989, 146–150   8 T. SPYROPULOS et al., Megalopolis. 2. Vorbericht. 1994–1995, in: AA 111, 1996, 269–286.; F. CARINCI, s.v. Arcadia, EAA 2, 1994, 337f.; A. PETRONITIS, Ἡ Μεγάλη πόλις τῆς Ἀϱκαδίας (Ancient Greek Cities 23), 1973; W. F. WYATT, s.v. Megalopolis, PE, 564f.   Y.L. E.MEY.

Megapanus (Μεγάπανος; *Megápanos*). According to Hdt. 7,62 commander-in-chief of the Hyrcanians on → Xerxes' Greek campaign, latter allegedly governor of Babylon, perhaps identical to the Bakabana of the PFT [1. 672]. A *Ba-ga-a-pa-ʾ* appears in Babylonian texts as satrap of Babylonia and Ebir Nāri or governor of Babylon, albeit for the year 503 BC.

1 R. T. HALLOCK, Persepolis Fortification Tablets [PFT], 1969   2 A. KUHRT, Babylonia from Cyrus to Xerxes, in: CAH2, vol. 4, 1988, 131, 136.   J.W.

Megapenthes (Μεγαπένθης/*Megapénthēs,* 'very sorrowful').
[1] Son of King → Proetus of Argos (Apollod. 2,29), father of Argeus and grandfather of Anaxagoras (Paus. 2,18,4) or father of Anaxagoras and Iphianira (Diod. Sic. 4,68,4; cf. also → Iphianassa [1]). M. exchanged kingdoms with → Perseus, so that he ruled over Argos and Perseus over Tiryns. According to Hyginus (Hyg. Fab. 244), he was said to have killed Perseus for the murder of his father.

[2] Son of → Menelaus [1] and a slave woman. It is the wedding of M. to the daughter of the Spartan → Alector [1] and that of the daughter of Menelaus to the son of Achilles that is being celebrated (Hom. Od. 4,1ff.) when Telemachus arrives at Sparta in search of information about his father Odysseus. Being illegitimate, M. and his brother Nicostratus are excluded from the throne, which leaves → Tyndareus' grandson Orestes next in line (Paus. 2,18,6). According to Rhodian legend, which deviates from the Spartan one, M. and his brother drive → Helene [1] from Sparta after the death of Menelaus and she seeks refuge with → Polyxo [3] in Rhodes (Paus. 3,19,9f.). On the throne of → Amyclae [1] M. and his brother are represented riding on horseback (Paus. 3,18,13).   AL.FR.

Megara

[1] (Μεγάρα/Megára, Μεγάρη/Megárē). Daughter of Creon [1] of Thebes, wife of → Heracles [1] (Hom. Od. 11,269–270), who had received her hand in thanks for the liberation of Thebes from tribute to → Erginus, and mother of some of the → Heraclidae. Whereas the Thebans according to Paus. 9,11,2 tell of the insane Heracles' infanticide (on his insanity Cypria p. 40,28f. PEG) as nothing other than what Stesichorus (= 230 PMGF) and Panyassis (= fr. 1 PEG) relate, the version of Pherecydes (FGrH 3 F 14) is that Heracles threw his five sons into a → fire, probably in fulfillment of a ritual of immortality. Thus, Pind. Isthm. 4,61–68 describes a nocturnal fire festival in Thebes, which took place on the eve of the Herakleia in honour of M.'s and Heracles' sons, the Alkaḯdai (= Alkeḯdai; schol. Pind. I. 4,104g. 110a). In Euripides's 'Heracles', by contrast, the hero is driven insane by Hera and kills not only his three children, but also M., with club and bow (based on this, with variants, Seneca, Hercules furens; only his children e.g. Diod. 4,11,1). Whereas Paus. 9,11,2 and schol. Pind. Isthm. 4,104a–110c harmonise the different versions, as perhaps does a calyx krater from Paestum ([1], c. 350–325 BC) on which Heracles carries one of his children to the funeral pyre under the eyes of → Mania [1], today two or three parallel versions are for the most part assumed. In the poem Megára ascribed to → Moschus [3] M. plays a rare leading role.

> TRENDALL, Paestum, 84, no. 127 fig. 46.; E. KRUMMEN, Pyrsos Hymnon, 1990, 33–97; M. SCHMIDT, s.v. Herakleidai, LIMC 4.1, 723–728; 4.2, 442–444; S. WOODFORD, s.v. Megara (1), LIMC 8.1, 828–829 (supplement).   T.H.

[2] (Μέγαρα/Mégara, in late antiquity also Μάγαρα/Mágara, inhabitant Μεγαρεύς/Megareús).
I. LOCATION II. CITY III. HISTORY

I. LOCATION
Principal city of the Megaris, a narrow land bridge connecting Attica and Corinthia. The → Gerania mountain range dominates the south. Its difficult terrain, in thrusting itself across the breadth of the → Isth-

mus, acts like a natural barrier. In the east the mountains → Cerata, Pateras and → Cithaeron block access to central Greece. Between the Gerania mountains and Mount Pateras there is a c. 15 km wide late-Tertiary massif. The region northeast of the Gerania range is hilly with partly stony and partly sandy soil. The fertile plain of M. stretches to the southeast. There were three ports in the Megaris: → Nisaea [1] on the Saronic Gulf, → Pagae and → Aegosthena on the Corinthian Gulf. There were other smaller places, such as Tripodiscus [1], Aegeirus, Ereneia and Cynosura [4] in the interior. Nature separates the Megaris from its neighbours by mountain ranges; politically these did not always form insurmountable borders [2]. Before the outbreak of territorial conflicts with its neighbours, M. controlled the peninsula of Perachora, regions southwest of the Gerania mountains and, intermittently, → Salamis [1]. A coast road on the Saronic Gulf, the Scironian Way, led from Corinth to Eleusis, in the west another route followed a pass over the Gerania range, the spurs of Mount Pateras and over Mount Cithaeron to → Plataeae. A difficult coast road on the Gulf of Corinth connected Pagae and Aegosthena with Boeotia.

After the losses in the archaic period the territory of M. was small, and apart from the plain around M. there were only few agriculturally usable areas. In the mountainous regions cattle breeding and husbandry were practised, in the plains intensive horticulture, and fishing in the coastal waters. The limited agrarian basis forced people to turn to the sea for their income and to trade, primarily in wool and textiles. Salt was extracted in the saltworks on the Saronian Gulf (Aristoph. Ach. 521–528; 760f.; Isocr. Or. 8,117; Xen. Mem. 2,7,6; Theophr. Hist. pl. 2,8,1; Diod. Sic. 11,18; Diog. Laert. 6,41; [3. 141]).

II. CITY
The urban centre of M. was 2 km from the coast in the southwest of the plain. The city extended southwards from two acropoleis, Caria and Alcathous. In the 5th century BC, the city centre was surrounded by a wall [4]. In the south two Long Walls built in the middle of the 5th century under Athenian guidance connected M. with its chief port Nisaea. These were demolished in 424/3 BC by the Megarians themselves and only rebuilt in about 340 BC. The results of excavations (a well system which is not the same as Theagenes' well house [5] mentioned in Paus. 1,40,1 and 1,41,2 and numerous building complexes) are regularly reported by P. ZORIDES in the journal Archaiologikon Deltion.

III. HISTORY
A. EARLY HISTORY B. FROM THE END OF THE 6TH CENTURY TO THE ROMAN CONQUEST C. THE ROMAN PERIOD D. THE BYZANTINE PERIOD

A. EARLY HISTORY
The Megaris had been settled by the Bronze Age [6]. The pre-Doric population probably maintained close

relations with Athens and Boeotia. It was not mentioned in the Homeric Catalogue of Ships. Whether Nisa (Hom. Il. 2,508 [7. 279f.]) can be identified with M. is disputed. M. became Doric under the influence of → Argos [II]. Five towns are supposed to have existed in the Megaris before the → synoikismos, the inhabitants of which called themselves *Herais*, *Piraeis*, *Megareis*, *Kynosurei*s and *Tripodiskioi* (Plut. Quaest. Graec. 18). The 7th century saw the beginnings of tensions with Corinth, leading to the loss of the Perachora Peninsula. A growing population, the search for farmland and an influx of refugees resulted in colonising expeditions (→ Colonization) from M. first to Sicily (*c.* 730 BC M. [3] Hyblaea, 650 BC Selinus [8]) and from 675 to 625 to the Propontis and the Black Sea region (Chalcedon, Selymbria, Astacus, Byzantium, Heraclea [7] Pontica, cf. [9]). After 650, Theagenes ruled in M. as tyrant (Aristot. Pol. 5, 1305a 24–26) [10. 225–230]. After his fall (Plut. Quaest. Graec. 18) there were further conflicts with Corinth and the Athenians, who after Spartan arbitration ultimately obtained Salamis. Internal tensions contined within the population [11. 98–111]. The political and social conditions in the archaic period come to life in the poems of → Theognis (according to Pl. Leg. 1,630a 4 a citizen of the Sicilian city of M. who described the conditions in the mother city, but cf. Didymus, schol. Plat. l.c.) [12].

B. FROM THE END OF THE 6TH CENTURY TO THE ROMAN CONQUEST

From the end of the 6th century, M. was a member of the → Peloponnesian League. In 480 BC, M. took part in the naval battles against the Persians at Artemisium and Salamis (→ Persian Wars) with 20 ships on each occasion. In 479 BC, → Mardonius [1] led an expedition into the Megaris (Hdt. 9,14; Paus. 1,40,2f.). 3,000 Megarian → *hoplitai* took part in the battle at Plataeae, suffering heavy losses. Whether the funerary epigram for Pollis is related to these campaigns is disputed [13]. After renewed border wars with Corinth, M. left the Peloponnesian League in 461 BC (Thuc. 1,103,4; Diod. Sic. 11,79,1f.). The Long Walls (→ Fortifications) to Nisaea were built. Several times a theatre of war in the First → Peloponnesian War (460–446 BC), M. soon rejoined the Peloponnesian League, but the Athenians did not give up Pagae and Nisaea until 446. The restrictions on access to markets in Attica imposed by the Megarian Decree contributed to the outbreak of the Second Peloponnesian War [14], which severely affected M. [15]. In 427 BC, → Minoa was occupied by the Athenians. A democratic overthrow in 424 with the aim of bringing M. over to the Athenian side failed after violent struggles [16. 106–109]. Athens was able to occupy the port of Nisaea, however, and it was not handed back to M. until 410. There is a list of the fallen from M. belonging to this period (SEG 39, 1989, 411).

Intelligent policy-making helped M. avoid most military conflicts in the 4th century (cf. Isocr. Or. 8,117; Xen. Mem. 2,7,6). It was able to free itself from Sparta in 394 and introduce a democratic constitution. Minting also began in the 4th century (HN 393f.). In 343, Philip II failed in his attempt to take M. against the resistance of the Athenians [16. 110]. Under → Stilpon, the → Megarian school of Philosophy, founded by Euclid [2], flourished. After the → Lamian War initially under the influence of Cassander, M. was then conquered by Ptolemy I in 308 BC, but fell to Demetrius [2] Poliorketes the following year. After 286, M. was autonomous, then came under Macedonian influence. In 243 BC it was a member of the Achaean Confederacy (→ Achaeans, with map); the ports of Pagae and Aegosthena joined as autonomous cities. In 224, M. crossed over to the Boeotian League (→ Boeotia, with map), but in 192 returned to the Achaean Confederacy.

C. THE ROMAN PERIOD

In 146 BC, an Achaean garrison in M. capitulated to the Romans, and M. escaped destruction (Paus. 7,15,7–11). Cornelius [I 90] Sulla used M. as a supply base for the siege of Athens. On the side of Pompey in the Civil War, M. was conquered by Caesar's legates and was largely destroyed. In the Imperial period M. was a small provincial town wich, as Pausanias' account (l.c.) shows, had preserved a stock of old buildings. Plin. HN 4,23 calls M. a Roman colony. Several honorary inscriptions to Roman emperors are extant, a phyle was named after Hadrian (IG VII 72; 74; 101). Affiliated to Boeotia in administrative terms, M. nominated → Boeotarchs in this period (IG VII 24; 106). According to an architectural inscription, a stoa was built in 259 AD [17]. In 395, M. was destroyed by the Goths (Zon. 5,6,3), but was rebuilt (IG VII 26; 93).

K.F.

1 K. J. RIGSBY, Megara and Tripodiscus, in: GRBS 28, 1987, 93ff. 2 C. ANTONETTI, I confini della Megaride, in: E. OLSHAUSEN, H. SONNABEND (ed.), Stuttgarter Kolloquium zur historischen Geographie des Altertums 4 (1990), 1994, 539–551 3 GEHRKE 4 P. ZORIDES, Τὰ ἀρχαῖα τείχη τῶν Μεγάρων, in: ArchE 1985, 217–236 5 TRAVLOS, Attika, 258–287 6 R. HOPE SIMPSON, O. T. P. DICKINSON, A Gazetteer of Aegean Civilization in the Bronze Age 1, 1979, 74ff. 7 E. VISSER, Homers Katalog der Schiffe, 1997 8 P. DANNER, Megara, Megara Hyblaea and Selinus, in: H. D. ANDERSEN et al. (ed.), Urbanization in the Mediterranean, 1997, 143–165 9 C. ANTONETTI, Megare e le sue colonie, in: Id. (ed.), Il dinamismo della colonizzazione greca, 1997, 83–94 10 L. DE LIBERO, Die archaische Tyrannis, 1996 11 U. WALTER, An der Polis teilhaben, 1993 12 T. J. FIGUEIRA (ed.), Theognis of Megara, 1985 13 J. EBERT, Neue griechische Epigramme, in: J. H. M. STRUBBE et al. (ed.), Energia. Studies on ancient history and epigraphy presented to H.W. Pleket, 1996, 19–25 14 B. R. MACDONALD, The Megarian Decree, in: Historia 32, 1983, 385–410 15 T. E. WICK, Megara, Athens and the West in the Archidamian War, in: Historia 28, 1979, 1–14 16 H. J. GEHRKE, Stasis, 1985 17 M. HEIL, Zwei spätantike Statthalter aus Epirus und Achaia, in: ZPE 108, 1995, 162ff.; F. BOHRINGER, Mégare. Traditions mythiques, espace sacré et naissance de la cité, in: AC 49, 1980, 5–22; K. HANELL, Megarische Studien, 1934; R. P. LEGON,

Megara. The Political History of a Greek City-State, 1981; E. MEYER, s.v. Megara, RE 29, 152–205; A. MULLER, Megarika I–VIX, in: BCH 104, 1980, 83–89; BCH 105, 1981, 203–225; BCH 106, 1982, 379–407; BCH 107, 1983, 157–179; BCH 108, 1984, 249–264; L. PICCIRILLI (ed.), Megarika. Testimonianze e frammenti, 1975. K.F.

D. THE BYZANTINE PERIOD

Apart from being pillaged by the Goths (in 395) and threatened by the → Slavs, the history of M. in the Byzantine period proceeded almost without incident until the Crusades. From the 4th to the 6th centuries there is evidence of a diocese, but it is only mentioned again after 1204 in connexion with Frankish rule, and in 1222 it was combined with that of Athens. Despite limited archaeological finds, the continued existence of M. as a modest provincial town in the periphery of Athens is certain, considering that it had always held a certain significance on account of its position on the road to → Corinth and because of its acropolis, the κάστρον/kástron. The late-mediaeval Albanian migratory expansion, which fundamentally altered the ethnic composition of → Attica, passed M. by.

TIB s.v. Megara, 215ff. J.N.

[3] (Μέγαρα/Mégara, Μέγαρες Ὑβλαῖοι/Mégares Hyblaîoi; Megara Hyblaea is modern; Lat. Megara, -orum and Megara, -ae; the region τὸ Μεγαρικόν/tò Megarikón or Μεγαρίς/Megarís). One of the oldest, if not the oldest Doric colony (→ Colonization) on the eastern coast of Sicily. According to the tradition in Thuc. 6,4,1, which is at least reliable in principle (i.e. most likely transmitted through → Antiochus [19] of Syracuse), M. was founded 245 years before its destruction by → Gelon [1] (in 484/481), i.e. in 729/726 BC. → Lamis and colonists from M. [2] in the mother country settled first at Trotilum above the River Pantacyas, then together with Chalcidians in Leontini. After that, driven out by the latter, on Thapsus, and finally, with the consent of the Siculan king Hyblon, in nearby Hybla in a place at the innermost part of the flat bay between modern Augusta and Syracuse.

What is certain is that according to archaeological findings (abundant ceramic yields from the 8th to the early 5th centuries BC) M. did exist by the second half of the 8th century (the first half according to some scholars). In 553 BC, M. took part in the conflict between Syracuse and Camarina (Philistus FGrH 556 F 5). Thuc. l.c. is probably reliable in claiming that, 100 years after its own founding, M. founded → Selinus under the leadership of Pammilus, who had been summoned from the mother city. However, this was perhaps less a demonstration of power than a sign of overpopulation in a small settlement area constricted by powerful neighbours (Syracuse, Leontini, Catane). In all likelihood this also caused the social tensions that according to Hdt. 7,156 gave Gelon [1] the opportunity

to conquer and destroy M., transplant the aristocracy to → Syracuse and sell the démos into slavery.

In 415, M. was deserted (Thuc. 6,49,4). The following winter Syracuse built a fort on the site of M. which the Athenians could not capture when they landed in the spring (Thuc. 6,75,1; 94,2; → Peloponnesian War). M. remained deserted (archaeological evidence supports this), but in 309 it was again called a pólis in connection with the siege of Syracuse by the Carthaginians (Diod. Sic. 20,32,3ff.). It had probably been restored to its former status in the course of → Timoleon's large-scale restoration of the free Greek communities (c. 340). The Hellenistic boundary wall would seem to support this, although it only encompassed a small part of the area of the former city. In 263 M. belonged to the kingdom of → Hieron [2] (Diod. Sic. 23,4,1), in 214 it was allied to Syracuse and was conquered and destroyed by → Claudius [I 11] Marcellus (Liv. 24,35,2; Plut. Marcellus 18,2). From then up until the present day M. has existed simply as an anchorage and village settlement.

Archaeological finds stretch back as far as the Neolithic (settlement with entrenchments). Settlement in archaic and classical periods. Noteworthy finds of ceramics from the Orientalising period and of archaic sculptures. Three necropoleis (earliest finds from the beginning of the 7th century BC), agora surrounded by porticos and cult buildings (temple with antae, temple with central colonnade, heroon (?) and residential areas). Among the evidence for the existence of a scaled-down city under Timoleon are fortifications, an agora with portico, cult buildings, baths and residential areas. From after the destruction by the Romans there are agricultural installations (late Hellenistic and Imperial periods).

G. VALLET, s.v. Megara Hyblaia, EAA, Supplement 3, 1995, 584–587; Id., s.v. Megara Hyblaia, PE 565f. Gl.F. K.Z

Megareus (Μεγαρεύς; Megareús).

[1] Son of Poseidon (Hyg. fab. 157), father of Hippomenes (Ov. met. 10,605). M. brings an army to the aid of → Nisus against → Minos and falls in the battle. The city of Nisa is renamed after M. to → Megara [2] (Paus. 1,39,5). According to others, M. is married to Nisus's daughter Iphinoe and succeeds him (ibid. 1,39,6; see also 1,41,3).

[2] Son of → Creon [1] and Eurydice. He saves Thebes by sacrificing his own life in war (Aeschyl. Sept. 474; Soph. Ant. 1303 with schol.). J.STE

Megarian School (Μεγαρικοί; Megarikoí). This word designates those philosophers belonging to the tradition of Socrates' pupil → Euclides [2], whose home town was Megara. How much they had in common beyond being pupils of Euclides, is hard to say. It seems there was neither an institutional organisation connecting them, nor a fixed place of teaching. Only Euclides and → Stilpo are known to have lived in Megara. Other

members of the School lived and worked in other places, at least temporarily (→ Eubulides [1], Alexinus, Diodorus [4]). As far we know, neither were there any dogmas recognised by all of Euclides' followers. One thing they did seem have in common, besides the derivation from Euclides, is a strong interest in dialectic questioning; hence the Megarians are also known as eristics and → dialecticians. SEDLEY [7] tried to prove that within the Euclidean tradition there were distinct Megarian and Dialectic Schools, and many have accepted this. The counter-arguments are compiled by DÖRING [3]. The earliest testimony mentioning the Megarian School as a group is a passage in the 'Metaphysics' (9,3,1046b 29–32), in which Aristotle rejects the view' of those who, like the Megarian School, state that only when a thing is active it has ability (sc. the ability of being active in the relevant sense), if however it is not active it does not have ability'. It is unknown whether Theophrastus's work *Megarikós* (Diog. Laert. 5,44; 6,22) had anything to do with the Megarian School. For details on the Megarian School see → Alexinus, Bryson, Diodorus [4], Dionysius [9], Eubulides [1], Euclides [2], Ichthyas, Cleinomachus, Philippus of Megara, Philo [I 7], Stilpo.
→ Dialecticians; → Logic; → Socratics

EDITIONS: 1 K. DÖRING, Die Megariker, 1972   2 SSR II A-S.

BIBLIOGRAPHY: 3 K. DÖRING, Gab es eine Dialektische Schule?, in: Phronesis 34, 1989, 293–310   4 Id., Eukleides aus Megara und die Megariker, in: GGPh2 2.1, §17   5 K. VON FRITZ, s.v. Megariker, RE Suppl. 5, 707–724   6 R. MULLER, Introduction à la pensée des mégariques, 1988   7 D. SEDLEY, Diodorus Cronus and Hellenistic Philosophy, in: PCPhS 203, 1977, 74–130.   K.D.

Megarian cups see → Relief ware

Megaron (μέγαρον; *mégaron*). Architectural feature mentioned several times in the Homeric epics (e.g. Hom. Od. 2,94; 19,16; 20,6). It was evidently the main room of the palace or house with the communal hearth in the centre. On later mentions of *megara*. in Greek literature (esp. Hdt. 7,140f.) cf. → Temple.

Scholarship on the archaic period contains considerably different ideas about the understanding of the term megaron and the derivation of the corresponding building forms connected with it at different times. On the one hand, the megaron, on the basis of the Homeric passages, was understood as an architectural feature, hence a room or group of rooms within a larger surrounding architectonic complex (cf. → House, → Palace); on the other hand it has been seen as an entire building complex. Whereas a constructional phenomenon which could be sufficiently precisely comprehended by the term megaron does not really survive in Greek architecture of the historical period, rectangular central rooms or a central groups of rooms arranged as a rectangle with a main room and attached ante-rooms, are encountered in the late-Neolithic and Bronze Age

cultures of Greece and Asia Minor in large numbers (→ Troy, Dimini, → Sesklo, → Poliochni; examples from Asia Minor and the Orient collected in [1]). The idea of the megaron, derived from Homer, as the main room of a palace or a ruler's house found a presumed correspondence in the archaeological evidence of Mycenaean palaces, esp. those at → Mycenae, → Tiryns and → Pylos. The function assigned to a megaron is also debatable, corresponding to the lack of consensus on the term as such. The idea of a fundamentally secular hearth room in the sense of an assembly building (→ Assembly Buildings) contrasts with the idea of a solitary cult building (→ Temple). Constructions in the historical period (1st millennium BC) which have been connected with the term megaron, occur in Asia Minor, e.g. in Gordion.

1 B. HROUDA, s.v. Megaron, RLA 8, 1993/1997, 11f.

A. MAZARAKIS AINIAN, From Ruler's Dwellings to Temples: Architecture, Religion and Society in Early Iron Age Greece, 1997; B. C. DIETRICH, A Religious Function of the Megaron, in: Rivista storica dell'antichità 3, 1973, 1–12; G. HIESEL, Späthelladische Hausarchitektur. Studien zur Architekturgeschichte des griechischen Festlandes in der späten Bronzezeit, 1990, 237–239; C. HOPKIN, The Megaron of the Mycenaean Palace, in: Studi miceni ed egeo-anatolici 6, 1968, 45–53; B. HROUDA, Die Megaron-Bauten in Vorderasien, in: Anadolu 14, 1970, 1–14; S. LAUFFER, Megaron, in: Stele. FS N. Kontoleon, 1980, 208–215; T. SCHULZ, Die Rekonstruktion des Thronpodestes im ersten großen Megaron von Tiryns, in: MDAI(A) 103, 1988, 11–23; K. WERNER, The Megaron during the Aegean and Anatolian Bronze Age, 1993.   C.HÖ.

Megas Logariastes see → Logariastes

Megasthenes (Μεγασθένης; *Megasthénes*). Diplomat and historian (c. 350–290 BC). An envoy sent out several times between 302 and 291 under Seleucus I, especially to northern India, where Chandragupta (→ Sandracottus) founded the Maurya kingdom.

His geographical and ethnographical work *Indiká*, three or four books, preserved only in fragments, was based on observation and information uncritically received through interpreters. For a long time it was the most detailed presentation of India and was used by→ Diodorus [18] Siculus, → Strabo and → Plinius the Elder, but primarily by → Arrianus [2] as the main source for his own *Indiké*. FGrH 715.
→ India

A. B. BOSWORTH, The Historical Setting of Megasthenes' Indica, in: CPh 91, 1996, 113–127; K. KARTTUNEN, India in the Hellenistic World, 1998.   K.BRO.

Meges (Μέγης/*Méges*). Son of Phyleus, sailed with 40 ships from Dulichium to Troy (Hom. Il. 2,625ff.), where he killed several enemies (e.g. ibid. 5,69; Q. Smyrn. 1,276ff.). He is one of Odysseus's men who fetched the propitiatory gifts for→ Achilles from Agamemnon's tent (Hom. Il. 19,238ff.), and one of those in the Wooden Horse (Quint. Smyrn. 12,326). M. is also mentioned as one of Helen's suitors (Apollod. 3,129). According to Apollod. *Epitome* 6,15a he is one of the many who died on Euboea during the return voyage.

J.STE.

Megiddo (Tall al-Mutasallim in the Plain of Jesreel) was settled from the Neolithic until the Persian period (6th–4th millennia BC). Archaeological finds include temples, palaces and installations for water supply, as well as worked ivory and a clay tablet fragment of the Epic of Gilgamesh (14th century BC). M. (Egyptian *m-k-t*) is first mentioned by name in the time of Thutmosis III (15th century BC) and in letters sent by Biridiya, the ruler of the city of M. (Akkadian URUMa-gi-id-daKI), to the Pharaoh (14th century BC; → Amarna Letters). The originally Canaanite city (Judges 1:27; cf. Jos 12:21) had been an important Israelite garrison since → Salomo (1 Kg 4:12; 9:15). It was conquered in the 10th century BC by the pharaoh Shoshenk (cf. 1 Kg 14:25f.), and in 733 BC Tiglatpilesar III turned it into the centre of the Assyrian province of Magidû. The significance of M. and the adjoining plain may be reflected in the name Harmagedon ('M. mountains') as the location of a final battle at the end of time in Rev 16:16.

Y. AHARONI, Y. SHILO, s.v. M., NEAEHL, vol. 3, 1003–1024.

R.L.

Megillus (Μέγιλλος/*Mégillos*). Spartan, one of three members of a legation which negotiated the release of prisoners of war in Athens in 408/7 BC (Androtion FGrH 324 F 44; [1. 50; 2. 395]). He was probably identical with a homonymous member of a legation sent by→ Agesilaus [2] II to→ Tissaphernes in 396 (Xen. Hell. 3,4,6), and with an interlocutor in Plato (Epin. *passim* and Leg. 642b), described there as a guest of the Athenians.

→ Peloponnesian War

1 D. J. MOSLEY, Envoys and Diplomacy in Ancient Greece, 1973   2 B. BLECKMANN, Athens Weg in die Niederlage, 1998.

K.-W.W.

Megiste (Μεγίστη/*Megístē*). Island off the Lycian coast near the city of Antiphellus. From the 4th century BC, it was a Rhodian naval base (Ps.-Scyl. 100; Liv. 37,24,1; 45,2), mentioned in Str. 14,3,7 as a *pólis* and in Plin. HN 5,131 as a 'former *civitas*'. Inscriptions so far only provide evidence of Rhodian military presence in a fortress (*pýrgos*) under a *hagemón* or *epistátēs* (SEG 14, 719; SGDI III 1, 4332).

MA.ZI.

Megisto (Μεγιστώ/*Megistó*). Wife of one Timoleon. In → Plutarchus' 'Bravery of Women' (which was probably inspired by → Phylarchos' 'tragic' school of historiography) she is a moral example and the leader of the

women's resistance against → Aristotimus, the tyrant of Elis for six months in 271/270 BC (Plut. Mor. 252b-e). After the tyrannicide, hers is the sole heroic voice raised on behalf of the tyrant's young daughters who are now at the mercy of the furious mob (Plut. Mor. 253c-e).

J.CO.

Megistonous (Μεγιστόνους/*Megistónous*). Spartan who supported the reforms of his stepson → Cleomenes [6] III (Plut. Cleomenes 7,1; 11,1). As the Spartan commander at Orchomenus (Arcadia) he was defeated and captured by → Aratus [2] of Sicyon after Cleomenes' coup (227 BC) at a time which has not been exactly determined (Plut. Aratus 38,1), and was sent by him to Cleomenes as a go-between (Plut. Cleomenes 19,5; Plut. Aratus 41,5). M. died in 224 while trying to prevent Argos being captured by Aratus and Antigonus [3] Doson (Plut. Cleomenes 21,1-3; [1. 374f.]).

1 S. LE BOHEC, Antigone Dôsôn, 1993.   K.-W.W.

Meherdates see → Mithradates

Meidias (Μειδίας/*Meidías*).
[1] Athenian demagogue. Nothing certain is known about his role in politics (Pl. Alc. 1,120a-b). Between 420 and 400 BC he was mocked by comedians for embezzlement of public funds, as a → sycophant and braggart, and for his breeding of quails and cockerels (Aristoph. Av. 1297f.; Metagenes fr. 12; Phryn. fr. 4; 43; Pl. fr. 85; 116 PCG).

PA 9714; TRAILL, PAA 637170.   W.S.

[2] Athenian rhetor, son of Cephisodorus of Anagyrus, born c. 400 BC, died before 330. He was a rich (mining, see Agora XIX P 26, 211, and estates 249), follower of → Eubulus [1] (Dem. Or. 21,206f.) and opponent of → Demosthenes [2]. M. undertook trierarchies (IG II² 1629d 770; 1631b 132) and other honorary offices (→ tamias of the trireme Paralus 358/7: Dem. Or. 21,171–174; IG II² 1612d 291), was a member of the→ híppeis and in 349/8 BC he proposed laws on the Athenian cavalry (Demosth. or. 21,173). Before 348/7 BC, he was *epimelētḗs* (→ epimeletai) of the Mysteries (→ mysteria; Dem. Or. 21,171) and instituted votive offering for Amphiaraus (SEG 15, 284). M., himself previously a *chorēgós* (Demosth. or. 21,156), tried to hinder Demosthenes's voluntary *choregeia* and gave him a box on the ear in the theatre during the Dionysia of 349/8 (Dem. Or. 21; Plut. Demosthenes 12,3–6; Plut. Mor. 844d). A speech by Demosthenes with personal attacks (*diabolḗ*) on M., which was not taken to court (Or. 21), is our main source for M. The conflict between Demosthenes and M. ended with an out-of-court agreement (Aeschin. In Ctes. 52), for in 340/339 BC he is one of the *pylagoroi* (→ Pylagóras) in Delphi.

DAVIES, 385–87; DEVELIN, nr. 1921; D. M. MACDOWELL, Demosthenes, Against Meidias (Oration 21), 1990

[3] Son of M. [2] of Anagyrus, he proposed a decree in honour of → Phocion, because of which he was successfully accused by → Hypereides (or in 305/4 BC (?) by his son Glaucippus) (Plut. Phoion 4,2; Plut. Mor. 850b; P Oxy. 3360). In 304/3, M. was a member of the Council of Five Hundred (Agora XV 61, 177), and after 322 made a votive offering for Amphiaraus (SEG 24, 351).

> c ;DAVIES, 387; DEVELIN, nr. 1922; J. ENGELS, Studien zur politischen Biographie des Hypereides, 1993², 215 note 444   J.E.

[4] Greek bronze sculptor. According to a decree and surviving foundations, before 202/201 BC M. created at least one larger-than-life statue of Antiochus [5] III in Delphi and a statue for the *démos* of Antiochy in Caria. There is an hypothesis that signature on a base from the Acropolis in Athens, which only survives in fragments, reads his name.

> J. MARCADÉ, Recueil des signatures de sculpteurs grecs, 1, 1953, 77; G. A. MANSUELLI, s.v. Meidias (2), EAA 4, 1961, 978; B. HINTZEN-BOHLEN, Herrscherrepräsentation im Hellenismus, 1992, 104, 213.   R.N.

Meidias Painter Painter of Attic red-figured vases, active c. 420–405 BC, named after the potter of the great *kalpis* (→ pottery, shapes and types of) in London, BM (E 224). Only three dozen vases and fragments of the most diverse form are ascribed to him; nevertheless he is the most influential exponent of the 'Rich Style'. His vase pictures abound in figures wrapped in richly embroidered clothes, whose jewellery – in relief and gilded – gracefully contrasts with the fineness of the relief lines. None of his contemporaries so often provided their figures with legends; it is through him that we know a whole series of personifications (e.g. *eutychia* and *eudaemonia*). His choice of pictorial themes became characteristic of the 'Rich Style': without exception, there are mortal or divine women at the centre; men occur only as their abductors, lovers, admirers or, like → Pentheus (Athens, Kerameikos 2712), as their victims. → Adonis and → Phaon lie in the bosom of their goddess and allow themselves to be surrounded by → Eros in all its forms (Florence, MA 81947–8). → Musaeus and → Thamyris too leisurely enjoy the company of Aphrodite and the Muses (New York, MMA 37.11.23; Ruvo, Museo Jatta 1538). M. never really leaves this paradisiacal timeless world, not even in the representations of the birth of → Erichthonius [1] (Cleveland, Mus. Art 82.142) or of the little → Asclepius, who, on the arm of personified Epidaurus, takes in the world around him (Leuven, Univ. 4615). A picture on a → Choes pitcher in New York (MMA 75.2.11) takes us into a house in which women, festively robed for the → Anthesteria, are awaiting the visit of the → Basilinna; while in a *Choes* representation in Athens (Kerameikos 4290), → Amymone is theatrically surprised by Satyrs. Many painters tried to copy the maestro in content and form, e.g. the representation on several levels, but these excursions into a subtle, intricate and honey-sweet world ultimately fail.

BEAZLEY, ARV2, 1312–1314; BEAZLEY, Paralipomena, 477; BEAZLEY, Addenda2, 361f.; L. BURN, The Meidias Painter, 1987.   A.L.-H.

Meilanion see → Melanion

Meilichios, Meilichioi Theoi (Μειλίχιος, μειλίχιοι θεοί/ *meilíchios, meilíchioi theoi*). The divine epithet *meilichios* was undoubtedly connected in Greek antiquity with a number of words (μειλίχιος/*meilíchios*, μείλιχος/ *meilíchos*, μειλίσσομαι/*meilíssomai*, μείλιγμα/*meíligma*, in EM 582,35f. even with μέλι/*méli*, 'honey') which convey the idea of kindness, soothing, propitiation. These words often imply a prior anger which must be appeased. Allusions to the epithet *meilíchios* show a similar fluctuation between two ideas: that the name belongs to a god who allows himself to be assuaged (Cornutus 11), or that the god is simply kind (Plut. De superstitione 4,166d; Plut. De Is. et Os. 48,370c). The assumption that the epithet is a matter of applying the adjective μειλίχιος/*meilíchios*, 'kind, favourably inclined' to a god raises no serious problems. However, if the epithet is connected with the Semitic root *mlk* (→ Moloch), the relationship with the adjective remains obscure.

In the cult, the epithet was applied to Dionysus on Naxos (Ath. 78c = FGrH 499 F 4); Athena in Epidaurus (IG IV 1², 282 – also a Zeus Meilichios) and Metapontum (SEG 38,997); Hera, as well as Zeus Meilichios, in Hierapytna on Crete (Inscr. Creticae III 3,14), to an anonymous group of (θεοί) μειλίχιοι/(*theoi*) *meilíchioi* in Locris in Ozolia (Paus. 10,38,8) and in Thebes in Phthiotis (IG IX 2, 1329), and perhaps to the → nymphs in Astypalaea (IG XII 3, 199 – the reading is uncertain). In literature, a few other powers (Leto, Hypnus, the Muses, Tyche) are given the epithet, and there are also further references to *Theoí Meilíchioi* as a class of gods (an oracle in Phlegum FGrH 257 F 37 p. 1190,26) and to Aphrodite Meilichia. The only known information on the details of the forms of the cult at the time is that sacrifices to the *Meilíchioi* in Locris in Ozolia took place at night and had to be completed before daybreak.

Of quite different significance is the cult of → Zeus Meilichios, for which there are hundreds of pieces of evidence in almost every region of the Greek world. The other *meilíchioi* may all be derived from this model. In → votive offerings Zeus is often referred to simply as Meilichios, or (as in → Lebadea) even as δαίμων μειλίχιος/*daímon meilíchios* [1] (→ Demons), and occasionally depicted on votive reliefs as a gigantic snake (e.g. [2. vol. 1 fig. 27,2]). A votive from → Thespeia connects him with a female *Meilíchē* (IG VII 1814). Zeus Meilichios is thus an example of how the combination of god and epithet can acquire a quasi-autonomous identity. His cult exhibits several unmistakable characteristics: temples dedicated to him are a rarity. Festivals are also almost unknown, with the exception of the *Diásia* in Athens, and even this was not financed by the polis, although participants gathered from the whole of

Attica for it, and they may have celebrated it in many small groups, all at the same place, yet separate [3. 78 note 41]. Objects, which are identified by inscriptions as 'Zeus Meilichios of the Kleulidai' or even 'Zeus Meilichios' of an individual, have been found in Selinunt (→ Selinus) [4] and elsewhere: apparently, Zeus Meilichios was worshipped by families or family-like groups, which gathered at the place of their own Meilichios, with each individual Meilichios being clearly differentiated from the others.

Zeus Meilichios is connected with purification, particularly of blood-guilt (Paus. 2,20,1; Plut. Theseus 12,1; Suda s.v. Διὸς κώδιον), perhaps because it allowed and required (re)admission into a social group. In votive reliefs, when appearing in human form, he is often carrying a cornucopia, a symbol of prosperity (e.g. [2 vol. 1 fig. 28,1]). In Xenophon (An. 7,8,1–6), he is explicitly described as a bringer of wealth. → Sacrifices to him often deviated from the strict Olympian pattern: holocaust sacrifice (Xen. An. 7,8,1–6), sometimes offerings without wine (LSCG 18 A 37–43), perhaps offerings without meat (Thuc. 1,126,6; [5]). The ritual of the Diásia was carried out 'with a certain grimness' (schol. Lucian. 107,15; 111,27f. RABE). Occasionally Zeus Meilichios is connected with forces of the Underworld such as the Eumenides (SEG 9,327; 20,723; → Erinys), Enodia (IG IX 2, 578; → Hecate) or the → Tritopatores (SEG 43,630), but is not himself a god of death or of the dead. His Athenian festival, the Diásia, was celebrated in the deme Agrae, where the 'Mother in Agrae' was also worshipped. In another Attic cult he was connected with Ge (IG I³ 1084; → Gaia), and in the official calendar of sacrifices a mysterious 'Melichos' (possibly = Meilichios; apparently a hero) is among a number of Eleusinian heroes who receive gifts ([6]; → Hero cult). Many of the traits stated here – connection with a purification ritual, with the Underworld, with the earth and with wealth, his form as a snake, unusual forms of sacrifice – show Zeus Meilichios as a typical example of a 'chthonic' divinity, a category, however, which in more recent research is discussed with great controversy (→ Chthonic Deities).
→ Polytheism; → Zeus
R.PA.

1 J. JANORAY, Nouvelles inscriptions de Lébadée, in: BCH 64–65, 1940–41, 36–59 2 NILSSON, GGR 3 R. PARKER, Athenian Religion, 1996 4 L. DUBOIS, Inscriptions grecques dialectales de Sicile, 1989, 55–60 5 M. H. JAMESON, Notes on the Sacrificial Calendar from Erchia, in: BCH 89, 1965, 159–172 6 F. GRAF, Zum Opferkalender des Nikomachos, in: ZPE 14, 1974, 139–144.

A. B. COOK, Zeus, vol. 2, 1925, 1091–1160; vol. 3, 1940, 1183–1189; M. H. JAMESON et al., A Lex Sacra from Selinous, 1993, 81–103, 114–116; F. PFISTER, s.v. Meilichioi Theoi, RE 15, 340–345. R.PA.

Meilichus (Μείλιχος; *Meílichos*). Mythical king of Spain, son of a → satyr and the nymph Myrice; with horns on his head was (Sil. Pun. 3,103–105). L.K.

Mekionike see→ Euphemus

Melaeneae (Μελαινεαί/*Melaineaí*, Latin *Melaenae*). Town in western Arcadia, north of the river Alpheius, 40 *stadia* (*c.* 7 km) west of Buphagium, abandoned by Pausanias's time (Paus. 5,7,1; 8,3,3; 26,8), perhaps near modern Kokkora, south of Kakouraeika (Kakouraei). There are some remains of an estate from the Roman period. Evidence: Plin. HN 4,20; Tab. Peut. 7,5; Steph. Byz. s.v. Μελαιναί.

JOST, 74–77; E. MEYER, Peloponnesische Wanderungen, 1939, 101–106. Y.L.

Melaina Akra (Μέλαινα Ἄκρα/*Mélaina Akra*). Bithynian foothills to the east of the northern end of the Bosporus, modern Kara Burun.

W. RUGE, s.v. Melaina Akra (2), RE 15, 387. K.ST.

Melambium (Μελάμβιον/*Melambion*). Philip V reached the region of → Scotussa at M. on the day before the battle of Cynoscephalae in 197 BC. The town, mentioned only in Pol. 18,20,6 and Liv. 33,6,11, is thought to have been to the east of Scotussa.

J.-CL. DECOURT, La vallée de l'Enipeus en Thessalie, 1990, 109ff.; F. STÄHLIN, s.v. Melambion, RE 15, 390f. HE.KR.

Melammu s. → Nimbus

Melampodia (Μελαμποδία/*Melampodía*). Early Greek hexametrical epic in at least three (fr. 277) books. Ancient testimonies ascribe it to → Hesiodus, only Paus. 9,31,5 claims it is pseudo-hesiodic. Its origin lies in the 6th cent. BC, probably in Corinth [2. 59]. Ten fragments survive, eight of which verbatim, with 24 hexameters in all (fr. 270–279 in [1]). The author makes use of Homer, Hesiod and the → Epic Cycle (Trojan and Theban legends including → Alcmaeonis [2. 58]). He presents Greek early history (Theban legend,→ Trojan legend, Corinthian cycle of legends) as a triumph of the cleverness of Greek seers, who supposedly descend predominantly from→ Melampus [1] (Adrastus, Amphiaraus, Calchas) and from→ Teiresias (Mopsus) (genealogy as a red thread and hence ascribed to Hesiod; the author of the Melampodia was himself probably a Melampodide). The Melampodia may well have been the source for most of the later 'accounts of seers'.

ED.: 1 R. MERKELBACH, M. L. WEST, Fragmenta Hesiodea, 1967.
LIT.: 2 I. LÖFFLER, Die Melampodia. Versuch einer Rekonstruktion des Inhalts, 1963. J.L.

Melampus

[1] (Μελάμπους/*Melámpous*). Mythical seer. Son of → Amythaon, brother of → Bias [1], husband of → Iphianassa [1], father of → Mantius, grandfather of → Amphiaraus, born in Pylus. As a child he received the

gift of interpreting bird songs when snakes licked his ears. Apollo granted him other prophetic gifts. He was considered a seer, a miracle healer and an expiatory priest, and also the founder of the cult of → Dionysus in Greece (Hdt. 2,48f.). When his brother Bias wooed → Pero, M. and Bias accomplished the posed task of retrieving Pero's mother's stolen cattle by snatching them from → Iphicles and curing the latter of his impotence. In addition he healed the daughter of→ Proetus (→ Proetids), who had been sent mad for her obstinacy against the cult of Dionysus (as in Hes. fr. 131 M.-W.) or for her disdain of Hera's cult image (as in Acusilaus FGrH 2 F 28). As a prize he received a third of the kingdom of → Argos. Bias received a further third. Since then the kingdom of Argus was divided into three (Hdt. 9,34; for the aetiology: schol. Pind. Nem. 9,13(30b)). The myths are alluded to in Hom. Od. 15,225ff.; 15,238ff.; 11,291, and related in detail in the → Melampodia [1], summarised in Apollod. 1,96ff.; 2,25ff. (cf. schol. Apoll. Rhod. 1,118; Eust. on Hom. Od. 11,292 p. 1685; Plin. HN 10,137; for the Proetids esp. Diod. 4,68; Paus. 2,18,4; Pherecydes FGrH 3 F 114; Bacchyl. 11; Pind. Pae. 4,28–30 [2; 3]). M. may have been one of such historical 'miracle men, expiatory priests and seers as there were in the archaic period' [4] (cf. Diod. 4,68: dating of M. in the time of Anaxagoras). M. had a sanctuary and a festival in Aegosthena [5].

1 I. LÖFFLER, Die Melampodie, 1963   2 L. KÄPPEL, Paian, 1992, 129–133   3 H. MAEHLER (ed.), Bakchylides, Siegeslieder I.2, 1982, 196–202   4 NILSSON, GGR 1, 613ff.   5 NILSSON, Feste, 460f.

E. SIMON, s.v. Melampus, LIMC 6.1, 405–410; TH. GANTZ, Early Greek Myth 2, 1993, 185–188, 312f.   L.K.

[2] Byzantine grammarian and commentator on the *Téchnē grammatiké* by → Dionysius [17] Thrax. Only a few parts of his scholia survive (on §§1–11 and §§19–20 of the *Téchnē*) [2], which are also ascribed, by a group of manuscripts, to an otherwise unknown Diomedes. The explanation that Diomedes copied M. verbatim [3. 18–26] is less plausible than the assumption that the scholia of M. and of Diomedes represent independent copies of an original which, as an excerpt of an earlier source, already shows the lacuna of §§12–18 [1. 403].

1 A. GUDEMAN, s.v. Melampus (8), RE 15, 399–404; 2 A. HILGARD, in: Grammatici Graeci 3, 1901 (reprint 1965), 10–67 (Commentarius Melampodis seu Diomedis)   3 W. HOERSCHELMANN, De Dionysii Thracis interpretibus veteribus 1, 1884.   GR.DA.

Melampyges see → Cercopes

Melanchlaeni (Μελάγχλαινοι; *Melánchlainoi*). Greek designation ('those dressed in black') of a tribe whose region of settlement was 20 days' journey from the → Pontos Euxeinos (Hdt. 4,101), bordering to the south the 'royal' Scythians (Hdt. 4,20), to the west the

Androphagi (Hdt. 4,100) and to the east the Geloni and Budini. North of them there were said to be only swamps and lakes. Although they were supposedly not Scythians (Hdt. 4,20, *contra* Hecat. FGrH 1 F 185), they are said to have lived according to Scythian customs (Hdt. 4,108). No more precise localisation or ethnicity is known.   I.v.B. S.R.T.

Melancholy (μέλαινα χολή/*mélaina cholé*, 'black bile'). The fourth humour in the tradition of Hippocratic medicine represented by *De natura hominis*, ch. 4, and later by Rufus of Ephesus and Galen. It was predominant in autumn, associated with the element earth, and cold and dry. It was viewed as the antithesis of blood, having many deadly properties [1]. According to Galen (De atra bile 5,104–148 K.) in its purest form it was highly destructive to everything it touched, and had its origin in the spleen. Not every believer in humours in the Hippocratic Corpus (→ Hippocrates [6]) accepted 'black bile' as a separate humour, or even mentioned it. Once integrated into the *Viererschema*, however, its Hippocratic origin and authentic existence was not challenged [2].

How the idea of 'black bile' arose is unclear. Physical causes could include any 'black' discharge, e.g. in vomit or the black urine of the fatal blackwater malarial fever, and 'black' in medical contexts frequently indicates something deadly or malignant, without implying any specifically humoral cause [3]. Since the author of *De natura hominis* refers to the 'so-called' black bile, the term may have been newly coined, and derive from the already existing terms, μελαγχολάω/*melancholáō*, –χολίη/-*cholíē*, μελάγχολος/*meláncholos*. Although these terms appear as disease conditions in the Hippocratic Corpus (e.g. Hippocr. Aph 3,22) their use is not confined to medical writers; cf. Aristoph. Av. 14; Aristoph. Eccl. 251; Soph. Trach. 573, where there is a clear link with a psychological state, whether anger or madness [4].

Aristotle (probl. 30,1; 953a 10–954a 41) asked why men of eminence in philosophy, politics or the arts were melancholic, easily affected by diseases of black bile [5]. His answer, that they had a natural excess of black bile, a mixture of hot and cold easily changing from one extreme to the other, was less significant than his initial assumption linking genius with melancholy, an idea that had a long existence in European culture [6]. Another notion of melancholy linked it specifically to old age, to sadness, depression, and hallucination, discussed at length by Rufus of Ephesus in a book lost in Greek but surviving in Arabic quotations [7]. Galen (De locis affectis 3,10 = vol. 8, 179–193 K.) added to Rufus' theory that melancholy was produced by an excess of black bile in the hypochondrium two further types of melancholy, one in which blood throughout the body turned to black bile, the other in which this altered blood was found only in the brain. Those who suffered from these forms of melancholy had both physical and mental symptoms, and were to be treated by a similar

mixture of somatic and psychological therapies.
→ Hippocrates [6]; → Humoral theory; → Melancholy;
→ Mental illness

1 H. FLASHAR, Melancholie und Melancholiker, 1966
2 E. SCHÖNER, Das Viererschema in der antiken Humo-
ralpathologie, 1964 3 F. KUDLIEN, Der Beginn des medizinischen Denkens bei den Griechen, 1967, 76–86 4 V.
LANGHOLF, Medical Theories in Hippocrates, 1990, 46–
50, 267–269 5 PH. J. VAN DER EIJK, Aristoteles über die
Melancholie, in: Mnemosyne 43, 1990, 33–72 6 R. KLI-
BANSKY, E. PANOWSKY, F. SAXL, Saturn and Melancholy,
1964 7 M. ULLMANN, Islamic Medicine, 1978, 36–38
8 J. PIGEAUD, La maladie de l'âme, 1981.   V.N.

Melanchrus (Μέλαγχρος; *Mélanchros*) was able to establish himself as tyrant during the internal conflicts in
→ Mytilene around 600 BC, probably with the support
of a → *hetairia*. Another of these aristocratic groups, to
which Pittacus and the brothers of the poet → Alcaeus
[4] belonged, however, soon managed to overthrow
him again (Alc. fr. 331 VOIGT; Strab. 13,2,3; Diog.
Laert. 1,74).

E.S.-H.

H. BERVE, Die Tyrannis bei den Griechen, 1967, vol. 1,
91f., vol. 2, 572; L. de Libero, Die archaische Tyrannis,
1996, 315.   E.S.-H.

Melancomas (Μελαγκόμας/*Melancomas*). Eponymous
priest of Alexander in 166/5 BC. Son of the Aetolian
Philodamus, served in 180–145 as garrison commander
and priest of the *theoí euergétai* (→ *euergétēs*) in
Citium, father of the garrison commander M. (PP VI
15119). PP III/IX 5194 (VI 15120?).

W. CLARYSSE, G. VAN DER VEKEN, The Eponymous Priests
of Ptolemaic Egypt, 1983, 24.   W.A.

Melanditae (Μελανδῖται/*Melandítai*). Greek name for
a Thracian tribe north of → Perinthus (Xen. An. 7,2,32;
cf. the name of the region in Steph. Byz. s.v. Μελανδία).
North of them was the tribal territory of the Thyni, in
the east the 'Thracian delta' of Byzantium. Their territory belonged to the Hellenistic *stratēgía* of Astikḗ.

T. SPIRIDONOV, Istoriceska geografija na trakijskite plemena, 1983, 40f., 111f.   I.v.B.

Melaneus (Μελανεύς/*Melaneús*). Son of Apollo (in
Pherecydes FGrH 3 F 82a of Arcesilaus), father of Eury-
tus [1] and Ambracia. A skilled archer who ruled over
the Dryopians and conquered Epirus by war (Antoni-
nus Liberalis 4,3). According to Paus. 4,2,2 the Mes-
senians claimed that he had been given the territory of
Oechalia by Perieres, the ruler of Messenia. The city of
Oechalia is supposed to have received its name from
M.'s wife. Eretria on Euboea was previously named
Melaneís after M. (Str. 10,1,10).   J.STE.

Melangea (Μελαγγεία/*Melangeía*). Town in the terri-
tory of → Mantinea in Arcadia at the exit of the Climax
Pass. Drinking water was led from here to Mantinea.
To be found at modern Pikerni (Paus. 8,6,4).   Y.L.

Melania

[1] M. the Elder, Roman Christian aristocrat, widow
and ascetic; left Rome in the autumn of 373 AD, and
together with → Rufinus [6] founded a monastic community on the Mount of Olives in Jerusalem. She was
also on intimate terms with → Evagrius [1] Ponticus. In
400 she returned to Rome.
[2] M. the Younger (born in Rome in 383), granddaughter of M. [1], related to → Marcella [1], used her
wealth for charity. She married Pinianus (in 396) and
after the death of two children in infancy she turned to
the Christian ascetic ideal. She travelled in southern
Italy, northern Africa and to Constantinople and Jerusalem, where she died on 31 December 439.
→ Ascesis/Asceticism; → Monasticism; →Vita Sanctae
Melaniae; →Woman (IV. Christianity)

D. GORCE, Vie de Sainte Mélanie (SChr 90), 1962; N.
MOINE, M., in: Recherches augustiniennes 15, 1980,
3–79.   S.L.-B.

Melanion (Μελανίων/*Melaníōn*, Μειλανίων/*Meila-
níōn*; Latin *Milanion; personal name from μέλας/
*méla*s, 'black'). An Arcadian, son of Amphidamas. In
the 'Arcadian' version of the myth, he is the suitor of
→ Atalante (according to Ps.-Apollod. 3,105 her cousin), with whom he has a son → Parthenopaeus (Hellanicus FGrH 4 F 99; Ps.-Apollod. 3,109; Paus. 3,12,9;
among the latter's alternative fathers none is the → Hippomenes [1] of the 'Boeotian' version). As a participant
in the games in honour of Pelias, M. was to be seen on
the → Cypselus Chest (*c*. 600 BC, according to Paus.
5,17,10; 19,2) and as a participant in the Calydonian
Hunt (→ Meleager [1]) he is shown on the François
Vase (*c*. 570 BC, now in Florence). A choral song by
Aristophanes (Aristoph. Lys. 781–796) stylises him as a
misogynous 'Black Hunter' of the → Hippolytus [1]
type (according to [3] an ephebic myth of reference). A
pupil of Chiron in hunting (Xen. Cyn. 1,2), M. wins
→ Atalante through his diligence (*philoponía*: Xen.
Cyn. 1,7; Prop. 1,1,9–16; Ov. Ars am. 2,185–192; the
motif is inverted in Eur. Hipp. 215–222), which also
earns him a wound by the centaur → Hylaeus (Prop.
1,1,13; Ov. Ars am. 2,191). There is clearly a conflation
of the two myths when M. wins the race with Atalante
instead of Hippomenes [1] (Ps.-Apollod. 3,105–108; cf.
Palaephatus, Perì apístōn 13).

1 J. BOARDMAN, s.v. M., LIMC 6.1, 404–405; 6.2, 205
2 J. FONTENROSE, Orion: The Myth of the Hunter and the
Huntress, 1981, 176–181 3 P. VIDAL-NAQUET, Le chas-
seur noir et l'origine de l'ephébie athénienne (1968), in:
Id., Le chasseur noir, 1991³, 151–175 (English in: The
Black Hunter, 1986).   T.H.

Melanippe (Μελανίππη; *Melaníppē*).

[1] Daughter of → Aeolus [1], the son of → Hellen, and of → Hippe [2], the daughter of the centaur → Chiron. Mother by Poseidon of the twins → Aeolus [3] and → Boeotus. M. was the protagonist in two fragmentarily surviving tragedies by Euripides: M. ἡ σοφή ('The Wise M.'; TGF 479–487) and M. ἡ δεσμῶτις ('M. Bound'; TGF 488–514). In the older '*Wise M.*' (set in Thessaly), it is told how in the absence of her father Aeolus, M. becomes the mother of two sons by Poseidon. Although she exposes the children, they survive and are discovered, for which reason an attempt is made to kill them as *térata* (i.e., 'monsters' that contravene the laws of nature, and were therefore considered bad omens). M. tries in vain to save the children by giving a long speech proving there has been no breach of natural laws. Ultimately she confesses that she is their mother, and is to be punished. Her mother Hippe, however, comes to her aid and saves both M. and her sons, who become the ancestors of the Aeolians and the Boeotians. In 'M. Bound' (set in Metapontium), M. is imprisoned by her enraged father and her children are exposed. They are saved, however, when Metapontius' childless wife passes them off as her own sons. When she herself has twins, she sets out to kill the other woman's children, but fails. With the help of Poseidon, the children then free their mother M., who becomes the wife of Metapontius. They found the cities of Boeotia and Aeolia in the Propontis. According to Diod. 4,67,4–6 it is Arne who is the mother of Aeolus and Boeotus (for further genealogies cf. Diod. 19,53,6 and schol. Hom. Od. 10,2).

[2] An Amazon (→ Amazons), sister of queen → Antiope [2]. M. was captured by Heracles on his Amazonian campaign, and released in return for the queen's girdle, which Heracles had to obtain (Diod. 4,16,3; Just. 2,4,21–26; cf. also Apoll. Rhod. 2,966–979).

[3] Daughter of → Oineus and → Althaea [1], transformed into a guinea-hen: Antoninus Liberalis 2.

W. LUPPE, Das neue Fragment aus der Hypothesis zu Euripides' M. Sophe, in: ZPE 89, 1991, 15–18; W. RUGE, s.v. M., RE 15, 418–422; H. W. STOLL, s.v. M., Roscher 2, 2576–2577.   K.WA.

Melanippides (Μελανιππίδης; *Melanippídēs*). Dithyrambic poet from Melos, whose main period of creativity was in the second half of the 5th century BC. A grandfather of the same name, also a poet, is mentioned in the Suda: there are no surviving fragments from this M. the Elder, who, according to information from the → *Marmor Parium*, won a victory in Athens in 494/93. In Pherecrates' *Cheírōn* (PCG VII 155), M. the Younger, who exercised considerable influence on the new musical style, is reprimanded by Music personified, because he was the first to misuse it. Various innovations are ascribed to him, including astrophic → anabolé (Aristot. Rhet. 1409b). Fragments of the *Danaídes*, a *Marsýas* and a *Persephónē* survive.

D. A. CAMPBELL (ed.), Greek Lyric, vol. 5, 1993; M. L. WEST, Ancient Greek Music, 1992; B. ZIMMERMANN, Dithyrambos, 1992.   E.R.

Melanippus (Μελάνιππος; *Melánippos*, Latin Melanippus).

[1] Son of Astacus, opponent of → Tydeus (Aesch. Sept. 407–414). At the defence of Thebes against the → Seven, he defeats → Mecisteus (Hdt. 5,67; Paus. 9,18,1) and mortally wounds Tydeus. When Tydeus himself (Stat. Theb. 8,716–766; Apollod. 3,6,8, perhaps interpolated; temple façade from Pyrgi, Rome, Villa Giulia [1. 43–45; 2]) or → Amphiaraus (schol. Hom. Il. 5,126; schol. Pind. N. 10,12; Paus. l.c.) kills M., Tydeus demands his head and sucks out the brain, thereby depriving himself of the immortality intended for him by Athena. According to Apollodorus, Amphiaraus induces Tydeus to this cannibalistic act out of revenge. M.'s grave was on the road from Thebes to Chalcis (Paus. l.c.). His cult was later relocated to → Sicyon for political reasons (Hdt. l.c.).

[2] One of the sons of → Agrius [1], who, for the sake of their father, overthrow his brother → Oineus, king of Calydon, and keep him captive, for which they are later killed by Oineus's grandson → Diomedes [1] (Apollod. 1,8,6).

[3] Son of Theseus and → Perigune, the daughter of the pine-bender Sinis. Victor in the footrace in the Nemean Games held by the Epigoni (Plut. Theseus 8,3; Paus. 10,25,7). He had a *heroon* in the Attic deme of → Melite [5] (Harpocr. s.v. Μελανίππειον; [3. 146f.; 4. 184]).

[4] Son of Hicetaon, honoured as his son by → Priamus, killed by Antilochus in the battle by the Greek ships (Hom. Il. 15,546–583). Apollod. 3,12,5 names a M. among the children of Priam. The same name is borne by two fallen Trojans (Hom. Il. 8,276; 16,695).

[5] One of the Greeks who fetch the propitiatory gifts for Achilles from Agamemnon's tent (Hom. Il. 19,240).

[6] Lover of → Comaetho [2], the priestess of Artemis. When their parents forbid their marriage, the couple desecrates the temple and are sacrificed in expiation. An aetiological legend for a mythical double human sacrifice said to have been held yearly in Patrae, which was suppressed by → Eurypylus [5] (Paus. 7,19,2).

1 I. KRAUSKOPF, Der thebanische Sagenkreis und andere griechische Sagen in der etruskischen Kunst, 1974   2 G. GIANGRANDE, Tideo, Melanippo ed il Frontone di Pyrgi, in: Siculorum Gymnasium 42, 1989, 41–45   3 U. VON WILAMOWITZ-MOELLENDORFF, Aus Kydathen, 1880   4 E. KEARNS, The Heroes of Attica (BICS Suppl. 57), 1989.

M. DELCOURT, Tydée et Mélanippe, in: SMSR 37, 1966, 139–188; A. KOSSATZ-DEISSMANN, s.v. M., LIMC 6.1, 410–11.   CL.K.

[7] see → Menalippus

Melanippus [7] see → Menalippus

Melanopus (Μελάνωπος; *Melánōpos*), son of Laches of Aexone. Member of the Athenian legation to Sparta in 372/1 BC (Xen. Hell. 6,3,2). He proposed a decree of the Council in 364/3 (IG II² 145,11–14) and in 355 was legate (possibly as *strategos* IG II² 150,5) to → Maussollus of Halicarnassus, and possibly also to Naucratis in Egypt (Demosth. Or. 24,12). M. was accused of corruption several times, primarily by → Demosthenes [2] (Demosth. Or. 24,127; cf. Aristot. Rhet. 1,14,1, 1374b 25), and was a political opponent of → Callistratus [2] of Aphidnae. However, he partially supported the latter's motions as a spokesman in the Assembly, either for political reasons or because he was bribed by Callistratus (cf. Plut. Demosthenes 13,3 and Anaxandrides fr. 41 PCG).

e; Develin, no. 1933; PA 9788; Traill, PAA 638765.   J.E.

Melanthium River flowing into the → Pontos Euxeinos to the east of Ordu, modern Melet Irmağı (Plin. HN 6,11).   E.O.

Melanthius (Μελάνθιος/*Melánthios*).
[1] (also Μελανθεύς/*Melantheús*). Son of Dolius [2], brother of Melantho [2], treacherous goatherd of → Odysseus, negative counterpart to the swineherd → Eumaeus and the cowherd → Philoetius (Hom. Od. 17,212–22,479).

G. RAMMING, Die Dienerschaft in der Odyssee, 1973, 15–17; 74–77; 142–145.   T.H.

[2] Athenian *strategos* who led the troops sent in support of the Ionians when they revolted in 499/8 (Hdt. 5,97).
→ Ionian Revolt

PA 9764; TRAILL, PAA 638260.   E.S.-H.

[3] An Athenian involved as a *strategos* in the fortification of the → Eetioneia Peninsula in 411 BC. As this allegedly had the function of allowing the Spartans into the city, it was demolished with Theramenes' consent (Xen. Hell. 2,3,46; Thuc. 8,90–92).

PA 9768; TRAILL, PAA 638280.   W.S.

[4] **M. from Athens** Tragedian and elegist of the late 5th century BC (TrGF I 23), much mocked by comic poets (T 3–5); from Aristoph. Pax 1012 'Medeia' can be inferred as a title. An elegiac distich survives (fr. II 70–73 GENTILI/PRATO).   B.Z.
[5] (also Melanthus) Distinguished representative of the second generation (*c.* 370–330 BC) of the Sicyonian school of painting. Both he and → Apelles [4], who also worked on a portrait ascribed to M. of the ruler Aristratus as the victor in a chariot race, were pupils of the esteemed master → Pamphilus [2]. No other themes or titles have been preserved, but it appears that by the early 3rd cent. several examples of his rich and universally prized *oeuvre*, as far as it can be traced, had found their way into the representative collections of the Pto-

lemies in Alexandria (Plut. Aratus 12f.; Athen. 196a). M.'s paintings, which are limited to four → pigments, were renowned for their special method of composition (Plin. HN 35,50; 80): it consisted in the balanced arrangement and the self-explanatory grouping of individual image elements. M. also wrote a now lost theoretical treatise on painting (Diog. Laert. 4,18), in which self-confidence and severity were demanded of the artist. Whether and how these characteristics shaped his works must remain speculation.

N. HOESCH, Bilder apulischer Vasen und ihr Zeugniswert für die Entwicklung der griechischen Malerei, 1983, 45ff.; N. KOCH, De picturae initiis, 1996; I. SCHEIBLER, Griechische Malerei der Antike, 1994.   N.H.

[6] **M. of Athens** Fourth-century BC author of an → *Atthis*, of which only a fragment survives (fr. 1), and a work 'On the Mysteries in Eleusis' (frr. 2–4). F. 3 (in schol. Aristoph. Plut. 845) contains the wording of the → *pséphisma* against the 'atheist' Diagoras [2].

FGrH 326 with commentary; F. JACOBY, Atthis, 1949; PA 9770; TRAILL, PAA 638285.   K.MEI.

[7] **M. of Rhodes** Second-century BC Academic philosopher from the circle of → Carneades [1] (Philod. Academicorum index 23,14; cf. also Cic. Acad. 2,16), who was a successful tragic poet before turning to philosophy. It may be that we know a tragic trimeter from his pen: τὰ δεινὰ πράσσει τὰς φρένας μετοικίσας (TrGF I 131 F 1). This has been interpreted as a reference to the dispute between the Academy and the Stoa about the → affects [1. 90–94]. According to Diog. Laert. 2,64, M. was also the teacher and lover of Aeschines [4] of Neapolis.
→ Academy

1 U. VON WILAMOWITZ-MOELLENDORFF, Der Tragiker Melanthios, in: Id., Kleine Schriften 2, reprint 1971, 90–94.; T. DORANDI, Filodemo, Storia dei filosofi, 1991, 74f.   K.-H.S.

Melantho (Μελανθώ/*Melanthố*).
[1] Daughter of → Deucalion, who gave birth to → Poseidon's son → Delphus, the eponym of Delphi (Tzetz. Lycoph. 208).

F. BÖMER, P. Ovidius Naso, Metamorphosen, Kommentar zu Buch 6–7, 1976, 42f.

[2] Unfaithful servant of → Penelope (Hom. Od. 18,320–340; 19,65–95), lover of → Eurymachus (cf. Diog. Laert. 2,79); brazenly sought to quarrel with the beggar Odysseus; reprimanded by Penelope.

O. TOUCHEFEU-MEYNIER, s.v. Melantho, LIMC 6.1, 412.   B.GY.

Melanthus (Μέλανθος/*Mélanthos*).
[1] M. of Messenia, descendant of → Neleus of Pylus (Hdt. 1,147; 5,65), son of Andropompus and Henoche (Paus. 1,3,3; 19,5; 2,187ff.; 7,1,9), father of → Codrus

(ibid. 8,18,7). Expelled from Messenia, he went to Attica (Eleusis), where he fought a duel on behalf of the king Thymoetes with Xanthus, the king of Boeotia. With the aid of Dionysus Melanaigis and by his own cunning he gained the victory. Dionysus received a sanctuary in reward, and M. became king of Athens.

[2] Mythical pirate of the Tyrrhenian Sea, turned into a dolphin by Dionysus (Ov. Met. 3,617; Hyg. Fab. 134; cf. H. Hom. 7).   L.K.

[3] Spartan, charged together with Alcamenes by → Agis [2] II with the task of leading 300 → neodamodeis to Euboea in support of a revolt against Athens in the winter of 413/2 BC (Thuc. 8,5). The troops did not see action there, however, owing to other pressing tasks [1. 60].

1 P. HUNT, Slaves, Warfare, and Ideology in the Greek Historians, 1998.   K.-W.W.

[4] See → Melanthius [5]

Melantias (Μελαντιάς/*Melantiás*, Melantiana). Last station before (and 150 *stadia* from) Constantinople on the → *via Egnatia*, where the Athyras flowed into the → Propontis (Agathias 5,14,20; It. Ant. 138; 230); its precise location is unknown. The emperor Valens spent several days at his *villa* in M. before the battle of Adrianopolis in AD 378 (Amm. Marc. 31,11,1; 12,1). In AD 558, M. was attacked by the Cutrigur Huns (Agathias 5,13).   I.v.B.

Melas (Μέλας/*Mélas*).
[1] Son of → Porthaon (Portheus) and Euryte in Calydon [3], brother of → Oeneus, → Agrius [1], → Alcathous [2], Leucopeus and Sterope (cf. Hom. Il. 14,115ff.; Apollod. 1,63). M.'s eight sons were killed by → Tydeus for pursuing their uncle Oeneus (Apollod. 1,76 = Alcmaeonis fr. 4 EpGF).
[2] Son of → Phrixus and → Chalciope [2], the daughter of → Aeetes, brother of → Argus [I 2], Phrontis and Cytis(s)orus (Apollod. 1,83). In the older myth M., like Argus, probably returned from → Aea before the → Argonauts' voyage, as his and Euryclea's son Hyperes is considered to be the → eponym of Hyperea (Pherecydes FGrH 3 F 101) [1. 213f.]. By contrast, In Apollonius Rhodius the brothers do not set out on the journey to Orchomenus until after Phrixus' death (at his command). They are shipwrecked on the island of Dia, sacred to Ares, from where they are rescued by the Argonauts and brought back to Colchis (Apoll. Rhod. 2,1093ff., 1141ff.; Hyg. Fab. 3,17–21) [1. 320f.].
[3] Son of Ops, from Teuthis in Arcadia, in whose form → Athena appears in Aulis, before the Greek fleet sails for Troy, and tries in vain to prevent the leader of the Arcadians, Teuthis or Ornytus, from returning home on account of a dispute with Agamemnon (Paus. 8,28,4ff. from Callim. Fr. 667 [2. 244]).

1 P. DRÄGER, Argo pasimelousa, vol. 1, 1993   2 U.v. WILAMOWITZ, Pausanias-Scholien, in: Hermes 29, 1894, 240–248.   P.D.

[4] Mistakenly introduced by Pliny as father of → Micciades and progenitor of the Chian school of sculpture. An extant epigram in Delos, presumably Pliny's source, does not name Micciades' father. Instead it describes Micciades' place of origin (Chios) by way of its mythical founder, M. son of Poseidon.

FUCHS/FLOREN, 335; L. GUERRINI, s.v. Melas (1), EAA 4, 1961, 983; LOEWY, no. 1; J. MARCADÉ, Recueil des signatures de sculpteurs grecs, 2, 1957, 66; 75; OVERBECK, no. 314 (textual sources).   R.N.

[5] Boeotian river (modern Mavropotamos). From its headwaters in the northern foothills of Mount Acontium near → Orchomenus [1] the M. flowed along the northern edge of the Copais basin and into the great *katavothra* on its eastern edge. Today it is canalised for irrigation and drainage. Allegedly the water turned sheep black. Sources: Theophr. Caus. pl. 5,12,3; Theophr. Hist. pl. 4,11,8; Vitr. De arch. 8,3,14; Str. 9,2,41; Plin. HN 2,230; Sen. Q Nat. 3,25,3; Plut. Pelopidas 16,3–6; Plut. Sulla 20,6f.; Paus. 9,38,6; Solin. 7,27.

J. KNAUSS et al., Die Wasserbauten der Minyer in der Kopais, 1984, 17–20; S. LAUFFER, Kopais 1, 1986, 148ff.; N. D. PAPACHATZIS, Παυσανίου Ελλάδος Περιήγησις 5, ²1981, 242f. (map); PHILIPPSON/KIRSTEN 1,2, 475f., 480–486; P. W. WALLACE, Strabo's Description of Boiotia, 1979, 78f.   P.F.

[6] Southern tributary of the → Spercheus from the Oete mountain range, flowing past Trachis (Hdt. 7,198) and Heraclea [1] (Liv. 36,22,8), modern Mavroneria or Mavropotamos.

F. STÄHLIN, Das hellenische Thessalien, 1924, 196f.   HE.KR.

[7] Modern Kavak Deresi, river flowing into the → Melas Kolpos. Lysimachea [1] was on its banks (Liv. 38,40,3). M. probably formed the border between the Apsinthii and the Dolonci (Hdt. 7,58; Scyl. 67; Str. 7, fr. 52). In Ov. Met. 2,247 described as *Mygdonius Melas* with geographically incorrect alliteration.
[8] Modern Karasu, small river to the west of Byzantium, joining the Athyras and flowing into Lake Büyükçekmece. Mentioned only in Byzantine sources (Nicetas Choniates 85,20 C NIEBUHR).   I.v.B.
[9] Modern Karasu, tributary of the Halys near Caesarea in Cappadocia. The breaking of a dam built by Ariarathes IV caused disastrous flooding (Str. 12,2,8).

[10] Modern Çark Dere, tributary of the Sangarius in Bithynia, rising in modern Lake Sapanca.

W. RUGE, s.v. Melas (19–20), RE 15, 440; HILD/RESTLE, 233.   K.ST.

Melas Kolpos ('Black Gulf') Now the Gulf of Saros between the Thracian Chersonesus [1] and the mouth of the River Hebrus (Str. 7, fr. 52). From the south it could be controlled from Alopeconnesus, and from the north from Aenus.   I.v.B.

Melchites
I. TERM II. HISTORY

I. TERM
Arabic *al-malakiyyūn* from Aramaic *malkā*, 'king', used in the sense of the Greek βασιλεύς/*basileús*. Syrians and Arabs used this (pejorative) term for the followers of the Council of → Calchedon (AD 451), which is even today not recognized by the Monophysites (→ Monophysitism) of the Middle East (Syrians, Copts, Armenians). The modern term they use to describe themselves is *Rūm* (Arabic for 'Byzantium', 'Byzantines'). By contrast, the use of Melchites in the sense of a 'United Church of the Syrian region' is comparatively recent (not before the schism of 1724).

II. HISTORY
Cf. [1; 2]. In late antiquity, the Hellenized class of Byzantine administrators and civil servants (→ *árchontes* [III] and others), who had remained faithful to the *basileús*, found itself in constant conflict with the Monophysites; however, this does not imply that the line of confrontation was between Monophysite 'Aramaeans' in the countryside and 'Greeks' in the cities – the situation was far more complicated, as proven by the existence of a → Christian-Palestinian literature. This phenomenon thus falls into the wider context of the → Hellenization of the Middle East. Following the Arab conquest of the Levant (*i.e.* after AD 634), this group was faced with an entirely new situation: their support of the emperor turned them into *a priori* suspects in the eyes of the Islamic regime. As early as the turn of the 7th to the 8th cent. AD (Damascan psalm fragment, cf [6]), the Melchites exhibited a noticeable tendency to break out of their isolation with a new – Arab – identity. The Melchites were in fact the creators of Christian Arabic, whereas Syrians and Copts tended to cling to the ancient languages for much longer [3; 4]. For that reason, it was the Melchites who in centres such as Damascus, Mar Saba, later Jerusalem and Alexandria, achieved the integration of their Hellenistic heritage into their own Christian-Arabic literature [5]. As already noticeable for → Iohannes [33] of Damascus, this 'middlemen minority' (with Nestorians – → Nestorianismus – as the other main group apart from the Monophysites) constituted an important link between the developing Islamic-Arabic literature and the tradition of the Hellenized Levant.

1 T. E. GREGORY, s.v. Melchites, ODB 2, 1332 2 E. CHR. SUTTNER, s.v. M., LMA 4, 499f. 3 G. GRAF, Geschichte der christlich-arabischen Literatur, 5 vols., 1944–1953 4 J. NASRALLAH, Histoire du mouvement littéraire dans l'église melchite du Vᵉ au XXᵉ siècle, 4 vols., 1979ff. 5 S. GRIFFITH, The Monks of Palestine and the Growth of Christian Literature in Arabic, in: The Muslim World 78, 1988, 1–28 6 B. VIOLET, in: OLZ 4, 1901, 384ff. J.N.

Meldi People of Gallia → Lugdunensis on the lower → Matrona (Strab. 4,3,5; Plin. HN 4,107; Ptol. 2,8,11). The capital was Iatinon ('Ιάτινον, Ptol. 2,8,15; = *Fixtinnum*, Tab. Peut. 2,4), later called *civitas Meldorum* (Not. Galliarum 4,7) or Meldis (Ven. Fort. 3,27), modern Meaux. In 55/4 BC, Caesar had the M. build him ships for the expedition to Britain (Caes. BG 5,5,2); however, there was possibly another people by this name on the sea coast. Archaeological finds: coins.; water pipe. Inscriptions: CIL XIII 3023f.; a theatre (discovered in 1993) [1. 197f.] was pledged by the Gallic [*flamen*] *Aug(usti)* Orgetorix on behalf of his fellow citizens and built by his sons in the 1st cent. AD (CIL XIII 3024).

1 J.-P. LAPORTE, Meaux gallo-romain, in: R. BEDON (ed.), Les villes de la Gaule lyonnaise (Caesarodunum 30), 1996, 179–224. Y.L.

Meleager (Μελέαγρος/ *Meléagros*, Lat. *Meleager*).
[1] Mythological hero. Hero from the generation before the Trojan War, from → Calydon [3], the capital city of the Aetolians. As one the Argonauts (→ Argonautae) M. participated in the funereal games for → Pelias (Stesich. PMG 179; Diod. 4,48,4). As the brother of → Deianeira he is also linked with the Hercules cycle (Bacchyl. 5,170–175; Pind. fr. 70b). First and foremost, however, he is associated with the local legend of Calydon.

In the archaic period there were two variations of the myth. According to one of these, M., the son of → Ares, was killed by Apollo while fighting the Curetes at Pleuron (Hes. fr. 25,1–13 M.-W.; cf. Apollod. 1,65; Hyg. Fab. 171); this version is also to be found in the → *Minýas* epic (Paus. 10,31,3, cf. Hes. fr. 280,10). Through Homer and Euripides the second variant became the better-known one. In Homer (Il. 9,528–599) M. is the son of → Oeneus, king of Calydon, and → Althaea [1], daughter of → Thestius, king of Pleuron. Oeneus angers Artemis because he refuses her the usual sacrifice. As punishment she sends the Calydonian boar which M. ultimately kills. Then a war breaks out between Calydon and Pleuron for the boar trophies, in the course of which M. kills Althaia's (nameless) brother. When she curses her own son, M. leaves the battle and only returns through the influence of his wife Cleopatra in order to save Calydon. He does not receive the promised reward, but dies as a result of Althaea's curse. It is generally assumed that Homer is referring to a well-known story which he changed so as to [1] create a more exact parallel with the situation of Achilles [1].

The theme of Homer's version is the problematical status of a wife and her loyalty in a patrilineal, patrilocal society. However, this problem does not arise in ancient iconographical material. Here, e.g. on the well-known François Crater (Florence 4209), the myth is depicted exclusively through the boar hunt, i.e. as a heroic fight [2]. Stesichorus' *Syothérai*, 'The Boar Hunters' probably had the same objective (Stesich. PMG

221f.). In later versions an additional motif is added to the story – the motif of the log to which → Moira Atropos (Hyg. fab. 171) has tied M.'s life. By burning this log that the mother had once saved from the fire and kept safely, she now extinguishes the life of her son. The motif of the log upon which M.'s life depends appeared for the first time in Phrynichus' *Pleuróniai* though certainly in a way that already appeared to presuppose that it was well known (Paus. 10,31,4 = TrGF I 65). The first extant text to use the motif (Bacchyl. 5,124–154, *c.* 475 BC) presents M. as the innocent victim of Althaea's maliciousness. Bacchylides uses as a framework Hercules' meeting with M. in Hades; as in Pind. I. 7,31f., the hero represents the warrior who dies young. → Polygnotus on the other hand depicted him in the Cnidic → *lesche* in Delphi (of c. 450 BC) as a bearded man (Paus. l.c.).

It is generally assumed that J.G. FRAZER [3] was correct when he identified the log as 'external soul'. However, the death of M. did not occur automatically. Althaea brings it about through an incantation while the wood is burning (Bacchyl. 5,140–144). Later the wood was often understood as a more direct representation of M.'s life, as the period in which it burnt was equated with M.'s life-span (Sen. Med. 779; Dion Chrys. 67,7).

Although → Atalante is present in many ancient depictions of the boar hunt, she does not appear there together with M. but with the Arcadian → Melanion. She first became the key figure of the tale in Euripides' lost tragedy *M.* (TGF 515–539; [4. 27]) the plot of which – Althaea's claim to the boar skin and M.'s quarrel with the two sons of Thestius (Thestiadae: the names vary) – shows only minor deviations in most later versions (Diod. 4,4,4f.; Ov. met. 8,267–546; Apollod. 1,65–71). An exception is Antoninus Liberalis 2, whose representation appears to go back to the lost *M.* of Sophocles (cf. TrGF III 401). The motif of the war between Calydon and Pleuron and M.'s wife Cleopatra fade in importance; the main interest is focused on the psychological plot motivation. In several versions M. and Atalante have a child together, → Parthenopaeus (Hyg. Fab. 70; 99; 270). Adaptations of Euripides' drama influenced pantomime performances in the Principate Period (Lucian. De saltatione 50, cf. Sen. Med. 643–646) as well as the many representations on sarcophagi. Here the motifs of the myth are removed from their narrative context and function as symbols, e.g. of noble death, of premature death (*mors immatura*) or of *vita activa*.

1 J. N. BREMMER, La plasticité du mythe: Méléagre dans la poésie homérique, in: C. CALAME (ed.), Métamorphoses du mythe en Grèce antique, 1988, 37–56   2 J. BOARDMAN, G. ARRIGONI, s.v. Atalante, LIMC 2.1, 940–950   3 J. G. FRAZER, The Golden Bough (abridged edn.), 1922, 874–917   4 D. L. PAGE, Greek Literary Papyri, 1942.

T. GANTZ, Early Greek Myth, 1993, 328–335; S. WOODFORD, I. KRAUSKOPF, s.v. M., LIMC 6.1, 414–435.   R.G.

[2] Commanded a troop (*ilé*) of → *hetaîroi* of → Alexandros [4] the Great at Gaugamela (Arr. An. 3,11,8; Curt. 4,13,27). Perhaps identical with M. [3].

[3] Friend of → Peithon (son of Crateuas) and after the latter's execution in 316 BC by → Antigonus [1], leader of the uprising planned by Peithon; fell in battle against the superior Macedonian-Persian armies (Diod. 19,47).

[4] Son of Neoptolemus, in 334 BC one of the young bridegrooms (Arr. An. 1,24,1) who were sent home in winter and who then led back a number of newly conscripted troops to the camp of → Alexander [4] the Great. As the least important of the → taxis leaders, M. fought in the Getic campaign on the → Granicus, at → Issus and at Gaugamela, then at the Persian passes in Sogdiana, Bactria und on the Hydaspes, where he did not take part in the actual battle. The only other mentions of him are on the return march from India under → Craterus [1] and at the feast of → Medius [2]. After Alexander's death, M. set himself up as the leader of the → phalanx, accused → Perdiccas, the son of Orontes, of setting his sights on the succession, and promoted the election of → Arrhidaeus[4]. After the latter's acknowledgement, M. gradually lost the support of the phalanx, was lured into a trap by Perdiccas and was killed along with 300 of his followers.

BERVE 2, No. 494.   E.B.

[5] Son of → Ptolemaeus I and of Eurydice [4], brother of → Ptolemaeus Keraunos and as the latter's successor, king of Macedonia in February/March 279 BC; deposed by the Macedonians after being defeated in a battle against the Celts because he was considered unworthy; nothing certain is known about his later life.

PP VI 14535; F. W. WALBANK, A History of Macedonia 3, 1988, 253f.   W.A.

[6] Milesian, probably the brother of the Seleucid envoy Apollonius [1. 480], served → Antiochus [6] IV in the 6th → Syrian War in 170 and 169 BC on several occasions as envoy to Rome (Pol. 27,19; 28,1,1–6; 22; [2. 213f.]; cf. [3. 176,17]).

1 F. GEYER, s.v. M. (4), RE 15, 479f.   2 E. OLSHAUSEN, Prosopographie der hellenistischen Königsgesandten, 1974   3 P. HERRMANN, Milesier am Seleukidenhof, in: Chiron 17, 1987, 171–190.

[7] Son of Apollonius and nephew of M. [6], lived like his brothers Menestheus and Apollonius in Rome as *sýntrophos* ('Foster-brother') of the Seleucid prince → Demetrius [7]whom he supported in 162 BC in his flight and seizure of power (Pol. 31,11–14, esp. 13,2) [1. 176].

1 P. HERRMANN, Milesier am Seleukidenhof, in: Chiron 17, 1987.   L.-M.G.

[8] M. of Gadara Outstanding epigrammatist and author of lost → satires in the style of his countryman → Menippus [4] (cf. Athens 4,157b; 11,502c), as whose successor he regarded himself; M. lived approximately between 130 and 70 BC. According to several autobiographical epigrams (Anth. Pal. 7,417–419; 421), he was born in Gadara but was educated in Tyre; he ultimately moved to Cos where he perhaps compiled his 'Garland ' (cf. → Anthology C.) and was given citizenship. He was simultaneously a Syrian, Phoenecian and Greek and so according to a cosmopolitan ideal held up by the Cynics, he was 'a citizen of the world' (Anth. Pal. 7,417,5f.). No further traces of → Cynicism are noticeable in his poems, which do not differ much from those of his Epicurean countryman → Philodemus (whose epigrams M. did not collect). M. gives an accurate definition of his own poetry when he boasts that he was able to unite 'Eros who makes sweet tears flow and the Muses with the smiling Charites' (Anth. Pal. 7,419,3f.), i.e. that he extolled the most varied aspects of love with grace and humour.

The 'Greek Ovid', as he has been called (cf. [1]), also takes his place among the greatest and best-represented poets in the Greek 'Anthology' (132 epigrams) as a result of other characteristics: apart from the elegance of his fluid style, however interwoven it is in his strict versification, M.'s talent lies in his outstanding imagination and resourcefulness: mimic scenes (5,182; 184), autobiographies, epitaphs (cf. 7,207, a witty reversal of animal epitaphs), riddles (7,428), echoes of mythological stories in a dramatic (16,134) or intellectually stimulating (9,331) tone. However M. knows above all how to express himself in love epigrams sensitively and brutally, jokingly and melancholically, sentimentally and vindictively, virtuously and obscenely (with regard to numerous hetaeras, esp. Zenophila and Heliodora, and boys; e.g. Myiscus the sun who with its radiance puts out the stars, 12,59). The conventional theme of love that consists of desire and betrayal, sighs and tears, is refreshed with the ingenious contamination by traditional elements (5,149; 7,195, etc.) or by reverting to new images. The cruellest tones are regularly reserved for the boys (12,95, etc.) and the sweetest for Heliodora, for whose death M. wrote his most famous poem (7,476) in which a new and intense pathos is expressed in spite of the pathos-filled and redundant style. It is this that predominates in M. who seldom dispenses with a cool and affected patina (cf. 5,57; 163; 176) or shows himself to be simple and concise (cf. 5,96; 172; 180; 12,70). M. is an artist who has at his disposal an extraordinary number of tools of expression, as well as above all being a virtuoso of form, and among others things also a creator of various *hapax legomena* (verbal and adjectival composita).

→ Satire

1 F. SUSEMIHL, Geschichte der griechischen Literatur in der Alexandrinerzeit, vol. 2, 1892, 556.

GA I 1, 214–253; 2, 591–680; J. CLACK (ed.), Meleager. The Poems, 1992; A. CAMERON, The Greek Anthology from Meleager to Planudes, 1993; K. J. GUTZWILLER, Poetic Garlands. Hellenistic Epigrams in Context, 1998.
M.G.A.

Meleager Painter One of the most prestigious and prolific Attic red-figure vase painters of the early 4th cent. BC. More than 110 works are ascribed to him, while less important painters in his circle copied his style. He painted large vessels, kraters of all kinds, amphorae, pelikai and hydriai, as well as bowls. Favoured themes include Dionysiac and mythical scenes, e.g. that of → Meleager [1] (hence his name) and → Atalante, but, most of all, his works deal with the idyllic worlds of the symposium and the wedding. Especially well known are the volute krater Vienna 158 and the bowl London E 129, with Dionysus and Ariadne as lovers on the internal tondo. In stylistic disposition, he descends from the generation of vase-painters thriving at the turn of the 5th century to the 4th (→ Pronomos Painter, → Talos Painter, Suessula Painter). He can be recognised by the rich botanical ornamentation of his vessels; the same wealth of embellishment is also evident on his figures, another characteristic deriving from the previous generation of vase painters. His compositions of few figures in the tondi of bowls contrasted with simple scenes on the exterior have proved particularly important.

BEAZLEY, ARV², 1408ff.; BEAZLEY, Paralipomena, 490; BEAZLEY, Addenda², 374ff.   S.DR.

Meles (Μέλης/*Mélēs*, also Μέλητος/*Melētos*). Athenian who, not returning the love of the metic Timagoras, drives him to suicide; after the latter's death, M. follows suit out of remorse: aition for the altar of → Anterus, which the → metoikoi erected in the city and venerated in memory of Anterus' having avenged Timagoras (Paus. 1,30,1). There is a similar story in Aelianus (fr. 72 DOMINGO-FORASTÉ = Suda s.v. Μέλητος μ 497): M. and Timagoras are both Athenian citizens of noble family. M., who is in love with Timagoras, accomplishes all the labours his beloved imposes upon him, e.g. acquiring rare birds for him. Timagoras, however, remains unmoved, and M. throws himself from the Acropolis. Timagoras follows him to death with the birds: aition for a statue of a beautiful, naked boy, plunging into the abyss with two roosters under his arms.   AL.FR.

Melesippus (Μελήσιππος; *Melésippos*). Spartiate, son of Diacritus, member of the last Spartan delegation to Athens in 431 BC before the outbreak of the → Peloponnesian War (Thuc. 1,139,3). In the same year, during the advance of the army of → Archidamus [1], he was again sent to Athens for negotiations, but was turned back at the city gates. On leaving Attica, he is said to have prophesied that that day would mark the beginning of great misfortune for the Hellenes (Thuc. 2,12).   K.-W.W.

Melete see → Exercitatio

Meletius of Antioch came from a wealthy family from → Melitene/Armenia Minor (Greg. Nyss. in Meletium, p. 444 SPIRA; Philostorgius, Hist. eccl. 5,5 = GCS 69,11 BIDEZ/WINKELMANN), was privileged with a thorough education and then apparently lived as an ascetic. He was elected to be the successor of the deposed Homoiousian → Eustathius [6], bishop of Sebaste, and advocated a theology in the tradition of → Eusebius [7] of Caesaria from AD 357 as well as supporting the ecclesiastical politics of his successor → Acacius [2]. M. could, however, not last in Sebaste. He lived in Beroea for a while and from there he took part in the synod of Seleucia/Isauria in 359. In 360 he succeeded Eudoxius as bishop in Syrian Antioch and at first advocated the Homoean course of the imperial church (Philostorgius, Hist. eccl. 5,1 = GCS 67,1f.). A witness of his theological orientation at that time (and at the same time his only completely extant text) is a sermon which he preached before the Emperor → Constantine [2] on Proverbs 13:22 (Epiphanius, Adversus haereses 73,29–33 = GCS Epiphanius 3, 303–308 HOLL/DUMMER or CPG 2, 3417). He was deposed after being in office for four weeks (the reasons remain unclear), exiled to his homeland and replaced by an old symapthizer of Arius, Euzoeus. Not a few members of the congregations remained loyal to the exiled bishop, the so-called Meletians (Ioh. Chrys. Hom. in sanctum Meletium = PG 50, 520 C/D; the creed texts come from this group CPG 2, 3415 and 3416).

When the Emperor → Iulianus [11] allowed the exiled bishops to return, → Lucifer [2] of Calaris ordained Paulinus as bishop of Antioch before M. could return; this started an extraordinarily momentous schism of the Antiochene church, which could only be settled in 415. → Athanasius' attempts in the spring of 362 to reconcile the Meletians and the followers of bishop → Eustathius [5] of Antioch, who was Nicene oriented already since 330/1 (*Tomus ad Antiochenos*, PG 26, 796–909), failed; but the Alexandrian bishop accepted the neo-Nicene creed of M. and the Meletians. M. was banned again to Armenia in under → Valens 365, returned at his own risk in 367 and was exiled again in 371/2 (Greg. Nyss. In Meletium, p. 449 SPIRA). After the death of Athanasius in the year 373, M. was the central figure of ecclesiastical politics in the East, but in the West he was considered to be an 'Arian' by individual Nicenes (Basil. Epist. 266,2; → Arianism); in the following years he developed into the undisputed leader of the neo-Nicene bishops, as is documented above all by his correspondence with → Basilius [1]. M. only returned to his bishop's seat in 378 and then became the most powerful Church leader in the East. In 379, M. led an important Antiochene synod and presided over the imperial council of Constantinople in 381 (Greg. Naz. De vita sua 1514–1524).

SOURCES: CPG 2, 3415–3418; A. SPIRA (ed.), Gregor von Nyssa, Oratio funebris in Meletium Episcopum (Opera 9), 343–416, 439–457; CH. JUNGCK (ed.), Gregor von Nazianz, De vita sua, 1974.

BIBLIOGRAPHY: H. CH. BRENNECKE, Erwägungen zu den Anfängen des Neunizänismus, in: D. PAPANDREOU et al., Oecumenica et Patristica. FS für W.Schneemelcher, 1989, 241–257; W. ENSSLIN, s.v. Meletius (3), RE 15, 500–502; F. LOOFS, s.v. Meletius von Antiochien, Realencyclopädie für protestantische Theologie und Kirche 12, 1903 (reprint 1971), 552–558; A. M. RITTER, Das Konzil von Konstantinopel und sein Symbol (Forschungen zur Kirchen- und Dogmengeschichte 15), 1965, 41–56.   C.M.

Meletus (Μέλητος; *Mélētos*).
[1] Athenian. In the year 415 BC he was denounced for having participated in the → profanation of the mysteries and the mutilation of the Herms (→ Herms, mutilation of the). He fled from Attica and was condemned to death *in absentia* (And. 1,12f.; 35; 63). Possibly the same as M., the great-grandson of the Alcmaeonid → Megacles [4] (IG II² 1579,19).

PA 9825; TRAILL, PAA 639290.

[2] Athenian; along with → Socrates and others he was ordered in the year 404 BC by the 30 tyrants (→ *triákonta*) to arrest Leon of Salamis in order to kill him. Only Socrates disobeyed the command. In 400, M. was one of the prosecutors of → Andocides [1] (Pl. Ap. 32c-d; And. 1,94). Maybe the same as the M. who took part in negotiations with Sparta after the overthrow of the 30 tyrants (Xen. Hell. 2,4,36), as well as with M. [3].

D. FURLEY, Andokides and the Herms, 1996; D. MAC-DOWELL, Andokides: On the Mysteries, 1962; TRAILL, PAA 639292.   W.S.

[3] Tragedian of the 2nd half of the 5th cent. BC (TrGF I 47), often ridiculed by Aristophanes (Aristoph. Ran. 1302, fr. 156,10 PCG), apparently of Thracian origin (fr. 453 PCG); lover of → Callias [5] (Aristoph. fr. 117 PCG); presumably the same as M. [2].
[4] Son of M. (presumably [3]) from the deme of Pitthus (Pl. Euthphr. 2b), prosecutor of → Socrates as representative of the poets (Pl. Ap. 23e), probably author of an Oedipus tetralogy. He was condemned to death by the Athenians according to Diog. Laert. 2,43.

D. M. MACDOWELL, Andokides. On the Mysteries 1962, 208–10; TrGF I 48.   B.Z.

Melia (Μελία; *Melía*). According to Hecat. (FGrH 1 F 11, with Steph. Byz. s.v. M.) a city in Caria, according to Vitr. De arch. 4,1,4–6 one of the ancient Ionian cities. It was destroyed by the Ionians around 700 BC, and the territory between Samos and Priene was divided up (IPriene Nr.37). Since [1. 78–167] the late Geometric/early Archaic hilltop enclosure on the Kale Tepe by Güzel Çamlı north of the Mycale (today's Samsun Dağı) is considered to be M. But it should rather be localized as the ruins on the → Mycale (ibid. also the archaic → Panionium? [2. 137¹]) discovered in 1999.

1 G. KLEINER, P. HOMMEL, W. MÜLLER-WIENER, Panionion und Melie, 23. Ergh. JDAI, 1967   2 U. WILAMOWITZ, Panionion, in: U. WILAMOWITZ, Kleine Schriften 5,1, 1971, 128–151.

F. LANG, Archaische Siedlungen in Griechenland, 1996, Index s.v. M., esp. 196f. fig. 69f.   H.LO.

Meliae (Μελίαι, Μελιάδες; *Melíai, Meliádes*). Tree, esp. ash nymphs, related to the dryads and → hamadryads [1; 2]. According to Hes. Theog. 176–187, they arose, like the Erinyes and Titans, from drops of blood from the castration of → Uranus, which fell to Earth (→ Gaia) and fertilized her. Hes. Op. 145 confines the descent of humans from tree divinities to the third age of iron (→ Ages). Some of these nymphs are linked in local legend with heroes: (1) a Theban nymph, daughter of → Oceanus, mother of Ismenius and → Tenerus (Pind. Pyth. 11,3–10; Lycophr. 1211; Paus. 9,10,5 and 26,1). (2) an Argive nymph, daughter of → Oceanus, mother, by → Inachus [1], of the first human → Phoroneus (Apollod. 2,1). (3) a Bithynian nymph, mother, by Poseidon, of → Amycus [1] (Apoll. Rhod. 2,4; Hyg. Fab. 17). (4) a Cyzician nymph, mother, by Silenus, of Dolion, progenitor of the → Doliones, and of the centaur Pholus (Str. 14,681; Apollod. 2,5,4).
→ Nymphs

1 WILAMOWITZ 1, 186   2 M. L. WEST, Hesiod: Theogony, 1966, 221.

NILSSON, GGR 1, 246.   K.v.S.

Meliboea (Μελίβοια/*Melíboia*, Latin *Meliboea*).
[1] Heroine, known within the Leto cult of Argos as → Chloris [2] (on the aition: Paus. 2,21,9f.). In the Demeter cult of → Hermion(e), Kore (→ Persephone) bears the byname M. (Ath. 14,624e, the passage is textually disputed). M. first appears in Hom. Od. 11,281–287 as the daughter of → Amphion [1], later also as the daughter of → Niobe (Apollod. 3,47) and spouse of → Neleus (Pherecydes FGrH 3 F 117). Ath. 13,557a mentions her as the spouse of → Theseus.

R. CARDEN, The Papyrus Fragments of Sophokles, 1974, 231–235; P. LINANT DE BELLFONDS, s.v. Chloris (1), LIMC 3.1, 271; J. TAMBORINO, s.v. M. (1), RE 15, 509–511.
ILL.: P. LINANT DE BELLFONDS, s.v. Chloris (1), LIMC 3.2, 218.   R.HA.

[2] Town on the east coast of the peninsula of → Magnesia [1], mentioned as early as by Homer as the home of → Philoctetes (Hom. Il. 2,717). Part of the Persian fleet ran ashore nearby in 480 BC (Hdt. 7,188). M. was known for its production of purple dye (Verg. Aen. 5,251). In the 4th cent. BC, M. was ruled by → Pherae, whose tyrant Alexander [15] had many citizens murdered (Plut. Pelopidas 29). In 344/3, M. became Macedonian along with the whole of Magnesia. It was presumably incorporated into the town of Demetrias [1], founded around 290. In 169, M. resisted a Roman

siege, and was pillaged after the Battle of Pydna (Liv. 44,13,1ff.; 46,3). Its location is not certain. There was probably a fortified harbour at the site of the modern Agiokampos, while the ruins of the town inland are not to be found at the modern Meliboia (formerly Athanatou), but approx. 6.5 km to the south west. There, at Skiti, is a ruined town which Emperor Justinian had refortified as Kentauropolis (Procop. Aed. 4,3,13).

F. STÄHLIN, s.v. M. (2), RE 15, 511ff.; KODER/HILD, 186; A. TZIAFALIAS, Αναζητώντας την αρχαία Μελίβοια, in: La Thessalie. Actes du colloque international 1990, 1994, 143ff.

[3] Settlement in western Thessaly, mentioned only in Liv. 36,13,6 as one of a number to have been jointly subdued in 191 BC by the Macedonian and Roman armies. Its existence and location are in question.

J.-CL. DECOURT, La vallée de l'Enipeus en Thessalie, 1990, 119; F. STÄHLIN, s.v. M. (3), RE 15, 514.   HE.KR.

Melicertes (Μελικέρτης; *Melikértēs*). Mythical son of → Athamas and Ino. Threatened by Athamas, Ino jumps with M. from a cliff into the sea (Eur. Med. 1284 ff.; Ov. Met. 4,48 1 ff.; schol. Lycophr. 229). She becomes → Leucothea, M. Palaemon. → Sisyphos, king of Corinth, finds his body at the Isthmus of Corinth and buries him. Leucothea and Palaemon are henceforth regarded as saviours for those in distress at sea. In Corinth, M./Palaemon was worshipped in cult; the Isthmian Games (→ Isthmia) were supposedly founded for him (Paus. 2,1,3). It is doubtful whether M. is the Greek form of → Melqart.   L.K.

Melingi see → Slavs

Melinno (Μελιννώ; *Melinnṓ*). Greek female poet who composed a hymn in five Sapphic stanzas to the goddess Roma. Stobaeus (ecl. 3,7,12), who cites her, gives Lesbos as her place of origin, probably on account of the metre because there are only hints of an Aeolian dialect in het poetry. Her date is much disputed: most scholars propose the Republican period because – despite some similarities in images and ideas – there is no reason to suppose that she was influenced by Latin poetry and because she made no mention of the *princeps* [1]; others assign her to the 2nd cent. AD by pointing to her pompous style and metric idiosyncrasies also known from Statius.
→ Women authors

1 C. M. BOWRA, M.'s Hymn to Rome, in: JRS 47, 1957, 21–28   2 SH 541.; R. Mellor, Thea Roma, 1975, 122ff.   E.R.

Melinophagi (Μελινοφάγοι/*Melinophágoi*; 'Millet-eaters'). Greek name of a Thracian tribe located between Salmydessus and Byzantium. According to Xen. An. 7,2, the M. settled to the east of the Melanditae, Thyni and Tranipsii (cf. Theop. FGrH 115 F 223).

T. Spiridonov, Istoriceska geografija na trakijskite plemena, 1983, 41, 108 f.   I.v.B.

Melissa (Μέλισσα/*Mélissa*, 'bee'). Epithet of priestesses, name of nymphs and proper name, sometimes in aetiological myths.

[1] *Mélissai* are the priestesses of → Demeter (Pind. Fr. 158; Callim. H. 2,110; [1. no. 91]; Apollod. FGrH 244 F 89, on Paros), and in schol. Theoc. 15,94 of → Persephone as well. The name probably derives from the association of bees and their behaviour, which was thought of as especially pure (Aristot. Hist. an. 4,535a 2 f.; schol. Pind. P. 4,106a), with idealised femininity (Semonides fr. 7,83–93) and sexual abstinence in particular (Aristot. Gen. an. 759a 8–761b 2; Verg. G. 4,197–209; Porph. De antro 18), as typical for the ritual of the → Thesmophoria [2]. According to Apollodorus, *Mélissai* are also women taking part in the festival. It is unclear whether the priestesses of → Artemis, in particular in → Ephesus, or indeed the goddess herself were called *Mélissai* as well (on bees in the cult of Artemis at Ephesus, see Aeschyl. TrGF 3 fr. 87; [3. 99 f.]). Pindar's 'Delphic M.' (Pind. Pyth. 4,60 f.: → Pythia) reflects the belief that bees had prophetic abilities; and bees are often associated with Delphi (Hom. H. 4,552–563; Paus. 10,5,9; Plut. De Pyth. or. 17; Philostr. Ap. 6,10) and with other oracle-cults (Pind. Ol. 6,45–47; Paus. 9,40,1 f.). The priestesses of → Rhea are called *Mélissai* as well; M. is also a by-name of → Selene (Porph. de antro 18).

In addition, *Mélissai* are → nymphs, whose life is supposedly as innocent as that of bees. The ancients thought that some bees carried water (Aristot. Hist. an. 9,625b 19; Ael. NA. 5,11; 1,10) comparable in purity to → honey (Mnaseas of Patara, FHG 3 p. 150, fr. 5; Porph. De antro 17; Hesych. s.v. ὀροδεμνιάδες). Finally the souls of the dead can also be called *Mélissai* (for bees in a funerary context, see Soph. TrGF Suppl. fr. 879; [4. 111–114]).

According to myth, M. is one of the two daughters of the Cretan king → Melisseus; she feeds honey to the new-born Zeus (Zeus Melissaios: Hesych. s.v. Μελισσαῖος), while her sister → Amalthea [1] gives him milk to drink. M. then becomes a priestess of Megala Mater/Rhea (Lactant. Div. inst. 1,22,19–21; cf. Columella 9,2,2–5). In local Peloponnesian tradition M. is the name of one of the women in the service of Demeter, who first found out how to collect and use honey; bees are named after her (Mnaseas of Patara loc. cit.). M. is also the name of an especially assiduous devotee of Demeter from the Isthmus (Serv. Aen. 1,430). M. is, finally, the name of the daughter of Epidamnus, the eponymous hero of → Dyrrhachium/Epidamnus (Philon FHG 3 p. 574, fr. 15; Steph. Byz. s.v. Δυρράχιον). M., wife of → Periander of Corinth, may also be legendary (Hdt. 3,50; 5,92; Diog. Laert. 1,94; Paus. 2,28,8); see however LGPN for M. as a historical proper name. For poets described as *Mélissai*, see → bee.

1 D. L. Page, Greek Literary Papyri, 1942   2 M. Detienne, Orphée au miel, in: J. LeGoff, P. Nora, Faire de l'histoire, vol. 3, 1974, 56–75   3 R. Fleischer, Artemis von Ephesos und verwandte Kultstatuen aus Anatolien und Syrien, 1973   4 R. Lullies, Zur Bedeutung des Kranzes von Armento, in: JDAI 97, 1982, 91–117.

L. Bodson, ΊΕΡΑ ΖΩΙΑ, 1978, 20–43; A. B. Cook, The Bee in Greek Mythology, in: JHS 15, 1895, 1–24; M. Davies, J. Kathirithamby, Greek Insects, 1987, 43–83; F. Diez Platas, s.v. M., LIMC 6.1, 444–446; W. Robert-Turnow, De apibus mellisque apud veteres significatione, 1893.   B.K.

[2] An author difficult to date, but judging from the language probably late (AD 100?), who wrote in the Doric dialect a supposedly Pythagorean, extremely banal letter, addressed to a woman, on the 'adornment' (*eukosmía*) of women. This, it claims, does not depend upon finery, expensive clothing and jewellery, but rather on modesty, good house-keeping and obedience towards her husband, whose wishes are unwritten law.

R. Hercher, Epistolographi Graeci, 1873, 607–608; H. Thesleff, The Pythagorean Texts, 1965, 115–116.
                                                          M.FR.

[3] 'Partner' of the philosopher → Carneades [1] (C.P.A. Val. Max. 8,7,5: *uxoris loco habebat*); thought to be identical to the *pallakê* ('mistress') mentioned in Diog. Laert. 4,63 f.; allegedly seduced by Mentor, a disciple of Carneades, who was in consequence publicly excluded from the lectures of his teacher (Cf. also Euseb. Praep. evang. 14,8,13).   K.-H.S.

[4] Village in central Phrygia in the wooded region of Arginusa (Aristot. Hist. an. 578b 27 f.), named after the characteristic white tufa, and located between Synnada and Metropolis to the north. In 404 BC, Alcibiades was killed there on the orders of Pharnabazus (Plut. Alcibiades 39). Hadrian had a statue of Alcibiades made from Parian marble placed upon his grave (Athen. 13,34,22–29 Kaibel).

in; L. Robert, A travers l'Asie Mineure, 1980, 257–299.
                                                          T.D.-B.

Melisseus (Μελισσεύς; *Melisseús*). Mythical king of Crete, father of the nymphs → Adrastea and → Ide [2] (Apollod. 1,5; Hyg. Fab. 182) or → Amalthea [1] and → Melissa [1] (Didymus In Lact. inst. 1,22,19 f.). After → Rhe(i)a gives birth to → Zeus in a cave of Mt Dicte on Crete, she hands them the baby and they raise him on goat's milk and honey. The names of M. and Melissa are derived from Greek *méli* (honey). According to Didymus (l.c.), M. was the first to sacrifice to the gods and to introduce rites and religious festivals. He appointed his daughter Melissa the first priestess of → Mater Magna.   AL.FR.

Melissus (Μέλισσος; *Mélissos*).
[1] M. of Thebes, son of Telesiades, addressee of Pind. I., 3 and 4 (→ Pindarus). Two victories are mentioned,

one in the horse or chariot race at Nemea (ibid. 3,9–13), the other in the → pankration (ibid. 4,44). The two metrically identical poems are not treated separately in all MSS. The race victory was probably later, I. 3 being appended to the longer poem I. 4 in regard to a single celebration [1. 202–203]. M.'s father belonged to the family of the Cleonymidae, his mother to that of the Labdacidae. The family had recently lost four members in a battle (ibid. 4,17), possibly that of Plataea.

1 A. TURYN, Pindari Carmina cum Fragmentis, ²1952.

E.R.

[2] M. of Samos Eleatic philosopher of the 5th cent. BC, successful *strategos* of the Samian navy, who in 441 BC foiled a fierce assault by the Athenians under the command of → Pericles (30 A 3 DK = Plut. Pericles 26ff.). It is not known what contacts, if any, M. had with → Parmenides.

M. presented his philosophical principles in a prose treatise probably entitled 'On Nature, or On What Is'. The work contains several omissions and innovations compared to Parmenides. M.'s essential argument is the fundamental Eleatic insight, namely that only Being (τὸ ὄν) is. Since nothing can impair Being, M. deduces that Being is limitless in both space and time (cf. 30 B 3; B 4 DK). Aristotle [6] inferred from this argument that M. had derived the spatially infinite extent of Being from its temporally infinite duration, and denounced this as an (elementary) error in M.'s reasoning. He also repeatedly condemned M.'s deduction of spatially infinite extent: M. was, he argued, constructing flawed inversions of his own argument, in deriving 'if q then p' from 'if p then q' (e.g. Aristot. Soph. el. 167b 13ff.). Two other modifications were criticized by modern interpreters: a) that M. diluted the temporality of Parmenidean Being in the cruder concept of omnitemporality (B 1; B 2 DK); b) that M. derived his thesis of Monism from the spatial infinity of Being (B 5; B 6 DK), and that this attribute could not therefore apply to Parmenidean Being (but cf. 28 B 8,6 DK). However, both objections depend upon dubious interpretations of Parmenides.

The fragments also allow further guiding ideas of M. to be reconstructed. Notably, M. stresses in his negative definition of Being that physical and mental pain are alien to Being, since they imply change, and therefore 'Non-existence' and incompleteness (B 7,4–6 DK). This statement stands in pointed contrast to Parmenidean Being, which is never – even negatively – defined in terms of a distinction between soul and body. Another illuminating realization of M. is that Being, owing to its uniqueness, is non-corporeal (B 9 DK). M.'s (counterfactual) assertion that, even if there were more things than the One, these would have to correspond to the requirements of Eleatic thinking, is surprisingly reminiscent of the arguments of the → Atomists concerning indivisible, inalterable and insensitive bodies (B 8 DK); however, there is not necessarily a direct dependence, since M. and the Atomists may equally have reached similar deductions independently based on Eleatic premises, while constructing their entirely contrasting philosophical structures of thought.

→ Eleatic School

FRAGMENTS: DIELS/KRANZ 1, 258–276; G. REALE, Melisso, 1970.
BIBLIOGRAPHY: J. BARNES, Parmenides and the Eleatic One, in: AGPh 61, 1979, 1–21; F. SOLMSEN, The 'Eleatic One' in Melissus, in: Mededeelingen der koninklijke Nederlandsche Akademie van Wetenschappen, Afdeeling Letterkunde 32, 1969, 221–233.   I.B.

[3] C. Maecenas. Roman grammarian of the Augustan period, from Spoletium, confidant and freedman of → Maecenas [2], later a favourite of → Augustus, who made him librarian of the library in the *porticus Octaviae* around AD 23 (Suet. Gramm. 21, from that Hier. Chron. p. 168 H. for AD 4.). His attempt to revive the Roman national comedy (→ *togata*) among the equestrian class (*trabeata*, cf. Ov. Pont. 4,16,30; Suet. l.c., from that Ps.-Acro, Ars 288) was apparently unsuccessful; neither fragments nor traces of an effect are evident. There are no definitive quotations from the *Ineptiae* or *Ioci* (Suet. l.c.), a collection of anecdotes in 150 vols. (?), but cf. Macr. Sat. 2,4 and the mention of M. in Plin. HN, index to bks. 7, 9–11 and 35, although reference to a scientific work cannot be excluded here (Serv. Aen. 7,66: *De apibus*). M. may also have composed a commentary on the *Aeneid* (frr. 2/3 FUNAIOLI, cf. also Serv. Aen. 10,304); frr. 4/5 refer to a grammatical piece, frr. 1 and 6 to another on the rhetorical *actio* (manner of speech), also Plin. NH. 28,62 [3. 215f.].

FRAGMENTS: 1 GRF, 537–540.
BIBLIOGRAPHY: 2 J. CHRISTES, Sklaven und Freigelassene als Grammatiker, 1979, 86–91 3 R. KASTER (ed.), Suetonius, De grammaticis et rhetoribus, 1995, 214–222.   P.L.S.

Melitaea (Μελιταία, Μελιτεία; *Melitaía, Meliteía*). Town of Achaea Phthiotis on the northern slopes of Mount → Othrys, its location near Avaritsa (officially modern M.) is confirmed epigraphically. The migrating Thessalians moved the earlier town of Pyrrha from the valley of the Enipeus to its historical location as M. (Strab. 9,5,6). → Brasidas stayed there in 426 BC (Thucyd. 4,78,1). One of the two → *hieromnémones* of Achaea Phthiotis generally came from M. (Syll.³ 314,5; 444,5). M. was a stronghold of the Greeks in the → Lamian War (Diod. 18,15,1). From approx. 260, M. belonged to the → Aetolian League, on whose behalf M. also often sent a *hieromnémón* to Delphi (Syll.³ 523,4; 538,6; 553,6). In 217, a siege attempted by Philip V. failed because the scaling ladders were too short (Pol. 5,97,5f.; 9,18,5). After the Roman victory over the Aetolians, and not later than 189, M. became a part of Thessaly, whose town constitution (administration by the → *tágoi*) M. adopted around 146. Sulla stayed in M. in 86/5 (Plut. Sulla 20). M. flourished under the Romans too, bearing the honorific name *Sebasté*. Numerous inscriptions bear witness to the regulation of frontier issues and relations with neighbouring towns, esp. Narthacium, Peraea, Peuma, Xyniae (IG IX,2, 89; 205 add.). M. survived into the Byzantine period.

J.-CL. DECOURT, La vallée de l'Enipeus en Thessalie, 1990, 84f.; G. DAUX, P. DE LA COSTE-MESSELIÈRE, De Malide en Thessalie, in: BCH 48, 1924, 343ff.; A. JOAN-NIDOU, Trial Excavations at Melitaea in Phthiotis, in: Archaiologika Analekta ex Athenon 5, 1972, 47ff.; E. MEYER, s.v. Kyrsilida, RE Suppl. 10, 355ff.; F. STÄHLIN, s.v. M., RE 15, 534ff.; KODER/HILD, 218.   HE.KR.

Melite (Μελίτη; *Melítē*).

[1] → Oceanid, playmate of Persephone's (Hom. H. 2, 419).

[2] → Nereid (Hom. Il. 18,42; Hes. Theog. 247; Verg. Aen. 5,825). She is present on Attic vases at the struggle between Peleus and Thetis [1].

[3] Naiad (→ Nymphs), daughter of the river-god Aegaeus. When Hercules comes to the land of the Phaeacians to atone for the murder of his children, he fathers a son, → Hyllus [2], by M. (Apoll. Rhod. 4,537ff.).

[4] Daughter of Myrmex or Dios, eponym of the Attic demes of M. [5] (Harpocr. s.v. M.). M. was a lover of → Hercules, who was initiated into the lesser mysteries in this demes and had a sanctuary dedicated to him (schol. Aristoph. Ran. 501) [2. 99, 184].

1 N. ICARD-GIANOLIO, s.v. M. (1), LIMC 6.1, 446
2 KEARNS.   J.STE.

[5] Major Attic *asty* deme of the Cecropis (307/6 to 201/0 Demetrias) phyle, allotted seven *bouleutaí*. Situated within the walls of Athens to the west of the Acropolis, and urban in character [4. 26], M. also included the Colonus Agoraeus and the Pnyx, and bordered on the demes of Collytus (Eratosth. at Str. 1,4,7; [2. 55; 4. 28]) and Cerameis. As well as an *oíkos* of the *demotai* and the residences of Antiphon (Pl. Prm. 126bc), Epicurus, Callias [5], Phocion and Themistocles, M. has evidence of more → *métoikoi* than any other → *dêmos* [2] [4. 83], also several cults and sanctuaries, including those of Eurysaces [3. 261f.], Melanippus (Harpocration s.v. Eurysakeion, Melanippeion), Artemis Aristoboule (Plut. Themistocles 22,2; SEG 22,116 [3. 121ff. figs. 164–167, 219]; [4. 79[54], 177]), Hermes Alexikakos (schol. Aristoph. Ran. 504; [3. 274ff. fig. 351–355]), with a statue of → Agelades, and Thesmophoria [4. 80]. Demedecrees: [4. 384 nos. 77–80].

1 E. HONIGMANN, s.v. M. (9), RE 15, 541f.   2 H. LOH-MANN, Atene, 1993   3 TRAVLOS, Athen   4 WHITEHEAD, Index s.v. M.

W. JUDEICH, Topographie von Athen, ²1931, 196, 390f., 396f.; TRAILL, Attica, 11, 50, 67, 111 Nr. 87 Tab. 7, 12; J. S. TRAILL, Demos and Trittys, 1986, 4f., 11, 14, 24, 110, 134.   H.LO.

[6] Island of the Adriatic south-east of → Corcyra [2] Melaina close to the Dalmatian coast, modern Mljet (Croatia, 99 km²). Probably a Greek settlement (Scyl. 23), conquered and cleared of its population in the Illyrian War by the future Augustus for alleged piracy in 35–33 BC (App. Ill. 16). Callimachus (fr. 579; in Plin. HN 3,152) mentions dog breeding.

J. J. WILKES, Dalmatia, 1969, 11, 49f.   D.S.

[7] (Μελίτη/*Melítē*) Scyl. 111; Diod. Sic. 5,12,2f.; Latin *Melita*, Cic. Verr. 2,4,103f.; Itinerarium Maritimum 518), the modern island of Malta. M. and its neighbouring island of Gaudus, modern Gozo, were of great importance in the Neolithic period and the Bronze Age, with the creation of megalithic constructions, subterranean burial sites and cultic sites above ground. The most important are Hal-Tarxien near Valletta, Hagar Qim and the nearby (approx. 500 m distant) temple of Mnajdra in the south of the island, and Ggantija on Gozo. The Phoenician settlement (8th/7th cents. BC) had its focus in the area of modern Rabat (necropolis of Mtarfa); at Tas-Silġ in the south-east of the island, on the site of a Bronze Age temple, an apparently important Astarte sanctuary was built [1]. M. was later under Carthaginian rule, falling to Rome in 218 BC and assigned to the province of Sicilia. The apostle → Paul was shipwrecked near M. and spent some time on the island (Acts 27,27–28,12). Extensive 3rd–6th cent. AD catacombs near Rabat suggest a large early Christian congregation. Remains of ancient villas. The Arabs conquered the island around 870. M. became a centre for the slave trade; cotton and citrus fruits were cultivated, and even today the Arabic influence is recognizable in language and placenames. Epigraphical evidence: CIS I 1, 122–132; IG XIV 600–604; CIL X 7494–7511; SEG 17, 438; Coins: HN 883.

1 A. CIASCA, Malte, in: V. KRINGS (Hrsg.), La civilisation phénicienne et punique (HbdOr 1,20), 1995, 698–711.

TH. ASHBY, Roman M., in: JRS 5, 1915, 23–49; G. HÖLBL, Ägyptisches Kulturgut auf den Inseln Malta und Gozo in phönikischer und punischer Zeit, 1989; M. CAGIANO DE AZEVEDO et al., Missione archeologica italiana a Malta, 8 vols., 1964ff.; CH. SELTMAN, The Ancient Coinage of M., in: NC 6, 1946, 81–90.   H.KAL. H.G.N.

Melitene (Μελιτηνή/*Melitēnḗ*; Lat. *Melitene*). Name of a town and region in eastern Cappadocia. M. controlled the access to Elbistan and the near-by Euphrates crossing at Tomisa. Remains of the ancient town are found in the ruin field of Eski Malatya, while the Ancient Oriental settlement (inhabited from the Chalcolithic) is located at Arslantepe. M. is attested in texts from the mid 2nd millennium BC, Hittite *Mal(i)dija*, Assyrian-Babylonian *Mi/elid(i)*, Urartian *Melite/ia*, Aramaic *mlz*, Luwian *Malizi*. The neo-Hittite dwarf state of M. (1st millennium BC; → Asia Minor III C.1.b), whose territory was also known as *Kammānu*, was temporarily controlled by → Urartu and Assyria (→ Assyria). In 712 BC, there was a short-term Assyrian occupation (palace of Sargon II). Str. 12,2,6 reports that a polis did not exist during his time at M. After AD 70/1, M. was a legionary camp of the *legio XII Fulminata* (Ios. BI 7,18) and under Trajan it became a metropolis. From the time of Diocletian, M. belonged to Armenia minor, from AD 386 to the province of Armenia II, later to Armenia III. In AD 575, Chosroes burnt it down. The episcopal see of M. was strongly fortified by Justinian (Procop. Aed. 3,4,12).

→ Armenia; → Cappadocia

J. D. HAWKINS, M. FRANGIPANE, s.v. Melid, RLA 8, 35–52; E. HONIGMANN, s.v. Malatya, EI 6, 230f.; T. B. MITFORD, Cappadocia and Armenia Minor, in: ANRW II 7,2, 1980, 1169–1228; W. RUGE, s.v. M., RE 15, 548f.   K.KE.

Melitius of Lycopolis Bishop of Lycopolis in Middle Egypt. († c. AD 327), originator of a schism in the Egyptian church at the time of the Diocletian persecution (→ Tolerance). Because of the frequent vacancies of episcopal sees, M. consecrated bishops in vacant bishoprics about 305/6 on his own initiative. Additional conflicts with bishop → Petrus of Alexandria over the treatment of → *lapsi* and the latent conflict between Alexandria and the rest of Egypt [2. 297] eventually resulted in his deposition. The numerically significant church of the Melitians (survey in [2. 303–319]) was only reintegrated into the Egyptian church with certain conditions at the Council of Nicaea in 325.

1 S. T. CARROLL, The Melitian Schism, 1991   2 A. MARTIN, Athanase d'Alexandrie et l'Église d'Égypte au IVe siècle (328–373), 1996, esp. 215–319   3 T. VIVIAN, St. Peter of Alexandria, 1988.   J.RI.

Meliton (Μελίτων; *Melítōn*).
[1] M. from Athens (?). According to fr. 1 (= Harpocr. s.v. κάθετος) author of a text called *Perì tôn Athénēsi génōn* ('On the Clans in Athens'). Date uncertain, in any case before → Harpocratio [2], who lived in the first or second century A.D.

PA 9842; TRAILL, PAA 639945.   K.MEI.

[2] Greek author of tragedies (TrGF I 182); there is evidence of a work called 'Niobe'.   B.Z.
[3] **M. of Sardes** Of the mostly lost works by M., who served as bishop of → Sardes during the Antonine era (2nd cent. AD), a sermon for Passover has come to light due to papyri found in the 20th cent. (Pap. Chester Beatty XII/Mich. inv. 5553/Bodmer XIII/Oxy. 13.1600). This rhetorically well-structured text with numerous biblical quotations and allusions is one of the most important sources for the (lunar) quartadeciman practice (that is, celebration of Easter on the 14th day of Nisan in the Jewish calendar) that was widespread in Asia Minor. A catalogue of lost writings and quotations from the aforementioned sermon (Περὶ τοῦ πάσχα or πρὸς τὸν αὐτοκράτορα sc. Ἀντωνῖνον) can be found in → Eusebius [7] of Caesarea (HE 4,26,2–14); the Syriac apologia [1] attributed to M., although definitely of pre-Constantinian origin, is not authentic.

1 W. CURETON (ed.), Spicilegium Syriacum, 1855, kb-la/41–51.

SOURCES: CPG 1, 1092/1093 (with postscripts in Suppl., 1998, 10f.).
BIBLIOGRAPHY: H. LIETZMANN, s.v. M. (4) von Sardes, RE 15, 553f.; H. DROBNER, 15 Jahre Forimalschung zu M. (1965–1980), in: Vigiliae Christianae 36, 1982, 313–333.   C.M.

Meliuchus see → Dead, cult of the; → Magical Papyri

Mella Small river system [2. 473 f.] in the foothills of the central Alps, with the river Ollius (today: Mella) as its tributary, which has its own tributary called Garza. In Catull. 67,32 poetically called *flavus* ('blond'). According to Verg. G. 4,277 f. it passes through sheep pastures near Brixia (Serv. Georg. ad l.c.). In Geographus Ravennas 4,36 it is wrongly called a tributary of the Padus.

1 NISSEN 2, 196   2 P. TOZZI, L'antico corso del fiume Garza e Catullo carmina 67, 32–3, in: RIL 107, 1973, 473–498.   A.SA.

Mellaria (Μελλαρία; *Mellaría*). The name of two cities. According to [3], it is uncertain whether it is Iberian, Celtic or Latin; according to [1; 2. vol. 8, 352] it is Latin for 'City of Honey').
[1] In the western part of the Strait of Gibraltar, between Traducta (near modern Tarifa) and Baelo, known from Sertorius' landing near M. in 80 BC (Plut. Sertorius 12; [2. vol. 4, 169]; cf. Strab. 3,1,8; Mela 2,96; Plin. HN 3,7; Ptol. 2,4,6; It. Ant. 407,2).
[2] M. (Baeturiae) near modern Fuente Ovejuna (CIL II 2344–2346).

1 A. SCHULTEN, s.v. Mellaria, RE 15, 557   2 Id. (ed.), Fontes Hispaniae Antiquae 4, 1937; 8, 1959   3 HOLDER, s.v. Mellaria

C. F. KONRAD, Plutarchs Sertorius 1994, 129; A. SCHULTEN, Sertorius, 1926, 54f.; TOVAR 2, 213f.   P.B.

Mellona see → Food

Melobius (Μηλόβιος; *Mēlóbios*). Athenian. In the course of the oligarchical overthrow of 411 B.C. M. gave the speech (in connection with the → *Pséphisma* of Pythodorus) proposing, among other things, that the number of authorized commisioners be stocked up from 10 (Thuc. 8,67,1) to 30 (Androtion FGrH 324 F 43; Philochorus 328 F 136; Aristot. Ath. pol. 29,1). In 404 he was one of the 'Thirty' (→ Triákonta; Xen. hell. 2,3,2; Hyp. fr. 61). He participated in Lysias' [1] arrest (Lys. 12,12).

A. W. GOMME, A. ANDREWES, K. J. DOVER, A Historical Commentary on Thucydides, Bd. 5, 1981, 212 (on Aristot. Ath. pol.); P. KRENTZ, The Thirty at Athens, 1982, 51ff.; PA 10102; RHODES, 370f.; TRAILL, PAA 648210.

Melon (Μέλων; *Mélōn*). A Theban. Together with → Pelopidas and other conspirators, he prepared from Athens for the overthrow of the oligarchy at Thebes in 379 BC. Having secretly returned, they killed the → *polémarchoi* and → Leontiades [2], one of the leading figures among the oligarchs (Xen. Hell. 5,4,2–9; Plut. Pelopidas 8–12; Plut. de genio Socratis 576a; 587d; 596d; 597a). They freed the political prisoners and proclaimed freedom, were honoured in the people's assembly and elected as → boeotarchs (Plut. Pelopidas 12,7–13,1). They succeeded in driving the Spartan occupants out of the Cadmeia [1. 177–180; 2. 72–80]. → Thebes

1 H.-J. GEHRKE, Stasis, 1985   2 R. J. BUCK, Boiotia and the Boiotian League, 432–371 BC, 1994.   W.S.

Melon Plant from the cucumber family (*Cucurbitaceae*) with two species, the elongated golden-yellow honeydew melon *(Cucumis melo L.)* and the rounded water-melon (*Citrullus vulgaris Schrad.*) with reddish flesh. It is known that they were cultivated early in Egypt and Greece. Greek testimonies, however, offer – aside from more or less incidental descriptions – various names (πέπων/*pépōn*, σίκυος πέπων/*síkyos pépōn*, σικύα/*sikýa*). According to Pliny (NH. 19,67), the golden-yellow *(aureus)* honeydew melon, *melopepo*, which he described as a → cucumber, first appeared in Campania. He differentiates (NH. 19,65) it from the especially large watermelon, *pepo*. Dioscurides (2,135 WELLMANN = 2,163 BERENDES) describes the flesh of the *pépōn* as a diuretic and its dried root, when drunk with mead (ὑδρόμελι/*hydrómeli*), as an emetic. The flesh is said to cure eye infections when used as a compress, whereas its skin is said to serve as a bandage, for example in the case of running eyes. Plin. NH. 20,11f. confirms these qualities and adds, among other properties, its cooling effect when eaten, and its cleansing effect on the skin. As *melones* (hence the name in English and elsewhere) the seeds, according to Pall. Agric. 4,9,6 should be sown in March (or April,: ibid. 5,3,5 or Mai: ibid. 6,5) in well-fertilised soil. If placed in mead and milk for three days, the later fruits will become sweet, and if stored for a longer period covered in rose-petals, also sweet-smelling.

A. STEIER, s.v. M., RE 15, 562–567; V. HEHN, Kulturpflanzen und Haustiere (ed.H. SCHRADER), ⁸1911, repr. 1963, 318f., 321–325.   C.HÜ.

Melos

[1] (Μῆλος/ *Mêlos*, Doric Μᾶλος/ *Mâlos*; Latin *Melos*, modern Milos). Name of the westernmost of the Cyclades islands, the fifth largest at 161 km². Included in the archipelago of M. are Kimolos off the northeastern point, Polaegus (modern Polivo) to the east, and Erimomilos to the west of M., plus a number of very small islands and rocks.

M. is the caldera of a Pliocene volcano; its relics are still present today in the sulphurous thermal springs in the northeast and southeast. The sea has access to the caldera of the crater through a cleft in the northwest, forming one of the best harbours in the Mediterranean. The north of M. is flatter and more fertile than the mountainous southwest (Profitis Elias, 748m). The non-volcanic, crystalline basement of the Cyclades, with deposited lime and marl, surfaces only in the south. All that remains of the former volcanic activity are weak fumaroles and thermal springs (Ath. 2,43a). Of particular significance in prehistory was the rich deposit of → obsidian, for which M. was the main supplier [1]; in addition, there were sulphur, clay, pumice and alum, honey, wine, and oil. The flat eastern part is the island's area of settlement in antiquity and modern times; there are no settlements, little precipitation, and little water in the rocky, inhospitable western section.

Because of the obsidian deposits, the island was already densely settled in the prehistoric era. The oldest permanent settlement is proven for the Early Cycladic period, especially in Pelos on the east coast. The economically and culturally most significant Bronze Age Cycladic city at Phylakopi on the northeast coast came under Minoan and Mycenaean influence in the 2nd millennium BC and, despite strong fortifications, was destroyed about 1100 BC. Afterwards, Doric immigrants from Laconia founded the *pólis* of M. in the eastern part of the island above the narrowest place in the entrance to the bay, but also settled in the southwest around the modern Profiti Elias. The Geometric pottery shows East Greek-Ionian influence; Archaic sculpture also appears to be Ionian-Cycladic influenced. However, the rest of the ancient town dates, for the most part, from the Roman period (theatres, necropoleis with many rock tombs, Christian catacombs [2]). Isoc. Or. 12,89 speaks of πολίχνια ('little towns') outside of the city. Among the numerous individual finds, the Aphrodite found in the ancient city is famous (now in the Louvre; → Venus de Milo).

Particularly prosperous in the 8th–6th cents. BC, the island minted its own coins, with the apple (Greek *mêlon/málon*, cf. the meaning of the place name) as a device, and was generally considered to be a Spartan colony (Hdt. 8,48; Thuc. 5,84,2; 112,2; Xen. Hell. 2,2,3; Diod. Sic. 12,65,2). M. took part in the battles of Salamis and Plataeae (→ Persian Wars), remained allied with Sparta, and did not join the → Delian League, a fact that the campaign of Nicias in 426 BC was not able to change. The assessment of a tribute of 15 talents in 425/4 was fictitious (ATL 1, 341; [3]). In 416, Athens conquered the island and punished the inhabitants severely (cf. the 'Melian dialogue' in Thuc. 5,85–113). Attic → *klēroûchoi* were settled on the largely depopulated island. In 405, Lysander freed the island and restored it to the surviving inhabitants. The economic strength of the island led to a new increase in prosperity in the 4th cent., which also continued under Roman rule (beginning *c.* the middle of the 2nd cent. BC). In the

1st cent. AD, Jewish merchants settled on the island. This facilitated the advent of Christianity (Jos. AI 17,12,327; Jos. BI 2,7,1,103; Christian inscriptions: IG XII 3, 1237–1239). Additional sources: Scyl. 48; Str. 10,5,1; Ptol. 3,15,8; Plin. HN 4,70; Solin. 11,32; Fest. 111 L; Isid. Orig. 14,6,8; inscriptions: IG XII 3, 1073–1258 with add.; 1267f. and p. 230; Suppl. 335f. no. 1661–1670; SGDI 3, 4871–4939; SCHWYZER, Dial. 207–213; CIL III 490; 14203; SEG 3, 737–739; 12, 366; 14, 523; coins.: HN² 486; 892; [4].

→ Aegaean Koine; → Minoan Culture and Archaeology

1 C. RENFREW et al., Obsidian in the Aegaean, in: ABSA 60, 1965, 225ff. 2 D. MACKENZIE, Ancient Sites in M., in: ABSA 3, 1896/7, 71ff. 3 M. TREU, Athen und M. und der Melierdialog des Thukydides, in: Historia 2, 1953/4, 253–273; Addendum in: Historia 3, 1954/5 4 J. G. MILNE, The M. Hoard, in: Numismatic Notes and Monographs 62, 1934, 1ff.

S. CASSON, The Baptistery at Kepos in M., in: ABSA 19, 1912/13, 118ff.; A. CHANIOTIS, Vier kretische Staatsverträge. Verträge zwischen Aptera und Kydonia, einer ostkretischen Stadt und M., Olus und Lyttos, Chersonesos und Rhodes, in: Chiron 21, 1991, 241–264; R. COOK, Greek Painted Pottery, ²1972, 29, 31, 106, 112ff., 294, 301, 304, 309f. 319, 327, 342f.; A. CORSO, A Short Note about the Aphrodite of M., in: Xenia Antiqua 1995, 27–32; R. M. DAWKINS, J. P. DROOP, The Excavations at Phylakopi in M., in: ABSA 17, 1910/1, 1ff.; D. FIMMEN, Die kretisch-mykenische Kultur, ²1924, 15; S. IMMERWAHR, Aegaean Painting in the Bronze Age, 1991, 4, 13, 18, 24, 33, 47f., 51, 54, 62, 80, 102, 159, 206 n. 4; H. KALETSCH, s.v. M., in: LAUFFER, Griechenland, 418–421; D. PAPASTAMOS, Melische Amphoren, 1970; PHILIPPSON/KIRSTEN 4, 185f.; A. E. RAUBITSCHEK, War M. tributpflichtig?, in: Historia 12, 1963, 78–83; C. RENFREW, M. WAGSTAFF (ed.), An Island Polity, 1982; Id., The Archaeology of Cult: The Sanctuary at Phylakopi (ABSA Suppl. 18), 1985; M. G. SEAMAN, The Athenian Expedition to M., in: Historia 46, 1997, 385–418; R. A. SONDER, Zur Geologie und Petrographie der Inselgruppe von M., in: Zeitschrift für Vulkanologie 8, 1924/5, 181ff. H.KAL.

[2] (μέλος; mélos). Greek: song, tune, or melody. The word melos is used by Homer in the plural in the sense of 'limbs, members'; the singular in the musical sense is likewise recorded early (Hom. H. 19,16; Alcm. 3,5 PMGF; Archil. 120 IEG). In later Greek, melos survives only in the musical sense. The constituent parts of a song – words, melody, and rhythm (cf. Pl. Resp. 398d) – were divided into 'members' or phrases; this connection between 'member' and 'song' also exists in other Indo-European languages [1]. The creation of an etymological relationship to μέλπειν/μολπή (mélpein/molpḗ, 'to sing/song', cf. for example Eur. Alc. 454) lacks any foundation. The term 'melic' poetry is sometimes used to refer to Greek → lyric poetry, because the lyre was not the only instrument which was used to accompany songs.

1 FRISK 2, 204. E.R.

Melpeia (Μέλπεια; Mélpeia). Settlement in the Nomian mountains with a sanctuary of Pan Nomios, south of → Lycosura (Arcadia). The exact location is unknown. (Paus. 8,38,11).

JOST, 178f.; K. KURUNIOTIS, Ἀνασκαφαὶ ἐν Νομίου Πανός, in: Praktika 1902, 1903, 72–75. Y.L.

Melpis River originating in the area of the Volsci (Latium) to the north-east of Atina. Between Fabrateria and Aquinum, in a distance of four miles, it flows in the river Liris. It is crossed by the via Latina (Melfel, Tab. Peut. 6,2), modern Melfa.

NISSEN 2, 669; MILLER, 330. G.U.

Melpomene (Μελπομένη/Melpoménē; Lat. Melpomena; descriptive name: 'she who sings'; cf. Diod. Sic. 4,7: M. because of the melody that affects the listeners). One of the nine → Muses (Hes. Theog. 77). According to → Achelous [2], she is the mother of the → Sirens (Apollod. Ep. 7,18). For a long time, M. remains the least specific and most rarely mentioned Muse. She is regarded as the patron of tragedy, especially of the lyric choral parts, and is depicted with, among other things, theatrical masks (cf. Anth. Lat. 664). In Horace (Hor. Carm. 1,24; 3,30; 4,3), however, she plays a central role as the most exalted of the Muses, as the inspirer of the great laments for the dead and lyric songs [1].

1 M. T. CAMILLONI, Le Muse, 1998, 156–166. C.W.

Melpum Wealthy, probably Etruscan town in upper Italy (Nep. fr. 56 HALM in Plin. HN 3,125), taken and razed by a Celtic coalition, allegedly on the same day → Veii fell (386 BC). Exact location unknown [1. 154], usually identified with Melzo, less probably with Marzabotto [2. 247].

1 M. PALLOTTINO, Etruscologia, 1984 2 G. A. MANSUELLI, in: M. PALLOTTINO e.a. (ed.), Popoli e Civiltà dell' Italia antica 3, 1974. A.SA.

Melqart Phoenician deity; originally *mlk qrt ('king of the city'), title of the city god of → Tyrus. The oldest documentary evidence is found on the Bar-Hadad inscription (KAI 201) dated around 800 BC from Brēdsh (Buraiğ), a village north of Aleppo. In the treaties of Asarhaddon [5. 27, IV 14] and Aššur-nēraris V. [5. 13, VI 22], written in cuneiform in the 7th cent BC, his name is recorded for the first time in connection with Tyre as ᵈMi-il-qar-tu. The name presupposes ancient concepts of a religious, god-worshipping kingdom. M. combined the features of a mythical and deified founder with those of a deity who protects the city. From the 5th cent. BC he clearly assumed traits of → Heracles [1]. In a 2nd-cent. BC Phoenician-Greek dictionary from Malta (KAI 47,1), he is also called bᶜl Ṣr ('ruler of Tyre') and ἀρχηγός/archēgos ('master, protector god'). The ritual worship of the god spread out over Syria-Palestine, in particular to the northern coast of Africa (→ Carthage), and as far as the Iberian peninsula, to Ibiza, Italy and the nearby islands and on to Cyprus and Greece.

The few pictorial representations, such as the image on the Bar-Hadad Stele, show M., according to a Syrian model, striding along wearing a conical cap and holding a battleaxe in his left hand and the anch sign (life loop) or lotus flower(?) in the right hand. He is also shown as Heracles (with a cudgel and a lion skin), as well as on coins (lion or eagle symbol). According to Eus. Pr. Ev. 1,10,10; CIS I, 122, M. was worshipped aniconically in the form of (dual) pillars (KAI 47). In late classical sources, festivals during the month of Peritios (spring equinox)are mentioned, that celebrated the reawakening of M., who was identified with Heracles (Ios. C. Ap. 1,119; Ios. Ant. Iud. 8,146), so that connections with the cult of → Adonis are inferred. Ios. Ant. Iud. 8,5,3 quotes a report by MenandER [5] of Ephesus, according to which → Hiram of Tyre had performed rites for the revival of M. in the 10th. cent. BC. In genealogy Heracles-M. is the son of → Hadad-Demarus and a descendant of → Uranus (Philo of Byblus, Eus. Pr. Ev. 1,10,27). Memories of M. might be preserved in the OT (1 Kg 16:31ff.) in so far as the Baal idol, worshipped by the Princess Jezebel, can be regarded as an epithet of M. Ez 26:11 (pillars) and the prophecy against the king of Tyre (Ez 28:14ff.) contain numerous allusions to M.

1 C. BONNET, Melqart: cults and myths of Hercules at Tyre in the Mediterranean, 1988   2 M. KREBERNIK, s.v. M., RLA 8, 52f.   3 H. NIEHR, Religionen in Israel's Umwelt. Einführung in die nordwestsemitischen Religionen Syrien-Palestinas, 1998   4 S. RIBICHINI, Poenus Advena. Gli dei fenici e l'interpretazione classica, 1985   5 S. PARPOLA, K. WATANABE (ed.), Neo-Assyrian Treaties and Loyalty Oaths (State Archives of Assyria 2), 1988.
TH.PO.

Meltas (Μέλτας; *Méltas*). His name is mentioned only by Pausanias (2,19,2): son of ('king'; Plut. mor. 89e) Lakedas, descendant in the tenth generation of Medon (the grandson of Temenos), the last king of the Argives (mostly identified with the last Temenid king mentioned but not named in Diod. 7,13,2). Non historical character, neither the son of Leokedes mentioned in Hdt. 6,127,3 or the son of → Pheidon (ca. 1st half of 6th.cent.BC) nor the magistrate (*basileús*) Melantas c. 450 BC (ML 42, Z. 43).

T. KELLY, History of Argos, 1976, 107f.; M. WÖRRLE, Examination of the Constitutional History of Argos in the 5th cent.BC, 1964, 86ff.
K.KI.

Membliarus (Μεμβλίαρος; *Memblíaros*, also Βλίαρος; *Blíaros*). Mythical Phoenician settler, member of the expedition undertaken by → Cadmus [1] in search of his sister → Europa [2]. He stayed behind on the island of Thera, whence he colonised the nearby island of → Anaphe (Hdt. 4,147; Paus. 3,1,7f.).
L.K.

Membrana see → Parchment

Memmius Roman plebeian *gens* name, whose bearers may have originated from the territory of the Volscians and who rose to prominence (in several branches) during the 2nd and 1st centuries BC. They rose to consular rank only with M. [I 4]. The descent of the *gens* from the Trojan Mnestheus (Verg. Aen. 5,117) is a late-Republican construction. An aedile called M. supposedly instituted the *Cerealia* (before 211 BC; RRC 427).

A. BIEDL, De Memmiorum familia, in: WS 48, 1930, 98–111; Id., Nochmals zur Familiengeschichte der Memmier, in: WS 49, 1931, 107–114; SCHULZE, 424; T. P. WISEMAN, Legendary Genealogies in Late Republican Rome, in: G&R 21, 1974, 157; Id., L. Memmius and His Family, in: CQ 17, 1967, 164–167.
K.-L.E.

I. REPUBLICAN PERIOD   II. IMPERIAL AGE

I. REPUBLICAN PERIOD

[I 1] M., C. Popular politician at the end of the 2nd century BC. His generally assumed identity with the eponymous *tr. mil.*, who fought at → Numantia (Frontin. Strat. 4,1,1; Plut. Mor. 201D) in 134 BC, is chronologically problematical [1. 85]. In 112 BC, as designated people's tribune, M. mobilized the plebs against the policies of the nobility towards Numibia, and achieved a declaration of war against → Jugurtha (Sall. Iug. 27,2–5). In 111, he criticized L. Calpurnius [I 1] Bestia and M. Aemilius [I 37] Scaurus in particular for rushing into peace agreements with Jugurtha and made sure that the latter was summoned to Rome for interrogation (Sall. Iug. 32f.). In 109, he successfully prosecuted Bestia in the special tribunal established by the *lex Mamilia* (Cic. De orat. 2,283). In 104 he was probably praetor and the following year he administered Macedonia with *imperium proconsulare* (MRR 1,564). Subsequently he faced prosecution for extortion under the *lex repetundarum,* but was acquitted despite an incriminating statement by Scaurus (Val. Max. 8,5,2; Cic. Font. 24; cf. [2. 174–6]). In 100 BC he stood for the consulate of 99, but was bludgeoned to death at the behest of L. Appuleius [I 11] Saturninus and C. → Servilius Glaucia at the *comitiae* (Liv. per. 69; App. B. Civ. 1,142).

According to Sallust, M. was famed for his eloquence (Sall. Iug. 30,4 *clara pollensque*). Cicero qualified this somewhat in that he considered M.'s abilities as defender no more than average (Cic. Brut. 136). The speech in Sall. Iug. 31 is not authentic, of course [3].

1 G. V. SUMNER, The Orators in Cicero's Brutus, 1973, 85f.   2 E. S. GRUEN, Roman Politics and the Criminal Courts, 1968   3 R. SYME, Sallust, 1975, 151.   W.K.

[I 2] M., C. In 81 BC he was governor for his brother-in-law Pompey in Sicily (Plut. Pompeius 11,2). From 79 he fought in Spain against → Sertorius. When he fell in battle at Saguntum in 75 (76?) BC, he was a quaestor (Plut. Sertorius 21,2; Oros. 5,23,12; Cic. Balb. 5). MRR 3,141.

[I 3] M., C. Born in about 98 BC, praetor in 58. In 56,
→ Lucretius [III 1] dedicated to him the didactic poem
De rerum natura (Lucr. 1,24–27; 5,8 etc.: *inclute
Memmi*). M.'s position in the dispute between the
→ *factiones* seems to be determined by his marriage (in
72?) to Sulla's daughter Cornelia [I 5] Fausta. For that
reason his apparent harsh changes of opinion following
his period as people's tribune (66) are quite surprising.
He failed in the prosecution of M. Licinius [I 27] Lucullus who was involved in Sulla's network of power and
also in his attempts to thwart the triumph of L. Licinius
[I 26] Lucullus (Plut. Lucullus 37,1f.; Plut. Cato Min.
29,3), but caused considerable stir and scandal as the
lover of both of these brothers' wives (Cic. Att. 1,18,3).
As praetor, he was an opponent of Caesar (Cic. Att.
2,12,2; Cic. Ad Q. Fr. 1,2,16). During his propraetors-
hip in Bithynia (57), M. was acclaimed imperator (coins
of his nephew C.M. [I 4]: RRC 427), but his administration was the cause of open resentment (even for the
younger poets of his *entourage*, cf. Catull. 10; 28).

During the year of his official separation from Cornelia (55), he switched allegiances yet again; Caesar
supported M.'s candidature for the consulate of 53 with
a horrendously corrupt campaign (Cic. Att. 4,15,7;
16,6; Cic. Ad Q. fr. 2,14,4; Suet. Iul. 73). Forced by
Pompey to reveal this unsupportable corruption, M.
was dropped by Caesar (Cic. Att. 4,17,2f.). His convic-
tion (in 52) for → *ambitus* (Cic. Ad Q. Fr. 3,2,3; App.
Civ. 2,90) marked the end of his political career. M.
Subsequently enjoyed a luxurious political exile in
Athens (for his plan to build a villa in Epicurus's famous
garden: Cic. Fam. 13,1). The historical trace of this
wealthy, politically unscrupulous bon vivant and con-
noisseur of Greek literature who liked to surround himself with artists and who had even dabbled in poetry
himself (Ov. Tr. 2,433f.; Plin. Ep 5,3,5) gets lost in the
early years of the Civil War (he died before 46: Cic.
Brut. 247).

MRR 2,203; SCHANZ/HOSIUS 1,310f.; J. H. NICHOLS,
Epicurean Political Philosophy, 1976, 41ff.; J. D. MINY-
ARD, Lucretius and the Late Republic, 1985, 25, 36f.,
74ff.

[I 4] M., C. People's tribune in 54 BC, prosecutor in
Pompey's trial for *repetundae,* supporter of A. Gabinius
[I 2] (Cic. Ad Q. Fr. 2,11,3; 3,1,15; 3,2,1) and against
C. Rabirius Postumus, who was defended by Cicero
(Cic. Rab. Post. 7). This C.M. was probably also the
master of the mint in 56, and (together with Paullus
Aemilius [I 16] Lepidus) suffect consul in 34 (Fasti
Venusini = CIL I² p.66). MRR 3,141; RRC 427. T.FR.

II. IMPERIAL AGE

[II 1] Senecio M. Afer Senator, probably from Africa.
Proconsul in Sicily and imperial legate in Aquitania during the late Domitianic period and under Nerva;; *cos.
suff.* in AD 99. Buried near Tibur (CIL XIV 3597 = ILS
1042). PIR² M 457.

[II 2] C.M. Fidus Iulius Albius Senator from Bulla
Regia in Africa. A lengthy senatorial career saw him as
proconsul in Hispania Baetica in *c. AD* 183, after that
as *praefectus Miniciae* in Rome, and *curator viae Flami-
niae* in Italy, he served as imperial legate in Noricum,
and was *cos. suff.* either at the end of 191 or in 192.
Consular legate in an unknown province. His daughter
was Memmia Aemiliana Fida. PIR² M 462.

M. CORBIER, in: EOS 2, 715.

[II 3] C.M. Regulus Son of [II 4]. M. was still quite
young when he accompanied his father to the provinces
of Moesia, Macedonia, and Achaia, where statues were
frequently erected in their honour. *Cos. ord.* in AD 63,
and *magister* of the *sodales Augustales Claudiales in 65*.
PIR² M 467.

[II 4] P.M. Regulus Senator, probably a → *novus homo*
(Tac. Ann. 14,47) but unlikely to have been a patrician,
cf. [2. 340ff.]. Served as quaestor to Tiberius and praetor. The office of *tr. pl.* or *aedilis* probably has to be
added in [1. 633]. On 1 October 31 AD he became suffect consul together with Fulcinius [II 4] Trio. Tiberius
entrusted M. with the task of bringing about the overthrow of → Aelius [II 19] Seianus, prefect of the Praetorian Guard, and Sutorius Macro. On 1 October 31 he
read Tiberius's letter to the Senate and, once one of the
senators had proposed the motion, had Seianus arrested. It is likely that he chaired the following day's session of the Senate and sentenced Seianus to death. M.
travelled to Tiberius, who was on Capri, to accompany
him back to Rome, but was sent back without success.
He became embroiled in violent disputes with his fellow
consul, who accused him of not having pursued Seianus's followers energetically enough. The dispute
dragged on into the following year (Tac. Ann. 5,11;
6,4,3f.).

In 35, M. was appointed by special order to succeed
Poppaeus Sabinus as legate in Moesia, Achaia, and
Macedonia, where he remained until AD 44, when
Achaia and Macedonia were restored as proconsular
provinces. In 38, M. was briefly recalled to Rome by
→ Caligula who forced him to give him in marriage his
wife Lollia [1] Paulina whom M. had married when
they where young. Although the emperor soon rejected
her, she was not permitted to live with M again. In AD
39 or early 40 M. returned to his provincial command.
He was honoured in numerous cities in Achaia and
Macedonia, and this may be taken as an indication of
the esteem in which he was held. When Caligula commanded him to bring the statue of Zeus from Olympia
to Rome, he delayed and so prevented the execution of
the order, as in the meantime Caligula had been murdered. M. was proconsul in Asia, probably in 48/9. He
was a member of the priestly college of the *septemviri
epulonum*, the *soldales Augustales* and the → *arvales
fratres*. The records of these show that during Nero's
reign M. probably spent all his time in Rome, but no
longer actively participated in politics to any great
extent. Tacitus (Ann. 14,47) refers to his policy of po-

litical inactivity (*quies*). Nevertheless, he was one of the 'elder statesmen' of the Claudio-Neronian era PIR² M 468.

1 VOGEL-WEIDEMANN   2 M. E. ESPÉRANDIEU (ed.), Inscriptions latines de Gaule (Narbonnaise), 1929.

E. GROAG, s.v. M. (29), RE 15, 626ff.; SCHEID, Recrutement, 213ff.

[II 5] M. Rufus Mentioned between AD 102 and 113 (Trajan was already Dacicus, but not yet Optimus) on a *fistula aquaria* (see → Water pipes) in the city of Rome with the formula *sub cura Memmi Rufi*, together with Silius Decianus and another Memnius [*sic*] Rufus. This function should not be connected with the *cura aquarum*. Presumably these senators held official positions in the city of Rome with the duty of constructing buildings and installing the required water pipes. PIR² M 471.

W. ECK, Überlieferung und historische Realität: Ein Grundproblem prosopographischer Forschung, in: Id. (ed.), Prosopographie und Sozialgeschichte, 1993, 387ff.

[II 6] L. M. Tuscellianus Mentioned in CIL VI 37326. Presumably of senatorial rank. PIR² M 475.

[II 7] L. M. Tuscillus Senecio Son of M. [II 1]. It remains unresolved whether he is identical with M. [II 6]. PIR² M 475.   W.E.

Memnon (Μέμνων; *Mémnon*).

[1] Mythical King of the Ethiopians, son of → Tithonus and → Eos, brother of Emathion (Hes. Theog. 984–5). His entry into Troy as an ally of the Trojans after the death of Penthesilea, his successful single combat with Antilochus, his death at the hands of Achilles and the immortality conferred upon him by Zeus at the behest of Eos were, as the summary of Proclus (Chrestomathia 172) shows, depicted in the lost Cyclic epic → *Aithiopís*. Hom. Od. 4,187–8 and Pind. P. 6,28–39 also refer to his single combat with Antilochus, as does Pind. N. 6,49–53 to his killing by Achilles. On several occasions, Pausanias mentions depictions of this fight in sculpture (thus Paus. 3,18,12 on the Throne of Apollo at → Amyclae [1] and 5,19,2 on the → Cypselus Chest in the Heraeum at Olympia). In Aeschylus' *Psychostasía* (→ 'Souls, weighing of') (Aeschyl. frr. 279–280a RADT = TrGF III 374–6), this combat was preceded by a weighing of fates (Plut. Mor. 17a-b), in the same way as the result of the combat between Achilles and Hector had been ascertained in advance by the weighing of their fates (Hom. Il. 22,209–13). The same Aeschylean trilogy may also have included the *M.* fragment (frr. 127–130 RADT), as well as some fragments not clearly assigned to any piece (frr. 300; 328–329 and 405 RADT). We do not know what material Sophocles used in his *Aithíopes* (frr. 28–33 RADT); only the title of a *M.* survives. Like Achilles, M. possessed weapons made by Hephaestus (Procl. Chrestomathia 172), which Ajax received after his death (Q. Smyrn. 4,456–459). M. may have faced Ajax in single combat (possibly suggested by

Alcman fr. 68 PMGF). According to Paus. 3,3,8, M.'s sword was exhibited in the Temple of Asclepius at Nicomedia.

Later aspects of the material are provided by sources including Diod. 2,22 (= Ctesias FGrH 688 F 1,22), which reports an ambush of the Thessalians, to which M. falls victim; Dion Chrys. 11,116–7, which has the dying Antilochus afflict M. with a mortal wound; and Q. Smyrn. 2,300–38 with a verbal duel between M. and Nestor, in which M. refuses combat with the older man. M.'s supposed geographical origins in Egyptian Ethiopia (thus Aeschyl. fr. 300 RADT or Plin. HN 6,182) is contradicted by his oft-cited close connections to the Persian → Susa: even Aeschylus (fr. 405 RADT = Strab. 15,3,2 p. 728) described M.'s mother as a Cissian (i.e. Susian); Her. 5,44 called Susa the city of M., Paus. 4,31,5 mentions the 'Memnonican Walls' there. According to Paus. 1,42,3, M. is said to have come out of Ethiopia towards Egypt and then gone to Susa, consequently M. did not start out for Ilium from Ethiopia, but from Susa (Paus. 10,31,5–7).

It is thus not surprising that various locations are also given for M.'s grave: Hes. fr. 353 M.-W. refers to a grave by the → Aesepus, as do Strab. 13,1,11 p. 587 and Q. Smyrn. 2,585–587 ('where the winds bear M.'), but it is elsewhere considered to be in Syria (on the river Badas: Sim. fr. 539 PMG = Strab. 15,3,2 p. 728), Belas (Aristot. fr. 641,62 ROSE; according to Plin. HN 6,182, Ethiopia ruled the whole of Syria) or in Susa (Diod. 2,22). Philostr. Ap. 6,4 even reports that M. died in Egypt as king, thus bringing about a distinction between a Trojan and an Egyptian M. (cf. M. [2]; Philostr. Heroikos 26,16–18). According to Philostr. Imag. 1,7,2, his grave is nowhere to be found, and according to Ael. NA 5,1, the grave on the Aesepus is only a cenotaph; this arises from the tradition of the immortality of M. bestowed by Zeus (Proclus Chrestomathia 172).

A. KOSSATZ-DEISSMANN, s.v. M., LIMC 6.1, 448–61 (with notes); figs.: LIMC 6.2, 230–239.   JO.S.

[2] Memnon Colossus Two seated quartzite statues ('colossi') of King Amenhotep III (→ Amenophis [3]) stand before his (now destroyed) mortuary temple in western Thebes; they were originally 21 m high. There is an architect's report describing their transportation from the quarry at Heliopolis. Figures of the king's mother and his wife Teje are displayed beside his legs. Owing to the similar-sounding praenomen, or throne name, of Amenhotep (Egyptian *Nb-mȝ't-Rˁ*, vocalized in Babylonian as *Nib/mmu(a)rea*), the Greeks identified him with the Homeric Memnon [1]; the mortuary temple was thus called the Memnon(e)ion, and the entire Theban left bank (as early as the Ptolemaic period) the Memnon(e)ia. Correspondingly, the name Memnonion given to the mortuary temple of Sethos' I. at Abydus (Strab. 17,813) comes from a re-interpretation of his praenomen (*Mn-mȝ't-Rˁ*, Babylonian *Minmuarea*). As is shown by graffiti, the royal tomb of Ramses VI. (whose praenomen was also pronounced *Nb-*

mȝ't-R') in the Valley of the Kings was considered to be the grave of M. The northern statue was severely damaged at an unknown time (whether by the earthquake of 27 BC is not known; it may have happened earlier) and, from this time forth, it issued particular sounds at sunrise (first mentioned by Strab. 17,816), which were interpreted as greetings to the Dawn from her son, M. The precise nature of the acoustic phenomenon is unclear, but it is attested by a great number of Greek and Latin graffiti (e.g. the poems of → Iulia [10] Balbilla; → Women authors B.). During the Imperial period, the Memnon Colossus was the main sightseeing attraction of Thebes, visitors including Germanicus (Tac. Ann. 2,61) and Hadrian, whose retinue left 27 graffiti. The statue was restored under Septimius Severus, after which it fell silent.
→ Thebae

    1 A. and E. BERNAND, Les inscriptions greques et latines du Colosse de Memnon, 1960   2 R. S. BIANCHI, s.v. M., LÄ 4, 23–24   3 A. H. GARDINER, The Egyptian M., in: JEA 47, 1961, 91–99.   K.J.-W.

[3] Rhodian, brother of → Mentor [3], brother-in-law of the Persian satrap → Artabazus [4]; after Mentor's death he married his widow → Barsine. The brothers received a fief in the Troad from Artabazus; they helped free him from imprisonment during his struggle with his rival → Ariobarzanes [1] and took part in his rebellion against → Artaxerxes [3]. After its failure, around 353 BC, M. fled with Artabazus to Pella in Macedonia. His brother Mentor won their return and amnesty in reward for his helping Artaxerxes in the conquest of Egypt (343 BC). They brought important news concerning the plans of → Philippus II (see → Hermias [1]).

    After Mentor's death, M. inherited his fief, but → Darius [3] dared not also entrust him with supreme command. A surprise attack on Cyzikus failed (Polyaen. 5,44,5), but M. was able to force back Philip's invading army in 335 and surround it at Abydus [1]. M. wanted to foil the invasion of → Alexander [4] the Great (334 BC) by means of a scorched-earth defence in the threatened areas, but the satraps would not agree. The annihilation of the Persian army by Alexander followed at the → Granicus. M. now sent his family as hostages to the Persian court, received supreme command in the west and attempted to organize resistance in the fortress of Halicarnassus. The situation, however, was hopeless, and he escaped with the bulk of his army. His next plan, since Alexander had discharged his fleet, was to reconquer the islands and cross to Greece; he made contact with → Agis [3]. However, he died during the siege of Mytilene (Spring 333) – 'incalculable good fortune' [1. 253] for Alexander.

    1 BERVE 2, no. 497.

[4] *Stratēgós* of Thrace under → Antipater [1]; in 331 BC, M. revolted against → Alexander [4], thus forcing Antipater to intervene, just as → Agis [3] was beginning his war against Alexander on the Peloponnese. Anti-

pater concluded an unfavourable peace with M. in order to devote himself to the dangerous war against Agis (Diod. 17,62,4–63,1). M. retained his office, certainly with further concessions. Late in 327, he supplied Alexander with troops to India. Since at this time the name M. only occurred in the family of M. [3], he must have belonged to it (cf. Diod. 16,52,4) and is probably identical with the grandson (?) of → Artabazus [4] honoured in Athens in the autumn of 327 (see TOD 2, 199). He probably wished to visit Athens before his march-off to join Alexander.

    E. BADIAN, Agis III., in: Hermes 95, 1967, 170–192; BERVE 2, no. 498 (wrong), 499.   E.B.

[5] **M. of Heraclea** [7] on the Pontus, wrote a local history of Heraclea (*Perì Hērakleías*). Vols. 9–16 are preserved among the papers of Photius (Phot. Bibl. 224): they cover the period from the beginning of the Tyranny at Heraclea in 364/3 BC to the return of Caesar to Rome in 47 BC; since Photius (ibid. p. 240a 9–11) speaks vaguely of 'the books after the 16th', the work's full scope and where it ended are unknown. M. certainly belonged to the Imperial period, and on stylistic grounds – Photius (ibid. p. 240 a 2) refers to the work's 'sober character' (*ichnós charaktḗr*) – the work cannot be considered later than the 2nd cent. AD.

    The first part is a pure city chronicle, whereas from approx. 335 BC events throughout the East are given stronger consideration. With vol. 14, Roman history too comes ever more into the foreground, not least due to the change in source material: M.'s model up to that point, → Nymphis of Heraclea, broke off at the year 247/6. Roman history is introduced in a digression covering events from the origins to the battle of Magnesia [3] in 190 BC (M., ch. 18,1–5). Historically of particular importance is the depiction of the third → Mithridatic War (chs. 27–37). In view of the total loss of Hellenistic local literature, M. is of great importance, being the only representative of this type.

    FGrH 434 with commentary.; H. BENGTSON, Römische Geschichte., ³1982, 206; M. JANKE, Historische Untersuchungen zu M. von Herakleia, 1963; K. MEISTER, Die griechische Geschichtsschreibung, 1990, 127f.   K.MEI

Memnonides (Μεμνονίδες/*Memnonídes*; Lat. *Memnoniae aves*).The legend of the birds of Memnon is closely associated with the grave of → Memnon [1] on the river Aisepus. According to Paus. 10,31,6 → Polygnotus had portrayed Memnon wearing a robe painted with birds in the picture of Hades on the Lesche of the Cnidians at Delphi. The extant versions probably date back to scholarly of Alexandrine poetry: according to Q. Smyrn. 2,642–655 it is the companions of Memnon who are turned into birds by → Eos (similar to Serv. Aen. 1,751, though with a fight motif). They cover the grave of their leader with dust; according to Ov. Am 1,13,3–4 and Ov. Met. 13,600–622, every year two groups of birds rise up from the ashes of Memnon and tear each other apart over the grave; the element of transformation is missing in Paus. 10,31,6 (only records the tending of the grave), Plin. HN 10,74 and Ael. NA 5,1 (each with the Ovidian element of combat).

A. Kossatz-Deissmann, s.v. Memnonides, LIMC 6.1, 461–462 (with bibliography). JO.S.

Memoirs see → Autobiography

Memor M. was a Moor placed in charge of the grain supply in Egypt In the reign of → Gallienus. Apparently he planned a coup. He was killed by soldiers on the orders of Theodotus ca. 262 AD, without having been proclaimed emperor (Zos. 1,38,1; Petrus Patricius, Excerpta de sententiis, p. 264 No. 160 Boissevain). PIR² M 490. T.F.

Memoriales Chancellery officials in the first division of the *sacra scrinia*, the imperial offices, who are attested in the Roman Empire from the latter part of the 3rd cent. AD. From *c.* 310, these were led by the→ *magister officiorum* and later by the *quaestor sacri palatii*. It was generally the task of the three *scrinia* (*memoria*, *epistolarum* and *libellorum*) to manage communication between the Empire's central administration and the provinces. The *memoriales* under the *magister memoriae*, attested in the eastern part of the Empire in particular, were, on the evidence of the → Notitia dignitatum, responsible for handling petitions, which they answered by writing out *adnotationes* in the name of the Emperor. From the latter part of the 5th cent. AD, however, the areas of competence of the three *scrinia* were no longer so clearly distinguished, and thenceforth their officers in general were described as *memoriales*.

M. Clauss, Der magister officiorum in der Spätant. (4.–6. Jh.), 1980. F.T.

Memory, Recollection
A. Etymology   B. Greece   C. Rome

A. Etymology
The semantic field memory/recollection can be traced back in Greek and Latin – apart from *recordor* and *recordatio*, both derivations from *cor* – to the Indo-European root *men*-. This dual etymology suggests an inner but not necessarily cognitive activity [1. 11, 20].

B. Greece
There is a correlation between μνήμη (*mnémē*), human memory, and Μνημοσύνη (→ *Mnēmosýnē*), the mother of the Muses: the Muses exist in an all-encompassing region of knowledge and truth (ἀλήθεια/ *alétheia*, is the opposite of forgetting, λήθη/*léthē*) and they inspire the Homeric bards, Hesiod and Pindar [1. 118f.]. With the discovery of techniques of mnemonics by → Simonides, the memory produces words that are no longer guaranteed by the Muses [2. 105f.].

Parallel to that, Pythagoras and Empedocles taught that the soul gains access to truth by recollection or ἀνάμνησις (*anámnēsis*)[3]. Platonic *anámnēsis* (Pl. Men. 81a–98a; Phd. 72e–77a), gained by way of dialectics, is influenced by that; sophistry (Pl. Hp. mi. 368) and writing (Pl. Phd. 274cf.) generate recollections which only come from the outside (ὑπομνήματα, *hypomnémata*). Like Plato (Pl. Phlb. 34b-c), Aristotle also distinguishes between *mnémē* and *anámnēsis*; through memory, time can be perceived and conceived of in images (De memoria 449b). For the process of memory storage, Plato and Aristotle introduce the metaphor of an imprint in the soul (Pl. Tht. 191c–192a; Aristot. De memoria 450a-b).

C. Rome
Livius Andronicus translated *Mnēmosýnē* by *Moneta* (Juno) and, with the etymology (*moneo*), alluded to the function of the goddess (reminding, recalling). *Memoria*, however, is not deified. No systematic distinction is made between memory and recollection (Cic. Tusc. 1,59–61; Plin. HN 7,24; Quint. Inst. 11,2,4f.). As a component of *prudentia*, recollection is also part of the citizen's *virtus* (Cic. Inv. 2,160); he has to remember the conditions of his social and historical status: his obligations to the gods [4] and to other humans beings (Sen. Ben.), his genealogy (Cic. Att. 6,1,17) and the *exempla* in family und people that constitute history (Cic. De or. 2,36; Sall. Iug. 4). Memory is the attribute of those who are familiar with the juridic and religious framework and are in possession of the archives: the senators (Cic. Leg. 3,18), legal scholars, priests and augurs (Cic. Cato 22). Finally, the orator has to master *memoria* as part of rhetoric (Cic. Inv. 1,9; → Memoria (Mnemonics)) in order to be able to recall his speech (Rhet. Her. 3,28) and the material needed for its composition (Cic. De or. 2,355; Quint. Inst. 11,2,1). As there were no central archives [5], these people were the guarantors of the collective memory. Many of them belong to the list of extraordinary 'masters of memory' [6. 51f.].

In the Christian period, memory is bound up with the problem of individual knowledge of God (Aug. Conf. 10,8–26).

1 M. Simondon, La mémoire et l'oubli, 1982   2 M. Detienne, Les maîtres de vérité, ²1990   3 J.-P. Vernant, Mythe et pensée chez les Grecs, 1965, 107–152   4 G. Dumézil, L'oubli de l'homme et l'honneur des dieux, 1985, 135–150   5 C. Nicolet (ed.), La mémoire perdue, 1994   6 F. Yates, L'art de la mémoire, 1975.

M. Carruthers, The Book of Memory, 1990; J. Coleman, Ancient and Medieval Memories, 1992; N. Loraux, L'oubli dans la cité, in: Le temps de la réflexion, 1980, 213–242. CA.BA.

Memphis City in Egypt, situated on the west bank of the Nile about 30 km south of the apex of the Delta. The name M. (Greek. Μέμφις; assyr. *Mempi*) derived from the name of the pyramid town of king Pepi I. (around 2300), Egyptian *Mn-nfr-(Pjpj)*. The older name, 'White Wall' (Egyptian *Jnb-ḥḏ*; *leúkon teíchos*/ λευκὸν τεῖχος in Hdt. 3,91 and Thuc. 1,104), probably referring to the particularly well-fortified centre of the settlement, was used interchangeably with M. until its latest time. From the time of the New Kingdom the city was also called *Ḥwt-kȝ-Ptḥ* ('House of the Soul of Ptah', Babylonian *Ḥikuptaḥ*), in reference of the main temple of Ptah. This later became the name of the whole country ('Egypt').

There are several sites near M. with finds from prehistoric civilisations (Maʿādī, Ḥalwān). According to Hdt. 2,99 the city itself was founded by → Menes [1], the mythical first king of Egypt, who also erected the first temple of Ptah. M. was already a royal city in early times: the 1st Dynasty royal burial ground is situated nearby and the first kings of the 2nd Dynasty were buried there. Several rites of the Egyptian kingdom, in evidence at an early date, are associated with M. Though it is doubtful whether M. or the respective pyramid city was the actual residence of the king during the Old Kingdom (3rd to 6th Dynasties), all the royal burial grounds of this period are in its immediate vicinity. M. was the capital of Egypt in most of the following times as well. During the Middle Kingdom the Pharaoh's residence (*Jtj-tȝwj*) was close to M. Besides → Thebes and later the city of Ramses, M. was the most important centre during the New Kingdom, as it was in the 25th dynasty, in the Saite Period (alongside → Sais) and in the Persian Period, when the satrap resided in M. After Alexandria was founded, M. was replaced as residence city, but it remained the capital of Egypt itself. It was not until Roman times, principally after the beginnings of conversion to Christianity, that M. lost significance. Because of its central position M. was in all periods the preferred administrative centre. It had one of the most important harbours, was the starting point for military campaigns in Asia and Libya and included the largest fortress in the country. It constituted the key to the possession of Egypt throughout. During the entire period of the Pharaohs, M. was the royal city par excellence, and also the city with the most extensive necropoleis.

The chief god of Memphis was Ptah (god of creation and patron of craftsmen); there is evidence of his cult dating back to the 1st Dynasty. Equally old is the worship of the sacred bull, Apis, whose shrine is near the temple of Ptah. Also prominent were the earth god Sokar and in the Late Period the cult of the deified sage Imhotep (→ Imuthes [2] (ʾΙμούθης), sometimes equated with Asclepius). From the New Kingdom until well into the Ptolemaic period M. was a distinctively multi-ethnic city, where foreign gods, such as Baal, Rešep, Astarte and Qadeš were also worshipped.

It is no longer possible to ascertain archeologically the extent and size of M.; there are details of dimensions in Hdt. 2,99, Diod. 1,50, Strab. 17,807–8 and in medieval Arabic descriptions, but all without a centre of reference. It is also uncertain whether or not they include the necropoleis. Only very little of the city has been preserved; the majority of the stone material was used in the extension of Cairo. The still existing ruins, especially the area of the temple of Ptah and the palace of Apries in the north, are today situated well to the west of the Nile, since the river has consistently shifted to the east starting in the New Kingdom. The main archeological remains are the extensive necropoleis, which stretch west of the city far to the south and north.

1 H. KEES, s.v. M., RE 15, 660–688 2 D. THOMPSON, M. under the Ptolemies, 1988 3 CH. ZIVIE, s.v. M., LÄ 4, 24–41.   K.J.-W.

Memphites see → Ptolemaeus Memphites

Memra (*mēmrā*). Name of a Syrian poetic form consisting of isosyllabic couplets, usually rendered in a combination of 7 + 7 or 12 + 12 syllables; the former combination is associated with the name of → Ephrem the Syrian, the latter with that of → Jacob [3] of Sarūg. Many *mēmrē* are homilies in verse form, a genre characteristic of Syrian literature and represented mainly through the 5th- to 6th-cent. AD authors → Narsai, Jacob of Sarūg and → Isaac [2] of Antioch.

A. BAUMSTARK, Geschichte der syrischen Literatur, 1922, 40 (reprint 1968).   S.BR.

Men Moon-god, primarily known from ancient inscriptions, coins and pictorial works; rarely mentioned in literary works [2, vol. 3, 115–118].
A. NAME B. CHRONOLOGICAL AND GEOGRAPHICAL SCOPE C. PICTORIAL REPRESENTATIONS D. GENERAL

A. NAME
Greek. Μείς/*Meís* or Μήν/*Mén*, Latin *Mensis* and → Luna [1] (abbreviated *L*). Often combined with the following epithets (as far as identifiable): cult founder, e.g. M. Φαρνάκου/*Pharnákou* ('M., whose cult goes back to Pharnaces', Strabo 12,3,31); geographical and other attributes, e.g. Μοτελλείτης/*Motelleítēs* ('from Motella'), Σωτήρ/*Sōtér* ('saviour'); distinctions, e.g. εἷς/ *heîs* ('[M. is] unique'), μέγας/*mégas* ('[M. is] great'). In addition to the epithets discussed in LANE [2, vol. 3, 67–80] there are also: M. Ἀκραῖος/*Akraîos* ('Castle M.', SEG 28,1168); M. Ἀξιοττηνὸς Περκον βασιλεύων/ *Axiottēnòs Perkon basileúōn* ('M. Axiottenos, ruling as king over Perkos (-on)', [6, no. 6]); M. (ἐξ) Ἀρτεμιδώ-ρου Ἀξιοττα κατέχων/*Artemidórou Axiotta katéchōn* or Ἀξιοττηνός/*Axiottēnós* ('M., whose cult goes back to Artemidorus and who rules Axiotta ', [6, on no. 79,1–2]); M. ἐξ Ἀττάλου/*ex Attálou* ('M., whose cult goes back to Attalus', EA 28, 1997, 70); M. Βασιλεύς/ *Basileús* (?, 'King M.', IK 9 [Nisaea], no. 43); M. Γαλληνός (ETAM 23, 1999, 89, no. 86); M. Κεραειτων (SEG 38,1321); M. Να[ν;]ν φ (dative; SEG 38, on 1310; 44,1061); M. Ουαραθω (dative; unpubl.); M.

Πετραείτης Ἀξετηνός [6, no. 38]; M. Πετραείτης ἐν Περ-ευδῳ/*Petraítēs en Pereudōi* ('M. Petraeites in Pereudos (-n)', SEG 34,1219); M. Πλονεάτης (SEG 34,1216).

B. CHRONOLOGICAL AND GEOGRAPHICAL SCOPE

Elements common to the Persian and M. religions may be indications of Persian origin [2, vol. 3, 113f.]. It remains uncertain whether the founding of its cult in Cabira in Pontus by Pharnaces (see below) [2, vol. 3, 67] around 600 BC is historical. Originating from the 4th/3rd cents. BC is a Colchic regulation, adherence to which is said to have been watched over by, i.a. 'the earth-goddess, the sun-god and the moon-god', [ἡ] Γῆ καὶ ὁ Ἥλιος καὶ ὁ Μείς/*[hê] Gê kaì ho Hélios kaì ho Meís* (SEG 45,1876,19). Further monuments, particularly from Attica, and coins representing or mentioning M., are of Hellenistic date. The majority of the evidence originates from the Imperial period [2, vol. 1, no. 25: AD 383]. The cult can be traced best in Asia Minor, especially in Lydia and Phrygia; → Antioch [5] near Pisidia, with numerous remains of the cult site of M. *Askaenus* [2, vol. 1 and 4; 4, vol. 2, 14 and 24f.; 5, 37–90], one of the two M. shrines mentioned by Strabo (12,3,31; 8,14), and → Sillyum (coins). There or in → Perge was a shrine to M. with right of asylum (IK 54, p. 27 note 29). Colchis (see above), Rome, Dacia and → Laodicea [2] in Lebanon mark the boundaries of the geographical extension of the cult.

C. PICTORIAL REPRESENTATIONS

See [10] for a detailed description. Men's main characteristic is the crescent moon, rising above his shoulders. The crescent moon alone often symbolizes the god, e.g. on steles or as a symbol at the head of processions at celebrations of mysteries (IK 17,1,3252,7–11). M. is nearly always depicted wearing a Phrygian cap, sometimes decorated with stars or a wreath, and a garment with sleeves and legs, a chiton and a cloak; he is also depicted wearing long garments. His hands are shown holding a sceptre (on the meaning cf. [6, on no. 3,2–4]) or a rod ending in the crescent moon, thyrsos or torch, a double axe (EA 11, 1988, 27 note 51), pine cone, dish (*patera*) or a plate of fruit. He rides on a horse, a ram or a cock (sacred to him [2, vol. 3, 116, T 7f.]). Like → Cybele he may be flanked by lions. In representations with a bull he often has one foot on the head of the subdued animal.

D. GENERAL

M. rules over places (see below; cf. M. *Týrannos*), watches over the law [7, 21 note 33], punishes and avenges ([6]; IK 52, no. 49; 57; 339–342; 351f and elsewhere), but also bestows wealth (e.g. as a river god [2, vol. 3, 107]) and healing. He is god of Heaven (*Uránios*) and the Underworld (see below). He was worshipped in conjunction with Greek, Egyptian and native deities; a 'mother of M.' and a joint cult with → Anahita are at-

tested ([2, vol. 3, 81–98]; SEG 28,1232: with → Leto). Combinations of several hypostases, e.g. M. *Petraeitēs* and M. *Labanas* [6, no. 35], are mentioned and also nine Μῆνες/*Mênes* of the Underworld (IK 52, on no. 351,4); the god also appears in connection with a group of twelve gods (→ Twelve (Olympian) Gods) (IK 52, on no. 51). M. manifested himself in epiphanies (→ epiphany), through messengers [7, 9–14], → oracles and dreams. Sacred dignitaries and slaves are attested for his shrines. Believers turned to the god as individuals or in association with families or cults (*Meniastaí* on Rhodes [2, vol. 1, no. 16f.], δοῦμος/*doûmos* et al). In the cult association founded in Attica by the Lycian slave Xanthus on the instruction of M. *Týrannos* (2/3rd cent. AD), the observation of purity and the organization of sacrifices were subject to precise rules (Syll.³ 1042; LSCG 55; [2, vol. 1, 7–10; vol. 3, 7–16]). M. mysteries were celebrated jointly (see above).
→ Moon deity

1 W. DREXLER, s.v. Men, ROSCHER 2, 2687–2770   2 E. LANE, Corpus Monumentorum Religionis Dei Menis, Vol. 1–4 (EPRO 19), 1971–1978   3 Id., Men: A Neglected Cult of Roman Asia Minor, in: ANRW II 18.3, 1990, 2161–2174   4 S. MITCHELL, Anatolia, vol. 1–2, 1993   5 Id., M. WAELKENS, Pisidian Antioch, 1998   6 G. PETZL, Die Beichtinschriften Westkleinasiens (EA 22), 1994   7 Id., Die Beichtinschriften im römischen Kleinasien und der Fromme und Gerechte Gott (Nordrh.-Westf. Akad. Wiss., Vorträge G 355), 1998   8 D. SALZMANN, Neue Denkmäler des Mondgottes Men, in: MDAI(Ist) 30, 1980, 261–290   9 Id., E. LANE, Nachlese zum Mondgott Men, in: MDAI(Ist) 34, 1984, 355–370   10 R. VOLLKOMMER, s.v. Men, LIMC 6.1, 462–473; 6.2, 239–255.   G.PE.

Mena According to Varro, Antiquitates rerum divinarum fragments 95 and 273 CARDAUNS (in Aug. Civ. 7,2–3; cf. ibid. 4,11), a daughter of → Jupiter; se was the Roman goddess of menstruation. M., recorded nowhere else, seems to be patterned on the Greek μήνη/*ménē*, 'Moon' (personified as *Ménē*/→ *Sélēnē*), or the linguistically and connotatively related Greek μήν/*mēn*, Latin *mēnsis*, '(lunar) month', and continues the customary association of menstruation with the monthly cycle and the influence of the moon. M.'s sphere of action overlaps those of other goddesses (Juno → Lucina or Flu(vi)onia, Paul Fest. 82,4f. L.). M. seems to be a scholarly construct rather then the object of an actual cult.
→ Antiquarians; → Menstruation   AN.BE.

Menaechmus (Μέναιχμος/*Ménaichmos*).
[1] M. of Sicyon Greek historian and antiquary of the 4th cent. BC. Author of a Pythian history (*Pythikós*), which was superseded by a list of victors of the Pythian Games at Delphi composed by Aristotle (T 3) and therefore must have existed in the early 330s (cf. Syll.³ 275). A history of Alexander, (*Historía hē katá ton Makedóna Aléxandron*) is entirely lost (T 1), while only fragments remain of a local history of Sicyon (*Sikyō-*

niká). Fragments of a treatise 'On Artists' (*Perí technítōn*, F 3–6; 9) deal primarily with problems of music history.

> FGrH 131 with commentary; B. MEISSNER, Historiker zwischen Polis und Königshof, 1992, 206f. K.MEI.

[2] see → Manaechmus

[3] The mathematician M. was a pupil of → Eudoxus [1] and a friend of Plato. He is said to have told Alexander the Great that there is no royal road to geometry (Stobaeus, Anthologium 2,228 WACHSMUTH). M. is regarded as the founder of the theory of conic sections. His work with these is connected to his solution of the problem of the duplication of the cube (the 'Delian Problem'): he proved that this solution can be obtained either by the intersection of two parabolas or of one parabola and one hyperbola. This follows because three equations result from the proportions $a : x = x : y = y : b$ to which the problem of the duplication of the cube leads (→ Hippocrates [5] of Chios): namely $x^2 = ay$, $y^2 = bx$ and $xy = ab$. The first two describe parabolas, the third a right-angled hyperbola. The point of intersection of the two parabolas, or of one parabola with the hyperbola, then delivers the solution x to the 'Delian Problem'. On M.'s method, see [1] and [3. Vol. 1, 253–255].

→ Mathematics

> 1 O. BECKER, Das mathematische Denken der Antike, 1957, 82–85 2 I. BULMER-THOMAS, s. v. Menaechmus, in: GILLISPIE, Vol. 9, 1974, 268–277 3 T. L. HEATH, A History of Greek Mathematics, Vol 1, 1921, 251–255; Vol 2, 1921, 110–116. M.F.

[4] Sculptor from Naupactus. M. and Soidas together made a chryselephantine statue of → Artemis Laphria at Calydon, which Augustus removed to Patrae. According to Pausanias 7,18,9–10, it dated from the early 5th cent. BC, and thus cannot have been the stylistically later Artemis depicted on local coins. M. may be identified with the sculptor of the same name who, according to Pliny, made a statue of a bullock in bronze and wrote about his work. Since → Athenaeus [3] (2,65b; 14,635b) also quotes the writings of a M. of Sicyon, 'On Artists', this may not necessarily be a case of confusion with the historian of the same name, M. [1].

> G. CRESSEDI, s.v. Menaechmo, EAA 4, 1961, 1013; OVERBECK, no. 479. R.N.

Menaenum, Menae (Μέναινον/*Ménainon*, Μέναι/*Ménai*). A *pólis* in Sicily, founded by → Ducetius in 459 BC (Diod. Sic. 11,78,5), modern Mineo, 15 km to the east of Caltagirone. In 396 BC occupied by → Dionysius [1] I (Diod. Sic. 14,78,7). After the Roman conquest first *civitas decumana* (Cic. Verr. 2,3,102), then *stipendiaria* (Plin. nat. 3,91). In late antiquity M. was a base of the Sicilian *thêma*. Taken by the Arabs in 830. – Small bronze finds from the time after the Roman conquest, as well as coins.

> G. V. GENTILI, Fontana-ninfeo di età ellenistica nella zona detta Tomba Gallica, in: NSA 1965, 192ff.; A. MESSINA, s.v. Menai, PE 571. AL.MES.

Menaḥem ben Yehuda Son (or grandson) of Judas Galileus, who (like his father Hezekiah) fought against Rome and Herod (Ios. Ant. Iud. 18,1,6; 14,9,2) [2]. Judas is described by → Iosephus [4] Flavius as the founder of the so-called fourth (nameless, later given the derogatory name of Sicarii, 'Dagger Men' = 'Murderers' [1. 50]) philosophical school, which differed from the → Pharisaei mainly in its love of freedom and its struggle for the absolute rule of God (Ios. Ant. Iud. 18,1,1; 18,1,6) [3. 599; 1. 85–93]. Bound to these convictions, M. was one of the leaders of the party of → Zealots in the Jewish-Roman War (AD 66–74) against the occupying Roman powers. At the outbreak of the war he conquered the fortress of → Masada and led the warfare in → Jerusalem, conducting himself with Messianic pretensions (Ios. BI 2,17,8; Babylonic Talmud Sanhedrin 98b; Jerusalem. Talmud Ḥagiga 2,2 (77d) [1. 296–307]; his identification in rabbinical sources is disputed [1. 339f.]). After the successful capture of the palace of Herod, M.'s troops murdered the surrendering Roman troops and the High Priest Ananias, who was working for peace and settlement (in AD 66). M. himself was murdered by the followers of → Eleazarus [9], Ananias' son (Ios. BI 2,17,9). The fortress of Masada remained in the hands of his followers, and was defended until the end of the war by → Eleazarus [12], a relative of M. (Ios. BI 7,9,1).

→ Zealots

> 1 M. HENGEL, Die Zeloten. Untersuchungen zur jüdischen Freiheitsbewegung in der Zeit von Herodes I. bis 70 n.Chr., 1961 (²1976) 2 F. LOFTUS, The Anti-Roman Revolts of the Jews and the Galileans, in: Jewish Quarterly Journal 68, 1977, 78–98 3 SCHÜRER 2, 598–606. I.WA.

Menalcas (Μενάλκας; *Menálkas*). Bucolic poet, protagonist of Theoc. 8 alongside Daphnis. Both → Hermesianax (fr. 2 and 3 POWELL) and → Sositheus (fr. 1a–3 SNELL) mention his unrequited love for Daphnis. In → Vergilius' *Bucolica* his name appears frequently as the poet's *alter ego* and as a figure associated with a tragic love story. M. is probably not a historical person.

> F. MICHELAZZO, s.v. Menalca, Enciclopedia Virgiliana, 3, 1987, 477–480 (with bibl.). S.FO.

Menalcidas (Μεναλκίδας/*Menalkídas*). Spartan, of radically pro-Roman disposition. He had been taken into custody in 168 BC at Alexandria for property offences, but was pardoned because he was a favourite of C. → Popillius Laenas (Pol. 30,16,2). In 151/0, as strategos of the Achaean League (→ Achaeans with map), during the corruption case concerning the Achaean commitment to Oropus, he betrayed → Callicrates [11], bribed → Diaeus and, condemned to death in the escalating Achaean-Spartan conflict, fled to Rome

(149/8). There, M.'s agitation furthered the outbreak of the Achaean War (Paus. 7,11,7–12,9; cf. Pol. 38,18,6), in the course of which his Spartan adversaries compelled him to take his own life (Paus. 7,13,7f.).

P. CARTLEDGE, A. SPAWFORTH, Hellenistic and Roman Sparta, 1989, 87–89; J. DEININGER, Der politische Widerstand gegen Rom in Griechenland, 1971, 220–222.
L.-M.G.

Menalippus (Μενάλιππος/*Menálippos*). Brother of → Tydeus, who accidentally killed him while hunting (Hyg. Fab. 69; schol. Stat. Theb. 1,402; 2,113; TRF I, 190ff., there also in the variant 'Melanippus').   CL.K.

Menambis According to Ptol. (6,7,38; 8,22,13, Μενάμβις βασίλειον; *Menámbis basíleion*) the capital of → Arabia Felix, on Ptolemy's map to the north west of the Κλῖμαξ ὄρος (*Klîmax óros*) and a day's journey from → Magulaba. It may have been a royal frontier fort of the Hadramauts (→ Ḥaḍramaut) against the Ḥimyār (Homeritae) and Sabaeans (→ Saba). There may be a connexion between the name and that of Banū Munabbih, who according to Arabic sources (Hamdāni, Ǧazīra 167 MÜLLER) settled there in the Islamic period.

H.v. WISSMANN, M. HÖFNER, Beiträge zur historischen Geographie des vorislamischen Südarabien (AAWM, Geistes- und Sozialwiss. Klasse), 1952, no. 4, 37, 40, 114; H.v. WISSMANN, Zur Geschichte und Landeskunde von Altsüdarabien (SAWW, Phil.-histor. Klasse 246), 1964, 416, 417 (map).   I.T.-N.

Menander (Μένανδρος; *Ménandros*).
[1] The Athenians M. and Euthydemus [1], who were already in Sicily, were chosen as joint *strategoi* of → Nicias towards the end of 414 BC, during the Sicilian Expedition, to support him until the relief expedition of Demosthenes [1] arrived (413) (Thucyd. 7,16,1; Plut. Nicias 20,2); re-elected 413/12 (Plut. Nicias 20,6–8; Thucyd. 7,69,4; Diod. 13, 13,2). Possibly identical with the M. who fought in Abydus in 409 (Xen. Hell. 1,2,16). He was *stratēgós* with → Tydeus (405/4) in the defeat at → Aigos potamoi (Xen. Hell. 2,1,16; 26; Plut. Alcibiades 36,6); nothing is known of his death.

DEVELIN 152f.; PA 9857; TRAILL, PAA 641065.   K.KI.

[2] *Hetaîros* of → Alexander [4] the Great. At first, M. led the Greek mercenaries, and in 333 BC he became satrap (→ *satrápēs*) of Lydia; however, he extended his territory up to Mysia (Syll.³ 302). In 324/3 he was recalled and brought reinforcements to Alexander at Babylon (Arr. An. 7,23,1; 24,1). He is said to have taken part in → Medius' [2] carouse. After the death of Alexander, M. regained Lydia, but in 321, when → Antigonus [1] landed in Asia, he joined him, serving under him as an officer against → Eumenes [1] (Plut. Eumenes 9; Diod. 18,59,1). M. had his portrait painted by → Apelles [4] (Plin. HN 35,93).
[3] *Hetaîros* of → Alexander [4] the Great, by whom M. is said to have been killed when he refused to accept a

garrison command (only in Plut. Alexander 57,3). The anecdote is unlikely to be true.   E.B.

[4] Menander, the most important poet of the New Comedy in Athens.
A. LIFE AND CAREER B. WORKS C. CHARACTERISTICS D. INFLUENCE

A. LIFE AND CAREER
M. was born in 342/1 BC [1. test. 2] and died at the age of 52 [1. test. 2, 3, 46], in 291/0 [27], allegedly by drowning in the Piraeus [1. test. *23]. He is said to have performed his military service as an Ephebe (→ Ephebeia) together with → Epicurus [1. test. 7]; it remains open to doubt whether the comic poet → Alexis, who was his teacher [1. test. 3], was also his uncle [1. test. 6]. There is evidence of connections to the → Peripatos: → Theophrastus is mentioned as M.'s teacher [1. test. 8], and the favour of → Demetrius [4] of Phalerum [1. test. 10] is even said to have put M. in political danger after Demetrius' fall [1. test. 9]. He had his first play, *Orgḗ* ('Wrath'), performed when in his early twenties (321; 1. test. 3, 49), and won his first competition victory (at the Dionysia?) in 315 [1. test. 48]; on the other hand, there is evidence that his *Dýskolos*, probably performed in 316, won a victory at the Lenaea [1. test. 50]. He took only fifth place, probably in 312 and 311, with *Hēníochos* and *Paidíon* [1. test. *51]. Only a few other pieces can be roughly dated (*Méthē*: before 318; *Olynthía*: soon after 314/3). In total, M. is said to have written 105 [1. test. 46], 108 [1. test. 1, 3, 63] or 109 [1. test. 46] pieces, but to have been victorious on eight occasions only [1. test. 46; cf. test. 98]; even in antiquity, the greater success of his rival → Philemon was found disconcerting [1. test. 71, 101, 114].

B. WORKS
Owing to the lack of chronological information, the following overview is arranged according to the state of rediscovery of M.'s dramas. At the present time, the following pieces are known entirely or in part:

1) Ἀσπίς (*Aspís*, 'The Shield'; approx. the first 60% preserved): A faithful slave of a master who has apparently died in battle as a mercenary uses wit and imagination to defend the master's sister from her acquisitive uncle, who wishes to marry her for her wealthy inheritance.

2) Δύσκολος (*Dýskolos*, 'The Grouch'; hitherto only piece almost completely preserved): A misanthropic farmer (title role) is persuaded by the initially unsuccessful efforts of several people and, above all, by suffering an accident, to give his daughter's hand in marriage to a wealthy city youth, who has fallen in love with her through the influence of the god Pan (prologue figure).

3) Ἐπιτρέποντες (*Epitrépontes*, 'The Court of Arbitration'; almost the whole of act 2, and parts of acts 1 and 3–5 preserved): Marital crisis of a pair of newlyweds, brought about by the husband's assumption that

the child born five months after the marriage is another's, until – above all through the influence of a 'good' hetaera – it turns out that the man himself was the progenitor; the child is the point of contention in the glorious court scene in the second act which gives the piece its name.

4) Κόλαξ (*Kólax*, 'The Flatterer'; approx. 140 verses or parts of verses from various scenes preserved): A soldier (supported by the title figure) and a young man (perhaps supported by a parasite) compete for a hetaera, who is in the power of a brothel-keeper.

5) Μισούμενος (*Misoúmenos*, 'The Hated Man'; thanks to numerous papyri from the 1st to 5th/6th cents. AD, which attest to the popularity of the work, a total of more than 590 verses exist in whole or in part): profound disagreement between a soldier (title role) and his concubine, a prisoner of war, who believes him to be the murderer of her brother, until the latter appears alive.

6) Περικειρομένη (*Perikeiroménē*, 'The Girl With Her Hair Cut Short'; approx. 450 verses from all acts preserved): a jealous soldier cuts off his lover's hair when she is apparently caught with another man, who, however, proves to be her twin brother.

7) Σαμία (*Samía*, 'The Woman of Samos', with more than 730 verses in existence, the second-best preserved piece): misunderstandings between father and son delay the wedding (desired by everyone in the play!) between the son and the neighbour's daughter, whom the son has made pregnant while his father was away; the helpful concubine (title role) of the father almost becomes an innocent victim of the crisis.

8) Σικυώνιος/-οι (*Sikyónios/-oi*, 'The Sicyonian(s)'; around 420, some very fragmentary, verses preserved, including a long quasi-tragic messenger's speech which clearly echoes Eur. Or. 866ff.): the theme here is the identity and good fortune in love of an officer (title role), who proves to be an Athenian and the brother of the man who seeks to vie with him for the favour of his beloved.

Individual scenes or parts of scenes have so far come to light from the following pieces: 1) Geōrgós ('The Farmer'); 2) Dís exapatón ('The Double Deceiver': POxy. 4407 contains 113 verses (some, however, very badly damaged), which correspond to Plaut. Bacch. 494–562); 3) Hḗrōs ('The Guardian Spirit'); 4) Theophorouménē ('The Woman possessed by a God'); 5) Karchēdónios ('The Man from Carthage'); 6) Kitharistḗs ('The Lyre Player'); 7) Kōneiazómenai ('Women Drinking Hemlock'); 8) Leukadía ('The Girl from Leucas'); 9) Perinthía ('The Girl from Perinthus'; according to Ter. Andr. 9–14, M.'s Andría, which he copied, was similar in many respects to this piece); 10) Phásma ('The Apparition').

C. CHARACTERISTICS

M. can be described as the zenith and the perfector of the New → Comedy: he was the master of all its conventions, and was therefore able to play with them –

and with the expectations of the audience. The figures appearing in the plays, with their archetypical characteristics, were developed before M., but he portrayed them supremely, so that to some extent they emerge as individuals; the soldiers here do not merely swagger, but are prone to noble feelings and faithful love (*Misoúmenos*, *Perikeiroménē*, *Sikyónios/-oi*), and the hetaeras are not merely avaricious and egotistical, but also well-meaning and insightful (*Epitrépontes*, *Samía*).The great realism with which M. brought the civic life of Athens (including its often subtle legal aspects) to the stage [28. 94–141] was already extolled in antiquity [1. test. 83]. Quintilian also pointed out how strongly M. was evidently inspired by → Euripides [1] [1. test. 101]; the juxtaposition – and sometimes merging together – of comic and tragic situations is typical of M.'s comedies. His language, too, was much admired [1. test. 101, 103f.]: it was more consistent than that of → Aristophanes [3], but succeeded also in attaining great wealth of nuance in the characterisation of individual speakers [30. 201–251].

M. is the first (though he probably did not invent the idea), to use the fixed five-act structure, which became obligatory in subsequent European theatrical history. The flexible structuring of exposition is noteworthy: actual prologues (e.g. of gods bringing a 'higher' perspective on events) often (*Aspís*, *Epitrépontes*?, *Hḗrōs*?, *Misoúmenos*?, *Perikeiroménē*, *Phásma*) occur only after an introductory dialogue scene. New dramatic developments are often introduced just before the ends of acts; towards the ends of pieces, farcical elements come to the fore [28. 59].

D. INFLUENCE

Interest in M. among literary historians began early: the probably anecdotic work (in 2 vols.) of his younger contemporary → Lynceus [1. test. 75] was followed by the important study of → Aristophanes [4] of Byzantium, who valued M. highly as a portrayer of human life [1. test. 83] and evidently undertook careful investigations into M.'s relationship to earlier authors [1. test. 76]. There is evidence of a commentary on M.'s Kólax by Timachides (=Timachidas of Rhodes) [1. test. 77], of complete commentaries by → Didymus [1] Chalcenterus [1. test. 78] and Soteridas [1. test. 79], summaries of the plays by Homerus Sellius [1. test. 80], by → Latinus [4] 6 bks. on M.'s borrowing from other poets [1. test. 81], and a commentary on the *Theophorouménē* by Nicadius (?) and Harmatius (?) [1. test. 82].

More than 70 images of the poet still survive; their archetype was erected in the Theatre of Dionysus at Athens at the beginning of the 3rd cent. BC [1 test. 25]. There is also a striking number of illustrations of M.'s plays; murals and mosaics (at Oescus, Pompeii, Mytilene, Cydonia, Ephesus) show scenes from *Achaioí*, *Encheirídion*, *Epitrépontes*, *Theophorouménē*, *Kybernḗtai*, *Leukadía*, *Messēnía*, *Misoúmenos*, *Perikeiroménē*, *Plókion*, *Samía*, *Sikyónios/-oi*, *Synaristṓsai*, *Phásma*.

These depictions also attest to the great posthumous success M. enjoyed on the stage, for although he was often overshadowed by Philemon during his lifetime (cf. above), his plays were later regarded as 'more dramatic' [1. test. 84]. A revival of *Phásma* in 262 or 258 won a 2nd prize [1. test. 53], another is reported from 167 [1. test. 55], and the *Misogýnēs* was revived in 193 [1. test. 54]. M.'s plays were favourite models for Roman dramatists [1. test. 62]: for → Plautus (*Adelphoí* αʹ/*Stichus*, *Dís exapatón*/*Bacchides* [29], *Synaristósai*/*Cistellaria*; *Ápistos* or *Thēsaurós*?/ *Aulularia*), → Caecilius [III 6] Statius (*Andría*?, *Andrógynos*, *Dárdanos*, *Ímbrioi*, *Karínē*?, *Naúklēros*?, *Plókion*, *Progamón*, *Pōlúmenoi*, *Synaristósai*, *Synéphēboi*, *Títyē*?, *Hymnís*, *Hypobolimaíos*?, *Chalkeía*), → Turpilius (*Dēmiourgós*, *Epíklēros*, *Thrasyléōn*, *Kanēphóros*, *Leukadía*), → Luscius [I 2] Lanuvinus (*Thēsaurós*?, *Phásma*), → Atilius [I 1] (*Misogýnēs*), → Terentius (*Adelphoí* βʹ, *Andría*, *Hautón timōroúmenos*, *Eunoúchos*; he also used parts of *Kólax* and *Perinthía*), → Afranius [4] (*Thaís*; cf. also [1. test. 66f.]). Emulators of the Imperial period included → Vergilius Romanus [1. test. 68] and → Pomponius Bassulus [1. test. 69].

To the Roman poets Ovid [1. test. 90–92], Manilius [1. test. 94] and Martial [1. test. 98], M. was the epitome of Greek comedy, as he was to many Imperial period representatives of rhetoric (Theon [1. test. 108], Quintilian [1. test. 10f.], Dion [I 3] of Prusa [1. test. 102], Apuleius [1. test. 114], Hermogenes [1. test. 116], Themistius [1. test. 126]). Plutarch clearly preferred M. to Aristophanes [1. test. 103f.], while for Ausonius he was the equal of Homer [1. test. 128]. The eagerness with which M. was read up to the end of antiquity (in the West, Sidonius was still reading the *Epitrépontes* in the original [3. I p. xxiii], and in the East, reading of M. demonstrably continued into the 7th cent. [3. ibid.]) is shown by the richness of the papyrus finds, exceeded only by those of Homer and Euripides. However, with the rise of the linguistic severity of → Atticism (2nd cent. AD), M.'s star began to wane: the grammarian → Phrynichus inveighed against the high renown accorded to M. among the educated men of his day [1. test. 119]; → Iulius [IV 17] Pollux, too, allowed him only limited acceptance as a linguistic model [1. test. 120]. This criticism caused M. to be removed from the syllabus of higher education, and therefore after the 'Dark Ages' there are no texts by M. left at Byzantium to be transliterated into minuscules. Only a collection of aphorisms (monosticha) from M.'s plays survives [24], adulterated with much inauthenticity, and around 900 (mostly brief) quotation fragments, many of them included by reason of their moralizing content in the anthology of Iohannes → Stobaeus. The first modest new discoveries were made in 1844, and since 1905 (discovery of the Cairo Codex), papyri have allowed ever greater portions of M.'s works to be won back (Details in [3. I p. xxvi-xxix]).

→ Comedy; → Comedy

EDNS.: TESTIMONIA AND QUOTATION FRAGMENTS: 1 PCG VI 2, 1998. TEXTS ON PAPYRUS: 2 F. H. SANDBACH, ²1990   3 W. G. ARNOTT, Vol. I: *Aspís – Epitrépontes*, 1979; Vol. 2: *Hḗrōs – Perinthía*, 1996. COMMENTARIES ON THE PAPYRUS TEXTS: 4 A. W. GOMME, F. H. SANDBACH, 1973. COMMENTED INDIVIDUAL EDITIONS: ASPÍS: 5 C. AUSTIN, 1969–70   6 F. SISTI, 1971   7 A. BORGOGNO, 1972   8 J.-M. JACQUES, 1998. DÝSKOLOS: 9 E. W. HANDLEY, 1965   10 J.-M. JACQUES, ²1976   11 ST. IRELAND, 1995. EPITRÉPONTES: 12 U.v. WILAMOWITZ, 1925   13 F. SISTI, 1991   14 A. MARTINA, 1997. MISOÚMENOS: 15 F. SISTI, 1985. PERIKEIROMÉNĒ: 16 M. LAMAGNA, 1994. SAMÍA: 17 C. AUSTIN, 1969–70   18 J.-M. JACQUES, 1971   19 F. SISTI, 1974   20 D. M. BAIN, 1983   21 M. LAMAGNA, 1998. SIKYÓNIOS/-OI: 22 R. KASSEL, 1965   23 A. M. BELARDINELLI, 1994. MENANDRI MONOSTICHA: 24 S. JAEKEL, 1964. LITERATURE: 25 A. G. KATSOURIS, Menander Bibliography, 1995   26 H.-D. BLUME, Menander, 1998; 27 ST. SCHRÖDER, Die Lebensdaten Menanders, in: ZPE 113, 1996, 35–48   28 N. ZAGAGI, The Comedy of Menander: Convention, Variation and Originality, 1994   29 O. ZWIERLEIN, Zur Kritik und Exegese des Plautus 1, 1990, 24–40; 2, 1992   30 M. KRIETER-SPIRO, Sklaven, Köche und Hetären: Das Dienstpersonal bei Menander, 1997.

H.-G.NE.

[5] M. of Ephesus said to be a pupil of → Eratosthenes [2] (T 1), approx. 200 BC. According to Josephus, (c. Ap. 1,116 = T 3c), M. described 'the events among the Greeks and Barbarians during the reigns of the individual kings, according to the indigenous sources', thus composing a universal chronicle on a chronographic and documentary foundation. Thanks to his 'Translation of the old records of the Tyrians' (thus T 3 a and b), he was an important source for the history of Tyre in particular. Of the seven surviving fragments, F 4 is particularly informative.

EDN.: FGrH 783. LITERATURE: O. LENDLE, Einführung in die griechische Geschichtsschreibung, 1992, 202–205; L. TROIANI, Osservazioni sopra l'opera storiografica di Menandro d'Efeso, in: S. F. BONDÌ et al (Ed.), Studi in onore di E. Bresciani, 1985, 521ff.   K.MEI.

[6] M.I. Soter One of the most important Indo-Greek kings, of around the mid–2nd cent. BC, known from Greek, Roman and Indian literature alike. According to Strabo (11,11,1), who was relying on Apollodorus of Artemita, M. was the real conqueror of India, along with → Demetrius [10]. Pompeius Trogus (41) deals with Indian history during the time of → Apollodotus and M. M.'s kingdom stretched from the Hindu Kush to the Punjab, but was divided after his death: in the east, his widow → Agathoclea [4] ruled with his son Strato. After M.'s death, his ashes were shared between several cities (Plut. Mor. 821). In his numerous coin

issues, M. is known by the Middle Indian name Menaṃdra Tratara, and in inscriptions as Mine(ṃ)dra. His fame lives on in India in the *Milindapañha*, a Buddhist work containing dialogues between M. (Milinda) and the Buddhist saint Nagasena.
→ India

BOPEARACHCHI, 76–88, 226–247; O. BOPEARACHCHI, Ménandre Sôter, un roi indo-grec. Observations chronologiques et géographiques, in: Studia Iranica 19, 1990, 39–85; G. FUSSMAN, L'indo-grec Ménandre ou Paul Demiéville revisité, in: Journal Asiatique 281, 1993, 61–138. K.K.

[7] Son of Melas, sculptor from Athens, active on Delos in the late 2nd cent. BC. Alongside dedications to Sarapis, he created a Poseidon statue, now lost, for the Institution of the Poseidoniasts. His signature on the pedestal of the Roma statue preserved there may not refer to that statue, as the pedestal was altered or reused at a later date.

L. GUERRINI, s.v. M. (1), EAA 4, 1961, 1016; A. LINFERT, Kunstzentren hellenistischer Zeit, 1976, 114; J. MARCADÉ, Recueil des signatures de sculpteurs grecs, 2, 1957, 67f.; Id., Au musée de Délos, 1969, 128–133; H. MEYER, Zur Chronologie des Poseidoniastenhauses in Delos, in: MDAI(A) 103, 1988, 203–220; A. STEWART, Attika, 1979, 65. R.N.

[8] **M. II. Dikaios** Indo-Greek King in → Arachosia and → Gandaritis, approx. 1st cent. BC, only known from coins. He can be distinguished from his great namesake and predecessor M. [6] I. Soter by his by-name and the entirely different style of coinage. M. is known on his coins by the Middle Indian name Menaṃdra Dhramika.
→ India

BOPEARACHCHI, 108f., 313–316. K.K.

[9] M. of Laodicea, cavalry officer of → Mithridates VI, with Taxiles and Diophantus [2] in the entourage of the king's son of the same name when he fought in the 1st → Mithridatic War of 85 BC against C. Flavius [I 6] Fimbria at the → Rhyndacus near Miletopolis in Bithynia (Memnon FGrH 434 F 1,24,4; [1. 175]). In the 3rd Mithridatic War of 71, M. was defeated by Sornatius, a legate of Licinius [I 26] Lucullus, at → Cabira in Pontus (Plut. Lucullus 17,1), and he was displayed in the triumphal procession of → Pompeius on 28./29.9.61 (App. Mithr. 573; [2. 409f.]).

1 L. BALLESTEROS PASTOR, Mitrídates Eupátor, 1996 2 TH. REINACH, Mithradates Eupator, 1895 (reprint 1975).

E. OLSHAUSEN, Zum Hellenisierungsprozeß am Pontischen Königshof, in: AncSoc 5, 1974, 153–170. E.O.

[10] Son of Diogenes, sculptor of Docymeum. A late Hellenistic seated statue of Zeus from Antioch in Pisidia bears his signature.

H. BUCKLER, Monuments from Iconium, Lycaonia and Isauria, in: JRS 14, 1924, 30f. no.9; L. GUERRINI, s.v. M. (2), EAA 4, 1961, 1016. R.N.

[11] Gnostic from Samara (Capparetaea), taught at Syrian Antioch around the turn of the 2nd cent. AD. Just. Mart. Apol. 1,26,4 describes him as a pupil of → Simon and a magician. According to Irenaeus (Adv. haereses 1,23,5) he purported to be able to exercise power over the world-creating angels. He made himself out to be the saviour (*salvator*) sent by the First Power; anyone baptized by him would attain immortality; his pupils were said to be → Satornil and Basilides. The credibility of all of this information is weak, since it arose from the attempt to create a lineage of heretics (→ Heresy). Later sources depend on Iustinus [6] and Irenaeus (= Eirenaios [2]).
→ Gnosticism

C. S. CLIFTON, Menander the Samaritan, in: Encyclopedia of Heresies and Heretics, 1992, 95. J.HO.

[12] **M. Rhetor** Greek rhetor of the late 3rd cent. AD, from Laodicea, by the Lycus. The texts ascribed to him in the Suda (commentaries on Hermogenes, Minucianus, probably also Demosthenes, etc.) are lost; two treatises in his name survive concerning types of epideictic oratory: the first deals with speeches praising gods, countries and cities, etc., the second gives rules for addressing high dignitaries and speaking on particular occasions (for the first time also for the funeral oration). Owing to linguistic and stylistic differences, many reject the possibility [2] that these two pieces shared the same author; a surviving variant of the title of the first treatise in the Cod. Parisinus of 1741 may indicate → Genethlius as its author; others [3] ascribe both treatises to M.

EDN. WITH TRANSLATION AND COMMENTARY: 1 D. A. RUSSELL, N. G. WILSON, 1981.
LITERATURE: 2 L. PERNOT, Les topoi de l'éloge chez M. le rhéteur, in: REG 99, 1986, 33–53 3 J. SOFFEL, Die Regeln Menanders für die Leichenrede, thesis Mainz, 1974. M.W.

[13] **M. Protector** Byzantine historian of the second half of the 6th cent. AD; lawyer; lived in Constantinople as an officer of the palace guard of the *protectores,* and continued the work of → Agathias, whose style he also imitated, in writing his *Historíai* ('History') of the period 558 to 582. No fewer than 70 excerpts of this work are preserved by → Constantinus [1] VII. Porphyrogenitus and in the → Suda; some anonymous excerpts in the Suda can also probably be ascribed to M. In his writings, M. betrays a clear preference for the east of the empire; he strove for objectivity, e.g. by using embassy reports (fragment 6,1 on the peace negotiations of 561 between the Emperor Justinian I and Chosroes I of Persia) and documents, and included many geographical and ethnological digressions. As the sole exhaustive contemporary source for the period in question, his work was much used by later Byzantine historians. M. is also the author of the epigram Anth. Pal. 1,101.

EDN.: R. C. BLOCKLEY, The History of Menander the Guardsman, 1985.
LITERATURE: O. VEH, Beiträge zu Menander Protektor, 1955; B. BALDWIN, Menander Protector, in: Dumbarton Oaks Papers 32, 1978, 99–125. AL.B.

Menapii People of the North Sea coast of what is now Flanders, originally also north of the Rhine delta (Caes. B Gall. 4,4,2; Strab. 4,3,4). In 56/5 BC, the Germanic → Usipetes and → Tencteri crossed the Rhine, driving the M. out of their homelands on the right bank of the Rhine (Caes. B Gall. 4,4). The frontier of the *Civitas Menapiorum* formed after their subjugation by Rome in 53 BC (stages of conquest 58 BC, Caes. B Gall. 2,4,9; 56 BC, Caes. B Gall. 3,9,10; 3,28f.; Cass. Dio 39,44; 55 BC, Caes. Gall. 4,22,5; 38,3; 53 BC, Caes. Gall. 6,5,6) ran along the coast in the north and west from the mouth of the Maas to the Aa, upstream on the latter to the east of St. Omer, meeting the Leie to the south and following it downstream to the mouth of the Dijle, then following this upstream to the south to Carvin and on through Orchie to the Scarpe. After the confluence of this with the Schelde, whose main branch in antiquity did not flow directly into the sea but into the Maas, the Schelde formed the frontier [1].

Prior to the Roman conquest, the M. had a scattered, socially egalitarian society, as archaeology confirms. The continuity of indigenous materials into the Roman period is, however, noteworthy. Rather than giving way to the development of Gallo-Roman *vici* or *villae rusticae*, autochthonous settlement units structured according to family bonds survived and small village-like structures developed (e.g. Asper, Eke, Sint-Martens-Latem). In many cultural spheres, the M. held on to pre-Roman traditions [2]. They developed economic activities in salt mining, the trading of salt (CIL XI 390 [3]) and in the marketing of their famous ham (Mart. 13,54; Edictum Diocletiani 4,8). Sparse remains of the main settlement of Castellum (Ptol. 2,9,5; Tab. Peut. 2,2; It. Ant. 376; CIL XIII 9158; modern Cassel, Département du Nord in France), which was abandoned in late antiquity [4], are preserved. The southern part of the *civitas* was more strongly Romanized. This is the modern Pévèle, between the Leie and the Schelde and between the Dijle and the Scarpe, with the Roman *vici* of Cortoriacum (modern Kortrijk), Gent (Ganda?), Kruishoutem and Turnacum. In Diocletian's and Constantine's periods, Turnacum was the capital, and the *civitas* was renamed the *civitas Turnacensium* (cf. Not. Gall. 6,8).

1 S. J. DE LAET, Les limites des cités des Ménapiens et des Morins, in: Helinium 1, 1961, 20–34 2 F. VERMEULEN, Moderate Acculturation in the Fringe Area of the Roman Empire... , in: Bull. de l'institut historique belge de Rome 62, 1992, 5–41 3 E. WILL, Le sel des Morins et des Ménapiens, in: M. RENARD (ed.), Hommages à A. Grenier 3, 1962, 1649–1657 4 P. LEMAN, Chef-lieu de la cité des Ménapiens, in: Les villes de la Gaule Belgique au Haut-Empire, Actes du colloque Saint Riquier 1982, 1984, 139–147. F.SCH.

Menas (Μηνᾶς; *Menâs*).
[1] One of the Spartiates who in 421 BC swore the Peace of → Nicias and the symmachy with Athens (Thucyd. 5,19,2; 5,24,1). In the interval between these treaties he was one of the emissaries who, by the terms of the peace, were to guarantee the transfer of → Amphipolis to Athens, but owing to the resistance of → Clearidas, the commandant there, failed (Thucyd. 5,21). K.-W.W.
[2] see → Menodorus [1]
[3] Son of Ajax, sculptor from Pergamum. According to the surviving signature, M. created the mid–2nd century BC statue of Alexander [4] the Great at Magnesia ad Sipylum (Istanbul, AM), the model for which stood at Pergamum.

L. GUERRINI, s.v. M. (1) (fig.), EAA 4, 1961, 1016; LIPPOLD, 271, 359; B. S. RIDGWAY, Hellenistic Sculpture, 1, 1990, 144. R.N.

[4] Egyptian martyr (?), died in AD 295 (296) at Cotyaeum (Phrygia). M. withdrew from Roman military service into the desert and preached his Christian beliefs in the Circus of Cotyaeum. He is said to have been executed after a trial. Legends, translated from Coptic into Greek and through Arabic into Ethiopic tell of frequent miracles around his cult site in Mareotis in Lower Egypt. His saint's cult spread to Alexandria [1] and Rome.

F. JARITZ, Die arabischen Quellen zum heiligen M., 1993. K.SA.

Menches Greek name: Asclepiades (*ho kaì Asklēpiádēs héllēn enchórios tôn katoíkōn*), son of Petesouchus, Greek: Ammónios (*toû kaì Ammoníou*), and grandson of Asclepiades (PTebtunis I 164). He is a typical example of how double Graeco-Egyptian names could be used in Ptolemaic Egypt, according to context. M. is mentioned again in August 119 BC as → *kōmogrammateús* of Cerceosiris. He served until 111 BC. M.'s 'archive' (PTebt I; IV) is the most important source for the office of *kōmogrammateús* in the Ptolemaic period. The necessary payments for M.'s official appointment were made by one Dorion, *tôn prótōn phílon*, of Alexandria, but the intention behind this cannot be determined nor can the extent of the custom be assessed.

A. VERHOOGT, M., Komogrammateus of Kerkeosiris, 1998. W.A.

Mende (Μένδη; *Méndē*). Town on the western coast of → Pallene [4] near the modern Kalandra on the Chalcidian Peninsula, a colony of Eretria [1] which owed its blossoming from the 6th century BC to a famous wine and the profits from its export. Images on the town's coins, which were minted from as early as the 6th century, also make reference to the wine. In the Athenian tribute quota lists, M. is recorded with a tribute fluctuating between five and nine talents. After the outbreak of the → Peloponnesian War in 431, M. initially remained on the side of the Athenians, only going over to the Spartans at the instigation of the Oligarchs in 423, but it was soon to be won back. In the first half of the 4th century, M. largely preserved its autonomy until its conquest by Philip II. Its decline began only with the foundation of the town of Cassandria (→ Potidaea), to the territory of which it subsequently belonged. M. is last mentioned in literature as a *maritimus vicus* of Cassandria in the year 199 BC.

F. PAPAZOGLOU, Les villes de Macedoine à l'époque romaine, 1988, 427–429; M. ZAHRNT, Olynth und die Chalkidier, 1971, 200–203. M.Z.

Mendes (Egyptian *'np.t* or (*Pr-bꜣ-nb*)-*Ḏd.t*; modern Tall al-Rubꜥ). Town in the north eastern Nile delta, metropolis of the 16th nome of Lower Egypt and cultic centre of the ram god *Bꜣ-nb-Ḏd.t* ('Ram, Lord of M.'). Recent excavations have unearthed extensive findings from as early as the Old Kingdom, including a cemetery for public officials from the 6th Dynasty (2290–2157 BC) and the 1st Intermediate Period (2154–2040). Other remains provide evidence of a temple of the New Kingdom. M. flourished particularly in the Late Period and the Ptolemaic Period (8th–1st cents. BC); in the Roman Imperial period, M.'s importance waned in favour of its neighbour → Thmuis (Tell Timai).

H. DE MEULENAERE, s.v. Mendes, LÄ 4, 43–45. S.S.

Mene see. → Selene

Menecleidas (Μενεκλείδας/*Menekleídas*). Theban orator and politician of the 4th century BC. The main source (Plut. Pelopidas 25, 290f–291d) does describe him as a man powerful in speech, but also as a man of intrigue, who forced → Epameinondas out of the boeotarchy, and who tried to disparage → Pelopidas by playing off Charon against him. In a paranomy lawsuit (accusation of proposing an illegal resolution), a large fine was imposed on Menecleidas, but this did not prevent him from further agitation against Thebes. Nepos (Epaminondas 5,2) lists two examples of Menecleidas's hostility to Epaminondas and the latter's quick-witted replies (cf. also Plut. Mor. 542b). Plut. Mor. 805c mentions Menecleidas as the paradigm of one who disparages a merited statesman out of envy. M.W.

Menecles (Μενεκλῆς/*Meneklês*).
[1] Athenian. In 350 and 347 BC he was → synegoros for Boeotus (→ Mantitheus [3]) and his mother → Plangon in two lawsuits (Dem. Or. 39,2; 40,9f.; 32). Allegedly a sycophant, Menecles was himself accused by Ninus's son. The prosecution speech (Din. fr. 33 CONOMIS) was attributed to → Dinarchus.

SCHÄFER, Beilagen 1885, 211–226
PA 9908; TRAILL, PAA 643135. J.E.

[2] Menecles from Barca in northern Africa, a Greek historian and antiquarian of the 2nd cent. BC. Of his 'history of Libya' (*Libykaí Historíai*) in four books only fragments (on Cyrene) survive. Menecles probably also wrote a compilation (*synagōgḗ*) with ethnographical content and a work explaining unusual words (*glōssókomon*). It is doubtful whether he is identical with → Menecles [3]. FGrH 270.

[3] Author or reviser of the periegetic work *Perí Athēnṓn* ('On Athens'), which must have appeared before the destruction of the city by Sulla in 86 BC. Fragments survive of a single book, introduced with 'Menecles and Callicrates' or perhaps 'Callicrates or Menecles'. Which of the two was the author and which the reviser must remain unsettled, as must identification with Menecles [2] from Barca. FGrH 370. K.BRO.

[4] Rhetorician of the 2nd and 1st cents. BC from Alabanda in Caria (Str. 14,2,26=661). Among his pupils were the teachers of rhetoric → Apollonius [5], who later moved to Rhodes, and → Molon (Str. 14,2,13=655). Cicero, who heard the latter in 78 on Rhodes, characterised the sort of Asianist style cultivated by Menecles and his brother→ Hierocles [2] as follows: preference for brilliantly worded but often superfluous and purposeless sentences (Cic. Brut. 325f.), and lack of variation of rhythm (→ Prose Rhythm) in clauses (Cic. Orat. 231). In all, however, he considers Menecles and Hierocles rather praiseworthy representatives of → Asianism (ibid.) and stresses their wide influence (De or. 2,95). A papyrus fragment of an accusation, modelled on the → Arginusae case, against the captain of a ship [1] may be attributed to Menecles.

1 K. JANDER (ed.), Oratorum et Rhetorum Graecorum fragmenta nuper reperta, 1913, 26–30. M.W.

Menecrates (Μενεκράτης; *Menekrátes*).
[1] Attic comic poet of the 5th cent. BC. Two titles of his plays have survived, Ἑρμιονεύς/*Hermioneús* (or Ἑρμιόνη/*Hermiónē*?) and Μανέκτωρ/*Manéktōr* (probably 'Manes as Hector') [1. test. 1], as well as an anapaestic tetrameter (fr. 1) from the latter. It is uncertain whether Menecrates was once victorious at the Dionysia [1. test. *2].

1 PCG VII, 1989, 1–2. H.-G.NE.

[2] Greek tragic poet, victor at the Great Dionysia in 422 BC (TrGF 35 T 1), perhaps identical with the successful actor who was victorious four times at the Dionysia (after 430) and once at the Lenaea (*c.* 431). B.Z.

[3] **Menecrates from Syracuse** Greek physician, fl. 350 BC. He believed the body was formed of four elements, two hot, blood and bile, and two cold, pneuma and phlegm (Anon. Londinensis 19) (→ Humoral Theory). An (allegedly unsuccessful) treatment for epilepsy is mentioned by Caelius [II 11] Aurelianus (Morb. chron. 1,140), but Athenaeus (7,289) claims that he made those whom he had cured of the illness attend him as his

slaves and answer to the names of gods. He was called Zeus, either because of his wonderful cures (Plut. Agesilaus 21) or because of his mad ideas, of his self-importance or his theomania (Ael. VH 12,51) [1]. Jokes about his strange behaviour in the presence of (or in correspondence with) Agesilaus [2] or Philip of Macedonia circulated for centuries after his death (Ael. VH 21; Athenaeus 7,289; Plut. Agesilaus 21; Plut. Apophthegmata regum 5; Plut. Apophthegmata Laconica 59). The respect shown by later medical writers for his views suggests that he was not always the mad fool described by the humorists.

1 O. WEINREICH, Menekrates Zeus und Salmoneus, 1933.
V.N.

[4] Menecrates of Xanthus Greek historian of the 4th cent. BC. M. wrote a 'history of Lycia' (Lykiaká) of at least two books in Ionic. Some fragments on the mythical period (F 2: Lycian farmers, F 3 Legend of Aeneas with stylistic exercise!) survive. FGrH 769.   K.MEI.

[5] At an unknown time – if in the Diadochi conflicts, then no later than 295/4 BC – M. tricked his soldiers, who were threatening to run away, into victory when besieging the Cypriot city of Salamis (Polyaenus, Strat. 5,20). It is uncertain whether he is identical with M. [7].

A. MEHL, Seleukos Nikator, 1986, 293f.   A.ME.

[6] Teacher of → Aratus [4], 3rd cent. BC, author of érga in the Hesiodic style in two or more books on agriculture and beekeeping (if the latter was not an separate poem like the Melissourgiká by → Nicander, whom Menecrates imitated). Menecrates was also a grammarian. He is one of the sources of → Varro and → Plinius the Elder.
→ Didactic Poetry

1 SH 542–550   2 H. DIELS, Poetarum Philosophorum Fragmenta, 1901, 171–172   3 M. GEYMONAT, Spigolature nicandree, in: Acme 23, 1970, 140–151.   S.FO.

[7] After Lysimachus's [2] defeat and death in the battle against → Seleucus I, M. led a rebellion in Ephesus in 281 BC and killed a woman he thought to be Lysimachus's widow Arsinoe (Polyaenus, Strat. 8,57). It is uncertain whether he is identical with M. [9].

A. MEHL, Seleukos Nikator, 1986, 293f.   A.ME.

[8] Son of M., Greek sculptor. According to a surviving signature he worked on the great frieze in → Pergamum (c. 180 BC), but assignation of his contribution has not been possible. → Apollonius [18] and → Tauriscus described themselves as his pupils and adopted sons.

EAA 4, s.v. Menekrates (2), 1961, 1017; C. BÖRKER, Menekrates und die Künstler des Farnesischen Stieres, in: ZPE 64, 1986, 41–49; P. MORENO, Scultura ellenistica, 1994, 437; D. THIMME, The Masters of the Pergamon Gigantomachy, in: AJA 50, 1946, 345–357   R.N.

[9] General (stratēgós) and negotiator for → Perseus in the Third → Macedonian War. In 169 BC, at Demetrias [1], he sounded out whether Eumenes [3] II king of Pergamum was prepared to remain neutral (Pol. 29,61; Liv. 44,24,9).

E. OLSHAUSEN, Prosopographie der hellenistischen Königsgesandten, 1974, 160f.   L.-M.G.

[10] Son of Sopater, sculptor from Thebes. Later, he lived at Delphi. On the evidence of two surviving bases with signatures, he and his son Sopater sculpted the statue of a boy victor in about 140 BC and about 110–106 BC a statue for Minucius Rufus after his victory over the Gauls.

L. GUERRINI, s.v. Menekrates (3), EAA 4, 1961, 1017; LIPPOLD, 340; J. MARCADÉ, Recueil des signatures de sculpteurs grecs, 1, 1953, 82f.   R.N.

[11] Freedman of Cn. Pompeius Magnus (Vell. 2,73,3) or his son Sex. Pompeius (Plin. HN 35,200; Cass. Dio 48,46,1). Under the latter, M. made a career as a naval commander around 40 BC. In 38 BC, M. initially gained the upper hand in a sea battle between Ischia and Cumae over admiral Menodorus [1], who had defected to Octavian, but was then severely wounded in a fight with his hated erstwhile colleague, had to surrender his flagship, and threw himself overboard (App. B Civ. 5,343–350; Oros. 6,18,21).   T.FR.

[12] Epigrammatist of the 'Garland' of Meleager [8] (Anth. Pal. 4,1,28). Three poems are ascribed to him: to 'M. from Samos' (Μ. Σάμιος) the epigrams Anth. Pal. 9,54 (= Stob. 4,50,62) and 55 (the alternative ascription to → Lucillius could be correct), two distichs on old age, to 'M. from Smyrna' (Μ. Σμυρναῖος) the poem 9,390 (with a pathos-filled description of an infanticide). To which M. Meleager is referring is impossible to say: the frequency of the name speaks against identification, which would assume a corruption in the ethnika.

GA I.1, 139f.; 2, 398f.   M.G.A.

[13] Interpreter of Homer from Nysa near Tralleis (cf. Str. 14,1,48), author of a comparative 'juxtaposition of the Odyssey and the Iliad' (Σύγκρισις Ὀδυσσείας καὶ Ἰλιάδος; cf. schol. B T Hom. Il. 24,804; FHG II 344–345). The author of περὶ Ὕψους (→ Ps.-Longinus) or → Caecilius [III 5] of Cale Acte probably used the writings of Menecrates (cf. [1]).

1 E. HEFERMEHL, Menekrates von Nysa und die Schrift vom Erhabenen, in: RhM 61, 1906, 283–303.   GR.DA.

Menedaeus (Μενεδάϊος/Menedáios). Spartan, in 426 BC a member of Eurylochus's [2] war council in Acarnania. After Eurylochus's defeat and death at Olpae, he became commander of the Peloponnesian troops there. In a secret agreement the Athenian commander Demosthenes [1] granted him free passage in return for surrender of the Ambraciots (Thuc. 3,100,2; 109,1–3; [1. 30].

1 J. ROISMAN, The General Demosthenes and His Use of
Military Surprise, 1993.   K.-W.W.

Menedemus (Μενέδημος; *Menédēmos*).

[1] sent by → Alexander [4] the Great in 329 BC, with a
1500-strong mercenary infantry, Caranus with 800
mounted mercenaries and Andromachus with 60 → hetairoi, to relieve the fortress of → Maracanda, which
was under siege by → Spitamenes. → Pharnuches, a
Lycian (but certainly descended from Persian settlers)
interpreter, was provided to them as he was familiar
with the inhabitants and their language (Arr. An.
4,3,7). Through the incompetence of the officers and
lack of co-ordination the troops fell into an ambush and
were annihilated by Spitamenes and his Scythian allies
(Arr. An. 4,5,3–9: from Ptolemy (?); otherwise 6,1:
from → Aristobulus [7]). Pharnuches is described by
Arrian (only An. 4,5,5, other passages are ambiguous)
as commander-in-chief. In the same sense he cites Aristobulus (Arr. An. 4,6,1ff.), who however has Pharnuches deny having supreme command. He should probably, as he says and Arrian intimates, be only the leader
and negotiator, but then this most serious debacle of the
campaign was ascribed to him in order to exculpate the
Macedonian officers. Curtius (7,6,24.7,31–39) names
only M., and his narration is novelistic.

A. B. BOSWORTH, A Historical Commentary on Arrian's
History 2, 1995, 23–25; 32–35 (with alternative interpretation).   E.B.

[2] from Croton: as a *strategos* in 317 BC he defeated
and annihilated the aristocrats, who had been driven
out from there, then became tyrant and fell during the
conquest of the city by → Agathocles [2] in 295 (Diod.
Sic. 19,10,3f.; 21,4).   K.MEI.

[3] Rhodian. In 304 BC he conducted a successful naval
war against → Demetrius [2] with three *trihemioliai*,
captured many supply ships and a quadrireme and
either sold the proceeds or sent them to Ptolemy I.

H. HAUBEN, Het Vlootbevelhebberschap in de vroege
Diadochentijd, 1975, 69f.   W.A.

[4] **M. of Pyrrha** Pupil of Plato, who, like Heracleides
[16] Ponticus, was defeated in the 339/8 BC election for
scholarch of the → Academy with only a few votes
against → Xenocrates (Philod. Academicorum index
6,37–7,9 = T 7 L.). He incurred, as did Speusippus and
Plato himself, the mockery of the comedian Epicrates
[4] (T. 5 L. = Epikrates fr. 5 PCG). Like many of Plato's
pupils he was politically active: according to Plut. Adv.
Colotem 32 (= T 6 L.) he developed a constitution for
his native city.

F. LASSERRE, De Léodamas de Thasos à Philippe
d'Oponte, 1987, 91–96, 305–309, 523–529.   K.-H.S.

[5] **M. of Eretria** born 350–45, died 265–60. After they
studied together, initially under → Stilpon in Megara,
then under → Anchipylus and → Moschus in Elis, he
was connected in lifelong friendship with → Asclepia-

des [3] of Phleius and later also by family relationship
after the two married mother and daughter (Diog.
Laert. 2,126; 137). Thanks to the excerpts surviving in
Diog. Laert. (2,129–132; 137–138) of the 'Life of M.'
by → Antigonus [7] of Carystus we know a series of
details of the life the two led together in Eretria and
elsewhere. From the beginning of the 3rd century M.
played a leading role in the political life of Eretria. Later
he enjoyed a close personal relationship with Antigonus
Gonatas. In 274/73 and 268 he held the position of a
hieromnemon in Delphi. Soon after that he had to leave
Eretria for political reasons. He set out initially for Oropus, then to the court of Antigonus [2] Gonatas in Pella.
There he is said to have ended his own life (Diog. Laert.
2,140–143). M. was friendly with the poets → Aratus
[4], → Lycophron and → Antagoras (Diog. Laert.
2,133). In a satyr play named after him by Lycophron it
is described how the chorus of satyrs invade one of M.'s
symposiums in which the richness of the conversation
compensated for the frugality of the food (TrGF 100,
2–4).

Antigonus of Carystus reports (bei Diog. Laert.
2,136) that M. wrote no works at all nor did he commit
himself to any particular form of teaching, but nevertheless was an extremely disputatious debater. According to Diog. Laert. 2,135 'M. took negative statements
and replaced them with affirmative ones, and of these
he accepted the simple ones, the others he removed'. It is
unclear what M. was aiming at with this doctrine. Probably as little was meant by it as the other one he adopted
from his teacher → Stilpon, that nothing can be said of
something other than pure statements of identity, because otherwise different things would be incorrectly
identified with each other by the word 'is' (Simpl. In
Aristot. phys. 91,28–31). In the area of ethics M., like
→ Eucleides [2] of Megara, represented the idea that
there was only one Good or one Virtue and that what
might be described as an individual good or virtue was
only another name for the one Good or Virtue (Plut. De
virt. mor. 440e). Cicero (Acad. 2,129) ascribes to M.
the opinion that this one Good is based 'in thought and
in the acuteness of the thought with which truth is recognised'.

→ Elis and Eretria, School of

EDITIONS: 1 D. KNOEPFLER, La vie de Ménédème d'Eré-
trie de Diogène Laërce, 1991   2 B. A. KYRKOS, Ὁ
Μενέδημος καὶ ἡ Ἐρετρικὴ σχολή, 1980   3 SSR III F.

Literature: 4 K. DÖRING, Menedemos aus Eretria, in:
GGPh2, 1998, 2.1, § 18 B.   K.D.

[6] 3rd century BC. Pupil of the Epicurean → Colotes
(Diog. Laert. 6,102), then of the Cynic Echecles of
Ephesus (ibid. 6,95). According to a proposed interpretation by [1] the section in Diog. Laert. 6,102 dedicated to him in reality refers to → Menippus [4], who is
treated in sections 6,99–101. The confusion here arose
as a result of the incorrect interpretation of the abbreviation Μεν. This hypothesis is corroborated in the
Suda s.v. Φαιός (4,180, p. 710, Z. 13–19 ADLER). In the

case of the M. spoken of by Athenaeus (4, 162 E) and Eus. Pr. Ev. 14,5,13), it is very probably a matter of M. [5] of Eretria.

PHercul. 208 and 1032 preserve excerpts of two works by Colotes (*in Plat. Lys.*, *in Plat. Euthyd.*), in which he polemicises against a M. Here it is probably a matter of the Cynic [2; 5] rather than the philosopher M. [5] from Eretria [3], who it is said left no writings (Antigonus of Carystus in Diog. Laert. 2,136).

→ Epicurean School; → Cynicism

EDITIONS: 1 W. CRÖNERT, Kolotes und Menedemos, 1906 (repr. 1965), 1–4, 167–170   2 SSR II 588f.; IV 581–583.
LITERATURE: 3 A. CONCOLINO MANCINI, Sulle opere polemiche di Colote, in: CE 6, 1976, 61–67   4 K. DÖRING, Sokrates, die Sokratiker und die von ihnen begründeten Traditionen, GGPh2 2.1, 1998, 305   5 M. ERLER, Zur Polemik des Epikureers Kolotes gegen Menedemos, GGPh2 4.1, 1994, 236–238   6 M. GIGANTE, Cinismo e Epicureismo, 1992, 74–78.   M.G.-C.

[7] M. from Alabanda Officer of → Antiochus [5] III, who in 218 BC took part as leader of a unit at the breaching of the Ptolemaic position on the River Lycus [15] or the narrow coastal fringe near Berytus, and in 217 as the commander of Thracians or a lightly armed force at the battle of → Raphia (Pol. 5,69,4; 5,79,6f.; 5,82,10f.). See also M. [8].

H. H. SCHMITT, Untersuchungen zur Geschichte Antiochos' des Großen, 1964, 19.   A.ME.

[8] M., identical with M. [7]?, is mentioned in inscriptions as a *strategos* of → Antiochus [5] III for Media and as a governor-general for the Upper Satrapies in 193 BC [1. 5–8; 2. 469–471].

1 L. ROBERT, Hellenika. Recueil d'épigraphie, de numismatique et d'antiquités grecques, in: Hellenica 7, 1949, 5–8   2 ROBERT, OMS 5, 1989, 469–471   3 H. H. SCHMITT, Untersuchungen zur Geschichte Antiochos' des Großen, 1964, 19.   A.ME.

[9] According to Caes. B. Civ. 3,34,4 the most powerful man (*princeps*) of 'free western' Macedonia (*pars quae libera appellatur*). He conveyed to Caesar the loyalty of his people in 48 BC and received Roman citizenship in return (Cic. Phil. 13,33). After the occupation of the province, the republican M. Iunius [I 10] Brutus had him executed at the end of 44 for (feared) lack of loyalty (Cic. Phil. 13,33).   W.W.

Menelais (Μενελαΐς; *Menelaḯs*). Town in Dolopia (→ Dolopes) reclaimed as formerly Macedonian by Philip V in 185 BC (Liv. 39,26,1). M. may have been on the northern slopes of Mount Itamos, where there is a ruin near Kasthanaia.

B. HELLY, Incursions chez les Dolopes, in: I. BLUM (ed.), Topographie antique et géographie historique en pays grec, 1992, 60, 81f.; F. STÄHLIN, s.v. M., RE 15, 806.   HE.KR.

Menelaus (Μενέλαος/Menélaos, Attic Μενέλεως/ Menéleos; Latin Menelaus).
[1] A significant character in the cycle of myths about the Trojan War (→ Troy: Cycle of myths). A younger brother of → Agamemnon, who ruled the most significant power centre in Greek myth, Mycene, by marriage to Zeus's daughter Helen (→ Helene [1]; their only child was a daughter, → Hermione) M. became king of a region in the Eurotas valley with its capital → Sparta and → Amyclae [1], which was significant in the pre-Doric period (description of his territory in Hom. Il. 2,581–590 [1]). As a son of → Atreus (in Bacchyl. fr. 15, 48, Aeschyl. Ag. 1569 and Serv. Aen. 1,458 also described as a descendant of → Pleisthenes [2]) M. was a member of the Tantalid family (→ Tantalus). By his being described, as was his brother Agamemnon, as an 'Atreid' (descendent of Atreus), this patronymic in the dual Ἀτρεΐδα (*Atreída*) combined the two brothers into a unit. It was essentially out of this combination with his 'big brother' Agamemnon that M.'s role in the dispute over Troy arose: after his wife Helen had left him for the son of the Trojan king, → Paris, it was his brother who formed an alliance of Greek princes against Paris's homeland and its ruler Priam and led it against Troy.

In his depiction of this struggle between Greeks and Trojans the poet of the *Iliad* has M. act as a figure whose claims are bigger than his abilities: in the assembly his voice plays a role of little significance, in battle he does not distinguish himself much, he often has the upper hand only thanks to his good armour (Hom. Il. 3,346–349; 13,601–617; 17,43–45), and he is the only one of the leading Greek combatants to retreat in the face of superior forces (ibid. 3,89–108) [3]. Only in the recovery of → Patroclus's corpse can he distinguish himself as a warrior (ibid. 17). In the '*Odyssey*' this depiction undergoes a certain change: having returned to Sparta with Helen, in the 4th book he is characterised almost in stereotype as a respectable householder and representative of a now aged generation of heroes in his palace. Indeed, by means of the comprehensive presentation of his wanderings, especially his stay in Egypt, M. is also given a more positive characterisation, particularly as in this presentation he simultaneously foreshadows Odysseus's return home [4].

In the cyclic arrangement (→ Epic cycle) of the Troy myth and in the lyrical genre, apart from his connection with Helen, M. hardly appears. By contrast, in the Attic tragedy he again plays a truly significant role. In 6 of the 31 surviving dramas the character of M. is represented: in the context of the sacrifice of → Iphigeneia (Eur. Iph. A.), the suicide of the son of Telamon, → Ajax [1] (Soph. Ai.), winning back his wife Helen (Eur. Hel.; Eur. Tro.) [5], and as the last great warrior of the Trojan War, who on his return is confronted with the effects of the victory in Greece (Eur. Andr.; Eur. Or.). In all these dramas the character traits M. has in the '*Iliad*' have become even more unpleasant: Sophocles presents him as vengeful and envious in his reaction to Ajax's attacks, Euripides generally as treacherous, cowardly, indecisive and opportunistic. The actions of M. in the 'Orestes' are extreme in this respect. It had already been suspected in antiquity that the characterisation of this Spartan king in Euripides was not unconnected with political relationships at the time of writing (→ Peloponnesian War; schol. Eur. Andr. 445).

The image of M. changes in Hellenistic and Latin literature. In the poetic representations it is no longer a matter of M. the warrior of the Trojan War, but exclusively of his love for Helen and his role in relation to Paris (Theocr. 18: epithalamion for Helen just arrived at M.'s palace; Ov. Epist. 13; 16; 17).

Probably because of his prominent role in the Troy myth and even more so because of the significance of Homeric poetry in Greece, M. enjoyed worship as a hero in Sparta (→ Hero Cult): in → Therapne there was a heroon, originally for Helen and the → Dioscuri, in which M. was included (Alcm. fr. 7 PAGE). From the Hellenistic period this heroon was described as a Menelaion [6]). It is presumably also this function that results in M.'s mention in Simonides's elegy on the battle of Plataeae, in which he and the Dioscuri are named as a symbol for Sparta's military strength as early as the heroic period (Sim. fr. 11 West).

The iconography of M. is dominated by two thematic areas: one on M.'s deeds as a warrior in the Trojan War, primarily his duel with Paris and his recovery of Patroclus's corpse (esp. significant is the presumably Hellenistic Pasquino group, which shows M. raising the upper body of the dead Patroclus [7]) and the other on M.'s actions against Helen, whom he initially pursues and threatens to kill after retrieving her from the Trojans.

1 E. VISSER, Homers Katalog der Schiffe, 1997, 479–507   2 E. FRAENKEL, Aeschylus, Agamemnon, 1950, 740   3 B. FENIK, Stylization and Variety. Four Monologues in the Iliad, in: Id., Homer: Tradition and Invention, 1978, 68–90   4 S. OLSON, The Stories of Helen and Menelaus (Odyssey 4, 240–289) and the Return of Odysseus, in: AJPh 110, 1989, 387ff.   5 D. HARBSMEIER, Die alten Menschen bei Euripides: Mit einem Anhang über Menelaus und Helena bei Euripides, 1968, 132–165   6 F. BÖLTE, s.v. Menelaion, RE 15, 803–806   7 R. WÜNSCHE, Pasquino, in: Münchner Jb. der Bildenden Kunst 42, 1991, 7–38.

W. VAN DE WIJNPERSSE, Menelaus (Odyssee 4 en Ilias passim), in: Hermeneus 37, 1966, 270–281; C. BARCK, Menelaos bei Homer, in: WS 84 (= N.F. 5), 1971, 5–28; I. M. HOHENDAHL-ZOETELIEF, Manners in the Homeric Epic, 1980, 143–183; L. KAHIL, s.v. Menelaos, LIMC 6.1, 834–841.   E.V.

[2] Son of Amyntas [3] III of Macedonia and his first wife Gygaia and half-brother of → Philippus II. Fleeing from the latter he and his brother Arrhidaeus [3] reached Olynthus no later than 349 BC. Philip took this as a pretext for war against the city and after its capture had the two brothers executed (Iust. 7,4,5; 8,3,10; Harpocr. s.v. Menelaos; Oros. 3,12,19f.).

→ Argeads (with stemma)

N. G. L. HAMMOND-G. T. GRIFFITH, A History of Macedonia II, 1979, 699–701.

[3] Pelagonian, son of Arrhabaeus, who in a position not further elucidated for providing help against the Chalcidians and Amphipolis in 363/2 BC was honoured by the Athenians as euergétēs ('beneficiary') (Syll.[3] 174). It seems that he was expelled, went to Athens, and a short time later was worshipped in Ilium as an Athenian (Syll.3 188).

N. G. L. HAMMOND, G. T. GRIFFITH, A History of Macedonia II, 1979, 19f.; 186; 207.   M.Z.

[4] Son of → Lagus [1], brother of → Ptolemaeus I. M. was sent on a military mission to → Cyprus in 315 BC. He remained on the island with → Nicocreon as a representative of Ptolemaic interests (as stratēgós?). In 310, M. took part in the removal of Nicocreon and became his successor as city king of Salamis [2] (and more?; see the evidence in [1. 61f.]). In 306, he was defeated by → Demetrius [2] at Salamis and besieged; he sent to Egypt for help, but could not prevent the defeat of Ptolemy I and had to cede Cyprus to Demetrius (Diod. Sic. 20,47–52). In 284/3, M. was an eponymous priest of Alexander. A city and a district in the northwestern Delta is named after him (PP III/IX 5196; VI 14537).

1 O. MØRKHOLM, Early Hellenistic Coinage, 1991.

R. BAGNALL, The Administration of the Ptolemaic Possessions Outside Egypt, 1976, 40ff.   W.A.

[5] Jewish high priest of the Temple in Jerusalem between 171 and 163 BC (his origin is unclear: according to 2 Makk 4,23–27 of non-priestly origin [4. 149]; otherwise according to Old Latin and Armenian MSS [2. 508f.], according to which M. may indeed be of priestly descent but not a member of the high-priestly family of the → Zadokids). M. presumably bought the office of high priest in his function as financial administrator of the Temple (or his brother) at the court of → Antiochus [6] IV and took the place of the Oniad Jason (→ Onias). M.'s assumption of office introduced the peak of the Hellenisation policy, which culminated in the plundering of the Jerusalem Temple supported by M., its conversion into a Zeus sanctuary and the building of the Akra, a Greek fortified polis within Jerusalem [2. 514]. He was probably supported in this by the lay-aristocratic Tobiad family (→ Tobiads), which had fallen out with the pro-Ptolemaic Oniads (Ios. BI 1,1,1; Ios. Ant. Iud. 12,5,1; [4. 151], cf. [2. 526ff.]). However, there is no mention in the sources of the precise role of M. in the 'Hellenisation' of the Temple, the Maccabaean uprising and the rededication (Ḥanukka) of the Temple in 164 BC. M. was removed from office in 163 BC after the peace between → Lysias [6] (guardian of Antiochus V Eupator) and → Judas [1] Maccabaeus and was executed in Aleppo or → Beroea [3] (2 Makk. 13,4–8; Ios. Ant. Iud. 12,9,7 [385]). Josephus and 2 Makk concur in their judgment of M., and with him of

the Tobiads who supported him, as the originator of religious persecution under Antiochus IV [2.527]. As the sources are scanty and polemic, however, the question remains whether religious persecution was a matter of 'an internal process among the Jews' (Hellenist party under M. versus traditionalists, i.e. *Asidaîoi*, *Ḥ^asīdîm* = 'devout') or of 'a political measure of the Seleucids' [3. 59] (not dealt with in [1. 12f.]).

1 K. BRINGMANN, Hellenistische Reform und Religionsverfolgung in Judäa. Eine Untersuchung zur jüdisch-hellenistischen Geschichte (175–163 v.Chr.), 1983   2 M. HENGEL, Judentum und Hellenismus, ²1973, 508–532   3 P. SCHÄFER, Geschichte der Juden in der Antike. Die Juden Palästinas von Alexander dem Großen bis zur arabischen Eroberung, 1983, 52–62   4 SCHÜRER 1, 137–163   5 V. TCHERIKOVER, Hellenistic Civilization and the Jews, 1959.   I.WA.

[6] **M. of Alexandria** Greek mathematician and astronomer. He was alive around AD 98, as two of his observations this year are mentioned by Ptolemy (Almagest 7,3). M. appears as an interlocutor in Plut-

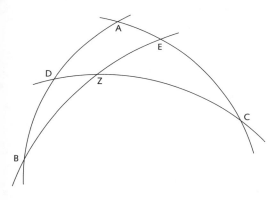

arch's *De facie in orbe lunae*. His main work was the 'Spherics', which (apart from a few theorems cited by Pappus) is lost in Greek, but survives in an Arabic version. His book on specific weights, mentioned by Al-Ḥācinī (12th cent.), is probably contained in the MS Escorial 960 (German translation in [4]). Proclus cites M.'s proof of a theorem of Euclid (Euclides [3], Elementa 1,25). Works on chord calculation, on the settings of the signs of the → Zodiac and on a transcendental curve are known only from citations.

The 'Spherics' (in Latin and Arabic versions) consists of 3 books. The following subdivision is according to Gerhard von Cremona's version (see below): book 1 transfers Euclid's theory of triangles to the surface of a sphere, book 2 gives a number of significant propositions in spherical geometry, and book 3 deals with spherical trigonometry. At the beginning of book 3 there is M.'s Theorem (also: 'Transversal Theorem'): crd 2CE : crd 2EA = (crd 2CZ : crd 2ZD) × (crd 2DB : crd 2BA). Here 'crd' is the chord (crd 2α = 2 sin α), and all arcs are part of great circles.

This theorem, which also appears in Ptol. Almagest 1,13, was the basis of spherical astronomy until the end of the 10th century and was also still much used after that. Ṭābit ibn Qurra (d. 901) wrote a treatise on the Transversal Theorem, in which he introduced *inter alia* a new proof. Of the ''Spherics'' geometry there are at least two independent Arabic versions: that of Al-Harawī (10th cent.), who adapted the texts by Al-Māhānī (9th cent.), and that of Abū Naṣr ibn 'Irāq (11th century), who presumably used another translation. The Latin translation by Gerard of Cremona (d. 1187) and the Hebrew translation by Jakob ben Maḥir (13th cent.) traces back to a hybrid of these two versions.

1 A. A. BJÖRNBO, Studien über Menelaos' Sphärik, in: Abhandlungen zur Geschichte der mathematischen Wissenschaften 14, 1902, 1–154   2 T. L. HEATH, A History of Greek Mathematics, vol. 2, 1921, 260–273   3 M. KRAUSE, Die Sphärik von Menelaos aus Alexandrien in der Verbesserung von Abū Naṣr b. 'Alī b. 'Irāq, 1936   4 J. WÜRSCHMIDT, Die Schrift des Menelaus über die Bestimmung der Zusammensetzung von Legierungen, in: Philologus 80, 1925, 377–409.   M.F. RI.L.

[7] Greek tragedian, son of Ariston, second half of the 1st century BC, emissary to Ariarathes V, the king of Cappadocia, (163–130 BC) and festival emissary from the Athenian *technitai* to Delphi in 127 BC (TrGF I 137).   B.Z.

[8] Colleague of → Callimander as emissary from the Alexandrians, who was to offer the Egyptian throne to a Seleucid prince in 56 BC.   W.A.

[9] **M. of Aegae** (which place this name refers to remains unknown), Author of an epic *Thēbaîs* in 11 books, of four fragments of which Stephanus of Byzantium transmits, each of one or two words (all toponyms). The dating is unclear. It is probably the same M. that the rhetor → Longinus [1] took as an example of a blameless but talentless poet. M. may also have been an author of Sotadics.

1 SH 551–557   2 FGrH 384   3 M. FANTUZZI, Epici ellenistici, in: K. ZIEGLER, L'epos ellenistico, 1988, LXXII–LXXIII (with bibliography).   S.FO.

[10] Greek sculptor, pupil of → Stephanus. According to its signature he created the early imperial period eclectic group of Orestes and Electra (Rom, MN) and is presumably identical with the M. Cossutius M. of a now lost signature.

G. CRESSEDI, s.v. Cossutius Menelaos (fig.), EAA 2, 1959, 871; Lippold, 386; Loewy, no. 375; P. MORENO, Scultura ellenistica, 1994, 758; B. PALMA, Museo nazionale romano. Le sculture, 1, 5, 1983, 84–89.   R.N.

[11] Town in the northwestern Nile delta, capital of the Menelaites (Μενελαίτης; *Menelaítēs*) district. It was newly founded to the west of the Rosetta branch of the Nile on the territory of the old Lower Egyptian 7th district at the beginning of the Ptolemaic period and was named after Ptolemy I's brother (Strab. 17,801). The statement in Ptol. 4,5,4 that the capital of the district

was → Canopus is probably a mistake. According to BERNAND, M. should be identified with Schedia (Strab. 17,800–803) near the modern Al-Karyūn.

A. BERNAND, Le delta égyptien d'après les textes grecs, 1, 1970, 381–442. K.J.-W.

Menemachus (Μενέμαχος/*Menémachos*).
[1] Pontic general. When → Mithradates [6] VI and Licinius [I 26] Lucullus faced one another at the Lycus in northern Bithynia in 71 BC, Mithradates had a unit under M. and Myron attack a Roman supply column under M. Fabius Hadrianus. The king tried to explain its heavy defeat (the two leaders and almost all the men fell) by the lack of experience of the generals (Plut. Lucullus 17; Sall. fr. IV 8 M.).
[2] Cavalry leader of → Tigranes II of Armenia. In 67 BC he defected to Marcius [I 23] Rex, the governor of Cilicia (Cass. Dio 36,17; Sall. fr. V 16 M.). M.SCH.
[3] Rich citizen of Sardeis, to whom → Plutarchus dedicated his works 'Political Advice' (*Politiká parangélmata*, Plut. Mor. 798a–825f) and 'On Flight' (*Perí phygḗs*, 599a–607f), and perhaps also 'Instructions for the Newly Rich' (*Protreptikós pros néon ploúsion*). K.MEI.

Menenius Name of a patrician family, but plebeian bearers of this name are also in evidence (attested for M. [2]). This *gens* gave its name to the *tribus Menenia*. In the 5th cent. BC, it produced a number of high-ranking officials, but died out during the 4th. cent. BC. Noteworthy is the use of the *praenomen* Agrippa, which later only appeared as a *cognomen* [1. 19f.].

1 SALOMIES.

[1] M., Agrippa In 442 BC, in the position of a *triumvir coloniae deducendae* (MRR I 54), M. led a *colonia* to Ardea. According to Livy (4,11,5f., he chose to remain there because of the unpopularity of his administration in Rome and the threat of a law-suit, but he is probably identical with the *cos.* 439.
[2] M., L. *Tr. pl.* 357 BC. Together with his colleague M. Duilius, M. introduced a law which – possibly to reform a clause from the *XII tabulae* cf. Tac. Ann. 6,16) – set the annual interest rate at 8¹/₃% (*fenus unicarium*).
[3] M., M. According to Livy (4,53,2–13), he introduced an agrarian law as *tr. pl.* of 410 BC on restoring illegally occupied land. Probably not historical.
[4] M., M. According to Livy (6,19,4–20,1; 20,12), as *tr. pl.* of 384 BC he pursued together with his fellow tribune Q. Publilius the prosecution and sentencing of T. Manlius [I 20] Capitolinus and carried out his execution.
[5] M. Lanatus, Agrippa Consul and *triumphator* over the Sabinians (or Auruncians ?) in 503 BC (MRR I 8). His fame is based on his alleged role during the first → *secessio* of the plebs on *mons sacer* in 494 out of resentment at their debts and at the despotic behaviour of the patricians. He is said to have convinced them to

return by citing the parable of the refusal of the limbs to feed the stomach (Liv. 2,32,8–12; Dion. Hal. Ant. Rom. 6,86; Florus 1,23; Plut. Coriolanus 6,2–5; Cass. Dio 4,17,10–13 cf. Zon. 7,14]; Vir. ill. 18,1–5). This parable, which reached the Roman tradition in the 2nd cent. BC at the latest (possibly during the Gracchan period: the ideal of → *concordia*) has its roots in Greek political theory (the organic structure of the state) and Stoic philosophy. When M. died in 493, he was allegedly so impoverished that his funeral was paid for by the state (Liv. 2,33,10f.; Dion. Hal. Ant.Rom. 6,96,1–4).

M. HILLGRUBER, Die Erzählung des M. Agrippa. Eine griechische Fabel in der römischen Geschichtsschreibung, in: A&A 42, 1996, 42–56; D. PEIL, Der Streit der Glieder mit dem Magen, 1985.

[6] **M. Lanatus, T.** Son of M. [5]; *cos.* in 477 BC (MRR I 26f.). According to Liv. 2,51,1f.; 52,3–5 and Dion. Hal. Ant. Rom 9,23; 9,27 (cf. also Cass. Dio fr. 21,3), M. suffered defeat against the Etruscans following the perishing of the Fabians on the banks of the → Cremera. He was sentenced in the following year because he did not give any aid to the Fabians, even though he and his army were in the vicinity (contradictory Liv. 2,52,1 and Dion Hal. Ant. Rom. 9,18,5, according to whom M. only heard of the Fabians' defeat just before he ordered his own army to march); he died from shame.
[7] **M. Lanatus, T.** *Cos.* 452 BC (MRR I 44f.). Because of illness, he allegedly left his fellow consul P. Sestius Capitolinus Vaticanus to carry out all official functions (Dion. Hal. Ant.Rom. 10,54,5; 55,3; Fest. p. 237 L.). Livy (3,33,4) described M. as an opponent of the appointment of the → *decemviri* [2]. C.MÜ.

Menerva, Menrva see → Minerva

Menes
[1] From the 19th Dynasty on (13th cent. BC), the Egyptian king lists mention a king M. (Egyptuan *Mnj*; Manetho: Μήνης/*Ménēs*) as the first ruler of the 1st Dynasty, and the authors of classical antiquity simply shaped his image into that of the founder par excellence. The construction of the residential city of → Memphis and its temple (Hdt. 2,99; Jos. Ant. Iud. 8,155), the invention of → writing (Plin. HN 7,56), the laying down of laws in writing (Diod. 1,94) and generally the introduction of civilised ways of life were ascribed to him (Diod. 1,43.45, Plut. Is. 8).

The identification of this ruler in contemporary sources of the early period, which always mention throne name but not birth name, remains controversial. Most probably, he is to be identified with Horus *ḥꜣ* ('the warrior'), whose burial site in the royal cemetery of → Abydos [2] is known, the successor and probably the son of king Narmer. The sources permit the sequence of Egyptian kings to be traced back even further. Nevertheless the government of Horus *ḥꜣ* can be recognised as a significant moment in political, social and cultural development. According to archaeological evidence, the relocation of the royal seat to Memphis does in fact fall in his period, and the extent of the use of writing in administration clearly increased at the time.

H. BRUNNER, s.v. Menes, LÄ 3, 46–48.   S.S.

[2] Son of Dionysius from Pella. After the battle of → Issus (333 BC) M. was admitted to the → sōmatophýlakes of Alexander [4] the Great (Arr. Anab. 2,12,2). In Susa (Arr. Anab. 3,16,9; in Curt. 5,1,43: Babylon) in 331 BC, he is said to have been appointed hýparchos of Syria, Phoenicia and Cilicia (in Diod. 17,64,5: stratēgós). He was provided with 3000 talents of silver (an escort had to accompany the procession, Arr. Anab. 4,7,2), which were made available to → Antipater [1] for the war against → Agis [3]. It is hardly possible that M. was satrap of the whole region: in 329 a satrap of Syria is mentioned (Arr. Anab. 4,7,2: the name is corrupted). Rather, he probably had a special command, running alongside that of the satraps, over the lines of communication. E.g., he had to supervise in 330 BC the embarkation for Greece of the contingents that had been dismissed in Ekbatana (Arr. Anab. 3,19,6).

J. E. ATKINSON, A Commentary on Q. Curtius Rufus' Historiae Alexandri Magni B. 5 to 7.2, 1994, 51–53 (with bibl.).   E.B.

Menesaechmus (Μενέσαιχμος; Menésaichmos). Attic rhetorician of the 4th cent. BC. → Lycurgus [9] (Ps.-Plut. Mor. 843d) succesfully charged him with neglecting his obligations as leader of the festival legation to Delos (Fr. in [1. 115–118]). M. succeeded Lycurgus as leader of the financial administration of Athens (Dion. Hal. de Dinarcho 11) and accused him shortly before his death (ibid. 842f) and afterwards his sons, who were temporarily arrested (ibid. 842e). M. was one of the accusers of → Demosthenes [2] in the Harpalos lawsuit (Ps.-Plut. Mor. 846c). Dion. Hal. De dinarcho 11 attributes to him three then still extant speeches under the name of → Dinarchus on the basis of stylistic deficiencies ('watery, weak, scattered-minded, frosty') and records the only two known verbatim citations.

1 N. C. CONOMIS (ed.), Lycurgi Oratio in Leocratem cum ceterarum Lycurgi orationum Fragmentis, 1970.   M.W.

Menestheus (Μενεσθεύς; Menestheús).
[1] Son of Peteus, great-grandson of → Erechtheus. M. led the contingent of Athenians with fifty ships at Troy. Only Nestor was his equal in marshalling horses and warriors for battle (Hom. Il. 2,552ff.). While → Theseus was detained in Hades, the Dioscuri conquered Aphidna and installed M. as king of Athens. Theseus's sons fled to Euboea. Because M. gained the favour of the Athenians, they ousted Theseus on his return (Paus. 1,17,5f.). According to Plut. Theseus 32f., M., the first demagogue, roused the Athenians against the absent Theseus and allowed the → Dioscuri into the city.

→ Lycomedes is said to have killed Theseus on Scyros to please M. (ibid. 35). M. is mentioned in Apollod. 3,10,8 and Hyg. Fab. 81 in the catalogue of the suiters of → Helene [1] (cf. Hes. Cat. 200). At Troy, M. took part in the battles against → Glaucus [4] and → Sarpedon (Hom. Il. 12,331). He was one of those in the Wooden Horse (cf. Paus. 1,23,8). Together with his Athenian companions, he founded the city of Elaea in Aeolis (Str. 13,3,5). After the destruction of Troy M. went to Melos, where he ruled as king after the death of Polyanax (Apollod. Epit. 15b). According to Dictys 6,2, M. returned to Athens, accompanied by → Aethra, and died there (his grave epigram is in Ps.-Aristot. peplos [fr. 640,34 ROSE]).

W. KULLMANN, Die Quellen der Ilias (Hermes ES 14), 1960, 74–79; E. SIMON, s.v. Menestheus, LIMC 6.1, 473–75.   J.STE.

[2] Son of the Athenian strategos → Iphicrates from Rhamnous and a daughter (or sister) of the king Cotys [I 1] (Nep. Iphicrates 3,4). He married a daughter of the strategos Timotheus (Dem. Or. 49,66). After the end of his term as strategos in the → Social War [1] in 356/355 BC, M. was indicted in Athens but acquitted (Isocr. 15,129; Dion. Hal. Dinarchus 13). As late as 333 BC, M., as strategos, took on a command in the Hellespont, when the Macedonians had seized corn ships at Tenedos (Dem. Or. 17,20). He was trierarch several times (IG II² 1622b 199; e 723 and 731f.; 1623a 47f.). He died before 325 (his heirs are mentioned in IG II² 1629, 486f.).

DAVIES, 250–251; DEVELIN, Nr. 1969; PA 9988; TRAILL, PAA 645115.   J.E.

[3] Attic comic poet of the 3rd cent. BC, who appears behind → Diodorus [10], → Eumedes and → Pandaetes on a list of winners in the Lenaea with one victory [1]. No more is known.

1 PCG VII, 1989, 3.   H.-G.NE.

Menesthius (Μενέσθιος; Menésthios).
[1] Son of Areithous and Philomedusa, from Ame in Boeotia, killed in → Paris in the Trojan War (Hom. Il. 7,9; Tzetz. ad Hom. Il. 132).
[2] Myrmidonian, one of → Achilles's generals in the Trojan War, son of Polydora and the river god Spercheus or the giant Pelor (Hom. Il. 16,173; Str. 9,433; Apollod. 3,168 with various genealogical and matrimonial variations for Polydora).   L.K.

Menestor (Μενέστωρ; Menéstōr). A Pythagorean from Sybaris, contemporary of Empedocles (5th cent. BC) and according to Iambl. VP 267 the earliest Greek botanist. Three citations in Theophr. Hist. pl., and the four in C. plant. [1. 375f.] show that he distinguished warm plants, i.e. evergreen ones such as → ivy and → laurel and water plants such as rushes and reeds (→ Kalamos [2]) from the other cold ones. He even took into account ecological factors such as different habitats, climate (see esp. Theophr. Caus. pl. 1,21,6) and maturation times.

1 DIELS/KRANZ no. 32 (22), fr. 1–7.

A. STEIER, s.v. M., RE 15, 853–855; W. CAPELLE, Zur Geschichte der Botanik, in: Philologus 69, 1910, 278ff.; C. VIANO, Théophraste, Ménestor de Sybaris et la »symmetria« de la chaleur, in: REG 105, 1992, 584–592.
C.HÜ.

Menestratus (Μενέστρατος; *Menéstratos*).
[1] One of the sons of → Niobe (Hellanicus FGrH 4 F 21 with commentary by JACOBY).
[2] M. of Thespiae, who sacrifices himself for his lover Cleostratus, by volunteering to take his place and be thrown to the dragon that on Zeus's instructions is fed a young man each year. Barbs on his armour kill the monster (Paus. 2,26,7f.) L.K.
[3] Athenian, one of 18 denounced by Teucer in connexion with the → Mutilation of the Herms in 415 BC (And. 1,35). He fled or was executed.

PA 9993; TRAILL, PAA 645405.

[4] Athenian from Amphitrope, denounced by → Agoratus in 403 BC. Set free by the 'Thirty' (→ Triákonta), he was arrested for murder in 400/399, condemned and 'drummed to death' (ἀπετυμπανίσθη; *apetympanísthē*, Lys. 13,55–57).

PA 10002; TRAILL, PAA 645570.

[5] Known from a speech by → Lysias [1] against him, the authenticity of which was already doubted in antiquity (fr. 89 TH., from Harpocration). Any two or all three M.s [3–5] may be identical.

TRAILL, PAA 645410.

[6] Eretrian *dynástēs* ('ruler'; → Dynasteia) 352 BC (Dem. 23,124). K.KI.
[7] Sculptor from Athens. He created a portrait, now lost, of a Learchis and highly praised marble statues of Heracles and Hecate at the Artemisium in → Ephesus (with site-plan). By him or a sculptor of the same there is a bronze statue of Herus Ptoeus in → Acraephia, of which the base and signature survive.

L. GUERRINI, s.v. M. (1), EAA 4, 1961, 1022f.; OVERBECK, no. 1610. 1611. R.N.

Menetekel Properly *Mene-tekel-ufarsin,* a cryptic Aramaic inscription in the literary context of Dan 5:25–28 (within an Aramaic apocalypse in Dan 2–7), written by a supernatural hand on the wall of the palace during a banquet given by → Belsazar, the heir to the Babylonian throne. The elements of this writing have been interpreted as cuneiform signs for weights (Neo-Babylonian *manû*'mina', *šiqlu*'shekel'; *mišlu/zūzu*'half'/'to share'), or as Aramaic terms in cuneiform script, in the order mina, shekel, half-shekel. Daniel interpreted the writing

as a play on the words *manû* 'to count' and *šaqālu* 'to weigh', and combined them into an oracle against Belsazar's regency. However, other interpretations based on Seleucid accounting formulas are also possible.

A. ANGERSTORFER, s.v. Mene-tekel-ufarsin, Neues Bibel Lexikon 2, 1995, 759–760. TH.PO.

Menexenus (Μενέξενος; *Menéxenos*).
[1] A son of → Socrates, still a child when his father died (Plat. Apo. 34d; Phd. 116b; Diog. Laert. 2,26). See → Socratics.

A.-H. CHROUST, A Comment On Aristotle's On Noble Birth, in: WS 85 N.F. 6, 1972, 19–32; PA 9975; TRAILL, PAA 644865.

[2] Pupil of the Sophist Ctesippus, a relative, and of Socrates, at whose death he was present (Plat. Lys. 206d; 211c; Plat. Phd. 59b). Plato named his dialogue 'M.' after him. See → Socratics.

PA 9973; TRAILL, PAA 644855. W.S.

Meninx (Μῆνιγξ; *Mêninx*). Island (modern Djerba) and city (modern al-Kantara) in the province of Africa Tripolitana (→ Africa [3]). Eratosthenes (fr. p. 308 BERGER, in Plin. HN 5,41) describes the island as 'lotus-eating' (λωτοφαγῖτις; *lōtophagîtis*). Sources: Ps.-Scyl. 110 (GGM 1,85–89); Pol. 1,39,2; 34,3,12; Str. 3,4,3; Mela 2,105; Ptol. 4,3,35; 8,14,13; Stadiasmus Maris Magni 103; 104; 112; 124 (GGM 1,465f.; 468; 471). In 253 BC the Roman fleet ran into diffilculties off M. ((Pol. 1,39,2). In 217 BC the island was laid waste by the Romans (Liv. 22,31,2). Marius [I1] landed on the island during his flight to Africa (Plut. Marius 40,4). Contrary to [Aur. Vict.] Epit. Caes. 30,1–31,1, M. was not the home of the emperors Trebonianus Gallus and Volusianus (251–253).

S. CHAKER et al., s.v. Djerba, EB, 2452–2460; S. LANCEL, E. LIPIŃSKI, s.v. Djerba, DCPP, 134. W.HU.

Menippe (Μενίππη; *Meníppē*).
[1] One of the → Nereids (Hes. Theog. 260) or → Oceanids (Hyg. Fab. praef.). Not mentioned among the Nereids in Hom. Il. 18,35ff. or Apollod. 1,11–12.

[2] Daughter of → Thamyris, mother of → Orpheus (Tzetz. Chil. 1,306; 8,9).
[3] Daughter of → Orion. M. and her sister Metioche learned the art of weaving from → Athena. They sacrificed themselves for → Aonia, which had fallen victim to the plague, and which, according to the Oracle of Apollo at → Gortyn, could only be redeemed by two virgins. To placate the gods of the underworld, they ripped open their throats with their weaving shuttles. Their corpses became invisible; two stars appeared, which people called comets (Antoninus Liberalis 25). According to Ov. Met. 13,685ff. they sacrificed them-

selves for Thebes. So that their line would not be extinguished, two youths emerged from their ashes; they were called the *Coronae*.

PRELLER/ROBERT I⁴ 556; II⁴ 410 note 2; I⁴ 454.   I.BAN.

Menippian Satire see → Menippus [4] of Gadara; → Satire

Menippus (Μένιππος; *Ménippos*).
[1] In Plut. Pericles 13,10 (cf. Plut Mor. 812d) mentioned as a friend and sub-commander of → Pericles (probably between 443 and 430 BC). Like the latter, he was mocked in the comedies. It is uncertain if M. really was a *strategos*. Plutarch's term for him (*hypostratēgón*) is the Greek equivalent of the Latin term *legatus* (DEVELIN, 103). Aristoph. Av. 1294 mentions a M., whom the scholias identify as a horse dealer.

PA 10033; TRAILL, PAA 646185 (vgl. 646190 und 646195).   W.W.

[2] Commander of → Philippus V during the 1st → Macedonian War: He is attested in the Peloponnese in 209 BC and in Euboea in 208 (Pol. 10,42,2; Liv. 27,32,10; 28,5,11).   L.-M.G.
[3] M. 'the Macedonian' In 193 BC, M. led a delegation on behalf of Antiochus [5] III to Rome (together with → Hegesianax) and another in 192 to Aetolia. As a commander, he conquered some towns in Perrhaebia in 191 and led soldiers to Stratus (Syll.3 601; Diod. Sic. 28,15; Liv. 34,57–59; 35,32,8–14; 50,7; 51,4; 36,10,5; 11,6; App. Syr. 6,23ff.).

E. BEVAN, The House of Seleucus, 1902.   A.ME.

[4] M. of Gadara (Syria). Cynical philosopher, first half of the 3rd cent. BC. The short, anecdote-rich biography in Diog. Laert. 6,99–101, according to which he was first a slave in Sinope and later a citizen of Thebes, charlatan and money-lender until he hanged himself for lack of money, is without credibility in large parts and copies the life of → Diogenes [14] of Sinope [1]. Within → Cynicism, M. is considered by some to be close to Crates [4], by others to Metrocles, and is held to be one of its main representatives (Eun. Vit. soph. 454,5; Varro, Sat. Men. 516).
Of M.' writings nothing is preserved except for four short fragments (Ath. 14,629e-f; 14,664e; 1,32e; Diog. Laert. 6,29). Diogenes [17] Laertius ascribes 13 works to him of which he quotes a few titles (6,101): *Nékyia* (probably a parody of the journey to the Underworld based on Hom. Od. 11 and Aristophanes' 'The Frogs'), from which the Suda derives a character description that is conferred on M. (cf. Suda s.v. Φαιός); *Diathḗkai* ('Testaments'); Ἐπιστολαὶ κεκομψευμέναι ἀπὸ τοῦ τῶν θεῶν προσώπου (fictional letters to the gods); one or more treatises 'Against Natural Philosophers, Mathematicians and Grammarians' (Πρὸς τοὺς φυσικοὺς καὶ μαθηματικοὺς καὶ γραμματικούς); two treatises against the Epicureans: 'On the Birthday of Epicurus ' (Γονὰς

Ἐπικούρου) and 'On the Observance of the Twentieth' (Τὰς θρησκευομένας ὑπ' αὐτῶν εἰκάδας), which alludes to the custom called for by Epicurus in his will that his students should gather on the 20th day of every month (Diog. Laert. 10,18; → Epicurean School). This catalogue of M.' works (ibid. 6,29) is supplemented by Διογένους πρᾶσις ('The Sale of Diogenes') [2], while Ath. 14,664e speaks of a treatise called 'Arcesilaus' (Ἀρκεσίλαος), which probably was directed against the head of the Academy and contemporary of M. bearing the name → Arcesilaus [5], as well as a *Sympósion* (Ath. 14,629e) [3].
M.' works were not just criticism and Cynical mockery of the most diverse trivialities of the world (Diog. Laert. 6,99; M. Aur. 6,47), but the epithet *spoudogéloios* refers to a blend of the 'serious and the merry' (Str. 16,2,29). Lucian [1], who makes M. the narrator of many of his dialogues, builds on this characteristic [4].
M.' treatises achieved literary significance through their peculiar mixture of prose and verse passages in various metres (Lucian Bis Accusatus 33; Prob. in Verg. Ecl. 6,31). This prosimetrum [5] became the genre characteristic of 'Menippean → Satire' [1; 6; 7]. The first imitations of this form are already found in → Meleager [8] of Gadara (Anth. Pal. 7,417,3–4.; 7,418,5–6), later in → Varro, whose satires are entitled *saturae Menippeae*, in → Seneca's *Apocolocyntosis*, and Lucian's satirical dialogues [8]. Regarding the genre development of Menippean satire in Petronius, Apuleius, Boethius, Martianus Capella to the Renaissance cf. [1; 9; 10; 11].
→ Cynicism; → Satire

1 J. C. RELIHAN, Ancient Menippean Satire, 1993, 39–44   2 R. HELM, Lukian und Menipp, 1906, 231–253   3 J. MARTIN, Symposion. Die Geschichte einer lit. Form, 1931, 211–240   4 J. C. RELIHAN, Vainglorious Menippus in Lucian's Dialogues of the Dead, in: Illinois Classical Studies 12, 1987, 185–206   5 D. BARTONKOVÁ, Prosimetrum, the Mixed Style, in Ancient Literature, in: Eirene 14, 1976, 65–92   6 H. K. RIIKONEN, Menippean Satire as a Literary Genre with Special Reference to Seneca's Apocolocyntosis, 1987   7 J. C. RELIHAN, On the Origin of 'Menippean Satire' as the Name of a Literary Genre, in: CPh 79, 1984, 226–229   8 J. HALL, Lucian's Satire, 1981, 64–150   9 F. J. BENDA, The Tradition of Menippean Satire in Varro, Lucian, Seneca and Erasmus, Diss. Austin 1979   10 E. P. KIRK, Menippean Satire: An Annotated Catalogue of Texts and Criticism, 1980   11 J. C. RELIHAN, Menippus in Antiquity and the Renaissance, in: R. BRACHT BRANHAM, M.-O. GOULET-CAZÉ (Hrsg.), The Cynics, 1996, 265–293.   M.B.

[5] M. Rhetor Greek orator of the 2nd and 1st cents. BC from Stratonicea in Caria (Str. 14,2,25=660; Diog. Laert. 6,101). He bore the epithet Katokas (Strabo, ibid.). Cicero, who heard him during his educational tour, regarded him as being above all other contemporary rhetors (Brut. 315; cf. Plut. Cicero 4,862f.).   M.W.
[6] M. of Pergamum Geographer. → Marcianus (GGM 1,566,6) lists him after Artemidorus [3] and Strabo, which suggests dating him to the 2nd half of the 1st cent. BC. *Terminus post quem* for his 3–volume 'Peri-

plus of the Inner Sea' (GGM 1,566,42) is probably 37 BC or later, when Polemon I had received the kingdom of Pontus from Antonius [I 9] and founded Polemonium ([5. 1218], but cf. [6. 427f.]), which is mentioned in the derivative *Anonymi Periplus Ponti Euxini* (GGM 1,409,13). The work was completed in 26/5 BC, the date of the second delegation of → Crinagoras of Mytilene to Augustus ([2. 863], [8. 573] with hesitations). In an epigram (Anth. Pal. 9,559), Crinagoras requested a → periplus for his journey from M., who had composed a 'Learned Tour' (ἴστωρ κύκλος). M.' work (according to Marcian, GGM 1,566,42) discussed the coasts of the Pontus Euxinus, the Propontis and the Hellespont (Bk. 1), the Mediterranean coast of Europe up to the 'Pillars of Hercules' (Bk. 2), then that of Africa and the rest of Asia (Bk. 3). Only a small part has been preserved in excerpts: 1) The incompletely preserved *Epitomé* of Marcian (GGM 1,63–573) covers Book 1 (and small parts of the other volumes), which describes the Asian coast to the Chadision river, 170 stadia east of → Amisus; 2) Fragments of this *Epitomé* in Steph. Byz. (s.v. Χαδισία, Ἑρμώνασσα, Χαλδία, Ἀχίλλειος δρόμος, Πόρθμιον – in Maeotis –, Χερρόνυσος, Χαλκηδών on the Propontis); 3) in the work of the *Anonymus Ponti Euxini* (GGM 1,402–423; [1. 118–146], → Arrianus [3]; [7. 68f.]), probably written after AD 576 [1. 102–106] and whose author relies apart from → Arrianus [2] especially on M. Other textual traditions possibly referring back to → Agathemerus [7. 65f.] and especially the anonymous *Stadiasmòs tês thalássēs* (GGM 1,427–514; [1. 149f., 154–156]), whose content is older than the 1st cent. BC, are unlikely to offer anything actually by M. [5. 1218; 4. 88f.].

Therefore, a clear impression can be formed only of Bk. 1 (from the form of the text in [1. 151–156]). It begins with a description of the → Pontus Euxinus at the sanctuary of Zeus Urios on the Asian shore of the → Bosporus and first deals with → Bithynia (its boundary is the river Billaeus, but according to other geographers the Parthenius river), → Paphlagonia up to the border river Euarchus, and the 'two [later] provinces of Pontus' (τῶν δύο Πόντων [1. 154,36]) to the border river Ophius. The text then follows the coasts of 'various Barbarian peoples' up to → Maeotis including Achilleion, which lies at the mouth of the Tanais (where Asia meets Europe), goes on to the mouth of the Ister and then to Thrace (→ Thrake) on the Pontus Euxinus to Therae, the NW border of Byzantium's territory and finally along the coast back to the entrance of the Bosporus. Internally, it is divided by titles such as *Períplous tês Paphlagonías* (Περίπλους τῆς Παφλαγονίας, 'Description of the Coast of Paphlagonia'). The second part of the 1st bk., which in turn begins on the Bosporus describing the → Propontis and → Hellespont [1. 163; 4. 89], is as good as lost.

M.' *Períplous* was mostly of nautical interest, as is still clearly evident in the *Epitomé* of Marcian [3; 5. 1219] and took a 'crow's nest view', which M. probably adopted from his models [4. 91f.]. As preserved, the book focuses on coasts, the quality of anchorages, distances between conspicuous coastal points (mouths of rivers, capes), but also longer distances while omitting way stations (4,520 stadia from the sanctuary of Zeus Urios to Amisus). M. also speaks of a *diáplous* (διάπλους, 'passage'; [1. 154,25]) when sailing past a bay. According to Marcian (GGM 1,566,6f.), M. also described journeys from coast to coast across the open sea [4. 87f.]. However, little is found in the *Epitomé* of the historical and geographical claims of M. reported by Marcian (GGM 1,566,43f.), at most a mention of inhabitants, boundaries and river mouths. Therefore, one can only conjecture (with [5. 1219]) that this combination of geographical and nautical aspects constituted the work's originality. Artemidorus in particular is thought to be among the numerous sources relating to the Pontus Euxinus that must have been available to M. [5. 1219].

→ Geography II; → Oikoumene; → Periplus

1 A. DILLER, The Trad. of the Minor Greek Geographers, 1952 (mit Textrekonstruktion des M., Komm. und ausführlicher Bibliogr.) 2 F. GISINGER, s.v. M. (9), RE 15, 862–888 3 R. GÜNGERICH, Die Küstenbeschreibungen in der griech.Lit., 1950 4 G. HARTINGER, Die Peripluslit., Diss. Salzburg 1992 5 F. LASSERRE, s.v. M. (6), KlP 3, 1217–1219 6 E. OLSHAUSEN, s.v. Polemion, RE Suppl. 14, 1974, 427f. 7 Ders., Einf. in die histor. Geogr. der Alten Welt, 1991 8 H. STADTMÜLLER (Hrsg.), Anthologia Graeca, 3,1, 1906.   H.A.G.

[7] Greek comedy writer of unknown dates, only attested in the Suda [1], which mentions Κέρκωπες 'among others' as the title of a work. Attempts to change the name to 'Hermippus' or to equate M. with the cynic writer → M. [4] remain uncertain.

1 PCG VII, 1989, 3.   H.-G.NE.

Menius (Μήνιος; *Ménios*). A small tributary of the → Peneius in the territory of the city of Elis, which Hercules was said to have diverted in order to clean the stables of → Augias. It cannot be identified with certainty as a tributary of the modern Revmata. Attested in Paus. 5,1,10; 6,26,1; Theoc. 25,15.   C.L.

Mennis Only Curtius Rufus (5,1,16) reports that Alexander [4] the Great reached the city M. after four days on the road from Arbela [1] to Babylon. A strong spring of naphtha was said to gush forth from a cave nearby. The city wall of Babylon was said to have been built of asphalt from M., which was probably located in the petroleum region of Kirkūk.

F. H. WEISSBACH, s.v. Mennis, RE 15, 896.   K.KE.

Meno (Μένων; *Ménōn*).
[1] For his support for the Athenians in their attack on → Eion [1] on the Strymon, M. of Pharsalus was, according to Demosthenes (Or. 13,23), awarded → *atéleia* or (Or. 23,199) Athenian citizenship [1. 20–23].

[2] M. of Pharsalus, was, like his ancestors, closely connected to the Thessalian dynasty of the → Aleuadai (M.
was the *erómenos*, 'beloved', of Aristippus) and bound
by paternal hospitality to the Persian ruling house (Plat.
Men. 70b; 78d). M. contributed 1000 hoplites and 500
peltasts to Cyrus the Younger [3] in his campaign
against → Artaxerxes [2] in 401 BC at Phrygian Colos-
sae (Xen. An. 1,2,6; Diod. Sic. 14, 19, 8). He facilitated
Cyrus' invasion of Cilicia. He was the first to cross the
Euphrates with his troops, for which Cyrus rewarded
him handsomely. He commanded the left wing at the
battle of → Kunaxa (Xen. An. 1,2,20f.; 1,4,13–17;
1,7,1; 1,8,4). According to Xenophon, he betrayed the
Greek generals, who were captured and executed by
Artaxerxes (Xen. An. 2,1,5; 2,2,1; 2,5,31; 2,5,38; Ctesias FGrH 688 F 27f.; Ath. 11, 505a-b). Initially spared,
M. is said to have been killed one year later by order of
the Great King (Xen. An. 2,6,29). In Xenophon (An.
2,6,21–29) and the Suda (s.v.) M. is characterized as
avaricious, ambitious, and greedy for power, perfidious
and dishonest. The image of him in Plato's dialogue
"*Menon*" is also critical [2; 3; 4; 5].

1 M. J. OSBORNE, Naturalization in Athens 3, 1983   2 T.
S. BROWN, Meno of Thessaly, in: Historia 35, 1986, 387–
404   3 O. LENDLE, Kommentar zu Xenophons Anabasis,
1995   4 D. P. ORSI, Il tradimento di Menone, in: Quaderni di Storia 16, 1990, 139–145;   5 J. HOLZHAUSEN,
Menon in Platons 'Menon', in: WJA 20, 1994/95, 129–
149.   W.S.

[3] Son of Cerdimmas. He is said to have been made
satrap of → Coele Syria by Alexander [4] the Great at
the end of 333 BC (Arr. Anab. 2,13,7). However, from
Egypt, a certain Arimmas [1. no. 114] was entrusted
with preparations for the march to the Euphrates, and
later removed for unsatisfactory fufillment of his orders
(Arr. Anab. 3,6,8: his successor was Asclepiodorus).
Curtius (4,5,9; 8,9–11) tells quite a different story:
either after the capture of Tyre or already after the vic-
tory at Issos, → Parmenion handed over command to
Andromachus, who was killed in a revolt in Samaria;
Alexander took vengeance on the culprits and made
Mémnōn his successor (Arr. Anab. 4,8,11; is this our
Meno?). The sources cannot be reconciled.

1 BERVE 2.

J. E. ATKINSON, A Commentary on Q. Curtius Rufus'
Historiae Alexandri Magni Vol. 3 and 4, 1980, 370f. (with
bibl.); A. B. BOSWORTH, A Historical Commentary on
Arrian's History 1, 1980, 224–5 (not unobjectionable
from a methodical point of view).

[4] In 330 BC. Satrap of Arachosia (Arr. Anab. 3,28,1;
according to Curt. 7,3,4–5 with a strong garrison). He
died in 325 BC. Sibyrtius was his successor.   E.B.

[5] Athenian from the deme of Potamus, sent to the
Hellespont as strategos in 362 BC, then recalled and
prosecuted by → *eisangelía* (Dem. Or. 36,53; 50,4 and
12–14). M. was nevertheless strategos once again on
Euboea in 357 BC (IG II² 124,10 and 21).

DEVELIN, Nr. 1994; P. M. FRASER, E. MATTHEWS, s.v.
Meno (2), A Lexicon of Greek Personal Names 2, 1994;
PA 10085; TRAILL, PAA 647070.

[6] of Pharsalus, proved himself militarily in the
→ Lamian War 323/2 BC as a Thessalian cavalry commander, and in 322 as hipparch of the Hellenic League.
He tried in vain to instigate peace negotiations between
the Hellenic League and Antipater [1] (Diod. Sic.
18,17,6). M. fell as archon of the Aetolians in battle
against → Polyperchon (Diod. Sic. 18,38,5–6). M.'s
daughter Phthia was the mother of → Pyrrhus of Epirus
(Plut. Pyrrhus 1,7).

J. ENGELS, Studien zur politischen Biographie des Hypereides, 1993², 357f.   J.E.

[7] Of Segesta. He became the slave of → Agathocles [2]
when his hometown was conquered in 307 BC. It seems
he caused the tyrant's death on the instigation of → Archagathos [2] in 289/8 BC, by handing him a poisoned
toothpick. He then tried to seize power over Syracuse,
had Archagathos killed and placed himself at the head
of the mercenaries. He subsequently fought beside the
Carthaginians against → Hicetas [2]. Nothing more is
heard of him after this (Diod. Sic. 21,16).

H. BERVE, Die Tyrannis bei den Griechen 1, 1967, 456,
458.   K.MEI.

Menodorus (Μηνόδωρος; *Mēnódōros*).
[1] M. (according to Appian, elsewhere Mena(s),
Μηνᾶς; *Mēnâs*), a freedman, previously perhaps a Cilician pirate, in about 40 BC S. → Pompeius' admiral in
the Tyrrhenian Sea. As an opponent of a settlement with
the Triumviri (Plut. Antonius 32,6f.), M. defended Sardinia and Corsica. When Pompey threatened to strip
him of his power at the instigation of his rival Menecrates [11], M. delivered the islands into the hands of
Octavian in 38 (App. B Civ. 5,78–80,330–337; a relationship to CIL X 8034 is disputed). M., now a Roman
equestrian and a legate of C. Calvisius [6] Sabinus, attacked Pompey's followers and killed Menecrates.
Overshadowed by → Agrippa [1], M. returned to
Pompey in 36 (App. B Civ. 5,96,400; Cass. Dio
48,54,7). The distrust with which he was treated there
drove him to commit treason for a third time (App. B
Civ. 5,102,422–426). Octavian pardoned M. but
posted him to Illyria where he was killed in a a river
battle near Siscia in 35 (Cass. Dio 49,37,6).   JÖ.F.

[2] Name of several Greek sculptors. According to base
inscriptions on Delos between 103 and 96 BC, M. of
Mallus, the son of Phaenander, created votive offerings
to Serapis, Apollo and Pistis, which are no longer
extant. In Thespiae, Pausanias (9,27,4) saw a copy by
M. of Athens of the Eros of → Praxiteles, which had
been taken to Rome. Pliny included this sculptor name
in a list (HN 34,91).

LOEWY Nr. 306, 307; G. A. MANSUELLI, L. GUERRINI, s.v.
M. (1.3), EAA 4, 1961, 1024f.; J. MARCADÉ, Recueil des

signatures de sculpteurs grecs, 2, 1957, 69; OVERBECK, Nr. 2259, 2260; C. PICARD, Manuel d'archéologie grecque: La sculpture, 3.2, 1948, 441f. R.N.

Menodotus (Μηνόδοτος; *Mēnódōtos*).

[1] M. of Perinthus In about 200 BC, he wrote a 'Greek History' (*Hellenikaì Pragmateîai*) in 15 books, probably a continuation of the work of Psaon of Plataeae (FGrH 78) and dealing with events after 218/17 (Diod. Sic. 26,4). He may be identical (see [1]) with M. of Samos (which was considered a colony of Perinthus). The latter was the author of a periegesis (→ *periēgētés*) on 'Notabilia of Samos' (*Tôn katà tèn Sámon endóxōn anagraphḗ*), from which Athenaeus (15, 671–699) relates an extensive passage on the pre-Hellenic history of the island.

1 FGrH 82 und 541 with comm. 2 O. LENDLE, Einführung in die griechische Geschichtsschreibung, 1992, 143. K.MEI.

[2] M. of Nicomedia Greek doctor active around AD 125. He was a leading member of the → Empiricist school and teacher of → Herodotus [3] (Diog. Laert. 9,115). M. wrote books of considerable scope, among them one dedicated to an otherwise unknown Severus, on which Galen wrote a commentary (Gal., De libris propriis 9; 19,38 K.). The view that he provided the impetus to Galen's *Protreptikós* is based on a corruption of the text (cf. CMG 5,1,1, p. 70). He strongly opposed the → Methodists, especially Asclepiades [6], and fought against them with strong language. Similarly, those who only followed a routine when healing were a thorn in his side [1]. He openly acknowledged that a doctor should seek fame and profit (Fr. 293 DEICHGRÄBER). He modified some points of Empiricist theory and espoused the view that analogy was a key only to the possible, not to reality, and that a simple original experience was to be modified by later subsequent continuing experiences. After memory and perception, he considered this way of thinking to be the third part of medicine. In his therapeutic writings he wanted to have phlebotomy reserved for cases of plethora (Fr. 294–296 DEICHGRÄBER).

1 DEICHGRÄBER, 213. V.N.

[3] Several Greek sculptors of the same name whose family tree has been reconstructed. According to signatures on the bases of lost works, M. was from Tyre, was the son of Artemidorus and was active with his father and his brother Charmolas in Rhodes and Halicarnassus in about 130–85 BC. In Athens he collaborated on a large-scale sculpture group for the athlete Menodorus. Four signatures by his nephew M., the son of Charmolas, between 85 and 50 BC are preserved in Rhodes. One of the two M.s left a lead label with signature inside the Apollo from Piombino (Paris, LV). Again in the Imperial period, a M. signed a portrait sculpture in Aphrodisias. A lost Hercules statue with the signature of a M., son of Boethus, from Nicomedia is suspected of being a fake.

V. C. GOODLETT, Rhodian Sculpture Workshops, in: AJA 95, 1991, 669–681; L. GUERRINI, A. DI VITA, s.v. M. (1–3), EAA 4, 1961, 1025; LIPPOLD, 371; LOEWY, Nr. 308, 309, 521; J. MARCADÉ, Recueil des signatures de sculpteurs grecs, 2, 1957, 72; B. S. RIDGWAY, The Bronze Apollo from Piombino in the Louvre, in: AntPl 7, 1967, 43–75; R. R. R. SMITH, Hellenistic Sculpture, 1991, 272; A. STEWART, Attika, 1979, 119. R.N.

Menoeceus (Μενοικεύς/*Menoikeús*, Latin *Menoeceus*).
[1] The father of → Creon [1] (Soph. Ant. 156 *et passim*).
[2] The son of Creon [1] who Tiresias prophesied had to be sacrificed to Ares to ensure victory for Thebes over the army of the Seven (→ Seven against Thebes). M. tricks Creon, who tries to persuade him to flee, and kills himself (Eur. Phoen. 834ff.; 1090ff.; 1310ff.; melodramatically elaborated by Stat. Theb. 10,610ff., where M. is spurred on to the act by the goddess Virtus and, after he has thrown himself from the wall being attacked by Capaneus, is caught by her and Pietas and rises to Heaven). Pausanias (9,25,1) was familiar with the tomb of M. by the Neitian Gate.
[3] A friend of → Epicurus and the addressee of his third letter. CL.K.

Menoetes (Μενοίτης; *Menoítēs*). The mythical herdsman of → Hades, who watches his herds on the island → Erythea near the entrance of the Underworld. He reports Hercules's theft of one of his cattle to the neighbouring herdsman → Geryoneus, but is killed by Hercules in a wrestling match (Apollod. 2,108; 125). L.K.

Menoetius (Μενοίτιος; *Menoítios*).
[1] Son of → Actor [1] and Aegina, who settled in Opus (Pind. Ol. 9,69f.); husband of Sthenele (or Periopis or Polymele), father of → Patroclus and Myrto (Apollod. 3,13,8; Plut. Aristeides 20,7). In the *Ilias* M. is designated as *hḗrōs* (Hom. Il. 11,771; 18,325). When Patroclus killed Cleitonymus, son of Aphidamas, in battle, M. fled with him to → Peleus in Phthia. From there, he sent his son to Troy, in support of → Achilles [1] (Hom. Il. 23,83ff.; 11,765ff.). M. himself remained in Phthia throughout the war. M. took part in the voyage of the → Argonauts (Apoll. Rhod. 1,69f.; Apollod. 1,9,16) and was a friend of → Heracles, whose cult he founded at Opus (Diod. 4,39,1). J.STE.
[2] Admiral of Ptolemy I, subordinate to → Menelaus [4], *naúarchos* at → Cyprus in 306 BC (Diod. 20,52,5). He may be identical with [1. no. 511] (PP V 13775).

1 BERVE 2.

H. HAUBEN, Het Vlootbevelhebberschap in de vroege Diadochentijd, 1975, 70f. Nr. 25. W.A.

Menogenes (Μενογένης; *Menogénēs*). Greek grammarian. In Eust. 2,494 (ad Hom. Il. 2,494) he is mentioned alongside Porphyry and → Apollodorus [7] as a commentator on the Homeric Catalogue of Ships. Nothing is preserved of his work, which was said to have encompassed 23 books. His dates are likewise unknown: [1] places him between Apollodorus and Porphyry.

1 A. GUDEMAN, s.v. Menogenes, RE 15, 917.   M.B.

Menologion (Μηνολόγιον; *Mēnológion*). A collection of the lives of Saints of the Orthodox Church, arranged according to the feast-day of the corresponding saint, in accordance with the ecclesiastical year (→ calendar). In contrast to the → Synaxarion, which provides only brief notices for each saint, and to the Menaion, which usually contains liturgical songs and prayers for the saint's festival, the βίοι/*bíoi* ('lives') of the Menologion are normally longer. It may have been mentioned first in → Theodoros Studites [1. vol. 1, 21], yet the first preserved copies date from the 9th cent. AD. However, the authoritative Menologion was the one by → Symeon Metaphrastes (10th cent. AD).

→ Saints, Veneration of the saints; → Martyrs

1 A. ERHARD, Überlieferung und Bestand der hagiographischen und homiletischen Literatur der griechischen Kirche, 3 vols., 1936–1939   2 G. BOTTEREAU, s.v. Menologion, Dictionnaire de spiritualité, 1024–1027   2 N. P. ŠEVČENKO, s.v. Menologion, ODB 1340f.   J.N.

Menophanes (Μηνοφάνης; *Mēnophánēs*).
[1] General of → Mithradates VI. In the first → Mithradatic War, in 88 B.C., he defeated Roman troops under M'. → Aquillius [I 4] (Memnon FGrH 434 F 1,22,7). It is doubtful whether this was the battle at Proton Pachion mentioned by Appianus (Mith. 72) [3. 1101²⁷]. According to Pausanias (3,23,3–5), in the same year, either on orders of the King or on his own initiative, M. conquered, plundered and destroyed → Delos, killed the foreigners and Delian men there, and enslaved their wives and children. In the service of divine vengeance, merchants who had been able to escape his attack subsequently ambushed M. and sank him, together with his ship (Paus. 3,23,3–5. There is a discrepancy with App. Mith. 108, according to whom it was Archelaus [4] that attacked Delos). According to Appianus (Mith. 524), at the end of the 3rd → Mithradatic War in 64 B.C., a certain M., general of Mithradates VI, advised him to spare → Pharnaces. For discussion of the problems of identification, cf. [1. 135; 2. 46–48; 3. 1101²⁷; 4. 271f.; 5. 118, 137].

1 L. BALLESTEROS PASTOR, Mitrídates Eupátor, 1996
2 M. JANKE, Historische Untersuchungen zu Memnon von Herakleia, 1963   3 MAGIE;   4 D. MUSTI, M. TORELLI, Pausania, Guida della Grecia 3, 1991, 271f.   5 TH. REINACH, Mithradates Eupator, 1895 (repr. 1975).   E.O.

[2] Grammarian, date unknown, called ἀρχαῖος and οὐκ εὐκαταφρόνητος by → Photius (Phot. 120a 11–12). According to Photius, M. delved into work of the historian → Theopompus [3] von Chios and advanced the

hypothesis that the twelfth book of his Histories was lost. Yet Photius still knew this book.

FGrH 115 T 18.

Menophantus Greek sculptor. A statue of Aphrodite (Rome, MN) bears his signature, with the additional note that the model is in the Troad. The work, which is a variation on the type of the Capitoline Venus, dates from the 1st cent. BC.

G. CRESSEDI, s.v. Menephanto, EAA 4, 1961, 1026; LOEWY, Nr. 377; B. S. RIDGWAY, Hellenistic Sculpture, 1, 1990, 356; O. VASORI, Museo nazionale romano. Le sculture, 1, 1, 1979, 109–111, Nr. 81.   R.N.

Menophilus of Damascus, known only from 15 hexameters cited by Stobaeus from his poem 'Tresses' (Πλοκαμῖδες/*Plokamîdes*), a song on the beauty of his beloved's hair.

SH 558.   S.FO.

Menorah The golden seven-branched candlestick (Hebr. *mᵉnôrāh*, Ex 25,31–40), which adorned the second Jewish → Temple, soon became the symbol of → Judaism. From the time of Mattathias → Antigonus [5] (40–37 BC), it appears occasionally on Jewish coins. The representation on the Arch of Titus in Rome shows how the menorah, looted from the Jerusalem Temple, was paraded triumphally through Rome together with other implements for the sacred service, thus documenting its symbolic meaning for all of Judaism. Since the 1st cent. AD, pictorial representations of the menorah, usually in combination with palm branches, incense shovels and shofar horns, have adorned → synagogues, Jewish funerary inscriptions, amulets, lamps, and glass vessels. Today, it stands at the center of the official emblem of the State of Israel.

M. HARAN et al., s. v. Menorah, in: Encyclopaedia Judaica 11, 1971, 1355–1371.   LUK.KU.

Mens Roman personification of 'prudence', wrongly classified as 'amorphous → numen' [1. 478]. The → *Sibyllini libri* decreed the introduction of its cult in 217 BC (Liv. 22,9,8): its temple was pledged as the result of the Roman defeat at the hands of → Hannibal at Lake Trasimenus by the Praetor T. Otacilius Crassus (Liv. 22,10,10; Ov. Fast. 6,241–248), and was dedicated on the Capitol, beside the temple of → Venus Erycina, in 215 BC (Liv. 23,31,9). It was renewed by → Aemilius [I 37] Scaurus (*cos.* 115 BC: Cic. Nat. D. 2,61). The early Imperial → Fasti record the 8th of June as → *natalis templi* (InscrIt 13,2 p. 467; Ov. Fast. 6,247f.). The instructions of the Greek *libri Sibyllini*, and M.'s connection with Venus Erycina (Liv. 22,9,10; Serv. Aen. 1,720), together with its acting as the Greek *Euboulía/Gnōmē* (Plut. Mor. 318e, 322c) have led to the erroneous assumption of Greek influence. Epigraphic evidence begins in the late Republican period

(e.g. [2. 9 no. 12]: *Bonai Menti*, late 2nd cent. B.C., cf. [3. 65–76]; AE 1975, 237: *Menti Bonae*). Dedications from slaves and freedmen stem primarily from the early Imperial period [4. 937]. M. was typically represented as a seated, anthropomorphic figure [1. 478f.].
→ Personification

1 E. SIMON, s.v. Mens, LIMC 6.1, 477–479   2 G. B. BRUSIN, Inscriptiones Aquileiae 1, 1991   3 F. FONTANA, I culti di Aquileia repubblicana, 1997   4 E. MARBACH, s.v. Mens, RE 15, 936f.

LATTE, 239f.; M. MELLO, Mens Bona, 1968; CH. REUSSER, s.v. Mens, LTUR 3, 240f.   C.R.P.

Mensa see → Table

Mensarius As a state magistrate, the mensarius exercized the function of a money-changer or banker, and was responsible above all for state payments and expenditures. Some Greek city-states, e.g. Tenos in the 1st cent. BC (Cic. Flacc. 44) had such official bankers constantly available: they were called δημόσιοι τραπεζῖται (*dēmósioi trapezîtai*). At Rome, this function existed only in exceptional situations, as during a debt crisis in the 4th cent. B.C. (352 B.C., Liv. 7,21,5ff.) and during the Second Punic War (*triumviri mensarii*, Liv. 23,21,6; 24,18,12; 26,36,8). In addition, the word *mensarius* sometimes also designated bankers who transacted private financial operations (Suet. Aug. 4,2), since the pay-table *(mensa)* was characteristic of the practice of their trade.
→ Argentarius [2]; → Banks

1 J. ANDREAU, La vie financière dans le monde romain, 1987, 224–246   2 R. BOGAERT, Banques et banquiers dans les cités grecques, 1968, 401–408   3 A. STORCHI MARINO, Quinqueviri mensarii. Censo e debiti nel IV secolo, in: Athenaeum, 81, 1993, 213–250.   J.A.

Mensis see → Calendar

Mensor was the Latin term for technical experts who carried out measurements in the broadest sense of the word. *Mensores agrarii* (*agrimensores, geometrae, gromatici*, → surveyor) were responsible in both civil and military domains for marking out surfaces, laying out → roads, → aqueducts, and building camps. This activity gained great importance during the 1st cent. BC, as a consequence of the allocation of land to veterans. According to the representation on the gravestone of L. Aebutius Faustus (CIL V 6786 = ILS 7736), their main instrument was the → groma. *Mensores aedificiorum* are found in the areas of house construction and supervision (Plin. Epist. 10,17b; 10,18,3). The funerary altar of the *mensor aedificiorum* Titus Statilius Aper shows the deceased holding a wax tablet with a measuring-sketch in his hands (CIL VI 1975 = ILS 7737).
Mensores frumentarii were active under the *praefectus annonae* in the Roman civic grain supply (→ cura annonae) (CIL XIV 172 = ILS 1429; CIL XIV 303 = ILS 6169; CIL XIV 309 = ILS 6163; CIL XIV 409 = ILS 6146), and were responsible in the military domain for supplying the troops with victuals (ILS 9091). Levelling was also a part of the technique of measurement, and was carried out by means of the chorobates (Vitr. 8,5; on the → *librator* in the Roman army, cf. ILS 2059; 2422; 5795). A *mensor sacomarius*, responsible for the maintenance of correct → measures and → weights at markets, is also attested epigraphically (CIL X 1930 = ILS 7739).

1 O. BEHRENDS, L. C. COLOGNESI (ed.), Die römische Feldmeßkunst (AAWG), 1992   2 K. BRODERSEN, Terra cognita, 1995   3 E. FABRICIUS, s.v. M., RE 15, 956–960   4 K. GREWE, Planung und Trassierung römischen Wasserleitungen, 1992², 13–23   5 ZIMMER, catalogue no. 141–142, 1982.   H.-J.S.

Menstruation In Hippocratic medicine, menstruation was regarded as essential not only to female health, but also to becoming a mature woman or *gynḗ*; menstruation is 'the most important sign of the radical difference between men and women.' [1.234] One of the Greek words for menstruation is *gynaikeîa*, while other terms – such as *kataménia* and *epiménia* – emphasise the ideally monthly pattern of loss. Due to the looser texture of their flesh and their sedentary way of life, women were thought to absorb more fluid from their diet than men did, needing to evacuate the blood which this generates regularly, so that their internal balance could be maintained (e.g. *Mul.* 1,1; 8,10–14 L.; see → Gynaecology). The age of menarche was believed to be the fourteenth year, as the network of internal channels in a girl's body developed sufficiently to allow the collection of blood. *Nat. Puer.* 15 (7,492–494 L.) suggests that the accumulated blood then moves to the womb 'all at once'. The amount of blood lost should be about half a litre over two to three days (*Mul.* 1.6, 8.30 L.). If the blood remained in the body, it could exert pressure on vital organs and cause first pain (*Mul.* 1.1, 8.12 L.), then disease (*Mul.* 1.3, 8.22 L.), and – if attempts to draw out the blood by using drugs, pessaries and fumigations were unsuccessful – death (*Mul.* 1,2; 8,16–18 L.).

In Aristotle's [6] model of the female body, menstruation became more fully a sign of inadequacy; only the male body was thought to be hot enough to concoct blood into semen (e.g. *Gen. An.* 775a 14–20). Parmenides and others apparently believed, by contrast, that women were hotter than men, on the grounds that women have more blood, and blood is humorally valued as 'hot' and 'wet' (Aristotle *Part. An.* 648a 28–30; *Gen. An.* 765b 19). Aristotle, Diocles [6] und Empedocles [1] believed that all women menstruated at the same time of the lunar month, with the waning moon (Aristotle *Gen. An.* 767a 2–6). As for the quality of menstrual blood, Greek writers in general thought that it was no different from other blood, although some argued that it was a cold, corrupt form (e.g. Plut. *Moralia* 651c-e).

Medically, menstruation could be welcomed as an indication of the ability to conceive, since it demonstrated that the womb was sufficiently open to receive the male seed. This meant that – in contrast to the Christian tradition – intercourse towards the end of a menstrual period was not seen as polluting, but was instead positively encouraged as providing the best opportunity for cnoception, since the womb was still open, there was sufficient blood remaining to provide the raw material to form a foetus, but there was not enough blood present to 'wash out' the male seed (Hipp. *Nat. Mul.* 8; 7,324 L.; *Mul.* 1,17; 8,56 L.; Aristotle *Gen. An.* 727b 12–25).

There is no evidence that the Greeks of the classical period attributed any malign influence to a menstruating woman: in contrast with many cultures, the Greeks did not believe that a menstruating woman should be segregated or forbidden to cook for men, or that she had any magical powers. However, later Greek sacred laws of the Hellenistic period do include menstruating women among those categories forbidden to enter a sacred precinct [2.74–103]. Pliny (HN 7,64–5; 17,266; 28,77–86) lists many malign powers of menstrual blood, including blunting knives and turning wine sour. Columella lists the effects of menstruation, particularly menarcheal blood, on the natural world; these powers can be used for good, for example by averting hail or killing caterpillars and other crop pests (*De re rustica* 10.357–63, 11.3.38,64; cf. Plutarch *Moralia* 700e). Even the gaze of a menstruating woman may be thought to have power (→ Magic). Columella (*De re rustica* 11.3.50) reports that it can blight cucumbers and gourds, while Aristotle (*Insomn.* 459b 24–460a 23) claims that it dims a mirror with a bloody haze which is difficult to remove. However, this passage may be an interpolation, as it does not otherwise conform with Aristotle's views on menstruation [1.229f.].

As menstruation is only discussed at length in medical texts, we know little about its management in the lives of ordinary women. Folded rags (*rhákea*) appear to have been used for menstrual protection (e.g. Plut. *Moralia* 700e; Hipp. *Mul.* 1,11; 8,42 L.); these could also be known as 'protection' (*phylakía*) [2.102 Nr. 113] The account of the life of the philosopher → Hypatia given in the *Suda* claims that she once threw one at an unwanted suitor [3.77]. MOMMSEN suggested that the term *rhákos* in the inventories of Artemis Brauronia should be understood as evidence of the dedication of menstrual rags to the goddess at puberty [4.343–347]; however, this is more likely to indicate that the garments offered had deteriorated to a 'ragged' condition [5.58].

→ Gender roles II. Medicine; → Gynaecology; → Woman

1 L. A. DEAN-JONES, Women's Bodies in Classical Greek Science, 1994   2 R. PARKER, Miasma, 1983 (²1996). 3 G. CLARK, Women in Late Antiquity, 1993   4 TH. MOMMSEN, Rhakos auf attischen Inschriften, in: Philologus 58, 1899;   5 T. LINDERS, Studies in the Treasury Records of Artemis Brauronia Found in Athens, 1972.

P. DIEPGEN, Die Frauenheilkunde der alten Welt, 1937; D. GOUREVITCH, Le mal d' être femme, 1984; H. GRENSEMANN, Hippokratische Gynäkologie, 1982; A. E. HANSON, Hippocrates: Diseases of Women I, in: Signs 1, 1975, 567–584; H. KING, Hippocrates' Woman, 1998; G. E. R. LLOYD, Science, Folklore and Ideology, 1983; P. MANULI, Donne mascoline, femmine sterili, vergini perpetue, in: S. CAMPANESE et al. (ed.), Madre Materia, 1983, 147–192; H. VON STADEN, Women and Dirt, in: Helios 19, 1992, 7–30.   H.K.

Mental illness
A. NEAR EASTERN   B. EARLY GREECE   C. MENTAL ILLNESS IN THE HIPPOCRATICS   D. PLATO AND ARISTOTLE   E. THE METHODISTS   F. RUFUS AND GALEN   G. LATE ANTIQUITY

A. NEAR EASTERN
Mental illnesses (MI) are described in both Jewish and Babylonian texts. Sometimes physical signs are indicated, as in epilepsy, sometimes behaviours are described as in 1 Sam 16:14–16; 21:13–15, but all MI are ascribed to the intervention of God, or, in texts from 500 BC onwards, of a variety of demons [1]. Treatment might be limited to confinement (Jer 29:26–8) or exorcism, including music, but the Jewish 'Therapeutae' took an approach that involved the entire lifestyle (Phil. De vita contemplativa 2). The fluid boundary between madness and divine inspiration is seen in attitudes towards prophecy.

B. EARLY GREECE
Early Greek attitudes to MI are similar: strange behaviour is ascribed to punishment by an offended deity. Similar explanations are current in Greek tragedy, e.g. Eur. Bacch.; Soph. Aj., and in other literature. Although Homer distinguishes between different souls or parts of the soul, madness in his poems does not lead to a derangement of any structure of the soul or of the relationship between its parts. Relief is sought in appeasing the deity, as well as in various activities such as prayer, exorcism, and the therapy of the word [2].

C. MENTAL ILLNESS IN THE HIPPOCRATICS
The Hippocratic author of De morbo sacro, c. 420 BC, offers a purely physical, non-theological explanation for → epilepsy and mania; both are caused by physical imbalances, epilepsy by excess phlegm blocking channels in the brain, mania by bile burning up the brain. Treatment is physical, by diet and drugs, e.g. hellebore. Other medical writers imply a similar somaticism, with disturbances in the brain region responsible for both physical and mental changes. Other MI, such as → hysteria or hypochondria, were ascribed to physical disorders in other regions of the body, and were described in both physical and mental terms. General character could also be affected by the physical conditions of life, according to the author of De aere, aquis, locis.

D. PLATO AND ARISTOTLE

Plato develops a concept of MI as the result of conflict within the organs of the body; the brain and its activities are affected by physical changes everywhere, e.g. through drunkenness. His persuasive mixture of medical, moral, and political analogies and explanations in the *De re publica* and the *Timaeus* depends on a holistic somaticism, in which moral failings, e.g. excess pleasure and pain, can be ascribed to physical causes. At the same time, by moral training, and occasionally diet, many of these conditions can be improved.

Aristotle also accepts a somatic explanation for certain mental states; in the later ps.-Aristotelian *Problemata* (30,1) a physical cause, black bile (→ Melancholy), produces the positive genius as well as the mentally disturbed [3]. The development of → physiognomics also associates certain types of unusual behaviour with physical conditions.

E. THE METHODISTS

Hellenistic doctors produced a more medical interpretation of MI as a sharply-defined collection of symptoms, with causes explained in physical terms, alongside popular and legal definitions in terms of unusual behaviour. Asclepiades of Bithynia and later Methodists offered sophisticated ideas on diagnosis and treatment which combined drugs and diet with psychotherapy, and which accepted the reality to the patient of what others might see as hallucination [4].

F. RUFUS AND GALEN

Rufus of Ephesus continued the tradition of somatic interpretations of MI, especially in his writings on melancholy, preserved in Arabic [5]. He was followed in this by Galen, who found his Platonic psychological theories confirmed by his own anatomical and clinical observations. He paid particular attention to stress-related diseases, explaining both their psychological and physical manifestations [6]. While accepting that some types of MI, e.g. phrenitis, were curable by physical means, he left others, e.g. mania, untreated except by psychological means. His doctrines gradually formed the basis for a general medical view of MI as largely physical in origin, and, later on, as a character trait largely determined by temperament.

G. LATE ANTIQUITY

The Christian Gospels talk of MI as involving demoniac possession, and curable by exorcism. While not excluding medical intervention, this belief strengthened the notion that MI were different from other diseases in cause and in treatment. Although doctors might deny this (Philostorgius VIII,10), and although lawyers refused to allow medical exorcists the same privileges as physicians (Dig. 50,13,1), there was an increasing tendency in Late Antiquity to believe in some form of possession for a variety of diseases (e.g. incubus, lycanthropy), as well as for MI (Paul of Aegina III 13–17). Treatment in such cases was by religious means, prayer

or exorcism, and the madman was usually kept confined within the family. At the same time, the boundary between madness and divine inspiration became more and more blurred, culminating in the story of St. Maro, a holy fool, who feigned madness in order to drive away his followers, but whose behaviour only convinced them of his sanctity (John Ephes. 68; [7]).

1 M. STOL, Epilepsy in Babylonia, 1993   2 P. LAIN ENTRALGO, The therapy of the word in Classical Antiquity, 1970   3 P. J. VAN DER EIJK, Aristoteles über die Melancholie, in: Mnemosyne 43, 1990, 33–72   4 J. PIGEAUD, Folie et cures de la folie, 1987   5 M. ULLMANN, Islamic medicine, 1978   6 M. DOLS, Majnun: the madman in medieval Islamic society   7 L. RYDEN, The holy fool, in: S. HACKEL, The Byzantine Saint, 1981.

J. L. HEIBERG, Geisteskrankheit im klassischen Altertum, in: Allg. Zeitschr. f. Psychiatrie 86, 1927, 1–44; W. LEIBBRAND, Der Wahnsinn, 1961; H. FLASHAR, Melancholie und Melancholiker in den Theorien der Griechen, 1966; O. TEMKIN, The falling sickness, 1971²; B. SIMON, Mind and Madness in Classical Greece, 1978; J. PIGEAUD, La maladie de l'âme, 1981; S. W. JACKSON, Melancholia and Depression, 1987.   V.N.

Mentes (Μέντης; *Méntēs*).

[1] Mythical commander of the → Cicones in the Trojan War. Apollo assumes his guise to spur Hector on to battle (Hom. Il. 17,13).

[2] Mythical Prince of the Taphiae. Athena assumes his guise to appear to Telemachus (Hom. Od. 1,105; 1,180; → Mentor [2]).   L.K.

Mentesa Name, possibly Iberian [1. 549], of two towns.

[1] **M. Bastitanorum** (CIL II 3377f.; 3380), modern La Guardia, south east of → Castulo (Plin. HN 3,9; 19; 25; It. Ant. 402,4). Mint and bishopric in the Visigothic period.

[2] (Μέντισα; *Méntisa*). Probably near the modern Villanueva de la Fuente, close to the source of the Guadiana Menor, in the *conventus* of → Carthago Nova (CIL II p. 434f.; Plin. HN 3,25; Ptol. 2,6,59; CIL XI 3281–3284).

1 HOLDER 2.

A. SCHULTEN (ed.), Fontes Hispaniae Antiquae 8, 59; 9, 451; TOVAR 2, 151f. and 178.   P.B.

Mentor (Μέντωρ; *Méntōr*).

[1] Father of → Imbrius of Pedaeum (Hom. Il. 13,171).

[2] M. of Ithaca, son of Alcimus (Hom. Od. 22,235), companion of → Odysseus, who on his departure to Troy hands over to M. the supervision of his household (ibid. 2,225ff.). In the People's Assembly M. firmly opposes the behaviour of the suitors (ibid. 2,224ff.). The goddess → Athena often takes on his form in order to help → Telemachus with her advice (ibid. 2,267ff.; 3,22ff.; 240ff.; 4,654ff.) or to support Odysseus (ibid 24,502ff., 545ff.; → Mentes [2]).   AL.FR

[3] Rhodian. He and his brother → Memnon [3] rendered outstanding service to the satrap → Artabazus [4]. The two were rewarded with a fief in th Troad. M. took part in Artabazus's uprising against → Artaxerxes [3] and found refuge with→ Nectanebus II in Egypt. Sent to Sidon with 4,000 mercenaries to support Tennes who was in revolt against Artaxerxes, he did however help with Tennes's plan to betray Sidon to Artaxerxes and for this he was taken into the service of the Persian king. In 343 BC in Egypt he did him valuable service and joined Bagoas [1] who supported him at court. Artaxerxes rewarded him generously, gave him supreme command in Asia Minor and had Memnon and Artabazus return with full amnesty (cf. → Memnon [3]). Informed by them of the plans of → Philippus II, he arrested → Hermias [1], occupied his territories without a fight and with Bagoas brought about his execution (Didymus, In Demosth. comm. 6,8f.). Soon after that he died (Diod. 16,42,2; 47,4; 49,7–50,8; 52,1–7).   E.B.

[4] Greek toreutist (→ Toreutics). The (exclusively Roman) records [3] of M. are always concerned with the value of his works for collectors, leaving his creative period unclear. Information about the actual or imaginary possession of works by M. dates to the 1st cents. BC and AD. By the Imperial period it was said that it had become practically impossible to get hold of genuine pieces by him. Four pairs of vessels were votive offerings in Ephesus before their destruction. Aside from silver vessels, statuettes by M. are also mentioned. His art was based on the invention of new types of vessel and relief images.

    1 G. BECATTI, Arte e gusto negli scrittori latini, 1951   2 L. GUERRINI, s.v. M., EAA 4, 1961, 1028   3 OVERBECK, no. 607, 1189, 1612, 2160–2181   4 M. PFROMMER, Griechische Originale und Kopien unter römischer Tafelsilber, in: The J.P. Getty Museum Journal 11, 1983, 135–146.
                                                    R.N.

Mentores Tribe of the northern Adriatic (Dalmatia), in Hecat. FGrH 1 F 62 neighbours but in Plin. HN 1,139 part of the → Liburni (together with the Himani, Encheleae, Peucetti). The M. were later ruled by the → Iapodes.

    G. ALFÖLDY, Bevölkerung u. Ges. der röm. Prov. Dalmatia, 1965; J. J. WILKES, Dalmatia, 1969.   H.SO.

Menyllos (Μένυλλος; *Ményllos*).
[1] After the Athenian defeat in the → Lamian War by → Antipater [1] in 322 BC, M. was appointed commander of the Macedonian garrison at the → Munychia fortress in Piraeus (Diod. 18,18,5; Plut. Phocion 28,1 and 7). He was on good terms with → Phocion who was then in charge of Athenian policy. After the death of Antipater, Cassander replaced M. with → Nicanor.

    W. S. FERGUSON, Hellenistic Athens, 1911, 20.   J.E.

[2] In 163/2 BC, M. of Alabanda went as the envoy of Ptolemy VI to Ptolemy VIII in Rome, where he helped his old and trusted friend, the historian → Polybios, arrange the flight of Demetrius [7] I Soter (Pol. 31,12,8f.; 14,8). In 162/1, M. was back in Rome although without achieving success for his king.

    E. OLSHAUSEN, Prosopographie der hellenistischen Königsgesandten, vol. 1, 1974, 74f. no. 51.   W.A.

Menysis (μήνυσις; *ménysis*). A 'charge' or 'application' in certain criminal proceedings The Greek polis functioned on initiatives of private citizens. In criminal law, too, the principle for accusations was considered to be 'no plaintiff, no judge'. In cases of high treason and blasphemy, which endangered the state, the Athenians nevertheless found ways of compensating for the lack of an official public prosecutor. Thus, in special cases state investigative commissioners (ζητηταί, *zētētaí*) were appointed and in others a reward was offered to encourage the lodging of a *menysis* (cf. And. 1,14). Accomplices were promised immunity (→ *aídesis*) from criminal proceedings if they issued a *menysis*. The cases of *menysis* are largely identical with those of an → *eisangelía* (literally also 'charge, application'), but the procedures cannot be considered in any way to be parallel. By means of a *menysis* an informer merely gives the state (the Council or the People's Assembly) the opportunity to initiate formal proceedings. The *eisangelía* could only be raised by a citizen plaintiff, whereas anyone could denounce with a *menysis*, even slaves (who were often promised freedom as a reward).

    BUSOLT/SWOBODA, 544; D. M. MACDOWELL, Andokides on the Mysteries, 1962.   G.T.

Mercello T. Mercello Persinus Marius. An equestrian from Cordoba, where he held municipal offices; *procurator Augusti*, probably in the first decades of the 1st cent. AD, possibly in Hispania Baetica (CIL II² 7, 311; II² 5, 1296).   W.E.

Mercenaries
I. GREECE II. ROME

I. GREECE

Mercenaries (μισθοφόρος/*misthophóros* or μισθωτός/*misthōtós*, ξένος/*xénos*) – soldiers who fought in foreign service as professional soldiers in exchange for payment (*misthós*) – had existed in Greece since ancient times. In the 6th cent. BC they served Egyptian or eastern kings (Egypt: Hdt. 2,154; ML, No. 7; Babylon: Alc. 350 LOBEL/PAGE); Greek tyrants like Peisistratus [4] or Polycrates [1] needed mercenaries to protect them (Hdt. 1,61; 3,45). Only from the → Peloponnesian War onwards did the poleis deploy, to a great extent, mercenaries alongside the citizen soldiers who, however, remained the military basis of their forces; among these mercenaries were Thracian → *peltastaí* (Thuc. 5,6,4; 7,27,1 f.; 7,29) or Cretan archers (Thuc. 6,43); as → pay each mercenary received one drachma per day (Thuc. 7,27,2).

During the 4th cent. BC, Greek mercenaries in the Persian empire and on Sicily had a wide field of work available to them: in the campaign of the younger Cyrus [3] in 401/400 (Xen. An. 1,6–2,3), in the satrap revolts after 370 BC, the battles for Egypt and finally in the defensive battles against Alexander [4] in 334–330, Greek → *hoplítai* were involved. Dionysius [1] I of Syracuse and his successors mainly relied on mercenaries. The Greek cities continued to enlist mercenaries primarily as specialists in a particular type of weaponry (→ *peltastaí*, → *toxótai*, → slingers) or as oarsmen and sentries. Even Athens relied on mercenary troops in the wars of this period (Isocr. Or. 7,9; 8,45 f.). The power of Jason [2] of Pherae was essentially based on an army of mercenaries (Xen. Hell. 6,1,2–16); a special case was also the mercenary army that the Phocians financed in 356–346 from the pillaged Delphic temple treasure (Diod. 16,25,1; 16,30,1). Philippus [4] II of Macedon also had mercenary troops at his disposal; the pinnacle was reached in the deployment of mercenaries in the campaigns of Alexander and in the Wars of the → Diadochi. In Alexander's [4] army the mercenaries were initially a contingent of 5,000 men (Diod. 17,17,3). The Hellenistic rulers, too, always remained reliant on mercenaries. The social standing of mercenaries was low (Isocr. Or. 4,168 ff.; 8,44 ff.; Plaut. Mil. *passim*), they were considered outsiders and often their social circumstances, particularly impoverishment and exile, forced men to become mercenaries. Overall, however, mercenaries only constituted the majority of the troops on rare occasions.

1 M. BETTALLI, I mercenari nel mondo greco, Bd. 1, 1995   2 L. A. BURCKHARDT, Bürger und Soldaten, 1996   3 Y. GARLAN, Guerre et économie en Grèce ancienne, 1989, 143–172   4 G. T. GRIFFITH, The Mercenaries of the Hellenistic World, 1935   5 H. W. PARKE, Greek Mercenary Soldiers, 1933   6 M. M. SAGE, Warfare in Ancient Greece, 1996, 147–157   7 G. SEIBT, Griechische Söldner im Achämenidenreich, 1977   8 D. WHITEHEAD, Who Equipped Mercenary Troops?, in: Historia 40, 1991, 105–112.   L.B.

II. ROME

Lat. *mercenarius* ('man who works for a wage', *merces*) is the term used in the military sphere to describe a man who fights in exchange for payment for a foreign city or a foreign ruler, in other words, for a matter that does not directly concern him. The army of the Roman Republic was recruited from among the citizens; however, the Romans lacked a real battle-ready → cavalry and also lightly armed troops, especially archers and → slingers. These troops were often recruited from outside Italy; some came from independent allies, others were levied compulsorily and still others were enlisted as mercenaries. In this way Hieron [2] of Syracuse supported the Romans at the beginning of the 2nd → Punic War by sending 500 Cretan archers to Italy (Pol. 3,75). In the battle of Zama, in 202 BC the Numidian cavalry under King → Massinissa played a decisive

part (Liv. 30,29,4; 30,33,2; 30,35,1–2). In the two subsequent centuries, the number of variously armed units of allied troops increased in the wars led by Rome; the cavalry of the Italian → *socii* is last mentioned in conjunction with the war against → Iugurtha (Sall. Iug. 95,1). → Caesar deployed Spanish and German cavalry in Gaul (Caes. BG. 5,26,3; 6,37,1; 7,13,1; 7,65,4 f.; 7,88). Aside from cavalrymen from Spain, archers from Crete and slingers from the Balearic Islands were highly regarded troop divisions. Normally each corps was commanded by leaders from its own tribe or by a Roman officer. During the Civil Wars, both Pompey [I 3], Iunius [I 10] Brutus and Cassius [I 10] on the one hand, and later Antonius [I 9] on the other, relied on armies and fleets provided by kings and cities in the east (cf. for instance App. Civ. 4,88).

The re-organisation of the Roman army under → Augustus then led to the real integration of such troops as → *auxilia* into the regular army units. It is certainly the case that troops also continued to be recruited on the periphery of the Imperium Romanum; they normally served under their own commanders. In this way Dacians, Palmyrians, Sarmatians and Moors took part in individual later campaigns.

In late antiquity this practice was retained; in the battle of Mursa in AD 351, Armenian archers fought on the side of Constantius [2] II (Zos. 2,51,4). From the 4th cent. AD onwards, the tendency became more and more entrenched of replacing the levy of Roman recruits by monetary payments; in this way the Imperium Romanum became increasingly reliant on the enlistment of foreign mercenaries. After the Goths defeated the Romans at Hadrianopolis [3] in AD 378, closed tribal units that were contractually bound to Rome (→ *foederati*), became obligated to serve in the Roman army. Contracts with barbarians normally included payment in gold, food supplies and settlement in the Imperium Romanum. The *foederati*, who continued to be under the control of their tribal leaders, fought on the borders of the Imperium Romanum, on the Rhine and the Danube as well as in Africa, mostly near the territory from which they originated; occasionally, however, they were also sent to more distant theatres of war. When the Roman army was ultimately in decline (5th cent. AD), the *foederati* as a whole were incorporated into the regular army as *auxilia*. It is still hard to assess to what extent the use of barbarian mercenaries weakened the fighting power or loyalty of the army.

1 H. ELTON, Warfare in Roman Europe AD 350–425, 1996, 128–154   2 JONES, LRE, 199–202; 611–613   3 P. SOUTHERN, The Numeri of the Roman Imperial Army, in: Britannia 20, 1989, 84–104.   J.CA.

Mercenaries' War Modern term ('Libyan War', for instance in Pol. 1,13,3; Diod. 26,23) for the uprising of the mercenaries employed by Carthage in the 1st → Punic War (241/0–238 BC). It plunged → Carthage into a serious crisis as the revolt of the mercenaries from various ethnic origins who still had to be paid despite the emptiness of the state coffers also provoked rebellion among the Libyans under the leadership of → Mathus. The general → Hanno [6] who had already fought against rebels in the Carthaginian hinterland around 247 was ordered to resolve the conflict, but the fact that he was replaced twice, namely by → Geskon [3] and Hannibal [4], as well as the appointment of → Hamilcar [3] Barkas as his joint commander, throws light on the internal political tensions (cf. [1. 258]). The 'national' Libyan War of Liberation (= 'Africans'; cf. [2. 87–113]) not only spread to the conquered Punic cities of → Hippo [5] and → Utica/Ithyca but in 239, with bloody pogroms also to Sardinia, where ultimately the rebellious mercenary troops were expelled to Italy by the Sardo-Punic populace. When the Carthaginians sought to reoccupy the island in 238, Rome demanded, contrary to the agreement (1st → Punic War), the ceding of Sardinia [1. 266–268; 3. 231–235] and 1,200 Talents.

The initial successes of the rebels under Mathus, → Spendius, → Autaritus and → Zarzas can be seen from the sieges of Utica, Hippo and Carthage itself; the victories above all of Hamilcar on the Bagradas River (239) and at Prion (238) were not least the result of the alliance with the Numidian Naravas, who was related by marriage to the → Barcids [1. 255–265]. The exact location of the decisive battle in which Mathus was taken prisoner cannot be pinpointed [2. 188].

The Mercenaries' War is poorly attested historiographically [1. 252]; the detailed depiction in Polybius (Pol. 1,65–88) is oriented towards the cliché of the disloyal mercenary so as to explain that the superiority of Rome rested on its citizens' army (cf. [3. 223–225]). Of particular value as a source is therefore the numismatic material that depicts not just symptoms of crisis in Carthaginian coin minting but also the diverse efforts of the rebels to mint their own coins (mostly with the legend ΛΙΒΥΩΝ) (cf. [4. 176–179]).

1 Huss;   2 L. Loreto, La grande insurrezione libica contro Cartagine del 241–237 A. C., 1995   3 B. Scardigli, I trattati romano-cartaginesi, 1991   4 H. R. Baldus, Zwei Deutungsvorschläge zur punischen Goldprägung im mittleren 3. Jahrhundert v. Chr., in: Chiron 18, 1988, 171–179.   L.-M.G.

Mercurinus (better known as Auxentius of → Durostorum in Moesia). Student of the Gothic bishop → Ulfila, perhaps a Goth himself. M. had to give up his bishopric in AD 380 after the edict of → Theodosius I with regard to the return of the churches to the Orthodox. Shortly afterwards he was consecrated as Arian bishop of Milan (→ Arianism). He was an opponent of → Ambrosius; he exerted great influence on the court of Valentinian II. His 'On the Life and Death of Ulfila' (*De vita et obitu Ulfilae*). (PL Suppl. 1, 703–707) has come down to us.

K. Gross-Albenhausen, Imperator christianissimus, 1999, 85–91; M. Meslin, Les Ariens d'Occident, 1967, 335–430, 1967, 44–58.   K.G.-A.

Mercurius
I. Greek (soldier saint)   II. Roman (the god Mercury)

I. Greek (soldier saint)
(Μερκούριος; *Merkoúrios*). Widely attested but legendary figure – a soldier saint who according to Soz. 6,2,3ff. is said to have killed Emperor → Iulianus [11] at God's behest by spearing him.

H. Ch. Brennecke, Studien zur Geschichte der Homöer, 1988, 96f.   K.SA.

II. Roman (the god Mercury)
A. Origin and functions   B. Republican and Augustan literature   C. Imperial period   D. Iconography

A. Origin and functions
The traditional view is that M. is the direct Roman transposition of the Greek god → Hermes (= H.) [1. 304–306]: According to this, M., by order of the → Sibyllini libri, was given a temple in Rome in 495 BC (Liv. 2,27,5). It is assumed that an indication of his Greek origin is that M. was part of → lectisternium celebrated according to Greek rites (*Graeco ritu*) in 399 BC (with → Neptunus: Liv. 5,13,6). From the point of view of Greek religious history as well, experts maintain that he was a Greek import [2.247]. However, Livy does not mention the Sibyllines for 495 BC, although the introduction of Greek deities into Rome could of course occur without their collaboration (e.g. Castor and Pollux: [3]; → Dioscuri). An even weightier argument against this theory is that the *Graecus ritus* describes a certain form of ritual but not the origin of the divine addressee of the cult [4; 5].

Historical arguments suggest that no direct borrowing from Greek religion occurred. Apparently the Roman Plebeians were affected by an economic crisis at the beginning of the 5th cent.: the sources speak of indebtedness, declining trade and food shortages (Liv. 2,9,6: 508 BC, Dion. Hal. Ant. 6,17,2–4: 496, Liv. 2,34,2–5: 492; [5; 6. 265–268]). The dedicant of the Temple of M., according to annalistic fiction a Plebeian by the name of M. → Laetorius, is said, by order of the people, to have organised food supplies and to have set up a → *collegium* of *mercatores* ('traders', 'merchants' Liv. 2,27,5f.; Val. Max. 9,3,6). Bad weather in 399 BC, in the year of the first Roman *lectisternium*, also resulted in economic depression (Liv. 5,13,4). Linguistic arguments substantiate the commercial background: Festus (111,10f. L.) suggests that M. is derived from Latin *merx* ('trade'). Faliscan inscriptions (cousin No. 264; cf. 136) connect the → *aediles* (*efiles*) with an offering for M. (*mercui*); this is probably a case of a loanword from the Latin as only this language has a root *merx* [7]. Later etymologies are Varronian speculation, e.g. *medius currens*, 'running in the midst' (Varro, Antiquitates rerum divinarum fr. 250 Car-

DAUNS) and *mirari*, 'to be amazed' (GL 7, 77,12–15). Despite assertions to the contrary [9], there are no clear indications for a commercial function of the Greek H., so here too Roman borrowing is out of the question: → Herms on Greek agoras do not constitute evidence of a connection between H. and trade, as the → agora was also a place where numerous non-commercial activities took place. Scattered literary (Diod. 5,75; Poll. 7,15; schol. Aristoph. Plut. 1153) and epigraphical testimonials (IEry 201a 59; [10]) linking the Greek god with trade are of late origin. Finally, on Delian inscriptions after 166 BC (IDélos 1709, 1711, 1713f., 1731–1733; [11]) the commercial function of H. is influenced by the Roman M.

Influence from the Etruscan Psychopompus ('escort of souls') *Turms*, supposedly, is improbable. M. only appears as the one who leads the dead into the Underworld in the Augustan period. It is a coincidence that the *dies natalis* of his temple (→ *natalis templi*) on 15th May (InscrIt 13,2 p. 458f.) and the celebrations of the *collegia* of merchants (Fest. 135,4f. L.; Macr. Sat. 1,12,19) followed the → Lemuria (9th, 11th, 13th May), which are associated with the cult of the dead. Of course knowledge of H. as psychopomp in Rome is possible from the 3rd century BC as a result of Livius Andronicus' translation of the 'Odyssey'; however, there are no translations of the relevant passage (Hom. Od. 24,1–14) available so it remains unclear whether Livius used M. instead of the Greek H.; he replaced *Moûsa* (Hom. Od. 1,1) with *Camena* (Livius Andronicus, fr. 1 FPL) and *Kronídēs* (Hom. Od. 1,45) with *Saturni filius* (Livius Andronicus, fr. 2 FPL), but also used the Greek name *Calypso*, fr. 13). Naevius perhaps mentioned M. in his Greek role as the messenger of the gods (Naev. fr. 7 FPL; [12. 130f.]).

B. REPUBLICAN AND AUGUSTAN LITERATURE

The Hellenisation of M. was in progress at the latest in the 2nd cent. BC. The *lectisternium* of 217 BC (Enn. Ann. 240f.; Liv. 22,10,9: M. with → Ceres), the link between the Roman Di → Consentes and the Greek → Twelve Gods , was the result of the greater familiarity of the Romans with the world of the Greek gods [13]. M.'s prologue in Plautus' *Amphitruo* includes both the roles of the Roman god of commerce (Plaut. Amph. 1–16) and of the Greek H. (ibid. 17–34). Accius' *Atreus* calls M. 'son of → Maia' (TRF fr. 1b); in Cn. Gellius there is a euhemeristic representation by (→ Euhemerus) of M. (fr. 2 PETER), perhaps from L. Cincius (fr. 1 PETER). The importance of trade in the late Republican Period explains the continued interest in the god of commerce. In at least two instances, a deity probably introduced to Rome by foreign traders is identified with M,. through → *interpretatio Romana*: the Carthaginian M. Sobrius, 'the sober M.' (Fest. 382,6–10 L.), and the Iberian M. Malevolus, 'the ill-disposed M.' (Fest. 152,22–25 L.) [12. 80–103, 142–144].

In Augustan poetry M. is the god Hellenised according to the Greek literary models [14]: messenger (e.g.

Verg. Aen. 4,239–241); guide (Hor. Carm. 1,10,13–16; 2,7,13–15 according to Archil. fr. 5 W., Hom. Il. 20,443f.; cf. Ov. Met. 8,626f.); Psychopompus (Hor. carm. 1,10,17–20; Verg. Aen. 4,242–244); orator (Hor. Carm. 1,10,1–3; Ov. Fast. 5,668; [15]); protector and symbol of poetry [16]. → Augustus' identification with M. (Hor. Carm. 1,2,41–49; ILS 5422) was based on the tradition of the Greek H. as the saviour and guarantor of a new beginning (Apollod. 1,7,2); this identification became important as a result of the programme of the Augustan Restoration after the civil wars [16. 445f.]. Although the Roman *Mercuriales* (Cic. ad Q. fr. 2,6,2; CIL XIV 2105), which since the Augustan period had been organised as part of the cult for the emperor, had an economic aspect to them, their significance for the → emperor cult was the result of the Hellenisation of M. [17]. Roman literature in this way spins a Greek thread that runs parallel to that of commerce without overlapping with it often, except in rare cases (e.g. CIL VI 520 *infra*). At the same time it documents the openness in the accumulation of various functions in one god that was typical of → polytheism.

C. IMPERIAL PERIOD

The various roles of M. can appear in the same author: Petron. 29,5f. (commerce), ibid. 140,12 (psychopomp). A bilingual inscription on a herm mentions Greek *Hermês* and among others Lat. *lucri repertor*, 'inventor of profit' (CIL VI 520). Normally the roles are, however, separated: messenger and orator (Apul. Met. 6,7); herald's staff of the messenger (*caduceus* and *virgula*: Apul. Met. 10,30); profit (Pers. 6,62; CIL V 6594); Psychopompus (Sen. Apocol. 13,1f.; Stat. Theb. 1,303–308; ILS 3961; [18. 528 No. 324]); orator (Apul. Met. 6,7); gambler (Fronto Epist. p. 233,6 VAN DEN HOUT). Greater religious permeability from the 2nd cent. AD onwards resulted in new connections e.g. with → Anubis (Apul. Met. 11,10) or with 'magical' interrelationships (Apul. Apol. 31,9; 42,6; [19]).

→ *Interpretatio Romana* numbers M. among the main gods of the Celtic or Germanic pantheon (Caes. Gall. 6,17; Tac. Germ. 9; Min. Fel. 6). Numerous inscriptions and pictorial representations from the 1st cent. AD onwards [20; 21] document his position in Roman Gaul and Germania: M. appears alone, without or with local epithets; with indigenous (above all → Rosmerta) or Graeco-Roman deities (Maia; the Bacchus child; Apollo and Minerva; Volcanus; Mithras; with Diana, shepherds and Silvanus (AE 1966, 272–275); as the focal point of the Twelve Gods [21. 172 No. 103]); in the cult of the emperor (CIL XIII 3013f.; M. Augustus: CIL XIII 577, 3183, 11037; AE 1976, 426).

D. ICONOGRAPHY

Roman M. frequently appears with one or several attributes of H. without following the Greek canon slavishly [18]: Greek attributes e.g. *caduceus*, winged helmet or sandals are suited to iconographical depiction whilst apart from the purse there is no simple pictorial symbol for commerce. Instead of merely imitating the Graeco-Roman canon, M. iconography in Roman Gaul and Germania connects indigenous attributes with it [21; 22]. A combination, e.g. M. with the helmet and *caduceus* as well as with the Bacchus child with the purse illustrates that the Graeco-Roman model (H. with the Dionysus child) was expanded to suit regional and provincial religious needs [23. 115–118].

→ Hermes

1 G. Wissowa, Religion und Kultus der Römer, ²1912 2 Burkert   3 E. M. Orlin, Temples, Religion and Politics in the Roman Republic, 1997, 97–105   4 J. Scheid, *Graeco Ritu*: A Typically Roman Way of Honoring the Gods, in: HSPh 97, 1995, 15–31   5 Id., Nouveau rite et nouvelle piété, in: F. Graf (ed.), Ansichten griechischer Rituale, 1998, 168–182   6 R. M. Ogilvie, A Historical Commentary on Livy, Books 1–5, 1965, 294, 309f.   7 T. J. Cornell, The Beginnings of Rome, 1995, 256–271 8 Dumézil, 439   9 Farnell, Cults, vol. 5, 26 10 Graf, 270–272   11 Ph. Bruneau, Recherches sur les cultes de Délos, 1970, 353f., 586–589   12 R. E. A. Palmer, Rome and Carthage at Peace, 1997   13 C. Long, The Twelve Gods of Greece and Rome, 1987   14 D. Feeney, The Gods in Epic, 1991, 141–155   15 A. E. Housman, Anth. Lat. Ries. 678, in: ClQ 12, 1918, 35 16 J. Rüpke, M. am Ende: Horaz Carmen 1,30, in: Hermes 126, 1998, 435–453   17 B. Combet-Farnoux, M. romain, les Mercuriales et l'institution du culte impérial sous le Principat augustéen, in: ANRW II 17.1, 1981, 457–501   18 Simon   19 A. Abt, Die Apologie des Apuleius von Madaura und die antike Zauberei, 1908, 117–120, 171–177   20 F. Heichelheim, s.v. M., RE 15, 982–1016 21 J. Hupe, Studien zum Gott M. im römischen Gallien und Germanien, in: TZ 60, 1997, 53–227   22 G. Bauchhenss, s.v. M., LIMC 6.1, 537–554   23 T. Derks, Gods, Temples and Ritual Practices, 1998.

B. Combet-Farnoux, Mercure romain, 1980; E. Simon, s.v. M., LIMC 6.1, 500–537.   C.R.P.

Mercury (ἄργυρος χυτός; *árgyros chytós*, ἀργύριον ὕδωρ; *argýrion hýdōr*, Latin *argentum vivum*).
First mentioned in Aristot. An. 1,3,406b 19. Theophr. De lapidibus 60 [1. 80] reports on its usual synthesis at the time in a copper vessel by pounding cinnabar (κιννάβαρ/*kinnábar*) with vinegar (ὄξος/*óxos*). Because of its toxicity, which was already known in ancient times, it was not used in medicine but it was used quite commonly in → alchemy to separate gold and silver for jewellery.

1 D. E. Eichholz (ed.), Theophrastus De lapidibus, 1965.

F. Rex, Q., in: Gmelins Handbuch der anorganischen Chemie, 34, ⁸1960, 1.80.   C.HÜ.

Merenda
[1] *Cognomen* of M. Antonius [I 13] and of the Cornelii family.

Kajanto, Cognomina, 340.   K.-L.E.

[2] see → Meals.

Meribanes M. III, king of → Iberia [1] in Caucasia, sent an embassy by Constantius [2] II in 360/61 to recruit him to the Roman side against the Persians (Amm. Marc. 21,6,8).

W. Ensslin, s.v. M., RE 15, 1028; PLRE 1, 598.   A.P.-L.

Meridarches (μεριδάρχης, *Meridárchēs*).
[1] Ptolemaic administrative official. The Egyptian district (→ *nomós*) of Arsinoites was divided up into three *merídes* ('parts'), which in turn consisted of *tópoi*. This subdivision is attested from 260/259 BC at the latest[1. 5]. A *meridarches* was in charge of a *merís* and hence of its toparchs; the title is attested from the end of the 2nd century BC (PTebtunis I 66), but the names of the *merídes* (Ἡρακλείδου, Θεμίστου, Πολέμωνος) may go back to the first *meridarchai*. The last *meridarchai* are attested for the 3rd century AD (list of the Ptolemaic *meridarchai*: PP I/VIII 871–5a).

1 P. Jouguet, P. Collar, J. Lesquier, X. Xoual, Papyrus grecs (Institut Papyrologique de l'Université de Lille), vol. 1, 1907 (repr. 1929, 1975).

E. van't Dack, Ptolemaica, 1951, 48f.

[2] In the closing years of the 1st cent. BC, the toparch of Heracleopolites was called *meridarches*, a title in Egypt that was used over-extensively.

E. van't Dack, La toparchie dans l'Égypte ptolémaïque, in: CE 23, 1948, 155.

[3] Title in the Seleucid territorial administration of Syria; probably not (*pace* [1.383 n.1]) taken over by the Ptolemies.

1 U. Wilcken, Gr. Ostraka, Bd. 1, 1893.

E. Bikerman, Institutions des Séleucides, 1938, 198.   W.A.

Meriones (Μηριόνης; *Mēriónēs*).
Cretan, son of → Molus (Molos). As a young soldier efficient in battle and a faithful and devoted follower of → Idomeneus [1], he takes part in the Trojan campaign (Hom. Il.). Together with the sons of Nestor, → Antilochus and → Thrasymedes, M. represents the second guard of the Greek army consisting of younger warriors. This guard performed duties suited to their age (e.g. night watch: ibid. 9,79ff.) and had to prove their worth on the battle field, mainly after the main heroes were wounded (ibid. B. 13–17). M. distinguishes himself with both bow and lance. In the funeral games for → Patroclus (ibid. B. 23) he is the only one to compete in three contests (chariot racing, archery, javelin throwing). Later sources (Q. Smyrn. 12,320) mention M. as one of those inside the wooden horse.

The verse formula Μηριόνης ἀτάλαντος Ἐνυαλίω ἀνδρεϊφόντῃ ('Meriones, of equal importance to Enyalios = Ares, the murderer of men': e.g. Hom. Il. 7,166) is prosodically correct only with 'proto-Mycenaean' phonology [1] and therefore indicates an ancient mythical figure. Similarly the boar's tooth helmet that → Odysseus (ibid. 10,261–265) borrows from M. (details on the story of this type of helmet [2]) in the → Doloneia. Possibly the name M. is related to Hurrian *maryannu*, 'elite chariot warrior' [3].

1 C. J. RUIJGH, D'Homère aux origines proto-mycéniennes de la tradition épique, in: J. P. CRIELAARD (ed.), Homeric Questions, 1995, 85–88   2 C. W. SHELMERDINE, From Mycenae to Homer, in: E. DE MIRO et al (ed.), Atti e memorie del secondo congresso internazionale di micenologia, vol. 1, 1996, 467–492   3 M. L. WEST, The East Face of Helicon, 1997, 612.

W. BECK, s.v. M., LFE (with bibliography).   RE.N.

Meris (ἡ μερίς; *merís*, 'part, portion', Verb μερίζειν; *merízein*). As a term in Greek administrative language, *meris* describes any type of systematic division and is used e.g. generally in Hellenistic administrative practice, especially e. g. in the Ptolemaic-Roman administration of Egypt in which the Arsinoite → *nomós* [2] was divided into three *merídes* (OGIS 177,8 f., 2nd cent. BC). There is another interpretation in the territorial administrative classification in Egypt which describes it as the smallest element in the series *nomós*, → *tópos* [1], → *kṓmē* (B.), *meris* and hence the basic unit of land area (cf. Str. 17,1,3). The term *meris* also describes the four governmental districts (Latin *regio*; cf. Liv. 45,29,5 f.) into which Rome divided the territory of the Macedonian (→ Macedonia II. D.) and Illyrian monarchies after the victory at → Pydna in 168 BC.
E.O.

Merismos (μερισμός; *merismós* from μερίζειν; *merízein* = 'to divide, distribute') in Athens the name for the 'distribution' of funds from tax incomes by the → *apodéktai* to the appropriate officials (→ *archaí*). The sums allocated were determined by the council of the polis (→ *boulḗ*) and had to be struck off immediately after distribution ([Aristot.] Ath. pol. 48,1–2). *Merismos* is not attested before the 4th century BC (→ Taxes III. B.).

RHODES, 557–560.   W.ED.

Mermerus (Μέρμερος; *Mérmeros*).
[1] Trojan, killed by Antilochus (Hom. Il. 14,513).

[2] Father of a mythical king, Ilius of Ephyre in Thesprotia, visited by Odysseus (Hom. Od. 1,259f.).
[3] One of the two sons of → Jason [1] and → Medea. He and his brother Pheres are killed by their mother in revenge on Jason (Eur. Med.). According to Paus. 2,3,7, he is killed by a lioness during a hunt on Corfu.   L.K.

Mermnadae (Μερμνάδαι; *Mermnádai*). Lydian lineage, presumably originating in the Mysian-Bithynian region (see → Dascyleion [2]). According to Andronius (apud Glossarium Oxy. 1802, Z. 46 [POxy book 15]), the name derives from the word for 'buzzard' (Indo-European root. *merh*, 'to grab, rob'). In *c.* 680 BC, the M. under → Gyges gained power in Sardis where it is said they deposed the Heracleidae, who may have been of Luwian origin (Maeones; → Maeonia [1]). The last ruler of the house of M. was → Croesus (Hdt. 1,6–7; 27–92).

S. MAZZARINO, Fra oriente e occidente, 1947, 171–187; O. SEEL, Herakliden und Mermnaden, in: Navicula Chiloniensis. FS F. Jacoby, 1956, 37–65.   P.HÖ.

Merobaudes
[1] In AD 363 Flavius M., presumably a Frank, served Iulianus [11]. Appointed *magister peditum* by → Valentinianus I (Zos. 4,17), M. fought in the war with the→ Quadi in 375. Acting on his own authority, he elevated → Valentinianus II to the rank of Augustus (Amm. 30,10; Zos. 4,19) and was Consul in 377 and 383 consul. In 377, M. withheld units of the army sent to Valens in Thrace (Amm. Marc. 31,7,4),and this probably contributed to → Mallobaudes's victory in Gaul. Presumably he took part in more of → Gratianus' [2] campaigns, but in 383 sided with Magnus → Maximus [7] and so sealed Gratianus' fate (Chron. min. 1, 461). It is a matter of contention whether Maximus left M. in office and appointed him *cos.* III for 388 or whether the inscription ICUR I 370 refers to *cos.* II (383) [3. 44], which would mean that M. had previously been forced by Maximus to commit suicide (Paneg. 12,28).

1 P. KEHNE, s.v. Gratian, RGA 12, 598–601   2 PLRE 1, 598–99   3 M. WAAS, Germanen im römischen Dienst, ²1971, 42–44, 93–98.   P.KE.

[2] **Flavius M.** 5th century AD Latin poet and panegyrist, of senatorial rank, perhaps born in Spain (Sidon. Carm. 9,297f.) as a descendant of the consul M. [1], who was of Frankish origin. He made a career for himself in the army, moved to the imperial city of Ravenna and as a writer there won the favour of Valentinian III and the commander-in-chief → Aetius [2]. The honorary inscription set up at the emperor's request in the Forum of Trajan in Rome on 30 July 435, together with a bronze statue, praises his bravery and his fine education (CIL 6,1724). After 435, M.'s career was shaped primarily by his patron Aetius: under his command with the rank of *magister utriusque militiae*, he fought succesfully against the rebellious Bagaudae in his Spanish homeland in 443 (Hydatius 128). He thanked Aetius in a panegyric prose speech (between 443 and 446) for arranging for him a 'very high office', perhaps the tile of *patricius*. He acclaimed him in a metric panegyric on the occasion of his third consulate in 446. No later information on M. has been found.

M.'s literary legacy, extant only in very fragmentary form at St. Gallen MSS 908 (5th–6th centuries, Clavis Latinorum auctorum 7, No. 953), were discovered and edited for the first time by NIEBUHR (1823) and are from the decade up on 446. Two poems in elegiac couplets are of ecphrastic content: *carmen* 1 describes a representational image of the imperial family (mosaics in the palace *ad laureta*), *carmen* 2 is on an ornamental fountain system (in the palace?) and again a ceiling painting (mosaic?) with representation of the imperial couple and their two daughters. *Carmen*. 3 (in elegaic distichs) depicts a forest-like park (in a *villa rustica*?), *carmen*. 4 (in hendecasyllables) is a poem for the first birthday of a son of Aetius (probably Gaudentius) in the style of Statius's *Genethliacon Lucani*. Panegyrics to Aetius follow: four fragments of a prose expression of thanks and 197 hexameters of the poem, written on the occasion of M.'s consulate, are extant. In all these works M. demonstrates his familiarity with literary language and the literary techniques of his time, the prerequisite for which was a thorough knowledge of the Roman classics and of the authors of the 1st century AD. Mythological comparisons and allegories of politically relevant concepts like *concordia*, *pax* and *fatum* indicate the style of late antique panegyrics (→ Claudianus [2]).

A hexametric poem *De Christo* is attributed to M. in early modern publications. It shows similarities to the Claudianus poem *De Salvatore* (Carm. min. 32) which is of disputed authenticity, and it quotes from Dracontius. Its authenticity can be neither proved nor refuted. The panegyric upon the first consulate of Aetius has been lost.

→ Panegyrics

EDITIONS: F. VOLLMER, MGH AA 14, 3–20, 1905.
BIBLIOGRAPHY: F. M. CLOVER, F.M., 1971; (translation, commentary); A. FO, Note a Merobaude, in: Romanobarbarica 6, 1981–82, 101–128; M. MAZZA, Merobaude, in: La poesia tardoantica, 1984, 379–430.   K.SM.

Merodachbaladan see → Marduk-apla-iddin(a)

Meroe (Μερόη/*Meróē*: Hdt. 1,29). Graeco-Latin rendition of the Meroitic *M/Bedewi*. Centre of the kingdom of Kush (Napatan period: late 9th cent. – c. 270 BC; Meroitic period: c. AD 270 BC – 350, → Nubia), between the 5th and 6th cataracts of the Nile, near present-day Begrawiyah. Building activity is attested from around 720 BC (western cemetery), and an administrative centre at least since Aspelta (c. 590 BC). 'Royal Enclosure' (excavated by J. GARSTANG, 1909–14 [3]): a royal city with palace complex, temples, and what is presumably a nymphaeum. There are numerous temples in the urban area, particularly of the god → Amun, as well as the so-called 'Temple of the Sun' (Temple M 250, previously compared to the Table of the Sun at Hdt. 3,18). Extensive slag piles and remains of smelting ovens attest to significant iron-work. East of the city are the cemeteries (excavated by G.A. REISNER, 1920–23 [1]: the southern (c. 270–250 BC) and northern cemetery (c. AD 250 BC – 350) of the royal family (pyramids with chapels attached), the western cemetery for high officials (pyramids with chapels), and private persons (simple shaft graves).

→ Candace; → Mandoulis

1 D. DUNHAM, The Royal Cemeteries of Kush, vols 1–5, 1952–63   2 D. EDWARDS, The Archaeology of the Meroitic State, 1996 (economy)   3 L. TÖRÖK, Meroe City, 1997   4 Id., Geschichte Meroes, in: ANRW II 10, 1988, 107–341   5 S. WENIG, Africa in Antiquity, 1978 (art)   6 J. W. YELLIN, Meroitic Funerary Religion, in: ANRW II 18, 1995, 2869–2892.   A.LO.

Meroitic National language of the kingdom of Kush. Literary language from the mid second millennium BC at the latest. Written with 18 single-sound characters (15 consonants and 3 vowel signs) and 4 syllabic signs in a hieroglyphic form and the usually employed cursive form. Decipherment of the script by F.L. GRIFFITH in 1911. Grammatical structure and vocabulary are still largely incomprehensible, but M. probably belongs to the North-Sudanese language family (as does Nubian). → Meroe; → Nubia

1 F. HINTZE (ed.), Sudan im Altertum (Meroitica 1), 1973, ch. IV: Sprachforschung   2 K. H. PRIESE, Meroitisch. Schrift und Sprache, in: D. WILDUNG (ed.), Sudanesische Antike Königreiche am Nil, 1996, 253–254.   A.LO.

Merope (Μερόπη/*Merópē*).
[1] One of the seven → Pleiades, daughter of Atlas, wife of → Sisyphus, mother of → Glaucus [2] (Apollod. 1,85; 3,110; Hyg. fab. 192; Ov. Fast. 4,175).
[2] Daughter of Oenopion and Helice, raped by → Orion (Apollod. 1,25; Hyg. Astr. 2,34).
[3] Daughter of → Cypselus [1], wife of → Cresphontes [1], mother of → Cresphontes [2]. In her son's attempt to avenge incognito his father's murder by his brother → Polyphontes, who had meanwhile married M., his mother nearly kills him. After mother and son recognize each other, the attempt is successful (thus in Eur. Cresphontes [1. 1–222 *passim*]).

1 A. HARDER, Euripides' Kresphontes und Archelaos, 1985.

[4] Wife of the mythical king → Polybus of Corinth, ostensible mother of → Oedipus (Soph. Oed. T. 775).   L.K.

Meropis (Μεροπίς; *Meropís*).
[1] Land of the *Meropes* (poet.: 'human beings'); a fiction created by Theopompus of Chios (Philippica B. 8), transmitted by Aelian [2] (FGrH 115 F 75c): Silenus instructs Midas about the cities of *Eusebés* ('pious city') and *Máchimos* ('city of battle'), then (the context is unclear) about M. and *Ánostos* ('place without return'). The nature of these cities points to Platonic myths (for instance, Plat. rep. 10,614c), while the opposition between the cities is reminiscent of Atlantis and Athens (Plat. Tim. 23c–25d). The story is neither utopian nor political allegory, but a literary confrontation with → Plato (parody [1]?; cf. Alexis PCG II fr. 151).

1 H.-G. NESSELRATH, Theopomps M. und Platon: Nachahmung und Parodie, in: Göttinger Forum für Altertumswissenschaften 1, 1998, 1–8.

[2] Epithet of → Cos (e.g., Thuc. 8,41,2). The inhabitants are often poetically called *Meropes* (e.g., Pind. N. 4,26); this was probably, in the first instance, the name of the pre-Doric population. An anonymous epic with the title *M.* (SH 903A) dealt with local myths (Heracles).

S. M. SHERWIN-WHITE, Ancient Cos, 1978, 47–50.
B.GY.

Merops (Μέροψ/Mérops).
[1] Mythical king of the Meropians on the island of Cos (Q. Smyrn. 8,6,71). From grief and longing for his spouse Echemeia, who had been sent to Hades, he is transformed into an eagle by Hera, and finally catasterized (Hyg. Astr. 2,16).
[2] Father of → Eumelus [2] (Antoninus Liberalis 15; → Agron [1]).
[3] Mythical king of the Ethiopians, husband of → Clymene [1] (Ov. Met. 1,755f.).
[4] Mythical seer, king of Rhyndacus, from → Percote on the Hellespont. His sons fall in the Trojan War; his daughters are → Cleite and Arisbe, the first wife of Priam (Hom. Il. 2,830ff.; Apollod. 3,147f.).
[5] Father of → Pandareus: Paus. 10,30,2; Antoninus Liberalis 36; schol. Pind. O. 1,90.
[6] Follower of → Aeneas [1], killed by → Turnus (Verg. Aen. 9,702). L.K.

Merovingians (Lat. *Merovingi*). The Frankish dynasty of the Merovingians achieved its position, which finally enabled it to found the Kingdom of the Franks, in the late Roman army and military nobility. However, the family's dynastic awareness of its origins first took gradual shape in their ancestor Merovech's claim of kinship with the Frankish warrior-king Chlodio. The widespread assumption of sacred origin of the Merovingian dynasty is to be rejected [17].

In *c.* 463, the first historically tangible Merovingian, Merovech's son King → Childerich († 481/2), stood at the head of an *exercitus Francorum*, allied with the Romans, in the Roman province of Belgica II (→ Belgica), which had been handed over to him by → Aegidius, the Roman *magister utriusque militiae per Gallias*. The foundation of the Kingdom of the Franks was not, therefore, based on occupation of territory by the Franks (→ Franci), but is to be identified with the takeover of civil administration by a military regime that had already been recognized by Rome [1]. In around 486 Childerich's son and successor King → Chlodwig (482–511), was able to prevail against Aegidius' son, the *rex Romanorum*→ Syagrius, who was residing in Soissons. In the following period, Chlodwig was able to considerably expand his area of dominion through victories over the → Visigoths, the Alemanni (→ Alamanni) and other Frankish kings [14]. Once Burgundy and Provence were added to it under his sons, the kingdom of the Franks included almost the entire area of the former Gaulish and Germanic Roman provinces, and reached as far as Thuringia. East Rome recognized Chlodwig's political and military position in 508 by granting him an honorary consulate and patriciate [3]. The Merovingians continued to issue coins with the portrait of the reigning East Roman emperor until the 7th century [4; 13].

With the foundation of their kingdom, the M. entered almost completely into the domain of the rights and responsibilities of the Roman emperors [13; 16]. Through their royal documents [5; 13] and general decrees [12; 13; 16], prepared in the tradition of Roman imperial rescripts and laws, they controlled the continuation and transformation of Roman institutions. The Roman system of taxes and *munera* (→ *munus*) continued to exist to a large extent [8], but the M. promoted the decentralization of imperial administration [9] through privileges of immunity (freedom from *munera),* so that parts of the Roman fiscal system and jurisdiction were gradually absorbed into feudal forms of organization [6]. Through the granting of privileges and domains, the M. integrated church institutions and secular personages within the realm's administration, and thus brought about the formation of a Romano-Frankish aristocracy of the kingdom [11].

The baptism of Chlodwig (498 or 507/8) and the conversion of the Franks to Catholic Christianity [14] ensured the M.'s acceptance among the Roman population and enabled a close co-operation with the episcopate, recruited from the Gallo-Roman senatorial nobility. This was reflected in the royal convocation of kingdom-wide synods, the continuation of imperial church legislation, and the delegation of administrative tasks to the Church, as well as in the Christianisation of the kingdom [7; 9; 10]. The M.'s practice of filling dioceses with former court officials represented an innovation, as did their monastery policy and promotion of missionary activities [13] (→ mission). In the 7th century, the monastery of St. Denis near Paris became the centre of their dynastic burial [13; 15].

The Merovingian kingdom was marked by a cultural and legal gap between the Romanic South and the Frankicized North [13; 15; 16]. This, together with regionalist tendencies [2], determined the formation of the three partial realms of Neustria, Austria, and Burgundy. In 613, King Chlothar attributed each division its own majordomo as a secondary authority. Beginning with the mid 7th century, the majordomos were no longer named by the king, but chosen by groups from the nobility [15]. They degraded the M. to the status of puppet-kings, yet usurpation by the Carolingians, which took place through the office of the majordomos, did not lead to the end of the Merovingian kingdom until 751.

1 K. F. WERNER, Die Ursprünge Frankreichs bis zum Jahr 1000, 1989 2 P. J. GEARY, Die Merowinger, 1996 3 M. McCORMICK, Clovis at Tours, Byzantine Public Ritual and the Origins of Medieval Ruler Symbolism, in: E. K. CHRYSOS, A. SCHWARCZ (ed.), Das Reich und die Barbaren, 1989, 155–180 4 S. E. RIGOLD, An Imperial Coinage in Southern Gaul in the Sixth and Seventh Centu-

ries?, in: NC 14, 1954, 93–133   5 P. CLASSEN, Kaiser-reskript und Königsurkunde, 1977   6 W. GOFFART, Merovingian Polyptychs, in: Francia 9, 1981, 57–77   7 M. HEINZELMANN, Bischof und Herrschaft vom spät-antiken Gallien zu den karolingischen Hausmeiern, in: F. PRINZ (ed.), Herrschaft und Kirche, 1988, 23–82   8 J. DURLIAT, Les finances publiques de Dioclétien aux Caro-lingiens (284–888), 1990   9 R. KAISER, Das römische Erbe und das Merowinger-Reich, 1993   10 E. EWIG, Die Merowinger und das Frankenreich, ³1997   11 M. WEI-DEMANN, Adel im Merowinger-Reich, in: Jb. des Röm.-germ. Zentralmuseums Mainz 40, 1993, 535–555   12 I. WOLL, Untersuchungen zu Überlieferung und Eigenart der merowingischen Kapitularien, 1995   13 Die Franken. Wegbereiter Europas (exhibition catalogue) 2 vols, 1996   14 M. ROUCHE (ed.), Clovis – histoire et mémoire, 2 vols, 1997   15 H. ATSMA (ed.), La Neustrie, 2 vols, 1989   16 S. ESDERS, Römische Rechtstradition und merowingi-sches Königtum, 1997   17 A. C. MURRAY, *Post vocantur Merohingii*: Fredegar, Merovech, and 'Sacral Kingship', in: id. (ed.), After Rome's Fall, 1998, 121–152.   S.E.

Merovingian scripts The term 'Merovingian' primari-ly designates the cursive script used in diplomas and documents of the royal Merovingian chancery (c. AD 457–751), but also specific bookhands, today denoted as 'pre-Carolingian', that developed under the influence of this document hand in the region that is now France. This → document hand derives in a direct line from Roman cursive (→ Script). It was modified, either by planned design or by gradual, unconscious transfor-mation, into a typical form that is still recognizable, in a diluted manner, even in royal documents of the 11th cent. This process must have been concluded before the end of the 6th cent., as is attested by a fully developed example from the year 625 [3. XIII, no. 852; 5. pl. 1]. Typical of this script are letters pressed together from the side with long up- and downstrokes, as well as nu-merous ligatures. Characteristic, for instance, are the *b* with a connecting stroke to the right, the *d* with a ver-tical stroke under the baseline, and the *h* with a left-slanting, rounded stroke. In the peculiar ligature *ex*, the tongue of the *e* is continued in the left leg of the *x*.

In the Merovingian period (→ Merovingians), nu-merous bookhands arose out of the later Roman cur-sive, either directly [6. vol. 5, no. 573], or indirectly, via the above-mentioned document hand. The earliest of the more widespread stylized Merovingian document hands was the 'Luxeuil' minuscule from the monastery of the same name, where it was probably created and used from the second half of the 7th cent. until well into the 8th cent. [6. vol. 6, xv–xvii]. A modification of the Luxeuil script from the 8th cent. is called *az* after the typical form of these letters: the *a* consists of two con-nected angles; the *z* draws its upper stroke clearly downwards, and draws its groundstroke likewise downwards in an arc. The derivation from the town of Laon has not been fully proven [6. vol. 6, xviii with no. 765, 766].

Two additional scripts of the same origin arose after the end of the Merovingian period. The so-called *b* script is a highly elegant script which exhibits the graph-ic flow of a document hand more strongly (the letter *b* maintains its connecting stroke to the right). This short-lived script probably arose in the convent of Chelles near Paris. In contrast, the so-called *ab* script (where the *a* resembles an *ic* ligature, and the *b* is that of the *b* script) is to be brought into relation with the abbey of Corbie near Amiens. It was used from the end of the 8th cent. until the third decade of the 9th cent. [6. vol. 6, xxv–xxvi and no. 743, 792].

1 B. BISCHOFF, Paläographie des römischen Altertums und des abendländischen Mittelalters, 1986², 140–147, 252–258   2 L. E. BOYLE, Paleografia latina medievale. Introduzione bibliografica, 1999, 144–174   3 A. BRUCK-NER, R. MARICHAL, Chartae Latinae Antiquiores: Fac-simile-Edition of the Latin Charters Prior to the Ninth Century, vols. 1–49, 1954 – 1998 (esp. vols. 13–19: France 1–7, 1981–1987)   4 G. CENCETTI, Lineamenti di storia della scrittura latina, 1997   5 PH. LAUER, CH. SAMARAN, Les diplômes originaux des Mérovingiens, 1908 (with 48 pls.)   6 E. A. LOWE, Codices Latini Anti-quiores: A Palaeographical Guide to Latin Manuscripts Prior to the Ninth Century, 11 vols. with suppl., 1934–1971 (esp. vol. 6, xiii-xxx)   7 R. MCKITTERICK, The Scriptoria of Merovingian Gaul: A Survey of the Evidence, in: H. B. CLARKE, M. BRENNAN (ed.), Columbanus and Merovingian Monasticism (British Archaeological Reports, Int. Series 113), 1981, 173–207 (with 16 plates and 9 ills.)   8 L. SCHIAPARELLI, Note paleografiche: Intorno all' origine e ai caratteri della scrittura merovin-gica, in: Archivio storico italiano, ser. 7, 16, 1931, 169–195 (with 2 pls.; reprint: Id., Note paleografiche (1910–1932), ed. by G. CENCETTI, 1969, 511–539).   J.J.J.

Merusium (Μερούσιον; *Meroúsion*). Settlement of unknown location, 70 stadia (Theopompos FGrH 115 F 189) from Syracuse, probably in the vicinity of a sanc-tuary of Artemis Meroessa (Steph. Byz. s.v. M.).

BTCGI 9, 567.   GI.F.

Merw (also → Alexandria [5], later → Antioch [7]), principal town of → Margiana; an oasis at the delta of the Murgab (or Margus); 30 km east of modern Mary in southern Turkmenistan. Inhabited since the Neolithic. First blossom in the 2nd millenium. The citadel of Erk-/Ark-Kala was built in the Achaemenid period; in Hel-lenistic times a town with rectangular grid pattern was attached to it. M. belonged to the Parthian and later to the Sassanid kingdom. It was conquered by the Arabs in 651 AD. Excavations have uncovered both Parthian and medieval remains.

G. A. PUGACENKOVA, Puty razvitija architektury juznogo Turkmenistana, in: Juzhno-Turkmenistanskoi archeolo-gičeskoi ekspedicii, 5, 1958, 42–60.   B.B.

Mesala (Masala, Plin. HN 6,158). City of the Home-ritae (Himyars) in → Arabia Felix, certainly identical with the port of Mesalum (Plin. HN. 12,69), from which white → myrrh was exported. It may be equated with the ruined town of al-ʿAṣala, dialect am-ʿAṣala (13° 13′ N, 45° 28′ E), in the delta of the Wadi Banā on the Arabian Sea northeast of Aden.

H. VON WISSMANN, s.v. Zamareni, RE Suppl. 11, 1325–1329.   W.W.M.

Mesambria/Mesembria

[1] (Μεσ(σ)αμβρία,   Μεσ(σ)ημβρία/Me(s)sambría, Me(s)sembría).
I. LOCATION II. HISTORY

I. LOCATION

A city on the west coast of the Black Sea (→ Pontos Euxeinos), situated at the northern entrance to the bay of Burgas, on a small rocky peninsula, 850 m long and 300 m wide, now known as Nesebâr (in modern Bulgaria). It is connected with the mainland by a narrow strip of land, 400 m long and 3 m high.

II. HISTORY

A. EARLY HISTORY UP TO ROMAN TIMES B. BYZANTINE TIMES

A. EARLY HISTORY UP TO ROMAN TIMES

Traces of Thracian settlements dating from before the Greek foundation are preserved. M. was founded either at the time of Darius' Scythian campaign (512 BC) or toward the end of the → Ionian Revolt (493 BC) by Byzantium and Calchedon (Hdt. 6,33), or by Calchedon and Megara (Ps.-Scymn. 737–742), or by Megara alone (Str. 7,6,1). The language of the inscriptions (IGBulg 1, 306–349) as well as the arrangement of the phylae and the city gods (Pythian Apollo, Demeter and Dionysus) prove that M. was a Doric colony (→ Colonization). The polis grew quickly between the harbours of Apollonia [2] and Odessus, and gained economic and political importance, as can be seen from the minting of coins beginning in the middle of the 5th cent. BC and the founding of a daughter-colony, Naulochus (modern Obzor) in the north. Trade with cities on the Pontos Euxinos, in southern Asia Minor, in Greece (esp. Athens) and with inland Thracia, as well as iron mining, were the most important sources of revenue. M. can probably be found in the Athenian tribute lists for 425 BC. It seems relations with the surrounding Thracian areas were good. M. concluded a treaty with Philip II (341 BC) which remained in force under Alexander the Great. The city lost its independence for a time under Lysimachus [2] (302–281 BC). M. does not appear to have suffered from the Celtic incursions; Antiochus II sent an envoy to assist Apollonia and M. against the Celts in 260 (or 255) BC (IGBulg 1, 388). War broke out in the 2nd cent. BC over the city of Anchiale [2], founded by Apollonia (IGBulg 1,388 bis). M. seems to have allied itself in 179 with Pharnaces I against kings Eumenes II, Prusias II and Ariarathes IV, who were friendly to the Romans (Pol. 25,2,12). In 72

BC the city surrendered to Licinius [I 26] Lucullus, and probably concluded a treaty with him (App. Ill. 30). M. was forced to wage war with the Bessi (IGBulg 1, 344) and the Dacian king Burebista (IGBulg 1,323). From 45 AD, M. was part of the Roman province of Thracia, while in the 2nd cent. it belonged to Lower Moesia (Ptol. 3,10,1; 8). Whereas M.'s importance declined in Roman times, it increased again in Byzantine times.

I. GĂLĂBOV, Nesabăr i negovite pametnici, 1961; I. VENEDIKOV (ed.), Nessebre 1, 1969; IGBulg 1², 255ff.; R. F. HODDINOT, Bulgaria in Antiquity, 1975, 317–323.   I.v.B.

B. BYZANTINE TIMES

The city expanded from the 5th cent. AD on (remains of a new water supply system as well as of three basilicas). Until the 9th cent. M. was a bishopric in the church province of → Hadrianopolis [3]; then an autocephalic archbishopric until the 12th cent., and later a metropolis without suffragan. However, before 680/1 AD no bishops are attested at councils [1. 894 l. 10]. Although Bulgarians and Byzantines fought over M. since the 8th cent., M. also made possible the exchange of goods and information between the two powers. Italian merchants also made use of M.'s role as an intermediary in the 13th and 14th centuries. Extensive archaeological remnants provide evidence of the expenses invested by the Byzantines in the city's development [2. 220–243, with map]. M. did not fall under lasting Turkish rule until 1453.
→ Anchiale [2]

1 R. RIEDINGER (ed.), Acta conciliorum oecumenicorum, ser. 2, vol. 2,2, 1992   2 P. SOUSTAL, s.v. Mesambria, RBK 6, 218–243 (with lit. to 1997).

R. BROWNING, A. CUTLER, s.v. Mesambria, ODB 2, 1347f.; H.-D. DÖPMANN, s.v. Mesambria, LThK³ 7, 155 (bibl.); P. SOUSTAL, s.v. Mesambria, TIB 6, 355–359; Id., s.v. Mesambria, LMA 6, 552; V. VELKOV, Mesambria zwischen dem 4. und dem 8. Jahrhundert, in: R. PILLINGER, A. PÜLZ, H. VETTERS (eds.), Die Schwarzmeerküste in der Spätantike und im frühen Mittelalter, 1992, 19–22.
                                                                                       E.W.

[2] (Μεσαμβρία; Mesambría). According to Arr. Ind. 39, a peninsula off the Persian coast of the Persian Gulf, rich in gardens and fruit trees, 200 stadia distant from Taoke. It is also mentioned in Plin. HN 6,99 as a nameless island (insula sine nomine), and by Marcianus, Periplus 1,24 as Chersonesus (Χερσόνησος/Chersónēsos. Ptol. 6,4,2 speaks of the Χερσόνησος ἄκρα/Chersonēsos akra.

F. H. WEISSBACH, s.v. Mesambria (3), RE 15, 1074f.
                                                                                       J.W.

Mesatis (Μεσάτις; Mesátis). One of three communities or regions from which the city of → Patrae in Achaea was founded. M. had a cult of Dionysus. It was possibly the hilly country to the east and north of Patrae, at the modern Ano Sychaina-Voundeni (Paus. 7,18,4–6; 19,1; 21,14).

A. D. RIZAKIS, Achaïe 1. Sources textuelles et histoire régionale (Meletemata 20), 1995, 164. Y.L.

Mesatus Greek tragedian, who enjoyed success at the Dionysia several times after 468 BC (TrGF I 11). B.Z.

Mescinius Roman *gens*, evident in the names of some individuals of the late Republican period, also in the Greak-speaking areas (CIL I² 2247).

SCHULZE, 193, 272, 288.

[1] M. Rufus, L. In 51 BC, M was assigned as quaestor to the proconsul → Cicero in Cilicia. Differences in their reports cast a shadow over their relations (Cic. Att. 6,3,1; 4,1; Cic. Fam. 5,20). Cicero attempted to cover up this resentment when he tried to win M. over as an adversary of Caesar (Cic. Fam. 5,21,1; 13,28,2). MRR 2,242. T.FR.

Mesene (Μεσήνη, Hebr. *Mēšān*, Syr. *Maišān*, Mid. Pers. *Mēšūn*, Arab. *Maysān*). A designation for southernmost → Mesopotamia, attested since → Hyspaosines and used into Islamic times (corresponding approximately to the 'Sealand' of the older period, that is, the 2nd and 1st millenium BC). It is also used to form an ethnic term for the inhabitants of the region. The precise extent of the area, located in the region of the confluence of the Tigris and the Euphrates, varies in the sources (Str. 2,1,31; 16,1,8; 16,3,3; Plin. HN 6,129; 131f.; Steph. Byz. s.v. Mesene; cf. also *Maisanítēs kólpos*, Ptol. 6,7,19 [1]) and cannot be precisely determined. The term M. is often used as synonymous with (the political entity) → Characene. Its linguistic origin is unclear (Iran. 'Land of the buffalo'? [6. 1095]; *mê šanû*, attested in cuneiform inscriptions [4. 216f., 278f., 282f.], gives the impression of a popular etymology: 'other = further? water'). According to Palmyrene inscriptions, Forat, together with → Charax Spasin(o)u, was an important center in M. for trade with India via the Arabian-Persian Gulf [2. 113f.].

1 A. GROHMANN, s.v. Maisanites, RE 14, 607f. 2 S. H. NODELMAN, A Preliminary History of Charakene, in: Berytus 13, 1959/6, 83–121 3 A. OPPENHEIMER, Babylonia Judaica in the Talmudic Period, 1983, 241–257 4 A. J. SACHS, H. HUNGER, Astronomical Diaries 3, 1996; 5 M. STRECK, [M. MORONY], s.v. Maysān, EI 6, 918–923 6 F. H. WEISSBACH, s.v. Mesene, RE 15, 1082–95. J.OE.

Mesengyema (μεσεγγύημα; *mesengýēma*), the 'thing entrusted': an item or money, which was entrusted jointly by several individuals to a third party. The *mesengyema* was then to be returned to one or to all depositors as agreed (Harpocr. s.v.). The procedure was suitable for safe-keeping during disputes, for stakes in bets and for secure keeping of documents (cf. Isocr. Or. 12,13; IG VII 3172,69: Boeotia; BGU 592 II 9 and MITTEIS/WILCKEN 88,13: both 2nd cent. AD; PAntinoopolis 35 II 14, 4th cent. AD: Egypt).

J. PARTSCH, Griechisches Bürgschaftsrecht, 1909, 336–340. G.T.

Mese stigme see → Punctuation

Mesoa (Μεσόα; *Mesóa*). *Ōbá* or *kṓmē* ('village') of → Sparta [1. 119]; specifically the urban region south west of the theatre (Str. 8,5,3; Paus. 3,16,9; Steph. Byz. s.v. Μεσσόα). The inscription IG V 1, 515 is a forgery [2].

1 N. F. JONES, Public Organization in Ancient Greece, 1987 2 A. J. S. SPAWFORTH, Fourmontiana. IG V 1, 515: Another Forgery 'from Amyklai', in: ABSA 71, 1976, 139–145. Y.L.

Mesogeia (μεσόγεια, *mesógeia*), the inland area of Attica. Since → Cleisthenes' reform of the tribes [4. 157ff.], each of the ten Attic *phýlai* consisted of one *trittýs* ('third') each of *démoi* from *asty*, *mesógeia* and *paralia* (Aristot. Ath. Pol. 21,4) [1; 2. 251ff.; 4. 159]. In classical times the 10 *mesógeia trittýes* included approximately 47 *démoi* [3. 125ff.].
→ Attica (with map); → Demos [2]

1 M. H. HANSEN, Asty, M. and Paralia, in: CeM 41, 1990, 51–54; 2 P. J. RHODES, A Commentary on the Aristotelian Athenaion Politeia, 1981 3 J. S. TRAILL, Demos and Trittys, 1986 4 K.-W. WELWEI, Die griechische Polis, ²1998. H.LO.

Mesolabium (μεσολάβιον; *mesolábion*). A mechanical device invented by → Eratosthenes [2] to establish graphically the two geometric means x and y between two given lines a and b (as in the relationship $a{:}x = x{:}y = y{:}b$). The mesolabium enabled the mechanical solution of the problem of the duplication of the cube ('Delian problem'): if $b = 2a$, then x is the desired solution of the equation for the duplication of the cube ($x^3 = 2a^3$).
→ Hippocrates [5] of Chios

mes; T. L. HEATH, A History of Greek Mathematics, Vol. 2, 1921, 258–260. M.F.

Mesomedes (Μεσομήδης; *Mesomḗdēs*). Cithara player and lyric poet from Crete, freedman of Hadrian (according to the Suda), main period of production AD 144 (according to Eusebius). Besides two poems in the *Anthologia Palatina* (14,63) and the *Anthologia Planudea* (16,323), 13 poems are transmitted by the manuscripts, four of which are provided with musical notation. They include hymns, animal fables, the description of a sponge and of a clock, as well as a poem on the manufacture of glass. There is a variety of metres, in particular anapaestic (apokrota, paroemiac, proceleusmatic). The dialect displays a Doric coloration.

E. HEITSCH, Die griechische Dichterfragmente der römischen Kaiserzeit, 1, 1961, 22–32 (1963², 24–32); E. PÖHLMANN, Denkmäler altgriechischen Musik, 1970, 13–31; M. L. WEST, Ancient Greek Music, 1992, 303–308; Id., Greek Metre, 1982. E.R.

Mesopotamia

I. GENERAL II. HISTORY FROM THE PALEOLITHIC
TO 1600 BC III. FROM THE MIDDLE BABYLONIAN
PERIOD TO THE END OF THE SASSANID PERIOD

I. GENERAL
A. NAME B. CHRONOLOGY C. ECOLOGY
D. POPULATION

A. NAME
The name M., i.e. '[land] between the rivers [→ Euphrates [2] and → Tigris]', first appears in Arrian (Arr.
Anab. 3,7,3; 7,7,3) as a designation for the area of what
is now eastern Syria and northern Iraq, probably corresponding to the Aramaic *beyn nahrīn* and the Akkadian
māt birīt nārim (both 'between the rivers'). However,
this expression designated only the region between the
bend of the Euphrates and Baliḫ/Ḫabur [1; 2]. Later, M.
could also refer to the entire region of the two rivers
(Plin. HN 5,86). In modern, imprecise usage, M. denotes the region of what is now Iraq, divided into northern and southern M., respectively → Assyria and → Babylonia, with the border above the narrowest point between the rivers. In earlier times, the modern name
Sumer was used for southern Babylonia, and Akkadia
for northern Babylonia.

B. CHRONOLOGY
An absolute chronology for the Mesopotamian area
beginning *c.* 1350 BC is provided by dynastic or
→ Kings' lists, → Chronicles, and other historical data.
A fragmentary tradition for the preceding period results
in an insoluble area of uncertainty ('Dark Age'), which
prevents the accurate connection of an internally confirmed (apart from small uncertainties) block of *c.* 740
years. Subject to the unproven assumption that
→ Ḫammurapi of Babylon reigned between 1792 and
1750, the oldest reasonably secure date is *c.* 2334
(accession of → Sargon of → Akkad [3; 4]); despite the
debate which has flared up recently [5], these dates will
form the basis of all Mesopotamia-related articles in
this encyclopaedia. For the older period, one must rely
on estimates of dynasty lengths, synchronisms with predynastic Egypt, and C14 dating.

C. ECOLOGY
M. is an essentially flat landscape, which stretches to
the east as far as the → Zagrus mountains and includes
some of its foothills. The broad floodplain of Babylonia
arose from the formation of the delta by the major rivers. While northern M. receives enough rain for reliable
crop production, throughout the south such cultivation
is only possible by using water from the Tigris and Euphrates. Here, the Tigris, which has more water, plays a
lesser role, because its channel runs so deep that water
can mostly only be removed by hoisting mechanisms.
After a moist, warm prehistory, a transition to a
slightly drier and cooler climate began in the 4th millennium, leading to a decline in irrigation water owing

to a decrease in precipitation at the headwaters of the
rivers. From the 3rd millennium on, therefore, water
had to be led through long canal systems to areas which
had previously been irrigated naturally. Canal irrigation is characteristic of Babylonia throughout the entire
historical period (→ Canals). From 2000 BC on, the climate appears to have remained more or less stable.

D. POPULATION
When we approach population groups beginning
with the mid–3rd millennium BC through their written
language, it becomes clear that we are always dealing
with a linguistic, and hence ethnic, mixture. This is also
true for the language underlying proto-cuneiform texts
from Babylonia from the end of the 4th millennium, the
main component of which was certainly → Sumerian
(→ Cuneiform script). Later waves of immigration
came primarily from the milieu of Semitic languages
(→ Akkadian; → Amorite; → Aramaic), but are also associated with languages of unknown affiliation (Cassite, → Cossaei; → Hurrian mainly in north M.).

II. HISTORY FROM THE PALEOLITHIC TO 1600 BC
A. PALEOLITHIC (TO C. 10000 BC) B. NEOLITHIC
(C. 10000–6000) C. CHALCOLITHIC
(C. 6000–3900) D. URUK PERIOD (C. 3900–3200)
E. EARLY DYNASTIC PERIOD (TO 2334) F. THE EM-
PIRE OF AKKAD (2334–2154) G. THE THIRD DYN-
ASTY OF UR (2112–2004) H. OLD ASSYRIAN PERI-
OD (1900–1700)

A. PALEOLITHIC (TO C. 10000 BC)
The small number of known find sites from this period (e.g. → Carmel, Israel; Beldibi, Turkey; Šanidar,
Iraq; Hotu, Iran) is a consequence of limited research.
Wherever intensive site investigations have taken place
in the Near East, ample remains of human existence
during the Paleolithic period have been found; this is
also true for the mountainous areas of M., as well as for
the southwestern desert (Abu Dibbis). As far as can be
discerned development proceeded parallel to that
known from Europe.

B. NEOLITHIC (C. 10000–6000)
Towards the end of the Paleolithic (about 10000
BC), the mountainous parts of the Near East witnessed
an increase in signs of the beginning of food production,
instead of the acquisition of food through gathering,
hunting, and fishing. At the same time, there is evidence
of early forms of permanent settlement. By the 6th millennium, a crucial share of food was provided by agriculture and animal husbandry carried out by a sedentary people. Because of the crescent-shaped formation
of the mountains of Palaestina, western Syria, the Taurus, and the Zagrus, surrounding the plains of Syria/
M., where this development took place, these areas are

collectively known as the 'Fertile Crescent'. In addition, the uncertainty of agricultural techniques, and consequently, the potential need for resorting to food gathering, demanded a preference for fragmented landscapes with the potential for a wide variety of uses.

C. CHALCOLITHIC (c. 6000–3900)

In the following periods of Ḥassuna, Samarra, and Ḥalaf in the north, Eridu and Ḥağği Moḥammed in the south, each characterized by a particular type of ceramic decoration, the great plains of M. remained largely unsettled, despite improved cultivation techniques. Not until the ʿObēd period (2nd half of the 5th millennium), again characterized by another type of ceramics, did settlements spread to the plains. Closer cohabitation gave rise to conflicts which were countered, in part, by the formation of settlement hierarchies. Division of labour, specialization, and, above all, an administration rapidly formed in the centres of the first settlement systems. Larger (cult) buildings are another sign of the consolidation of central functions in specific locations. The architectural form of temples on elevated terraces (→ Ziggurat), which would later be characteristic of all M., is first attested in southern M.

D. URUK PERIOD (c. 3900–3200)

A slight shift in climate at the beginning of the 4th millennium left large parts of the southern Mesopotamian plain free of water and, thus, suitable for settlement over a broad area. Within a short time in the mid–4th millennium, the number of settlements in the hinterland of the central town of Uruk rose from c. 11 to more than 100, with a simultaneous increase in the variety of size and number of hierarchical levels. Around 3200 BC, → Uruk itself covered at least 250 ha and was thus almost twenty times larger than the largest towns known previously. Although the stages of development remain unclear, since the early layers of the Uruk period were determined only in one narrow sondage, the consolidation of the so-called 'Early Advanced Civilization' apparently took only a short time. The numerous innovations in this period (monumental architecture, the first large-scale art, cylinder seals, new ceramic techniques, and, last but not least, writing) are probably connected with the efforts to manage the formidable problems brought about by the rapid increase in size and density of the population.

The appearance of cylinder seals (→ Gem cutting) and other means of data storage are indicative of the difficulties experienced by an economic administration in dealing with large quantities of information. In this context, the earliest → Writing eventually appeared about 3200 BC. Approximately 80% of the more than 5000 clay tablets from the period down to c. 3000 BC contain data pertaining to a central economic administration; the remaining 20% belong to the genre of so-called lexical → Lists, each of which give the names and concepts of a semantic category. No literary, cultural, or historical texts are known. Because no syntactically complete texts have been transmitted, the language used (most probably → Sumerian) is not unambiguously clear, nor are the contents known in individual detail [6]. Nevertheless, there is no doubt that the basic structures of the society that characterized all later Mesopotamian history were formed in this period. Although changes are apparent in northern M. as in Syria, Anatolia, and western Iran (proto-Elam) – partly driven by developments in southern M.- the corresponding (cultural) concentrations did not occur there [7].

E. EARLY DYNASTIC PERIOD (TO 2334)

Scant archaeological information allows little more to be discerned than that the characteristic systems of → Canals developed due to increasing water shortage. The complete historical tradition does not begin until about 2600 BC, when cuneiform signs with their syllabic values were used, enabling the grammatical details of the language to be written down (→ Cuneiform script). Sources include primarily literary texts and texts with historical content. Apart from the Sumerian language (with countless loan words from Akkadian and other languages), we witness the first writing of Akkadian (Semitic) names (see also → Eblaite).

It is difficult to reconstruct the political situation, because, for example, the so-called 'Sumerian King List' propagates the idea that individual cities took turns ruling, while the historical texts record that the dynasties reigned alongside each other (for instance, → Lagaš; → Ur; Kiš) and fought and vied with one another in changing alliances. The religious centre and residence of the chief god of the pantheon (→ Enlil) was → Nippur. In addition, almost all historical inscriptions come from Lagaš, so that, due to the lack of further evidence, the conditions there were considered representative not only of earlier periods, for which information is lacking, but also of the entire region. A form of theocracy was deduced from these texts, commonly considered the most important form of society in the early Babylonian period. More recent research has adopted a more differentiated approach, and considers the 'temple city' as only one of several possibilities. It is beyond dispute that near the end of the early dynastic period, there was an increase in attempts by individual rulers to gain sovereignty over all of Babylonia through the conquest of other city-states. Owing to a lack of written evidence, almost nothing is known about northern M. → Assur [1] was probably another city-state which stood in close connection to the south; the same is true of → Susa.

The discovery of the royal tombs of Ur in the 1920s was spectacular, because of their abundance of precious metals and stones as well as other burial goods.

F. THE EMPIRE OF AKKAD (2334–2154)

With his victory over Lugalzagesi, a southern Babylonian ruler who already commanded a large territory, Sargon, from the north Babylonian city → Akkad (not yet located), was able in a short time to unite all of Babylonia under his rule, and consolidate this central-

Overview of selected rulers in Babylonia and Assyria

BABYLONIA		ASSYRIA	
about 2500	Urnanše of Lagaš		
about 2350	Urukagina (Uru'inimgina) of Lagaš		
2334–2279	Sargon (Šarru-ukīn) of Akkad		
2254–2218	Naramsin (Narām-Sîn) of Akkad		
2111–2095	Urnamma of Ur		
2094–2047	Šulgi of Ur		
2017–1985	Išbi'erra of Isin		
		1813–1781	Šamšī-Adad I of Assur
1792–1750	Ḫammurapi of Babylon		
1626–1595	Samsu-ditana of Babylon		
1595	Destruction of Babylon by the Hittite Mursili I		
		1425–1418	Aššur-nirārī I
about 1415	Kara'indaš	1418–1409	Aššur-bēl-nišēšu
		1409–1401	Aššur-rīm-nišēšu
about 1400	Kurigalzu I	1401–1391	Aššur-nādin-aḫḫē
1374–1360	Kadašman-Enlil I	1391–1364	Erība-Adad I
1360–1333	Burnaburiaš II Karahardaš/Nazibugaš	1364–1328	Aššur-uballiṭ I
1333–1308	Kurigalzu II		
1328–1318	Enlil-nirārī		
		1318–1306	Ārik-dēn-ili
1308–1282	Nazimaruttaš	1306–1274	Adad-nirārī I
1282–1264	Kadašman-Turgu	1274–1244	Salmanassar I (Šulmānu-ašarēd)
1264–1255	Kadašman-Enlil II		
1255–1246	Kudur-Enlil		
1246–1233	Šagarakti-Šuriaš	1244–1207	Tukultī-Ninurta I
1232–1225	Kaštiliaš IV		
1225	Tukultī-Ninurta I in Babylon		
1225–1223	Enlil-nādin-šumi Kadašman-harbe II		
1223–1217	Adad-šuma-iddin		
1217–1187	Adad-šuma-uṣur	1207–1203	Aššur-nādin-apli
		1203–1197	Aššur-nirārī III
		1197–1192	Ellil-kudurrī-uṣur
1187–1172	Melišipak	1192–1179	Ninurta-apil-Ekur
1172–1159	Marduk-apla-iddina	1178–1133	Aššur-dān I
1559–1158	Zababa-šuma-iddin		
1158–1155	Enlil-nādin-aḫi		
1158–1140	Marduk-kābit-aḫḫēšu		
1140–1132	Itti-Marduk-balāṭu		
1132–1126	Ninurta-nādin-šumi	1133–1115	Aššur-rēša-iši I
1126–1104	Nebukadnezar I (Nâbû-kudurrī-uṣur)	1115–1076	Tiglath-Pileser I (Tukultī-apil-Ešarra)

(Subsequent Babylonian kings to the middle of the 8th cent. BC and Assyrian rulers to the 2nd half of the 10th cent. BC are omitted).

		935–912	Aššur-dān II
		912–891	Adad-nirārī II
		891–884	Tukultī-Ninurta II
		884–859	Assurnaṣirpal II (Aššur-nāṣir-apli)
		859–824	Salmanassar III
		824–811	Šamšī-Adad II
		811–783	Adad-nirārī III
		783–773	Salmanassar IV
		773–755	Aššur-dān III

BABYLONIA

748–734	Nabonassar (Nabû-nāṣir)
729–727	Pulu (= Tiglath-Pileser III)
727–722	Ulūlaja (= Salmanassar V)
722–710	Marduk-apla-iddin II
710–705	Sargon II
705–703	Sennacherib
703	Marduk-zākir-šumi II
703	Marduk-apla-iddin II
703–700	Bēl-ibni
700–694	Aššur-nādin-šumi
694–693	Nergal-ušēzib
693–689	Mušēzib-Marduk
689–681	Sennacherib
681–669	Asarhaddon (Aššur-aḫa-iddina)
669–668	Assurbanipal
668–648	Šamaš-šuma-ukīn
648–627	Kandalānu
627–626	Interregnum/Sin-šumu-līšir
	Dynasty of the Chaldaeans:
626–605	Nabupolassar (Nabû-apla-uṣur)
605–562	Nebukadnezar II
652–560	Amēl-Marduk
560–556	Neriglissar (Nergal-šarra-uṣur)
556	Lābāši-Marduk
556–539	Nabonid (Nabû-nāʾid)

ASSYRIA

755–745	Aššur-nirārī V
745–727	Tiglath-Pileser III
727–722	Salmanassar V
722–705	Sargon II (Šarru-ukēn)
705–681	Sennacherib (Sîn-aḫḫē-erība)
681–669	Asarhaddon
669–631	Assurbanipal (Aššur-bāni-apli)
631–627	Aššur-etel-ilāni
627–612	Sin-šarra-iškun
612–610/09	Aššur-uballiṭ II

For later rulers in Babylonia, cf. → Achaemenids; → Parthians; → Sassanids; → Seleucids.

ized hegemony so that the central state lasted four generations, despite strong attempts to restore the sovereignty of the city-states. Both Sargon and his grandson → Naramsin were considered by later generations to be outstanding figures of rulers. Thus, → Sargon II of Assyria explicitly named himself after the older ruler.

Campaigns on the southern coast of the Persian Gulf ('Magan') as well as the Mediterranean (conquest of → Ebla) and perhaps southeastern Anatolia delimit Akkad's sphere of influence, rather than indicating a lasting rule. An example of a strong outpost is Tell Brak on the → Ḫabur, with its palace built by Naramsin. Sargon's daughter Enḫeduana, high priestess of the moon god of Ur, is known by name as the author of numerous Sumerian poems.

G. The Third Dynasty of Ur (2112–2004)

After a poorly attested phase in which power was divided among individual cities, characterized in reports by the reign of terror by the Guti, who came from the Zagrus, Babylonia was once again united around Ur by → Urnamma in about 2112 BC. Through strengthening central institutions, a stabilization of centralized rule was achieved, which enabled the reign of the third dynasty of Ur to last for five generations. Yet when it collapsed, it did so from excessive centralization; in addition, the Amurrite peoples massively

pressed Babylonia from the west, and conquered the cities (→ Amurru [1]). The Ur III period saw the climax of the agricultural crisis caused by water shortage. A solution was attempted through expanding the written monitoring of all resources, which produced an enormous increase in written material from the 21st year of King Šulgi. A side effect was an increase in the number of literary and legal texts ('Codex Urnammu'), and the genre of royal hymns (→ Songs) emerged.

H. Old Assyrian period (1900–1700)

Northern M. remained, as before, in the sphere of influence of the third dynasty of Ur; however, there are scarcely any sources for this period. Beginning c. 1900 BC, → Assur became an important centre of trade between Anatolia, the Zagrus, and southern M. The activities of Assyrian traders are known primarily from the thousands of documents found in Assyrian trading colonies (kārum) in Anatolia (→ Commerce; → Kanesh; → Asia Minor III.A.4.).

J. Old Babylonian period (2017–1595)

After the end of the third dynasty of Ur, another distribution of power occurred to the cities now ruled by the Amorites: Isin, Larsa, and → Babylon. Around 1790 BC, all of Babylonia was finally reunified under → Hammurapi of Babylon. Ḫammurapi's realm reached beyond the borders of Babylonia, but with the conquest of Eshnunna and → Mari he also destroyed the buffer zones against the attacks of the Cassites (→ Cossaei) and Hittites (→ Ḫattusa II). In 1595 BC, Babylon was destroyed by the Hittite Mursili I.

Northern Mesopotamian sources are largely mute for this period as well, but numerous finds of texts from throughout Syria testify to relative cultural and political autonomy and intensive exchange within the Near East. It is significant in this context that the Hittite cuneiform script was taken not from M., but from → Aleppo.

K. RELATIONS BETWEEN ELAM AND MESO-POTAMIA

The relative geographic similarity of the Elamite and Babylonian floodplains resulted in similar political, cultural, and economic structures (for the 4th millennium see [7]). The sparse written record from → Elam obscures the fact that this region sometimes had greater political influence on M. than we can infer from the Mesopotamian sources. Whenever the political structure of Babylonia, and later also Assyria, appeared weak, Elam was ready to assert its claim for power. This is even true for the period of Ḫammurapi, where letters found in Mari indicate that Elam was able to gain a foothold in the area of east Syria, not to mention the fact that it occasionally took power in Larsa. (For a later example, see below III.A.)   H.J.N.

III. FROM THE MIDDLE BABYLONIAN PERIOD TO THE END OF THE SASSANID PERIOD

A. MIDDLE BABYLONIAN PERIOD: CASSITES/ 2ND DYNASTY OF ISIN (C. 1570–1027) B. THE MIDDLE ASSYRIAN EMPIRE (C. 1390–1076) C. ARAMAEAN STATES (FIRST CENTURIES OF THE 1ST MILLENNIUM BC) D. THE NEO-ASSYRIAN EMPIRE (935–609) E. THE NEO-BABYLONIAN EMPIRE (626–539) F. THE ACHAEMENIDS (C. 640–331) G. MESOPOTAMIA UNDER ALEXANDER THE GREAT (330–323) H. THE SELEUCIDS (311–141)

A. MIDDLE BABYLONIAN PERIOD: CASSITES/ 2ND DYNASTY OF ISIN (C. 1570–1027)

The 2nd half of the 2nd millennium BC was a period of close international relations between Near Eastern states. This development was initially dominated by the state of the → Mittani (→ Hurrians), which had emerged in northern M.; by the Hittites (→ Ḫattusa II), who had advanced from Asia Minor into Syria; and by the Egyptians of the New Kingdom, who had extended their rule to Palestina and southern Syria (→ Egypt). After a gap during which the names of kings are almost the only record, the sources in Babylonia and Assyria become more abundant from the end of the 15th cent.

In Babylon meanwhile, the dynasty of the Cassites (→ Cossaei) had come to power. Since the time of Kara'indash, who built a temple in → Uruk (façade with figurative representations made of carved bricks), and Kurigalzu I, who had a new residence built at Dūr-Kurigalzu (modern ʿAqar Qūf, west of Baghdad), until the end of the dynasty in the mid–12th cent., an established political system can be discerned in inscriptions, clay tablets (legal and administrative documents, letters, literary texts), and last but not least the so-called *Kudurru* inscriptions (stone stelae with records of legal acts, frequently gifts of land by the ruler). In the 14th and 13th cent., the culturally Babylonized Cassite kings participated in diplomatic exchanges (gifts, embassies, dynastic marriages) with the surrounding states. In the 13th cent., Assyria occasionally succeeded in gaining a foothold in Babylonia. The 12th cent saw confrontations above all with westward-advancing → Elam, which led to the plundering of the capital → Babylon under Šhutruk-Naḫḫunte.

The Cassite dynasty was replaced by the second dynasty of Isin, whose most significant ruler → Nebuchadnezzar I (1126–1104) for his part attacked Elam and plundered → Susa. During his reign, there were important changes in religion: → Marduk, the city god of Babylon, became the ruling deity of the Babylonian pantheon (Song of the creation of the world → *Enūma ēliš*). Already toward the end of the second dynasty of Isin, however, and then under the succeeding second Sealand dynasty, the central Babylonian power largely collapsed, caused primarily by the invading → Aramaeans. A renewed consolidation of the region did not occur until centuries later.

B. THE MIDDLE ASSYRIAN EMPIRE (C. 1390–1076)

The interruption in Assyrian records after the end of the dynasty of Šamši-Adad I indicates that at that time → Assur [1] had merely local significance. The city was temporarily dependent on → Mittani, whose influence stretched east of the Tigris (Arrapḫa, → Nuzi). However, beginning in the later 15th cent., Assur also participated in diplomatic exchange with Near Eastern powers. Under Assur-uballiṭ I (1364–1328), Adad-nirari I (1306–1274), and above all Salmanassar I (1274–1244), Assur had become so strong that it was able to expand militarily and eliminate the Mittani rump state Ḫanigalbat. Assyrian territory now stretched to the Euphrates and bordered on the Hittite empire. The practice of deporting prisoners and settling them in other areas of the empire, which would later become characteristic of Assyrian warfare, began at that time.

Tukulti-Ninurta I (1244–1207), who built a new capital on the Tigris opposite the city of Assur (Kār-Tukultī-Ninurta), not only subjugated additional territories in the east and north, but also advanced as far as Babylon (1225). Because Babylonia influenced the culture of Assyria in fundamental areas, there was a close relationship between the two regions, however, it was not free from tensions.

After a period of limited foreign policy activity, → Tiglath-Pileser I. (1115–1076) resumed the policy of

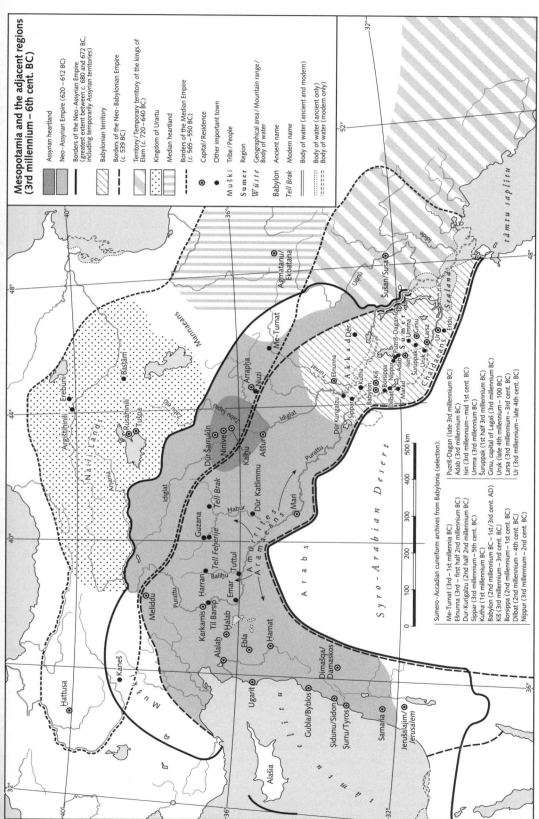

Mesopotamia and the adjacent regions (3rd millennium – 6th cent. BC)

Assyrian heartland

Neo-Assyrian Empire (620–612 BC)

Borders of the Neo-Assyrian Empire (greatest extent between c. 680 and 672 BC, including temporarily Assyrian territories)

Babylonian territory

Borders of the Neo-Babylonian Empire (c. 539 BC)

Territory / Temporary territory of the kings of Elam (c. 720–640 BC)

Kingdom of Urartu

Median heartland

Borders of the Median Empire (c. 565–550 BC)

●   Capital / Residence

●   Other important town

Muški   Tribe / People

Sumer   Region

Wüste   Geographical area / Mountain range / Body of water

Babylon   Ancient name

Tell Brak   Modern name

Body of water (ancient and modern)

Body of water (ancient only)
Body of water (modern only)

Sumero-Accadian cuneiform archives from Babylonia (selection):

Me-Turnat (3rd – 1st millennia BC)
Ešnunna (3rd – first half 2nd millennium BC)
Dur-Kurigalzu (2nd half 2nd millennium BC)
Sippar (3rd millennium – 5th cent. BC)
Kutha (1st millennium BC)
Babylon (2nd millennium BC – 1st / 3rd cent. AD)
Kiš (3rd millennium – 3rd cent. BC)
Borsippa (2nd millennium – 1st cent. BC)
Dilbat (2nd millennium – 4th cent. BC)
Nippur (3rd millennium – 2nd cent. BC)

Puzriš-Dagan (late 3rd millennium BC)
Adab (3rd millennium BC)
Isin (3rd millennium – mid 1st cent. BC)
Umma (3rd millennium BC)
Šuruppak (1st half 3rd millennium BC)
Girsu, capital of Lagaš (3rd millennium BC)
Uruk (late 4th millennium – 100 BC)
Larsa (3rd millennium – 3rd cent. BC)
Ur (3rd millennium – late 4th cent. BC)

expansion. The fall of the Hittite empire (→ Ḫattusa II. B.4.) left no serious opponent that could have prevented an expansion to the west. Soon after his accession to power, he turned against the Muški, who had emigrated to eastern Asia Minor; there followed campaigns in the Naʾiri regions (Lake Van area) and as far as the Mediterranean. Finally, in the later years of his reign, even Babylonia was attacked. With this, Assyria reached its greatest extent. However, this height of Assyrian power in the late 2nd millenium BC, combined with a cultural ascendency (among other things, extensive reports on the deeds of the king), did not outlast the reign of Tiglath-Pileser.

C. ARAMAEAN STATES (FIRST CENTURIES OF THE 1ST MILLENNIUM BC)

The Assyrians had been forced to confront the → Aramaeans (initially under the name Aḥlamu) since the 13th cent. BC. These tribes, still nomadic at the time, in the area west of Assyria, from the middle Euphrates to → Karchemish, succeeded at the beginning of the 1st millennium in forming several small states: in Syria: Bīt Agusi, Samʾal (Jaʾudi), Ḥamat, Aram/Damascus; in northern M.: Bīt Bahiani on the upper Ḫabur with the chief towns Guzana/modern Tell Ḥalaf and Sikani/modern Tell Feḥerije (whence there are royal statues with bilingual Assyrian-Aramaic inscriptions, late 9th cent.), as well as Bīt Adini farther west [8; 9]. They were the target of Assyrian expansion in the 9th and 8th cent., and were finally incorporated into the empire.

Aramaic tribes also penetrated southern M.; however, they can be found, like the Chaldaeans (→ Chaldaei), who must be distinguished from them, primarily in the area outside the old cities, where they formed tribal principalities with fluctuating boundaries. They stood in close association and exchange, but also in confrontation, with the city dwellers. Their representatives succeeded several times in being acknowledged as kings of Babylon. It is ultimately due to them that Babylonia played no economic and political role in the waning 2nd and 1st centuries of the 1st millennium must.

D. THE NEO-ASSYRIAN EMPIRE (935–609)

Assyria regained its strength at the end of the 10th cent. BC. We can speak of a 'Neo-Assyrian empire', beginning with kings Assur-dan II (935–912), Adad-nirari II (912–891), and Tukulti-Ninurta II (891–884).

The first peaks are represented by the reigns of Assurnaṣirpal II (884–859) and → Salmanassar III (859–824). These rulers had their deeds glorified, inter alia by decorating the palaces with (originally painted) relief panels; first in → Kalḫu (modern Nimrūd), and later in Dūr-Šarrukīn (modern Ḫorsabad), and Niniveh (modern Kouyunjik, → Ninus [2]). In the provinces, the palaces were embellished in the same way, although with less costly wall paintings (Til Barsip/modern Tell Aḥmar). Under Salmanassar III, the Arabs, who were to

appear more and more often in subsequent times, are documented in the sources (→ Arabs; → Arabia) for the first time.

It was above all Assurnaṣirpal II and Salmanassar III who succeeded, through numerous campaigns, in securing Assyrian power from Cilicia and Syria in the west to the Zagrus mountains and Lake Urmia in the east. In the north, the kingdom of → Urarṭu, which came into being in the 9th cent., represented a powerful opponent, that would only be decisively weakened by Sargon II in 714 BC.

Although its expansive vigour subsequently dwindled, Assyria nevertheless continued to be the only major military power in the Near East. Over the course of time, both the Aramaean nations and the Hittite successor states (→ Asia Minor III. C. with map) in northern M., eastern Asia Minor, and Syria as far as Palaestina fell victim to Assyria and were transformed into provinces. These regions rebelled against their subjugation in numerous revolts that were brutally suppressed.

Three stages can be distinguished in the establishment of Assyrian rule: 1. the creation of a vassal relationship with regular payment of tribute; 2. the removal of vassal kings upon suspicion of disloyalty, and the appointment of princes loyal to Assur, often associated with a reduction in territory; 3. eventual military occupation and creation of a province [10. 293]. Military actions were connected with the deportation of the population of the conquered region.

The provincial system was organized in detail by → Tiglath-Pilesar III (745–727), under whom expansion efforts regained intensity. From then until the end of its existence, Assyria ruled practically all of the Near East. Babylonia also became once again the target of Assyrian interests. Tiglatpilesar made use of the dual monarchy, but assumed the throne name Pulu as king of Babylon. Under his successor Salmanassar V (727–722; as king of Babylon: Ululayu), the state of Israel in northern Palaestina was conquered (722); only Judah in southern Palaestina initially retained its political independence under Assyrian hegemony (→ Judah and Israel).

The final cent. of Assyrian history was determined by a new dynasty. Under the usurper → Sargon II (722–705) and his successors → Sennacherib (705–681), → Asarhaddon (681–669), and → Assurbanipal (669–631, not to 627), the largest extent of the empire was achieved. However, internal tensions also became discernable. Sargon reached Cyprus and weakened Urarṭu; while under Asarhaddon and Assurbanipal, the Assyrians, after a few failed attempts, temporarily occupied Egypt as far as Thebes (671–655). Other targets included Elam and the Iranian territory east of Assyria, where new states had already begun forming some time earlier (Mannaeans; in the 7th cent., the → Medes also increasingly appear). The Cimmerians (→ Cimmerii) and → Scythians) also appeared in the north at this time as new opponents.

Special relationships with Babylonia, dependent on Assyria since Tiglatpilesar III, arose through cultural associations, but Babylonian endeavours for independence led to tensions. At the end of the 8th cent., the Chaldaean → Marduk-apla-iddin [2] II temporarily succeeded in gaining independence. In 689, Sanherib destroyed the city of Babylon as a retaliation. However, his son Asarhaddon began its reconstruction, and also rebuilt temples in other Babylonian localities. Under Assurbanipal, a special Babylonian kingdom was established, and its throne occupied by Šamaš-šuma-ukin, the king's older brother (668–648). His rebellion against Assurbanipal (652–648) was put down after years of struggle, and Kandalanu became the new king of Babylon (648–627).

With the conquest of the entire Near East, all the economic resources of the region became available to the Assyrians, including the manpower for massive construction projects. The cruel warfare, ideologically founded on the claim to world power of the city god Assur, on whose behalf the ruler acted, led to a broad political integration which not only produced strong cultural interactions, but also, and at the same time – with the help of the deportation policy – a blending of populations.

After the major expansion of power, the collapse occurred within a few years under the onslaught of the → Medes, in alliance with the Babylonians under the Chaldaean → Nabupolassar, who had placed himself on the throne of Babylon in 626 BC. In 614, Assur was conquered and destroyed; in 612, Nineveh; in 609, the last refuge → Ḥarran. The once mighty empire was divided between the two victors. In the following period, the Assyrian heartland scarcely appears in the sources for centuries, although it continued to be inhabited. The lack of sources probably mostly reflects that the → Cuneiform script was abandoned as a means of communication, and written records in → Alphabet script have not been preserved. Interestingly, only vague notions of Assyria are to be found in the Greek tradition.

E. The Neo-Babylonian Empire (626–539)

The final phase of Babylonia's political independence began with the consolidation of power by → Nabupolassar (626–605). The near century-long rule by the new dynasty, traditionally called the Chaldaean dynasty (→ Chaldaei), represented a period of cultural and economic prosperity. The sphere of influence extended from the lower Euphrates and Tigris, across northern M., Syria, and Palaestina, to the borders of Egypt (the borderline with Median territory cannot always be clearly identified). In 596 and 587/586, → Jerusalem was conquered and the sovereignty of → Judah brought to an end; the population was deported to Babylonia (2 Kgs 24,14). → Nabonidus (556–539) drew Arabia as well into the Babylonian sphere of influence. During his ten-year stay in → Ṭeima, his son → Belsazar managed the empire. The expansion of the capital city → Babylon, already begun by Nabupolas-

sar, was continued above all under his son → Nebuchadnezzar II. (602–562) (palaces, processional street, and → Ishtar Gate).

A wealth of records provides insights into the social and economic system. Because hardly any royal archives have been found so far, the presumed → Palace economy remains largely obscure. However, temple archives from Uruk (Eanna) and → Sippar (Ebabbar) show that, as before, the sanctuaries formed powerful economic units, though they were controlled by royal functionaries. From a number of private archives (the most comprehensive is that of the Egibi family at Babylon), it becomes clear that from this period on the private economy played an important role. The importance of slaves in economic life also grew, particularly in the → Crafts, but also in → Commerce. It was not uncommon for them to work on their own account, paying a fee to their masters.

F. The Achaemenids (c. 640–331)

In October 539, Babylon was captured without resistance by the troops of the Achaemenid ruler → Cyrus [2] (→ Achaemenids, with map). In the Babylonian record, Cyrus is praised as a liberator, while Nabonid is severely reproached. In the background were tensions between the priesthood of → Marduk and the king's preference for the cult of the → Moon deity Sin of Ḥarran. With this end of its centuries-old political independence, M. was incorporated into a national entity of massive proportions: the former New Babylonian empire became the administrative district *Babilu u ebir nāri*, 'Babylon and [the territory] on the other side of the river (i.e. the Euphrates)' under → Gobryas [2] (→ Assyria; → Babylonia; → Syria; [11. map 28–29]; cf. also TAVO map B IV 23).

Although the transition from the New Babylonian empire to the rule of the Achaemenids occurred without major disturbances, usurpers with national-Babylonian ambitions appeared briefly upon the death of → Cambyses [2] and the transfer of the government to → Darius [1] I in 522/21 (→ Gaumata; Nebuchadnezzar III/IV), and again a few decades later (Bēl-šimanni; Šamaš-erība). The later unrest in the Achaemenid empire finds no echo in the Babylonian texts, any more than the campaign of Cyrus [3] the Younger, described by → Xenophon in the *Anábasis*. M. remained undisputedly in Achaemenid hands until the end of the dynasty.

Southern M. formed one of the economically productive parts of the Achaemenid empire. At first, little changed socially and economically. According to the texts, life continued to be determined by the temple and private economies. The aforementioned larger archives were continued without change into the Achaemenid period, but then end abruptly. New research has shown that this is clearly not connected with external influences (such as destruction of the sanctuaries [12]), but was rather brought about by internal organization (storage of texts). The beginnings of the so-called 'feudal system' (the granting of larger or smaller estates in exchange for fees and services, primarily military) clearly go back to the time of the Neo-Babylonian empire [14], but the economic situation was altered by its broad proliferation (archive of the Murašû family from Nippur, 2nd half of the 5th cent.).

Although no larger temple constructions are known from the Achaemenid period, the Babylonian → Religion remained alive, but internal adjustments are to be considered (stronger henotheism [15]). Particularly in the area of → Astronomy, the 5th and 4th cent. BC proved to be an intellectually productive period (development of the → Zodiac; beginnings of mathematical astronomy).

G. Mesopotamia under Alexander the Great (330–323)

Following his victory at → Gaugamela (331 BC), → Alexander [4] the Great marched into Babylon. Returning there after his Indian campaign, he died in the city on 10 June, 323. Just as the transition from the New Babylonian kings to the Achaemenids hardly represented a break, the social, economic, and cultural-religious situation in Babylonia changed only little now. This is shown both in the cuneiform sources and in the Greek work of → Berosus, which is preserved only fragmentarily. Scarcely any sources are available for the other regions of M., i.e. the area between the Euphrates, Baliḫ, Ḫabur, and Tigris.

During the conflicts between the Diadochi (→ Diadochi and Epigoni, with map) battles were partly fought out in M., but after the consolidation of the Seleucid Empire (→ Hellenistic states, with map), the fighting was mostly carried out outside this region; the location of battles in the → Syrian Wars was the western Euphrates region.

H. The Seleucids (311–141)

→ Seleucus, initially installed as satrap of Babylonia by Ptolemy, assumed the title of king in 305 BC and expanded his sphere of influence. → Seleucia on the Tigris arose southwest of modern Baghdad at the end of the 4th cent., after Hellenistic cities had already been founded in the country since Alexander. It developed into one of the most important metropolises in antiquity, as well as a centre of → Hellenism.

In the old Babylonian cities, the centuries-old local culture, largely unaffected by external problems, experienced a final cultural flowering under favourable economic conditions. Here, → Hellenization occurred only to a limited extent among the upper classes, while on the other hand, the rulers participated in indigenous cults [16; 17]. The large temple constructions in traditional Babylonian style in Uruk and other localities (Babylon, Borsippa) are an outward expression of this prosperity. Numerous cuneiform texts of astronomical-astrological content, chronicles, legal and administrative documents, letters, and copies of literary-religious compositions, attest the continuation of tradition and the existence of older social structures. Major activity is attested, particularly in the area of astronomy (observations, mathematical calculations).

J. The Parthians (and Rome, 141 BC – AD 226)

The whole of M., including Babylonia, remained part of the Seleucid empire until the westward advance by the Parthians (also Arsacids; → Iran, → Parthia) under → Mithradates I (171–139/8); they entered Babylon in 141 BC. The → Seleucids succeeded once again (129) in briefly advancing as far as Babylon under Antiochus [9] VII, and in 127 BC → Hyspaosines of Charax was even temporarily acknowledged as king of the city. But the entire east Euphratean area was Parthian from the time of Mithradates II (124/3–88/7). The river long formed the border between the Parthian and Roman empires, as was confirmed by treaty several times from 96 BC on. Until the end of the Parthian era, the extreme south of M., now designated as → Mesene, formed a vassal state under the kings of → Characene, an important station in trade with India (→ India, trade with) (with map). The Parthians built → Ctesiphon [2] as their new capital opposite Seleucia on the other bank of the Tigris.

M. was the site of a number of military confrontations between Parthia and Rome. While the former initially succeeded in holding position (53 BC, victory at Carrhae/→ Ḫarran), the latter was able to extend its territory to the east as far as the → Ḫabur and to → Dura-Europos (AD 164). The attempt to incorporate all of M. into the Roman empire (AD 115) by emperor Trajan must be considered a failure. The newly founded provinces of Assyria and Mesopotamia were consequently given up again by his successor Hadrian (AD 117). Ctesiphon and Seleucia on the Tigris were conquered in a new advance (AD 165/66), and the Romans finally advanced once again as far as Babylonia and northeastern M. under Septimius Severus (197/98) and Caracalla (216/17) (→ Adiabene; → Limes VI. with map).

Repeated sieges by the Romans of the Arab desert city → Ḫatra in northern M. (AD 117, 199), where an Arab dynasty ruled under Parthian sovereignty in the 2nd and 3rd cent. AD, were unsuccessful. In the Parthian era, Babylonian deities (Bēl, Nabû, Nergal, and others) can be detected in the pantheon of Ḫatra, as well as of → Palmyra, Dura-Europos, and other localities [18]. After centuries in which almost no information is preserved, Assur also reappears in the later Parthian era. According to Aramaic inscriptions, the cult of the homonymous city god and other local deities were still alive at this time.

In Babylonia, the transition to the Parthian era occurred without disruption. The cuneiform record did decrease quantitatively during the course of the 1st cent. AD, but it is attested in the city of Babylon down to the end of the Arsacid era (beginning of the 3rd cent. AD) [19]. A temple in Babylon style may have been built in → Nippur in the 1st cent. AD [20].

Contrary to the description by Greco-Roman authors (e.g. Strab. 16,15), Babylon was at that time in no way a derelict city [21]. Together with → Borsippa and Kutha, it formed the centre of this latest detectable Babylonian culture.

K. The Sassanids and Rome (226–642)

In AD 226, the → Sassanids succeeded in occupying the Parthian capital Ctesiphon [2]. Their numerous military confrontations with Rome in the 3rd cent. AD were frequently fought in M. In the course of these conflicts, the Sassanids also conquered Ḥatra (around 240) and Dura-Europos (256). On the other hand, the Romans advanced as far as Ctesiphon and succeeded in conquering→ Nisibis farther to the north. In 262, → Odaenathus [2] of Palmyra was likewise able to penetrate deep into Sassanid M. Relations between the two powers were also determined by struggles in the following cent. The Roman author → Ammianus Marcellinus left an impressive description of the war in 363 between the Roman emperor → Iulianus [11] Apostata and → Sapor/Šābuhr II (309–379), with a wealth of topographical information about M. Only a few indigenous sources from M. itself are available for this period. Except for the capital complex in Ctesiphon and the surroundings, archaeological finds are not very numerous (large buildings outside the old city wall at Uruk, as well as at Kiš). Administratively, Babylonia – at this time also the most important centre of → Judaism – belonged to the Sassanid province of Asōrestān. A good deal of information about the area is contained in the Babylonian Talmud (→ Rabbinical literature), as well as in Christian literature. Christianity is traceable outside of → Edessa [2] in M. since the later 2nd cent. (mostly Nestorians in Sassanid M.; → Nestorianism). There is practically no more direct evidence for the old Babylonian culture since the 2nd half of the 3rd cent. AD. Presumably, a certain Iranization took place. On the other hand, however, new religious tendencies arose, in whose works information about M. can be found and which also assimilated aspects of the old Babylonian culture: → Mandaeans and Manichaeans (→ Mani).

L. Mesopotamia under the Arabs

The Arabs, who are named in the sources since the time of the New Assyrian empire, clearly played a role in M. in the later 1st cent. BC and in the first centuries of the 1st millennium AD. Not only were they able to establish independent kingdoms in → Edessa [2] and → Ḥatra [1], they were also repeatedly mentioned in texts from southern M. until the end of the cuneiform record. In southern M., the tribal group of the Tanukh formed a nation under the Lakhmid dynasty (→ Lakhmids), traceable since the 3rd cent. AD, with the capital al-Ḥira near modern Kerbela, which was at the same time a centre of ancient Arab culture with influence on the Arabian Peninsula. They stood on the side of the Sassanids. In the conflicts of this period, similar to the

way in which a buffer state independent of Byzantium existed farther west under the Ghassanids (5th/6th cent.; → Arabia with map).

With the defeat of the Sassanids by the Arab-Islamic army at the battle of Qadisija (642), their rule over M. came to an end. The territory between the Euphrates and the Tigris fell completely into Arab hands and, over the course of time, was largely Islamized (→ Islam).
→ Assyria; → Babylonia; → Rulership; → Rulers; → Literature; → Myth; → Religion; → Ancient oriental philology and history

1 J. J. Finkelstein, Mesopotamia, in: JNES 21, 1962, 73–92 2 W. Röllig, s.v. Mesopotamia, RLA 8, 94 3 J. A. Brinkman, Chronology, in: A. L. Oppenheim, Ancient Mesopotamia, 1968 4 H. J. Nissen, Geschichte Altvorderasiens, 1999, 15–20 5 H. Gasche, et al., Dating the Fall of Babylon, 1998 6 H. J. Nissen, P. Damerow, R. K. Englund, Frühe Schrift und Techniken der Wirtschaftsverwaltung im alten Vorderen Orient, 1990 7 G. Algaze, The Uruk World System, 1993 8 H. Sader, Les états Araméens de Syrie depuis leur fondation jusqu' à leur transformation en provinces assyriennes, 1987; 9 P.-E. Dion, Les Araméens à l'âge du fer, 1997 10 H. Donner, Geschichte des Volkes Israel und seiner Nachbarn in Grundzügen, 1986² 11 J. Seibert, Die Eroberung des Perserreiches durch Alexander den Grossen auf kartographischer Grundlage (TAVO Beiheft B 68), 1985 12 M. Dandameyev, Was Eanna Destroyed by Darius I?, in: AMI NF 25, 1992, 169–172 13 R. Rollinger, Überlegungen zu Herodot, Xerxes und dessen angeblicher Zerstörung Babylons, in: Altoriental. Forsch. 25, 1998, 339–373 14 M. Jursa, in: NABU 1998, 116f., no. 124. 15 J. Oelsner, Henotheistische Tendenzen in der spätbabylonischen Religion?, in: H. Preissler (ed.), Gnosisforschung und Religionsgeschichte. Festschrift K. Rudolph, 1994, 489–494 16 S. Sherwin-White, Ritual for a Seleucid King at Babylon?, in: JHS 103, 1983, 156–159 17 A. J. Sachs, H. Hunger, Astronomical Diaries and Related Texts, 2, 1989, No. 187A Rs. 10'–12' 18 S. Dalley, Bel at Palmyra and Elsewhere in the Parthian Period, in: Aram 7, 1995, 137–151 19 M. Geller, The Last Wedge, in: ZA 87, 1997, 43–95 20 E. J. Keall, Parthian Nippur and Vologases' Southern Strategy: an Hypothesis, in: Journ. of the American Oriental Society 95, 1975, 620–632 21 S. R. Hauser, Babylon in arsakidischer Zeit, in: Colloquien der Deutschen Orientgesellschaft 2, 2000.

CAH, vols. 1–4; Cambridge History of Iran, vols. 1–3; Fischer-Weltgeschichte, vols. 3–8, 1965ff.; B. Hrouda (ed.), Der Alte Orient, 1991; A. Kuhrt, The Ancient Near East, c. 3000–300 BC, vol. 2, 1995; A. Kurth, S. Sherwin-White (ed.), Hellenism in the East, 1987; H. J. Nissen, Geschichte Altvorderasiens, 1999 (extensive bibliography); J. Oelsner, Materialien zur babylonischen Gesellschaft und Kultur in hellenistischer Zeit, 1986; W. Orthmann, Der Alte Orient (PropKg Bd. 14), 1985; G. Widengren, Geschichte Mesopotamiens, 1966, 1–31; J. Wiesehöfer, Das antike Persien, 1994.
Maps: TAVO B I, 1–12, 14–18, II, 7–9, 12, 15; III, 7, 8; IV, 8, 10, 13, 22, 23; V 1–5, 7–9, 11–13; VI 1–7, 11, 18.
J.OE.

Mesotes (μεσότης, *mesótēs*: 'middle', 'mean', understood in the positive sense). Key concept of a Greek ethical (and resulting political) maxim, which – according to the classical definition of Aristotle (see below) – postulates an orientation toward the mean between 'too much' (*hyperbolé*) and 'too little' (*élleipsis*). A diffuse *mesótēs* ideal is perceptible since the Archaic period, and was already propagated by → Hesiodus (Op. 694) and ascribed primarily to the Delphic → oracle or the → Seven Sages (*mēdén ágan*: 'nothing too much', supporting documents in [1. 11f.]). About 600/590 BC, → Solon called on the nobility for moderation (fr. 5 GENTILI/PRATO) and sought a balance between the interests of rich and poor in his reforms (fr. 7 and 8 G./P.). Seminal for later *mesótēs* theories was their role in Hippocratic medicine and dietetics as the mean between extremes (cold/warm, moist/dry, etc., cf. [1. 35–38]; → Hippocrates C. 4.). In → Plato, *mesótēs* then becomes a basic principle, above all in ethics and politics [2. 146ff.].

Mesótēs teaching reached its ultimate development in the 'Nicomachean Ethics' of → Aristotle (cf. Eth. Nic. 2, 1106a 13–1109b 27), where, following Democritus (68 B 102 DIELS/KRANZ) and the Corpus Hippocraticum [3], the ethical virtues are defined as a mean between a respective 'too much' and 'too little' [4]. Even political theory was not untouched by these ethical categories: according to Aristotle, the so-called *politeía* (polity), as a mixture of → oligarchy and → democracy, is the best constitution for most poleis, because it is based on an (economically defined) 'middle class' (*mésoi*) of equals (*ísoi*) whose members do not know the disadvantages either of excessive poverty or excessive wealth. They therefore act according to political reason (i.e. which is not led by the extremes), thus providing stability to the → polis (Aristot. Pol. 1295a 25–1297a 12; 1304a 38ff.; 1309b 18; cf. [5. 428f.; 6. 58ff.]; → Mixed constitution).

The *mesótēs* principle underwent a re-evaluation in the Stoa (→ Stoicism), where median things and behaviours (*adiáphora*) were defined by the fact that they have the least possible portion of the extremes 'good' and 'bad' (cf. Zeno SVF 1, fr. 190f.). In the Roman era, the *mesótēs* ideal continued to function as a popular philosophical maxim for life (cf. e.g. Anth. Gr. 10,102); thus, Horace also oriented himself with regard to *aurea mediocritas*, 'Golden Mean' (Hor. Carm. 2,10). *Medietas* also appears subsequently in early Christian literature as a principle of virtue (e.g. Jer. Ep. 130).
→ Ethics

1 H. KALCHREUTER, Die M. bei und vor Aristoteles, Diss. 1911 2 H. J. KRÄMER, Arete bei Platon und Aristoteles, 1959 3 F. WEHRLI, Ethik und Medizin, in: MH 8, 1951, 36–63 4 U. WOLF, Über den Sinn der Aristotelischen M.-Lehre, in: Phronesis 33, 1988, 54–75 5 P. SPAHN, Aristoteles, in: I. FETSCHER, H. MÜNKLER (ed.), Pipers Handbuch der politischen Ideen, vol. 1, 1988, 397–437 6 W. NIPPEL, Mischverfassungtheorie und Verfassungsrealität in Antike und früher Neuzeit, 1980 7 H. SCHILLING, Das Ethos der M., Thesis, Cologne 1930. M.MEI.

Mespila
[1] (Μέσπιλα; *Méspila*). In 401 BC, M. is mentioned in Xen. An. 3,4,10 as an abandoned city of ruins, surrounded by a shell stone wall, 50 feet high and just as wide, 6 parasangs in length, on top of which was a brick wall 100 feet high. Xenophon was told that M. had been inhabited by → Medes who had fled the Persians, among them the wife of the Medean king. The city – allegedly almost impregnable to the Persian king – is said to have been conquered through the terror Zeus caused by his thunder. This can only refer to the ruins of → Nineveh. The etymology may be based on the Akkadian *mušpalu* 'deep-lying land'.

J. READE, Greco-Parthian Nineveh, in: Iraq 69, 1998, 65; F. H. WEISSBACH, s.v. Mespila, RE 15, 1163. K.KE.

[2] The Latin *mispela* can mean both the bush and the fruit of the → medlar as well as other thorny plants from the related genus Crataegus, as in Theophrastus (Hist. pl. 3,12,5f. = Plin. HN 15,84) μεσπίλη ἡ ἀνθηδών/ *mespílē hē anthēdōn* = *Crataegus orientalis* and μεσπίλη ἡ ἀνθηδονοειδής/*mespílē hē anthēdonoeidēs* = *C. oxyacantha L.*, the English hawthorn

J. WILDE, Kulturgeschichte der Sträucher und Stauden, 1947, 114–122. C.HÜ.

Mesrop Known as Maštocʿ in the older MSS and in the *vita* written by his student Koriwn. His date of birth (*c.* AD 360/364) and his descent from the influential family of the Mamikonians are uncertain. Born in Katzikkʾ in the Armenian province of Tarawn, M. received a Hellenic education. After military service under the Armenian king – either Chosrov III (→ Chosroes [4]) or his lieutenant Arawan – in Vagharshapat, he became a secretary at the Armenian royal court between 385 and 389. Between 390 and 395, the Armenian Patriarch → Sahak [Isaac] the Great (*c.* 457–438) made him a monk. After the Romans and Persians had divided Armenia, Persarmenia gained a leading role in the political, ecclesiastic, and cultural life of the country, thanks to the invention of the Armenian alphabet by M. and other scholars, with the support of the Patriarch and King Vramshapuh (401–408/9; → Vahram). The intense translation activity which was just beginning (the Bible; Greek and Syrian Patristic literature), together with the introduction of an Armenian liturgical language, led to a national and religious autonomy which, thanks to M.'s missionary travels in the Byzantine part of Armenia, included both parts of the country. It is not certain whether M. led the Armenian church as patriarch in the brief period after the death of Sahak (†438/9) and before his own death on 7 February 440, nor if the 23 letters and homilies which bear the name of Gregory the Illuminator stem from M. The so-called 'Teachings of Gregory' in Agathangelus [2], however, probably derive from his pen.
→ Armenia; → Armenians, Armenian literature; → Armenian

G. Winkler, Koriwns Biographie des Mesrop Mastoc'. Übersetzung und Kommentar (Orientalia Christiana Analecta, 245), 1994.   K.SA.

Messaliani (Μασσαλιανοί; *Massalianoí*). The Messaliani (Syrian *mṣallyēnē* for 'prayer'; Greek Euchites, Εὐχῖται/*Euchîtai*), as they were known to their enemies, referred to themselves as 'Pneumatics' (Πνευματικοί/ *Pneumatikoí*, 'endowed with spirit'), or '(true) Christians'. The participants of the 4th- and 5th-cent. Christian synods who condemned the Messalians took offense at their prayer, regarding it as immoderate and as a challenge to baptism, because the Messalians claimed prayer to be the essential path to perfection. In contrast to baptism, prayer was supposed to completely eradicate sin (e.g. Theod. Hist. Eccl. 4,11). Further accusations against the Messalians included contempt of the Church, of the sacraments, and of work; an over-emphasis on visions, the notion that evil could be exorcised, and that the Holy Ghost could enter into man, which was indicated by sensually perceptible phenomena (Theod. l.c.; Timotheus of Constantinople, De receptione haereticorum PG 86, 45–52; Iohannes Damascenus, De haeresibus 80).

At first, the Messalians were an amorphous movement that became noticeable from the 60s of the 4th cent. AD on. Adelphius of Edessa soon emerged as their leader. He relied on the works by Macarius (→ Symeon), the ascetic Desert Father. Adelphius strengthened the tendencies contained in these works that were aimed at an ecstatic sensing of the Holy Ghost and at a consequential separation of social and ecclesiastic norms, thus giving rise to the criticism detailed above. Soon after 381, Adelphius and other Messalians were excommunicated as heretics by Bishop Flavianus of Antioch, but by then the movement was already spreading into Asia Minor. In 390, in Side, the excommunication was renewed, followed by further condemnations. At the Council of Ephesus in 431, the Messalians were condemned in the entire empire and their ascetic handbook, the *Askētikón*, extant only in fragments, was rejected [1].

Following the excommunication, the movement gradually died out. The name 'Messalians', however, as the tried and true label for heretics, was transferred to movements in Syria and Byzantium that were regarded as analogous; primarily to monks who stood in opposition to the hierarchy of the Church. Beginning in the 11th cent., this name for heretics was increasingly adopted; it was applied to the → Bogomils and finally to Hesychasm, which advocated an internal experience of God in prayer.
→ Ascesis; → Heresy; → Prayer.

1 E. Schwartz, Acta Conciliorum Oecumenicorum I,1,7, 1929, 127.

K. Fitschen, Messalianismus und Antimessalianismus, 1998.   K.FI.

Messalina

[1] Statilia M. Born between AD 30 and 40, daughter of T. Statilius Taurus (*cos.* 44), married her fourth husband M. Atticus Vestinus (= M. → Iulius [II 147] Vestinus Atticus, *cos.* 65) in 63/4. In 65, emperor → Nero forced Vestinus to commit suicide so that he could take M. as his (third) wife in 66 (Tac. Ann. 15,68,3; Suet. Nero 35,1; IG IV 1402 and IV² 604: M. as Nero's wife). In the same year, she was installed as *Augusta*. As a widow, she was courted by Otho in 69 (Suet. Otho 10,2). M., who was deified during her lifetime (as noted in the Acts of the Arval Brethren from the year 66, CIL VI 2044c), died after 69. For the honours bestowed upon her cf. ILS 8794 and RPC I, 2061.

U. Hahn, Die Frauen des römischen Kaiserhauses, 1994, 223–227; 358; Kienast², 100; PIR² S 625; Raepsaet-Charlier, 730; Vogel-Weidemann, 288; 618; 639.
ME.SCH.

[2] Valeria M.
A. Historical figure B. Reception

A. Historical figure
Daughter of M. Valerius Messalla Barbatus and of Domitia [5] Lepida; b. in *c.* AD 25, from *c.* 39 third wife of future emperor → Claudius [III 1] with whom she had two children: → Octavia [3] (b. in early 40) and → Britannicus (b. in early 41; Suet. Claud. 26,2.27,1–4). She was denied the title of *Augusta* (Cass. Dio 60,12,5; on the coins [4. 268]), but was granted the → *prohedría* of the Vestal Virgins in 43 (Cass. Dio 60,22,2).

Ancient literature depicts M. as a greedy, cruel and, above all, sexually profligate woman (Juv. 6,115–132: the emperor's wife as a prostitute in a brothel; Plin. HN 10,172; Tac. Ann. 11,30,2; Cass. Dio 60,18,1–2) who wantonly (*per lasciviam*) toyed with the state (Tac. Ann. 12,7,3) [3. 399–423]. These character traits were seen as the motivation behind her alleged involvement in the elimination of several – and in some cases politically important – figures, such as C. Appius [II 4] Iunius Silanus in 42 (Cass. Dio 60,14,2–4), Iulia → Livilla [2] in *c.* 42 (Cass. Dio 60,8,4–5), → Iulia [8] Drusi and Catonius Iustus in 43 (Cass. Dio 60,18,3–4; Tac. Ann. 13,32,3), → Valerius [II 1], Mnester, and Cn. Pompeius Magnus in 47 (Tac. Ann. 11,1–3; 11,36,1; Cass. Dio 60,29,6a). Research has revealed, however, that M. should be regarded in the context of the early Principate, with its dynastic and power-political conflicts at the imperial court. In this light, her actions can be better understood as an attempt to secure her position as an imperial wife, which was not unthreatened, and her son's succession as *princeps* with all means at her disposal [1. 53–67; 2. 123–169]. M.'s marriage to C. Silius in 48 was a formality serving the same goal [2. 132–169] but it ultimately resulted in her downfall and her death (Tac. Ann. 11,12–38). M. suffered → *damnatio memoriae* (CIL VI 918; AE 1948, 16). On her coins cf. [4. 265; 267–269]; on her portraits, esp. a sardonyx cameo in the National Library in Paris see [5. 1079f.].

1 B. LEVICK, Claudius, 1990   2 E. MEISE, Untersuchungen zur Geschichte der Julisch-Claudischen Dynastie, 1969   3 C. QUESTA, Messalina, meretrix augusta, in: R. RAFFAELLI (ed.), Vicende e figure femminili in Grecia e a Roma, 1995, 399–423   4 H. COHEN, Description historique des monnaies frappées sous l'empire Romain, vol. 1, ²1955   5 M. FLORIANI SQUARCIAPINO, s.v. Messalina (1), EAA 4, 1961.   H.S.

B. RECEPTION

The figure of M. as *femme fatale* drew the attention of painters in France during the Second Empire (G. MOREAU, *Messaline*, 1874; Paris, Musée Gustave-Moreau). It also inspired operas, (ISIDORE DE LARA, *Messaline*; premiere in Monte Carlo, 1901) and literature (A. JARRY, *Messaline*, a novel, Paris 1901). During the *fin de siècle*, she became a cipher for the lascivious upper-class woman who descends into the gutter in her greedy pursuit of sexual adventures. The medium of film has exploited the material since 1910, sometimes adopting a similar slant. Four versions appeared until 1930, seven more have been made since 1949; none of them by outstanding directors or with notable actors.

> TH. HIRSBRUNNER, Isidore de Lara, in: Pipers Enzyklopädie des Musiktheaters 3, 1989, 412–414; B. ERULI, Jarry's Messaline, in: L'Esprit Créateur 24, 1984, 57–60; J. SOLOMON, The Ancient World in the Cinema, 1978; M. WYKE, Projecting the Past. Ancient Rome, Cinema and History, 1997.   W.ED.

Messalinus Originally, a *cognomen* in the family of the Valerii (→ Valerius), from them it passed over to the family of the Aurelii (Aurelius [II 13]); epithet of C. Prastina Pacatus M. (*cos.* AD 147).   K.-L.E.

Messalla *Cognomen* in the family of the Valerii (→ Valerius). The best-known bearers are Manius Valerius Maximus M. (*cos.* 263 BC), a commander in the Second Punic War, Marcus Valerius M. Rufus (*cos.* 53), a follower of Caesar and antiquarian, and Marcus Valerius M. Corvinus (*cos. suff.* 31), a supporter of emperor Augustus, who promoted → Tibullus and other contemporaneous poets.   K.-L.E.

[1] Valerius M. Avienus As a member of an old consular family (Rut. Nam. 1,271f.; Macr. Sat. 1,6,26), he became *legatus senatus* in *c.* AD 396/398 (Symm. Epist. 6,49) and *praefectus praetorio* for *Italia* and *Africa* in 399/400. He frequently appears as the latter in the Cod. Theod. gen. (in the period from 13 May 28 [16.2.399] to 5 January 13 [27.11.400]). He corresponded with → Symmachus [2] (Symm. Epist. 7,81–92). The fact that he appears in → Macrobius' [1] 'Saturnalia' as an interlocutor indicates his traditional religious orientation and emphasizes his literary and rhetorical education and skill, which are also evident in other sources (Sidon. Carm. 9,305; Rut. Nam. 1,267–276: ecphrastic *carmen*; M. as orator ibid.).

PLRE 2, Messalla 3.   J.R.

Messalla's Circle see → Valerius Messalla; → Cirkle, literary

Messana, Messene

[1] (Μεσσάνα/*Messána*, Ionian Μεσσήνη/*Messḗnē*, Lat. *Messana*). Town in northeastern Sicily, modern Messina. The original name Zancle (Ζάγκλη/*Zánklē* = Siculan: 'sickle') is derived from the topographically suggestive shape of the natural harbour (Thuc. 6,4,5).

A. FOUNDATION B. 5TH AND 4TH CENTS. BC
C. 3RD CENT. BC AND THE ROMAN PERIOD
D. BYZANTINE PERIOD

A. FOUNDATION

The site was settled at an early time because of its outstanding strategic situation on the strait between Sicily and Italy. Piracy is attested by Thuc. 6,4,4 and Paus. 4,23,7. Its actual foundation occurred in the context of Greek → colonization after the mid 8th cent. BC by Chalcidians from → Cyme [2] in Campania (Thuc. 6,4,5f.). The oldest traces of settlement are located on the south side of the harbour [1]. Because the town lacked agricultural resources, → Mylae [2] (716 BC according to Eus. Chronicon p. 90b H) and → Himera (649 BC according to Diod. Sic. 13,62,4) were founded.

B. 5TH AND 4TH CENTS. BC

After the → Ionian Revolt (early 5th cent. BC), settlers immigrated from → Miletus [2] and → Samos. The tyrant → Anaxilaus [1] of Rhegium [2] played a significant role in this process though the details are unclear. He eventually assumed power and renamed Zancle to M., allegedly in remembrance of the Peloponnesian origin of his family (Thuc. 6,4,6; cf. Hdt. 6,23). This was associated with the immigration of Messenians (→ M. [2], Messene) from the motherland (Str. 6,2,3). The successors of Anaxilaus were able to retain power over Messene until 461 BC.

After a confrontation with Athens over the colony of Mylae, M. was briefly under Athenian control in 426 BC (Thuc. 3,90). However, M. sided with → Syracusae, the Sicilian hegemonic power, in the following year (Thuc. 4,1). A military campaign against the neighbouring town of Naxos led to a conflict with the Leontinians and Athens (Thuc. 4,25). Despite advances by Alcibiades (Thuc. 6,50), M. remained for most part neutral during the great Sicilian expedition of the Athenians at the time of the → Peloponnesian War, but had to struggle with internal political differences (Thuc. 5,5).

As an ally of Syracusae, M. like many other Sicilian towns was a target of Carthaginian military actions in the early 4th cent. BC. In 396 BC, the Carthaginians destroyed the town (Diod. 14,59,1), but Syracusae had already rebuilt and resettled it by 395 BC. The tyrannis of Hippon, which suggests a volatile political and social situation, was deposed in 337 BC by the Corinthian → Timoleon.

C. 3RD CENT. BC AND THE ROMAN PERIOD

In the 3rd cents. BC, the Campagnian → Mamertini, former mercenaries of the tyrant → Agathocles [2], took over the rule of M. (which was renamed *Mamertina*; cf. Cic. Verr. 2,2,13). Their organized raids into eastern Sicily led to the outbreak of the 1st → Punic War in 264 BC, in which the Mamertini, who were pressed by Hieron [2] II first turned to → Carthage and then to Rome for help (Pol. 1,10–12) [3]. During the war, M. was a loyal ally of the Romans. After the war, M. was granted the status of a *civitas foederata* (Cic. Verr. 2,2,13). M. stayed aloof from the great Sicilian → slave revolt late in the 2nd cent. BC. As an important naval base and a prospering centre of commerce, M. experienced a significant economic and demographic upswing in the Roman period. Because of later construction only few ancient remains (archaic sanctuary, chamber tomb of the classical period, two Hellenistic-Roman necropoleis, traces of residential buildings and the Mamertinian defences) have been uncovered [4].

1 J. BOARDMAN, Kolonie und Handel der Griechen, 1981, 201f. 2 H. BERVE, Die Tyrannis bei den Griechen 1, 1967, 155–157 3 K.-W. WELWEI, Hieron II. von Syrakus und der Ausbruch des Ersten Punischen Krieges, in: Historia 27, 1978, 573–587 4 G. SCIBONA, s.v. Zankle, PE 998f.

P. FAURE, Die griechische Welt im Zeitalter der Kolonisation, 1981; A. SCHENK GRAF VON STAUFENBERG, Trinakria, 1963; G. VALLET, Rhégion et Zancle, 1958; Id., La colonisation chalcidienne et l'hellénisation de la Sicilie orientale, in: Kokalos 8, 1962, 30–51 H.SO.

D. BYZANTINE PERIOD

In 550, M. briefly came under the Ostrogothic rule of → Totila. After its reconquest by → Iustinianus [1], the town shared the fate of → Sicilia, including in ecclesiastical terms. It owed its prosperity in the Byzantine period both to its geographical position and its sericulture. The onset of the Arab conquest of the entire east of Sicily (→ Syracusae) was decisive for M. (fell in 843) because the political and economic focus shifted to the west (→ Panormis). However, the Greek element withstood and was still active in the Norman period (after 1061) [1].

1 A. GUILLOU, Les actes grecs des S. Maria di Messina, 1963.

S. TRAMONTANA, s.v. Messina, LMA 6, 562f.; A. KAZHDAN, D. KINNEY, s.v. M., ODB 2, 1350f. J.N.

[2] (Μεσσάνα/*Messána*, Μεσσήνη/*Messénē*; the Greek region of Messenia).
I. THE REGION II. HISTORY

I. THE REGION

M. is the southwesternmost region of the → Peloponnese. In the historical period, its boundaries were formed by the Neda in the northwest towards Triphylia (Elis), by the mountain ranges running towards southeast towards Arcadia, by the Taygetus towards the east and by the gorge of the Choerius (Sandava), which runs from the Taygetus to the Gulf of M., towards Laconia in the southeast. The region is divided into the fertile coastal plain on the Messenian Gulf (Macaria), the smaller upper plain of Stenyclerus, which is surrounded on all sides by mountains, and the western Messenian upland (only in the northwest up to 1,222 m altitude) with the broad West Messenian coastal plain. Low, broad passes link this plain to both the upper interior plain and that of the Messenian Gulf. The West Messenian uplands consist of limestone and chert with overlying conglomerate and large adjoining tertiary plates formed from sandy marls. The plains were formed from alluvial deposits. The upper plain is crossed by three rivers that merge in the southwest (ancient names not certain) and to form the → Pamisus [1. 46–48], which then crosses the lower plain. In Antiquity it was not this river system that was considered to be its upper course, but the eastern tributary emanating from a vigorous spring in Agios Floros. The Nedon flows from the Taygetus and enters the sea near Pherae, while numerous other streams flow through the lower and the western coastal plain. M. is rich in springs and several rivers flow all year round. Together with the relatively rich precipitation and the favorable soils, they result in the abundant fertility of the landscape. Important settlements on the west coast are → Cyparissia [1], → Pylos in Messenia (→ Coryphasium), and → Methone, on the Messenian Gulf → Asine [2], → Corone with the southern sanctuary of Apollo Korythos, in the lower coastal plain → Thuria and → Pharae, and in the upper plain → Messene [2] and the sanctuary of the mysteries at → Andania, which was to become famous. Convenient access to M. is only granted in the western coastal plain towards Triphylia and towards the northeast over some easy passes to Arcadia (→ Megale Polis).

II. HISTORY

A. EARLY HISTORY B. THE AGE OF SPARTAN RULE C. FROM THE REFOUNDING TO THE ROMAN IMPERIAL PERIOD D. BYZANTINE PERIOD

A. EARLY HISTORY

In numerous locations the earliest finds are from the Neolithic period and there is a strong increase of finds for the MH period. During the Mycenaean period, western M. was one of the most densely settled and richest regions of Greece with a palace at Ano Englianos (→ Pylos) and numerous tholos tombs. Other important Mycenaean settlements are Muriatada and Peristeria in the hill country north of Ano-Englianos, Malthi in the southeastern plain of Kokla, Katarrachaki 8 km northeast of modern Pylos near Kukunara, and Nichoria 2 km west of the northwestern end of the Messenian Gulf [2] (→ Mycenaean culture). This early flowering was broken by the migrations of around 1200 BC and then the Spartan conquest. Therefore, M. as such does not occur in Homer. Cyparissia was part of

→ Nestor's Triphylian kingdom in the catalog of ships (Hom. Il. 2,593), while the seven Pylian towns (Il. 9,149–152; 291–294) [3] are located in the southeast outside of M. and already belonged to Sparta. The single mention of M. in Hom. Od. 21,15 is based on the mislocation of Ortilochus to Pherae in M. instead of to Pharae in Arcadia. In the early Geometric period, cults developed at several Mycenaean tombs (e.g., in Kukunura, Volimidia, Akurthi, and Mila). Settlement remains have been found in Kardamyle, Volimnos, Nichoria, Kato Englianos, Karpophora and Tragana. A celebration of Zeus Ithomatas took place at an altar on Mount Ithome (Eumelus, 8th/7th cents. BC, in Paus. 4,32,2). There is a literary tradition of the expulsion of the Neleids by the Dorians (→ Doric Migration).

B. THE AGE OF SPARTAN RULE

On the conquest by Sparta, see the → Messenian Wars. The coastal areas became desolate or towns of Spartan *perioikoi* were founded (→ *períoikoi*). The region was mostly under Spartan rule with an unfree population. Two uprisings of → helots are known; the historical reality of the uprising of 500/490 BC with a long siege of Hira in the Arcadian borderland remains questionable. Part of the population migrated to Rhegium and Zancle (later M. [1]/modern Messina: Ephorus in Diod. Sic. 15,66,5; Paus. 4,23,6–10 [4]). Another uprising after the Spartan earthquake of 464 BC occasioned a long siege of Ithome by the Spartans (Thuc. 1,101,2–103,3; Diod. Sic. 11,63,1–64,4; 84,8; Plut. Cimon 16,4–17,2) [5. 131–135]. After their capitulation, the Athenians settled the besieged at Naupactus. During the many years of the Athenian occupation of Pylos (Coryphasium) after 426 BC, some of the Messenian people were settled there and in Cranii on Cephallenia. After the Spartan reconquest of Pylos in 410 BC, the Messenians were expelled from there, likewise in 399 BC from Cranii and Naupactus. The exiles found refuge in Sicily and Cyrene. Sources: Thuc. 4,9; 32,2; 41,2; 5,35,6; 56,2f.; 7,57,8; Xen. Hell. 1,2,18; Diod. Sic. 12,63,5; 13,64,5ff.; 14,34,2ff.; 78,5f.; Paus. 4,26,1ff.

C. FROM THE REFOUNDING TO THE ROMAN IMPERIAL PERIOD

In 369 BC, M. was liberated from Spartan rule with Theban help and a new state with its capital at → Messene [2] near Mount Ithome was founded. Corone was also refounded at the same time. The new state initially only comprised the upper Messenian plain and the coastal plain west of Pamisus. Cyparissia and Pylos were apparently won about 365 BC with Arcadian help (Diod. Sic. 15,77,4; on this, see Xen. Hell. 7,4,27), while Thuria had also become Messenian by 365 BC. (SGDI 2619). Sparta persisted in not recognizing the new state and repeatedly attempted to reconquer it. Scylax still includes Asine and Methone (GGM 1,40 § 46; 4th cent. BC) in Laconia. They presumably only became part of M. under Philip II (on Asine cf. also

Xen. Hell. 7,1,25). At Mantinea (362 BC), the Messenians fought on the Theban side (Xen. Hell. 7,5,5; Diod. Sic. 15,85,2). M. then joined Philip II (Demosth. 6 *passim*; Paus. 4,28,2), who through Greek arbitration obtained the border region of the Denthalii in the Taygetus and the coast from Pharae to Leuctrum in the southeast, which were disputed with Sparta, for the Messenians (Pol. 9,28,7; Str. 8,4,6; Tac. Ann. 4,43). In 342 BC, M. concluded a federation with Athens (Dem. Or. 16,9; IG II² 225). During the wars of the → Diadochi, M. repeatedly changed rulers.

About 245 BC, M. joined the Aetolian League (→ Aetolians, with map) and arranged an → *isopoliteía* with Phigalia (Pol. 4,6,11; IG V 2,419; Syll.3 472), which was prepared through personal relationships. This did not spare M. from acts of violence and raids by the Aetolians about 220 BC (Pol. 4,3,5–6,12). The consequence was an alliance with the Achaean Confederacy (→ Achaeans, with map) and inclusion in the Hellenic League by Philip V (Pol. 4,7ff.; 15,8–11; 16,1). As a result, M. was involved in the → Social War [2] (Pol. 4,31,1–33,10, with a general summary of M.'s history; 5,1ff.; 5,3,3; 20; 92,2ff.). In 215/4, severe and bloody social unrest occurred, in which Philip V and Aratus [2] intervened (Pol. 7,12; 13,6; 9,30,2; Plut. Aratus 49f.). Philip initially resisted the temptation to use the event to occupy the town, but a later attempt to seize M. led to its estrangement with the Achaean Confederacy (Pol. 8,10;14; Plut. Aratus 51,2f.). M. again allied itself with the Aetolian League (Pol. 9,30,6; Liv. 27,30,13) and then with Rome (Liv. 29,12,14; 34,32,16). In 201, → Nabis attacked the town and occupied it except for the acropolis, but then immediately vacated it when → Philopoemen rapidly approached (Pol. 16,13,3; 16f.; Liv. 34,32,16; 35,6; Plut. Philopoemen 12,4–6; Paus. 4,29,10; 8,50,5). Nevertheless, the relationship with the Achaean Confederacy, which already possessed Asine and Pylos, remained unfriendly (Pol. 18,42,7; Liv. 27,30,13). In 191 BC, the Achaean Confederacy violently forced M. to join (Liv. 36,31,1–9), with the towns of the western upland becoming independent members and M. being restricted to the two main plains with Thuria and Pharae. Particularly, confrontations with the returned exiles led to new tensions and armed occupation by the Confederacy's troops. Philopoemen was captured in 182 BC and murdered in prison (Pol. 23,12; Plut. Philopoemen 18–20; BLiv. 39,48,5–50,11; Paus. 4,29,11f.). A new expedition by the Confederacy enforced submission (Pol. 23,16f.; Plut. Philopoemen 21,1–5). The town received a garrison, and Abia, Thuria and Pharae were separated off as independent confederates (Pol. 23,17,1f.).

The situation after 146 BC is unclear. The ownership of the Dentheliatis remained disputed with Sparta until Tiberius definitively assigned the land to the Messenians (Tac. Ann. 4,43). The towns of the southeast, which in any case no longer were part of M., were assigned to Sparta by Augustus (Paus. 4,30,2; 31,1f.; 3,26,7). Important finds and inscriptions of the Roman period have been found, and in the wealthy western coastal plain a number of large estates existed. A few honorary inscriptions for Roman emperors are preserved, the latest one for Constantine (IG V 1,1420). The towns again minted their own coins under the Severi, for whom there are honorary inscriptions, and a fragment of the Diocletian price edict was found at Pharae: IG V 1, 1359; SEG 22,311. Literary sources: Scyl. 45f.; Str. 8,4; Paus. B. 4 [6]; Ptol. 3,14,31; 42). Inscriptions: IG V 1, 1351–1502; coins: HN² 418; 431–433.

1 R. BALADIÉ, Le Péloponnèse de Strabon, 1980   2 W. A. McDONALD, N. C. WILKIE (ed.), Excavations at Nichoria in Southwest Greece 2: The Bronze Age Occupation, 1992   3 B. SERGENT, La situation politique de la Messénie du Sud-Est à l'époque mycénienne, in: RA, 1978, 3–26   4 N. LURAGHI, Pausania e la fondazione di Messene sullo stretto, in: RFIC 122, 1994, 140–151   5 J. DUCAT, Les Hilotes (BCH Suppl. 20), 1990   6 D. MUSTI, M. TORELLI (ed.), Pausania. 4: La Messenia, 1991.

N. KALTSAS, s.v. M., EAA2, 636–639; E. MEYER, s.v. Messenien, RE Suppl. 15, 155–289; C. A. ROEBUCK, A History of Messenia from 369 to 146 B.C., 1941; M. N. VALMIN, Études topographiques sur la Messénie ancienne, 1930.   Y.L.

D. BYZANTINE PERIOD
Gothic and Avaro-Slavic incursions occurred in 395 and the early 6th/7th cents. respectively. The latter resulted in a fundamental restructuring of the area (disappearance of ancient settlements and the appearance of Slavic toponyms [1. 160–164; 2. 57ff.]), while Byzantine rule largely collapsed in the 7th/8th cents. The ecclesiastical and secular reorganization of the 9th cent. occurred in the framework of the → thema Peloponnesus while the regional name M. only appeared in archaizing texts. Apart from the fortresses Korone (→ Asine [2]) and Modon (→ Methone), also known as the 'Eyes of the Republic of Venice', the towns of Arkadia (→ Cyparissia) and Kalamata (→ Pharae) gained regional importance [2. 162].

1 M. VASMER, Die Slaven in Griechenland, 1941 (Abh. der Preuss. Akad. der Wiss. 1941, 12)   2 A. BON, Le Péloponnèse byzantin jusqu'en 1204 (Bibliothèque byzantine. Ét. 1), 1951.

A. KAZHDAN, N. PATTERSON ŠEVČENKO, s.v. M., ODB 2, 1350; J. KODER, s.v. Morea, LMA 6, 834–836.   E.W.

Messapeae (Μεσσαπέαι; Messapéai). Region around the sanctuary of Zeus Messapeus, south west of Sparta, possibly on the hill of Agios Georgios east of Lele on the road to Gythium or near modern Katzarou or Antochori (Paus. 3,20,3; Theop. FGrH 115 F 245).

D. MUSTI, M. TORELLI (ed.), Pausania, vol. 3: La Laconia, 1991, 254f.   Y.L. E.MEY.

Messapian pottery Messapian pottery originated on the Italian peninsula of Salento (in Antiquity → Messapia or → Iapygia) around the mid–7th cent. BC as an independent genre. For the most part, geometric patterns (circles, squares, diamonds, horizontal lines, → swastikas, etc.) were sparsely distributed over vessels; later, under Greek influence → maeanders were added. Preferred vessel forms were the → olla, pitcher and trozzella (→ nestoris). Early in the 5th cent. BC, figurative representations, which also included new ornaments (ivy and other leaf motifs), appeared under the influence of imported Attic ware. The painting covered the entire surface area of the vessels. In the 4th cent. BC, the geometric patterns returned but with floral elements that were borrowed from Attic and Lower Italian vase painting, especially → Gnathia ware; the paintings were divided by metope frames. The → pyxis and the → krater were new forms, but the trozzella continued to be the characteristic form until the disappearance of Messapian pottery in the first third of the 3rd cent. BC.

D. YNTEMA, Messapian Painted Pottery. Analyses and Provisory Classification, in: BABesch 49, 1974, 5–84; M.

Vessel shapes in Messapian pottery

1 Olla   5 Pitcher
2 Trozzella   6 Kalathos
3 Trozzella   7 Stamnos
4 Krater (Messapian)   8 Pyxis

A. TIVERIOS, Kapaneus auf einer Messapischen Vase, in: AA 1980, 511–523; M. MAZZEI, Le trozzelle messapiche, in: J. SWADDLING (ed.), Italian Iron Age Artefacts in the British Museum (Papers of the 6th British Museum Classical Colloquium), 1986, 357–361; J. W. HAYES, Greek and Greek-Style Painted and Plain Pottery in the Royal Ontario Museum, 1992, 135–140.   R.H.

Messapians, Messapia (Μεσσάπιοι/*Messápioi*, Μεσσαπία/*Messapía*). A people and region in the extreme southeast of Italy. According to Str. 6,3,1; 6,3,5, these are Greek terms for the → Iapyges and Iapygia, south of the isthmus between Taras/Tarentum and Brundisium (Str. 6,3,1; 5). Their indigenous name was partly *Salentinoi* (on the southern tip and the Ionian coast), partly *Kalabroi*. According to most sources, the terms designated all of southeastern Italy, including the Daunii (or → Daunia), the → Peucetii (or Peucetia), and the Iapyges or Iapygia (Pol. 3,88; Nicander FGrH 271/272 F 25; Str. 6,3,2; cf. Thuc. 7,33; Steph. Byz. s.v. Μεσσαπία, χώρα Ἰαπυγίας) [1; 15]. Only Pol. 2,24,10 differentiates between the Iapyges and the M. In the Roman period, the terms Calabri or → Calabria and → Sal(l)entini are usually used instead of M. (Plin. HN 3,99; 105; Ptol. 3,1). However, in 266 BC the Romans triumphed *de Sallentineis Messapieisque* [19]; cf. [14; 17].

The name *Messapia* is also found in many places of the Balkan peninsula, but neither the etymological (from *met + *ap* = *aqua*?) nor the linguistic (Illyrian?) origin [2; 11; 14] can be proved. Messapia was said to have been named after the Boeotian → Messapus (Strab. 9,2,13; Solin. 2,12; Isid. Orig. 15,1,58; Serv. Aen. 7,691; Steph. Byz. s.v. Μεσσάπιον; Paul. Fest. 112,12 L.; Plin. HN 3,99; Lydus, Mens. 1,6). The M. are first mentioned by Hdt. 7,170 as the *Iépyges Messápioi* (Ἰήπυγες Μεσσάπιοι) of Cretan origin in the Minoan period, but of Illyrian descent. Their land bordered immediately on the town of Taras (Paus. 10,10,6; Steph. Byz. s.v. Μεσσαπία), with which they had repeated military confrontations (in the 5th cent. BC: Paus. l.c.; Hdt. l.c.; cf. Aristot. Pol. 5,3,7; Diod. Sic. 11,52; in the 4th cent. BC: Aristox. fr. 30 W.; Plut. Agis 3; Str. 6,3,4). In 244, the Latin colony of → Brundisium (Vell. 1,14,8) was founded; later the *via Appia* was extended to Brundisium (as early as 50 BC according to Cic. Att. 6,1,1?, Vir. ill. 36). The M. belonged to the second Augustan region (Plin. HN 3,99). Brundisium (Scymn. 364) was considered the port of Messapia.

Economy: sheep (Nicander FGrH F 25) and horse breeding (Liv. 24,20,16; cf. Paus. 10,10,6; Serv. Aen. 8,6); pastures and woodlands (Str. 6,3,5); olive groves (Dion. Hal. Ant. 1,37).

From the 8th cent. BC, many hut villages are archaeologically attested in M., especially near the coast (exceptions include Oria). Some of them were already in contact with Greek towns in the 6th cent., and most by the 4th cent. BC. The existence of defensive walls, houses, necropolises and sanctuaries (e.g., Oria, Caval-

lino, Ugento, Manduria, Alezio, Rudiae) has been confirmed for the cities of M. All were under strong Greek influence, though independent (e.g., graves inside the towns since the 6th cent. BC) [7; 9; 10; 12; 14; 17; 18]. Significant craft industries are recorded, esp. pottery, mainly with native forms (e.g., *trozzella*, → Messapian pottery) and decoration, but also, especially in the 4th–3rd cents. BC, Greek types (red-figure and → Gnathia ware) [9; 10; 12; 13; 14; 17].

→ Messapic

1 NISSEN 2, 872f.   2 O. PARLANGÈLI, Studi messapici, 1960   3 C. DE SIMONE, Die messapischen Inschriften, in: H. KRAHE (ed.), Die Sprache der Illyrier 2, 1964, 7–151   4 G. UNTERMANN, Die messapische Personennamen, in: H. KRAHE [3], 135–213   5 C. DE SIMONE, La lingua messapica, in: A. STAZIO (ed.), Atti XI Convengo di Studi sulla Magna Grecia, 1972, 125–201   6 C. SANTORO, Nuovi Studi Messapici 1–3, 1982–1984   7 C. PAGLIARA, Materiali iscritti arcaici del Salento, in: ASNP 13, 1983, 21–73   8 C. DE SIMONE, Su 'tabaras' (femm-'a') e la diffusione di culti misteriosofici nella Messapia, in: SE 50, 1984, 178–197   9 F. D'ANDRIA, Messapi e Peucetii, in: G. PUGLIESE CARRATELLI (ed.), Italia omnium terrarum alumna, 1988, 653–715   10 E. DE JULIIS, Gli Iapigi, 1988   11 C. DE SIMONE, Gli studi recenti sulla lingua messapica, in: G. PUGLIESE CARRATELLI (ed.), Italia omnium terrarum parens, 1989, 655–658   12 F. D'ANDRIA (ed.), Archeologia dei Messapi, 1990   13 D. YNTEMA, The Matt-Painted Pottery of Southern Italy, 1990   14 A. STAZIO (ed.), I Messapi. Atti XXX Convegno di Studi sulla Magna Grecia, 1991   15 M. LOMBARDO, I Messapi e la Messapia nelle fonti letterarie greche e latine, 1992   16 D. YNTEMA, In Search of an Ancient Countryside, 1993   17 J.-L. LAMBOLEY, Recherches sur les Messapiens, 1996   18 G.-J. BURGERS, Constructing Messapian Landscapes, 1998.   19 DEGRASSI, FCap. XX.   M.L.

Messapic Pre-Roman language of the Daunians (→ Daunia), Peucetians (→ Peucetii), Iapygians (→ Iapyges) and → Sal(l)entini in the territory of modern Apulia, the ancient regions of → Apulia and → Calabria. It is recorded in 600 mostly very short inscriptions and a few glosses; according to modern convention named after the people of the → Messapii who were listed in Antiquity without clear demarcation together with the Sallentinians and Iapyges. The inscriptions have been dated to the period from about 500 BC to the beginning of the 1st cent. AD. They used the Greek alphabet of the town of Taranto (→ Taras) to which a few special symbols were added. The locations of the finds are widely scattered throughout ancient Apulia between Monte Gargano and the Taranto – Brindisi line, but are densely concentrated on the Sallentinian peninsula, the most important sites being Ceglie, Oria, Lecce, Alezio and Vaste.

There are a few longer texts (up to 20 words) that are only known from copies. The preserved linguistic monuments are primarily funerary inscriptions and statements of ownership. An epigraphic sensation occurred in the 1980s with the discovery of the Grotta

della Poesia on the coast southeast of Lecce. Its walls are covered with numerous votive texts in Messapic, but difficulties of access have resulted in only a small extent being recorded and edited. The language of the inscriptions is part of the Indo-European family but has not been assigned to a known subfamily. Links to the east coast of the Adriatic, which are recognizable in similar proper names, have supported the theory that Messapc is an 'Illyrian' language. However, this remains without substance as long as it is impossible to clearly identify characteristics of pre-Roman and pre-Greek languages in the Balkan peninsula. Some etymological links are the foundation of the still very incomplete decipherment: *klaohi zis venas* 'listen, Zeus, Venus,' as the introduction to a longer text; *tabara* 'priestess' linked to the name of a deity in the genitive: *damatras*, or in adjectival derivations: *damatria*, *aproditia*. Some certain data can be gained from the formulas of giving personal names for inflections and word formation; the finds of recent years have provided new records for verbs other than the previously mentioned, familiar imperative form *klaohi*, e.g., *apistaθi*, *ligaves*, and the preverb *niligaves*.
→ Italy, languages (with map); → Messapii; → Messapia

EDITIONS OF THE INSCRIPTIONS: O. PARLANGÈLI, Studi Messapici, 1960; C. DE SIMONE, Iscrizioni messapiche della Grotta della Poesia, in: ASNP 3,18,2, 1988, 325–415. J.U.

Messapium (Μεσσάπιον; *Messápion*). Mountain chain (modern Ktypas) in the northeast of → Boeotia, the eastern edge of which separated the mainland territory of Chalcis on Euboea from the rest of Boeotia. Sources: Aeschyl. Ag. 293 (with schol.); Aeschyl. fr. 55,10 METTE; Strab. 9,2,13; Paus. 9,22,5; Steph. Byz. s.v. M.

S. C. BAKHUIZEN, Salganeus and the Fortifications on Its Mountains, 1970; PHILIPPSON/KIRSTEN 1,2, 497f.; P. W. WALLACE, Strabo's Description of Boiotia, 1979, 61. P.F.

Messapus (Μεσσάπος; *Messápus*, Latin *Messapus*). Son of → Neptune (Verg. Aen. 7,691), from → Boeotia where the mountain Messapius/→ Messapium on the coast of → Anthedon is named after him (Serv. Aen. 8,9; Steph. Byz. s.v. Μεσσάπιον). He migrated to Italy, and on his arrival in Apulia (Paul. Fest. 112,12 L.) or Iapygia (Strab. 9,2,13), he gave the region the name of → Messapia. Ennius [1] purports to be descended from him (Serv. Aen. 7,691; Sil. 12,393).

F. ALTHEIM, Messapus, in: ARW 29, 1931, 22–32. I.BAN.

Messe (Μέσση; *Messē*). One of the Laconian villages mentioned in Hom. Il. 2,582. Its ruler was → Menelaus (cf. Stat. Theb. 4,226). Str. 8,5,3 reports that a village called Messe could nowhere be shown, but that some held Messe to be an abbreviated form of → Messene [2].

Paus. 3,25,9 locates Messe on the road from Taenarum to Oetylus on the coast of the Messenian Gulf. At the other hand, the identification with Messoa found in Strabo cannot be excluded.

E. VISSER, Homers Katalog der Schiffe, 1997, 483–488. J.STE.

Messeis (Μεσσηίς; *Messēís*). A spring mentioned in Hom. Il. 6,457. → Hector prophesies to → Andromache, that one day she will fetch water from the springs Messeis and Hypereia in Argos. According to Strab. 9,5,6, the inhabitants of → Pharsalus pointed out a town, Hellas (cf. Heraclides 3,2), entirely in ruins, which was 60 stadia from their own town and in whose vicinity the two springs were to be found. Plin. HN 4,8,30 locates a spring Messeis in Thessaly, whereas Paus. 3,20,1 claims to have seen a well Messeis at Therapne in Laconia. J.STE.

Messene (Μεσσήνη/*Messénē*).
[1] Daughter of Triopas of Argos (Paus. 4,1,1; other genealogy: schol. Eur. Or. 932). She married Polycaon, son of the Laconian king Lelex, and incited him to conquer the country that was later named after her, Messenia (→ Messana [2]) (Paus. 4,1,2). There, they founded → Andania, among other cities, and built a palace. It is believed that through → Caucon, M. established the Eleusinian Mysteries (→ Mysteria) in Andania (Paus. 4,1,5; 1,9). In historical times she was honoured as a heroine and even had a temple dedicated to her (Paus. 4,3,9; 31,11). RA.MI.

[2] The capital of the Messenian state (→ Messana [2] [1. 110f.]), founded in 369 BC, located in a saddle between the mountains of → Ithome [1] and Eua, where it was protected on all sides by the terrain. The territory of M. included the entire upper Messenian plain up to the crests of the surrounding mountain ranges, the Kokla basin and the western portion of the lower plain. The centre of the ancient city was near modern Mavromati. Its original name in the 4th century BC was Ithome (Scyl. 45; Diod. 19,54,4).

The 9 km-long ring wall is famous, the best preserved in Greece (mid 4th cent. BC). Worthy of note is the almost completely preserved 'Arcadian Gate' in the northern section of the wall, which has a round inner courtyard. Remains of an older wall were found at Mount Ithome. In the city area, there are remains of a theatre and a stadium (with a nearby heroon). On the slope of Ithome there was a sanctuary of Artemis Limnatis. A small sanctuary to the northeast from it dates from the Hellenistic period. A large square courtyard surrounded on all sides by a double-columned hall and buildings has been identified as an Asklepieion (late Hellenistic period; see site plan). At the northern edge of this building complex there are rooms for the imperial cult (sebasteion; see site plan No. 12), on the east side there are a small theatre and a square meeting room and on the west side is a closed series of rooms measuring

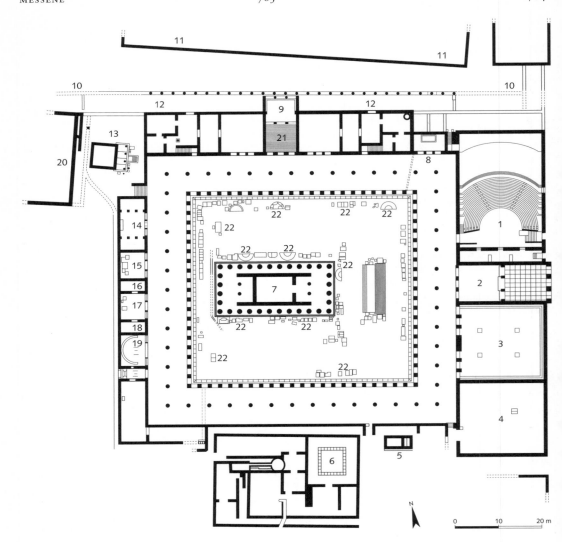

Messene, Asklepieion (ground-plan)

1 Ekklesiasterion (Odeion)	9 North Propylon	17 Oikos of Epaminondas
2 East Propylon	10 Late Roman Stoa	18 Oikos with the statue of Heracles
3 Bouleuterion	11 South wall of the Agora complex	19 Oikos of Apollo and the Muses
4 Hall of the Archive	12 Sebasteion terrace	20 Temenos of a goddess
5 Heroon with cist grave	13 Heroon	21 Staircase
6 Baths	14 Artemision	22 Bases of statues
7 Great Doric temple with altar	15 Oikos with the statue of Tyche	::::::: Conjectural outlines
8 Oikos of Asclepius	16 Oikos of the Theban city goddess	

5.80 m deep (see site plan Nos. 14–19), the first four of which were cultic rooms. The Temple of Asclepius was located within the courtyard (Doric peristyle temple; see site plan No. 7). The → agora was where Mavromati is now, to the north of the Asklepieion (the south wall has been identified; see site plan No. 11). A large number of buildings are mentioned in an inscription from the time of Augustus (SEG 23,207; 41,327) [2]: temples of Demeter, Hercules and Hermes in the gymnasium, a *bouleíon* ('council building') with a stoa, the

logeíon ('speaker's platform') of the *deiktérion* ('exhibition hall') and several other stoai. A *prytaneíon* ('town hall') is mentioned in IG V 1,1390, l. 112, and an underground, dark *thēsaurós* ('treasure chamber') is referred to in connection with the capture of Philopoemen (Plut. Philopoemen 19,3).

The primary god of the city and state was Zeus Ithomatas, whose priest was the eponym of the city; the goddess of the city was M. [3; 4]. The springs mentioned by Pausanias are probably the large spring at the village of Mavromati (Klepsydra [1]) and a spring near the northern stoa at the agora (Arsinoe). There is a great deal of instructive information on the constitution of M. in the inscription concerning the Andania mysteries (IG V 1,1390) of 92/1 BC. Cf. also Str. 8,4,8; Paus. 4,31,4–33,3 [5. 251–262]. Inscriptions: IG V 1,1425–1496; SEG passim. Coins: HN² 418; 431f. [6]). For information on new excavations, cf. [7].

→ Messana [2]

1 N. H. DEMAND, Urban Relocation in Archaic and Classical Greece, 1990   2 L. MIGEOTTE, Réparation de monuments publics à Messène au temps d'Auguste, in: BCH 109, 1985, 597–607   3 Y. MORIZOT, Le hiéron de Messéné, in: BCH 118, 1994, 399–405   4 S. MAGGI, Sul tempio di Messene a Messene, in: Athenaeum 84, 1996, 260–265   5 D. MUSTI, M. TORELLI (ed.), Pausania, vol. 4: La Messenia, 1991   6 C. GRANDJEAN, Monnaies et circulation monétaire à Messène, in: Topoi 7/1, 1997, 115–122   7 P. THEMELIS, Ἀνασκαφὴ Μεσσήνης, in: Praktika 141 (1986), 1990, 74–82; 142 (1987), 1991, 73–104; 143 (1988), 1991, 43–79; 144 (1989), 1992, 63–122; 145 (1990), 1993, 56–103; 146 (1991), 1994, 85–128; 147 (1992), 1995, 60–87.

E. MEYER, s.v. Messene, RE Suppl. 15, 136–155; P. THEMELIS, s.v. Messene, EAA², 625–635.   Y.L.

Messenger scenes Longer rhesis in drama, in which other characters or the chorus are informed, either behind or off scene, of events that have taken place before or during the dramatic action and that could not represented on stage either because of the means or the conventions of Attic drama. These reports, furnished with all available rhetorical means, are usually presented by a main or a supporting figure (Eur. Heraclid. 389ff; Soph. El. 68off.), but often by a nameless messenger specifically introduced for this purpose (ἄγγελοι/ángeloi or ἐξάγγελοι/éxangeloi, if the message comes from inside the house; more rarely a κῆρυξ/kêryx [Aischyl. Ag. 503ff, in a ritual context Aristoph. Av. 1271ff]).

In *Aeschylus'* tragedies, messenger scenes (MS) primarily occur in the overall context of the plot at points where certainty follows a slowly built-up uneasy expectation: Pers. 302ff. (defeat of the Persian army), Sept. 375ff. (report of the spy, seven pairs of speeches), Supp. 605ff. (Danaos' report about the Argive people's assembly), Ag. 503ff. (the herald's report). Sophocles uses messengers particularly in closing scenes to describe catastrophes that have occurred behind the scenes: Trach. 749ff. (the death of Hercules), 899ff. (Deianira's suicide), Ant. 1192ff. (the deaths of Antigonus and Haemon), OT 1237ff. (Iocasta's suicide and Oedipus' self-blinding), OC 1586ff. (Oedipus' disappearance). Special cases are the false report of the pedagogue in El. 68off. and the anticipated report on the war in the chorus' vision in OC 1044ff. In Euripides' tragedies, catastrophe reports are found at: Alc. 152ff. (Alcestis' imminent death), Med. 1135ff. (the deaths of Creon and his daughter), Hipp. 1173ff. (Hippolytus'

death), Hec. 518ff. (sacrificial death of Polyxena), HF 921ff. (Hercules' deed), Bacch. 1043ff. (Pentheus' death). A MS may report the outcome of an intrigue: Ion 1122ff., Hel. 1526ff., El. 774ff., IT 1327ff. MS describing battles occur in Supp. 650ff., Phoen. 1090ff. (cf. Aischyl. Sept. 375ff.); the outcome of the Argive people's assembly is reported in a MS in Or. 866ff. Cf. also IT 260ff. (capture of Orestes and Pylades), Bacch. 677ff. (doings of the Bacchantes). Or. 1369ff. is a lyrical form of the MS (the Phrygian slave's lyrical monody). In Aristophanes'comedies, MS occur in a paratragic context (catastrophe report: Ach. 1174ff., intrigue: Thesm. 574ff.) and, as in tragedy, to describe events behind and outside the scenes (Equ. 624ff., Vesp. 1292ff. 1474ff., Av. 1122ff. 1168ff. 1271ff., Lys. 980ff., Eccl. 834ff. 1112ff., Plut. 627ff. 802ff., likewise in Menander: Dysk. 666ff., Epitr. 249ff.).

→ Comedy; → Tragedy

I. J. F. DE JONG, Narrative in drama: The art of the Euripidean messenger-speech, 1991; M. HOSE, Studien zum Chor bei Euripides I, 1990, 196–215; B. MANNSPERGER, Die Rhesis, in: W. JENS (ed.), Die Bauformen der griechischen Tragödie, 1971, 143–181; M. PFISTER, Das Drama, 1977, 122148; P. RAU, Paratragodia. Untersuchungen einer komischen Form des Aristophanes, 1967, 162–168; G. A. SEECK, Dramatische Strukturen der griechischen Tragödie: Untersuchungen zu Aischylos, 1984.   B.Z.

Messenian Wars Conflicts between the Spartans and the Messenians (→ Messana, Messene [2]) are already attested at the end of the 8th cent. BC (Paus. 4,4,2f.). Repeated assaults by Spartan nobles against Messenians culminated ca. 700/690–680/670 (the older date, based on the list of Olympic victors for 736–716 [1. 9ff.; 2. 34] is not tenable, cf. [3; 4. 91ff.]) in the 1st Messenian War, which resulted in Spartan control over large parts of Messenia [4. 70–91]. A Messenian uprising ca. 640/30–600, the 2nd Messenian War, represented a danger to Sparta's existence, but eventually all of Messenia was successfully subdued. Most Messenians were made into → helots, and the arable land was divided among the Spartiates. From that moment, Sparta always had to fear helot uprisings [5. 176f.], which had considerable political and social consequences and explains, among other things, the Spartan regime of the classical period. The main source for the two wars is Tyrtaeus fr. 2–10 GENTILI/PRATO. The long reports in Pausanias (bk. 4), which are based on Hellenistic material, are mostly romantic embellishments (→ Aristocrates [1], → Aristomenes [1]).

A Messenian War ca. 490 BC mentioned by Plato (Leg. 698e) is probably not historical (despite [1. 106f.; 2. 88ff.], and may have been intended to justify Sparta's late arrival at the battle of → Marathon (for discussion [6. 139ff.]). However, there was a serious Messenian revolt after the severe earthquake of 464 BC in Sparta (3rd Messenian War). It took years to put down, and led to severe tensions with Athens, whose support expedition under → Cimon [2] was first reque-

sted and then abruptly sent home (Thuc. 1,102). In 370/369 BC Messenia was liberated by Thebes. Many Messenians whose ancestors had fled (especially to Lower Italy and Sicily) were able to return home [1].
→ Messana, Messene [2]

1 F. KIECHLE, Messenische Studien, 1959   2 G. L. HUXLEY, Early Sparta, 1962   3 V. PARKER, The Dates of the Messenian Wars, in: Chiron 21, 1991, 25–47   4 M. MEIER, Aristokraten und Damoden, 1998   5 P. CARTLEDGE, Sparta and Lakonia, 1979   6 P. OLIVA, Sparta and Her Social Problems, 1971.   M.MEI.

Messiah (griech. Μεσσίας; *Messías*, from Aramaic. *mᵉšiḥa* and Hebrew. *mašiaḥ*, 'the Anointed'; Greek. χριστός/*christós*, vgl. Jo 1,41).
I. JUDAISM II. CHRISTIANITY

I. JUDAISM

Whereas in the pre-Exile period this term was used primarily for reigning kings of the dynasty of David (before David for Saul 1 Sam. 24:7 etc., for the dynasty of David cf. the Psalms of David Ps. 2,2; 18,51; 132,10 *et passim*; for David: 2 Sam. 19:22, 23:1 *et passim*), who were enthroned by anointing (e.g. 1 Sam. 16:1–13, 1 Kgs. 1:28–40), Exile and post-Exile Israel and early Judaism linked it with the expectation of a future saviour figure. The origin of this development was the idealization of David's kingship (Ps 72) and the expectation of a righteous king of peace (Mic. 5:1–5, Isa. 9:1–6, 11:1–16, but without the term in question). But there are diverse usages of the term: the prophet Deutero-Isaiah, who lived during the Exile, uses the title in referring to the contemporary Persian king → Cyrus [2], who would allow Israel to rebuild the Temple (Isa. 45:1), whereas the prophets Haggai and Zechariah, who after the return from Exile in the year 520 BC called for the rebuilding of the Temple, look to the returning prince Zerubbabel from David's line to restore Israel's greatness (cf. Hag. 2:20–23, Zech. 4:1–14, 6:9–14). In the figure of the high priest Joshua, moreover, Zechariah recognises a priestly Messiah (cf. Zech. 4:14, 6:9–15).

Against this background, the conceptions of the Messiah in records from subsequent centuries (apocryphal, pseudepigraphic and Qumran texts) are characterised by their variety and variability: often not entirely differentiated from the royal David liberator figure (e.g. PsSal 17,21.32; 4QFlor 1,10–13; 4QPatr V; ApcEzr 12,31–34), we also have the expectation of an eschatological priest (TestLev 17–18; CD 12,23; 14,19; 19,10f.; 20,1: 'anointed out of Aaron and Israel') or judge (4QpIsaᵃ fr. 8/9; Z. 11ff.; cf. the tabular collation of the numerous sources in [4. 291–301]). Closely associated with the early Judaic hope for a Messiah is the expectation of a 'Son of Man' (Dan. 7:13f., Enoch 1–46:3–5, 48:2–7, ApcEzr 13). This is taken up by the various Messiah concepts in the NT, which, while professing the redemptive influence of → Jesus of Nazareth, emphasize decidedly un-kingly and non-militant

elements such as humility and meeknes (e.g. Mt. 11:29, cf. Zech. 9:9).

In opposition to increasing political pressure from their Roman masters, supposed Messiah figures came forward before the 1st Jewish War (AD 66–74), prophesying or foretelling by signs speedy liberation from Roman rule under an ideal theocracy (Jos. BI 2,57–65; 258ff; Jos. AJ 20,97), or raising messianic claims, for example, during the Jewish uprising itself the leaders → Menahem ben Jehuda (cf. Jos. BI 2,444) and Simon bar Giora (4,575).

The expectation of an apocalyptic messianic saviour figure also played an important role after the destruction of the Temple in AD 70. In 132–135 came the second uprising against Rome, under the leadership of one Bar Kosiba, the messianic implications of whose movement were made manifest when he changed his name to → Bar Kochba ('Son of the Star'; cf. yTaan 4,8 [48d]), implying a clear reference to Num. 24:17. After this uprising, too, had been put down by the Romans, with radical consequences for the population of Judaea (→ Judah and Israel), the majority of rabbinical texts display clear reticence with regard to concrete messianic expectations. Of significance are the reinterpretation of the name Bar Kosiba as Bar Koziba ('Son of Lies') and the firm renunciation of any imminent messianic expectation (e.g. BSan 97a-b), directed at any kind of political activism. Typically, moreover, the coming of the Messiah, regarded by the majority of sources as the 'Son of David', is made contingent upon Israel's repentance or its obedience to the commandments (e.g. BSan 97b). The messianic period is characterised by concrete political and religious expectations, such as liberation from foreign rule by the Romans, the rebuilding of the Temple, and the return from the → Diaspora to Jerusalem (cf. the 'Eighteen Blessings'), accompanied by the restoration of the conditions of Paradise (e.g. BKet 111a–112b). Not until the transition from Christian to Arab rule in the 7th century as well as later in the conflict with the crusaders, do we again find a upsurge of acutely messianic expectations in the Holy Land (cf. e.g the apocalyptic text *Sefer Zerubbabel*).

1 J. H. CHARLESWORTH, The Concept of the Messiah in the Pseudepigrapha, in: ANRW II 19.1, 1979, 188–218   2 M. HENGEL, Die Zeloten (Arbeiten zur Gesch. des ant. Judentums und des Urchristentums 1), ²1976   3 J. MAIER, Die messianische Erwartung im Judentum seit der talmudischen Zeit, in: Judaica 20, 1964, 23–58, 90–120, 156–183, 213–236   4 G. OEGEMA, Der Gesalbte und sein Volk. Unt. zum Konzeptionalisierungsprozeß der messianischen Erwartungen von den Makkabäern bis Bar Koziba, 1994   5 L. H. SCHIFFMAN, The Eschatological Community of the Dead Sea Scrolls, 1989, 1ff.   6 G. SCHOLEM, Zum Verständnis der messianischen Idee im Judentum, in: Judaica 19, 1963, 7–70   7 A. H. SILVER, A History of Messianic Speculation in Israel, 1959   8 G. STEMBERGER, s.v. M./Messianische Bewegungen II. Judentum, TRE 22, 622–630 (Lit.)   9 S. TALMON, Typen der M.-Erwartung um die Zeitwende, in: H. W. WOLFF (Hrsg.), Probleme der biblischen Theologie. FS Gerhard von Rad, 571–588   10 J. H. CHARLESWORTH, H. LICH-

TENBERGER, G. S. OEGEMA (Hrsg.), Qumran-Messianism. Stud. on the Messianic Expectations in the Dead Sea Scrolls, 1998 (Lit.). B.E.

II. CHRISTIANITY

The term Messiah occurs only twice in the NT (Jn. 1:41, 4:25). *Christós; χριστός* is used instead (*chríein*: 'to coat with colours', 'to make up', 'to anoint'). Concepts of the Messiah are inconsistent in the NT. → Jesus probably did not describe himself as Messiah, but he did claim the title 'Son of Man', which takes on messianic and apocalyptic expectations [1]. The Gospels lead us to assume that the title *Christós* was applied to Jesus by others (Mk 8:29, 10:46ff., 11:10). Calling Jesus 'Son of David' gave expression to the expectation that Jesus would seize power as a royal Messiah in → Jerusalem. The label 'King of the Jews' on the cross also shows that Jesus was executed as a pretender to the messianic crown. Pauline formulas, on the other hand, associate the title of Christ with a soteriological interpretation of Jesus's death and resurrection (Rom 5:6, 5:8, 8:34 etc.) [2. 468f.]. It may be that pre-Christian ideas of a suffering Messiah also played a part. → Paul certainly took up early Christian interpretations of the Cross and Easter. In them, messianic expectations of a historical Jesus which had been frustrated by the Crucifixion were transformed into a messianic interpretation of the Cross and the Resurrection. In this context the titles *hyiòs theoû* ('Son of God') and → *kýrios* ('Lord') were added to the title of Christ [2. 481]. The original premiss of the soteriological interpretation of the death and resurrection of Jesus in association with the title 'Son of God' and the divinity of Jesus are probably early Jewish interpretations of the sacrifice of Isaac (Gn 22:1–19) [3. 180–206].

→ Isaac; → Isaiah; → Jesus; → Mark; → Paul

1 V. HAMPEL, Menschensohn und histor. Jesus, 1990 2 G. THEISSEN, A. MERZ, Der histor. Jesus, 1996 3 L. KUNDERT, Die Opferung/Bindung Isaaks, Bd. 1, 1998 4 E. W. STEGEMANN (Hrsg.), M.-Vorstellungen bei Juden und Christen, 1993. LUK.KU.

Messius *Gens* name of Oscan origin. During the Republican period there is evidence of individuals bearing this name in Campania (e.g. ILS 5347) and in the Greek areas (IG XII 9,845).

SCHULZE, 33, 193, 424.

I. REPUBLICAN PERIOD   II. PREHISTORY AND EARLY HISTORY   III. CLASSICAL ANTIQUITY

I. REPUBLICAN PERIOD

[I 1] **M., C.** In 57 BC as people's tribune, M. called for → Cicero's return from exile (initially without success: Cic. P. red. in sen. 21). Partisan of Pompey (Cic. Att. 4,1,7; 8,11D,2). 55 (plebeian?) aedile (organizer of the → Floralia: Val. Max. 2,10,8). In 54 subsequently discovered irregularities in his application resulted in

charges being brought against M. (defender: Cicero; Cic. Att. 4,15,9) and prevented him being sent to Gaul. In 46 as Caesar's officer in North Africa, M. held the besieged Acylla (Bell. Afr. 33,2; 4; 43). MRR 2,202; 2,216.

[I 2] **M. Cicirrus** Oscan whose quick temper (cf. cognomen 'fighting cock') in a dispute with the freedman Sarmentus was described by Horace (Hor. sat. 1,5,51–69). T.FR.

II. Imperial Rome

[II 1] **T. M. Extricatus** Equestrian, possibly from Leptis Magna. *Praefectus annonae* AD 210 (AE 1977, 171), *cos. ord. II* in the year 217, thus probably awarded the *ornamenta consularia* before that time. May have been a *praef. praet.* under Caracalla and identical to the M. of Dig. 49,14,50. PIR² M 518.

B. SALWAY, A Fr. of Severan History: The Unusual Career of...atus, Praetorian Prefect of Elagabalus, in: Chiron 27, 1997, 148ff.

[II 2] **Q. Herennius Etruscus M. Decius** see → Herennius [II 3]

[II 3] **C. Valens Hostilianus H.M.Quintus** Son of Emperor Decius [II 1], see → Hostilianus

[II 4] **L. M. Iu[– – –]** Prefect of one of the two fleets in Italy under Hadrian, possibly identical with a M. Iunianus who was prefect of an *ala* (documented in the year 103 in Egypt) [1. 243ff.].

d   1 P. WEISS, in: ZPE 126, 1999, 243–245.

[II 5] **M. M. Rusticianus Aemilius Lepidus** From Siarum in Baetica, son of the senator M. [II 9]. *Praef. urbi feriarum Latinarum* in AD 135, the consular year of his father and his father-in-law → Burbuleius Optatus Ligarianus. M. died a *tribunus plebis designatus* and was honoured with an equestrian statue in his homeland (AE 1983, 517). PIR² M 520b.

CABALLOS, Senadores 1, 213f.

[II 6] **L. M. Rusticus** Senator from Baetica, probably from the city of Siarum, member of the Senate perhaps as early as the reign of Domitian. *Cos. suff.* in AD 114, documented as a *curator alvei Tiberis* (official responsible for the bed of the Tiber) in the years 121 and 124. PIR² M 521.

CABALLOS, Senadores 1, 215.

[II 7] **M. M. Rusticus Aemilius Papus** Probable full name of the Papus who was documented as a friend of Hadrian (HA Hadr. 4, 2). Possibly a brother of M. [II 6]. PIR² M 524.

CABALLOS, Senadores 1, 217f.; G.-H. PFLAUM, Un ami inconnu d'Hadrien: M. Aemilius Papus, in: Klio 46, 1965, 331–337.

[II 8] **M. Rust[icus Aemilius] Papus A[rrius? Procl]ianus Iu[lius Af]er** Related to M. [II 5] and [II 7]. Senator, possibly made a patrician. Probably quaestor of Antoninus Pius and legate of Asia. Honoured in Ephesus (IEph III 697b). PIR² M 525.

CABALLOS, Senadores 1, 218; W. ECK, Epigraphische Untersuchungen zu Konsuln und Senatoren des 1.–3. Jh.n.Chr., in: ZPE 37, 1980, 41ff.

[II 9] M. M. Rusticus Aemilius Papus Arrius Proculus Probably a son of M. [II 7], senator from Siarum in Baetica. Worked through the usual lower offices of a senatorial career: after praetorate and *cura viae Latinae* in the years AD 128 to *c*. 130, he became legate of the *legio XX Valeria Victrix*, then *praef. aerarii Saturni* and *cos. suff.* in the year 135 [1. 249ff.]. *Curator operum publicorum* in the year 138, finally legate of the province of Dalmatia, documented in the year 147. Father of M. [II 5]. PIR² M 526.

1 M. M. ROXAN, Two Complete Diplomas of Pannonia inferior, in: ZPE 127, 1999, 249–274.

CABALLOS, Senadores, 1, 220ff.

[II 10] P. M. Saturninus Equestrian whose lengthy career as a procurator is documented in [1. 250]. M. came from Pheradi Maius in Africa. After being tribune with the *legio II Adiutrix* in Pannonia superior and prefect of an *ala* he became a procurator. He carried out all of his duties in Rome, in which his rhetorical and legal capabilities were clearly important. It remains uncertain whether he is identical with the jurist M. mentioned in the Digests (49,14,50) (see M. [II 1] above). PIR² M 514; 527.

1 A. MERLIN (ed.), Inscriptions latines de la Tunisie, 1944.   W.E.

Mes(s)ogis (Μεσ(σ)ωγίς; *Mes(s)ōgís*). Central range of a chain of mountains stretching westwards from near → Celaenae in southwestern Phrygia to the → Mycale, and reaching heights of over 1,600 m (Strab. 13,4,12f.), modern Aydın Mountains, the watershed between the → Cayster and the → Maeander [2], originally the frontier between Lydia and Caria (Ptol. 5,2,15). The best wines of the M. was said to be from grapes grow on Mount Aroma (Strab. 14,1,47; Steph. Byz. s.v. ᾿Άρωμα).

J. KEIL, s.v. M., RE 15, 1100ff.; MAGIE, 783.   H.KA.

Messor A Roman deity who, according to Serv. Georg. 1,21 belongs to a circle of twelve gods invoked by the *flamen Cerialis* (→ Flamines) in the *sacrum Cereale* for → Ceres and → Tellus. M. and the other deities of the circle are linked by protective functions for specific agricultural activities. The etymology of the name M. indicates a rural deity that presides over the 'reaping' (i.e., the harvest) of the grain. Whether the twelve deities originally had an independent significance is disputed; their age is uncertain (on this problem cf. also → Adolenda). However, the lists in Varro, Rust. 1,5f. and Verg. G. 1,7–20, which mention additional cycles of twelve agrarian deities, may indicate priestly systematization and classification.

→ Indigitamenta; → Sondergötter; → Twelve (Olympian) gods   HE.K.

Mestleta (Μεστλῆτα; *Mestlêta*, Ptol. 5,10,8; Agathias Scholastikos 2,22,5: Μεσχιθά, Georgian in Kartlis Cxovreba [1]: *Mcʿetʿa*). Capital of Caucasian → Iberia [1] from the 3rd cent. BC until the end of the 5th cent. AD (elevation of Tbilisi to capital by → Vaxtang Gorgasal) located at the confluence of the → Aragus and the → Cyrus [5]. Starting-point of the road to the *Portae Caucasiae* (→ Kaukasiai Pylai), after Christianization in the 4th cent. seat of the head of the Georgian Church. The city was surrounded by walls, which were reinforced by Vespasian in AD 75 (cf. ILS 8795). M. extended over a large area: on the right bank of the Cyrus, at the foot of the residence of → Harmozice, on the tributaries Armazi and Karsni was the *pitiaxši*'s (*vitaxa* = 'governor') residence of Armazisxevi from the Roman period, with a palace, (row-type) thermal baths and a necropolis with nine stone sarcophagi and a rich inventory (including silver bowls with a portrait of Antinous and a bust of Tyche), comparable to the Harmozice necropolis, and the Hellenistic-Roman settlement of Karsnisxevi with residential and farm buildings of rough stone and mud-brick masonry and with tiled roofs. On the left bank of the Cyrus there were royal gardens and the extensive necropolis of Samtavro (2nd millenium BC – 7th/8th cents. AD) with stone chests, tiled tombs and burial sites. Excavations began in 1937.

1 R. W. THOMSON, Rewriting Caucasian History, 1996, 10–13 *et passim*   2 A. HERRMANN, s.v. Μεσχῆτα, RE 15, 1076   3 A. APAKIDZE (ed.), Mccheta. Archeologiceskie raskopki, 1958ff.   4 C. TOUMANOFF, Studies in Christian Caucasian History, 1963, 89, 371–373   5 O. LORDKIPANIDSE, Archäologie in Georgien, 1991, 158–70.   A.P.-L.

Mestor (Μήστωρ; *Méstōr*).
[1] The son of → Perseus and → Andromeda; the husband of Lysidice, a daughter of Pelops; and the father of Hippothoe. His great-great-grandson, the son of Pterelaus, was also named M. (Apollod. 2,4,5).
[2] The son of → Priamus, killed by Achilles on Mount Ida (Apollod. Epit. 3,32); Priamus laments his death in Hom. Il.24, 255ff. [1. 283f.]. In Dictys 6,9, M. accompanies Pyrrhus as a prisoner.
[3] A son of Locrian Ajax who is not mentioned in literary sources. M. is depicted on a Homeric cup of the Hellenistic period as a companion of Agamemnon at the latter's murder (according to the inscription, he is mentioned in the lost epic of the *Nóstoi*; EpGF Nostoi T 2) [2].

1 W. KULLMANN, Die Quellen der Ilias (Hermes ES 14), 1960   2 P. MÜLLER, s.v. M., LIMC 6.1, 559.   J.STE.

Mestra (Μήστρα; *Méstra*). Daughter of Helios's son → Aethon [2]. According to Hes. Cat. fr. 43c, Mestra received from Poseidon the gift of transforming herself. The legend was first recorded in detail at the time of the Roman Empire: Mestra helps her father, whose punishment from Demeter makes him suffer ravenous hunger, by allowing him to sell her, but she uses Poseidon's gift to turn herself into an animal and return to her father to be sold again (Ov. Met. 8,738f.; cf. also schol. Lykophr. 1393; Antoninus Liberalis 17; Palaephatus 23). In Ovid, however, her father is → Erysichthon. The earliest document in support of identifying Aethon with Erysichthon is Hellanicus FGrH 4 F 7. The Erysichthon legend without M. is found in Call. h. 6,24–117. In Antoninus Liberalis 17 M. is called Hypermestra.

W. Luppe, Poseidons Verwandlungsgabe für M. PHerc. 1609 II, Hesiod fr. 43 c M./W., in: CE 26, 1996, 127–130; K. Scherling, s.v. M., RE 15, 1289–1291.   K.WA.

Mestrius

[1] L.M. Son of M. [3]. PIR² M 529.
[2] L.M. Autobulus Son of → Plutarch, who was revered in Chaeronea as a Platonic philosopher (Syll.³ 844). His father dedicated his work on the Platonic *Tímaios* to him (Plut. mor. 1012a–1030d). PIR² M 530.
[3] L.M. Florus Senator. Probably entered the Senate as a *novus homo* under Nero. At the beginning of the year AD 69 he was in Rome. When Otho set out for northern Italy to fight against the troops of Vitellius, he was accompanied by M. and numerous other senators, and M. took part in the battle of Bedriacum. It is not known whether he came into contact with Vitellius. He later had a close relationship with Vespasian. In about 75 he was a suffect consul, about 88/9 proconsul of Asia (IEph II 234; [1. 315]). It is likely that during his career he also carried out official duties in the province of Achaea. In any case he was acquainted with → Plutarch and obtained Roman citizenship for him. Plutarch took on the name of his senatorial friend and visited the site of the battle of Bedriacum with him. Plutarch frequently mentioned M. as an interlocutor in his *Quaestiones Convivales* [2. 48f.]. PIR² M 531.

1 W. Eck, Jahres- und Provinzialfasten der senatorischen Statthalter von 69/70–138/39, in: Chiron 12, 1982   2 C. P. Jones, Plutarch and Rome, 1971.   W.E.

Meta

[1] (Μήτα; *Méta,* = Melite: Schol. Eur. Med. 673), first wife of → Aegeus (Apollod. 3,207).   L.K.
[2]
A. Definition   B. Meta in the Roman circus
C. Meta Sudans

A. Definition
The etymology of the Latin term *meta* is unclear. Basically it describes cone- or pyramid-shaped objects of stone, or sometimes wood, with various functions. In stone as a *meta molendaria*, the conical lower stone of ancient mills (*mola asinaria,* → Mill), on top of which the upper stone, the *catillus*, turned (Dig. 33,7,18,5).

B. Meta in the Roman circus
In the Roman → circus the term *meta* usually occurs in the plural, as three conical *metae* marked each of the two turning points of the track. They were arranged in a triangle or next to one another on a semicircular platform bounded by a *euripus*. The *metae* were surmounted by egg-shaped objects, and they were normally subdivided into three horizontal bands and decorated with mostly religious motifs. A common material for the ornamentation was gilt bronze sheet or stucco. The form of the *metae* possibly refers to movable land markers in the context of Roman settlement, but could also derive from the area of burials: very similar conical objects quite often marked Etruscan and Roman graves. Although they are one of the oldest elements of the Roman circus, literary mentions (of the *metae* in the Circus Maximus in Rome) are not found until the early 2nd century BC. The earliest depictions of *metae* are found on decorated objects from the late 1st century BC. Original *metae*, although very common in antiquity, have not survived.

C. Meta Sudans
Meta sudans describes the type of an ancient fountain whose central element was a conical *meta* standing in a basin, with water flowing from its highest point into the basin. The most celebrated of these *metae sudantes* was the fountain in Rome near the → Colosseum. It survived in part until 1936, but was then demolished. Although written sources from late antiquity (e.g. the → Chronographer of 354, Chron. 1 p. 146,20) associate the construction of this fountain with the emperor Domitian, the *meta sudans* can be seen on coins of AD 80/1 together with the completed Colosseum. Late 1980s excavations appear to confirm that date. The *meta sudans* possibly originated as a monument marking a crossroads where four or five of the *regiones* of the city of Rome had met since Augustan times. The foundations of the Flavian *meta sudans* were up to 10 m deep, and may have destroyed traces of predecessors. The fountain itself comprised two concentric cement foundations on which was mounted a *meta* about 17m high (diameter approximately 7 m) in a basin of nearly 16 m in diameter. Ancient coins and other figurative representations show that the *meta sudans*, which was lavishly clad in marble in the fashion of an → incrustation, was in three parts; the middle part had niches, and the top was crowned with a spout. The *meta sudans* was restored in the 4th century, the basin was surrounded by a balustrade and extended to a diameter of about 25 m.

J. Humphrey, Roman Circuses, 1986, 255–260; C. Panella (Hrsg.), M. Sudans, vol. 1. Un'area sacra in Palatino e la valle del Colosseo prima e dopo Nerone, 1996; Ead., M. Sudans, in: LTUR Bd.3, 1997, 247–249.   I.N.

Metabus see → Camilla

Metagenes (Μεταγένης; *Metagénēs*).
[1] Attic poet of the last years of the Old Comedy (end of the 5th and early 4th cent. BC), listed among the winners at the Lenaea with two victories, immediately before → Theopompus [1. test. 2]. The Suda mentions the titles of five plays: Αὖραι ἢ Μαμμάκυθος, Θουριοπέρσαι, Φιλοθύτης, Ὅμηρος ἢ Ἀσκηταί (or Ὅμηρος ἢ Σοφισταί [1. fr. 11]) [1. test. 1]. The plays have been lost, except for a few fragments. In the most extensive fragment (11 V. from the Θουριοπέρσαι) the narrator rhapsodizes about the Cockaigne-like rivers near Thurii (fr. 6).

1 PCG VII, 1989, 4–13.   T.HI.

[2] 6th-century BC architect, son of → Chersiphron of Knossos on Crete, named, along with his father, by Vitruvius (7 praef. 16) as the builder of the archaic → dipteral temple of Artemis in Ephesus. The relationship between Chersiphron and M. remains uncertain, as does the differentiation of their activities. In comparison with his famous father, M. is only seldom mentioned in ancient literature.

H. SVENSON-EVERS, Die griechischen Architekten archaischer und klassischer Zeit, 1996, 67–100 (with further bibliography).

[3] Classical period architect from the Attic deme of Xypete. According to Plutarch (Plut. Pericles 13), after the death of → Coroebus (Koroibos) he and Xenocles completed the telesterion of → Eleusis.

H. SVENSON-EVERS, Die griechischen Architekten archaischer und klassischer Zeit, 1996, 237–251.   C.HÖ.

Metagonium (Μεταγώνιον; *Metagṓnion*).
[1] Promontory in → Mauretania Tingitana, east of Rusaddir and west of the mouth of the Mulucha (Str. 17,3,6.9; Ptol. 4,1,7), modern Cabo de Agua. The name *Metagōnîtai* (Μεταγωνῖται, in Pol. 3,33,13 and Ptol. 4,1,10) does not appear to be derived from this promontory. The Metagonitae probably inhabited Libyan towns and localities lying between Cape Spartel and Ceuta ([1. 36], otherwise [2. 97]), but not Libyo-Phoenician cities; cf. also Pol. 3,33,12 (τὰ Μεταγώνια τῆς Λιβύης; *tà Metag?nia tês Liby?s*) and Str. 3,5,5 (ἐν τῷ Μεταγωνίῳ, Νομαδικῷ ἔθνει; *en tôi Metag?ní?i, Nomadikôi éthnei*, 'among the M., a nomadic tribe').

Hecataeus (FGrH 1 F 344) mentions a *pólis* by the name of M., but its locality, if it ever existed, is unknown.

1 J. DESANGES, Catalogue des tribus africaines ... , 1962
2 HUSS.

M. SCHWABE, s.v. Metagonium (1), RE 15, 1320f.

[2] Promontory in Numidia, north-west of Chullu (Mela 1,33; Plin. HN 5,22), the modern Cape Bougaroun. M. can probably be identified with the Τρητὸν ἄκρον; *Trētòn ákron* in Ptol. 4,3,3.

M. SCHWABE, s.v. Metagonium (2), RE 15, 1321.   W.HU.

Metalla
[1] see → Mining
[2] Modern technical term for small Roman bronze coins, formerly described as mine tokens [1], from the period between Trajan and Antoninus [1] Pius, bearing in the obverse the head of the emperor, Roma, or one of the metal gods Apollo (gold), Diana (silver), Mars (iron), and Venus (copper). On the reverse there are circumscriptions such as *metalli Ulpiani, m(etalli) U(lpiani) Delm(atici)*, or *Pann(onici)*, with only Illyrian mines being named. Depictions include a woman and ears of corn, Aequitas (personification of justice), and armour. The *SC* on many coins indicates that they were minted in the city of Rome [2; 3]. Judging from the locations of finds, *metalla* circulated in Rome and Italy, and not, as assumed by some, in mining areas [2]. The legends on the reverse may indicate that mines formerly run by leaseholders were taken over by the emperor [3].

1 SCHRÖTTER, s.v. Bergwerksmarken, 71   2 H. CHANTRAINE, s.v. M., KlP 3, 1969, 1259   3 GÖBL, vol. 1, 32.
                                                          GE.S.

Metallurgy
I. ANCIENT NEAR EAST   II. PREHISTORY AND EARLY HISTORY   III. CLASSICAL ANTIQUITY

I. ANCIENT NEAR EAST
A. METAL EXTRACTION   B. METALWORKING

A. METAL EXTRACTION
Metals are extracted from ores (smelting). Precious metals: → gold, → silver, → elektron; base metals: → copper, → tin, → lead, → iron. The beginnings of metallurgy can be found in mineralogically favourable regions, particularly near the (copper-)ore deposits of Anatolia. Elements of pyrotechnology have been identified in aceramic neolithic settlements of the early 7th millennium BC, in particular products of metallurgy based on the smelting of copper ore. The analysis of slag has provided evidence for the use of oxide and carbonate copper ores in the 6th millennium BC. The existence of lead objects (e.g. from Çatal Höyük) points to the smelting of galena. Since there is always a certain silver content in lead ores, silver metallurgy probably also began in the 6th millennium BC. To improve its characteristics, copper was alloyed with other metals from the second half of the 5th millennium BC onwards, initially mostly with arsenic compounds (arsenic bronze), from the early 3rd millennium BC increasingly with tin (→ Bronze) and from the early 1st millennium BC with zinc(-ore) to produce → brass. Although early iron metallurgy can be dated to the first half of the 3rd millennium BC, probably as a 'by-product' of early copper metallurgy, the greatest advances were made at the end of the 2nd/beginning of the 1st millennium BC.

In addition to artefacts, archaeological evidence for the history of metallurgy is provided by the raw materi-

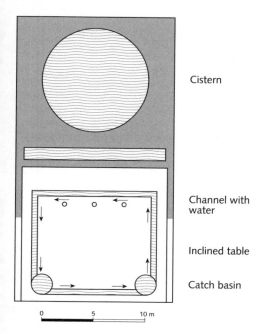

Cistern

Channel with
water

Inclined table

Catch basin

0   5   10 m

Ore-washing plant at Laurium (ground-plan)

made of two or more parts and lost-wax moulds. To
retain hollow spaces in the castings (e.g. sockets in tools
and weapons, holes in beads and pendants) removable
'cores' were placed in the mould; an early example is a
copper object from Can Hasan (southern Turkey; 6th
millennium BC). From the 3rd millennium BC, hollow
as opposed to solid casting facilitated the manufacture
of larger and more complex objects. The many methods
for cold and hot working of metal into decorated thin
sheet may largely have corresponded to modern techniques. Joining techniques such as riveting, groving, ful-
lering or dovetailing, were known, as were various
decorative techniques: e.g. raising or beating from the
reverse side (repoussé), chasing (embossing), engraving,
wire-inlay work, stamping/striking, openwork and polishing. The main attested techniques for hot working
are forging, welding and hard and soft soldering. Various goldsmithing technologies (such as granulation,
plating, incrustation, gilding using thin gold foil, fili-
gree, cloisonné) first flourished as early as the 3rd millennium BC.

F. JOANNÈS, J. SIEGELOVÁ, P. CALMEYER, s.v. Metall und
Metallurgie, Met.-Gefäße, RLA 8, 96–147; P. R. S.
MOOREY, Ancient Mesopotamian Materials and Indus-
tries. The Archaeological Evidence, 1994, 216–301.
R.W.

II. PREHISTORY AND EARLY HISTORY
A. CYPRUS B. ETRURIA

A. CYPRUS
In → Cyprus the use of metal for manufacture goes
back to the Chalcolithic, because rich copper deposits
were easily accessible and highly concentrated [1. 15–
17]. Their exploitation increased into the Late Bronze
Age, when Cyprus was the main supplier of → copper in
the Mediterranean world. Oxhide ingots, so called because of their shape, were found on the Greek mainland, in → Sardinia, and also in the shipwrecks at Uluburun (14th cent. BC) and Cape Gelidonya (12th
cent. BC; off the Lycian coast of Asia Minor) [5. 235–
240]. They weighed 10 to 37 kg and were fundamental
for the manufacturing of bronze and thus the entire
economy of the Bronze Age [3. 197–239]. A visible
expression of the significance of copper is the figure of
the 'Horned God' from → Engomi, armed with a spear
and round shield and standing on an ox-hide ingot
[2. 74–77]. The rise of → iron and the Iron Age brought
a marked change to the situation; however, the distribution of 12th- and 11th-cent. Cypriot iron knives
throughout the entire eastern Mediterranean suggests
that Cyprus continued to play an important role in the
spread of the new technology [6. 85]. This has been
confirmed by recent finds [4. 159].
→ Cyprus; → Kypros

1 G. CONSTANTINOU, Geological Features and Ancient
Exploitation of the Cupriferous Sulphide Orebodies of
Cyprus, in: J. D. MUHLY et. al. (ed.), Early Metallurgy in
Cyprus, 1982, 13–23   2 J.-C. COURTOIS, J. und E.

als (lumps of ore, crude metal), waste products (e.g.
slags), semi-manufactured articles, equipment and
pyrotechnical installations. In the Ancient Near East
smelting was done on simple hearth fires, which were
sufficient for metals with a low melting-point (e.g. lead
at 327°C) without the artificial introduction of oxygen,
and with smelting furnaces, which reached the temperatures of approx. 1100°C required for the smelting of
non-ferrous metals with a natural airflow. Installations
that used bellows for artificial ventilation (initially
drum bellows made of pots covered with skin or leather; blow tubes, with ceramic nozzles or tuyéres, verifi-
able from at least the 5th/4th millennia BC), crucibles
(from the 5th millennium BC), moulds (from the late
4th/early 3rd millennium BC) and various tools aided
the smelting process. Metal was transported to the
place of use as ingots produced in various forms (slab,
tongue, bun and oxhide ingots) and as blanks for further processing.

R. J. FORBES, Studies in Ancient Technology, vols. 8–9,
²1971–²1972; A. MÜLLER-KARPE, Anatolisches Metallur-
gie-Handwerk, 1994.

B. METALWORKING
During the 7th millennium BC, native copper was at
first worked cold by means of simple hammering, bor-
ing, scoring or splitting. There is evidence for first pyrotechnical procedures (melting, heating) from much the
same period. The development of metallurgical techniques – smelting, refining, alloying – gave rise to various
casting techniques, using open moulds, piece-moulds

LAGERCE, Enkomi et le bronze récent à Chypre, 1986
3 N. H. GALE, Copper Oxhide Ingots: Their Origin and
Their Place in the Bronze Age Metals Trade in the Medi-
terranean, in: N. H. GALE (ed.), Bronze Age Trade in the
Mediterranean, 1991   4 A. B. KNAPP, M. DONNELY, V.
KASSIANODOU, Excavations at Politiko-Phorades 1997,
in: RDAC 1998, 149–160   5 C. PULAK, The Uluburun
Shipwreck, in: S. SWINY, R. L. HOHLFELDER, H. W.
SWINY (ed.), Res Maritimae – Cyprus and the Eastern
Mediterranean from Prehistory to Late Antiquity, 1997,
233–262; 6 S. SHERRATT, Commerce, Iron and Ideology:
Metallurgical Innovation in the 12th–11th Century
Cyprus, in: V. KARAGEORGHIS (ed.), Cyprus in the 11th
Century B.C., 1994, 59–106.

A. B. KNAPP, J. F. CHERRY, Provenience Studies and
Bronze Age Cyprus. Production, Exchange and Politico-
Economic Change, 1994.   K.GIE.

B. ETRURIA

Central Italy and the offshore island of Elba (→ Ilva)
are rich in natural resources. The ores most important
for metallurgy – → copper and → iron – occur naturally
in the → Tolfa Mountains (between → Tarquinii and
→ Caere) and in northern Etruria (between → Populonia, → Volaterrae, and → Arretium) as well as on Elba.
The Tolfa Mountains also produce lead, silver and tin,
and to this day are rich in wood and water. The prerequisites for metal extraction were thus present, and they
led to a rising level of high-quality metal production.
However, it is doubtful whether all the ore deposits
known today were already being mined (→ Mining) in
antiquity. The first indications of a metals trade from
the end of the Bronze Age are small pieces of copper in
the area around Populonia. Various → hoard finds from
this period and from the → Villanovan culture point to
bronze casting. → Sardinia suggests itself as a trading
partner and purveyor of technical knowledge, as it had
a long tradition of the mining and trading of copper
from the Bronze Age onwards. Imports of crude metal
from the British Isles, Spain or the Danube area, as well
as the adoption of processing techniques from the eastern Mediterranean, may be assumed.

Direct evidence of metal smelting in the form of slag
and furnaces essentially confirms ancient written tradition. Primarily the slag-heaps on the Golfo di Baratti
and in the hinterland at Campiglia Marittima, and in
particular also the buildings of the workers' quarter in
Populonia, confirm that from the 6th cent. onwards this
city increasingly benefited from the iron deposits of
Elba. Finds of tuyères and outlet pipes as well as the
waste products of metalworking point to the activities
of the former inhabitants. The iron ore was heated in
furnaces to which charcoal was added, it was then
taken out of the destroyed furnace and separated from
slag and other materials, and purified further by hammering. The iron residues in the slags (approx. 30 to
60%) indicate decreasing care in the monitoring of furnace temperatures in the context of the increasing 'in-
dustrialisation' of iron extraction. Fragments of the furnace base were re-used many times. The much smaller

settlement on Lago dell'Accesa (near Massa Marittima)
on the other hand bears evidence to occasional exploitation of the surrounding ore deposits during the 7th
and 6th cents. BC.
→ Etrusci, Etruria (with maps); → Lead; → Silver; → Tin

G. CAMPOREALE (ed.), L'Etruria mineraria (conference
proceedings), 1979; G. Camporeale (ed.), L'Etruria
mineraria (exhibition catalogue), 1985; A. ZIFFERERO,
Miniere e metallurgia estrattiva in Etruria meridionale, in:
SE 57, 1991, 201–241.   C.KO.

III. CLASSICAL ANTIQUITY
A. METAL EXTRACTION   B. METALWORKING

A. METAL EXTRACTION
1. DEPOSITS   2. PREPARATION   3. SMELTING

1. DEPOSITS

Metals are only rarely found in pure form; there are
occurrences of pure or virtually pure → gold in rivers
(placer gold) or in deposits at the edge of watercourses
(alluvial gold), and of virtually pure → iron (meteoric
iron, often with a very small proportion of nickel). At
the beginnings of iron processing such iron deposits
were of greater significance, since they did not necessitate the production of pig iron from iron ore by smelting. Metals are usually a component of chemical compounds; these minerals in turn occur in combination
with other rocks. The metal content of ores is often very
slight: galena, the most important silver ore, reaches at
most a content of 0.5 % silver. Under these circumstances it was necessary to enrich ores, so as to be able
to extract as much metal as possible in the smelting
process with an economic use of fuel.

2. PREPARATION

The ore was prepared in two stages: first the ore and
accompanying gangue that had been obtained by
→ mining were mechanically broken up, then the metal-bearing ore was separated from the dead rock by
washing. Both processes are described in detail in the
ancient literature with respect to the gold-mines of the
Ptolemies in Nubia and the Spanish silver-mines. In
Nubia, where prisoners worked in the mines, the ore
was first pounded with iron pestles in stone mortars
until the individual pieces were the size of beans, and
then milled in rotary mills. The small grains obtained in
this manner were spread onto a slightly inclined wood-
en board over which water was repeatedly directed, so
that the lighter material was washed away while the
heavier gold dust remained on the wood (Diod. Sic.
3,13f.). A slightly different process was used in Spain;
here the broken-up fragments of ore were plunged into
water in large sieves, which caused the metal-bearing
material to be separated from the dead rock. The process was repeated many times, with the metal-bearing
components being reduced into ever smaller fragments.
The final product was an ore which produced pure
silver when smelted (Str. 3,2,10).

Many installations for the preparation of argentiferous lead ores have been found in the mining area of → Laurium (with map). Among these were large rectangular washing tables, with sluices along their sides into which the water could be channelled. When the broken-up material was poured into the water stream the heavy, metalliferous ore settled in the receiving basin or in depressions, while the lighter dead rock was washed away (see fig.). There were also remains of circular washing devices with sluices into which closely set holes were cut; this was doubtless more efficient than the washing table. As water was scarce in the Laurium region, these installations were often associated with covered cisterns; the used water was collected and re-used.

3. SMELTING

The enriched ore was smelted in furnaces; different processes were used for the extraction of different metals. On the one hand the slag had to be smelted out, and on the other the metals had to be reduced from their combinations with other elements. In extracting silver, the slag was first separated from the argentiferous lead by smelting; in a second smelting process oxygen was introduced into the furnace. The lead oxidised differently from the silver and flowed out of the furnace as yellow litharge (PbO), from this the silver was finally extracted.

Unlike other metals, → iron could not be melted in antiquity, as its melting-point ($1,539°C$) is higher than the temperatures that could be achieved by smelting. Iron oxides (hematite, Fe_2O_3, and magnetite, Fe_3O_4) were the main sources of pig iron. They were reduced by roasting before the actual smelting process: the ore was heated without the slag being removed. The slag was then melted out during smelting, leaving the iron behind in the form of a bloom (a large, sponge-like block). This iron was freed of slag residues by repeated heating and hammering, and processed into pig iron and shaped into ingots. However, the heavy lead ingots (weighing approx. 80 kg) of the time of the Principate were cast.

The ores were prepared and smelted in the immediate vicinity of the mines; transportation of ores over long distances was avoided. In Attica washing installations and smelting-furnaces are located directly within the Laurium mining district, and in Diodorus' description of the Nubian goldmines the mine and the facilities for preparing the ore formed one complex (Diod. Sic. 3,12–14; cf. for Elba: Diod. Sic. 5,13; for Spain: Str. 3,2,10). The mining regulations (FIRA 1,104) for the mining district of Vipasca (Portugal) show that in the 2nd cent. AD the district had its own smelting installation. The metal was transported as ingots to centres of production, which were often located at a great distance from the mines. → Tin and → lead were brought to the Mediterranean from Britain; traders sold pig iron from Elba to smiths in Puteoli (Diod. Sic. 5,13,2). Pig iron from different regions could possess entirely different characteristics owing to the varying components of the iron ore; for special articles smiths preferred high-quality iron (e.g. *ferrum Noricum*). In addition the iron had to be hardened by quenching in cold water (Hom. Od. 9,391ff.). The technique of influencing the quality of the iron by enriching it with carbon in a charcoal fire was already known.

B. METALWORKING

1. TECHNIQUES 2. THE USES OF PARTICULAR METALS

1. TECHNIQUES

The techniques of metalworking depended on the one hand on the characteristics of the metal or alloy, and on the other hand on the products of a particular workshop. The smith worked the iron while red hot with a hammer while an assistant held the piece in place with a long pair of tongs; a smith's equipment also included an anvil (Hdt. 1,68). Bellows were used to direct oxygen at the fire so that high temperatures could be achieved for heating the iron. → Silver and → copper or → bronze on the other hand could be worked cold by hammering (raising); this process is completely different from the working of iron. Copper and bronze were also melted in large crucibles. In solid casting, which was used from the Archaic period onwards for making small figurines (votive offerings), bronze was poured into a mould formed over a wax core which melted during the casting process (lost-wax method). Hollow casting (late 6th cent. BC) may be regarded as one of the most significant technical advances in antiquity. Here parts of the figurine were cast separately in the space between the mantle and the core of a mould and then joined together. Bronze was now the preferred material for the creation of life-size statues.

2. THE USES OF PARTICULAR METALS

Iron was mainly used for making weapons, → tools for cutting (knives, sickles, axes) and for metalworking (hammers, tongs) and implements for → agriculture (hoes, iron ploughshares) (cf. Plin. HN 34,138f.). Bronze was used for a wide variety of items, such as household objects (vessels, keys, → household equipment) and esp. precision instruments such as → surgical instruments. Characteristic of the Roman period was the increasing use of lead, a soft metal with a low melting point ($327°C$). Lead was well suited to the production of pipes, which were used for water-supply installations (pressurised systems, inner-city supply networks). → Minting (→ Coin production) was an area of metalworking that had extreme economic importance in antiquity.

Production for consumption beyond the local area was confined to a few high-quality products; the local demand for items made of iron, bronze as well as precious metals was met by workshops that were located even in small country towns or villages (Hes. Op. 492). Smiths also operated on large country estates, producing or repairing tools and agricultural implements (Varro, Rust. 1,16,4).

Smiths and bronze founders at work as well as their workshops are depicted on numerous Attic vase paintings (such as [1. 426,9; 2. 400,1]); Roman funerary reliefs (esp. [16. no. 122]) also provide important information on smiths, their tools and products.

→ Bronze; → Copper; → Fuels; → Gold; → Iron; → Laurium; → Lead; → Mining; → Silver.

1 BEAZLEY, ABV   2 BEAZLEY, ARV   3 BLÜMNER, Technik 4, 1–378   4 P. C. BOL, Antike Bronzetechnik, 1985   5 P. T. CRADDOCK, M. J. HUGHES (ed.), Furnaces and Smelting Technology in Antiquity, 1985   6 W. GAITZSCH, Römische Werkzeuge, 1978   7 B. GRALFS, Metall verarbeitende Produktionsstätten in Pompeji, 1988   8 B. GRALFS, Metall verarbeitende Werkstätten im Nordwesten des Imperium Romanum, 1994   9 J. F. HEALY, Mining and Metallurgy in the Greek and Roman World, 1978, 139–198   10 LAUFFER, BL, 36–46   11 J. RAMIN, La technique minière et metallurgique des anciens, 1977 (Coll. Latomus 153)   12 H. SCHNEIDER, Einführung in die antike Technikgeschichte, 1992   13 STRONG/BROWN;   14 TRAVLOS, Attika, 203ff.   15 WHITE, Technology, 113–126   16 ZIMMER, Katalog, Nr. 112–140   17 G. ZIMMER, Antike Werkstattbilder, 1982   18 G. Zimmer, Griechische Bronzegußwerkstätten, 1990.   H.SCHN.

Metamorphosis Terminology: Greek μεταμόρφωσις (*metamórphōsis*; 'transformation'); Latin *transfiguratio*, *mutatio*, with the verbs *mutare*, *refigurari*, *transformare*.
A. DEFINITION   C. INTERPRETATION

A. DEFINITION

Metamorphoses are specific types of myths, particularly widespread in Ancient Greece, whence they found their way into Roman literature. Two types may be distinguished: (1) temporary transformations of gods (for instance → Zeus in various erotic adventures), magicians, or tricksters for deceptive purposes, etc.; (2) lasting transformations of human beings into animals, plants, stones, water, landscape features, etc. (the transformation of animals into human beings is rare: Myrmidons, Ov. Met. 7,614ff.). The second type is metamorphosis in the significant sense.

There are various theories concerning the origins, shrouded in darkness, of metamorphosis, which is found in the folktale repertories of almost all cultures (cult, animism, etc.: for a survey of the scholarship, cf. [2. 1–95]). It is difficult to make any statements, particularly because metamorphoses are known exclusively from literary texts.

Although metamorphoses are not among the dominant or even more important themes of Homeric epic, this is nevertheless where they first become tangible for us in the Graeco-Roman cultural sphere; in the stories of → Circe (Hom. Od. 10,238f: transformation of Odysseus' companions into swine; cf. Plut. Mor. 12 for the perspective of one of the transformed victims) and of the transformation artist → Proteus (Hom. Od. 4,355ff.) they are limited to the realm of → magic and

the extraordinary capacities of the gods. In the transformation of a snake (Hom. Il. 2,319ff.) and of the Phaeacians' (→ Phaeaces) ship into stone (Hom. Od. 13,163f.), metamorphoses are simultaneously the expression of divine power and warning signs. However, metamorphosis of type (2), which was to be dominant from Hellenistic literature on, is already present in brief mentions or comparisons (metamorphosis as punishment, as in the case of Niobe (→ Nioba): Hom. Il. 24,610ff.; → Aedon: Hom. Od. 19,518ff.). No metamorphoses occur in the Hesiodic didactic poems "Theogony" and "Works and Days", yet there are several in the "Ehoiai" and the pseudo-Hesiodic poems. Metamorphosis also played a prominent role in the Attic tragedians Aeschylus, Sophocles and Euripides [2. 12ff.]. At any rate, most metamorphosis-stories are first attested beginning with Alexandrian literature, which seems to have developed a particular interest in metamorphosis: in his '*Heteroioumena*', → Nicander [4] describes the most various transformations into animals, plants, or inanimate objects, while Boeus, in contrast, limited himself in his '*Ornithogonia*' (probably translated into Latin by Aemilius [II 10] Macer) exclusively to metamorphosis of human beings into birds, even noting that every bird had once been a human being. Ovid's "Metamorphoses" provide what is for us the most extensive and enchanting collection of approximately 250 metamorphoses (most of them of type 2), which constitute an inexhaustible storehouse of motifs for European literature and art [3]. The mythographer → Antoninus [2] Liberalis also provides a catalogue of metamorphoses, probably following Nicander and Boeus. In his novel 'Metamorphoses', → Ap(p)uleius of Madaura describes the un-Ovidian, temporary metamorphosis of a human being into an ass.

C. INTERPRETATION

In most cases it cannot be decided whether a poet has taken a metamorphosis from an oral tradition that had not previously reached a literate public, or else 'invented' it himself. However, metamorphosis as a type of story is productive in principle [1], as is shown for instance by KAFKA's 'Die Metamorphosis' (1915) or the transformation of two washer-women into a tree and a rock in JOYCE's 'Finnegan's Wake' (1939, 1, chap. 8).

In most metamorphoses of the Hellenistic and later periods, specific recurring structures of metamorphosis (type 2) can be identified: all metamorphoses take place through the action of the gods, who punish or reward those who are transformed. Sometimes, however, a decision on the meaning and goal of an ambivalent metamorphosis cannot be reached. Characteristic of metamorphosis is its final nature (that is, there can be no reverse transformation, and the transformed object remains part of the visible world forever), but also a continuity, however it may be articulated, between the person transformed and the object into which he or she is transformed. Metamorphosis provides the opportunity to break through the natural order of things: at the cost of the loss of human form and identity, the transformed persons can continue to indulge in their insatiable grief or love (e.g. Niobe (→ Nioba); → Ceyx and → Alcyone [2]) or else escape an unbearable situation (→ Daphne [2]). Here, the metamorphosis presents itself as a kind of *tertium quid* between death and life. Building on a tendency of Alexandrian collections of metamorphoses, the metamorphosis in Ovid becomes a kind of (poetic) explanation of the world, embracing the whole of visible nature [4]. Metamorphosis gives poets the opportunity to describe exceptional mental states and transformations of the physis.

→ Metamorphosis

> 1 H. D. EDINGER, s.v. metamorphosis, in: J.-C. SEIGNEU-RET (ed.), Dictionary of Literary Themes and Motifs, 1988, Bd. 2, 842–850   2 P. M. C. FORBES IRVING, Metamorphosis in Greek Myths, 1990   3 M. MOOG-GRÜNE-WALD, Metamorphosen der 'Metamorphosen'. Rezeptionsarten der ovidischen Verwandlungsgeschichten in Italien und Frankreich im XVI. und XVII. Jahrhundert, 1979   4 E. A. SCHMIDT, Ovids poetische Menschenwelt. Die Metamorphose als Metapher und Symphonie, 1991.
> C.W.

Metaneira (Μετάνειρα; *Metáneira*).
[1] Wife of the Eleusinian king → Celeus (according to schol. Eur. Or. 964 of Hippothoon), mother of → Demophon [1] and of several daughters. Metaneira takes → Demeter, who is looking for Persephone, into her house and entrusts her little son, Demophon, to her care. However she unwittingly disturbs the goddess who is trying to make the child immortal in the fire, and Demeter pulls away from him (Hom. h. 2,185–291; Ov. fast. 4,507ff., in which Metaneira and Celeus are just ordinary people). Paus. 1,39,1f mentions a sanctuary to Metaneira between Eleusis and Megara.   J.STE.
[2] One of the → hetaerae in 4th-century BC Athens, famous for her beauty and wit. She was a slave of Nicarete and mistress of → Isocrates and of → Lysias [1]. The latter initiated her into the mysteries of Eleusis (→ Mysteria) (Athen. 3,107e; 13,584f; 587d; 592b; 593f; [Demosth.] or. 59,19–23). Letters, allegedly from Lysias to her are considered to be fake (Lys. fr. 111f. THALHEIM).   W.S.

Metaphor (μεταφορά/*metaphorá*, 'transference'; Latin loan translation: *translatio*).
A. DEFINITION OF THE PROBLEM AND ITS CLASSIFICATION IN THE RHETORICAL SYSTEM
B. HISTORICAL OVERVIEW OF DEFINITIONS
C. PROBLEMATICS AND FUNCTIONS

A. DEFINITION OF THE PROBLEM AND ITS CLASSIFICATION IN THE RHETORICAL SYSTEM
The discussion of metaphor and other forms of figurative speech, which today is taking place with great emphasis in various fields (linguistics, neurophysiology, psychology, and philosophy), has its origin in Aristotle, who dealt with metaphor in the 'Poetics' and

'Rhetoric'. In keeping with these origins, metaphor finds its place in the rhetorical system that later established itself firmly, as the most important of the → tropes, which all sought to systematize the phenomenon of 'artistically altered speech' (Quint. Inst. 8,6,1). Metaphor is a trope in which a word or phrase is displaced from its normal usage into a foreign context, where it evokes new meanings. Although the discussion of metaphor was to become independent in modern times, in ancient rhetoric it was indissociable from the system of tropes, and must be seen in its demarcation from the other tropes: metonymy, periphrasis, synecdoche, antonomasia, emphasis, litotes, hyperbole, and → irony.

B. HISTORICAL OVERVIEW OF DEFINITIONS
In his presentation of metaphorics in the 'Rhetoric', Aristotle starts off from the observation of the Homeric epics. He defines metaphor as 'the transference of an alien name', and sees metaphor, as opposed to the simile, as an 'abbreviated' comparison, which he supports with the famous comparison of Achilles to a lion (Aristot. Rhet. 3,4ff., 1406b: Hom. Il. 20,158–177). The distinction consists in the omitted comparative particle ὡς/*hōs* ('as/like'; Aristot. Rhet. 3,10,3, 1410b 17ff.; cf. Quint. Inst. 8,6,8f.). An object can be named not only by a concept, but also by an 'image', which is a higher, sensory form of picturing things; at the very least, this variation in denomination causes pleasure in the recipient. In the 'Poetics', the function of metaphor is to lend dignity to the style, insofar as a puzzling expression is used which points out similarity, or creates a previously non-existent name for something. Aristotle also posits that comparison and simile are more suitable for poetry, while metaphor is appropriate for prose (Aristot. Rhet. 3,3,4). Depending on the direction of the transference of meaning, he distinguishes four types, which nevertheless belong to only two structural types (Aristot. Poet. 21, 1457b, 6ff.; cf. Tryphon, Peri tropon 1,1, vol. 3, 192, 11ff. SPENGEL). The first three (from genus to species; from species to genus; from species to species) follow the model of substitution; the fourth is analogy. This very broad definition corresponds overall to the tropes, which here are still subsumed under the concept of metaphor. Only the fourth type, as the most important one designated, corresponds most closely to the modern understanding of metaphor. Here, analogy means primarily proportionality ('...as old age is to life, so evening is to the day. Thus, one will call the evening 'old age of the day' and old age 'evening of life'). In the 'Rhetoric', Aristotle deals with metaphor in the context of persuasive strategies, a fact that is responsible for the later negative image of metaphor, for instance in logic. In subsequent tradition, metaphor is treated within the narrowly-drawn borders of rhetoric as an ornament of speech, or as one of the tropes.

The → *Rhetorica ad Herennium*, where the concept of 'tropes' is still unknown, places metaphor among the *exornationes* ('ornamentations', 4,34,45f.), which, for the sake of beauty, deviate from a word's usual meaning and express an idea through another related or similar word. The anonymous author holds that metaphors occur when 'a word is transferred from one thing to another 'on the basis of similarity (l.c.). Cicero (De orat. 3,157) defines metaphor, in contrast to the simile (*similitudo*) as 'the short form of a comparison, compressed into a single word'.

Quintilian (Inst. 8,6,4–67), Tryphon (Peri tropon 1, vol. 3, p. 191,15ff. SPENGEL) and Anaximenes [2] (Rhet. Alex. 23,1f.; 1434b 33f., 40) classify metaphor under the tropes, which are canonized differently in each author. Quintilian designates metaphor as the most-used and most beautiful trope, supplied by nature and almost universally applicable, since 'almost everything we say is figurative'. Metaphors are used even by the uneducated, for instance peasants (cf. Cic. Orat. 24,81f.; Cic. De orat. 3,155). Quintilian defines metaphor as a shorter simile, and distinguishes (Quint. Inst. 8,6,9f.) four types of metaphor, which – unlike in Aristotle – build upon the dualism between animate and inanimate (animate-animate; inanimate-inanimate; inanimate-animate; animate-inanimate). Particularly when a kind of animation is attributed to inanimate things, a 'marvelous loftiness '(*mira sublimitas*, l.c.), arises, since here the degree of unusualness is at its highest.

Certain faulty applications (*vitia*) are contrasted with both the heuristic potential and the decorative function of metaphor. Thus, metaphor should never be taken from a different stylistic level, or from sordid or ugly figurative domains (Quint. 8,6,14ff.); this leads us to the sphere of *decorum*, or seemliness. Metaphors that are overly bold or harsh should be mitigated by such formulas as *ut dicam* ('so to speak'; Cic. De orat. 3,165; cf. Quint. Inst. 8,3,67). Over-frequent use generates obfuscation (→ *obscuritas*) or tedium. On the other hand, a metaphor should be clearly recognizable as such, and therefore not be too puny or weak, nor too far-fetched.

C. PROBLEMATICS AND FUNCTIONS

In ancient discussions of metaphor, 'possibilities for increase are seen in the need for verbalization' [1. 39]: metaphor is no mere stylistic adornment. Anticipating modern discussions of the basically metaphorical nature of language in general, Cicero points out at Orat. 92–94 that metaphor must often be used because no appropriate expression is available for many things (metaphors used out of necessity are called *katáchrēsis*, Lat. *abusio*). Indeed, many states of affairs, for instance intellectual processes, can only be explained by means of metaphor. In this perspective, language often consists of faded or 'dead' metaphors, which are no longer perceived as such.

The effects of metaphor depend on use and context (Quint. Inst. 8,3,38). In its aesthetic function, it directs attention to something and makes the description more lively; in its pragmatic function, it can contribute to the

specification of a state of affairs, insofar as it renders the inexpressible expressible. The distancing synthesis of states of affairs has a cognitive function, in that it gives the recipient access to a fresh experience of the object: through metaphor, complex abstractions may achieve concrete semantic reality. In this process, the speaker makes use of the associations of the deviant element (the vehicle, in modern terminology), which go beyond the limited domain of a comparison and thus enable a broadening of the semantic field. Accumulations of images for intensifying an idea are also possible, whereby a metaphor that is continued over a long stretch of text (*metaphora continuata*) may become an → allegory.

Whereas in antiquity metaphor enjoyed high esteem in the dynamic-creative process of speech, especially in poetry, in modern times it is often either discredited as pure decoration, or even as a 'lie'. Alternatively, it is ennobled in the context of a discussion of the 'productivity of the figurative ' and as a 'world-opening achievement', or as 'an intellectual activity that is important beyond the question of → its content' [1. 12]. → Allegory; → Metaphor; → Rhetoric; → Simile; → Tropes

1 K.-H. GÖTTERT, Einführung in die Rhetorik, 1994² 2 J. NIERAAD, »Bildgesegnet und bildverflucht«. Forschungen zur sprachlichen Metaphorik, 1977 3 J. MARTIN, Antike Rhetorik (Handbuch der klassischen Altertums-Wissenschaft 2,3), 1974, 266–268 4 P. RICOEUR, The rule of metaphor, 2003. C.W.

Metaphysics

A. INTRODUCTION B. METAPHYSICS OF ORIGIN (PRESOCRATICS) C. METAPHYSICS OF UNITY (PLATO) D. THE METAPHYSICS OF BEING (ARISTOTLE) E. THE METAPHYSICS OF MIND (NEOPLATONISM) F. POSTERITY

A. INTRODUCTION

Since the → commentators on Aristotle from Late Antiquity, the word metaphysics designates the most prominent and fundamental part of philosophy. It concerns itself with the highest and ultimate principles and the cohesion of reality as a whole. It derives from the book title – controversial both in origin and original meaning – Τὰ μετὰ τὰ φυσικά ('What comes after physics ', that is, probably, in the course of philosophical education in the Aristotelian school) from → Aristotle's lecture manuscripts concerning fundamental philosophy, compiled in the 1st cent. BC by Andronicus [4] of Rhodes. Aristotle himself speaks of 'first philosophy' (πρώτη φιλοσοφία/*prótē philosophía*), 'theology' (θεολογική/*theologikē*), or 'wisdom' (σοφία/*sophía*) and designates as their object 'the first causes and principles' (Aristot. Metaph. 981b 27ff). This definition is broad enough to include Platonism and its Presocratic precursors. Plato designates basic philosophy, understood as the theory of principles, as 'dialectics' (Resp. 511b). In later Platonic tradition the name 'epoptics' (→ *epopteía*), borrowed from the terminology of the

Mysteries, is also used, since the first and highest principles can be observed only by the *noûs* (cf., for instance, Plut. De Is. et Os. 382d; Theon, Expositio rerum mathematicarum 14 HILLER; Clem. Al. Stromata 1,28,176). A decisive influence on the entire later understanding of metaphysics is the speculative interpretation of the term as the knowledge of that which, as transcendental reality and pure spirit, lies 'beyond' (*epékeina*) what is natural and sensible. According to this interpretation, by the Neoplatonic commentator → Simplicius (Simpl. in Aristot. Ph. 1 Diels), metaphysics refers to something beyond the realm of physics, and it is performed in transcendence. The modern polemical use of 'metaphysical' in the sense of 'superficial', 'rash' or even 'baseless' is derived from this understanding of metaphysics.

An understanding of metaphysics as transcendence is already present in → Plato, who in his 'simile of the cave' defines the task of philosophy as to turn thought away from the merely shadow-like reality of the sensible, and lead it 'beyond this' (*met' ekeína*) towards the true being of the Ideas and their principle, itself even beyond being (Plat. Resp. 516c; → theory of ideas). For the goal of 'dialectics' is to 'transcend '(*ekbaínein*) all determinations, presuppositions and conditions in order to reach the absolute or 'unconditioned' (*anhypótheton*) as the 'origin of everything' (*archḗ tou pantós*) (Plat. Resp. 511a-b).

In the Latin world, there is no genuine transcendental metaphysics prior to the Christian reception of Neoplatonism (see F below). Here, the decisive influence, despite individual Platonic reminiscences, especially in → Cicero and → Seneca, was the Stoa, whose materialistic philosophy (→ Materialism; → Stoicism) has no place for metaphysics.

B. METAPHYSICS OF ORIGIN (PRESOCRATICS)

If metaphysics is defined as the knowledge of origins, then → Presocratic thought is metaphysics, for it begins with the question of the Milesian natural philosophers regarding the → principle or origin (ἀρχή/*arché*) from which all things arise and in which, according to the conception of → Anaximander, they also pass away (Anaximand. fr. B 1 DK). The fundamental idea here is that despite its apparent multiplicity, reality constitutes a whole that is united through a single origin. This one origin makes possible, determines, and dominates the entire multiplicity of things. Hence it is that which genuinely is (→ Milesian School). The fundamental idea 'that all is one' was formulated explicitly by → Heraclitus (22 B 8; 10; 50 DK).

Eleatic monism radicalises the view that the origin is the only thing that genuinely *is*. For → Parmenides, only Being (ἐόν/*eón*) is is truly real and knowable. It excludes from itself all forms of Non-Being, and is therefore not only ungenerated, imperishable and immutable, but also represents a unity, undifferentiated in itself and completely single and homogeneous, since any kind of multiplicity and difference implies Non-Being (Par-

menides 28 B 8 DK). This one Being is accessible only to pure thinking (νοεῖν/*noeín*), i.e. thought turned away from all sense experience. Being includes intuitive thought within itself as an all-embracing whole, since outside of it nothing can be or be known (fr. B 3 DK). Thus, Parmenides discovers the dimension of the intelligible as true, i.e. eternal Being. This is the object of metaphysics (→ Ontology).

C. METAPHYSICS OF UNITY (PLATO)

→ Plato departed from Parmenides' discovery of intelligible being and its knowledge through the *noûs* (νοῦς), but he modified Eleatic monism into a metaphysics that postulates a graded order of Being proceeding from the One (ἕν/*hen*), as the origin of Being, yet itself beyond Being. Deviating from the → Eleatic School, Plato asked how it is possible that Being (ὄν/*on*), although characterized by unity, can only be understood and known through a multiplicity of determinations, such as Being, wholeness, and unity. (Pl. Soph. 244b ff). He solved this → aporia by distinguishing between One and Being, yet connecting them as origin and effect. The One itself is not Being but the origin of Being and therefore absolutely transcendent 'beyond Being' (*epékeina tēs ousías*). In itself, it is nothing but pure unity, since a determination would draw it into multiplicity (Pl. Prm. 137d–142a, Testimonia Platonica 50, 52 GAISER; cf. also Pl. Resp. 509b). This absolute beyond Being can only be grasped in a negative theology, through the exclusion of all determinations of being and thought. It is the origin that bestows unity, wholeness, completeness, and hence Being and knowability on everything that exists. Therefore the absolute One is the Good itself (cf. Pl. Resp. 508a ff; Aristot. Metaph. 1091b 13ff).

Being at the other hand is always a unity in multiplicity (ἐν πολλά/*hén pollá*). As the complete One and whole of various determinations (ἐν ὅλον τέλειον/*hén hólon téleion*), Being is an Idea, or rather, a unified multiplicity of Ideas, since every one of its determinations is an Idea, being identical to itself and in itself (Pl. Prm. 157e ff.). Multiplicity (*pléthos*) – or its basic form, indeterminate duality (*aóristos dyás*) as the second principle – is therefore the basis for the unfolding of the One, from which everything that is proceeds. Yet multiplicity in itself is null and void, because that which lacks all unity is no longer something determinate, but nothing (οὐδέν/*oudén* = οὐδὲ ἕν/*oudé hén*) (Pl. Prm. 144c; 166c; Pl. Resp. 478b). Hence, both Being as a whole and every individual Idea participates (*metéchei*) in the One beyond Being, and owes its Being (οὐσία/*ousía*, εἶναι/*eînai*) to this participation.

All this results in Plato's famous 'ontological comparative', stating that Ideas have 'more Being' (*mállon on*) than do phenomena (Pl. Resp. 515d 3). This is so because the Ideas, as perfect, eternal, and immutable forms of unity in multiplicity, are 'True Being' (ὄντως ὄν/*óntōs ón*). The phenomena at the other hand, in all their pluriformity and alterability, make up the domain of Becoming (γιγνόμενον/*gignómenon*). Because of its low degree of unity, this domain can be called Being only in a homonymous sense, since it possesses a derivative and transitory Being through its participation in the Ideas (cf. Pl. Ti. 27d f. with 52a). Here the metaphysics of unity assumes a twofold → transcendence, in which the intelligible Ideas transcend the phenomena as the ground of their Being, and the one transcends the Ideas as their principle (cf. e.g. Aristot. Metaph. 988a 10 f.).

D. The metaphysics of being (Aristotle)

→ Aristotle [6] followed Plato in his gradation of Being, and also in the view that all Being is Being to the extent that it is one. However, he no longer conceives of the One as the principle of Being, but as the determination that necessarily follows from it. It is the undividedness that belongs to every being as such. Because it is undivided, everything that exists is identical with itself. One and Being are interchangeable, even though they are different concepts (Aristot. Metaph. 4,2). Hence, the proper theme of metaphysics is 'being *qua* being' (Metaph. 1003a 21). Being has no unified meaning, but a multiple one, systematized through the → categories. Therefore an enquiry is made into the one fundamental meaning underlying these categories. This is substance (οὐσία/*ousía*), the highest level of which is the transcendent and divine *noûs* (νοῦς). It alone actualises in a perfect way the formal aspect (εἶδος/*eîdos*) to which substance owes its substantiality (cf. Aristot. Metaph. 12,1; 7; 9). As a theory of substance, Aristotelian metaphysics is as much → ontology as it is → theology: a theory of the paradigmatic divine substance, mind (Metaph. 6,1).

E. The metaphysics of mind (Neoplatonism)

The Aristotelian definition of true Being, i.e. substance, as Mind (*noûs*), was taken up and radicalised by → Plotinus, and linked to Plato's metaphysics of unity. The One is the principle of Being: 'all being is through the One' (Plot. Enneades 6,9,1). In its absolute transcendence, the One itself is withdrawn from all Being and all thought (*exhēireménon, epékeina pántōn*). In its absolute repletion (*hyperplērés*) the Absolute, in an inconceivable way, lets the *noûs* emanate as the original form of Being, which remains entirely determined by unity. In Mind, every multiplicity is taken up into a higher unity, so that each individual Idea is at the same time the whole of Being. Mind, in its self-unfolding into the Ideas, simultaneously returns to itself and to the fullness of its unity. Thus, Mind thinks itself as the unity of all Ideas. This absolute intellectual self-relation is the fulfillment of Being. That is why the deficient forms of Being, which proceed from the *noûs,* exist. The soul, which temporalises itself, and nature, which manifests itself to the senses, are also characterised by self-relation: the soul through reflective consciousness, and nature, in its being-alive, through a kind of pre-conscious reflectivity (Plot. Enneades 3, 8,1–8).

F. Posterity

With → Neoplatonism, Christian thought of Late Antiquity absorbed the other forms of ancient metaphysics contained within it. A decisive influence here was the attempt, prepared by → Porphyry and carried out in different but closely connected forms by → Marius [II 21] Victorinus, → Augustine and → Boethius, to think the One together with its first and most perfect form of manifestation in the Mind that thinks itself, and thereby to conceive of the triune God of Christianity (→ Trinity). This resulted in the discovery of the 'ontological difference': 'Being itself' (*autò to eînai*, lat. *esse ipsum*), identified with the One beyond all Being, is distinguished from all everything that is. As the moment of origin of the divine Mind, this being constitutes the other moments of the mind within its self-related, trinitarian unity, simultaneously immanent and transcendent. All later forms of metaphysics remain indebted to the models developed paradigmatically in Antiquity.

→ Metaphysics

P. AUBENQUE, Études sur la Metaphysique d'Aristote, 1979; W. BEIERWALTES, Denken des Einen, 1985; Id., Platonismus im Christentum, 1998; F. P. HAGER (ed.), M. und Theologie des Aristoteles, 1979; J. HALFWASSEN, Der Aufstieg zum Einen, 1992; Id., Hegel und der spätantike Neuplatonismus, 1999; G. W. F. HEGEL, Lectures on the history of philosophy, 3 vols., 1892–1896, new ed. 1995; G. HUBER, Das Sein und das Absolute, 1955; H. J. KRÄMER, Arete bei Platon und Aristoteles, 1959; Id., Der Ursprung der Geistmetaphysik, ²1967; C. ZINTZEN (ed.), Die Philosophie des Neuplatonismus, 1977.   JE.HA.

Metapontum (Μεταπόντιον, *Metapóntion*; Lat. *Metapontum*). A lower Italian city in Lucania, on the Gulf of → Taras/Tarentum, said to have first been founded by the Pylians under → Nestor upon their return from Troy (Strab. 6,1,15). The continuity of the Achaean substrate between the Mycenaean period and the great → colonisation seems to have continued in the cultic domain (Artemision by the Venella and Artemision of Lusi). At the beginning of the 7th century, M. was founded a second time on the initiative of Achaeans from → Croton and → Sybaris (Strab. l.c.). However, the presence of Achaeans is dated archaeologically to the mid 7th century B.C. The conquest of the *chóra* was accompanied by the destruction of the Graeco-indigenous settlement of Incoronata, which depended on → Siris, as well as the erection of shrines in the region of Tavole Palatine, S. Biagio alla Venella and Pizzica Pantanello, and by the establishment of the *phroúrion* ('fortress') of Cozzo Presepe. The organization of the territory between the rivers Bradano, Basento and Cavone developed quite early, with the help of two large-scale cadastral systems. Investigations of aerial photography and surveys made M. into a model case for the analysis of settlement structures of colonial *póleis* with primarily agricultural characteristics. The foundation of the city centre is characterised by the emergence of sacred enclosures, which was followed by the realization of the urban site.

The city reached its zenith in the 4th cent. B.C., and gradually fell into the sphere of influence of Taras. The second → Punic War dealt the life and economy of M. a crushing blow: by the end of the 3rd century B.C., a large part of the city area was deserted, and the settlement became concentrated in the *castrum* southeast of the agora. In the 2nd century AD, Pausanias reports (6,19,11) that only the theatre and a few sections of the walls of M. were still standing.

In the sacred enclosure stood five temples, oriented perpendicular to the current network of streets: their first construction phases go back to 580–570 BC (Temple C, A, B).The following phases are attributed to the years between 530 B.C. and 470 BC (Temple D). To the east rose the agora complex, dominated by the theatre and datable to the second half of the 4th cent. BC. On a circular plan, not clearly visible because of the theatre, stood the *ekklēsiastérion* ('assembly building') built ca. 470 BC on an initial site datable to c. 550 BC. Inscriptions enable several attributions. In the sacred enclosure stood a temple of Apollo (Temple A) and a temple of Hera (Temple B). The *argoì líthoi* ('white stones'), reminiscent of the aniconic cult of Phara in Achaea, also refer to Apollo. Outside the city at Tavole Palatine is a Heraion, and there is an Artemision at S. Biagio alla Venella. The numerous cult-sites in the *chóra* exhibit close relations with cults connected with water.

Metaponto, Atti del XIII Convegno di Studi sulla Magna Grecia, Taranto (1973) 1974; D. ADAMESTEANU et al., Metaponto 1 (NSA Suppl. 25), 1980; F. G. LO PORTO, Metaponto, in: NSA ser. 8, 35 (1981), 1982, 289–391; D. MERTENS, A. DE SIENA, Metaponto, in: Bolletino d'Arte, 16, 1983, 1–60; G. CAMASSA, I culti delle poleis italiote, in: V. MARCHI (ed.), Storia del Mezzogiorno 1, 1991, 471–478; M. OSANNA, Chorai coloniali da Taranto a Locri, 1992, 39–84; BTCGI 10, 1992, 65–112; J. C. CARTER, Insediamenti agricoli, in: G. PUGLIESE CARRATELLI (ed.), I Greci in Occidente, 1996; J. C. CARTER, Sanctuaries in the Chora of Metaponto, in: S. E. ALCOCK, R. OSBORNE (ed.), Placing the Gods, 1994, 161–198; A. MUGGIA, L'area di rispetto nelle colonie magno-greche e siceliote, 1997, esp. 89–92; J. C. CARTER, The Chora of Metaponto, 1998; L. GIARDINO, A.DE SIENA, Metaponto, in: E. GRECO (ed.), La città greca antica, 1999, 329–363.   A.MU.

Metatron One of the highest princes of angels in Jewish mystical literature. There are several etymological explanations for M.'s name. ODEBERG [2. 137 ff.] had already pleaded for the Greek words *metá* and *thrónos*, '(he who sits)next to the throne (of God)' (similarly [1]; negatively [5. 75]). In addition, a tradition of 70 secret names is linked with M. [3], including 'Youth', 'Servant', 'Yahoel' and 'little Yahweh'. He is given a central role in late antique → Hekhalot literature [5]. In the so-called Third Book of Enoch (between c. 500 and 850 AD [5. LIII f.]), which is based on earlier traditions, the transformation of → Enoch into the angel M., as well as

his service at the Throne of God, stand at the centre [2. 79 ff.; 6. 72 ff.]. Another tradition identifies him with the archangel → Michael, who protects the people of Israel. In addition to esoteric literature, M. is also mentioned in → rabbinic literature (Babylonian Talmud, Ḥagiga 125a; Sanhedrin 38b) and in magical texts [4. 29]. The figure of M. is further developed in Medieval mysticism (Kabbala and Ḥaside Aškenaz, or the so-called 'deutsche Fromme') [7].

1 S. LIEBERMAN, M., the Meaning of His Name and His Functions, in: I. GRUENWALD, Apocalyptic and Merkavah Mysticism, 1980, 235–241   2 H. ODEBERG, 3 Enoch or the Hebrew Book of Enoch, 1928, esp. 79–146 (edn., transl. and commentary)   3 C. ROHRBACHER-STICKER, Die Namen Gottes und die Namen M.s: Zwei Geniza-Fragmente zur Hekhalot-Literatur, in: Frankfurter Judaistische Beitr. 19, 1991/2, 95–168   4 P. SCHÄFER, Der verborgene und offenbare Gott, 1991   5 Id., K. HERRMANN (ed.), Übersetzungen der Hekhalot-Literatur 1 (§§ 1–80), 1995   6 G. SCHOLEM, Die jüdische Mystik in ihren Hauptströmungen, 1980 (1st ed. 1957), esp. 72–76 (Major Trends in Jewish Mysticism, 1974³)   7 E. WOLFSON, M. and Shiʾur Qomah in the Writings of Ḥaside Ashkenaz, in: K. E. GRÖZINGER, J. DAN (ed.), Mysticism, Magic and Kabbalah in Ashkenazi Judaism, 1995, 60–92.   I.WA.

Metaurus

[1] see → Mataurus

[2] (Liv. 27,47; *Mataurus*, Tab. Peut. 5,2). River rising in the Umbrian Apennines, flowing past Tifernum and Urbinum through the Ager Gallicus and into the Adriatic to the south of Fanum Fortunae, modern Metauro. In 207 BC it was on the M. that the battle between the Romans and → Hasdrubal [3] took place.

N. ALFIERI, La battaglia del M., 1994.   G.U.

Metelis (Μέτηλις; *Métēlis*). Town in the north-western Nile delta, east of Alexandria; the precise location of M. and its Arab successor settlement of Maṣil remains unclear, but probably near Fuwwa (Kom el-Aḥmar?). In the Roman period, M. was the capital of a new *nome* of Metelites on the territory of the former 7th Lower Egyptian district. Its chief deity was Hathor/→ Isis, who was honoured in the shape of a falcon (Egyptian *bjk*); the placename Bechis (Βῆχις; *Bêchis*), given by Steph. Byz. for M., is derived from this. In the Byzantine and Arab periods (until the 11th cent.), M. was a diocesan town.

1 A. BERNAND, Le delta égyptien d'après les textes grecs, 1970, 443–489   2 S. TIMM, s.v. Maṣil, Das christlich-koptische Ägypten in arabischer Zeit 4, 1988, 1604–1610.   K.J.-W.

Metella see → Caecilia

Metellus Roman *cognomen* in the family of the Caecilii Metelli (→ Caecilius [I 10–32]; → [II 16]).   K.-L.E.

Meteon (Μετεών; *Meteón*). Town of the Illyrian → Labeates in the territory of Labeatis (Pol. 29,3; Liv. 44,23,3; 32,3), near modern Podgorica (Montenegro). M. achieved political significance in 168 BC as the meeting place of → Pantauchus, an emissary of the Macedonian king → Perseus, and the Illyrian prince → Genthius (Pol. loc.cit.; Liv. loc.cit.). Towers of the 3rd-cent. BC town walls are preserved; no systematic excavations.

J. J. WILKES, Dalmatia, 1969, 26f., 166.					H.SO.

Meteorology
I. ANCIENT ORIENT   II. CLASSICAL ANTIQUITY

I. ANCIENT ORIENT
Meteorology in the sense of a systematic study of the weather is found in Babylon in the form of omens, for instance in the omen collection *Enūma Anu Enlil* (→ Astrology). Thunder ('the call of the god Adad') and lightning were particularly important; for instance, the date, time of day, direction, and number of their occurrence were observed. For rain, the time and the way it appeared were considered ominous, as were rainbows, the colour and position of the clouds in the sky, as well as twilight and fog. Predictions derived from the weather were usually general, yet sometimes referred to weather events themselves. In two texts from the Hellenistic period, weather predictions are derived from observations of the planets, and periods for the return of weather phenomena are determined.

Astronomical diaries (2nd half of the 1st cent.; → astronomy) report on the weather, especially when it prevents astronomical observations, in a terminology that is only partially comprehensible. Various kinds of cloud cover and rain are recorded, as are thunder and lightning; among other things thunderclaps are counted (as far as three). Wind is usually connected with indications of its direction. Perhaps the collected weather observations were to serve for predictions by means of omens or for calculations; however, such interpretations are not attested.

Egyptian texts (most of which are still unpublished) give only scant information on meteorological terminology. Isolated allusions to → divination based on meteorological events are found in texts from the Old Kingdom until the Late period [3].

1 G. VAN DRIEL, Weather, in: D. J. W. MEIJER (ed.), Natural Phenomena, 1992, 39–52 2 H. HUNGER, Astrologische Wettervorhersagen, in: ZA 66, 1976, 234–260 3 A. ROCCATI, Lessico meteorologico, in: H. ALTENMÜLLER (ed.), Studien zur Sprache und Religion Ägyptens, vol. 1, 1984, 343–354 4 E. WEIDNER, Die astrologische Serie Enūma Anu Enlil, in: AfO 22, 1968/69, 65–75.					H.HU.

II. CLASSICAL ANTIQUITY
A. DEFINITION   B. PRESOCRATICS   C. ARISTOTLE
D. HELLENISTIC AND ROMAN METEOROLOGY

A. DEFINITION
In Greek natural science, the concepts of μετεωρολογία (*meteōrología*) or τὰ μετέωρα (*ta metéōra*) originally comprised all events that occurred above the earth. They included atmospheric and astronomical phenomena (wind, rain, snow, lightning and thunder; planets, fixed stars, comets, manifestations of celestial light, etc.), as well as a range of terrestrial phenomena (earthquakes, volcanism, springs and rivers, sea currents, salinity of the sea, etc.), which were attributed to the same causes as atmospheric processes. The μετεωρολόγος (*meteōrológos*), who investigated 'what is above and what is beneath the earth ' (τὰ μετέωρα καὶ τὰ ὑπὸ γῆς/tà metéōra kaì tà hypò gês, Plat. Apol. 23b) was considered to be a 'blatherer about phenomena on high' (Aristoph. Nub. 1,223–274; Diog. Laert. 2,18; Plat. Phaedr. 270a; Plat. Apol. 18b) from the 5th cent. BC. The designations *meteōrología* and *meteōrologiká* (μετεωρολογικά) are first attested in Aristotle [3. 318f.] as a specific sub-branch of the investigation of nature.

B. PRESOCRATICS
Of the Presocratic natural philosophers, those who were particularly interested in atmospheric events were → Anaximander, → Anaximenes [1], → Xenophanes, → Heraclitus [1] and → Anaxagoras [2] (→ Pre-Socratics). Explanations of individual phenomena are attested from → Empedocles [1], → Leucippus [5] and → Diogenes [12] of Apollonia. A theory of the formation of rain is found in the Hippocratic work Περὶ ἀέρων ὑδάτων τόπων/Perì aérōn hydátōn tópōn ('Airs Waters Places') [3. 333, 335–337].

Anaximander supposed that the entire surface of the earth was originally moist (ὑγρός/*hygrós*) or flooded. Part of this moisture was evaporated by the sun (DIELS/KRANZ 1,88,7f.). The remaining (salty) part of the original moisture, which had been transformed through 'decoction', formed the sea. The evaporated part, called ἀτμίς (*atmís*), and later ἀναθυμίασις (*anathymíasis*) is the 'primary substance' of meteorological phenomena. From the *atmís* the winds (ἄνεμοι/*ánemoi* or πνεύματα/*pneúmata*) originate, when the finest exhalations dissociate, accumulate, and are set in motion by the sun (DIELS/KRANZ 1,84,17–19; 1,88,8). The πνεῦμα (→ *pneûma*), consisting of compressed air under pressure, is the cause of lightning and thunder. When it is surrounded by a cloud and forces its way out, the tearing of the cloud causes a crash (ψόφος/*psóphos*) and a flash (διαυγασμός/*diaugasmós*; DIELS/KRANZ 1,87,24–27). At the same time, the *atmís* serves as food (τροφή/*trophḗ*) for the heavenly bodies, and so is the cause of the turning (τροπαί/*tropaí*) of the sun and moon (on these concepts, cf. [1. 169 n. 40,15]). The 'consumption' of terrestrial moisture by the stars also leads to a gradual desiccation of the sea (DIELS/KRANZ 1,88,9f.).

For Anaximenes, air is the ultimate cause from which everything originates through condensation (πύκνωσις/*pýknōsis*) and rarefaction (ἀραίωσις/*araíōsis*) (DIELS/KRANZ 1,91,25–7). Through rarefaction of the air arises → fire, while through respectively increasing condensation wind, clouds, water, and earth come into being, and through extreme condensation stone. Hail and snow form when water descending from the clouds freezes, while lightning arises as a bright, fiery ray when the clouds are torn by the force of the *pneûma* (DIELS/KRANZ 1,92,21–28).

Xenophanes emphasizes the heat of the sun as the moving cause of meteorological events (μετάρσιοι/*metársioi*). It draws moisture up from the sea, whence clouds form through condensation of the 'sweet' components and from these arise rain showers and winds (πνεύματα/*pneúmata*; DIELS/KRANZ 1,125,20–23). Lightning is generated through illumination of the clouds as a result of motion (DIELS/KRANZ 1,125,18f.); further heating makes the clouds glow and the heavenly bodies come into existence (DIELS/KRANZ 1,124,28).

For Heraclitus, *anathymíasis* is the 'end product' of a series of elemental transformations out of fire (DIELS/KRANZ 1,141,25–29). He distinguishes between a bright, pure exhalation of the earth, and a dark exhalation of the sea. Fire and the heavenly bodies arise from the former, and moisture from the dark exhalation (DIELS/KRANZ 1,141,29–31).

Anaxagoras declared the sun as the determining factor of atmospheric phenomena. It engenders the winds by diluting the air, at which point heated particles of light escape to the pole, whence they are repelled once again (DIELS/KRANZ 2,17,1–3). The heavenly bodies are 'glowing masses of rock', which were torn loose from the earth and carried about by the ether (αἰθήρ/*aithḗr*; → *aether*) (DIELS/ KRANZ 2,16,17f; 2,23,23).

C. ARISTOTLE

According to the Pythagorean/Platonic determination of the sphere beyond the moon as the region of immutable, eternal order (cf. [4. 83]), → Aristotle [6] defined the *meteōrologiká* as those phenomena which occur naturally, yet which, compared to the first elements of bodies, are nevertheless more irregular (ἀτακτότερος/ *ataktóteros*; Aristot. Mete. 1,1,338 a 26–b 2). Likewise, → Plato had differentiated his discussion of the origin of rain, hail and snow as probable (εἰκότες/*eikótes*) reflections on the process of development from the investigation of eternally existent things (Plat. Tim. 59c-e). In Aristotle, too, several astronomical phenomena (comets, shooting stars, auroras, → Milky Way, etc.) remain as part of meteorology, since he attributed them to the sublunary sphere. More clearly than in his predecessors, terrestrial phenomena appear as the subject of meteorology. Earthquakes and minerals (ὀρυκτά/*oryktá*) have the same causes as winds, thunder and shooting stars, i.e. dry *anathymíasis* (Aristot. Mete. 2,9,370a 25–28).

Aristotle rejected the assumption that the heavenly bodies were 'fed' by the *atmís* or the *anathymíasis*, and so arrived at the concept of a completely terrestrial water cycle: the moisture drawn upwards is constantly sent back to earth as water, and although the quantities do not correspond precisely in every season and in every region, nevertheless everything the atmosphere receives is given back to earth in fixed periods (ibid. 1,2,355a 25–29).

Decisive for Aristotelian meteorology was the distinction between two kinds of exhalation, one moist (ἀναθυμίασις ὑγρά/*anathymíasis hygrá*) and one dry and warm (ἀ. ξηρά θερμή/*a. xērá thermḗ*, ibid. 1,7,344a 10; 2,4,359b 28f.) – Aristotle also mentions a fiery exhalation (ἀ. πυρώδης/*a. pyrṓdēs*, 3,3,372b 32–33) –, as well as the causal attribution of *meteōrologiká* to individual spheres (cf. ibid. 2,2,354b 23–25). Both kinds of *anathymíasis* are always to be understood as a combination (σύγκρισις/*sýnkrisis*), that is, each is potentially contained (δυνάμει/*dynámei*) within the other (ibid. 2,9,369a 12–15). Winds do not extend beyond high mountains (ibid. 1,3,340b 36–341a 1); the sphere of fire reaches down to the highest mountain peaks (cf. ibid. 1,3,340b 19–22). In the sphere of ἀήρ (*aḗr*, that is, air) the processes of combination and condensation of (moist) *anathymíasis* (cf. ibid. 2,4,359b 2–4) take place, as well as that of the excretion (ἔκκρισις/*ékkrisis*) of the moist *anathymíasis* in the form of rain, snow and hail, and of the dry exhalation as thunder and lightning (cf. ibid. 2,9,369a 25–27; 3,1,370b 3). The sphere of fire, the most extreme of the earthly spheres, consists of a highly inflammable material, the ὑπέκκαυμα (*hypékkauma*, ibid. 1,4,341b 19); this is the region of the (brief) combustion of the dry exhalation (ἐκκαομένη ἀναθυμίασις/*ekkaoménē anathymíasis*), in which shooting stars, comets, and other fiery celestial phenomena arise (cf. ibid. 1,4,342a 16–20). A further class of manifestations in the sphere of air are phenomena of 'reflection' (ἀνάκλασις/*anáklasis*, cf. ibid. 3,4,373a 32) of light or the rays of the sun, which include rainbows and halo effects, among others (cf. ibid. 3,4,373b 35–374a 3).

D. HELLENISTIC AND ROMAN METEOROLOGY

After Aristotle, meteorology was further developed by → Theophrastus and → Posidonius. The *Naturales quaestiones* by → Seneca the Younger, which were the main source for meteorology in the Latin Middle Ages, were based on Posidonius. From the "*Meteorology*" of Theophrastus, a fragment on the winds is preserved [9. 376–389]. He interpreted atmospheric events conceptually as μεταρσιολογικά (*metarsiologiká*) and thus differentiated them from the οὐράνια (*Ouránia*, 'heavenly phenomena') (DIELS, DG 364a 9–12). In Posidonius, meteorology (once again) embraced both atmospheric and sidereal events. His works entitled Μετεωρολογικὴ στοιχείωσις (*Meteōrologikḕ stoicheíōsis*, 'Elements of Meteorology'), Περὶ μετεώρων (*Perì meteṓrōn*, 'On supraterrestrial things') and

Μετεωρολογικά (*Meteōrologiká*, 'Meteorology') discussed the entire arrangement of heaven and earth (Diog. Laert. 7,138; see also [6. fr. 14, fr. 18,5–8]; cf. also [3. 323]). Whether Posidonius interpreted comets as sidereal events, that is, as condensed air, 'forced upwards' from the atmosphere into the region of the ether (as is attested by Diog. Laert. 7,152; [6. fr. 131b 12–14]), cannot be decided unambiguously (Sen. Q. Nat. 7,22f., cf. [4. 651f.; 3. 348]). As in Aristotle, earthquakes and volcanic events were attributed to *pneûma* (cf. [6. fr. 12,3]; see also Diog. Laert. 7,154). In any event, Posidonius understood the latter as the ' life-giving breath' of the world: Θεός ἐστι πνεῦμα νοερὸν διῆκον δι᾽ ἁπάσης οὐσίας ('God is the rational pneûma that permeates all being', [6. fr. 100,3f.]; cf. also Sen. Q. Nat. 6,16,1; cf. [3. 350]).

After Posidonius, the further development of Greek meteorology was limited to commentaries on the '*Meteorology*' of Aristotle (→ Alexander [26] of Aphrodisias, → Olympiodorus [4] and Iohannes → Philoponus).

In addition to Seneca, → Lucretius [III 1], Vitruvius, → Plinius the Elder and → Isidorus [9] of Seville were also important for the history of the reception of ancient meteorology. They essentially transmit the views of Aristotle and Posidonius, and deal with the winds (Lucr. 6,423–494; Vitr. 1,6,2–5; Plin. nat. 2,114–116; Isid. orig. 13,11,1–22; Isid. nat. 36,1–37,5), clouds and rain (Lucr. 6,495–523; Vitr. 8,2,1–4; Plin. HN. 2,111; Isid. Orig. 13,7,1–2; 13,10,2–3; Isid. Nat. 32,1–2; 33,1–3), snow and hail (Lucr. 6,527–534; Isid. orig. 13,10,5–6; Isid. nat. 34,1–35,2), lightning and thunder (Lucr. 6,96–378; Plin. HN. 2,133–141; Isid. Orig. 13,8,1–9,2; Isid. Nat. 29,1–30,5), the rainbow (Lucr. 6,524–526; Isid. Orig. 13,10,1; Isid. Nat. 31,1–2), volcanoes (Lucr. 6,639–702; Isid. Orig. 14,6,36–38), hot springs (Vitr. 8,3,1–4; Isid. Orig. 14,6,40–41) and earthquakes (Lucr. 6,535–607; Plin. HN. 2,191–200). Lucretius explains rain by the union of atoms of water (*semina aquarum*, Lucr. 6,507–510). The cause of lightning is the finely distributed atoms of fire, as well as the atoms of the warm exhalation (*vaporis semina*, Lucr. 6,275–276), which can easily penetrate within all bodies. This explains the powerful effects of lightning (Lucr. 6,352–356; see also Isid. Nat. 30,4).

In the Church Fathers, individual Biblical representations, with their roots in Babylonian or Jewish cosmology, continued to have an effect: so, for instance, the idea of heavenly waters (Gn 1,6–7; Isid. Nat. 14,1–2; cf. [5. 5–13]). Aristotle had already turned indirectly against this doctrine: atmospheric precipitation first comes into being in the atmosphere, and does not exist there pre-made (Aristot. Mete. 2,9,369b 31–34). Aristotle's '*Meteorology*'was first translated into Latin by Gerard of Cremona in the 12th century, from an Arabic source dating from the 9th century. The first Latin commentary was composed by Albertus Magnus, while the most important later commentary was written by the Milanese scholar Francesco VIMERCATI (1556).

Although attempts are repeatedly made in the discussion of the concept of ancient and medieval Meteorology to identify in it a limitation, albeit implicit, to the physics of the atmosphere in the modern sense (cf. [3. 321]), such a limitation first becomes tangible only in modern times. R. DESCARTES' *Les météores* (1637) is still marked by the Aristotelian concept of meteorology. → Astronomy; → Earth-quake; → Fixed stars; → Moon; → Nature; → Sun; → Volcanoes; → Winds; → METEOROLOGY

1 H. STROHM, Aristoteles, Meteorologie. Über die Welt, ³1984 (transl., introd., notes) 2 W. CAPELLE, μετέωρος, μετεωρολογία, in: Philologus 71, 1912, 414–448 3 Id., s.v. M., RE Suppl. 6, 315–358 4 O. GILBERT, Die meteorologischen Theorien des griechischen Altertums, 1907 (repr. 1967); 5 I. HOFFMANN, Die Anschauungen der Kirchenväter über Meteorologie, 1907 6 L. EDELSTEIN (ed.), Posidonius, Bd. 1 (The Fragments), 1972 7 F. SOLMSEN, Aristotle's System of the Physical World, 1960 8 G. GASPAROTTO, Isidoro e Lucrezio, 1983 9 F. WIMMER (ed.), Theophrasti Eresii opera, 1866 10 W. CAPELLE, Die Vorsokratiker. Die Fragmente und Quellenberichte, ⁴1954 (transl. and introd.) 11 P. L. SCHOONHEIM, Die arabisch-lateinischen Überlieferungen der aristotelischen Meteorologie, in: G. ENDRESS, R. KRUK (ed.), The Ancient Tradition in Christian and Islamic Hellenism, 1997, 239–258.

L. TAUB, Ancient Meteorology, 2003 B.FR.

Meter see → Cybele

Methana (ἡ Μεθάνα; *hē Methána* or τὰ Μέθανα; *tà Méthana*). Peninsula and city on the north coast of the Argolid peninsula. The circular peninsula, about 9 km across and with a highest elevation of 743 m, is linked to the mainland by a 300 m wide isthmus. It consists almost entirely of young volcanic rocks and lava flows. The last known eruption, to which a crater and a lava flow on the northwestern coast still bear witness today, took place at the time of Antigonus [2] in the 3rd cent. BC (Strab. 1,3,18). There are several hot carbonic acid and sulphurous springs. In antiquity the chief town was in the southwest near modern Megalochori, which still has remains of the city walls. There are further remains of ancient settlements, baths and fortifications at various locations, finds from the prehistoric period, archaic dedications (IvOl 247). Occupied and fortified by Athens during the → Peloponnesian War (Thuc. 4,45,2; Diod. 12,85). In the 3rd cent. it was a Ptolemaic garrison and renamed Arsinoe (IG IV 72; 76). There are inscriptions and coins dating from the Imperial period. M. is also mentioned in Hierocles, Synecdemus 646,11 (cf. Strab. 8,6, 15; Paus. 2,34,1–4; Ptol. 3,14,33). Inscriptions: IG IV 853–871; SGDI 3369–3377; SEG 37, 315–321; 38, 326f.; 39, 363–366, coins: HN 442.

C. MEE et al., Rural Settlement Change in the M. Peninsula, Greece, in: G. BARKER, J. LLOYD (Ed.), Roman Landscapes, 1991, 223–232; Ders., H. FORBES (Ed.), A Rough and Rocky Place, 1997; N. PHARAKLAS, Τροιζηνία, Καλαύρεια, Μέθανα (Ancient Greek Cities 10), 1972. Y.L.
E.MEY.

Methodists 1st-century AD medical school. Its representatives explicitly defined themselves as Methodists (μεθοδικοί; *methodikoí*), as it was their goal to base the practice of medicine on a single simple method (μέθοδος; *méthodos*) that they could teach to anyone in just a few words.

Extant are only the gynaecological treatise of → Soranus, a Latin translation of his pathological writings by → Caelius [II 11] Aurelianus and doxographic fragments, e.g. POxy. 3654 [1. 382–386, 388–390], probably a medical textbook from the time of → Galenus. The Methodists are often mentioned in Galen, statements that can be evaluated only with difficulty because of his opposition to the Methodists, and also in the medical history of → Celsus [7] (cf. [4]) and in → Sextus Empiricus.

At present it is estimated that the school was established about the middle of the 1st century AD by → Thessalus of Tralles. The foundations of his thought are to be found in the theories of → Asclepiades [6] of Bithynia and primarily those of → Themison of Laodicea, the originator of the basic concept of 'common features, or generalised states' [7. 35]. Apart from Thessalus and Soranus, little is known of the members of the school (for some cf. [2. 60f.]). In spite of their strong individualization they can nevertheless be divided up into 'ancient' (*veteres*, Caelius Aurelianus, Chronicae passiones 1,171) and 'younger 'Methodists, corresponding to the 1st and 2nd centuries AD. The 'younger' Methodists were more receptive to other medical schools. In the period after Galen, the Methodist school appears to have disintegrated, even though its doctrine outlived it.

The Methodists, who undoubtedly had a negative view of theory, limited medicine to the treatment of disease by basing their actions on the concept of 'common features '(κοινότης/*koinótēs*) in the state of the body. However divergent the definition may have been because of the differences (διαφωνία/ *diaphōnía*) amongst the Methodists so strongly criticized by Galen, 'the *koinótēs*' is a a state present in all diseases, while these are not themselves defined any further.

For the Methodists, the identification of pathological conditions is based on direct observations triggered by the 'koinótētes' themselves (this means the ἔνδειξις/ *éndeixis*, or 'indication' of the disease by its characteristics) [7. 15–18] without any speculation at all, although at least at a later stage, Methodists based their diagnosis on anatomical and physiological concepts. Treatment was aimed at restoring balance in the particles according to the principle of opposites and by means of a limited spectrum of medical substances which were adapted to the patient individually. Accompanying this, measures such as fasting for three day (*diátriton*) or physical exercise were prescribed, in order not only to have an effect on the disease but also, where applicable, make a change in the patient's constitution. The therapies had to be employed at the most favourable time (although this does not correspond to

the Hippocratic copncept of *kairós*), work gently and slowly and also be pleasant [6. 23–28].

The Methodist school was so successful in the 1st century AD in Rome that its approach was practised even at the imperial court [6. 20]. Its teachings spread as far as Egypt, not only in Alexandria, where Soranus is said to have learnt them [3. 992f.], but also further inland. It was later criticized fiercely by Galen, but it survived, as can be seen not only from Caelius Aurelianus's translation of Soranus but also from the influence on → Theodorus Priscianus [5], in the Latin translation of → Oribasius [8. 245–251] and even in the Ravenna commentaries on the Galenic treatise *De sectis* [8]. It may owe this continuity to its simple and practical nature.

1 I. ANDORLINI, Papiri e medicina: POxy II 234 + POxy LII 3654, in: A. H. S. EL-MOSALAMY (ed.), Proc. of the XIXth International Congress of Papyrology, vol. 1, 1992, 375–390   2 D. GOUREVITCH, La pratique méthodique, in: P. MUDRY (ed.), Les écoles médicales à Rome, 1991, 51–81   3 A. E. HANSON, M. H. GREEN, Soranus of Ephesus: Methodicorum princeps, in: ANRW II 37.2, 1994, 968–1075   4 P. MUDRY (ed.), La préface du De medicina de Celse, 1982   5 P. MIGLIORINI, Elementi methodici in Teodoro Prisciano, in: P. MUDRY (s. [2]), 231–240   6 V. NUTTON, Therapeutic Methods and Methodist Therapeutics in the Roman Empire, in: S. SAKAI (ed.), History of Therapy, 1990, 1–35   7 J. PIGEAUD, Les fondements du méthodisme, in: P. MUDRY (s. [2]), 7–50   8 M. E. VAZQUEZ BUJAN, Isti methodici constabilitatem non habent. Remarques sur la persistance tardive du méthodisme, in: P. MUDRY (see [2]), 241–254.

G. BENZ (ed.), Caelius Aurelianus, in: CML 6, 1–2, 2 Bks., 1990–1993; P. BURGUIÈRE (ed.), Soranus Ephesius, Maladies des femmes, 3 books, 1988–1994; L. EDELSTEIN, s.v. Methodiker, RE Suppl. 6, 358–373 (English in: Ancient Medicine. Selected Papers of L.E., 1967, 173–191); V. NUTTON, Ancient Medicine, 2004; J. SCARBOROUGH, The Pharmacy of Methodist Medicine, in: P. MUDRY (see [2]), 203–216; M. M. TECUSAN, The Fragments of the Methodists, vol. 1, 2004; A. TOUWAIDE, La toxicologie dans le De medicina: un système asclépiado-méthodique?, in: P. MUDRY (ed.), La médecine de Celse, 1994, 211–256.

A.TO.

Methodius (Μεθόδιος; *Methódios*).

[1] Bishop of Olympus (late 3rd – early 4th cent. BC). Little about his life is known for certain. According to Jer. Vir. ill. 83 he was bishop of Olympus in Lycia, but Tyre, Patara, Myra and Philippi are also mentioned as his see. His martyrdom, also reported by Jerome, is equally disputed. M., who preferred the dialogue form in imitation of Plato, wrote numerous works (CPG 1810–1830) in an elegant style. His main work *Sympósion ē Perí hagneías* (Συμπόσιον ἢ Περὶ ἀγνείας [2]) celebrates virginity as an anticipation of Heaven. A hymn to Christ in the form of an alphabetical acrostic is inserted into it [2. 310–321]. In the dialogue *Perí tou autexousíou* (Περὶ τοῦ αὐτεξουσίου), later frequently cited by the Armenian → Eznik of Kolp, M. regards the human free will as the origin of evil. Further works are

preserved mostly in Old Slavonic translation [1]. In his late work *De resurrectione* (CPG 1812) M. defends the identity of the resurrection body with the present body against → Origenes, whose allegorical exegesis he adopts (→ allegoresis) [5. 15–55]. A work against → Porphyry is lost. The Apocalypse (CPG Suppl. 1830; (Ps.-)→ Methodius [3]), popular in the Middle Ages, stems from the late 7th cent. AD.

EDITIONS: 1 G. N. BONWETSCH, 1917 (GCS 27, complete edition) 2 H. MUSURILLO, V. H. DEBIDOUR, 1963 (SChr 95) 3 A. VAILLANT, Le *De Autexusio* de Méthode d'Olympe, in: Patrologia Orientalis 22, 631–888.
BIBLIOGRAPHY: 4 L. G. PATTERSON, Methodius, 1997; 5 E. PRINZIVALLI, L'esegesi biblica di Metodio di Olimpo, 1985 6 R. WILLIAMS, s.v. Methodius, TRE 22, 680–684.
J.RI.

[2] Lexicographer, whose life time, given his use of → Orus and Cassius → Longinus, is to be situated in the 5th cent. AD at the earliest [3. 1381]. M. composed a strictly alphabetically arranged etymological lexicon, now lost, whose sources included the pseudo-Herodian Homeric → Epimerismi and Homeric scholia [2. 11–44]. Excerpts from Letter A of his extensive work are found in the *Etymologicum Genuinum*, in the first part of the Αἱμωδεῖν-Etymologicon ([1]: α 1–75; 76?; 144?) and in the Oxford Homeric Epimerismi ([1]: α 205; 305–359).

1 A. R. DYCK (ed.), Epimerismi Homerici: Pars altera. Lexicon AIMΩΔEIN, 1995 2 R. REITZENSTEIN, Geschichte der griechischen Etymologika, 1897 (repr. 1964) 3 C. WENDEL, s.v. Methodius, RE 15, 1380–1381.
GR.DA.

[3] Unidentified author of an Apocalypse composed in Syriac ca. 690 AD. Through his pseudonym, transmitted unanimously by the Syriac, Greek and Latin traditions, the author links his prophesy of the imminent end of Arab domination with M. [1] of Olympus. The Christian bishop's millenarianism is connected with the structure of the anonymous Syriac 'Book of the Cave of Treasures', which undertakes a division of world history into millennia. For M., the end of days began with the march by the → Arabs out of the wilderness of → Yatrib; he stresses the preeminence of → Christianity and warns against conversion to → Islam.
→ Apocalypses

G. J. REININK (transl.), Die syrische Apokalypse des Pseudo-Methodius (CSCO, Scriptores Syri, 221 und 541), 1993.
K.SA.

[4] (810/820 – 6 April 885). Saint, known as the second of the two apostles of the Slavs → Cyril [8] and M. (*Kiril i Metodij*). M. governed a principality inhabited by Slavs (ἀρχοντία, *knęženije Slověnsko*: Vita Methodii 2,5; Vita Constantini 4,13), presumably Strymon [2. 17], before he retired, ca. 850, to the monastery of Polychronion (?) on the Olympus (Vita Methodii 3), where he was named abbot (ἡγούμενος, *igumen*: Vita Methodii 4,6). During his mission in Moravia, he twice went to Rome with his brother Cyril (Constantine),

and, on his second visit (869/870), was consecrated as *Pannonicus archiepiscopus* 'to the chair of St. Andronicus' by Pope Hadrianus II (Vita Methodii 3,17), i.e. appointed [4. 228²⁹]. It seems that in establishing M.'s diocese the Pope harked back to older canonical rights of Sirmium as *caput Illyrici* and *civitas Pannoniae*, later renamed as *civitas sancti Demetrii* (today Sremska Mitrovica) [5. 9f.]. According to legend, it was at Sirmium that Andronicus (Rom. 16,7) was active as the first bishop [2. 251–253; 3. 22], although Eirenaios (Irenaeus) was the first demonstrable bishop of Sirmium [5. 9]. In the writings of Iohannes VIII (873) and the bull of Hadrianus II (869), three Slavic principalities (Rastislavs, Sventopulks, Kocels) are designated as Pannonia, which renders precise localisation difficult [1; 3. 23]. Apart from the liturgical 'books' and the *Nomocanon*, which he composed together with his brother, he devoted, together with his students, a Slavic canon to St. Demetrius (*sv. Dimitrij*: Vita Methodii 15,4) [4. 234⁴]. M. was also supposed to have established the annual commemorative festival in honour of St. Demetrius at the place where he suffered his martyr's death († 9.4.304 at Sirmium) [6. 513].

1 I. BOBA, The Episcopacy of St. Methodius, in: Slavic Review 26, 1967, 85–93 2 F. DVORNIK, Les légendes de Constantin et de Méthode vues de Byzance, 1933 3 M. EGGERS, Das Erzbistum des Method, 1996 4 F. GRIVEC, F. TOMŠIČ, Constantinus et Methodius Thessalonicenses. Fontes, 1960; 5 G. GYÖRFFY, Ein Güterverzeichnis des griechischen Klosters zu Szászentdemeter (Sremska Mitrovica) aus dem 12. Jahrhundert, in: Studia Slavica Academiae Scientiarum Hungaricae (Budapest) 5, 1959, 9–74 6 J. VAŠICA, Původní staroslověnský liturgický kánon o sv. Dimitrijovi Soluňském, in: Slavia (Praha) 35, 1966, 513–524.

S. NIKOLOVA, Metodij, in: P. DINEKOV, Kirilo-Metodievska Enciklopedija 2, 1995, 632–650.
L.D.

Methone (Μεθώνη/*Methōnē*, Μοθώνη/*Mothōnē*).
[1] A city on the west coast of → Messana [2]. Its indigenous name was *Mothōnē* (Μοθώνη on coins), after the reef called *Móthōn* which rose in front of it; hence the medieval and modern name Modon, Mothoni, Methoni (Μεθώνη in Thuc. 2,25,1ff. and Strab. 8,4,3). There are few ancient remains: isolated bases of city walls under the Venetian fortress and the breakwater wall in the harbour, some remains of columns, and in addition some graves. The modern city lies north of the Venetian fort, which marks the site of the ancient city. There are Mycenaean finds. In Homer it is not called M., but is identified with Pedasus, one of the seven cities Agamemnon offers to angry Achilles (Hom. Il. 9,152; 294; Strab. l.c.). In historical times it was a Spartan city of perioeci (→ Perioikoi), where displaced inhabitants of Nauplia were settled. There was an Athenian attempt to conquer the city in 431 BC (Thuc. 2,25,1ff.; Diod.12,43,2f.). It was first annexed to Messana in 338 BC (Paus. 4,27,8; Scyl. 46), but was an independent member of the Achaean League from 191 BC on

(→ Achaeans, Achaea, with map). In 31 BC, Agrippa annihilated the fleet of → Bogudes [2] at M. (Strab. l.c.; Cass. Dio 50,11,3). M. was declared free by Trajan (Paus. 4,35,3). Coinage was issued under the Severi (193–235). There was a devastating earthquake and tidal wave in 365 AD (Amm. 26,10,19). In 533 AD, it served as the base of the fleet of → Belisarius (Procop. Vand. 3,13,9ff.). M. is still mentioned in Hierocles, Synekdemos 647,17, and is attested as a diocese (Not. Episc. 3,471; 10,578; 13,428). It was one of the strongest fortresses in Greece in the Middle Ages and modern times, and an important Venetian stronghold. There was important viticulture in the neighbouring plain in antiquity (Paus. 4,35,1–12; Ptol. 3,14,31; Mela 2,41; Plin. HN 4,15; Tab. Peut. 7,5). Inscriptions: IG IV 619,2; V 1,1417; SEG 11,1001; coins: HN 433.

J. C. Kraft, S. E. Aschenbrenner, Palaeogeographic Reconstructions in the Methoni Embayment in Greece, in: Journ. of Field Archaeology 4, 1977, 19–44; E. Meyer, s.v. Messenien, RE Suppl. 15, 200f.   Y.L. E.MEY.

[2] Locality on the west coast of the Magnesian peninsula. Named as a possession of Philoctetes in the Homeric Catalogue of Ships (Hom. Il. 2,716), it existed until Hellenistic times. In the 4th cent. BC, M., together with Homole, appointed the *hieromnēmōn* (→ Hieromnemones) of Magnesia at Delphi (Syll.³ 239; 315; 444). It was incorporated c. 290 BC into the newly founded city of Demetrias [1]. M. is located on the Nevestiki Hill near Lechonia, where the Byzantine successor settlement Liconia stood.

F. Stählin, s.v. M. (6), RE 15, 1384f.; Koder/Hild, 201f.   HE.KR.

[3] A city in Macedonian Pieria (its precise location near modern Eleftherochori has not yet been identified), a foundation of → Eretria [1] (Plut. Quaest. Graec. 11). In the 5th cent. BC, it was a member of the first → Delian League, and received trading privileges c. 430 (IG I³ 61). M. accepted Macedonian refugees in 417/6 (Thuc. 6,7,3f.); it probably became independent after the → Peloponnesian War. C. 360 it received *theōroí* (→ Theoria) from Epidaurus (IG IV² 94), and provided sanctuary for the fleeing Attic politician → Callistratus [2] (Demosth. or. 50,48). Probably only then was the city occupied by the Athenian Timotheus (Demosth. or. 4,4; Din. or. 1,14), and served in 359 as the base for Argaeus' attempted seizure of power in Macedonia, which was carried out with Athenian help, but failed (Diod. 16,3,5f.). It was conquered and destroyed by Phillip II In 355/4 (Diod. 16,31,6; 34,4f.).

Errington, 27f., 48f.; HM 2, s. Index.   MA.ER.

Methora see → Mathura

Methydrium (Μεθύδριον/*Methýdrion*, locally Μετίδριον/*Metídrion*). City in northern Arcadia with a small number of ruins near the modern M. (formerly Nemnitsa), south of Vytina (at a height of approximately 1000 m). Originally independent, M. belonged to Orchomenus, probably from 400/368 BC, and to Megale Polis from 369/360 BC (?). Border inscription: [5. 664; 1; 2]. Remains of a circular wall dating from the 4th cent. BC. [3]. M. was several times temporarily independent (Syll.³ 490,18ff., c. 234/3 BC; Syll.³ 559,61; coins). The place is mentioned in Theoph. FGrH 115 F 344 as an example of rural frugality. M. is often mentioned in military histories owing to its position on important roads (last stage of the road leading from Megale Polis through Eutresia to central Arcadia). Several shrines have been attested [4]. M. was the *kṓmē* ('village') of Megale Polis at the time of Pausanias, possibly from the time of Augustus (Paus. 8,12,2; 27,4; 35,5; 36,1–3; Strabo 8,8,2; Plin. HN 4,20; Steph. Byz. s.v. M.). Inscription.: Syll.³ 90,6; coins: HN 418; 451.

1 A. Plassart, Détermination de la frontière entre Orchomène et Methydrion, in: BCH 39, 1915, 53–97   2 S. Dusanic, La délimitation d'Orchomène, in: BCH 102, 1978, 346–358   3 G. S. Korres, Δίπαλτος καὶ Ὅρκιος Ζεύς, in: AE 1972, 208–233   4 Jost, 213–216; 5 Schwyzer, Dial.   Y.L.

Methylium (Μεθύλιον; *Methýlion*). Town in western Thessaly, mentioned on coins and in a Delphic list of *theorodókoi*. Its location can only be approximately identified, between Cierium and Metropolis [4] in the region of Karditsa.

B. Helly, Incursions chez les Dolopes, in: I. Blum (ed.), Topographie antique et géographie historique en pays grec, 1992, 85ff.; F. Stählin, s.v. Methylion, RE 15, 1391.   HE.KR.

Methymna (Μήθυμνα; *Méthymna*). City on the north coast of the island of → Lesbos, formerly Molivos, today again officially M., on a hill jutting into the sea. M. was one of the five *póleis* of Lesbos (Hdt. 1,151; Strab. 13,2,2) with a considerable amount of territory after the subjugation of Arisbe (c. 600 BC). The ancient history of M. was dominated by continual rivalry with → Mytilene.

M. was involved in the founding of Assus in Asia Minor (Strab. 13,1,58) and, like Mytilene, was one of the cities in the → Delian League that provided ships instead of paying tribute (Thuc. 6,85,2; 7,57,5; 8,100,5). In 428 BC, M. was the only Lesbian city to take no part in the movement organized by Mytilene to break away from Athens (Thuc. 3,2,1). In the final stages of the → Peloponnesian War (from 406 BC), the city was controlled by the Spartans (Xen. Hell. 1,6,12–15). In 377 BC, M. returned to the Athenian side and became a member of the second → Athenian League. As in other Lesbian cities, tyrants (Cleomis) ruled here around the middle 4th century BC.

In the Hellenistic period, M. was initially under Ptolemaic rule. During the 2nd century BC, M. followed a policy of increasing friendship with Rome, which the Romans rewarded in 167 BC by granting M. the territory of Antissa (Liv. 45,31,14; Plin. HN 5,139). The Romans also came to the aid of M., after the devastation caused there by → Prusias of Bithynia in about 156 BC, by forcing Prusias to pay reparations (Pol. 33,13,8). In about 129 BC a formal alliance was made with Rome (IG XII 2,510 = Syll.³ 693). After that, M. became less important, because Roman protection now also extended to its rival Mytilene. From the Roman Imperial period no significant evidence remains. In the 4th century AD, M. became a bishopric. In the Byzantine period there was a noticeable reduction in the area of the city.

M. was famous for its wine (Sil. 7,211). It was the home of the poet → Arion and the historian → Myrsilus (both end of the 7th century BC.). There are very few ancient remains, but parts of the archaic city wall, solitary tombs and remains of the harbour mole are extant.

H.-G. BUCHHOLZ, M.: Arch. Beitr. zur Top. und Gesch. von Nordlesbos, 1975; M. DREHER, Der Eintritt Thebens und M. in den Zweiten Att. Seebund, in: Liverpool Classical Monthly 15, 1990, 51–53; W. GÜNTHER, s.v. M., in: LAUFFER, Griechenland, 430–432; H. J. MASON, Mytilene and M.: Quarrels, Borders and Topography, in: Échos du monde classique 37, 1993, 225–250; H. PISTORIUS, Beitr. zur Geschichte von Lesbos im 4. Jh.v.Chr., 1913.
H.SO.

Metics see → Metoikos

Metilius Roman *gens* name, probably of Latin origin with Etruscan parallels (the patrician *gens* in Dion Hal. Ant. Rom. 3,29,7 is invented), historically attested no earlier than the 3rd century BC.

J. REICHMUTH, Die latinischen Gentilicia, 1956, 111; 117; SCHULZE, 290.
K.-L.E.

I. REPUBLICAN PERIOD   II. IMPERIAL PERIOD

I. REPUBLICAN PERIOD

[I 1] In 220–219 BC, at the instigation of the censors C. Flaminius [1] and L. Aemilius [I 27] Papus, a *lex Metilia* was passed on the professional status of fullers (*fullones*) (Plin. HN. 35,197; MRR 1, 236). Its exact purpose, its creator and his office remain as unclear as his identity with M.M., who in 217, as people's tribune, was instrumental in having M. Minucius [I 10] appointed alongside Fabius [I 30] Maximus as second dictator for the same duties. The extant details of this process are all inventions by late annalists.   TA.S.

II. IMPERIAL PERIOD

[II 1] Praetorian legate in Galatia under Tiberius. PIR² M 534.

[II 2] Son of Marcia Cordus's daughter Marcia [6]. Raised by his mother, as his father, who is unknown, died young. It is impossible to say wether he can be identified as the only M. [II 1] who can definitely be dated to the appropriate time. Senator, as he was a *pontifex* (Sen. Dial. 6,24,3). He did not take up a position in the army. When he died, Seneca sent a letter of condolence to his mother (Sen. Dial. 6). PIR² M 535.

[II 3] **M. M. Aquillius Regulus Nepos Volusius Torquatus Fronto** Patrician, who went through the customary *cursus*, becoming *consul ordinarius* in AD 157. M. held three priestly offices: *augur, salius collinus, sodalis Flavialis* (CIL XIV 2501 = ILS 1075). PIR² M 540.

[II 4] **M. Atilius M. Bradua** cf. → Atilius [II 9]. *Cos. suff.c.* AD 133, proconsul of Africa under Antoninus Pius. PIR² M 541.

THOMASSON, Fasti Africani, 95f.

[II 5] **P. M. Nepos** M. is probably the *cos. suff.* in the → *Fasti Ostienses* for the year AD 103. (FO² 46). A consular governorship can be deduced from Pliny (Ep. 4,26), perhaps in Pannonia (cf. also [1. 237; 251; 345f.; 699f.]). Evidently designated as *cos. iterum* for the year 128, but died before that. PIR² M 545.

1 SYME, RP, vol. 2.

W. ECK, s.v. M. (19), RE Suppl. 14, 282; N. LEWIS, The Documents from the Bar-Kokhba Period in the Cave of Letters. Greek Papyri, 1989, nos. 17–19.

[II 6] **P. M. Sabinus Nepos** Suffect consul in the year AD 91, consular legate of Britain approximately 95–97/8 [1. 324ff.]. He can probably be identified with the *frater Arvalis* who died a short time before February 118. PIR² M 547.

1 W. ECK, Jahres- und Provinzialfasten der senatorischen Statthalter von 69/70–138/139, in: Chiron 12, 1982.

BIRLEY, 83ff.; SCHEID, Collège, 40f.; 361f.

[II 7] **P. M. Secundus Pon[tianus?]** M.'s career, recorded in CIL XI 3718 = ILS 1053, began under Trajan. He commanded the *legio XI Claudia* and from 121 to 123 the *legio III Augusta* in Africa. Suffect consul in AD 123 or 124. Subsequently *curator operum publicorum* and legate of an unknown consular province. *Frater Arvalis*. Son of M. [II 5](?). PIR² M 549.

SCHEID, Collège, 44f., 373ff.; THOMASSON, Fasti Africani, 142ff.   W.E.

Metiochus (Μητίοχος; *Mētíochos*). Eldest son of Miltiades [2], half-brother of Cimon [2]. Commanded one of the five triremes used by Miltiades to flee from the Chersonesus [1] to Athens in 493 BC at the end of the → Ionian Revolt. It was the one the Persians seized, but Darius [1] gave him a fief and a wife and children were regarded as full Persians (Hdt. 6,41,2–4; non-Herodotean tradition in Marcellinus, Thucydides Vita 12, but cf. e.g. [1. 302]). Nothing is known of his probably Athenian mother or any siblings.

1 DAVIES   2 PA 10132   3 TRAILL, PAA 650600.   K.KI.

Metion (Μητίων; *Mētíōn*). Son of → Erechtheus and Praxithea, brother of → Cecrops (Apollod. 3,15,1). His sons, the Metionids, drive → Pandion, the son and heir of Cecrops, from power in Attica, but are in turn overthrown by his sons (Paus. 1,5,3f.; Apollod. 3,15,5). → Daedalus [1] was both M.'s grandson, as the son of Eupalamus (Apollod. 3,15,8), and M.'s son (Pherekydes FGrH 3 F 146; Diod. 4,76,1 with M. as the son of Eupalamus and grandson of Erechtheus).   J.STE.

Metis (Μῆτις/*mêtis*, literally 'cleverness', 'clever advice'). M. first appears as an attribute of → Zeus (*Mētíeta*' gifted with wisdom', e.g. Hom. Il. 1,175 etc.) and is personified as a goddess for the first time in Hes. Theog. 358 as one of the daughters of → Oceanus. She becomes the first wife of Zeus (ibid. 886ff.). But → Gaia and → Uranus warn Zeus that M. will bear dangerously clever children and advise him to swallow her. By doing this he prevents the birth of a son, but not the birth of → Athena, who ultimately springs from his head. By swallowing M., Zeus acquires her wisdom. Two motifs are merged into one in this myth. (1) The new ruler Zeus is in danger of being overthrown by his own son, as he himself had deprived his father → Cronus of power and Cronus his own father Uranus. To stop the chain at Zeus, the succession has to be broken. In other versions it is → Thetis who threatens to bear the stronger son (→ Peleus, → Achilles [1]). The motif of swallowing is also a repetition of the Cronus episode. In a third version the threatening successor is → Typhon. (2) The birth of Zeus's daughter from his head is originally an independent story. Athena's famous cleverness obviously suggested making M. her mother (cf. Hom. Od. 13,299; Hom. h. 28,2). The linking of the two motifs is designed to document the continuity and stability of Zeus's new world order: new gods are created (in this case Athena), who are to represent in the new order the values (in this case cleverness) symbolised in the old order by their mothers (in this case M.), now as children of Zeus (cf. → Themis as mother of → Dike [1], → Eirene [1] and Eunomia: Hes. Theog. 901f.; → Mnemosyne as mother of the → Muses: ibid. 915–917 etc.).

Chrysippus SVF fr. 908 quotes some lines following on from Hes. Theog. 926 which offer a slightly modified version (M. is only the mistress of Zeus, with Hera). They derive possibly from the → 'Melampodeia' [1. 401–403].

1 M. L. WEST (ed.), Hesiod, Theogony, 1966 (with comm.).   L.K.

Metochites style Greek style of writing dated to the first half of the 14th cent., employed in the eastern territories of the Byzantine empire; its use probably remained restricted to Constantinople and its close environs. The style owes its name to the fact that it is primarily attested in MSS of works by Theodoros Metochites, the Great Logothete (→ Logothetes) and personal friend of the emperor Andronikos II. This style is characterised by an exceptional concern with calligraphic effect, achieved by separating the individual letters, shrinking the size of accents, aligning upper and lower strokes at perpendicular angles, and by sparing use of abbreviations. All of this – although associated with the moderate enlargement of individual letters, distinctly recognisable as the influence of the → Greasedrop script – gives a harmonious and elegant look to any page written in the Metochites style. One hand from among those writing in this style belongs to a copyist who has been called the 'Metochites scribe', because he appears to have been the personal copyist of Theodoros Metochites. A copy of the latter's works in the order of their composition was written in this hand between *c.* 1311 and 1332 (the year of Metochites' death); its MSS are the Cod. Vindob. Phil. gr. 95, Vat. gr. 1365, Paris. gr. 1776, and Paris. gr. 2003. The scribe belonged to the imperial chancellery, and some of the chrysobulls issued in 1311, 1314, 1317, and 1321 from the chancellery of Andronikos II are attributed to him; several of the most important MSS of the Palaeologan period, such as the celebrated Cod. Crippsianus of the Attic orators (Lond. Burney 95), are also said to have been written by him. The Metochites scribe has recently been identified with the imperial notary Michael Klostomalles.

1 H. HUNGER, Griechische Paläographie, in: Id., Geschichte der Textüberlieferung der antiken und mittelalterlichen Literatur, vol. 1, 1961, 102 and fig. 23   2 G. PRATO, I manoscritti greci nei secoli XIII e XIV: note paleografiche, in: D. HARLFINGER, G. PRATO (ed.), Paleografia e codicologia greca. Atti del II Colloquio internazionale (Berlin – Wolfenbüttel 1983), 1991, 131–149, esp. 140–149 (Repr. in: G. PRATO, Studi di paleografia greca, 1994, 115–131, esp. 123–131 and fig. 9–24)   3 E. LAMBERZ, The Library of Vatopaidi and its Manuscripts, in: The Holy and Great Monastery of Vatopaidi. Trad. – History – Art, vol. 2, 1998, 562–574, 672–677, esp. 567 and 676 n. 78.   G.P.

Metoikos (μέτοικος; *métoikos*).
I. DEFINITION   II. SOCIAL AND LEGAL STATUS
III. THE NUMBER OF METOIKOI   IV. METOIKOI IN POLITICS AND IN POLITICAL LITERATURE
V. METOIKOI OUTSIDE ATHENS

I. DEFINITION

Métoikoi, or metics, immigrant foreigners who lived in a Greek city without possessing rights of citizenship, were clearly distinguished from the citizens of a → *pólis* in 4th cent. BC political theory, as is shown by the following: 'But these are only citizens in the manner in which children who are as yet too young to have been renrolled in the list and old men who have been discharged.' This statement by Aristotle (Aristot. Pol. 1275a 14–16), who is the most famous *metoikos* of antiquity, being a citizen of Stagira living in Athens only as a resident alien, can be taken as convincing evidence that *metoikoi.* actually held a politically inferior status in the world of the classical *pólis*; their social status, on the other hand, may have varied from place to place and from individual to individual.

From an etymological standpoint, a *metoikos* had either changed → *oíkos* (preposition μετά/*metá* with accusative) or, from the standpoint of the new group that had accepted him, was someone who had come to live together with (*metá* with genitive) the people of this social and political grouping. The word *metoikos* is first attested in Aeschylus (Aeschyl. Pers. 319, 472 BC); but the history of the group of people categorised under the term *metoikos* goes back to the reforms of → Cleisthenes [2], who in 508/7 set up the → *phylai* and created democracy in Athens (Hdt. 6,131); in so doing, he formally excluded from the *phylai* those who lacked the required family origin and/or permanent residency, and so could not be registered as members of a deme.

II. SOCIAL AND LEGAL STATUS

The dividing line in the 5th cent. BC between visitors from foreign cities and places (ξένοι; *xénoi*) and *metoikoi* appears to have been more or less fluid. The status of *metoikos* brought with it a series of legal advantages, such as the right under certain conditions to raise a complaint before an Athenian court; the polemarch (→ Polémarchoi) was responsible for private proceedings (δίκαι ἴδιαι, *díkai ídiai*) affecting *metoikoi* or *próxenoi* (→ *proxenía*) (Aristot. Ath. pol. 58,2). For *metoikoi*, however, economic and social burdens predominated, especially the requirement for paying a regular, presumably monthly, poll-tax (μετοίκιον; *metoíkion*: one drachma for an adult male, half a drachma for an independent adult female). In addition, prosperous *metoikoi* were obliged to perform military service as hoplites (→ *hoplítai*); at the invasion of the Megarian territory at the beginning of the Peloponnesian War (431 BC) *metoikoi* provided 3,000 hoplites (Thuc. 2,31,2). Military service in particular was probably experienced by the *metoikoi* as a burden.

By the 4th cent. the granting of the status of *metoikos* had become a routine affair, and was largely the subject of a bureaucratic procedure. After continuous residency of one month, a foreign visitor or resident had to register in a → demos – usually Piraeus – as a *metoikos;* an Athenian citizen would stand as official legal representative (προστάτης; *prostátēs*) of the *metoikos*. A foreigner who failed to register was liable to civil trial (ἀπροστασίου δίκη; *aprostasíou díkē*); if a *metoikos* was accused of illicitly claiming the status of an Athenian citizen, he could be prosecuted under public law (ξενίας γραφή, → *xenías graphé*).

The negative social implications associated with the status of a *metoikos* in Athens were rendered still more severe by the fact that this status was also regularly granted to freed slaves. In Athens some Athenian *metoikoi* (such as the freeborn Syracusan immigrant Cephalus and his sons Lysias and Polemarchus, as well as the former slave → Pasion, before being granted citizenship in an unprecedented *ad hominem* procedure)

were known for their wealth, and probably associated with the citizenry on an equal footing (on Cephalus cf. Plat. Rep. 328bff.). Thus women with the status of *metoikos* were seen by some citizens as potential marriage partners; in this may reside the reason for the fact that the law on Athenian citizenship was repeatedly tightened, and the corresponding regulations vigorously enforced. The first law of this nature went back to the initiative of → Pericles, and restricted Athenian citizenship to children both of whose parents were Athenian citizens (Aristot. Ath. Pol. 26,3; Plut. Perikles 37,3). It was renewed immediately after the Peloponnesian War (*c.*400 BC; Isaios 8,43); later, marriage between citizens and foreigners was forbidden in general (Demosth. Or. 59,16, on → Neaera). A few *metoikoi* only were treated on an equal footing with Athenian citizens in matters of taxation (ἰσοτέλεια, → *isotéleia*), which meant that they were freed from the demeaning *metoíkion*; a similar privilege was the legally granted right to possess land (γῆς ἔγκτησις, *gês énktēsis*), allowed not to individuals, but to entire groups of *metoikoi*: thus the Phoenicians and Egyptians in Piraeus were granted permission to erect sanctuaries to Aphrodite/Astarte and Isis (IG II² 337,44f. = Syll.³ 280,44f.). However, most *metoikoi* could not acquire land, and were consequently excluded from agricultural activities, being active more in the areas of crafts, trade, and money-lending; they often performed low-status functions, e.g. that of a donkey-driver.

III. THE NUMBER OF METOIKOI

As the biggest *pólis* in the Greek world, Athens attracted the most foreigners: in around 313 BC the number of officially registered *metoikoi* is said to have reached virtually one half of the entire population, which had been severely curtailed shortly before (10,000 *metoikoi* and 21,000 citizens: Athen. 272c); a century earlier the proportion of *metoikoi* to the free population was perhaps higher still.

IV. METOIKOI IN POLITICS AND IN POLITICAL LITERATURE

Athenian ideology as regards the *metoikoi* remained extremely ambivalent, in spite of – and doubtless in part owing to – their economic and military significance. The expectations of Athenians in respect of *metoikoi* are clarified by an extract from the '*Hiketides*' of Euripides; here it is said of the Arcadian Parthenopaeus, who had lived in Argos as a *metoikos*, that he was never resentful or quarrelsome, that he had fought in the army and defended the country like an Argive, always rejoiced at the victories of Argos and lamented its defeats (Eur. Suppl. 889–900). This portrayal describes the behavioural norm for *metoikoi*: the *metoikos* must above all cause no strife in the community and be loyal to the *pólis*, especially in time of war. At about the same period in an anti-democratic text the equal standing of citizens and *metoikoi* was brusquely denied (Ps.-Xen. Ath. pol. 1,10–12); prejudices against the *metoikoi* found their expression in the measures of the Thirty (→ Triakonta), who in 404 BC had rich *metoikoi* killed, and their wealth seized (Xen. Hell. 2,3,21; 2,3,40). One of the victims of this reign of terror was the orator → Lysias [1], who managed with difficulty to flee to Megara; his brother Polemarchus was killed, and the family's possessions lost (Lys. 12,4–34). In the clashes that followed, many *metoikoi* fought for the restoration of democracy; some *metoikoi* were granted Athenian citizenship after the end of the fighting: the resolution of the popular assembly survives in fragmentary form (Aristot. Ath. pol. 40,2; Lys. 31,29; IG II² 10 = Syll.³ 120). In the 4th cent., Xenophon saw the presence of *metoikoi* in Athens primarily from an economic point of view: the taxes of the *metoikoi* brought the *pólis* high returns, while the *metoikoi* received no payments in return from the *pólis*; to attract more foreigners to settle as *metoikoi* in Athens, Xenophon advised that the *metoikoi* should be allowed more rights and privileges (Xen. Vect. 2). Plato on the other hand wanted residency of any individual *metoikos* restricted to 20 years, so as to prevent the permanent integration of foreigners (Plat. Leg. 850aff.); he saw an essential function of the *metoikoi* precisely in those retailing activities from which citizens should be excluded (Plat. Leg. 920a).

V. Metoikoi outside Athens

The status of the *metoikoi* is best attested for Athens, but they were by no means confined to that city. Their existence is attested in some 70 cities of the Hellenistic as well as the classical periods, although under various names (*époikos*, *kátoikos*, *pároikos*, *sýnoikos*). Sparta, on principle inimical to *xénoi*, was, not surprisingly, an exception; but the status of some *períoikoi*, as well as that of those *xénoi* known as τρόφιμοι (*tróphimoi*) (Xen. Hell. 5,3,9), is in some respects entirely comparable to that of the *metoikoi* of other regions.
→ Politeia

1 A. BOEGEHOLD, Perikles' Citizenship Law of 451/0 B.C., in: Id., A. C. SCAFURO (ed.), Athenian Identity and Civic Ideology, 1994, 57–66   2 A. CHANIOTIS, Ein diplomatischer Statthalter nimmt Rücksicht auf den verletzten Stolz zweier hellenistischer Kleinpoleis (Nagidos und Arsinoe), in: EA 21, 1993, 33–42   3 M. CLERC, Les méteques athéniens, 1893 (reprint 1979)   4 Id., s.v. Metoikoi, DS 3, 1876–1886   5 R. DUNCAN-JONES, Metic Numbers in Periclean Athens, in: Chiron 10, 1980, 101–109   6 PH. GAUTHIER, Symbola, les étrangers et la justice dans les cités grecques, 1972   7 M. H. HANSEN, Democracy & Demography, 1986; 8 HANSEN, Democracy, 116–120   9 A. H. M. JONES, Taxation in Antiquity, in: JONES, Economy, 151–186   10 E. LÉVY, Métèques et droit de résidence, in: R. LONIS (ed.), L'étranger dans le monde grec, 1987, 47–67   11 C. PHILLIPSON, The International Law and Customs of Ancient Greece and Rome, 1911, 157–179   12 S. C. TODD, The Shape of Athenian Law, 1993   13 D. WHITEHEAD, Aristotle the Metic, in: PCPhS 21, 1975, 94–99   14 Id., Immigrant Communities in the Classical Polis, in: AC 53, 1984, 47–59   15 Id., The Demes of Attica 508/7 – ca. 250 B.C.: A Political and Social Study, 1986   16 Id., The Ideology of the Athenian Metic, 1977   17 Id., The Ideology of the Athenian Metic: Some Pendants and a Reappraisal, in: PCPhS 32, 1986, 145–158   18 U. VON WILAMOWITZ-MOELLENDORF, Demotika der attischen Metöken, in: Hermes 22, 1887, 107–128, 211–259.   P.C.

Meton (Μέτων; *Métōn*).

[1] Meton came from Acragas, he was the son of one Empedocles who won a victory at Olympia in 496BC, and father of the famous philosopher → Empedocles [1]. After the overthrow of the tyrant Thrasydaeus in 472/1 Meton was a highly regarded figure in Akragas (Diog. Laert. 8,51–53; 8,72 = DIELS/KRANZ 31 A 1; Suda s.v. Empedocles = DIELS/KRANZ 31 A 2).   K.MEI.

[2] Astronomer and geometrist from Athens, son of Pausanias. At the end of. 5th cent BC, next to → Euctemon, he played a leading role in the reform of the Athenian lunisolar → calendar. The 19 year cycle was named after him (Ἐννεακαιδεκαετηρίς/*Enneakaidekaetērís*, ἐνιαυτὸς Μέτωνος/*eniautós Métōnos* or ἐνιαυτὸς μέγας/*eniautós mégas*: Diod. 12,36,2–3; he is described without being named in Geminus 8,50–56). Meton observed the solstice of 28 June 432 BC. (Ptol. syntaxis mathematica 3,1 p. 205,21). As a protest against the Sicilian expedition (→ Peloponnesian War) he is said to have feigned madness and to have set fire to his house (Plut. Nikias 13,7–8; Plut. Alkibiades 17,5–6; Ael. VH 13,12). In the lost *Monótropos* of Phrynichos and in the 'birds' of Aristophanes (Av. 992–1010) he appeared as a geometrist; the problem of the quadrature of the circle which was topical at the time, is satirized there (compare it with the detailed scholion).

F. GINZEL, Handbook of mathematical and technical chronology 2, 1911, 388f.; W. KUBITSCHEK, s.v. M. (2), RE 15, 1458–1466; A. REHM, Parapegma studies, 1941, 7–9.   W.H.

[3] In the year 280 BC M. from Tarentum is supposed to have warned his fellow citizens against calling on → Pyrrhus for help against the Romans, by acting as a drunkard to gain their attention (Plut. Pyrrhus 13,6).The historicity of this M. is disputed with regard to the feigned madness of M.[2].

P. LÉVÊQUE, Pyrrhos, 1957, 248, n. 3.   L.-M.G.

Metope

[1] In Greek building inscriptions μετόπιον/*metópion* i.e. μετόπη/*metópē* (supporting documents: [1. 29–32]), in Vitruvius *metopa* (cf. [2]) is the opening or gap, which in Greek columned buildings is framed by two triglyphs (→ triglyphos) in a Doric → Frieze. In wooden buildings metopes were openings next to the projecting beam ends that were finished as carved triglyphs and probably served to ventilate the roof truss. The space between the triglyphs was already closed up in early Greek temple buildings with panels made from clay or stone which were decorated with painted designs or

reliefs. The metope now changed conceptually from a space between two triglyphs to a representational structural element enclosing this space. Initially it was square; later it became rectangular, slightly higher than wide. The limestone reliefs of the peripteral temple at Mycenae (late 7th cent. BC) and the painted clay metopes from Thermus (early 6th cent. BC) rank among the oldest preserved metopes of this kind. Relief-work on metopes reached its high-point with the temple of Zeus at → Olympia and the → Parthenon on the Acropolis in Athens (→ Architectural sculpture).

1 EBERT   2 H. NOHL, Index Vitruvianus, 1876 (repr. 1983), s.v. μετόπη.

H. KÄHLER, Das griechische Metopen-Bild, 1949; D. MERTENS, Der Tempel von Segesta und die dorische Tempelbaukunst des griechischen Westens in klassischer Zeit, 1984, Index s.v. M; W. MÜLLER-WIENER, Griechisches Bauwesen in der Antike, 1988, Index s.v. M.   C.HÖ.

[2] (Μετώπη; *Metópē*). River in the area around → Stymphalus in Arcadia; cannot be located more precisely. References: Pind. Ol. 6,84; Callim. H.. 1,26; Ael. Var. 2,33.

H. LAMER, E. MEYER, s.v. M. (1), RE 15, 1466f.   C.L.
E.MEY.

Metragyrtai (Μητραγύρται; *Mētragýrtai*). Wandering 'beggars of the *Métēr*' (according to Aristot. rhet. 1405a 20f. and later sources; older terms are *kýbēbos*: Semonides frag. 36 WEST; *agersikýbēlis*: Kratinos frag. 66 PCG); they spread and and carried out the rituals of the *Métēr*/→ Kybele by dancing ecstatically to the sound of the *týmpana* and *kýmbala* followed by begging, apparently as early as the 7th century BC in Greece, later also in Rome (→ Mater magna, compare. e. g. Cic. leg. 2,40). Castration probably only took place occasionally (e.g.. Anth. Pal. 6,218; compare. Plut. Nikias 13,3f.). A tale which traces the building of the Athenian shrine of the *Métēr*, the *Mētróon*, to the killing of one of the Metragyrtai (e.g. Jul. or. 5,159a; a notable variation in schol. Aristoph. Plut. 431), scarcely appears to be historical fact.

In the time of the emperors the → Syria Dea was also worshipped by this type of wandering beggar (Pseudo.-Lukian. Lukios 35ff.; Apul. met. 8,24). An inscription from Syria [2. 59 No. 68; 1. Vol. 3, 347–349] records the income of one of her 'servants'.

→ Cybele; → Mater Magna

1 F. BÖMER, Investigation into the Religion of the Slaves in Greece and Rome, Vol. 3, 1961, 347–349; Vol. 4, 1963, 10–17, 122, 131   2 CH. FOSSEY, Syrian Inscriptions, in: BCH 21, 1897, 39–65.

PH. BORGEAUD, The Mother of the Gods, 1996; W. BURKERT, Classical Mysteries, ³1994, 40; R. PARKER, Athenian Religion, 1996, 189–193.   T.H.

Metre
I. PRELIMINARY REMARK   II. MESOPOTAMIA
III. EGYPT   IV. OLD TESTAMENT AND UGARIT
V. GREEK   VI. LATIN   VII. BYZANTINE

I. PRELIMINARY REMARK
Originally sung poetry, often accompanied by dance, metric literature was obviously subject to other formative conditions than poetry intended from the outset for spoken presentation or for reading. Texts of such kinds still show traces of their earlier sound form (→ Music). Accordingly the form ranged from simple 'melodic lines of sound', as can be presumed for the ancient Orient and Israel (*parallelismus membrorum*, strophic poetry, sometimes with rhythmic accent order, congruence of form and language syntax) to the complicated 'rhythmic-melodic sound strophes' of Greek → lyric poetry (quantitative rhythms with an abundance of verse and strophic forms with strict responsion, often incongruence of form and syntactic division). From the mid 5th cent. BC the transformation of the poetic metre by musical → rhythm can be observed.

F.Z. J.LE.

II. MESOPOTAMIA
For Akkadian as a reconstructed dead language, arguments from the language itself and more rarely also from orthography permit to infer an expiratory, i.e. a heavy stress accent, which among other things does not allow a sequence of three short syllables and drops the vowel of the middle syllable. The main stress is on the penultimate syllable if it is long, otherwise on the antepenultimate one. The end of the sentence is also mostly emphasized through a pause accent on the syllable before last. As poetic texts, in comparison with prose, do not show any significant orthographical particularities from which metrically conditioned accent shifts could be deduced, all investigations on metre take as their starting-point the layout of the cuneiform texts, which always shows the ending of lines and often also caesuras (according to the pattern a – b | c – d in four-line verses or a – b | c in three-line verses) or even single cola. As enjambement remains the exception, the line mostly ends on a pause (a so-called trochaic line ending); starting from this fact, scholars look at the interior of the line too, counting syllables and looking for metres of a classical-antiquity type, from which conclusions are again drawn with regard to metrically determined unusual stresses (*Gilgámeš*, *kakkábu* instead of the prose forms *Gílgameš*, *kákkabu*). But the significantly varying length of individual lines in one and the same epic clearly suggests that there is no regularly recurring and predictable pattern of a syllable-counting, accentuating or quantifying kind in Akkadian poetry. An alternative approach to describing Akkadian poetry therefore argues from colotaxy instead of colometry, allowing individual cola to be understood as prose.

At present it is still hard to reconstruct the metre of Sumeric texts [1].

Metrical terms

Acephalia, acephalic: absence of a metric element at the beginning of a line

Anaclasis: exchange of two *elementa* that follow each other consecutively (particularly in the ionicus)

Antepaenultima (sc. *syllaba*): third last syllable of a word

Aphaeresis: loss of the second vowel when two vowels come together at a word boundary (only relevant in Latin prosody)

Arsis: 'rising', in Greek metrical theory mostly the shorter part of a foot, in Roman metrical theory always the first part of a foot

Base, Aeolic: the first two syllables in an Aeolic line. In Greece and still in the early Phalaeceans of Catullus one of them (rarely both) can be short; from Horace on, always in the stereotyped form with two longs

Brevis in longo: licence to fill in a long element with a short syllable (symbol for the end of a period)

Caesura: preferred but not obligatory word ending in the middle of a foot (see diaeresis).

Catalexis, catalectic: absence of a metric element at the end of a line

Colon: metrical unit that is larger than a metron and smaller than a line (e.g. half of the hexameter up to the caesura); between two cola no period end occurs

Diaeresis: preferred or (as in the case of the middle diaeresis in the pentameter) obligatory word ending between two metres, feet or cola without a period end. If the word ending is merely preferred, it is not functionally different from the caesura

Elementum anceps: Element that can be occupied either by a short or a long syllable (sometimes also by a double short)

Elementum (also: **Locus**): smallest unit in a metre; as an abstract entity, it is to be distinguished from the actual syllable with which it is filled. An *elementum longum* requires a long syllable while an *elementum breve* demands a short syllable; in some metres, *elementa longa* and (more rarely) *brevia* can also be filled with a double short

Elision: loss of the first vowel when two vowels come together at the word boundary; barely distinguishable in Latin metre from synaloepha

Foot: smallest rhythmic unit, consisting of arsis and thesis

Hephthemimeres: caesura after seven half-feet

Hiatus: coming together of two vowels at the word boundary without slurring occurring

Ictus (Lat. *ictus*, 'beat'): artificial word stress in the recitation of quantitative verse at a particular point or points of the foot without taking account of the natural word stress so as also to make the line pattern audible even without quantitative articulation. Only introduced into recitation practice in the modern period; the term has been used since G. HERMANN. The only thing comparable (but not identical) in Antiquity is scansion (see below), which was however limited to metrical teaching

Metre: a) verse type; b) Building block of lines consisting of one or two feet

Paenultima (sc. *syllaba*): second last syllable of a word

Penthemimeres: caesura after five half-feet

Period: metrical unit (mostly a line, but in the Greek poets of choral lyric it sometimes takes up several book lines); at its end the word ending is obligatory and a hiatus or *brevis in longo* can occur

Prosody (Greek literally 'song sung to…'): originally the term for the word accent or the theory of word accent; already extended in antiquity into a comprehensive term for articulation phenomena (quantity, slurring, aspiration etc.)

Scansion (from Lat. *scandere*, 'stride'; cf. arsis and thesis): didactic breaking down of a verse into metra and feet for analytical and teaching purposes

Stichic (from Greek *stíchos*, 'verse line '): line-by-line repetition of a metre

Synaloepha: slurring of two vowels at the word boundary; barely distinguishable in Latin metre from elision

Synaphia: prosodic continuity, particularly two verse lines following each other without a period end in between

Synizesis: slurring of two vowels in the interior of a word resulting in one syllable

Thesis: 'setting down', in Greek metric theory mostly the longer part of the line foot, in Roman metric theory always the second part of the line foot   M.L.W.

1 D. O. Edzard, s.v. Metrik, RLA 8, 148f.   2 K. Hek-ker, Untersuchungen zur akkadischen Epik, 1974, 101–169   3 W. von Soden, Untersuchungen zur babyloni-schen Metrik, I., in: ZA 71, 1981/82, 161–204; II., in: ZA 74, 1984, 213–234   4 M. L. West, Akkadian Poetry: Metre and Performance, in: Iraq 59, 1997, 175–187
                                                                                    K.HE.

III. Egypt

For ancient Egypt the analysis of metre is still highly contentious although structuring of elevated literature is in itself plausible and is occasionally marked in the MSS with red line points. A key problem is the absence of vowels in the script that makes it impossible directly to count the syllables. Aside from researchers who pri-marily wish to reconstruct the poetic texts through par-allelism [1], there are also theories that apply strict met-ric rules. Generally an accentuating, non-quantitative metre is assumed in keeping with the 'expiratory' accent (strong emphasis on the main syllable while neglecting the auxiliary syllables/accents) of ancient Egyptian. The most common basic line pattern would probably be the two-liner but the existence of units of three is highly probable.

The approach by Fecht [2] is based on the recon-struction of accent units (cola) that are constituted through the reconstructed rules of historical phonol-ogy: according to this, two or three cola would consti-tute a line, formations with only one colon being rare and those with four cola practically non-existent. The basis for metre is hence the accent of the sentence, and the elementary line formation is very simple. In this theory, artful poetry only develops on the higher level as groups of lines give rise to structures that are numeri-cally significant. A problem with this theory is its fre-quent disregard for the line points. Suggestions for modification water down the importance of the accent units by introducing 'values' and in this way permitting lines that would not have been permissible in Fecht's theory as single-footers, i.e. lines with only one primary accent [5]. On the other hand, new research – while on the whole respecting traditional line points – is opening up the possibility of setting up criteria governing for which syntactic structures single-footed lines are per-missible [6].

Opposed to this is the theory of Mathieu who on the basis of rather intuitively constituted rules assumes as the basic pattern the heptametric and the enneame-tric distichon [3]. Exceptions and *ad hoc* explanations render this approach quite problematical. It is plausible that Coptic poetic texts partly continue the tradition of Egyptian metre, but they are themselves difficult to ana-lyze.

1 G. Burkard, Überlegungen zur Form der ägyptischen Literatur, 1993   2 G. Fecht, The Structural Principle of Ancient Egyptian Elevated Language, in: J. C. de Moor (ed.), Verse in Ancient Near Eastern Prose, 1993, 69–94   3 B. Mathieu, Études de métrique Égyptienne I–III, in: Rev. d'Égyptologie 39, 1988, 63–82; 41, 1990, 127–141; 45, 1994, 139–154   4 T. Säve-Söderbergh, Studies in the Coptic Manichean Psalm-Book, 1949   5 I. Shirun, Parallelismus Membrorum und Vers, in: J. Assmann (ed.) Fragen an die altägyptischen Literatur, 1977, 463–92   6 N. Tacke, Verspunkte als Gliederungsmittel in ramessi-dischen Schülerhandschriften, 2001.
                                                                                    JO.QU.

IV. Old Testament and Ugarit

With respect to ancient Hebrew poetry, scholars by and large assume an accentuating metre. The stress is usually on the last (ultimate) syllable of the word, fre-quently on second last (penultimate) and rarely on the third last (antepenultimate). This gives rise on many occasions to 'stichoi' (→ Stichometry) in a rhythm of two and three that as elements of the *parallelismus membrorum* form the poetic verse, which does not have to be identical with the numerical verse count of the Hebrew Bible. Parallelisms of structure 2+2, 3+3 or 3+2 are common. The latter is called a *Qinah*-metre and is a stylistic element of lament literature. As the poetic texts hardly ever keep to only one metre, the metre is repeat-edly the subject of general linguistic and literary-histori-cal discussions.

The existence and nature of a system of metre in the Ugaritic poetic texts are a matter of debate. The method of colometry or stichometry determines the length of the poetic units by counting the consonants and in this way achieves average line lengths and symmetrical (par-allel) verse structures. The relationship between Ugari-tic and Hebrew metre is unclear to a large extent.
→ Colometry; → Literature

1 O. Loretz, I. Kottsieper, Colometry in Ugaritic and Biblical Poetry, 1987   2 W. G. E. Watson, Classical Hebrew Poetry. A Guide to Its Techniques, 1986.   TH.PO.

V. Greek
A. General   B. Basic terms   C. Prosody
D. Metres   E. Ancient theory   F. Reception

A. General

From the beginnings to the early Byzantine period, Greek metre was quantifying, i.e. based on sequences of long and short syllables. From the late Hellenistic peri-od onwards, when the original purely musical word stress of Greek ('musical stress'; → Accent) gradually developed a dynamic, i.e. expiratory (stress) compo-nent, it began to play a subsidiary role in versification in the works of many poets, but it was not until the 4th or 5th cent. AD that verses were written in which only the stresses and not the quantities were regulated.

The quantitative principle goes back to the Indo-European period. Vedic verse theory heeds prosodic rules that are very similar to those of Greek verse theory and uses metres that show a clear relationship with sev-eral Greek metres (especially with those of Aeolic verses) [6]. It appears that originally the number of syl-lables in the verse was fixed but their quantities were prescribed only for the clausula. In Greek, the quan-tities were fixed proceeding from the end to the begin-ning of the line as early as the prehistoric period [8]. As

Table with an overview of Greek and Latin metre

⏑	short element/short syllable
–	long element/long syllable
×	elementum anceps (short or long syllable)
⏑⏑	long element that can be resolved into two short ones
⏓⏓	elementum biceps (double short that can be represented by a long syllable)
∘ ∘	Aeolic base (one of the two syllables can be short)
∧	missing element (initial: acephalia; final: catalexis)
¦	frequent word ending
|	required word ending
‖	end of period
‖‖	end of strophe
⁀	bridge (forbidden word ending)

Feet and metra

⏑ –	ia	iambus (metron: ×–⏑–)
– ⏑	tro	trochaeus (metron: –⏑–×)
– ⏑ ⏑	da	dactylus (= metron)
– –	spo	spondeus (not metron-creating)
⏑ ⏑ –	an	anapaest (metron: ⏑⏑–⏑⏑–)
⏑ – –	ba	baccheus (= metron)
– ⏑ –	cr	creticus (= metron)
⏑ ⏑ – –	io	ionicus (a minore; = metron)
– ⏑ ⏑ –	cho	choriambus (= metron)

Basic metres

dactylic hexameter: 6da∧

– ⏓⏓ – ⏓⏓ – ⏓⏓ – ⏓⏓ – – –

pentameter – ⏓⏓ – ⏓⏓ – | – ⏑ ⏑ – ⏑ ⏑ –

iambic trimeter: 3ia ×–⏑– ×–⏑– ×–⏑–

Common patterns of Aeolic metre

∘∘–⏑⏑–⏑–	Glyconeus (gl)
∘∘–⏑⏑–⏑⏑–⏑–	Asclepiadeus (ascl = gl^c)
∘∘–⏑⏑––	Pherecrateus (pher = gl∧)
∘∘–⏑⏑–⏑––	Hipponacteus (hipp)

Sapphic strophe (Latin form with stereotyped Aeolic base)

–⏑––⏑⏑–⏑––	Sapphic hendecasyllable
–⏑––⏑⏑–⏑––	(repeated
–⏑––⏑⏑–⏑––	(repeated)
–⏑⏑––	Adoneus

Alcaeic strophe (Latin form with stereotyped Aeolic base, ancipitia mostly long)

×–⏑––⏑⏑–⏑–	Alcaeic hendecasyllable
×–⏑––⏑⏑–⏑–	(repeated)
×–⏑––⏑––	Alcaeic enneasyllable
–⏑⏑–⏑⏑–⏑––	Alcaeic decasyllable

Phalaecean hendecasyllable (with stereotyped base; gl ba)

–––⏑⏑–⏑–⏑––

J.LE.

several set formulae are extant in Homer that (according to linguistic criteria) go back to the 14th or 15th cent. BC, we can assume that the development of the epic hexameter had been to a large extent completed in this period. Even if several idiosyncratic rhythms may have been adopted from foreign peoples (creticus: Minoan?; dochmius: Balkan?), it is plausible that the other Greek verse measures emerged from the internal development of inherited prototypes.

B. Basic terms

Greek verse measures are analysed according to feet (e.g. dactylic: –⏑ ⏑), metra (e.g. iambic: ×–⏑–), cola, lines (i.e. periods) and strophes. In some rhythms, foot and metron are identical, in others (iambus, trochaeus, anapaest) a metron comprises two feet; an iambic 'trimetre' therefore has six feet. The colon is a metric phrase of up to about twelve syllables that can be recognized by its characteristic sequence of long and short syllables. One characteristic of Greek poetry is that it is based on a foundation of common cola even when these can be combined in many and varied ways; at times they are delineated through word separation and relatively frequent syntactic pauses.

The basic independent unit of metric composition is the line or the period (consisting of one or several cola): its boundaries must coincide with word boundaries. Similarly, *synápheia* (prosodic continuity, see below) applies within the period but is disrupted at the end of the line or period. The final position of each period (long according to the nominal time value) can be occupied either by a long or by a short syllable (*brevis in longo*) because of the metric pause between the periods. In 'stichic' verse, single lines of a certain form (e.g. iambic trimetres or epic hexameters) are endlessly repeated; larger repeated units (strophes) are on the other hand constructed in sung poetry through the compilation of similar or different periods. In choral lyric verse from Stesichorus (around 550 BC) on, strophes were usually arranged in triads of the AAB type: two strophes of a corresponding metric form (that were sung to the same melody) were followed by a third strophe of a different kind. Whilst in the case of the non-dramatic poets the entire structure repeated itself (AAB AAB ...), in drama the usual sequence is however AA BB CC(D) or something similar.

C. Prosody

In Greek, almost all vowels had a fixed quantity, either long or short. A syllable was long if it contained a long vowel (or diphthong) but also if it was closed by a consonant, even if the vowel was short. Thus, in the line σκότος ἐμὸν φάος (*skótos emòn pháos*) all the vowels are short, the syllables μον and ος (at the end of the line) are however long; the syllable τος of σκότος, on the other hand, is not long because the syllables are separated as σκό-το-σε-μον (*skó-to-se-mon*) because of the effect of *synápheia* in the interior of the line. With two consecutive consonants, the syllable separation normally falls between them (including the consonants that are represented by the letters ζ ξ ψ = s+d, k+s, p+s), with the exception that combinations of plosive + liquid/nasal (πλ, τρ, κν etc., so-called *muta cum liquida*) are often regarded as inseparable, especially in Attic metres, which is why πα-τρί/*pa-trí* (˘ ˘) instead of πατ-ρί/*pat-rí* (‒˘) applies (so-called *correptio Attica*). In epic, elegy and part of the lyric, a long vowel or a diphthong can be shortened before another vowel, particularly at the end of the word, e.g. in Hom. Od. 1,2 πλάγχθη ἐπεί/ *plángchthĕ epeí* (so-called *correptio epica*; also Vedic). On further details of → prosody cf. [9. 7–18].

D. METRES

1. GENERAL RULES   2. HEXAMETER AND PENTAMETER   3. IAMBS, TROCHEES, ANAPAESTS 4. OLD LYRIC   5. STAGE LYRIC   6. LATER LYRIC 7. DECLINE OF THE QUANTITATIVE METRE

1. GENERAL RULES

Despite all the differences, Greek metres are generally based on the following principles: each line is characterized by a certain number of set long positions (*loci principes*) that are separated from each other either by two short positions or by a short position or by an *anceps* (i.e. either long or short). Each *princeps* is normally filled in by a long syllable but this can in some metres be replaced by two short ones. Each *princeps* must have at least one short position beside it but this can become unclear if two short positions are replaced by one long syllable (‾˘ = *biceps*). These principles mean that the basic rhythmic movements are ... ‒˘˘‒ ˘˘‒... and ... ‒˘‒×‒˘‒ ... (symmetrical rhythms) or a combination of these two ... ‒˘˘‒×‒˘‒ ... and. ‒˘‒× ‒˘˘‒ ... (asymmetrical rhythms). The start of each sequence can be either 'rising' (‖×‒˘ or ‖˘˘‒) or 'falling' (‖ ‒˘) and it can end either 'blunt' (˘‒‖) or 'pendant' (˘ ‒×‖).

The alternation of these alternatives sometimes has the function of differentiating one line from another one within a strophe. In lines in which the rhythm is regular enough for analysis according to metres (e.g. iambic¹×‒˘‒²×‒˘‒..., trochaic ¹‒˘‒×²‒˘‒×...), the last metre of the period is often shorter by one or two syllables: the line shows catalexis or is catalectic. A line without shortening of such kind is called acatalectic. Thus, × ‒˘‒×‒˘‒˘‒‖ is a catalectic iambic trimeter (3ia₍ₐ₎) whilst ‒˘‒×‒˘‒×‒˘‒˘‒⸗ is a catalectic trochaic tetrameter (4tr₍ₐ₎).

In certain lyric forms it is possible to alternate between ‒˘ and ˘‒ so that e.g. ⤫‒˘˘ (an iambic metron) can be regarded as interchangeable with ‒˘˘ ‒ (choriambus); this is called anaclasis and reflects musical syncopation. The ionic dimeter ¹˘ ˘‒‒²˘ ˘‒‒ through anaclasis becomes an anacreonteus ˘˘‒˘‒˘ ‒‒ which can no longer be divided into two equal metres.

Syntactical segments frequently but not inevitably coincide with metrical segments. Meaning-related pauses rarely occur before the end of the line or shortly before or after a caesura (= colon pause inside the line at which the word ending is regular). Also, a caesura or line ending normally must not separate a clitic word (prepositions, καί, με etc.) from the word it is connected with.

2. HEXAMETER AND PENTAMETER

Most Greek poetry is written in stichic verses, above all in the dactylic hexameter (standard for → epic and → didactic poetry) and in the iambic trimeter (the usual spoken-dialogue metre in drama). The hexameter comprises six dactylic feet or metra of the form ‒ ‾˘ (*princeps* + *biceps*) whose last one is catalectic (‒ ⤫). It is relatively rare to fill the fifth *biceps* with a long syllable, whilst word separation within the fourth *biceps* is even rarer (so-called 'Hermann's Bridge'). In the third foot, there is always a caesura (³‒| ‾˘   or   ³‒˘ | ˘) unless a long word stretches beyond this foot to include the fourth *princeps* (³‒ ‾˘⁴‒| ‾˘). Through the caesura the line is divided effectively into two balanced cola: ‒ ‾˘‒ ‾˘‒| ‾˘‒ ‾˘‒ ‾˘‒×| or ‒ ‾˘‒ ‾˘‒˘ | ˘‒ ‾˘‒ ‾˘‒×⤫.

These cola are also to be encountered independently of this in other metres and constitute the actual structural units; the traditional formulae of the epic are for the most part constructed in such a way that they either fill the one or the other colon.

Homeric verse shows a greater degree of prosodic freedom than any other form of Greek poetry: this includes the lengthening of vowels in certain classes of words so that they fit into the metre, hiatus (omission of the elision of vowels) as well as the lengthening of non-plosive consonants in the initial or final position (λ μ ν ρ σ) in order to close and thereby lengthen the preceding syllable (normally in the *princeps*; e.g. Hom. Il. 9,520 ἄνδρας δὲ (λ)λίσσεσθαι, *ándras de (l)líssesthai*). Many apparent irregularities are based on language changes dating from the pre-Homeric tradition and disappear when the older forms are restored. Later poets refined the technique of versification.

The elegiac distich was used in antiquity for various purposes, in particular for inscriptions and epigrams. It consists of a hexameter followed by a so-called pentameter (2×2½ feet) with two strictly distinct hemiepes-cola, ‒ ‾˘‒ ‾˘‒| ‒˘˘‒˘˘‒|. The caesura is unchanging, and the *bicipitia* (˘ ˘) in the second colon must always be bisyllabic.

3. IAMBS, TROCHEES, ANAPAESTS

The iambic trimeter (3ia) [3] (main types: Ionic iambus and drama) normally has a caesura in the third foot or else in the fourth foot:×‒˘‒×⫫ ‒˘: ‒×‒˘‒‖. As in the hexameter, this caesura divides the line into two balanced but not completely identical cola, one with a rising and the other with a falling arsis. In the Ionic iambus and in tragedy (but not in comedy), each line that does not have a caesura in the third or fourth foot has a caesura at the end of the third foot, usually with elision; and the *anceps* of the third metron does not permit a long final syllable of a word of two or more syllables ('Porson's Law'), as is the case e.g. in Menander's Dyskolos 1: τῆς Ἀττικῆς νομίζετ᾽ εἶναι τὸν τόπον. Each of the first five *princeps* positions can be resolved (× ⏗ ⏖ ⏗ ⏗ ...): Whilst the poets before Euripides used this freedom only sparingly, the latter makes increasing use of it in his later plays. In drama each of the first five feet can take the form of an anapaest (⏑ ⏑ –), although this is rare outside comedy and is limited in tragedy to the first foot (except when a proper noun has to be fitted in the line).

The catalectic trochaic tetrameter (likewise in iambus and drama) has similar characteristics: it resembles an iambic trimeter with the prefix – ⏑ – and a caesura normally after the second metron. → Hipponax and Old Comedy also use a catalectic iambic tetrameter. Hipponax and his imitators also regularly use 'choliambic' or 'scazonic' versions of 3ia and 4tr₍ₓ₎ in which the short penultimate position of the line is replaced by a completely false-sounding, 'scazonic' long one (choliambus = scazon): ἐμοὶ γὰρ οὐκ ἔδωκας οὔτε κω χλαῖναν (Hipponax 34,1).

The anapaest is a characteristic metre of drama, in comedy particularly in catalectic tetrametres: ‾‾ – ‾‾ –| ‾‾ – ‾‾ –| ‾‾ – ‾‾ –|⏑ ⏑ –⏗. The *principes* can be split, in which case the *bicipitia* are usually contracted: |⏓ ⏑ ⏓⏑–|. In tragedy the chorus and others marched to long sequences of anapaestic metres with catalexis at irregular intervals; each metre corresponded with a double step.

4. OLD LYRIC

Lyric (i.e. sung) verse of the 7th cent. BC shows an amazing regional diversity. The Lesbian lyric of → Sappho and of → Alcaeus [4] appears to be the most archaic (similarities to Vedic metres are obvious here): here the substitution of ⏑ ⏑ by – and vice versa is avoided so that the number of syllables per line is unchanging. In some metres, the line begins with two *ancipitia*, the so-called 'Aeolic base'. The songs are composed in short strophes of 2–4 lines. The cola are for the most part asymmetrical, as for instance the glyconeus ×× – ⏑ ⏑ – ⏑ – and its catalectic equivalent, the pherecrateus ×× – ⏑ ⏑ – –. In the Epodes of the Ionian → Archilochus we find on the other hand only symmetrical elements like hexameters, hemiepes (D; – ⏑ ⏑ – ⏑ ⏑ –) 4da, 4da₍ₓ₎, 3ia, 2ia, penthemimeres (× – ⏑ – ×) and ithyphallicus (– ⏑ – ⏑ – –) that are variously combined into simple stanzas of 2–3 lines.

The Doric choral lyric from → Alkman (7th cent. BC) onwards is characterized by far longer strophes: writers use not just Aeolic but also dactylic and other symmetrical cola; each song had a unique metrical pattern. The triadically structured lyric epics of → Stesichorus were mainly dactylic in rhythm but in several, iambic-trochaic cola are also encountered, especially at the end of the period. This mixture points forward to the 'dactylo-epitritic' verse type was frequently used by → Pindarus and → Bacchylides; it can for the most part be divided into the units d (– ⏑ ⏑ –), D (– ⏑ ⏑ – ⏑ ⏑ –), D² (– ⏑ ⏑ – ⏑ ⏑ – ⏑ ⏑ –), e (– ⏑ –) and E (– ⏑ – × – ⏑ –), which are

put together with or without a connecting syllable (usually long) before, between or after the units. Otherwise these poets mainly use cola of an Aeolic type that are combined into often highly complex strophic structures. The *princeps* in such cola now sometimes allows for resolution whilst the Aeolic Base assumes a form that is represented as ∘ ∘, meaning that at least one of the two positions has to be filled by a long syllable.

5. STAGE LYRIC

The line measures of the tragic Greek lyric can be sub-divided into eight categories: iambic-trochaic, cretic-paeonic, dochmiac, Aeoliac, anapaestic, ionic, dactylic, dactylo-epitritic. Sometimes different types are combined with each other, especially in the long astrophic monodies and lyric dialogues that characterize the late plays of Sophocles and Euripides. With regard to the first three of the above-mentioned categories, it should be noted that in lyric iambs the metre can not only appear in the form × – ⏑ – but also as – ⏑ – (creticus, ₍ₓ₎ia), ⏑ – – (baccheus, ia₍ₓ₎) or – – (spondeus, ₍ₓ₎ia₍ₓ₎). In these 'syncopated' metres, the missing short ones have to be absorbed in the adjacent *princeps* and in this way give it a time value of three instead of two shorts; ancient theory acknowledged such τρίσημα (*trísēma*, three-time lengths) and noted them with the symbol ⌐ or ⌐. The creticus of the iambic lyric (⌐ ⏑ –) is therefore distinguished from the cretic- paeonic lyric (– ⏑ –) whose metre corresponds with only five, not six short ones; the 'paeon' is a resolved creticus, e.g. – ⏑ ⏑ ⏑. Aristophanes often uses cretic-paeonic tetrametres. The dochmius, a typically tragic metre with an urging or emotional tone, is based on the curious metre ⏑ – – ⏑ – from which – through resolution or cramming of a long syllable into a short position – numerous variations can be created.

6. LATER LYRIC

Tragic lyric verse is (like the lyric verse of Pindar) often complex and difficult to analyse metrically. After 400 BC poets tended to simplify and narrow the spectrum of metres still in use. While some types (e.g. the dactylic lyric metre and the dochmius) stopped being used, others became stereotyped. There were hardly any significant innovations. The Alexandrian poets imitated metres of archaic models (Archilochus, Hipponax, the Lesbian poets Sappho and Alcaeus) and at times combined them in new ways, but they limited themselves to stichic use or short, clearly structured stanzas. The most important stichic metres (the dactylic hexameter, the elegiac distich and the iambic trimeter) became increasingly predominant in Greek poetry. Two lyric forms that continued to be popular were the hemiamb (2ia₍ₓ₎) and the anacreonteus; both, strophic or non-strophic, were used extensively in the Ps.-Anacreontea.

7. DECLINE OF THE QUANTITATIVE METRE

The influence of the new dynamic word stress on line structure can be discerned for the first time in the Hellenistic elegy, where an increasing tendency to finish a pentameter not with a stressed syllable is manifest. Before AD 100 we find occasional poets who regularly prefer a stress on the penultimate syllable of the line, e.g. this always occurs with → Babrius in his choliambs. Restrictions with regard to the accent can be observed in many different ways in the hexameters of → Nonnus and his successors. Although their prosody continues to be carefully composed, in the language of their time the old distinction between long and short syllables was barely noticeable any more because of the new opposition between stressed and unstressed syllables. Less educated poets from the 3rd cent.AD onwards wrongly treated stressed short syllables as long or unstressed long syllables as short.

E. ANCIENT THEORY

The study of metre commenced in the time of the Sophists (2nd half of the 5th cent. BC). Herodotus was already able to use terms like ἐν ἰάμβωι τριμέτρωι and ἑξαμέτρωι τόνωι ('in a trimetric iambus'; 'in the hexametric measure'). The Peripatetics and Alexandrians further developed technical vocabulary and analytical methods [11. 58–79] (→ Colometry). Our knowledge of ancient metrical theory mainly stems from writers of the Roman and Byzantine period, especially from the Epitome of → Hephaistion [4]. The ancient metricians made numerous astute observations but many basic facts also escaped them that were only discovered when scholars like A. BOECKH and G. HERMANN set themselves free from traditional theory. New insights required the introduction of new metrical *termini technici* that are used today along with many old terms.

F. RECEPTION

Greek metres decisively influenced the Latin ones and almost completely superseded local measures (see below VI.). The imitation of Classical metres in the national-language literatures of Europe was primarily based on Latin and not on Greek models [4]. The popularity of the Ps.-Anacreontea led from the 17th cent. onwards in various countries to imitation with more or less faithfulness to the line measures of the original (→ Anacreontics), whilst Abraham COWLEY (1656) and numerous imitators took Pindar as the authority for a new type of irregular wide-ranging poetry (that is known in English by the term 'Pindarics'), as KLOPSTOCK and the *Sturm und Drang* poets did in the 18th cent. in Germany [4. 280].

→ Lyric; → Metric symbols; → Music; → Phonetics; → Prosody; → Rhythmics; → Stichometry; → METRE

1 A. M. DALE, The Lyric Metres of Greek Drama, ²1968 2 Ead., Metrical Analyses of Tragic Choruses (BICS Suppl. 21), 1971–1983 3 J. DESCROIX, Le trimètre iambique, 1931 4 M.L. GASPAROV, A History of European Versification, 1996 5 P. MAAS, Greek Metre, 1962 6 A. MEILLET, Les origines indo-européennes des mètres grecs, 1923 7 L.P.E. PARKER, The Songs of Aristophanes, 1997 8 M. L. WEST, Indo-European Metre, in: Glotta 51, 1973, 161–187 9 Ibid., Greek Metre, 1982 10 Ibid., Introduction to Greek Metre, 1987 11 U. v. WILAMOWITZ-MOELLENDORFF, Griechische Verskunst, 1921

D. KORZENIEWSKI, Griechische Metrik, 1968; C. M. J. SICKING, Griechische Verslehre, 1993; B. SNELL, Griechische Metrik, ⁴1982; A. WIFSTRAND, Von Kallimachos zu Nonnos, 1933; T. ZIELIŃSKI, Tragudomenon Libri Tres, 1925.   M.L.W.

VI. LATIN
A. GENERAL B. PROSODY C. METRES
D. ANCIENT THEORY E. RECEPTION

A. GENERAL

The Latin metre has been a conscious imitation of the Greek since the late 3rd cent. BC; this was possible because the prosodic basis of the Greek metre (set vocal quantities, lengthening of the syllable through consonants following the vowel as the 'Position length', slurrings) also in principle existed in Latin [4; 21]. Of the Old Italian line measures, only the Saturnian used by → Livius [III 1] Andronicus and → Naevius [I 1] that → Ennius [1] finally replaced with the hexameter according to the Greek model is comprehensible in a literary sense; it is still hardly possible to clarify whether the Saturnian (formation principle contentious) was purely quantitative or whether other structural features were additionally or even primarily decisive here (overview in [5]).

B. PROSODY
1. DIFFERENCES FROM GREEK 2. HISTORICAL DEVELOPMENT 3. METRE AND WORD ACCENT

1. DIFFERENCES FROM GREEK

Despite the common basic rules, Latin prosody clearly deviates from the Greek in several points: *muta cum liquida* (e.g. *tr*) spanning the word boundary never involves positional lengthening (always *essĕ tristem*), in Old Latin the same applies in the interior of the word. Furthermore, *s*+consonant in initial position (*essĕ scelus*) does not lead to positional lengthening in Plautus; in later poetry such a word beginning is avoided after a short vowel [10]. With the word forms *est* and *es* slurring resulting in aphaeresis occurs (*Latino est > Latinost*); an *-m* at the end of the word was obviously pronounced so weakly before a vowel that slurring took place just as when two vowels met (*bell(um) et*).

2. HISTORICAL DEVELOPMENT

As a result of the canonizing (→ Canon [1]) of Augustan and post-Augustan literature, the prosody that we encounter in the poems of this period gained acceptance in the tradition as the 'normal' one. From the oldest poetry until this period a clear development of the prosodic rules can be observed, but it is hard to determine in detail what goes back to the (undeniable) change in living-speech articulation and what can be traced back to standardization processes of the poets. The most important particularities of the time until → Lucretius [III 1] are: an iambic syllable sequence can be measured short ('iambic shortening'), if the word stress falls on the first syllable (*ăpŭd forum*) or follows the iambus directly (*vŏlŭptátem*). The letter *s* at the end of the word can, after a short vowel, be prosodically omitted before a consonant (*opu' fuit*), and when followed by *est* or *es*, lead to aphaeresis (*ausus est*, see above). A long final vowel can before a word beginning with a vowel can be shortened as in the Greek, if it results in a double short (*quĭ amat*; prosodic hiatus). Real hiatuses also occur, and synizesis is used more freely (*mẽo, cũĩus*).

After Virgil and Ovid, the prosodic consequences of the further development of the living language, particularly the very significant fading of the syllable quantities as early as the 3rd cent. AD, only very occasionally finds its way into literary prosody (e.g. final -*o* measured short except in the dative and ablative, [19]). The growing tension after the 1st cent. AD between living prosody and literary tradition is probably also partly responsible for the fact that between the early 2nd cent. (→ Iuvenalis) and the time of Diocletian (around 300) – apart from individual products and scholarly poetry – no noteworthy Latin poetic literature was written [24]; an idea of the real prosodic conditions of the 3rd cent. is provided by the hexameters of → Commodianus [23]. The Classical prosody in the poetry of late antiquity that flourished again (since the end of the crisis of the Empire in the 3rd cent.) is therefore an artificial product from the schools – obviously sustained by a broad educated class and as such bringing forth works of art – with little support in the living language [12]. The transition to the non-quantitative verse forms appropriate to the living Latin articulation of late antiquity, is only to be found in ancient literature at a late stage and only in single cases, e.g. in Augustins *Psalmus in partem Donati* [11].

3. Metre and word accent

In the earliest period, the word accent possibly played a greater part in Latin versification than in Greek. In the artistic recitation of Lat. verses, word stresses and line structure were however, as in Greek, simultaneously audible. Artificial word stresses to clarify the line structure (called since G. Hermann 'ictus', in the hexameter e .g. *Músa mihí causás memorá*) existed in antiquity only (and probably in another way from the modern use of ictus) in metre instruction for didactic purposes [20; 6]. In the recitation of poetry, the verse's stucture emerged solely as a result of the correct placement of the syllable quantities (the rhythm of which may have been consciously 'overdone'). Strictly to be separated from the issue of the practice of recitation is the phenomenon that in Latin, as opposed to Greek, the → accent correlates strongly with the quantity sequence and hence there is a tendency for fixed stress patterns to emerge according to the type of verse [22].

C. Metres

1. General 2. Hexameter and pentameter 3. Iambs and trochees 4. Other lines structured 'kata metron' 5. Aeolic metre 6. Combined forms

1. General

Latin metres are almost without exception copies of the Greek ones, be it that in Latin almost solely the strongly regulated line measures really gained wide acceptance; only in the → cantica of the Old Latin drama (as can be gleaned from → Plautus) are there freer forms like those in the older Greek choral lyric; dactyloepitrites (see above V.4.) are absent even there. There is no evidence of the creation of strophic systems in Latin either. As in prosody, in the metres from Plautus up to the end of the 1st cent. BC, a development from freer to set rules more precisely tuned to the Greek model can be observed. Around the middle of the 1st cent. BC, a reorientation centred on Classical Greek models takes place, in the course of which → Horatius [7] in using the epodic forms of the Greek iambographers and the Aeolic metres (after first attempts by Catullus) introduced new metres to Latin literature. After the Augustan period, the introduction of new line measures barely occurs any more through the adoption of previously unknown Greek forms but rather through a combination of already established lines and building-blocks of lines.

2. Hexameter and pentameter

The dactylic hexameter takes over from the saturnian as the epic metre from → Ennius [1] onwards. As in Greek, the first 4 dactyls can be replaced regularly by a spondeus whereas this can only occur with the 5th as an exception. The frequency of spondees decreases from Ennius to Ovid so that the lines become lighter. Common word endings ('caesuras') are to be found after the 3rd *longum* (penthemimeres), after the 4th *longum* (hephthemimeres) and after the 4th foot (bucolic diaeresis), and – different from the Greek – seldom in the middle of the third double-short (*infandum regina iubes*: '*katà ton tríton trochaîon*'). The word ending after the 2nd *longum* (trithemimeres) was not regarded as a caesura until recently. The pentameter always has a middle diaeresis; the tendency towards a two-syllable final word becomes compulsory from Ovid onwards. The pentameter does not end in a genuine *elementum anceps*, but almost without exception in a long or at least a closed syllable.

3. Iambs and trochees

Iambic and trochaic measures are encountered for the first time in the Old Lat. drama (in the tragedy as well as in comedies); the most common are the iambic senarius (×-×-×-×-×- ⏑ -; with the exception of the two last ones, each element can also be resolved into a double short) and the trochaic 'septenarius' (-×-×-×-×-×-×-× - ⏑ -; actually a catalectic octonarius; resolutions as in the senarius). In these metres, there is an *elementum anceps* in place of the *elementum breve* in each foot so that the foot and not the metron appears to be the smallest unit (×-×- etc.); hence also the (already ancient) names senarius, septenarius, octonarius (instead of trimeter etc.). The statistics for the comedy texts show, however, that every second *elementum anceps* is realized much more frequently with a short syllable, so that there is a general tendency towards division according to metra (×-⌣- etc.) after all [18]. The iambic senarius (Plautus: 38%, Terence: over 50%) is a pure speech line; the trochaic septenarius and the other longer lines (above all the iambic octonarii) were associated with music (→ Canticum, → Diverbium). Iambs that according to the Greek type are strictly structured *katà métron* are first used by → Catullus [1]; → Horatius [7] combines in the Epodes – following Archilochus – iambic lines with each other or with dactylic elements; he is followed in this by the author of → *Catalepton* (→ Appendix Vergiliana). The choliamb used by Catullus (see above V.D.3.) is not adopted by Horace but it is by → Martialis [1]. In the tragedies of → Seneca (comedy gradually dies out after the 1st cent. BC) the speech line is the iambic trimeter according to the Greek model in which the second and fourth foot have a pure *elementum breve* (×-⌣- etc.); deviating from the Greek, the pure iambus is avoided in the 5th foot. The pure trimeter (all *elementa ancipitia* short, no resolution) found from Catullus and Horace on, the models of which (if any) are unclear, is probably no more than a metrical play. The four-line stanza in iambic dimeters introduced by → Ambrosius became of very great importance for late antiquity and beyond as a metre for the Christian → Hymn.

4. OTHER LINES STRUCTURED 'KATA METRON'

Other metres structured *katà métron* are to be found particularly in the cantica of Old Lat. drama, in evidence to us almost exclusively from Plautus. In them either a basic metre (the most common: baccheus, creticus, anapaest) or a mixture of different metres (including iambs and trochees as well as single Aeolic components) are combined in a free manner. In many cases, an exact analysis or even a reliable colometry is now no longer possible [7; 16]. Outside Old Latin drama, traces of various types of metre are still demonstrable in → Varro (Menippean satire) and in → Lucilius [I 6]. In later poetry only the anapaests in the choral songs of Seneca's tragedies have attained importance; the metra mostly appear there to be linked with synaphia so that separation of the lines is often problematical. In addition the various manifestations of the ionicus is of some importance. Pure ionics are only attested for Varro; Horace uses them uniquely in carm. 3,12. The 'galliambus' that is based on ionics and very free in structure is used by Varro and once by Catullus (carm. 63). 'Sotadeans' (i.e. ionics mixed with trochees) are, after occasional occurrences in → Petronius and → Martialis [1], to be found particularly in → Terentianus Maurus. Anacreontics (ionic dimeters with anaclasis) are attested in isolated cases from Petronius onwards. All other metres are almost no longer used in Latin literature outside the

drama cantica (about the lyric forms of → *poetae novelli* of the 2nd cent. little is known). Choriambic metre is once used by → Martianus Capella.

5. AEOLIC METRE

After the first attempts by Catullus – phalaecean hendecasyllable (---⌣-⌣-⌣-⌣--), sapphic strophe – Horace introduces Aeolic metre after Sappho and Alcaeus [4] to Rome in a programmatic way (carm. 3,30). The Aeolic base (see above V.D.4.) is always created by two long syllables from Horace onwards; the strophes almost always comprise 4 verse lines ('Meineke's Law') between which however there is to some extent a tendency to synaphia (above all V. 3/4). Most commonly Horace uses the alcaeic strophe, aside from asclepiadeus (gl[c]), both stichically and in various combinations with other Aeolic elements. In an arrangement that is partly new, Aeolic components – particularly sapphics, asclepiadei and glyconei – constitute, alongside the anapaests, the metres in the choral songs of Seneca's tragedies.

6. COMBINED FORMS

As an imitation of the older, free Greek choral lyric, polymetric chorus songs are to be found in Seneca's *Oedipus* and *Agamemnon* that are formed almost completely through an irregular, constantly changing combining of Horatian line components, not resulting in strophic systems as in Greek verse; possibly their creation can be traced back to ideas from contemporary theory regarding metre. Above and beyond Seneca, the new combination of lines and line components becomes the most important stimulus for innovation in the later period. In this field as well, the metrical experiments of the → *poetae novelli* are scarcely documented. The metrical forms in the *Consolatio philosophiae* of → Boethius, however, in which traditional forms like hexameters and distichs are used alongside artificial combinations – e.g. glyconeus with the alcaeic decasyllable (3, m. 4) or asclepiadeus with 2ia (3, m. 8) – proved to be quited influential.

D. ANCIENT THEORY

Ancient Latin theory of metre is closely dependent on the Greek and barely reflects Roman peculiarities. Apart from a fragment by → Caesius [II 8] Bassus and perhaps the writing of → Terentianus Maurus, complete writings are only extant from the end of the 3rd cent. AD onwards, with works particularly by Marius → Plotius Sacerdos, → Asmonius (→ Marius [II 21] Victorinus), → Diomedes [4] and Atilius Fortunatianus. Caesius Bassus and Terentianus Maurus represent the so-called derivation theory that derives all metres from the iambic trimeter and dactylic hexameter; all other authors blend with it the theory supported by → Heliodorus [6] and → Hephaistion [4] of *métra prōtótypa*, which starts from eight or nine basic metres.

E. RECEPTION

The quantitative Latin metre, which was already preserved in late antiquity despite developments in language, remained right through to the modern period the unquestioned form of expression in Latin poetry. In addition, from late antiquity onwards, a rhythmic poetry developed that was based on word stress and (or) syllable number. In the Renaissance, quantitative poetry once again came to be regarded as practically the sole Latin form of poetry; since this time imitations of ancient metres also developed in the European vernacular languages. The ancient texts served as a model for versification rules and → prosody in Latin poetry, as did to a lesser extent the ancient theory of metre as well. There were no major differences, be it that in → Prosody, after antiquity the slurring of *est* and *es* was always treated in poetry as normal synaloephe; the fact that aphaeresis occurs was not rediscovered until the 19th cent. [13]. Measuring a short syllable as long before a caesura, which was – particularly before the penthemimeres in the hexameter – only exceptionally permitted in the Classical period, became normal in the Middle Ages. In the choice of metres, poets limited themselves to the forms evidenced in antiquity; new developments on the basis of theoretical considerations was exceptional.

After the decline in knowledge of metre in the 6th and 7th cents., significant poetry in correct quantitative prosody and metre is again to be found from the → Carolingian Renaissance onwards. In the course of Late Antiquity, the hexameter, distichon, iambic dimeter (hymn strophe), phalaecean hendecasyllable and sapphic strophe established themselves as the most important line measures that then also determined the further Latin poetic tradition until the modern age. Right through to the 18th cent., Latin quantitative poetry had an important role in European literature and by no means produced only school poetry but also artistically highly sophisticated verse that had a significant influence on the poets of its time. The writing of Latin verse as a stylistic exercise was part of instruction in Latin right through to the 19th cent. and in Great Britain even almost up until the present.

→ Lyric poetry; → Diacritical signs; → Music; → Prosody; → Rhythm; → METRE

BIBLIOGR.: 1 F. CUPAIUOLO, Bibliografia della metrica Latina, 1995   2 L. CECCARELLI, Prosodia e metrica latina arcaica 1956–1990, in: Lustrum 33, 1991, 227–400.
LIT.: 3 W. S. ALLEN, Accent and Rhythm, 1973   4 Id., Vox Latina, ²1978   5 J. BLÄNSDORF, Metrum und Stil als Indizien für vorliterarischen Gebrauch des Saturniers, in: G. VOGT-SPIRA (ed.), Studien zur vorliterarischen Periode im frühen Rom, 1989, 41–69   6 S. BOLDRINI, Prosodie und Metrik der Römer, 1999   7 L. BRAUN, Die Cantica des Plautus, 1970   8 F. CRUSIUS, H. RUBENBAUER, Römische Metrik, ⁸1967   9 J. HALPORN, M. OSTWALD, Lat. M., ³1983 (Engl. original: The Meters of Greek and Latin Poetry, 1963, ²1994)   10 H. M. HOENIGSWALD, Language, Meter and Choice in Latin: Word-Initial Stop and Liquid, in: K. PIEPER (Ed.), Studia linguistica diachronica et synchronica. Festschrift W. Winter, 1985, 377–383   11 P. KLOPSCH, Einführung in die mittellateinische Verslehre, 1972   12 J. LEONHARDT, Dimensio syllabarum. Studien zur lateinischen Prosodie- und Verslehre

von der Spätantike bis zur frühen Renaissance, 1989   13 Id., Die Aphärese bei *est* in der Geschichte der lateinischen Metrik, in: Glotta 66, 1988, 244–252   14 G. MORELLI, La metricologia nel basso impero, in: La cultura in Italia fra Tardo Antico e Alto Medioevo (Atti del convegno tenuto a Roma 1979), 1980, 411–421   15 C. QUESTA, Introduzione alla metrica di Plauto, 1967   16 Ibid., Titi Macci Plauti Cantica, 1995   17 J. SOUBIRAN, L'élision dans la poésie latine, 1966   18 Ibid., Essai sur la versification dramatique des Romains. Sénaire iambique et septénaire trochaïque, 1988   19 L. D. STEPHENS, The Shortening of Final -o in Classical Latin. A Study in Multiple Conditioning and Lexical Diffusion of Sound Change, in: IF 91, 1986, 236–258   20 W. STROH, Arsis und Thesis, in: M. VON ALBRECHT et. al. (ed.), Musik und Dichtung, 1990, 87–116   21 H. STURTEVANT, R. G. KENT, Elision and Hiatus in Latin Prose and Verse, in: TAPhA 46, 1915, 129–155   22 E. ZINN, Der Wortakzent in den lyrischen Versen des Horaz, 1940 (repr. 1997)   23 E. HECK, in: HLL, § 498   24 K. SALLMANN, in: HLL, § 482.   J.LE.

VII. BYZANTINE

Aside from the ancient quantitative line measures that lived on in Byzantine poetry and that gradually – with the exception of the hexameter – developed into metres based on word accent, there appeared from the 10th cent. AD in funerary poems to the emperors → Leo [9] VI and → Constantinus [1] VII whose presentation was by chant, the 'iambic' pentecaidecasyllable (15-syllable) or 'political verse' (πολιτικὸς στίχος/ *politikòs stíchos*) [1]. This genuine Byzantine verse was primarily used in the courtly and religious sphere (panegyrics to the emperor, hymns, didactic poems); from the 12th cent. it also predominates in vernacular literature. This new type of verse, in which → prosody plays no part at all, is based solely on the regulated alternation of stressed and unstressed syllables. Apart from the syllable number that remains constant, the 'caesura' after the eighth syllable and the paroxytonizing (i.e. the stress on the penultimate syllable) of the line ending represent its most important features. The first half line must either close proparoxytonically (dominant type until the 11th cent.) or oxytonically; its beginning and/or that of the second half can also occasionally be 'trochaic' or 'anapaestic'.

The early history of the pentecaidecasyllable still remains obscure today. The prevailing view is that it should be regarded as a distich metre, consisting of an octosyllable and a heptasyllable derived from it. These two 'parts' can be recognized along with occasional, regular pentecaidecasyllables both in early hymnography (kontakion) [2] and in acclamations that are closely associated with the imperial court and its ceremonials [3].

In Byzantine church poetry, accent-based metre was also dominant and was always subordinate to the music. Based on the model of the Biblical → psalms, smaller chants first arose that later, among other things under the influence of strongly rhythmic prose sermons, developed into strophic systems of stressed-rhythmic lines (→ Kontakion, → Canon).

836

1 ODB 3, s.v. Political Verse, 1694f.   2 M. J. JEFFREYS, The Nature and Origins of the Political Verse, in: Dumbarton Oaks Papers 28, 1974, 141–195   3 J. KODER, Kontakion und politischer Vers, in: Jahrbuch der österreichischen Byzantinistik 33, 1983, 45–56   4 M. JEFFREYS, Byzantine Metrics: Non-Literary Strata, in: Jahrbuch der österreichischen Byzantinistik 31/1, 1981, 322–334   5 J. GROSDIDIER DE MATONS, Liturgie et hymnographie: kontakion et canon, in: Dumbarton Oaks Papers 34–35, 1980–1981, 31–43.   I.V.

Metretes (μετρητής; *metrētḗs*) is the Greek name for the largest unit of measurement for fluids, synonymous with → *kados*, a volume of 12 *chóai* (→ Chous [1]), corresponding to 144 *kotýlai* (→ Kotyle [2]). It is equivalent to approximately 39,4 litres, according to HULTSCH, whereas NISSEN puts it at approximately 38,9 litres.
→ Measures of Volume

1 F. HULTSCH, Griechische und römische Metrologie, ²1882 (reprint 1971), 101f., 703 table X A   2 M. LANG, M. CROSBY, Weights, Measures and Tokens (The Athenian Agora 10), 1964, 56ff.   3 H. NISSEN, Griechische und römische Metrologie, in: Hdb. der klassischen Altertumswiss. 1, ²1892, 834–890, esp. 843 table XI.   H.-J.S.

Metric Lengthening see → Prosody

Metrics see → Metre

Metrocles (Μητροκλῆς/*Mētroklês*). From a rich family in Maronea in Thrace, 3rd cent. BC. In turn a pupil of the Peripatetic → Theophrastus, the Academician → Xenocrates and the Cynic → Crates [4] of Thebes, who married his sister → Hipparchia (Teles, Diatribe 4 A). M., who was accustomed to luxury, learned under Crates to lead a simple and economical life, sleeping in temples in the summer and in the baths in the winter. His saying that wealth was damaging if it was not put to appropriate use indicates a moderate → Cynicism (Diog. Laert. 6, 95). According to Hecaton of Rhodes, 'Chreiai', M. burnt his own writings, but according to others, the notes he had made under Theophrastus (Diog. Laert. 6,95). M. is considered the inventor of → *chreiai*, short anecdotes or sayings which were learnt by heart and which could be drawn on in difficult situations in life (cf. Diog. Laert. 6,33). The pupils attributed to him in Diog. Laert. 6,95 were probably rather those of Crates. M. died at an advanced age, allegedly by holding his breath. Stilpon wrote a dialogue 'M.' (fr. 190 DÖRING), which may be the origin of a passage in Plut. *De tranquillitate animi* 6, p. 467 F–468 A (= SSR 5 L 2).

EDITIONS: SSR II 581–583; IV 101 (in the fragments and testimonies to M. Diog. Laert. 6,33 is lacking).
BIBLIOGRAPHY: K. DÖRING, Sokrates, die Sokratiker und die von ihnen begründeten Traditionen, in: GGPh² II.1, 1998, 304–305; P. P. FUENTES GONZÁLEZ, Les diatribes de Téles, 1998; M.-O. GOULET-CAZÉ, Une liste des disciples de Cratès le Cynique en Diogène Laërce VI 95?, in: Hermes 114, 1986, 247–252.   M.G.-C.

Metrodora (Μητροδῶρα; *Mētrodôra*). According to the manuscript Flor. Laur. 75,3 (12th cent. AD), the author of surviving extracts under the title 'Diseases of the Womb' (Περὶ γυναικείων παθῶν τῆς μήτρας). Although M. has been identified with various male or female physicians, his/her identity remains unknown, even enigmatic. It is possible that M. never existed, if the name (*mētròs dôra*, 'gifts of the mother') really is only an erroneous interpretation of the title of a collection of advice given to young women of marriageable age by their mothers.

The text, which is based on a gynaecological treatise in the *Corpus Hippocraticum* and on works of disputed authorship (e.g. Cleopatra, → Moschion [4]; cf. → Mustio), begins with gynaecology in the narrower sense, then therapeutics, and at the end there are excerpts from → Alexander [29] of Tralleis.

The manuscript probably originates in southern Italy (where a Latin translation of some Greek treatises on gynaecology circulated). The text belongs to the genre of Byzantine *iatrosóphion*, which is characterised by the accumulation of recipes in successive layers and an interest in folk medicine. It was partially published during the Renaissance (*Gynaecia*, Basel 1566 and 1586–88; Strassburg 1597).

A. P. KOUZES, ΙΑΤΡΙΚΟΙ ΚΩΔΙΚΕΣ – Metrodora's Work According to the Greek Codex 75,3 of the Laurentiana Library, in: Praktika tes Akademias Athenon 20, 1945, 46–6; M.-H. CONGOURDEAU, 'Metrodora' et son œuvre, in: E. PATLAGEAN (ed.), Maladie et société à Byzance, 1994, 57–96; H. PARKER, Women Physicians in Greece, Rome, and the Byzantine Empire, in: L. FURST (ed.), Women Physicians and Healers, 1997, 131–150.   A.TO.

Metrodorus (Μητρόδωρος/*Metródōros*).
[1] M. of Chios Democritan philosopher (→ Democritus [1]) of the 5th–4th cent. BC who recognised Fullness and Emptiness, Being and Non-Being as the first principles. This orthodoxy, however, does not go beyond the fundamental theoretical views of → Atomism: M. is said to have had his own views in other matters (70 A 3 DK). M. propounds the uncreatedness of the universe (τὸ πᾶν) in the Eleatic manner (→ Eleatic School) because a created universe must be formed from that which is not (A 4 DK = [Plut.] Strom. 11). He goes on to claim that the universe is 'infinite, because it is eternal', agreeing with → Melissus's [2] correlation of the spatial and temporal unboundedness of the universe. This unlimited universe is populated by an unlimited multiplicity of probably different worlds, based on the thought that it would be unreasonable for an enormous field to produce just one ear (A 6 DK). This, it seems, is a special application of the atomistic argument of 'nothing more' (sc. nothing more this than that; οὐδὲν μᾶλλον). Another reference to the principle of fullness may be the Eleatic sounding principle that whatever someone thinks also is (70 B 2 DK, cf. 28 B 3 and 28 B 6,1f.). The proto-Pyrrhonic formulation ('we know nothing and neither do we know whether we know anything') of

Sextus Empiricus and Philodemus (A 25 DK), Cicero and Eusebius [7] (B 1 DK) is attributed to Metrodorus. This is best understood as a broadening of the sceptical tendencies in Atomism.

FRAGMENTS: DIELS/KRANZ 2, 231–234.   I.B.

[2] Handed over to the Sarmatian Ixomati by his father → Satyrus I under duress as a hostage for him and Hecataeus, the king of the Sindi. Tirgatao, the latter's Maeotic wife, had him murdered (Polyaen. Strat. 8,55).
I.v.B.

[3] Epicurean philosopher, born in 331/330 BC in Lampsacus. He met → Epicurus during his stay in Lampsacus and became his pupil. He died in 278/7 BC, seven or eight years before his master. His brother → Timocrates became famous for his polemic against Epicurus, and their sister Batis married → Idomeneus [2]. M., together with Epicurus, → Hermarchus, and → Polyaenus, formed the Group of 'Masters' (καθηγεμόνες/kathēgemónes or ἄνδρες/ándres) of the 'Garden' (→ kepos, → Epicurean School). In Diogenes Laertius there is a long list of titles of works by M., but none of these writings has survived complete. KÖRTE's old collection [1] is inadequate.

In philosophical theory M. had evidently not greatly distanced himself from Epicurus (paene alter Epicurus: Cic. Fin. 2,28,92 = fr. 5 K.). We know about individual aspects of his thought. In a dialogue with Epicurus, M. occupied himself with linguistic problems: at the end of Book 28 of Epicurus's 'On Nature' (De natura/Περὶ φύσεως; Perì phúseōs) after defending a radical linguistic conventionalism, at the end of which is the formation of an artificial philosophical language, M. again approaches the position of his teacher. In 'Against those who claim that physiology produces good rhetors', Metrodorus's definition and view of rhetoric is used polemically against Nausiphanes: rhetoric must be differentiated from physiology, and only sophistic rhetoric, not forensic or political rhetoric is to be regarded as a téchnē. Wealth and economy were dealt with in M.'s writings 'On Riches' (scanty remains in PHercul. 200) and 'On Economy' (a longish fragment in Philodemus, De Oeconomia, col. 12,45–21,35 JENSEN), in which he defends the view of 'natural riches' (πλοῦτος κατὰ φύσιν) in accordance with Epicurus's theses. M. wrote a number of polemical works against Plato ('Against Plato's Euthyphron', 'Against the Dialectians' and 'Against the Sophists'). SPINELLI [3] recognized probable fragments of 'Against the Dialectians' in some remains of a severely damaged roll of the → Herculanean Papyri (TEPEDINO [4] assigns them to 'Against the Sophists'). Fragments of his letter collection also survive. Sentences 10, 30–31, 47 and 51 of the Gnomologium Vaticanum can be ascribed to him ([5]; Sentence 51 is from a letter to Pythocles). The text PHercul. 831, which KÖRTE attributes to M., is regarded today as being more likely by → Demetrius [21] Lacon.

EDITIONS: 1 A. KÖRTE, Metrodori Epicurei fragmenta, 1890 (new edition announced by A. TEPEDINO GUERRA).

BIBLIOGRAPHY: 2 M. ERLER, in: GGPh² 4.1, 216–222 3 E. SPINELLI, Metrodoro contro i dialettici?, in: CE 16, 1986, 29–43 4 A. TEPEDINO GUERRA, Metrodoro contro i dialettici?, in: CE 22, 1992, 119–122 5 A. BLANCHARD, Epicure, Sentence Vaticane 14: Epicure ou Metrodore?, in: REG 104, 1991, 394–409.   T.D.

[4] Emissary, accompanied by → Morcus and Parmenion, for → Perseus during the Third → Macedonian War in the spring of 168 BC. He negotiated with the Rhodians their entry into an anti-Roman alliance with Macedonia (Pol. 29,4,7; 29,11,1; Liv. 44,34,10).

E. OLSHAUSEN, Prosopographie der hellenistischen Königsgesandten, 1974, 161f.   L.-M.G.

[5] Poet of the New Comedy, who, according to the single (inscriptional) piece of evidence, was the winner at Rhomaea in Magnesia on the Maeander in the second half of the 2nd cent. BC with his play Ὅμοιοι [1].

1 PCG 7, 1989, 14.   T.HI.

[6] M. from Stratonicea Academic philosopher from the circle around → Carneades [1] (Philod. Academicorum index 24,9), probably born in about 170 BC. He was still said to be teaching as late as 110 (Cic. De or. 1,45, cf. Acad. 2,16). Before attaching himself to Carneades, Metrodorus was an adherent of Epicurus, according to Diog. Laert. 10,9 the only one ever who was unfaithful to this school. M. advanced the claim that he alone understood his teacher Carneades correctly (Philod. ibid. 26,9), and apparently openly represented a position which sought to mollify the radically Sceptic point of view. Therefore, under the scholarch Cleitomachus [1] he probably only taught outside the → Academy.
K.-H.S.

[7] Practical astronomer (parapegmatist). Ptolemy (Phaseis p. 14,15) cites him as the authority for star phases as → weather signs. According to Lyd. De ostentis p. 275,10 M. established observatories in Italy and Sicily. His date is uncertain. He is mentioned together with → Euctemon and → Eudoxus [1]. His unfavourable characterisation of the ides of March (Lyd. Mens. 50 p. 106,13) does not necessarily place him after Caesar's assassination. The astronomical and geometrical work in five books on the → Zones mentioned by Serv. Georg. 1,129, in which M. defended poets against the accusation of astronomical ignorance, is probably by another M.

W. KROLL, s.v. Metrodoros, RE Suppl. 7, 448f.; A. REHM, Parapegmastudien, 1941.   W.H.

[8] Hippocratic commentator at Alexandria, a pupil of → Sabinus, active around 150 AD (Gal., CMG V 10,2,2). He claimed to be able to be a much more accurate expositor than his predecessors. Galen denies this (CMG V 10,2,1), pointing to various errors in his interpretation of the 'Epidemics' (CMG V 10,1). He is condemned by implication by Galen for the medical failure of one of his students, → Philistion of Pergamum, who

had followed only too literally a recipe in 'Epidemics II', and who subsequently lost his reputation and his livelihood (CMG V 10,1). V.N.

[9] Various epigrams survive under this name, which can probably be ascribed to three different authors whose precise date can not be established with certainty: the epideictic epigrams Anth. Pal. 9,360 (reply to Posidippus ibid. 9,359, from Julian [20] ibid. 9,446 counterfeit) and 9,712 (by 'Metrodorus, a grammarian in Byzantium' on a lawyer called John) and a series of arithmetical problems (Anth. Pal. 14,116–146), to which 14,2; 3; 6; 7, which trace back to → Diophantus [4], should be added. M. was probably the compiler rather than the author of these.

FGE 71–73; P. TANNERY, Diophantus 2, 1895, X–XIII, 43–72; A. CAMERON, The Greek Anthology from Meleager to Planudes, 1993, 268.   M.G.A.

Metrological Relief see → Relief

Metron (Μήτρων; *Métrōn*). One of the → *basilikoi paides*, responsible for the arsenal of → Alexander [4] the Great in 330 BC. He heard of the conspiracy of Dimnus from Cebalinus, and reported it to Alexander (Curt. 6,7; Diod. 17,79,4–5). He is not to be identified with a trierarch of the Hydaspes fleet (Arr. Ind. 18,5).   E.B.

Metronax Philosopher, known only through → Seneca the Younger ([1] suspects a Stoic), first half of the 1st cent. AD; Seneca visited his school in Naples as *senex* (Sen. Ep. 76,1–4). M. died at the age of eighty (ibid. 93,1f.).

1 W. KROLL, s.v. Metronax, RE 15, 1485   2 M. T. GRIFFIN, Seneca, 1976, 339, 445.   MA.D.

Metronomoi (μετρονόμοι; *metronómoi*) were a group of market supervisors who inspected the weights and measures (μέτρα; *métra*) on the → Agora (ἀγορά; *agorá*) at Athens and the → Emporion in the Piraeus. According to Aristotle, five *metronomoi* were chosen by lot for the city and the Piraeus respectively (Aristot. Ath. pol. 51,2). Excavations of the Athenian *agorá* have brought to light measuring vessels and weights from the 6th cent. BC to the Hellenistic era. Some, dating from the 4th cent. BC, are provided with counterstamps, probably intended to guarantee the accuracy of the measure. This find suggests that the position of *metronomoi* was not created until the 4th cent. BC, to support the → agoranomoi, who were responsible for monitoring weights and measures in other cities. In an inscription [4] found in 1967 near the southern Stoa of the Agora which records the transfer of the weights and measures of the previous year from 222/1 BC, five *metronomoi* are mentioned, as well as two secretaries, one of whom was determined by lot while the other was elected. At this time, two additional secretaries probably belonged to the *metronomoi*, corresponding to the increase in the

number of Athenian *phylai* from 10 to 12 at the end of the 4th cent. BC.
→ Market

1 J. M. CAMP, Die Agora von Athen, 1989, 141–147   2 M. LANG, M. CROSBY, Weigths, Measures and Tokens (The Athenian Agora 10), 1964; 3 P. V. STANLEY, Ancient Greek Market Regulations and Controls, 1976   4 E. VANDERPOOL, Metronomoi, in: Hesperia 37, 1968, 73–76.   S.v.R.

Metrophanes (Μητροφάνης; *Mētrophánēs*). An official under → Mithradates [6] VI. During the 1st→ Mithradatic War (89–85), he transported Pontic troops to Greece in 87 BC [2. 89, n. 318], at the same time as → Neoptolemus [10] and Archelaus [4]. M. conquered Chalcis [1] in Euboea, and laid waste to the Magnesian coast as far as Demetrias [1], where the Roman *proquaestor* Braetius [1] inflicted some losses on his fleet (App. Mithr. 113, cf. Memnon FGrH 434 F 1,20,10; [1. 140]). M. may have been one of the envoys who in 79 negotiated an agreement with → Sertorius in Spain on behalf of the king (Sall. Hist. fr. 4,2; cf. Plut. Sertorius 23f.; App. Mithr. 286–288; Cic. Verr. 1,1,87; Cic. Manil. 9f.; [1. 203–210]). In the first year of the 3rd Mithradatic War (74–64), he – together with the Roman Fannius [I 3] who had gone over to the Pontic side – was defeated in the Roman province of Asia by Mamercus, a legate of Licinius [I 26] Lucullus. He subsequently fought his way through to the king, together with 2,000 horsemen (Oros. 6,2,16; Liv. fr. 20 WEISENBORN; [1. 226]).á

1 L. BALLESTEROS PASTOR, Mitrídates Eupátor, 1996   2 A. MASTROCINQUE, Studi sulle guerre Mitridatiche, 1999.   E.O.

Metropolis (μητρόπολις/*mētrópolis*, literally 'mother city').

[1] Since the so-called Great Colonisation (c. 750–500 BC, → Colonization IV, cf. the overview there), in numerous Greek communities an *oikistḗs* ('founder') and further *ápoikoi* ('settlers', 'colonists') were selected from the citizenry of the future metropolis as starting point for a colonisation enterprise (or they left on their own initiative) and entrusted with the establishment of an → *apoikía* outside the territory of the metropolis. Sometimes the group of settlers consisted of members of different communities, yet only one *pólis* was regarded as the metroplis.

The usually carefully prepared process (consultation of an oracle, performance of religious ceremonies, provision of ships, etc.) could serve to alleviate socio-economic problems (e.g. at the foundation of → Cyrene by Thera c. 630 BC, Hdt. 4, 150–158) and to generate trading posts [1]. It could also help to remove people who endangered the internal order of the metropolis, see for instance the foundation of Taras by Sparta c. 650 BC. In this case the *oikistḗs* was → Phalantus, the leader of a band of followers consisting mainly of nobles, who were forced to leave the community after a failed coup attempt [7. 121ff.]. The Spartan Dorieus [1] saw at the end of the 6th cent. BC no other way to escape the mounting pressure of his half-brother Cleomenes [3] I but to take on the leadership of a – ultimately failed – colonisation enterprise, thus sparing the metropolis further internal tensions (Hdt. 5,41–48).

In the archaic period, the *oikistḗs* often enjoyed almost unlimited power within the group of settlers [5. 95]. (Miletus seems to be something of an exception; hardly any oikists are known for its many *apoikíai*, cf. [3]). This arose from the *oikistḗs'* noble origins and from the sanctioning of the enterprise by a divine oracle [6. 17ff.], and after his death he was venerated in cult in the *apoikíai* (cf. Hdt. 6,38; [5. 98ff.; 6. 189ff.]). In the 5th cent. BC, the *oikistḗs* acted increasingly as an 'official of foundation' who carried out the colonisation on official instructions of the metropolis and then returned to his home town (e.g. Hagnon [1], cf. [5. 128ff., in particular 148ff.; 6. 228ff.]). In the general framework of the development of institutional structures in the Greek *póleis*, it can be observed that structures dominated by individuals – personified by independent oikists – were gradually replaced by an increasingly institutionally structured metropolis.

Usually, the *apoikíai* adopted the cult, dialect, script, and calendar from the metropolis. In the archaic period, they, with their newly constituted communal organisation, often influenced the institutional development of the metropolis in their turn. While the connection between metropolis and *apoikía* in the cultic field is for the most part clearly recognisable (cf. [8]), the political influence of the metropolis on an *apoikía* could vary [4; 9; 10]. A relationship of dependence was not absolute and often very difficult to enforce (as is shown, for instance, in the relations between Corinth and its *apoikíai*). War between metropolis and *apoikía* was regarded as particularly reprehensible, however, while mutual military assistance occurred repeatedly. The simultaneous possession of civil rights in both metropolis and *apoikía* seems to have been comparatively rare. If a colony in its turn wished to establish an *apoikía*, the *oikistḗs* of the original metropolis did so [5. 95ff.].

→ Apoikia; → Klerouchoi; → Colonisation IV. (with map and overview)

1 J. BOARDMAN, Kolonien und Handel der Griechen, 1981   2 P. DANNER, Megara, Megara Hyblaea and Selinus, in: H. D. ANDERSEN e.a. (eds.), Urbanization in the Mediterranean, 1997, 143–165   3 N. EHRHARDT, Milet und seine Kolonien, 1983   4 A. J. GRAHAM, Colony and Mother City in Ancient Greece, 1964   5 W. LESCHHORN, Gründer der Stadt, 1984   6 I. MALKIN, Religion and Colonization in Ancient Greece, 1987   7 M. MEIER, Aristokraten und Damoden, 1998   8 P. REICHERT-SÜDBECK, Kulte von Korinth und Syrakus, 2000   9 J. SEIBERT, Metropolis und Apoikie, 1963   10 R. WERNER, Probleme der Rechtsbeziehungen zwischen Metropolis und Apoikie, in: Chiron 1, 1971, 19–73.   M.MEI.

[2] Hellenistic-Ptolemaic administrative centre. Already in the times of the pharaohs, each Egyptian district had its centre where the administration was concentrated, and which had its own administration separate from the rest of the region. The Ptolemies adopted this and designated the main town of a district (→ *nomós*) as metropolis. The legal status of the metropolis was not that of a → *pólis*, but of a → *kṓmē*. The metropolis was the seat of the district administration and the urban centre of culture, commerce and industry. Augustus gave the metropolis its own officials (probably following the Alexandrian model; ditto for the → liturgies), as a result of which they distinguished themselves from the villages (*kṓmai*) and developed their own sense of identity. The metropoleis were accountable to the provincial administration and only received a first form of autonomy when every metropolis was entitled to a → *boulḗ* under Septimius Severus (199/202 AD); this was done to relieve the provincial officials of municipal duties. Under Diocletian (late 3rd cent. AD) the territory of the district became an *enoría* ('municipal area') of the metropolis, which now completely resembled a → *municipium* and lost its old function of administrative centre.

Ever since the Ptolemies, but especially since Augustus, the metropolis increasingly took over the functions of the cities; the difference between the metropolis and the Egyptian *póleis* became ever slighter, causing the metropolis to disappear in the end.

A. K. BOWMAN, D. RATHBONE, Cities and Administration in Roman Egypt, in: JRS 82, 1992, 107–127; H. A. RUPPRECHT, Kleine Einführung in die Papyruskunde, 1994, 60 (Bibl.).   W.A.

[3] (Ματρόπολις/*Matrópolis*). City in → Acarnania, close to Paleomanina, on the right bank of the Achelous. Since c. 270 BC member of the Aetolian League (→ Aetolians), but belonging to the Acarnanians again after the capture by Philippus V in 219 BC. Imposing layout of the city with a residential part and separate acropolis. Mycenaean [2. 322] and geometric graves [1] were found in the surrounding area, as well as archaic inscriptions. Inscriptions: IG IX 1²,1, 3 B; IG IX 1²,2, 418; [2; 3. 323]. Thucydides mentions an, as yet, unlocated place M. in Amphilochia 3,107,1; [4].

1 I. A. PAPAPOSTOLOU, in: AD 34 B, 1979, 208 (Archaeological report)   2 E. MASTROKOSTAS, in: AD 16 B, 1960, 195 (Archaeological report)   3 Idem, in: AD 22 B, 1967, 322f. (Archaeological report)   4 PRITCHETT 8, 25–27, 45.

PRITCHETT 7, 8–15; D. STRAUCH, Römische Politik und griechische Tradition, 1996, 323f., 344.   D.S.

[4] Μητρόπολις/*Mētrópolis*; Ματρόπολις/*Matrópolis*. One of the four fortress cities of Thessalia Hestiaeotis (Strab. 9,5,17), localized on the basis of inscriptions at c. 8 km to the south-west of Karditsa close to present-day M. (formerly Paliokastro). The city came into being

through → *synoikismos*. It was first mentioned in 360 BC in connection with a donation to the temple in Delphi (Syll.³ 239). The first coins date from this time as well (HN 302). In 198 BC an Aetolian raid ended at the walls of M. The surrender to the Romans took place in the same year (Liv. 32,13,11; 15,3). From 196 onwards M. played an important role in the newly founded league of the Thessalians. In 191 M. had to submit to Antiochus [5] III for a short time (Liv. 36,10,2; 14,6). The city flourished well into the 1st cent. BC (inscriptions). In the year 48 M. surrendered to Caesar (Caes. B Civ. 3,81). In Tiberius' time M. lost a border dispute with the neigbouring city of Cierium (IG IX 2, 261). Justinian renovated the city walls (Procop. Aed. 4,3,5).

Steph. Byz. s.v. M. mentions a further city M. in northern Thessalia, i.e. in the districts of Pelasgiotis or Perrhaebia. This assumption rests on a misconception.

A. ARVANITOPULOS, Ein thessalischer Gold- und Silberfund, in: MDAI(A) 37, 1912, 73ff.; B. HELLY, Incursions chez les Dolopes, in: I. BLUM (Ed.), Topographie antique et géographie historique en pays grec, 1992, 64ff.; F. STÄHLIN, s.v. Metropolis (1), RE 15, 1491ff.; KODER/HILD, 219. HE.KR.

[5] City in Ionia on the road from Ephesus to Smyrna (Roman milestones: [1. 3603, 3606]) in a region rich in wines (Strab. 14,1,2; 15), named after the Mother of gods (Meter Gallesia? cf. [1. 3401]), close to present day Yeniköy. Traces of settlement in the early and middle Bronze Age on the acropolis. Evidence of a Greek settlement from c. 750 BC has been found (subgeometric, orientalising and eastern Ionic ceramics). The city flourished under the Attalides in the 3rd and 2nd cents. BC (Ptol. 5,2,17; Ael. NA 16,38). The minting of coins can be shown to have existed from Augustus onwards (HN 583f.). The location of various imperial temples is unknown (Zeus Kresimos, Hera, → Twelve gods). A temple to Ares is located on the walled acropolis (a column drum bears the name of the cult figure [1. 3417]). More ancient remains: theatre, stoa, bouleuterion, baths, gymnasium. In Byzantine times, M. was the seat of a bishopric (cf. Hierocles, Synecdemus 660,19). Considerable remains of late Byzantine fortifications have been preserved.

1 R. MERIÇ e.a., in: IEph VII,1, 1981, 236ff.

H. ENGELMANN, Der Kult des Ares im ionischen Metropolis (Denkschriften der Akad. der Wiss. Wien, Philos.-histor. Kl. 236), 1993, 171–176; J. KEIL, s.v. Metropolis (8), RE 15, 1497; Id., A. VON PREMERSTEIN, Bericht über eine Reise in Lydien ..., in: Denkschriften der Akad. der Wiss. Wien 53,2, 1908, 101ff.; R. MERIÇ, Metropolis in Ionien (Beitr. zur Klass. Philol. 142), 1982; Id., Metropolis. Excavations: The First Five Years 1990–1995, 1996. R.M.

[6] City in southern Phrygia to the north-east of Apameia [2]; located on a hill close to Tartarlı in the *Metropolitanus campus* (present day Gülovası, previously Çölovası), through which Manlius [I 24] Vulso passed during his campaign against the Galatae (Liv.

38,15,13); located on the road between Apameia and Phrygia Paroreios (Strab. 14,2,29), in the *conventus* of Apameia (Plin. HN 5,106), and later likewise part of the province of Pisidia (Hierocles, Synecdemus 673,3) and the suffragan diocese of Antiochia [5]; to be distinguished from the city of the same name in northern Phrygia. Coins were only minted under Philippus Arabs and Traianus Decius; among the inscriptions (especially honorary inscriptions), the letter of the legate of a Roman *proconsul* that mentions the name of the city, the epitaph of a publican from Sinope, and various agonistic texts should be mentioned.

BELKE/MERSICH, 339f.; L. ROBERT, A travers l'Asie Mineure, 1980, 262f. T.D.-B.

Mettius The → *praenomen Mettus* is known for only two people in the early history of Rome (7th/6th cents. BC), for the Sabine Mettus Curtius [I 2], a contemporary of → Romulus (Dion. Hal. Ant. 2,42,2; 46,3; Lib. de praenominibus 1), and for Mettus Fufetius, the dictator of → Alba Longa at the time of Tullus → Hostilius [4] (Varro in Non. 2,443 L., Verg. Aen. 8,642 etc.). The form *Mettius* is also transmitted for both, albeit less reliably (Enn. Ann. 126 V.; almost always in Liv., and so on). No etymology of the name suggests itself; the doubled *tt* indicates a shortened form of the name. → *Metellus*, used only as a → *cognomen* (as in the case of the → Caecilii), is a diminutive.

SALOMIES, 105; SCHULZE, 463. H.R.

I. THE REPUBLICAN PERIOD II. THE EMPIRE

I. THE REPUBLICAN PERIOD

[I 1] M., M. Sent by Caesar to Ariovistus in 58 BC, together with C. Valerius Procillus. The mission seemed to be without danger, since M. had enjoyed the *hospitium* (→ Hospitality III. Greece and Rome) of the leader of the Suebi in the past, yet the Romans were taken prisoner and not freed until Caesar's victory (Caes. Gall. 1,47,4–6; 1,53,8). M. was probably *IIIIvir monetalis* in 44 BC (RRC 480/2; 3; 23; 28). MRR 3,142. T.FR.

II. THE EMPIRE

[II 1] M. Carus One of the informers (→ *delator*) under Domitian, who became notorious in the post-Domitianic era. He accused Herennius [II 11] Senecio in AD 93, and also denounced Pliny the Younger, according to the latter's own testimony (Epist. 7,27,14). His true identity, however, does not emerge clearly from the tradition. PIR² M 562.

[II 2] (M.) [Mo]destus Suffect consul in AD 82; probably related to M. [II 3] and M. [II 4]. He was presumably identical with M. Modestus, who was exiled by Domitian (Plin. epist. 1,5,5.13f.). PIR² M 565.

W. ECK, Epigraphische Untersuchungen zu Konsuln und Senatoren des 1.–3. Jahrhunderts n. Chr., in: ZPE 37, 1980, 31–68.

[II 3] M. M. Modestus Procurator, possibly in Syria, where his seal was found (AE 1973, 548); probably related to M. [II 2] and [II 4] [1. 9f.]. However, he was not *praefectus Aegypti*, as has been deduced from the Suda (s.v. Epaphroditus). PIR² M 566.

1 PFLAUM, Suppl.

F. CAIRNS, Epaphroditos, Φαινιανοχορίοις and 'Modestus', in: ZPE 124, 1999, 218–222.

[II 4] C. Trebonius Proculus M. Modestus Governor of Lycia-Pamphylia under Trajan, probably AD 99–103. [1. 332f.]. There, the people of Patara honoured M., together with other members of his family, with individual statues on an arch (TAM 2, 421). He was suffect consul in 103, and finally proconsul of Asia 119/120 [2. 214]. PIR² M 568; for the arch in Patara see [3].

1 W. ECK, Jahres- und Provinzialfasten der senatorischen Statthalter von 69/70 bis 138/39, in: Chiron 12, 1982, 281–362 2 Id., Jahres- und Provinzialfasten ... (II), in: Chiron 13, 1983, 147–237 3 B. BURELL, Neokoroi. Greek Cities and Roman Emperors, Leiden, etc. 2004.

[II 5] M. M. Rufus An *eques*, father of M. [II 4]. For his origins in Arelate or Petelia in Italy, see [1; 2. 220]; perhaps also from Lycia [3. 59]. He was *praefectus annonae* under Domitian; *praefectus Aegypti* AD 89–91/92; he was accompanied by the poet Peon of Side during a visit to the statue of Memnon. M.'s name was erased from Egyptian inscriptions, which may have been connected with the exile of M. [II 2]. He was honoured at Patara, like other members of his family (TAM2, 421 Bc, Bf); cf. M. [II 4].

1 PIR² M 572 2 F. CAIRNS, Epaphroditos, Φαινιανοχορίοις and 'Modestus', in: ZPE 124, 1999, 218–222; 3 W. ECK, Epigraphische Untersuchungen zu Konsuln und Senatoren des 1.–3 Jahrhunderts n.Chr., in: ZPE 37, 1980, 31–68.   W.E.

Metulum Main settlement of the Illyrian → Iapodes, now Cakovac near Ogulin (in modern Croatia). It was destroyed in 35 BC by the future Augustus (App. Ill. 19–21; Cass. Dio 49,35,2–4). In the Roman period, M. had the status of a *municipium* (CIL III 10060).

J. J. WILKES, Dalmatia, 1969.   H.SO.

Metus *Metus*, 'fear' of a concrete threat (FREUD'S *Realangst*), which activates defensive reactions or precautionary measures, can be rational and hence was not considered as negative [6. 7] as Latin *timor* ('fear'). *Timor* as an irrational emotional state of general expectation of disaster and without relation to a concrete threat (theories of fear and anxiety: cf. [4]) was considered unseemly in Roman thought (e.g. Sen. Ep. 88,26: *cautio illum decet, timor non decet*); yet Roman authors often blurred the boundary between *metus* and *timor* [3. 18f.]. Typical objects of *metus* were war, political turmoil, tyranny, social unrest, loss of freedom and possessions [3]. The Imperial propaganda opposed *metus*

with the theme of 'security' (*pax* and *securitas*) [3. 217ff.].

Particularly influential politically were the complexes of fear cause by major defeats in war: 1. *Metus Gallicus* resulting from the Celtic assaults on Rome in 387 BC. In fact it did not become manifest until the wars with the Celts of Upper Italy from 228 BC, and was projected back on to the Celtic attacks [1. 9–19; 9.]; 2. *Metus Punicus*, unleashed by the Battle of Cannae in 216 BC [1]; 3. fear of the *furor Teutonicus*, which arose through the wars against the → Cimbri and the Teutons from 113 BC and was reinforced by the Battle of Teutoburg Forest (→ Varus) in 9 AD (Iuv. 15,124; Lucan. 1,254–257, see [1. 36–40; 8]). These three forms of *metus* in particular were used in Roman politics to justify expansionist aims.

Metus Gallicus and *metus Punicus* were mutually strengthened by the alliance of Celts and Carthaginians in the war against → Hannibal [4] so that even decades after his defeat, imperialist forces in the Roman Senate could still exploit the *metus Punicus* politically: the Third → Punic War (149–146 BC) ended with a militarily unjustified excess, the physical destruction of Carthage, but abolished *metus Punicus* [1. 26–35]. Similarly, → Caesar exploited *metus Gallicus* to justify the Gallic War [1. 41–43]. Senatorial opposition recognised the questionable legality, and M. → Porcius Cato the Younger proposed handing Caesar over to the Germani (Suet. 24,3; see [2]).

Unlike Carthage, the Gauls were conquered but not destroyed. Consequently a latent *metus Gallicus* awoke when political unrest arose in Gaul [10], sc. in the uprisings of 21 AD (cf. Tac. Ann. 3,44,1; 45,2) and 69 AD. In the nightmare vision of an *Imperium Galliarum* Tacitus emphasised the danger that the Gauls and the Germani could unite and destroy Rome and seize world dominance (Tac. Hist. 4,54,2; 59,2). This bellicose theme still characterised the separate kingdom of Gaul in the 3rd century (Eutr. 9,9,3). *Metus Gallicus* was probably also responsible for an internal distance between the Gauls and the Roman Empire, which was generally reflected in senatorial opposition to the emperor Claudius's motion to allow leading Gauls the senatorial → *cursus honorum* (ILS 212; Tac. Ann. 11,23,1–25,1), and in the below-average representation of Gaulish members in the Roman Senate.

In the late Roman Empire *metus Gallicus* was superseded by a new source of fear, the fear of the Germani. Originally it represented a variety of *metus Gallicus*, as the (Germanic) Cimbri and Teutones were initially considered Gauls (Sall. Iug. 114,1; [1. 36–40]). Only when Caesar bundled the peoples beyond the Rhine together under the (foreign) designation 'Germani' [5. 36ff.], did the Germani become the object of a Roman fear complex in its own right, which, after the trauma of the Battle of Teutoburg Forest in AD 9 was overcome, continued in the Roman subconscious and was openly revived in the 'Age of Migrations'. After the Gothic invasion of Thrace (AD 375), *metus Gothicus* raged (Marc.

Amm. 30,2,8) as the most recent, eventually insuperable variant of Roman fear of the northern barbarians (comprehensively treated in [7]).

1 H. BELLEN, Metus Gallicus – Metus Punicus (AAWM 1985,3), 1985   2 M. GELZER, Der Antrag des Cato Uticensis, Caesar an die Germanen auszuliefern, in: E. KAUFMANN (ed.), FS P. KIRN, 1961, 46–53   3 A. KNEPPE, Metus temporum, 1994   4 H. W. KROHNE, Theorien zur Angst, 1976   5 A. A. LUND, Die ersten Germanen, 1998   6 H. MENGE, Lateinische Synonymik, ⁶1977   7 D. TIMPE, Rom und die Barbaren des Nordens, in: M. SCHUSTER (ed.), Die Begegnung mit dem Fremden, 1996, 34–50   8 CH. TRZASKA-RICHTER, Furor Teutonicus, 1991   9 B. L. TWYMAN, Metus Gallicus. The Celts and Roman Human Sacrifice, in: The Ancient History Bulletin 11, 1997, 1–11   10 R. URBAN, Gallia rebellis, 1999.   TH.GR.

Mevania Umbrian city above the Plain of Foligno (modern Bevagna), *municipium* of the *tribus Aemilia* traversed by the *Via Flaminia*. Ancient remains: city walls, forum with a pseudoperipteros temple, theatre (1st cent. AD), amphitheatre, thermal baths (mosaics, 2nd cent. AD) and aqueduct. In the territory of M. there was viticulture and cattle breeding.

C. PIETRANGELI, Mevania (Bevagna), 1953; P. FONTAINE, Cités et enceintes, 1990, 223–244; A. E. FERUGLIO, Mevania, 1991.   G.U.

Mevius
I. REPUBLICAN PERIOD   II. IMPERIAL PERIOD

I. REPUBLICAN PERIOD
[I 1] Supposedly a poet (Porph. in Hor. Sat. 2,3,239) of the Augustean period, brother of → Bavius, with whom he allegedly quarreled over a woman (Domitius Marsus fr. 1 M.). M was a critic of Virgil (Serv. Georg. 1,210), which made the poets of the circle around Maecenas count him among their opponents (Verg. Ecl. 3,90; Hor. Epod. 10; Domitius Marsus fr. 5 M.). Some notes may have been obtained from Suet. De poetis via the life of → Domitius [III 2] Marsus. The possibility of guild banter can not be excluded.

A. ROSTAGNI (ed.), Suetonius, De poetis, 1944, 123–126; W. KRENKEL, in: J. IRMSCHER (ed.), Römische Literatuur der Augusteischen Zeit, 1960, 36–38.   P.L.S.

II. IMPERIAL PERIOD
[II 1] C. M. Donatus Iunianus Senator, probably in the 3rd cent. AD. *Quaestor* in Sicily, *aedilis, praetor; curator civitatium universarum* probably in Sicily, imperial legate for Cilicia and lastly suffect consul. PIR² M 575.

F. JACQUES, Les curateurs des cités dans l'occident romain: de Trajan à Gallien, 1983, 213ff.

[II 2] M. Honoratianus Equestrian official. *Praefectus classis* probably of the Ravenna fleet in 226 AD (RMD 3, 196) and prefect of Egypt from 232 to 237 AD. PIR² M 576.

[II 3] P. M. Saturninus Honoratianus Probably related to M. [II 2]. Procurator under Septimius Severus. He also bore the title *clarissimus vir*. M. was probably admitted to senatorial status together with his son of the same name. PIR² M 580; cf. M. 579.

[II 4] (P.?) M. Surus Probably related to M. [II 2] and M. [II 3]. Perhaps a praetorian legate for Raetia in the year 195 AD, then in *c.* 196 suffect consul and finally consular governor of Dacia in about 198/9. PIR² M 582.

PISO, FPD, vol. 1, 156ff.   W.E.

Mevulanus, C. As military tribune of the consul C. Antonius [I 2] in 63 BC, he conspired with the Catilinarians (→ Catilina) at Pisaurum (modern Pesaro). He was later attacked by the quaestor P. Sestius near Capua (Cic. Sest. 9; homonym: ILS 2994).

MRR 2,170; SCHULZE, 215.   T.FR.

Meydancıkkale Site of finds in the Cilician mountain zone near Gülnar in Turkey. Aramaic inscriptions record *KRŠ* as its ancient name. Possibly identical with a *Kiršu* mentioned in a Neo-Babylonian chronicle, the old royal seat of the land of Pirindu, which was later removed to Ura. In the Achaemenid period it was fortified [1]. Fragments of orthostatic reliefs with representations of servants and soldiers indicate a intensive orientation towards courtly models from the centre of the Persian Empire. In the Hellenistic period too there was a military base here. Significant hoards of coins have been found (3rd century BC).
→ Asia Minor

1 A. LEMAIRE, H. LOZACHMEUR, Bīrah/Bīrtā'n en araméen, in: Syria 64, 1987, 261–266.

A. DAVESNE a.o., Le site achéologique de Meydancıkkale (Turquie): Du royaume de Pirindu à la garnison ptolémaïque, in: CRAI 1987, 359–381; Id. a.o. (ed.), Gülnar 1: Le site de Meydancıkkale, 1998; Id. a.o., Gülnar 2: Le trésor de Meydancıkkale, 1989; HILD/HELLENKEMPER, 349.   BR.JA.

Mezentius (Mezenties) Ruler of → Caere, eponym of a *gens Mezentie(s)* living there, as attested by the inscription of a *Laucie Mezentie(s)* from Caere in the second quarter of the 7th century BC [1]. As king of the Etruscans (Liv. 1,2,3; Dion. Hal. Ant. 1,64,4; InscrIt 13,2,130f.), or ruler or king of Caere (e.g. Liv. 1,2,3; Fest. 212,20 L.), M. is said to have fought → Aeneas in Latium (Cato Orig. 1,10f. CHASSIGNET; Verg. Aen. 8,472–503). From the Rutuli (Cato Orig. 1,12 CHASSIGNET) or the Latini (Plut. Quaest. R. 45) M. is said to have demanded delivery of the wine harvest of a whole year (Varro in Plin. HN 14,88), the harvests of all further years (InscrIt 13,2,130f.) or only the *primitiae* ('first fruits') of the wine harvest (Cato Orig. 1,12 CHASSIGNET; Fest. 322,15–17 L.). The consecration of these *primitiae* to Jupiter by Aeneas after his victory over M. served as *aition* for the institution of the → Vinalia.

Despite the origin of the events surrounding M. in Roman mythology, a basic stock of independent tradition is available: A *gens Mezentie(s)* may have occupied a significant position in Caere in the 7th cent. BC [2], and, at the beginning of the 5th cent. and during the 4th, Caere was a city state with individual rulers [3]. It was only in the disputes with Caere in the 4th cent. BC and at the beginning of the 3rd that the Romans may have made the ancestor of the Mezentii the opponent of their own progenitor. M. as blasphemer (Cato Orig. 1,12 CHASSIGNET; Verg. Aen. 7,648) and adversary of *pius Aeneas* was then also brought in to explain the Vinalia.

1 D. BRIQUEL, A propos d'une inscription redécouverte au Louvre, in: REL 67, 1989, 78–92   2 H. RIX, Zum Ursprung des römisch-mittelitalischen Gentilnamensystems, in: ANRW I 2, 1972, 700–758   3 M. PALLOTTINO, Le iscrizioni etrusche, in: ArchCl 16, 1964, 76–117.

E. GABBA, Considerazioni sulla tradizione letteraria sulle origini della repubblica, in: Entretiens 13, 1966, 135–169; A. LA PENNA, s.v. Mezentio, EV 3, 1987, 510–515; M. SORDI, Il mito troiano e l'eredità etrusca di Roma, 1989; G. VANOTTI, L'altro Enea, 1995, 254ff.   L.A.-F.

Mezetulus Numidian prince, who in 206 BC rose violently to power as regent of the → Massyli. M. sought support from Carthage, marrying a niece of → Hannibal [4]. Late in 206, M. was defeated by the pretender → Massinissa, his kinsman, on the latter's return from Spain, but his life was spared (Liv. 29,29,6–30,12). In 202, he – if he is to be identified with the Mesotylus mentioned by Appian (App. Lib. 33,141) – rebelled, and fought for Hannibal. He presumably fell at Zama. → Punic Wars   JÖ.F.

Micali Painter An important Etruscan vase-painter of the black-figure style (→ Vase painting, black-figured) with a workshop at Vulci (ca. 530–500 BC); attribution by BEAZLEY, refined by SPIVEY. He displays a penchant for ornamental motifs and winged creatures such as sirens, sphinxes and pegasi. The figures are often elongated and drawn with expressive gestures: they are initially under strong Ionian, later Attic influence. Battle scenes are dominant among motifs of mythical imagery. The workshop continued, at a lower level of achievement, until the early 5th. cent. (SPIVEY).

BEAZLEY, EVP, 1947, 12–16; N. J. SPIVEY, The Micali Painter and His Followers, 1987.   F.PR.

Micare see → Guessing games

Miccalus (Μίκκαλος; *Míkkalos*). Antiochene, brother of the provincial governors Evagrius and Olympius. He was himself administrator of Thrace in AD 362. Libanius describes his dispute with his brother Olympius (Lib. Or. 63,30–35; cf. also Lib. Epist. 97–99, 149). PLRE 1, 602.   W.P.

Micciades (Μικκιάδης; *Mikkiádes*). Father of → Archermus, of Chios. Pliny (HN 36,11) places him at the head of a Chian family of sculptors, erroneously giving him as the son of one → Melas [4]. However, the source which Pliny misread (and which survives), a votive epigram from Delos, dated to approx. 550 BC, does not say that M. was a sculptor.

OVERBECK, No. 314; LOEWY, No.1; J. MARCADÉ, Recueil des signatures de sculpteurs grecs, Vol. 2, 1957, 75; B. S. RIDGWAY, The Nike of Archermos and Her Attire, in: J. BOARDMAN (ed.), Chios, 1986, 259–274.   R.N.

Michael (Μιχαήλ/*Michaél*; Mîkā'ēl).
[1] **Archangel** One of the most prominent angels (cf. the description *archistratēgós*, 'supreme commander' of the heavenly host, Joseph of Aseneth 14,8, cf. Slavonic Hen 22,5; 33,10), one of the seven (Ethiopic Hen 20,5) or four (Ethiopic Hen 9,1; 10,11) archangels (cf. [1]). The name means 'who is like God' or 'who is victorious like God'. M., who was first mentioned in the 'Book of Watchers' (Ethiopic Hen 1–36, end of the 4th/beginning of the 2nd cent. BC), played an important role in early extra-canonical Judaic scripture, primarily on account of his collective and individual protective and intercessive functions. He was the patron of the people of God ('set over Israel', Ethiopic Hen 20,5), fighting for Israel against the angels of other peoples (Dan 10,13; 10,21; cf. also 1QM 17,6f.) or interceding on behalf of the people of God (Testament of Levi 5,6; Ethiopic Hen 68,4), and in the final hour standing up for Israel as 'a great prince' (Dan 12,3). In Apc 12,7 M. fights → Satan and his angels. In the context of individual eschatology, M. is a psychopomp who escorts the souls of the dead to God, protecting them against external danger (cf. e.g. Testament of Abraham A 8ff; Vita Adae et Evae 46ff.; Jud 9, according to which M. fights the Devil over the soul of Moses). In → Rabbinical literature, where M. can be identified with the angel → Metatron, he appears primarily in close connection with the patriarchs (cf. the rescue of Abraham from the furnace, or the appearance in → Mamre). He also acts as a priest who offers sacrifice in the heavenly sanctuary (Babylonian Talmud, tractate Hagiga, folio 12b e.g.) or, in a spiritualised version of the motif, offers up prayers or the souls of the righteous (Midrash Rabba on Numbers (Bamidbar) 12:12, folio 49a).

In Christian literature M. appears as a patron saint of the people of God (Apc 12,7–17; Herm. Sim.). The representation of M. as dragon-slayer or as accompanier and weigher of souls in the Final Judgment is typical of Christian iconography, which stands in the context of a widespread Christian worship of M. (cf. e.g. the numerous churches and places dedicated to M. from Constantinople on Monte Gargano through the Castel Sant'Angelo in Rome to Saint Michael's Mount in Normandy).

1 K. E. GRÖZINGER, s.v. Engel. III. Judentum, TRE 9, 586–596.

B. EGO, Der Diener im Palast des himmlischen Königs, in: M. HENGEL, A. M. SCHWEMER (ed.), Königsherrschaft Gottes und himmlischer Kult im Judentum, Urchristentum und in der hellenistischen Welt, 1991, 361–384; W. LUEKEN, Michael. Eine Darstellung und Vergleichung der jüdischen und morgenländisch-christlichen Tradition vom Erzengel Michael, 1898; M. MACH, s.v. Michael, in: K. van der Toorn e.a. (ed.), Dictionary of the Deities and Demons in the Bible, 1995, 1065–1072 (bibl.); J. P. ROHLAND, Der Erzengel Michael. Arzt und Feldherr. Zwei Aspekte des vor- und frühbyzantinischen Michaelkultes (Beihefte der Zeitschr. für Rel.- und Geistesgesch. 19), 1977; M. THEOBALD, s.v. Michael I: Biblischer Befund, LThK 7, 227f. (bibl.).   B.E.

[2] **M. Syncellus** Born in about 761 AD in Jerusalem. According to his *vita* he was of Arabian Christian origin. In ca. 786 AD monk of Sabas-Laura (→ Laura), in 798 priest, in 811 *sýnkellos* ('closest collaborator', originally 'cell companion') of Thomas, patriarch of Jerusalem. In 813 he and the brothers Theodorus and Theophanes Graptus set out on an ambassadorial journey to Constantinople and Rome, but on the way they were arrested during the second outbreak of iconoclasm (→ Syrian dynasty) in Constantinople in the year 815 and later banished to various places. After the restoration of the cult of icons in 843 he was abbot of the monastery of Chora and *sýnkellos* of Methodius, patriarch of Constantinople. He died in 846 AD.

M. was one of the most significant defenders of icon veneration in the early 9th cent. AD. His *vita* was written some time after his death and is of little value as a source. A great number of sermons and hagiographic encomiums, some poems in anacreontics and a treatise on syntax (which in fact deals with morphology) in his name survive, but it is disputed whether these should be attributed to him or to another *sýnkellos,* similarly named M. and living in Constantinople in the 9th cent. AD.

EDITION: D. DONNET (ed.), Le traité de la construction de la phrase de Michel le Syncelle de Jérusalem, 1982.
VITA: M. B. CUNNINGHAM (ed.), The Life of Michael the Synkellos. Text, Translation and Commentary, 1991.
BIBLIOGRAPHY: R. BROWNING, A. KAZHDAN, s.v. Michael, ODB 2, 1991, 1369f.   AL.B.

[3] **M. I Raggabe** Byzantine emperor 811–813 AD. Died on 11 January 844, married before 794 to Procopia, daughter of the later emperor → Nicephorus I (802–811), and rose under him to → Kouropalates. In July 811 Nicephorus fell in battle against the Bulgars, and his son, the co-emperor → Stauracius, was seriously wounded. He did succeed but on 1 October 811 was forced to abdicate, and M. was proclaimed emperor. Under his government, in the summer of 812 AD in Aachen, Byzantine ambassadors conceded to Charlemagne the title of *basileús* (*imperator*), whereas the Eastern Roman emperor thenceforth styled himself officially *Basileùs tôn Rhōmaíōn*. After a defeat by the Bulgars at Versinika, M. abdicated on 11 July 813 in favour of → Leo [8] V and became a monk.

ODB 2, 1362; P. SCHREINER, s.v. Michael (3), LMA 6, 597.

[4] **M. II.** Byzantine emperor 820–829 AD, founder of the → Amorian dynasty, born in Amorion (Asia Minor) to a modest family and died in Constantinople on 2 October 829. His rise in the imperial court was due primarily to the emperor → Leo [8] V. When the latter imprisoned him in 820 for participation in a plot, M.'s conspirators assassinated him and proclaimed M. emperor. In 823 he managed to assert himself against the usurper Thomas the Slav. In the following years the Arabs invaded Crete and gained a foothold on Sicily. M. continued in moderate form his predecessor's renewed policy against the veneration of cultic images. On iconoclasm see → Syrian dynasty.

ODB 2, 1363; P. SCHREINER, s.v. Michael (4), LMA 6, 597.

[5] **M. III** Byzantine emperor in 842–867 AD of the → Amorian dynasty. Born on 19 January 840 and died on 23/24 September 867, both in Constantinople. After the death of his father Theophilus (20 January 842) he was subject first to the regency of his mother until 856, then of her brother, the *kaisar* (Caesar) → Bardas, until 866. Lastly, he was domineered by his favourite Basilius, who assassinated him in 867, ascended the throne as → Basilius [5] I and later distorted the memory of M. through systematic propaganda. M. had (almost) no influence on important events during his reign (sanctioning of icon veneration in 843, elevation of the scholar → Photius to patriarch in 858, Christianisation of the Bulgars in 864, naval action against the Arabs on Crete and in Egypt). Nevertheless there is no doubt he campaigned actively and successfully against the Arabs in Asia Minor in 859 and 863.

ODB 2, 1364; P. SCHREINER, s.v. Michael (5), LMA 6, 597f.

[6] **M. IV** Byzantine emperor 1034–1041 AD, born in Paphlagonia, died in Constantinople on 10 December 1041. He was introduced in the imperial court by his brother, the court eunuch Iohannes Orphanotrophos, and became the lover of the empress → Zoe, heiress of the → Macedonian dynasty, who married him after the assassination of her first husband → Romanos [4] III Argyros and had him proclaimed emperor. He was only fit to rule in a limited way, being an epilectic. Internal politics were set by his brother Iohannes, who introduced new taxes to increase the state income and also brought into circulation gold coins of reduced standard. Nevertheless M. personally led a successful campaign against a rebellion by the Serbs in 1040/1. After the triumphal celebration of the victory he abdicated, withdrew to a monastery and died there shortly afterwards.

ODB 2, 1365f.; P. SCHREINER, s.v. Michael (6), LMA 6, 598.

[7] M.V Byzantine emperor from 10 December 1041 to 20 April 1042 AD, called 'the Caulker' after his earlier occupation, nephew of → Michael [6] IV. He was designated by → Zoe, the childless heiress of the → Macedonian dynasty, as the successor of M. IV. He was adopted, given the title of Caesar and ascended the throne after M's IV abdication and death. He attempted to banish Zoe in order to deprive her of power, but the people of Constantinople revolted and helped Zoe, together with her sister → Theodora, take over the rule. M. was blinded and died in a monastery shortly after afterwards.

ODB 2, 1366; P. SCHREINER, s.v. Michael (7), LMA 6, 598. F.T.

[8] M. Chartophylax (M. Χαρτοφύλαξ). Editor (10th cent. AD) of a presumably abridged copy of an anthology by Cephalas, which was used by the corrector (C) of the *Anthologia Palatina* (→ Anthology A, E). A single epigram by M. survives: three iambic trimeters in praised of a picture of the Madonna and child (Anth. Pal. 1,122).

A. CAMERON, The Greek Anthology from Meleager to Planudes, 1993, 111f., 116–120, 151, 325. M.G.A.

[9] M. Syrus Syrian Orthodox patriarch of → Antioch [1] (1166–1199 AD). Before M. became patriarch, he was abbot in charge of the important monastery of Barṣaumā near → Melitene. He was the author of the most important and most comprehensive of all Syrian world chronicles (up to the year 1194/5), in which he preserved numerous original documents and used older, otherwise lost sources, such as the chronicle of → [Ps.]-Dionysius [23] of Tell-Maḥrē (died 845). There are two recensions of an abridged Armenian adaptation of his chronicle. Chief among his other activities is the reform of the Syrian Orthodox pontifical ritual.

J. B. CHABOT (ed.), Chronique de Michel le Syrien, 4 vols., 1899–1924 (repr. 1963); V. LANGLOIS (ed.), Chronique de Michel traduite sur la version arménienne, 1868; W. HAGE, s.v. Michael, TRE 22, 1992, 710–712; A. SCHMIDT, Die zweifache armenische Rezension der syrischen Chronik Michael des Großen, in: Le Muséon 109, 1996, 299–319; E. TISSERANT, s.v. Michel le Syrien, Dictionnaire de Théologie Catholique 10/2, 1929, 1711–1719. S.BR.

Michaelios Grammatikos Otherwise unknown author of an epigram praising the image of → Agathias (whom he extols as an orator and poet), of his brother and of his father Memnonius (Anth. Pal. 16,316). The poem will presumably have been affixed to the base of a statuary group in Myrina [4] (the town in l. 1), perhaps not long after the death of Agathias (after AD 580). Identification with later poets of the same name is improbable.

Av. and A. CAMERON, The Cycle of Agathias, in: JHS 86, 1966, 8, Note 18. M.G.A.

Micines (Μικίνης; *Mikínēs*). An Athenian, whose name is known only because he was murdered in the streets of Athens one night between 403 and 380 BC. Lysias wrote a speech for the ensuing trial, which subsequently became famous (Fragment 90 THALHEIM, hypothesis of Antiphon 2a). M.W.

Micion (Μικίων; *Mikíōn*). Son of M., from Cephisia. Shortly after 230 BC he and his brother → Euryclides saw to it that the Macedonian troops in → Piraeus under Diogenes [1] were paid and hence left (IG II² 834, 10ff.; [1. 79ff.; 118ff.]). He had helped Athens before (in 248/7; at the time perhaps *agōnothétēs*: IG II² 1705), when it was threatened from outside (Agora XVI 213 I 35, cf. [2. 26ff.]). From the 240s until the 220s M. and his brother rejected an alliance with → Aratus [2] on ground of neutrality (Plut. Aratus 24; 33–34; 41; Pol. 5,106; [3. 235–240]). In the state cult of Demos [1] and the Charites (cf. [5]) they introduced, the two presumably practiced a hereditary priesthood [2. 183]. As benefactors of Athens (cf. IG II² 834) they were still alive in the last decade of the 3rd century ([1. 120ff.]: IG II² 844, 33ff.) and were allegedly poisoned by → Philippus V (Paus. 2,9,4). The family (genealogy: [1. 182]; to be supplemented from Agora I 7529, l. 99) retained political influence until the last quarter of the 2nd century [2. 288] and so is exemplary of the class of honoratiores in Athens which started forming in 230.

1 CHR. HABICHT, Studien zur Geschichte Athens in hellenistischer Zeit, 1982 2 HABICHT, 154–196 3 B. DREYER, Review of [2], in: GGA 250, 1998, 207–250 4 J. D. MIKALSON, Religion in Hellenistic Athens, 1998, 168–207 5 LGPN 2, 313, Nr. 19. BO.D.

Micipsa (Μικίψας/*Mikípsas*). Eldest heir of → Massinissa. He, → Mastanabal and → Gulussa were regents after Massinissa's death in 148 BC. He was in charge of the royal residence of → Cirta (App. Lib. 106; Zon. 9,27 D.). After the death of his two brothers M. ruled alone (Sall. Iug. 5). In the Iberian theatre of war and in Sardinia M. and Mastanabal supported Rome with troops and supplies (App. Lib. 111; Sall. Iug. 7–8; Vell. 2,9,4; Plut. C. Gracchus 23,5). In 134 M. sent → Iugurtha with auxiliary troops to Numantia, allegedly to expose him to danger (Sall. Iug. 6–7). M. continued Massinissa's policy of urbanisation and settled Greek merchants in Cirta (Strab. 17,3,13), but there were natural catastrophes and crises in supplies (123/2: Liv. Periochae 60; Oros. 5,15; Aug. Civ. 3,21; Obseq. 90). M. raised Mastanabal's son Iugurtha with his own sons, adopted him in about 121 and made him and his sons → Adherbal [4] and → Hiempsal [1] his heirs (Sall. Iug. 5–11). On his death they succeeded him, ruling as a threesome (Liv. Periochae 62).
→ Numidae

M. R.-ALFÖLDI, Die Geschichte des numidischen Königreiches und seiner Nachfolger, in: H. G. HORN, C. B. RÜGER (eds.), Die Numider, 1979, 43–74; C. SAUMAGNE, La Numidie et Rome. Masinissa et Jugurtha, 1966. B.M.

Micon (Μίκων/*Míkōn*). Greek painter and sculptor (Plin. HN 34,88) from Athens, active between 475 and 440 BC. He and → Polygnotus belonged to the first important generation of the Attic painting school in the early classical period, which broke ground for the development of the great Greek → painting. None of the wall paintings in Athens known from numerous written sources of various periods survives, but frequent mention does allow us to infer his great significance. His main patron was → Cimon [2] of Athens, whose political and ideological ambitions must have influenced M.'s works (→ Historical subject, paintings of). In ancient literature, a painting of the return of the Argonauts in the anaceum, a sanctuary of the Dioscuri on the agora in Athens, is mentioned (Paus. 1,18,1). M. also worked, with others, on the decoration of the → Stoa Poikile. His specific contribution can not be determined precisely; he is generally credited as the painter of an Amazon battle which alluded to the recent → Persian Wars. There were further paintings by M. illustrating various myths from the life of Theseus in the Theseion, the Attic hero's cult site. These paintings cannot be attributed with certainty to him either, because of differing traditions. M.'s style can be inferred rudimentarily from vase paintings on similar themes by the → Niobid Painter and other contemporaries, and from later Etruscan bronze cists and vases. These indicate that he strove to convey the impression of objects placed behind each other within the pictorial space. Sources also emphasise his skill in a special blending of → pigments and a particular love for the representation of details, e.g. of horses.

B. Cohen, Paragone: Sculpture Versus Painting, in: W. G. Moon (ed.), Ancient Greek Art and Iconography, 1983, 171–188; P. Moreno, Pittura greca da Polignoto ad Apelle, 1987, 64ff., passim; F. Prost, Miltiades et le lièvre, in: M.-Chr. Villanueva-Puig (ed.), Céramique et peinture grecques, 1999, 245–255; A. Reinach, s.v. Micon, Textes grecs et latins relatifs à l'histoire de la peinture ancienne: Recueil Milliet, ²1985; M. Robertson, The Art of Vase Painting in Classical Athens, 1992, 180ff.; I. Scheibler, Griechische Malerei der Antike, 1994; S. Woodford, More Light on Old Walls, in: JHS 94, 1974, 158–164.   N.H.

Micythion (Μικυθίων; *Mikythíōn*) from Chalcis [2], son of Mikylion (Syll.³ 585, 235f.), an influential friend of the Romans, who in the years 198–192 BC stopped a pro-Aetolian or a pro-Seleucid movement in Chalcis but then had to flee before the Seleucid king → Antiochus [5] III. (Liv. 35,38,1–12; 46,9–13; 50,10; 51,4; 6; Diod. 29,1) [1. 81–84; 130]. He returned after the Roman victory and continued to be part of the *principes* (compare IG XII 9,904).In 179/8 BC he acted as *próxenos* in Delphi (Syll.³ 585,235f.). In 170 BC, in spite of his great age and difficulty in walking, he was in Rome as an envoy denouncing the brutal attacks of Roman officials in Chalcis (Liv. 43,7,5–11).

1 J. Deininger, The Political Opposition against Rome in Greece, 1971.   L.-M.G.

Micythus (Μίκυθος; *Míkythos*). Son of Chirus, from the house of the tyrant Anaxilaus [1] of Rhegium. For nine years after Anaxilaus' death around 476 BC he was governor (ἐπίτροπος; *epítropos*) of Rhegium for his sons who were not legally of age (Hdt. 7, 170; Iust. 4,2,5; Diod. 11,48ff.). M. helped the people of Tarentum against the tribes of the Iapyges but suffered huge losses to his army. Probably after an intervention of → Hieron [1] of Syracuse he handed over control to Anaxilaus' sons and went to Tegea in Arcadia. From there he dedicated numerous votive offerings at Olympia for saving one of his sons who was seriously ill (Paus. 5,24,6; 26,2ff.; IvOl, Nos. 267–269).

N. Luraghi, Tirranidi achaiche in Sicilia e magna Grecia, 1994.   B.P.

Midaeum (Μίδαιον/*Mídaion*; Μιδάειον/*Midáeion*). City named after its legendary founder king → Midas (on coins from M.). Near the River Tembris (Porsuk Çayı; on coins from M.) in → Phrygia Epictetus (Str. 12,8,12) at Karahöyük on a high hill. Inhabited from Phrygian until Byzantine times. To the east of Dorylaeum on the road to Pessinus (Tab. Peut. 9,3). As early as the 5th cent. BC mentioned by Hellanicus (FGrH 4 F 17). Sextus Pompeius was captured here in 36 BC (Cass. Dio 49,18,4). M. was in the *conventus* of Synnada (Plin. HN 5,105). It minted coins from Augustus until Philippus Arabs. It later belonged to Phrygia Salutaris (Hierocles, Synekdemos 678,3). Suffragan bishopric of Synnada.

H. von Aulock, Münzen und Städte Phrygiens 2, 1987, 30–34, 99–111; Belke/Mersich, 341f.   T.D.-B.

Midas (Μίδας/*Mídas*).
I. Historical
II. Graeco-Roman literature

I. Historical

King of Phrygia, son of Gordius [1]. Assyrian sources document him as *Mit-ta-a*, 'king of the land of Muski,' for 718–709 BC. In the epichoric inscriptions of Yazılıkaya ('city of Midas') the name M. is found in conjunction with the titles laϝagtei and ϝanaktei. The name M. is more likely Old Anatolian than Phrygian.

According to Assyrian sources M. conspired with the Luwian kings of Atuna (Tyana), Karkemiš, Gurgum and Malida against Sargon II, until he – snubbing Urarṭu and fearing the Cimmerians – placed himself under Assyrian rule in 710/9. According to Herodotus (1,14) he established a throne at Delphi, which was not unusual within oriental royal diplomacy. M., it seems, developed the Phrygian script, inspired by Phoenician inscriptions such as those of Warpalawa of Atuna (e.g. in İvriz) north of the Taurus. He may also have adopted the cult of → Cybele from Luwian territory (→ Karkemiš). According to Eusebius's chronicle (Versio Armenica 84 Schoene) M. died in 696/5 BC. A skel-

eton found in 1957 in an undisturbed burial chamber under the 'Great Tumulus' in Gordium may be his.
→ Asia Minor (III. C.)

C. Brixhe, M. Lejeune, Corpus des inscriptions paléophrygiennes, 1984, 8; J. D. Hawkins, s.v. Mita, RLA 8, 1994–1997, 271–273; M. J. Mellink, Bilinguals, in: G. Arsebük (ed.), Light on Top of the Black Hill. FS H. Çambel, 1998, 495–498; Idem, in: CAH III 2, ²1991, 622–634.
P.HÖ.

II. Graeco-Roman literature

The historical Phrygian king became an important figure in Graeco-Roman literature. As a son of Gordius [1] (Hdt. 8,138) he was integrated into the genealogy of the Phrygian kings (described as *rex* in Ov. Met. 11,92 and Hyg. Fab. 191). As a wise man and pupil of → Orpheus (Ov. Met. 11,92–93) he traps → Silenus (Hdt. 8,138), by adding wine to a well and getting him drunk (Xen. An. 1,2,13; Theop. FGrH 115 F 75a). Silenus tells M. what his goal was and shares his knowledge (similar to the capture of Faunus and Picus by Numa in Ov. Fast. 3,291–328 and Plut. Numa 70c-d, likewise the enforced confrontation of Menelaus with the sea-daemon Proteus in Hom. Od. 4,384–570): the pessimistic and in antiquity frequent insight that it would be best never to be born and second best to die as soon as possible (Cic. Tusc. 1,48; Ael. VH 3,18 = Theop. FGrH 115 F 75c). M. entertains Silenus festively and takes him with him in pursuit of → Dionysus, who in return grants M. his wish that everything he touches should become gold. As a result M. soon is no longer able to eat or drink, but, on the advice of Dionysus, he takes a bath in the → Pactolus (aition for its gold content) and loses the curse-bringing gift (Ov. Met. 11,100–145; Hyg. Fab. 191; schol. Aristoph. Plut. 287).

M. withdraws into the mountains and becomes a witness to the musical competition between the cithara-playing of → Apollo and the flute-playing of → Pan (Marsyas in Hyg. Fab. 191). The mountain god Tmolus had awarded the first prize to Apollo, but M. associates himself unbidden with the contrary assessment. As a punishment for his inappropriate judgment he receives from Apollo the ears of an ass, which he hides under a tall hat (in Graeco-Roman interpretation, aition for the tall Phrygian caps). Only his barber knows about it, but collapses under the burden of not being able to tell anybody, and in relief tells a hole in the ground of the king's disfigurement. However, reeds growing on this land wave in the wind and whisper the truth to the world (Ov. Met. 11,146–193; grotesque reflections on this: schol. Lycophr. 1401).

As an important mythical figure of Phrygia, M. is also associated with the cult of → Cybele (see above I), as her son (Hyg. Fab. 191) and as the founder of her temple in → Pessinus (Diod. 3,59,8), similarly, connections with → Attis are reported (Arnob. 5,7). Hellenistic constructions make → Lityerses, the singer of the Phrygian harvest song, his son (schol. Theocr. 10,41). According to Hyg. Fab. 274 M. was the first to discov-

er/invent lead (*plumbum nigrum*) and tin (*plumbum album*), Paus. 1,4,5 also ascribes to him the invention of the anchor (in contrast to Plin. HN. 7,209: the Tyrrhenian Eupalamus).

The musical competition is a theme of many modern operas [1. 449–451].

1 E. M. Moormann, W. Uitterhoeve, Lexikon der antiken Gestalten, 1995.

F. Bömer, P. Ovidius Naso, Metamorphosen, B. 10–11, 1980, 259–263; M. C. Miller, s.v. Midas, LIMC 8.1, 846–851; 8.2, 568–572.
JO.S.

Middle Comedy see → Comedy

Middle Greek see → Greek

Middle Platonism

A. Definition   B. External circumstances C. Theory of principles   D. Constitution of reality   E. Cosmogony   F. Fate and providence   G. Theory of the soul   H. Ethics   J. Significant representatives K. Influence

A. Definition

Since K. Praechter, Middle Platonism has been the term for the period of ancient Platonism from the return of the Platonic → Academy to dogmatism under → Antiochus [20] of Ascalon (died 69 BC) until the beginning of Neoplatonism under → Plotinus (died 270 AD; → Dogmatists [1]; → Neoplatonists). The term is modern, but the periodization is ancient in as far as the Neoplatonists themselves distinguished between the 'old exegetes' before Plotinus and the 'new ones' (Procl. in Pl. Ti. 1,218,2ff.; 2,104,17ff.; 212,12ff./213,8ff.; 3,234,9ff.; 245,19ff. Diehl; Hierocles in Phot. Bibl. cod. 251, 461a 30ff.; Simpl. in Aristot. Ph. 790,30f. Diels; cf. [1. 655f.; 2. 165 with note 1]).

B. External circumstances

Middle Platonism fell in a period of philosophical blossom. It was taught as a subject in all the larger cities; philosophers were often legally and materially supported by the state or the cities and publicly honoured [3. 2ff., 121ff.]. The period is methodically characterised by a meticulous philological and philosophical exegesis of → Plato's works, both in teaching and in literary production. Following Plato's teaching and practice, oral teaching was the main form of mediation, and almost all written work by the Platonists arose out of it. These included biographies of Plato, the classification and epitomisation of Plato's dialogues, the presentation of the whole of his theory, introductory writings of various kinds, Plato lexicons, remarks on Plato's style, special treatises in individual problematic areas, and, above all, comprehensive commentaries on Plato's dialogues. Most of this rich literary production has been lost; we know of it only through excerpts and fragments. Only a few of the Platonists' writings survive, in whole or in part [3. 20ff., 162ff.]. The body of thought of Middle Platonism, very diverse in content, can be divided under the following headings.

C. THEORY OF PRINCIPLES

The principles (ἀρχαί, *archaí*) are an answer to the question of where things come from, and are therefore the origins or causes (αἴτια, *aítia*) on which all Being and Becoming are founded. Middle Platonists usually assumed three principles, the divine *nous* as the effective cause, the Ideas as the paradigmatic causes and matter as the material cause [4. 118ff., 387ff.]. Other Platonists added the form attached to matter as the formal cause, tools as the instrumental cause and the goal or purpose as the final cause [4. 132ff., 414ff.; 5]. In addition, still other variants of the theory of principles were represented [4. 124ff., 152ff., 399ff., 439ff.].

D. CONSTITUTION OF REALITY

Reality as a whole is divided into two areas: pure Being and mere Becoming. The first constitutes the intelligible cosmos (κόσμος νοητός/*kósmos noētós*), the second the perceptible cosmos (κόσμος αἰσθητός/ *kósmos aisthētós*) [4. 38ff., 256ff.; 6. 105f.; 7. 86⁶⁷].

1. THE INTELLIGIBLE COSMOS 2. THE PERCEPTIBLE COSMOS

1. THE INTELLIGIBLE COSMOS

At its head is an immaterial and transcendental god, identical with the Idea of the Good and the Platonic → *demiourgos* [8. 12ff.; 9. 30ff., 262ff.]. This god is usually regarded as pure mind (νοῦς, *noûs*), but occasionally also as mind in a divine soul [9. 245, 257]. The Ideas are often equated with the thoughts of this god. Like the god himself, they are divine, immutable, perfect and eternal. Their metaphysical location is usually seen as the god's mind, sometimes also its soul. The god is therefore the encompassing cause of the Ideas, producing them in an eternal act of creation. The Ideas for their part form an intelligible cosmos structured in itself, an intelligible living creature which is the model for the visible cosmos. The objects of this pure, perfect Being exist outside time and space in pure self-identity. Hence their life (βίος, *bíos*) is timeless eternity (αἰών, *aión*) [9. 367ff.].

The objects of → mathematics occupy a position halfway between the intelligible cosmos and perceptible world in as much as they, like the Ideas, are non-physical objects of thought, though, unlike the Ideas, they are not completely invariable [4. 84ff., 271f., 334ff., 350ff.; 9. 353, 359]. Because of this mid-position of its objects, mathematics is considered preparatory training (προγυμνάσματα, *progymnásmata*) for work on the Ideas [3. 100, 365; 4. 216¹, 229, 360, 491; 7. 93¹¹⁹, 140⁴⁶⁶].

2. THE PERCEPTIBLE COSMOS

The perceptible cosmos is characterised by constant Becoming and genesis [4. 38ff., 256ff.]. This cosmos is but an image of the intelligible cosmos – the most perfect image, but nevertheless only an imitation on a lower level. It can represent the Being of the intelligible cosmos only through its constant Becoming, and eternity only through passage in endless time. The perceptible cosmos is therefore the temporal expansion of the concentrated abundance of eternal Being in the intelligible cosmos [9. 369f.]. Like the intelligible cosmos, the perceptible world is a living creature, consisting of a world-body and a world-soul. The world-soul is ontologically prior to the world-body and follows in rank immediately after the divine *nous* and the ideas. It too stands in the middle between the two cosmoses and mediates between them [4. 62, 277ff., 322]. It is immaterial and transcends the world-body. It is the means by which the god steers the fate of the world, and by which the cosmos itself becomes a deity [4. 435, 446; 6. 55; 9. 110, 385, 389f., 413]. Other deities are the stars and the earth, also composed of body and soul [9. 281, 578f.].

The perceptible cosmos is a great sphere bounded by the sphere of the fixed stars. Inside it are the paths of the seven → planets then known (Saturn, Jupiter, Mars, Mercury, Venus, Sun, Moon – mostly in that order) [6. 90f.]. From this supralunar region, in which all motions remain (essentially) equal, the sublunar region is separated, stretching from the moon to the earth, which lies in the middle of the cosmic sphere [4. 272ff., 511f.; 9. 140f., 457f.]. Here, the order of movements is continually interrupted by irregularity; here alone evil and wickedness have their place [3. 334; 4. 162, 186ff., 188, 460, 463, 508ff.]. In the space between moon and earth → demons are located. They too consist of a soul and a (airy) body. Their task is mediation between gods and humans in sacrifices, prayers and prophecies. There are good and evil demons. The souls of the latter do not possess a perfect mind and hence are not emotionless like those of the gods, rather they are subject to passions. Hence they are responsible for wizardry and magic (→ demonology).

After demons come human beings. By their rational souls they are related to the world-soul and the gods. Yet they also possess an irrational part of the soul (τὸ ἄλογον, *to álogon*) – sometimes called irrational soul (ἄλογος ψυχή/*álogos psyché*) – consisting of the hot-tempered and the covetous (θυμοειδές/*thymoeidés* and ἐπιθυμητικόν/ *epithymētikón*), tempting them into moral misbehaviour. It is this irrational part of the soul that together with the etheric or pneumatic vehicle of the soul (αἰθηρῶδες/πνευματικὸν ὄχημα ψυχῆς; *aithērô-des/pneumatikòn óchēma psychês*) mediates between the rational soul and the body (Gal. De placitis Hippocratis et Platonis 474,25ff. DE LACY; Procl. in Pl. Ti. 3,234,8ff. DIEHL). After death, the soul is separated from the body, has to undergo judgment and is eventually reincarnated, either in a human being or an animal (Alcinous, Didascaliae 25 = 178,33ff. WHITTAKER-

Louis). Hence, animals are relatives of people and may, generally, not be killed. The lowest level of living creature (ζῷα/*zóia*) is formed by plants, which also possess souls. These correspond to the lowest part of the irrational souls of human beings, the *epithymētikón* [10]. The basic components of lifeless nature are the four or five elements, which consist of the 'Platonic solids': fire from the tetrahedron, air from the octahedron, water from the icosahedron, earth from the cube and the sky from the dodecahedron. These regular polyhedrons comprise formless and qualityless → matter (ὕλη/*hýlē*, as the Platonic χώρα/*chóra* was called). The elements are distributed in the cosmos in such a way that earth and water are in the centre, with the air around them, extending as far as the moon and above that the fire of the heavens. This was the customary theory of Middle Platonism. Some Platonists however assumed that the stars consisted of a fifth element, the aether [9. 180ff., 535ff.] (→ Elements, theories of the).

E. Cosmogony

The cosmos resulted from the interaction of the above-mentioned principles, with the true cause, god, utilising the other causes. Looking at the intelligible model, the god moulds the pre-cosmic matter and structures it in accordance with mathematical laws. The genesis itself had been expounded by the Platonic dialogue *Timaeus* and was not disputed. What was disputed was whether the cosmos had been formed once in a single (temporal) act (thus Plutarch, Numenius [6], Cronius [1], Atticus, Harpocration [1], in a modified form Severus) or was being produced by the god in an eternal act of creation (most Platonists). The problem was explosive because its answer had consequences for the eternality of the divine world-soul, the inner-cosmic gods, the demons, mankind and the human soul, and also for the immutability of the god himself. The aporias raised by the Platonists against the production of the world were countless, but their opponents were equally inventive in their solutions [9. 84ff., 373ff.].

F. Fate and providence

Although the world is structured in accordance with fixed mathematical laws, it is not subject to an absolute natural necessity, rather – as a consequence of refractory matter – at times accident and chaos have their place, but only in the sublunar sphere and only until they are bound anew by the laws of nature. In the sublunar sphere only the human → soul, endowed with reason, is excluded from the strict causal nexus of natural law. The soul is free in its decisions, but the consequences of its decisions are subject to the inexorable law of nature, → fate. Watching over everything is divine providence, reaching down in grades from the heavens to the earth [3. 320ff., 324f.; 7. 133⁴¹⁴; 11].

G. Theory of the soul

According to the Middle Platonists, the rational souls were created by god, but it was disputed whether this happened in a single act, as Plutarch, Atticus and their adherents believed, or in continuous creation. The latter was assumed by the majority of Platonists. According to them the rational soul – in human beings the upper part of the soul, the λογιστικόν/*logistikón* – is eternal. Whether this was also the case for the irrational parts of the soul, the θυμοειδές/*thymoeidés*, the ἐπιθυμητικόν/*epithymētikón*, and the pneumatic vehicle of the soul, was controversial (Procl. in Pl. Ti. 3,234,8ff. Diehl; Damascius in Pl. Phd. 1,177 Westerink). The rational soul in any case had existed before its birth and in this preexistence had seen the Ideas. In the turbulences of its incarnation it forgot this perception. However, in its earthly life the soul is reminded of this perception by copies or images of the Ideas. Only through this recollection (ἀνάμνησις/→ *anámnēsis*) can the soul achieve true understanding of reality, because only in this way can it recognise true Being and hence understand the image of this Being, the perceptible cosmos (Alcinous, Didascaliae 25 = 177,45ff. Whittaker-Louis; → Ontology). After the death of a human being the soul is separated more or less completely from its body (according to some Platonists also from the lower parts of its soul and its pneumatic vehicle), is judged and is rewarded or punished (Plut. De sera 23ff. [563f ff.]; De facie 28ff. [943c ff.]). After the appropiate time, the soul must descend into the cosmos again, either as punishment for its former life or with the task of establishing divine order on earth (Plut. De sera 32 [567e ff.]; Iamblichus on Stob. 1,378,25ff. W.) [10].

H. Ethics

It is the task of human beings and the highest goal of → ethics, to bring about the order demanded by the gods all in areas of life. This can happen in manifold ways, for example by the institution of states (Ammonius, Plutarch, Longinus etc.) [3. 129f., 201ff., 346, 380], but also by being active in philosophical communities, in philosophical schools, which for their part – primarily through the education of young people who later enter public life, but also through their authority – exerted great influence on the spiritual, cultural and political life of the period. In realizing this order, human beings attain a likeliness to the god (ὁμοίωσις θεῷ/*homoíōsis theōi*) and this is considered the goal of Platonic ethics: people should become like the god, in thought and in behaviour, so that they live like a god on the earth and thus in turn become models for others [7. 77²³, 137⁴⁵¹; 9. 56, 307ff.]. In order to achieve this goal they will allow their affects very limited freedom (μετριοπάθεια, *metriopátheia*) [7. 145f.⁵⁰²ff.] and seek perfection of the soul (ἀρετή, *aretḗ*, → Virtue) (Alcinous/ Albinus, Didascalicus 29ff. = 182,15ff. Whittaker-Louis). This leads to the best possible state (εὖ ἔχει, *eu échei*) of the divine portion of the soul (the δαίμων/ *daímōn*) and thus to human bliss (εὐδαίμων, *eudaímōn*) (ibid. 27f. [180,16ff.]).

J. Significant representatives

Among the most renowned Middle Platonists are Aelianus [3], Albinus, Alcinous [2], Ammonius [5], Apuleius [III], Atticus, Democritus [2], Dercylides, Eudorus [2], Gaeus, Harpocration [1], Hierax [4], Celsus, Longinus [1], Lucius [3], Manaechmus, Nicostratos [9], Origenes, Plutarchus of Chaeronea, Ptolemaeus, Severus, Taurus, Theon of Smyrna, Thrasyllus and Timaeus [12. 52ff.; 13].

Middle Platonism can not always be distinguished from → Neopythagoreanism, as some of its representatives (Numenius, Cronius, Nicomachus of Gerasa and perhaps also Moderatus) can be viewed equally as Neopythagoreans and as Middle Platonists [3. 149f., 217f., 269, 312, 313, 365f.; 12. 341ff.].

K. Influence

Out of Middle Platonism developed Neoplatonism. Many Neoplatonic ideas are already present or can be understood as further development of Middle Platonic ideas. Middle Platonism had a great influence on → Philo [I 12] of Alexandria and Christian theology in its various forms [15; 16], and on Hermetism [17] (→ Hermetic Writings) and the so called Chaldaic Oracles [18] (→ Oracula Chaldaica).

→ Plato;   → Neoplatonism;   → Neopythagoreanism; → Platonism

1 M. BALTES, Rezension zu C. ZINTZEN (ed.), Die Philosophie des Neuplatonismus, 1977, in: Gnomon 51, 1979, 655–657   2 A.-P. SEGONDS, Les fragments de l'Histoire de la philosophie, in: É. des Places (ed.), Porphyre, Vie de Pythagore. Lettre à Marcella, 1982, 163–197   3 DÖRRIE/BALTES 3, 1993   4 DÖRRIE/BALTES 4, 1996   5 R. W. SHARPLES, Counting Plato's Principles, in: L. AYRES (ed.), The Passionate Intellect. FS I.G. Kidd, 1995, 67–82   6 M. BALTES, Timaios Lokros, Über die Natur des Kosmos und der Seele, 1972   7 J. WHITTAKER, P. LOUIS (ed.), Alcinoos, Enseignement des doctrines de Platon, 1990 (with commentary and translation)   8 M. BALTES, Is the Idea of the Good in Plato's Republic beyond Being?, in: M. JOYAL (ed.), Studies in Plato and the Platonic Tradition. FS J. Whittaker, 1997, 3–23   9 DÖRRIE/BALTES 5, 1998   10 W. DEUSE, Untersuchungen zur mittelplatonischen und neuplatonischen Seelenlehre, 1983   11 W. THEILER, Tacitus und die antike Schicksalslehre, in: Phyllobolia. FS P. von der Mühll, 1946, 36–90 (= Forsch. zum Neuplatonismus, 1966, 46–103)   12 J. DILLON, The Middle Platonists, ²1996   13 S. LILLA, Introduzione al Medio platonismo, 1992   14 D. T. RUNIA, Philo of Alexandria and the Timaeus of Plato, 1986   15 J. H. WASZINK, Bemerkungen zum Einfluß des Platonismus im frühen Christentum, in: Vigiliae Christianae 19, 1965, 129–162 = C. ZINTZEN (ed.), Der Mittelplatonismus, 1981, 413–448   16 W. FAUTH, Philosophische Tradition und geistige Begegnung mit der Antike im Schrifttum der Patristik, in: GGA 230, 1978, 69–120   17 A.-J. FESTUGIÈRE, La révélation d'Hermès Trismégiste, vol. 1, ³1950; vols 2–4, 1949ff.   18 H. LEWY, M. TARDIEU, Chaldaean Oracles and Theurgy, 1978.

M. BALTES, Was ist antiker Platonismus?, in: Studia Patristica 24, 1992, 219–238; DÖRRIE/BALTES 1ff., 1987ff.; S. GERSH, Middle Platonism and Neoplatonism. The Latin

Tradition, vol. 1, 1986; C. ZINTZEN (ed.), Der Mittelplatonismus, 1981.   M.BA.

Midea (Μίδεια; *Mídeia* or Μιδέα; *Midéa*).
[1] City in Argolis City in → Argolis, in mythology (cf. Paus. 2,16; 25) one of the most important cities in the region. It had a Mycenaean citadel and palace on a steep hill about 1 km from modern Dendra in the northeast of the Argolian plain. Already abandoned in the Mycenaean period. Tholos tombs with rich finds, several burial chambers. New excavations started in 1983. The site of the historical village of M., incorporated into Argos and already abandoned by the Hellenistic period, has not yet been found. Sources: Str. 8,6,11; Paus. 2,16,2; 25,9; Steph. Byz. s.v. M.; Pind. Ol. 10,66; Theocr. 13,20; Apollod. 2,4,4; 6. Archeology: [1].

1 OpAth 16, 1986, 19–25; 17, 1988, 7–11; 18, 1990, 9–22; 19, 1992, 11–39; 20, 1994, 19–41; 21, 1996, 13–32 (excavation reports).

P. ASTRÖM a.o., The Cuirass Tomb and Other Finds at Dendra, 1–2, 1977–1983; K. DEMAKOPOULOU, Mycenaean Citadels, in: BICS 40, 1995, 151–176; A. PERSSON, The Royal Tombs at Dendra near Midea, 1931; Id., New Tombs at Dendra near Midea, 1942; G. WALBERG, Excavations on the Lower Terraces at Midea in the Argolid, in: E. de Miro a.o. (ed.), Atti e memorie del secondo congresso internazionale di micenologia, 1996, 1333–1338.
Y.L. E.MEY.

[2] Boeotian city mentioned in Hom. Il. 2,507 (Str. 8,6,11; Stat. Theb. 7,331; Nonnus Dion. 13,60; Steph. Byz. s.v. M.). According to Str. 1,3,18 and 9,2,35 it was inundated by Lake Copais. According to Paus. 9,39,1, it was an early settlement of → Lebadea.

FOSSEY, 336–318; J. M. FOSSEY, The End of the Bronze Age in the South West Copaic, in: Id., Papers in Boiotian Topography and History, 1990, 62–64.   P.F.

Midian
[1] Son of Abraham and Keturah in the genealogy of Genesis (Gn 25,2).
[2] (Hebrew *midyān*, Arab *madyān*). In the OT, name of a region south of → Edom and east of the Gulf of ʿAqaba. The region is presumably the homeland of the later Israelite national god → Yahweh. Settlement, trade, pottery making and camel breeding are attested archaeologically since the 13th/12th cent BC. From the 8th cents. BC., the Midianites were also involved in Arabian trade along the → Incense Road.
→ Maesaimanes

1 E. A. KNAUF, s.v. M. and Midianiter, Neues Bibel Lexikon 2, 1995, 802–804   2 G. E. MENDENHALL, s.v. M., Anchor Bible Dictionary 4, 1992, 815–818.   TH.PO.

Mididi (Punic *M(j)ddm*). An ancient Berber locality southwest of → Mactaris, the modern Henchir Meded. M. came under strong Punic influence. Some 25 Neo-Punic inscriptions dating from around the 1st cent. BC have been found to date, including votive inscriptions for Baal Hamon, who was replaced by Saturnus from about the 2nd cent. AD. Cf. also CIL VIII Suppl. 4, 23356 (*Mars patrius*). Other inscriptions: CIL VIII 1, 608–618; 2, 11772–11778; Suppl. 4, 23357–23394 a; AE 1985, 902 (?).

Some; E. LIPIŃSKI, s.v. M., DCPP, 292; F. VATTIONI, M. e le sue epigrafi, in: Studi epigrafici e linguistici 11, 1994, 113–128.   W.HU.

Midrash see → Rabbinical Literature

Midwife
I. ANCIENT ORIENT   II. GREECE   III. ROME

I. ANCIENT ORIENT
In Babylonia and Egypt midwives are only known from allusions found in literary texts. In the → Atraḥasis myth the mother goddess opens the womb, lets the woman deliver the baby 'on the birth brick' (cf. Ex 1,16) and determines the child's fate while cutting the umbilical cord.

E. BRUNNER-TRAUT, s.v. Hebamme, LÄ 2, 1074f.; M. STOL, Zwangerschap en geboorte bij de Babyloniërs en in de Bijbel, 1983, 84–86.   MA.S.

II. GREECE
The story of Agnodike (Hyg. Fab. 274), the first midwife, who allegedly went, dressed as a man, to study with a certain Herophilus, is obviously a foundation myth of the midwife profession [3. 52–85]. One may assume that women have always assisted other women in the process of birth, and it is not surprising to find female helpers in the *Corpus Hippocraticum* (Carn. 19 = 8,614 L.; for the abbreviations of treatises in the *Corpus Hippocraticum* see the table under → Hippocrates [6]). In legend, Athena acted as midwife to Leto and later taught Artemis, the goddess of childbirth, all her art (Aristid. 37,18). The midwife might be responsible for cutting the umbilical cord (Aristot. Hist. an. 587a9), hence the Ionic term for midwife, *omphalētómos*, (Hippoc. Mul. 1,46 = 8,106 L.; Hipponax Fr. 19 WEST). Socrates (in claiming to be the son of a midwife (Pl. Tht. 149b-e), describes the midwife (*maîa*) as an elderly woman who uses chants and charms as well as drugs in order to induce labour and ensure a successful birth. Midwifes might also write books of recipes dealing with problems of conception (Plin. HN 28,23). The description of Phanostrate in the 4th cent. BC as a midwife and doctor (IG II/III,3²,6873) suggests that midwives and female doctors had separate responsibilities, and that the *maîai* confined themselves entirely to midwifery while the female doctor ranged more widely, but this is far from certain [1. 275–290; 5]. Male healers appear also in the birth process (e.g., Hippoc. Foet. Exsect. 15 = 8,484 L.; note the male midwives on Paros in the 1st cent. AD, IG 12,5,199), and requently male

and female healers co-operate at a birth [1. 212f.]. The gynaecological texts of the *Corpus Hippocraticum* presuppose a male readership, as indeed do later writings on gynaecology.

III. ROME
The major ancient text on childbirth, Soranus' 'Gynaecology', early 2nd cent. AD, describes the excellent midwife as, among other things, sober, discreet, not superstitious, hard-working, literate and trained in diet, surgery and pharmacology. The 25 *obstetrices* named in CIL are mainly slaves or freed-women [4; 5. 515–518], and literary sources reveal a great variety of social statuses and expertise. Galen praised highly the midwives attending the wife of the consul Boethus (De praecogn. 8, CMG 5,8,1,110); he would not have been so complimentary about the bar-maid who according to Eunapius (Eunap. VS 463) acted also as the local midwife. But comparatice historical evidence suggests that the latter may have been the more typical midwife, combining medicine with other activities.
→ Birth; → Gynaecology; → Soranus

1 L. A. DEAN-JONES, Women's Bodies in Classical Greek Science, 1994   2 N. DEMAND, Monuments, midwives and gynecology, in: P. J. VAN DER EIJK et al., Ancient medicine in its socio-cultural context, 1995, 275–290   3 H. KING, Agnodike and the profession of medicine, in: PCPhS 12, 1986, 53–75   4 J. KORPELA, Das Medizinpersonal im antiken Rom, 1987   5 D. NICKEL, Berufsvorstellungen über weibliche Medizinalpersonen in der Antike, in: Klio 61, 1979, 515–518.   V.N.

Mieza (Μίεζα; *Mieza*). An ancient Macedonian town between Beroea [1] and Edessa [1], probably near modern Naoussa, its exact location is unknown. → Aristotle [6] taught the young Alexander the Great at the Nymphaeum of M. (Plut. Alexander 7). Peucestas, the *triērárchēs* of Alexander, came from M. (Arr. Ind. 18,6; [2. 318f. no. 634]). In the 3rd cent. BC, M. had the status of a polis, and received *theōroí* from Delphi [1. 17 l. 59]. Cf. also Plin. HN 4,34; Ptol. 3,12,36.

1 A. PLASSART, Inscriptions de Delphes. La liste des Théodorokes, in: BCH 45, 1921, 1–87   2 BERVE 2.

F. PAPAZOGLOU, Les villes de Macédoine, 1988, 150–152.   MA.ER.

Migonium (Μιγώνιον; *Migónion*). A locality on the Laconian coast south of Gythium, with a sanctuary of Aphrodite Migonitis (Paus. 3,22,1f.).

V. PIRENNE-DELFORGE, L'Aphrodite grecque (Kernos Suppl. 4), 1994, 212f.   Y.L. E.MEY.

Migration Migration denotes the more than temporary transfer of the residence of individuals and groups to another location. A uniform concept was lacking in antiquity, which elaborated only individual aspects of the associated concept: sedentarism was considered the

norm. This resulted in a fundamental contrast to nomadism (→ Nomads), which was conceived as anti-civi-
lization. Phenomena such as → *synoikismos* and → Colonization were perceived as the constitution, enhancement or expansion of one's own cultural space, i.e., as
fundamentally different from a migratory existence. It
was always groups understood as peoples or tribes that
appeared as migrants. When political borders were
crossed, migrations by individuals or families were
indeed subject to legal regularization (e.g., → *metoikoi*,
→ *isopoliteia*, → *commercium*, → *conubium*), or received due consideration as internal migration in administrative acts (e.g., the declaration *idía*) or legal developments (as in the doctrine of *origo*), but were not
associated with the aforementioned ones as phenomena
of migration. Only in foundation legends could there be
an overlap, for nomadism served not only as the epitome of a counter-world, but also as a stage of one's own
civilising development that had been overcome, i.e., an
objectified paradigm of the fear of regression and
decline. Migration was the subject of historical reflection particularly in this respect.

Hence, one model for the interpretation of the origins and decline of antiquity as the consequence of
population migrations stems from antiquity itself. Ibn
Ḥaldūn (1332–1406) was later to use it to sketch a
theory of history as the tension between sedentarism
and its menace by non-sedentary peoples [16]. However, the core of the modern conception is constituted
by the fact that a 'mechanism' of historical development
can be described in terms of a conflict between 'peoples'
competing for 'space' [8]. Such clichés are being broken
down by modern research on migration, which has its
roots in demography and the population history that
has grown out of it, as part of a combined social and
cultural history. E. G. RAVENSTEIN's 'laws' [14] provided an initial theoretical foundation which, however,
continued to rely on a mechanistic sociology ([14; 15],
cf. [6]). The overcoming of the prejudice of the allegedly
static nature of pre-modern societies led to the discovery of migration as a field of research for these periods
as well. Attention was thereby directed toward a complex nexus of conditions for historical change through
the transfer of technologies and ideas, but also of patho-
gens, with innovative or destructive consequences respectively [2; 3; 7; 11; 12; 13; 18. 21–62]. In order further to develop this nexus, there was a need – not only
because of the bulkiness of the material relating to these
questions – for a methodically and theoretically wide-
ranging interdisciplinary horizon, against which the
unity of the phenomenon is to be constituted, boundaries are to be defined against simplifying generalizations
that merely reproduce prejudices [10], typologies and
periodizations are to be achieved [9], and at the same
time the significance of empirical studies [1; 4; 5; 17]
should be made evident.

→ Citizenship; → Deportation; → Exilium; → Husbandry;→ Mercenaries; → Migration of peoples; → Mobility; → Town planning; → Traffic

1 M. BEER et al. (ed.), M. und Integration (Stuttgarter
Beitr. zur Histor. M.-Forsch.3), 1997   2 H. BRAUNERT,
Die Binnenwanderung, 1964   3 P. CLARK, D. SOUDEN
(ed.), M. and Society in Early-Modern England, 1987
4 A. GESTRICH et al. (ed.), Historische Wanderungsbewegungen (Stuttgarter Beitr. zur Histor. M.-Forsch. 1),
1991   5 Id., et al. (ed.), Ausweisung und Deportation
(Stuttgarter Beitr. zur Histor. M.-Forsch. 2), 1995   6 D.
B. GRIGG, E.G. Ravenstein and the 'Laws of M.', in:
Journ. of Historical Geography 3, 1977, 41–54   7 G.
JARITZ, A. MÜLLER (ed.), M. in der Feudalgesellschaft,
1988   8 A. and E. KULISCHER, Kriegs- und Wanderzüge,
1932   9 J. and L. LUCASSEN (ed.), M., M. History, History, 1997   10 W. H. McNEILL, Human M.: A Historical
Overview, in: id., R. S. ADAMS (ed.), Human M., 1978,
3–19   11 L. P. MOCH, Moving Europeans, 1992   12 A.
MÜLLER, I. MATSCHINEGG, M. – Wanderung – Mobilität
in Spät-MA und Frühneuzeit, in: Medium Aevum Quoti-
dianum 21, 1990, 3–92   13 C. P. POOLEY, I. D. WHYTE
(ed.), Approaches to the Study of M. and Social Change,
in: Ead., Migrants, Emigrants and Immigrants, 1991,
1–15   14 E. G. RAVENSTEIN, The Laws of M. (1), in:
Journ. of the Statistical Society 48, 1885, 167–227
15 Id., The Laws of M. (2), in: Journ. of the Statistical
Society 52, 1889, 214–301   16 B. D. SHAW, 'Eaters of
Flesh, Drinkers of Milk'. The Ancient Mediterranean
Ideology of the Pastoral Nomad (1982–83), in: Id., Rulers, Nomads and Christians in Roman North Africa,
1995, no. VI, 5–31 (with sources)   17 L. WIERSCHOWSKI,
Die regionale Mobilität in Gallien nach den Inschriften
des 1. bis 3. Jahrhunderts n.Chr., 1995   18 W.
WISCHMEYER, Von Golgotha zum Ponte Molle, 1992.
TA.S.

Migration of peoples

I. HISTORY OF THE TERM II. TIME-FRAMES AND
HISTORICIZATION III. HISTORY OF RESEARCH
IV. OUTLINE OF THE MIGRATION OF PEOPLES

I. HISTORY OF THE TERM

As a distinctive term for a specific period of history,
the German word *Völkerwanderung* first appears in the
title of SCHILLER's study *Über Völkerwanderung,
Kreuzzüge und Mittelalter* ('On the migration of peoples, the Crusades and the Middle Ages'; 1792). Earlier,
in 1778, M. I. SCHMIDT, in the introduction to his
Geschichte der Deutschen ('History of the German people'), had spoken cautiously of the 'so-called German
Völkerwanderung', and in 1791 J. G. HERDER in the
16th book of the *Ideen zur Philosophie der Geschichte
der Menschheit* ('Thoughts on the Philosophy of the
History of Humanity') had drawn a distinction between the 'long Völkerwanderung' and earlier 'barbarian' incursions into the Mediterranean (Ch. 6, 1985,
438). The distinctive use of the term migration of
Germanic peoples then quickly caught on. F. HEGEL
used it in 1822 in the 4th part of the *Philosophie der
Geschichte* ('Philosophy of History'; first section, vol.
12, 1970, 419) and F. SCHLEGEL in 1828 in the 11th
lecture of the *Philos. der Gesch.* ('Philosophy of History'; vol. 9, 1971, 254). Likewise, in 1828 HEINE noted
in the 3rd part of the *Reisebilder* ('Travel Pictures'; ch.

23, vol. 2, 1969, 205) on Verona that the city had been 'the first stopping-place for the migrating Germanic peoples' in a phase of history 'called by historians the *Völkerwanderung* or the Migration of Peoples'. RANKE, on the other hand, did not like the term or, like SCHMIDT, qualified it with 'so-called' (*Aus Werk und Nachlaß* ('From his Published and Unpublished Work') 4, 1975, 434; 460).

The construct Migration of Peoples (MP) was formed by analogy with the non-ancient compounds *populorum migratio* and *migratio gentium*. In → Eugippius' *Vita S. Severini*, that he composed in 511, the terms *populi migratio* and *populi transmigratio* are used for the move to Italy by the population of Noricum (Vita 40,6; 43,9; Ch. 40; 44). The term 'barbarian invasions', commonly used in Anglo-Saxon and Romance languages to designate this historical period, derives from the late Latin *invasio barbarica*, which also reflects the perspective of the Greek and Latin sources [4; 7].

II. TIME-FRAMES AND HISTORICIZATION

MP or invasion by the barbarians – both terms really apply only to the initial phase of a development that led to autonomous regimes being established under Germanic kings on the territory of the Western Roman Empire, in Gaul, Spain, North Africa and Italy. Although Rome had for centuries repelled, subdued or integrated intruders that penetrated the Roman Empire from the huge hinterland beyond the Rhine and Danube, it was no longer in a position to do so in the 5th and 6th cents. AD, as imperial central control grew weaker and weaker in the West and finally came to an end. The first to impose their autonomy on Iimperial territory were the → Tervingi or → Visigoths, who made way for the → Hunni in 376 and thrust across the Danube, where Emperor Valens [2] initially granted them territory for settlement in Thrace but was crushingly defeated by them in 378 at Adrianople (→ Hadrianopolis [3]). These events are generally regarded as the beginning of the MP, which had an acknowledged conclusion in 568, when the → Langobardi moved from Pannonia to Italy. They were the last to create their own dominion in the West.

The Roman historian → Ammianus Marcellinus saw the invasion of the → Goti in c. 390 as simply another link in the chain of large-scale Roman-Germanic clashes that had begun with the incursions of the → Cimbri and → Teutoni at the end of the 1st cent. BC and continued with the Marcomannic Wars of Marcus [2] Aurelius in AD 166–180 and the Gothic assaults of the 3rd cent. (cf. Amm. Marc. 31,5,12–17). Ammianus (14,6,3) also agreed with many non-Christians that *victura dum erunt homines Roma* ('the city of Rome, ever victorious while mankind exists') would meet the new danger just as it had met the earlier challenges. His Christian contemporaries Ambrose (De fide 2,137–138; expositio evangelii secundum Lucam 10,10), Jerome (Epist. 60,16) and Tyrannius Rufinus [6] (Historia ecclesiastica 11,13), on the other hand, saw the downfall of the *urbs aeterna* ('the eternal city') approaching. Both optimistic and pessimistic points of view continued in the following period and stood in the way of an appreciation of the MP as a distinct historical period. Its historicization did not come about until a long time afterwards, first of all in the retrospective survey with which the Langobard monk Paulus [4] Diaconus opened his *Historia Langobardorum* in c. 795 [7. Ch. II]. Even with RANKE's 'so-called 'migration of peoples'', however, there remains the methodological objection that no new epoch began in 376, as Rome had already had to deal with the Germani for centuries beforehand (→ Germani).

III. HISTORY OF RESEARCH

Academic interest in the migration of the MP began with Humanist scholars who were excited by the discovery in 1455 of the *Germania* of → Tacitus [1]. In 1530 W. PIRCKHEIMER published a *Germaniae ex variis scriptoribus perbrevis explicatio*, and in 1557 the Viennese doctor W. LAZIUS composed his work *De gentium aliquot migrationibus*. Tacitus' view that the Germani were a homogenuous, indigenous people, 'unlike any other', consisting of various but homogenuous tribes (Tac. Germ. 4,1) had a wide and sustained effect lasting into the 20th century. The etymology of the Latin → *gens* and *natio* and the term 'tribe' encouraged biological concepts going as far as to posit a Germanic race [2. 135]. Thus, whenever the transmission speaks of migrating tribes, it conjures up the image of a compact column of people sharing a common ethnic origin and a homogenuous culture and lifestyle. Individual doubts that entire peoples should have marched off 'with bag and baggage, the whole kit and caboodle' [20], did not circulate until classical philology had worked out the many topical elements in ancient historiography and ethnography [8; 15].

Further progress was made after the Second World War by non-ideological analysis of the transmission, taking into account the temporal bias of the written sources, reviewing philological-historical criticism against the archaeological evidence, and examining new questions raised by social history and comparative ethnography. Pioneering work was done by R. WENSKUS, who in his book [9] carried forward earlier hypotheses and demonstrated from a broad range of sources that a tribe was scarcely ever the fixed unit, which it is depicted in the non-Germanic transmission. Very often there were only 'kernels of tradition', which in transmission preserved the tribal name but which constantly underwent change themselves and which changed their environment through accumulation and acculturation. To understand the MP, new hypotheses emerged that were reflected in the intensive research of the last decades [5; 6]. They also disposed of the cliché, especially popular in earlier German thought, that young German tribespeople had delivered the death-blow to an aged empire, a senile population or an effete culture [3].

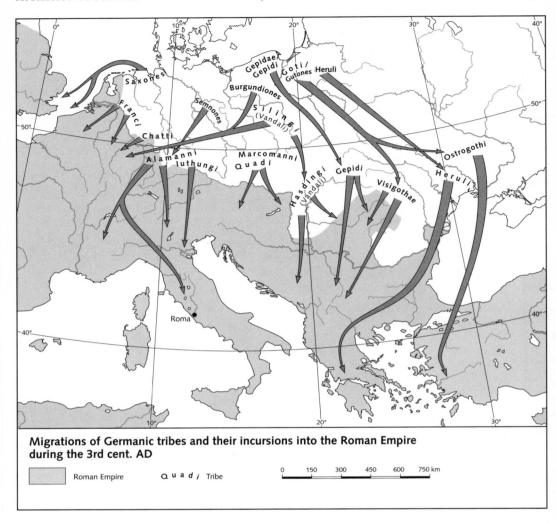

Migrations of Germanic tribes and their incursions into the Roman Empire during the 3rd cent. AD

Roman Empire   Q u a d i Tribe   0   150   300   450   600   750 km

IV. OUTLINE OF THE MIGRATION OF PEOPLES

The objective that the → Visigoths were seeking in 376 was the same as for earlier Germanic groups who were not just seeking to benefit from the wealth of the border provinces by raids of pillage and plunder. They were striving to find a place to live in the Imperium Romanum, in the hope of finding better living conditions and greater security there (→ Alaricus [2]; → Ataulfus; → Vallia). The objective remained unchanged in the following period. The → Suebi, → Vandali and → Alani, who pushed across the Rhine in 406 and across the Pyrenees in 409, were seeking that objective, just like the Burgundians (→ Burgundiones), who settled around Worms in 413, and the → Franci, who soon afterwards settled in northern Gaul. The → Angles (Angli), Jutes (Eutii/Euthiones) and → Saxons (Saxones) established themselves in southern Britain around 430. The → East Goths (Ostrogothi) and the → Langobardi sought a new homeland in Italy, the former in 489 (→ Theoderic [3] the Great), the latter in 568. The same objective characterised internal migrations like

those of the Vandals, who moved to North Africa in 429. Initially, the target area for settlement was always some region of the Empire. The only exception to that was the king of the Huns, Attila, when he sought to take the emperor's sister, → Honoria, as his wife in 450 and claimed half of the Western Empire as dowry [18. 93–97].

Throughout the Imperial Period, Rome had taken Germani in and had also constantly benefited from them. That was the case with the many thousand settlers and → prisoners of war granted land by the emperor but it was especially true of the Germani serving in the Roman army. Their influx started in the early Principate and reached its climax in the 4th cent., when the overwhelming majority of the troops under Constantine [1] I were of German origin. Constantine opened up the officer corps to the Germani: competent soldiers were able to rise to the upper ranks, or the emperor conferred officer appointments to the members of German nobility [14. 9–29, 30–53; 16]. Under his son Constantius [2] II, there then began the never-ending

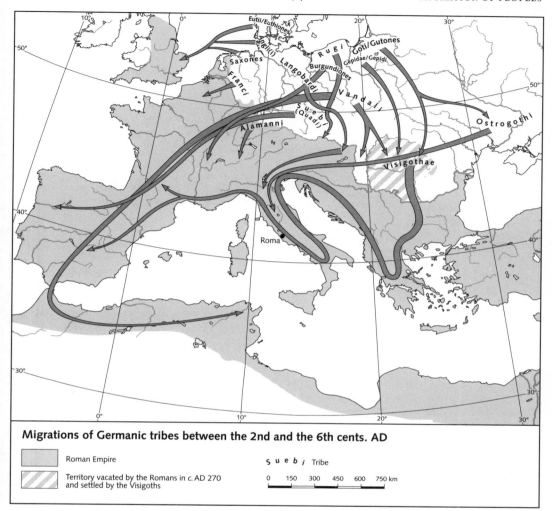

Migrations of Germanic tribes between the 2nd and the 6th cents. AD

Roman Empire

Territory vacated by the Romans in c. AD 270
and settled by the Visigoths

s u e b i   Tribe

0   150   300   450   600   750 km

series of German masters of the soldiers (→ *magister militum*; Aëtius [1]; Arbogastes; Bauto; Merobaudes [1]; Ricimer; Stilicho). No feelings of pan-Germanic nationalism constrained these 'Imperial Germans', if they were dispatched against other Germans, within or beyond the borders. Their loyalty to emperor and empire was ensured not only by their military career but even more so by the maintenance entitlements that they and their relatives could expect at the end of military service. Imperial policy after 376 also had precedents in earlier settlement and military service policy. The orator → Themistios, had this in mind when he predicted to emperor Theodosius that the West Goths, who had been settled in 382 with extensive autonomy, would one day become good Roman citizens (Them. Or. 16,211 C-D).

Such integration, however, did not take place, either with the West Goths or with later intruders. The reasons lay with both the Romans and the Germani. Peaceful integration ran counter to the ambition of the Germanic leaders and their followers' lust for booty. Even if, to

integrate them into their policy, the emperors granted high office to the leaders, who were military rather than tribal kings, they did not abandon their plan of establishing their own area of territorial sovereignty, in which they were autonomous lords rather than willing → *foederati*. Thir plans were supoorted by the fact that the series of strong emperors who had ensured the security of the empire, internally and externally, in the 4th cent. were succeeded in the 5th cent. by mere weak incumbents (→ child emperors). Working even more against integration was the fact that both halves of the empire grew further apart after 395 and the German leaders frequently had the opportunity to exploit the differences between East and West for their power-struggle that was constrained more by their German neighbours than by Roman resistance. Consequently, integration increasingly became an illusion.

However, even the contrary policy to integration, namely warding off and driving the attackers away, failed, starting with Adrianople in 378 (→ Hadriano-polis [3]), when Rome suffered one of the heaviest

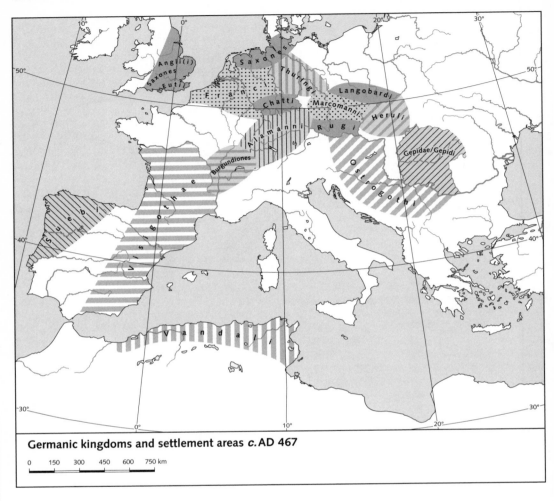

Germanic kingdoms and settlement areas *c.* AD 467

0   150   300   450   600   750 km

defeats in its history: about two thirds of the army of the eastern half of the empire perished in the battle against East and West Goths. Initially, the western half had greater military capability, and if the energetic Valentinianus [1] I, who had driven back the → Alamanni on several occasions, had been succeeded by an Emperor of similar stamp, Gaul would not so easily have become a playground of several Germanic forces in 406, and Spain and North Africa would probably never have seen a single German. The prospect of successfully expelling the invaders was all the greater as they were not as numerous as claimed in ancient transmission – following historiographic tradition [7. 99–101]. After Theodosius, though, no emperor, least of all any of the 'child Emperors', undertook the duty of an *Imperator Augustus* in ensuring the *securitas* ('security') of the empire at the head of an army. Many masters of the soldiers did admittedly achieve partial success, but they were unable to halt the emergence of Germanic territorial dominions. The old Roman tactic of playing off the German kings against one another contributed to their consolidation, for as a result the downfall of one led to the strengthening of another. The 'multi-ethnic

coalition' that Aëtius [2] brought together against Attila in 451 (→ Campi Catalauni) and that put an end to the expansion of the Huns remained an exception.

Thereafter, in the West, when the monarchic head disappeared there was no-one left to pursue a major strategy for restoring the empire. What a central imperial power in the West might have been able to achieve, if it had the resolve, was demonstrated in the East by → Iustinianus [1] I, whose re-conquest put an end to first the Vandal Kingdom in North Africa in 534 and then the East Goths' dominion of Italy in 555 (cf. → Belisarius; → Narses). The end of West Goth control of Spain came about not through any Roman emperor but through the → Arabs in 711 (→ Rodericus), and in 776 Langobard autonomy was ended by Charlemagne, whose Franks became the principal heirs of the MP.

→ Alamanni;   → Alani;   → Angli;   → Burgundiones;
→ Franci;   → Germani;   → Goti;   → Greuthungi;
→ Hunni; → Langobardi; → Migration; → Ostrogoths;
→ Roma (II. E.3.a); → Saxones; → Suebi; → Tervingi;
→ Vandali; → Visigoths; → EPOCHS;
→ HISTORIOGRAPHICAL MODELS

1 RGA   2 W. CONZE, Rasse, in: Geschichtliche Grundbegriffe 5, 1984, 135–178   3 DEMANDT   4 E. DEMOUGEOT, La formation de l'Europe et les invasions barbares, 1979   5 D. GEUENICH (ed), Die Franken und die Alemannen bis zur 'Schlacht bei Zülpich' (496/97). Suppl. vols. to RGA 19, 1998   6 A. KRAUSE, Die Geschichte der Germanen, 2002   7 L. MUSSET, Les invasions: Les vagues germaniques, 1969   8 E. NORDEN, Die germanische Urgeschichte in Tacitus' Germania, 1920; ⁴1959   9 W. POHL (ed.), Kingdoms of the Empire. The Integration of Barbarians in Late Antiquity, 1997;   10 Id., Die Germanen (Enzyklopädie deutscher Geschichte 27), 2000   11 Id., Die Völkerwanderung, Eroberung und Integration, 2002   12 K. ROSEN, Die Völkerwanderung, 2002   13 TH. SCHIEFFER (ed.), Europa im Wandel von der Antike zum MA (Hdb. der Europäischen Geschichte 1), 1976; ⁴1996;   14 K. F. STROHEKER, Germanentum und Spätantike, 1965   15 K. TRÜDINGER, Studien zur Geschichte der griechisch-römischen Ethnographie, 1918   16 M. WAAS, Germanen im römischen Dienst, ²1971   17 R. WENSKUS, Stammesbildung und Verfassung. Das Werden der früh-mittelalterlichen gentes, 1961; ²1977   18 G. WIRTH, Attila. Das Hunnenreich und Europa, 1999   19 H. WOLFRAM, Das Reich und die Germanen. Zwischen Antike und Mittelalter, 1990;   20 Zedlers Universallexikon, Bd. 63, 1750, s. v. Züge ganzer Völker.

MAPS: B. KRÜGER, Die Germanen, vol. 2, 1983; W. POHL, Die Völkerwanderung, 2002; O. MAENCHEN-HELFEN, Die Welt der Hunnen, 1978; L. KWANTEN, A History of Central Asia 500–1500, 1979; RGA, see the individual ethnic groups.   K.R.

Migration of the soul see → Soul, migration of the

Milanion see → Melanion

Milesia (ἡ Μιλησίη/*hē Milēsíē*, Str. 14,1,8; ἡ Μιλησίη χώρα/*hē Milēsíē chōra*, Hdt. 5,29).
A. GEOGRAPHY B. HISTORICAL TOPOGRAPHY
C. SETTLEMENT HISTORY

A. GEOGRAPHY
Peninsula of → Miletus [2] between the Latmian Gulf in the north and the Gulf of Akbük (*basilicus sinus*, Mela 1,16–17; Plin. HN 5,112) in the south, not identical with the entire polis territory of Miletus, which changed repeatedly [2. 13ff.]. After its exploration had been initiated by TH. WIEGAND [13; 14], M. and the development of its landscape have been systematically investigated since 1992 [1; 4; 5; 6]. Sections of the eastern upland settled by → Cares (Carians), *Milesia Hyperákria* (Hdt. 6,20), around Akbük have been studied by VOIGTLÄNDER [11; 12].

B. HISTORICAL TOPOGRAPHY
Apart from the large city of Miletus, M. comprised several small towns and villages: *Argasa on the Gulf of Akbük, Assessus in the northeast of Mengereb Dağ, Teichiussa (modern Saplı adası) near Akbük, Panormis near modern Mavişehir. → Didyma apparently was a sanctuary without settlement in the archaic period, but politically it belonged to Miletus (cf. [3]) and was linked to it by a Sacred Road [9]. M. ended at the Poseidion, the Poseidon altar at Cape Monodendri (modern Tekağaç Burnu according to Str. 14,2,1. The Limeneion (Hdt. 1,18), Pyrrha (modern Sarıkemer?) and the former islands Dromiscos and Perne (Plin. HN 2,204) have not been located. It is uncertain if the Milesian *démoi* of Argaseis, Katapolitai, Lerioi, Plataieis and Tichiesseis, which in the Imperial period functioned as electoral districts for the election of the prophet in Didyma, also represented settlement units [5. 302f.; 7; 8].

C. SETTLEMENT HISTORY
Dense settlement first in the late Chalcolithic, but late prehistoric settlement sites are rare and usually located on the coast or small peninsulas and islands before it. In the archaic period, M. had a hierarchical settlement structure that along with the metropolis of Miletus included urban sub-centres such as Assessus, Pyrrha and Teichiussa, probably some villages (*Argasa? [5. 299ff.]) and numerous individual farms (Hdt. 1,17 [4. 307ff.; 5. 291]). Only the southern shore of the Latmian Gulf was densely settled at that time, the waterless Milesian plateau only with growing population pressure from the Hellenistic period. Assessus and Teichiussa were fortified no later than the classical period, also two smaller fortifications on the coast near Taşburun secured the *chōra*. The Hellenistic period saw a social and demographic shift: Teichiussa became desolate, Miletus flowered, and (for the first time?) a settlement formed about Didyma [8. 283ff.; 9. 24]. Monumental tombs indicate a concentration of property. Differing from shepherds' camps in M., which are evidence of a highly developed pastoral economy - Milesian wool has been famous since the archaic period – the archaic compounds [5. 292f.] in Carian Grion were permanent settlements of Carian shepherd clans with which the Greek population had an intense economic exchange. A decline occurred in the late Hellenistic and Imperial periods; a widely branched network of water pipes was created in the 1st/2nd cents. AD to supply Miletus [10. 85ff.], but settlement sites of the Imperial period are rare.

M. only experienced another flowering in the early Byzantine period. The settlement forms included, apart from the metropolis of Miletus, the entire range from individual farms of modest smallholder operations to large estates, monasteries and monastic estates as well as villages and small towns. → Iustinianopolis, which is attested in inscriptions, is possibly a new foundation of Justinian's reign. The approximately 100 large estates mostly practiced an intensive, export-oriented oil production. This last ancient flowering ended abruptly in the 7th cent. The middle Byzantine period from the 8th to the 10th cents. AD is entirely shrouded in darkness; in the 11th to 13th cents. AD, fortified towers were built, which were mistakenly considered to be military bases. They disappeared with the Turkish settlement, which is not evident in archaeology, and with the foundation of the emirates of Menteşe and Aydın about 1300, which in turn were absorbed in 1425 and 1426 into the Ottoman empire [15; 16. 1ff.].

1 H. BRÜCKNER, Coastal Research and Geoarchaeology in the Mediterranean Region, in: D. H. KELLETAT (Hrsg.), German Coastal Geographical Research. The Last Decade, 1998, 235–257   2 N. EHRHARDT, Milet und seine Kolonien, ²1988   3 Ders., Didyma und Milet in archa. Zeit, in: Chiron 28, 1998, 11–20   4 H. LOHMANN, Survey in der Chora von Milet, in: AA 1995, 293–333   5 Ders., Survey in der Chora von Milet, in: AA 1997, 285–311   6 Ders., Survey in der Chora von Milet, in: AA 1999, 439–473 und Kartenbeilage   7 M. PIÉRART, Athènes et Milet. 1. Tribus e dèmes milésiens, in: MH 40, 1983, 1–18   8 Ders., Athènes et Milet. 2. L'organisation du territoire, in: MH 42, 1985, 276–299   9 K. TUCHELT, Branchidai-Didyma (Sonderh. Ant. Welt 22), 1991   10 G. TUTTAHS, Milet und das Wasser, 1998   11 W. VOIGTLÄNDER, Umrisse eines vor- und frühgesch. Zentrums in der kar.-ion. Küste, in: AA 1986, 613–667   12 Ders., Akbük-Teichioussa, in: AA 1988, 567–625   13 TH. WIEGAND, Milet 2,2. Die miles. Landschaft, 1929, 1–18   14 P. WILSKI, Milet 1,1. Karte der miles. Halbinsel, 1906   15 P. WITTEK, Das Fürstentum Mentesche, in: MDAI(I) 2, 1934.   16 K. WULZINGER, P. WITTEK, F. SARRE, Milet 3,4. Das islamische Milet, 1935.   H.LO.

Milesian School Although we do not know in what manner the first three natural philosopher – → Thales, → Anaximandros and → Anaximenes [1] (end of the 7/6 cent. BC.) – interacted and collaborated with each other, it is remarkable that they originated from and were active in the same town, Miletus [2], on the coast of Asia Minor. However, they do not constitute a 'school' proper (despite [4], cf. [2]). Each of them specified a basic stuff or ἀρχή (*arché*), of which all the phenomena of the natural world are modifications only. The three *archaí* – water, the 'unlimited' (ἄπειρον/*ápeiron*) and air respectively – could fulfil this role in different ways. Anaximander's extra-cosmic *ápeiron* apparently controlled the processes of the → cosmos by being the source of the original matrix of the world. The two intracosmic principles – water in the case of Thales and air in the case of Anaximenes – could be intimated by the diverse and various forms in which they can be present in other bodies: all the major components of animal and vegetable bodies are permeated by water, whereas air can freely infuse all sorts of porous bodies, and apparently human and animal souls are also constituted by the airy breath (→ *pneúma*) of these living beings.

Control, governing and rule are the key concepts of the Milesian philosophers: the *arché* holds every process in the world in its sway. Thus, she is the deity that replaces all the mythical gods [3]. The testimonies about Thales add that the principle is also basic by being able to transform into all the other materials in the world (Aristot. Metaph. 983b 6ff.). Even if one were inclined to doubt this testimony, it is clear that for Anaximander, the key position of the *arché* rests on the

processes which bound the principle to the other substances, and these to each other. As the *ápeiron* is extracosmical, it cannot exert any direct rule on the processes of the world (other than containing and holding it together). Hence it can be said that the first two Milesians held an – at least implicit – theory of change. Anaximenes, however, already formulated an explicit – albeit still rudimentary – theory of change, specifying the processes – condensation and rarefaction – which link different stuffs to each other and to air, the *arché* in his philosophy. → Hippon and → Diogenes [12] of Apollonia in the 5 cent. BC revived the Milesian fundamental teachings about *arché*. The knowledge of the dependency of the universe on a superior deity, the source and governing principle of all things, passed over to the entire Greek philosophy.

→ Metaphysics; → Natural philosophy; → Presocratics; → Presocratics

1 K. ALGRA, The Beginnings of Cosmology, in: A. A. LONG (ed.), The Cambridge Companion to Early Greek Philosophy, 1999, 45–65   2 H. DIELS, Über die ältesten Philosophenschulen der Griechen, in: Philosophische Aufsätze, E. Zeller gewidmet, 1887 (repr. 1962), 239–260   3 W. JAEGER, Theologie der frühen griechischen Denker, 1953   4 G. E. R. LLOYD, The Social Background of Early Greek Philosophy, in: idem, Methods and Problems in Greek Science, 1991, 121–140.   I.B.

Milesian Tales (Μιλησιακά; *Milēsiaká*). Title of a work by one → Aristides [2] with the epithet 'of Miletus' (his actual origin is unknown). The text is not extant; all we know for certain is that it had an obscene character. The ancient references are difficult to interpret and do not allow precise categorization: it may have been a novel [1] or, as is more widely accepted, a collection of novellas, possibly integrated into a framework structure.

Modern literary studies favour the latter hypothesis, which was forcefully argued by E. ROHDE [3; 4]. This is linked to a wider use of the term *Milēsiaká* (or *fabulae Milesiae*) and the adjective 'Milesian' to refer to ancient short stories of erotic content: the *Milēsiaká* in this sense are thought to have been a Greek literary form transposed to Rome by a certain Sisenna. According to Ov. Tr. 2,443, he translated Aristides' work; identification with the historian → Sisenna from the time of Sulla has wide acceptance but is not expressly attested by any source (cf. also [5]). MT in that sense would include the stories of the 'Widow of Ephesus' and the 'Ephebe of Pergamon', found in the *Satyrica* of → Petronius [5], as well as some of the → 'Novellas' inserted in the *Metamorphoses* of Apuleius (→ Ap(p)uleius [III.]): the 'Milesian' origin of Petronius' stories would then be confirmed by the setting in Asia Minor and the obscene character of both tales. In the case of the *Metamorphoses*, this is articulated at the beginning of the text (Apul. Met. 1,1: *at ego tibi sermone isto Milesio varias fabulas conseram*, 'I shall, however, weave together for you varied stories in that Milesian style'; ibid. 4,32: *propter Milesiae conditorem*, within the story of Amor and Psyche). The interpretation of both passages is, however, controversial. It is also not clear whether Apuleius is referring to the *Metamorphoses* as a whole or to the secondary stories inserted into the novel.

It is true that in Late Latin there are instances of the term *Milesia* (or related) applied to fictitious stories, generally in a pejorative sense, and in one case there even appears a reference to Apuleius, but the sense of the term is rather obscure (SHA Alb. 12,12 *Milesias Punicas Apulei sui*, 'the Punic *Milesiae* of his Apuleius'; cf. further: ibid. 11,8; Tert. De anima 23,4; Mart. Cap. Ce nuptiis Philologiae et Mercuri 2,100; Hier. Contra Rufinum 1,17; Hier. Comm. in Isaiam 12; Sidon. Epist. 7,2). Whether this was an allusion to novels or short stories cannot be determined (contrary to ROHDE, no firm conclusion can be drawn from the diminutive *fabella* in Hier. Comm. in Isaiam 12, where it clearly has a derogatory sense).

→ Novella; → Novel

1 K. BÜRGER, Der antike Roman vor Petronius, in: Hermes 27, 1892, 345–358   2 Id., Studien zur Geschichte des griechischen Romans, vol. 1, 1902, 24–28   3 E. ROHDE, Über griechische Novellendichtung und ihren Zusammenhang mit dem Orient, app. to: Id. Der griechische Roman und seine Vorläufer, ⁴1960   4 Id., Zum griechischen Roman, II, in: RhM 48, 1893, 125–139   5 E. RAWSON, L. Cornelius Sisenna and the Early First Century BC, in: CQ 29, 1979, 327–346.

FGrH 495; Q. CATAUDELLA, La novella greca, 1954, 126–164; P. FERRARI, G. ZANETTO (ed. and trans.), Le storie di Mileto, 1995; C. RUIZ-MONTERO, The Rise of the Greek Novel, in: G. SCHMELING (ed.), The Novel in the Ancient World, 1996, 59–64.   M.FU. L.G.

Milestones
A. FUNCTION AND FORM   B. REPUBLIC   C. IM-
PERIAL PERIOD   D. MILESTONES AS A PROPAGAN-
DA TOOL   E. PATTERN OF DISTRIBUTION

A. FUNCTION AND FORM
As indicators of distance, milestones were a characteristic feature of Roman imperial roads. Erecting milestones as indicators of distance on significant inter-re-
gional roads was known even before the Romans, e.g.
in Assyria, in the Persian Empire and at various places
in Greece.

The term milestones (Latin *miliarium*) is first attested in 132 BC (CIL I² 638). As a special form of → building inscriptions, the mostly cylindrical columns were
termed *miliarium* (ThlL VIII, Sp. 946–949) in antiquity,
often also simply as *lapis* ('stone', ThlL VII, Sp. 951f.).
The height of Republican milestones was between 1.1
and 1.9 m, of which *c.* 0.5 m were sunk in the ground as
plinth.

B. REPUBLIC
In the Republic, the inscriptions on milestones
named in each case the supervising magistrate (in the
earliest instances, aediles, or praetors, consuls or pro-

consuls) with his title of office, and ideally the end-point
of the road (*caput viae*) with an indication of distance
expressed in *milia passuum* ('1,000 [double] paces';
1 mp = 1481 m). The oldest known milestone (253 BC
?) comes from the *via Appia* (CIL I² 21: *P. Claudio(s)
A[p. f.]/C. Fourio(s)/aidiles /(a Roma milia passuum)
LIII /(a Foro Appii milia passuum) X*). According to
Plutarch (Plut. C. Gracchus 7), road construction and
the erection of milestones received a marked impetus
from C. → Sempronius Gracchus. That statement appears to be supported by the fact that the milestones of
M. → Aemilius [I 10] Lepidus (CIL I² 617–619) do not
date from the year of construction of the *via Aemilia*
(187 BC) but only from the 2nd half of the 2nd cent. BC.
In the provinces, too, the first milestones date from the
middle of the 2nd cent BC (e.g. AE 1957, 172; AE 1992,
1532; CIL I² 647–651; 823; 840; CIL XVII 2, 294), and
this suggests a general evolution in road works. In this
context, Plutarch (in the 2nd cent. BC) probably erred
in linking surveying activity with the Gracchian agrarian reforms. The scant number of Republican milestones known today (30 specimens) is explained by
milestones probably being erected only at distinctive
locations.

C. IMPERIAL PERIOD
Under Augustus, who assumed oversight of road
works (*cura viarum*; → *cura, curatores*) in 20 BC, a fundamental, qualitative change in road works is discernible. It found visible expression in the erection of the
'Golden Milestone' (*miliarium aureum*) in the Forum
(Cass. Dio 54,8,4) and led to an increase in the number
of milestones erected; *c.* 6,000 specimens from the Imperial period are known to us today. These milestones
also show a new abundance of offices (e.g. CIL II 4868:
*Imp(erator) Caesar divi f. Aug(ustus)/pont(ifex) maxi-
mus imp(erator) XV consul/XIII trib(unicia)
potest(ate) XXXIV pa/ter patriae (a) Brac(ara) /(milia
passuum) IIII*). In the eastern provinces, milestones
sometimes carry bilingual inscriptions. Details that are
missing from the milestones today – very often the distance details – were probably painted on. The milestones of the 1st/2nd cents. AD are of significantly
larger dimensions (height: 2.5–3 m, diameter: 0.4–
0.5 m).

D. MILESTONES AS A PROPAGANDA TOOL
Even under Augustus and Tiberius, milestones were
used as a monopolistic means of propaganda: from then
on, the *principes* appear on milestones as the only or
principal construction sponsors. The only exceptions
known to us are from Africa up to AD 10, with just the
name of the governor, e.g. A. Caecina Severus (AE
1987, 992). Occasionally – and with distinct regional
differences – governors take second position. This subscription of governors, then, generally reflects their
direct supervision of construction. Italian *curatores
viarum* are never named on milestones before the 4th
cent. Even during the Imperial period, milestone in-

scriptions undergo further change, as the *principes* increasingly bear their victory titles as well as the classical offices. In the 1st cent., the emperor's title is generally shown in the nominative case. This shows the *princeps* basically as the sponsor of the road building or the repair work. On the basis of the source material, though, it is difficult to establish whether any direct personal influence was involved. From the time of Caligula (AD 37–41 , cf. CIL II 4639f.), and more strongly with the → adoptive emperors, inscriptions appear in which the names of the emperors are in the dative case, and this gives the milestone inscriptions the character of a votive inscription. From the end of the 1st cent. AD, there is a steady increase in the number of milestones dedicated without reference to any construction or repair work. From the end of the 2nd cent., moreover, the titles are provided with distinct dedicatory formulae (e.g. CIL VIII 10307) that are widely used in the 3rd and 4th cents.

Apart from the use of case in inscriptions, however, it is not possible to draw any authoritative conclusions from milestones as to evidence of construction or dedication (cf. CIL XVII 2, 572; 574). In the provinces in particular a change in attitude seems to have taken place: for details of the construction authorities, the communities increasingly used dative formulae to highlight their own role, without encroaching on the emperor's position as principal builder. Chronological classification of milestone details is therefore of great significance.

E. PATTERN OF DISTRIBUTION

Apparently milestones were not erected on all imperial roads. Thus, on the *via Domitia* (between the Pyrenees pass at Le Perthus and the Rhône) a series of milestones of individual Emperors can be found (CIL XVII 2,204–296), whereas milestones are only rarely encountered on coastal roads otherwise. In the 2nd and 3rd cents., milestones also record repair details (e.g. *restituit, refecit*) that can offer extensive information (cf. AE 1951, 208; CIL VIII 10335; CIL III 14110).

A peculiarity of the Gallic-Germanic provinces is the adoption of the → *leuga* (= 1,5 mp) which did not, however, lead to the German term *Leugenstein* (league-stone) (cf. CIL XIII 4549). It appears for the first time on one of Trajan's milestones (CIL XVII 2,426) in → Aquitania and spread from there until the reign of Septimius Severus (AD 193–211). The province of Gallia Narbonensis, however, together with some neighbouring areas, retained the measurement in miles. The causes for this are unexplained but may lie in some regional idiosyncrasies.

In late antiquity, milestones were written on several times over. The old inscription was not completely deleted but the milestone was turned around or stood on its head, with the result that in some instances up to four inscriptions are discernible. The practice of erecting milestones dropped off markedly in the 4th cent. and disappeared completely in the 5th cent.

→ Roads; → Roads and bridges, construction of

I. KÖNIG, Zur Dedikation römischer Meilensteine, in: Chiron 3, 1973, 419–427; K. SCHNEIDER, s.v. Miliarium, RE Suppl. 6, 395–431; G. WALSER, Meilen und Leugen, in: Epigraphica 31, 1969, 84–103; Ders., Bemerkungen zu den gallischgermanischen Meilensteinen, in: ZPE 43, 1981, 385–402.; Z. MARI, s.v. Miliarium Aureum, LTUR 3, 1996, 250f.; CHR. WITSCHEL, Meilensteine als historische Quelle? Das Beispiel Aquileia. in: Chiron 32, 2002, 325–393   M.RA.

Miletupolis, Miletopolis (Μιλητούπολις/*Milētoúpolis*, Μιλητόπολις/*Milētópolis*). City in Mysia. M. lay on the 'lake of M.' (Μιλητοπολῖτις λίμνη) and has been located near Melde, a town in the neighbourhood of modern Mustafa Kemalpaşa; cf. Tab. Peut. 9,3 (20 *milia* from Apollonia [6]); Steph. Byz. s.v. M. (περὶ τῶν Ῥύνδακα). M. was founded by Athens at the end of the 7th/beginning of the 6th cent. BC [1. 102ff.], was a member of the → Delian League from no later than 410/409 BC (ATL 1,342f.; 520; ATL 2,81; 86; 25; 204). M. minted coins from the 4th cent. BC. It was destroyed in the 3rd/2nd cent. BC, with its residents being partly resettled in → Gargara (Str. 13,1,58). It was in M. that the battle between Mithradates' son and Flavius [I 6] Fimbria took place in 85 BC (Oros. 6,2,10). M. lost all significance in late antiquity after the founding nearby of Lopadion (modern Uluabat).

1 E. SCHWERTHEIM, Die Inschriften von Kyzikos und Umgebung. Part 2: M. (IK 26), 1983.

W. RUGE, s.v. Miletopolis (1), RE 15, 1583–1585.   E.SCH.

Miletus (Μίλητος; *Mílētos*).

[1] Mythical founder of the city of M. [2]; from Crete; son of Apollo and Areia, daughter of Cleochus whose tomb was in the sanctuary of → Didyma [1. 165f.] (Apollod. 3,5f.), or of Apollo and Deione (Ov. Met. 9,443ff.) or of Apollo and Acacallis, daughter of Minos (Antoninus Liberalis 30). → Minos fell in love with M., but M. fleed to Caria, establishds M. there [2] and married Eidothea; the children of their union are → Byblis and → Caunus [1]. According to Ephorus FGrH 70 F 127 M. was founded by → Sarpedon.

1 J. FONTENROSE, Didyma, 1988.   L.K.

[2] (Ionic Μίλητος/*Mílētos*, Doric Μίλατος/*Mílatos*, Aeolic Μίλλατος/*Míllatos*, non-Greek place name, Hittite *Millaṷa(n)da-*). City in western Asia Minor on the southern coast of the Latmian Gulf, opposite Priene and Mycale, modern Balat (based on the medieval name *Palatia*); today 9 km from the sea.

I. History II. Topography and archaeology

I. History
A. Chalcolithic Age to the Bronze Age
B. Hittite Period (14th–13th cents. BC)
C. Development right through to the 7th cent. BC D. Archaic Period E. Classical and Hellenistic Period F. Roman Period

A. Chalcolithic Age to the Bronze Age
Traces of habitation go back to the Chalcolithic Age. The oldest architecture found to date comes from the level hill at the temple of Athena above the theatre bay, and consists of three building phases from the late Bronze Age (→ Aegean Koine): a Minoan settlement from the 16th cent., a first Mycenaean settlement from the 14th cent. and of a fortified second settlement from the 13th/12th cent. BC.   J.CO.

B. Hittite Period (14th–13th cents. BC)
The identity of M., the sole significant Mycenaean place of settlement in Asia Minor, with the Millawa(n)da which according to Hittite sources belonged in the 14th–13th cent. BC to → Achijawa/Ahhijawa (Greece) may now be regarded as certain [1; 2. 452⁴⁹; 3. 26–28]. Its territory – which in view of a permanent Mycenaean presence [1. 40] (not improbable for Müsgebi [4] either) may approximately have covered a narrow coastal strip to the Halicarnassian Peninsula – bordered directly on → Mira (heartland of → Arzawa and later a Hittite vassal state) as well as on → Lukkā (cf. → Hattusa II, map). The burnt layer between the two Mycenaean settlements of M. can be linked to the conquest by the Hittite army commanders Gulla and Malazidi at the beginning of the large-scale Arzawa campaign in the third year of the reign of Mursili II (c. 1318–1290 BC) [5. 36–39].
In the first half of the 13th cent., Millawa(n)da was the basis from which the Arzawa prince Pijamaradu – who lived in Ahhijawian exile and was related by marriage to the Ahhijawan representative there – entered into numerous political and military ventures directed particularly against Mirā, which detrimentally affected the entire coastal region of western Asia Minor [2. 453–455] (→ Sēha, → Wilusa). These are also the main subject of the (Hittite) letter from Hattusili II ('III', c. 1265–1246 BC) to the king of Ahhijawa. This 'Tawaglawa Letter' [6. 2–194] received its (traditional) name (< Mycenaean *Etewoklewes) from the brother of the king of Ahijawa mentioned therein (see in this regard [7]). To the late years of the reign of Tudhalija III ('IV', c. 1240–1215 BC) belongs the fragmentary 'Milawada Letter' [6. 198–240; 8] from the Great Hittite king to the King of Mirā (probably Tarkasnawa). It refers, among other things, to a border regulation affecting the territory of Millawa(n)da, mentioning in a broader context several towns belonging to Lukkā, among them Awarna (= Xanthus) and Pinala (= Pinara) in the Xanthus Valley.

→ Aegean Koine; → Mycenaean culture and archaeology

1 W.-D. Niemeier, The Mycenaeans in Western Anatolia and the Problem of the Origins of the Sea Peoples, in: S. Gitin e.a. (ed.), Mediterranean Peoples in Transition, 1998, 17–65   2 F. Starke, Troia im Kontext des historisch-politischen und sprachlichen Umfeldes Kleinasiens im 2. Jahrtausend, in: Studia Troica 7, 1997, 447–487; 3 J. D. Hawkins, Tarkasnawa King of Mira, 'Tarkondemos', Karabel, and Boğazköy Sealings, in: AS 48, 1998, 1–31   4 F. Prayon, A.-M. Wittke, Kleinasien vom 12. bis 6. Jh.v.Chr. (TAVO Beih. B 82), 1994, esp. 150 s.v. Müsgebi   5 A. Götze, Die Annalen des Muršiliš, 1933 (repr. 1967)   6 F. Sommer, Die Ahhijavā-Urkunden, 1932 (repr. 1975)   7 H. G. Güterbock, Wer war Tawagalawa?, in: Orientalia 59, 1990, 157–165   8 H. A. Hoffner, The Milawata Letter Augmented and Reinterpreted, in: AfO, Beih. 19, 1982, 130–137.   F.S.

C. Development right through to the 7th cent. BC
The second Mycenaean settlement was destroyed at the end of the 12th cent. A stratigraphic sequence for the early Iron Age is still missing. According to some, ceramics already reappeared in the submycenaen period, and they certainly did in the protogeometric period. Architecture in the city area dates from the 8th cent. and on the Kalabaktepe from the 1st half of the 7th cent. BC. In the geography of Asia Minor in the catalogue of Trojans in the Iliad no Achaeans are mentioned; here M. belongs to the Carians (Hom. Il. 2,867–870). The myth was later based on two acts of city founding. According to the chronology of the legends, two generations before the fall of Troy, settlers came from M. [3] on Crete under Sarpedon (Ephor. FGrH 70 F 127 = Strab. 14,1,6). Alternatively, a M. [1], who had fled with Sarpedon from Minos, founded the city (Apollod. 3,1,2). Within the context of the construction of the Ionian migration (→ Colonisation), four generations after the fall of Troy, → Neileus, son of Codrus of Athens, founded M. (Hdt. 9,97; Hellanicus FGrH 125 F 10) as the southernmost of the Ionian cities (Hdt. 1,142); the Ionians came without their women and took those of the Carians whose fathers they had killed (Hdt. 1,146).

D. Archaic Period
Ioniae caput, 'head of Ionia', was the name given to archaic M. in view of its 'over 90 colonies' (Plin. HN 5,112). However, we know of almost 40, and with subsequent foundations not quite 70, colonies in the Propontis and on the Pontos Euxeinos, which since the 670s emanated from M., e.g. Abydus, Istria, Olbia, Panticapaeum and Sinope. Around 650, the city of M. was the co-founder of Naucratis on the Canopic Nile. The coins of M. belong to the early minting of electrum at the beginning of the 6th cent. BC.
In the early 6th cent., M. was the centre of Ionian natural philosophy (→ Milesian School) with Thales, Anaximander and Anaximenes [1]. In their geographi-

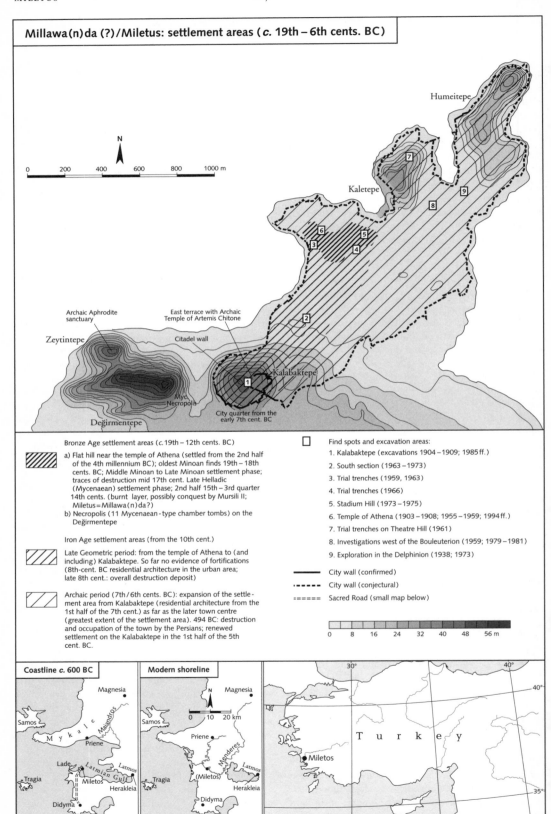

Millawa(n)da (?)/Miletus: settlement areas (c. 19th – 6th cents. BC)

Bronze Age settlement areas (c.19th – 12th cents. BC)

a) Flat hill near the temple of Athena (settled from the 2nd half of the 4th millennium BC); oldest Minoan finds 19th – 18th cents. BC; Middle Minoan to Late Minoan settlement phase; traces of destruction mid 17th cent. Late Helladic (Mycenaean) settlement phase; 2nd half 15th – 3rd quarter 14th cents. (burnt layer, possibly conquest by Mursili II; Miletus = Millawa(n)da?)
b) Necropolis (11 Mycenaean-type chamber tombs) on the Değirmentepe

Iron Age settlement areas (from the 10th cent.)

Late Geometric period: from the temple of Athena to (and including) Kalabaktepe. So far no evidence of fortifications (8th-cent. BC residential architecture in the urban area; late 8th cent.: overall destruction deposit)

Archaic period (7th/6th cents. BC): expansion of the settle-ment area from Kalabaktepe (residential architecture from the 1st half of the 7th cent.) as far as the later town centre (greatest extent of the settlement area). 494 BC: destruction and occupation of the town by the Persians; renewed settlement on the Kalabaktepe in the 1st half of the 5th cent. BC.

Find spots and excavation areas:

1. Kalabaktepe (excavations 1904 – 1909; 1985 ff.)
2. South section (1963 – 1973)
3. Trial trenches (1959, 1963)
4. Trial trenches (1966)
5. Stadium Hill (1973 – 1975)
6. Temple of Athena (1903 – 1908; 1955 – 1959; 1994 ff.)
7. Trial trenches on Theatre Hill (1961)
8. Investigations west of the Bouleuterion (1959; 1979 – 1981)
9. Exploration in the Delphinion (1938; 1973)

———— City wall (confirmed)

- - - - - City wall (conjectural)

====== Sacred Road (small map below)

| 0 | 8 | 16 | 24 | 32 | 40 | 48 | 56 m |

Coastline c. 600 BC

Modern shoreline

cal world view, which speculatively divided the → oikoumene into three parts of the earth (Hecat. FGrH 1;
Hdt. 4,36–45), M. formed the centre (Hdt. 1,142).
From Herodotus we know of the hazards faced by M.
since the 670s as a result of the raids of the → Cimmerii
(Hdt. 1,6) and of the expansion by the Lydian kings
onto the Ionian coast (Hdt. 1,5–94) from → Gyges [1]
onwards. Just before 600, M. stood up to → Alyattes
thanks to its fleet; a peace treaty was ascribed to the
powerful tyrant → Thrasybulus (Hdt. 1,22). Under
→ Croesus and, after 547, under → Cyrus [2], M. was
able to assume a privileged position in Ionia (Hdt.
1,141; 143; 169). At the end of the 6th cent. BC, M. was
'flourishing and the jewel of Ionia' (Hdt. 5,28). Only
scanty information has been passed down to us regarding the conflicts between the cities, e.g. a naval venture
of M. with Erythrae against Naxos in the 7th cent.
(Andriscus FGrH 500 F 1) or the 'Battle at the Oak', a
victory of Samos and M. over Priene in the early 6th
cent. (IPriene 37). We have even less information about
the situation in M itself. Thoas and Damasenor are the
names of two tyrants of the early 6th cent. BC, after
whose fall the country was plunged into civil war (Plut.
Quest. Graec. 32; Hdt. 5,28f.). After M.'s fleet had
played an important part in Darius's Scythian campaign around 513 (Hdt. 4,137), the tyrants → Histiaeus
[1] and → Aristagoras [3] led the city in 499 BC into the
→ Ionian Revolt. In 494 the Persians destroyed M. and
deported the inhabitants (Hdt. 6,18–22).

E. CLASSICAL AND HELLENISTIC PERIOD

There are signs of direct continuity, like the prosopography of aristocratic families and the resettlement
on the eastern terrace of the Kalabaktepe. After 479 BC,
M. was part of the → Delian League; in the tribute list of
450/449 the high contribution of 10 talents is recorded
(IG I³ 263, V. 18). After an attempt to break free just
before the mid–440s, M. was occupied by an Athenian
army (Ps.-Xen. Ath. pol. 3,11; IG I³ 21). In the Ionian
War, M. broke free in 412 and became the base of operations for the Spartan navy (Thuc. 8,17ff.). In 405
BC, Lysander [1] in an alliance with Cyrus [3] the
Younger brought the 'oligarchs' to power (Diod.
13,104). In 402, the 'democrats' were reinstalled by
Tissaphernes, to whose field of power, Caria, M. then
belonged (Xen. An. 1,1,7). The same thing happend
later under Mausolus and between 323 and 312 under
Asander. The satrap Struthas mediated just before 390
between M. and Myus [9. 9]. In 334 BC, Alexander the
Great defeated a Persian garrison, laying siege to and
conquering M. (Arr. Anab. 1,18–20; Diod. 17,22). In
the Hellenistic period, M. maintained a certain independence amidst the changing guarantors of 'freedom
and autonomy' (first in 312 Antigonus [10. 123]);
agreements of → isopoliteía with Tralleis (212), Mylasa
(209), Pidasa (188) and Heraclea [5] (185) strengthened its own position in its rivalry with Magnesia und
Priene [10. 143, 146, 149f.].

F. ROMAN PERIOD

Even before the battle of Magnesia in 190 BC, M.
was in contact with Rome (Liv. 37,16) and was favoured in the Treaty of Apamea in 188 (Pol. 21,48;
[10. 150]). A cult law for the populus Romanus and the
dea Roma [11. 203] dates from the time when the province of → Asia [2] was set up. M. honoured Pompeius,
the victor over the pirates, with a statue in 63 BC
[13. 21]. In the year of the Secular Games in Rome in
17/6 BC, a new list of epomyms for M. started with the
→ aisymnêtês Augustus [10. 127]. In the Imperial period, M. was a wealthy city, but not in the same league as
Ephesus. A Jewish community [12. 940 III] and, already
at an early time, a Christian one (Acts 20,15 [12.
959ff.]) are attested. For protection against the Goti,
the walls of M. were renovated around AD 262. Iustinianus's building inscription of AD 538 [11. 206] dates
the alteration of the market gate into a city gate for a
city that had become very much smaller. The church of
St. Michael from the 4th cent., built on top of the temple
of Dionysus, was renovated around 600. In the 7th/8th
cents., a fort was built above the theatre. In the 12th
cent., a wall was constructed around the entire theatre
hill; this settlement was called ta Palátia. M. was a bishop's seat right through to the 14th cent. From the beginning of the 14th cent. onwards, M. belonged to the
Seljuk emirates, first of Aydın, then to that of Menteşe
of Milas; Eliasbeg as the dominus palatie concluded
treaties with Venice in 1403 and 1414. In the course of
the Imperial period the harbours silted up, but Cyriacus
of Ancona in 1412 (being scriba minor on a trading ship
of the Alfieri) could still reach the harbour of Palatia via
a canal.

                                                          J.CO.

II. TOPOGRAPHY AND ARCHAEOLOGY
A. EARLY HISTORY   B. GEOMETRIC AND ARCHAIC PERIOD   C. CLASSICAL PERIOD TO LATE ANTIQUITY

A. EARLY HISTORY

M. owed its power particularly to the favourable
position (like a ram) on an open gulf reaching far into
the interior of the country, according to the latest research even right through to modern Aydın. In this way
the city had access to all the sea routes as well as to the
land route through valley of the Upper Maeander into
Anatolia. Sufficient territory in the form of the Milesian
Peninsula (→ Milesia) ensured economic development
along with trade.

The earliest finds inside the city area go back to the
late Chalcolithic period of the 5th/4th millennium BC.
Recent geomorphological investigations support the
view that the finding places from that time below the
later Heroon III and at the temple of Athena were then
not yet any contingent land mass but formed smaller
islands.

The longest continuity of settlement is proven for the
temple of Athena. Here the excavations have shown an
uninterrupted stratigraphy from the Chalcolithic Age

Miletus (7th cent. BC – 6th cent. AD)

1. Temple of Demeter on the Humeitepe (Hellenistic)
2. Baths on the Humeitepe (Imperial period)
3. Delphinion (as of the Imperial period)
4. Small harbour monument (Imperial period; built over with the synagogue in the 4th cent. AD)
5. Harbour stoas (Hellenistic), in front of them large harbour monument (Imperial period)
6. Roman theatre
7. Heroon I (Hellenistic)
8. Colonnaded square (Hellenistic)
9. North Agora (Hellenistic)
10. Capito Baths (Imperial period)
11. Temple of Dionysus (Hellenistic), built over with the church of St. Michael and the bishop's residence (c. AD 600)
12. Ionic Stoa (Imperial period)
13. Hellenistic Gymnasium
14. Bouleuterion (mid 2nd cent. BC)
15. Nymphaeum (Imperial period)
16. Large church (1st half 6th cent. AD), in front of it Roman propylon (3rd cent. AD)
17. Heroon III (early 3rd cent. AD)
18. Hellenistic warehouse
19. South Agora (Imperial period)
20. Stoa of Antiochus (Hellenistic)
21. Baths of Faustina (post-AD 164)
22. Serapeion (3rd cent. AD)
23. Stadium (Hellenistic?)
24. West Agora (Hellenistic)
25. Hellenistic courtyard house
26. Temple of Athena (Archaic)
27. Round church (early 6th cent. AD)

28. Sacred Gate (as of the Imperial period)
29. Lion Gate (Late Hellenistic?)
30. Archaic sea wall (based on 1999 prospection)
31. Archaic city wall? (prospection 1995, excavation 1997/98)
32. East terrace of Kalabaktepe (early Classical settlement)
33. Kalabaktepe excavations 1986–95 (Archaic settlement)
34. Sacred Road to Didyma
35. Roman aqueduct

Street grid of northern part according to B. F. Weber (Milet 1.10, fig. 87), confirmed by geophysical measurements made by H. Stümpel (bolder outlines).

Street grid of southern part according to A. v. Gerkan (Milet 2.3, plate 1), confirmed by geophysical measurements made by H. Stümpel (bolder outlines).

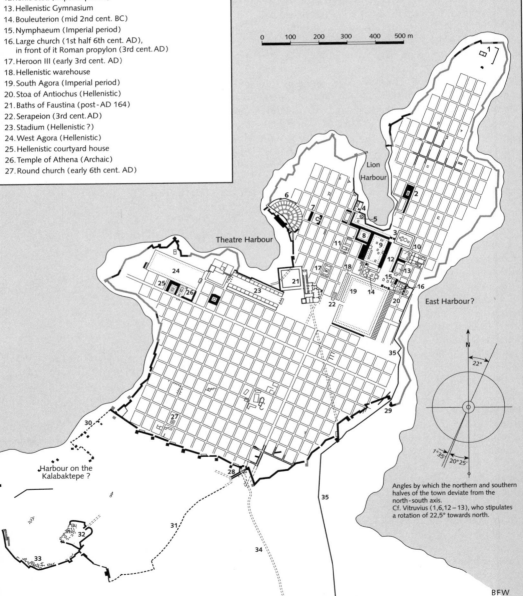

0   100   200   300   400   500 m

Lion Harbour

Theatre Harbour

East Harbour?

Harbour on the Kalabaktepe?

N

22°

1°35'   20°25'

Angles by which the northern and southern halves of the town deviate from the north-south axis.
Cf. Vitruvius (1,6,12–13), who stipulates a rotation of 22,5° towards north.

BFW

via the various phases of the Bronze Age to the Archaic period whilst the finds also stretch right through to the Byzantine period. Obsidian finds from → Melos [1], one of the Cyclades, which have come to light in Aphrodisias in the valley of the Upper Maeander, as well as ceramics with links to Inner Anatolia and the Aegean area, show that M. was already an important centre for trade between the Aegean and Anatolia in the late Chalcolithic period (→ Aegean Koine, with maps). This role continued in the early Bronze Age as is demonstrated by finds. At the beginning of the middle Bronze Age, a strong Minoan component appears. Aside from fine Kamares ware, we also encounter in the layers from that time locally produced Minoan household and cooking ceramics; finds of seals prove that there was an administration of a Minoan kind. At the beginning of the late Bronze Age, the finds of Minoan fresco fragments, cult vessels and inscriptions in Minoan → Linear A indicate a predominant Minoan presence. In the 1st half of the 15th cent. BC, the Minoan city fell victim to destruction. After it was rebuilt, the settlement was dominated by Mycenaeans who built their necropolises at Değirmentepe. Many indicators from the excavations lend support to the view that the Mycenaean city is identical to the *Milla-wa(n)da* mentioned in the Hittite sources, which was conquered and destroyed just before the end of the 14th cent. BC by troops of Mursilis II (see above I.B.; → Minoan culture and archaeology).

B. Geometric and Archaic Period

The arrival of → Ionians is documented by the presence of Protogeometric ceramics. Building remains from that period are still lacking. For the late Geometric period, an area of habitation can be shown to have stretched south from the temple of Athena, including the Kalabaktepe. In this period, we encounter two types of houses: rectangular and oval buildings. A Geometric city fortification has not yet been found. As a continuous destruction layer proves, the city must have been gripped by war-like occurrences at the end of the 8th cent. BC.

In the Archaic Period of the 7th and 6th cent. BC the city obviously extended from the Kalabaktepe to the later city centre, thus encompassing a much larger area than in the Hellenistic and Roman periods. The area of the Minoan-Mycenaean city remained one centre; here, in the 7th cent. BC, the first temple of Athena was built (site plan no. 26). The Kalabaktepe in the south-west of the city became another centre. On its eastern terrace stood the temple of Artemis Chitone, whose cult, according to written evidence, stretched back to the Ionian foundation phase of the city. In the south around the hill, there was a closed city quarter, existing since the early 7th cent. BC, with spacious houses with courtyards, in which various types of trades were carried out, e.g. pottery. On the summit of the Kalabaktepe, excavations have provided evidence of remains of a 'citadel wall' (no. 33). In keeping with its special hierarchy, the Kalabaktepe appears to have had its own harbour at its northern foot. Among the sanctuaries of the city in the Archaic period, the sanctuary of Aphrodite 'of Oecus' had a special status, along with the already mentioned sanctuaries and the Delphinion, which was probably already in existence in this period but has not yet been examined in greater detail. The sanctuary of Aphrodite was rediscovered in 1990 on a hill directly above the city (Zeytintepe) and since that time it has provided a major part of the ancient finds from M. At the end of the Archaic period, a new temple was built for Athene at the old location, a temple whose enormous gneiss foundations had previously been wrongly dated to the Classical period. The matter of the ancient city wall has not yet been conclusively clarified. We have to assume a ring that encircled the entire later city area, but which also surrounded the Kalabaktepe fortification. Geophysical prospecting was carried out on an eastern shank wall by which the Kalabaktepe fortification was linked to the 'Sacred Gate', with probes confirming its existence.

C. Classical Period to Late Antiquity

The re-founding of the city after the catastrophe of 494 BC was preceded by a clean-up campaign, with large parts of the rubble being piled up on the Kalabaktepe, forming an artificial mound. At least partial resettlement appears to have occurred almost immediately after. Whether and to what extent → Hippodamus of M. was personally involved in the re-planning of the city remains a matter of debate. It is evident, however, that in large parts of the city, e.g. around the temple of Athena, the area of the bouleuterion (no. 14) and probably also of the Delphinion (no. 3), the Archaic orientation of buildings was adopted by the new city plan, which could explain several of its slight inconsistencies.

The 'Hippodamian' city developed slowly. Right from the outset, space was probably left in the city centre for the laying out of markets and public buildings that then only gradually took their places. According to recent geophysical research, the *insula*-system also stretched to the Humeitepe, whilst in the south even within the late Hellenistic defence ring relatively large areas appear to have remained open. M. once again achieved urban elegance with large Roman buildings like the theatre, the Baths of Faustina (no. 21), the Nymphaeum (no. 15) and the Market Gate in the southern agora (no. 19), so that these, together with the facade of the bouleuterion, created an impressive square in the middle of the city. During this period however, other cities like Ephesus had already surpassed M. in status. Despite the unfavourable location now caused by the river deposits of the Maeander, M. remained a minor municipal centre right through to the Seljuk-Venetian age, in whose harbour goods could be transferred.

→ MILETUS

1 J. COBET, Die Mauern sind die Stadt, in: AA 1997, 249–284   2 N. EHRHARDT, Milet und seine Kolonien, ²1988

3 V. V. GRAEVE u.a., Milet 1992–1993, in: AA 1995, 195–292   4 Ead., Milet 1994–1995, in: AA 1997, 109–188   5 F. HILLER V. GAERTRINGEN, s.v. Milet (1), RE 15, 1586–1622   6 G. KLEINER, Die Ruinen von Milet, 1968   7 B. and W.-D. NIEMEIER, Milet 1994–1995. Projekt 'Minoisch-mykenisches bis protogeometrisches Milet', in: AA 1997, 189–248   8 TH. WIEGAND e.a., Milet. Ergebnisse, vols. 1,1–6,2ff. 1998ff.   9 H. KNACKFUSS, Das Rathaus von Milet (Milet. Ergebnisse 1,2), 1908;   10 G. KAWERAU, A. REHM, Das Delphinion (Milet. Ergebnisse 1,3), 1914   11 H. KNACKFUSS, A. REHM, Der südliche Markt (Milet. Ergebnisse 1,7), 1924   12 P. HERRMANN, Inschriften von Milet 2 (Milet. Ergebnisse 6,2), 1998   13 TH. WIEGAND, Vierter vorläufiger Bericht über die Ausgrabungen der königlichen Museen zu Milet, in: AA 1906, 1–41.   J.CO. V.v.G.

[3] City on the north-eastern coast of Crete, locally Μίλατος/*Mílatos*. Mythical birth place of → Pandareus (Paus. 10,30,2). Under the leadership of → Sarpedon, M. is said to have been involved in the foundation of the city of M. in Asia Minor [2] (Ephor. FGrH 70 F 127). According to Hom. Il. 2,647, M. was one of the Cretan cities that took part in the Trojan War (→ Troy; → Homerus). Mycenaean habitation is evidenced by the cliff chamber graves with clay sarcophagi. In the Hellenistic period, M. was one of the Cretan cities which concluded a legal assistance treaty with the city of M. in Asia Minor (around 260 BC, StV III 482). In 220 BC, it was still attested as an autonomous political unit (Syll.³ 527 l. 144), M. was annexed after 200 BC by the neighbouring city of → Lyctus (Strab. 10,4,14). Its further existence into Roman times, not confirmed by archaeological evidence, is suggested by M.'s inclusion in the Cretan Catalogue of Cities in Plin. HN 4,59.

H. BEISTER, s.v. Milatos, in: LAUFFER, Griechenland, 436; I. F. SANDERS, Roman Crete, 1982, 141; D. VIVIERS, La cité de Dattalla et l'expansion de Lyktos en Crète centrale, in: BCH 118, 1994, 229–259.   H.SO.

Mileu(m) Numidian settlement, 50 km northwest of Cirta, today's Mila. M. came under strong Punic influence, was given to the mercenary leader P. Sittius by Caesar and as *colonia Sarnia Milevitana* it was one of the four *coloniae* of the *res publica Cirtensium*. Sources: App. B Civ. 4,54; Ptol. 4,3,28; It. Ant. 28,3; Tab. Peut. 3,3; Iulius Honorius, Cosmographia A 44; Anon. Cosmographia 1,44; Geogr. Rav 39,26. In the Roman period the village-like settlement attained metropolitan character. In the Byzantine period it was expanded into a fortress. Inscriptions: CIL VIII 1, 3266; 6700; 6710; 6711; 7013; 7098; 7103; 7115 (?); 7125; 7130; 8201–8238; Suppl. 2, 19973–20075; AE 1972, 694; 1989, 886. Bishops of M. are mentioned from AD 256 (Cypr. Sententiae episcoporum 13). The most famous were Optatus, who wrote *Contra Parmenianum Donatistam*, and Severus. Both were friends of Augustine (Aug. Epist. 34,5 *et passim*).

C. LEPELLEY, Les cités de l'Afrique romaine ... 2, 1981, 438f.; E. LIPIŃSKI, s.v. Milev, DCPP, 293; H. TREIDLER, s.v. M., RE 15, 1659f.   W.HU.

Miliarensis (Greek μιλιαρήσιον/*miliarésion*). Late Roman silver coin of $^1/_{72}$ Roman pound = 4.55 g (light *miliarensis*) and $^1/_{60}$ Roman pound = 5.45 g (heavy *miliarensis*; it is uncertain whether *miliarensis* was the ancient name [3. 15]); minted from AD 324. The *miliarensis* is first mentioned in the year 384 (Cod. Theod. 6,30,7 = Cod. Iust. 12,23,7). Dardanius gives the *miliarensis* the value of 1,000 (bronze) *oboli*, which would mean a 1:125 ratio of silver to bronze [1. 125f.]. A gold to bronze proportionate value from the year 396/7 of 1 → *solidus* = 25 pounds of bronze – that is 1:1,800 (Cod. Theod. 11,21,1), and 5 *solidi* = 1 pound silver (Cod. Theod. 13,2,1 = Cod. Iust. 10,76,1) – yields a gold-silver ratio of 1:14.4 [1. 126]. According to the early Byzantine *Glóssai nomikaí*, the *miliarensis* would be $^1/_{1000}$ gold pound [4; 1. 128] or $^1/_{14}$*solidus*, which would mean a proportionate value of gold to silver of 72:1,000 = 1:13.88. According to the same glosses one *miliarensis* was 1 $^3/_4$ (exactly 1.728) → *siliquae* at $^1/_{1728}$ gold pound and later (only since 615? [1. 130]) $^1/_{12}$*solidus* and thus 2 *siliquae*. The minting of the light and heavy *miliarensis* ended in the west under Honorius [1], in the east (Byzantium) only at the beginning of the 7th century. There the miliarensis was replaced by the heavier *hexagrammon* in the year 615, but remained the weight standard in the form of the *dikeraton* (for 2 *siliquae*, attested from the beginning of the 8th century) until into the 11th century.

→ Siliqua

1 J.-P. CALLU, Les origines de »Miliarensis«, in: RN 1980, 120–130   2 G. DEPEYROT, Le système monétaire de Dioclétien à la fin de l'Empire Romain, in: RBN 138, 1992, 33–106   3 C. E. KING, The Fourth Century Coinage, in: L. CAMILLI (ed.), L'»inflazione« nel quarto secolo D.C., 1993, 1–87   4 K. REGLING, s.v. M., RE 15,2, 1661f.   5 SCHRÖTTER, 390.   DI.K.

Miliarium see → Milestones

Military camps
[1] **Canabae** The canabae ('hutments') were civilian settlements that grew up round legionary bases. The long-term presence of a military unit in one location attracted people who expected to profit from the soldiers – traders, artisans, providers of food and drink, prostitutes, and also women with whom soldiers had formed unofficial liaisons and regarded as their 'wives'. Often there were also the children of such unions. Up to the reign of Septimius Severus soldiers were forbidden to marry, and accommodation for dependents will not usually have been available in barracks. Veterans too settled in the *canabae* as legionary bases became permanent fixtures. *Canabae* therefore marked an important interaction between civilians and soldiers in frontier areas. Since *canabae* were originally situated on land assigned to the army, they were under local military control. Over time what had been a kind of shanty town of temporary wooden structures began to assume a more sophisticated form. First, more buildings were

constructed of stone and some public amenities were established. Second, an administrative framework developed.

Canabae are found at many military sites, for example at → Carnuntum, base of XIV Gemina and seat of the governor of Upper Pannonia, → Deva (Chester), base of XX Valeria Victrix, → Isca (Caerleon), base of II Augusta. At Carnuntum the *canabae* grew up round three sides of the camp, about a mile away. Eventually the civilian settlement moved westwards to a larger site and developed its own amenities including an amphitheatre. At Chester the *canabae* were grouped along the road from the east gate, on the west between the rampart and the river Dee, and in the south. The amphitheatre could accommodate 7000 (presumably including local civilians). By the first half of second century AD stone buildings had appeared, including some with private bath suites. At Caerleon a civil settlement with urban characteristics spread round the west, south, and east of the camp.

The local military commander was best placed to influence the early development of *canabae*. He could determine how close to the camp they were located. In many cases a legionary legate was probably responsible for the day-to-day running of the legionary territorium and the canabae. He often turned to Roman citizens, especially veterans, to take on the role of *de facto* magistrates. They employed the terminology of self-governing communities in describing themselves as e.g. aedile or decurion. *Canabae* that developed into separate and distinct communities and had sufficient standing and resources were assimilated into the structure of Roman local government. For example, Carnuntum was granted municipal status by Hadrian in AD 124 and in 194 Septimius Severus established Colonia Septimia Carnuntum, after he had launched his successful bid for the purple from here.

[2] see → Castra

Military clientela

Modern term (e.g. [1. 28]) for the Roman professional armies of the late Imperial period (→ Roma I. D.), which had an especially close relationship to their commander and thus let themselves be detailed as his *clientela* (→ *cliens*) for his goals interior politics. This 'militarization of home politics' began with C. → Marius [I 1] and L. → Cornelius [I 90] Sulla, who used the professional army created by Marius to further their own power claims in the civil war of 88–81 BC. They had to promise the soldiers material gains, especially a large part of the → spoils of war and allocation of land at the end of their terms of duty. → Caesar created an army that was loyal to him in the Gallic War (58–51) with which he was militarily superior to his rival Cn. → Pompeius [I 3] in the Civil War (49–44).

The special loyalty of the troops tied them personally to the commander and thus continued for each respective → veteran as well (thus with Marius and Sulla) or could be passed on to the heirs (thus with Caesar's heirs

→ Octavianus [1]/Augustus). But the idea entailed in the term, of a unique relationship of closeness and loyalty between army and commander, which rests on reciprocal duties (*fides*) ought to be rejected, for the actual *clientela* relationship did not contain the right of the → *patronus* to a military muster of his *clientes* (but this was indeed possible in rare individual cases as the military conscription of Pompey in Picenum in 83 show). The soldier's oath (→ *sacramentum* III.) always bound the individual soldier only to the respective bearer of *imperium* as the representative of the state. The troops' strong ties to their respective commander can thus more readily be explained by the material interests of the soldiers, which only a successful commander could meet (so especially [2. 435–438]).

1 M. GELZER, KS 3, 1964   2 P. A. BRUNT, The Fall of the Roman Republic, 1988, 435–438.   K.-L.E.

Military diplomas

Modern term for a type of Roman document introduced by the emperor Claudius (AD 41–54) and later widespread. Military diplomas (MD) are bronze double documents consisting of two rectangular, closed, and sealed tablets. On the two inner sides is the actual text of the document, with the same text on the outside of *tabella* I. On the outside of *tabella* II, the names of seven witnesses (licenced by the state since Vespasian) flank the seals secured to the central wire closure by a capsule soldered onto the document.

MD are notarized copies of *ad personam* imperial orders, prepared in the central administration, which granted Roman citizenship (→ *civitas*) to the soldiers of specific troops – mostly after the end of their term of service and/or after the → *missio honesta*, but also as an award (as it occurred to some extent in the late Republic as well), insofar as they did not already have it – as well as the right of → *conubium* with a foreign woman. In most cases, this was recognition of an already existing marriage-like relationship and existing children were included in the citizenship grant (more restrictive rules beginning AD 140). Thus, the MD are evidence (*instrumenta*) of personal legal privilege earned through service, not discharge documents. Formally, they represent to a certain extent miniature copies of the original orders, published in Rome on bronze tablets, which have not been preserved.

The citizen units of the → *praetoriae cohortes* and the → *urbanae cohortes* (for whom only the *conubium* applied) were covered by such constitutions (and as a result there were MD for the soldiers), as were the two imperial fleets at Misenum and Ravenna, the → *equites singulares Augusti*, and – by far the most important in terms of numbers – the auxiliary units from all the provinces, with their *alae* and cohorts, possibly also the provincial fleets and *numeri*. The legions given that they consisted of Roman citizens (with exceptions caused by the civil war around AD 69), on the other hand, are not represented on MD. Despite the stereotypical pattern, both the different forms and the format of the MD underwent changes over the course of time.

With increasing mass production beginning in the reign of Trajan (98–117), the quality declined: size and weight decreased (from 1 kg and more in the 1st cent. to *c.* 200 g around 150/160); the actual document texts inside deteriorated, in part strongly. For reasons that are not clear, the issuing of MD for *auxilia* came almost to a standstill after *c.* 180 (last known record from 203). For the other troops, MD – even after the → *Constitutio Antoniniana* (212) – were produced until *c.* 255. The last isolated examples come from the period of the → Tetrarchy.

MD (and the numerous fragments) are an important source for the Principate in general and in particular for citizenship policy, the central bureaucracy, dating, questions of military history, and for the prosopography of the *equites* and senators (up to the consuls and consular governors). Until 1994, *c.* 400 military certificates had been published; since then, the material has once again increased tremendously. The finds occur most frequently in the military provinces in the Balkan area.

→ Diploma; → Diptych; → Navies

EDITIONS: H. NESSELHAUF, CIL XVI, 1936 (essential), and supplement, 1955.
LITERATURE: 1 W. ECK, H. WOLFF (ed.), Heer und Integrationspolitik. Die römischen Militärdiplome als historische Quelle, 1986 2 M. M. ROXAN, Roman Military Diplomas 1954–1977, 1978; 1978–1984, 1985; 1985–1993, 1994 (with corrigenda and updated lists) 3 Id., P. WEISS, Die Auxiliartruppen der Provinz Thracia, Neue Militärdiplome der Antoninenzeit, in: Chiron 28, 1998, 371–420 4 P. WEISS, Neue Militärdiplome, in: ZPE 117, 1997, 227–268. P.W.

Military feriale see → Feriale Duranum

Military lands Inheritable lands owned by Byzantine soldiers, intended to enable them to defray their cost of living and maintain their accoutrements and a horse during times of peace. The institution of ML probably goes back to the 7th cent. AD, when the Byzantine state, as a result of economic necessity resulting from the wars against the Arabs, was forced to remunerate soldiers by land grants instead of cash [3. 619–621]. The term ML (στρατιωτικὰ κτήματα/*stratiōtikà ktémata*) first appears in the 10th century in a novella of Constantine [9] VII (944–959), through which a legal framework was to be provided for ML, which had previously been based largely on customary law. ML were registered officially, and a minimum value of 4 pounds of gold was established for the inalienable part. The minimum value of the land was raised to 12 gold pounds under Nicephorus II Phocas (963–969). However, this did not stop the decline of ML, nor the gradual replacement of the system with mercenary armies. ML are no longer mentioned after the 10th century.

1 J. HALDON, Recruitment and Conscription in the Byzantine Army, ca. 550–950 …, 1979 2 Id., Military Service, Military Lands, and the Status of Soldiers, in: Dumbarton

Oaks Papers 47, 1993, 1–68 3 M. F. HENDY, Studies in the Byzantine Monetary Economy c. 300–1450, 1985.
AL.B.

Military law Military service in Rome was controlled by a variety of laws, the development of which was strongly influenced by established religious beliefs and collective mindsets. From the early days of the city, Roman citizens were obligated to perform military service; the ranks of the citizens were reinforced by the → *auxilia* (auxiliaries) of the → *socii*. When a citizen was drafted as a soldier, he was no longer subject to paternal authority (→ *patria potestas*), but rather had to subordinate himself to the → *disciplina militaris*. The conditions of military service (minimum age, provision of weapons, pay) could be altered by law – as in 123 BC, by a *lex Sempronia militaris* of C. → Sempronius Gracchus (Plut. C. Gracchus 5). The soldiers had a set of rights, including above all the right to have property. Everything which they acquired during their term of service was designated as *peculium castrense* (Dig. 49,17); this included primarily the *bona castrensia*, i.e. the property acquired as a result of military service, such as by → soldiers' pay, → *donativa*, or → spoils (Dig. 37,13). As *possessor*, the soldier could bequeath his possessions (Dig. 29,1; 49,37,13). As the existence of the → *peculium* and the right to draw up a testament show, the tendency was to grant the soldier all the rights of a free citizen not subject to the *patria potestas*. Furthermore, soldiers were exempt from taxes.

Soldiers were granted new rights beginning in the Severan period (193–235): Septimius Severus allowed the formation of religious *collegia* (→ Associations) and expressly permitted soldiers to cohabit with women outside the legionary camp (Herodian. 3,8,5); however, this cannot be equated with the right to conclude a valid marriage (→ *concubinatus*). In late antiquity, armies and military service were regulated by a multitude of imperial edicts; thus, the provisioning of the soldiers (*annona*) was precisely established (Cod. Theod. 7,4). This was meant to protect the provincial population from unauthorized demands of the soldiers (Cod. Theod. 7,4,12). There were detailed regulations for the provisioning of clothing for the army (Cod. Theod. 7,6), for the right to pasture animals used by the army on private land (Cod. Theod. 7,7,5), for quartering (7,8–10), and for furlough (*commeatus*: 7,12). The recruitment of troops is the object of a variety of provisions which range from the requirement for a minimum height of the recruits (Cod. Theod. 7,13,3) to threats of punishment for self-mutilation with the goal of not being recruited as a soldier (Cod. Theod. 7,13,4), to the permission to pay money rather than supplying recruits (Cod. Theod. 7,13,13f.). → Veterans were granted widespread privileges (Cod. Theod. 7,20); however, it was expected that they either farmed or were active as traders (Cod. Theod. 7,20,3).

Military service ended with the legal act of discharge, which could be honourable (*honesta* → *missio*), for reasons of health (*causaria missio*), or dishonourable (*ignominiosa missio*), depending on the circumstances. In the latter case, there was no legal claim to the privileges of the *veterani*. Soldiers received a written document (→ Military diplomas) upon discharge. At the same time, insofar as they were not Roman citizens, they were granted citizenship and the → *conubium*.

In times of war, the soldier had the right to spoils; as a prisoner of war, he lost his citizenship, though he regained it as a result of *ius postliminii* (Dig. 49,15) if he escaped and returned to his unit or home.

→ Armies; → Disciplina militaris; → Military penal law; → Prisoners of war

1 C. E. BRAND, Roman Military Law, 1968   2 O. BEHRENDS, Die Rechtsregelungen der Militärdiplome und das die Soldaten des Prinzipats treffende Eheverbot, in: W. ECK, H. WOLFF (ed.), Heer und Integrationspolitik, 1986, 116–166   3 V. GIUFFRÈ, Testimonianze sul trattamento penale dei 'milites', 1989;   4 H. HORSTKOTTE, SB 7523 und der Veteranenstatus, in: ZPE 111, 1996, 256–258   5 A. MAFFI, Ricerche sul postliminium, 1992;   6 E. SANDER, Das Recht des röm. Soldaten, in: RhM 101, 1958, 152–191, 193–234   7 J. VENDRAND-VOYER, Normes civiques et métier militaire à Rome sur le principat, 1983.

Y.L.B.

Military penal law The → penal law in effect in the Roman army recognized two different categories of malfeasance. The first category concerned those offences which were also punished in the civilian world, such as theft or *crimen maiestatis* (→ *maiestas*). The second category included specific misconduct in military service, above all disobedience toward superiors, absence from the unit without leave, desertion (→ *desertor*), and treason (→ *perduellio*). The composition of the military tribunal and the punishments changed in accordance with the general political development: for serious offences, though, the *consilium* (the staff of the commanding general) had to convene to pronounce judgment. During the Republic, for which Polybius offers important information (Pol. 6,37–38), a commander who held the → *imperium* had the right to determine life and death over the → *socii* through the *ius gladii* (cf. the case of T. Turpilius Silanus: Sall. Iug. 69,4); however, Roman citizens had the right of appeal (→ *provocatio*) based on the *lex Porcia*. The *centuriones* and the *praefectus castrorum* had general disciplinary power over the soldiers.

In the Principate, military jurisdiction for capital crimes was held by the supreme commander or, as a last resort, the *princeps*. The *praefectus praetorio* pronounced judgement on the Praetorians stationed in Rome (Tert. De corona 1); however, the *legati Augusti pro praetore* normally lacked the authority to impose capital punishments on the soldiers of the legions in the provinces (Dig. 2,1,3). A legal dispute between a member of the Roman army and a Roman citizen was decided by the *praetor*, but from the 3rd cent. by a military court (cf. for this Cod. Theod. 2,1,2). There were a variety of punishments (Pol. 6,37–38; Polyaenus, Strat.

24,1–4; cf. also Suet. Aug. 24); units could be collectively punished for cowardice in the face of the enemy by → *decimatio* (Tac. Ann. 3,21,1) or disbandment; punishments imposed on individual soldiers for this were often degrading; corporal punishments were carried out by the *centuriones*. Punishments for lesser offences also included deductions from pay. The death penalty was imposed for serious offences, disobedience to superiors, or desertion (Jos. BI 5,124). Punishments were made more severe in late antiquity, and there were new forms of penalty: mutilation, burning (Cod. Theod. 7,13,5), hanging, or condemnation to death by wild animals (*ad bestias*) (Dig. 49,16,4); soldiers escaped only forced labour in quarries and mines (*ad metallas*), which was seen as unworthy (Dig. 49,16,3).

→ Crimen; → Disciplina militaris; → Military law

1 C. E. BRAND, Roman Military Law, 1968   2 J. B. CAMPBELL, The Emperor and the Roman Army, 31 BC-AD 235, 1984, 300–314   3 A. DEMANDT, Die Spätantike, 1989, 265ff.   4 V. GIUFFRÈ, Testimonianze sul trattamento penale dei 'milites', 1989   5 T. KISSEL, Kriegsdienstverweigerung, in: Antike Welt 27, 1996, 289–296   6 Y. LE BOHEC, La troisième Légion Auguste, 1989   7 MOMMSEN, Strafrecht   8 E. SANDER, Das römische Militärstrafrecht, in: RhM 103, 1960, 289–319   9 M. VALLEJO GIRVES, Sobre la persecución y el castigo a los desertores, in: Polis 5, 1993, 241–251.

Y.L.B.

Military technology and engineering
I. ANCIENT ORIENT II. EGYPT III. CLASSICAL ANTIQUITY

I. ANCIENT ORIENT
For Mesopotamia, as for the Near East in general, we are poorly informed by both written and archaeological sources about military organization, techniques, and engineering. The isolated case of the 'Vulture Stele' (about 2500 BC, from Tello, southern Babylonia; [1. pl. 91]) points to differences between heavily and lightly armed soldiers. The war chariots depicted there and on the 'Ur Standard' (somewhat older, from Ur; [1. pl. VIII]) were probably static symbols, rather than influential in battle, due to their clumsiness, but particularly because the land around the Babylonian cities was cut through by irrigation canals without bridges. The actual → war chariot technology with the use of horses began under the → Mittani. Only from the 1st millennium, primarily from the Assyrian area, is numerous written and archaeological information preserved, especially on the Assyrian palace reliefs. The creation of greater mobility (e.g. war chariot technology: three horses instead of two) necessary for the vast steppe regions and various measures to cover the army logistically in advanced positions were crucial to Assyrian military successes from the 9th cent. BC on. For weapons, see → Armies I.C.

1 W. ORTHMANN (ed.), Der Alte Orient (PropKg 14), 1975.

Y. YADIN, The Art of Warfare in Biblical Lands, 1963; W. MAYER, Politik und Kriegskunst der Assyrer, 1995 (with detailed bibliography).   H.J.N.

II. EGYPT

From the emergence of the Egyptian state (about 2650 BC), expeditions into the bordering desert regions, Nubia, the Levant, and Syria were common; they required the organized use of large numbers of people and logistics, for which the army and navy were responsible as early as the Old Kingdom (2650–2160 BC). The Egyptian army recruited through conscription of the populace, who were commanded by representatives of the higher administration in the event of a campaign. These troops were supplemented by, special military units constituted by → prisoners of war who had been settled in Egypt, as well as later (1st millennium) by mercenary units, composed primarily of Nubians and Libyans,. The armies of the Graeco-Roman era (323 BC – AD 395) were composed primarily of foreign mercenaries, above all Greeks.

Siege warfare, rather than battles in open territory, became the prevalent form of combat with the appearance of fortified settlements in the Early Bronze Age (3rd millennium). Only in the Late Bronze Age (2nd half of the 2nd millennium) did open battle between two large armies prevail. The armament of the Egyptian army consisted of bows and arrows, axes, spears, bronze knives, staves, shields, and mobile scaling ladders. At the beginning of the New Kingdom (c. 1640–1070 BC), light → war chariots drawn by two horses were introduced to Egypt from the Near East. In addition, technical achievements, that can be traced back to influences from the Near Eastern and Aegean regions, included composite bows, scimitars, duck-bill axes, and later iron long swords, sophisticated projectiles, shields, and bronze coats of mail and helmets,

A. M. GNIERS, War and Society in Ancient Egypt, in: K. RAAFLAUB, N. ROSENSTEIN (ed.), War and Society in the Ancient and Medieval Worlds, 1999; J. K. WINNICKI, Das ptolemäische. und das hellenistische. Heerwesen, in: L. CRISCUOLO (ed.), Egitto e storia antica dall'Ellenismo all'età araba. Atti del Colloquio Internazionale Bologna 1987, 1989, 213–230.   A.M.G.

III. CLASSICAL ANTIQUITY
A. GREEK   B. ROMAN

A. GREEK

The dependence of a hero fighting in war on the technical expertise of craftsmen was recognized already in the epics of Homer: when Achilles [1] also loses his weapons and armour through the death of Patroclus, he must rely on → Hephaestus to forge a shield, armour, helmet, and greaves for him (Hom. Il. 16,64; 16,130ff.; 17,125; 18,82ff.; 18,187ff.; 18,450ff.). Due to the steadily growing significance of → naval warfare and fleets in the Archaic and Classical eras (6th and 5th cents. BC), the interconnection between → crafts

and technical skills on the one hand and the military on the other became even clearer; it is significant that → Thucydides illustrates the change in warfare from the Archaic era with the example of the development of → navies and shipbuilding. The construction of a fleet of triremes, of ships of one type, was a prerequisite for the Greek victory over the Persians at Salamis (Thuc. 1,103ff.; Plut. Themistocles 4); in the late 5th cent. BC, it was possible to express the opinion that the conduct of naval warfare could be counted among the τέχναι (téchnai; → Art) (Thuc. 1,142,9). However, → technology did not just play a role in the arming of soldiers and battle, rather it often created the conditions for the advance of an army; during the campaign of → Xerxes against Greece in 480 BC, a canal was dug across the Athos peninsula and a bridge built across the Hellespont (Hdt. 7,22ff.; 7,39ff.; cf. the bridge of → Mandrocles Hdt. 4,85ff.).

A new epoch of Greek military technology began in 399 BC with the campaign of Dionysius [1] I of Syracuse against the Carthaginians; it is said that during the preparations for the war – for which he brought the most skilled engineers from all of Greece to Syracuse – the → catapult was invented and a large number of efficient weapons were developed (Diod. Sic. 14,41). Since the conquest of fortified cities and places was now decisive in war, Dionysius had large siege engines built, such as six-storey high siege towers on wheels (→ Siegecraft). War became a field of activity for engineers, who now took part in the decisions on the process of a siege; engineers were present in the theatre of war from this time on (Diod. Sic. 14,48; 14,51ff.). The changes in military technology and their effects on warfare were quite noticeable to contemporaries: when a catapult was demonstrated for the Spartan king Archidamus [2], he is said to have proclaimed that valour was thus condemned to ruin (Plut. Mor. 191e; 219a). In view of the progress in siege technology, Aristotle considered it imperativel for a city to erect extraordinarily solid walls to protect against attack (Aristot. Pol. 1330b–1331a).

The new possibilities in military technology were also used effectively by the Macedonian kings → Philippus II and → Alexander [4] the Great on their campaigns; of the engineers in the Macedonian army, Vitruvius names Polyeidus, Diades, and Charias – capable figures who were able to improve siege engines significantly and construct new devices; they wrote books about their achievements, which were still known to Vitruvius (Vitr. De arch. 10,13,3ff.; cf. 7 praef. 14). The superior military technology of the Macedonians contributed decisively to the successes of Alexander; the rapid conquest of the strategically important cities on the coasts of Asia Minor and Phoenicia were the prerequisite for the advance to the east. The technical aspects of the siege of → Tyrus (332 BC), which was considered particularly spectacular, were led by Diades, who connected the town, which was located on an island, with the mainland via a monumental causeway and had the walls bombarded by ballistae placed on ships (Arr. Anab. 2,16ff.).

The technical costs of warfare ultimately reached previously unheard-of levels during the Diadochi period (323–281 BC; → Diadochi). The general Demetrius [2] Poliorcetes for example had a genuine interest in military technology; the presentation of his novel ships and siege engines served as a means of impressively demonstrating his military potential (Plut. Demetrius 20). Sieges in this period became a virtual competition of engineers. Thus, during the siege of Rhodes (305 BC), the architect Epimachus built a mobile tower, circa 40 m high, that was moved forward by 800 men; numerous catapults were placed on its nine storeys. The size of such siege engines did not necessarily lead to success: Diognetus, an engineer from Rhodes, was able to prevent the tower from being advanced to the city wall with countermeasures (Vitr. De arch. 10,16,3,ff.; cf. Diod. Sic. 20,95ff.; Plut. Demetrius 21). The siege of Syracuse by the Romans in 213/212 BC was famous; the effort of the mathematician Archimedes [1], who constantly built and used new defensive weapons, rendered the military capture of the city impossible; the Romans were finally able to capture it only through treachery (Pol. 8,5–9; 8,37; Plut. Marcellus 14–17).

The construction of effective → catapults proved to be extraordinarily difficult technically; above all, the mechanicians from Alexandria [1] tried to solve this problem theoretically and through testing in the 3rd cent. BC. Thus arose a new technical discipline, the *belopoiikê* (manufacture of catapults), which was perceived as a branch of mechanics. The effort to formulate the technical problems precisely by means of mathematics was characteristic of the approach of the mechanicians. Their goal was to build catapults with a long range and major penetrating power. Of the works on *belopoiikê*, the texts by Philo of Byzantium and → Hero of Alexandria have been preserved; Vitruvius also devoted a longer section to this field (Vitr. De arch. 10,10ff.). The function of military technology was seen by these authors essentially as protection against attacks from the outside (Vitr. De arch. 10,10,1; Heron, Belopoiika W71–72).

B. ROMAN

The Romans adopted the Hellenistic achievements in military technology; from the time of the late Republic, the → legions had siege engines and catapults, with specialized engineers responsible for their construction and repair (Vitr. De arch. 1, praef. 2; cf. Tac. Hist. 3,23; Jos. BI 3,121; 5,270; for late antiquity, cf. Veg. Mil. 2,25; Amm. Marc. 23,4). The technical accomplishments of the Roman army lay essentially in the construction of transportation infrastructure, in the construction of → roads and bridges; in this way, the rapid appearance of the legions in the theatre of conflict and the supply of the troops was supposed to be ensured (Plin. Ep. 8,4,2; on roadbuilding by the legions cf. ILS 151; 2478; 2479; 5835; 5865). During the Dacian Wars of Trajan, the famous bridge across the Danube was built by the architect Apollodorus [14] in order to con-

nect the conquered territories with the Imperium Romanum (Cass. Dio 68,13; Procop. Aed. 4,6,11ff.). This aspect of Roman warfare is also emphasized in the iconography of Trajan's Column. It is clear that Rome's technical intelligence was primarily present in the legions, and the civilian sphere also relied occasionally on help from military engineers (cf. the aqueduct of Saldae ILS 5795).

→ Catapult; → Siegecraft; → Technology;→ Weapons

1 J. G. LANDELS, Engineering in the Ancient World, 1978, 94–132   2 O. LENDLE, Texte und Untersuchungen. zum technischen Bereich der antiken. Poliorketik, 1983;   3 E. W. MARSDEN, Greek and Roman Artillery, Historical Development, 1969   4 Id., Greek and Roman Artillery, Technical Treatises, 1971.   H.SCHN.

Military tenure is the ownership of land – perhaps better described as → 'soldiers' tenure' – to which military obligations were attached: whether armed service by the owner or the recruiting and equipping of soldiers (as representatives of the owner, so to speak). Military tenure (MT) in this sense occurred particularly in the Ancient Orient. It is relatively well recorded for the Persian empire of the → Achaemenidae [2] (6th–4th cents. BC) and the Hittite empire (→ Hattusa II.); Egyptian military colonies probably also consisted of active soldiers. One can only speak of MT (and not merely land tenancy) when there are hereditary rights and duties, as is recorded at any rate for Persia and then again in the Byzantine empire from the time of the Arab invasion in the 7th cent. into the 11th cent. The Byzantine MT was called *stratiōtiká ktḗmata* ('soldiers' property').

There is no MT when the military is based on purely citizen or professional armies. This applies to Classical Greece and the Roman empire. However, in Rome from the beginning of the 1st cent. BC, the problem of providing soldiers with land after their term of service (→ Veterans) arose. The resulting military colonies (cf. → coloniae) had nothing to do with the services by the owner typical for tenure, since they were allocated only after the end of service as a 'reward' (remuneration).

G. CARDASCIA, Armée et fiscalité dans la Babylonie achéménide, in: Armées et fiscalité dans le monde antique (colloque no. 936 du C. N. R. S.), 1977, 1–11; W. HELCK, s. v. Militärkolonie, LÄ 4, 134 f.; M. GREGORIOU-IOANNIDOU, Les biens militaires et le recrutement en Byzance, Byzantiaka 12, 1992, 215–226.   G.S.

Military writers The intellectual education of the future officers of the Roman army was based on the reading and interpretation of the works of historians such as Polybius and Livy, as well as the military regulations put into force under Augustus and Hadrian, which were still valid under Severus Alexander (Veg. Mil. 1,27: *Augusti atque Hadriani constitutiones*; Suet. Aug. 24f.; cf. Cass. Dio 69,9,4). Alongside these, works by Cato, Marius [I 1], Rutilius Rufus (Val. Max. 2,3,2), and Arrius [II 5] Menander were also read. Under Constantinus [1], these readings were largely abandoned. Furthermore, there was a series of works on the military which were influenced by Greek models and bore little relation to Roman reality.

Greek authors worthy of mention include, above all, → Xenophon, who described a model general in the person of the Persian king → Cyrus [2] (Xen. Cyr. 1,6,9–43; 8,1,1–5, 8,5,8–16) and composed a work on the duties of a cavalry commander (Xen. Hipp.), as well as → Aeneas [2] Tacticus, a fragment of whose work on defending a city has been preserved, and the engineers who wrote primarily about siege engines in the Hellenistic era (Vitr. De arch. 10,13,3; → Siegecraft). From a comment in Sallustius, it can be assumed that Roman military leaders were expected to have read *Graecorum militaria praecepta* (military instructions of the Greeks) (Sall. Iug. 85,12); Xenophon was read by Roman senators in the 2nd and 1st cents. BC (Cic. Ad Q. Fr. 1,1,23).

In the Roman era, authors such as → Asclepiodotus [2] (1st cent. BC) and → Arrianus [2] (2nd cent.) dealt with → tactics; stratagems (→ Strategemata) were the subject of the work by → Frontinus (1st cent.), who had extensive military experience as the governor of Britain (Tac. Agr. 17,2), and → Polyaenus (2nd cent.), who primarily drew upon Greek historians. Questions of military technology also attracted interest. Catapults and siege engines were described by → Vitruvius, who was one of Caesar's military engineers (Vitr. De arch. 1, praef. 2; 10,10–16), → Athenaeus [5] Mechanicus (probably of the Augustan period), → Heron of Alexandria (1st cent.), and → Apollodorus [14] of Damascus (2nd cent.). → Onasander [2] wrote a manual on military leadership which was geared toward higher-ranking officers of the Roman army (1st cent.). The construction of a Roman camp is described precisely by (Pseudo-) → Hyginus (2nd/3rd cents.). In late antiquity, → Vegetius summarized the knowledge of the Roman military in a systematic manual, describing, however, not the army of the 4th cent., but rather that of the early Principate: the selection and training of recruits (Veg. Mil. 1), the legion and the duties of the higher-ranking officers (Mil. 2), the legion on the march and in battle (Mil. 3), and the siege of cities and naval warfare (Mil. 4).

1 B. CAMPBELL, Teach Yourself How to Be a General, in: JRS 77, 1987, 13–29   2 V. GIUFFRÈ, La letteratura 'de re militari', 1974   3 Y. LE BOHEC, Que voulait Onesandros?, in: Y. BURNAND et al. (ed.), Claude de Lyon, empereur romain, 1998, 169–179   4 A. A. SCHILLER, Sententiae Hadriani de re militari, in: W. G. BECKER u.a. (ed.), FS U. von Lübtow, 1970, 295–306.   Y.L.B.

Milk (Greek γάλα/*gála*; Latin *lac*). The milk of various mammals (donkey, camel, cow, sheep, mare, goat) was used in ancient times; the concept was thus not, as today, limited to cow's milk. Cow's milk was rather unpopular in the Mediterranean region, and was consumed in large quantities only in northern regions of the ancient world (Aristot. Hist. Ant. 3,20). The favourite kind of milk among the Greeks and Romans was that of sheep, also the only kind to appear in the → Edictum [3] Diocletiani (6,95 LAUFFER); goat's milk was similarly popular. Camel's milk, on the other hand, was only of regional significance, while the milk of donkeys and mares was used specifically for medicinal and cosmetic purposes in the Mediterranean region.

Milk, which spoils rapidly unless cooled, was only a significant contribution to nutrition (Colum. 7,2,1f.) in the countryside. In cities, it was much less consumed, not least due to sometimes extremely high prices (on sheep's milk, cf. Edictum Diocletiani 6,95 LAUFFER). Milk served primarily as a drink (→ Beverages), consumed either pure, flavoured, or sweetened. However, it was also used as an ingredient in bread, porridge, casseroles, cakes and desserts (Apicius 7,13). The nutritional and healing aspects of milk were wellknown to physicians; they prescribed it for various internal and external uses (Dioscurides, De materia medica 2,75 WELLMANN; Plin. HN. 28,123–130; Gal. De alimentorum facultatibus 3,14). In the early Greek and Roman periods, milk was very highly valued as a cheap libation (Plin. HN. 14,88; Eur. Or. 114f.). Later, wine became more popular for this purpose (Macr. Sat. 1,12,25). It was regarded as proof of their cultural backwardness that peoples on the margins of the ancient world drank mostly milk (Herodotus 1,216; Caes. Gall. 4,1,8).

J. ANDRÉ, Essen und Trinken im alten Rom, 1998; A. BAUDRILLART, s.v. Lac, DS 3, 883–886; A. DALBY, Essen und Trinken im alten Griechenland, 1998; G. HERZOG-HAUSER, s.v. Milch, RE 15, 1569–1580.   A.G.

Milky Way
I. ANCIENT ORIENT   II. CLASSICAL ANTIQUITY

I. ANCIENT ORIENT
The expression for the MW in ancient Mesopotamia has not yet been discovered. However, it is possible that it referred to milk; in hymnal texts, the stars were described as the 'cattle herds of the → Moon deities'. In Egypt, too, the MW was perceived as a phenomenon; its designation is still discussed in modern scholarship [2].

1 W. HEIMPEL, The Babylonian Background of the Term 'Milky Way', in: H. BEHRENS (Ed.), FS A.Sjöberg, 1989, 249–252   2 O. NEUGEBAUER, R. A. PARKER, Egyptian Astronomical Texts I, 1960, 50.   H.HU.

II. CLASSICAL ANTIQUITY
The MW – Greek γάλα/*gála*, ὁ τοῦ γάλακτος (κύκλος)/ *ho toû gálaktos (kýklos)* etc., Latin *circ(ul)us (orbis) lacteus, via lactea* – is the only visible sphere of heaven and one of the seven great spheres (→ *kýkloi*). Because of its irregularity, its division into two branches (between Altair in Aquila and Cygnus) and its fluctuating breadth on the threshold between ἀήρ/*aér* and αἰθήρ/*aithér*, Aristotle and the Stoics located it together with the comets, below the lunar sphere, but usually in the sphere of the fixed stars. The course of the MW, which cuts across the → zodiac in Gemini and Sagitta-

rius, is described in detail in Ptol. Syntaxis mathematike 8,2. It was seldom depicted on globes (Geminus 5,69; examples in [1. 1022–1024]); the only extant ancient example showing the MW was discovered only recently [2. 56–58].

In Graeco-Roman mythology, the MW was explained as the spilt milk of Ops (Hyg. Astr. 2,43) or Juno (Eratosth. Katasterismoi 44) from suckling Heracles, Mercury or Bacchus. It was also said to be the course of the straying chariot of Helios (→ Sol) or → Phaethon (Manil. 1,729–749) or the pathway of the gods (Ov. met. 1,168–171). In religious tradition, it was interpreted as the path of the souls to heavenly Hades (Heracl. Pont. In Philop. in Aristot. Mete. 117,31 HAYDUCK), or the habitat and nourishment of astral souls before their birth and after their death (Pythagoras in Porph. De antro Nympharum 28 in connection with the gates of heaven: → Zodiac; Procl. in Plat. Rep. 2,129,25 KROLL). To the Romans, the MW was the residence of souls of outstanding personalities (Cic. Rep. 6,16; Manil. 1,758–804; Mart. Cap. 2,211–213). In physical interpretations (predominantly among the Pythagoreans, Aet. 3,1) it was the trail of a fallen star, the former path of the sun, an optical illusion, an emanation (ἀναπνοή/*anapnoé*) of fire (Parmenides A 37 p. 224,11 DK), a conglomeration of many dim stars (the correct explanation from Anaxagoras and Democritus in Aristot.), the refraction (ἀνάκλασις/ *anáklasis*) of starlight (Hippocrates of Chios, A 6 p. 397,9 DK), a mist of dry, flammable vapours (Aristot. Mete. 1,8,345a 11 – 346b 15), a rip in heaven or its cicatrisation (Manil. 1,718–728). The image of a river, common in other cultures, is absent in Graeco-Roman antiquity. The texture of the MW was imagined to be misty, composed of particles of the finest matter. Among the individual → constellations, particularly auspicious portents were Aquila in the north and Canis Major in the south (Plin. HN. 18,281f.).

1 F. BOLL, W. GUNDEL, s.v. Sternbilder, in: ROSCHER 6, 1021–1029   2 E. KÜNZL, Der Globus im römisch-germanischen Zentralmuseum in Mainz, in: Der Globusfreund 45/6, 1997/8, 7–80.

P. CAPELLE, De luna stellis lacteo orbe animarum sedibus, 1917; H. DIELS, Doxographi Graeci, 1879; W. GUNDEL, s.v. Galaxias/Γαλαξίας, RE 7, 560–571.   W.H.

Millet see → Grain

Mills

I. ANCIENT ORIENT AND EGYPT   II. CLASSICAL ANTIQUITY

I. ANCIENT ORIENT AND EGYPT

In the Near Eastern and Egyptian cultures, only grinding mills were used. These consisted of an oblong grindstone and a running stone that was moved back and forth on top of it. Rotary mills, the upper stone of which turned on an axis, did not appear until Roman

influence made itself felt. The grinding stones were mostly of basalt, imported from afar when necessary. The terms for the grinding and rubbing stones are *NA₄.ARÀ* in Sumerian, *erûm* and *narkabum* in Akkadian, *bnwt* in Egyptian.

Mills could be found in every household; large-scale mill works were part of the large households of palaces and temples. Thus in Palace G (3rd millennium) in → Ebla, an arrangement was found consisting of grindstones set in a row and embedded in a bank of clay. To our knowledge, work in the mills was done mostly by women; from the Hittite region there are reports of blind prisoners of war also being used. Detailed information comes from the large state-owned enterprises of the time of the 3rd dynasty of Ur (21st cent. BC), which employed their own permanent personnel. Each worker was expected to produce 8 sila of fine flour or 10 sila of coarsely-ground meal per day (1 sila = 0.84 l). In addition to cereals, nuts, olives and spices were processed in smaller quantities.

L. MILANO, H. A. HOFFNER, R. S. ELLIS, s.v. Mühle, RLA 8, 393–404; CH. MÜLLER, s.v. Mühlstein, Müllerin, LÄ 4, 212.   H.J.N.

II. CLASSICAL ANTIQUITY

A. PUSH AND LEVER MILLS   B. THE ROTARY MILL C. THE DONKEY MILL   D. THE WATER MILL E. ARCHAEOLOGICAL EVIDENCE

A. PUSH AND LEVER MILLS

There are records of various types of mills (Gr. μύλη/ *mýlē*; Lat. *mola*) in Classical Antiquity. Beginning with the Neolithic period, the simple saddlestone mill (grinding mill) was used for the grinding of grain. This mill consisted of a fixed lower stone (bed stone) and a smaller, movable upper stone (runner stone) held in both hands while grinding. Such mills were still common in the Archaic era in Greece. Not until the 5th cent. BC, an important improvement on the mill was introduced in Greece: the rubber received a round hopper for the continuous introduction of the grist. In the next stage development (end of the 5th cent. BC), a wooden lever was affixed to the upper stone; one end of the lever was moved back and forth, while the other end pivoted on a vertical axle. Thus, the original pushing movement was replaced by a turning movement. This was the beginning of the mechanization of the mill. This significantly more efficient lever mill, also called 'Olynthian mill' after the most important place where it was found, became prevalent in the eastern region of the Mediterranean and then spread to Lower Italy, Sicily and southern France. From the 4th cent. BC, it was increasingly replaced with the rotary mill, but there is evidence of its use into the 1st cent. BC, mainly in the eastern Mediterranean.

Ancient mills

Prehistoric
saddlestone mill

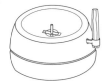

Late Hellenistic
hand-mill

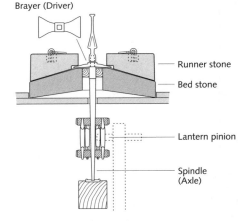

Fast-turning grinding mechanism, its components
based on the find at Zugmantel, Taunus (2nd half
2nd cent. AD).

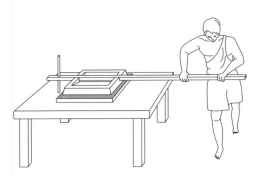

Lever mill (reconstruction)

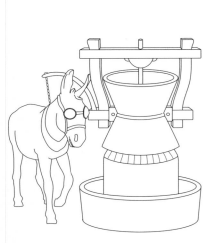

Donkey mill, 1st cent. AD (reconstruction)

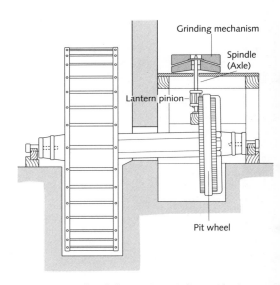

Water-mill with fast-turning grinding mechanism
(from 2nd cent. AD onwards); reconstruction.

B. THE ROTARY MILL

The rotary mill originated in the western Mediterranean in the 4th cent. BC as a further development of the lever mill. The oldest revolving mills had steeply sloping grinding surfaces and were proportioned so that they could be operated by a person walking around them. Thus, the next stage of mechanization was attained. From this early rotary mill derived the development of the small revolving hand mill, turned by a single person with one hand, as well as the large donkey mill (the 'Pompeian mill' or 'hourglass mill'). To ensure a precise running of the mill, both the hand mill and the donkey mill were equipped with a centering axle for the running stone.

The revolving hand mill probably appeared in the 3rd cent. BC in the western Mediterranean. There, it was used by non-Greek peoples as well – the Carthaginians, Italic peoples, Iberians, and Celts. Numerous variants of this mill arose in the course of the following centuries. The diameter of these small mills was between 30 and 45 cm; its grinding surfaces were less steeply positioned than those of the oldest rotary mills.

From the Hellenistic period, hand mills belonged to the equipment of troops, in the case of the Roman army, from the 2nd cent. BC at the latest. Along with other types of mills, the rotary hand mill remained in use in Europe into modern times.

C. THE DONKEY MILL

The donkey mill was designed to be powered directly by draft animals and therefore ran slowly. Its grinding surfaces were sloped at a very steep angle. The heavy running stone was suspended in a frame of beams at adjustable height ('hanging runner') and so could easily be lifted; otherwise, one could not have set the mill in motion because of the friction of the grinding surfaces. Further, it was possible to change the gap width between the lower stone and the upper and by this means of set the grinding fineness. Mills of this construction can be shown to exist from the 2nd century BC; they were used on country estates (Cato Agr. 10,4; 11,4: *mola asinaria*). In the cities, donkey mills were part of the equipment of a *pistrina* (combination milling enterprise and bakery, as for example in Pompeii) because of their productivity. Donkey mills spread throughout the entire Mediterranean region from the 2nd century BC, and can be shown to exist into Late Antiquity. They were also driven by horses (Anth. Gr. 9,19–21; Apul. Met. 9,13). Rotary mills were also used for the grinding of ore. In the north of the Roman Empire, hand mills were most common, in addition to large mills of different construction types. A special development of the slow-running mills were the oil mills (edge mill, *trapetum*). Besides donkey mills, other large mills (larger than hand mills) are known from Pompeii, the grinding parts of which show a compact cylindrical shape. Mills of similar form have been found at other Roman sites as well, dating from around the beginning of the Common Era and the 1st cent. AD. Like the donkey mills, these mills turned slowly, using a direct capstan drive. As was the case with the donkey mills, the running stones of these mills were suspended.

Not until the 2nd cent. AD do we find archaeological evidence for large mills with running stones with holes for the mill rind (or rhynd). Finds of iron mill axles (spindles), mill rinds and components of axle gears also date from this time. The running stone of such a mill was not suspended but rested upon the mill rind and spindle. The mechanical parts served the purpose of turning the grinding stone and raising it to allow start-up of the grinding mechanism and regulate the fineness of the grinding. This important technical invention of the Roman Imperial period made possible the construction of significantly faster-running mills with greater milling efficiency. In order to reach the required rotation speed, transmission gearing was necessary, driven either by water power or by means of a capstan.

D. THE WATER MILL

According to Strabo, Mithridates [5] V. Euergetes (150–120 BC) owned a water mill at his palace in Cabira (Pontus) (ὑδραλέτης/*hydralétēs*, Strab. 12,3,30). A high point in the mechanization of the mill in Antiquity was reached with the use of water power for grinding. In the time of Augustus (Antipater of Thessalonica, Anth. Pal. 9,418), the water mill was still being acclaimed as an innovation. The only detailed description that has come down to us is in Vitr. De arch. 10,5,2; according to this text, the water mill was equipped with a mitre gear that lowered the speed of rotation of the waterwheel, resulting in a slowly turning grinding mechanism. Since water mills were located mostly outside of settlements, they promoted the rise of specialized milling businesses without a bakery. Water mills served not only to grind grain, they were also used to de-husk the spelt cereals popular with the Romans (*far*; Plin. HN 18,97). After the 2nd cent. AD, fast-operating grinding mechanisms prevailed among water mills.

There were probably numerous water mills of this type in the Roman Empire, but the archaeological evidence is not sufficient to allow a more precise statement regarding their distribution. There were large works with several water mills, e.g. in Barbegal (France, near Arles) and in Rome (Baths of Caracalla, the Ianiculum). In Barbegal and on the Ianiculum, these mill complexes received their water from aqueducts; in the 6th cent. AD, all the grain required to meet the city's needs was milled on the Ianiculum (Cod. Theod. 14,15,4; Prok. Goth. 1,19,8). By the 4th/5th cents. at the latest, a water mill belonged to the equipment recommended for a country estate, if there was sufficient water available (Pall. Agric. 1,41). Especially in the arid regions of the Mediterranean, however, the water mill could not replace the old donkey mill. In many parts of the Roman Empire, the technology of the water mill survived beyond the end of Antiquity and the era of the Migration of Peoples. From the time of the waning of the Middle Ages, this mill technology served as a starting-point for the development of industry in Europe.

There is evidence of a water mill dating from the early 4th century AD in Chemtou (Algeria) which must have possessed a turbine-like paddle wheel that turned on a vertical axle and propelled a fast-working grinding device directly without gears. During the siege of Rome by the Goths (537), the Roman commander Belisarius had mills set up on ships moored on the Tiber beneath the *pons Aemilius*. Such ship-mills had the advantage of being located within the city and of adapting easily to the fluctuating water level (Prok. Goth. 1,19,19ff.). Ship-mills existed in many cities during the Middle Ages; in Rome, they existed until the early 19th cent.

E. ARCHAEOLOGICAL EVIDENCE

In addition to the numerous finds of millstones (Olynthus; Pompeii), Roman reliefs belong to the most important archaeological evidence regarding the history of ancient mills, particularly the reliefs on the tomb of Eurysaces near the Porta Maggiore and in the Museo Chiaramonti (Rome, MV); these depictions show in a detailed manner the beam framework for the suspension of running stones.

→ Bakeries; → Flour; → Oils for cooking

1 M. C. AMOURETTI, Le pain et l'huile dans la Grèce antique, 1986, 138–147   2 D. BAATZ, Die Wassermühle bei Vitruv X 5,2, in: Saalburg-Jb. 48, 1995, 5–18;   3 J. F. HEALY, Mining and Metallurgy in the Greek and Roman World, 1978, 142f.   4 J. HENNING, Mühlentechnologie und Ökonomiewandel zwischen Römerzeit und Hochmittelalter, in: Saalburg-Jb. 47, 1994, 5–18   5 A. HUG, s.v. Μύλη, RE 16, 1821–1831   6 L. A. MORITZ, Grain-Mills and Flour in Classical Antiquity, 1958 (repr. 1979)   7 D. P. S. PEACOCK, The Mills of Pompeii, in: Antiquity 63, 1989, 205–214   8 J. u. G. RÖDER, Die antike Turbinenmühle in Chemtou, in: F. RAKOB (ed.), Simitthus, vol. 1, 1993, 93–102   9 Ö. WIKANDER, Archaeological Evidence for Early Water-Mills, in: History of Technology 10, 1985, 151–179;   10 Id., Exploitation of Water-Power or Technological Stagnation?, 1984   11 Id., The Use of Water-Power in Classical Antiquity, in: Opuscula Romana 13, 1981, 91–104.   D.BA.

Milo see → Annius [I 14] Milo, T.

Milon

[1] see → Medon [7]

[2] Milon (Μίλων) of Croton. A wrestler, one of the most famous athletes of Greek antiquity, with 32 victories at Panhellenic competitions (→ Sports festivals). No other ancient athlete won six times at Olympia as he did (540; 532–516 BC) [1. no. 115, 122, 126, 129, 133, 139]; he was also a six-time *periodonikēs* (→ Periodos, Periodonikes) [2. 16–18; 3. 340]. His countryman Timasitheus [1. no. 145] thwarted his attempt at a seventh Olympic victory. Legend ascribes gigantic stature and incredible feats of strength to M. E.g., he is said to have brought his victory statue from Olympia into the Altis, the grove and courtyard of the temple of Zeus, on his own. The story of his deeds of strength reported by Pausanias (6,14,6–7) seems to have been inspired by his victory statue, remnants of which may have been preserved [4. 116f.; 5; 6]. We also know the text of the victor inscription on it [7. no. 61]. Doubt is cast on his alleged aristocratic origins [8. 83–87] by the tradition that he was the father-in-law of a physician [9. 153f.]. At the head of his native town's army, he is said to have led his countrymen to victory in the battle against Sybaris in 511/10 BC (Diod. 12,9,5–6). He was said to be connected to the circle surrounding the philosopher → Pythagoras [10. 118f.].

1 L. MORETTI, Olympionikai, 1957   2 R. KNAB, Die Periodoniken, 1934, repr. 1980   3 E. MARÓTI, ΠΕΡΙΟΔΟΝΙΚΗΣ. Anmerkungen zum Begriff Perioden-Sieger bei den panhellenischen Spielen, in: Acta Antiqua Academiae Scientiarum Hungaricae 31, 1985–1988, 3–4, 335–355   4 H.-V. HERRMANN, Olympia, 1972;   5 Idem, Die Siegerstatuen von Olympia, in: Nikephoros 1, 1988, 144 n. 39   6 E. GHISELLINI, La statua di Milone di Crotone ad Olimpia, in: Xenia 16, 1988, 43–52   7 J. EBERT, Griechische Epigramme auf Sieger an gymnischen und hippischen Agonen (Abh. der sächsischen Akad. der Wiss.

zu Leipzig. Philol.-histor. Kl. Bd. 63 H. 2), 1972;   8 A. HÖNLE, Olympia in der Politik der griechischen Staatenwelt, 1972   9 D. C. YOUNG, The Olympic Myth of Greek Amateur Athletics, 1984   10 M. B. POLIAKOFF, Combat Sports in the Ancient World, 1987.

W. DECKER, Sport in der griechischen Antike, 1995, 131–133; A. MODRZE, s.v. Milon (2), RE 15, 1672–1676.
                                                                    W.D.

Milonia Caesonia Daughter of Vistilia [2], born around 5 AD. Although she was not exceptionally beautiful and was already the mother of three daughters, → Caligula had a relationship and a close personal bond with her. He married her when she was pregnant, shortly before the birth of a daughter who was given the name Iulia [14] Drusilla. However, Nero did not grant M. the name *Augusta*. She was murdered together with Caligula and her daughter at the beginning of the year 41 by a *centurio*. Nothing in CIL VI 32347 (Acts of the Arval brethren) points to the deletion of her name.

J. SCHEID (ed.), Commentarii fratrum Arvalium, 1998, 39, Nr. 14; PIR² M 590.   W.E.

Miltas (Μίλτας; *Míltas*). Thessalian, seer and occasional member of the Platonic academy (→ *Akadēmeia*); in 357 BC he took part in the campaign of → Dion [I 1] against → Dionysius [2], and interpreted the lunar eclipse (August 8) which preceded departure as a portent of the fall of Dionysius (Plut. Dion 22,6f.; 24,2–4).

K. TRAMPEDACH, Platon, die Akademie und die zeitgenössische Politik, 1994, 111.   HA.BE.

Miltiades (Μιλτιάδης; *Miltiádēs*). From the 7th (Paus. 4,23,10; 8,39,3) to the 4th cent. BC, a name belonging to the family of the Philaïdae in Athens.

[1] **M. the Elder** Son of Cypselus (archon 597/6 BC), grandson (?) of the tyrant Cypselus [2] of Corinth, relative ([7. 7]: adoptive son) of → Hippocleides (archon 566/5); from the same mother as the three-time Olympian victor Cimon [1]. M. was victor in the four-horse chariot race at Olympia (548?). 'Dynast' alongside → Peisistratus. Not in exile in 546, unlike Cimon, M. took control of Thracian Chersonesus [1] for Athens, together with Athenian settlers, on advice from Delphi. M. was taken prisoner in the war against → Lampsacus, but released at the urging of → Croesus. M. died childless, his heir being his nephew Stesagoras 524 (?) [14. 250]. A founder cult is attested for M. in the Chersonesus (Hdt. 6,34–38; Marcellinus, Life of Thucydides 3–10; not attested in Nep. Miltiades 1; [7. 109–120]).
→ Peisistratids; → Peisistratus; → Philaïdae

BIBLIOGRAPHY DAVIES, 299f.; PA 10209; TRAILL, PAA 653685.

[2] **M. the Younger** Victor at the battle of → Marathon. Son of Cimon [1], nephew of M. [1], father of Cimon [2]. Born c. 555 BC, his career in Athens culminated in the archonship for 524/3 (Dion. Hal. 7,3,1; IG I³

1031a) and membership in the → Areopagus conjointly (Hdt. 6,39,1) with the Peisistratids. In the interest of Athens, M. took over the position of his murdered brother Stesagoras on the Chersonesus (Hdt. 6,39) c. 520, fled (to Athens?) before the invasion of the Scythians, but was recalled to the Chersonesus c. 518 (Hdt. 6,40). M. conquered Lemnos (probably also Imbros and Tenedos) for Athens (Hdt. 6,136–140; Nep. Miltiades 1f.). His second marriage was to → Hegesipyle (mother of Cimon [2], Hdt. 6,39,2); the dating of these events in M.'s life between 523 and 493 is disputed.

In 514/13 M., now a Persian vassal tyrant, took part 'loyally' (against Hdt. 6,137f.; Nep. Miltiades 3) in Darius' [2] great Scythian campaign, thus gaining important insights into the command structure of the Persian army. Whether, how frequently, and how long he lived in Athens is unclear, but his family is registered in the deme of the Lakiadae after 507. After the failure of the → Ionian Revolt in 493, M. fled to Athens (loss of his son → Metiochus, Hdt. 6,41).

Accused by 'enemies' of contemplating tyranny, but acquitted and elected as *stratēgós* (Hdt. 6, 104), in 490 M. became the spokesman of uncompromising resistance to the Persian invasion under the command of Datis and Artaphernes [3]. A proposal by M., comparable to the → *pséphisma* of Themistocles, to surrender and abandon the city (*deîn exiénai*), is attested only in literary evidence (first mention in the 4th cent.: Aristot. Rhet. 1411 a 10; Demosth. 19,303). The Persians, who had landed on the plain of → Marathon on the advice of Hippias [1] (on the topography of the now destroyed landscape [10; 5]), were encircled; the attempt by the Persian cavalry to break out to the sea (Suda s.v. χωρὶς ἱππεῖς, h'orsemen apart'), with the intention of taking Athens, enabled and forced the Athenian attack. Their → phalanx of approx. 10,000 hoplites, supported by 1,000 Plataeans, was victorious (before mid September 490) with minimal losses (192 dead, buried in the grave at Marathon, the modern Soros). The Spartans, alerted by the runner → Phidippides (Hdt. 6,105f.; Nep. Miltiades 4,3), arrived late, delayed by a religious festival (Hdt. 6,106,3; 120) or by a revolt of helots (Plat. leg. 698e). The → 'Marathon' to Athens is described only from the 4th cent. [15. 161]. The army marched back to Athens on the same day; the Persians gave up their plans of attack and sailed away (Hdt. 6,116). The Cimon-like painting in the Stoa Poikile (c. 560) [6] shows M. as the main figure.

At the peak of his influence, M. now commanded a pillaging expedition seeking Persian treasures in the Aegaean, but, after a setback, and having been winjured at Paros, he broke off the expedition on his own initiative (Hdt. 6,132–135; Ephorus; cf. [8]). Already at death's door, he was arraigned by → Xanthippus; although acquitted of high treason, for betrayal of the people he was condemned to pay the enormous costs of the expedition (Hdt. 6,136; Nep. Miltiades 7,5f.), costs which his son Cimon [2] then took on.

→ Marathon; → Persian Wars

DAVIES, 301f.; PA 10212; TRAILL, PAA 653820.

[3] Descendant of M. [2], son of a Cimon [3?], from Lakiadai. Father of Euthydice, who married Ophellas (Alexander's [4] → *hetaîros*, later tyrant of Cyrene) and in 307/6 BC Demetrius [2] Poliorcetes. In the spring of 324, M. was charged with securing Athens' grain route in the Adriatic as founder of an → *apoikía* (IG II/III 1629; TOD 200).

DAVIES, 309; DEVELIN, 403; PA 10213; TRAILL, PAA 653830.　　　　　　　　　　　　　　　　　　K.KI.

[4] 2nd-cent. rhetorically trained Greek Christian apologist from Asia Minor (Tert. Adversus Valentinianos 5,1; Hier. vir. ill. 39). His writings have all been lost. He wrote against Valentinian → Gnosis and → Montanism (Eus. HE 5,17,1); he also wrote an apologetic text against the pagan Greeks and one against the Jews, and a defence of the Christian way of life against the rulers of this world (Eus. HE 5,17,5). The last-mentioned text may have served as a model for → Tertullianus' *Apologeticum*.

→ Apologia

R. M. GRANT, Five Apologists and Marcus Aurelius, in: Vigiliae Christianae 42, 1988, 1–17.　　　　　　K.P.

[5] Bishop of Rome from 2 July 310 to 10 January 314. Under → Maxentius he received back the ecclesiastical property confiscated during the Diocletianic persecution (303). After the indictment directed against → Caecilianus [1] by the *pars Maiorini/Donati* (party of Maiorinus,or of Donatus [1]), Constantine appointed M., along with three Gallic bishops as *iudices dati* ('commissioned judges'), to settle the dispute among the African bishops (→ Donatus [1]). M. called upon 15 additional Italian bishops, who in three sessions from 2.10. to 4.10.313 decided in favour of Caecilianus. In this way the new model of state/ecclesiastical jurisdiction was created. M. is buried in the San Callisto catacomb on the Via Appia.

K. M. GIRARDET, Das Reichskonzil von Rom (313) – Urteil, Einspruch, Folgen, in: Historia 41, 1992, 104–116; E. PAOLI, s.v. Miltiade, Dictionnaire Historique de la Papauté, 1994, 1109–1110 (lit.); CH. PIETRI, Roma christiana, 1976, vol. 1, 4–14 and 159–168 (lit.).　　O.WER.

Miltocythes (Μιλτοκύθης; *Miltokýthēs*).
[1] Thracian leader of mercenaries under → Cyrus [3] the Younger, defected to the side of the Great King → Artaxerxes [2] II after the Battle of → Cunaxa in 401 BC (Xen. an. 2,2,7).　　　　　　　　　　　　U.P.
[2] Thracian aristocrat, treasurer (?) of → Cotys [I 1] I, with whom he broke around 362 BC, seizing the → Hieron oros [1]. M. sought the aid of Athens, but the diplomatic skill of Cotys I thwarted the conspiracy in 361 (Demosth. Or. 23,104; 115). In 359 M. again attempted rebellion, this time against → Cersobleptes, but the Greek Smicythion betrayed M., and → Charidemus [2] handed him over to Cardia. He and his son were murdered there (Demosth. Or. 23,169, 175; Ana-

ximen. FGrH 72 F 5–6; Theop. FGrH 115 F 307; Philochorus FGrH 328 F 42).   U.P.

Milvus This flying fish, mentioned by Pliny in HN 9,82 together with the flying gurnard (*hirundo*, Dactylopterus volitans, Aristot. Hist. an. 4,9,535b 27–29; cf. Opp. Hal. 2,459 and Ael. NA 2,50) and often confused with it, is identical, it seems, with the *hiérax* (two-winged flying fish, Exocoetus volitans Cuv., Opp. Hal. 1,427f.; Ael. NA 9,52) [1. 140 and 145f.]. Further information is lacking, apart from the fish's wariness of hidden hooks (Hor. Epist. 1,16,50f.: *cautus ... metuit ... opertum milvus hamum*).

1 LEITNER.   C.HÜ.

Milyas

[1] Milyas (Μιλύας; *Milýas*), a confidant of → Demosthenes [2], administered his inheritance. In a legal dispute between Demosthenes and his guardians, the latter accused M. of irregularities. → Aphobus demanded that the presumed slave M. be handed over for interrogation under torture. Demosthenes refused, on the grounds that M. had already been freed by his father (cf. Dem. Or. 29).

SCHÄFER, Vol. 4, supplements, 1885, 82–85; TRAILL, PAA 653990.   J.E.

[2] Milyas (Μιλυάς; *Milyás*). Region in southern Asia Minor with an indigenous population (Μιλυαδεῖς/ *Milyadeís*), whose identification with the Hittite *Millawanda* remains uncertain, despite traces of Bronze Age settlement. Geographical identification is hampered by the fact that ancient authors assigned the name M. to various parts of the region, which stretched from Comba in Lycia to Phrygian-Pisidian Apameia. The political organization of the *commune Millyadum* (Cic. Verr. 2,1,95) was rather loose, although the *Milyadeis* undertook a dedication for Rome and Augustus together with Thracian military settlers and Roman traders in 5/4 BC (SEG 36, 1207), by which time the south belonged to *Lycia*. Last mentioned in the 6th cent. AD (Hierocles, Synekdemos 680).

A. S. HALL, The Milyadeis and their Territory, in: AS 36, 1986, 137–157.   MA.ZI.

Milye (Μιλύη; *Milýē*). Daughter of Zeus, sister and wife of Solymus, eponym of the Lycian people of the → Solymi, who were called Milyae after M. (Hdt. 1,173; 3,90; 7,77); later wife of Cragus, after whom Mount → Cragus was named.   L.K.

Milyian see → Luwian

Mimaces (Μίμακες; *Mímakes*). Libyan nomads living near the Machyni, Machryes and Gephes (between the Tunisian Dorsale and the Chott el-Jerid) (Ptol. 4,3,26 and Steph. Byz. s.v. M. = Philistus of Syracuse). According to Ptol. 4,6,20f., M. also lived in the Libyan interior, not far from the *Thála óros* (Θάλα ὄρος; the modern Tahela Ohat in the Ahaggar mountains?) and near the *Noubai* (Νοῦβαι).
→ Libyes, Libye

J. DESANGES, Catalogue des tribus africaines..., 1962, 115, 224; H. TREIDLER, s.v. Mimakes, RE 15, 1711f.
                                                                W.HU.

Mimallones see → Dionysos

Mimas (Μίμας).
[1] → Giant, killed either by Zeus' thunderbolt in the fight to rule Olympus (Eur. Ion 212ff.), or by Ares' lance, after M. had torn the island of → Lemnos out of the sea and hurled it at the god (Apoll. Rhod. 3,1227 with scholia). The field of battle was Phlegra on the Macedonian peninsula of Pallene; the struggle of M. and the Giants against other gods such as Pallas Athena and Hera was equally fruitless (schol. Apoll. Rhod. loc. cit.; Hor. Carm. 3,4,53ff.). M. was imprisoned under Mount Erythrae (schol. Hom. Od. 120,50ff.) or under the island of Prochyte near Cumae (Sil. Pun. 8,540).

[2] → Centaur in the battle against the Lapiths (Hes. Sc. 184ff.).
[3] Man of the Bebrycian tribe, killed by Castor the Argonaut (Apoll. Rhod. 2,105).
[4] Trojan in the army of Aeneas, killed in the battle against → Turnus by Mezentius (Verg. Aen. 10,689ff.).
                                                                AL.FR.
[5] Thracian promontory of unidentifiable location, possibly in the Rhodope mountains (Alexander of Myndus, FGrH 25 F 4; Sil. Pun. 3,494; Lucan 7,450). At Ov. Met. 2,222, the Ionian mountain range of the same name is probably meant.   I.v.B.

Mime (μῖμος/*mîmos*, lat. *mimus*).
I. GREEK II. ROMAN

I. GREEK
A. GENERAL REMARKS B. HISTORICAL DEVELOPMENT TO THE END OF THE 5TH CENT. BC C. HELLENISM AND IMPERIAL PERIOD

A. GENERAL REMARKS
Mimos signifies in the first place the actor in the popular theatre, then the play itself in which he – alone or with a small number of others – portrays human types by word and gesture (cf. μιμέομαι,*miméomai*: imitate) in for the most part comic or coarse scenes. Relying on the Aristotelian concept of → mimesis, Diomedes gives the definition (GL I p. 491): Μῖμός ἐστιν μίμησις βίου τά τε συγκεχωρημένα καὶ ἀσυγχώρητα περιέχων, 'Mimos is an imitation of life encompassing what is allowed and what is forbidden'. *Mimoi* performed their plays unmasked (αὐτοπρόσωπος), in booths or on improvised stages, before large and small audiences in streets, in the theatre, at popular festivals (cf. Clearchus fr. 93 WEHRLI), and at symposia.

Plutarch (Mor. 712e) knows two kinds of mime: the longer (ὑποθέσεις, *hypothéseis*), and the shorter, lascivious (παίγνια, *paígnia*). The former he rejects because its length renders it unsuitable for providing entertainment at the symposium; the latter because its effect on the disposition is 'more exciting than wine'. An Attic lamp (3rd cent. BC) depicts a scene with three *mimológoi* ('mime actors'), who, to judge from the title (ἡ ὑπόθεσις ἑκυρά) are giving such a 'hypothesis' entitled 'The mother-in-law' [15]. *Mimoi* were on the whole accorded scant esteem; Demosthenes (or. 2,19) rebukes Philip of Macedon for gathering 'Mime actors and composers of vulgar songs' (μίμους γελοίων καὶ ποιητὰς αἰσχρῶν ᾀσμάτων) about him. Similarly, Plutarch decries Sulla's association with mimes and suchlike 'rabble' (Plut. Sulla 2,3: μῖμοι, γελωτοποιοί; ibid. 2,5: μιμῳδοὶ καὶ ὀρχησταί). As a guild, *mimoi* were on the same level as dancers (ὀρχησταί; *orchēstaí*), comic actors (γελωτοποιοί; *gelōpoioí*), and 'conjurers' (θαυματοποιοί; *taumatapoioí*) (cf. Athen. 19c–20b). Everyday scenes constituted the stock in trade of *mimoi*: drunkenness, violence, sex, and betrayal were favourite themes, extemporised by means of stereotypical characters (such as the fool, the adulterer, the flatterer, the mistress) with all the trappings of vulgar entertainment. Theophrastus (3rd cent. BC) mentions several performances (πληρώματα, *plērōmata*) of such street varieties (θαύματα, *thaúmata*) per day (Theophr. Char. 27,7); entrance was by means of a token (→ *sýmbolon*), which suggests a closed or at least partitioned-off auditorium (ibid. 6,4).

B. HISTORICAL DEVELOPMENT TO THE END OF THE 5TH CENT. BC

This kind of popular theatre existed before, during, and after the heyday of the Attic drama (5th cent. BC). The earliest instances go back to the Peloponnesian popular farce, played by → *deikeliktaí* ('burlesque actors'), who performed plays such as the 'Fruit Thief' (Sosibius in Athen. 621d-e) or the 'Meat Thief' (Poll. 4,105) as comic interludes at cult celebrations [4; 8]. A Corinthian Krater from before 550 BC shows a flute player and a masked dancer adjacent to such a 'theft scene' and the punishment of the thieves, indicating a possible choral accompaniment to the play [9]. At first restricted to the Doric language area, mime had its first high point in Syracuse with the metric plays of → Epicharmus and the *mimoi* of → Sophron (5th cent.BC), written in rhythmic prose (cf. schol. Greg. Naz. CGF 153) and supposed to have been admired by Plato (Duris of Samos, FGrH 76 F 72; fr. on both in [3]). Sophron's *mimoi* were apparently divided into 'female' and 'male' plays; of the former, we have titles such as 'The Sempstress', 'The Sorceress' (ταὶ γυναῖκες αἳ τὰν θεόν φαντι ἐξελᾶν) 'Spectators at the Isthmia;' of the latter 'The Messenger', 'The Fisherman to the Farmer', 'The Tunnyfisher'. A longer papyrus fragment, probably from 'the 'Sorceress', depicts preparations for the cult/magical invocation of a goddess, with vivid instructions to various individuals (fr. 17 πότνια) [3. 70]. According to

WIEMKEN's convincing theory, during the 5th and 4th cents. BC, Greek mime was displaced by the all-powerful Attic drama (tragedy and comedy) and its influence, while Western Greek. Doric mime survived into the Roman period in the lower-Italian *phlyakes* farce (→ Phlyakes) and the → atellana.

C. HELLENISM AND IMPERIAL PERIOD

Mime gained new literary significance in the *mimiamboi* of → Herodas (3rd cent. BC) and the mimetic poems of → Theocritus (pastoral poems and e.g. Theocr. 15 'Women Celebrating the Festival of Adonis': schol. Theocr. 2 speaks of Theocritus' 'transfer' (μεταφέρει) of material from Sophron: the *Adoniázousai* itself could go back to a known title from Sophron, 'Spectators at the Isthmia'), and Callimachus (Hymns 2,5,6); ALBERT [5] describes a poem as 'mimetic' if the character acting as narrator '... refers to a continuous action taking place in the present by which s/he is affected': the distinction between this and *mimos*, which signifies performed drama, is evident. Herodas' *mimiamboi* are a bold attempt to combine popular, in part obscene material with a refined artificial language (literary Ionic). Whether the plays, which typically present two or three characters in sometimes lively action, were merely recited by a single performer or actually performed by a mime ensemble remains a matter of dispute. But the distance between the literary claims of Herodas and genuine popular theatre, which is characterised by improvisation and popular, non-metric language (see below), remains unmistakable.

We also have some fragments of Hellenistic poems that, although belonging within the ambit of 'mimetic poetry', are not *mimoi* in the real sense of the word (most recent edition of the texts [1]). The most important of these is the lengthy passage written in various meters and known as 'The Maiden's Lament' [1. no. 1], containing a long monodic lament by a woman deceived in love [17. 209f.]; neither she nor her faithless lover are mentioned by name, but there are frequent allusions to Aphrodite (Cypris) as instigator of the unfortunate liaison. The frankness with which the unknown woman portrays her inner feelings, confused between love, disillusionment, and jealousy, is scarcely paralleled in Greek literature (Sappho fr. 31 portrays her physical, not her psychic symptoms), although perhaps in Latin love elegy (→ Ovid).

Two papyrus fragments of some length (POxy 413: 1st/2nd cent. AD) provide valuable evidence for style and performance practice in the popular theatre, sources for which are otherwise few and far between ([1. nos. 6–7]; good discussion but inadequate text in [4]). The first, called 'Charition' [1. no. 6], appears to represent a mimetic reworking of the tragic material from Euripides' 'Iphigenia in Tauris' [12]. The papyrus itself, according to [4. 75], comprises only a 'director's sketch' of the whole play, short cues being provided for the players to elaborate upon by means of appropriate improvisation (apart from metric verses and song parts, which are fully written out), but it is possible to reconstruct the main outlines of the action: a leading character, Charition, who serves an indigenous goddess in India, succeeds in fleeing the barbaric land along with her brother. They evade the attacking Indians (whose language is reproduced in a genuine, though difficult to attribute, Indian dialect), partly by means of a comic character's secret weapon (his fart), partly by means of the drunkenness motif well known in literature (→ Polyphemus myth; the Greeks give the barbarian king and his retinue unadulterated wine, thus rendering them harmless). Euripides' tragedy is reduced to the level of a vulgar farce, all that is mythic and heroic being entirely displaced by the absurd, the grotesque, and the comic. In a newly discovered papyrus fragment Jarcho [10] sees 'new evidence for the travesty of myth and tragedy', i.e. a Heracles/Omphale satire.

The second play, the 'Poisoner' [1. no. 7], is as roughly crafted as the Charition mime, but contains only the lines of the main character, who to a large extent determines the action (an 'excerpt in' [4]). The papyrus indicates responses from fellow players and stage directions only by an oblique stroke. The main character is revealed as a cruel and unscrupulous mistress who condemns a slave by the name of Aisopus to death, because he refuses to supply her with sexual services; she has him led away to a terrible death along with his beloved Apollonia. Up to this point the play shows a striking resemblance to Herodas' 5th *mimiambos*, the 'Jealous Mistress'. By a ruse of the guards the couple succeed in escaping; they have to feign death (according to the reconstruction in [4]) so that the vengeful mistress will give up further pursuit. The mistress then devotes her attention to her next victim (her husband or possibly her father); she prepares poisoned wine, having the household *parasitos* administer it to the master of the house. This attempt too, however, fails through an intrigue of the cunning servant Spinther ('Spark'). The play's entertainment value may have resided in the audience's satisfaction at the failure of the main character's repellent designs. This mime lacks a (known) literary model, although vengeful female figures (Clytaemnestra, Phaedra, Medea, Hecuba) are not rare in tragedy. [4] compares the plot of this mime with a mime play that might be reconstructed from Apul. Met. 10,2–12, also dealing with the murderous demands of a *matrona* frustrated in love.

For the performance of these two plays from Oxyrhynchus, [4] estimates an ensemble of seven actors; to these are added in the Charition mime a chorus of Indian men and women, who at one point perform a drunken dance to musical accompaniment; the 'Poisoner' possibly involves a chorus of servants. Structurally, both plays comprise a series of individual scenes following rapidly one upon another, the setting remaining unchanged (as in the Attic theatre) in front of a building (temple or house). The Charition mime contains metric lines in the choral sections and the closing scene; but many spoken lines are close to the comic trimeter,

which may reflect either the predominating influence of Attic comedy or the supposedly rhythmic character of Sophron's prose.

EDITIONS: 1 I. C. CUNNINGHAM, Herodas, Mimiambi, 1987 (with an Appendix on the mime frr. on papyri). 2 Id., Herodas, Mimiambi, 1971 (edn. w. comm.) 3 A. OLIVIERI, Frammenti della commedia greca e del mimo nella Sicilia e nella Magna Grecia, 1947, vol. 3: Frammenti del mimo siciliano 4 H. WIEMKEN, Der griechische Mimus. Dokumente zur Geschichte des antiken Volkstheaters, 1972.
LITERATURE: 5 W. ALBERT, Das mimetische Gedicht in der Antike Geschichte und Typologie von den Anfängen bis in die augusteische Zeit (Beitr. zur Klass. Philol. 190), 1988 6 U. ALBINI, Il mimo a Gaza tra il V e il VI sec. d.C., in: SIFC 15, 1997, 115–122; 7 L. BENZ, Dramenbearbeitung und Dramenparodie im antiken Mimus und im plautinischen Amphitruo, in: TH. BAIER (ed.), Studien zu Plautus' Amphitruo (Scriptoralia 116), 1999, 51–85 8 L. BREITHOLZ, Die dorische Farce im griechischen Mutterland vor dem 5. Jahrhundert Hypothese oder Realität? (Studia Graeca et Latina Gothoburgensia 10), 1960; 9 F. DÜMMLER, De amphora corinthia caere reperta, in: Id., KS 3, 1901, 22, fig. 29 10 V. N. JARCHO, Zu dem neuen Mimos- Fragment. POxy vol. 53, 3700, in: ZPE 70, 1987, 32–34 11 H. REICH, Der Mimus. Ein literar-entwicklungsgeschichtlicher Versuch, vol. 1, 1903 12 S. SANTELLA, Chariton Liberata (POxy 413), 1991 13 A. SWIDEREK, Le mime grec en Égypte, in: Eos 47.1, 1954, 63–74 14 R. G. USSHER, The Mimic Tradition of Character in Herodas, in: Quaderni Urbinati 50, 1985, 45–68 15 C. WATZINGER, Mimologen, in: Ath. Mitt. 26, 1901, 1–8 Taf. 1 16 H. WIEMKEN, Der Mimus, in: G. A. SEECK, Das griechische Drama, 1979, 401–433 17 U. v. WILAMOWITZ-MOELLENDORFF, Des Mädchens Klage, in: Id., KS 2, 1941, 95f. 18 E. WÜST, s.v. M., RE 15, 1727–1764.
W.D.F.

II. ROMAN

A. HISTORY   B. CHARACTER   C. SCRIPTED MIME AND LITERARY FORM   C. LATER DEVELOPMENT D. MINERVA IN THE ROMAN EMPIRE

A. HISTORY

Next to the → *Atellana fabula, mimus* was the form of farce that immediately appealed of itself to the Romans, without any period of probation [1, 149ff.]: after its debut in Sicily (6th/5th cents.BC) and its blossoming in the Greek East and in the Orient (*c.*5th–3rd cent.BC), mime found its third home in Rome. The mime players came out of Lower Italy with the rise of Rome and the opening of the *viaAppia* in the 3rd cent. BC; at this time too began the direct influx of mime actors from the Hellenistic East, which was to last into the 6th cent. AD. Evidence of the mass appeal of mime immediately after its arrival in Rome is amongst other things its admittance from the public squares and streets into the *ludi florales*, which were inaugurated in 238 BC and celebrated annually from 173 (→ *ludi* III.C.): here, mime ruled the *scaena levis*. It celebrated its real triumphs in the Greek area after the final decline of the Attic drama at the end of the 3rd cent., and in Latin after the dying days of the Roman artistic theatre at the beginning of the 1st cent. Mime, which had occupied a secure place in entertainment in the street and at the banquet as well as at the popular → Floralia (presumably also in the → Saturnalia and → Compitalia), at this time also reached the theatre, from which it had up to then been excluded by the dominance of classical drama. It featured as an entracte (*interludium* or *embolium*, Fest. 436/438 L., Plin. HN 7,158), primarily comprising mimetic dance, and as an exuberant comic epilogue (*exodium*) to performances of tragedies, in which function in Cicero's time mime displaced the Atellana (Cic. Fam. 9,16,7). Mime rose to become the leading comic genre of the outgoing Republic, and in the Imperial period along with → pantomimus definitively dominated the stages of Rome and the Roman Empire.

B. Character

Improvisation and lack of pretension are the main characteristics of mime. Even where the stand-alone sketch was complemented by the fully composed stage mime, the interest lay in the individual scene; mime with its colourful interplay of speech, song, dance, and clowning was largely unconcerned with consequential logic (Cic. Cael. 65). Nothing was sacred to the mime actor in his mocking caricatures of everyday life. There was a particular predilection for adultery and seduction (Ov. Trist. 2,493ff., Juv. 6,44; [8]); also popular were intrigues and deceptions of all kinds (Cic. Rab. Post. 35, Artem. 1,76). Mime was notorious for its gross obscenities (Ov. Trist. 2,497), for its riotous action comedy (Juv. 8,186), for altercation and biting mockery, not sparing even the mighty (Suet. Dom. 10,4; SHA Aur. 29,1ff.), let alone the gods (Tert. Apol. 15, Arnob. 4,35), including the Christian religion (baptism and martyrdom [11. 93ff.]); it was notorious too for its increasing brutality (Mart. Liber spectaculorum 7) and immorality, denounced by the Church Fathers [4; 12]; but, on the other hand, also for its whimsical verbal wit (Cic. De orat. 2,259) and wise aphorisms (Sen. Epist. 8,8). The actors performed barefoot (thus the term *planipes* for the mime actor, Fest. 342 L.), in simple costume and as a rule without masks (exceptions: Athen. 10,452f., [11. 87ff.]); also not infrequently with the stage phallus (Schol. Juv. 6,65).

C. Scripted mime and literary form

From the 1st cent. BC, mime was also set in written form. Some players were also writers; they usually belonged to the class of freedmen, and their crudely drafted outlines, in which only selected parts, perhaps the → *cantica* and the prologue, were fully written out, could scarcely be said to have had literary pretensions. But members of the elite also tried their hand at being mime writers. The most celebrated representatives of these two groups were, on the one hand, the former Syrian slave → Publilius Syrus, and on the other the Roman equestrian D. → Laberius [I 4]; in 46 BC these two met head to head in an impromptu competition, from which Publilius emerged the victor [5]. Although the tendency to written form persisted in the Imperial period, it was still as before in its improvised form that mime celebrated its real triumphs.

By virtue of its popularity, mime exerted an influence (materials, motifs, types, and techniques) on other popular literary genres such as the → palliata [1. Ch. 3; 2], the → satire [3], the → elegy [3; 6], and the → novel [10].

→ Catullus [2] Mimographus; → Laberius [I 4]; → Lentulus [1]; → Pantomimus; → Publilius Syrus

1 L. Benz, Die römisch-italische Stegreifspieltradition zur Zeit der Palliata, in: ead., E. Stärk, G. Vogt-Spira (ed.), Plautus und die Tradition des Stegreifspiels, 1995, 139–154   2 Ead., Dramenbearbeitung und Dramenparodie im antiken Mimos und im plautinischen Amphitruo, in: T. Baier (ed.), Studien zu Plautus' Amphitruo, 1999, 51–95   3 R. E. Fantham, Mime: The Missing Link in Roman Literary History, in: CW 82, 1988, 153–163   4 H. Jürgens, Pompa Diaboli, 1972   5 W. A. Krenkel, Caesar und der Mimus des Laberius, 1994   6 J. C. McKeown, Augustan Elegy and Mime, in: PCPhS N.S. 25, 1979, 71–84   7 H. Reich, Der M., 1903   8 R. W. Reynolds, The Adultery Mime, in: CQ 40, 1946, 77–84   9 R. Rieks, M. und Atellane, in: E. Lefèvre (ed.), Das römische Drama, 1978, 348–377   10 M. Rosenblüth, Beiträge zur Quellenkunde von Petrons Satiren, 1909   11 G. J. Theocharidis, Beitr. zur Geschichte des byzantinischen Profantheaters im IV. und V. Jahrhundert, 1940   12 W. Weismann, Kirche und Schauspiele, 1972   13 H. Wiemken, Der griechische Mimus, 1972   14 E. Wüst, s.v. M., RE 15, 1727–1764.

M. Bonaria, Romani mimi, 1965.   L.BE.

Mimesis (μίμησις/*mímēsis*, Lat. *imitatio*, 'imitation'). The Greek term denotes action (to do something like, or to make something similar to something else), the product of the action or both at once; it also means reproduction or representation, but not expression as an immediate sign of what is interior. *Mimesis* makes 'appearances reappear' [6, 77], initially as 'making oneself similar to another in voice or gesture' (Pl. Resp. 393c; Soph. 267a) in poetry, music and dance (the ancient Greek unity of → *mousiké*) as an artistic representation, then also in the fine arts by means of colours and shapes (Hom. h. 3,163; Pind. P. 12,21; Xen. An. 6,1,5–13; Hdt. 2,78; 2,169). Drama is mimetic in the strongest sense. Representation goes beyond the individual appearance covering the gamut from ideal image (*parádeigma*) to caricature; the interior (thinking and emotion) is represented as it manifests itself (Xen. Mem. 3,10,1–8; Xen. Symp. 2,21–23 [9. 80]).

Mimesis becomes a pivotal concept in → Plato. He examines the problems of the action of the artist, who can apparently produce anything by *mimesis*. Whereas a carpenter, for example, imitates the unique god-created idea of the table (→ Ideas, theory of) and produces a usable table, the artist imitates not the idea [9, 133–145], but imitations, thus producing a third creation, the image of the appearance of the table, and hence of everything else (Pl. Resp. 597e). The *mimesis* that represents all kinds of things, or rather everything, is banished from Plato's ideal state, and only the more rigorous *mimesis* of the good and beautiful is included (Resp. 398ab; 401b-d; but cf. Leg. 816de). This is demanded not only out of didactic considerations ('lest from enjoying the imitation, they come to enjoy the reality': Pl. Resp. 395cd; 424c), but because according to the Platonic principle of justice, each individual can do only *one* thing well. Thus, even *mimesis* must fit in with the principle of division of labour if it is to be an art (*téchnē*) (Pl. Resp. 394e) [10. 212–222].

→ Aristotle explains *mimesis* by human nature: that is, by mankind's first learning through *mimesis* and its pleasure in representations (Arist. Poet. 4,1448b). He differentiates the imitative arts by medium, subject and type of *mimesis* (Poet. 1,1447a). In the case of poetry, he describes the subject (the action) as what is possible in the sense of the probable or necessary. It does not record the particular like historiography, but focuses more on the general (Poet. 9,1451b [8. 31]). With regard to an ideal image, later authors speak of imitation of the idea. Thus, → Cicero says that → Phidias did not create the figure of Zeus after a model, but after an ideal, inherent in his mind, of extraordinary beauty (Cic. Orat. 2,8–3,10). → Plotinus goes even further: Phidias fashioned Zeus by taking him as he would be seen if he deigned to appear before our eyes (Plotinus Enn. 5,8,1,38–40). However, even the simple *mimesis* of nature is for Plotinus not to be despised, since nature also imitates something else, namely the spirit (νοῦς/*noûs*). In addition, he says, the arts transcend what has been imitated and reach the rational forms from which they derive, and, since they are in possession of beauty (ibid. 5,8,1,32–40, cf. 4,3,11; 5,9,11; Arist. Ph. 2,199a 15–17) they supplement what is lacking.

The concept of 'imitation of nature' remained an ambiguous topic of art theory (→ Art, theory of) until well into the 19th cent. *Mimesis* relates to the arts in other respects too: the creative *mimesis* (*imitatio*) of authors (Quint. Inst. 10,2), long practised in ancient poetry after Homer (to be distinguished from → plagiarism, became an important basis for post-Aristotelian rhetoric [2. 86] and to some extent characterizes Roman artistic creation [7. 5, 7f.] (→ Canon; → Literary history; cf. Hor. Ars P. 268f.). It consists in a free emulation of great figures from the past, drawing on its own era and increased to the point of rivalry (*aemulatio*). According to Lucretius [III 1], this *mimesis* is the result of reverential love (Lucr. 3,5f.; cf. Pl. Resp. 500c). In Ps Longinus (De sublimitate 13f.) it is given the same status as inspiration and leads to the stimulating 'concept of a public of all times' [2. 88].

→ Art; → Art, theory of; → Literary Theory; → Nature; → Rhetoric; → Techne; → Mimesis

1 H. BLUMENBERG, Nachahmung der Natur, in: Studium Generale 10.5, 1957, 266–283 2 W. BÜHLER, Beiträge zur Erklärung der Schrift vom Erhabenen, 1964 3 K.

FLASCH, Ars imitatur naturam, in: Id., Parusia, 1965, 265–306 4 G. GEBAUER, Mimesis, 1992 5 H. KOLLER, Die Mimesis, in der Antike, 1954 6 A. B. NESCHKE, Die 'Poetik' des Aristoteles, Vol. 1, 1980 7 A. REIFF, Interpretatio, imitatio, aemulatio, 1959 8 A. SCHMITT, Mimesis bei Aristoteles und in den Poetikkommentaren der Renaissance, in: A. KABLITZ (ed.), Mimesis und Simulation, 1998, 17–53 9 G. SÖRBOM, Mimesis and Art, 1966 10 U. ZIMBRICH, Mimesis bei Platon, 1984.   U.ZI.

Mimiambs see → Herodas

Mimnermus (Μίμνερμος; *Mímnermos*) of Colophon or Smyrna, 2nd half of the 7th century BC. One of the earliest writers of Greek → elegy. In antiquity, he was viewed, along with → Callinus [1] and → Archilochus as its possible 'inventor'. The Suda dates M. to the 37th Olympiad (632–629 BC), but the opinion of scholars is divided: that M. was still living around 600 cannot be proved by citing Solon (20 W., purporting to be a reply to M.) (*contra* [7]); praise of a victor from an earlier generation over the Lydians (14 W.), as well as a poem about a battle against → Gyges [1] (Paus. 9,29,4; 13 W.), fit well with a date of *c.* 640 BC.

This poem, which later bore the title *Smyrnēís* (Σμυρνηΐς; 13a W.), contained a complex prooemium to the Muses (13W.): it was presumably a long narrative elegy that commemorated not only the wars of the recent past with Lydia (cf. the elegy on Plataea by → Simonides) but perhaps also the foundation of Smyrna [6]. The *great lady* (μεγάλη γυνή) of Callimachus (fr. 1,11–12 'Pf.') was perhaps an allusion to this SMYRNĒÍS, one of the two books in which the Hellenistic edition of M. circulated (cf. Porph. Hor. comm. epist. 2,2,101).

The other book named by Callimachus, αἱ κατὰ λεπτόν [sc. ῥήσιες] ('finely composed discourses'), probably bore the title *Nannó* (Ναννώ), and was preferred not only by him but by other ancient readers as well. The character Nanno is not mentioned in any of the fragments, but the statement by Hermesianax that 'M. was aflame with love for Nanno' (καίετο μὲν Ναννοῦς, CollAlex 7,37) suggests that he was familiar with love poems by M. in which she played a role (cf. her description as an *aulós* player, Athen. 13,597a). The *Nannó* was perhaps a collection (compiled by Antimachus [3]?) of symposiac elegies by M., which had in common the fact that some of the poems were addressed to Nanno (cf. Perses in Hesiod's *Erga*, Cyrnus in Theognis). Verse citations from the *Nannó* by later writers deal with various themes, such as a declaration of love lamenting the brevity of youth and the frailty of old age (5 W., likewise 1 W. and 2 W.), with Tithonus as an example (4 W.). The tale of 'our' ancestors from Pylos, who settled in Colophon and migrated from there to Smyrna (9–10 W.), suggests that M. dealt with this theme in his short elegies as well as in the *Smyrnēís*, rather than that the *Smyrnēís* was part of the *Nannó* (opposing view in [8]). A short myth tells of the sun's return from the west to a golden bed in the east (12 W.). Other fragments locate the palace of the sun in eastern Oceanus, and that of Aeetes nearby (11; 11 a W.). The mention of a Trojan Daites (18 W.) and of the Niobids (19 W.) indicate that M. drew on panhellenic myths to a greater extent than other early elegists.

Many of M.'s love poems were pederastic (cf. 1,9 W., Alexander Aetolus fr. 5,1–5 CollAlex), and a certain Examyes may have played a role in this context (Hermesianax CollAlex 7,35–40). The few iambic verses attributed to M. (24–26 W.) are generally considered inauthentic, but invective poetry by M. was known in antiquity (Hermesianax CollAlex 7,35–40).

The *Nannō*, which → Antimachus [3] perhaps drew upon as a model for his *Lýdē*, was admired by Callimachus (fr. 1,11–12 Pf.), while Poseidippus (Anth. Gr. 12,168), Hermesianax (CollAlex 7,35–40) and Propertius (1,9,11–12; cf. Hor. Epist. 1,6,65–66) praised M. as a love poet. M.'s work was excerpted for the anthology on which our *Theognidea* (→ Theognis) are based (5,1–6 W. = Thgn. 1017–22, 7W. = Thgn. 795–6), as well as by Stobaeus (1; 2; 3; 5,4–8; 8; 14 W.) and the compiler of the *Anthologia Graeca* (7 W.). M. was known to Hipponax, Strabo, Plutarch, Pausanias, Diogenes [17] Laertius, Athenaeus [3] and Aelian [2]. A gymnasium was named after him in Smyrna the 1st cent. AD. (CIG 3376).

→ Elegy

BIBLIOGRAPHY: 1 D. E. GERBER, in: Lustrum 33, 1991, 152–163 (for 1921–1989).
EDITIONS: 2 IEG   3 B. GENTILI, C. PRATO, Poetarum et elegiacorum testimonia et fragmenta, vol. 1, 1988²   4 D. E. GERBER, Greek Elegiac Poetry, 1999.
COMMENTARIES: 5 A. ALLEN, The Fragments of Mimnermus, 1993.
LITERATURE: 6 E. L. BOWIE, Early Greek Elegy, Symposium and Public Festival, in: JHS 106, 1986, 28–30   7 A. DIHLE, Zur Datierung des Mimnermos, in: Hermes 90, 1962, 257–275   8 C. W. MÜLLER, Die antike Buchausgabe des Mimnermos, in: RhM 131, 1988, 197–211.
E.BO.

Min (Μίν/*Mín*; Egyptian *Mnw*). Egyptian god, chief deity of → Coptus and Achmīm, was responsible for the desert regions accessible from Coptus. Colossi of M. are preserved from Coptus from early times (3rd cent) [6], demonstrating the classical iconography – they are anthropomorphic, with relatively unstructured bodies, ithyphallic, with a tall plume on the head. One arm is raised and bears a scourge. This figure became the model for the ithyphallic form of → Amun. The written character for M. may be interpreted as a thunderstone (or belemnite fossil). Behind portrayals of M., a bed of lettuce (reference to the milky sap of the plant as semen) and a round hut with an emblem of bulls' horns are depicted.

The Egyptians' own connection of their god with the land of Punt, the regular appearance of 'Nubians' at the god's festivities, esp. at the erection of the tent poles associated with M., and the presence of linguistically non-Egyptian sections in the festival scenes have sometimes been advanced as arguments for M.'s non-Egyptian origin, but it has not been possible to substantiate these. At the main festival of M. [3], ceremonial included the presence of a white bull, the ritual harvesting of a bundle of ears of grain and the sending out to the points of the compass of four birds to emphasize the legitimate rule of the Pharaoh. The Greeks usually equated M. with → Pan (Diod. 1,98; Plut. Is. 14), but Herod. 2,91 identifies him with → Perseus, probably owing to the homoeophony with the M. epithet (*p³*) *wrš* [6]; reasons of content may also be significant in the context of a possible Oriental origin of the Perseus legend [5].

1 C. J. BLEEKER, Die Geburt eines Gottes, 1956   2 F. FEDER, Das Ritual *s'ḥꜥ kꜣ šn.t* als Tempelfest des Gottes M., in: R. GUNDLACH, M. ROCHHOLZ (ed.), Feste im Tempel. 4. Ägyptologische Tempeltagung, 1998, 31–54   3 H. GAUTHIER, Les fêtes du dieu M., 1931   4 A. McFARLANE, The God M. to the End of the Old Kingdom, 1995   5 S. MORENZ, Die orientalische Herkunft der Perseus-Andromeda-Sage, in: Forschungen und Fortschritte 36, 1962, 307–309   6 S. SAUNERON, Persèe, dieu de Khemmis, in: Rev. d'Égyptologie 14, 1962, 53–57   7 B. WILLIAMS, Narmer and the Coptos Colossi, in: Journ. of the American Research Center in Egypt 25, 1988, 35–59.
JO.QU.

Mina

[1] The *mina* (μνᾶ/*mná*), with its multiples and divisions, was the most common Greek unit of weight alongside the *stater*. It was set on the one hand by the theoretical weight of the drachma coin minted in the city concerned, and on the other hand by the number of → Drachmai which equated to a *mina*. The view long current in research that every *mina* weighed 100 *drachmai*, has been refuted. On Aegina, the *mina* (coin and weight) amounted to 70 *drachmai* (70×6.237 g = 436.6 g); the Corinthian *mina* was probably commensurate to it, equating to 150 *drachmai* (150×2.911 g = 436.6 g). The Attic *mina* coin was part of this system, equating to 100 *drachmai* (100×4.366 g = 436.6 g). However, the *mina* weight in Athens weighed almost 105 *drachmai* at first (= 458.4 g). In the course of time, it rose to 110 (= 480.2 g), 138 (= 602.5 g) and finally 150 (= 654.9 g) *drachmai*. The last value listed corresponded to exactly two Roman pounds. Almost all the enumerated *minai* are attested by surviving weights. There is evidence of a heavy, Hellenistic *mina* of around 600 g at Delphi and Corinth. The Greek cities of Asia Minor seem to have used the Oriental sexagesimal system, in which the stater coin must be understood as a double piece. The sixty-fold weight of the halved → stater produced a *mina* which probably usually weighed less than 500 g. The Persian *mina*, on the other hand, can be calculated at slightly over 500 g. Very few weights that might contribute to our knowledge of the system have as yet been retrieved from Asia Minor.
→ Weights (Greece)

1 K. Hitzl, Die Gewichte griechischer Zeit aus Olympia (OlF 25), 1996 2 M. Lang, M. Crosby, Weights, Measures and Tokens (Agora 10), 1964, 2–38. K.H.

[2] Town in → Mauretania Caesariensis on the Oued Mina, modern Relizane. Ruins of the walls, as well as a church, cisterns and a water pipe are preserved. References: Itin. Anton. 37,4; cf. Geogr. Rav. 41,21. Inscriptions: CIL VIII 2, 9726; Suppl. 3, 21535–21540. An *episcopus Minnensis* is mentioned for the year 484 AD (Notitia episcoporum Mauretaniae Caesariensis 49).

AAAlg, Folio 21, no. 36; H. Treidler, s.v. Mina (2), RE 15, 1764. W.HU.

Minaean see → Ancient Southeren Arabian; → Minaei

Minaei (Μιναῖοι; *Minaîoi*). Eratosthenes mentions the M., who lived beside the Erythraean Sea, as the first of the four nations of South Arabia (Strabo 16,768). According to Plin. HN 6,157 the Minaei were descendants of → Minos, king of Crete. Ptol. 6,7,23 still presents the M. as an important nation. In Ancient South Arabian inscriptions the people and the kingdom of M. were called *m'n* or *m'nm*, Ma'īn or Ma'īnum. The heartland of the M. was the large oasis of the River Madāb, which extended north-west of Mārib (→ Mariaba) and since the Islamic period has been called al-Ǧauf.

The kingdom of Ma'īn arose in the course of the 7th cent. BC and existed until the last quarter of the 2nd cent. BC, when, weakened by the invasion of Arabian nomads, it was incorporated into the Sabaean kingdom (→ Sabaei). The names of numerous kings of Ma'īn are also known to us from this period. The most important centres of the Minaean city alliance were the capital Qarnāwu (Carna as the M.'s largest city in Strabo 16,768; today named after the destroyed kingdom of Ma'īn) and the cities of Yaṭull (whose inhabitants are mentioned in Cass. Dio 53,29,8 as Ἀθλούλου/Athluloi; modern Barāqiš), Kamināhū (Caminacum in Plin. HN 6,160; modern Kamnā) and Naššān (modern al-Baydā'). The majority of the inscriptions, written in Minaean, a separate Ancient South Arabian language (→ Ancient South Arabian), originate from these places.

From the second half of the 6th cent. BC until the 2nd cent. BC, the M. controlled the major part of the trading route by which the South Arabian caravans travelled to the Mediterranean. According to Plin. HN 12,54 the Minaean people were the first to trade in incense (→ Incense Road), for which reason, in the Roman empire, it is called Minaean incense. The M. are reputed to have brought incense and aromatic herbs from upper Arabia as far as the territory of the Nabataean Arabs and Palestine (Agatharchides, De mari Erythraeo 89 = Diod. 3,42,5; Strabo 16,776). The M. also had settlements in other regions of ancient South Arabia. To secure this trade route the M. set up a far-off colony in the north-western Arabian oasis of Dedān,

from which numerous Northern Minaean inscriptions have been preserved. The youngest of the three non-Israelite friends of Job, Zophar the Naamathite, is called king of the M. in the LXX version of the Book of → Job (Job 2,11; 42,17c) and in three further passages Μιναῖος/*Minaíos* (Job 11,2; 20,1; 42,9). It is also probable that the tribe of the Me'īnīm mentioned in 1 Chr 4,41 are identical to the M. living in north-west Arabia, especially as they called M. in the LXX. Light is shed on the struggle for command of the trade routes by an inscription dating from the mid 4th cent. BC (Répertoire d'Épigraphie Sémitique 3022), in which the leaders of the Minaean community in Dedān thank their national god 'Attar Dū-Qabdim for saving them and their possessions from attacks by the Sabaeans on the caravan road. The connections of the M., very far-reaching for the period, are reflected in the mention of Gaza, Egypt, Assur, Syria, the Phoenician cities of Tyre and Sidon, Yaṯrib and other places in the area of the Incense Road in inscriptions testifying to the trade activities, as well as in lists of names of foreign wives. Even on the island of Delos, with its cult sites of Apollo and Artemis, two M. erected an altar to their native god Wadd, with a Minaean-Greek inscription (Répertoire d'Épigraphie Sémitique 3570).

1 S. F. Al-Said, Die Personennamen in den minäischen Inschriften, 1995 2 Inventaire des inscriptions sudarabiques, Bd. 1: Chr. Robin, Inabba', Haram, al-Kāfir, Kamna et al-Ḥarāshīf, 1992; Bd. 3: F. Bron, Ma'īn, 1998; Bd. 4: A. Avanzini, As-Sawdā', 1995 3 Chr. Robin, Les premiers états du Jawf et la civilisation sudarabique, in: Id. (ed.), Arabia Antiqua. Early Origins of South Arabian States, 1996, 49–65 4 H. v. Wissmann, Die Geschichte des Sabäerreiches und der Feldzug des Aelius Gallus, in: ANRW II 9.1, 1976. W.W.M.

Mincius Tributary of the Padus/Po, modern Mincio; sluggish (Liv. 24,10,7; Plin. HN. 2,224; 3,131; Verg. Ecl. 7,12f.; 10,205f.; Verg. Georg. 3,14f.; 2,198f.; Sidon. epist. 1,5,4; Claud. Carm. 12,12f.) outflow of → Lacus Benacus (Verg. Aen. 10,205f.), prehistoric [2. 532] trade route, navigable to Mantua. Formed the boundary between the → Cenomanni [3] and the → Veneti (Pol. 34,10,19 = Strab. 4,6,12). From the 5th cent. BC, centre of Etruscan expansion between roads converging from the Adriatic, the Apennines and the Alps [3. 18].

1 Nissen 2, 188–190 2 P. Tozzi, s.v. Mincius, EV 3, 531f. 3 R. De Marinis, in: R. Bussi (ed.), Misurare la terra: il caso mantovano, 1984. A.SA.

Mindarus (Μίνδαρος; *Míndaros*). A Spartan, *naúarchos* (fleet commander) in 411/410 BC. In September 411, he set out from Miletus for the Thracian Chersonesus, in order to strike at the most important Athenian supply route, but was defeated soon afterwards at → Cynossema by a smaller Athenian fleet under → Thrasybulus [3] (Thuc. 8,99–107), as well as in a

second battle at Abydus [1] (Oct./Nov. 411), after
→ Alcibiades [3] unexpectedly led reinforcements to
the Athenian forces (Xen. Hell. 1,1,2–7; Diod. 13,45,1–
47,2). With the support of the satrap → Pharnabazus,
M. succeeded in taking → Cyzicus, but his forces were
annihilated there in March or April 410 by the Athenians under Alcibiades, → Theramenes and Thrasybulus. M. himself fell in this battle (Xen. Hell. 1,1,11–19;
Diod. 13,49,2–51; Plut. Alcibiades 28). Xenophon and
Diodorus propound different reasons for the Athenian
victory, but neither lays the blame with M.

> B. BLECKMANN, Athens Weg in die Niederlage, 1998, 42–
> 72; R. J. BUCK, Thrasybulus and the Athenian Democracy,
> 1998, 33–39.   K.-W.W.

Mindius Uncommon Roman family name; a few *gentiles* are identifiable as merchants in Greece (Delos, Asia
Minor) during the later Republican period, e.g. a M.M.
who died in Elis (Cic. fam. 5,20,2; 20,8; 13,26,2; 28,2).
[1] M. Marcellus, M. From Velitrae, the home of Octavian (→ Augustus), whom M. probably knew from his
youth (App. civ. 5,422). Speculated in property with the
encouragement of Caesar (Cic. fam. 15,17,2). Under
the latter's adoptive son Octavian, a career as officer of
the fleet from 38 BC: M. promoted the reconciliation of
Octavian with the admiral → Menodorus [1], who refused to take sides (App. civ. 5,422ff.), and acted – even
before the Battle of → Actium – as *praefectus classis* in
the Adriatic (honorific inscriptions, cf. [1]).

> 1 G. MANCINI, in: NSA 21, 1924, 511–513   2 MRR
> 2,405   3 D. R. SHACKLETON BAILEY, Two Studies in
> Roman Nomenclature, ²1991, 33.   T.FR.

[2] L.M.Balbus Proconsul of Pontus-Bithynia under
Claudius. PIR² M 597.

> G. STUMPF, Numismatische Studien, 1991, 150ff.

[3] M. Aurelius M. Mattidianus Pollio Knight from a
province of Asia Minor, either Bithynia or Asia (Ephesus). M. was leaseholder of the 2.5% duty in Asia for
over 30 years, and Imperial procurator at the same
time: *praefectus vehiculorum* with a salary of 200,000
sesterces, *procurator patrimonii*, → *dioikētēs* in Egypt,
procurator XX hereditatium and – presumably simultaneously – *procurator summarum rationum*. In Asia he
also took on the functions of asiarch (→ Asiarchy), and
in Bithynia those of bithyniarch (IEph III 627; VII 1,
3056). PIR² A 1559.

> PFLAUM, Vol. 1, 523–531.

[4] L.M.Pollio Proconsul of Pontus-Bithynia under
Claudius. PIR² M 598.

> W. AMELING, in: Gnomon 1995, 695; G. STUMPF, Numis-
> matische Studien, 1991, 146ff.   W.E.

Mine Coins see → Tessera

Mineral Resources
I. GEOGRAPHY   II. ECONOMY AND POLITICS

I. GEOGRAPHY
Compared with Europe as a whole and other continents, the mainlands and islands of the Mediterranean
are poor in valuable mineral resources; furthermore,
deposits of precious metals and marble are limited to
only a few regions. Many of the deposits were exploited
in antiquity or during the Middle Ages, especially wherever they were easily accessible along the coasts. The
Phoenicians traveled to obtain tin ore from Iberia as
early as the Bronze Age, and the Greeks transported this
ore, so important to ancient civilization, from Cornwall
to Massilia by way of Gaul.

The distribution of mineral resources can be explained by the geological development of the region,
type of rock formation, and the processes of ore enrich-
ment. In areas where sediment was left behind by the
Miocene and Pliocene seas, limestone, sandstone, clay,
gypsum (alabaster) and sulphur have been extracted
from earliest times; in volcanic areas, tuff, basalt and
obsidian; and in karst areas, calc-tufa and calc-sinter
(travertine). Older rock was shifted or completely
transformed (metamorphosis) during the Tertiary or in
earlier phases of mountain formation. Under high pressure and temperatures, limestone was consolidated in
greater depths and transformed into crystalline marble,
e.g. the marble of Carrara in the interior beyond the
foldbelt of the Apennine Mountains, the marbles of
Mount Pentelicon, those of Paros and Naxos in the
Cyclades Islands, of western Turkey, the Alps (Carin-
thia) and the marble of Chemtou (Tunisia). The banded
marble of Thasos before the Thracian coast was repeatedly thrust layer over layer. The mountain ranges with
marine sediments of the Tertiary, Jurassic, and Creta-
ceous periods that were folded upward and/or raised
generally contain ores only where older masses in the
depths were involved in the formation of mountains.
Examples are the iron ores of the Iberian rim mountains of the Sierra del Moncayo (Mons Caius), the iron
and copper ores of the central zone of the Eastern Alps
(Hüttenberg, Mitterberg), the gold of the Hohe Tauern
range and the ores of the Atlas mountain chains. Hot
water forced its way up into the channels and crevasses
and left the dissolved minerals behind as ores (hydro-
thermal deposits).

The most valuable mineral resources (metal ores of
copper, tin, gold, silver, lead and zinc) are found in the
margins of those mountain ranges classified as belonging to the old masses; these boundary areas are especially prone to tectonic disturbances. The old masses include granite massifs, e.g. in northwestern Spain, northern Portugal, Morocco (Oulmés) and Sardinia with tin
ore, and metamorphic rock from the Palaeozoic era as
in the Sierra Morena in southwestern Spain and southern Portugal, where copper, lead, zinc and silver are
associated with pyrites. In the eastern portion of the
mountain range one finds the mercury ores (cinnabar)

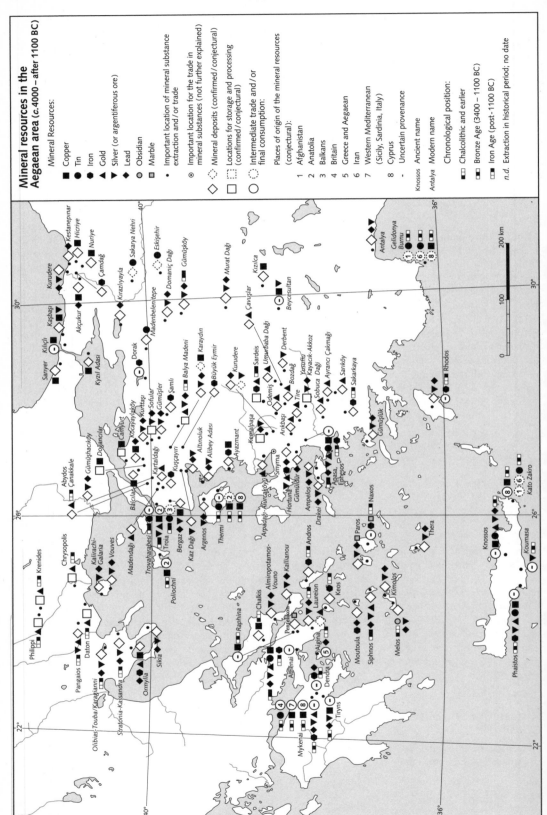

Mineral resources in the Aegean area (c. 4000 – after 1100 BC)

of Almaden (Sisapo). Some ores occur in close proximity, as for example lead and zinc in the Iglesiente in southwestern Sardinia, copper and iron ores as well as granite on the island of Elba and in the Metallifere Colline of Tuscany. The mining district of → Laurium has argentiferous lead ore, zinc ore and iron ore. Further, the once significant silver-lead ores of the island of Siphnos in the Cyclades are associated with iron ore in channels in the limestone.

Deposits of valuable ores occur in narrow zones that stretch along the margins of old continents and can be traced back to regions of former oceans, in this case the Tethys Ocean. They contain mainly ultrabasic rocks (e.g. serpentine, gabbro, peridotite) thought to have been part of the oceanic crust. With the drift of the continents and individual plates, oceanic crust material was thrust over the edges of those continents (obduction), whereas in other instances the crust descended below the continents (subduction). The iron and copper mining area of Tuscany belongs to a serpentine and ophiolite zone; another such zone traverses central Albania with chrome nickel, copper, and iron ores. We find its continuation on the Chalcidic peninsula as well (with chrome, magnesite, lead, zinc, copper, gold). Ophiolite zones surround the Anatolian Massif Range (chromite, lead, silver, copper, gold, iron) and include Cyprus in the south. The Troodos Mountain, with its ultrabasic core, supplied rich copper ore as well as gold and iron from 3000 BC. Gold was mined in the ophiolite zone of Egypt, between the Nile and the Red Sea, as were copper, lead, and tin ores. The Semail ophiolite of the Oman Mountains also supplied copper. In the Mediterranean region, copper has been extracted since the beginning of the Metal Age, followed by gold, silver, lead and iron. The tin ore necessary for the production of bronze had to be mostly imported – in early times probably from the Ore Mountains among other places. The small deposits in the vicinity of the Etruscan copper smelters near Campiglia Marittima may have been mined, as well as some deposits in Sardinia. The Hittites were probably able to extract some tin in Anatolia (in the region of Eskisehir), or they imported it from Afghanistan where tin ores are known to exist near Kandahar and south of Herat. Probably the ores were transported over trade routes to the Levantine Coast, Crete and Egypt. The tin deposits of Europe are linked to late Variscan granite and are found mainly in Galicia, western Brittany and Cornwall. In the contact zone, tin-stone (cassiterite = tin oxide) was formed pneumatolytically and hydrothermally in veins of quartz. Mainly it was placer deposits that were worked, as for example on the 'Cassiterides', the Tin Islands of ancient reports, probably those in the rias of Arosa, Pontevedra and Vigo (Spain), and also on the coasts of Brittany and Cornwall. The three tin regions of Europe probably formed a contiguous complex whose parts achieved their present-day locations through the divergent drifting of plates and a rotation of the Iberian mass to the left.

1 E. BEDERKE, H. G. WUNDERLICH, Atlas zur Geologie, 1968   2 C. DE PALMA, Le vie dei metalli. Le rotte commerciali nel Mediterraneo antico, L'Universo 65, 1985, 578–593   3 A. DWORAKOWSKA, Quarries in Ancient Greece, 1975   4 Id., Quarries in Roman Provinces, 1983   5 J. HEALY, Mining and metallurgy in the Greek and Roman World, 1978   6 R. D. PENHALLURICK, Tin in Antiquity: its mining and trade throughout the ancient world with particular reference to Cornwall, 1986   7 S. SCHÖLER, Mineralische Rohstoffe in vorgeschichtlicher und geschichtlicher Zeit. TAVO A II 2, 1990   8 R. SHEPHERD, Prehistoric mining and allied industries, 1980   9 R. F. TYLECOTE, The early history of metallurgy in Europe, 1987   10 VITTINGHOFF.   F.TI.

II. ECONOMY AND POLITICS

Access to the most important mineral resources and exploitation of the relatively few deposits of gold, silver, copper, tin and iron ores had a decisive influence on political and economic developments in the ancient world; ancient writers themselves saw the relevance that control over precious metal resources had for gaining and consolidating political power, and cities as well as rulers strove to achieve control over the mining districts and organize the mining of ore. With the rise of a money economy in the centres of the ancient world, extraction of gold and silver ores became a basic prerequisite for coinage and thus determined to a certain extent the financial power of a polis or a ruler. Herodotus explained the wealth of individual islands like Siphnos and Thasos (Hdt. 3,57; 6,46f.) by citing their gold and silver mining, and he emphasized that the financing of naval construction in Athens was possible only with the help of revenue from the mines of Laurium (Hdt. 7,144; cf. Aeschyl. Pers. 238). The political position of Athens in the 5th century BC and the dominance of Attic silver currency in the Greek world are undoubtedly due in part to the extraction of silver in the mining district of Laurium. The prominent role that silver mining played in the political and social structure of Athens also finds expression in Xenophon's Póroi; the crux of the proposals that Xenophon submitted for a solution to Athen's social problems in the 4th century BC was an intensification of silver mining, with the polis itself supplying the unfree labourers necessary to do this. In the course of Macedonian expansion in the north Aegean region, Philip II was able to bring the gold mines of the Pangaeum Mountains in Thrace into his sphere of power and at the same time considerably increase yield from the mines through improvements; revenues were said to amount to 1,000 talents a year and to have contributed to a great extent to financing the king's aggressive politics (Diod. 16,8,6–7).

The Romans, too, were quick to organize the excavation of ores and alluvial gold after conquering and annexing a region in which deposits of precious metals were to be found. In 195 BC, M. Porcius Cato set down rules for the administration of iron and silver mines in Spain and fixed high taxes (Liv. 34,21,7); exploitation of the gold deposits in northwestern Spain also began immediately after conquest of the region under Augustus, and during the time of the Principate, exploitation of lead deposits was initiated in Britain as early as under Claudius. As the increase in the amount of silver currency in circulation shows – from 35 million denarii in the mid-second century BC to over 400 million denarii in the mid-first century BC – development of the Roman money economy was dependent in large measure on exploitation of Spanish silver deposits. There can be no doubt that metals belonged to the most important items of trade, and commercial relations like those between Greece and Etruria can be explained in the light of Greek ambitions to acquire high-quality iron.

Marble, too, which was a sought-after material for sculpture in the Archaic Period as well as during the Principate, and which was the preferred stone in both Greek and Roman architecture for the construction of representative buildings, is to be found in only relatively few areas. For the construction of its prestige buildings in the 5th century, Athens had at its disposal the marble of the → Pentelicon, and Carrara marble was used to a great extent during the expansion of Rome under Augustus. In general, it can be said that from the 6th century BC on, marble had to be transported over great distances to the construction sites or to the places where sculptures were to be erected.

Mineral resources, and in particular the extraction of precious metals, received much attention in the historiographic and geographic literature ever since the 2nd century BC. Polybius described the extraction of silver, so lucrative for the Romans, near Cathago Nova (Strab. 3,2,10), and Posidonius devoted lengthy comments to this topic in his regional and cultural writings; interest in mineral resources is also manifested in the works of Diodorus, Strabo, and Pliny (cf. for example Diod. Sic. 3,12–14; 5,13; 5,27; 5,35–38; Strabo 3,2,8–10; 9,1,23; Pliny HN 33;34).
→ Marble; → Mining

1 Cary   2 A. M. Snodgrass, Heavy Freight in Archaic Greece, in: Garnsey/Hopkins/Whittaker, 16–26.
H.SCHN.

Minerva (Menerva, Menrva).
I. Cult   II. Iconography

I. Cult
A. The earliest findings   B. Minerva in Roman literature until the Augustan period   C. Later development   D. Minerva in the Roman Empire

A. The earliest findings
1. General   2. Linguistic findings   3. Historical and topographical findings

1. General
M. is traditionally considered an Etruscan deity that came to Rome as part of the Capitoline Triad of → Jupiter, → Juno and M., who had their temple on the → Capitolium ([1; 5]; undecided [6. 163f.]). Thus, on the basis of representations of M. on Etruscan mirrors as a martial goddess [2] modelled on the Greek → Athena, it is assumed that she was a Hellenic goddess introduced via Etruscan trade contacts with Greece. Besides taking as evidence the form *Menrva*/*Menerva* in Etruscan, but also *Menerva* in Italian and Old Latin inscriptions – this view is based on the assumption that the Romans possessed only a few of their own great deities prior to Etruscan influence, that resulted in an influx of new deities and shaped Roman religion. This assumption, however, is dubious: while there was an Etruscan influence it was less decisive than has long been thought, and it was not limited to the era of Etruscan rule in Rome from 626 to 509 BC [3]. Linguistic, historical and topographical reservations also cast doubt on the traditional interpretations (see below); the question of the origin of M. cannot be answered conclusively.

2. Linguistic findings
Linguistic discoveries point to derivation of the name *Menerva*/M., especially the root √*men-*, from the Indogermanic. [4. 197, note. 4]. Fest. 109,27–29 and 222,24f. L. imply derivation from the Latin *promenevare* (hardly plausible, with the ancient interpreters = *monere*, 'to remind', perhaps rather 'a sanctification *pro Menerva*' [5]), which they relate to the *Carmen Saliare*. This connection could be an indication of the age of this etymology (even if it were popular etymology) [6. 164, note 1]. The appearance of M. in an Etruscan context could thus be explained by means of Etruscan adoption from Indoeuropean Italian dialects.

3. Historical and topographical findings
Varro (Ling. 5,74; cf. Dion. Hal. Ant. 1,14) assumes a Sabine origin for M. Sabine influence in Rome can be dated to Rome's early royal period. Loose Etruscan contacts with Rome (e.g. Liv. 1,14,4–15 – as well as with other Italian communities) at this early time, and thus early Etruscan knowledge of M., are corroborated by the existence of the → Vicus Tuscus in one of the oldest areas of the city of Rome and early Etruscan links with the → Caelius Mons [1] (Varro Ling. 5,46). The temple of M. Capta, mentioned in an (early?) description of the itinerary of the → Argei in the *libri sacerdotum* 'Minervium' (Varro Ling. 5,47; [7]), was located there. This temple has long been erroneously dated to the year 241 BC because of the supposed connection with the fall of → Falerii [1] (Ov. Fast. 3,835–846; Lat. *capta* – 'the captive'); it must, however, be significantly older [8. 112–115]. Thus it remains unclear whether Falerii with its Sabine cults [9] was the place where both Etruscans and Romans could have learned early on about a native Italian M.

Based on Etruscan knowledge of the Greek → Athena conveyed via Greek trade relationships, the image of M. may have first developed further in Etruria Etruscan amphorae from the early 6th cent. BC represent the Hesiodic myth of Athena's birth from Zeus head (Hes. Theog. 820–880, 886–900) [10]. Familiarity with the Greek tradition suggests that additional aspects of Athena (e.g. *Prónoia, Ergánē, Prómachos*) could also have been known. Athena's connection with Zeus, the hurler of lightning-bolts, led to her association with lightning at an early stage (Hom. Od. 24,533–544); M.'s lightning-bolts were to occupy an important place in Etruscan → divination (Serv. Aen. 1,42). In the tradition of the city goddess Athena Polias, M. as a protectress of the state took her place beside Zeus/Tin/Jupiter and his wife Hera/Uni/Juno. Due to increased Etruscan contacts beginning in the late 7th cent. this M. – enriched by a Hellenistic dimension – returned to Rome and there encountered the Italian goddess associated with crafts. The influence of Hellenic (Etruscan?) ideas on the M. figure is illustrated, as early as the middle of the 6th century BC, by the statue programme of the Roman city sanctuary of San Omobono, that, just as in Greek myth, represents → Hercules [1] together with his protectoress Athena/M., the latter as a warrior [11] (see II. below). The fusion of Greek and Italian traditions influences later developments: by the time of the → *lectisternium* of 217 BC (Liv. 22,9,10) at the latest, a Hellenic M., with Etruscan and Greek influence, was accepted in the official cult along with the indigenous goddess of crafts.

The → *natalis templi* of M.'s temple on the Aventine was June 19; the temple itself was most likely founded in the middle of the 3rd century BC [8. 109–112]. *Quinquartus*, the festival of craftspeople dedicated to M., took place on June 19. That day was also a sacred day of → Mars (InscrIt 13,2 p. 173); Roman antiquarian writers attempted an implausible association of both deities with → Nerio (Gell. 13,23). Musicians honoured M. on the *Minusculae Quinquartus* (June 13) (Fest. 134,3–6 L., Varro Ling. 6,17). Up until the early 2nd cent. BC, her temple on the Aventine was the meeting place of the → *collegium* [2] *poetarum* (Fest. 446f. L.). M.'s function as warrior and patron of musicians linked her with the → *tubilustrium* on March 23 (Ov. Fast. 3,850).

It is worth noting that M. never really became established as protectoress of the political system (analogous to Athena Polias) in Republican Rome because Jupiter together with Juno Sospita already occupied that role [6. 166f.]. M. was also honoured in Rome as Medica '(the physician)' (CIL VI 30980; ILS 3135; Cic. div. 2,123). However, the localization of her temple on the Esquiline and the assignation of the votive offerings found there to M. Medica are disputed ([8. 115–117]; differently: [12]). Both the healing cult of M. Medica and the account about hairdressers in the service of the Capitoline Juno and M. (Sen. De superstitione fr. 35–37 HAASE) call into question the strict division between an official and a private cult of M.

B. MINERVA IN ROMAN LITERATURE UNTIL THE AUGUSTAN PERIOD

Livius Andronicus' translation of Homer's 'Odyssey' in the late 3rd cent. BC spread knowledge of Athena and the Greek aspect of M. Accius' *Deiphobus* portrays M. as a warrior (TRF 127). Ennius' *Eumenides* adapt a portion of Athena's speech in Aeschyl. Eum. 741, 752f. (TRF 136; [13]). Clodius' insinuation that Cicero regarded M. as his sister (Cic. Dom. 92) suggests her function as a personal protectress which the latter claimed for himself. The Augustan poets combine the various aspects of M. (e.g. Prop. 1,2,30; 2,9,3–6; Virg. Georg. 1,18f.; 4,246f.) and alternate freely between Athena, → Pallas and M. (Virg. Aen. 2,15,31,615–617; Ov. Met. 6,1–145; 2,563, 567).

C. LATER DEVELOPMENT

→ Domitianus [1] favoured M. (Philostr. Ap. 7,32; cf. Mart. 5,2,8); the reasons are more complex [14] than mere philhellenism [15]. It is likely that Domitian emphasized M.'s martial aspect in order to legitimize his own military achievements in the face of senatorial criticism (Tac. Agr. 39,2). Even before that, M. appears in propaganda [16.100f.] in times of military insecurity. Among women of the Augustan and Flavio-Trajanic dynasties, M. appears only in association with → Plotina; the connection with → Vesta remains the usual one [17]. M.'s martial aspect is frequently emphasized during the military crises of the 3rd cent. AD: às M. Victrix, for instance, on coins during the Severan era (RIC 4,1 p. 381), in the → Feriale Duranum, in inscriptions (ILS 31331, Severan). M. is frequently associated with the reigning emperors (e.g. Aurelian, RIC 5,1, Nr. 334). During the Tetrarchy she appears as a patroness *(comes;* Paneg. 9,10,2 MYNORS; [18]), usually subordinated to Hercules (e.g. [19.239 with pl. XI; 20]).

D. MINERVA IN THE ROMAN EMPIRE

The starting-points for the introduction of the Roman M. to the provinces were frequently the Roman → *coloniae* [21. 115–124] and, especially during the Imperial era, the army. Despite M.'s prominent function as one of the Capitoline Triad, also honoured in the provinces, the goddess' multiple character continued to prevail [21. 124]: she appeared frequently as a divinity of war and crafts (e.g. Roman Inscriptions of Britain 91, together with → Neptunus; [22]). In the army, M. was revered by musicians, training instructors and scribes, among others [23]. The → *interpretatio Romana* of native divinities played a part, e.g. in Gaul (Caes. BGl. 6,17,1f; in general: [24]), but was less important than in the case of → Mars and → Mercury: for example, M. was assimilated to an indigenous divinity known as M. Sulia in → Aquae [III 7] Sulis (Bath) [25].
→ Etrusci; → Sabini

MINERVA 1 C. THULIN, M. auf dem Capitol und Fortuna in Praeneste, in: RhM 60, 1905, 256–261 2 U. W. SCHOLZ, Studien zum altitalischen und altrömischen Marskult und Marsmythos, 1970, 141–151 3 T. CORNELL, The Beginnings of Rome, 1995, 151–172 4 P. KRETSCHMER, Einleitung in die Geschichte der griechischen Sprache, 1896 5 WALDE/HOFMANN, vol. 2, 90f.; 6 LATTE 7 R. E. A. PALMER, The Archaic Community of the Romans, 1970, 84–97 8 A. ZIOLKOWSKI, The Temples of Mid-Republican Rome and Their Historical and Topographical Context, 1992   9 E. Evans, The Cults of the Sabine Territory, 1939, 159–164   10 H. Cassimatis, s.v. Athena, LIMC 2.1, 986f. no. 346 pl. 743, no. 334 pl. 742   11 R. Holloway, The Archaeology of Early Rome and Latium, 1994, 68–80   12 R. Ch. Häuber, in: M. Cima, E. La Rocca (ed.), Horti Romani, 1998   13 H. Jocelyn, The Tragedies of Ennius, 1967, 283–287   14 J.-L. Girard, Domitien et M.: une prédilection impériale, in: ANRW II 17.1, 1981, 233–245   15 C. Gmyrek, Römische Kaiser und griechische Göttin, 1998, 57–59, 154   16 S. Weinstock, Divus Iulius, 1971;   17 H. Temporini, Die Frauen am Hofe Trajans, 1978, 110f.   18 A. D. Nock, The Emperor's divine comes, in: JRS 37, 1947, 102–116   19 E. M. Wightman, Roman Trier and the Treveri, 1971   20 J. Boardman, s.v. Herakles, LIMC 5.1, 131 Nr. 2938   21 F. Fontana, I culti di Aquileia repubblicana, 1997   22 A. Bodor, Die griechisch-römischen Kulte in der Provinz Dacia und das Nachwirken der einheimischen Tradition, in: ANRW II 18.2, 1989, 1094–1096   23 A. v. Domaszewski, Die Religion des römischen Heeres, 1895, 29–33   24 J.-L. Girard, La place de M. dans la religion romaine au temps du principat, in: ANRW II 17.1, 1981, 203–232   25 B. Cunliffe, P. Davenport, The Temple of Sulis M. at Bath, vol. 1, 1985.   C.R.P.

II. Iconography

Already in the oldest known Etruscan-Roman evidence, M. is depicted in accordance with the Greek iconographic tradition of Athena: in her long chiton and peplos (→ Clothing), with a (Corinthian) helmet and aegis, frequently with lance and shield; the representational themes correspond to Greek myth. As one of the Capitoline Triad (her cult statue in the temple on the Roman Capitol has not survived), she is represented on reliefs and coins at Jupiter's left side, either standing or seated on a throne, with or without lance and shield; sometimes her hand is raised to her pushed-back helmet in an → epiphany-gesture. On official monuments she is relatively seldom portrayed; not until the end of the Republic does M. gain greater importance through the reproduction of the (Trojan) → Palladion (cult image of Athena) on coins, gems and official cameos, and, beginning with the Julio-Claudian era, frequently on armor reliefs: the old cult image, in small format and mostly an attribute of emperors or of the goddesses Vesta, Roma, and Victoria, is propagated for the purpose of legitimizing the imperial claim to power and in accordance

with the aeternitas imperii Romani. Many of the various types of portrayals, as found on coins up until the 3rd cent. AD, can be traced back to the emperor Domitianus [1], who proclaimed M. to be his special protecting goddess; the attica relief on the M. temple in the Forum Transitorium in Rome (AD 97/98) possibly shows up this relation with unusual depitction of a → paludamentum; in the era of Domitian, M. is shown for the first time on a state relief, in prominent position next to the emperor (Cancelleria frieze A, Rome, VM, AD 94/96).

In her function as patroness of craftsmen (corresponding to Athena Ergane), M. is present on votive and altar reliefs as well as wall paintings depicting scenes with craftsmen (see above I.). The statue of M. preserved on several coins from the 1st cent. AD, with her raised left hand resting on her lance and an owl on her outstretched right hand, could refer to the cult image in her chief sanctuary on the Aventine. The cult image in the temple of M. Chalcidica on the Field of Mars has been identified as belonging to the type of the long-striding M. with a shield and, often, a lance in her left hand (statue, Rome, MC; Cancelleria frieze A: see above). For other Roman copies and/or transformations of Greek statues of Athena, see → Athena E. Iconography.

F. Canciani, s.v. Athena/M., LIMC 2, 1074–1109 (with further bibl.); Th. Köves-Zulauf, M. Capta. Eine gefangene Göttin?, in: J. Dalfen (ed.), Religio Graeco-Romana. FS W. Pötscher, 1993, 159–176; W. Schürmann, Typologie und Bedeutung der stadtrömischen M.-Kultbilder, 1985.   A.L.

Minervius

[1] Consular before AD 370/1; at this time a member of a Senate deputation to the court of → Valentinianus I, protesting against the use of torture on senators; possibly the M. of Trier mentioned by Symmachus (ep. 4,30) (→ Augusta Treverorum). PLRE 1, 603, 1.

[2] Possibly a son of M. [1]. probably magister epistularum in AD 394/5, thereafter active in Gaul; comes rerum privatarum in 397/8, comes sacrarum largitionum in 398/9; addressee of several letters of → Symmachus, who described him as an expert critic of his writings. PLRE 1, 603, 2.   K.G.-A.